Y0-BBW-116

THE BLUE GUIDES

Countries **Austria**
Belgium and Luxembourg
Channel Islands
Corsica
Crete
Cyprus
Egypt
England
France
Germany
Greece
Holland
Hungary
Ireland
Northern Italy
Southern Italy
Malta and Gozo
Morocco
Portugal
Scotland
Sicily
Spain
Switzerland
Turkey: Bursa to Antakya
Wales
Yugoslavia

Cities **Boston and Cambridge**
Florence
Istanbul
Jerusalem
London
Moscow and Leningrad
New York
Oxford and Cambridge
Paris and Versailles
Rome and Environs
Venice

Themes **Churches and Chapels of Northern**
England
Churches and Chapels of Southern
England
Literary Britain and Ireland
Museums and Galleries of London
Victorian Architecture in Britain

An early 16C bench-end signed by Robart Daye in St. Nonna's, Altarnun, Cornwall

BLUE GUIDE

CHURCHES AND CHAPELS OF SOUTHERN ENGLAND

Edited by Stephen C. Humphrey

A & C Black
London

W W Norton
New York

First edition 1991

Published by A & C Black (Publishers) Limited
35 Bedford Row, London, WC1R 4JH

© A & C Black (Publishers) Limited

Published in the United States of America by
WW Norton & Company, Incorporated
500 Fifth Avenue, New York, NY 10110

Published simultaneously in Canada by
Penguin Books Canada Limited
2801 John Street, Markham, Ontario LR3 1B4

ISBN   0–7136–3029–9

A CIP catalogue record for this book
is available from the British Library.

ISBN   0–393–30725–5 USA

Stephen Humphrey was trained as an historian. In 1979 he was
elected Hon. Secretary of the Ecclesiological Society, an old-
established body then in decline. He has invested considerable time
and effort to restore its reputation as a respected society, especially
as a publisher. Over the years he has written numerous pamphlets
and papers in journals on architecture and local history. He has often
lectured and guided parties on tours. He has lately embarked on the
publication of an annotated list of all churches and chapels which
have ever existed in England, the most comprehensive such list ever
to be attempted.

With five drawings by the **Reverend Brian Roy**.

Typeset by CRB Typesetting Services, Ely, Cambs.
Printed and bound in Great Britain by
William Clowes Limited, Beccles and London

PREFACE

The pair of volumes, of which this is one, describes a selection from the many thousands of churches and chapels in England. To a large extent, the buildings chosen are those widely considered to be 'the best' in terms of their antiquity, their historical associations, and the magnificence of their architecture and fittings. The choice was influenced by a wish to represent all periods of architecture. There was in addition a need to give recognition in a touring guide to some much-visited churches which are not always 'the best' architecturally. An attempt has been made to draw attention to private chapels and to non-Anglican churches, for such buildings are omitted in traditional books on parish churches. Finally, there are a few special pleadings, such as any compiler would doubtless wish to make.

The volumes are arranged largely by the traditional counties of England. The popularity of these counties is obvious enough, but it should also be remembered that they usually correspond with the Church of England's diocesan boundaries, which are equally ancient. The county texts are the work of 17 writers; entries initialled 'S.C.H.' are the work of the editor.

ACKNOWLEDGEMENTS

A work of this sort requires the help of innumerable people. My thanks go first and foremost to Miss Freda Gould, who arranged in advance so many of my tours of the churches described, and who assisted too during some of the tours themselves. Miss Anna Zaharova fulfilled a similar role for my early tours. I gladly thank the staff of Top Grade Services of Barrett Street, London for typing much of the text so efficiently, and the staff of Mercury Secretarial Services Ltd of New Cavendish Street, London for endless copying (and especially to Mr Jack Coachworth for his unfailing pains to secure the best results). The staff of the Redundant Churches Fund kindly helped me to gain access to numerous churches in their care and commented on my text. I also gratefully acknowledge my debt to the National Monuments Record, whose staff have provided much help over illustrations. Gratitude is due too to Mr David Williams, formerly of the Council for the Care of Churches, to my mother (Mrs G.L. Humphrey) for reading and commenting on much of the text and for valuable further help, to Mr John Warbis for matters photographic and for driving me round Suffolk in 1987, to Miss Mary Boast and Miss Pauline Casey. I must also express my thanks in general to fellow-members of the Ecclesiological Society for information and advice over the years, with special mention of the late Gordon Barnes, sometime Chairman, who taught me so much about Worcestershire and Gloucestershire in many splendid tours, Mr T.F. Blood, also formerly Chairman, and the late Mr Maurice Henley, Vice-President, who helped me with illustrations and other matters. The worthy contributors to the text all deserve my gratitude for what they have done *beyond* writing their counties. Hospitality, information and advice have been freely provided.

Incumbents, churchwardens and caretakers throughout England have been agreeably helpful. A number of particular debts need to be mentioned. I was specially fortunate in Yorkshire in the help I received. Canon C.J. Hawthorn of St. Martin's, Scarborough was very helpful over his distinguished Bodley church and on related Bodleian matters. The Reverend H.E. Hutchinson read my text for the East Riding and made useful comments. Canon Barry Keeton of Howden Minster corrected my information on statues and effigies in that church. Canon J.H. Armstrong of All Saints', Pavement, York has been very helpful on more than one occasion. Mr John Hutchinson suggested subjects for entries in the West Riding, and made comments on my choices for the East Riding. The Reverend R.M. Harvey opened Wadworth Church for me at no little inconvenience to himself, and gave me much information. Mr Leslie Hayes took great pains to show me round St. John's, Leeds and to discuss its history. In Rotherham, Mr Martyn Taylor specially opened the medieval bridge chapel and explained various features. Mr B. Heath was an exceptionally agreeable guide at St. Wilfrid's, Cantley. At Fulneck, Mr J. Ingham enabled me to see the Moravian Church and explained its history. My visit to the church at Adel near Leeds led me to meet Mr Brian Roy, who not only discussed that church in detail but went on to provide some admirable drawings for this work. Much useful information was provided by the Reverend S.M. Hind about Womersley Church and elsewhere.

In Lancashire, where so many churches are locked outside services, special access was gladly afforded at Mossley Hill;

Warrington; St. Agnes's at Sefton Park, Liverpool; at St. Helen's, Sefton (by Canon O.J. Yandell, who discussed the church in detail); St. John's at Lancaster; St. Walburge's at Preston (by Father Leo Caton, who gave me much of his time in explaining features in the church); and at the Friends' Meeting House in St. Helen's, where Ada Williamson, Clerk of the Meeting, was my guide. Miss Margaret Hodge, Domestic Bursar of Manchester Polytechnic, kindly allowed me to see the former Christian Science Church which is now in her care.

At Dukinfield, Mr Norman Stephens introduced me to the Unitarian Church at no more than a moment's notice. Much farther north, at Crosby Ravensworth, Westmorland, Canon R.H. Gurney welcomed me and discussed his church in the busy circumstances of a flower festival. In County Durham, the Reverend Michael Waters was exceptionally helpful at Ushaw College, again at just a moment's notice. In the same county, Canon A.H. Nugent of Brancepeth made detailed and valuable comments on the entry for his church. The Reverend T.J. Ganz gave much information about Tutbury Church, Staffordshire. I was guided and made very welcome at St. Chad's, Stafford (by Mrs Joan Eley) and St. Michael's, Lichfield (by the Reverend D.A. Smith). Mr Bruce Scott was notably helpful at St. Mary's, Clumber, Nottinghamshire, in the difficult circumstances of a major restoration. The late Mr Vivian Leleux was most helpful concerning Holy Sepulchre Church, Northampton. The Archdeacon of Northampton gave useful comments on St. Peter's in that town. In Huntingdonshire the Reverend P.J. Shepherd was informative and welcoming at Yaxley, as was Canon K.S.S. Jamal at Fletton.

For information on Essex I am indebted to Mr C.R. Starr. At Harlow I was enabled to see the Baptist Church, Potter Street by Mr Percy White. Mr R.J. Lloyd welcomed me at Radwinter Church on more than one occasion and gave me much information. At Blackmore, Mrs Skrimshare specially opened the church and discussed its history. In Suffolk I was helped at Blythburgh by Mr R.I. Collett, and at Bury St. Edmund's, admission to the Unitarian Chapel was made possible by Mr Ben Johnson (Chairman of the Trustees) and Mr Philip Orchard, who explained its history and the works proposed for it. I am grateful to the Reverend L.J.H. Hard for help with All Saints', Cambridge over many years. In Hertfordshire, Mr A.G. Trower was helpful and hospitable in respect of the old church at Stanstead Abbots. I acknowledge too the permision granted me to view the chapel of All Saints' Pastoral Centre, London Colney. On the churches of Bedfordshire, I have learned much from Mr C.J. Pickford, the County Archivist. At Edlesborough in Buckinghamshire I was enabled to view the church by Mrs J.C. Horne.

The late Mr John Pinder commented on my entry for St. George the Martyr, Southwark, and gave me other useful information. The Reverend Nicholas Richards commented in considerable detail on the entry for St. Mary's, Rotherhithe. My text for St. George's, Hanover Square was much improved by the advice of the Reverend W.M. Atkins. Mr Ian Anstruther and Mr Robert Elleray both read my text for Sussex and made valuable comments. At St. Nicholas's, Arundel Mr David Robinson opened the church specially and provided much information, and at St. Michael's, Brighton the Reverend D.G. Hewetson kindly unlocked the church when I visited in 1986 and explained various features. In the same year I went to All Saints', Selsley, Gloucestershire, where the Reverend I.E. Burbery was markedly helpful and most agreeable.

A NOTE ON BLUE GUIDES

The Blue Guide series began in 1918 when Muirhead Guide-Books Limited published 'Blue Guide London and its Environs'. Finlay and James Muirhead already had extensive experience of guide-book publishing: before the First World War they had been the editors of the English editions of the German Baedekers, and by 1915 they had acquired the copyright of most of the famous 'Red' Handbooks from John Murray.

An agreement made with the French publishing house Hachette et Cie in 1917 led to the translation of Muirhead's London Guide, which became the first 'Guide Bleu'—Hachette had previously published the blue-covered 'Guides Joanne'. Subsequently, Hachette's 'Guide Bleu Paris et ses Environs' was adapted and published in London by Muirhead. The collaboration between the two publishing houses continued until 1933.

In 1931 Ernest Benn Limited took over the Blue Guides, appointing Russell Muirhead, Finlay Muirhead's son, editor in 1934. The Muirheads' connection with Blue Guides ended in 1963 when Stuart Rossiter, who had been working on the Guides since 1954, became house editor, revising and compiling several of the books himself.

The Blue Guides are now published by A & C Black, who acquired Ernest Benn in 1984, so continuing the tradition of guide-book publishing which began in 1826 with 'Black's Economical Tourist of Scotland'. The Blue Guide series continues to grow: there are now more than 40 titles in print with revised editions appearing regularly and many new Blue Guides in preparation.

'Blue Guides' is a registered trade mark.

CONTENTS

HISTORICAL INTRODUCTION

Beginnings in the Roman Empire

On July 25th in the year 306 the Roman Emperor, Constantius Chlorus, died at *Eboracum*, the Roman city of York. On the same day and in the same city his son, Constantine, was proclaimed Emperor in his place. The proclamation probably took place at the main entrance of the Roman military headquarters, which directly underlies the S transept of York Minster. This was where a disastrous fire occurred in 1984. The equally dramatic proclamation of 306 was an event of marked significance in the earliest Christian record of this island. The accession of Constantine was one of the most momentous events in Christian history, for less than 20 years later he became the first Christian to be the sole ruler of the Roman world. Without Constantine, the future of Christianity might have been very different, as its story outside the Roman Empire suggests. Although Constantine's conversion is normally dated to 312, he might have become a Christian in some sense long before then. It is possible that he might have been drawn to Christianity in York itself, for just eight years after his proclamation a bishop from the city attended the Council of Arles. No doubt a Christian community was an obvious part of the York which Constantine knew.

These events of 306 took place in a city which was the military capital of a Roman province. *Londinium* was its commercial and administrative capital. At that time the English nation was still living in Angel and elsewhere across the North Sea. The Christian history of this country thus predates the change from Roman Britain to the English kingdoms. It goes back not merely beyond the Reformation, when the Church in western Europe was still united, but to that much remoter period when the Latin West was in full communion with the Greek East; in other words, when Christendom was one and when it acknowledged (with minor exceptions) the civil power of the Roman Emperor. The Christian world of Constantine's day was in fact centred much more in the Greek East than in the Latin West. The great Council of Nicaea in 325 was attended by only a handful of bishops from the Roman Empire's western provinces (and none from Roman Britain) in contrast to hundreds from the East. Egypt, Syria, Asia Minor: these were the Christian heartlands of the 4C, and they were also the richest parts of the Roman Empire. Constantine's church building schemes took place in Nicomedia, Antioch, Jerusalem and Constantinople as well as Rome; and even in Rome, where he built the two great basilicas of St. Peter on the Vatican Hill and St. Paul outside the walls, the East was recalled in their largely Egyptian endowments and in their further income from Antioch in the case of St. Peter's and Tarsus in that of St. Paul's, both sources being entirely appropriate in view of the connections of the two saints with those cities. In the course of time, all the major Christian cities of the East (Jerusalem, Antioch, Alexandria and Constantinople) fell under the power of Islam, leaving Rome in an unrivalled position. Rome, however, had another major advantage: it was acknowledged to be the burial place of St. Peter and St. Paul. This fact was to be of continuing importance long after the Roman Empire had faded.

A few traces of Christianity in Roman Britain are familiar as rather disconnected facts. The first English historian, St. Bede the Venerable, wrote in the 8C of 'an old church, built in honour of St. Martin during the Roman occupation of Britain', which stood in his day on the E side of Canterbury and which had been brought back into use in the late 6C. From an earlier period—the early 4C at the latest—may be recalled the martyrdom of St. Alban at *Verulamium*. The record of the Council of Arles in 314 shows that *Londinium* then had a bishop called Restitutus and that there were bishops in York and Lincoln too. Archaeological evidence which has received publicity includes the Water Newton hoard of Christian silver in Huntingdonshire; lead baptismal tanks, including the one found at Caversham, Berkshire, in 1988; the Christian mosaic from Hinton St. Mary in Dorset; the 'country house chapel' in the villa at Lullingstone in Kent; and, above all, the basilican church at Silchester in Hampshire. To these one can add the multitude of objects stamped with the *chi-rho* symbol (✗)—which the Emperor Constantine made a Christian symbol—or with an *alpha* and an *omega* (∝,Ω). All these facts speak of a Christian Church in Roman Britain whose bishops were in full communion with those elsewhere in the Empire. It was of course a Church which moved from being persecuted into the toleration which Constantine's success bestowed; and, later in the 4C, a Church which became an integral part of the Roman establishment.

From the days of persecution there were martyrs to recall and honour. Over their graves in the cemeteries (which always stood outside Roman towns), shrines were built. In Continental cities a clear connection has been shown between such shrines in late Roman cemeteries and later churches (which are often cathedrals). Xanten, Cologne and Trier are principal examples. In England, one such early shrine is known: that of St. Alban, an inhabitant of the Roman town of *Verulamium* who was martyred there at an unknown date in the 3C or early 4C. His cult is the earliest of a local saint in this country for which there is evidence. In 429 St. Germanus of Auxerre visited St. Alban's shrine. We do not know whether the shrine was continuously maintained; a gap in the post-Roman period is possible. Knowledge of the site was clearly never lost.

It is wrong to assume that churches in the Roman Empire were necessarily poor, even in the days of persecution. 'Primitive poverty' or 'primitive simplicity' are erroneous labels. In the year 303, during Diocletian's persecution, a record was made of the belongings of a house-church at Cirta in N Africa. The clerk of the court listed two golden chalices, six silver chalices, a silver bowl, seven silver lamps, seven short bronze candlesticks with their lamps, two torches, eleven bronze lamps and chains, and innumerable items of clothing, apparently for use in baptism. The hoard of silver from Water Newton appears to have belonged to a comparable church. One major difference between the early Church and later times was that a bishop would have regular, direct dealings with *all* the worshippers of his diocese, before the pressure of numbers overwhelmed the Church's early practice. The word *parochia*, a parish, originally meant a diocese. Subsequently, when places of worship multiplied, there was still a sense of belonging to one, central congregation. One reflection of this is the Italian tradition of baptism not in a local church but in the central church or cathedral. Hence, for example, the very prominent baptistery next to the cathedral in Florence.

Baptism in general had a prominence in the early Church which it later lost. Many people, including the Emperor Constantine himself, were not baptised until the ends of their lives. Adults (not infants) would become full members of the Church in the presence of all its existing members.

The history of the Church in this country suffered much discontinuity as Roman Britain became England. The economy, population and towns of Roman Britain all decayed. A new pagan English population settled in large areas of the country. Surviving Christianity must have rubbed shoulders with paganism in many districts. Elmet, near Leeds, remained non-English territory, and probably Christian, until the 7C, by which time the conversion of the English was beginning. The SW (Devon and Cornwall), Wales and the NW remained non-English for centuries and therefore preserved Romano-British or Celtic Christianity alongside that of the new English Church. It has become academically normal in recent years to emphasise continuity between Roman Britain and the English kingdoms. Specific instances of sites in continuous occupation, however, are few, although archaeology will doubtless reveal more in the future. The church at Rivenhall in Essex is an unsuspected example yielded by excavations in recent years.

The Early English Church

The English Church began at the very end of the 6C. Pope Gregory I (reigned 590–604) had wanted to lead a mission to England in person, but in the event he sent a group of evangelists under a Roman monk called Augustine. The group had the good fortune to arrive in Kent when its ruler, King Aethelberht, was the most important ruler in England. In early English history, there were a number of distinct kingdoms in this island and at any given time one of them was usually recognised as suzerain of the rest. King Aethelberht happened to have a Frankish Christian wife, Bertha. According to Bede, she had worshipped since her arrival in Kent in a church which had been built in Roman times, that is, in a building which had presumably survived from the 4C. Posterity identified her church with that of St. Martin, which still stands on the E side of Canterbury and thus claims to be the oldest church in continuous use in England. Augustine and his missionaries made much headway in Kent; King Aethelberht's capital, Canterbury, became the centre of the new English Church, and Augustine himself became the first Archbishop of Canterbury in 601. The spread of Christianity throughout England was substantially a matter of politics. Kent directly influenced Essex (in which kingdom London lay) and Northumbria. In each case there was a setback after an initial success, and then renewed evangelisation produced a more permanent result.

Northumbria was arguably the key to the conversion of England in the mid-7C. Three successive Kings of Northumbria—Edwin, Oswald and Oswy—held suzerainty in most of England. Their power and their marriage alliances allowed them to influence religion in other kingdoms. Although both Edwin and Oswald were ultimately defeated in battle by the notorious pagan King of Mercia, Penda, Northumbria recovered on each occasion to ensure the survival of Christianity in the N and to oversee its introduction into Mercia itself.

A marriage alliance between Penda's son, Peada, and a daughter of King Oswy led to a mission by four priests in the E part of Mercia, around Peterborough, where Peada ruled in his father's lifetime. Penda himself died in battle in the year 654. The favourable background for Christianity under Peada and his queen continued under the next king, Wulfhere, another of Penda's sons. Wulfhere was King of Mercia from 657 to 674. He achieved dominance in England S of the Humber, and in his day, the great Mercian abbey of Peterborough began to set up daughter-houses in the Midlands and southern England. The evidence for these foundations constitutes an interesting account of evangelisation in the first century of English Christianity.

A 12C monk of Peterborough, Hugh Candidus or Hugh White, wrote a chronicle in which he stated that from Peterborough 'many other monasteries were founded and from that house monks and abbots were constituted at Ancarig, which is now called Thorney, at Brixworth, at Breedon-on-the-Hill, at Bermondsey, at Rippingale, at Woking and at many other places'. Bermondsey and Woking are both S of the Thames; their early connection with Peterborough speaks of King Wulfhere's control of southern England. Breedon-on-the-Hill in Leicestershire has a church of St. Mary and St. Hardulph which possesses significant pre-Conquest sculptures. Brixworth in Northamptonshire is even more notable, for its church of All Saints is a famous pre-Conquest building, which might date from the late 7C, or at least from the 8C, and excavations there have yielded evidence which must relate to the monastic foundation from Peterborough. The church is the principal survival of the story of Mercian evangelisation in the age of Bede and a reminder of the way in which the early English Church grew.

Dedications

Peterborough's name reminds us that in the 7C and 8C, St. Peter was by far the most frequent choice among known dedications of churches. Bede's 'Ecclesiastical History of the English Nation', which was completed in 731, mentions 25 dedications in total, of which eight are of St. Peter and three are of St. Peter and St. Paul together. An ancient dedication to St. Peter is one indication that a church might be of particularly early foundation. In Bede's time, St. Peter was held in great honour throughout the western Church. A famous manuscript of the Bible, the 'Codex Amiatinus', which is now in the Laurentian Library in Florence, was written in Bede's monastery of Jarrow in Northumbria and was taken to Rome by Abbot Coelfrid in 716. It was given to the Pope, but its dedication was strictly to the shrine, or indeed the relics, of St. Peter. Similarly, the pallium or scarf of office which Roman consuls had once worn and which, in due course, Popes sent to archbishops, was considered all the more important from the fact that before being granted by the Pope, it had been laid on St. Peter's tomb. The pallium still appears in the arms of the See of Canterbury.

The antiquity of other dedications is less consistent. There are some indications that All Hallows (or All Saints) and St. Martin might have had above-average early use. The Apostles and prominent Roman martyrs clearly formed the majority of early dedications.

Local saints in England were not commemorated until long after their deaths, in some cases centuries later. So, for example, a dedication to St. Augustine of Canterbury does not imply an early 7C foundation; more than likely it would be 10C, 11C or 12C. It is sometimes stated that churches dedicated to the Virgin Mary are of early foundation; this is not so. Comparatively few are recorded as bearing her name in the first couple of centuries of English Church history. Her over-whelming popularity over all other saints arose as late as the 12C. The original form of a dedication to her was 'Holy Mother of God', which reflects the title of *Theotokos* (literally 'God-bearer') which had been bestowed on her at the Council of Ephesus in 431.

The Danish Invasions

It is conventional to put together all churches from the time of St. Augustine to the Norman Conquest as pre-Conquest. Yet in many ways it is unsatisfactory to consider as one group buildings whose origin may be up to four and a half centuries apart. It would be ludicrous to put into one group churches built in the comparable span from Elizabethan times to the 20C. Although developments in pre-Conquest architecture, liturgy and Church government were relativ-ely very gradual, there were nevertheless clear differences between one century and another. The most obvious division in pre-Conquest Church history is before and after the Danish or Viking invasions of the 9C. Many monasteries, which had been founded in the 7C and 8C, did not survive the onslaught. The daughter-houses of Peter-borough which were discussed above, did not preserve their original status. Some, such as Brixworth, remained as parish churches with-out Peterborough connections. Others, such as Bermondsey, disap-peared entirely, to be re-founded under quite different patronage at a later date. Peterborough itself, which was attacked in 870, was not re-founded as a Benedictine monastery until 972. It was one part of the great Church renewal which took place in the reign of King Edgar (959–75) and under St. Dunstan, St. Ethelwold and St. Oswald.

Shrines and Relics

If the Danish invasions represent the great divide, what were the common factors from the 7C to the 11C? Above all, there was a common emphasis on shrines and relics, which continued until the Reformation. We are familiar with the subject of pilgrimage to a great shrine such as that of St. Thomas Becket at Canterbury, but much less so with the innumerable minor shrines throughout England and with the existence of quite small relics in parish churches. Churches were sometimes built to a plan which was chiefly geared to the circulation of pilgrims. The early crypts which survive at Hexham and Repton and under Ripon Cathedral were all designed to display relics and to ensure an orderly passage of pilgrims. St. Edmund's Abbey at Bury St. Edmund's was a typical example of the same thing on the most grandiose medieval style.

Relics divide into two groups: the bones of saints; and objects associated with them (or, in exceptional cases, objects reputedly associated with Christ). The first group would range from the entire remains to just one small fragment. All Saints' at Brixworth, for example, seems to have had a throat-bone of St. Boniface, which was as treasured in its reliquary as the entire mortal remains of an Apostolic martyr. It is true that pilgrims brought money to a church and especially to cathedrals and abbeys, and that there was some hankering for a local saint in places where no local martyr had existed, but it is very wrong to look upon the movement as mercenary. In the 10C, King Aethelstan—who had all the power and riches a king could have wanted—collected relics incessantly for what he clearly considered to be their spiritual worth. Rome achieved its pre-eminence in the western Church because it could claim the shrine of St. Peter, and it was the accepted site of his burial which led to the building of St. Peter's basilica halfway up the Vatican Hill. Such an awkward site was used for Constantine's great church, and for its successor, only because the principal Apostolic martyr was considered to be buried there. The word martyr comes from the Greek for a witness: a witness to belief in the Resurrection of Jesus. No more revered position in the early Church could exist than that of a martyr, whose death was recorded for posterity in a *passio*. The date of his martyrdom, known as his birthday in Heaven, was reverently recorded in liturgical calendars and marked more or less widely in Christendom. Not all saints, of course, were martyrs. Local English saints were often bishops, or founders or foundresses of churches and monasteries. But martyrdom was a special crown. So St. Thomas Becket was honoured more than St. Anselm, and St. Edmund more than St. Dunstan.

Pre-Conquest Buildings

Surviving pre-Conquest churches have been described in minute detail in many books and articles. Yet much that has been written has been oblivious or neglectful of the liturgy and customs of the early English Church. Buildings have been considered with little reference to their use. Shrines and relics, as discussed above, form just one subject which needs emphasis. Church organisation must also receive attention, for its history from St. Augustine's mission to the fully-established parochial system of the Middle Ages is a very long and complicated one. Monasteries loom large in much of the pre-Conquest period, especially for the influence they had on what survives of pre-Conquest art and architecture. Peterborough's scattered daughter-houses form just one small part of the story. In County Durham, it has been argued persuasively that almost all surviving pre-Conquest fabric and sculpture was monastic in origin, with a considerable number of monastic sites arranged in loose clusters. The word 'monastery' is used a little vaguely in relation to the early English Church. Monasteries existed in the absence of a modern parochial system; they were mission centres which were bound to remain prominent and influential long after a network of local churches had appeared.

Archaeology has added much to our knowledge of pre-Conquest churches in recent decades, even in cases where documents and standing fabric have been eloquent. Sometimes, standing fabric which was considered of much later date has been identified as pre-Conquest. The church at Rivenhall in Essex, now seen to be substantially pre-Conquest, was previously thought to be 19C. Archaeology has often revealed a succession of churches, beginning with a small pre-Conquest plan, which would typically be enlarged and rebuilt down to the 15C. Occasionally, there would be contraction—aisles would be demolished and arcades filled in—but medieval expansion was more usual.

Various pre-Conquest features are distinctive. They include 'long-and-short work', or quoins which were laid alternately vertical and horizontal; pilaster strips or lesenes; tall, narrow naves, and doorways of like proportions; central towers with re-entrant angles (that is, towers which are wider than their naves, chancels and transepts); very small windows, often with a single stone at the head; lateral chambers or *porticus*, sometimes placed side by side as if to form an aisle, but prevented from being one by transverse walls; doorways placed high up in towers, presumably affording access to W galleries; and triangular-headed windows and doorways. Some features are found equally in pre-Conquest and Norman churches, such as the reuse of Roman materials, the use of small, paired belfry windows, and E apses. In the case of apses, however, some very early pre-Conquest churches do have the distinctive feature of an arcade to separate the E end from the nave (examples are Reculver, Brixworth and St. Paul-in-the-Bail, Lincoln). A few pre-Conquest features seem very strange to us today. One is the turriform nave, whereby a tower's lowest stage formed a nave. This is strange because the proportions of such a church are very different from those which we consider normal. W galleries in churches seem normal enough, but pre-Conquest ones clearly emerged from towers and not at all in the manner familiar from the 18C and early 19C. Divisions in pre-Conquest churches seem odd, too: upper storeys apparently occurred quite frequently, and a ground-plan may be divided into distinct rooms as at St. Peter's, Barton-on-Humber, Lincolnshire. The influences which dictated these arrangements are not nearly so obvious as they are for the High Middle Ages; they were probably much more varied. If we knew as much about pre-Conquest Church life as we do, say, of the 15C, I suspect that the influence of the Greek East would be much more prominent than we have allowed.

The Norman Conquest

The Norman Conquest of 1066 and later was not an absolute divide in architecture or in Church life. Some 'Norman' churches had been built in England before the Conquest (such as the Westminster Abbey built by King Edward the Confessor), and some bishops in King Edward's reign were Normans. Conversely, some churches built after 1066 followed pre-Norman conventions—we label them 'Saxo-Norman'—and a few Englishmen remained as leaders of the Church amidst many newcomers. Some features shared by pre-Conquest and Norman churches were mentioned above. Nevertheless, there was a significant change in the scale of church building. Existing cathedrals and churches were rebuilt to dimensions which greatly exceeded those of their predecessors. Norman design has a regularity and a heaviness which we would not connect with earlier times. *'Ponderosum opus'* was the label given in the Middle Ages to the Norman Barnwell Priory Church in Cambridgeshire: heavy, ponderous work.

Norman churches often feature endless courses of small, squared ashlar, such as we see at St. Andrew's, Weaverthorpe, in Yorkshire. St. Andrew's is a most attractive example of the plainest Norman design, featuring little more than some small single-light windows, which are deeply-splayed within. Usually, there would be flat buttresses, possibly a stringcourse, a decorative corbel table just below the roof, shafting and mouldings round windows and doorways, and perhaps figurative carving in the capitals of the main doorway and in the tympanum above it. Within a Norman church, the piers of arcades were round and squat in the earliest buildings, supporting square abaci and round unmoulded arches. The abaci later became octagonal and eventually round; the piers became less heavy; capitals changed from the 'cushion' type to scallops and then to waterleaf; and, gradually in the 12C, zigzag and other mouldings appeared over arches, doorways and windows, becoming quite lavish by c 1175. A special type of Norman church was the 'round church', in which a round nave or rotunda derived from the Holy Sepulchre in Jerusalem. This type was prompted as much by pilgrimage to the Holy Land as by the Crusaders.

The Foundation of Churches

The Norman period of the 11C and 12C is distinguished also by the number of new church foundations. Although we do not know when most ancient churches were first built, documents and archaeology tell us of enough to allow us to gauge the whole picture. More ancient churches—and this is particularly clear in towns—were founded in the 11C and 12C than at any other period. It may be said that the great majority of English churches were founded either in those centuries, or in the 19C and 20C. In towns, it was a combination of merchant wealth and a keenness to build churches which explains the great wave of Norman foundations. The number of monasteries founded in Norman England in contrast to other periods speaks very clearly of the vast scale of giving to churches at that time. The Church has been the recipient of money and land in every century, but it must not be forgotten that the scale of giving has fluctuated very markedly from one age to another. In England, the Norman period and the 19C have been the two great periods of giving.

The Parochial System

The practice of each church building serving a defined area called a parish has been part of the English scene for so many centuries that it is difficult to imagine earlier arrangements. Those arrangements centred on 'minster churches', which served wide areas, far larger than normal parishes. The word 'minster' comes from the Latin *monasterium*, which also gives us 'monastery'; but minsters were not often the same as monasteries. Minsters were gradually complemented by a spread of local churches, whose means of financial support were to cement the parochial system as we know it. Ancient parishes were more or less fixed permanently in the 12C, in the Norman period and just after. At the time of Domesday Book (1086), the older arrangements were still apparent; by 1200, the 'modern' system had effectively been reached. The parish of that time was not merely a geographical area, within which one priest had the 'cure of souls'. It was instead a grouping of legal and financial rights—the right to collect tithe, the right to bury (and to collect fees from burials) and the right to baptise. Churches had to be supported from their own income, and so it was important that their exclusive rights within their parishes were safeguarded. The result was that from c 1200 the parochial system was largely set fast. It became exceedingly difficult to create a new parish, for there were enough already, and all of them defended their rights. Even a chapel of ease which had long existed could not become a parish church without great difficulty. The great church of Holy Trinity at Kingston-upon-Hull, for example, was originally a chapel of ease to All Saints' at Hessle, further up the River Humber; Hessle was the more ancient place, and Hull was a medieval 'new town'. Consequently, Holy Trinity Church had no burial ground for many generations; burials took place at Hessle. Not until 1661 was Holy Trinity Church constituted a full parish church, by which time Hull was a major and prosperous port and was many times larger than Hessle. Market Harborough's main church lacked a burial ground for the same reason. In later centuries (from the 17C to the 19C), the division of an ancient parish was usually effected by Act of Parliament, because by then a parish had *civil* purposes as well as ecclesiastical ones. It was only in the 19C that the Church was enabled to create new parishes more easily, allowing the division of those inherited from the Middle Ages.

The Ownership of Churches

Although many major churches were founded and endowed by kings and given to bishops, the great majority of ancient churches were founded by layfolk for their own use. They were not given to bishops or to a diocese or any other ecclesiastical authority; they were private properties or 'proprietory churches'. Such churches could be bought and sold like a house or a farm, and it was possible for one to be owned by two or more people (or by two or more institutions). Divisions of ownership led to the use of technical terms such as 'mediety', 'moiety' and 'portioner', which lingered for centuries in some places. The proprietory church was normal in late pre-Conquest and Norman times, but was gradually brought within the Church's system of government. As the Middle Ages proceeded, the idea of the absolute lay ownership of a church faded, to be replaced by the lesser notion that an individual had the 'advowson', the right to present a priest. Ownership by institutions—by which is chiefly meant monasteries—was also modified so that resident priests had defined rights to complement those of the institutions.

The rights over a church largely concerned the entitlement to its income, which derived from tithes, surplice fees and its real estate (or 'glebe'). The issue at stake was always the division of that income between the owner and the resident priest. Certain parts of the income were always reserved to the priest, but the Church eventually legislated to ensure that parish priests received a fixed and adequate share. Bishops were said to 'ordain a vicarage' when they stipulated such fixed shares. The priest on the spot became a 'vicar', or substitute for the non-resident 'rector'. The owner, who came to be called the 'patron', still had some property rights (which depended on the local historical circumstances), but they were not exclusive as they had once been, and moreover he had certain duties, of which the upkeep of the chancel was the most common.

The proprietory church and the existence of innumerable small parishes (especially in towns) both resulted from lay initiatives. They produced a system which bishops had not planned and which was only gradually assimilated into Church government. A system planned by the Church itself would have been very different.

The position of the medieval clergy as literate men in a largely illiterate world led to their being recruited by kings for the purposes of civil government. Bishoprics were often filled by the equivalents of today's cabinet ministers. Numerous Bishops of Winchester, for example, held the office of Lord Chancellor, which was the nearest equivalent of the modern position of Prime Minister. Lesser officials received Church offices, too, to give them an ecclesiastical income to support their civil duties. Popes also had an administration to pay for, as large as any king's and of much longer standing; and so its officials were supported from the revenues of cathedrals and parishes throughout Europe. 'Papal provisions', or the appointment of (non-resident) papal officials to Church positions, were very numerous in the Middle Ages.

The Gothic Styles

From the late 12C until the 16C the Gothic styles of architecture were in use; and Gothic design continued, alongside Classical buildings, into the 18C in some places, by which time the Gothic Revival got under way, to ensure the use of Gothic styles into the 20C. So on any reckoning, Gothic forms are central to English church architecture; a Gothic church is the normal English idea of a church. By Gothic we mean one of the various styles which succeeded the Norman and preceded the revived Classicism of the 16C and later. In the early 19C, the architect Thomas Rickman labelled those styles 'Early English', 'Decorated' and 'Perpendicular', and English architectural writers have kept to those labels ever since. They are precise enough for most purposes, but it must always be remembered that architectural style is constantly changing, and that there are no firm boundaries by date. Between the heydays of any two styles there will always be a transitional style, or a series of them. 'Transitional' is in fact a formal label applied to late 12C buildings, which begin to show the supersession of Norman design by the Early English style. The crucial change was the arrival of the pointed arch in the last quarter of the 12C to replace the round arch of the Normans. All Gothic styles use the pointed arch, whether shallow or steep.

The Early English style is very roughly the style of the 13C. It is sometimes called the 'lancet style', because its chief characteristic is the tall, narrow, pointed window we call a lancet. Usually they are single-light, but at the E end of a parish church there may be a group of three (which are said to be 'graduated' if the middle one is taller); and very occasionally there will be more. The chancels of Eccleshall in Staffordshire and Haltwhistle in Northumberland are good examples of a simple lancet style. In the middle of the 13C, plate tracery came into use. Typically, two lancets would be placed side by side, with a quatrefoil added above them in the centre. All these elements would pierce the full thickness of the wall, rather than being divided by relatively thin mullions and transoms as in later centuries. Tracery formed by such internal divisions, or bar tracery, superseded plate tracery in the later 13C. By c 1300 three forms had developed. One was Geometrical tracery, in which foiled circles and triangles predominate. Elaboration quickly developed, as one may see in the windows of Howden Minster in Yorkshire. Another form was Y-tracery, in which a mullion divides into a Y-shape at the head of a two-light window. Thirdly, there is intersecting tracery, which is really Y-tracery repeated and overlapped so that a series of straight intersections are formed in the head.

Within an Early English church, it is normal to find round piers with round capitals and round abaci. The capitals developed out of the late Norman forms into what is called 'stiff-leaf' design. Arches, which had often acquired a shallow chamfer as well as a pointed shape in the late 12C, were normally given two full chamfers in the 13C, and sometimes they became very steeply pointed. For doorways, sedilia and blind arcading, the trefoil-headed arch was frequently used. Purbeck marble, which had appeared in some 12C Norman churches (e.g. Iffley, Oxfordshire), became very widely used in the 13C. The E parts of Beverley Minster in Yorkshire exemplify its lavish use. Finally, mention must be made of dogtooth moulding on nave arches, chancel arches and windows. Dogtooth is as characteristic of the 13C as zigzag is of the 12C and ballflower of the 14C. West Walton Church in Norfolk is a foremost example of the Early English style in all its elements.

In the 14C, the ogee curve appears, and this is the most characteristic element of the Decorated style. It is a double-curve, one part of which is convex and the other concave. Above the apex of an ogee arch, over doorways, belfry windows, etc., there will often be a crocketed upright. The ogee curve is the crucial element in 'flowing' or curvilinear tracery, in which all manner of patterns are created. A more regular pattern is found in Reticulated or net-like tracery, whereby cusped circles are pulled into ogee shapes on two sides to create the semblance of a net.

The Decorated period is known for some elaborate chancels, in which the regular features of sedilia, piscina and doorways are joined by an Easter sepulchre and a benefactor's tomb. A full set of these features in a lavish ogee style is found at Hawton in Nottinghamshire, Patrington in Yorkshire and Heckington in Lincolnshire. 14C naves will generally have octagonal piers and octagonal moulded capitals, with double-chamfered arches. Adornment might come in the form of ballflower moulding.

The Perpendicular style is the normal style of the later 14C and the 15C. Its name comes from the upright panel tracery which windows of that period reveal. Perpendicular windows were the largest of all medieval windows, regularly comprising several lights at the E end of a parish church or in other principal positions, and reaching as many as 15 lights in exceptional cases such as the W window of St. George's Chapel, Windsor. With the use of buttresses, it became possible to create walls of glass, as in King's College Chapel at

Cambridge or at Holy Trinity Church, Hull. The large medieval windows always have one or more transoms (which are sometimes battlemented) to divide the lights horizontally. The lights in Perpendicular windows are sometimes almost round-headed rather than pointed; and arches themselves are typically four-centred or shallow-pointed. The main windows of a church were often supplemented in the 15C by a substantial clerestory above the nave arcades (and very occasionally in the chancel too). Such a clerestory was typically part of a 15C remodelling of an earlier church, which would also include the replacement of some windows (especially the main E window), the rebuilding or heightening of the tower, and the addition of chancel chapels. The top of the tower would be given crocketed pinnacles, and they would appear also above buttresses to the nave and chancel.

Perpendicular arcades are formed most usually of piers of clustered shafts, perhaps with additional mouldings in the angles, and with capitals which are small and of limited detail. Sometimes there are no capitals at all, or they are just decorative bands (as in All Saints', Rotherham, Yorkshire). Octagonal piers of 14C type continued in use in the 15C in many places, and occasionally they will have concave faces (as at Northleach, Gloucestershire). 15C arcades are frequently very tall.

Spires

Medieval spires range from the 13C to the 16C. Norman churches had usually been given flat-topped towers or low, pyramidal caps. The earliest spires were of the broach type, whereby the transition from tower to spire—from a square to an octagon—is achieved by placing half-pyramids at the four corners, perhaps with gabled lucarnes in between. Later, it became normal for spires to be recessed behind ornamented parapets. Sometimes the two types are mixed; and in any case recessed spires began in the 13C, not so very long after the broach type. Pinnacles became more elaborate and more numerous as the Middle Ages advanced, and they are sometimes connected with the spire by flying buttresses.

Medieval Fittings

Most surviving medieval fittings tend to be 15C or 16C. Very few go back to the pre-Conquest and Norman periods. Fonts are exceptional. They were very often preserved when the church for which they were made was replaced in the later Middle Ages. Most fonts are of stone, but some attractive early ones are of lead. Norman fonts are particularly numerous, and they may display carvings which are as valuable as tympana and capitals. 15C fonts are also frequent, but decoration is generally limited to quatrefoils. 15C covers are often more notable, amounting to intricate, spire-like works in the best East Anglian examples such as that at Ufford, Suffolk. A 'Seven Sacrament' font will bear carvings to represent the Sacraments recognised throughout the medieval Church. Fonts are often placed near the main door of a church, or at least at the W end, to symbolise the entry into the Christian family at baptism. The octagonal shape which they frequently possess is also symbolic—of regeneration—for the Resurrection was looked upon as having occurred on the 'eighth day'.

Most medieval woodwork tends to be 15C and 16C. Screens in particular date from the late Middle Ages because churches were more likely to be divided up by that period. It was the great age of the guild chapel and the chantry chapel, which were often divided by screens from the rest of the church. The principal screen would be the chancel screen, which could extend across the aisles where they continued alongside the chancel. The chancel screen was usually the Rood screen, for above the loft would be placed the Rood—a carving of the Crucifixion, flanked by the Virgin Mary and St. John and sometimes by further figures. The Rood loft would be reached by stairs at one end of the screen; the entrances to such stairways remain in many places where Rood and screen have long gone. Beneath the loft, chancel screens will usually comprise an enclosed base and openwork tracery above, arranged as in windows. The base was sometimes painted, typically with portraits of saints. They have rarely survived in great clarity, but enough generally remains to recognise St. Catherine from her wheel, St. Edmund from his crown and arrows, etc. All these saints were painted according to late medieval fashions and practice. Thus St. Edmund will look like a 15C king, not a 9C one, and St. Martin will be vested like a 15C bishop, not a humble 4C pastor; both are far from their historical realities. So numerous are these later medieval depictions, and so regularly were they copied in the 19C, that we take them as 'correct'. It must therefore be remembered that they are quite anachronistic. St. Martin would not have worn a mitre, St. Gregory would not have had a triple tiara, etc. Their times were worlds away from what the 15C knew.

Guilds were very numerous and important in late medieval times. They are usually thought of as *trade* guilds, but many of them were unconnected with trades. They offered their members spiritual benefits, especially the saying of Masses after their deaths. The belief in Purgatory, in which forgiveness is sought after death for unforgiven venial sins and temporal punishment is undergone until complete expiation is achieved, excited in the late Middle Ages a conspicuous level of allusion to death and to the need for expiatory prayer. Guilds in late medieval town churches often acquired their own chapels, which were sometimes new additions and sometimes adapted parts of the existing fabric. Rich individuals might found and endow a chantry, and this too might have its own chapel. The minimum endowment would be for a priest to say Mass regularly, especially on the 'obit' or anniversary of a person's death. A chantry would do for the individual what a guild would achieve collectively. The grandest chantry chapels were elaborate stone enclosures, comprising a tomb, an altar and an intricate vaulted canopy. Winchester Cathedral has an exceptional number of these.

Further categories of medieval woodwork which are also predominantly 15C and 16C are pulpits and seating. Pulpits survive from the 14C; but they were often introduced into a church for the first time in the late Middle Ages. Their panels may be painted in the manner of screen bases, or they may have niches for statues. Devon is the county for colourful pulpits, as it is for colourful screens. Seating for layfolk is chiefly of interest for the carved finials of benches (such as poppyheads), and the straight-topped, carved bench-ends which are so much a feature of West Country churches. The Instruments of the Passion are the favourite subjects of carvings on bench-ends. It should be noted that they very often date from the 16C, and sometimes from after the Reformation. Seating for the clergy may include medieval stalls, and stalls may incorporate misericords or small tip-up seats which often bear carvings. They tend to represent secular subjects, and, as with bench-ends, sometimes involve satire against abbots and bishops. Misericords were provided to relieve clergy who would otherwise have to stand through long choir offices.

Rarer items of woodwork which might be found in a chancel are sedilia, pyx-canopies, and aumbries or small cupboards. Sedilia are nearly always of stone and form part of a chancel's S wall, but very rarely they are wooden and detached. A fine four-seat example exists in Beverley Minster. Medieval pyx-canopies (to hold the Reserved Sacrament) are also very rare. Only one is in use today—at Dennington, Suffolk. The grandest is found at Milton Abbey in Dorset, a four-stage example with tracery and a spire which is now fixed to the chancel's N wall. Aumbries were used to store precious items and were normally placed on the N side of a chancel.

It should be noted that fittings which are normally wooden may sometimes be of stone. There are a few stone chancel screens (examples are Compton Bassett (Wiltshire) and Great Bardfield (Essex)), and pulpits are sometimes made of stone (including a canopied 15C case at Arundel in Sussex, and also some colourful Devon examples, as in St. Saviour's, Dartmouth). Early seating is also normally of stone, in the form of a continuous sill along the outer walls and occasionally around pier bases.

Medieval ironwork is usually a matter of decorative ironwork on door leaves. Hadstock in Essex has the only pre-Conquest example, but Norman cases are more numerous and later medieval work is fairly frequent. The earliest work comprised C-shaped hinges. Subsequently, the curls split and gradually became barbed straps and fleur-de-lis. The hinges themselves became scroll-shaped rather than C-shaped. Elaboration on later doors is marked. A few churches have medieval wrought-iron screens or grilles; there is a fine example at Arundel in Sussex. Also of wrought-iron are closing-rings on doors, and the occasional sanctuary ring. They typically show an animal head holding the ring in its mouth. Sanctuary in medieval churches did not give permanent freedom from arrest and punishment; it was a prelude to exile overseas as an *alternative* to trial and punishment in England.

The familiar eagle lecterns began in the 14C in wood, but many from the 15C onwards are of brass.

Wall paintings often formed an important feature of medieval interiors, sometimes covering the entire wall surfaces in one or more series. Most of them have a predominantly orange-red colour, but blues and greens may appear too. The Infancy and Passion of Christ, the life of the Virgin, and the lives (but particularly the martyrdoms) of saints formed the principal subjects. The saints appear in the dress and attributes of the time they were painted (as discussed under screens, above). Over the chancel arch there would normally appear the Last Judgement or 'doom painting', in which the Risen Christ presides over the judgement on the last day or 'doomsday'. To his left will be the 'goats'—the damned—and to his right (or place of honour) the 'sheep', or the blessed, all as in Chapter 25 of St. Matthew's Gospel. St. Michael will be weighing souls, and the Virgin Mary will be pleading for mercy on their behalf. The mouth of Hell and the New Jerusalem will receive those who have been judged, and all around will be the general resurrection, heralded by angels with trumpets. The power of that scene in the restricted world of a medieval village, where death was never far away, needs no emphasis. The 'doom' at Wenhaston in Suffolk is perhaps the most celebrated example. Another subject which tended to have a fixed place in a church was that of St. Christopher carrying the Christ Child, which was usually found on the wall opposite the south door. Most of the series or 'cycles' depicted in medieval wall paintings are ubiquitous, but some are rare. Battle in Sussex, for example, has an unusual series about St. Margaret of Antioch. Here we must remember that artists used both historical and legendary lives of the saints, and the apocryphal New Testament as well as canonical Scripture. The whole body of writings which was widely known in the Middle Ages must be familiar to the interpreter of medieval art.

Medieval stained glass is present in few parish churches in more than fragmentary form. Only a handful of churches in a county, on average, will have complete windows or a series of them. Even where there are such windows—most notably, in various York churches—the glass has often become jumbled through incorrect replacement in the past, or it is obscure for want of cleaning and restoration. Nevertheless, medieval stained glass is an important subject, for it was certainly central to the appearance which a late medieval church was intended to have. It performed the same didactic role as mural painting, but it also had a memorial and expiatory function too. A window's inscription will seek mercy for the soul of a donor, who will appear as a kneeling figure in the lower part of a light. Sometimes a window derived from collective giving. The delightful series of windows at St. Neot in Cornwall resulted from donations by different groups in that village. Depictions of Biblical scenes and of saints are most usual, with the larger schemes often presenting New Testament subjects alongside or opposite their Old Testament prefigurations. Some windows were purely decorative, with patterns of greyish glass known as *grisaille*. Tabernacle or canopy work became more prominent as the Middle Ages proceeded. In the very late medieval period, Flemish artists took the lead in stained glass design, most notably at King's College Chapel, Cambridge.

Medieval Monuments

Monuments are found in and around churches from the 7C to the present, but few survive from before the later Middle Ages. Pre-Conquest standing crosses are known to be memorials in many cases, and there is the very occasional named monument such as that to Herebericht the priest at Monkwearmouth in County Durham. Almost all early monuments, however, are anonymous. They comprise slabs with a raised cross or with incised decoration. Often they have been referred to in guides—wrongly—as 'coffin-lids'. Gradually, figures began to appear on slabs. The earliest are of abbots and bishops; most cathedrals have an example. The next stage, reached in the 13C, was to have the effigy raised on a tomb-chest, whose sides would be decorated with blank tracery, heraldry and small figures. These figures were usually 'weepers' or mourners. Occasionally there will be a 'bedesman', a figure praying for the deceased's soul. Medieval monuments were highly coloured, but little colour remains on most of them today. Even if effigies are never portraits, they are obviously valuable sources for medieval armour and civilian dress. The old story that a knight's crossed legs indicate a Crusader, incidentally, is fiction; it was merely a fashion of c 1300. Inscriptions are not widespread until the late Middle Ages, a fact which contributes to the anonymity of many monuments.

From the 13C another form of memorial existed: brasses. England is exceptional in Europe for the number of its brasses. They occur more in the E counties than elsewhere, nearer the Continental source of the latten from which they were made. Brasses are sometimes reused or engraved on the reverse; they are then known as 'palimpsests'. A brass will often be quite small and was clearly an inexpensive memorial in contrast to a stone tomb-chest with effigy.

In the late Middle Ages both stone and brass memorials sometimes show a skeleton or a decaying corpse. Such reminders of death accorded with the pessimistic mood of the late Middle Ages. A call to repentance in view of ever-imminent death was the intention of such memorials. Inscriptions often underlined the point.

Here and there a heart burial will be seen in the form of a small plaque, with a heart clasped by two hands.

The Reformation

The Reformation in the 16C divided the Church in western Europe permanently for the first time. It divided not only the Church in one country from that in another, but also produced in due course different Churches or *denominations* within each country. The Reformation in England was not eventually so drastic as that which occurred, say, in Switzerland or the Netherlands. King Henry VIII broke with the Pope but he did not repudiate the doctrines in which the Pope believed. So long as Henry lived, the Latin Mass continued, bishops remained as before, and even the chantry chapels survived. The king was responsible, however, for major acts of destruction in carrying out the Dissolution of the Monasteries and in stripping cathedrals and other churches of their shrines.

If we take together the century and a half after King Henry VIII's initial break with the Papacy, the continuities in the English Church are as obvious as the discontinuities. Above all, the Church retained its bishops, whereas in many reformed Churches elsewhere, the episcopate was abolished. With the bishops there survived in England the full panoply of medieval Church government, with the exception, of course, that appeals from Church courts no longer went to Rome. Nevertheless, the Reformation brought with it no little destruction to church fabric. Under King Henry VIII all the monasteries in England were dissolved; their lands and possessions were confiscated and passed permanently into lay ownership (which is why some country houses have names such as Woburn *Abbey* and Nostell *Priory*). In addition, the rich and magnificent shrines which existed in the country's major churches were plundered and dismantled. Pilgrims could no longer see the bejewelled and gilded monuments which stood over such tombs as those of St. Thomas

Becket in Canterbury Cathedral or of St. Edmund at Bury St. Edmund's. In the reign of King Edward VI (1547–53), destruction went much further. All the chantries and colleges were dissolved. The fabric of many chantry chapels survived, but their entire reason for existence had gone. No longer were prayers and Masses said for the souls of the deceased. The Latin Mass itself was superseded by the English service in Archbishop Cranmer's new Prayer Book of 1549. Plate, vestments and 'images' of all sorts—especially Rood groups on screens—were destroyed, sold, melted down or otherwise reused. By and large, 16C destruction ended when King Edward VI died. The Elizabethan Church more or less kept what it had inherited. The lurch towards Continental Protestantism around 1550 was followed by a more stable period under Queen Elizabeth I, in which the mainstream Church saw itself as following a middle way between Puritans on the one hand and Catholics on the other.

Mention of Puritans introduces the struggles of the 17C, which were ultimately just as destructive as those of the mid-16C. The Puritans were those who tried, from the late 16C, to push the Church of England even farther away from the medieval Church towards the more extreme Continental models of the Reformation. Ultimately they failed, but during the 1640s and 1650s—when the Civil War occurred and when Oliver Cromwell was in power—they did achieve ascendancy in England. It was during these years that some particularly appalling destruction occurred. Stained glass and sculptures especially suffered. It was during the Civil War too that the one break in the episcopate occurred. The office of bishop was abolished and all the property of the country's bishoprics was forfeit to the state. The Anglican Church's privileged position was replaced by a Presbyterian ascendancy. Parish churches usually lost their Anglican incumbent; almost all lists of Rectors and Vicars which one may see displayed in churches will mention 'Commonwealth intruders'. In 1660, upon the Restoration of King Charles II, these Cromwellian changes were reversed. Bishops once again presided over the Church of England, which resumed its status as the Established Church. Property which had been confiscated under Cromwell was restored. In 1662, a new Act of Uniformity reaffirmed the beliefs and liturgy of the Anglican Church, automatically removing the 'Puritans' and like-minded men from the parish churches of the land. Nonconformity was thus distinguished from the New Anglican order and gradually crystallised into a number of formal denominations. Initially, these groups were persecuted, but in 1672 a measure of relief was allowed, and in 1689, after the 'Glorious Revolution', toleration of worship was generally permitted to Protestant Nonconformists, subject to their registering their chapels and meeting houses. Right down to the 19C, however, they were still excluded from public offices and from the ancient universities. None of this toleration in the late 17C was extended to those who maintained an allegiance to the Pope. It is true that judicial executions or martyrdoms ceased in 1681, but imprisonment remained normal until the late 18C, when Catholic Relief Acts gave Catholics the same rights which Protestant Nonconformists had enjoyed for a century.

Nonconformity

Nonconformity or Dissent—the 'Free Churches' of today—is generally considered to divide into two strands: the denominations surviving from the 17C ('Old Dissent') and those arising from the
evangelical awakening of the 18C ('New Dissent'). There were also
the Unitarians, whose emergence in the later 18C was a dynamic
element in the ranks of Old Dissent. The Unitarians became particularly important in Birmingham, where their members in the
Victorian age included many influential figures, above all Joseph
Chamberlain. Old Dissent proper comprised the Religious Society of
Friends (the Quakers), Independents (later Congregationalists), Baptists, and Presbyterians. The last of these declined in 18C England,
when many Presbyterians became Unitarians or Independents. The
Baptists were divided into Particular and General streams down to
1891. Both streams were chiefly found in southern England. The
Friends have always been a small but influential group, seen as one
of the more subversive parts of Nonconformity in the 17C, but
appearing to be the least evangelistic sect by 1800. The Independents shared with the Baptists a belief in autonomous churches (or
congregational government), but disagreed with them over baptism.
Baptists practise believer's or adult baptism, as opposed to infant
baptism. In theology the Independents were Calvinist, a position
they shared with the Presbyterians and Particular Baptists.

The evangelical awakening of the 18C led to the formation of the
various Methodist Churches by John Wesley (1703–91) and others in
the century or so after 1738. Wesley launched his life's work from
within the Church of England and he viewed his ministry as comple-
mentary to that of the Established Church. He wished to concentrate
on those areas where the Anglican presence was weak. Subsequent
to his death, the Methodists divided into a number of separate
groups. The mainstream Wesleyan Methodists remained the largest
group. Second to them were the Primitive Methodists, who
pioneered 'camp meetings' in the early 19C. Smaller Methodist
groups were the New Connexion, the Independent Methodists and
the Bible Christians. Each of these denominations, or 'connexions' as
they called themselves, consisted of societies or churches which were
grouped into circuits. The circuits were in turn grouped into
districts—roughly equivalent to dioceses—and were ultimately gov-
erned by an annual conference. Ministers were stationed in a circuit
for three or four years, and were thus expected to serve (or 'travel in')
a number of circuits during their active ministry. The Methodists
therefore put an emphasis on central government, quite unlike the
organisations of Baptists and Independents. In theology, they have
always been Arminian (like Anglicans and Catholics) and not
Calvinist.

The maximum division between Methodists was reached in 1849.
The groups began to reunite in 1857, when some of the smaller
groups joined to form the United Methodist Free Churches. The new
denomination merged in turn in 1907 with the Bible Christians and
the New Connexion to create the United Methodist Church. Finally,
in 1932 the Wesleyans, the Primitive Methodists and the United
Methodists came together in full Methodist reunion.

16C and 17C Churches

Very little church building took place in the century or so after the
Reformation. There was some revival in the second quarter of the
17C, but not until the Restoration did church building occur on any
significant scale. The style used until the mid-17C was almost always
a late form of Perpendicular. Windows would usually be square-
headed and they would have arched and uncusped lights. It was a
matter of medieval forms without much of the detail which makes a
genuinely medieval church interesting. Inside a late 16C or early 17C
church, the story is normally as much Classical as Gothic. Such new
fittings as there had been since c 1540 would display some Classical
features. Early 17C pulpits form the most frequent category, following a canon or order to install pulpits in all churches. They invariably
feature blank arches. Communion tables replaced medieval stone
altars following the Reformation, and so they are frequently Elizabethan, with distinctive bulbous legs. Screens of the period are
largely parclose screens, built to surround a private pew. Such
pews—which could be substantial structures—were in a sense the
successors of the old chantry chapels. Many communion rails remain
from the 16C and 17C, for they were inserted to protect the altar
either where screens had gone or where propriety considered the
post-Reformation arrangement inadequate. In the N of England, a
number of churches were given woodwork which is associated with
Bishop Cosin of Durham. It was fitted from the 1620s until the later
17C. Brancepeth and Haughton-le-Skerne in County Durham and St.
John's in the centre of Leeds are the best examples of the style. Cosin
(1595–1672) was a younger contemporary of Archbishop Laud (Archbishop of Canterbury (1633–45) and previously Bishop of London),
who attempted to embellish churches in the decade before the Civil
War. He sought, in common with other influential Churchmen, an
Anglican ideal in opposition to both Catholics and Puritans, but at
that time the Puritans were strong, and Laud became their enemy,
suffering execution in 1645. The 17C Anglican divines were to
become important again in the 19C, when their example was
attractive to the proponents of the Oxford Movement.

Stained glass was by no means absent in the 17C, but it was
substantially heraldic. This did not offend the Puritan zeal against
'images', which reached such a destructive peak in the 1640s.

Post-Reformation monuments form an immense subject, involving
foremost works of sculpture. The contribution of the Elizabethan and
Stuart periods was to introduce the new Classical style and to
develop a number of different forms of monument. Recumbent
effigies on tomb-chests now mingled with reclining or semi-reclining
effigies. The grandest monuments had large arched canopies on
Classical columns, with long inscription plates and much heraldry.
More modest and thus frequent types were of two kneeling figures
facing one another, often across a prayer-desk, or of figures kneeling
in a line, the standing figure in a niche, and the frontal bust or half-
figure framed by Classical columns and a pediment. Shakespeare's
monument at Stratford-on-Avon is the best-known example of this
last type. It is also typical of its time in being the work of a Flemish
sculptor, for in the late 16C and early 17C Flemish designers
became markedly prominent in monumental sculpture, and many
of them formed the 'Southwark School' (see the introduction to

London South of the Thames). Nicholas Stone was the one notable English exception to the Flemish rule.

Amidst the Perpendicular Survival of the early 17C, there was one undisputed Classicist: Inigo Jones. His Queen's Chapel in Marlborough Gate, London (built 1623–27) was the first completely Classical church in England, totally different from its contemporaries. Jones also designed St. Paul's, Covent Garden (1631–38). Not until Wren's time in the later 17C were there further Classical churches, and even then they had Gothic contemporaries (most notably in Oxford).

The Great Fire of London of 1666 provided the opportunity for Sir Christopher Wren to design a new St. Paul's Cathedral and no fewer than 51 parish churches. A summary of their features is found in the introduction to The City of London. A few churches with affinities to Wren's were built outside London, such as All Saints', Northampton. These late 17C Classical buildings are of particular note for their fine woodwork and for their plans. It is a commonplace that Wren's churches were 'fitted for auditories', meaning that the pulpit was as much a focus as the altar, and that the longitudinal plan of the Middle Ages was superseded. It would be wrong, however, to say that the altar was regarded as a minor fitting. Chancels may have been shallow—mere alcoves—or absent altogether, but almost always in the late 17C (and the 18C) a large and ornate reredos would be placed behind the altar, which would probably be all the more prominent for the absence of a deep chancel and a chancel screen.

By the late 17C the 'box-pew' was the normal new seating of a church: high, enclosed pews, set amidst panelled column bases, wainscoted walls, doorcases, pulpit and reredos, would create a sea of dark woodwork at ground level. Above would be round-headed windows with plain glass and cobweb ironwork, and walls with small memorial plaques. The ceiling might be embellished with plasterwork, and a little colour would be given by the prominent royal arms. In the larger cities (London, Norwich, Bristol) civic grandeur and merchant wealth would be represented by upright sword-rests and ornamented mayoral pews or seats. All this presented a very different scene from a pre-Reformation church, but it was still a seemly and sumptuous setting for worship.

The 18C

The 18C has usually been portrayed as a somnolent backwater in Church history, a static phase in the building and upkeep of churches, and in the wider life of the Church. Anglican churches have been considered neglected, 'Old Dissent' has been seen as declining and lacking fire, and Catholics viewed as dwindling in numbers. As with so many traditional accounts, all this is substantially inaccurate. Georgian churches were portrayed as neglected and inadequate partly because the Victorians wished to emphasise and justify their new ideas in architecture and in worship. It was part of their polemic to paint their predecessors as neglectful. They wished to stress that because their arrangements were 'proper', 'Christian' and worthy, those of previous generations were inadequate and unworthy. It is true that the scale of new church building in the 18C was only a fraction of the 19C's achievement, but England's 18C population rose very little, whereas in the 19C there was a colossal increase. In fact, new Anglican churches were built in all the major towns, and there were innumerable new non-Anglican buildings. 'Old Dissent' was less thrusting than it had been in the 17C, but it was certainly alive and building as much as the Church of England. 'New Dissent', by which is chiefly meant the Methodists, was immensely energetic and successful. These 18C churches and chapels were built in or near the centres of what were then much smaller towns; their surroundings have become depopulated over the last century and thus so many of these buildings have been demolished. Their absence today should not lead us to picture Georgian neglect of church building.

Nobody who has studied 18C vestry minutes and churchwardens' accounts from different parts of the country could conclude that neglect of church fabric was normal. Repairs and 'beautifications' were as numerous as at any other period. Sometimes, as at Beverley, buildings were saved from collapse. In most cases, work was relatively minor. Apart from the reinstatement of ancient fabric, refittings were common. The stereotype of an 18C interior is a familiar one: box-pews, a three-decker pulpit standing in the centre, benches for the poor also in the centre, a reredos at the E end with inscribed panels of the Creed, the Lord's Prayer and the Commandments, the royal arms prominently displayed, galleries to N and S for worshippers and at the W end for the organ and singers, and sometimes upper W galleries for the 'charity children'. Pulpits were not always in the centre, but often they were moved there to provide more space for pews at the sides. They were almost always very tall ('six feet above contradiction') so that the preacher could address the congregation in the galleries as well as those in the nave. Smaller churches in the country would often lack the N and S galleries but perhaps they would have an elaborate box-pew, reserved for the local landowner, complete with fireplace and wig-pegs. Examples of interiors of smaller 18C churches are Tong near Bradford and King's Norton in Leicestershire. The grander interiors were urban ones and trace their descent from Wren's designs for St. Andrew's, Holborn and St. James's, Piccadilly. Pews in all these churches were bought and sold as private possessions. This was regarded as normal, even if it was strictly contrary to Church law.

Of the buildings themselves, virtually all the early 18C ones were Classical, and so too were the majority of the later ones. At the beginning of the century the Gothic Survival was still more notable than the Gothic Revival. Nicholas Hawksmoor consciously revived Gothic for his towers at St. Michael's, Cornhill and at Westminster Abbey, but far more ubiquitous were the towers of rural churches which were rebuilt on late medieval lines, in a style which their builders had received as standard, not 'revived'. Very few parishes outside the major towns would think of employing a well-known architect or 'gentleman surveyor'; a local master mason would be employed instead. By the end of the 18C all Gothic work was revived. The revival, however, amounted to no more than a decorative use of medieval features on normal 18C shells. Pointed windows (often without tracery or cusping), ogee labels over windows and doorways, battlements and quatrefoils were all applied without much or any attention to medieval precedents. It is usual to label all this 'Gothick', reserving Gothic for later work. The plans of 18C churches, whether Classical or Gothic, generally followed the medieval precedent of an E–W rectangle. Only a few Classical works had centralising plans, such as Joseph Bonomi's St James's at Great Packington in Warwickshire and Nicholas Revett's church at Ayot St. Lawrence in Hertfordshire. 18C plans did not neglect chancels, as is traditionally claimed. In new churches, a chancel would perhaps be shallow in contrast to medieval examples, but it was not excluded. A Greek cross plan would automatically have a chancel in one of its arms. In existing churches, chancels were rebuilt or refitted in many cases, as at Bruton in Somerset, St. Clement's in Cambridge and St. Paul's Walden in Hertfordshire. It must be recalled that in the 18C the Sacrament was taken relatively infrequently. The chancel was not the permanent honoured focus of a church as it was for the Victorians. It was a part of the building which had a specific but intermittent use. It was not adorned in the 19C manner with coloured tiles, mural painting, gleaming brass and so forth; but in many cases it did have a reredos (or a religious painting) to give due honour to the communion table, and in a surprising number of 18C churches there was stained glass in the E window.

From the churches' financial viewpoint, the 18C was a different world to subsequent times. Royal briefs could be sought to collect money throughout England for rebuilding or repairs. Church rates could be levied on a regular basis, as normally as the poor rate or the highway rate. Pew-rents were regularly collected. Finally, in the cases of rebuildings, Acts of Parliament were often obtained, and by their authority loans could be raised on the security of parochial income, such as that from burial dues. By 1900 all these sources of income were either unknown or were highly unusual. In the case of London in the 18C, there was an exceptional source of income for church building, and one which resulted in some exceptional churches. An Act passed in 1711, known as the 'Fifty Churches Act', provided Government money for the building in London of some very grand parish churches in districts which had little or no church provision. Barely a quarter of the intended fifty churches were built, but most of them were of the first significance: Nicholas Hawksmoor's St. George's, Bloomsbury, St. George's-in-the-East, St. Anne's, Limehouse, and Christ Church, Spitalfields; Thomas Archer's St. Paul's, Deptford and St. John's, Westminster; and James Gibbs's St. Mary-le-Strand. Hawksmoor, Wren's chief successor, was a master of Baroque, as was Archer; Gibbs was closer to Wren himself, especially in his steeples.

18C monuments could claim a book by themselves. They tend to be the tallest and grandest of all church monuments. In the Gothic 19C they were looked upon as 'pagan' for their Classical obelisks and urns, and for their trumpeting of their subjects' worth in the place of the medievalising piety which the Victorians favoured. Standing figures, which had appeared in the 17C, became frequent in the 18C, and sometimes there are two or three in aedicules. A full architectural surround, sometimes from floor to ceiling, was normal. Of the sculptors, the three who are notable in the early 18C were all foreign: L.F. Roubiliac, Peter Scheemakers and J.M. Rysbrack. The last two were Flemish, like their Elizabethan predecessors in the Southwark School. Of English sculptors, Thomas Green and Edward Stanton must be mentioned. Peter Scheemakers's son, Thomas, and his pupil, Joseph Nollekens, were prominent later in the 18C. The late 18C and the early decades of the 19C may be taken together. They formed the age of the two John Bacons, father and son, Sir Francis Chantrey, John Flaxman, and the three generations of Richard

Westmacotts. Their works appear frequently in these volumes. Smaller monuments of note—in the form of busts or profiles in medallions—were more numerous by this time than the huge works of the earlier 18C.

Non-Anglican Churches

By the beginning of the 19C non-Anglican churches were both numerous and significant. Their earliest examples in the 17C were almost all domestic in character: see the Friends' Meeting Houses at Brigflatts (Yorkshire, West Riding) and Thakeham (Sussex), and the Unitarian Chapel at Ipswich (Suffolk). Their use for worship is shown only in the arrangement of windows. During the 18C a more ecclesiastical character appeared. The typical form was that of the Classical oblong, with two tiers of arched windows along the sides, and a W or entrance front with a pediment and perhaps an ornamented doorway. What would be missing in Anglican terms would be a tower. The non-Anglican interior, however, would differ very little from a contemporary Anglican one. Catholic churches of the late 18C and early 19C used the same general designs as those of the Protestant Nonconformists.

Two particular strands of non-Anglican design in the 18C need to be mentioned. Thomas Ivory's Octagon Chapel of 1756 in Norwich set off a fashion, mainly among the Methodists, of octagonal buildings. The other strand concerns the churches of the Countess of Huntingdon's Connexion. Selina, Countess of Huntingdon (1707–91) set up chapels, with chaplains to serve them, which were nominally still Anglican (like Wesley's arrangements), but which in time formed a separate denomination (of Calvinistic Methodists—Calvinist in theology but Methodist by government). Her chapels were stately affairs, grander than most non-Anglican buildings and evangelical Anglican in character.

Classicism stayed in the non-Anglican denominations long after the Established Church had abandoned it. The Gothic Revival was only beginning to enter the picture in the 1840s, in a manner which Anglican churches had known in the 18C. For long after the 1840s, however, the Baptists in particular continued to use the grandest Classical manner. Most denominations did turn to Gothic in time, and by the end of the 19C many of their churches were indistinguishable externally from Anglican ones. Internally, however, they differed. Free Church E ends were dominated by a platform for the preacher, behind which a large organ would be placed. A plain communion table would stand in front of, and below, the platform. In a separate category were the Catholics, who, despite Pugin, never adopted Gothic exclusively; some late 19C Catholic churches—above all, the London Oratory Church at Brompton—were entirely Classical. In the Victorian period, the main non-Anglican development was perhaps less the triumph of Gothic than the immense size and grandeur which some non-Anglican buildings reached. Sir Titus Salt's Congregational (now United Reformed) Church at Saltaire (Yorkshire, West Riding), the Unitarian Church at Todmorden (ditto) and the great Free Church buildings of Birmingham reflected their patrons' wealth and influence, which would have been unimaginable to their fellow-religionists of the 17C and 18C.

This was especially true in the industrial cities. Rochdale had 15 mayors who belonged to the United Methodist Free Churches, a denomination which was markedly strong in that town. The national position of the Free Churches was transformed by the end of the 19C. After the General Election of 1906, there were no fewer than 157 Free Church MPs; in the 18C none of them would have been eligible in the first place.

The 19C

When the 19C opened, the Industrial Revolution was beginning to increase the national population. The growth in population in the 19C was unprecedented in English history. The first national census of 1801 recorded nearly nine million in England and Wales; by 1901 the total was 32½ million. So it is not surprising that church building was often undertaken to increase accommodation for worshippers; to provide more 'sittings', as it was put. But it was not merely a matter of more seats in more churches for more people. The 19C was a rare period in which gifts for church building sharply increased. It is a fact that although donations for church purposes are common to all periods, they rise and fall without proven reasons. The 11C and 12C constituted a peak; and so too did the 19C. Initially, generosity was the Government's also. Parliamentary grants were made in 1818 and 1824. But these were not repeated. Royal briefs were abolished in 1828. Church rates ceased to be compulsory in 1868. The great engine of 19C church building was personal giving.

It is the scale of church building in the 19C that needs to be stressed. A large town which had two or three Anglican churches by 1800 would have 30 or 40 by 1900, not to speak of up to double or treble that figure in Free Church buildings and mission halls. The ancient parish of St. Mary, Newington, in S London, for example, had just one Anglican church in 1800. Two more were built in the 1820s. By 1892 there were 15. In Bournemouth, Alexander Morden Bennett built eight churches as well as the main church of St. Peter. Schemes of Victorian church building spoke regularly in tens or dozens. Bishop Thorold launched a Ten Churches Fund in S London in 1882, and Bishop Blomfield's Metropolis Churches Fund built or helped 78 churches.

Free Church congregations either grew up in newly-populated areas, or they were formed from disputes in existing congregations. In most cases such disputes concerned the choice of a new pastor. A preacher would be invited to supply the pulpit for a few weeks, after which half the congregation would want him as their permanent pastor and half would not. The dispute would be resolved by a division into two congregations; one would keep the existing church building and the other would build a completely new one. In 1818, a new pastor was needed for the Camden Chapel at Camberwell, S London. Two candidates appeared: Joseph Irons and Edward Andrews. In the event, neither of them was appointed, with the result that their supporters formed two new congregations and built *two* new churches—the Grove Chapel for Irons and the Beresford Chapel for Andrews. Camden Chapel itself later became Anglican.

Church Building in the 19C

The early 19C was a period in which the Classical and Gothic styles co-existed more or less equally. Classicism went through a Greek phase in the 15 years after Waterloo and produced such notable churches as New St. Pancras' in London. Gothic became much more widespread than it had been in the late 18C. The main Greek Revival architects of the day were just as ready to turn their hand to Gothic. The churches built by the Commissioners under the parliamentary grants of 1818 and 1824 often used a simple Perpendicular style, with tall, thin windows, equally thin pinnacles and the use of crocketed hoodmoulds over doorways and windows. A few contemporary churches, such as St. Luke's, Chelsea, London (by James Savage, 1820–24) were of much better quality; the money needed for them was usually raised locally and not given by the Commissioners. Outside London, there were similar churches in scholarly Gothic, such as Pensax, Worcestershire. After c 1840 this scholarly Gothic became widespread and normal. Overlapping with its onset, there was a brief neo-Norman phase. Neo-Norman may be found from the 18C into the 20C, but only c 1840 did it become a normal style for a few years.

The Victorian Gothic Revival differed from its 18C and early 19C antecedents in both style and conviction. Earlier Gothic churches almost all used Gothic forms in ways which were not medieval. They were built without a belief in Gothic as the *only* appropriate Christian style. A.W.N. Pugin (1812–52) was the great proponent from the 1830s of the view that Gothic was synonymous with Christian, and that there must not be a random use of Gothic elements but a scholarly copying of medieval precedents. The Cambridge Camden Society of 1839, which became the Ecclesiological Society in 1845, similarly argued for faithfulness to medieval Gothic and for its exclusive worth, such that we speak of churches designed in Gothic before the 1840s as 'pre-Ecclesiological'. At the same time the Oxford Movement, a movement of theology and Church order which began in 1833, taught its hearers to claim a Catholic inheritance for the Church of England as well as one derived from the Reformation. These various lines of argument came together from c 1840 to prompt, in due course, profound changes in the Victorian Church.

Obviously, widespread change was not immediate. Just as, in one direction, scholarly Gothic had been used in some places well before 1840, so in the other it must be stressed that the impact of the Oxford and Ecclesiological Movements on the Church of England was by no means as immediate and strong as past comment has alleged. The new movements eventually secured widespread acceptance and influence, but for long after 1840 the number of Anglican churches which were built or reordered in precise accordance with their teachings did not comprise a very large proportion of the whole. A church which followed high fashion in its architectural style could still have a plan and fittings which owed as much to old ideas as to new. For example, Sir Gilbert Scott's St. Giles's, Camberwell, in S London, was a Gothic work of the new scholarly type when it was built in 1842–44, but inside it was given galleries and an altarpiece which included the usual inscribed panels of 18C convention. Architectural change preceded liturgical change as a general rule.

The Victorian Church Interior

The Victorian Gothic Revival was not merely one of architecture. It revived a wide range of medieval fittings and practices. Open benches replaced box-pews. Tiles were laid down, most frequently in the chancel and less often throughout a church. Mural paintings were reintroduced. Memorials once again took the forms of recumbent effigies on tomb-chests, and of brasses. Sedilia were duly placed on the S side of a chancel, and occasionally an Easter sepulchre would appear on the N. Side chapels, with their own furnishings, reappeared. Fonts, pulpits and reredoses were made by the thousand in wood, marble and alabaster, featuring in their carvings the standard iconography of the High Middle Ages. Chancel screens were revived, either in wood or in brass; but the Roods to go above them were only beginning to appear at the end of the 19C, and they tend to be 20C additions. Choirstalls in the chancel are characteristically Victorian, for choirs were no longer placed in the W gallery. A large new organ would typically be placed at the E end, too, in a N or S chapel or special chamber. In a similar position there would often be a new vestry. Above all in a Victorian church, there would be new stained glass. The art of making stained glass had never completely disappeared after the Reformation, but the quantity and quality of its production after c 1840 overwhelmed that of the previous three centuries. A small number of firms supplied the greater part of the market. William Warrington, Thomas Willement, Clayton & Bell, Morris & Co., John Hardman & Co., William Wailes, Heaton, Butler & Bayne, the Gibbs family, Ward & Hughes, James Powell & Sons, the O'Connor family, Lavers, Barraud & Westlake, Burlison & Grylls, and C.E. Kempe were the principal designers. Many of them also undertook mural painting, and sometimes woodwork and brasswork too. Very few churches in England do not possess some of their work.

Victorian Restorations

The installation of all the above fittings almost always accompanied a restoration. 'Restoration' was no neutral term in Victorian usage, but implied the *improvement* of a church and a revival of its presumed appearance in the High Middle Ages; or, if it were a later and Classical building, changes to mitigate a style and plan which were considered disagreeable. Victorian restoration was no once-for-all effort; a church could undergo a number of intermittent changes. 'Restoration' should imply conservative repair, but in Victorian days it involved much radical replacement. Decorated window tracery would replace Perpendicular work; porches, arcades, aisles and entire chancels were rebuilt; roofs were totally replaced; walls were 'scraped' of their plaster; and serviceable fittings—even medieval screens—were swept away for new ones. Towards the end of the century a more conservative view began to emerge. See how St. John's, Leeds, a 17C church, was drastically altered in the 1860s but carefully reinstated from the 1880s onwards. William Morris's Society for the Protection of Ancient Buildings (1877) was founded specifically to stop radical restorations.

Victorian Church Architects

A.W.N. Pugin. Although Pugin was the major early theorist of the scholarly Gothic Revival, he was not the most significant designer of its churches. For one thing, he was a Catholic who was almost never employed by Anglican parishes. Unfortunately too, his fellow-religionists rarely had the money to build according to his ideals, and often they did not share his passion for Gothic at all. Only the 16th Earl of Shrewsbury was a rich and wholehearted Catholic patron of Pugin, and together they built St. Giles's at Cheadle, Staffordshire, which, after cleaning and restoration in recent years, is a splendid example of what Pugin advocated. The style is Decorated; the fittings are designed and placed as they would appear in a lavish 14C church; and every surface is painted. St. Giles's is a magnificent work, but it was unique in Pugin's career.

Sir Gilbert Scott and his Contemporaries. Sir Gilbert Scott (1811–78) was the most prolific of all Victorian architects. He was regarded as the Wren of his day, and was consulted on the restoration of innumerable cathedrals and major churches. Countless parish churches were designed in his office, but his personal contribution to many of them is difficult to judge. He regarded All Souls', Haley Hill, Halifax as his best parish church, and it is certainly among the most magnificent 19C churches, lavish in its architecture and in its fittings. Scott's hallmark was the use of the late 13C Geometrical style.

Scott's chief contemporaries among church architects were William Butterfield (1814–1900), J.L. Pearson (1817–97), G.E. Street (1824–81), William Burges (1827–81) and G.F. Bodley (1827–1907). These architects were, with Pugin and with Scott himself, the leading figures in Victorian church building. Their combined church output was immense, for the great wave of 19C church building allowed architects to design churches almost exclusively. Butterfield was noted for his 'structural polychromy'—the use of bands of coloured brick or stone. His masterpieces were All Saints', Margaret Street, London, and the chapel of Keble College, Oxford. J.L. Pearson's churches show the influence of 13C French Gothic; they generally have apsidal E ends and, unusually for the Victorians, they are vaulted. The best examples of his work are St. Michael's, Croydon (Surrey); St. Stephen's, Bournemouth; St. Agnes's, Sefton Park, Liverpool; St. Augustine's, Kilburn; St. Peter's, Vauxhall, in S London; and, last but not least, Truro Cathedral.

G.E. Street wrote important books on Continental Gothic after much travelling in the 1850s and 1860s. His early use of medieval English precedents thus gave way to French and Italian models. He tended to favour an earlier Gothic style than his contemporaries; not for him the complexities of 14C 'flowing' tracery. Many of Street's churches are rather small—such as those he designed for the Sykes family in the East Riding of Yorkshire; larger and more significant ones are St. James's, Pimlico, London; St. Peter's, Bournemouth; and the church of St. Philip and St. James, Oxford. William Burges shared with Pearson a love of 13C French Gothic, but he often showed an extravagance of material and detail which distinguishes his work from Pearson's. His churches at Studley Royal and Skelton-on-Ure in Yorkshire (West Riding) are his best parish churches. G.F. Bodley practised for more than 50 years as a Gothic architect. He had been Scott's pupil, but reacted against Scott's Geometrical style. He shared in the use of French and Italian models in the 1850s and

1860s, but then moved to an English 14C and 15C style, to which he kept for the rest of his career. His early, 'Continental' works include All Saints', Selsley (Gloucestershire), St. Martin's, Scarborough, and St. Michael's, Brighton. All Saints', Cambridge (1863–64) was his first 'English' work. The masterpieces of his mature style were Holy Angels, Hoar Cross (Staffordshire), St. Augustine's, Pendlebury, Manchester, and St. Mary's, Clumber (Nottinghamshire. The Gothic Revival never reached so attractive a phase as it did in Bodley's hands.

Further Victorian Architects

So huge was the field of Victorian church building that there are countless architects of lesser standing to add to the seven already mentioned. R.C. Carpenter was a designer of some attractive Decorated churches c 1850. William White, another of Scott's pupils and close to the Ecclesiologists, designed a few important churches in London and elsewhere. S.S. Teulon, for long labelled a 'rogue architect' for his independent Gothic style, designed innumerable churches, of which St. Stephen's, Hampstead, London ranks as the most important. James Brooks designed notable churches in London, chiefly in Haggerston. Butterfield's pupil, Henry Woodyer, was responsible for Holy Innocents, Highnam (Gloucestershire). S.W. Dawkes was a notable architect in the same county, who also built St. Andrew's, Wells Street, London, now removed to Kingsbury, Middlesex. J.D. Sedding produced the two very different London churches of Holy Redeemer, Clerkenwell and Holy Trinity, Sloane Street—the one Italianate and having an early baldacchino, and the other an Arts and Crafts ensemble. Among Victorian provincial architects, the works of W.H. Bidlake in Birmingham demand attention, and in Lancashire the firm of Paley & Austin designed numerous churches of considerable merit.

After c 1875 a number of architects moved away from the mainstream Gothic of the previous and their own generation. G.G. Scott, Jr (1839–97) produced in St. Agnes's, Kennington and All Hallows', Southwark, both in S London, two churches which were notable for their use of Perpendicular, a medieval style which the High Victorians had tended to regard as 'debased'. Norman Shaw, better known for his secular works, designed St. Michael's, Bedford Park in a style which borrowed from Classicism. J.F. Bentley turned to Byzantine models for his Westminster Cathedral. For the Methodist Central Hall in London in the early 20C, Lanchester & Rickards used a French Classical style. Mainstream Gothic continued in this period in the hands of Sir Arthur Blomfield, Temple Moore, Charles Hodgson Fowler, F.A. Walters (for Catholic churches), Ninian Comper, and the heirs of Sir Gilbert Scott (his son, J.O. Scott and his grandson, Sir Giles Gilbert Scott). Comper lived until 1960 and, although he turned increasingly to Classicism in the 20C, represented the Gothic tradition well into the days of the Modern Movement.

The 20C

In the 20C, the great cities have lost much population from their centres. It has been a familiar pattern in all denominations for churches to be closed in city centres and in the inner suburbs. It would not be hard to show that for every 'inner-city report' of recent years, half a dozen inner-city churches have been closed. The more historic churches in the ancient city centres and in country villages have almost all been retained and cherished, at ever-increasing costs of maintenance. The Free Churches have contracted most markedly, but all denominations have lost clergy in large numbers. Long gone are the days when an Anglican parish might have had an incumbent and up to six curates, and not be unusual. Such a parish, with a church built in 1863 in a teeming district, may well have been suppressed in 1963 and be absent today as if it had never existed.

From the First World War onwards, churches drew away from the Victorian mould. Interwar Gothic became more and more diluted—as in the work of Sir Edward Maufe—although traditional plans tended to remain. After 1945 all 19C and early 20C models were widely abandoned. It was claimed in so many cases that a totally new plan had been devised, or that a building was a product only of the 20C and borrowed nothing from past ages. In reality, no plan is ever new; there is always a precedent. The real mark of a mid-20C church was a complete absence of decorative detail. It was surely this fact, in churches no less than in secular buildings, that has brought so much popular hostility to 20C design.

It would be wrong to underestimate the extent of new church building in the 20C, especially for new suburbs and to replace buildings bombed in the Second World War, but most church work of the last half-century has been a matter of repair and reordering. 'Reordering' is to recent decades what 'restoration' was to the 19C, a compelling fashion which has removed much of value in fabric and in fittings from the past. The crucial element in many reorderings has been to introduce a 'central' altar—at the E end of the nave, or under the crossing, and certainly well away from the traditional E end. Such a position was not unknown in past ages, but it has become normal in the later 20C. The drawback in so many reorderings has not been the new plan but the aesthetic nullity of so many new fittings. Often they are discordant in their settings, and remarkable for their starkness. The Second Vatican Council (1962–65) prompted in the Catholic Church the same changes which the Liturgical Movement had brought to the Church of England. If only that Council had occurred in 1865, or 1905, rather than 1965, its artistic results would not have been so dismal.

Much has been said about the 20C retreat from 19C teachings. It must be remembered, nevertheless, that Gothic and Classical churches continued to be built by some architects. Mention has been made of Sir Ninian Comper's work. His great churches of St. Cyprian, Clarence Gate, London and St. Mary, Wellingborough (Northamptonshire) in the early 1900s were followed between the wars by the chapel at All Saints' Convent, London Colney (Hertfordshire) and St. Philip's, Cosham (Hampshire). The Anglican cathedral at Liverpool, begun under Sir Giles Gilbert Scott in Edwardian days, was completed only in 1980 in a full Gothic style. Perhaps the foremost mid-20C Gothic architect has been S.E. Dykes Bower, designer of the E parts of St. Edmundsbury Cathedral (Suffolk) and the postwar additions to Lancing College Chapel in Sussex. H.S. Goodhart-Rendel designed a few notable churches in a style which sometimes veered to the Romanesque and included enough detail to be attractive in traditional terms.

Conclusion

All churches might be called ripples of the Resurrection. The faith which they express is reflected in the styles and customs of every age since Christianity began. The many and diverse subjects which the history of the Christian Church in England encompasses are linked together over the centuries by the basic tenets of Christian belief, shared by innumerable individuals whose craftsmanship, memorials and local connections we may see and appreciate today. In St. Ethelburga's, Bishopsgate, in the City of London, we see inscribed in the pavement the words *'Bonus intra, melior exi'* (enter a good person, leave a better one); who could fail to be moved in that way by the message we see of countless ages of faith in our churches?

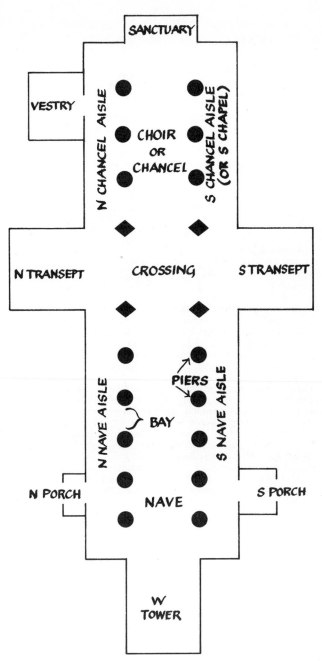

SANCTUARY

VESTRY

N CHANCEL AISLE

CHOIR
OR
CHANCEL

S CHANCEL AISLE
(OR S CHAPEL)

N TRANSEPT

CROSSING

S TRANSEPT

PIERS

N NAVE AISLE

BAY

S NAVE AISLE

N PORCH

S PORCH

NAVE

W
TOWER

Standard ground plan of a church

GLOSSARY

ABACUS: The uppermost part of a column, above the capital: a thin, flat slab of various shapes and treatments.

ABBEY: A monastic house under an abbot, or a church which was once monastic but is now parochial (e.g. Tewkesbury Abbey) or a cathedral (e.g. St. Alban's Abbey) or a royal peculiar (e.g. Westminster Abbey). The name also applies to country houses in private ownership which occupy the sites of medieval monasteries (e.g. Woburn Abbey).

ACHIEVEMENT OF ARMS: A full work of heraldry, consisting of the shield or coat of arms, the supporters, crest and motto.

ADVOWSON: The right to nominate a priest for a benefice.

AGNUS DEI: Latin for the *Lamb of God*, a title which St. John the Baptist accords to Christ in the first chapter of St. John's Gospel. It is also used as the title of a prayer (based on St. John's Gospel) which is said (or sung) before the distribution of Holy Communion. In art, a lamb is often shown carrying a cross or a crossed flag.

AISLE: From the Latin *insula*, an island. A lateral and subsidiary part of a nave, a chancel or (more rarely) a transept, and running parallel to it. An arcade usually separates the two. The word is also used to mean a space between pews or benches, which is also called an *alley*.

ALTAR: A stone table, or a wooden one with a stone slab set into it, which is the focus of a Communion service. In the Middle Ages everywhere, and in the Catholic Church still, an altar will contain a relic of a saint. A 'high altar' is the main altar of a church.

AMBO: A reading-desk or pulpit.

AMBULATORY: A processional way round the E end of a larger church, comprising the choir or chancel aisles and the retrochoir E of the high altar.

ANGEL: From the Greek word for a messenger. An angel is an intermediary between God and Man. Medieval writers arranged them into nine orders, or three hierarchies of three choirs each: Seraphim, Cherubim and Thrones; Dominations, Virtues and Powers; and Principalities, Archangels and Angels. The Nine Orders of Angels sometimes form a subject in medieval Church art.

ANTECHAPEL: The W portion of a chapel, which is subsidiary to the rest and from which it may be divided by a screen (e.g. in King's College chapel, Cambridge) or by being the crossbar of a T-shaped building (e.g. in New College chapel, Oxford).

APSE: A rounded or polygonal termination to a church or chapel, most usually of the entire E end, less often of the transepts or subsidiary chapels. In early churches, apses were built at the W end too. The adjective is apsidal.

ARCADE: A line of arches. A *Blind* arcade is fixed to a wall.

ASHLAR: Stone cut to squared shapes and smooth faces and laid in regular courses.

ASSUMPTION: The belief that the Virgin Mary was assumed into Heaven. The date of the feast is August 15th. In 1950 the belief was proclaimed to be a dogma of the Catholic Church, although it had been widespread since the early Middle Ages.

AUMBRY: A free-standing cupboard or a recess in a wall, used for storage, normally of sacred vessels or of books. Also known as an *armarium*.

BALDACCHINO: A canopy, usually supported on four or more pillars, which stands over an altar and occasionally over a font. In late 19C and 20C England, a number of architects favoured the baldacchino, above all Sir Ninian Comper. Also known as a *ciborium*.

BAPTISM: The initiatory Sacrament of the Christian Church. From the Greek word meaning a dipping. The form of baptism has varied in Christian history. It can be immersion (the submersion of the head), full submersion, affusion (a pouring) or aspersion (a sprinkling). A baptistery may be a detached building.

BARTIZAN: A projecting turret at the top of a tower.

BASILICA: A Roman public hall, aisled and with an E apse, which gave its name to churches which were built according to a similar plan. The word is loosely used for some early churches in England.

BATTLEMENT: A parapet which has a regular pattern of gaps between higher portions. The gaps are known as loops or crenellations, the flanking higher walls as merlons. Crenellated is a synonym for battlemented.

BAY: A division of an arcade, elevation or roof, which is marked out by piers, pilasters, buttresses, windows, ribs, etc.

BEAKHEAD: A moulding which resembles a succession of beaked heads.

BEDESMAN: One who prays for the soul of a deceased. The word is applied to small figures which may sometimes be found at the feet of recumbent effigies.

BELLCOTE: An open frame or turret, usually placed on the gable end of a church, to contain bells.

BILLET: A moulding consisting of short cylindrical or square blocks placed at intervals, sometimes in two parallel lines whereby the blocks of one line are positioned above the spaces of the other.

BOSS: A carved stone or piece of woodwork, placed at the junction of ribs in a vault or at the junction of members of an openwork wooden roof.

BOX-PEW: A bench in a church which is surrounded by high panelled sides and by a door; or a group of such benches.

BROACH SPIRE: An octagonal spire which sits on a tower without a parapet has angles which are covered by half-pyramids known as broaches. Broach spires generally date from the 13C and 14C.

BUTTRESS: An attachment to a wall which supports and strengthens it. A clerestory above an aisle roof sometimes needed a *flying buttress* to take the thrust of the upper wall over the aisle. Towers are more regularly buttressed. There are *angle buttresses*, in which the lines of the walls continue to create a 90° angle at each corner; *set-back buttresses*, also at 90° to each other, but placed away from the corner so that the angle of the buttressed fabric is visible; *clasping buttresses*, which encase the corners in a square of masonry; and *diagonal buttresses*, which extend from the corners at equal angles of 135° from each face.

CADAVER MONUMENT: A 15C practice, sometimes found at later dates too, to remind the living of the decay of the body and so to prompt them to seek salvation. Also known as a *memento mori*, a reminder of death.

CAPITAL: The upper part or capping of a column or pilaster, and usually its most decorative part.

CARTOUCHE: A mural monument with an elaborate curling frame.

CATHEDRA(L): A cathedral is a church in which is placed a bishop's chair or *cathedra*. A chair was the symbol of a teacher or philosopher in the

BROACH SPIRE · St MICHAEL AND ALL ANGELS · HALLATON · Leics.

Drawing by the Reverend Brian Roy

ancient world; a bishop has one to symbolise his position as an authoritative teacher of the Christian Faith.

CATHOLIC: A Greek word meaning 'universal'. Originally, it implied orthodoxy or views which were shared universally. After the Reformation, it implied traditional beliefs, which Protestants questioned. It is used as a title by those in communion with Rome and also by members of the Church of England and the Eastern Orthodox Churches.

CHALICE: From the Latin *calix*, a cup used for the Communion wine. Usually made of precious metal.

CHAMFER: An edge is chamfered when the square angle between two surfaces is cut, usually at half a right angle to each.

CHANCEL: The E part of a church, often thought of as being beyond the screen or *cancella*.

CHANTRY: An endowment for the saying or chanting of Masses

for the soul of a deceased. A chantry chapel, usually a small, enclosed chapel within a church, was sometimes specially built, and staffed by one or more chantry priests. All chantries were dissolved under King Edward VI, but many chantry chapels survive, for example the magnificent group in Winchester Cathedral.

CHAPEL: A small detached place of worship, especially one which is private rather than parochial or public, or a subsidiary part of a church. The word derives from the diminutive of the Latin word for a cloak: it was first used for the place where St. Martin's cloak was kept by *capellani* or cloak-keepers. In recent centuries in England, the word has been applied to buildings of the Free Churches in contrast to Anglican churches. 'Chapel' is sometimes used as a synonym for Nonconformity. A chapel of ease is a building which is dependent on a parish church.

CHAPTER (HOUSE): The governing body of a larger church, or a meeting of such a body. Originally, a chapter of the Rule (or statutes) would be read aloud at each meeting. A monastic chapter house will almost always be found to the S of the S transept.

CHEVRON: A zigzag decoration, especially in Norman architecture, or a V-shaped design in heraldry.

CHOIR: The body of singers in a church, or the part of the church in which they sing, usually towards the E end between the nave and the sanctuary.

CIBORIUM: Another word for a baldacchino, q.v.

CLERESTORY: An upper or 'clear' storey, designed to provide natural light in a church, most usually in the nave, but sometimes in the chancel as well. More often than not a clerestory will be a 15C addition to the fabric.

CLOISTERS: A covered walk around three or four sides of a quadrangle, with windowless outer walls and pierced (but often unglazed) inner walls, usually but not exclusively associated with cathedral and monastery churches. Each arm of the walk is known as an alley. The enclosed space within the quadrangle is the cloister garth and is sometimes known as a paradise.

COLLEGE: In its ecclesiastical sense, the word refers to a body of clergy living in an endowed community, but whose members are not monks or friars. Very often such a community was one of chantry priests. A collegiate church, however, is usually grander than this implies, being a larger church served by a body of canons or prebendaries.

COMMUNION TABLE: A wooden table for the celebration of the Eucharist or Holy Communion, which was originally distinguished from a stone altar. The terms are often used loosely today as if they were synonyms. A wooden table can have an inserted stone slab.

CONSECRATION: The word is used in speaking of the solemn hallowing or dedicating of a church. In the Church of England, this is usually the date of opening. In Catholic churches, it follows long after, sometimes a century or more later. The word is also used in the consecration of the water and wine in Holy Communion. Finally, it can refer to the consecration of a new bishop. In all these cases, the word means 'to make sacred or holy'.

CONVENT(UAL): Any monastic house, not merely of nuns, is a convent. Thus, it is proper to speak of the 'Prior and Convent of Christ Church, Canterbury' in the Middle Ages for the predecessors of the present Dean and Chapter. Conventual is an adjective which refers to a monastic house, particularly to its domestic buildings.

CORPORAL WORKS OF MERCY: In chapter 25 of St. Matthew's Gospel, these are given as feeding the hungry, giving drink to the thirsty, sheltering the homeless, visiting the sick, visiting prisoners and clothing the naked. The Church added a seventh, the burial of the dead.

CREDENCE: A small table or shelf near an altar, on which the bread and wine are placed before consecration.

CRENELLATED: See Battlement.

CROCKET: An embellishment in Gothic design which is applied to spires, gables and pinnacles. The shape is usually of a stylised leaf or a knob.

CROSSING: The junction between the E–W axis of a nave and chancel, and the N–S axis of N and S transepts. Often there is a crossing tower, which creates a quite distinct space beneath it.

CRYPT: A vaulted underground room in a church (or in a secular building), which usually underlies only a part of the superstructure. Crypts in early English churches were often used as shrines for relics. Later, they came to be used for burial, especially in the 17C, 18C and early 19C. Also called an undercroft.

CUPOLA: A small domed lantern, sometimes placed on a church tower in the absence of a steeple, and occasionally placed on the roof of the body of a church or chapel in the absence of a tower, e.g. over an almshouse chapel.

CUSP: The point formed where two foils meet in Gothic tracery.

DECALOGUE: The Ten Commandments. From the 17C to the 19C it was normal for an Anglican church to have the Commandments inscribed on a board at the E end, usually as part of the altarpiece.

DOOM PAINTING: See Last Judgement.

DOSSAL: A backcloth, normally behind an altar or on the N and S walls of a chancel.

EASTER SEPULCHRE: A specially-built recess, or a tomb used or adapted for the purpose, almost always on the N side of the chancel, which served to represent Christ's tomb during the celebration of Easter. Special recesses were most often built in the 14C. Today an altar of repose for the Reserved Sacrament fulfils the same function at Easter.

EMANCIPATION: The removal of restrictions on Catholics in 1829, but also used loosely of Catholic Relief Acts in the late 18C.

ENTABLATURE: The horizontal superstructure of a Classical design.

EUCHARIST: The Sacrament of the Lord's Supper or Holy Communion. From a Greek word which means 'to give thanks'.

FALDSTOOL: A small prayer desk, folding and portable.

FILLET: A raised band. The term is usually applied to those found on columns in a church.

FLEURON: A stylised flower carved in stone as an enrichment.

FLOWING TRACERY: 14C Decorated tracery, in which the ogee or curving element is dominant. Also called Curvilinear.

FLUSHWORK: A decorative chequerwork of black and white pebbles, often seen in East Anglian churches.

FOIL: A leaf, referring to the leaf-like shapes between the cusps of a Gothic window. Trefoil means with three foils, quatrefoil with four, cinquefoil with five, and sexfoil with six.

FRIARS: From the Latin fratri, meaning 'brothers'. The word was used from the 13C to distinguish groups of religious who worked amongst layfolk and without endowments from monks who lived in endowed

14TH CENTURY EASTER SEPULCHRE
ALL SAINTS' ❖ HAWTON ❖ Notts ❖

Drawing by the Reverend Brian Roy

institutions quite detached from lay life. The principal Orders of friars were Franciscans (Greyfriars), Carmelites (Whitefriars), Dominicans (Blackfriars) and Augustinian or Austin Friars.

FRIEZE: A horizontal band of decorative carving.

GALILEE: A W porch or chapel. Famous examples exist at Durham and Ely Cathedrals.

GALLERY: The term refers either to a wooden gallery which is separate from the structure of a church (and whose purpose is to provide additional seating) or a stone gallery which is part of the structure. The latter type will rise above the aisles but be below the clerestory and will be open to the nave or chancel; it is also called a *triforium*. Wooden galleries are ubiquitous, especially in churches from the 17C to the early 19C, but a triforium will usually be found only in cathedrals and monastic churches, or in exceptionally substantial parish churches.

GARGOYLE: A grotesque waterspout, intended to throw water off a wall.

GEOMETRICAL TRACERY: Tracery of the late 13C which consists of circles and foils.

GREEK CROSS: A cross with arms of equal length.

GREEN MAN: *See* Wodewose.

GREYFRIARS: A name for the Franciscans, whose habit was grey (but is now usually brown).

GRISAILLE: Clear glass which is painted in geometric patterns and with leaf decoration within those patterns. It cuts out glare but admits more light than stained glass.

HALL CHURCH: A church in which the nave and aisles are of equal height.

HAMMERBEAM: A type of roof in which beams project from the side walls but do not cross the roof-space as tiebeams do. Instead, they carry posts or struts which support the rafters. There may be one or two tiers of hammerbeams.

HATCHMENT: A diamond-shaped board bearing a shield of arms, placed in a church after a funeral.

HIERATIC: Priestly.

ICONOSTASIS: An icon or image screen, normal in Eastern Orthodox churches.

INTERSECTING TRACERY: A form of tracery common in c 1300, in which mullions intersect as they curve in the window head.

JAMB: The side of a doorway, an archway or a window.

JESSE TREE: A genealogical tree of Christ's descent from Jesse via St. Joseph, often depicted in a Jesse window.

LADY CHAPEL: A chapel named in honour of the Blessed Virgin Mary, which was commonly added to medieval churches but which is not found in very early churches. In larger churches, a Lady chapel will often be found E of the high altar.

LANCET: A relatively thin, single-light window, characteristic of the Early English style.

LAST JUDGEMENT: The judgement of each individual at the end of time (at the Last Trump), as described in chapter 25 of St. Matthew's Gospel. Christ will divide the sheep from the goats, that is the righteous from the unrighteous, the former on his right, the latter on his left. A depiction, also known as a Doom Painting, was often placed above the chancel arch of a medieval church.

LATIN DOCTORS: St. Augustine of Hippo, Bishop of Hippo in N Africa, a foremost theologian of the early Church; St. Jerome, the translator of the Latin Vulgate, a standard 4C Latin text of the Bible; St. Gregory the Great, Pope from 590 and 604 and Apostle of England; and St. Ambrose, Bishop of Milan. A frequent group in medieval and Gothic Revival art, especially on chancel screens and pulpits. St. Jerome is always depicted as a cardinal and St. Gregory is shown wearing a triple tiara (both anachronistically).

LESENE: A pilaster strip (q.v.).

LIGHT: A vertical division of a window, divided from its neighbour by a mullion.

LINENFOLD: A wavy pattern, usually found in 16C and 17C woodwork, which resembles in a stylised way the folds in linen.

LONG-AND-SHORT-WORK: A feature of pre-Conquest churches in which quoins are alternately small and large, that is, laid horizontally and vertically.

LOUVRE: An arrangement of small horizontal boards which are placed in a sloping position one above the other. They take the place of glass in belfry windows to allow the sound of the bells to carry but to exclude rain.

LOW-SIDE WINDOW: A window found in chancels, usually on the S side at the W end, but sometimes on the N side. Its sill will be markedly low and its lower part will often be shuttered rather than glazed. No undisputed explanation has ever been given for this feature. Also called a lychnoscope.

LUCARNE: An opening in a spire.

LYCHGATE: A gate to a burial ground. From the Old English word *lych*, meaning a corpse or a dead body.

MARTYR: The Greek word for a witness; a person who had witnessed to the Christian Faith by suffering death in its name.

MEMENTO MORI: *See* Cadaver Monument.

MINSTER: A large church, originally one which had more than just a local or parochial responsibility. Minsters were normal from the 7C until the 11C and then ceased to have a formal status as the parochial system was completed. The word remains in use for certain large churches, such as the cathedrals at York, Lincoln and Ely, and collegiate churches such as Beverley and Southwell. Although minster derives from *monasterium*, a minster was not necessarily a monastery.

MISERICORD: The Latin word for mercy, which is applied to tip-up seats found in the choirs or chancels of churches. These seats were designed to provide relief during the long hours of standing during the daily offices of the medieval Church. They attract attention for their carvings, which usually reflect a mixture of piety and humour. Also known as a miserere.

MULLION: A vertical division of a window.

NAILHEAD: A moulding in which low miniature pyramids are repeated in a line, for example above an arch.

NARTHEX: A vestibule at the W end of a church.

NAVE: The main body of a church, which takes its name from the Latin *navis*, a ship, on account of a rectangular building with a pitched roof seeming like an upturned ship.

NICHE: An alcove or recess, usually intended for a statue.

OGEE: A double curve, one convex and the other concave, which was introduced in the early 14C as a characteristic part of Decorated design.

ORIENTATION: The siting of a church so that its altar is at the E end, facing the Orient.

PARCLOSE: A screen which separates the main part of a church from a subsidiary part, e.g. a chancel from its aisle.

PARISH: A defined district whose cure of souls is assigned to a particular priest.

PEDIMENT: A triangular or segmental gable over a portico, window, E end, W end, etc., of a Classical building. An open pediment is one in which the sloping sides do not meet at the apex. A broken pediment has the horizontal member interrupted in the centre.

PELICAN IN HER PIETY: A depiction of a pelican biting her breast, symbolic of self-sacrifice and thus of the Eucharist.

PERPENDICULAR TRACERY: Tracery from the later 14C onwards, in which upright panels are the main element. Also called Rectilinear.

PIER: A solid upright, often used loosely as a synonym for column.

PILASTER: A flat pillar placed against a wall, with a base and capital of a Classical order. A pilaster strip, found on the exteriors of pre-Conquest churches, has no base or capital.

PINNACLE: A decorative upright above a parapet, most usually on a tower but often on a nave or a chancel or their aisles. A pinnacle will frequently rise out of a buttress. It may itself be decorated with crockets.

PISCINA: A stoup with a drain, usually on the S side of a chancel, used for the ritual washing of chalices.

PLATE TRACERY: Tracery in the 13C which is pierced through the wall rather than forming parts of a continuous window.

POPPYHEAD: An ornamental finial on a bench-end.

PORCH: A roofed space immediately outside an exterior

PERPENDICULAR WINDOW ◆ S. TRANSEPT
St PETER & St PAUL ◆ LANGHAM ◆ Leics.

Drawing by the Reverend Brian Roy

doorway, usually single-storey but sometimes higher. The word is also used to translate *porticus*, which applies to chapels or chambers in pre-Conquest churches. Such *porticus* do not normally have exterior doorways.

PREDELLA: The term usually refers to a shelf at the base of an altarpiece.

PRESBYTERY: The word has three uses. Firstly, it refers to the entire E end of a church, more usually to a cathedral or monastery church. Secondly, it is used of a priest's house in the Catholic Church. Thirdly, it describes an essential part of the government of a Presbyterian Church, especially in Scotland.

PRIORY: A priory is a monastic house which is dependent on an abbey, either because it is a daughter-house of the abbey in question or because it is part of an order in which member houses are subordinate to the central one.

PULPITUM: A screen placed between a nave and a choir, with an opening in the centre, and usually with an organ in the gallery above. A feature of cathedrals and larger churches.

PYX: A receptacle for the Reserved Sacrament, especially when it is suspended over an altar.

QUOIN: A dressed stone at the exterior angle of a church.

RECTOR: The clergyman who had the right to receive the full endowments of a benefice. The title in use today no longer has implications of income. *See also* Vicar.

RELIQUARY: A container for relics, very often an oblong and gable-topped box, elaborately embellished.

REREDOS: A stone or wooden screen behind an altar, often arranged in arches or panels and adorned with painting or sculpture.

RETICULATED: Meaning 'net-like', this word refers to tracery of the early 14C in which circles are pulled at the ends into ogee shapes to create the appearance of a net.

RETROCHOIR: 'At the back of the choir', referring to the space at the E end of larger churches, behind the high altar. Such a place is usually reached by the choir aisles, which, together with the retrochoir, form an ambulatory (q.v.).

RIDDEL (POSTS): A riddel is a curtain at the sides or back of an altar. Up to four riddel posts are used as supports. An altar thus curtained is known as an English altar, for it was normal in late medieval England. In the late 19C and early 20C the arrangement was revived under the influence of Percy Dearmer and Sir Ninian Comper.

ROOD: A Crucifix. The Rood group, comprising the Crucified Saviour flanked by the Virgin Mary and St. John the Evangelist and sometimes by further figures, was placed above the Rood screen of a medieval church. A Rood loft was a small gallery above the screen. Revived in the 19C and 20C.

SACRAMENT: A rite in which God's grace is active. St. Augustine of Hippo wrote of a 'visible sign of an invisible reality'. The word is often used to refer solely to the Eucharist or Holy Communion. All Christians recognise the Eucharist and Baptism as Sacraments. Catholics and the Eastern Orthodox add another five: Holy Orders, Matrimony, Penance, Confirmation and Extreme Unction.

SACRING BELL: A bell rung at the consecration of the water and wine in Holy Communion. Also known as a saunce or a sanctus bell.

SALTIRE CROSS: A cross with diagonal arms, almost always used as a symbol of St. Andrew, who suffered crucifixion on such a cross.

SANCTUARY: The part of a church, usually its easternmost part, enclosed by the communion rails. In most churches it will be the E part of the chancel. The word also refers to the place of (temporary) refuge for criminals, which was recognised to exist in churches in the Middle Ages.

SEDILIA: Three seats (occasionally more) on the S side of the sanctuary, usually a prominent architectural feature of the S wall but sometimes a wooden structure placed against or near the S wall. The sedilia were intended for the use of the priest, deacon and sub-deacon during parts of the medieval Mass. Stepped sedilia are on different levels or steps. In some cases the sedilia are formed from the sill of a chancel S window.

SEE: A bishopric or diocese. From the Latin *sedes*, a seat or bishop's throne, which is a symbol of his right and duty to preach the Christian Faith authoritatively.

SEVEN DEADLY SINS: Pride, covetousness, lust, envy, gluttony, anger and sloth.

SHAFT: A small circular upright which is a subsidiary part of a larger feature such as a pier or a window. It can also refer to the upright portion of a standing cross (a cross-shaft). A shaft-ring is a decorative band which encircles a shaft.

SHRINE: A receptacle for sacred relics, normally a highly enriched tomb of a saint.

SPANDRELS: The wall space between two arches or between a single arch and a square-cut frame above it. The word usually applies in churches to the nave arcades.

SPLAY: A slanted side, especially to a window. Very early churches often had markedly narrow windows, which would light their interiors better by being splayed. Double-splayed means splayed inside and out.

SQUINCH: A supporting arch in an angle.

SQUINT: An opening in a wall, often at an oblique angle, which enabled a person to see the high altar from an aisle or from a room next to the church proper. Also known as a hagioscope.

STALL: A seat, especially in the choir or chancel of a church, usually with arms and often with misericords (q.v.).

STEEPLE: The word is normally used to refer to a Classical tower and its superstructure, or to the superstructure alone.

STIFF-LEAF: A term applied to carved decoration of capitals, which is particularly characteristic of the Early English period.

STOUP: A receptacle for holy water, usually near a door.

STRAPWORK: Characteristic 16C and 17C decoration which consists of curving and interlaced bands like straps.

STRINGCOURSE: A horizontal moulded course of stonework which is often to be seen on exterior walls and particularly on towers. Sometimes a stringcourse which was originally external will now be found within a church as a result of expansion.

TABERNACLE: The word has four uses. Firstly, it refers to a Sacrament house or receptacle for the Reserved Sacrament (especially in Catholic churches). Secondly, it was used in the 17C and 18C to mean a temporary church. Thirdly, it is used by Baptists as a title for some of their churches. Finally, it can mean any niche or canopied recess.

TERM: A support for a bust or similar carving, which tapers towards the base.

TESTER: A canopy over a pulpit, which is also called a Sounding Board.

TETRAGRAMMATON: Greek for 'four letters', applied to the Holy Name, especially as written in Hebrew as the central feature of a painting in a church.

THREE-DECKER PULPIT: A term used for a type of pulpit found in churches from the 17C to the 19C, which comprised three parts at different levels. The highest was the pulpit proper; below it was a reading-desk; and at the bottom came the clerk's pew.

TRANSENNA: A screen of lattice work.

TRANSEPT: If a church is built in the shape of a cross, its N and S arms are known as transepts. Sometimes only a N or only a S transept exists.

TRANSITIONAL: A halfway stage between one style and another, used most frequently to refer to the change between the Norman and Early English styles in the later 12C.

TRANSOM: A horizontal division of a window, found in late

Y-TRACERY ~ NOSELEY Leic's.
EXTERIOR

Drawing by the Reverend Brian Roy

Gothic designs. Transoms are sometimes embattled.

TRIFORIUM: *See* Gallery.

TYMPANUM: The space between the horizontal lower edge of a pediment and its sloping sides, or between the lintel of a door and an arch above it. A Norman doorway often has carving in its tympanum and this is perhaps the most frequent use of the word concerning churches.

UNDERCROFT: *See* Crypt.

VENETIAN WINDOW: A motif in Classical design by which an arched and taller middle light is flanked by two lower square-headed lights.

VESICA: The shape of an oval with pointed ends, which was occasionally used as a feature in wall paintings (to surround a figure of Christ or of the Virgin Mary) and more rarely for windows.

VICAR: From the Latin *vicarius*, a

deputy. A vicar was a deputy or substitute for a rector.

WEEPERS: Small figures in mourning on the sides of a tomb-chest.

WODEWOSE (or Woodwose or Woodhouse): A wild, hairy man, often carrying a club, who was the subject of many medieval carvings. He is very similar to the Green Man.

Y-TRACERY: Characteristic of 13C windows, in which a mullion divides into two in the window head.

BEDFORDSHIRE

Bedfordshire, as all the guidebooks tell you, is a small county that people travel through rather than to. The guidebooks go on to point out that the visitor will find many things to interest and delight him and this is true of the churches as well as other attractions. The county forms a kind of architectural bridge between the Home Counties and the Midlands. In the N are large, grand churches like Felmersham, Odell or Turvey that are in no way inferior to the greater churches in Northamptonshire. Several like Souldrop, Swineshead and Wymington have stone spires that are such a feature of the Northamptonshire landscape. In the S one meets features associated with Home Counties' churches—the appearance of flint and those curious lead-covered spikes that are so common in Hertfordshire.

It is therefore quite difficult to speak of characteristics of Bedfordshire churches. They change from one part of the county to another. To a large extent geology is responsible, as there are marked differences in building materials throughout the county. Generally it is not blessed with good stone, apart from where the Jurassic ridge spills over from Northamptonshire to provide limestone but even this is rather platy and not used in large blocks. Further S is the greensand ridge which contains very variable stone. The most commonly used in churches is a dark, gritty ironstone known as carstone. A real curiosity is Husborne Crawley because, although 'greensand' is not usually green, here much of the fabric is a real rich green. In the S the chalk of the Chilterns was the source of the famous 'clunch' from Totternhoe. Although this is a marvellous material for carving, this advantage has turned to disadvantage outside, as the stone has weathered terribly. At Studham the only answer was to roughcast the exterior. Some places like Chalgrave and Lower Gravenhurst had to make do with rubbly material. The most attractive use of materials is undoubtedly the chequerwork of stone and flint in the S as at Luton.

Another noticeable characteristic is that from the Bedford area and S almost every church tower has a stair turret which rises above the parapets. Also, Bedfordshire churches seem to have a good survival rate of medieval screens and benches though the latter are usually quite plain. Stoups are common and so is that most attractive feature, the angle piscina.

Bedfordshire has a good cross-section of medieval church building. Pre-Conquest work is represented at four churches in the NW—Clapham, Stevington, Turvey and St. Peter's, Bedford. Clapham is notable for the height of its tower and Stevington for the survival of a mid-wall wooden board in a window. The most substantial Norman remains are from two monastic sites—Dunstable Priory and Elstow. In each case what survives is part of the nave. Dunstable is certainly the best 12C work in the county. At Elstow the three 12C bays of the Benedictine nunnery give some idea of Norman work at its most elementary. St. Mary's, Bedford is a Norman cruciform church and at St. Peter's the top of the tower was added in the 12C to the pre-Conquest structure.

The 13C is well-represented, sometimes by work of the highest order. Pride of place must go to Felmersham with its beautiful W front and majestic interior. There are some fine arcades too, notably at Eaton Bray, Chalgrave, Sundon and the two W bays at Elstow. At

Eaton Bray the 13C work is concealed in what is otherwise a Perpendicular church; the S arcade is earlier though the N one with deeply-cut roll-moulding and excellent stiff-leaf is lovelier. Eaton Bray also has a notable cauldron-type font with more rich stiff-leaf (Leighton Buzzard has a similar font but without the stiff-leaf). Leighton Buzzard and Toddington both have 13C crossing towers. The former, together with Eaton Bray and Turvey, are notable for retaining some wonderful ironwork of the 13C on their doors. It has been attributed to Thomas of Leighton, who made the railings for the monument to Queen Eleanor in Westminster Abbey in 1293. It could, however, be older.

Decorated work of the highest quality is less plentiful though there was much remodelling and rebuilding. Dean and Swineshead are largely early 14C. Wymington is interesting in that it is known who paid for it: John Curteys, whose brass records that he died in 1391 and was a merchant of the Calais Staple. The church was built in one campaign in the third quarter of the 14C and is a fascinating blend of Decorated and early Perpendicular. The builder of the small church at Lower Gravenhurst is also known; he died in c 1360 and the building predates this. The most unusual and attractive architectural feature of this time is the vaulted stone canopy over the font at St. Mary's, Luton, a poised design without any of the excess that Decorated was all too capable of reaching. As in the rest of the S Midlands, Perpendicular times were ones of remodelling and alteration rather than wholesale rebuilding. There are, however, a few wholly Perpendicular buildings such as Odell, built to a spacious plan with slender piers and a typically tall tower arch. More important is Willington, probably all built by Sir John Gostwick, who acquired the manor in 1529 and died in 1545.

Of church building between the Reformation and Queen Victoria, what little was done continued in the medieval tradition as at Elstow in 1580, Blunham in 1583 and Holcot in 1590. Even in the 17C, work at Knotting in 1615 and Campton in 1649 was still in the Perpendicular spirit. A most appealing church is Whipsnade, which has a 16C brick tower and a delightful small nave of 1719 with brick chequerwork. Obviously the Victorians liked it too since they added a chancel in 1860 in a totally sympathetic style. Undoubtedly the most pleasing building of all is the Congregational church at Roxton. It is thatched, the overhang of which is supported by tree trunks as a rustic Gothick verandah.

In the revival of true Gothic in Bedfordshire, Silsoe Church of 1829–31 is a remarkable achievement. The architect was either Earl de Grey, first President of the Royal Institute, or T. Smith of Hertford. Smith's later Clophill (1848–49) also attempts medieval seriousness but is more a product of its time. Another interesting work is by the young Benjamin Ferrey, his East Hyde of 1840–41. The entrance façade is a pretty Romanesque composition, drawing on a Norman porch and stair to the N hall at Canterbury though the red brick gives it an Italianate feel. Moving on in time the most concentrated expression of mid-19C architecture is Gilbert Scott's chancel at Turvey (1852–54), a big work filled with enough cusps, crockets, Purbeck marble and general seriousness to delight any High Victorian. Scott also did Ridgmont on the Bedford estate in 1854–55, but he was displaced by Henry Clutton as architect to that prolific builder, the eighth Duke. There is more work by Clutton than any other major 19C architect. In all his work here he is assured and individualistic. Everywhere his detailing is imaginative. The first commission was rebuilding Steppingley Church for the Duke in 1859–60. This was followed by the nave and chancel at Souldrop and then the masterpiece, Woburn Church in 1865–68. Then came Aspley Heath in 1867–68, which has some inspired touches, and finally a restoration at Willington in 1876–77. Edward Haycock of Shrewsbury built the N aisle at Clifton in 1862; strong High Victorian stuff that would not have shamed a Street or a Butterfield. Sir Arthur Blomfield is to be remembered for Caldecote (1867–78) and forgotten for everything else. Caldecote shows him in his exciting early phase and he uses a free Byzantine-cum-Romanesque with lots of brick polychromy. Here is an early use of a properly articulated W baptistery, a favourite Blomfield device which was taken up by many late 19C architects. G.E. Street created the chapel at Luton Hoo in the 1870s in a Byzantine style but little can be seen of his work now: the chapel ceased to be used as such in 1940. The best place of worship from the turn of the century is G.F. Bodley's Bedford School chapel of 1907–08.

Bedfordshire has a considerable amount of interesting old wood-work. A good church for this is Upper Dean which retains its Perpendicular screen and its medieval roofs which include angel figures. Also there is a 15C pulpit and bench-ends, 18C altar rails and an old almsbox and chest. Oakley has a screen with a loft with quite a lot of painting. Over the entrance is a rather naive Christ seated on a rainbow against a red background and with the orb of the world at his feet. Other screens include 14C work at Lower Gravenhurst and Campton and, probably very late in the century, at Dunstable. A few screens, e.g. at Clifton, retain painted figures in the wainscot. At Leighton Buzzard there is a good display of 27 misericords, probably from St. Alban's Abbey; others are at St. Paul's, Bedford. At Odell the screen in the tower arch is dated 1637 and has two tiers of balusters; it is heavy work but a good example of its time. The pews date from 1686–87 and the 17C pulpit has an hourglass stand. There are many medieval roofs but among the best are those at Leighton Buzzard, where the nave roof was given by Alice de la Pole, Duchess of Suffolk, who held the manor between 1467 and 1475.

The two most extraordinary churches for woodwork are Old Warden and Cockayne Hatley, which contain extensive collections brought in during the early 19C, mainly from Belgium. At the latter it arrived in the 1820s thanks to the squarson, Henry Cockayne Cust, whose long incumbency lasted from 1806 to 1861. He purchased stalls of 1689 from Aulne Abbey and these line the walls of the chancel and extend into the nave. The collecting activities of Robert Henley, third Baron Ongley of Old Warden, were yet more prolific. He restored the church in 1841–42 and stuffed it full of ornate Continental work from the 16C to the 18C. It is interspersed with rather more than a sprinkling of contemporary Gothick. However, his lordship successfully rivals the Baroque weightiness of the furniture with the florid Gothick of his nave roof. The scheme at Cockayne Hatley is the more successfully arranged; at Old Warden it fails through over-indulgence. The only notable item of modern woodwork is the eagle lectern of 1955 at Cardington by Sir Albert Richardson, a very individual though hardly attractive piece.

Returning to Cockayne Hatley, this church has four fine early 14C stained glass figures (brought from a Yorkshire church) and some rare early 19C glass. There are three windows by Thomas Willement in the chancel: E, 1829 and two side ones, 1839. In the S aisle at

Northill there is a remarkable example of mid-17C glass, mostly in sunny yellow tones. It used to be in the E window and was put there in 1664 by the Grocers' Company, the patrons of the living. The royal arms were in the centre originally, a clear celebration of the newly restored monarchy. They were flanked by the arms of the Grocers (note the camel bringing spices) on one side, and of Lady Margaret Slaney, who had re-endowed the living, on the other. The work is signed by John Oliver. As for 19C glass, one of the best displays is the C.E. Kempe glass at Leighton Buzzard, including work brought from other churches. At St. Paul's, Bedford, there is engraved glass of 1982 by David Peace and Meinrad Craighead. It is interesting but rather sentimental and one hopes it does not date terribly. There are some interesting medieval wall paintings in the county. Chalgrave has late 13C Apostles and a 14C heraldic scheme. Wymington and Marston Moretaine both have Dooms. The latter is a rare dated example, for money was left for it in the will of William Wodill who died in 1505. Houghton Conquest has a Christ in Majesty over the chancel arch. Artistically, the best painting of all is an early 14C Crucifixion at Turvey.

Monumental brasses occur in some numbers, notably at Dunstable, Cockayne Hatley, Ampthill and Wymington. St. Paul's, Bedford has the slab to Simon de Beauchamp (died 1208) S of the altar and which, had it retained its brass, would have been by far the earliest in England. The most spectacular place for monuments must be Flitton (see gazetteer). For quality perhaps the best group is at Turvey to the Mordaunt family. Other good monuments are at Clifton (a fine early 16C work with angels bearing shields), Cardington (between the chancel and chapels and then in the N transept to the Whitbread family), Luton (the Wenlock monuments), Sutton (by Grinling Gibbons to Sir Roger Burgoyne, died 1679) and Eyeworth (a 17C series to the Anderson family).

There are a few miscellaneous features worth seeking out—two vast hooks for pulling burning thatch off houses at Eaton Bray, a medieval sanctus bell at Dunstable, and a three-tier bread cupboard at Milton Ernest, 'The Gift of Mrs Susanna Rolt and Tho: Rolt in Twelve, Two-Penny loaves, Weekly to the Poor of the Said Parish for Ever'. The surfaces of stone piers seem to have inspired would-be Bedfordshire artists for centuries for there is a remarkable preponderance of graffiti, the best examples of which are in the crossing at Leighton Buzzard—Geometrical tracery, a bird, a chalice with a face and a 3-D representation of the old story of Simon and Nell, the putative inventors of the simnel cake.

By far the most famous person connected with Bedfordshire churches was John Bunyan (1628–88), son of a tinker and born and baptised at Elstow. His spiritual awakening came in Bedford in the 1650s (see St. John's, Bedford). Dunstable Priory's Lady chapel was the scene in 1533 of the proceedings for the divorce of King Henry VIII and Catherine of Aragon. Joseph Paxton, designer of the Crystal Palace, was born the son of a poor farmer in Milton Bryan; there is a memorial window to him in the church. At Northill there is a plaque to Thomas Tompion (1639–1713), the 'father of English watch-making', who was born in the parish and who is buried in Westminster Abbey. Samuel Whitbread (1720–96), the founder of the great brewing dynasty, was born at Cardington and is buried in the N transept. In the churchyard at Cockayne Hatley lies Margaret Henley, who died aged five in 1894, and who was the inspiration for Wendy in J.M. Barrie's 'Peter Pan'. She was able to refer to Barrie only as the 'Fwendie' of her father, the poet W.E. Henley. Henley himself died in 1903 and was buried with his daughter.

(I am grateful to Mr C.J. Pickford for suggestions for this introduction.)

Bedford

St. John the Baptist, St. John's Street. St. John's main claim to fame is its part in the life of John Bunyan under the Commonwealth. In 1653 there was established within it the Independent Bedford Gospel Church of which the Rector was John Gifford. He appears to have been a reprobate but completely changed his ways on turning to religion. It was Gifford who was responsible for the spiritual awakening of Bunyan in 1653 during their discussions in the old rectory, which still stands N of the church. John Bunyan had been born in 1628 at Elstow a few miles S of Bedford and had led the life of a tinker. After his momentous conversion, Bunyan was appointed, in 1657, open-air preacher for the town and county. With the Restoration three years later, the Independent Gospel Church was thrown out of St. John's and Bunyan found himself in prison, as he refused to give up his outdoor preaching. His imprisonment lasted 12 years and during this time he wrote 'Pilgrim's Progress'. The Bunyan Meeting in Mill Street is the direct successor of the Independent Gospel Church. It has bronze doors illustrating scenes from 'Pilgrim's Progress'. Bunyan was pastor here in his later years. He died in 1688.

St. Mary, St. Mary's Street. This is the old parish church S of the Ouse, now vested in the Redundant Churches Fund. It has grown around an unaisled Norman cruciform structure, the tower and S transept of which survive little altered. The most striking external feature is the tower, in which the third stage includes broad, two-light openings with a central shaft. At the top two-light Perpendicular windows have been inserted and beside them are filled-in Norman arches. The S transept contains herringbone masonry, which the tower does not have, and in its E wall there is a blocked Norman window. This was cut into by a later one, perhaps in the early 13C, which in turn was blocked when the chancel was enlarged in the 14C (these windows are best seen inside). The S aisle was added in 1853 by T.J. Jackson and answers the one on the N which seems to have been erected in the early 16C. Jackson was also responsible for further extensive work in 1874–82. On the clerestory are attractive rainwater heads dated 1804. Inside, the nave has four-bay arcades—though more accurately the S one has three and a half. The half, at the E end, arose because at its construction in 1853, a crack in the SW part of the tower prompted the retention of a short stretch of wall for buttressing.

St. Paul, St. Paul's Square. St. Paul's lies in the town centre and sits comfortably as the town's main church, large, spacious and containing within its fabric remains of Newnham Priory, founded E of Bedford in c 1165 but now vanished.

The church, surrounded by elegant 18C gatepiers and railings, has a reconstructed crossing tower supporting a low stone spire in the style of its 14C predecessor. The crenellated tower has on each side a pair of two-light openings with trefoils, and the spire has similarly styled lucarnes. The main body of the church is predominantly Perpendicular and the form is known as a 'hall church' because the aisles reach the same height as the nave. The aisle walls display the clerestory. The fabric was heavily repaired in the last century; the most important external feature which remains is the two-storey 15C S porch, with statue niches over the doorway and stone quatrefoil panels at ground level. The N aisle is Victorian; care was taken to make the new exterior wall resemble its predecessor. St. Paul's has transepts N and S of the tower and a S chancel chapel (1415). N of the chancel lie the sacristy and vestry designed by G.F. Bodley in 1899.

Entering through the W door, the visitor finds himself beneath the gallery in the narthex, now converted into meeting rooms, kitchen etc. The broad hall of the nave and aisles may be seen ahead; the columns of the S arcade are quatrefoil, dating from c 1300, and have been copied in the N arcade of 1884. The roofs of the nave and the S aisle are 15C, and a roof of similar date may be seen in the S porch beneath a priest's room. A stone staircase leads to this 'parvise' from a low door E of the porch. A new chapel has been opened in the NW porch. At the W end of the nave there are galleries built in the 18C manner in 1982; they are well worth a visit for their view over the whole church and for a closer look at the ceiling carvings and the glass. The tower crossing is supported on four columns of c 1300, with arches rebuilt in 1865–68. The N transept was built in the 15C. The choir and sanctuary have their origins in the 13C; a door in the N wall dates from the same period but the wide arcades with their low capitals date from 1878–79. Before this date, the N wall contained Perpendicular windows; now, the organ stands above a screen in a new arcade, behind which a large, walk-through passage leads from the N transept to the new vestries. The choir roof is 15C and was raised in 1879 without dismantling the timbers; the angels date from this time. S of the choir, the Trinity chapel of 1415 was built for the Guilds of the Trinity and Corpus Christi. The ceiling is contemporary with the chapel fabric but some of the carved stone corbels are Norman in origin.

The choir fittings were reordered from a maze of old pews and stalls in 1899 under G.F. Bodley. New screens were created from old fragments to fit the arcades of the choir, whilst some clever splicing together of medieval and new work created a fine set of choirstalls facing each other in front of the screens. Rattee & Kett of Cambridge were in charge of the carpentry and only a close examination of the woodwork, dark for the old and light for the new work, reveals the difference between them. The misericords and the faces on the arm rests are also notable. Bodley provided the black and white floor, the roof gilding and painting, and stencil patterns on the E wall, although these last have been covered with whitewash. The organ to the N was built in 1898 by Norman & Beard. Within the sanctuary, the high altar with its riddel posts and curtains was set up by F.C. Eden in 1900; the reredos now lies against the N wall of the sanctuary. Fortunately, the Persian carpet, 17C chairs and pair of large bronze candlesticks (copied by William Bainbridge Reynolds from Italian originals) have not been removed. S of the altar may be found the tomb of Simon de Beauchamp (died 1208), who founded the Priory of Newnham. Unfortunately, the brass has been removed from its matrix, for it would have been the oldest in England.

On the S side, a plaque commemorates the National Day of Prayer held in this church and broadcast by the BBC in 1941. In the Trinity chapel, S of the choir, the two brasses to Sir William Harpur and his second wife Dame Margaret lie beside a chancel column. Sir William, who died in 1573, displays an unusual combination of dress, wearing his robes as Lord Mayor of London over a suit of armour. Sir William and his wife were important benefactors of Bedford, providing moneys for several schools and almshouses. Nearby stands the obelisk monument to the later Sir William Harpur (died 1768) and his wife Dame Alice (commemorated also by the school which still bears her name). The colour-glazed roundel is a 19C copy of a 16C Della Robbia original. Near the altar, a chair was constructed from two 15C bench-ends.

The chapel is divided from the S transept by a parclose screen which used to be a five-panel 15C Rood screen across the choir but was removed here in the last century. Outside the screen and against the S wall are the mid-19C Mayor's stalls. Beneath the NW tower arch stands a stone pulpit which used to form part of the reredos in the Trinity chapel, but which was skilfully converted to its current use with the addition in 1680 of a spiral staircase. From here, firstly John Bunyan and later John Wesley gave some of their powerful and influential sermons.

Turning to the E, the richly carved Rood screen forms the chief work at St. Paul's of G.F. Bodley; it was made by Rattee & Kett. It was Bodley's last work for the church (1906) and one of his last works altogether before he died in 1907. The beautiful screen shows his sensitive proportioning and knowledgeable use of the Gothic style after more than 50 years' practice; it was coloured by F.C. Eden in 1938. The font in the N aisle has a medieval base and Victorian basin, and a cover by J.P. White (1936). Notice also the window of 1892 by C.E. Kempe. By ascending the stairs into the gallery at the W end one can obtain an unusually close view of the interesting Te Deum window dating from 1932, which bears a description on its right side. On leaving the church, one passes through the engraved glass doors by David Peace and Meinrad Craighead, showing symbols of Genesis and the Resurrection.

St. Peter de Merton, St. Peter's Street. St. Peter's derives its name from Merton Priory in Surrey, to which the church belonged. It is pleasantly set across a green N of the centre and presents an interesting spectacle, with its early tower and striking—albeit modern—gables to the W. The tower, now at the centre of the church, was originally a W one to a late pre-Conquest church, parts of the nave of which survive in the present chancel: see the long-and-short quoins (N, visible only inside). Traces of a rounded apse to the early church have been found below ground. The main external feature of the tower is the twinned belfry openings beneath a recessed enclosing arch. Further Norman evidence is the impressive S door, which came from St. Peter de Dunstable, another Bedford church demolished in 1545. It has three richly decorated orders. The church is entered through a W porch of 1885 by J.P. St. Aubyn. Inside, the main interest is the pre-Conquest evidence—see the long-and-short quoins of the tower either side of the W arch. The present nave and aisles are of six bays. The N aisle was erected in 1846, probably by J.T. Wing, and it was extended westward, together with the nave and S aisle, in 1882. It is a pity about the bare stonework and red ribbon-pointing. In the windows on the N of the chancel are extensive fragments of old stained glass.

Bedford School, *Chapel.* The chapel was commissioned from G.F. Bodley at the end of his long career. Although Bodley died during its construction, its external appearance remains much as he originally intended, while the interior fittings sometimes show the hand of his assistant, Cecil Hare, who took over its completion after Bodley's death.

The chapel, built in 1907, lies on high ground away from the main school buildings, and is constructed of red brick with stone dressings in the long, tall style so much favoured by Bodley. A low square tower forms the main accent on the W front, and a wide flight of steps leads up to the W door. On the second stage of the tower is a stone niche, and above this a crenellated belfry; to the SW lies a narrow turret, and two small windows complete the W elevation. Eight buttresses support each side of the chapel. Note how they do not break the roofline. Between them lie small three-light windows, whilst the E window is kept high, together with those above the N and S vestries.

Inside, the N and S walls are lined the full length with stalls in the manner of an Oxford or Cambridge college. The roof is of the wagon type and displays gilded bosses which conceal ventilation holes, allowing air to clear from inside the chapel into the open via the tower. The E wall is divided into the sanctuary arch and the two low vestry-passage archways; two empty statue niches stand above the smaller arches. A wooden gallery lies across the W wall beneath the windows. The interior resembles Bodley's other academic chapels at Marlborough and at Queens' College, Cambridge, which employ the same long, narrow plan; at Bedford, however, the roofline is broken inside by the use of a separate space for the high altar.

The stalls are executed in pale oak and are placed in front of panelling and beneath carved wooden coving. The bench-ends at the rear were designed by Bodley and were carved locally to show heraldic beasts. The panelling supports memorials, mostly to old boys who lost their lives in the First World War. More pews were added in later years to the designs of Cecil Hare and were placed in front of Bodley's. Only the painted decoration of the tiebeams survives in the nave, the original stencil work on the roof having been obliterated in 1960 by the present scheme. The roofs of the sanctuary and its N and S passages, however, still maintain their elegant Edwardian colours and also contain some lettering. The sanctuary floor is made of black and white tiles, and it was a favourite concept of Bodley's to contrast the flowing lines of his Gothic tracery with the rigid geometry of this type of flooring. The stone altar (1928) is by Oswald P. Milne, an old boy who became an architect and who subsequently designed buildings for the school. The altar frontals are by Watts & Co., the church furnishing firm which Bodley helped to found in the 1870s. The E window contains glass fitted as a Boer War memorial, while the glass in the N sanctuary passage (1909) is probably by Kempe & Co. The lectern and pulpit in the nave, together with the reredos, are by Cecil Hare but they betray Bodley's influence.

Chalgrave, *All Saints.* The great interest here lies in the medieval wall paintings, largely uncovered in the 1930s. The earliest paintings date from the very end of the 13C and are to be found at the W ends of the aisles where the walls were left blank to receive them. This was a scheme of almost life-size representations of the 12 Apostles beneath tall canopies. The figures extend to the side walls where they have been interfered with by later windows. On the N and S walls there are also two separate figures, that on the S perhaps representing St. Thomas Becket. The most complete series, however, is the heraldic work, paralleled on such a scale only at Hailes in Gloucestershire. In the spandrels of the arches there are, or were, shields with armorial bearings. Those facing the nave are set among leafy tendrils and hang, picture-like, from a tendril hook suspended from an ornamental border. Dr E. Clive Rouse points to the scheme as celebrating the Loryng family, who were lords of the manor, and their connections. Theirs is the only coat to be repeated. Rouse dates the work to after 1352 and before 1382 on the heraldic evidence. Later medieval work (of c 1400) includes, over the S doorway, St. Martin on a white horse dividing his cloak with a beggar, and, on the E wall of the N aisle, part of an Annunciation. There are also considerable traces of 18C texts.

There are two good 14C effigies of knights on tomb-chests. One, placed under the N arcade, is probably of Sir Nigel Loryng. He died in 1385 or 1386, was noted for his courage at the Battle of Sluys in 1340 and was a founder of the Knights of the Garter in 1348. The other, also to a Loryng, is slightly earlier, perhaps of 1360–65. Other features to note are the remains of the double piscina in the S aisle, a nice 14C piscina in the chancel, the old roofs and ceilings and two very attractive Victorian metal chandeliers.

A late 18C incumbent, Dr William Dodd, was executed for forgery in 1777.

Dunstable Priory, *St. Peter.* St. Peter's is all that now remains of the major monastic foundation in Bedfordshire. It was founded in 1131 as an Augustinian priory and stands as one of the finest examples of Norman work in the county.

Most of the priory buildings were dismantled during the Reformation, but to the SW lies the 15C gateway which led into the outer court. S of the church, mounds under the grass are all that remains of the cloister walls which connected with the S side. At the E end there are the blocked archways which indicate the doors connecting the nave inside with the choir, now gone. The brickwork and windows and the E wall are modern; the appearance of the N wall is largely the result of Victorian restoration, including the aisle windows in the Perpendicular style and most of the Norman doorway. This doorway was surrounded by a porch until the 16C. Only the capitals are definitely original.

The history of the sumptuous W front is complicated by a series of removals and additions, beginning in the 12C and ending with the 19C restoration. The large, round-headed portal to the S of the façade dates from c 1170–90 with four richly carved arches of diminishing size. The tympanum of three niches and the doorway itself with its square-headed mouldings are 15C. Immediately N of the portal lies a small length of four intersecting arches, framed within a gently pointed arch about 20ft high, all of which dates from the end of the 12C. Next, a little further N, a richly decorated doorway, also late 12C, is surmounted by arches and capitals of five orders, some displaying different varieties of stiff-leaf moulding. Surrounding the arch, a light overall diaper relief provides a subtle enrichment for this highly decorated façade. Seven pointed arches, with brackets for a line of statues, lie above the small doorway, whilst above these niches, an arcade of six taller, cusped arches protect the deep recesses which lie behind them. In 1222, before the rest of this

W front could be completed, a storm blew down the two towers N and S of the façade. Rebuilding started at the top of the W end, and an asymmetrical elevation appears to have been developed over the next 30–40 years. Two tall lancet windows with a smaller arch between them provides what normally would be seen as the centre of the elevation, whilst a single 15C buttress was placed further S. A NW buttress, complete with statue arcading and of substantial proportions, replaced the old tower. Further alterations were made in the 15C. The Totternhoe stone from which the church was built is soft and thus requires renovation from time to time. This wall was sensitively restored in 1900 by G.F. Bodley, followed by further attention in the 20C by Sir Albert Richardson.

Inside, the wide Norman nave has seven-bay arcades with scalloped capitals; one shaft runs up the side of the columns to support the roof, which rests on carved wooden figures of the Apostles. Another two shafts run on each side of the roof shaft and stop at the springing of the outer arch of the old triforium arcade, now the clerestory level. The old clerestory was removed after the parishioners were given the right to use the nave in 1392, and windows were placed in the triforium. The roof dates from 1871 but it is a copy of the Perpendicular original. The S aisle vaulting is largely an 1852 copy of the two original E ones and was made by George Somers Clarke, Sr.

The most important fitting is the beautiful screen dating probably from c 1400, having five open bays to the floor and cusped arches within ogee gables beneath a long beam. The E wall contains a tall crocketed canopy over a statue of Christ in Majesty, with a figure of the Archangel Gabriel on the left and the Virgin Mary on the right, all dating from 1962, when G.F. Bodley's Rood screen was removed to St. John's, Tue Brook in Liverpool (q.v.). The two doorways on each side of the niches led into the choir. In the easternmost bay of the N arcade stand unusual 16C pillars; these are ten carved wooden banisters depicting, for instance, symbols of the Passion, the royal badges of England and the arms of Castile. Also on the N side, W of the screen, is the square font, which dates from 1852 and is made of red marble.

There are many funerary monuments in the S aisle, for example, a fine incised tomb-slab dating from the 13C, which probably depicts a Canon called Richard Darant, floor brasses to Richard Pynfold and his wife (1516), and memorials to 18C Londoners who had second homes in Dunstable. The glass in the W windows represents King Henry I, founder of the priory and Bernard, the first Prior; it was designed in 1972 by John Hayward. Near the W entrance, the old font was reconstructed in the 19C from Norman fragments.

One leaves at the W end by modern doors, but passing the old ones which are peppered with shot fired at them during the Civil War. In the original Lady chapel, now gone, a significant event occurred when the annulment took place of the marriage between King Henry VIII and Catherine of Aragon.

Eaton Bray, St. Mary the Virgin. A Norman baron, William de Cantelou, began to build the present church in c 1200. It is celebrated for its excellent stonework, particularly in the N aisle. The building material used is Totternhoe stone (a hard band in the chalk strata), quarried from the village of that name which lies a little E of Eaton Bray.

The exterior is a 15C remodelling of an earlier building. Thus while the basic structure was begun in the early 13C, most of the windows date from the Perpendicular rearrangement. The low tower with its spike was enlarged in c 1500 by the Lord of the Manor, Sir Reginald Bray, adviser to King Henry VII; the tower was rebuilt again in the early part of the present century. The nave roof was raised in the 15C when the clerestory windows were added. The roofs are low-pitched and have plain parapets. The chancel is partially off-set from the main body of the church, while 'transepts' are formed by two low chapels to the NE and SE of the nave aisles. N and S porches abut the W ends of these projecting chapels. Inside the S porch, fine 13C scroll ironwork forms a pattern covering almost the whole door, the timber body of which was renewed in 1900.

Inside the church, a superb rhythm is established by the five-bay arcades. Deeply cut roll-mouldings enliven the beautiful outlines of the N arcade dating from c 1220; the piers have eight shafts, some of them detached, with shaft-rings just below the stiff-leaf capitals which are boldly undercut. Here, the early medieval stonemasons demonstrated the fresh imagination and spirited execution of a new style, the spontaneity of which the 19C revivalists were so often unable to imitate. Behind the arches in the N aisle, notice the truncated springings above each capital which were intended to form a low aisle roof. It is doubtful, however, whether this feature was ever built. The S arcade is a little later in date and plainer; the piers are unshafted, octagonal in section and with simpler moulded arches. The responds at the ends of the arcades are conical and are carved with foliage decoration similar to that of the capitals. Over the arcades, the line of the old roof is visible on the nave walls and above each arch lies a small clerestory window; between these windows lie the corbels supporting the roof, the majority of them carved with human faces. The N chapel and the Lady chapel, although originally 13C or 14C, were rebuilt in the 15C in the Perpendicular style. The fine E window in the Lady chapel, which has a partly blocked central transom to hold a statue (replaced in the last century), the stone niches and the low stone reredos above are all late 15C work. They were probably designed by Sir Reginald Bray, whose building mark may be found on the S wall of the chapel. On each side of the chancel arch lie two more niches, this time probably contemporary with the arch which is dated to 1320. The chancel was also rebuilt in the 15C, but the piscina, with its two sturdy columns, is 13C.

The fittings in the chancel have been added over several centuries. The altar-tomb beneath the NE window belongs to Jane, Lady Bray (died 1539), who married Edmund, the nephew of Sir Reginald Bray. The choirstalls, of the same date, were reconstructed during the Victorian period, while the E window by Heaton, Butler & Bayne commemorates the Silver Jubilee of King George V in 1935. In the nave, the wooden pulpit is 18C, while the organ commemorates the completion of the conservative restoration of the church between 1890 and 1916 by Robert William Edis. The long-handled tools on each side of the organ are thatching hooks, which were used to tear down the blazing thatch from burning cottages. In the N chapel may be seen the beautifully executed record of Vicars which shows also the coats of arms of benefactors. The reredos in the N chapel dates from the 15C and was repainted and donated in 1979. In the Lady chapel may be seen the brass to Jane, Lady Bray, mentioned above, who is buried in the chancel tomb-chest. The brass is a palimpsest and was taken from the tomb of a bishop or an abbot at the Reformation; Lady Jane's son and her ten daughters are depicted together with their mother, who kneels before a prayer book. The inscription contains a *momento mori*: 'For as ye ar so I was, and as I am so shalt ye be'. In the S aisle, the stout font is 13C, and judging by its short columns, which have similar stiff-leaf capitals, probably dates from the same period of construction as the N arcade; the wooden cover dates from 1923.

Felmersham, *St. Mary.* At Felmersham one finds that poised elegance which is the mark of Early English architecture at its very best. There are few façades in the whole of England to compare with the W one here. Inside, the majestic crossing ranks favourably with those in the greatest churches. Why this splendour at Felmersham? In the 12C the church had been granted to Lenton Priory (near Nottingham), but there is no reason to suppose that Lenton would have felt the need to erect such an ambitious structure. It was probably built between c 1220 and 1240 but the only documentary evidence is the grant of 25 oaks for the tower in 1235. The building consists of a chancel, crossing tower, asymmetrical transepts, nave, aisles and a S porch. It is largely unaltered from the early 13C, except for the heightening of the tower, the addition of a clerestory and new windows in the aisles. Restorations took place in 1848, 1853–54 (both by T.J. Jackson of Bedford) and 1867–69.

Starting on the S, the Perpendicular additions of the tall embattled clerestory and top stage of the tower have undue prominence. Later work is also met with in the two renewed square-headed 14C windows in the S aisle. Otherwise all is 13C. The tower has two 13C stages before the present top and looks as though a spire may have existed originally or at least was planned. The original belfry stage has different treatment on each face, the basic design being two openings flanked by two large blind arches (not on the N). The S transept arrangement is unusual. The gabled part is not wide and either side of it are lean-to roofs against the tower. The E window contains modern Reticulated tracery but within 13C jambs: was there a triple-lancet arrangement originally? The N transept is larger and more conventional than the S and has three equal lancets on the N. The N wall of the aisle has three-light Perpendicular panel tracery windows. But the climax is the W front. It is arranged in three tiers with vertical proportions of, very roughly, 3:1:2, starting at the top. The upper stage was altered in Perpendicular times by the insertion of a large three-light window but this does not destroy the composition. On either side of it are single shafted lancets. Shafts appear in profusion in the row of seven arches that divide the upper from the lower tier. They are remarkably delicate. Each cluster is arranged as a line of three with a further shaft set in front of the middle one. In the ground stage is a W portal of extraordinary richness. It has no fewer than 18 rolls or similar devices which stand proud of very deep cutting (up to c 2ins). On either side of the doorway are double blind arches with a quatrefoil in the head. The W ends of the aisles in no way try to rival the nave, having only small shafted lancets to enliven them.

The dominating feature of the interior is the mighty crossing. Its arches and piers are all finely moulded. The inner order consists of a large roll which, on the arch to the nave, dies into two corbels. The nave arcades have four bays and, oddly, the two E ones are wider than the others. Another oddity is that although the alternation of octagonal and round piers is common enough in an E–W direction, here each pier has the different shape opposite it on the other side of the nave. None of this, however, is unduly troubling to the eye. Each arch has moulding on the outer order and a chamfer on the inner one. The nave is well-lit by the large clerestory windows and is thus a marked contrast to the dark, 13C atmosphere of the chancel. From the S transept half-arches lead up to the tower walls.

The vaulted screen was given, as the inscription says, by 'Ricardi Kyng et agnet' his wife. Particularly attractive is the way nine angel figures have been devised to take the place of normal crockets over the entrance to the chancel. Sadly, the Rood loft was removed in 1853. In the chancel is a double piscina. There is a chest dated 1628.

Flitton, *St. John the Baptist.* Flitton Church presents an extra-ordinary spectacle. At the E end are white, stuccoed structures attached to a conventional nave, aisles and a W tower, all built in dark brown sandstone. The explanation for the eastern parts is that they represent a remodelled chancel and the vast mausoleum of the de Grey family which contains a huge array of monuments. The de Greys were Earls of Kent and had their seat at Wrest Park two miles to the E.

The medieval parts include a standard Perpendicular tower with an equally standard Bedfordshire stair turret. Less usual is the turret for the Rood loft stairs projecting above the clerestory. The S porch used to bear the arms of Edward de Grey, who succeeded as fourth Lord Grey de Ruthyn in 1440 and was created Earl of Kent in 1465. As he died in 1489 the porch and, it is usually presumed, the rest of the medieval church, date from between 1440 and 1489. The nave is of three bays and has slim piers of standard section. The de Grey mausoleum is a vast construction built on a cruciform plan so that one can wander from room to room as if in a museum. It is organised so that its 'nave' flanks the chancel of the church on the N. From its crossing its S transept wraps round the E end of the true chancel. Yet this is not very clear from the S side because of a remodelling of the chancel to harmonise with the mausoleum. Both the chancel and mausoleum are stuccoed—the latter is built mostly of brick (see the E wall of the N transept)—and finished with battlements and shaped gables. The original part of the mausoleum was built N of the chancel to house an early 17C monument to Henry, fifth Earl of Kent (see below) and has two contemporary three-light windows. Then, as an inscription in the crossing declares, an addition was made in 1705. A further inscription mentions 'Further alteration' and it was no doubt then that the chancel and the mausoleum took their final form. On the date evidence of the monuments this cannot have been later than c 1740. The N and E arms have wooden windows.

The earliest monuments are in fact in the N aisle of the church—a fragmentary brass to Alianora Conquest (died 1434) towards the W end and in the centre a brass to Elizabeth Waren (died 1544). The mausoleum is entered through a pair of fine wrought-iron gates (a pity about the Victorian woodwork just beyond them). Taking the monuments room by room, one starts N of the chancel with a brass to Henry Gray [sic] (died 1545) in armour on the floor towards the W and obviously not *in situ*. Facing the gates is the monument that started the enterprise, the tomb-chest for Henry, fifth Earl of Kent (died 1614) and his wife, Mary (died 1580). To the E are the white marble effigies of Henry, ninth Earl (died 1651) and Amabella his wife (died 1658). This tomb is altogether more ambitious and the back is enriched with allegorical figures. On the W wall Elizabeth Talbot, Countess Dowager (died 1651) is commemorated by a large curved black marble tablet flanked by pink marble columns. Jane Hart (died 1671) has a monument dated 1673 against the S wall. Her figure rests in a semi-reclining position on a black and white monument. In the crossing are a pair of very similar monuments in which tall pyramids embrace broken pediments and arms; there are no figures. They are to Amabella de Grey (died 1727) and Anne de Grey (died 1733). In the N arm lie Henrietta de Grey (died 1717) and Henry de Grey (also died 1717) on separate tombs. The tall pyramid motif reappears but here girt with a garland. Anthony de Grey, Earl of Harrold is in Roman dress and a semi-reclining pose; the monument is by John Dowyer and was paid for in 1726. The smallest and simplest monument of all is a white urn to Mary Gregory (undated). The biggest and finest, however, is in the E arm to Henry de Grey, Duke of Kent (died 1740) and his two wives. It is signed by Edward Shepherd. The Duke's semi-reclining effigy is in Roman costume and has been attributed to J.M. Rysbrack. His first wife, Jemima, is at a lower level but, though there is space for her, there is no effigy of the second. Also in this area are Philip, Earl of Hardwicke (died 1790) with a sorrowing woman beside an urn, and, in a style by then becoming old-fashioned, Amabel, Baroness Lucas of Crudwell (died 1833). In the S transept are the latest monuments starting with Henrietta, Countess de Grey (died 1848) which was made by Terence Farrell in 1853. It shows the disconsolate family round the coffin while above an angel spirits her soul to heaven. Against the E wall is Thomas de Grey (died 1859) by Matthew Noble.

At the E end of the S aisle there is some very charming glass by Christine Boyce (1978), showing the creatures, flowers and fruits of the fields and hedgerows.

Leighton Buzzard, *All Saints*. This large 13C church stands at the far end of Church Square, with the pedimented old school to the left. In 1189 the Bishop of Lincoln granted the church to a Prebendary of his cathedral, under whose 'peculiar' jurisdiction it remained until the 19C. The church was rebuilt from c 1277 in ironstone. It was consecrated in 1288 and the building was completed shortly afterwards with the construction of the spire, 191ft high. Remodelling occurred in the 15C, when Perpendicular windows replaced the Early English ones, and when the nave was given a clerestory and a new 'angel roof'. In the 16C a two-storey vestry was added, and in the 17C the heavy porches were built or rebuilt. Further high quality decorative work and fittings were provided in the Victorian period, notably some fine stained glass. On the 13th April, 1985, the church was badly damaged by a fire which was begun by an intruder. The exterior was restored by the end of 1987 and the interior by late 1988, under the direction of Paul Reynolds.

The church comprises a nave with aisles and W, N and S porches, a crossing tower and spire, transepts, a chancel, a NE vestry and a choir vestry (of 1906) which is placed like a N chancel aisle. The lower parts of the ironstone walls of the cruciform building, together with the central tower and limestone spire, remain from the 13C. The upper parts of the walls, their roofs and crenellations (a wall plate in the N side of the chancel shows the division), and the windows throughout, date from the 15C. The chancel is the same width as, and only a little shorter than, the nave; the former connects with a two-storey vestry to the N, dating from c 1500, which originally was entered only from the chancel, and with the choir vestry. The ironstone tower has belfry openings of louvred central lancets, with a blind lancet and trefoil decoration on each side; each corner has a narrow buttress which is apparently only decorative. Above the buttresses and in front of the spire's broaches rise small corner pinnacles, which were added in 1842. The spire has a set of three narrow lucarnes on the cardinal faces, the lowest having two paired openings. The gargoyles around the church are also from this period, while the sundials post-date the Civil War. The W wall, with Decorated doorway, was restored by G.F. Bodley at the end of the

Famous 13C ironwork by Thomas of Leighton on the W door at All Saints

19C. The 13C hinges of the W door (which is of modern wood) were probably designed by Thomas of Leighton, who was responsible for the grille which screens the tomb of Queen Eleanor in Westminster Abbey. The hinges at All Saints' have scroll decorations which end in stylised flowers and leaf fronds.

The tall, narrow, four-bay nave has octagonal piers and moulded capitals, and double-chamfered arches. The three-light clerestory windows are paired above each bay. The wooden roofs are 15C. The present nave roof was built by Alice de la Pole, Duchess of Suffolk, who owned the manor from 1467 to 1475. It is East Anglian in style, bearing carved wooden angels and, on the stone corbels which support the heavy timber beams, more angels who hold symbols of the Passion. Both transepts have a late 13C statue niche in the E wall, with roll-mouldings and a trefoiled arch. On the S wall of the chancel there are the 13C sedilia, with fine Purbeck marble shafts, and the contemporary piscina; but these and the frieze above them are much restored.

One of the oldest fittings is the Early English font of local white limestone, of c 1240, in the SW corner, which has a tubby round bowl supported by a substantial central column and four tall, thin shafts at the corners, whose tops provide flat projections to the rim of the bowl. In the nave are the pulpit of 1638 and the fine oak eagle lectern which is of the late 14C. It owes its survival to the quick actions of the church architect, who rescued it during the fire in 1985. Other woodwork that survived includes the elegant screen (15C), with some painted decoration, the late 14C stalls with 27 misericords (probably from St. Alban's Abbey), and G.F. Bodley's panelling and paving in the sanctuary. The reredos, of c 1900, is a good example of Bodley's later work, displaying a Crucifixion and two accompanying figures beneath carved alabaster canopies, parts of the latter being highlighted in gold. The side panels of angels are made from embossed leather and were produced locally. Bodley's choir organ of 1888 perished in the fire; he also designed the loft for the main organ in the N transept in 1906, but not the organ case. The new instrument is by Harrison & Harrison. Bodley was responsible, too, for bringing inside the ancient iron hinges onto the vestry door in the N chancel wall; the hinges used to be on the small S chancel door. The hinges have recently been identified as being probably by Thomas of Leighton or by his masters. The splendid glass dates from between 1863 and 1905 and is mostly by C.E. Kempe. Work by Kempe may be seen in the W window of 1887, in the S aisle (of the same date), in the N aisle (1889 and 1905), in the S transept (1888), and soon, the S transept's S window will contain four newly-donated Kempe archangels to replace glass removed in the 1960s. Also worth noting is the pictorial N transept N window of 1865. The E window of 1870 by Goddard & Gibbs was damaged by the fire and will probably have to be replaced.

The oldest memorial is on the N side of the chancel. It is of Purbeck marble, with the brass missing, and it probably commemorated John Prophet (died 1416), Dean of Hereford and York and Prebendary of Leighton. Joshua Pulford, a former Vicar and founder of the old school in Church Square, is commemorated by a plaque on the W wall of the N transept. Two important examples of medieval graffiti are on the crossing piers; on the SE pier is a scratched drawing of a fine pointed window with Geometrical tracery; on the SW pier is a deeply carved representation of a man and a woman, which probably represents Simon and Nellie from the medieval story of the Sim-Nel cake; the woman, to the right, is waving a mixing-spoon at the man. The scene provides an indication of the kind of clothes worn by those who used the medieval church.

Lower Gravenhurst, *St. Mary the Virgin.* This church, on top of a small hill, is interesting for two reasons. First, there is a documentary date for its building, and second, it has an interesting selection of fittings. S of the altar is a brass tablet which records that Robert de Bilhemore had the church built anew (*fiet faire cette eglise de nouele*). He died in c 1360 and this would fit the Decorated building. It is small, with a W tower and the nave and chancel in one. The interior has that pleasing, somewhat decrepit air of unrestored churches. This lack of 19C attention no doubt explains the survival of the furnishings. These are a late 14C square-headed screen with traces of painting in the wainscot, a Jacobean pulpit and tester, 17C altar rails and 15C benches. There is also the medieval altar slab with its five consecration crosses, a 15C shelf S of the altar with four holes for candles, a piscina in the SE part of the nave and a kingpost roof. A rare survival is a couple of tussock kneelers in a case on the N side. N of the altar is a small monument to Benjamin Pigott (died 1606), who had three wives and, if you count them, no fewer than 14 children. The monument was altered later. The church is now vested in the Redundant Churches Fund.

Luton

St. Mary. The earliest known church on this site was completed in 931, but in the 12C it was replaced by a cruciform building, parts of which still survive. In the 13C and 14C, the church was rebuilt largely in the form we see today, with its characteristic flint and stone chequer pattern on the exterior and the fine 15C stonework of the Wenlock chapel and Barnard chantry inside.

The exterior is largely 15C, but the lower parts of the tower are early 14C, including the W doorway and the window above with cusped tracery; the tower is crenellated, with small angle turrets, short spire and with buttresses containing early 20C statues by Taylorson on their first and second stages. The first and second stages of the tower itself contain single-light openings in each face, surrounded by the overall chequer-pattern, which covers most of the church. The Perpendicular aisles and clerestory have five bays and are crenellated. The S porch (14C) has a turret stair leading to a parvise and, inside the porch, a door which is known to date from 1530—the Wolsey door—named after the Cardinal who was a patron of the church. The N and S transepts each has an E chapel; off the N transept is the Wenlock chapel of the 14C, enlarged in 1461, and off the S transept, the narrow Hoo chapel. E of the Wenlock chapel is the early 15C sacristy, which Lord Wenlock dismantled and rebuilt one bay further E in order to enlarge his own private chapel; access to the room above the sacristy is through the NE stair turret. The chancel has late 14C origins; while restoring the church in the mid-19C, G.E. Street discovered the remains of a Perpendicular E window. Instead of reconstructing the original window, however, he inserted the present Early English lancets, which he particularly favoured.

Inside, most of the nave piers date from the Perpendicular rebuilding, but the tower responds of the two arcades, like the tower itself, are early 14C, and the roofline of this earlier date may be seen above the tower arch. The three W columns of the N arcade are 14C also. Walking to the E end of the S aisle, one may see the oldest surviving fabric: a Norman arch leading into the transept, its plainness contrasting with the slightly later Early English arch between the N aisle and N transept with its crisply carved, stiff-leaf capitals. The remainder of the nave dates from the first half of the 15C; also at that time, the transepts were raised and provided with new roofs. The arcades leading from the transepts into their respective chapels are 14C, while the screens between the chapels and the chancel date from the 15C. The more modest of the two, the S screen into the Hoo chapel, was constructed in the late 15C; on the opposite side, the double-arched Wenlock screen dates from the enlargement of the chapel in 1461 by Sir John Wenlock. With its well-proportioned height and depth, this screen remains the dominant feature of the E end. The Wenlock chapel was restored in 1914 by Lady Wernher of nearby Luton Hoo. Through the E doorway one enters the Decorated sacristy, comprising four bays of a rib-vaulted stone roof supported by a single, free-standing column and six wall supports. The N wall of the chancel preserves some 13C arcading near a 14C Easter sepulchre; the wall opposite contains the early 15C four-seat sedilia with elaborate canopy panels and, to its W, the low chantry to Richard Barnard (Vicar, 1477–92). The shallow recess has carved relief in the spandrels of the arches, delicate vaulting and small windows.

The choirstalls in the chancel date from the early 15C and display armrest carvings of animals. The chancel screen was dismantled in the late 18C and now fills the arcading between the S transept and the Hoo chapel. In 1864, G.E. Street discovered some painted panels in the S porch which he considered were originally from the screen, and so he placed them in the position we see today. The medieval screen which divides the Wenlock chapel from the N transept came from Luton Hoo; beneath the stone screen lie the tombs of William Wenlock (died 1392) and Lady Alice Rotherham, with a brass of c 1490. Inside the Wenlock chapel, the many brasses are mostly from the 15C; the helmet and gauntlets are said to be those worn by Sir John Wenlock. In the upper sections of the E window of the chapel are remnants of medieval glass, while the Gothic Revival reredos dates from Lady Wernher's restoration in 1914. The W wall of the N transept displays the fine brass to John Acworth (died 1513), below which are eight brothers and nine sisters of the Luton guild which he founded. The windows in the nave clerestory show the arms of 20 English dioceses, those on the S side having been designed by George Pace; notice the 15C corbel heads in between the windows. The 14C Totternhoe stone baptistery at the W end of the nave was probably presented by King Edward III's wife, Phillippa, when the crown held the living; it is divided into eight arched sections with Decorated canopies and is unique in this country. The Purbeck marble font inside was the gift of the Vicar in c 1330 and has carved faces around the bowl. In the S aisle, the recess holds the somewhat damaged effigy of Richard Barnard, donor of the font. E of the doorway lies a pre-Conquest corbel of a man with a moustache, and below, a 14C stoup.

Union Chapel, Castle Street. The Baptist Church was founded in Luton in 1675 and this important Greek Revival building dates from

1836–44. It has three bays with a Doric entrance portico of two fluted columns rising above a flight of steps from the street; the exterior is stuccoed and painted, with the words 'Union Chapel' carved on the pediment above the metopes. The doorway lies within a recessed entrance bay. Victorian additions of brick lie at the rear. The future of the building is uncertain.

Roxton, *Congregational Church.* There can be few more delightful places of worship in the country. A church was established here in 1808 by C.J. Metcalfe of Roxton Park. It started in a barn and did not become independent till 1822. The barn still forms the core of the church but wings were built on for day and Sunday schools. As a result the building is T-shaped. It is wholly covered by thatch, which overhangs the walls considerably to make a verandah, supported by tree trunks. By the entrance to the church these even have struts as if to form a kind of rustic tracery. The windows of the building are Gothick and the walls are covered by whitened roughcast. At the tip of the S wing is a timber-lined alcove with a prospect over Roxton Park. On the S of the church is a projection for the Metcalfe pew. The internal arrangements have changed little, with a gallery in the first bay and simple benches. This building is in character with others in the village, especially one near the main road with a high thatched roof and supporting timber columns—one expects a little old witch to pop out at any moment! There is no definite dating for the remodelling of the church, but it may have occurred shortly after 1822.

Swineshead, *St. Nicholas.* Practically the whole church is Decorated. It seems to have been started about a third of the way through the 14C and, apart from the clerestory and vestry, was complete some 30 or 40 years later. The plan is of the standard aisled variety though it seems that the tower, now placed in the conventional W position, was originally destined for the NW corner.

The tower has paired belfry openings and a parapet of pierced quatrefoils, behind which rises a spire with two tiers of lucarnes. The most distinctive feature is the W entrance consisting of a shallow porch under a battlemented gable with flanking pinnacles. This arrangement no doubt derived from Northamptonshire, where related examples can be seen at Higham Ferrers and Oundle. It covers the original 14C doors which are ornamented with large tracery patterns. Proceeding to the S side, a Decorated trail runs round the aisle, porch and on to the chancel. N of the chancel comes an odd arrangement. The E end of the vestry, which contains two tiers of small single-light windows, seems to be a slight eastward extension of the N aisle. This vestry had two storeys but the curiosity is that it is connected to the chancel by a low, narrow passageway—and with unhappy results as will be seen inside. Was this unusual idea adopted as a cheaper expedient than a new vestry in the usual position at the NE corner? At the NW end of the aisle is another strange feature. The masonry here is thickened and apparently a NW tower was intended. However, the extra width near the N doorway was achieved only by butting the masonry up to the aisle wall—hardly a recipe for structural stability. Also, why is there some moulding at the NE angle of this area? It is almost as though a doorway was projected and abandoned.

Inside, there is more evidence for the proposed tower. There is the trace of springing from the NW pier for an arch and also a slight enlargement of this pier. But it is dubious that this would have been sufficient to carry a tower and it seems that the whole idea was abandoned for reasons of safety. The chancel arch is wide and rises from two well-carved, agonised figures. The entrance to the chancel is through a Perpendicular screen with some pretty detail in the trail over the wainscot (N side) and the head of the entrance arch. Within the chancel, distinction and interest arises from the shafting to the windows, the double graduated sedilia (formed in the windowsill), the enterprising if awkwardly organised angle piscina and the tomb-recess on the N with lovely double cusping. This recess no doubt doubled as an Easter sepulchre but was interfered with when the vestry and passage from it were constructed. The low, stone-roofed passage emerges in the W part of the recess through a doorway under a shouldered lintel. The grave-slab that probably occupied the recess is now laid in the floor in front of it. The stalls have simple misericords. Back in the nave the simple buttressed bench-ends are medieval. At the E end of the S aisle there is a niche for a statue and around this considerable traces of painting. The outline of two angel figures flanking the niche can be picked out.

Turvey, *All Saints.* Set attractively next to the grounds of Turvey House, All Saints' is a spacious church, to be visited for its monu-ments, a lovely 14C wall painting, pre-Conquest work and an elaborate mid-19C chancel.

The church was expanded eastwards in 1852–54 by Gilbert Scott for Charles Longuet-Higgins. The medieval chancel probably did not extend much beyond the E wall of the S aisle. What can be seen outside, other than the 19C work, is a 13C porch heightened probably in the 15C, a tower 13C in origin but with a 15C top (the pyramidal roof is modern), a late 16C extension to the N aisle into a chapel, and a further extension for the 19C vestry. In the angle between the S aisle and the tower are old vestries, perhaps built in 1593, a date suggested by a stone over the S doorway. The doors in the S porch are probably original and bear wonderful, ornate swirling ironwork along with the old closing rings.

To see the oldest work it is best to stand in the nave. In the SW part can be traced the heads of two late pre-Conquest double-splayed windows (only one is visible from the S aisle). It has been suggested that the blocked doorway to the right of the big glazed opening in the tower is pre-Conquest. (Is the triple-glazed opening Scott's?) This seems highly debatable, as there seems no reason why it should not be one of the normal 13C openings between a tower and the nave roof space. Moving towards the E end, evidence for the eastward extension is clear in the second pier from the E: the vertical joint indicates this. The medieval part of the arcades is 13C with the S one being slightly earlier than the N. The design and furnishing of the chancel is archetypal High Victorian work—a brooding roof com-plete with double cusping between each of the four bays, a porten-tous triple arch on the N (complete with Purbeck marble columns), the mighty organ and a wealth of contemporary furnishings. Only the panelling at the E end seems later. In the S aisle recess is a particularly lovely early 14C painting, depicting the Crucifixion against a green background. On either side of the cross stand the Virgin Mary and St. John with expressions of intense grief. Further E are triple graduated sedilia and a piscina from the 13C. At the W end of the S aisle is an old weathercock bearing the date 1630. The font is an unusual piece of c 1200 or very early 13C: it has four corner shafts rising to enlarged caps which cluster together to make up the bowl. At the W end under the tower arch is an unusually good example of modern church furnishing: a screen given in 1972, with a crown of thorns motif in the divisions.

Monuments. There are three brasses in the S chapel, two to a member of the Mordaunt family and a priest (both c 1500) and one to Alice Bernard (died 1606). But the key monuments at Turvey are four to the Mordaunt family, spanning 100 years from the early 16C. The earliest is to Sir John (died 1506) and his wife Edith. Sir John's head rests on a helmet crowned with an extraordinary shrieking man. The next, by T. Kirby, is to John (died 1560), who was created first Baron Mordaunt in 1532, and his wife Elizabeth. This vast monument lies between the chancel and S chapel. At the E end of the N aisle is a large monument to John, second Baron (died 1571) and his two wives, Eleanor and Joan. He was a Knight of the Bath and attended the coronation of Anne Boleyn in 1533. His bequest of £250 paid for the monument and the extension to the N aisle in which it is housed. The last monument is, in its simplicity, the most surprising. It has no figures and commemorates Lewis, third Baron (died 1601), and his wife Elizabeth. It is a tomb-chest with a black painted alabaster pall and a black marble slab. He was a most reluctant judge at the trial of Mary Stuart and also commanded troops to resist the expected invasion by Spain in 1588.

Woburn, St. Mary the Virgin. Between the attractive town and the entrance to Woburn Abbey stands this mighty piece of mid-Victorian church building, erected in 1865–68 by William, eighth Duke of Bedford at a cost of £35,000. It was even grander before 1890, when the spire was removed for reasons of safety. The architect, Henry Clutton, built on a large scale both inside and out. At the SW corner is the tower which doubles as a porch. The five-bay nave and aisles are the same height and under separate gables. The main inspiration is early French Gothic. Clutton has broad, shafted one-light windows and handles his details in a bold, innovative manner that is poised somewhere between the vagaries of Rogue Gothic and the more subdued freedom of the late 19C. No medieval Goth would have treated, say, the capitals of the E window as Clutton does. The overall impression, however, is unostentatious and only the belfry stage of the tower has an extensive display of ornament. The one real concession to local idioms is the stair turret poking up above the tower. Note the sinister creatures peering over the corners of the tower like devils in a Gothic nightmare. Another good touch is the elongated gargoyles that throw the water out beyond the big buttresses.

The interior is solemn and serious. It is quadripartite-vaulted throughout and the equal height of the nave and aisles gives the feel of a large Low Countries' church. Yet despite the fact that the slender twinned columns of the arcades are tall, the overall atmosphere is of spreading size rather than great height. The chancel is set unusually high above the nave with seven steps at the entrance. There is a surprising lack of colour in this church, which arises from the bare stonework and the absence of stained glass. There are some good furnishings and fittings, notably the massive circular Bath stone font, and the furnishings in the chancel. The latter were given in 1902 by the 11th Duke, who also provided the large organ in 1903.

BERKSHIRE

Berkshire is one of the prettiest of the SE counties. The Thames running through the deep chalk cutting between Streatley and Reading, the Downs with some lovely villages nestling under their slopes, the valleys of the Lambourn and Pang, and the Vale of the White Horse towards which the Downs sweep—all these features mean that Berkshire can easily rival any of the Home shires. It has also been one of the great through-routes from E to W. The ancient Ridgeway runs through it into Wiltshire. The Romans drove three great roads through Berkshire from Silchester to London, Gloucester and Bath. In the 18C there came the road from London to Bath, and in the 19C the railway from Paddington to Bristol. The Thames has always been a highway through the county. It is surprising, therefore, that there are few fine churches, and no great cathedral, although the ruins of the Benedictine abbey at Reading point to its former glory as the third biggest monastic foundation in England. Apart from St. George's Chapel, Windsor, the best medieval architecture is to be found away from the main routes in the W amongst the small downland villages.

Pre-Conquest remains are scanty, but South Moreton and Aston Tirrold have pre-Conquest doors. The best Norman work is at Avington, with good details at Catmore and Padworth. Blewbury is an early Norman church which was rebuilt in c 1170–80 and given a central tower and transepts. It retains a number of Norman features, and also has a good collection of brasses. Lambourn, too, is a large, late Norman church, with fine nave arcades and central crossing arches, and a W door with a circular window in the gable above. It contains a good collection of brasses and monuments, mostly to the Estbury and Garrard families.

The best Early English work is at Uffington, but there are good Early English chancels at Baulking, Cholsey and Chieveley. Tidmarsh has a rare 13C polygonal apse. The principal churches of the Decorated period are North Moreton, with the late Geometrical Stapleton chapel, and its fine E window which contains contemporary glass showing 15 scenes from the lives of Christ, the Virgin, St. Nicholas, St. Peter and St. Paul. Its founder, Miles de Stapleton, was steward to King Edward II's household and was killed at Bannockburn. Shottesbrooke, Sparsholt, Steventon and Aldworth contain fine tracery and carving, especially the former two. (See the Easter sepulchre, sedilia and piscina at Sparsholt, with the tomb-recess containing an early 14C knight with crossed legs, and 14C oak effigies in the S transept). Warfield too, is a very rewarding church with a Decorated chancel and N chapel. St. George's, Windsor is the major example of the Perpendicular period, begun by King Edward IV and completed by King Henry VII, and a magnificent example too. Other good Perpendicular work can be seen at Abingdon, Childrey and Newbury.

There are interesting towers and a few spires, including Shottesbrooke and the rebuilt Early English one at Welford. The round towers at Welford and West Shefford are Norman. Uffington has an octagonal Early English tower, while Farnborough has a fine 15C limestone tower. East Shefford has a circular tower of 13C flintwork, topped by an octagonal 15C storey.

The finest series of early monuments are the tombs of the de la Beche family at Aldworth, locally known as 'the giants' because of their huge size. Other 13C effigies are at Childrey, Sparsholt, Burghfield, Didcot and Long Wittenham. There are fine Perpendicular chantries in St. George's Chapel, Windsor, and a good series of alabaster monuments ranging from Wantage, 1361, Little Shefford, 1442, to St. George's and Aldermaston, 1526. There is a fine cadaver to Sir John Golafre, 1442, at Fyfield. The county is not outstanding for its memorial brasses, the best collections being at Blewbury, Bray, Childrey, West Hanney, Lambourn, Shottesbrooke, Sonning, Wantage and St. George's Chapel. At Bray, Sir John de Foxley stands on a fine bracket with the remains of a canopy, at Shottesbrooke a 14C layman and priest lie side by side in solemn splendour, and at Hurst, on a rectangular plate of 1600, Alice Harison is shown in the four-poster bed in which she died giving birth to her only son.

The best medieval glass is at Aldermaston (two 13C panels), North Moreton, showing a 14C Crucifixion, Childrey and St. George's Chapel, Windsor. Other fragmentary remains can be found at Buckland, Compton Beauchamp, East Hagbourne, Long Wittenham, Warfield, East Shefford and Stanford in the Vale.

There is little of interest from the Elizabethan and Jacobean periods, apart from Bishop Jewel's W porch at Sunningwell and towers at Wargrave, Hurst, Purley, Winkfield and Ruscombe. However, there are some fine monuments from this period, especially in the Hoby chapel at Bisham, and at Coleshill, Sonning, Faringdon, Shinfield, and Shottesbrooke. There are few churches of the Renaissance period, but Shrivenham has a fine building of 1638, oblong, with Tuscan columns and lovely floor slabs, Jacobean pulpit and sounding-board, 18C brass candelabra and royal arms. In the 18C All Saints', Pusey was built by J.A. Pusey, an Italianate building housing a stately monument to Jane Pusey, 1742, by Peter Scheemakers, showing her seated below the bust of her late husband. Another Scheemakers bust is at Kintbury, but the best of this type is John Hickey's monument to Elizabeth Hawkins, 1782, at St. Helen's, Abingdon, showing six portraits of members of her family. Englefield contains a fine monument by Thomas Carter to Mrs. Mary Benyon, 1777.

Before passing on to the Gothic Revival we must note examples of Nonconformist church architecture, especially the Baptist Chapel at Abingdon, 1841, a Classical building with impressive attached portico; the Methodist Chapel, Abingdon, 1845, by James Wilson of Bath, of early Gothic style; the Congregational Chapel, Hungerford, 1840; the grand Congregational interior in Broad Street, Reading (now closed); and the Friends' Meeting House in Wallingford of 1724.

Turning to the early phase of the Victorian revival, Berkshire has some good examples of Commissioners' churches in Windsor (1820–22), Hungerford (1816), Sunninghill (1826) and Bear Wood (1846). While these betray Georgian and Rococo features, the first reasonably accurate neo-Gothic church is Holy Trinity, Theale, in the Early English style, by E.W. Garbett, with massive details and mouldings borrowed from Salisbury Cathedral. It is a stately and impressive building, inside as well as out, and contains the chantry chapel of Bishop Waynflete, removed from Magdalen College, Oxford, in 1830 by the long-lived Dr. Routh.

Most of the well-known Victorian church architects have left their mark on Berkshire. A.W.N. Pugin built St. James's, Reading, 1837–40, in a rather unsuccessful Norman style (since much altered), and the church at Tubney (1844–47) in the Middle Pointed style with a

Tractarian interior. It is chiefly noteworthy for the fact that a Catholic architect could design an Anglican church at this period, especially one so near to Oxford. Sir Gilbert Scott was employed by the Rector of Bradfield, Thomas Stevens, in 1847, to restore the parish church. It is vast inside, severe and angular, with interesting glass by William Wailes of 1849. There are good vistas inside and from the church-yard. St. John's, Moulsford was also rebuilt by Scott in 1846. George Edmund Street, who lived for some years at Wantage, designed the dark little church at Fawley, 1866, with its vaulted chancel, low stone screen and pulpit. Note, too, the reredos by Thomas Earp and Salviati of Venice, and a window of c 1866 by William Morris. Street also designed the fine group of buildings of All Saints', Boyne Hill, Maidenhead, 1854–65. The church, parsonage, school and alms-houses form three sides of a quadrangle, built of red brick with bands of stone. The church has a detached tower and spire.

Other churches by Street are at Tilehurst, 1855, Brightwalton, 1862, Sandhurst, 1864, Purley, 1869, and White Waltham, 1869. Henry Woodyer designed three major buildings: Christ Church, Reading (1862), with its traceried chancel arch; St. Paul's, Wokingham (1864), more ornate with an effective N entrance and lofty rich interior; and the chapel of the House of Mercy at Clewer, dating from 1881. It is large and lavish, and Woodyer never asked a penny for it. There is a carved stone reredos, the stained glass is by John Hardman & Co. of Birmingham, and there is a brass to the foundress, Harriet Monsell (died 1883), on the chancel floor; also a recumbent alabaster effigy to Canon T.T. Carter, Rector and first Warden of Clewer (died 1901), designed by G.F. Bodley. Other Victorian churches worth mentioning are Leckhampstead, by S.S. Teulon, 1856—spiky and polychromatic; Welford by T. Talbot Bury, 1852–55, done in the Early English style, and paid for by the Reverend William Nicholson, who is commemorated by a large brass set in a canopied wall recess; and Wickham by Benjamin Ferrey, 1845, richly decorated, with splendid papier-maché elephants sup-porting the N aisle roof.

Wickham also contains some attractive Belgian glass of c 1850, in the S aisle, and in fact the county is well-endowed with good glass of the Victorian period. Bradfield College contains the earliest pre-Raphaelite glass made, designed by Sir Edward Burne-Jones in the 1850s and made by James Powell & Sons. It is striking and powerful in composition and colour. Other glass of the 1850s can be seen at Brimpton (Crucifixion by Thomas Willement, c 1856), Steventon (E window by Warrington & Co., c 1850), Bear Wood (chancel by William Wailes) and Uffington. Morris & Co. glass of the 1860s can be found at Dedworth, Cranbourne and Tilehurst, and of the '70s at Eaton Hastings and Easthampstead. Other notable glass is in the window by the font in Brightwalton by Ford Madox Brown; the E window at Sunningwell, designed by J.P. Seddon, a friend of Morris and the pre-Raphaelites; and the Arts and Crafts E window at Longworth by Heywood Sumner, c 1900.

Stained glass was not the only craft to be revived during the last century. There was also a Victorian revival of memorial brasses, stimulated by the archaeological zeal and polemical writings of A.W.N. Pugin who had seen many medieval brasses during his numerous Continental tours, and who wished to re-establish them as a fitting form of memorial for the day. Thereafter a number of firms rapidly sprang up to satisfy the great demand for the memorials and some excellent examples of this craft were produced. Berkshire contains a number of good Victorian and modern brasses, the best of which can be seen at Theale (Sophia Sheppard, 1848), All Saints', Boyne Hill, Maidenhead (Reverend William Gresley, 1876), St. George's Chapel, Windsor (Duchess of Gloucester, 1859) and St. Peter's, Earley, Reading (the Dunlop Brothers, 1913). A good collection of 20C brasses by the artist and sculptress, Julian Allen, can be seen at Denchworth and Longworth.

Finally, we cannot leave Berkshire without noticing the numerous religious communities which were revived in the 19C and which are architecturally well-served. In 1846 the Reverend W. J. Butler was appointed Vicar of Wantage and soon (1854) founded the sisterhood whose convent lies on the W side of the town. The buildings were designed by G.E. Street, including a small chapel, which was replaced by a larger one designed by J.L. Pearson in 1887. Street also restored and extended the parish church in 1857 and 1877, and it contains a fine Street pulpit, glass by Thomas Willement and John Hardman & Co., and some C.E. Kempe fittings. The Society of the Holy Trinity, founded by Priscilla Lydia Sellon, a friend of Pusey's, in 1848, moved to Ascot Priory, built by Charles Buckeridge in 1861. The chapel is by William Butterfield, 1877 onwards, and has a short nave with aisles in the Norman style and a long Early English chancel. There is glass in the E windows by J. N. Comper. There is also a separate Lady chapel of 1935 in a simple but effective neo-Gothic style. Douai Abbey Church at Upper Woolhampton was begun in 1928 in massive style, designed by J. Arnold Crush, a pupil of Sir Giles Gilbert Scott. It would have been an impressive, if conventional building, but only the sanctuary and Lady chapel were completed by 1933. Nothing more has been done, and although it soars above the other monastic buildings, it looks sadly incomplete, a poignant reminder of ever-rising building costs in the 20C, and a lack of the zeal for building that motivated and inspired those who built the churches of former centuries.

Abingdon, _St. Helen._ The church acts as a focal point for the town with its tall 13C spire and flying buttresses. It is squeezed into a constricted site by the River Thames and consequently its width exceeds its length. Around the churchyard there is a most delightful collection of buildings, the earliest, 'Long Alley', dating from 1446. Inside the church the immediate impression is of great breadth. It is in fact the second widest church in England and still looks much as it did in the 16C.

The oldest part of the exterior is the N tower with its lancet windows, and the N aisle. The spire has been rebuilt several times, lastly in the 19C. The main part of the church dates from the 15C and 16C, during Abingdon's prosperous days. Through an Elizabethan archway you enter the churchyard, bounded by ancient almshouses. On the N side of the church there is a small house between the tower and the N porch, which may have housed a guild priest. The S porch was added c 1550, possibly by Thomas Reade.

In addition to the N aisle, four more aisles were added side by side; the S aisle was completed in 1539. The chancel was redesigned by Henry Woodyer in 1873 at a cost of £7000 and is totally out of character with the rest of the building. Much of the interior and exterior was heavily restored in the 19C.

The church has many furnishings of note. The font is by H.P. Peyman of Abingdon, and was shown in the 1851 Exhibition. The reredos (1897) is by G.F. Bodley, as is the altar in the inner N aisle. There is an impressive pulpit of 1636, and the Mayor's Seat of 1706 includes a small iron sword-rest. The rarest item inside is the painted ceiling of c 1390 in the Lady chapel. It consists of three sections: a central (unpainted) horizontal one, flanked to the N and S by two sloping portions. Originally there were 52 panels, each with a full-length figure, representing Old Testament prophets and kings, all standing above branches of a vine stem and comprising an elaborate and unusual Tree of Jesse, unique in England.

There are three windows containing stained glass by C.E. Kempe: the nave, 1889, inner N aisle, c 1914, and outer S aisle, 1893. There are a number of brasses, including a demi-figure of Geoffrey Barbour, a merchant (died 1417), in the inner S aisle. At the end of the N aisle there is a massive monument to Elizabeth Hawkins (died 1780), a wealthy spinster and local benefactress who lived for 90 years in Abingdon. The monument is by John Hickey.

Aldworth, St. Mary the Virgin. This is an attractive, mainly 14C church containing the famous group of stone effigies of the mid-14C which represent members of the de la Beche family—seven knights and two ladies. Six are set under high, richly carved Decorated canopies (much restored in the 19C), three against the S wall and three against the N wall. The others (a married couple and a single knight) are on tomb-chests under the arcade arches between the nave and S aisle. All have been mutilated, some very badly, apparently during the Commonwealth. Nevertheless, they were clearly of fine quality originally, with much elegance and accomplished carving, and several still preserve interesting details, especially of armour. Note particularly the E knight on the N side, of almost giant proportions, in reclining posture (extremely rare in the Middle Ages), the beautiful figure of the lady on the S side, the single knight under the arcade (with fascinating detail of lacing of surcoat, or jupon/surcoat), and the knight of the couple E of the last (note details of the surcoat and small dogs curled up under his legs). All except one, which is reduced to a rather shapeless lump, repay careful inspection, particularly of their undamaged parts.

Bisham, All Saints. The church is delightfully situated by the River Thames, especially when viewed from the opposite bank. It stands near the remains of the abbey just outside the park. It is not of great architectural interest except for the Norman W tower and the Hoby chapel with its outstanding Renaissance monuments of the 16C and 17C. The three most important which retain much original colour and gilding are: Sir Philip (died 1558) and Sir Thomas Hoby (died 1566), erected after the latter's death by his widow, Elizabeth. This consists of two effigies on a tomb-chest against an arched back-plate. This is the first example of reclining effigies in England since the Middle Ages, probably due to French influence; Margaret, Lady Hoby (died 1605). This is an exceptionally interesting and important monument consisting of a free-standing plinth, with a tall obelisk topped by a heart and surrounded by four heraldic swans; Elizabeth, Lady Russell (died 1609), widow of Sir Thomas Hoby (see above), and secondly of John, Lord Russell (died 1584). She kneels under a canopy with her husband behind her and wears much the same coiffure as in her picture by Holbein. They are represented in the newly-fashionable kneeling posture, at prayer, with a baby lying in front of Lady Russell. She was a very remarkable woman, one of the most learned ladies of the age and fluent in Greek and Latin. Of later monuments the most interesting is the substantial one to George Vansittart (died 1904, aged 14), showing him kneeling at prayer with a pet dog beneath a Gothic Revival canopy.

Buckland, *St. Mary.* The church is surrounded by fine beech woods on the Berkshire Ridge. It is a cruciform building with an Early English central tower and an early 12C nave. The N and S doorways are also of the same period. The S door has a rebuilt porch with a Decorated niche. The chancel is of the early Decorated period, with exceptionally beautiful sedilia and piscina. Unfortunately the building was hacked about in the 18C, parts of it probably being repaired even prior to that. There are two Decorated tomb-recesses with ballflower decoration. The S transept is resplendent with a mosaic decoration made in the 1890s by Powell's. The stained glass is also by Powell's. There is a Jacobean gallery and pulpit and a number of box-pews. The octagonal font is Perpendicular with nice sculptured motifs. There is a memorial to William Hobcot, who died in 1570. He had been a Protestant lay preacher to King Edward VI, but had recanted under Mary Tudor, to resume his preaching under Queen Elizabeth I. He made a will, stipulating that his heart should be kept in a casket in the niche which is in the N wall of the chancel. There are tombs to Edward Yeat, 1648, Sir John Yeat, 1658, and Elizabeth Perfect, 1802. There are also a brass to John Yeat, 1578, in civilian dress with his wife, now fixed to the wall in the N transept, and an indent for a 14C floriated cross.

Childrey, *St. Mary the Virgin.* The stone church sits on the edge of this attractive village, which lies under the N slope of the Berkshire Downs in the Vale of the White Horse. The village was for many centuries one of the chief homes of the Fettiplace family, and in 1526 William Fettiplace founded a chantry and an almshouse here.

The church is a cruciform building with a W tower, unaisled nave, S porch, N and S transepts and chancel. It is not architecturally outstanding but nevertheless attractive and enjoyable, and chiefly rewarding for its atmosphere and interesting contents. The earliest part is the nave, originally late 12C, but the walls were largely rebuilt in the 15C when Perpendicular windows were inserted. It was then heightened in the 16C, when the clerestory windows were added. Evidence of the earlier building remains in the N and S doorways. The S doorway has a hoodmould of dogtooth decoration (c 1200). Next in date comes the chancel, late 13C, as shown by the side windows, although the E window is a large Perpendicular replacement of five lights with good panel tracery in its head. There is no chancel arch. The transepts were originally added in the early 14C, as is shown by the arches opening into them and by the E window of the N transept and the monument in its N wall. But the N transept was provided with a Perpendicular window and the S transept was remodelled as a chantry chapel in the early 16C. This was founded by William Fettiplace in honour of the Holy Trinity, Our Lady and St. Catherine. The W tower is a 15C Perpendicular addition of three stages with the crenellated top and W doorway. The S porch of the nave was added in the 16C.

There are numerous contents of note. The circular lead font of c 1200 at the W end of the nave is a rare piece, enriched with a line of 12 standing bishops in relief all round it. The nave roof is largely 19C but retains at the E end a panelled late medieval section over the former Rood. The S transept roof is early 16C, resting on a good set of carved stone corbels representing angels bearing shields. In the chancel there are fine late 13C sedilia and a piscina on the S side, beautifully carved under pointed-arched canopies, very restrained and elegant. Also in the chancel there is an Easter sepulchre on the N side, probably late 14C, but exhibiting some Decorated characteristics in its carving. From the base, which has Perpendicular panels, rises an elaborate canopy which shelters the recess, consisting of a cusped and sub-cusped cinquefoiled arch under a crocketed ogee gable. Above this rises more Perpendicular panelling with crenellated bands. Between the arch and gable is a circle containing a cusped and sub-cusped quatrefoil and, to each side of this in spandrels of cusping on the arch, much attractive Decorated style foliage and animal carving. There are considerable pieces of late 15C glass in the N window of the N transept, although it is very damaged. The scenes include the Coronation of the Blessed Virgin Mary, the Annunciation and the Nativity. Also in the E window of the S transept there are fragments of early 16C glass, including shields of arms. In the N wall of the S transept there is a Decorated canopied recess consisting of a cusped and sub-cusped cinquefoiled ogee arch, with ballflower decoration and crocketing, which shelters a full-length effigy of a cross-legged knight in mail and surcoat, wearing a shield and holding his scabbard with his left hand and about to draw his sword with his right hand. The monument is somewhat damaged and worn but still of great interest. The date is approximately 1325.

There is a large and interesting collection of brasses in the chancel and S transept. Note especially: William Fynderne (died 1444) and his wife: two large figures under canopies, with long marginal inscription. The great interest is that much of the knight, who wears a tabard, is of lead, and nearly all the lady is of lead. Of brass are the two heads, two pairs of hands, the knight's forearms, and the knight's legs, feet and lion on which his feet rest (see illustration in Morley, *Brasses of Berkshire*, p.68); Thomas Walrond (died 1480) and his wife (died 1477), but the brass is probably of c 1510–20. S transept on S wall. Two figures kneel beneath a representation of the Trinity (God the Father wearing triple crown seated, with crucified Son between His knees and the Holy Ghost as a Dove on the bar of the Cross), to which scrolls ascend from the deceased asking for mercy; Jane Strangbon, daughter of Thomas Walrond (died 1477). In the S transept. A shrouded corpse in a coffin beneath an extremely fine and beautiful Trinity; John Kingston (died 1514) and his wife. Chancel. The man in contemporary armour and his wife in contemporary dress with pedimented (or kennel) head-dress, with a Trinity above (no Dove for the Holy Ghost); William Fettiplace and his wife Elizabeth (latter died 1517). Small-scale, set into back-plate of a canopied recess of Purbeck marble in the S transept. Very interesting and unusual, showing the two deceased in shrouds rising from their coffins and uttering prayers to the Trinity on ascending scrolls (no depiction of the Trinity).

Faringdon, *All Saints.* This fine cruciform church is of first-rate importance for its architecture and monuments. It has an aisled nave, transepts, a central tower which lost its spire in the 17C, chancel and N chapel. Its chief architectural importance lies in the excellent Transitional and Early English features, which are very instructive for architectural and carving developments of the late 12C and the early 13C. The nave arcades have round, moulded arches on cylindrical piers with rich, varied and well-carved stiff-leaf capitals. The crossing arches, also of c 1200, pointed and moulded, rest on many-shafted supports with numerous stiff-leaf capitals equally varied and well-carved. The effect is one of considerable elegance and refinement. The chancel is very fine, long and noble Early English with tall lancets. The N wall of the chancel has been broken into by the 15C arcade to the N chapel. There are a large Early English piscina, sedilia in Transitional style with dogtooth ornament, and three aumbries. The S transept was destroyed in the Civil War, but rebuilt in the original style in 1853. Note also two large and good six-light and transomed Perpendicular windows in the N aisle.

The church contains a very important collection of monuments. There are 14C and 15C brasses in the chancel. In the N transept there is a good collection of 16C monuments to the Unton family; especially noteworthy are Sir Thomas Unton (died 1533) and his wife, two recumbent effigies of alabaster on a tomb-chest of Renaissance style. The sides and ends of the chest are enriched with heraldic shields in circular wreaths set in shell-headed panels and surmounted by a tun (or barrel), the Unton rebus (one tun). Another tomb-chest under a flat-topped canopy in late Perpendicular style with brasses set against the back commemorates Sir Alexander Unton (died 1547) and his two wives. There is a large wall tablet of alabaster to Sir Edward Unton (died 1583), who married a daughter of the Protector, Somerset. Lastly, there used to be a fine monument to Sir Henry Unton (died 1596), originally erected in 1601 by his widow, but destroyed in 1646 during the Civil War. There is a depiction of it in the remarkable composite painting of Sir Henry's life and death in the National Portrait Gallery. There is a large female alabaster effigy in late 16C dress, which has long been identified as the figure of Sir Henry's widow from his former monument. In the N or Pye chapel there are three good 18C monuments to members of the Pye family, each of different coloured marbles. Jane Pye (died 1706) is commemorated by a large inscription plate, flanked by black marble columns supporting a pediment on which sit two cherubs, flanking a heraldic achievement with a flaming urn above. This is by Edward Stanton. Henry Pye (died 1749) has a sarcophagus with an inscription on its front supporting a garlanded urn, set against a pyramidal back-plate with a medallion portrait of the deceased. There is good Victorian glass in the E window and in the S aisle by William Wailes.

Newbury, _St. Nicholas._ Newbury is an important town in the Kennet Valley and features in the history books because of the Battle of Newbury in 1460 in the Wars of the Roses, and two battles in the Civil War. It has for centuries been a prosperous town as a result of the cloth trade. One of the chief merchants in the Middle Ages was John Smallwood, later John of Winchcombe (died 1519)—Jack of Newbury—an apprentice who married his master's widow and became a leading citizen. He was on good terms with King Henry VIII and out of his wealth rebuilt the parish church.

It is a large, early 16C building, Perpendicular throughout, built between c 1500 and 1532. Jack of Newbury's monogram, 'JS', is on the roof. Note inside the clustered columns from which rise the arches that support the 20C roof. Henry Woodyer restored the building in the 19C and the chancel arch and roof are by him. The Jacobean pulpit is dated 1607 and is a splendid example of its type.

There are a number of brasses, including one to John Smallwood and his wife and children (1519). The stained glass is all by John Hardman & Co. and makes the interior very dark.

St. Nicholas's: an impressive Perpendicular church with a late 18C gateway

Reading. Until the 12C there was only one parish church, St. Mary's in St. Mary's Butts, the head of a large early parish extending S and W of Reading. St. Mary's is possibly of very ancient foundation (? 7C). The church in its present form is largely Victorian, with the exception of a rather fine W tower of the 1550s (black and white chequered effect of flint and stone), built of materials from the dissolved Reading Abbey. There is a Norman door on the N side. The S arcade is Early English and was evidently brought wholesale from the abbey. The N arcade and the whole of the chancel are modern Early English. In the chancel is a Decorated Easter sepulchre which must be original.

In the 12C Reading's two other medieval parish churches appeared—St. Giles' in Southampton Street, and St. Laurence's in Old Market Place. St. Giles', much damaged in the Civil War, was almost entirely rebuilt by J.P. St. Aubyn in the 1870s, with a rich High Victorian chancel in Early English style. The main features of interest inside are the numerous 18C and early 19C tablets of various designs.

St. Laurence's began life as the *capella ante portam* of Reading Abbey, being built at the abbey's main gate. It developed into a parish church in the 13C to serve the new residential and commerical area which soon grew up in the vicinity of the abbey. Architecturally it is the most important and interesting of Reading's old churches with Norman fragments, an attractive Early English chancel, the E wall of which has three shafted lancets, and an arcade of the same date to the N chapel. It gives an atmosphere of peace in the bustling town centre. The N aisle arcade was rebuilt in 1522 and has high four-centred arches. There is a good Perpendicular nave roof and a fine, tall Perpendicular W tower (in design, cf. Henley-on-Thames, Oxfordshire).

There are interesting brasses (15C and 16C, including a palimpsest) and varied collections of wall monuments, among which note especially: John Blagrave (died 1611), mathematician and astronomer. Frontal demi-figure in a recess lined with books, surrounded by allegorical figures holding geometrical solids—an accomplished piece; Anne Haydon (died 1747), a late survival of its type, with the deceased kneeling in prayer at a *prie-dieu*. By Peter Scheemakers; Dr. Richard Valpy, Headmaster of Reading School (1838), a standing figure set in the lofty tower arch. Designed by Edward Charles Hakewill and executed by Samuel Nixon.

The W window commemorates the principal benefactors of the town, i.e. Archbishop Laud, Sir Thomas White, and three kings—Henry I, Henry VII and Charles I.

Of the later churches, Christ Church in Christ Church Road in the S part of the town is a fine High Victorian church by Henry Woodyer (of 1861–74), with commanding tower and spire and absorbing interior. Of special note are the arcade piers and capitals and open tracery in the head of the chancel arch. St. Bartholomew's, London Road, a brick church without a tower, is by two distinguished architects—the nave by Alfred Waterhouse (1879) and the chancel by G.F. Bodley (1898). St. James's, Forbury Road, near the abbey ruins, is mainly of 1837–40 by A.W.N. Pugin in Romanesque style, but with 20C S and N aisles. The font is made from a large, carved 12C stone found on the abbey site.

Shottesbrooke, *St. John the Baptist.* This church is a celebrated example of Decorated architecture, although it has been altered by Victorian restorers. It is, however, still an unusually impressive building, dating almost entirely from the mid-14C. It appears to be the work of a single imaginative architect and shows great simplicity and exactness of proportion. With St. Leonard's, Wallingford and St. George's Chapel, Windsor it is one of three collegiate churches in Berkshire. It was built in 1337 for Sir William Trussell as a chantry in which a Warden and five priests were to pray for his soul.

Today the college and most of the other houses in the parish have disappeared. The church now stands in parkland next to Shottesbrooke Park, a 16C house Gothicised in the 19C. It is cruciform in shape with a crossing tower carrying the slender ribbed spire, giving an impression of soaring height. The walls are of flint, and there is deeply-moulded curvilinear tracery in all the windows.

Inside, the walls are white and some of the glass is clear, giving an impression of airy spaciousness. In the chancel there are ogee-headed sedilia and a piscina, and in the N transept is the founder's tomb, from which the effigies have disappeared. The tomb is slightly wider than the transept, perhaps because it was prepared elsewhere and brought to the church ready-made.

The font is 14C. The pulpit is by G.E. Street (1854) and there is a nice E window by John Hardman & Co. of Birmingham. The church contains a fine series of brasses, including a late 14C brass to a priest and layman, showing them standing under a double canopy. This may commemorate the first Warden of the chantry and his brother. Sir William Trussell's daughter also has a brass in the N transept floor. There are an alabaster 'coffin' monument (1535) in the chancel

*Canopied brass figures of a priest (left, with a maniple
over his arm) and a layman, c 1370, at St. John's*

to William Throckmorton, priest, and a number of wall tablets to the
Cherry and Vansittart families.

The manor of Shottesbrooke has two peculiarities. First, it was the
only manor in Berkshire not taken away from its English owner at the
Norman Conquest. The Domesday Book tells us that 'Aelfward the
Goldsmith holds Shottesbrooke...', Secondly, the manor was
held by the extraordinary form of grand serjeantry, that is the right of
refashioning the crown for each coronation, which Aelfward was
presumably qualified to carry out. His descendants sold the manor to

the Trussells. Since then it has been held by the de Veres of Oxford, by the Cherry family and by the Vansittarts.

Shrivenham, *St. Andrew*. A large and important church, comprising a central tower, nave and aisles, chancel and chapels. Its interest lies in the fact that, apart from the central tower, it dates wholly from King Charles I's reign, when rebuilding round the late medieval central tower was carried out by Lord Craven, beginning in 1638, a rare time for building or rebuilding churches in England. The building is in a most interesting hybrid style between late Perpendicular and Classical. Note the uniform series of windows in 17C Perpendicular style (a late case of Perpendicular survival) with cusped lights but no tracery. Inside, of interest are the arcades running the length of the church (embracing the N and S crossing arches) and consisting of unorthodox round arches with double chamfers on Tuscan columns. Note also the fine 17C pulpit and tester, heraldic glass in the E window (including a late medieval heraldic shield of an Abbot of Cirencester, with his kneeling figure in glass—his abbey possessed the church until the Dissolution), and a number of rewarding, mostly modest-sized monuments, though none of great importance.

Sonning, *St. Andrew*. The church is located in a large and beautiful churchyard in this famous and attractive Thames-side village. It is of ancient foundation, in pre-Conquest times being the head of a very large parish extending as far as Sandhurst and Arborfield.

The building was heavily restored in the Victorian period by Henry Woodyer and not much medieval work remains in its original state other than the Perpendicular W tower. There is a good Victorian pulpit, an extremely rich Victorian reredos and chancel decorated by G.F. Bodley. In the chancel floor there is a good collection of brasses, including a 15C knight (Laurence Fyton, died 1434) and a number of the 16C. In the equally good collection of other monuments special note should be made of: Lady Anne Clarke (died 1653), with a bust of the deceased by John Stone; Sir Thomas Rich (died 1667) and his son Thomas, comprising two large urns upon a slab carried by four standing cherubs, of black and white marble. It is now under the tower, to which it was moved in the 19C; William Barker, a very early work by Sir Richard Westmacott, dating possibly from c 1796; Canon Hugh Pearson, Vicar (died 1883), by Frederick Thrupp, a recumbent effigy at prayer, set under a restored and richly carved medieval arch N of the high altar.

Uffington, *St. Mary*. Uffington, in the Vale of the White Horse, is a pretty village beneath White Horse Hill, where Tom Brown went to school before being sent off to Rugby. The parish church is a cruciform building dating from the first half of the 13C, the most complete Early English building in the county. It retains pebble-dash walls, a rose window over the N door, three transept chapels with gabled roofs of stone, a SE porch, moulded circles for consecration crosses, original oak doors and ironwork.

Externally the building consists of a chancel, tower, N and S transepts, nave, and porch with chamber above. There are two E 'chapels' in the N transept. The central tower is octagonal and used to have a spire until it fell in the 18C. The S porch is a grand affair with stiff-leaf capitals to the outer and inner doorways. The doorway into the S transept may have been an entry from a house nearby.

From the deepness of the mouldings and excellence of proportion the church was probably designed by a master mason, perhaps one working on Salisbury Cathedral.

The interior is all mid-13C, although a little bare. The chancel is divided into three bays, each being lighted by two original windows on each side, except the middle bay on the N which was occupied by the sacristy where there are two blank arches. The E window of the bay consists of a triplet of lights, the middle light higher than the others. The E bay forms the sanctuary and is divided from the rest of the chancel by a pointed arch, springing from the wall shafts resting on corbels. The arch above the springing dates from 1852. There are original sedilia and piscina, and many interesting mouldings over the arches at the tower crossing.

The priest's doorway has unusual mouldings around the arch. The carved oak reredos dates from 1902, and the rest of the chancel fittings are modern. The chancel was re-roofed by G.E. Street, who did other restoration work in 1850. The transepts are lighted by windows similar in style to the side windows in the chancel. The N transept contains two altar recesses, each lighted by a triplet of lights. The piscinae are situated on the S side of each recess and have decorated heads. In the N wall is a large square aumbry divided into four compartments and hinged for a door. There are some pieces of 15C screen which have been turned into bench-ends. Also here are the works of an old clock, a 15C parish chest and a 17C monument to Edward Archer. On the N wall there is a brass tablet, with semi-relief bust, to Thomas Hughes, QC, sometime MP for Lambeth and Frome, County Court judge, and author of 'Tom Brown's Schooldays'. He spent his childhood in the parish and was baptised in the church, of which his grandfather was Vicar. To the right of the tablet are two letters of his mounted in a frame. In the S transept is a painted semi-reclining effigy of John Saunders (1638), and in the N transept stained glass by Alexander Gibbs.

The nave is lighted by a triplet of windows at the W end and double windows on both walls at the E end. During rebuilding work in the 17C the heads of these windows were removed and the windows taken up to the eaves. The S door preserves original ironwork. The porch is vaulted, with ribs springing from angle shafts with moulded capitals. Above is a chamber which was originally reached by a stairway from the nave. With the building of the gallery the position of the steps was altered to give access from the porch to both the gallery and chamber above.

The church was appropriated to Abingdon Abbey in 1343, but the tithes had been owned by the abbey since the time of Abbot Faritius, who was appointed by King Henry I. Faritius had been cellarer at Malmesbury Abbey, and was also a skilled doctor, a distinguished scientist and scholar. To him is owed the eventual magnificence of Uffington Church, one of the finest examples of the Early English period.

Wallingford. This is an old and attractive market town beside the Thames at a stategic crossing point for early travellers and invaders. It is guarded by the Thames on one side, the castle on another and by huge pre-Conquest earthworks on yet another, and so was a perfect site for a medieval town. In the 12C it had no fewer than 11 parish churches and a priory, but now there are only three churches, of which one is redundant.

St. Mary's lies in the heart of the town. Apart from the W tower rebuilt in 1653, the church is very largely Victorian, reconstructed and enlarged in 1854 by David Brandon. Inside, note the pulpit erected as a memorial in 1888, of Italian marble with bronze relief panels of saints, by E. Onslow Ford. There is also an interesting group of modest wall tablets in the chancel, including Thomas Renda (died 1723) by Edward Stanton and Christopher Horsnaile (note the winged skull at the bottom), and John and Elizabeth Cottingham (died 1746 and 1748), with a nice pair of winged cherub heads at the bottom. Also at the W end of the S aisle there is a tablet to Walter Bigg (died 1659), one of the founders of Wallingford Grammar School.

St. Leonard's in the SE part of the town, near the river, has the most attractive interior of the town churches. It was originally a Norman church but was converted into barracks by the Cromwellian forces during the siege of Wallingford in 1646. It was left roofless and ruinous but was restored to worship in the early 18C and was then heavily restored in 1849–50 by J. H. Hakewill, who rebuilt the destroyed S aisle, S arcade and apse. Nevertheless, much interesting Norman work remains. Note especially the herringbone work on the exterior N wall of the nave, the Norman N doorway and, most importantly, the two splendid round arches, one behind the other, between nave and sanctuary. Each has much small-scale relief carving up the sides and round the arches, and the capitals of the W arch are enriched with interlace or basketwork carving, while those of the E arch have carved heads and scrolls.

St. Peter's in the High Street, near Wallingford Bridge, was destroyed during the Civil War and rebuilt in 1763–69 by an unknown architect. The tower and spire were added in 1776–77 to the designs of Sir Robert Taylor. He had given an estimate for completing the interior in 1767 and so the entire work has sometimes been attributed to him. The spire is the chief feature and makes a very attractive addition to the town's skyline. The extremely slender Gothick spire, of elegant openwork stone construction, stands on an octagonal belfry with tall open cusped arches, all resting on a plain square tower. A churchwarden at the time of rebuilding was Sir William Blackstone, author of 'Commentaries on the Laws of England'. He was buried in a vault below the church in 1780. St. Peter's was declared redundant in 1971 and passed into the care of the Redundant Churches Fund in 1972.

Windsor Castle, *St. George's Chapel.* This imposing building, which dominates the Lower Ward of Windsor Castle, was built by King Edward IV on the site of two previous chapels. The building began in 1475 and is wholly late Perpendicular in style. The impression is one of tremendous space and light in view of the length of the building, the wide interior, and the tall aisle and clerestory windows. The great W window is especially fine and shows some 75 kings, princes, saints and popes. The chapel serves the College of St. George and the Order of the Garter.

The S front is the show front, which is immediately visible to visitors who enter Windsor Castle by King Henry VIII's Gateway. Nave and choir are each of seven bays. They have two tiers of tall, four-light windows with embattled transoms, separated by flying buttresses. From the middle of the front there projects a substantial, two-storey polygonal transept. The symmetry of the front is broken, however, by the quite different polygonal chapels which project from the E and W ends. The E chapel has three tiers of relatively small windows and a flat roof, whereas the W one is single-storey and has an ogee dome. Both nave and choir, with their aisles, have openwork parapets with pinnacles. The N front mirrors the S in its windows, its central transept and in its W chapel, but some of the details are omitted, such as the niches which appear in the S buttresses. The great W front, so familiar from photographs of royal occasions, comprises a 15-light window with four transoms, two flanking polygonal turrets, the low nave aisles, and the ogee-domed polygonal chapel at each corner.

Within the chapel, the nave is divided from the choir by an organ screen under the central crossing. The choir is rich in its fittings and relatively enclosed, whereas the nave is relatively open. The crossing and the aisles are fan-vaulted; the nave and choir have complex vaults which are flat in the centre. There are no capitals to the piers. The vault is so shallow and the clerestory windows so tall that the latter seem to be partly cut out of the vault.

The principal visitors' entrance is just W of the central S transept. Turning left, the Beaufort chapel is found in the SW corner, at the W end of the S nave aisle. It contains the alabaster tomb of Charles Somerset, Earl of Worcester (died 1526), and his wife, forbears of the Dukes of Beaufort. In the aisle outside the chapel stands a font of 1888 by J.L. Pearson. At the W end of the N nave aisle there is a memorial to King Leopold I of the Belgians (died 1865). He was Queen Victoria's uncle, whose first wife was Charlotte, the daughter and only child of King George IV, who would have become the reigning monarch but for her death in childbirth in 1817. Her large marble monument stands in the Urswick chapel in the NW corner of the building and just N of King Leopold's monument. Next to the N nave arcade is the tomb of King George V (died 1936) and Queen Mary. The saracophagus was designed by Sir Edwin Lutyens and the effigies of *bianca del mare* stone were carved by Sir William Reid Dick. The modern pews and altar in the nave are unattractive additions and are out of character with the building. The stained glass in the great W window is very largely of the early 16C. Some figures were added by Thomas Willement in 1842. The order of figures was re-arranged in 1920–30 under the advice of Dr M.R. James, the great antiquary who was then the Provost of Eton.

The main transept on the N side is the Rutland chapel. It contains the tomb of George Manners, Lord Roos (died 1513) and his wife, forbears of the Dukes of Rutland. The tomb has figures under arcades on all sides. Also in the chapel is a brass memorial of Sir Thomas St. Leger (died 1483) and his wife, Anne, Duchess of Exeter, the sister of King Edward IV (died 1476). On the walls are five embroidered tapestries of Gospel themes by Beryl Dean, completed in 1974.

The N choir aisle runs E of the Rutland chapel. Immediately on the left is the memorial chapel and tomb of King George VI (died 1952), containing the words quoted by him in his Christmas broadcast of 1939: 'I said to the man who stood at the gate of the year/Give me a light that I may tread safely into the unknown/and he replied/Go out into the darkness and put your hand into the hand of God, that shall be to you better than a light and safer than a known way'. The chapel was dedicated in 1969. Further on, on the right, is the Hastings chantry, containing wall paintings of the late 15C, depicting the martyrdom of St. Stephen, and the tomb of Lord Hastings who was executed in 1483 under King Richard III. A little further E, on the right, is the tomb of King Edward IV (died 1483), builder of the present chapel, separated from the choir by an elaborate iron screen.

Notice too the Tudor wooden oriel window built by King Henry VIII as a gallery for his first Queen, Katharine of Aragon.

The choir is flanked by the stalls of the Knights of the Garter. Their order of chivalry was founded by King Edward III in 1348. The Garter stalls contain several hundred brass plates with the names and arms of previous occupants, over which are hung the present knights' swords, helmets and banners. The stalls themselves were made in 1478–85; William Berkeley was the main carver. They were carefully repaired by Henry Emlyn in 1782–92 for King George III. The stalls include a large set of carved misericords. The black and white marble floor of the choir is 17C. In the centre of it is a stone stating that in the vault below are buried Jane Seymour (King Henry VIII's third wife), King Henry VIII himself, and King Charles I. A little further to the left is the entrance to a second royal vault, containing three Hanoverian kings, George III, George IV and William IV. At the E end the alabaster reredos by J.B. Philip, 1863, is an elaborate composition. It was given, together with the stained glass in the E window above, by the Dean and Canons in memory of the Prince Consort. The E window is of 15 lights, with two full transoms and a third across the central group of lights. The stained glass is by Clayton & Bell.

In the ambulatory at the E end, notice the E doors, which were originally the W doors of King Henry III's chapel. They bear beautiful 13C ironwork. In the SE corner is the Lincoln chantry, which contains the tomb of Edward, Earl of Lincoln (died 1585) and his third wife. He was Lord High Admiral of England. His effigy depicts him in armour with a greyhound at his feet. Notice the FitzGerald ape at his wife's feet. This chapel was previously the shrine of Master John Schorn (died 1314), which had been a place of pilgrimage on account of his reputation as a healer. Notice the illuminated book of hours, containing prayers used by pilgrims.

Proceeding W into the S choir aisle, there may be seen the tomb of King Edward VII (died 1910) and Queen Alexandra. The King's favourite dog, Caesar, lies at his feet. To the W is the slab of black marble which covers the grave of King Henry VI. He was originally buried at Chertsey, but his body was transferred here by King Richard III. The nearness of his grave to that of King Edward IV inspired Pope's well-known lines: 'The grave unites where even the great find rest,/and blended lie the oppressor and the oppressed'. Further W on the right is the Oxenbridge chantry, founded in 1522 and commemorating Master John Oxenbridge, who was a Canon from 1509 to 1522. Over the door can be seen an ox, an N and a bridge. Inside, there are three paintings by a Flemish artist of the Passion of St. John the Baptist, and also the screen and monument to Dean Urswick, removed from his chantry in the NW corner. Opposite is the chapel of Oliver King, Canon of Windsor in 1480–1503 and then Bishop of Bath and Wells. He was secretary to four royal masters, including King Edward V, the boy king whose crown is shown suspended over him.

The main S transept is the Bray chapel, founded by Sir Reginald Bray (died 1503). His badge, the hemp-bray for crushing hemp, is reproduced ten times along the top of the stone screen. There is also a memorial in the chapel to the Prince Imperial who was killed in the Zulu War in 1879. He was the only son of the Emperor Napoleon III.

E of the Chapel proper is the Albert Memorial chapel, which dates probably from King Edward III's time, with alterations under King Henry VII. It is aisleless and has a polygonal apse, tall four-light windows with two transoms, and a lierne-vault. The windows are set high in the walls and below them runs a dado of coloured marbles. This dado was part of the works by which Queen Victoria turned the existing chapel into an overpoweringly elaborate memorial chapel for Prince Albert, between 1863 and 1873. Marble, mosaic and painting were lavished on the building. Sir Gilbert Scott designed the reredos, Salviati of Venice the mosaic work, and Clayton & Bell the stained glass.

In an E–W line in the centre stand three large monuments: a cenotaph to Prince Albert (E end); the tomb of Prince Leopold, Duke of Albany, Queen Victoria's youngest son (died 1884) (W end); and, between the other two, the much larger tomb of the Duke of Clarence, eldest son of the future King Edward VII and thus due to succeed to the throne himself, who died in 1892. This tomb, with its 12 bronze statuettes and elaborate ironwork, is a remarkable example of the work of Sir Alfred Gilbert.

(Acknowledgement is made to Dr Brian Kemp for assistance with some entries.)

THE CITY OF BRISTOL

Bristol has always been one of England's greatest cities. The number of medieval churches, as in Norwich and York, proves this. Many were destroyed in the last war, but fortunately Bristol Cathedral and the churches described in the gazetteer have survived. Bristol Cathedral is the surviving church of a medieval Augustinian monastery, to which G.E. Street added the present nave and W towers in 1868–88. Across the river, the church of St. Mary Redcliffe vies with the cathedral in grandeur. St. Mary's was built with merchant wealth, for Bristol was a great port, closely associated with North American trade and the voyages of Cabot. The Lord Mayor's Chapel (or St. Mark's), which stands on College Green opposite the cathedral, is basically a 13C building which has received many later additions and alterations, and which is notable for its monuments. St. Mary's and St. Mark's are both described in detail in the gazetteer. The third description is of Wesley's New Room, built in 1739, which is humble architecturally but of much historical interest for being the earliest of all Methodist churches and for its close association with John Wesley himself.

Of churches which are not described in the gazetteer, we can still recommend visits to several of them. From the Middle Ages there are St. Stephen's, with its fine Perpendicular tower (attributed to John Hart), whose parapet and pinnacles are based on Gloucester Cathedral; the church of St. James's Priory (closed in 1984), which has fabric from the 12C; St. John's in Quay Street (in the hands of the Redundant Churches Fund), of the 14C and 15C, whose tower and spire sit above the city's only surviving medieval gate; and the church of St. Philip and St. Jacob, near Old Market Street. In addition the famous leaning tower of the Temple Church still stands, although the body of the church has been destroyed; its most remarkable fitting, a 14C candelabrum with figures of the Virgin and Child and St. George, was fortunately saved and is now in the cathedral.

The 18C has left many interesting churches besides Wesley's New Room. There are Christ Church in Broad Street (1786–90), attributed to William Paty; St. Michael's, a Gothick work of 1775–77 by Paty but retaining a 15C tower; and Lewin's Mead Meeting, a Unitarian church of 1787–91 by William Blackburne, an impressive Classical design comprising a pediment over a semicircular portico, rusticated lower walls and tripartite arched windows high up in the walls. N of Bristol's centre a further worthy 18C church stands: Redland Chapel, built in 1741–43 by William Halfpenny as a proprietory chapel for the owner of Redland Court. The exterior is typical of the period, and the interior has all its original fittings with sumptuous woodwork, and there are several busts by J.M. Rysbrack. From the 19C one may note the church of St. Mary on the Quay, built by R.S. Pope for the Catholic Apostolic Church in 1839, but taken over by the Roman Catholic Church in 1843; St. Mark's, Lower Easton , convincing neo-Norman of 1848 by Charles Dyer (redundant from 1984); and Cotham Parish Church of 1842–43, William Butterfield's first work, which he built as the Highbury Congregational Church.

St. Mark, College Green (generally referred to as the Lord Mayor's Chapel). It was built as the chapel of the Hospital of St. Mark which was founded in 1220, and was purchased by Bristol Corporation in

1541. It has been the official place of worship of the Lord Mayor and Corporation since 1721. It stands a little to the N of Bristol Cathedral.

The core of the building, that is the nave, dates from the 13C, but there have been many alterations to the medieval structure throughout the centuries. The W window of the S chapel with ballflower is 14C, the E tower can be dated 1487, and the Poyntz chantry chapel with old Spanish floor tiles and a fan-vault is of 1536. The 14C S chapel was an addition to the W end, but it was later given a Perpendicular extension to the E. The E end of the chancel is also Perpendicular. The major 19C restoration was carried out by J.L. Pearson in 1887–90, who rebuilt the W front and altered windows.

Inside, the massive timber roof is 16C with about 100 carved panels with bosses. The E end has 19C fittings. On the S side of the nave there is a sword-rest of 1707 by William Edney which was brought from the Temple Church in 1948. Also on the S wall are the arms of King Charles II. There is much 15C to 17C Continental glass bought by the Corporation in 1823. Some of it came from the sale of William Beckford's property at Fonthill in Wiltshire. The figure of St. Thomas Becket in the E window of the S aisle was designed for Fonthill by Benjamin West. The visitor will, however, come to see the numerous monuments. They range in date from the 13C to the 19C. On the N side of the sanctuary there are two monuments: the larger one, with an ogee canopy, has effigies of Sir Maurice Berkeley (died 1464) and his wife; the other commemorates Bishop Miles Salley (died 1516). At the W end of the N nave wall a memorial to William Bird (died 1590) comprises a canopy with four fluted Ionic columns over a crude tomb-chest. The majority of the monuments are placed in the S aisle. In its E part, the large table-tomb in the centre has effigies of Robert de Gourney (died 1260) and Maurice de Gaunt (died 1230). On the N side of the aisle, the following memorials are placed, beginning at the W: George Upton, 1608, with an effigy on its side under an arch supported by two Corinthian columns; Sir Baynham and Lady Throkmorton, 1664 and 1635, with two effigies in a deep recess framed by two Corinthian columns; and John Aldsworth, 1615, and his son Francis, 1623, comprising two kneeling figures (which face E) under a square-cut Gothic canopy. At the E end of the aisle Dame Mary Baynton (died 1667) kneels in a central niche, the drapes of which are held back by her two sons, who kneel at the sides. The W end of the S aisle has a number of Classical monuments, from the 17C onwards. Amongst them, however, is a large ogee recess with a tomb-chest and an unidentified effigy.

St. Mary Redcliffe, Redcliffe Way. Queen Elizabeth I called this church 'the fairest, goodliest and most famous parish church in England'. It is built on a cathedral scale, paid for by the merchant wealth of Bristol's port. The upper part of the NW tower is 14C with characteristic ogee windows, crocketed gables and ballflower. The spire suffered from lightning in the 15C and was only completed in 1872. It is 292ft high. The 14C N porch is most original, for instance in shape, which is hexagonal. It has the exuberant foliage of the period, nodding ogee arches, niches and gables. The doorway is quite oriental. The interior of the porch is equally remarkable with six piers against the six angles and a vault. The inner N porch is earlier, of c 1200. The S porch is also notable, but later (14C) and with a liernevault. The 14C S transept windows are again notable, and its clerestory and the aisles introduce the Perpendicular style. The chancel E window is of seven lights and the W window is of five transomed lights. The clerestory has 34 six-light Perpendicular windows and requires flying buttresses throughout. The exterior, with projecting Lady chapel, is dominated by the clerestory, pierced parapets of trefoils in triangles and large windows. There is cusped panelling between the clerestory windows and the parapets. The transepts have E and W aisles, which are only found in large churches. The exterior has been floodlit since 1984.

The interior is all vaulted and it is as glorious as the outside. The nave is of seven bays. The S aisle is early 14C, based on Bristol Cathedral and with a lierne-vault. The S transept is slightly later and then all is Perpendicular, late 14C or 15C. The N aisle is of the latter period and it should be compared with the S aisle. The nave and the chancel are similar, except for the vaulting. Indeed, the variety of vaulting patterns is amazing. There are about 1200 bosses, all different; to study them, field glasses are recommended. One, which depicts a maze, has been copied in a fountain in Victoria Park, Bristol. Between the arcades and the clerestory windows there is cusped panelling as on the exterior. The E window is placed high up, over the arch which leads into the Lady chapel. Under the sacristy and N transept there is a crypt. In the S nave aisle there are three large recesses, each surmounted by a concave arch with ogee sides. There is cusping and sub-cusping, cresting and elaborate finials. They are based on those at the E end of Bristol Cathedral.

The font at the W end is Perpendicular, octagonal and with panelling. The wrought-iron screen under the tower is of 1710. The space beneath the tower forms the chapel of St. John the Baptist (or the American chapel). In it is placed a painted wooden figure of Queen Elizabeth I, possibly made after her visit in 1574. She holds an orb and sceptre. Nearby is a large whalebone, brought back to Bristol by the explorer, John Cabot. The brass eagle lectern to the right of the crossing is of 1638. Near it, at the E end of the nave on the S side, there is an 18C sword-rest. Mayors of Bristol used to live in Queen Square, not far from the church, and so St. Mary's has long had close civic links. There are Stuart royal arms over the S nave door. In the Lady chapel there is a 17C brass chandelier, which was copied throughout the Church in the 19C. The pulpit, screens and choirstalls are all 19C. The pulpit was carved by William Bennett in 1856. In the W window of the tower there are eight large 15C figures. In the S window of the S transept is glass by Sir Ninian Comper, 1914. It depicts famous figures in Bristol's history. A *Messiah* window in the N ambulatory, 1859, is in memory of Handel, who was often in the church. The Lady chapel has good glass in three windows, by H.J. Stammers, 1965. The E window of the chapel depicts the Nativity with the Magi and Shepherds (above) and a Pietà (below).

There are some significant memorials. One major benefactor, William Canynge (or Canynges), has two monuments in the S transept. He is shown with his wife Joanna in a large canopied and painted monument in the centre of the S wall. She died in 1467. After her death he took Holy Orders, celebrating his first Mass here on Whit Sunday, 1468, and he has another monument, 1474, showing him as Dean of Westbury College, with two angels at his head and a bearded bedesman at his feet. John Lavyngton, a chantry priest of the early 15C, is commemorated by a worn effigy in a S nave aisle recess. In the N transept there is an effigy of a knight with crossed legs, perhaps of the 13C. He might be Robert de Berkeley, who was a notable benefactor at the end of the 12C.

Two adjoining recesses at the E end of the N chancel aisle have effigies of Philip Mede and his wife, Isabella, 1475, and brasses of Richard Mede (the son of Philip) and his two wives. There are brasses too for Sir John Juyn, Chief Justice, and his wife and daughter, 1439 (in the Lady chapel); John Jay, Sheriff, his wife and 14 children, 1480; and John Brook, Serjeant at Law, and his wife, 1512. A memorial is placed high on the N nave wall by the tower to Admiral Sir William Penn (died 1670), the father of the founder of Pennsylvania. His naval pennants and armour hang above. He lies buried in the S transept. The large monument of 1839 to the NE of the church commemorates Thomas Chatterton and his family. Chatterton, a minor poet, died in 1770.

The New Room (John Wesley's Chapel), The Horsefair. This church was built by John Wesley himself in 1739, and it is the oldest Methodist church in the world. It was enlarged in 1748. Restoration took place in 1929–30 under Sir George Oatley. It has been only slightly altered from its 18C appearance, which was substantially domestic. Above and adjoining the church proper are the original house and the stables. The exterior is rather austere, with windows only at gallery level. In the forecourt on the Broadmead side is the statue of John Wesley on horseback by A.G. Walker, 1932 (well-known for his statue of Florence Nightingale in London). The forecourt at the Horsefair end has a statue of Charles Wesley, by Brook Hitch, 1939. The two forecourts have been considerably altered in the 20C.

The interior of John Wesley's New Room, the earliest surviving Methodist church (1739)

The interior has six Tuscan columns with an octagonal lantern in the centre. There are galleries along the E and W sides. The pulpit and lower reading desk at the N end have pretty staircase railings. They form in effect a N gallery which connects with the side galleries but not directly with the body of the church. Box-pews stand in a block in the centre of the church; there is no central alley. Simple benches which face towards the centre are placed under the side galleries and, of course, within them. The Snetzler organ of 1761 at the N end of the E gallery was bought in 1930. The subdued green colour of the interior is a 20C revival of the original.

The second Methodist Conference, of 1745, was held here. Charles Wesley lived in the house in 1748–49 and elsewhere in Bristol until 1771. For many of those years he was the minister of the New Room. John Wesley spent a part of each year on the premises, which served as the early Methodist headquarters for SW England.

BUCKINGHAMSHIRE

What it lacks in size Buckinghamshire more than makes up for in a rich diversity of landscape. The principal division is marked by the crest-line of the Chiltern system that runs across the county at its narrowest point along a line, above Princes Risborough and Wendover, no more than a dozen miles in length. Though there are water-meadows around the Thame and the Ouse and ranges of low hills and even a few nearly isolated hills, such as Brill Hill, rising boldly to over 600ft, the land N of the Chiltern escarpment is scenically part of the Midlands and still essentially agricultural. To the S, the land is almost all hilly as the Chilterns, clad in beech and penetrated by narrow valleys, tumble gently through 'stockbroker belt' towards Burnham Beeches (remnant of an ancient forest), the Thames Valley and the suburbs of London.

The building materials are no less varied than the landscape. Nowhere is there much building stone—just a little in the numerous outliers covering the Kimmeridge Clay that lies in the Vale of Aylesbury and a little more (and better) where the N of the county, around Westbury and Thornborough, penetrates the oolitic limestone belt that stretches across England from Somerset to Lincolnshire. It was from this source indeed that the main supplies of building stone were obtained and it is noticeable that some of the churches in the N and W of the county succeed in having something of the splendour of those in neighbouring Northamptonshire and Oxfordshire. But, otherwise, what tells is the great variety of building materials and their different colours and textures: soft white clunch, grey chalk rubble, hard black flints, mellow brown bricks and warm red tiles. It is this and, especially near London, their over-zealous restoration that more than anything else characterise the county's churches and chapels. For Buckinghamshire contains no ecclesiastical building of the first rank. It has never had a cathedral and monastic remains are scanty; there are no big towns with grand parish churches and not many churches even of more than local interest. Nor is there any Buckinghamshire 'type' of feature except the well-known Aylesbury fonts.

Buckinghamshire is not a medievalist's dream county. But Wing would find a place in even the briefest survey of pre-Conquest architecture. Its apse, polygonal within and without like that at Deerhurst, Gloucestershire, is decorated with the familiar narrow strips (or lesenes) and the arcade inside consists of no more than the unadorned pieces of wall left when the arches were cut through. Fingest sports the most memorable Romanesque tower in the county, so huge as perhaps to have been used as nave to what now is nave but might once have been chancel. Stewkley and Upton are two perfect examples of the Romanesque parish church. Both consist of nave, central tower and straight-ended chancel (Upton's S aisle, of course, is 19C) and the chancel of both is rib-vaulted. Stewkley is richly, if somewhat monotonously, decorated and Upton has within recent years been shamefully deprived of all character inside.

The Early English style is represented by Haddenham's tower and a number of more or less restored chancels especially (for example, Aylesbury) but by nothing so splendid as the body of Chetwode Church, itself originally the chancel of an Augustinian priory church. Admittedly, some of the work has been reset and restored, but it is undoubtedly the best 13C work in the county. Edlesborough's E

window is much restored but shows perfectly the coming of the
Decorated style of the early 14C in the way in which its centre light is
wider than its outer lights and projects above them to force apart, as
it were, the foiled circles above. The 14C itself is on the whole but
poorly represented. Emberton is a basically Decorated (though
textureless) church related to Olney, from which it is indeed distant
but a couple of miles. Also not far from Olney is Hanslope. Both have
splendid spires reminiscent of those across the border in Northamptonshire. With Hanslope's tower and spire (rebuilt in 1804) we
are in the Perpendicular age and here there is something really to
report. Maids Moreton to the N, and Hillesden to the S, of Buckingham are two wonderful churches even if they are no match in
either scale or splendour for the late medieval wool churches of the
Cotswolds and East Anglia. But in the chapel of Eton College the
county can at last boast one of the great monuments in the history of
English medieval architecture. And finally, though in an entirely
different class of course, there are the three detached medieval
domestic chapels that still exist at Creslow Manor, Great Hundridge
Manor, Chesham, and Widmere, Marlow.

The post-medieval churches are again on the whole not especially
remarkable. Willen is no great architectural masterpiece and
Gayhurst is interesting rather as the work of a lesser man attempting
the English Baroque. Of Browne Willis's Fenny Stratford little is now
left and the same, alas, is true also of Henry Keene's Hartwell. This
was designed in 1753, so the Gothick Revival appears early in
Buckinghamshire's churches. St. Lawrence's at West Wycombe is in
a class of its own. When dealing with religious buildings of the 18C,
Nonconformist chapels must for the first time be included. Buckinghamshire has at Jordans the most famous of all Friends' meeting
houses. It and the Baptist Chapel at Winslow are models of reticence,
humble in scale, modest in materials and domestic in appearance.
The neo-Romanesque Revival, usually associated with the years
around 1840, appears as early as 1815 at Old Wolverton by Henry
Hakewill. The turn to a real respect for the Middle Ages and
consequently to an archaeologically correct Gothic came, nationally
speaking, only with A.W.N. Pugin and Gilbert Scott. None of Scott's
churches has any special interest and Pugin is represented none too
worthily by St. Peter's, Marlow of 1845–48; so the simple, handsome
cruciform church of 1849 at Penn Street by Pugin's biographer,
Benjamin Ferrey, must stand as perhaps the best expression of the
new Gothic ideal. It was one that in 1859 Sir William Tite's church at
Gerrards Cross was hailed as a welcome reaction against. At Prest-
wood E.B. Lamb had introduced his 'roguish' reaction ten years
earlier and in 1866 William Butterfield used at Dropmore his own
harsh brand of novelty. The following year, G.E. Street, arguably the
greatest architect of the age, is seen less to react against, than to
create from, Gothic principles: his church at Westcott is marvellously,
brutally, austere, dependent upon stark geometry rather than upon
either richness of materials or prettiness of detail. The chancel added
in 1871 to Lacey Green Church by J.P. Seddon is typical of his
generally colourful style. Considering how rich the county was, it is
perhaps surprising that the architects of the Arts and Crafts movement are not represented, and the story ends with the chapel at
Stowe School by Sir Robert Lorimer, Scotland's answer to Lutyens.

So far as Buckinghamshire is concerned, medieval fittings are no
more important really than are its medieval churches. The tympana
of the Romanesque S doorways of Dinton and Water Stratford are

especially interesting, the one decidedly more pre-Conquest looking than the other, which has a Christ in Majesty flanked by angels in the manner of the Prior's Door at Ely. Romanesque also is the series of fonts centred on that at Aylesbury which have for their bases an inverted scalloped capital and their bowls decorated with fluting and foliage. About a dozen of them are known either complete or with either stem or bowl only; Great Kimble is an especially fine one, and that at Bledlow might have been altered and also recut. In the chancel at Little Kimble there are a number of very fine 13C tiles of the Chertsey type with each roundel of figures composed of four quarter tiles. There are two pairs of oaken knight and lady of c 1300 at Clifton Reynes and at Taplow is one of the very earliest surviving brasses to a civilian, a small bearded figure in the head of a foliated cross, c 1350. Also as early as the 14C probably is the pulpit at Upper Winchendon. That at Edlesborough is (like the tall Rood screen there) 15C and, though much restored, retains—most unusually—its lofty canopy. Also 15C and even greater rarities are the vestment cupboard at Aylesbury, with its brackets swinging outwards to receive the vestments, and the Doom at Penn.

Stained glass and wall paintings are less satisfactorily included in any such chronological listing because so fragmentary. In the chancel S window of Chetwode, Buckinghamshire has some of the most important later 13C stained glass in England: there are grisaille, a couple of figures and some of the very earliest heraldic glass in the country, and all very enjoyable too. Also at Chetwode there is an early 14C saint carrying a book and in the E window at Weston Underwood there are some late 14C figures of Christ and his angels and saints. At Hitcham there are more remains of 14C glass and, finally, at Hillesden there are fragments of saints in the tracery of the E window that must be about contemporary with the body of the church and in the E window of the S transept scenes from the life of St. Nicholas that are early 16C. The later date of the scenes is shown by the modelled figures and the way they are placed in architectural settings in the late 15C Flemish manner. The most important wall paintings are without doubt those of 1479–88 in Eton College chapel, where those on the N wall display similar Flemish characteristics. Otherwise, the wall paintings of Buckinghamshire are generally more numerous than enjoyable. At Little Kimble there are some especially impressive figures among the early 14C paintings and at Little Missenden it is still possible to admire the large 15C St. Christopher and gain some idea, too, of the appearance of the church in the 17C with all its texts and frames.

Hillesden's St. Nicholas glass and the Eton wall paintings have brought us almost to the arrival of the Renaissance. In architectural terms it first appears significantly enough in a monument, that to Margaret Gyffard (died 1539) at Middle Claydon which, though still medieval in its conventions, now has coarse Renaissance corner balusters to the tomb-chest. But, again, the county has relatively little of importance to offer in the way of post-medieval fittings and monuments. Langley Marish with its wooden arcade of 1630 and Kederminster pew and library is unquestionably the principal monument. After that, items like the Ivinghoe pulpit and Chetwode's painted wooden triptych of 1696 are very minor things. The interiors of the Friends' meeting house at Jordans and of the Baptist Chapel at Winslow (where the fittings are apparently mostly of the early 19C) are movingly simple; those of Willen and of Fawley are less genuine than they at first seem to be, and those at Gayhurst are overshadowed by the great Wrighte monument. But before turning to monuments, we must mention the utterly egregious font and pulpit (it is in fact an armchair with a desk in front of it) at West Wycombe; there really is nothing like them anywhere. Chronologically next in importance after the Gyffard monument is the Dormer monument of 1552 at Wing, which in style belongs to the circle round the Lord Protector Somerset and the Duke of Northumberland. The medieval type with effigy or effigies on a tomb-chest is to be found as late as 1611 in the monument to Elizabeth, Lady Russell of Thornhaugh at Chenies, where there is an exceptionally complete run of Bedford monuments from 1555 to the present day. The Kederminsters are shown at Langley Marish in a monument of 1599 of the common Elizabethan type with figures facing each other across a *prie-dieu* and other common, but larger, Elizabethan and Jacobean types of monument are represented by the two Dormer monuments N (1590) and S (died 1616) of the chancel at Wing and another Dormer monument (1626?) at Long Crendon, where the deceased are por-trayed with their families beneath elaborate canopies.

But new types of monument were beginning to appear. The three Wheeler tablets of 1626–36 at Datchet have busts on top of them and the wonderful monument to Henry Curwen (died 1636) at Amersham shows the deceased standing in a shroud and within an arched recess whose doors are held open by angels. The Wheeler monuments have been attributed to an assistant of Hubert Le Sueur, one of the foreign artists working in England at the time to whose influence the loosening of the conventions of funerary monuments may in part be attributed. The Curwen monument is an important Mannerist piece by Edward Marshall who worked under Nicholas Stone and it is he who above all others brought about that relaxing of iconographical constraints that is characteristic of the early 17C in monuments. The change is clearly demonstrated in the plain slab of marble supported on columns that commemorates Lady Fraunces Bourgchier, 1612, at Chenies. Equally remarkable and original are the monuments to Elizabeth Hampden (died 1634) at Great Hampden and to Lady Boys, 1638, at Great Missenden, two fine purely Classical designs with open pediments, the later one by Nicholas Stone himself. The semi-reclining effigy accompanied in a Baroque way by asymmetrically placed figures and associated with John Bushnell and C.G. Cibber is found first in the monument to Sir Thomas Tyrril (died 1671) at Castlethorpe and again in the monument to Richard Winwood, 1689, by Thomas Stayner at Quainton where there is another exceptional collection of monuments.

The 18C opens with éclat at Chenies with the first Duke of Bedford and his Duchess seated under a baldacchino against surrounding architecture. Of the great trio, Peter Scheemakers, J.M. Rysbrack and L.F. Roubiliac, whose arrival in England from the Continent opens a new era in English funerary sculpture, Scheemakers is well repres-ented, Roubiliac not at all and Rysbrack by only one monument (and that, at Addington, 1753, a relatively minor one). The quality of Scheemakers's work is variable and there is no denying that the quality of the carving in his monument to John Piggott (died 1751) at Grendon Underwood is nowhere near as good as it is in his grandly Classical monument to the first Earl of Shelburne of 1754 at High Wycombe. Scheemakers signs the monument to Mountague Drake (died 1728) at Amersham, which is illustrated in James Gibbs's 'Book of Architecture' (1728) as having been designed by him. The design of monuments was not indeed always that of the sculptor:

Sir Richard Pigott's at Quainton, for example, is signed by the architect Giacomo Leoni but not by the sculptor. Two other monuments, both by unknown sculptors, must find a place in any survey of post-medieval monuments in Buckinghamshire: that to the Wrightes at Gayhurst of c 1728 and, far better in every way, that to Mr Justice Dormer at Quainton of c 1730. No less excellent, finally, is William Woodman's masterpiece at Drayton Beauchamp, the monument to Lord Newhaven (died 1728) and Lady Newhaven (died 1732). Sir Henry Cheere, that master of the colourful smaller monument and of Rococo ornament, appears at Hillesden (Sir Alexander Denton and his wife (died 1733), not at all Rococo yet), at Great Hampden (John Hampden, 1743) and at Amersham (Mrs Elizabeth Drake, died 1757, with her children in lively array behind her). The reaction against Rococo that takes place c 1760 is splendidly heralded in Buckinghamshire by the fine monument to the second Duke of Bedford and his Duchess at Chenies made in 1769 by Joseph Wilton to a design by Sir William Chambers. But the county is not rich in monuments by any of those other sculptors who later lived and worked in Italy, Nollekens, Flaxman, Westmacott, Chantrey and Gibson and nor in their oeuvre are any of the monuments of more than slight interest. There is indeed no more sculpture really to be noticed until the monument, also at Chenies, to Lord Arthur Russell (died 1892). It is by Alfred Gilbert, the most gifted of the New Sculptors of the post-1870 period. It is highly original in design (taking the form of a candelabrum) and displays well the sculptor's enormous repertory of ornament from Mannerist and Baroque to his own convoluted version of Art Nouveau.

And so, finally, a review of post-medieval stained glass. There is so much of it, especially Victorian of course, that it is difficult to make a selection. There are many panels of 16C and 17C Flemish glass at Addington and more 17C foreign glass in the E window at Amersham. Heraldic glass, of the earlier 18C, is to be found at Fenny Stratford (N aisle) and Bradenham (N aisle, E window) and, of the later 18C, at Wotton Underwood where in the S aisle there are some 200 reset panels by Francis Eginton. The E window at Chetwode by William Holland has been mentioned in the gazetteer. Sir Robert Frankland Russell made the interesting E window of Great Kimble in 1844, George Hoadley the W window of Fulmer in the pictorial style of Sir Joshua Reynolds's New College, Oxford windows in the same year, and Thomas Willement the panels of New Testament scenes in the E window of the S aisle at Turweston in 1851. Thereafter, most of the big names of the Victorian Age are well represented, especially C.E. Kempe. John Hardman & Co.'s glass is to be seen in the E window at Frieth, of 1849, and at St. Peter's, Marlow of about the same time as well as at Cadmore End rather later. William Butterfield restored Wavendon Church in 1848–49 and all the glass there was made by the O'Connors, whose work is also to be seen at Datchet. Clayton & Bell can be seen at their early best in a N aisle window of c 1865 at Edlesborough; the W window there of 1867 by Ward & Hughes can in no way compare with it. Later Clayton & Bell work can be seen at Bradwell and Hughenden. The Gibbses' work is to be seen at Aylesbury, Boarstall and Broughton. The E window of Little Marlow of 1866 by Heaton, Butler & Bayne expresses the changing style of the later 19C, as do Henry Holiday's window of 1868 at Bletchley with its pre-Raphaelite character and Burlison & Grylls's easternmost window in the S aisle of Ellesborough of 1875. Holiday (and Harry Wooldridge) also designed some windows at Latimer

Church which were executed by James Powell & Sons in 1873, using paint with water-soluble borax so that they are now but a shadow of their former glory. Kempe's glass is too widespread even selectively to record. It varies in date from the early window of 1877 at Upton beyond his death in 1907 and down almost to the closing of the business in 1934 with the right-hand light of the easternmost window of the N aisle of St. Mary's, Slough, having a date of death of 1933. But St. Mary's must mean not Kempe, whether early or late, but A.A. Wolmark whose W window of 1915 is a triumphant landmark in stained glass design—even if its strong colours and Expressionism are to some extent anticipated by Gerald Moira's window of 1898 in the N aisle of New Bradwell. Both windows make utterly irrelevant M.E. Aldrich Rope's belatedly pretty-pretty Arts and Crafts window in the S aisle of Edlesborough with its date of death of 1932.

Buckinghamshire's churches are quite rich in associations. John Schorne (late 13C) and his shrine have been mentioned under North Marston and the poet John Milton (1608–74) and William Penn (1644–1718), the founder of Pennsylvania, under Jordans. Browne Willis (1682–1760), the antiquary, restored Bletchley and Great Brickhill Churches as well as rebuilding the church at Fenny Stratford. John Newton (1725–1807), the hymn-writer, and the poet William Cowper (1731–1800) both lived at Olney and the architect Sir Gilbert Scott (1811–78) was born at Gawcott. St. Thomas Cantelupe (c 1218–82), Bishop of Hereford, was born at Hambledon. William Grocyn (1449–1519), the scholar and friend of Erasmus, was priest at Newton Longville and William Warham (c 1450–1532), Archbishop of Canterbury, priest at Great Horwood. John Hampden (1594–1643), famous for his refusal in 1636 to pay the ship money exacted by King Charles I, was born at Hampden. Edmund Waller (1606–87), the poet, was baptised in Amersham Church and is buried at Beaconsfield, as is Edmund Burke (1729–97). The churchyard at Stoke Poges may be that of the famous 'Elegy' by Thomas Gray (1716–71). Benjamin Disraeli (1804–81), the Prime Minister and novelist, lived at Hughenden and is commemorated in the church there by a monument erected by Queen Victoria. The architect G.F. Bodley (1827–1907) lived in Bridgefoot House, Iver, from c 1895 until his death.

Buckinghamshire has dedications to St. Laud at Sherington, a unique dedication in England, which refers to a 6C Bishop of Coutances in France who is better known as St. Lo; and to St. Firmin at North Crawley, one of only two English cases, recalling another saint from France, a 4C Bishop of Amiens.

Chenies, *St. Michael*. Chenies came to the Russells by marriage in 1526 and remained in their possession until 1954. The benevolent overall control of the Bedford Estate Office is gone; but the village still remains a typical estate village. The 15C church was very much restored in the 19C and is of little interest—especially in comparison with the Bedford chapel, which has a magnificent series of monuments from the 16C to the 19C. The chapel is not normally open to the public, but much may be seen through glazed screens. Bathed in Kempeian light, the House of Russell sleeps, robed in alabaster and painted, reflected in the black and white marble floor and beneath a hammerbeam roof bedecked with banners. It is a splendid if somewhat chill scene.

At the E end of the chapel, on steps as though an altar within its chancel, lies he who first acquired Chenies and was the founder of the wealth and greatness of the house, John, first Earl of Bedford (1486–1555). Well-carved in alabaster, he lies with his wife, Elizabeth, on a tomb-chest decorated with Venetian Renaissance motifs. In the nave, on the far side, is his grand-daughter, Anne, wife of Ambrose Dudley, Earl of Warwick (died 1604), in peeress's robes and then, on the near side, Francis, second Earl and his wife, Margaret. He died in 1585, but the monument was not erected until 1619. Both monuments are still in the medieval form of a tomb-chest with recumbent effigies, though the second Earl's tomb has a big back plate rising behind his and his wife's heads. Further W in the nave come two monuments brought from Watford Church: first, Bridget, Dowager Countess of Bedford (died 1600) and then, Elizabeth, Lady Russell of Thornhaugh (died 1611). Both are still in the medieval tradition; but the Dowager Countess's monument shows a first gentle departure from that tradition in having, either side of the tomb-chest, a male figure kneeling on a little stand. The monument is very likely to be by Isaac James, who, despite his name, was, significantly enough, a foreigner. Next, and best seen through the glazed screen at the W end of the church, is Lady Fraunces Bourgchier (died 1612). Now at last the medieval tradition is really set aside—no tomb-chest, no effigy, just a slab of black marble supported by white Doric columns and forming a canopy to a lower slab of black marble, itself with no more than a white lozenge and two shields of arms. Behind it is the bronze candlestick-like monument to Lord Arthur Russell (died 1892) by Sir Alfred Gilbert and in his own inimitable Art Nouveau style and, to its right, the monument to the first Earl Russell, the Prime Minister (died 1878), very similar to Lady Bourgchier's but with only a white marble coronet on its lower slab. To the extreme left and filling the whole nave wall is what must be the largest monument in the county, that to William, fifth Earl and first Duke of Bedford (died 1700) and his wife. They are seated beneath a large medallion portrait of their son who was executed after the Rye House Plot in 1683. The Duke sits in an ungainly—and improbable—pose wearing his Garter robes; the Duchess leans outwards for symmetry and is dressed in timeless robes. Outside and above is a huge Classically derived reredos background of white and grey-veined marbles with coupled Corinthian columns carrying an entablature and big segmental pediment. Four a side, between the columns, are portrait medallions of their other children and, within the pediment, a cartouche of arms and three cherubs. The monument, not a little pompous, funny even, is always ascribed to Francis Bird, though on no firm evidence. Finally, of the monuments that can be seen through the glazed screens, there are in the immediate foreground two late 14C clunch effigies of a Cheyne and his wife, she much defaced, he in armour and for some reason entirely uncut from the waist down.

Among the monuments that cannot be seen are those against the S wall to Frances, Lady Chandos (died 1623), with the effigy stiffly propped on its side; Francis, Lord Russell of Thornhaugh and fourth Earl of Bedford (died 1641), his wife and two daughters, still essentially medieval in type though against the wall and having an architectural background with two arched recesses, open pediment and obelisks; and, finally, the second Duke and his Duchess, made in 1769. This last was designed by Sir William Chambers and executed by Joseph Wilton, whose masterpiece it perhaps is. It is in the English tradition but much influenced by the Baroque of 18C France and Rome, where Wilton had lived.

Chetwode, *St. Mary and St. Nicholas.* Chetwode, like Hillesden, is only about four miles from Buckingham and yet could be miles from anywhere. But there the similarity ends; for its church is no complete splendour and the style is Early English rather than latest Perpendicular. The present structure is in fact the chancel only, so it seems, of the church of an Augustinian priory that was founded in 1245; it became parochial c 1480 when the monks had become impoverished and the old parish church of St. Martin ruinous. The building and its fittings show considerable evidence of 17C and 18C work and the church was further repaired in 1868.

The exterior prepares one not at all for the glorious display inside. Everything is deliciously humble: a simple stone rubble box with chaotic array of (often reset) windows and a NW tower scarcely more than 8ft square with modest 17C details to outer doorway and inner arch and a low pyramidal roof. The interior, by contrast, boasts perhaps the best Early English work in the county. The superiority of the chancel over the nave of the parish church is marked—most effectively—by a magnificent array at the E end of three groups of stepped lancets: one group of five in the E wall and one group of three in each of the N and S walls. All the windows are shafted and have their elaborately moulded arches stilted to follow the height of the individual lancets. The capitals of the shafts of the E window are moulded only, those of the shafts of the N and S windows have foliage instead. But this grand display is not enough. In the S wall there are, too, the piscina and sedilia linked in a single composition, with dogtooth ornament between the shafts as well as foliage in the capitals. It all seems to have been tampered with, however, especially the complex mouldings of the arches (can the 'stray' lengths of moulding in the apexes of the arches really be of c 1250?) and the central, wider recess of the sedilia has been converted, perhaps in the 17C, into a doorway. Presumably it is all reset and restored. After this grand show, there is little really to note and it may be taken chronologically. First, the two windows with bar tracery high up in the nave S wall, then the part single late 13C window in the wall opposite with shafts with naturalistic foliage and a lintel in place of the former traceried head, the reset W window with Y-tracery and, finally, the early 14C N chapel with excellent corbel stops to the arch leading into it.

This chapel is now the manor pew complete with reused 17C and 18C panelling, fireplace in the corner and thin Gothick vault. But it is the stained glass at Chetwode that must first demand attention. It is a remarkable collection—and enjoyable, too. In the chancel S window there is much partly restored later 13C glass, including grisaille with geometrical patterns in colour as well as, for example in the centre light, a shield with the arms of England and a St. John the Baptist and an Archbishop each in a vesica. In addition, in the lower parts of the outer lights there is some splendid early 14C glass including, in particular, a saint with a book under a canopy and against a marvellous blue background. The E window is in its own very different way hardly less remarkable. It is of 1842 and one of the earliest commissions of William Holland of Warwick who, inspired by the grisaille and medallions of Chetwode's own medieval glass, produces his own decidedly convincing version of it. Beneath the window and in a recess in the chancel N wall is a wonderfully bold scrollwork design in red and yellow; it looks, much of it, very well gone over. At the W end, a wooden triptych with verses from the Bible in illusionistically painted cartouches records the carrying out of repairs in 1696. The organ case is a pretty Gothick piece and the font, too, could also be 18C.

Clifton Reynes, St. Mary the Virgin. The village lies S of Olney, delightfully isolated at the end of a lane that seems to be leading nowhere and then comes to a stop in front of the uniformly embattled church. This is of great interest and has an immensely high and narrow nave with beautiful arcades. What makes a visit especially worthwhile, however, is the splendid series of 14C Reynes family monuments in the N chapel. Wooden effigies are always something of a rarity yet here there are two pairs of them. Both are of oak and date from c 1300. One knight and his lady (said to be Thomas Reynes and his wife Joan) now lie within a recess in the N wall whose cusped and sub-cusped arch suggests a date of c 1330. The other knight and lady, perhaps Ralph Reynes and his first wife Cecilia, lie on a tomb-chest under the W arch of the arcade between chapel and chancel. Against the knight, legs crossed and hand on sword, the lady cuts a particularly handsome figure, long and slender, in her tight-sleeved gown and wimple. The effigies lie on a stone tomb-chest, a made-up piece perhaps, that is decorated with shields in elongated quatrefoils. The last of the Reynes family monuments (which have all been conserved within recent years) is of c 1380 and of an inferior quality. It is under the adjoining arch, all of stone and somewhat mutilated. The effigies lie on a tomb-chest against each long side of which stand in niches eight alternately male and female weepers with, above them, an important display of heraldry in shields.

Dinton, St. Peter and St. Paul. Dinton is an attractive village whose church has a Romanesque doorway as elaborately carved as it is interesting. It consists of one order of barley-sugar-like twisted shafts, lintel, tympanum and continuous outer zigzag and billet mouldings, all vigorously, not to say crudely, carved and primitive in its iconographical arrangement. The doorway is, indeed, the perfect exemplar of that early 12C English sculpture whose origins are to be found in the Viking style and in the pre-Conquest English tradition of figure work. Here the lintel shows a tiny St. Michael with typically large wings valiantly thrusting a cross down the throat of a large and menacing dragon. The dragon, representing Satan, is of Scandinavian type. Its stylised curled-up tail, like those of the animals in the tympanum, and the band of interlace enclosing the tympanum, are a pre-Conquest English feature. Exceptionally, an inscription explains the symbolism: that pardon and the remission of sins are to be had only through the sacraments.

Edlesborough, St. Mary the Virgin. Edlesborough is a large village under the Chilterns, four miles from Tring. At its W end stands the church in about as exposed and isolated a position as may be imagined. Though considerably restored, it is a handsome building and one, moreover, that will pleasurably engage the visitor awhile as he unravels its complicated architectural development. And, if that is not enough, there are the unusually rich and varied fittings to enjoy, especially the remarkable woodwork. The church was vested in the Redundant Churches Fund in 1977.

From outside the church is much spoilt by having been heavily rendered. Still, it is a fine sight, its lowish embattled form spreading comfortably over the great mound on which it is set. The sturdy W tower is mid-14C and of two stages, the one tall and buttressed at the angles, the other with, in each wall, two bell openings with simple Decorated tracery. The tower originally carried a small lead spire but that was lost when the church was struck by lightning in 1828 and the bells fell and the tower was greatly weakened. The chancel had been rebuilt in the late 13C and of that period the best feature is the splendid five-light E window. Though unfortunately much restored, it is splendid not only in itself but as showing, too, that gentle relaxation of the evenness of Geometrical forms which presages the coming Decorated style. So the central light is taller and broader than the other four. For the rest, the body of the church is mostly mid-13C though now with later windows, mainly of early 14C date but with modern tracery inserted in their heads.

Inside, one can see that the church is in fact older than it seems. The four-bay arcades are both 13C, though evidently of two builds, the division being marked by the short length of wall that converts the third pier from the E on each side into two responds—and it will be noticed that there are slight differences of detail between the three bays to the E and the single bay to the W. This bay might represent part only of the second build; for, instead of another respond, there is to the W a complete pier. So there might have been—or might still be, incorporated in the tower masonry—one or more other bays. The short length of wall will represent the W wall of an earlier—perhaps Romanesque—church. The weatherings over the tower arch show that the nave roof of the 13C church was steeply pitched; but in the 15C the clerestory was built and the present almost flat roof behind parapets substituted. At the same time, the aisle walls were heightened and shallow transverse arches thrown across the aisles to support their new flatter roofs. Also 15C are the N and S porches and the small single-light westernmost window in the N wall of the N aisle. It is set low down in the wall and, with the fireplace and remains of a flue set high up in the W wall of the aisle, might suggest that there was a two-storeyed lodging here in the NW corner of the building.

The church is decidedly rich in fittings and especially in 15C woodwork. Pride of place must go to the pulpit and its canopy. Though of course much restored, they are a wondrous piece: the pulpit of elegant 'wine glass' shape, its sides lavishly decorated with niches with vaulted and gabled canopies and above it, a very great rarity, the canopy, a tall and glorious confection with vaulted underside and four diminishing tiers of traceried and pinnacled decoration. The screen, too, is much restored but, again, an unusually handsome piece with the top rail of its centre gates forming with the arch above a big open vesica shape. The screen preserves its ribbed coving only to the E side and there it forms a continuous canopy over the six old stalls below. These have the usual little heads at the elbows but misericords too, carved with grotesque beasts and so on. And their desk fronts are original as well, as are most of the fronts to the modern stalls against the N and S walls of the chancel. The font and its cover are of common enough types, the one 15C, the other 18C but with a finial that is certainly again 15C. Except those of the S aisle and its porch, the roofs are all of the same general 15C type, low-pitched with heavy chamfered tiebeams and carved struts; the chancel roof is appropriately a little more elaborate in having the spandrels traceried.

After the woodwork, the fittings may best be listed in chronological order. A few 14C patterned tiles were suffered to remain when the floor was completely relaid in the 19C. Of the 15C there are the *ex situ* corbels in the N chapel in the shape of angels with shields, a chalice, crowned heads and so on, a couple of niches, one in each of the aisles, a couple of piscinae, that in the chancel more elaborate than that in the S aisle, and the St. James of Compostela in the small single-light window in the NW corner of the church. A communion table (though now grained and varnished), a chair and a couple of chests are 17C and the painting of Aaron is 18C. The firm of Clayton & Bell did much wall painting in the nave in 1867 and there is a good early Clayton & Bell window in the N aisle which both in colour and drawing is much superior to Ward & Hughes's glass in their W window of the same year. (The guide book sold at the church attributes the wall painting to 'Messrs Bell of London' and adds, 'apparently not the well-known firm of Clayton & Bell'. The painting, however, is entirely consistent with Clayton & Bell's work and is listed in Peter Larkworthy's 'Clayton & Bell, Stained Glass Artists and Decorators' (1984).) The two windows of 1867 make a nice contrast with the belated Arts and Crafts window of c 1932 by M.E. Aldrich Rope in the S aisle. The splendidly convoluted wrought ironwork over the entrance to the vestry should not be overlooked.

Among the monuments, those worthy of notice are all brasses and the finest of them is also the earliest, that to John de Swynstede, last Rector of Edlesborough (died 1395). He is shown in Mass vestments, a very beautifully drawn figure. The 'rose brass' in the chancel floor (S side) has long been associated with Sir John Killyngworth (died 1412/13) who in fact seems to have been commemorated by a brass demi-figure in the N aisle where now only the inscription plate remains. Other rose brasses are known to have existed, but Edlesborough's is now unique. It consists of a four-petalled flower with the petals inscribed with Latin tags that might be translated as 'What I have spent, I have had; What I have given, I have; What I have refused, I am being punished for; What I have kept, I have lost'. As an ecclesiastical emblem, the rose is symbolical of the transitory nature of the life of man who 'flourisheth as a flower of the field'. Set in an indent of earlier date next to the vestry is the palimpsest brass to Sir John Rufford (died 1540). His three wives were on a separate palimpsest plate (recently stolen) and the reverse of the two plates made up part of an early 15C lady. The inscription plate, too, is palimpsest and has on its reverse another inscription referring to John Ingleby, Bishop of Llandaff (died 1499).

Eton College, *Chapel of St. Mary.* 'The King's College of Our Lady of Eton beside Windsor' was founded in 1440 by King Henry VI. The following year, on the model of William of Wykeham's twin foundations at Winchester and Oxford of some 60 years earlier, the King founded a sister college, King's College, at Cambridge. Besides a Master, Usher and 70 Scholars and the maintenance of a number of poor infirm men (an idea early given up), the foundation at Eton provided for the establishment of a college of secular priests. The collegiate chapel was begun in 1441, but pulled down in 1448 to make way for the present building. Work on this began in 1449 and was nearly finished by c 1459. In 1461 King Henry VI was deposed by the Yorkist Edward IV, who viewed the college with disfavour and work was not taken up again until 1469. In 1475 contracts were arranged for the furnishing of the chapel; but an idea of adding tower, transepts and nave was abandoned and, instead, in 1479 the antechapel was begun and, probably with its N and S porches, completed c 1482. So the plan of the present building is that

T-shaped one familiar from Oxford college chapels and consisting of a choir or chapel proper plus an antechapel running across the W end. At Eton, there are in addition a porch about halfway down the N side plus, to the E of it, a former vestry (now the Memorial chapel) and Lupton's chapel added c 1514 between two of the buttresses.

Porch, vestry and chapel in no way detract however from the uncomplicated nature of the building, which is one of the great royal chapels of the later Perpendicular style. It stands—very rightly—all but isolated on the S side of School Yard, its W end facing the street, its S and E walls, a small churchyard. It is from here that the sheer rationality of the building may best be appreciated. The chapel proper is divided into eight bays by deep buttresses that reach up to the battlemented parapet and then terminate in crocketed pinnacles. Within each bay is a single tall transomed window whose five lights are arranged as two intersecting three-light windows under the one arch. The windows stand on a moulding high above a blank wall, behind which the floor is raised some 13ft above the external ground level as a defence against flooding. The E end is flanked by octagonal stair turrets that rise above parapet and pinnacles to finish in little wooden lanterns. The huge (and again transomed) E window is of nine lights arranged as one central panel and two outer three-light windows and has for its arched head a bodge-up of stones reused probably from the building begun in 1441. The antechapel is clearly expressed in a matter-of-fact way: it is lower than the chapel proper and, to indicate that it runs transversely, has battlemented gables to its N and S walls. These each have a large seven-light window and the W wall, facing the street, has three five-light windows. The usual entrance for the public is by way of a mighty wooden staircase of 1694–95 in the two-storeyed N porch. The S porch is generally similar to that on the N but has in its W wall an entrance for the townspeople.

Inside, the division between antechapel and chapel proper is marked by a screen. Once through this, the full force of the extreme simplicity of the design is felt: the long, tall, narrow box is utterly devoid of spatial excitement, wholly filled with the powerful no-nonsense spirit of its unknown designer. The distinction between sanctuary and choir is made by bringing the vaulting shafts and the elaborately moulded and panelled window reveals down to ground level in the sanctuary but only to windowsill level in the choir, where a flat wall was needed for the canopied stalls. Equally rationally, the sanctuary is enriched by decorating the lower part of its walls with blank stone panelling to reflect, as it were, the grid-like windows above. The former timber roof was in 1959–61 replaced by Sir William Holford's ceiling resembling a fan-vault but in fact suspended from light metal girders; it is visually satisfactory if not archaeologically convincing.

The fittings are really very disappointing, except the 15C wall paintings and the 20C stained glass. There is a 15C brass lectern with double bookrest engraved with the signs of the Evangelists. There are also a Snetzler organ built in 1760 for King George III and a surprisingly sentimental statue of King Henry VI by John Bacon of 1786. Only a couple of all the brasses are worth a second look: that in the antechapel to Provost Henry Bost (c 1503), under a triple canopy, and that in his chapel to Provost Roger Lupton in his mantle as Canon of Windsor (c 1536). The monuments include one N of the altar to Thomas Murray (died 1623), with a frontal demi-figure of the Provost small in relation to its setting which, though so late, incorporates a skeleton; and the recumbent effigies of two 19C headmasters, Edward Hawtrey (died 1862), in a Gothic arched recess that one would never associate with Henry Woodyer, and Edward Balston (died 1891), all alabaster and black marble. The screen that divides antechapel from chapel proper is dull in its busy Decorated style; it is by G.E. Street and was erected in 1882, after his death. On it in 1885–87 was raised the great organ with J.L. Pearson's huge case all brightly coloured in orange, red, green and gold.

But it is the wall paintings and stained glass that one will want to see among the fittings. The former occupy the three W bays of the N and S walls of the chapel proper. They were executed in 1479–88 and the names of two painters, Gilbert and William Baker, are known. There were two bands of paintings, each divided into panels showing scenes from the Miracles of the Virgin and separated one from another by single figures in niches. The paintings were whitened out in the 16C, discovered in 1847 when the rather mechanical choirstalls were put in, and finally uncovered and restored in 1923 (when the canopies of most of the stalls were removed to expose the paintings). The upper bands on both walls had been almost wholly destroyed; the centres of the two lower bands could be replaced by copies. The remaining paintings, though much deteriorated, are the most important remaining examples of 15C wall painting in England. They are executed in oil on a gesso base in monochrome with a little yellow and less red. At first sight, the paintings on the two walls match quite well. But closer inspection reveals a decided difference in style of painting. Those on the N wall exhibit a keen sense of space with individual figures well modelled and placed in architectural settings, all in the late 15C Flemish way; those on the S wall are altogether flatter and lacking in depth.

The 20C stained glass is the happy result of bomb damage in 1940. The great E window depicts across the centre five lights the Crucifixion with the Last Supper below and Old Testament figures left and right. It is of 1949–52, by the Irish glazier, Evie Hone, and shows admirably her blunt, even primitive, style and wonderfully strong colours. Such conviction matches the architecture perfectly. The N and S windows of the four E bays date from 1959 and the 1960s and were designed by John Piper and made by Patrick Reyntiens. They make an interesting contrast with Evie Hone's glass with which they neither clash nor compromise. The windows on the N side depict various miracles, those on the S, various parables. All eight windows are almost abstract in composition, some of them, like the Multiplication of the Loaves and Fishes, powerful, others, like the Parable of the Sower, pretty, but all of them beautiful in their colours.

Fenny Stratford, _St. Martin._ This church is something of a curiosity in more ways than one. It was built at the instance of the antiquary, Browne Willis (1682–1760), in memory of his grandfather, the anatomist and physician, Dr Thomas Willis, who had died on 11 November, St. Martin's Day, 1675 at his home in St. Martin's Lane, London. Hence the dedication and hence, too, the early use of a Gothic style for the windows of what is now the N aisle. Willis's architect was Edward Wing of Aynho. Work began in 1724 and, after an appeal in 1728 for more funds to enable the work to be completed, the church was opened in 1730. Little now remains of this church: only the tower, the N wall with its symmetrical arrangement of door and 'Gothic' windows and, inside, the 40 remaining panels with the arms of the subscribers to the appeal incorporated in a new ceiling after the original collapsed in 1957. In 1866 a new chancel and nave were built to the designs of William White. Willis's church became the N aisle and later still, in 1907, a S aisle was added.

White's work is as hectic in its polychromy as Willis was odd in character. His eccentricities included the firing of six little cannon, called Fenny Poppers, each year on St. Martin's Day in memory of his parents and grandparents. He was a staunch High Churchman and not above showing his displeasure at the building of a dissenters' chapel in the town by buying its site and then demolishing the building. Yet he was so generous in the erection and repair of churches and so full of largesse to his family that he reduced himself to penury and was often taken for a beggar. He was one of the founders of the Society of Antiquaries of London and a man of prodigious energy. In his 'Surveys' of a dozen or more English cathedrals, he followed the tradition established by Dugdale in his 'Monasticon Anglicanum' (1655–73) and relied less on speculation than on facts won from medieval documents.

Fingest, *St. Bartholomew.* The beauty of Fingest Church lies in its setting, the interest in its tower. The church stands in lovely countryside at the top of the Hambleden Valley on the S edge of the Chilterns. The extraordinary tower is Romanesque and gargantuan in size, wider even than the nave and so huge that it is roofed with a pair of saddlebacks, believed to be 17C reproductions of the originals. It has been suggested that, as in some pre-Conquest churches, the tower was used as the nave and that the present nave (in its masonry also Romanesque) was originally the chancel. The present chancel is 13C.

Gawcott, *Holy Trinity.* The church is a Classical building in stone with arched windows, a polygonal apse and a W tower whose parapet has ball finials. It was built in 1828 to the designs, it is said, of the Reverend Thomas Scott whose monument, however, says no more than that 'by the assistance of friends, tho not without considerable expence [sic], he ... erected this Edifice, on the site of the former Chapel which had fallen to decay'. All the genteel painting of pews in brown, of walls in yellow and of ceiling in blue cannot add to the interest of so plain a building. That derives from the fact that Mr Scott was father to the future architect, Sir Gilbert Scott.

Gayhurst, *St. Peter.* There is no village of Gayhurst. The church stands—on an ancient site—near Gayhurst House. In 1724 George Wrighte applied for a faculty to build a new church. That seems to have been completed by 1728. Its architect is unknown; but the name of Edward Wing, carpenter and master builder of Aynho, Northamptonshire, has been suggested. Certainly, the church has all the signs of being the work rather of a lesser man seeking to work in the manner of the major early 18C architects. The church stands on a high rusticated plinth, employs the giant order outside and in and has pediments and cupola; in plan there is a cross-axis to the nave and, inside, there is much elaborate plasterwork and good joinery. Yet there is a certain gaucheness about it all: the bulk of the tower (which is perhaps only the recladding of the medieval one?) derides the power of the aedicule and flanking pilasters of the S, show, front; the centrepiece of the N side is a bizarre 'putting together' of motifs; and, inside, there is a denial of scale and volume in the giant pilasters with their strange 'scooped-out' channels and frothy capitals—and see how the cornice must be terminated and carried on volutes to permit the placing of the royal arms over the chancel arch. The monument to George Wrighte and his father is, like the building, important rather than really good.

The church is built of a beautiful golden coloured stone. The squat tower is surmounted by a cupola and has on its N and S sides arched recesses and unClassical blank hexagons. The W doorway is of French derivation. The windows with their Y-tracery suggest a date of c 1300 and the urns seem to provide only the corners of a battlemented parapet. But it is the nave that steals the show. On both N and S sides it is so treated as to seem detached alike from tower and chancel. On the S side giant Ionic columns and pilasters stand on a rusticated podium and tall pedestals to divide the wall into five bays, the central one wider than the others, pedimented and containing the entrance. All the openings are round-arched, but the door has its own eared outer frame on which sits, rather uncomfortably, a segmental pediment. The painful relation between entrance and pedimented bay should especially be noticed—as should the way in which 'every feature in the book' seems to be distributed about the building. On the other side, for example, the bay marking the cross-axis is rusticated and exhibits quite another mixture of ill-digested ingredients.

Inside, the nave again dominates. It is a spacious room, airy and all white, with giant pilasters, a frieze of mitres and open books, and a ceiling of late 17C rather than early 18C style. Through the tall narrow chancel arch may be glimpsed the chancel, unusually large and treated spatially as a quite separate room. Its ceiling is coved and appropriately richer in its plasterwork, with baskets of fruit and none too beautiful cherubs and a rayed Host over the altar.

The fittings are almost complete and but little altered. Few will worry that the organ case is not original, that the pulpit is a cut-down three-decker and that the font is 19C Gothic.,But it is unfortunate that the box-pews have been altered on the N side just enough to obscure inside the N–S axis that had been so deliberately expressed outside. There are fine wrought-iron altar rails and the reredos is a handsome piece with its fluted Corinthian columns and pilasters and wide segmental arch. Dominating the interior in every way, though, is the Wrighte monument erected c 1728. Sir Nathan, Keeper of the Great Seal, and his son, George, stand almost identical in pose and appearance beneath a baldacchino and in front of a big reredos. The monument is grand in composition rather than accomplished in carving (see, for example, the cutting of the Wrighteses' wigs), so that an attribution to one of the Carters, with whom he worked when first he came to England, seems perhaps more reasonable than that it should be the work of L.F. Roubiliac himself, as sometimes is said.

Gerrards Cross, *St. James.* The church stands in its walled enclosure by the Common as isolated from life today as it was in style distant from the Gothic required of churches when it was built in 1859. It is of brick—white for the structural elements, yellow and red for the decorative infill—and was erected by his two sisters in memory of Major-General George Reid, MP for Windsor. His 'valued friend', William Tite, was the architect. He won much praise from his contemporaries for eschewing Gothic in favour of a mixture of styles broad enough to encompass an Italian campanile, a crossing with Byzantinesque dome (with dormers!) and Chinese-capped angle turrets and, inside, the most gargantuan scagliola columns ever seen—complete with Early English stiff-leaf capitals! But the interior with its shed-like roofs is really rather uninspired.

Hartwell, *St. Mary.* The ruins of the former church on its eminence within the grounds of Hartwell House are a melancholy sight. For it was a highly important example of that rarity, a rococo Gothick church, and until as recently as 1950 was in good estate. The church was built in 1753–55 for Sir Thomas Lee. His architect was Henry Keene (1726–76), remarkable as one of the earliest of the early Gothic Revivalists. But his interest in the style was romantic rather than scholarly. The plan of the church—an octagon with E and W towers—is symmetrical, or Classical, while its proportions and the archaeological inaccuracy (and decorative distribution) of its details show that Keene had no real understanding of Gothic either as a style or as a system of construction. The principal feature of the interior was an extremely pretty fan-vault of plaster, probably the work of the great stuccoist, Robert Moor.

High Wycombe, *All Saints.* High Wycombe has been a place of importance since earliest times. Today, it is an industrial town and a suburb of London. In the 18C it was a market town. High above that town's principal remaining buildings, the Guildhall and the Market Hall, rises the church tower. It is of ashlar and, in its lower part, Perpendicular; but the dainty Gothick upper part is, like the Guildhall, the work of Henry Keene, 1755. The rest of the church is, from the outside, mostly of the later 13C when the original cruciform Romanesque church was enlarged. The flintwork was all so gone over and the stonework all so much renewed in 1887–89 that the most enjoyable of the later 13C work is now to be seen within the S porch. This is vaulted and has blank arcading along its side walls and an inner doorway with lush stiff-leaf capitals and richly moulded arch.

Inside the church one again senses that want of ancient textures noticed outside: the interior was indeed over-tidied in 1873–75. But it is a beautifully spacious interior, the result of a 15C heightening of the aisle walls and the erection of a lofty clerestory on rebuilt tall nave arcades. Not that the architectural development of the building is quite that simple. The old central tower was taken down only in 1509 and that necessitated the insertion at the E end of the nave of another higher and wider bay of arcade with clerestory above, so that the nave should meet the chancel. The observant visitor will notice that these later bays marking the place of the old crossing tower differ in detail from the more westerly 15C bays. And then, finally, there was the construction of a new tower at the W end. The tower arch was built behind and within the shafted arch of what must have belonged to the original late 13C spectacular W window of the nave.

The furnishings are much less interesting than the monuments. The grandest of these—and, indeed, one of the grandest of all 18C Classical monuments—is that in the N chapel to Henry Petty, first Earl of Shelburne (died 1751). He and his Countess are shown against a tall draped pyramid semi-reclining on a bulky sarcophagus high on a plinth that behind its railings provides, as it were, a stage on which the whole of the family can present themselves to us in the guise of an ancient Roman family. Noble attached and detached Corinthian columns support a broken pediment to create a pros-cenium arch and, in the wings, are groups of the deceaseds' children, on the left, their standing son and his seated wife with child on her lap and, on the right, the standing figures of two daughters and a boy. The *dramatis personae* are shown life-sized, nobly grouped about the stage in quiet dignity. The monument is the work of Peter Scheemakers and undeniably as brilliantly carved as it is consciously Classical. At the other extreme is the modest wall tablet in the S aisle to Jacob Wheeler (died 1621). Wheeler was a shoemaker and the alabaster frame of his monument is decorated with foliage and the tools of his craft. In the S chapel, finally, are the monuments to Sophia, Countess of Shelburne (died 1771), and Mrs Sarah Shrimpton (died 1783). Both are quite large and have that characteristic 18C feature, a pyramid, as background. But there the similarity ends: the one is heroic in scale, the other delicate in detail. The Countess is shown by Agostino Carlini, a Genoese who settled in England, more than life-sized and in profile as a Roman matron. Mrs Shrimpton's monument by the elder Richard Westmacott, by contrast, has an allegory of Victory standing on a daintily fluted sarcophagus beside an elegant urn. The differences in the treatment of the draperies and in the shape even of the pyramids in the two monuments should be observed.

Hillesden, *All Saints.* Hillesden is a lovely place, apparently miles from anywhere yet not four from Buckingham. Its parish church (which Gilbert Scott sketched when he was 15 and later, in 1875, restored) is one of the glories of the Perpendicular style in Buckinghamshire. The plan suggests that its transepts incorporate parts of an earlier cruciform church but what now one sees is, except for the stone rubble W tower of c 1450, entirely of the latest 15C and all beautifully ashlar-faced.

That no expense was spared on the late 15C work is indeed at once evident: the earlier tower looks too small in scale, rather plain and decidedly mean in its materials as compared with the body of the church. This is wonderful, especially as one approaches from the N. Here, there is a splendid progression from tall embattled porch to N aisle with two large three-light windows with serried ranks of cinquefoiled lights grouped in three sets of five in the clerestory high above; then the N transept and part of the N chapel with even larger four-light transomed windows and their embattled parapet reflected in the now embattled nave parapet; and, finally, the two-storeyed vestry with its polygonal stair turret crowned by an amazing confection of embattled, panelled and pinnacled parapet and ogee-shaped openwork flying buttresses all richly cusped and crocketed.

After this the interior perhaps comes as a disappointment—partly because of the emphasis on straight lines, endless panelling and that general want of fantasy in the Perpendicular style, partly perhaps because of Scott's thorough restoration and partly, no doubt, because of the painting of the flat plaster ceilings in tasteful blue and white like some café of the 1950s. Still, the interior is filled with an extraordinarily even light and is undeniably impressive in its proportions. As outside, there is some increase in display as one progresses E. Nave and aisle walls are without panelling and the slender piers of the arcades each have only four shafts. At the E end, however, the two-bay chancel N arcade has a pier with eight shafts and eight hollows and the upper part of the walls of the chancel are panelled in stone and have, right up beneath the ceiling, a frieze of demi-angels, some bearing musical instruments and others scrolls. The E window is largest of all, of five lights with a transom, and alone has tracery in its head; it is further distinguished by having a statue bracket either side of it.

The fittings include an unusual amount of stained glass and woodwork and a number of more than ordinarily interesting monuments. Most of the stained glass is late 16C, including many fragments of saints and canopywork in the chancel windows (in the tracery of the E window there is a figure of a Pope wearing a red cope), various buildings and parts of a God the Father from a Trinity and of an Annunciation scene in the windows of the N chapel and, in the windows of the S aisle, a couple of mitred heads. Much more enjoyable, however, is the later glass in the S transept. Here, in the upper part of the four-light E window are two rows of scenes from the Life of St. Nicholas. Canopies are now dispensed with and, instead, the scenes fill all the available space. Aping this early 16C glass, in style if not in colours, is Burlison & Grylls's glass of c 1875 in the adjoining S window.

Most of the woodwork is early 16C and unfortunately well worked over. This is particularly true of the various benches with their linenfold panelling. The Rood screen is considerably restored, especially in its coving, and the screen to the N chapel is about as much Victorian as original. Perhaps the best item is the later 17C family pew in the N transept with its two tiers of cartouches and pedimented aedicules. Under the tower are an 18C painted royal arms and the contemporary Moses and Aaron from a reredos.

In the N chancel chapel there are three interesting monuments. The earliest is that to Thomas Denton (died 1560) and his wife. It is of alabaster and in its conception as a tomb-chest with recumbent effigies and black-letter marginal inscription still entirely medieval. But the tomb-chest has shields in roundels separated by Early Renaissance type pilasters with flat baluster decoration. The monument to Alexander Denton (died 1576) and his second wife (died 1574), is quite different and, indeed, a remarkable piece of three-dimensional architecture, without effigy and wholly top-heavy. Its form with pediment and its details (especially the tall narrow sarcophagus) link it with the monuments to the first Lord Mordaunt (died 1563) at Turvey, Bedfordshire, and to Anthony Cave at Chicheley in this county, erected 1576. All three have been unconvincingly compared with the details of Hill Hall, Essex, and wrongly ascribed to a Thomas Kirby, apparently a mistake for Richard Kirby, master carpenter at Hill Hall in 1576. Thomas Isham died in 1676. His monument is no masterpiece but interesting in having its oval inscription tablet surrounded by oddly stylised seaweed-like foliage. Finally, on the S wall of the chancel is the monument to Sir Alexander Denton and Lady Denton (died 1733). It is signed 'H. Cheere Fec't' but shows nothing yet of that charming Rococo type of monument which is perhaps usually associated with him.

Jordans, *Friends' Meeting House.* The meeting house, humble in scale and modest in materials, is yet the most famous of all Quaker meeting houses. It sits quietly in its garden-cum-burial ground against a backdrop of gentle hills and glorious woods and was built for its purpose in 1688. It remains but little altered, complete with a cottage for the caretaker inside and some stabling behind.

The walls are of brick laid in Flemish bond and the hipped roof is tiled; glazed black headers impart a sobriety to the rich red colour that contrasts so well with the white-painted joinery of windows and doors. The principal front has a central doorway with window above. To its left, two cross-windows light the meeting room; to its right, two storeys of windows represent the caretaker's quarters. All the windows have leaded lights and external shutters.

The division noticed outside is made inside by a screen that rises the full height of the building. To one side of it is a small room, with little more in it than a fireplace, a door into a library beyond and some stairs leading to a room above. On both floors shutters in the screen open on to the meeting room with its brick floor and coved ceiling. The fittings are humble in the extreme: a plain panelled dado, the stand with ball finials to its newels as the only 'decorative feature' of the room, and simple wall and open-backed benches.

In the burial ground, and erected in 1862 on the approximate site of the burials, are headstones to William Penn (died 1718), founder and first Governor of Pennsylvania, and his two wives; Isaac Penington (died 1679) and his wife; and Thomas Ellwood (died 1713), friend of Milton, for whom he obtained what is now Milton's Cottage in Chalfont St. Giles.

Langley Marish, *St. Mary the Virgin.* Amid the featureless sprawl of the E suburbs of Slough rises the tower of Langley Church, the centrepiece of a group of buildings that are as interesting as they are unexpected. Opposite the church is the 'Red Lion' public house, timber-framed and with oversailing upper storey, and N and S of the church are ranges of almshouses, both 17C and of warm red brick. The S range was built by Sir John Kederminster in 1617, the N range by Sir Henry Seymour some time after 1669. The church is interesting enough in itself but is remarkable in its fittings and unique in its Kederminster pew and library.

The exterior of the church shows a great variety of materials: Romanesque masonry in the W wall and elsewhere, much knapped flint and stone rubble everywhere, brick buttresses with tiled cappings, and, of course, the 17C brickwork of the tower and large gabled S transept or Kederminster chapel with its adjoining library. Most of the windows have been renewed and there is some more recent, appalling, stone replacement around the priest's door into the chancel.

Inside, the great surprise is the three-bay N arcade. It is most remarkable: of wood, dated 1630 and with Tuscan columns set two-deep. Only a little less surprising (at any rate at first sight) is the chapel or whatever it is that rides high above us more or less opposite. The rest of the church is Decorated in style and, to judge by such remaining details as the shafted chancel windows and the piscina and sedilia, was no doubt of high quality.

The fittings are numerous, varied and delightfully jumbled. In the N aisle there are, towards the chapel, three excellent corbels of 'green men' and, in one of the windows, fragments of 15C and 16C stained glass. Font and chancel screen are Perpendicular in style. Jacobean are the pulpit and the gallery front (painted duck-egg blue!) under the tower and with the big carved royal arms on it as well as the bread charity shelf under the arms. The two-tiered chandelier with its handsome iron hanging is dated 1709 and the gallery into the N aisle, 1831. Among the monuments there are the somewhat unusual one in the N chapel signed 'T. Burnell Fleet Street' and, of course, the Kederminster monument in the chancel. This is of a common Jacobean type and is sculpturally of no great quality. At top right kneel John Kederminster (died 1588) and his wife with, below, their children. The eldest of them, Edmund, is again shown, upper left, with his wife and, again, their children below, one of them being John, later Sir John and founder of the Kederminster pew and library.

These deserve detailed description: they can safely be called unique. The pew lies against the back wall of a chapel which, approached from the nave up a flight of stairs, has since the late 18C been used as the mortuary chapel of the Bateson Harvey family. It was Sir Robert who in 1792 erected the charming Coade-stone Gothic vaulted arcade that encloses the chapel with its fine monuments and interesting 19C brasses. The walls are painted with coarse strapwork patterns that perhaps go with those of the arcade pilaster responds; so the date of the pew might be c 1630. Its front is a subtly coloured and marbled screen with central door, fielded panels below and windows above, all crowned by obelisks and a shield of arms within elaborate open strapwork. Behind the lattices the Kederminsters could pray unseen in a room whose walls and ceiling are panelled and marbled, with heraldic achievements at one end and everywhere texts and the all-seeing Eye of God.

W of the chapel is the Kederminster library. It was perhaps installed and decorated a little earlier than the pew, in 1613–23. The library is an amazing sight. The walls of the smallish room are entirely covered with white-bordered painted panels that contain, most of them, strapwork cartouches (some of them incorporating standing figures), but those at the top of the walls, landscape views based apparently on engravings. Dominating the room is a big fireplace, elaborately decorated and with an overmantel showing on a convex oval the Kederminster family alliances. Much of the panelling opens as doors to reveal the bookcases in the walls behind, and the backs of the doors are painted with more books in *trompe l'oeil* as well as, in one case, with portraits of Sir John Kederminster and his wife Mary. There are nearly 300 books, mostly theological works of the early 17C and in their contemporary calf leather bindings.

Little Kimble, *All Saints*. This small basically 13C church evidently had a 'face-lift' in the early 14C from which date belong most of the door and window openings and, most importantly, the wall paintings. These, though for the most part imperfectly preserved, are remarkable not least for being all of one period and they include some particularly fine and impressive figures. The E window in the N wall has in its E splay St. Francis Preaching to the Birds and in its W, a woman wearing a wimple. Between this and the next window (whose splays retain little more than the remains of figures and canopywork) is a large St. George with the Princess behind him on the right. His loose surcoat and small shield have his cross on them and he holds a long lance in his right hand. At the W end of the wall are the upper part of a St. Christopher and the remains of a Doom. On the S wall is a wonderfully impressive figure swathed in voluminous draperies and, over the door to the left, an Entombment of St. Catherine.

Little Missenden, *St. John the Baptist*. The humble church stands hard by the Manor House, the perfect example of a pre-Conquest church grown by accretion over the centuries, a multitude of textures without and of arched vistas within. Its wall paintings, discovered in 1931, are alas fragmentary. But they are of unusual interest and, some of them, of unusual beauty as well. They show that the whole church was apparently painted with a scheme of painting in the 13C and that, as usual, that scheme was in the course of time to a greater or lesser extent itself overpainted. There are, too, numerous post-Reformation fragments of texts in elaborate frames and these enable some idea to be formed of the appearance of a church in the 17C. To the first medieval scheme of paintings belong the band of scroll ornament across the feet of St. Christopher and the beautiful and strongly silhouetted Crucifixion with the Angel of the Annunciation facing it within the westernmost arch of the N arcade. Remains of 14C wall paintings appear in the N chapel where there are, on the N wall, scenes from the Infancy of Christ including an angel appearing to the shepherds and, in the tomb-recess, a later Christ in Majesty flanked by censing angels. Of about the same time is the life of St. Catherine of Alexandria cycle of paintings immediately to the right of St. Christopher. He dates from the 15C and is uncommonly large and complete and in his usual position, of course, opposite the entrance to the church.

North Marston, *Assumption of the Blessed Virgin Mary.* North Marston Church stands high above the village and is a prominent feature in the landscape. The first recorded priest here died in 1233 and his church probably consisted of an aisleless nave about the same size as the present nave plus, of course, a chancel. A 13C N aisle and 14C S aisle have made the body of the church effectively square in plan and the 15C saw the replacement of the chancel by one that is as long as the nave and even more splendid, as well as the addition of the W tower and N vestry. As one approaches the church, one is reminded of Hillesden: there are the same smallness of the tower in relation to the rest of the church, the same continuous band of lights for a clerestory, the same wondrously ambitious chancel and the same battlemented and pinnacled skyline. And if the vestry lacks the stair turret of Hillesden's with its beautiful 'crown', North Marston's is also on the N side, grand and two-storeyed.

Inside, the three-bay N arcade is clearly 13C with its quatrefoil piers with (slightly differently) moulded capitals carrying double-chamfered arches with nailhead decoration in the hoodmoulds. The S arcade is likewise of three bays but more complicated in its history, the two W bays with their concave-sided pier and respond being a later 15C rebuild using the original early 14C arches and the E bay mid-14C with its pier and respond being but roughly articulated and having big fleurons in their circular capitals. In the wall a little further E than the respond is the first evidence of the great elaboration of the chapel at the E end of the aisle, a small arched opening from chapel to nave liberally enriched with fleurons. More fleurons surround the E window with its flowing tracery and flanking niches with nodding ogee canopies and more again appear in the moulding that is carried around the inside of the chapel at sill level.

After this, the fittings are on the whole few and poor. The best of them are the result of a restoration and embellishment of the chancel in 1855 by Sir Matthew Digby Wyatt at the expense of Queen Victoria in memory of John Camden Neild, who had left her considerable property. The reredos with its flanking niches all in a Decorated style is nothing outstanding, but the stained glass window above it made by Ward & Nixon is quite a stunner with which none of the later windows (all 20C) can in any way compare. The brass to Mrs Elizabeth Saunders (died 1613) was erected by her son, who was a physician, and has as the opening lines of its verse: 'Though nor my skill nor prayers could save/Thy self Grave matron from the grave/ yet ile take care thy vertues ly/engravn in brasse and never dy'. The stone tablet to John Virgin (died 1694) has quite one of the most barbaric inscriptions ever encountered; no wonder it is usually misread. It ought to read, 'He lise gust (i.e. just) doune thare' and a hand points down to 'thare' and the floor below.

John Schorne, who reputedly conjured the devil into a boot, was priest here in the late 13C and the shrine at the E end of the S aisle erected over his body became in the 14C a great resort of pilgrims, especially those afflicted with the ague. Schorne was never canonised, but his shrine became so famous and profitable that in 1478 the Dean and Chapter of Windsor, the patrons of the living, transferred it to St. George's Chapel, Windsor.

Olney, *St. Peter and St. Paul.* The church at Olney, the Olney of Pancake Race fame, is large and over-restored, its spacious interior marred, moreover, by a welter of hanging things, speakers from capitals, heaters from arches and lights from everywhere. The church is Decorated in style and with its 'tall spire, from which the sound of cheerful bells just undulates upon the listening ear' is characteristic rather of Northamptonshire than of Buckinghamshire. The 185ft-high spire with its *four* tiers of lucarnes and slight entasis presides with quiet strength and dignity over the attractive little town and surrounding gentle countryside. These and their everyday life have been intimately and tenderly portrayed by that most unworldly of poets, William Cowper, who spent at Olney an on the whole happy and productive 19 years (1767–86). With his friend John Newton, he wrote the Olney Hymns.

Penn, *Holy Trinity.* The church, though perhaps a little too self-consciously 'cared for', is a quite wonderful sight with its variety of textures and multiplicity of gables. It was much altered by the Curzon family in the 18C and has a joyously cluttered interior with fine pulpit, doored pews, several brasses, royal arms and hatchments, monuments and many wall tablets, all embraced by a particularly fine late 15C wooden roof. It was here that in 1938 was found the great rarity of the church. The Doom is one of only four or five in the whole country painted in oil on oak boards. It was painted originally—in the early 15C—perhaps to go in the chancel arch above the Rood screen. Later in the same century, it was cut down, coarsely overpainted to represent a Christ great in glory rather than awful in judgment, and then set up over the chancel arch where it was found.

Quainton, *The Blessed Virgin Mary and the Holy Cross.* It is a pleasant walk from the village green eastwards to the church and a happy sight, the old Georgian rectory on one side of the road and the church tower rising up behind the homely and unClassical Winwood Almshouses of 1687 on the other. But the church was cruelly treated in 1877 when it was very thoroughly restored (and in no small measure rebuilt) by William White. The nave and aisles were built in the 14C, but the proportions were spoilt already in the 15C when, among other things, the arcades were heightened and a clerestory was added. Also added then was the W tower. Today, the church wears a rather sad and neglected look with ivy growing up the tower walls, drains blocked, tiles and old radiators stacked against the outside walls and disconnected and rusting oil tanks in the churchyard.

The interior is curiously devoid of feeling principally because of White's restoration (and, indeed, of his fittings) and the lanky proportions of the arcade but also partly, no doubt, because of the evident lack of care and respect for the building. The easternmost windows in the outer walls of the N and S aisles, though admittedly restored, provide one of the most enjoyable features of the church. They are each of three cinquefoiled lights and have prettily cusped vesicae in the tracery beneath their square heads. The SE window, moreover, has an angle piscina in its E jamb.

But it is for the monuments that one will visit Quainton Church. The fittings pale beside them. There are part of the dado of the 15C Rood screen painted in the East Anglian way and a contemporary font with Georgian cover. The chancel with boldly coloured and oddly arranged tiles, curiously blunt, take-it-or-leave-it choirstalls, reredos, sedilia and big E window with handsome surrounding wall paintings in an orange-brown colour is all White's, interesting certainly but hardly appropriate for a 'restoration'. Next come the insensitively displayed brasses. An interesting trio set in chronological order at the back of the sedilia shows the use in inscriptions first of Norman French (girl with long hair, c 1360), then of Latin (priest in cassock, kneeling, 1422) and finally of English (man in a cloak, 1510). Two larger but less interesting brasses are on the chancel N wall.

The late 17C and 18C monuments are as interesting as they are varied, an exceptional collection in more ways than one. The earliest of them is that under the tower to Fleetwood Dormer (died 1638) consisting of an inscription tablet and urn flanked by Corinthian columns that carry an open segmental pediment with shield of arms. It seems later to have been enlarged into a standing wall monument to commemorate also his son John (died 1679) and Fleetwood Dormer (died 1696) by being given a panelled and moulded base with two large urns on it supported by chubby cherubs and flanking garlanded obelisks on which there are more shields and apparently less chubby cherubs' heads. At the W end of the N aisle is a large inscription tablet to Lady Susan Dormer (died 1673) and her husband (died 1675). It is signed by William Stanton, quite a prolific mason-sculptor whose generally rather conservative style of design is shown here by his still placing busts at the top of the tablet. The monument to Richard Winwood, founder of the almshouses, was put up by his wife in 1689. He is shown dressed in armour and semi-reclining relatively at ease on a rolled-up mat (an exceedingly late date for this Netherlandish idea). She looks out over him towards us, her dress rumpled yet curiously metallic and inflexible. The monument is by Thomas Stayner and shows that, while he might have known something of Baroque tricks, he knew little about Baroque design.

Over in the opposite aisle is the grey and white marble monument to Sir Richard Pigott (died 1685) and Ann his wife (died 1686) and to other members of the family, so that it was not made until after 1735. It is prominently signed 'I. Leoni Archi'. For all that Giacomo Leoni knew Palladio's buildings at first hand and had published an edition of Palladio in 1715–20, the monument is less an essay in pure Palladianism than a Gibbsian synthesis of Baroque and Palladian ideas. The bulbous black sarcophagus on gargantuan feet owes as much to the Baroque as the reredos background generally does to Gibbs's 'Book of Architecture' (1728). Back under the tower, the big veined marble Dormer monument of c 1730 is exceptional for the earlier 18C in having a recumbent effigy: the lifeless corpse gave too little scope for the drama the Baroque Age sought. But here the son, face calm in death, is yet animated, his head propped on pillows, knees bent and all turbulently draped, while his parents grieve, the father standing composedly in his judge's robes, the mother kneeling, distraught and weeping bitterly. Cool and detached from the drama on the stage before it, a big reredos background with pilasters and pediment enframes three cherubs and a shaft of light—or is it the usual obelisk? The monument is almost of quality enough to make understandable an untenable but often repeated attribution to Roubiliac.

Quainton can lay claim to a double literary distinction. Dr Richard Brett (1595–1637), Rector here for 42 years, was one of the translators of the Authorised Version of the Bible, 1611. He is commemorated by a monument in the S aisle of the common Elizabethan type with two kneeling figures facing each other across a *prie-dieu*. It has a long inscription and ends in English: 'Instead of weeping Marble weepe for him/All ye his flock whom he did strive to winn/To Christ, to lyfe: so shall you duly sett/the most desired stone on Doctor Brett'. George Lipscomb (1773–1846), historian of Buckinghamshire, was born at Quainton and is commemorated by a 20C tablet on the chancel N wall.

Stewkley, *St. Michael and All Angels.* Stewkley provides a large and fine example of a three-celled Romanesque church with nave, axial tower and chancel. Here, the chancel is square-ended and rib-vaulted. The church is also unusually lavish in its decoration. There is everywhere that most characteristic of Romanesque decoration, the chevron or zigzag, but none yet of those other more florid forms of enrichment that, appearing c 1140–50, contribute so much to the exuberance of later Romanesque work. So the date must be c 1140. That the church appears to complete—and perhaps sterile—as it does is the result of G.E. Street's restoration of 1862. He restored to the church the steeply pitched roofs it had been deprived of in 1684, inserted an oculus in the heightened W gable and built a more correct porch.

Outside, it is the massive central tower that one first notices. It has a single small bell opening in each face hidden almost by a band of intersecting blank arches with zigzag in their heads. The top of the tower and its N stair turret are 14C. Next it will be the W front that is noticed. It is a rich and even beautiful composition of which the doorway is the centrepiece. Left and right of it is a single blank arch. These arches rise to meet, and the central arch to break into, a band of zigzag that runs all around the church and on which all the windows stand. There are nook-shafts with capitals of scallops, foliage and beasts, all without apparent order or reason—and, of course, the arches also have zigzag ornament, two rows of it. The tympanum to the doorway has its face covered with dragons and foliage trails and two lunettes cut in its lower edge. Above the doorway is an arched window, again with zigzag, and then there is Street's matching circular window in the gable. The S doorway, within Street's porch, has one order of shafts, zigzag in the arch and a hoodmould with pellets terminating in dragons' heads.

Inside, too, there is a band running around the walls beneath the windows—though of nutmeg decoration. But the windows again all have zigzag ornament as they had outside. Otherwise, the interior is curiously characterless and lacking in textures—even if the progress from nave to crossing, to vaulted chancel and zigzag-edged E window is not without splendour. Both tower arches are the same as well as surprisingly spacious. They have two orders of shafts with scalloped capitals and arches with an inner order of beakhead and an outer one of zigzag and then a hoodmould with yet more zigzag. The chancel itself is low and vaulted and suitably darker than the rest of the church. The vault (which was largely rebuilt in 1844) is quadripartite and the intersecting diagonal ribs are decorated each with a band of lozenge-shaped ornament.

The chancel of St. Michael's showing a quadripartite vault and windows enriched with zigzag moulding

The fittings are hardly worth noting. Most conspicuous among them is Street's more Romanesque than Romanesque stone pulpit in the nave. Much smaller and less mechanical are the alabasters found at the time of the restoration and now set in the chancel N wall. They are 15C and probably originally formed part of a reredos. One shows a crowned Queen of Heaven standing between censing angels and holding the (headless) Christ Child on her right arm and a sceptre in her left hand. The other shows the upper part of an unidentified figure, perhaps St. James of Compostella. Both fragments retain a considerable amount of their original colouring. The stained glass of the E window shows scenes from the Life of Our Lord and is excellent—especially considering its date, 1844.

Water Stratford, *St. Giles.* What is interesting here are the two doorways with their tympana reused when the church (apart from the tower) was rebuilt in 1828. They must both date from c 1150. The S doorway has one order of shafts with capitals with interlace and an arch with zigzag embracing a tympanum of Christ in Majesty within a mandorla attended by angels, all in a linear style exactly as though copied from some contemporary manuscript. The lintel on which the tympanum is set is decorated with a row of delicate intersecting arches with background diaper. This, like the draperies that hang convincingly over the bodies of Christ and angels alike, are Romanesque in feeling. But the interlace of the capitals and the contrived pose of the angels are pre-Conquest. The simpler chancel N doorway is a similarly interesting example of the fusion of pre-Conquest and Romanesque motifs: the Agnus Dei and diaper pattern of the tympanum are Romanesque whereas the dragons on the lintel are Viking.

West Wycombe, *St. Lawrence.* St. Lawrence's is the medieval church of a lost village called Haveringdon transmogrified in 1763 by Sir Francis Dashwood, Bt. It sits within an Iron Age earthwork dramatically sited high above the village of West Wycombe in the valley below. Dashwood was born in 1708. He succeeded to the title at the age of 16 and later went on the Grand Tour, earning a wide reputation for his learning and good taste. He proved a disastrous failure as Chancellor of the Exchequer in 1762. The following year, he became Lord Le Despencer and spent the rest of his life in retirement entertaining friends and continuing with the remodelling of his house, its grounds and the church. In 1736 he had been one of the founders of the Society of Dilettanti of which he remained a leading light until his death in 1781. But he is, no doubt, best known as the founder of that other club usually known today as the Hell Fire Club. The original members, of whom there were 12, called themselves a fraternity and the 'brothers' were known variously as Dashwood's Apostles, the Monks of Medmenham (from the abbey on the Thames where they met) and the Brotherhood of St. Francis of Wycombe. The motto of the club, *Fay ce que voudras,* has permitted more to be supposed about what the members got up to than the known facts will support. But it seems that about twice a year, when the full 'chapter' met, a week or more was spent in wining and whoring and it certainly seems, too, that members took pseudonyms, dressed up and indulged in some kind of black magic.

Dashwood the man of taste and lover of the arts and Dashwood the notorious rake and dabbler in magic converge in St. Lawrence's, the 'temple', as Charles Churchill, his fellow member of the Hell Fire Club, called it, 'built aloft in air/That serves for show if not for prayer'. In fact, though, the chancel and lower part of the tower are medieval. But Dashwood it was who heightened the tower and gave it its big, gaunt and open arches and famous golden ball which John Wilkes, another member of the Hell Fire Club, called 'the best Globe Tavern I ever was in'—for the ball opens to admit half a dozen people. Though there is nothing so odd about the nave, that too is Dashwood's. His architect is unknown. That is a pity, for there is nothing provincial about either the conception or the decoration of the room. In conception, the nave is decidedly secular, pagan even, deriving not a little from Vitruvius's Egyptian Hall. As to the decoration, that is as rich as it is well-executed. The floors are beautifully paved in marble and the walls are articulated by noble attached Corinthian columns of porphyry; there are richly carved friezes, painted ceilings and much dainty plasterwork.

The fittings are no less wonderful, though they perhaps show, some of them, the other side of Dashwood's character. The font is perhaps the single most extraordinary church fitting in England. A bold tripod carries a slender shaft, up and around which writhes a serpent. It makes for a dove that stretches up towards the tiny bowl around which four other doves perch, as though font were bird-bath. The pulpit is a capacious mahogany armchair in Chippendale style with a desk in front of it in the form of an eagle on a fluted stem. Chair and desk are raised high upon a movable platform complete with handles. There are two stalls en suite with it. After this, the rest of the fittings are unremarkable if excellent in quality.

Willen, *St. Mary Magdalene.* Willen Church is the sole remaining certain work of Robert Hooke (1635–1703), friend and colleague in science of Sir Christopher Wren. It was built in 1678–80 at the expense of Dr Richard Busby, the famous headmaster of Westminster School in whose house Hooke had lodged as a boy, and must then have seemed a City church planted in the country. The spread of Milton Keynes makes it less easy now to appreciate this—and less easy, too, to appreciate that, with its avenue of lime trees leading to the Rectory (destroyed by fire in 1947), the church in fact forms part of an interesting small-scale formal layout.

What is immediately clear, though, is that Hooke was no outstanding architect. The composition is a most disjointed affair: a thin tower, over-busy in its upper part and flanked by single-storeyed little rooms naively tied to it by rising curves, is put in front of a high yet short nave with three bare arched windows. All the angles have quoins except the tall upper storey of the tower and that has Corinthian angle pilasters—and two tiers of windows awkward in their relation one to another. The W door is set within an apsidal recess in the French fashion. The chancel is—especially for the 1860s—an unbelievably reticent addition and much less obtrusive as such, either inside or out, than are the screaming green of the copper roof of the 1950s and many of the later brick and stone repairs.

Little need be said of the inside. It has a tunnel-vault with penetrations and stucco panelling with shells, open books and the date 1680. In the apse the windows are neo-Romanesque rather than Classical in their proportions and the flower scrolls are just that little thicker, richer, than the 1680 work. The fittings are not as complete as at first they might seem. The altar rails are dated 1931 and well match the stall fronts which have evidently been remodelled—as must also surely have been the reader's desk and pulpit. And can the pew-ends with their curious, almost Jacobean-looking, tops be original? Apparently to hold light fittings, each alternate end has beside it in the seat a brass socket with brass ring above. Can they be original even to the (Victorian?) pew-ends? The best of the fittings are undoubtedly the font and its cover, though even they are evidently not in their original position. The former is chalice-shaped with (renewed?) black baluster and white marble bowl carved with cherubs' heads and drapery. The wooden font cover has fruit and foliage cascading down over its angles and is surmounted by an urn.

Wing, *All Saints.* For all its largely Perpendicular appearance from outside, Wing is one of the most important and interesting pre-Conquest churches in the country—on account of its aisled nave, its polygonal apse with crypt beneath and, not least, its sheer size. And there is also much of interest of later date including a remarkable series of Dormer monuments, one of which must appear in any history of funerary monuments in England.

The architectural development is not clear. Originally, in the early 9C, the church might have consisted only of the existing nave and an apsed chancel represented by the outer walls of the crypt. Whether or not the church was then already aisled is uncertain. Perhaps the (now late 13C) easternmost arches of the arcades represent openings into porticus, or side chapels, and the cutting into the nave walls of the three-bay arcades and the addition of the two aisles is late 10C work? Certainly of this later date is the creation within the open crypt of a central chamber with surrounding outer passage and the vaulting of the remodelled crypt as well as the rebuilding of the chancel apse above it. In the early 14C the present S aisle was built and in the 15C the clerestory was remodelled and the W tower added. N and S porches were also added in the 15C but that on the N was rebuilt from the old materials in the 19C.

The most striking external feature of the pre-Conquest church is the chancel apse, high, seven-sided and one of the most elaborate surviving examples of decoration with narrow strips, or 'lesenes', and arcading. The lesenes at the angles rise to carry first round arches and then, high up, straight-sided arches. In two of these on the S side may be seen, now blocked up, a couple of the original clerestory windows; but most of the evidence at this upper level was destroyed when, in the 15C, the chancel walls were lowered and the main windows below (traces of which may still be seen) were replaced by larger ones. Beneath the enlarged windows are arched openings lighting the crypt below. Each is opposite an arch in the later wall that forms a central chamber within the roughly vaulted crypt. A blocked doorway in the E wall of the N aisle suggests that the passage around the chamber (which is an elongated octagon in plan) was approached from the church perhaps by steps at the E end of each aisle.

The rest of the exterior is easily described. The embattled clerestory with its range of Perpendicular windows rides so high above as to make aisles and W tower alike seem relatively low. The N aisle is pre-Conquest in its masonry but has 14C and 15C windows. The S aisle is an early 14C rebuild of the pre-Conquest aisle. Its windows are all of two lights each except the E window. That is of three lights and characteristically Decorated in its tracery of a single exceedingly complex lobed motif. The window belongs in fact to a chapel—as will here perhaps be surmised from the slight projection between the two easternmost windows: it contains part of the staircase that led to the loft of the chapel screen. The tower is 15C and, like the clerestory, has an embattled parapet. Its best feature is to be seen inside the church.

Here, standing in the nave, we gain—really for the first time—an idea of how very large already the pre-Conquest church must have been. The spacious chancel arch is about 20ft wide and by far the largest pre-Conquest arch in England. The great height of the nave is shown by an offset in the walls at clerestory level and by the presence high above the chancel arch of a two-light window with turned baluster shaft, discovered in 1892. The great height enabled the 15C builders to create an airy clerestory and to give the interior perhaps its finest feature, the wonderfully soaring tower arch. The richness of its mouldings contrasts dramatically with the completely unmoulded arches of the arcades cut from the walls as though with a pastry cutter. Above the arcades, at the W end of the nave, two doorways were uncovered in 1954. They must have led to a W gallery. And over all is an unusually fine roof.

The fittings are as interesting as they are numerous and there is a fine series of Dormer monuments. One of these, the monument to Sir Robert Dormer, might for its supreme importance take precedence over everything else. It stands towards the E end of the N aisle. It is an early example of the large and purely architectural tomb and consists of a sarcophagus decorated with finely carved bucrania and garlands standing beneath a wide, flat canopy that is supported on coupled Corinthian columns on tall bases decorated with trophies. The columns are matched on the wall behind by similar pilasters and the underside of the canopy is decorated with strapwork. This and the over-wide canopy are the least purely Classical features of a monument whose authorship, derivation and date even are surrounded by mystery. For one thing, the monument is quite out of the ordinary, without any close parallel in England. Its materials are local yet its style is perhaps French in origin. And the date '1552' on the sarcophagus might be less the date of erection than record of the year in which, on 8 July, Sir Robert died. After this must come the two Dormer monuments in the chancel, that on the N side to Sir Robert's son William and his second wife Dorothy, finished in 1590, and that on the S side to his grandson Sir Robert, first Lord Dormer (died 1616) and his wife. Both are proud pieces eminently typical of their period, generally Netherlandish in style and with the deceased and his family portrayed beneath canopies all coloured and gilded and with an impressive display of heraldry. Both monuments retain their original iron railings. The last of the Dormer monuments is one to Lady Ann Sophia (died 1695). As late as this she appears still as a pedestal bust (between putti) above an inscription tablet. The monument to Henry Fynes (died 1758) is better in quality of carving but still hardly good enough for Roubiliac to whom it has been attributed. Of the brasses, that to Thomas Cotes (died 1648) is, with its quaint inscription, the most appealing.

The screens to both the chancel and the SE (St. Katharine's) chapel are more or less restored early 16C work and the pulpit, a simple early 17C wooden one with the inevitable blank arches, is also in part a made-up piece. The Bible of 1842 on the lectern has been rebound in an interesting mid-18C red leather tooled cover. The gilded decoration is in the English Rococo chinoiserie taste and incorporates, besides the Sacrament being borne in a kind of palanquin, the arms of the Earls of Chesterfield who presented to the living in the 18C and from whom the cover no doubt came. The stained glass in the chancel windows all commemorates members of the Ouvry family, and that in St. Katharine's chapel is by C.E. Kempe and dates, no doubt, from c 1904 when the chapel was restored. The E window shows St. Andrew, the Virgin and Child and St. Matthew with, below, Christ teaching in the Temple. In the tracery is some early 14C glass, apparently a Coronation of the Virgin with a shield of arms hanging from a tree wrongly set between Christ and the Virgin. The SE window shows the Prophet Samuel and King David.

Winslow, *Baptist Church.* A General Baptist church was in existence in Winslow by 1654 and a few years later Benjamin Keach was preaching in the area. In 1695 the meeting house was built. Apart from its walled burial ground in front, it looks like a little brick cottage with shuttered windows and a much renewed timber-framed porch. Inside, the fittings are all exquisitely humble: at one end, the communion table with pulpit behind and box-pews either side, at the other, Sunday school desks below the gallery and some open-backed benches. Except the communion table, which is 17C, the fittings are apparently all early 19C.

CAMBRIDGESHIRE

Cambridgeshire as a whole contains over 300 churches, and is three counties within a county; for the purposes of this book, however, two of them, the former counties of Huntingdonshire and the Isle of Ely, are treated in separate sections. Along its S perimeter, Cambridgeshire is bounded by the long chalk ridge known as the East Anglian Heights, wherein the Gog Magog hills rise to just over 300ft on the borders of the city of Cambridge, whilst the ground further to the SE rises to about 400ft. The valley of the River Rhee or Cam runs SW to NE from the source of the river at Ashwell, just over the border into Hertfordshire, whence it flows through Cambridge, joining the River Ouse near Ely. From the old Norman fortification mound known as Castle Hill on the rising ground above the original ford where once stood the precursor of Cambridge, it is sometimes possible to see Ely Cathedral 15 miles away. The flat lands in the N part of the county have churches which show a consistently high quality (and some which are exceptional), having been built under the influence of the numerous places of pilgrimage nearby. Notable among them was the monastery of Ely, whose tradition of learning probably was the *raison d'être* for the migration of scholars from Oxford to Cambridge in 1209. The only native building material which could be quarried was the chalk-marl, or clunch as it is known locally, a soft material which is unable to resist the weather and is seen at its best only when used for carved decoration inside buildings. Stone from Barnack and Ketton in the counties N of Cambridge was brought along the waterways, but after the Middle Ages the S of the county used brick from the local clays, whilst reed thatch from the waterlogged Fens to the N has been employed for roofing right down the ages. Timber for roofs came frequently from the uncleared forest areas in the S.

The oldest surviving stone construction is the tower of St. Bene't's in Cambridge, with three stages and long-and-short work at the corners, narrow, round-arch lancets at the top, and a crude tower arch inside, all dating from c 1000. Examples of Norman work may be seen in Cambridge at St. Peter's (with an original font) and at St. Giles's with its dogtooth moulding, and outside the city at Hauxton (which originally had a semicircular apse). Two Norman towers survive at Snailwell and Bartlow, and Norman tympana displaying figures may be seen at St. John's, Duxford, Kirtling and Pampisford. Several monasteries were founded in the later Norman period, such as the Benedictine house at Isleham and the nunnery of St. Radegund at Cambridge, the remains of whose chapel now form part of Jesus College (nave and transepts completed c 1175).

The simple and moving quality of the 13C Early English style in a parish church is perhaps best displayed by the chancel at Cherry Hinton (c 1250), with tall, unshafted lancet windows, at Histon with wall arcading (c 1275) and at Madingley (c 1300). The chancel of St. Radegund's in Cambridge (Jesus College chapel) remains the highest achievement of the style in the county, displaying slender-shafted lancets in the side walls, and dates from the mid-13C; the E lancets by A.W.N. Pugin in the 19C are probably reconstructed from the originals. Other examples are to be found in St. Andrew the Less at Barnwell in Cambridge, with some Purbeck marble detailing, in Bottisham's tower, Bourn's W doorway, Teversham's unusual clerestory and corbels, and at Linton, which is a large example of the later phase of the style. One of the earliest and most complete examples of the Decorated period in Cambridgeshire is the church of St. Mary and St. Michael at Trumpington, which was built almost entirely in one piece in the early 14C. Another is St. Mary the Less in Cambridge, with its fine window tracery. Over is also notable; it betrays financial assistance from nearby Ramsey Abbey in the form of beautiful window tracery, sumptuous ballflower decoration and a tall spire. Further examples are Bottisham, Elsworth and Isleham. The large chancels at Soham, Balsham and Grantchester are also important, the last making fine use of the ogee arch. The octagonal upper storeys which are a feature of some towers are probably derived from the W tower and octagon of Ely Cathedral and may be seen at Burwell, Cheveley and Wood Ditton. Willingham has a 14C spire and a N sacristy of note.

The three major Perpendicular churches in the county, King's College chapel and Great St. Mary's in Cambridge, and St. Mary's at Burwell, are mentioned in the main text; Great Chishall and Over should also be seen and, in addition, the chancels of Orwell and Swavesey, which indicate the new display of light and spaciousness arriving after recovery from the Black Death. In the 15C, a special feature of this area was the fine oak roofs, such as at Willingham. Two towers are worth seeing, Haslingfield with its excellent proportions, and Soham with a finely carved parapet.

The years of the Reformation and the Civil War took their toll when over-zealous iconoclasts and Cromwell's ruthless assistant, William Dowsing, destroyed in the space of 100 years the larger proportion of medieval craftsmanship throughout the county. Meanwhile, the period saw the change from Gothic to Renaissance in such buildings as Peterhouse chapel in Cambridge (1632; E face, 1665), whose free mix of Gothic and Classical styles contrasts with the contemporary but more sophisticated use of the purely Classical style at Pembroke College (1665) on the opposite side of the street. Not only was the latter Sir Christopher Wren's first work of architecture to be built, but it also introduced the Classical idiom into Cambridge. Of the 20 or so chapels which now exist in the colleges, only six—Pembroke, King's, Queens', St. Catherine's, Jesus and Gonville and Caius—are of pre-Reformation date, and only King's and Jesus have not been altered out of all recognition at a later period. The most splendid 18C ecclesiastical interior must be the chapel of Clare College with its noble antechapel, built in 1763–69 by Sir James Burrough and by James Essex. There are no 'Gothick' churches of interest, perhaps because the study of medieval architecture was so far advanced under the distinguished scholarship of William Cole, leading antiquarian and Vicar of Milton, and through the merit of the Cambridge architect, James Essex. Cole produced a massive and thorough catalogue of Cambridgeshire's churches, whilst Essex designed convincing late Gothic style woodwork for King's chapel in the late 18C.

By the 1840s, Ambrose Poynter had introduced the plain 'working' Gothic style at St. Andrew's and St. Paul's in Cambridge, and in 1863–64 G.F. Bodley built All Saints', with its archaeologically correct details, in the same city. Meanwhile, Sir Gilbert Scott added his over-assertive chapel to St. John's College after pulling down the old chapel, but after further demolition at Pembroke College by Alfred Waterhouse, a reaction set in with G.G. Scott, Jr's sensitive E extension of Pembroke chapel in 1878. The century closed with Bodley's Queens' College chapel (1890), which is in keeping with its ancient brick surroundings. Of 20C buildings, note T.H. Lyon's remodelling of the chapel at Sidney Sussex College in 1912 with splendid neo-Baroque woodwork; the attractive 'Wrenaissance' Unitarian Chapel and hall of 1928 in Emmanuel St by Ronald P. Jones, which is of mellow red brick with white woodwork outside, and rich panelling inside; and the chapel of Robinson College of 1981, by Andrew MacMillan and Isi Metzstein, with Piper windows.

Church furnishings remain from the medieval period in the form of screens such as those at Balsham, Guilden Morden and a stone example at Bottisham from the Perpendicular period. Stained glass is to be found at Meldreth, Landbeach—where an 18C Vicar, Robert Masters, collected medieval glass for the E window—King's College chapel, for 16C Flemish display, and Jesus College chapel, where glass from the 1860s was designed by the Morris group. The 20C is represented by J.E. Nuttgens at Soham. Hauxton contains a fresco of St. Thomas Becket from c 1200, whilst Trumpington contains one of the oldest surviving brasses in England—that to Sir Roger de Trumpington (died 1289). The most comprehensive groups of monuments may be seen at St. Andrew's, Isleham, at Wimpole Church and in Trinity College chapel, Cambridge; the last two contain statues of importance from the 18C and 19C, including two by James 'Athenian' Stuart at Wimpole. Eric Gill represents the best of the 20C with monuments at Trumpington. Notable lecterns appear at King's College chapel (c 1515), at Landbeach, where an unusual 17C Dutch example in wood awaits, and at Jesus College chapel, mid-19C and probably by A.W.N. Pugin.

Many connections between churches and chapels and eminent men and women survive from their short stays at Cambridge. Newton, Tennyson and Byron are duly recorded at Trinity in the form of statues in the chapel, whilst it is known that Erasmus preached in Holy Trinity Church. St. Edward's, Cambridge took a part in the Reformation with preachers such as Barnes and Latimer. The 18C Evangelical preacher, Charles Simeon, was Vicar of Holy Trinity in Cambridge for 54 years, and after overcoming strong opposition early on, he drew large congregations with his radical views. At Granchester, where he lived for a while, the poet Rupert Brooke made the church famous with the line 'Oh! yet Stands the Church clock at ten to three...'. Today, King's College chapel is celebrated for its wonderful acoustics, organ, choir school and the Festival of Nine Lessons and Carols which is heard on Christmas Eve across the world thanks to the radio broadcast by the B.B.C.

Bottisham, *Holy Trinity.* The church possesses perhaps the best late 13C/early 14C composition in Cambridgeshire. The exterior is marked by the unusual W porch adjoining the tower whilst the interior is noted for the quality of the overall design and richness of its stone carving.

The double-height W porch dates from the 13C and possibly derives from Ely Cathedral's example known as the Galilee. The flint-filled recessed arch was probably designed as a simple and interesting form of wall decoration. The 13C tower is constructed from clunch, trimmed at the corners with quoins of the stronger Barnack stone. Recent brick patching and a limestone wash have strengthened the fabric of the tower, which has plate tracery windows in the upper storey and later medieval battlements. The aisles display an imaginative Decorated composition and, together with the nave, mark the later phase of building in the first quarter of the 14C.

On the wall of the S aisle, the simple cusped arches of the windows are bordered above by a course of raised stone, whilst beneath the windows there runs a thicker course passing around the doorways. On the S wall also there are flattened arches raised from the wall containing knapped flint spandrels. N and S porches occupy the third bay W of the two aisles. The tall nave is early 14C but the windows to N and S are 15C; the E window is late Victorian.

Entering the W door, a long approach is made through the darkness of the Galilee, the tower base and beneath the organ gallery before reaching the open space and lightness of the main body of the church. Columns, each comprised of four slender shafts and without bands, support five bays of powerful yet graceful arcading along each side of the nave. The original height of the nave may be seen clearly above the organ on the tower wall. The new and more ambitious nave was designed as a single concept, and the finance possibly came from a single source. If this was the case, the most likely donor was Elias de Beckingham, a judge in the reign of King Edward I. Judge de Beckingham was a Bottisham man and died in c 1305, a date which coincides with the estimated date for the nave (1300–20). Towards the furthest E end of each aisle an unexplained extra window of a sophisticated nature breaks the rhythm of the windows, where the pointed arch lights are framed internally with a square-headed opening divided into two by a detached mullion.

The arcading of the nave is elegantly continued onto a third side by a chancel screen of three simple arches dating from c 1475, a date later than one might assign to it at first sight. Behind the screen, the chancel displays three features from the third quarter of the 13C, the piscina, sedilia and the priest's doorway, their chaste, modest simplicity imparting a sense of great antiquity. Our own century has provided a major rearrangement of the W end. In 1952, Lord Fairhaven, of nearby Anglesey Abbey, donated screens to form a Lady chapel (S) and a baptistery (N). The quality of craftsmanship in these oak screens and other fittings is immediately appreciated when one turns the beautifully made door handles. Sir Albert Richardson designed the chapels in a revived 18C manner.

One of the earliest monuments is the floor memorial stone to Elias de Beckingham (died c 1305) in the centre of the nave, but the brass has been removed from the matrix. At the E end of the N aisle a 14C parclose screen protects the tomb of Sir William Allington (died 1479), Speaker of the House of Commons; the table-tomb is made from Purbeck marble and would have been surmounted originally by a stone canopy. Amongst other tomb fragments behind this screen lie two early medieval coffin-lids. In the S aisle another, matching screen may be seen. These screens probably comprised a single screen which crossed the nave before being divided and moved to their present positions in 1839. The S aisle screen encloses the monument in white marble to Sir Roger Jenyns (died 1740) of Bottisham Hall, and his wife. The two sculptures are arranged picturesquely as though in conversation. Further commemorations of the Jenyns family are monuments on the aisle walls, the choirstalls (1867), the E window and the reredos. The last two items are memorials to Colonel Soame Gambier-Jenyns (died 1873), who was a survivor of the Charge of the Light Brigade. Notice too the hatchments on the S aisle wall which are probably 18C. The baptistery contains a font with possibly 12C origins. The Lady chapel contains a brass chandelier, Dutch, 1760, and also a wall plaque to Lady Fairhaven, to whom the W chapels are dedicated. Lady Fairhaven, née Cara Rogers, was the wealthy American heiress who presented Runnymede to the nation.

Burwell, *St. Mary.* St. Mary's is one of the most noble late Perpendicular churches in the county. The large building has a generous churchyard and not far from the W tower the neighbouring castle earthwork is bordered by a stream fed by the 'bur-well'. The name of the 15C master mason, Reginald Ely, has been linked with St. Mary's, for the gatehouse at Queens' College and also King's College chapel, Cambridge, both of which were his projects, exhibit notable similarities in window tracery and an overall refinement of detail.

The tall nave, comprising five bays, adjoins a mainly Perpendicular tower in which the lower walls of the N face contain evidence of an earlier building by way of round-headed Norman lights, now blocked. The top section is octagonal in the manner of Ely Cathedral's W tower; a small stair turret protrudes from one corner, and, in the centre of the tower, an open lantern holds a lead spirelet dated 1799. The nave and chancel, whose flint and rubble exterior walls are pierced by large shallow-arched Perpendicular windows, both date from the late 15C.

One enters by the N porch which has a stone fan-vault and leads into a typically airy and spacious Perpendicular interior, enhanced here by the bright off-white of the local clunch, a chalk soft enough to facilitate the high quality carving of the interior surfaces. Tall, lightly moulded nave piers extend upwards into moulded shafts which rise to mid-height of the clerestory windows, where arched roof beams spring to support the splendid wooden roof embellished by richly carved bosses. Precisely worked and skilfully proportioned stone fretwork in panels beneath the clerestory windows and above the chancel arch enliven the upper wall surfaces. Immediately below the circular window on the E wall of the nave, a Latin inscription provides the information that the nave roof and the E wall were completed in 1464 by John, Joan and Alice Benet. The chancel contains a roof corbel with the shield of John Higham, Vicar from 1439 to 1467, and therefore may be considered contemporary with the nave. Ramsey Abbey provided funds to build the chancel; it is decorated by tall niches displaying elaborate canopies and angel corbels in stone, whilst figures in wood provide the support for a timber roof whose quality admirably complements that of the nave. Two other features of fine woodwork must be noted: the screen and the 15C stall backs fixed against N and S chancel walls. Originally the screen would have supported a Rood loft, as indicated by the small doorway on the chancel arch. Below the windows of the N wall, another door leads down to a small, clunch-vaulted crypt.

The octagonal font is 15C and is decorated in harmony with the overall scheme inside the church. The chancel contains a palimpsest or reused brass, showing the last Abbot of Ramsey, John Laurence de Wardboys (died 1542); on its reverse may be seen the remaining portions of the brass's original depiction, that of a canon who lived over 100 years earlier than de Wardboys. Most of the other fittings are Victorian.

Cambridge

All Saints, Jesus Lane. The church was built in 1863–64 and 1869–71
to the designs of G.F. Bodley. It replaced a medieval building in St.
John's Street, opposite St. John's College, where a tall memorial
cross stands in the surviving churchyard. All Saints' is an important
church in Bodley's career because it marks the time when he
dropped his preference for an early French Gothic style and adopted
English models of the 14C and 15C instead. All Saints' is also notable
for its stained glass, fittings and decorations, some of which were the
results of Bodley's early connection with Morris & Co. The church
was declared redundant in 1973 and passed to the Redundant
Churches Fund in 1981.

All Saints' is built of brick, which is externally faced in dressed and
ashlared Casterton stone. Ancaster stone was also used, most notably
for the internal arcade. The church comprises a nave and S aisle of
equal width and with separate pitched roofs, giving a W elevation of
two gables; a chancel and sanctuary, which are adjoined on the S
side by a chancel aisle and a vestry respectively; a tower and spire
which stand above the chancel; and a N porch. The tower and spire
were copied from 14C originals at Ashbourne in Derbyshire, but
battlements were substituted for Ashbourne's low parapet. The
octagonal spire has three tiers of dormers in the cardinal faces. A
crocketed spirelet stands next to it at the NE corner. The sanctuary
reaches the same height as the nave and has an E window whose
tracery is apparently based on the model of Temple Balsall in
Warwickshire. All the windows have Geometrical and intersecting
tracery; the aisle windows are set high in the walls between buttresses. Within, the arcade between nave and S aisle is of five bays,
with octagonal piers and octagonal moulded capitals, a standard 14C
arrangement.

The fittings and decorations were added over 40 years as funds
permitted. The E window was made by Morris & Co. in 1865–66 for
£351 10s 0d in memory of Lady Affleck, the wife of the Master of
Trinity College. She had laid the foundation stone in 1863. The
window is light and appealingly silvery in effect. The figure of Christ
in Majesty at the top of the central light was designed by Sir Edward
Burne-Jones. Figures from the Old Testament and early Christian
saints fill the remaining panels. The first window from the E in the N
nave wall is filled with stained glass of 1891 by C.E. Kempe. The two
lights depict two SS. Margaret in honour of Margaret Luckock, the
wife of the Vicar at the time of the rebuilding. The next window, of
1905, is also by Kempe. This window, and its E neighbour, possess
Kempe's characteristic colouring and canopy work and also his
wheatsheaf mark. The third window from the E, of 1923, is by Kempe
& Co., 16 years after C.E. Kempe's death. Its subject is 'three great
Cambridge Christians'—George Herbert, Bishop Westcott and
Henry Martyn. The final window in the N wall is of 1944, by Douglas
Strachan. It is a little strident in contrast to its neighbours. The pair of
two-light windows at the E end of the S aisle wall are of 1893, by
Ward & Hughes. They depict the Evangelists and a series of scenes
on the subject of the Good Shepherd. The other pair of two-light
windows in the S aisle, plus the aisle's E window (beyond the organ),
are by Morris & Co. The windows comprise diagonal bands of text in
Gothic lettering set against quarries of clear and light blue glass,

some with floral patterns, and with borders decorated with signs of the Zodiac with red and blue fragments.

The chancel screen is of 1904, by John Morley, an architect who was also a member of the congregation. Bodley designed the screen which was placed between the S aisle and the organ in 1879. The pulpit was painted in c 1875 to C.E. Kempe's design by Wyndham Hope Hughes. It depicts St. John Chrysostom, St. Peter and St. John the Baptist. At the W end are two fonts: one of 1864 and the other (in the S aisle) of the 15C, octagonal and made of clunch, which came from the old All Saints'. The painted decorations were executed in 1864, 1870, 1878–79 and 1904–05. A limited amount of painting was undertaken by Morris & Co. in the sanctuary when the church was new. In 1870 C.E. Kempe supervised the painting of the nave roof. The phase of 1878–79 was Bodley's own work, comprising Planta Genista pods and flowers and dark yellow and green canopies and crowns. The final phase of 1904–05 was largely one of cleaning and restoration, at a time when electric light was replacing gas in the church, but the restorers, F.R. Leach & Co., painted the SE corner for the first time. In the 1980s much restoration work has been undertaken in the church, but more remains to be done, most notably on the painted decorations.

S.C.H.

Holy Sepulchre. The church is usually known as the 'Round Church' and makes a charming punctuation at the junction of the two major roads through the city centre. Dating from c 1130, it is one of only four surviving round churches in England. The small round building with its conical roof and W entrance facing the street resembles a beehive, whilst the intimacy and quaint appeal is accentuated by the tall buildings which closely border it on two sides. The origins of the circular form are to be found at the Holy Sepulchre in Jerusalem.

Looking from the outside, one may best understand the important changes which the overall structure underwent in 1841–44. A major restoration was carried out by the Cambridge Camden Society under Anthony Salvin. The most obvious alteration was the replacement of a medieval belfry stage by the present conical roof. The belfry was too heavy for the building beneath it and the church was considered unsafe. On the N side, Salvin constructed a bell tower which connects onto the late 14C or early 15C N aisle.

Entering by the W door with its bold Norman carving (apparently rebuilt by Salvin to the original design), one is almost overwhelmed by the eight massive piers which support the two upper stages of the tower. To add to this sensation of weight bearing down, there is rib-vaulting in the ambulatory. Two of the bays contain stone ribs with heavily carved zigzag mouldings. On stepping into the centre of the ring of columns, the full variety of their narrow capitals may be seen, each one scalloped in differing patterns. Above the main arches lie eight more piers with two arcaded openings in between each pair of columns. Fixed over the capitals of the short columns may be seen the carved heads, dating from the restoration of 1841. Higher still, eight windows in the Norman style open from deep, chamfered recesses. Above is a small, undecorated dome supported by eight slender shafts. E of the Norman work, the contrasting rectangular space of chancel and two aisles provides breadth and light. Two bays of wide arches divide the chancel from the aisles, comprising Early English work with 15C remodelling. The 15C roofs rest on supports decorated by an angel choir.

Much controversy surrounded the restoration which was thought by many to have gone too far, and that too much original work had been replaced. All the windows in the Norman part of the church were renewed and the medieval E portions were substantially rebuilt. The glass in the N, S, E and W windows was designed by Thomas Willement (1786–1871), 'artist in stained glass' to Queen Victoria, and show the Venerable Bede, St. Etheldreda of Ely, the Lamb of God, and the Pelican in her Piety respectively. The other four windows contain some 15C portions of glass. In the ambulatory, further glass by Willement provides points of bright colour in the dim light of the interior; the S window is by William Wailes.

Further controversy surrounded the restoration when a stone altar was set up in the chancel. The Vicar of Holy Sepulchre, R.R. Faulkner, objected to the stone altar and, after serious debate and a lawsuit, it was removed. It was considered by the Court of Arches to have resembled too much a sacrificial slab and so a wooden communion table took its place. This table, which is still used, dates from 1843 and was made by Josiah Wentworth who worked in Cambridge. The E window above the table shows Christ Crucified with St. Andrew and St. John standing on either side (1946). The previous window was destroyed by a Second World War bomb which hit the nearby Union Debating Society. The communion rails, made from oak in 1845, comprise Gothic Revival tracery and take the form of a low chancel screen. The floor tiles are also 19C.

Other fittings include the Perpendicular style font and wooden cover of 1843, and the tables which are fixed to the W wall of the N aisle and which depict the Creed, Decalogue and the Lord's Prayer. They date from the early 19C.

King's College Chapel. King's College was founded in 1441 by King Henry VI and was called initially the College of St. Nicholas. In 1443, the king altered the title to the King's College of the Blessed Mary and St. Nicholas, and stipulated that scholars should come from his earlier foundation, Eton College. The first stone of the chapel was laid on 25th July 1446 but 69 years were to elapse before the stonework was completed. The royal founder supplied white magnesian limestone from Yorkshire and with his master mason, Reginald Ely, planned and built the lower portion of the walls; the building was completed by 1515 in Weldon stone, provided from King Henry VII's funds.

The exterior is noted for the regular rhythm and upward thrust of its Perpendicular style, the N and S walls being partitioned by narrow buttresses and tall windows. Side chapels lying between the buttresses provide stability in relation to the tall proportions of the exterior.

The interior shows how the rigid geometry of the exterior undergoes spectacular transformation into a towering and dramatic enclosure. The unusual nature of the dimensions, narrow, long and tall, provides the powerful perspectives which make this unique European masterpiece so memorable. The ceiling leads the eye along the full length of the chapel and the tall shafts glide upwards 80ft to the swathes of vault ribs bound together by strong transverse arches. The interior is divided by the screen into two large areas: the antechapel to the W and the choir to the E, the latter containing both the stalls and altar. The two compartments provide different visual qualities. The first, the antechapel, displays a worldly dignity in the form of regal heraldry where carved stone beasts and coats of arms are reminders of its royal benefactor. Below these panels, pierced screens admit light into the side chapels. The narrative sequence displayed in the glass begins in the westernmost window of the N side with the birth of the Virgin, thus initiating the life of the Virgin and the life of Christ which are the two themes related in the glass throughout the chapel. Passing beneath the massive dark oak screen of 1532–36, the more sober choir contrasts the darkness of the stalls below with the highly coloured transparent glow of the glass above. This contrast, effective and clearly marked, highlights the disparity between the old woodwork and the Spartan appearance of the new arrangements at the E end to accommodate the painting by Rubens of the Adoration of the Magi (1633–34). Here, the stripping away of panelling in 1964 during these rearrangements revealed much blank wall and so removed some of the strong sense of enclosed space in the choir. Sited over the altar, this painting, with its swirling drapery and rich oil colours, is in competition with the earlier glass above whose acid blues, reds and yellows seem cool when seen in such close proximity.

The magnificent screen, probably by French woodcarvers, is best appreciated by turning W. Notice in particular the tympanum on the SW side representing the Descent of the Rebel Angels. The lower parts of the 118 stalls are the same age as the screen (1536), whilst the coats of arms of English monarchs from Henry V to James I, in elm, were added in 1633 and the canopies in 1675–78. Above the screen, the organ dates from the remodelling by Renatus Harris in 1688 but he probably used portions of previous instruments. The gold angels holding trumpets on the W side were added when the organ was enlarged in 1859. The lectern of c 1515 was given by Robert Hacumblen, Provost of King's from 1509–28.

The easternmost chapel on the S side was set aside as a memorial to those members of the college who gave their lives in the First World War. The work was carried out from the designs of T.H. Lyon, and contains portions of 15C and 16C glass.

25 of the 26 windows contain glass executed between 1515 and 1531, begun by the King's Glazier, Barnard Flower, and completed by the Netherlander, Galyon Hone, and his assistants. Scenes from the Old Testament are displayed next to corresponding illustrations from the New Testament; thus, on the N side, in the 11th window counting from the W, Noah mocked by Ham is matched with Christ mocked before Herod. The narrative scenes are separated by lights containing 'messengers' holding a device which explains the adjacent pictures. The E window depicts the Crucifixion and the Judgement of Pilate. The W window shows the Last Judgement; it is by Clayton & Bell, 1879. The S side chapels contain mainly 16C and 17C glass, together with brasses and monuments honouring past members of the college. The N side chapels contain an excellent permanent exhibition showing the architectural history of the chapel.

The Festival of Nine Lessons and Carols was devised by Eric Milner-White, Dean of King's, and was first held on Christmas Eve, 1918. Enjoyed through radio and television broadcasts, many other churches throughout the country now hold a similar service.

St. Mary the Great. The dual purpose of this church, the largest in Cambridge, which serves as both the principal city church and the University Church, is emphasised by its location. The E end faces Market Hill and the W tower overlooks the Senate House. From the

113ft-high stone tower—following the climb of its 123 steps—may be obtained a view of the whole city centre and most of the colleges.

The earliest record of a church on this site was made in 1205, but only the chancel walls date from the 13C, and they are all that remain to reveal its early medieval origin. All else was replaced after the existing building was started in 1478, so that the exterior now is a competent, if somewhat pedestrian example of East Anglian late Perpendicular Gothic. The work went very slowly because the last years of the Wars of the Roses caused great financial difficulty. In fact, the university went so far as to send its Proctors throughout England with 'Notices of Appeal' for funds. The rebuilding of the nave was accomplished by 1508. The W window was finished in 1593 and at the same time a temporary thatched roof was placed on the tower, awaiting the completion of the belfry and the construction of a tall spire. The spire was never built, but finally, the belfry section was completed in 1608 to the design of Robert Grumbold.

Additional work on the exterior followed in Victorian times. The W door (1851) was built to the design of Sir Gilbert Scott; the S porch replaces the original and was built in 1888; the tower was restored in 1892. Above the W door may be seen the 17C clock-face. The 1793 mechanism cost £300, a quite considerable sum of money in those days. The clock strikes the quarters on four bells, whilst the hours chime is derived from Handel's Aria, 'I know that my Redeemer liveth'; it was later copied for 'Big Ben'. Until 1939 the nightly curfew was rung from 9 to 9.15 pm.

The interior, 142ft long and 65ft wide, has five bays of tall arches which lead into two broad aisles. Immediately on entering the nave, one is faced by the large open space of the chancel, framed by its tall, wide arch, seen today without a screen or Rood. The slender nave piers flow into arches having spandrels filled with delicate enriched tracery; the nave roof, dating from 1505, is made from 100 oak trees provided by King Henry VII and brought from nearby Chesterford.

Many early fittings since removed must have made the interior appear quite different from the one we see today. In the early years of Queen Elizabeth I's reign (1558–1603), Archbishop Parker of Canterbury removed all the church ornaments and plate, and also ejected the 16C chancel screen and elaborate Rood loft. That the interior now may appear somewhat melancholy and seem not to encourage the visitor to warm to it may be owing in part to the dark galleries which interrupt the soaring arches of the aisles. The galleries were built when the university's Commencement ceremonies moved to the new Senate House whilst the church was given over entirely to the preaching of sermons; they were completed in 1735 to the designs of James Gibbs, architect of the Senate House and of the Fellows' Building at King's College. At the same time, a large three-decker pulpit (which became known as 'The Pit') was placed centrally in the nave. In 1754, a new gallery was made for the chancel and a throne (later nicknamed 'Golgotha') was introduced over the replacement screen for the Vice-Chancellor of the university. In 1863, the chancel throne and the old pulpit were removed, leaving once again neither chancel screen nor Rood, the old pulpit being remodelled to separate the chancel chapels from the aisles. A new pulpit, the one which exists today, was given by the university in 1872, specially designed to be moved along on three rails so as to occupy a position in the centre of the nave for the University Sermons. The chancel stalls and some of the nave benches are 19C. St. Andrew's chapel in the NE corner of the church was refitted in 1984.

None of the original stained glass survives and much of the present glass dates from the late 19C. Twenty clerestory windows by Powell's were donated by a mix of town and gown; they show 24 Prophets, the 12 Apostles, and 24 martyrs. 42 coats of arms appear in the aisle windows representing the contributors to the rebuilding of the nave between 1478 and 1519; these were given in 1892 by Samuel Sandars of Trinity College.

In 1697, an organ by 'Father' Bernard Smith was bought by the university to become the sole instrument in the church until joined by the parish organ in 1869. The case of the university organ is a fine, 17C example with two gilded cherubs' heads, and is placed in a stone gallery in the tower arch. The parish organ, reserved usually for parochial service only, is situated in the choir.

Several other important features should be mentioned. In the N aisle is kept the King Henry VII Hearse Cloth, 16C velvet on cloth of gold, depicting the royal arms, always used originally on the anniversary of the king's death in 1509. At the E end of the church, the eagle lectern dates from 1867. The font is late Gothic in its overall shape although its date is 1632; the ornamentation, however, is Jacobean, displaying strapwork and cartouches. On the E wall of the chancel, above the altar, stands the quite incongruous 'Majestas' of 1959, a sculpture in gilded wood of Christ in Majesty.

On the N wall of the chancel rests the effigy and memorial to Dr William Butler, the distinguished physician who died in 1618 aged 82. Three early 17C plaques in the N aisle commemorate local people and provide interesting examples of calligraphy on brass plate. A memorial to an undergraduate of Trinity Hall, Robert Booth-Campbell (died 1893), is situated on the tower arch. It was executed in brass in the Arts & Crafts style by Paton Wilson. On the outside E wall of the chancel lies the monument to those who died in the South African War, 1899–1902. Most local men were in the Suffolk Regiment. One final feature must be mentioned. Since 1732 a stone circle at the base of the tower buttress has been the datum point from which all mile distances from Cambridge have been recorded.

St. Mary the Less. The church of St. Mary the Less, or Little St. Mary's, was originally known as St. Peter-without-Trumpington-Gate. The earlier dedication was given to a 12C church on this site, of which some fragments may still be seen inside the porch. The first church gave its name to the adjoining college of Peterhouse, founded in 1284 and the earliest college in Cambridge; the scholars worshipped in the church until the opening of the present college chapel in 1632.

The church, built in 1349–52, hugs the N wall of Peterhouse, and a covered gallery may be seen connecting the college to the church. Looking from Little St. Mary's Lane, one is able to see the patchy, unfaced W wall with the wooden-framed bellcote (19C) below which chime the hours; there is no clock-face. The far W bay is mid-15C and incorporates the remains of a NW tower which predates the rest of the church. The church is dressed with ashlar on the N side but unfaced patches of stone and brickwork may be seen on the S and E walls. The tracery in the massive windows derives from work at Ely Cathedral in the early 14C and forms an especially beautiful feature of the church. On the E wall, two canopied niches, now much worn, are set low down on each side of the large window. To the S, two twin-light openings with square-headed drip courses provide light for the sacristy. To the right of the N door, through an iron gate, lies the gloriously overgrown graveyard. Tombstones and tomb-chests lie half-hidden along winding paths amongst briars and semi-wild flowers which are carefully tended to provide an illusion of 'pleasing decay'.

The spacious white interior is without aisles and the chancel is not structurally divided from the nave. From the architectural evidence surviving principally in the external appearance of the SW bay and buttress, it is clear that the first five bays of the present church formed the collegiate chancel built by Peterhouse in 1352, and historians have conjectured that a larger collegiate antechapel was planned, as at Merton College, Oxford. The doorway on the N side and the 20C chapel on the S side mark the sites of two small chantry

Near this Place lyeth the Body of the Late Rev.d M.r GODFREY WASHINGTON of the *County* of *York. Minister* of this Church and *Fellow* of S.t Peter's Colledge Born July the 26.th 1670. and Dyed the 28.th day of Sep.r 1729.

Monument to Godfrey Washington (died 1729), great-uncle of the first American President

chapels, given in the 15C by Masters of Peterhouse. In 1931, on the site of the S chantry, the modern chapel of the Holy Sepulchre, St. Mary and All Saints was designed by T.H. Lyon in a Classical style, contrasting with the Gothic of the main church. To the S, near the altar, may be seen the staircase leading up to Peterhouse and the steps down into the 14C crypt, now a chapel. Originally, the present sacristy doubled as a vestry chapel, whilst the vaulted chamber below probably served as a strong-room or treasury (these were added 30 years after the main building).

Fittings include the Perpendicular font with a cover dated 1632, the pulpit and sounding-board of inlaid oak (1741), and the altar posts and riddels (1913) by Sir Ninian Comper, these last being the memorial to John Willis Clark (died 1910) a churchwarden and Registrary of the university who wrote on the architectural history of Cambridge. Behind the font lies the old 19C reredos which has been placed against the wall. At the entrance to the SW porch of 1892, two wickets have been constructed from remains of the 15C chancel screen. No medieval glass remains. The W and E windows contain glass from 1892 by C.E. Kempe, together with armorial glass in the lower parts of the E window by Comper. The organ case was given in 1978. Before the altar steps lie memorial brasses to John Holbrook, Master of Peterhouse (died 1436), and to an unknown figure, probably a college Fellow, who died in 1480. Through the glass doors, to the immediate left of the W entrance, is the wall tablet to Godfrey Washington, Vicar 1705–29, who was the great-uncle of George Washington. It is believed that the 'Stars and Stripes' of the United States' flag were derived from the Washington arms which are depicted on this tablet, erected in 1736.

Since the 19C the church has maintained a high standard of worship and preaching in accordance with the Catholic tradition of the Church of England.

Hildersham, _Holy Trinity._ Holy Trinity Church is notable for the mural paintings in the chancel, which were undertaken in 1890 by the firm of Clayton & Bell. They were restored in 1973 by Messrs. Campbell, Smith & Co. under S.E. Dykes Bower. The paintings comprise a complete 19C chancel scheme, which is already a comparatively rare survival in the late 20C. Notice in particular the Entry into Jerusalem over the vestry door. The paintings formed the culmination of nearly four decades of work on the fabric under Robert Goodwin (Rector and patron, 1847–99). The chancel was substantially renewed by him and entirely refitted. Note the choirstalls, floor tiles, alabaster reredos and stained glass (some of which is also by Clayton & Bell).

The rubble-built church has an unbuttressed 13C W tower and a two-bay 14C nave. Almost all the windows were renewed in the 19C. Of interest is the brass of c 1530 which shows a skeleton in a shroud: a typical late medieval _memento mori_, to prompt the living to repentance. Further brasses, in the chancel, are a large military brass of Henry Paris (died 1466) and early 15C figures of Robert de Paris and his wife, kneeling at the foot of a cross. Until 1977 this church also possessed two 14C oaken effigies, unique Cambridgeshire examples of an Essex type and thought to be of Sir William Busteler and his wife. Unfortunately, they were stolen in 1977 after resting in Hildersham for 600 years.

S.C.H.

Ickleton, *St. Mary Magdalene.* This ancient church contains the most important Norman nave in the county together with a rare cycle of 12C wall paintings.

The exterior is distinguished by a lead broach spire over the crossing tower. The N face of the tower has a stair turret, and above the S and E bell openings, which date from the early 14C, may be seen two patonce crosses of black flint set into the wall. The spire, like the tower, is 14C and supports a small sanctus bell on its exterior. The church is built from flint and pebbles, and was originally cruciform; but during the Middle Ages, when the S aisle was enlarged, the N transept was demolished and the S transept was incorporated into the main body of the church. The chancel was rebuilt in the late Victorian period reusing old materials. The W door of the nave has a plain, wide semicircular archway (c 1100) and betrays the Norman origins of the church. The Perpendicular window above this door lies in the Norman fabric of the W wall which incorporates still earlier building materials. Significant alterations were made during the 14C when the roofs of the nave and aisles were raised; the narrow N aisle contains 14C and 15C windows, whilst clerestory windows from this period may be seen in the newer, heightened nave walls; the S aisle was made wider as well as taller and a porch was extended to the S. The porch has a handsome groined roof with original bosses.

Entering by the S porch, the early origins of the nave are clearly visible. The four columns at the furthest W and E ends of the nave are monoliths of Barnack stone and probably derive from a pre-Conquest church which once stood on the site. The central columns are composed of reused Roman tiles and Barnack stone, rendered over in the 19C to emulate the solid monoliths. The apparently makeshift piers support cushion capitals and semicircular arches, the arches decorated on both sides by alternating fan-shaped portions of Barnack stone and Roman tiles, the latter crudely rendered by stucco made from crushed Roman brick. Above the arcades may be seen the original Norman clerestory with its tapering openings left unblocked but now redundant below the raised roofs of the aisles; the ten medieval (upper) clerestory windows have faintly ogee heads on the S side and circular lights on the N. Turning towards the tower, the original Norman shafts continue up to the capitals, but a 14C pointed arch takes over above this level. The same style is repeated in the other three tower arches and again from the S aisle into the S transept. This last arch is a modern replacement, however, which was constructed after a major fire on the night of 24th August 1979. Fine new roofs now protect the S transept, chancel, the crossing and part of the S aisle. The S transept window also dates from the restoration which, remarkably, was completed in under two years. The N transept is 19C. The chancel was rebuilt by the Ecclesiastical Commissioners in 1882–83 but retains some old Perpendicular features such as the blocked doorway and broad arch on the N side which once led into a long-vanished chantry chapel. The much-restored piscina and sedilia together with a low window on the S side also remain from the 15C chancel.

The wall paintings in the nave date from the 12C and should be given close attention. The oldest lie above the two furthest bays to the E of the nave whilst the 14C 'Doom' painting over the tower arch was added when the nave was heightened. All these paintings were discovered as a result of cleaning after the fire in 1979 and are some compensation for the loss of medieval paintings destroyed with the

tower ceiling. The colour of the nave paintings matches approximately the plaster which covers the alternating Roman tiles over the
arcades described earlier. The upper level depicts scenes from the
Passion: reading from left to right, the Last Supper with the long
table and Judas in front stealing a fish (a traditional representation);
immediately to the right of the Norman window, the Betrayal,
showing the kiss of Judas; next, the Flagellation of Christ tied to a
column between two figures; and lastly, seen to the right of the
second window, Christ carrying the Cross. Below these scenes,
within the spandrels of the two arches, lie three martyrdoms: that of
St. Peter (on the left below the Last Supper and partly hidden by a
wall monument) shows him being crucified head downwards; that of
St. Andrew, with hands outstretched on the diagonal cross and the
hand of God touching his halo, is set between the arches; finally, to
the far right and somewhat damaged, the figure which probably
represents St. Laurence on the gridiron. The Doom painting shows a
bearded Christ seated on a rainbow with the Virgin Mary to the left,
baring her breasts in supplication, and St. John to the right. Little
remains of the saved and the damned who would have appeared
below the feet of Christ.

Amongst the fittings, notice the oak pews and the six remaining
poppyheads, one showing St. Michael weighing souls. The surviving
carvings were restored by the Victorians but many have been cut off
over the years. The delicate Rood screen is late 14C, the lower panels
painted on the W side with the symbols of the Evangelists, probably
in the 19C. The 16C pulpit, now located near the organ, was replaced
in the 19C by a new one on the opposite side of the nave. In the
chancel, situated within Gothic Revival panels on each side of the
altar are the Ten Commandments, probably dating from the 1880s.
The iron light fittings seem appropriate in a church of such great
antiquity. Three memorials commemorate the Herbert family: the
window in the N aisle to the Hon. Algernon Herbert (died 1855);
secondly, almost hidden in the S transept and damaged by the fire, a
wall monument in the manner of the early Italian Renaissance shows
St. Leger Algernon Herbert, a war correspondent who was killed in
the Sudan in 1885; and thirdly, the rich, late pre-Raphaelite style
window with complex imagery was installed in 1906 for Sir Robert
Wyndham Herbert.

Finally, on the churchyard wall may be seen carvings of animals;
although most of them are very worn, a fox carrying a goose is still
quite visible.

Stourbridge, *St. Mary Magdalene.* The two-cell chapel near Barnwell railway station, little more than 50ft long and 20ft wide, once
belonged to a leper hospital. The ancient Stourbridge Fair, which
became one of the largest wholesale markets and horsefairs in
Europe, lasted for three weeks in September, and was held on the
common opposite the chapel until the 19C. The fair levied tolls which
King John granted in 1211 to the Friars of Bethlehem, who minis-
tered to the lepers, and must have provided a substantial income for
several centuries. After the disappearance of the hospital, the chapel
was used both as a store for the fair and as a barn. The building,
which consists of flint rubble in the nave and dressed Barnack stone
in the chancel, appears to date from the first half of the 12C,
displaying familiar Norman features such as zigzag mouldings. After
300 years of secular use, the chapel was restored to provide a place of
worship for the builders working on the nearby railway. St. Mary's

was placed into the care of the Cambridge Preservation Society in 1951, which today maintains the ancient but sturdy fabric.

St. Mary Magdalene's Chapel, Stourbridge: a 12C two-cell leper chapel

Wimpole Hall, *Chapel.* The chapel may be viewed from the family gallery to the right of the entrance hall; it occupies five bays at the front of the E wing which was built to the design of James Gibbs by Lord Harley, second Earl of Oxford, in 1713–21. The construction of a chapel displaying such bold splendour was intended to complement the Earl's lavish way of life; a life which included not only grand schemes for buildings but also a great landscaping project in the park, a passion for book collecting and the maintenance of a large household including his Master of Music, Dr Tudway. The chapel was probably constructed as a type of concert hall for the presentation of anthems and services set to music by Tudway. The old Gothic church near the house would not have been considered satisfactory for such Baroque performances before its enlargement, which was not effected until after Harley's death. The highly elaborate formula devised for the chapel by Gibbs and the artist Sir James Thornhill employed a combination of plain, Palladian symmetry for the architecture and woodwork together with walls enlivened by paintings to provide a sense of depth and movement. The articulation of the ceiling and walls with *trompe l'oeil* coffering and niches, the latter filled by gilded figures of the Latin Doctors, culminates in an E wall painting showing a Nativity of heroic proportions; the drama is heightened by a deceptively realistic treatment of architectural features, drapery and winged putti. The high quality of the painted decoration is matched by the impressive craftsmanship which distinguishes the oak panelling, the pews and an elaborate iron communion rail.

CORNWALL

The glorious West Country lives up to its name, both in scenery and buildings. If one stands on Saltash road bridge all day and all night at the week-end in the summer, one would think that everyone in England was travelling to and from Cornwall (and this is only one of several roads). By rail one immediately sees the beauty of Cornwall inland and at the coast around St. Germans. Mining has made an impact upon some inland parts, but others are as beautiful as anywhere, for instance, around St. Neot and Luxulyan. For coastal scenery the county is unrivalled, and no other county has so much seaboard. It is, however, for its creeks and estuaries that Cornwall really comes into its own. What could be more beautiful than the church of St. Anthony-in-Meneage on the Helford River or the setting of the church of St. Just-in-Roseland? Around the old church is usually the best part of any village. So in visiting old churches, well-known beauty spots can also often be visited. For instance, in visiting the most westerly church in England, Sennen, Land's End can be included, and in visiting the most southerly church in England, Landewednack, the Lizard Point and Kynance Cove, noted for the rich colours of its serpentine rocks, can be included. Perhaps the most windswept church is Tintagel. It is partly pre-Conquest, and it has withstood the Atlantic gales since that early time. It is a grand coastline, and nearby is delightful Boscastle, with its church of Forrabury in an unrivalled situation.

Cornwall is exceptional in its building materials. Granite and slate are dominant. Of the former, moorstone (loose blocks on the moors) was used as much as quarried stone. The church at Altarnun, for example, uses moorstone in its piers. Despite the difficulty in carving granite, St. Mary Magdalene's at Launceston presents an astonishing display of decoration in that material, carved in the 16C. Rare or unique stones in this county are Pentewan, Polyphant, St.Stephen, Catacleuse and serpentine. They derive from restricted parts of Cornwall, but they are quite widely found. Sometimes a number of stones are found within one church, reflecting different building phases. Brick is absent.

All the medieval churches or churches of medieval foundation (some 209 in number) are of above-average interest, both with regard to structure and fittings. A prominent tower always makes the perfect English scene, and Cornwall abounds in examples. The typical exterior of a Cornish church is a tall W tower and low horizontal blocks of nave and aisles without any break in height, and ending in three gables. The interiors, with homely wagon roofs, enclose ancient arcades and fonts and particularly fine woodwork. Arcades often have piers of local style, which comprise four half-round shafts separated by hollows. Many screens have disappeared, but bench-ends survive in profusion, stressing the Instruments of Christ's Passion. Good series survive at Mullion, Launcells, Altarnun, Goran, St. Winnow, Kilkhampton and Mawgan-in-Pydar.

Numbers of pre-Conquest crosses remain, chiefly with wheel-heads, but no pre-Conquest churches, unless one counts two early oratories, at St. Gwithian and St. Piran. Norman remains are quite ubiquitous. St. Germans has a splendid W doorway, Kilkhampton has a notable S doorway and Morwenstow retains part of a Norman N arcade. Norman doorways survive too at Cury, Manaccan and Landewednack. Norman fonts are innumerable. 13C and 14C fabric is not prominent in Cornwall; the 15C and the 16C offer far more. St. Anthony-in-Roseland and Manaccan, however, have notable Early English fabric and the Decorated style appears at Wendron (chancel E window), St. Germans (S aisle windows) and St. Just-in-Penwith (E windows of aisles).

All ancient churches should be visited, but really only a very few are detailed in this book. Mention must be made, however, of the following. The finest tower is at Probus, obviously built by Somerset masons, who only went outside their county twice (here and at Chittlehampton in Devon). The tower of Probus is beautifully proportioned with double belfry windows and eight pinnacles and niches for statues, as was usual in Somerset. The finer local type of Cornish tower with four prominent pinnacles with spirelets is most attractive and is based on the tower of Widecombe in Devon. Very good examples are at St. Cleer, Stoke Climsland, Pillaton, Cardinham and Poughill. Some early towers are detached, as at Gunwalloe on the coast and Feock on its creek. The church of St. Enodoc near Padstow in the middle of the golf links at the mouth of the River Camel into the ·Atlantic Ocean will now be known for all time as the burial place of Sir John Betjeman, who died in 1984. The church has a charming small 13C stone broach spire. A church in a garden is always delightful and this applies to Lanhydrock in the grounds of the great manor house. The medieval tower of St. Ives dominates the flourishing seaside resort of that name. Inside the church, the modern baptistery has been designed by the well-known 20C Gothic architect, S.E. Dykes Bower. The best ancient Rood screen is at St. Ewe, but a fine one also remains at the collegiate church of St. Buryan, which possesses in addition a fine tower. The painted panels of saints on the screen of St. Budock are reminiscent of those in Norfolk and Suffolk and S Devon. A fine modern screen, which usually gives a devotional atmosphere to a church, is at Crantock, near Newquay, by E.H. Sedding. Travellers by train will notice an unusual 14C stone spire at Lostwithiel. In the church an unusual font of the same century, with a Rood group, huntsmen and various animals. There is also a wooden almsbox in the shape of a standing figure with a shield, dated 1645. Another rarity is that the church has some clerestory windows. A clerestory and a chancel arch are almost unknown in Cornwall.

Two gaily recoloured wall paintings of St. Christopher can be seen at Poughill (pronounced Poffil). The subject can also be seen at Breage, together with a local favourite, a warning to Sabbath breakers. The latter occurs again (with St. George) at St. Just-in-Penwith Church, which also has two remarkable stones, one with the Chi-Rho monogram and inscribed *Ni Selus Iacit* (5C or 6C), and the other is part of the cross-shaft with Hiberno-Saxon interlace (8C or 9C). In ancient glass, one will certainly visit St. Neot Church, but in addition St. Kew has a beautiful window of 1469, showing the whole of Christ's Passion and the donors who gave the glass. Lanreath has the most remarkable monument. It is of 1623 and its towerng height is all in wood. It is to Charles and Agnes Grylls and they are shown as doll-like kneeling figures, with their chaplain and steward on brackets in the background. Below are their eight children. The canopy has coat-of-arms and cherubs and Father Time with his scythe.

A good example of a 17C church is Falmouth's King Charles the Martyr, built in 1662–64. The strong 17C Royalist connection of the county is shown by a number of churches with painted panel copies of the celebrated letter of 1643 of King Charles I, expressing his gratitude for the loyalty of Cornwall. For an 18C church, St. Michael's at Helston, built in the 1760s, is typical. Redruth (1768) is similar. The 19C was the great age of refitting and renewal. Its greatest monument in Cornwall is of course J.L. Pearson's Truro Cathedral of 1880–1910, with its three stone spires, which replaced all but an aisle of St. Mary's Church in that town. Its stained glass by Clayton & Bell forms the most ambitious scheme undertaken by that firm. St. Mary's, Par, by G.E. Street, 1848, is perhaps the most interesting 19C parish church. Street was to give fame to Lostwithiel's spire by adapting it for new churches elsewhere in England. Of 19C restorations, F.C. Eden's work at Blisland is particularly notable.

Non-Anglican churches in Cornwall are largely those of the Methodists, who established a strong position in this county. Their buildings are chiefly of the 19C, Classical in the early decades, Gothic later. The Friends' Meeting House, Come to Good (q.v.), of 1710, is a notable early example, typically domestic in character. Even earlier, and equally domestic, is the meeting house at Marazion (1688).

Cornwall's saints merit a book to themselves. No other county has so many unusual or unique dedications. Many of the local saints are shadowy figures, but enough is known to suggest strong links in the 6C and 7C with Wales, Brittany and Ireland. St. Petroc was Welsh, for example, linked first with Padstow and then with Bodmin. His relics were apparently kept from the late 12C in a reliquary which survives at Bodmin. St. Nonna (patroness of Altarnun) was the mother of St. David. At a later date, St. Neot secured an association far from Cornwall by giving his name to a town in Huntingdonshire.

Altarnon (or Altarnun), *St. Nonna.* Dedicated to St. Non or St. Nonna, the mother of St. David of Wales, who lived in the 6C. It is the largest parish in Cornwall. The church, which is known as the 'Cathedral of the Moors', stands in a sloping churchyard above a stream. The tower is 109ft high, notably high for Cornwall. It is of three stages with four pinnacles and a stair turret rising above the parapet. The church has a five-bay nave with aisles, the S being notably wide. There are standard Cornish piers and capitals, each pier being a monolith—made from a single block of moorstone, as are the capitals and bases. The Perpendicular windows follow the usual Cornish design. There are N and S porches, both porches having their original wagon roofs. Repairs to the church were undertaken in 1986 after a pinnacle had fallen through the roof.

The notable Norman font of Purbeck marble was often copied in this county. It has carved faces at the corners, with large circular designs between them. The Perpendicular Rood screen with three gates runs right across the nave and aisles to enclose the E bay. There are two-light bays in the screen, with blank tracery at the base. Although the screen incorporates old work, it is largely of the 1880s, including the coving at the N and S ends. The bench-ends, some 79, make a marvellous collection. In addition to the Instruments of the Passion, there are figures of St. Michael with an inscription, 'Robart Daye, Maker of this Work', a jester with cap and bells, a man playing the bagpipes, St. Veronica with a veil showing the face of Christ, angels with shields, the five wounds, a sword dance, sheep on hills, and sheaves of corn which grow into a face. As their date is mid-16C, the detail is Renaissance. The altar rail of 1684, by John Gard, is remarkable for stretching across the width of the church. Inscribed on it are the names of the Vicar and churchwardens of 1684. There is a 17C chest with three locks. The E window includes a small medieval depiction of St. Nonna.

The church and parish feature prominently in Daphne du Maurier's novel, 'Jamaica Inn'.

Blisland, *St. Protus and St. Hyacinth.* The patron saints were two Roman brothers of the 3C and this is the only church dedicated to them in England. Blisland is a village on the edge of Bodmin Moor, and the church stands by the green. The church has the familiar Cornish E elevation of three gables. The plan comprises a nave with a S aisle, N and S transepts, a NE (or Lady) chapel, plus the tower and porch. The tower with a rectangular stair turret is in a most unusual position—at the end of the N transept. The walls are mainly Norman, but the S aisle and the porch (with wagon roof) were added in the 15C and are of granite.

The beautiful interior is most striking, owing to the late 19C screen with its colour. The plaster wagon roofs with angels and the leaning granite columns also enhance the interior. There is a six-bay S arcade of Cornish type. There are two fonts. One is Norman, is of St. Stephen stone and has ornamentation; the other is 15C, of Polyphant stone, octagonal, with shields, and has a tall, wooden lantern canopy which shelters a statue of the Virgin and Child. The pulpit, with tester, is late 17C with carving in the style of Grinling Gibbons. The glory of the church, however, is the Rood screen by F.C. Eden and erected in 1897, with a great crucifix showing Christ redeeming the world, and the attendant figures of His Mother and St. John the Evangelist. This will give one a very good idea of most of our churches before the Reformation. The altar, equally beautiful, is in Classical style. The monuments to note are a brass to a Rector, John Balsham (died 1410), and a slate monument of 1624 with six kneeling figures of the Kemp family. A monument to John Kemp of 1728 begins most appropriately with the words 'here's peace and rest'. Also to be noted are a stoup in the S porch, a piscina in the S chapel, Rood loft stairs, the arms of King James VI and I over the N door, and outside, the head of the Norman N doorway. The E window is an Early English triplet of lancets, and the N chapel has a typical four-light Perpendicular E window.

The church has followed the Anglo-Catholic tradition of worship for many years: hence the atmosphere of devotion.

Bodmin, *St. Petroc.* St. Petroc was a 6C abbot, originally from Wales and closely linked with Padstow, whose religious community later moved to Bodmin. 14 English churches are dedicated to him, all in Devon and Cornwall. This is the largest church in Cornwall and it was mostly rebuilt in 1469–72. The tower is on the N side at the junction of nave and chancel, and is Norman up to the third storey and Perpendicular above. The S porch is two-storeyed, with niches for sculpture and a fan-vault inside it.

The nave has arcades of six bays of St. Stephen stone with tall piers, and the chancel has similar, but lower, three-bay arcades. The outstanding feature is the very large 12C font. It is very often copied in the county. The bowl has interlaced foliage and beasts. This rests on a stout mid-shaft and there are four corner shafts with heads as capitals. A lantern cross with the Crucifixion is now inside the church. There are three piscinas, one now used as a money-box. The screens across the chancel aisles, pulpit, lectern and Corporation seats are mostly modern, but with some old fragments. There are two old carved chairs, one with the symbols of the Evangelists, and the other with Adam and Eve and the apple. The glass is modern but the E window of the N aisle should be noted. It shows King Arthur, Sir Percivale, Richard, Coeur de Lion, and King Edward I in chain armour with heraldic tabards. The roof of the S chapel is noteworthy.

Of monuments, there is a 13C cross-slab outside the S wall with an inscription in Norman French. Particularly fine is the monument to Thomas Vyvyan, Prior (died 1533), between the chancel and N chapel and brought from the Priory Church. It is of black Catacleuse stone and grey marble. The inscription is very clear. The recumbent effigy in vestments and mitre lies on a tomb decorated with balusters and figures of the Evangelists, and cherubs with shields. There is a slate slab on the wall in the SW corner to Richard Durant (died 1632), with two wives and 20 children, and there is an incised slab to Peter Bolt (died 1633).

In the S aisle wall there is displayed the reliquary of St. Petroc, a splendid ivory casket of Sicilian craftsmanship. It was probably given in 1177 by Walter of Coutances, a minister of King Henry II.

Come To Good, *Friends' Meeting House.* Named by corruption from the Cornish words, Cwm-ty-coit ('the combe by the dwelling in the wood'), this isolated place between Truro and Falmouth has a famous Friends' Meeting House of 1710. The building is a cottage of whitewashed cob, entirely thatched. Its original cost was £53 8s 3d. Entering by a W porch of 1967, the interior is seen to have a W gallery, which was added in 1717 and which is supported on rough, thin posts; a dais at the E end; and plain benches which have the most sparing backs. The present narrow stairway to the gallery replaces one which stood in the body of the room. The entrance was originally on the S side.

S.C.H.

Cotehele House, *Chapels.* Cotehele House is chiefly of the 15C and 16C. It belonged to the Edgcumbe family from 1353 to 1947, when it passed to the National Trust. Its main chapel is in the NE corner of Retainers' Court, which is itself reached through the W side of Hall Court, the entrance to the property. A dedication to St. Cyricus and St. Julitta is recorded for the house's earlier chapel, but no later record gives a dedication. The present chapel dates from the end of the 15C, from the time of Sir Richard Edgcumbe (died 1489), who had supported King Henry VII at Bosworth. The interior is divided by a 15C and later screen, which has cusped openings and most attractive carved tracery at the foot of the openings and as a cresting. There is a ceiled wagon roof. The three-light E window is restored. The central light has a 19C Crucifixion by John Fouracre. The armorial glass below is probably 16C. The S window, however, is original and has 16C glass of St. Anne and St. Catherine, probably of Flemish manufacture in Southwark, London. The most distinguished fitting in the chapel is a clock of 1485–89, which stands in a niche at the W end. It is a pre-pendulum clock and works by a verge escapement and foliot balance. It used to ring two bells in the pinnacled W bellcote. The clock was restored in 1962 by Messrs Thwaites & Reed.

In the woods below Valley Gardens is the 'Chapel in the Woods', c 1485, built by Sir Richard Edgcumbe in thanksgiving for his escape from King Richard III's agent. It is a single-cell chapel with some original bench-ends.

S.C.H.

Kilkhampton, *St. James.* It is rather rare to find an ordinary dedication in this county, but this indicates an English settlement, or at least an English connection, because medieval Kilkhampton was associated with the Priory of St. James in Bristol. The church is a dignified building with a tall W tower, with set-back buttresses, battlements and corner pinnacles, a S porch, and a continuous aisled nave and chancel of seven bays, all with wagon roofs. There was a church here in Norman times, as is proved by the fine Norman S doorway with beakhead and zigzag in its four orders. The present church was probably built by Sir Thomas Grenville (died 1513) and/ or two of his sons, Roger (died 1524) and John, who was Rector from 1524 to 1580. John's arms appear on the S porch and he clearly inscribed on it the date 1567 and the words 'gate of Heaven' in Latin.

The main feature of the interior is the wonderful array of bench-ends, for which Cornwall is so notable. Here they depict the Instruments of the Passion, such as the seamless robe, the 30 pieces of silver, a spear, a ladder, a hammer and nails. There is also some heraldic scroll work and a few grotesques and mermaids. All the borders of the bench-ends are different. The screen work is not medieval, but of 1860, the same date as the pulpit and choirstalls. The Rood was added in 1906. The organ is reputed to have come from Westminster Abbey in 1859; whatever its origin, it has been much altered and rebuilt since. The church is notable for its wealth of 19C and early 20C stained glass—in no fewer than 17 windows. Note the third window W of the screen in the N aisle, which depicts four saints of Cornish connection: Neot, Piran, Petroc and Germanus of Auxerre. The fifth window from the W in the S aisle shows Sir Richard Grenville and Sir Bevill Grenville, who lived nearby at Stow House. Sir Richard Grenville (died 1591), the hero of the 'Revenge' in the Battle of the Azores, was the squire of Kilkhampton and the patron of the benefice, one of a long line. Lord John Thynne, the church's restorer in 1859–60, appears in the S aisle's W window, holding a model of the church, together with Archbishop Benson (the first Bishop of Truro, 1877–82). The five-light E window of the chancel shows Christ in Glory, with the Virgin Mary and St. James, the church's patron. The 18C sculptor, Michael Chuke (a pupil of Grinling Gibbons), executed monuments to Sir Bevill Grenville (died 1643, but the monument executed in 1714), John Warminster (died 1700), Richard Westlake (died 1704), and John Curtis (died 1705), and he also carved the arms of King George II. The modern bronze figure of Algernon Carteret Thynne on horseback was made by Goscombe John.

Launcells, *St. Swithin.* St. Swithin was the Bishop of Winchester from 852 to 862 and has 58 churches of old foundation dedicated to him. St. Swithin's Well exists opposite the S entrance of this church, which has a most attractive wooded setting. The church itself is equally delightful and unspoilt. It was entirely reconstructed in the 15C and the windows are therefore all Perpendicular. The tower is attractive, being unbuttressed and having the typical local tall octagonal pinnacles. The S porch retains its holy water stoup.

The interior is as a church should be—very light with white walls and roofs. The nave arcade of five bays has Cornish shafts with capitals with fleur-de-lis cresting. The N arcade is of Polyphant stone. The wagon roofs of the aisles have carved beams and bosses. The stairway to the former Rood loft may be seen on the N side. There are over 60 bench-ends in the church. As elsewhere, the Instruments of the Passion predominate. There are the 30 pieces of silver, nails and whipping cord as usual, but what are unusual are the terse symbols, for example the empty tomb, grave clothes, and spice boxes for the Resurrection, and, for the Ascension, two footprints on earth and higher up, two feet at the bottom of a robe enclosed in a cloud. Box-pews from the 18C remain in the N aisle. The polished marble reredos is of the 18C, being a Gothick frame for the usual inscribed boards, which runs below and to the sides of the E window. Also notable are the 15C encaustic tiles at the E end which show flowers, Tudor roses, griffins, lions and a pelican. There is a plain Norman font with cable moulding and a Jacobean cover. Of the 17C also are the communion table and the arms of King Charles II with strapwork decoration (on the N wall next to the Rood stairs). Much earlier is the very old door with an immense lock. There is a faint 16C wall painting of the Sacrifice of Isaac on the W wall of the S aisle. There is a wall monument on the S wall, at the E end, to Sir John Chamond (died 1624), with a semi-reclining effigy in armour and delightful small figures at the head and feet.

Launceston, *St. Mary Magdalene.* Launceston was originally the main town of Cornwall with one of the most important castles and one of the richest priories. The largely 16C church of St. Mary Magdalene is in the centre of the town. It is an English and not a Celtic dedication, as also are those of the other two churches here, St. Thomas the Apostle and St. Stephen, with its fine tower with the usual four prominent pinnacles.

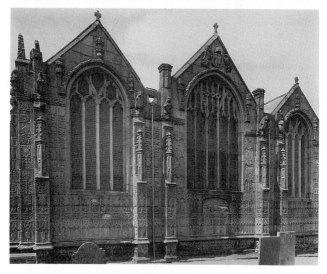

The 16C E end of St. Mary Magdalene with lavish carvings, all in granite

The exterior is said to be the most spectacular W of Exeter. The 14C SW tower, with higher stair turret, set-back buttresses and battlements, is the only survival of the earlier church. The remainder of the present church was entirely the work of Sir Henry Trecarrel (died 1554), who built it between 1511 and 1524 wholly of granite. The exterior is profusely carved, notwithstanding that difficult material. The ornamentation consists of coats of arms and fleur-de-lis, and an inscription, reading from the chancel door E *'Ave Maria gracia plena! Dominus Tecum. Sponsus amat sponsam. Maria optimam partem eligit. O quam terriblis et metuendus est locus iste. Vere aliud non est hic nisi Domus Dei et porta celi'*. (Hail Mary full of grace! The Lord is with thee. The bridegroom loves the bride. Mary chose the best part. How dreadful is this place! This is none other than the House of God and this is the gate of Heaven.) Above is some rose and thistle ornament. The large windows are flanked by ornamented buttresses, and by the sides of the windows are palm leaves with roses in the spandrels. The parapet has more thistle and pomegranate. Below the E window is a recumbent figure of the patron saint, St. Mary Magdalene, with angels playing musical instruments. In the E gable are the arms of King Henry VIII. The S porch is particularly notable. It has an upper storey. In front are carved (in granite, of course) the date 1511, the arms of Trecarrel and Kelway (Sir Henry married Margaret Kelway), and reliefs of St. George and the dragon, and St. Martin dividing his cloak with the beggar. The outer side walls of the porch are lavishly panelled with Cornish fern ornament. In the churchyard is an ancient cross with a carved head.

Inside, the arcade is of eight bays and there are N and S aisles, which extend as long as the nave and chancel. The piers are of an unusual type for Cornwall: slender, with four groups of three attached shafts; but the capitals are usual. The slightly wider arch might indicate a transept. The wagon roofs are new, but can be seen clearly as the large four-light windows give plenty of light. There are numerous angels and saints and about 400 bosses. The chancel screen is of 1911 (by Rashleigh Pinwell), and the bench-ends are of 1893–94 and are well carved (by Arnold Fellows). The finest fitting is the 16C wooden pulpit, which is splendidly carved. It is the best pulpit in the county. The font is of c 1525. There are three 17C chairs, an organ front of the 18C, and carved arms of King George I. The five-light E window has stained glass of 1858, depicting the Ascension. All the S aisle windows have 19C and early 20C stained glass.

The best monument is to Granville Pyper (died 1717) and Richard Wise (died 1731), in the N aisle. Both were Mayors of Launceston. There are busts of the two deceased on top and standing allegorical figures in two tiers.

Morwenstow, *St. Morwenna and St. John the Baptist.* This is the only church dedicated to St. Morwenna, who lived perhaps in the 6C. The parish is famous for its Vicar from 1834 to 1875, the Reverend Robert Stephen Hawker, one of the most celebrated characters of the 19C Church. The church itself is of particular interest for its Norman work.

The W tower is unbuttressed, but it has the four fine pinnacles of local type. The church is in a marvellous position above a combe facing the sea, which is why there are no belfry windows on the W face of the tower. Cornwall does not have much Norman work remaining in its churches, but Morwenstow is an exception. The S doorway is of that period with the usual zigzag ornament, a dragon and lamb, and a mermaid, dolphin and whale; one of the capitals has two birds and one fir-cones. There are crude heads of men and beasts on the porch. Three N bays of the five-bay arcade are Norman, with round arches and the usual ornament, but what is unusual are the remarkable heads of men and beasts in the spandrels of the arches, including a hippopotamus, antelope, head of a monk and a grinning face. The other two N bays are Early English, with circular piers and pointed arches, one of which is taller than the other. By contrast the S arcade and S aisle are Tudor (built during the incumbency of Thomas Kempthorne, Vicar 1560–1594 and partly rebuilt, as one capital bears the date 1564 (not 1664 as sometimes stated). What must be noticed is the capital with the words 'This is the house of God' cut upside down for the benefit of celestial readers proving that our churches were built first and foremost for the glory of God rather than for man. The wagon roofs of nave and aisles are of c 1564 with a mile of timbers and hundreds of bosses, and tiny angels on the wall plates. The chancel, which projects beyond the aisles, is not structurally separated from the nave.

Typical Cornish 15C piers (in the foreground), typical bench-ends, and rare (for Cornwall) Norman arches in the background

The font should be noticed; it is massive early Norman with cable ornament. There are a large number of bench-ends with early Renaissance motifs, indicating a late date. The Rood screen is of 1575, but it has been much restored with cast-iron tracery. The Rood itself (1934) marked the centenary of Hawker's incumbency. The reredos is of 1908 by Edmund Sedding, with four paintings, and there are two bronze reliefs of the Last Supper and Christ with the Crown of Thorns. There is a faint wall painting of St. Morwenna blessing a priest on the N wall. A delightful four-light window (1904) in the S aisle, the Hawker memorial window, is a history of the parish, showing the churchyard, font, the figurehead of the 'Caledonia' (wrecked here), and St. Morwenna holding her church with her brother, St. Nectan, holding his from the next parish, Welcombe (but which is in Devon). A 16C slate monument has the incised figure of John Kempthorne with hands clasped in prayer.

Robert Stephen Hawker was one of the most talked-of parsons, interesting everyone, looking after shipwrecked sailors, beautifying his church, and writing poems and books. Tennyson visited him here. He was a claimant to be the first to introduce Harvest Festival (in 1843). He built the vicarage nearby, and its chimneys are based on the towers of various churches with which he had been connected. A memorial slab to his first wife, Charlotte (died 1863), lies in front of the pulpit.

Mullion, *St. Mullion.* Mullion Cove is well-known. It is most delightful and is the Cornish coast at its best, visited by numbers of tourists who should also visit the church of St. Mullion or St. Melan, which is equally delightful. The patron saint was a 6C Welsh missionary. The church was re-erected in 1500, but 13C work remains in the chancel and tower. The W tower is built of blocks of local granite and local serpentine. It is of two storeys and has battlements and tall corner pinnacles. Above an upper window is a representation of the Crucifixion, with God the Father behind Christ. The S porch has panelled jambs and a holy water stoup. Mullion shares with other Cornish churches a pattern of three E gables with the chancel slightly projecting.

On entering, the doors should certainly be noticed: both the N and the S doors are original, the former having wooden studs and the latter iron studs, but the latter is unique in having near its base a small latchet door, probably for the ejection of dogs. The seven-bay arcades are identical and typical of late medieval Cornwall. The benches and bench-ends are profuse. Their date is mid-16C and they therefore show Renaissance influence. There are the usual Instruments of the Passion, but unusual is Jonah inside the whale. There are also grotesques, initials, and two cherubs with a chalice and a barrel. The most prominent object in the church, as intended, is the Rood screen. It is partly original but mainly 20C. The new work was begun by F.C. Eden in 1925. It has fan-vaulting, a loft and a modern Rood group of Christ on the Cross, redeeming the world, with St. Mary and St. John the Evangelist on either side. The Rood stairs still remain in the N wall. The lectern has two 16C panels with sibyls, formerly being bench-ends. The royal arms in plaster are of King Charles II. The 15C font is octagonal, with blank arcades and a serpent. The three-light E window has old stained glass which was collected together in 1840. Above all this are the typical West Country roofs, the wagon roofs, which are original: the chancel roof has five small angels on each side. In general, Mullion is a good example of a typical old West Country interior.

St. Germans, *St. Germans of Auxerre.* The house, Port Eliot, the seat of the Earls of St. Germans, was the Priory of St. Germans, of which an undercroft with 13C lancet windows and refectory remain. Most of the remainder of the house is 19C by Sir John Soane and H. Harrison. The grounds were laid out by Humphry Repton in the 18C, and, with the grounds surrounding the church, are very beautiful. It is a very large parish. The church is dedicated to St. Germanus, who was Bishop of Auxerre in France from 418 to 448 and who came to Britain in 429 and 447 to oppose the heresy of Pelagius concerning grace, freewill and baptism. Fifteen ancient churches are dedicated to him. The original church was the cathedral of Cornwall in pre-Conquest times, until the See was transferred to Crediton in 1027 and then to Exeter in 1050. The present 12C and 13C church is the church of the Augustinian priory which succeeded the earlier monastery, and is complete except for its E end, and has more Norman work than any other in Cornwall.

The W front will first be noted: two towers and an enormous Norman doorway between them, with seven orders of arches and much zigzag. It is built of local stone. Above, there is a gable with a cross. There are several Norman windows on the W front. The Norman N tower turns into a 13C octagon, and the S tower has the only Norman staircase in the county. Both towers have battlements and wide, flat buttresses. Inside, the transitional Norman bays that remain have short circular piers with scalloped capitals. The arches are slightly pointed. The blocked S clerestory windows have rich zigzag ornament. The very wide S aisle has work of various periods. Its E end was enlarged in the 14C to house a shrine for relics of the patron saint obtained from Auxerre. The rest of the aisle was widened later, in Perpendicular style. The S porch of that aisle is handsome, with a tunnel-vault and granite ribs. There is no N aisle. The five-light E window of the chancel is original Perpendicular and it was put into the present E wall when the medieval chancel disappeared. The N transept is 19C and was built as the Port Eliot family pew.

The font is of c 1200, of Purbeck marble. It is square and stands on one large central support and four rounded supports at the angles. There is one 14C choirstall with a misericord of a man punished for hunting on Sunday. The reredos shows the Last Supper with Judas stroking his beard as he holds the bag. There are carved figures of St. Nicholas and St. Anthony. The roofs are not original, but 19C. Repair work was needed after a fire in 1966. The Burne-Jones glass is an excellent example of the work of Morris & Co. In the E window (1896) we see ten large figures, including Christ and the centurion, the Evangelists, St. Paul and St. Stephen. In a S window are the six virtues—Faith, Justice, Hope, Charity, Praise and Joy (1902).

The following monuments should be noted. John Moyle (died 1661), has a memorial with a heraldic device on a black marble slab. Edward Eliot (died 1722), whose large monument by J.M. Rysbrack is in the S aisle, is shown as a reclining figure in Roman costume, with one mourning wife and another wife on a medallion. There are also several cherubs. The monument is most ambitious. The first Earl of St. Germans (died 1823) has a monument by Sir Richard Westmacott which shows a sad female and an urn.

St. Just-in-Roseland, *St. Just.* Dedicated to St. Just, of whom little is known. He may have lived in the 6C. Only one other church is dedicated to him, also in Cornwall, at St. Just-in-Penwith. The church lies at the bottom of a wooded combe where a creek from Carrick Sound reaches the churchyard. From the lychgate one looks down on the roofs of the church and one stands about level with the top of the tower. Could any setting be more remarkable? Moreover, there is no fairer churchyard in England with its exquisite flowers (particularly hydrangeas and polyanthus) and giant beeches and palm trees. It is for this charm that the church will be visited and remembered.

The 14C W tower of slate has a SE stair turret rising above the parapet, battlements and diagonal buttresses. The N transept and chancel have windows of the period when the church was built in 1261, but in the S aisle they are all Perpendicular. The jambs of the S porch show panelling, and the roof is original. The seven-bay S arcade rests on Perpendicular granite piers with four plain capitals and nearly semicircular arches, a common local feature. There is no N aisle. The N transept appears elongated because a modern vestry extends it to the E. The octagonal 15C font has quatrefoil panels. The benches have carvings of the 19C. The Rood stairs still exist and now lead to the pulpit. A winged lion from a misericord is worked into the lectern. The piscina in the chancel is 13C. Brasses are not common in Cornwall, but there is a brass here S of the chancel to a priest in a cope, of c 1520.

St. Mawgan-in-Pydar, *St. Mawgan (or St. Maucan).* The church, the Elizabethan manor house (Lanherne, home of the Arundells, and now a convent) and village are in a delightful wooded valley N of Newquay, and nearby is all the grandeur of the Cornish coast at Bedruthan Steps. The church, whose patron may have been a 6C Welsh abbot, comprises a nave, a S aisle which is as long as the nave, a N transept, a S porch, a S tower and a NE vestry. The S transept is incorporated within the aisle. The fine tower with higher NE stair turret is 15C in its upper part and 13C at its base, and is in an unusual position S of the S transept. It has thin, set-back buttresses, battlements and hexagonal corner turrets surmounted by knob-ended spirelets. Within, two arches of the S chapel of the chancel of Catacleuse stone are of c 1375, but the nave arcade of St. Stephen stone, with leaves on the capitals, and most of the rest of the church, with the S porch, is 15C. The nave W window is of c 1300, but the others are Perpendicular. There is a squint from the N transept to the chancel. The E end of the S aisle is now used as the Lady chapel. William Butterfield restored the church in 1860–61.

The Norman style font is of Pentewan stone on four corner supports of Devon marble (renewed in the 19C) and one central Bath stone pillar. It has faces at the corners, and its four sides have zigzag above and shields below. The pulpit carved with Instruments of the Passion is of a rare date, 1553. The fine Rood screen is tall and retains its loft. Most churches in Cornwall would once have had such an example. The Arundell arms are in the centre of the cornice. The 15C bench-ends should be noted. As usual, they have shields and the Instruments of the Passion. Modern glass in the five-light E window shows King Alfred, St. Augustine, St. Columba, St. Patrick and St. George (by Percy Bacon, 1902). In a S aisle window are St. Mawgan and St. Nicholas with two children (by G. Maile, c 1931). The W window of the nave and the E window of the S aisle are by Clayton & Bell. There are some brasses: a 15C priest in a cope; George Arundell (died 1573) and his wife (a palimpsest, the other side being early 16C Flemish work); and Cyssel Arundel (died 1578) in typical Elizabethan dress. There is a 17C slate monument to Henry Stephen and his wife (died 1611 and 1650).

Note the 15C lantern cross in the churchyard, SW of the church, carved with the Annunciation (W), the Crucifixion (E) and two bishops. The carvings stand within crocketed ogee arches in each of the four faces.

St. Neot, *St. Neot or St. Anietus*. St. Neot was a 9C monk and hermit who founded a monastery here. He was buried here, but later most of his relics were taken to Eynesbury in Huntingdonshire, which was renamed St. Neot's. This is a very large parish, and a lovely piece of Cornwall, the Glynn valley. The church dominates the village, and is visited by thousands to see the old glass. The oldest part is the W tower which is Decorated and has a tunnel-vault. It is embattled and has short pinnacles and diagonal buttresses. The belfry windows have intersecting tracery. The W window is also intersecting and there is a tower S window of two ogee lights. At the top of the tower may be seen a sprig of oak, placed there each year on the 29th May to keep in mind King Charles II's escape after the Battle of Worcester by hiding in an oak tree. The money for this purpose was left by an elderly man centuries ago. The rest of the church is Perpendicular. The spectacular S aisle and the two-storey S porch are built of large blocks of granite with battlements and pinnacles and typical Cornish windows of c 1525: four cusped ogee lights. The S porch has a tunnel-vault with ribs and five bosses, the central one having four heads conjoined. Both doors to the upper room are original. The N aisle windows are straight-headed of c 1520. There are the usual three E gables, with the chancel slightly projecting.

There are seven-bay arcades within. The wagon roofs should be noted, particularly that of the S aisle with shield-bearing angels. The chancel roof has coloured bosses and painted angels. Note a squint at the E end of the N aisle to the chancel. The font has a square, low 15C bowl of Pentewan stone with traceried panels (four ogee lights to the E, eight trefoils to the W) on 13C shafts. The pulpit is modern, with St. George and the dragon, St. Neot and his doe, and the servant with two fishes for St. Neot. On the reredos we can see the Annunciation and the Three Wise Men. The Rood screen is also modern, but the original stairs can be seen on the N side. There is a slate monument to William Bere (died 1610), showing the kneeling figures of himself, his wife, two daughters and a son; also a grinning skull. On the N side of the sanctuary there is an ogee tomb-recess, thought to be the shrine of St. Neot, but no doubt used too as an Easter sepulchre.

Visitors, however, will come chiefly for the glass. There are 15 windows with about 350 figures, and about one half are of the 15C and the early 16C. They give, of course, an excellent idea of the interior of a medieval church originally. They also show the devotion of parishioners to their parish church. A full description will help the tourist to appreciate this beauty. The great restoration was carried out by John Hedgeland in c 1830, and a few of the windows are his own. More repairs were undertaken in the 1930s and the windows were cleaned in 1970. We begin at the W window of the S aisle and walk round the church anti-clockwise.

W end of S aisle. By Hedgeland, c 1830. Armorial, with the arms of the Gryll family who restored the windows at that time.

Sixth from E. St. Paul, St. Peter, Christ with orb and sceptre, and St. James. In the tracery, the Annunciation. The arms are those of the Tubbe and Callaway families.

Fifth from E. St. Lulluwy, St. German (vested as a bishop), St. John the Evangelist and St. Stephen. In the tracery, the Resurrection, and below, the Callaway family and a priest.

Fourth from E. The Evangelists—St. Mark (lion), St. Luke (ox), St. Matthew (angel) and St. John (eagle). The donor was John Motton.

Third from E. The Virgin and Child, the Crucifixion, St. John the

Evangelist and St. Stephen. The donors, the Martyn family, appear below.

Second from E. St. Christopher, St. Neot, St. Leonard and St. Catherine. Below are Nicholas Borlase and his family: the parents and 12 children.

First from E. The Noah window in eight panels, with fascinating pictures of the Ark and Noah with the animals and his family and finally, his drunkenness and his death.

E end of S aisle. In the tracery, orders of angels, and below, the story of Creation. The Creator with compasses divides land from water and creates Adam and Eve and all living things. Adam and Eve are then seen in the garden with the green serpent at the tree. The Expulsion then follows and human toil begins (Adam with a spade and Eve with a distaff). Cain and Abel represent the beginning of human evil. The coming of death is shown by the death of Adam under a green counterpane, and Seth puts under his tongue the three apple pippins which would become the Tree of Life.

E window. The Last Supper by Hedgeland. St. John is asleep on Christ's lap and Judas has his hand behind him.

E end of N aisle. The Acts window is by Hedgeland. In the tracery are the Annunciation and the Coronation of the Virgin. Below are shown Pentecost, the stoning of St. Stephen, the Conversion of St. Paul (his horse equally startled) and St. Luke writing down the event.

First from E. The Redemption window, also by Hedgeland. In the tracery is the Resurrection. Below are the Descent from the Cross, the Burial, the Resurrection and the Ascension.

Second from E. St. John the Baptist, St. Gregory, St. Leonard and St. Andrew. Given by the Harys family who are shown below.

Third from E. The Wives' window, 1530. St. Mabena, Our Lady of Pity (pietà), Christ and St. Mawbred. Below are 20 of the wives kneeling.

Fourth from E. The Maidens' window. St. Patrick of Plymouth, St. Cleer, St. Manacus and St. Brechan in ermine robe in which are ten heads. Many maids kneel below.

Fifth from E. The St. Neot window, 1528, given by the young men of the village. The life of the saint is shown in 12 scenes—resigning his crown to a younger brother, taking his vow as a monk, rescuing a doe from the hunter, the angel pointing out the fishes in the well, of which the saint was to have one a day (and the supply would not then cease), but a disobedient servant brought two (one on a plate and one on a gridiron), and he is sent back and we see all the fishes revived. A thief then carries off St. Neot's oxen, a ploughman offers his stags to replace them, whereupon the thief returns them and becomes a monk.

W end of N aisle. The St. George window, also with 12 scenes in his exciting life. He fights the Gauls and is beheaded by them, but is restored to life. He is then seen on his white horse, slaying the dragon, the king and queen looking on and the princess in the distance with her little dog. Later, on a charge of treason, he is bridled on all fours as a horse upon which the king's son could ride. Finally, he is tortured in many ways (hung on a gibbet, thrown into a furnace of lead, dragged by a wild horse and beheaded), with the king looking on.

In the churchyard by the S door there is a pre-Conquest granite cross-shaft with interlaced work.

St. Winnow, *St. Winnow.* This is the only church with such a dedication. Winnow (or Winnoc) was a 7C and 8C evangelist who

died in France in 717. The church has a most beautiful situation by
the River Fowey, built on rising ground near a very wide expanse of
water. There are Norman remains on the N side, and some 13C work,
but otherwise it is the usual Cornish Perpendicular, with an embattled W tower, a nave and S aisle of equal length, a N transept and a S
porch. The church was restored by J.D. Sedding and by E.H. Sedding
in the 19C and early 20C.

The six-bay granite arcade has capitals of St. Stephen stone, with
ornamental carving. The arch to the N transept and the two-light
window W of it are 13C rebuildings of Norman work. The wagon
roofs are old, with bosses and wall plates. The Perpendicular font is
of granite, with carvings of shield-bearing angels and the inscription
Ecce charissimi de Deo vero baptizabuntur Spiritu Sancto. The
church is noted for its bench-ends, some Perpendicular and some
Elizabethan. In particular, note a ship in a storm (N side of nave), a
man drinking (by the S door) and a St. Catherine's wheel (S aisle).
The pulpit is also Elizabethan, elaborately carved and standing on
low, bulbous legs. The communion table is Jacobean. The church is
fortunate to retain its Rood screen of c 1520, which separates the two
E bays. It is original, except for the coving and cornice. It stretches
across the nave and aisle. The narrow panels are carved with flowers
or leaves above each other. The original stairs to the loft can be seen
in the N transept. Ringers' rhymes dated 1810 are in the tower. The
church is also notable for its old glass. In the E window is the
Crucifixion, and there is more old glass in the E window of the S aisle.
It is 15C or early 16C. The kneeling figures represent donors. The
upper row of figures are St. George, the Virgin and Child, St.
Christopher and St. Michael, and the lower row are St. Winnow, the
Virgin and Child again, St. Mary Magdalene and St. Leonard.
Among the coats-of-arms are those of the Courtenay family. In
modern glass we can see St. Winnow, St. Elizabeth of Hungary, and
the three women at the Empty Tomb. The slate monument to William
Sawle (died 1651) at the E end of the S aisle has good engraved
borders.

DEVON

Devon is the largest county in England not administratively divided. It is not surprising, therefore, that the geology is complex and the building material varied. The rocks range from the Devonian—345 to 395 million years old and one of the most ancient formations found in Britain—to the younger rocks of the SE comprising the Jura chalk of Beer. Devonian rock appears as dark slates and slaty limestone N of a line from Newton Abbot to Tavistock and also in the N of the county above a line running from Barnstaple to South Molton and Bampton. In between is Dartmoor, a granite plateau rising to over 2000ft and, further N, Culm—a belt of dark shales and often siliceous sandstone, unattractive with heavy clays on top and poor soil. There remains the rest of the SE where the spectacular rocks of the Triassic New Red Sandstone produce the red cliffs of the coast from Torquay to Seaton and the red earth on both sides of the River Exe up to Tiverton and N of Crediton. Flint is occasionally found in the Axminster neighbourhood but a far more attractive material and one that approaches more closely to true marble than any other English stone, which was once quarried at a number of places but now only at Ashburton, is a stone which polishes brilliantly and often shows the characteristic veining and figuring generally associated with true marble. When employed with discretion, it can be a great embellishment. Unfortunately, Devon is devoid of the oolitic limestone which is England's best building stone.

Apart from a few crosses or cross fragments of which Colyton is the best, some fonts (Hatherleigh, Spreyton) and Dolton, where parts of crosses have been made into a font, the only notable pre-Conquest survival is the plain crypt at Sidbury dating from c 670. Even before the Normal invasion, the See of Crediton was merged with that of St. Germans (Cornwall) to form the See of Exeter. With the advent of the Normans there is much more to see although the only major structural survivals are the transeptal towers of Exeter Cathedral (copied later by Bishop Grandisson at Ottery St. Mary) and the four-bay arcades at St. Mary Arches, Exeter. Single towers, however, S doorways and especially fonts (of which over 100 survive in the county) are to be seen in plenty. The towers are usually W ones but between 15 and 20 single transeptal ones occur (notably at Barnstaple, Braunton and Ilfracombe); central towers can be seen at a few churches, including Crediton and Tawstock among the gazetteer entries. The most eminent of the Norman towers is the W tower of Sidbury, although rebuilt in 1884; it has shallow buttresses and retains a rib-vaulted room on the ground floor. The body of the church is also Norman.

The S doorways are generally far more restrained in decoration than their counterparts elsewhere. The most richly decorated are at Bishopsteignton with a rare (for Devon) example of a carved tympanum, showing the three Magi approaching the Virgin, all under arches with a small palm tree above. Others of very similar design occur at Buckland Brewer and Shebbear with rows of heads and beaks, a beast at Shebbear having a fish in its mouth. The fonts fall into a number of categories, the simpler ones being circular or square with limited decoration. Elaboration comes in the form of corner supports and more ambitious carving. At Luppitt, the font has vigorous spirited carving showing a centaur fighting two dragons and two men fighting each other with nail-shaped clubs, and at

Stoke Canon four figures on the faces of the stem and four figures on the corners hold up the bowl from which four beasts crouch down to bite off their heads. There are a number of routine fonts of a type seen elsewhere with square, shallow bowls and sides decorated with plain shallow friezes of round-headed arches, made of Purbeck marble. Bondleigh, in addition to a Norman S doorway and a Norman font, has two well-executed and preserved Norman capitals built into the wall.

Gothic made an inauspicious start in Devon for, apart from Exeter Cathedral Chapter House, and Branscombe Church which has Early English transepts, it would need a long search among the moors and combes to find even one group of medieval lancets. The Decorated style, however, started with a flourish with the rebuilding of Exeter Cathedral between c 1275 and 1360; its incomparable vault, 300ft long, is the longest unbroken stretch of Gothic vaulting in the world. The new work was completed up to the crossing by 1327, when Bishop Grandisson took over and ran the diocese until 1369. Under him, the exquisite nave was built. He was also responsible for Devon's most notable Decorated church, Ottery St. Mary, which he founded as a college. The chapel of St. Blaise at Haccombe, a largely 14C building, since reconditioned, was also consecrated by Grandisson. Bere Ferrers, Hartland and Tawstock are other mainly 14C churches which have retained their Decorated character. On the whole, the new forms were applied conservatively in Devon and there is nothing of the full flowing tracery seen in other areas; the best tracery is in the W window at Cullompton and in the E window of the Dorset aisle at Ottery St. Mary.

It was, on the other hand, the Perpendicular period which made by far the biggest impact on Devon church architecture. Nevertheless, although impressive in some architectural details (e.g. the chancel capitals at Swimbridge), and often in its furnishings, there is a lack of individuality. Towers, usually at the W end, have much dignity to show as in the outstanding example at Chittlehampton and the picture-postcard Widecombe-in-the-Moor, and many are fine and austere, sometimes very lofty. Arcades are unadventurous. Windows and tracery are relatively uniform although not so standardised as the piers. Roofs are usually of wagon form, most pleasing when they are infilled with plaster. Nave and chancels are nowhere vaulted except at Exeter and Ottery St. Mary. Clerestories are rare—only ten in all. Instead, when churches were enlarged in the 15C and 16C, the usual practice was to add an aisle or aisles so that nearly all Devon places of worship are hall-churches with aisles of the same height as the nave. Where two aisles were built, they were often carried right through to the E end of the chancel in the form of chancel chapels, thus creating a three-gable effect (as in Cornwall). Normally, there is no structural division between nave and chancel, the wagon roof running continuously through the building, and a wooden screen, extending right across nave and aisles, often taking the place of the chancel arch.

This brings us to furnishings, for which Devon is justly famed, especially for its Rood screens. Frequently coved with ribs, shaped into fan-vault patterns and richly carved, the majority still coloured and gilded, they are more sumptuous in many ways than the more restrained East Anglian type but not necessarily more beautiful as works of art and with painting of lesser quality on the wainscot panels; the painting is found in S but hardly ever in N Devon. Devon screens place more emphasis on the horizontal than the vertical; the openings are lower and wider, and filled with tracery similar to that of stone Perpendicular windows. The earliest and the most luxurious, dating from the Decorated period, are of stone (pulpitum at Exeter Cathedral, and a screen to the Lady chapel, renewed in 1842, at Ottery St. Mary) and there are excellent 15C stone examples at Awliscombe, Colyton, Culmstock (now used as a reredos) and especially Totnes, which stretches right across nave and aisle. Among screens made of wood, there are notable ones at Atherington (a rare example in England of a screen which preserves its Rood loft complete), Chulmleigh, Cullompton, St. Saviour's at Dartmouth, Hartland, Plymtree and Swimbridge—the last two especially fine. The area W of the Exe estuary is rich in screens with painted wainscots (e.g. Ashton, Bovey Tracey, Kenton) whilst Bridford has charming small carved figures only 8ins high in the wainscoting.

Pulpits of the Perpendicular period are more notable in stone than in wood. Often they are highly coloured, with tall, thin panels of decorative carving placed between bowed ogee niches housing coarse figures. St. Saviour's at Dartmouth and Harberton are two examples found in the gazetteer. Fonts of the later Middle Ages are mostly octagonal, very often with quatrefoil decoration; Swimbridge has a lead bowl in octagonal panelled early 18C casing and folding cupboard doors, whilst Shaugh Prior has an octagonal cover of lantern shape, two-storeyed, its tapering sides set with little monkish figures and a bishop crowning the whole. Bench-ends are plentiful, square-headed and featuring blank tracery (especially in S Devon), Saints, Instruments of the Passion, initials (sometimes inverted) and heraldry—all as in Cornwall. Good sets are at Braunton, High Bickington and East Budleigh.

Amongst other items, Ottery St. Mary has a notable reredos, restored in 1884. A furnishing of considerable interest is the small wooden pyx case (c 1500) or ciborium at Warkleigh; measuring $7^{3}/_{4}$ x $7^{1}/_{4}$ ins, the sides are painted with roses, a sun in a circle and leaves in the spandrels. The colours are green, red, white and gold. From post-Reformation dates, special pews are important. The one at Tawstock shows early Renaissance decoration and dates from c 1540–50; the Bluett Pew at Holcombe Rogus is early 17C and the Portledge Pew at Alwington is also Jacobean and was brought from Portledge Hall.

Among Elizabethan and Jacobean furnishings, Pilton has a comely font cover with concave crocketed sides and finial and a communion rail with each alternate arch resting on a short column; there are Jacobean screens at Colyton (in stone), Rose Ash (1618) and notably Washfield (1624) and an Elizabethan pulpit at Shebbear with three tiers of crude little figures in blank arcades.

Some of the wagon roofs have celures or canopies of honour, boarding panels between the main timbers above where the Rood once stood; the boards may be decorated with suns, stars or other motifs. Stained glass of medieval date is seldom found, the most interesting being at Doddiscombsleigh and Littlehempston. There are five 15C windows in the N aisle at Doddiscombsleigh; the E window of the aisle depicts the Seven Sacraments.

More needs to be said about towers. Combe Martin, St. Andrew's at Plymouth and Widecombe-in-the-Moor have tall crocketed pinnacles. Salcombe Regis and Stockland have stair turrets rising above the parapets and a number in the S (e.g. Ashburton, Harberton and Torbryan) have a peculiarly local feature in that the turrets are placed in the middle of one side, usually the S (but the N at

Ashburton). Among notable towers not already mentioned are Cullompton, Kenton and Totnes, all of bright red sandstone, Hartland (at 128ft, one of the highest in Devon), and South Molton. Spires are not common but Barnstaple, Braunton and Swimbridge have lead-sheathed ones. Bishop's Tawton has a crocketed octagonal stone spire, unique in Devon. Other spires are to be seen in the Kingsbridge/Modbury/Totnes triangle (Diptford, Holbeton and Modbury) and, further N, at Buckfastleigh. Uffculme, near Cullompton, has a spire rebuilt in 1846–48.

Late medieval sculpture is not outstanding, but chantry chapels, Easter sepulchres and monuments in recesses may be impressive architecturally. Brasses are conspicuous by their absence, Devon being a long way from the source of the latten used for making them; the best are those to John Hanley (died 1408) and his two wives at St. Saviour's, Dartmouth and to Sir Peter Courtenay in Exeter Cathedral (1409).

Elizabethan and 17C monuments are present in all their various forms. Tawstock's monument to Frances, Lady Fitzwarren (died 1586) is a particularly important Classical work, the effigy still recumbent. Later came semi-reclining effigies (Tavistock, John Glanville, died 1600) and many frontal half-figures, and, at Berry Pomeroy (to the Seymour family) rows of figures like passengers on an old-fashioned steamer. There are a number of memorials in which a figure is supported on an arm with cheek in hand, such as Dulcebella Hodges (died 1628) at Kenton. Kneeling figures, often in facing pairs, are common in the 17C. Members of the Drake family kneel in line at Musbury. Among less typical forms is the standing figure of John Northcote (died 1632), showing him in high boots with sword and baton, at the curiously dedicated church of St. Cyriac and St. Julitta at Newton St. Cyres, and the standing figure of Susan Calmady in a shroud at Tamerton Foliat (after John Donne in St. Paul's Cathedral).

The largest monuments are those to Sir John Pole (died 1658) and his wife (died 1628) at Colyton, to Sir Thomas Wyse (died 1629) at Marystow—one of the most ambitious monuments in the county, to Sir Simon Leach, his second wife, son and daughter-in-law at Cadeleigh (erected c 1630), and to Sir John Hele (died 1608) and his family at Wembury. Of later date are the grand monuments to the fifth Earl of Bath of c 1680 at Tawstock and at Wembury to Lady Narborough who died in 1678, 'Mightyly Afflicted with a Cough and Bigge with Child'. Tawstock's numerous monuments are described in the entry for this church. In general, however, it must be stated that Devonshire's varied monuments are not so well-executed as in other counties.

18C church architecture shows no distinctive pattern and is not well represented. St. George's, Tiverton, which was consecrated in 1733 after the fire of 1731, has a good reredos and altar rails and, at Werrington, there is a curious early Gothic Revival church of 1743. Village churches often have the chancel separated from the nave by a tympanum in the form of a solid wall to fill in the chancel arch on which are displayed the Creed, Commandments and the Lord's Prayer; this is seen at Molland which has a delightful interior with box-pews and three-decker pulpit. Other furnishings include a fine screen (possibly pre-1700) at Cruwys Morchard, a reredos at Morchard Bishop and font cupboard at St. Maurice's, Plympton. 18C monuments are not numerous, the best being at Dunchideock (to Major General Stringer Lawrence—died 1778—bearing the

inscription, 'The desparate state of affairs in India becoming prosperous by a series of victories endeared him to his country'),
Georgeham, Stowford and Tawstock. There is work by John Flaxman at Buckland Filleigh, Dawlish and Kingsbridge and by John
Bacon and his son at Widworthy, Buckland Monachorum, Buckwell
and Ottery St. Mary. At Holbeton, Plympton and Teigngrace there
are artificial Coade & Sealy stone monuments.

The Victorian great names are thinly represented. A.W.N. Pugin
built a mausoleum at Bicton, William Butterfield designed All Saints',
Babbacombe, Torquay and Yealmpton Church, and G.E. Street built
St. John's, Torquay and the chancel of St. Peter's, Plymouth. The last
two churches were principal centres of the Anglo-Catholic movement in Devon, which found a palatable home in the county because
Bishop Henry Philpotts (Bishop of Exeter, 1831–69) was a notable
High Churchman. He sparked off the 'surplice riots' in Exeter in the
mid-1840s by his very moderate request to his clergy to wear a
surplice for preaching. R.C. Carpenter, an early leader of the 'accurate' Gothic Revival, designed St. John's, Bovey Tracey, for the
brother of the Earl of Devon. Butterfield and Henry Woodyer restored
Ottery St. Mary Church around 1850 and Butterfield returned there
in the late 1870s to decorate the Coleridge transept. Butterfield's font
in that church, 1850, was given by Alexander Beresford Hope, the
leading Ecclesiologist. Sir Gilbert Scott is not found much in Devon,
save for major restorations in his last years, especially at Exeter
Cathedral. Local architects were prominent in the 19C. John Hayward was the principal one; he was consulting architect to the Exeter
Diocesan Architectural Society (founded 1841) and undertook many
important restorations, such as at Crediton. His pupil, Robert Medley
Fulford, was important later. G.H. Fellowes Prynne, the son of the
Anglo-Catholic incumbent of St. Peter's, Plymouth (George Rundle
Prynne), looms large into the early 20C. Finally, J.P. St. Aubyn (who
worked from Plymouth) and the Seddings (from Penzance in Cornwall) both worked in many Devon churches. 19C stained glass is
found in quantity in the larger churches, such as Ottery St. Mary,
Tawstock and in Torquay, especially in St. John's. Especially noteworthy at the turn of the century are W.D. Caroë's St. David's, Exeter
of 1897–1900, which led into the current century with two excellent
churches by Nicholson & Corlette at St. Matthew's, Chalston, Torquay and St. Paul's, Yelverton. In the 20C, mention must also be
made of Buckfast Abbey Church by F.A. Walters, 1907–32, a remarkable revival of the medieval monastery on the site, built by the monks
and lavishly furnished.

To conclude, Devon has a few churches of distinction (e.g. in towns
where wealthy merchants or munificent nobility provided the where-
withal for sumptuous additions (Cullompton—Lane aisle, Ottery St.
Mary—Dorset aisle, Tiverton—the Greenway S porch and S chapel).
These three churches each have a clerestory and yet Totnes, which in
the 16C was one of the richest towns in Devon and was well-off in the
15C when the church was built, does not have a clerestory and
Tavistock, which was a prosperous centre of the cloth trade, preferred to extend aisles with chancel chapels.

The saints of Devon's churches show a strong Cornish and Welsh
element—such as Petrock (at Dartmouth, Parracombe, etc.), Brannock (at Braunton), Nectan (at Hartland) and Urith (at Chittlehampton). Such saints tend to be 6C or nearly as early. In c 675
Crediton was the birthplace of St. Boniface (Winfrith), an international figure in the Church of his day. Among later associations of

note are the claimed baptism of Sir Francis Drake at Tavistock, his definite marriage in 1569 in St. Budeaux, Devonport, the building of Bulkworthy Church by Sir William Hankford (Chief Justice under King Henry V, whom some claim to be the judge who imprisoned the king when he was Prince of Wales), the baptism of the poet Coleridge at Ottery St. Mary, and four remarkable incumbencies— Robert Herrick at Dean Prior in the 17C, Augustus Toplady (author of 'Rock of Ages') at Harpford in the 18C, Jack Russell at Swimbridge in the mid-19C (he was the hunting parson par excellence) and Sabine Baring-Gould, novelist, hymn-writer and traveller, at Lew Trenchard, 1881–1924. Finally, Queen Victoria gave a window to St. Nicholas', Sidmouth in 1860 in memory of her father, the Duke of Kent, who had died in the town in 1820.

Braunton, *St. Brannock*. St. Brannock's is one of the oldest churches in Devon, originally built by the Celtic missionary and priest who probably came from Pembrokeshire; his body still rests in the church that bears his name. In 1225, the Deanery of Exeter took over the Rectory of Braunton and the Deans were Rectors and Lords of the Manor until 1880. The present building is almost entirely 13C with furnishings of later dates. The nave is aisleless but there are indications that aisles which once existed were removed in Perpendicular times. The nave is now impressively wide with a wagon roof 34ft across.

The most striking external feature is the short stunted tower, buttressed centrally on the S side and completed with a lead-sheathed broach spire, slightly out of true like the two neighbouring ones of Swimbridge and Barnstaple (the last more pronouncedly so). The general impression externally is plain and severe.

The interior, which has a S chancel chapel with two-bay arcade added in Perpendicular times is, on the contrary, replete with admirable furnishings, starting with a probably Norman square font with faces at the corners and later tracery. The wide wagon roof has a number of interesting bosses, the most popular being the sow and litter boss above the font (symbolic of St. Brannock). And suspended from the roof are three candelabra of Flemish workmanship with beautiful wrought-iron stars above, dating from 1833, the middle one especially fine with coats of arms. But the crowning pleasure of the nave is the splendid set of carved bench-ends. Each one is different and even the thickness and size vary. Nearly all are of one piece of timber. They are 16C, the subjects including Instruments of the Passion, shields, initials (by far the most numerous and some inverted), and figures of saints among whom (no. 3 on the N side) appears St. Brannock himself with his cow (sic) under him. No. 6 on the S side depicts an hourglass in one panel and the 30 pieces of silver in the other. There are 46 in all. Other woodwork consists of a lectern and excellent pulpit (former dated 1636), organ gallery (1619), screen (not up to the best Devon standard) with modern Rood by Herbert Read, installed in 1938, altar screen of 1563 and communion rails with balusters like threads of beads, of the early 17C.

The Lady chapel, restored after the 1914–18 War, contains a notable Portuguese dower chest and the monument with the kneeling figure of Lady Elizabeth Bourchier (died 1548), daughter of the Earl of Bath (see Tawstock). It is in the form of a small brass and is a palimpsest. Other monuments include a grand and ornamental Classical memorial to the Incledon family (father died 1736 and son died 1746). A tombstone in the churchyard bears the inscription 'Death is the common treasury at which we all pay tax'.

Chittlehampton, *St. Hieritha*. St. Hieritha (or St. Urith) was a local Celtic girl saint who was murdered with scythes in the 6C. This is a church completely dominated by its 115ft W tower. The building consists of nave with aisles, chancel with two chapels, and two transepts. The S aisle and the transepts are embattled. There was a general renewal in 1872. The main furnishing is the font and there are one or two monuments.

The church stands in a shallow valley with the village spread before it, making the tower still more commanding. It is of Somerset type with large bell openings and of four stages. It is beautifully proportioned, tapering gently upwards and battlemented with eight pinnacles on the elegant crown; there are pinnacles also on the six buttresses and much quatrefoil decoration. A *tour de force*, it is the finest tower in the county. The windows are of three and four lights and the S porch with original door has fleuron decoration in the doorway and a niche above.

The five-bay nave and the two bays in the chancel opening into the Giffard and Rolle chapels are all usual 15C Perpendicular except that, on the N side, the main shafts have concave octagonal capitals and one of the piers on the N side has an elaborate niche for an image. A small arched recess leading to a narrow chamber in the N chancel now contains a sarcophagus with inscription of 1550; the recess formerly contained the shrine of St. Hieritha with her image. Her 'portrait' may be seen in a figure in the pulpit carrying a palm to signify her martyrdom. The early 16C pulpit is of stone with tall, thin panels finely carved.

On the floor near the pulpit is a small brass to John Cobleigh with his two wives of c 1480–90. A 17C monument in the N transept commemorates John Giffard, who lies on a tomb-chest, against which two figures kneel. On the back wall are two heads in profile in medallions. A fragment of another monument is in memory of Grace Giffard (died 1667), who is in a semi-reclining position.

The importance of shrines before the Reformation is shown by the fact that as late as 1539–40 the Vicar's share of the offerings to St. Urith's shrine was three times the value of his tithes and glebe.

Crediton, *The Holy Cross*. Successively monastery, cathedral, collegiate church and then parish church, Crediton's main place of worship has seen many changes and is in fact at least the fourth church to be built on or near the site. The monastery dated from 739 when, doubtless due to the influence of St. Boniface, land was granted for its construction. Born in c 675 and named Winfrith, he grew up in Crediton and became famous for his missionary work in what are now the Netherlands and Germany; he was given the name of Boniface ('doer of good') by Pope Gregory II and later was created Archbishop of Mainz, a position from which he subsequently resigned to resume his missionary work but was murdered at Dokkum in the Netherlands in 754.

Early in the 10C, the See of Sherborne was divided and when the new See of Devon was moved to Crediton, Bishop Eadwulf obtained a charter from King Athelstan in 933 to dedicate a new building as a cathedral. It was probably completed at the end of the century, but Crediton only remained a separate See until 1050 when Bishop Leofric, Chancellor of England, succeeded in transferring it to

Exeter. This was followed in less than 100 years by the formal foundation of a college and work started on the erection of a new collegiate church, initially in Norman but later in Gothic style. By the beginning of the 15C, however, the nave was in such a poor condition that it was decided to embark upon a fourth building and this is substantially the church we see today.

At the Dissolution, the townspeople raised sufficient funds to retain the building as the parish church but no Vicar was appointed until 1580 and the Lady chapel had to be restored to its former use as a school, which then became the Free Grammar School, remaining there until 1860. The 18C brought major changes. In 1723, galleries with access staircases were erected at the W end and in the transepts whilst, in 1788, the medieval wooden roofs of the choir, nave and aisles were plastered over to provide a flat ceiling; walls and even the piers were plastered over and whitewashed, box-pews were installed and the floors lowered. In the 19C, under John Hayward, the church was largely restored in a sensitive and restrained manner to something like its former appearance; a stone pulpit was substituted for the former wooden wine-glass one and the floors of the nave and S transept were restored to their original level. Since then, the extraordinary monument to General Sir Redvers Buller has been erected by W.D. Caroë, an uninspired stone reredos was placed by G.H. Fellowes Prynne before the high altar and a permanent but removable nave altar and rails were installed in 1927. The church consists of an aisled nave and chancel with a clerestory, central tower, N and S transepts, N and S nave and choir aisles, Lady chapel, Chapter House (Governors' Room and Vestry) and SW porch, together with three notable monuments and various furnishings of interest.

Although low-lying, the colourful red sandstone cruciform church is prominent in the town. A large spreading building, 230ft long with nave, chancel and aisles all battlemented, it is a good example of Devon Perpendicular work. Except for the Lady chapel (which nevertheless has later Perpendicular windows), the Chapter House and all but the crown of the tower, it is a complete church of the early Perpendicular style with three-light clerestory windows in the nave and wider four-light ones in the chancel. There is a two-storeyed S porch. The lower stage of the tower dates from the Norman period, the belfry stage is Early English and the battlemented crown with large pinnacles is Perpendicular. The Lady chapel dates from c 1260 but was extended E c 40 years later. The Governors' Room and Vestry on the S side are slightly later with more recent windows, the Vestry having originally been a chapel.

On entering, one is immediately struck by the huge and lavish memorial to General Sir Redvers Buller, which fills the whole of the E wall above the tower arch at the end of the six-bay nave. With a frieze of Victoria Crosses at the base, panels of armorial bearings, warrior saints, etc. and a line of martial saints on either side of Christ in Glory at the top, it is indeed a flamboyant affair. The central tower obstructs the vista through to the chancel, behind which is a wall. Beyond, at a lower level, is the Lady chapel, entered from the aisles by one of a pair of screens which have taken the place of the Decorated arches to the former ambulatory, now part of the chapel. The Governors' Room is probably little altered from when it may have served as the meeting place of the collegiate clergy and contains many items of interest. The S transept has excellent corbels in the form of human heads.

The furnishings include a square Norman font bowl with an elaborate cover of 1904. Of especial note is the very fine but damaged tomb-recess in the S choir aisle and an outstanding 15C Flemish merchant's chest used as an altar in the N aisle, with a beautifully-carved centre panel of the Nativity. There are remains of sedilia of c 1415 in the SE corner of the chancel with panelling on the backs and intricate thin vaulting above two of the seats but lacking pinnacles. A rare type of double piscina with two gables was restored to the Lady chapel in 1921. Modern furnishings comprise a lectern said to have been carved from a live model of an eagle (1894), a Victorian pulpit in Mansfield stone (1887–89) and a modern statue of St. Boniface by Witold Kawalec in the nave N aisle (given in 1979). Lavers, Barraud & Westlake designed the E window (1897), whose lower panels show scenes of St. Boniface's life.

The monuments vary from the tomb-recess in the S aisle to the huge memorial of 1911 by Caroë to General Sir Redvers Buller which dominates the W wall of the nave. The earliest is that at the E end of the S choir aisle with full-length figures of probably Sir John (died 1387) and Lady Isobel Sully; reputed to have lived to the age of 105, he is in armour and she in costume of the period on a tomb-chest. On the N side of the sanctuary are two 17C monuments, one of pink marble to Sir William Perryam (died 1605), a judge at the trial of Mary, Queen of Scots, shown recumbent and leaning on his elbow with his family kneeling in relief on the chest below; the other to John and Elizabeth Tuckfield and son. Father and son died in 1630 and are shown in medallions on either side of Elizabeth, who is a seated figure with head propped up by her arm, with cheek in hand. The three parts are separated by black columns, and a broken pediment crowns this notable monument.

Cullompton, St. Andrew. This mainly red sandstone church is one of the finest in Devon. It is typical in being entirely Perpendicular (dating from 1430), in having a wagon roof running the full length of the church and in possessing a screen between nave and chancel which spans the full width including the aisles. It is especially distinguished, however, in having a clerestory (one of only ten in the county), in the richness of the decoration of roof and screen and particularly in the late-addition show pieces, the 100ft high tower and the Lane aisle.

Externally, St. Andrew's W tower with stair turret dominates not only the church but the surrounding countryside. Not added until 1545–49, it is divided into four stages by stringcourses and has set-back buttresses with many set-offs, each stage having a crocketed shaft in Beer stone terminating downwards with a grotesque. The battlements are pierced and there are numerous pinnacles in the crown which is decorated with a line of quatrefoils, all in Ham Hill stone. Above the main W window there are three large panels with figures also in Beer stone, the Crucifixion in the middle flanked by much-worn figures of St. George and of King Edward VI, framed by ornamented shafts and overhead canopies. The clock dates from 1685. On the S side are the four-light windows of the Lane aisle separated by buttresses decorated with sheep-shears, monograms and some well-detailed medieval ships. Above each window and at the ends of the aisle are John Lane's initials, seen in profusion on the inside also. Running below each window is an inscription commemorating the donor. Below the parapet there are carvings of the life of Christ. The downpipes date from 1724. On the N side are the six windows of the N aisle in Beer stone terminating in the Moorhayes chapel. The E end of the chancel was rebuilt in 1849.

One enters through the tower by the W door and is immediately struck by the splendid roof and screen. The former—on angel brackets—is divided into four main bays by four-centred arched braces, enriched with quatrefoil decoration and a pendant boss at the apex of the roof. These main bays are subdivided by secondary ribs and purlins into 24 bays and 144 panels, each panel retaining its original blue and red colouring, having cross-ribs normally only found above celures or canopies of honour above a Rood. The highly-coloured screen of 11 bays, with tracery closely resembling that of the windows, is coved on the E and W sides. The fan tracery of the coving with ornamental bosses supports a finely-carved cornice of three orders, each of which is stepped proud of the one below. Above this the Rood beam survives. This once supported the Rood, of which a rare survival at the W end of the Lane aisle is the wooden carved Golgotha in the form of rocks with skulls and bosses; this formed the base of the Rood above the central door of the screen.

The arcades are of six bays with late medieval piers of Beer stone which have half-shafts at the angles and capitals decorated with foliage, heads and figures. The E bay beyond the screen forms the chancel (as usual in Devon, there is no chancel arch). The sanctuary extends slightly E of the aisles. Looking back towards the W door, one sees the oaken Jacobean gallery, one of the longest in Devon, supported on five fluted columns with Ionic capitals and, like the screen, stretching across nave and aisles. The E bay of the N aisle with windows of Beer stone forms the Moores chantry or Moorehayes chapel; this is separated from the chancel by a parclose screen with square-headed bays and surmounted by a double-sided cresting of seven feathered angels supporting the armorial shields depicting various marriages of the More family. There is a similar parclose screen on the S side.

This brings us to the Lane aisle, dating from 1526, one of the last chantry chapels to be built before the Reformation. John Lane was a wealthy wool merchant and was doubtless influenced in building it by the slightly earlier Dorset aisle at Ottery St. Mary (1520) and the Greenway aisle of 1517 at Tiverton. It was built by taking down the walls of the old S aisle except the E bay and creating two aisles with new piers which have structurally unnecessary buttresses facing the Lane aisle decorated with small figures of saints. Its great glory lies in the fan-vaulted roof, possibly inspired by the Dorset and Greenway aisles, with pendants decorated with emblems of the Passion and, as on the external buttresses, sheep-shears and John Lane's mark; it consists of four full fans and two half-fans on either side with a straight rib running the full length of the roof.

The furnishings are of limited interest for there is no old stained glass and the murals uncovered in 1849 have been covered up again, whilst the reredos of Caen stone in the chancel and the two-manual organ are 19C. There are, however, box-pews and a squire's pew in the Moorehayes chapel and a window (second from E in the Lane aisle) made by Morris & Co. depicting Samuel, Enoch, John the Baptist and Timothy. The royal arms above the Rood beam are those of Queen Victoria.

The only memorials are John Lane's tombstone (which has lost its brass effigy) on the floor at the E end of the Lane aisle and various tomb-slabs on the chancel floor together with a slab with foliated cross in the S porch.

Dartmouth, *St. Saviour.* Dartmouth was long important as a port and had a leading interest in the wine trade with Bordeaux from the 12C to the 15C. Being far from St. Clement's, the town church, King Edward I gave leave in 1286 for a chapel to be built on the shore. This chapel, now the church of St. Saviour, was dedicated on 13th October 1372. It is probable that the work of c 1372 was added to some existing fabric, and such earlier fabric seems to survive at the W end and perhaps in the transepts too. The church of 1372 was then remodelled in the late Middle Ages and in the 17C.

At the Dissolution, the control which Torre Abbey had over St. Saviour's ceased; the Corporation took over in 1586 and this continued until 1835. The town renewed the chancel in 1614–16 and further improvements were carried out in the 1630s by successive mayors whose arms appear on the front of the 1633 W gallery. In the 17C, special seats were carved for the mayor and his wife but the present Corporation seats date from c 1815. There was a major restoration in 1891–93 when the chancel lost its 17C furnishings. Nevertheless there are many fittings of interest, especially the S door, the Rood screen, the pulpit and the W gallery. And the brass to John Hawley and his two wives is of particular interest in a county notably devoid of brasses.

The church is especially attractive when viewed from the NE. The W tower is unbuttressed but is embraced by the aisles. The tracery of the large windows is post-Reformation, mainly 17C, with the E window dating from 1890. The S porch is embattled, leading to the notable S door. Despite carrying the date 1631, its remarkable ironwork, depicting two leopards guarding the Tree of Life, dates from the late Middle Ages and was probably renewed in 1631. The arcades are irregular; the three E bays are Perpendicular, with fleurons round the arches, but those to the W are earlier. These W

The Rood screen and painted pulpit of St. Saviour's, a richly furnished town church

arches, and also the N and S transepts may even date from the 13C. The W gallery spans the nave and aisles E of the tower, thus separating the first bays of the N and S aisles. There is a Lady chapel.

Of the internal furnishings, the Rood screen with simpler tracery than usual is nevertheless impressive with excellent coving and exceptionally well-carved friezes in the cornice. The parclose screens have unusually good cornices. The 15C stone pulpit is lavishly decorated with panels no wider than the encrusted uprights and a frieze of very large leaves, all supported on a slender stem; it is richly coloured. The W gallery is approached by a fine early 18C staircase and in it are kept the former large reredos with the Commandments and, above, a huge painting; the old fire engine is also housed by the staircase in the SW corner. Other furnishings include an altar table of 1588 with legs carved and painted with figures of the Evangelists, combined sedilia and piscina with crocketed ogee tops, and brass candelabra of 1708 in the nave.

The brass to John Hawley (died 1408) and his two wives in the chancel floor shows him in armour. He was three times Mayor of Dartmouth and gave much money for the building of the church. The three figures lie below ogee canopies.

Exeter. St. Mary Arches is the most normal of the medieval parish churches in its plan and, internally, is of interest in having arcades of four Norman bays on each side (unique in Devon). The SW tower of St. Mary Steps, approached by a steep and quaint lane of medieval steps, opens directly into the church through two arches. The small tower-hall of St. Olave's gives access to the chancel and, despite its diminutive size, has the pulpit compressed into it. It has two aisles on the N side. St. Pancras', said to be the earliest church, consists of nave and chancel only. St. Petrock's has the strangest plan of all, the present chancel being at right angles to the older part of the church. St. Stephen's has an appealing raised E chapel on an arch under which a narrow street runs. An internal 13C arch leads into this chapel from the church.

St. Martin's is richest in furnishings, although not of high quality—reredos of c 1700, 17C communion rail and W gallery. St. Mary Arches also has a 17C communion rail. St. Mary Steps has a Norman font and a screen but its most striking feature is the early 17C clock outside, called Matthew the Miller and his sons. The three figures are placed under an ogee-headed niche, one seated and the others standing, and the dial has the seasons in the four spandrels. St. Pancras' has the simplest type of Norman font and a pulpit of c 1600 with caryatids.

The noteworthy monuments are to Thomas Andrew, twice Mayor of Exeter (died 1518), and Thomas Walker (died 1628) and his wife, at St. Mary Arches. The former is a recumbent figure on a tomb-chest and the latter are life-size kneeling figures facing each other. St. Petrock's has a late 17C monument to William Hooper (died 1683) with two busts in round-headed niches.

W.D. Caroë's St. David's of 1897–1900 is one of his best works. The outstanding feature is the NE tower with clustered buttresses. The W front has two turrets with spirelets and the interior has a wide nave with a wooden tunnel-vault and tall narrow aisles.

Harberton, *St. Andrew.* A mile or two SW of Totnes, this dignified, largely Perpendicular church is typical of the county, embattled on both sides, long, without a clerestory and having a fine screen and wagon roofs. Externally, the church shows the normal Devon L-shape and is at the top of the hill which climbs up through the cottages of the small village. The W tower is 78ft high, with very tall corner pinnacles. The two-storey S porch is 14C (note the ogee sundial above and the ogee stoup to the left).

Internally, this is a six-bay church with large aisles on both sides; the *pièce de résistance* is the very impressive screen. Its wainscot was repainted in 1871 with appealing new designs (some of the old paintings can be seen in the N aisle). The screen stretches across nave and aisles, and is highly coloured in red and gold. There are parclose screens between the aisles and the chancel. The screen is supplemented by a notable 15C stone pulpit with 17C figures in its niches. The circular font in the SW corner is Norman. The arms of Queen Anne are placed over the S door. The 19C reredos of alabaster and mosaic depicts Christ enthroned in the centre, flanked by the four beasts of Revelation. Finally, the 14C sedilia are carved in a typically Decorated style.

In a recess in the N wall there is an interesting effigy in alabaster of a boy known as 'Tito', who died in 1895.

Hartland, *Stoke, St. Nectan.* Situated in a lonely upland spot away from the town, the church is near some of the finest coastal scenery in England. It is one of Devon's most notable places of worship, aisled, with N and S porches and a tower with tall, thin pinnacles which is one of the highest in the county. Without a clerestory but with a Lady chapel, St. Nectan's is more impressive within than without, possessing one of the best-preserved screens, spanning the whole width of nave and aisles, an unusually tall tower arch and a Norman font of interesting design and symbolism. There is a roundel of 14C glass and two others of similar style in the Lady chapel but otherwise, with one exception, the glass dates from 1848. An excellent tomb-chest made of Catacleuse stone survives.

The exterior, dominated by the W tower, reflects the isolation of the site. It is of four stages in late Perpendicular style and, with its tall thin pinnacles, reaches a height of 128ft. In the E wall is a large statue which is original, except it is believed for its head, of St. Nectan, one of 24 children born to the wife of a Welsh prince named Brecannus after he had returned home after 24 years in Ireland; Nectan set forth in a boat which took him to Devon, arrived there in c 550 and became a hermit until he was murdered by robbers. The church is embattled on both N and S sides, is 137ft long and has transepts and a chancel which extends E of the aisles. The N and S porches, which date from the same period as the aisles, retain their original roofs and the S doorway has two orders of moulding with the hollow between decorated with small carved rose bosses. The N porch retains its original outer doorway.

The interior is tall and spacious with a wide-arched four-bay nave, the piers of which are made of buff limestone and the arches with what may be Catacleuse stone, blue in colour. This was before granite came into general use for this purpose, St. Nectan's being built c 1360. The 15C screen is one of the finest in N Devon, 45ft long, 16ft tall and 6ft wide at the top, with four bands of decoration in the coving, and iron cresting; there is also decoration between the ribs, not usually seen. It has never been restored. The parclose screens date from 1848. The wagon roofs are another source of pleasure; they are varied, with some ceiled, others unceiled and the part of the nave adjoining the chancel ceiled and painted with large stars in the panels. Perhaps the finest roof is that of the Lady chapel (N of the chancel) with its 14C work and which has most of the original bosses and each panel of a different design. The S transept has boarded panels with carved bosses. Colouring, once rich but now faded, still remains.

Of the furnishings, the font dated c 1170 is the main feature. The bowl and case are joined by a stem with cable moulding separated by zigzag said to represent the Lake of Gennesaret. Carved heads at the corners of the bowl and base represent the baptised or saved looking down on the unbaptised or damned, from whom they are separated by the waters of the lake. The altar reredos was erected as a war memorial in 1931 and is carved with figures of saints. They represent the patrons of ten chapels in the parish of Hartland. The E window by Christopher Webb, 1950, depicts Christ in Glory. The Pope's Chamber entered from the N porch houses preserved panels of a Jacobean pulpit. Seats in use in the chancel aisle were provided by Hugh Prust in c 1540 at his own expense for the St. Mary Guild in the N chancel aisle; they were transferred to their present position in the mid-17C.

The oldest monument is in the chancel, an excellent altar tomb which was brought from Hartland Abbey in 1848. Of late 14C date, it is made of Catacleuse stone. It served as an altar and communion table until 1931. Also in the chancel is the original altar stone (with five incised consecration crosses) which was found buried under the base of the old churchyard cross. A brass in the chancel commemorates Ann Abbot (died 1610), a small kneeling figure with inscription.

Kenton, *All Saints*. The church lies in lush country near the River Exe and is a red sandstone building but with Beer stone used for decorative work. The church seems wholly Perpendicular, with a 120ft high W tower, aisled nave, projecting sanctuary and a battlemented, two-storeyed S porch. The tower has set-back buttresses, battlements, pinnacles and transomed three-light belfry windows. The aisles are also embattled; on the S side there is a turret for the Rood stairs, with a sundial outside. The charming red sandstone exterior is richly embellished with image niches, fleurons and gargoyles.

The interior is 140ft long and has seven-bay arcades of local Perpendicular type. Furnishings consist chiefly of screen, pulpit and a door made up of bench-ends leading into the Lady chapel in the NE corner. 19C additions include stained glass in the six-light E window by Clayton & Bell (showing Passion scenes) and a large sculpture of 1868 in the chancel of 'The Raising of the Widow's Son'. The screen is a notable one, with original painted panels of 1455 on the wainscoting. There are 40 figures of saints and prophets. The upper parts are much restored. The silver cross upon the screen, by Henry Wilson, 1923, was once placed on the high altar of Exeter Cathedral. The 15C pulpit has tall, thin painted panels. It was put together by Sabine Baring-Gould (see Lew Trenchard), who found it in pieces in 1888 in a schoolroom cupboard. It was restored in 1890 with the help of a drawing Baring-Gould had made in the 1850s, before its removal. The eight paintings, all of saints with local links, are modern. The folding reredos dates from 1893 and was made by

Sebastian Zwinke of Oberammergau. The Crucifixion is shown in the centre, Christ appearing to St. Mary Magdalene to the left, and the Supper at Emmaus to the right. The font is a usual 15C type, with quatrefoils on its octagonal bowl. The word 'Free' is written in quatrefoil panels at the ends of some benches, reminding us of the former distinction between free and rented seats.

The memorials include one to Dulcebella Hodges (died 1628), showing a seated figure, and another to the Reverend John Swete, the diarist (died 1821), by J. Kendall of Exeter.

Lew Trenchard, *St. Peter.* St. Peter's reflects the character of an eccentric and self-willed man of great energy, Sabine Baring-Gould (1834–1924), who went his own way despite criticism. He was a member of the Gould family who had made their home at Lew Trenchard for 400 years.

After becoming squire and Rector of Lew Trenchard, he embarked upon a plan to restore the early 16C church, using his encyclopaedic knowledge to collect whatever he thought would beautify his beloved St. Peter's. Acquiring furnishings from various Continental sources, he removed the unsightly mustard yellow deal pews installed by his uncle and made his greatest contribution by reconstructing the screen shamelessly destroyed by his grandfather over 50 years earlier. He did this with the aid of bits and pieces he had found in different places many years before and which he had stored away for future use; he was also helped by a painting made before the screen was taken down. Work began on the reconstruction in 1889 and was completed in 1915. Clergy stalls were reconstructed from old woodwork and nine of the bench-ends (the ones that Sabine saved in his youth) are old, but the Rood screen, even though some may say that it is over-large for the church, was Sabine's greatest achievement.

Although architecturally St. Peter's is not outstanding, it bears the imprint of an extraordinary man who was his own arbiter of taste. On his tombstone in the churchyard are the words which translate as 'I have prepared a lantern for my Christ'. Among his manifold interests, he was a hymn-writer and will long be remembered for 'Onward Christian Soldiers'.

(Bickford H.C. Dickinson, 'Sabine Baring-Gould' (1970).)

Ottery St. Mary, *St. Mary the Virgin.* The church occupies an inconspicuous position in the town and does not dominate like Cullompton, but it is one of Devon's major churches, built over three main periods and witnessing to the influence of Bishop Grandisson, who took over the manor and parish from Rouen Cathedral in 1335 and proceeded to make St. Mary of Ottery collegiate.

The origin of worship on this site is uncertain and the earliest record is the consecration of the 'Ecclesie de Otery Sce. Marie' on 4th December 1259. It would seem that the transepts and perhaps the outer walls of the chancel aisles belong to that date. The famous transeptal towers, however, copied from those of Exeter Cathedral, were the creation of Bishop Grandisson, who unroofed the original transepts to raise them to the towers that we see now. It is largely to him that we owe the stature of the present building. He obtained a Royal Licence from King Edward III to make the church collegiate, consisting of 40 members. Considerable alterations were made to the fabric in the Decorated style in vogue at the time, which, with its liturgical arrangements, was closely modelled upon those at Exeter Cathedral. The work was completed c 1342, whereupon the church entered upon its 200-year heyday. During this period the Dorset aisle and the two-storeyed S porch were added. The Dissolution and the Puritans wrought great havoc and it was not until William Butterfield took over restoration in 1849 that the church recovered some of its glory.

St. Mary's consists of an aisled five-bay nave and six-bay chancel, one of which is behind the reredos where the ambulatory runs. The Lady chapel is to the E with a stone screen (restored by Henry Woodyer in 1842) and a minstrels' gallery above the entrance. On either side of this are the small chapels of St. Stephen (S) and St. Lawrence (N). The sumptuous fan-vaulted Dorset aisle, entered from the N transept, was added in 1520. There are many furnishings and monuments of interest in the church. St. Mary's, built of low-toned red, buff and grey sandstone, drapes itself over a hill in the Otter Valley, and, although the transeptal towers (the N with a small lead-sheathed spire) are a focal point of interest and there is a clerestory, the exterior has a muddled appearance. The W end is unco-ordinated and the eight cusped lights of the Lady chapel at the E end lack any noteworthy tracery, whilst the whiteness of the lead roofs is almost shrill, reflecting far too much light.

It is the interior which impresses, although again it lacks cohesion. The influence of Bishop Grandisson is everywhere apparent—all the central bosses in the aisles carry his arms and these alternate throughout the entire length of the main vaulting of the church; a boss showing him in full pontifical vestments is in the ceiling at the centre of the crossing. For a parish church to possess a Lady chapel, it can only have been a man of the Bishop's influence and munificence who could have provided it. Many of his kinsmen appear on bosses in addition to the monument to Sir Otho de Grandisson (see below). The most interesting features of Grandisson's work are the vaults and the furnishings. The vaults show a variety not normally found in a parish church, those in the chancel using curvilinear forms to create a notable reticulated pattern but serving no structural purpose. In contrast, most of the other vaults are rectilinear in design. The bosses of the Lady chapel are worth close inspection. The nave is of five bays, the main arches being in early Perpendicular style. The highlight of the interior is the Dorset aisle which, unlike the Lane aisle at Cullompton, is on the N and not the S side. It is so named after the wife of King Henry VII's brother-in-law, Cicely, Marchioness of Dorset, who was a direct descendant of Bishop Grandisson's sister, the Countess of Salisbury, and it was due to her munificence that the aisle was built c 1520, with its rich heraldic decoration and fan-vaulting. As at Cullompton, it creates a double aisle. The vaulting has five large pendants of open tracery but these are not the equal of those in the Lane aisle at Cullompton. At the W end there is a colourful window of six lights divided into two tiers depicting the Apostles with their emblems, by William Wailes and dating from the mid-19C. Lovable features are two corbels of the nave aisle arcade capitals—one at the W end, in the form of two owls, is the rebus of Hugh Oldham, Bishop of Exeter and the other, a most engaging elephant's head. The church was thoroughly restored by William Butterfield in 1849–50 when he lowered the ground-level of the transepts, the W bays of the chancel and crossing to that of the nave.

The furnishings include the mid-14C reredos which was cruelly defaced at the Reformation and was restored by Edward Blore in

1829–33. He provided the ornamental niches and hoods but it was not until 100 years later that the three panels and 23 niches were filled with scenes and figures (the panels depicting the Crucifixion and, on either side, the Annunciation and the Nativity). The gabled sedilia are of the same date (14C) as are the misericords in the Lady chapel and chancel. There are also sedilia in the Lady chapel. The Rood screen was removed in the 16C and the present parclose screens, although dating from c 1350 and among the earliest preserved in Devon, are not in their correct position. The most notable furnishing is the gilded wooden eagle lectern in the Lady chapel; it stands on a globe decorated with the arms of Bishop Grandisson who presented it, and it is therefore one of the earliest in England. Also of this time is the famous astronomical clock above the gallery on the W wall of the S transept; it is still operated by what is largely its original mechanism. Some of the original encaustic tiles remain in the ambulatory, the best showing a knight on horseback. There is no medieval glass but plenty of Victorian glass by Warrington, Hardman and O'Connor. The elaborate font of inlaid multi-coloured marble (which came from Devon and Cornwall) in the nave opposite the S porch dates from 1850 (the gift of Alexander Beresford Hope) and is decorated with a chequer-board pattern on the sides of the bowl and has a cover with finial and, at the sides, pyramid-capped turrets. The pulpit dates from 1722 and has well-carved small figures of the Evangelists.

The monuments consist of two richly canopied tombs opposite each other under the nave arcades to Sir Otho de Grandisson (died 1359), the bishop's younger brother, who is shown in full armour, and his wife, Beatrix (died 1374); they are outstanding examples of monuments of the Decorated period. Between chancel and aisle there is an Elizabethan tomb-chest with quatrefoil panels to John Haydon (died 1587), without effigy, built upon the Purbeck marble slab of the former Easter sepulchre. Other memorials are to John Coke (died 1632) at the E end of the Dorset aisle, a life-size standing figure in armour; also a Jacobean monument on the S wall of St. Lawrence's chapel at the E end of the N choir aisle to Humphrey Walrond who was buried here in 1637; to William Peere Williams by John Bacon, Jr, dating from 1794 in the N transept and to Jane Fortescue, Baroness Coleridge, in white marble and shown recumbent with two angels at her head and an otter at her feet, dating from 1879 (by Frederick Thrupp), in a recess in the S transept. Rare (for Devon) brasses, to members of the Sherman family, are to be seen at the E end of the S aisle, two of which are dated 1542 and 1583.

Samuel Taylor Coleridge, the poet, was baptised here in 1772.

Parracombe, St. Petrock. Owing to the fortunate circumstance of a new church being built in a more convenient location in 1878, the Victorians left the old building alone and St. Petrock's has come down to us as an unspoilt example of a small, unassuming Georgian village church.

Situated away from the village in a narrow valley within the W boundary of Exmoor National Park, St. Petrock's has a squat early medieval NW tower with battlements, tiny corner pinnacles and round-headed belfry windows, a 13C chancel, and a late medieval nave and S aisle with square-headed windows and an internal arcade of depressed Perpendicular arches. There are also a S porch and a N vestry, and the roofs are of the usual wagon-type.

St. Petrock's, left in its Georgian state when a Victorian church was built nearer the village

The font, which may be Norman, is the earliest furnishing: it has a small, plain, circular bowl. It was brought here from Martinhoe. The screen separating nave and chancel is of an early type and has ten narrow lights, each with a cusped ogee arch; it has a straight top, above which is a solid tympanum repainted in 1758 with Commandments, Creed and Lord's Prayer, and with the royal arms centrally placed above. The pulpit is a three-decker, panelled and with a sounding-board. The pews, which may be 16C, are plain but at the W end, 18C box-pews, where the band of musicians sat, are raked as in a theatre. One pew has a piece cut out to allow room for the bow of a bass viol. The altar has rails on three sides.

St. Petrock's, whose dedication derives from a Cornish saint who died on 4th June 564, was declared redundant in 1969 and is now happily vested in the Redundant Churches Fund.

Swimbridge, *St. James the Apostle.* Until comparatively recent times, St. James's was only a chapelry but it now serves one of the largest parishes in N Devon. The church consists of nave, N and S aisles, N transept, chancel, N and S chancel chapels, vestry, S porch and W tower with lead-sheathed spire. Only the steeple survives from the building which preceded the present one. The nave is thought to have been started in c 1460, and the rest to have followed mainly in the 15C and 16C. It is, therefore, like so many Devon churches, a basically Perpendicular building but of modest size. The steeple is c 90ft high and the church is 71ft long. There was a thorough restoration in 1880.

The church lies in a broad valley in the middle of the attractive village. Its dominant feature is its lead-sheathed spire which was re-leaded in 1897 as a Diamond Jubilee memorial, although a leaden plate (now fixed to the wall of the choir vestry) discovered at the time bears the date 1674, demonstrating its weathering properties.

Barnstaple and Braunton have the only other lead-sheathed spires in Devon.

The nave arcade is of three bays to the screen with piers and capitals of local Perpendicular type; the chancel has more elaborate capitals. There is a noteworthy head-corbel on the arch between the N aisle and N chancel chapel. But the main pleasures of the fabric reside in the wagon roofs. The nave roof has bosses and, before the 1880 restoration, was ceiled; a celure with cross-ribs survives above the screen. The screen itself is one of the most splendid in Devon—high praise in such a county. Spanning nave and aisles, it is 44ft long and over 10ft high, with notable carving on the W side. The coving is intact. Openings remain in the upper portion; the N one is original and probably marks the site of a former altar of St. Katherine, but the other seems to date from 1880. It is surmounted by a modern Rood. The font is chiefly noteworthy for its extraordinary covering of c 1540, which gives it the appearance of a pulpit at first sight. The lead bowl is encased in an octagonal oak base, which is surmounted by a cupboard with a folding door and then by a more elaborate upper part ending in an open crown. Still higher there is a tester, whose support has carved panels resembling those of the folding door. The details are mixed Gothic and Renaissance. The stone pulpit of c 1490 has tall, thin panels with figures of St. Peter and St. Paul, and the Latin Doctors less St. Gregory. Early colouring remains. The altar rails are of the Restoration period.

The memorials include one to a lawyer, John Rosier (died 1685), whose long inscription speaks of his hopes of salvation in allusion to his profession. Another memorial, to Charles Cutliffe (died 1670), features an oval portrait painted in oils on copper.

Swimbridge will always be associated with Parson Jack Russell, the stalwart hunting Vicar who, when he came to the parish in 1833, found that there were already 20 parsons in the Exeter diocese who kept their own packs of hounds. He is best known for breeding the strain of fox-terriers which bears his name. His hunting brought him into contact with the Prince of Wales who invited him to Sandringham, where he preached. Russell remained as Vicar of Swimbridge for 46 years until 1879. The E window of the S aisle commemorates him.

Tavistock, St. Eustachius. Throughout the medieval era, this church came under the neighbouring Abbey of St. Rumon which entrusted clerical duties to a poorly paid vicar. Of the church dedicated in 1318, when both abbey and church were reconstructed by Abbot Robert Champeaux, only the lower part of the walls and tower remain, plus a recess in the N aisle. Most of the building dates from an enlargement and rebuilding between 1425 and 1450 (when Tavistock was a flourishing centre of the cloth trade) and is therefore Perpendicular in style. The unusual second nave aisle, known as the 'Clothworkers' aisle', added in 1445 and given by the widow of a wool merchant, underlines whence the money came.

The W tower, aisled chancel and nave with simple four-light windows, Lady chapel, St. George's chapel, Clothworkers' aisle and S porch make up the plan of the church. Faced with the local sea-green volcanic Hurdwick stone, the external appearance must have altered little since it was built, but inside there have probably been many changes. Apart from the granite piers of St. George's chapel, the interior is built of Roborough elvan. Entrance is through the tower porch at the W end but there are also large openings on the N and S sides which may have been used for processional purposes since the S arch led directly to the abbey. The chancel does not extend beyond the chancel aisles so that the three equal-height gable effect of SW England is created. At Tavistock, the three windows all have five lights. The arcades are tall and slender with clustered piers and four-centred arches, creating a wide spatial effect. The wagon roof of the chancel is lower than that of the nave.

The 15C font in the SW corner is octagonal, with shields in quatrefoils. Although there is no documentary proof, it is believed that Sir Francis Drake was baptised in it. Other furnishings, except for a beautiful Elizabethan altar table in St. George's chapel and two chests in the tower porch, are modern; particularly noteworthy amongst these are the oak bench-ends of the choir, copied from ancient work, and also the 1876 William Morris window at the E end of the N aisle.

There are two tombs—one of modest achievement to John Fytz (died 1590) and his wife and son (died 1605). It comprises a tomb-chest with two effigies, whose canopy is supported at the front on five columns, one in the centre and pairs at the corners. Above the canopy is a display of heraldry. The son, who killed three people before running himself through with his own sword, kneels behind the couple in profile against the back wall. The other tomb is to Sir John Glanville (died 1600) and his wife. He lies on his side in his robes, resting on his left elbow, with his hand resting on a skull on a tomb-chest. His wife kneels in front on the floor and faces the altar. This is an excellent tomb and the portraits are fine. Sir John was a Justice of the Common Pleas. Small effigies of five of their seven children, unfortunately mostly headless, kneel behind their mother.

Tawstock, *St. Peter.* Lying snugly in a hollow and once under the shadow of a great house, St. Peter's is a rare example in Devon of a mainly 14C church built in the Decorated style. It is also unusual in possessing a central tower.

The plan is of a three-bay nave with N and S aisles, crossing tower, transepts, chancel with S aisle and vestry. In c 1480, the nave aisles were raised to admit more light. At the same time, the W window was shortened to give extra height to the door, on the architraves of which are carved label stops in the form of two pigs' faces. The S chancel aisle and the vestry were added later; these, plus the tower bell openings, are the only Perpendicular additions. St. Peter's has one of the most complete set of monuments in the county and several furnishings of interest.

The picturesque site and the influence of the families who once lived in Tawstock Court overlooking the church create a place of visual attraction and social interest. With its pinnacles the central tower is 76½ft high and has four stages with twin lights in the belfry stage. Outside on the N side, old steps lead to the belfry door. The aisles break the cruciform plan but the overall design is compact and harmonious. The builders were favoured in having Ham Hill stone with which to construct the church. The porch, added in the 17C, has a fine ceiling with attractively carved bosses. Above the porch is an unusual sundial made in 1757 by John Berry which shows the time in places across the world, including Port Royal in the West Indies, with which nearby Barnstaple traded.

Although many say that the font is all that remains of the earlier church, probably built soon after the Norman Conquest, there is reason to believe that the square piers of the nave, chancel and crossing arches are also Norman and that the pointed arches and moulded sub-arches on ornamented corbels were later Decorated alterations. The predominant style reflects the forms in use between 1340 (or possibly earlier) and 1348, from which time the bulk of the fabric dates. There are good wagon roofs in the nave, chancel and chancel aisle; these are unceiled but the transept roofs are ceiled, that on the S side (once a chantry chapel) being attractively decorated. The N transept has a wooden gallery with some of the finest carving in the church; this may have come from Tawstock Court after the 1787 fire. The inside of the tower changes from square to octagonal and then back to a smaller square.

The Norman font has a square bowl with a single thick supporting stem; the crocketed cover was probably added c 1400 and has a good wrought-iron bracket above for supporting the pulleys. The Victorian pulpit was probably installed in 1867; it has the interesting feature of an hourglass held up by a wrought-iron arm. The reredos is also Victorian, made of Beer stone and dating from 1888. The bench-ends at the crossing are of older date, one bearing the arms of King Henry VIII and another, opposite, a 'hinky-punk': according to legend, hinky-punks were the original inhabitants of Dartmoor and had only one arm and leg. Looking like a four-poster bed with a canopy, an intricately carved 16C structure which was probably a private pew used by the third Earl of Bath, lies alongside the N transept door. The Rood screen and parclose screen are mid-16C, given by the second Earl of Bath; the parclose screen has some Renaissance carving in its doorway.

The monuments are numerous. The most appealing is a wooden effigy of a lady in a recess in the N chancel wall, recumbent with her hands folded on her breast and wearing a wimple and mantle. There is doubt about her identity: she may have been a 14C Martyn whose family held Tawstock, or Thomasin Hankford whose marriage to Sir William Bourchier brought Tawstock to his family. Thomasin died in 1461 when she was scarcely 30 years of age. On the NE wall of the chancel aisle, an arresting monument in the form of a six-poster with recumbent effigy commemorates Frances, Lady Fitzwarren (died 1586), a woman of strong character. She was the widow of the heir to the second Earl of Bath.

On the NE wall of the N transept there is a large monument to Sir John Wrey (died 1597) and Blanche Killigrew his wife, brought here in 1924. (The Wreys inherited from the Bourchiers only in 1680). The monument is rather clumsily Classical, with an enormous wall plate rising behind a tomb-chest. The wall plate features two small kneeling figures, much heraldry and some elaborate surrounds. On the tomb-chest lies a chained copy of Jewel's 'Apologie', a standard 16C Anglican text. Above the wooden effigy on the N side of the chancel there is a canopied monument to the kneeling figure of Maria St. John (died 1631). Beyond the altar railing and at the E end of the chancel aisle are the two most sumptuous monuments—to the third and fifth Earls of Bath (the third Earl succeeded in 1561 and died in 1623, and the fifth died in 1654). The third Earl's tomb is a magnificent monument of alabaster. The Earl and his wife lie on a sarcophagus, at the ends of which their children kneel. Two decorated square pillars frame the back plate and support a cornice which has a semicircular central section. The monument to the fifth Earl is quite different and unusual, being in the form of a white and black marble sarcophagus supported by four griffins; four obelisks at the corners have coronets around them, resembling quoits. To the right of the altar stands Lady Rachel Fane, the widow of the fifth Earl (died 1680), a statue in white marble on a tall pedestal, given by the clergy of the Diocese of Bath and Wells. She was the outstanding figure of the family, caring devotedly for clergy expelled from their livings during both the Commonwealth and Restoration periods. The figure is not a likeness of Lady Rachel herself because the sculptor—to save himself trouble—copied a model of a statue of a Countess of Shrewsbury, completed by his father in 1672. The Bourchier Earldom of Bath finally died with her.

The memorial to Ann Chilcot (died 1758), wife of an organist of Bath in the N transept, is notable: an attractive tablet on the S wall with portraits of her and her husband in profile. She was a Wrey from Tawstock.

Tiverton, *St. Peter.* The church stands high above the River Exe and the tall, slender 99ft high W tower and chancel display the red sandstone typical of the area, although the N and S aisles are built of a grey stone (limestone on the S side). St. Peter's, which in medieval times was collegiate, is a monument to merchant wealth and particularly to John Greenway, the richest merchant in town who—in 1517—contributed the opulent S porch and S chapel making no bones as to who paid for them as, above the inner doorway of the porch, there is a representation of the Assumption with the kneeling donor and his wife, and marked I.G. The N aisle was rebuilt in 1856 when a very drastic restoration was carried out. The interior is spacious with slim piers to the arcades. Furnishings and monuments are not especially noteworthy.

The exterior, particularly on the S side, is very showy. The tall tower has eight pinnacles and the red sandstone of the two extremities (tower and chancel)—the oldest parts—contrast with the grey stone of the aisles. The tower is fairly simple in design but with a most attractive clock. The Greenway S porch and chapel are covered with rich decoration containing niches and figures even on the battlements but unfortunately much patched and decayed. Above the windows of the chapel is a frieze of ships which appear also on the buttresses showing the source of the wealth which built them. A Norman doorway is built into the N aisle.

The interior is much restored and less spectacular than the exterior but is spacious, with aisles both to the six-bay nave and the two-bay chancel; both chancel and tall tower arches are panelled whilst each pier has a niche (now without a figure). The attractively vaulted Greenway chapel with pendants is separated from the S aisle by a low stone screen and is also accessible from the S porch by a 16C door; the chapel was restored in 1829 and again in 1952. Furnishings consist of a mayor's pew with plaster figures of a lion and unicorn of 1615, a rebuilt Christian and Bernard Schmidt organ installed in 1696 with attractive upper part, a candelabrum of 1707 and two paintings. The old screen went to Holcombe Rogus where it is now the chancel screen. The stained glass includes E and W windows by William Wailes (both 1856).

Two large brass figures are all that remain of the Greenway monument in the S chapel. There are tomb-chests to John Waldron (died 1579) and to George Slee (died 1613) on either side of the sanctuary, the former Gothic and the latter Jacobean in style, and a few further 17C and 18C memorials.

Torquay, *All Saints, Babbacombe,* **and** *St. John, Montpellier Road.*
The Victorian age in Devon is represented at Torquay by two leading
architects, William Butterfield and G.E. Street.

All Saints', Babbacombe was built by Butterfield in 1865–74. The
plan is of a W tower, a five-bay nave with narrow aisles, a chancel
with N and S chapels and a S porch. S of the chancel is the Lady
chapel; N of it stands the organ. The grey exterior with buff dressings
is more conventional than the interior, well-designed and attractively
decorated. The well-proportioned W tower is reinforced with clustered buttresses and a spire with tall, thin pairs of gabled lights. The
tower has capped octagons at the corners. The tiny clerestory
windows have attractive wavy gables whilst the S porch has a
pagoda roof with Butterfield's typical patterned tiles.

The interior is a powerful essay. The broad nave has arcades borne
on short columns of polished marble with circular moulded capitals.
The surface decoration above the arches is a mixture of diaper
patterns and incised tiles. Coloured marbles, polished alabaster (in
the sanctuary) and coloured brick banding all attract the eye. A very
clear case of mid-19C 'structural polychromy'. The red marble came
from Petit Tor near Babbacombe, the white from Sicily, and the black
from Belgium. At the E end, a disproportionately large double-arch
opens into the aisle from the chancel with over-size plate tracery.

The pulpit is an unprepossessing furnishing with arches masked
by a wide band and standing on several colonettes with staircase also
supported on colonettes, which are coupled. The colonettes have
annulets and moulded bases. The mosaic work of the reredos is by
Salviati of Venice. Butterfield designed the lectern. There are beautiful brass gates into the chancel and seven sanctuary lamps hang
before the altar.

Street's **St. John's** (1861–71) is a very prominent church in Torquay, its SW saddleback tower, added by A.E. Street in 1884–85,
being clearly visible from the harbour. The S nave aisle is plain, but
the clerestory with varying-height lancets under arches is better.

Inside, the church is spacious and has coloured marbles like
Babbacombe. Street's usual wrought-iron and brass fittings abound.
There is stained glass by Morris & Co. (to designs by Burne-Jones)
and by Clayton & Bell. The font is an immersion font, an unusual
fitting. The Lady chapel was decorated by J.D. Sedding in 1890; he
also designed the statues over the S door.

This parish was a significant early centre of the Anglo-Catholic
movement in Devon.

Widecombe-in-the-Moor, *St. Pancras.* This delightful church in its
incomparable setting is a notable example of man working in
harmony with Nature. Set with Glebe House (dating from 1527) and
Church House, it is not surprising that it is a magnet for tourists,
popularised as the village is by the song 'Widecombe Fair'. Except
for the loss of the upper part of the chancel screen, St. Pancras' is the
epitome of a Devon church, long and low, built of granite in
Perpendicular style, with a tall W tower—particularly fine and
ashlar-built—and wagon roofs in nave and chancel.

The church lies in a fold of Dartmoor which rises up behind the
church, making a magnificent backcloth. It dates mainly from the
late 14C (during the 1878 restoration a wall plate was removed which
bore the figure of a white hart—the badge of King Richard II), but the
tower is evidently later—probably early 16C—and does not bond
well with the main fabric. The building consists of a six-bay nave and

chancel (without division), two aisles, two transepts and S porch. Externally, the 135ft high W tower with large polygonal pinnacles, set-back buttresses and three-light bell openings, dwarfs everything beside it. All is of granite except the S transept with its large window constructed of a red sandstone (?). The churchyard is neat and compact.

The interior is 104ft long and more spacious than the exterior might give one to expect, due to the floor level being below that of the churchyard. The piers are octagonal granite monoliths and the ceiled wagon roofs are at a lower level in the chancel than in the nave. The general effect is one of uncluttered order. There are many fine carved bosses, one of the most interesting being the third from the E above the communion rails in the form of three rabbits, each with one ear which form a triangle—a Trinitarian symbol but also a symbol connected with tin mining. Only the early 16C wainscoting (containing paintings of saints and martyrs in varying degrees of preservation but retaining their colour) remains from the screen. In the N chancel aisle there is a newel staircase in excellent state which must have led to the Rood loft. There are the remains of a reredos with large paintings of Moses and Aaron at the W end and also a painting of Abraham sacrificing Isaac. An altar stone with incised consecration crosses discovered in the floor is now used as an altar table in the chapel of St. Catherine. The pulpit is modern, made of granite. At the E end there are splendid 19C lamps on tall brass supports.

Of the floor tablets, one (and possibly the one next to it) close to the chancel steps commemorates victims of a very severe thunderstorm which struck the church on October 21st 1638. The NE pinnacle fell through the roof and, according to contemporary record, a meteorite also passed through the church. Many were killed and injured.

DORSET

Dorset is a county of largely unspoilt countryside, with a large pocket of sandy heathland in the SE. It has a varied coastline which emphasises its geological diversity. With the exception of Poole, and to a lesser extent Weymouth, it has few large towns and man's impact on the landscape is not one of industrialisation.

Geologically, Dorset is a county singularly well-endowed with good building materials. Two of its stones have been quarried on a vast scale and exported nationally, namely Purbeck stone and the stone from Portland which is amongst the best-known of building materials. Purbeck stone when polished produces Purbeck marble, so widely used in the medieval period and even more so in the 19C. There were many small localised limestone quarries in Dorset and in the N stone was brought across the county boundary from the nearby Ham Hill quarries in Somerset and used most notably at Sherborne. In the NE greensand has been regularly used. Dorset also has much rolling chalk downland and as a result flint has often been pressed into use. Finally, in the SE and E, clay deposits have led to the production of varying-coloured brick, tiles and pottery.

Christianity is evidenced in a major way as early as the Roman period by the 4C mosaics at Hinton St. Mary and Frampton, the former including the earliest known image of Christ and the latter using the chi-rho symbol. Buildings of the English Church before the Conquest survive at Canford and at Wareham (St. Martin's). Until the 1840s another church at Wareham, Lady St. Mary's, was the largest surviving pre-Conquest church in England; now, with everything swept away, it can provide only the largest collection of pre-Conquest inscriptions in a parish church. They are sub-Roman, or British in the ancient sense rather than English; they were found when the pre-Conquest church was demolished. The early remains at Sherborne are tantalising, with a characteristic doorway and some long-and-short work all that survives of what was one of the most important pre-Conquest churches. The present nave piers at Sherborne are thought to encase pre-Conquest fabric, and the re-entrant angles of the crossing speak of a very early plan. The same seems to apply to the crossing of Wimborne Minster. Further fragmentary pre-Conquest work can be seen at Bere Regis.

The Norman period provides a number of examples. Studland is a complete small church, comprising nave, tower and chancel in line. Winterborne Tomson is single-cell and apsidal, dating from the 12C and restored in 1931 by A.R. Powys in memory of Thomas Hardy. Canford Magna has a two-bay Norman nave. Even smaller than these buildings are St. Catherine's Chapel, standing in the grounds of Milton Abbey, a well-preserved two-cell 12C chapel, and St. Aldhelm's Chapel on St. Aldhelm's Head, also 12C, which may not have been built as a chapel. Bere Regis has Norman arcades with notable carved capitals. Charminster has arcades of the later 12C and other Norman features. Worth Matravers is very largely Norman, with corbel tables, carving over the S doorway and a chancel arch to be noted. On a much grander scale are the nave and crossing of Wimborne Minster, and much of the transepts.

Fabric of the 13C is most rewarding at Whitchurch Canonicorum, where the N arcade has attractive capitals and where the transepts and chancel have much ringed shafting. The E end of Wimborne Minster and the Lady chapel at Sherborne Abbey are also principal

13C examples. The 14C is represented at Gussage All Saints (including an Easter sepulchre), at Milton Abbey (where, however, the details are very simple, save for the Reticulated S transept S window), and at St. Andrew's, Trent, where there is a fine 14C spire. In general, 14C work in Dorset is very subdued, with an absence of 'flowing' tracery. It is the Perpendicular style which is prominent in the county. First and foremost is Sherborne Abbey, which has magnificent mid-15C fan-vaulting in the choir (not totally distinct from lierne-vaulting), and slightly later fan-vaulting in the nave, N transept and crossing. Milton Abbey's tower has a fan-vault of c 1500. The finest tower in Dorset is Beaminster's, early 16C, akin to the great towers of Somerset. Bradford Abbas has a 15C W tower with niches which still contain statues. Buckland Newton is mainly 15C and 16C, with large windows and surviving benches of the period. The E part of Lyme Regis Church (the present nave and chancel and their aisles) is totally Perpendicular: a late 15C and early 16C new church added E of a Norman and 13C one, parts of which were kept. At Bere Regis the nave roof is a splendid late 15C work. The use of Perpendicular, as elsewhere, continued into the later 16C and 17C; Folke is a notable example from 1628.

It was not until the 18C that significant church building resumed, and then, of course, largely in Classical style. Horton has a tower of 1722 and Wimborne St. Giles one of 1732 which is attributed to John and William Bastard. St. George's, Portland (1754–66 by 'Thomas Gilbert of this island') is a distinguished Georgian church, naturally of good Portland ashlar, with a prominent tower in the Wren tradition. Most important of all in 18C Dorset is the rebuilding of Blandford Forum in 1733–39, which was definitely by John and William Bastard. A curiosity from a slightly earlier period, Frampton, has a tower of 1695 which is basically still Perpendicular but which has two tiers of Tuscan columns acting as clasping buttresses. By the late 18C revived Gothic was quite frequent. Of note are the delightful Gothick church at Moreton (1776) and the new estate church at Milton Abbas (1786). A much later building, the church at Fleet (1827–29), contains plaster vaulting and decoration in an 18C Gothick manner. Finally, in the 18C non-Anglican churches begin to be notable. There are the former Congregational Chapel at Lyme Regis, built in 1750–55, and the Catholic church at East Lulworth, built in 1786–87 by John Tasker. It was one of the earliest Catholic churches to be built since the Reformation and was typically reticent.

The 19C left few existing interiors untouched, but on the positive side it added a number of fine buildings. Certainly not in the positive category was the demolition at Wareham of the pre-Conquest Lady St. Mary's and its replacement by the large nave in Commissioners' Perpendicular by T.L. Donaldson in 1841–42. The fine Victorian buildings are these. At Melplash Benjamin Ferrey built in 1845–46 a powerful neo-Norman church; its crossing arches seem based on Wimborne Minster's. Cattistock is a large work by Sir Gilbert Scott (1857), with a magnificent W tower added in 1874 by G.G. Scott, Jr. At Kingston in 1873–80 G.E. Street built a large-scale church which he considered one of his best works. G.F. Bodley partly rebuilt Wimborne St. Giles in 1886–87, only for it to be largely destroyed by fire in 1908 and to be restored by Comper. Bodley's pupil, E.P. Warren, designed a competent church at Bryanston (1895–98). E.S. Prior built a major Arts and Crafts church at Bothenhampton in 1887–89 and he was also responsible for St. Osmund's, Parkstone, Poole, built in 1913–16, which was his final work, in a free interpretation of

Byzantine style. Byzantine too was the Catholic church at Chideock, built in 1870–72 by Charles Weld and extended by J.S. Hansom in 1884. The Welds were the long-standing Catholic landowners of Chideock. The church (and particularly its E end) is distinctive in style and falls outside the usual Victorian categories.

Amongst medieval fittings, carved Norman fonts are prominent. They include those at Stoke Abbott (with heads under arches and an hexagonal pattern below), Puddletown (beaker-shaped, with a consistent pattern), Toller Fratrum (with crude figures) and Lady St. Mary's at Wareham, which has an hexagonal lead font, very fine, with two figures under arches on each face. From the 13C there is the unique survival in an English parish church of a saint's shrine complete with relics: the shrine of St. Wite at Whitchurch Canonicorum. Milton Abbey has a 14C pulpitum—much restored—and Wimborne Minster has an 24-hour astronomical clock, made in c 1320 by Peter Lightfoot, a monk at Glastonbury. Stone reredoses of the 15C remain at Sherborne Abbey and Milton Abbey. Milton also possesses a 15C hanging pyx-canopy, one of only four pre-Reformation English examples, and two 15C paintings; further paintings once at Milton are now in Hilton Church. Cranborne has a circular wooden pulpit of the late 14C or early 15C and Okeford Fitzpaine possesses a 15C stone pulpit with ogee niches. A fine 15C font may be seen at Winterborne Whitechurch. Trent has a spectacular Rood screen which has been ascribed to Glastonbury Abbey. In the same place there are 16C carved bench-ends. Sherborne Abbey has a notable series of stalls, misericords and carved elbow-rests.

Medieval wall paintings may be seen at Whitcombe (13C, and a 15C St. Christopher), Wimborne Minster (13C and later), and Tarrant Crawford (mainly 14C; including some on the S wall of St. Margaret of Antioch's legend). Medieval stained glass is slight, with fragments at Sherborne and Milton. There is some 15C Flemish glass, installed in the 19C, in Wimborne Minster.

17C furnishings are numerous. Folke has a good collection, installed when the church was built in 1628. Lyme Regis has a pulpit dated 1613 (with a similar one at Abbotsbury), and a W gallery of 1611. Good 17C pulpits also remain at Holt (with Corinthian columns), West Parley (two-decker Jacobean), Beaminster and Trent (Dutch, c 1650). Puddletown has a whole range of 17C fittings: box-pews, a gallery of 1735, pulpit, etc. Wimborne Minster has stalls of 1608 and a famous chained library of 1686. At Iwerne Courtney the Freke chapel has an ornate screen of 1654. Sherborne Abbey possesses the earliest dated brass chandelier, 1657. From the 18C, the tiny church at Winterborne Tomson contains a complete set of furnishings installed by William Wake, Archbishop of Canterbury. Chalbury preserves an 18C interior, including a special pew. Blandford Forum, rebuilt in 1733–39, retains many contemporary fittings. Victorian furnishings of outstanding merit are few. At Kingston there are good wrought-iron screens by G.E. Street and at Wimborne Minster Thomas Earp carved the notable pulpit. At Cattistock the baptistery has wall paintings ascribed to Burlison & Grylls. 19C glass is of course well-represented, with good collections at Sherborne and Wimborne. Sherborne has work by A.W.N. Pugin and John Hardman and by Clayton & Bell. Pugin and Hardman also did good work at Milton Abbey. Cattistock has some of the finest glass by William Morris. William Wailes has work at Lyme Regis and at Trent. Kingston has a complete set of windows by Clayton & Bell. From the 20C, there is a group of windows by Sir Ninian Comper at

Wimborne St. Giles. Christopher Webb designed glass at Sherborne, where there is also an engraved glass reredos by Laurence Whistler. Whistler's finest work, however, is the complete set of engraved glass windows at Moreton.

Of Dorset's church monuments, the best medieval examples are seen at Sherborne, Wimborne and Bere Regis, with further good examples at Trent, Abbotsbury, Puddletown, Dorchester (St. Peter's) and Wareham. The monument of Abbot Clement at Sherborne (c 1160) is particularly early. Later notable tombs occur at Marnhull (three alabaster effigies, c 1470), Wimborne Minster (to the Duke of Somerset, died 1444), St. Peter's at Dorchester (two knights, late 14C), and Puddletown (Sir William Martyn, 1503, an alabaster effigy). There are a number of late medieval canopied tomb-chests, made of Purbeck marble, set against walls, and often including small brass figures on the back plate. An example is the monument to John Clavell (1572) at Church Knowle. Medieval brasses are few; Langton Long Blandford has one to John Whitewood and his two wives (1457 and 1467) and Thorncombe one to Sir Thomas Brook and his wife (1419 and 1437).

17C monuments are relatively frequent and good examples may be seen at Wimborne Minster, Wimborne St. Giles, Whitchurch Canonicorum and Longburton. One to Sir Edmund Uvedale (died 1606) in Wimborne Minster might be singled out. The monuments at Wimborne St. Giles are of the Ashley family, Earls of Shaftesbury from 1672. Later 17C works of note include memorials by John Nost at Sherborne Abbey and Silton; a monument of 1698 at Beaminster; and the Freke memorials at Iwerne Courtney, whose heraldry resembles the American flag and was supposedly a source of inspiration. Good 18C examples include a monument by Robert Adam and Agostino Carlini at Milton (1775), and works by Peter Scheemakers at Beaminster, by Thomas Scheemakers and by J.M. Rysbrack at Wimborne St. Giles, and by various hands at Gillingham. These are largely rather grand monuments, but most 18C memorials are in the form of cartouches and tablets. There are many late 18C and early 19C signed tablets, by John Bacon, Sir Francis Chantrey, etc. One notable statue, to Robert Gooden at Over Compton (1825), is unattributed. From very much more recent times, note must be made of the two monuments by Eric Kennington to T.E. Lawrence, a recumbent effigy at Wareham (St. Martin's) and an inscribed gravestone at Moreton (1935).

The historical associations of Dorset's churches are particularly strong from the days of the pre-Conquest Church. Sherborne was the seat of a diocese from 705 to 1075—from the time when the original West Saxon See was divided (and when St. Aldhelm became its bishop) to the time when the See was moved to Salisbury. King Alfred's brothers, Ethelbald and Ethelbert, were buried at Sherborne; another brother, Ethelred, was buried at Wimborne Minster. The foundress there, St. Cuthburga, was the sister of a far earlier King of Wessex, Ina (reigned 688–726). King Alfred's daughter, Aethelgeofu, was the first Abbess of Shaftesbury, which was to become the richest nunnery in England. At a humbler level and from an unknown date in the pre-Conquest period, Whitchurch Canonicorum has held the shrine of St. Wite, who possibly lost her life in the Viking invasions.

The poet, Sir Thomas Wyatt, was buried at Sherborne in 1542. Sir James Thornhill, the great painter of church interiors, was born in Weymouth in 1675 and was buried at Stalbridge in 1734. He was MP for Weymouth; painted the altarpiece in St. Mary's, Weymouth, in 1721; and served as a Commissioner for rebuilding Blandford in 1732. In the 19C and 20C, Thomas Hardy was a prominent son of Dorset. The future novelist and poet was born at Higher Bockhampton, near Stinsford, in 1840. He worked for John Hicks, the Dorchester architect, from 1856; a plan drawn by Hardy in that year hangs on the S wall of St. Peter's, Dorchester. After his death in 1928, his heart was buried at Stinsford. A younger contemporary, T.E. Lawrence ('Lawrence of Arabia'), was buried at Moreton.

The dedications of Dorset's churches include some very rare examples. The county has one of only two ancient cases in England of each of St. Hubert (at Corfe Mullen; the saint was an 8C Low Countries' bishop), St. Basil (at Toller Fratrum; one of the Greek Doctors), and St. Hippolyte (at Rime Intrinseca; a 3C martyr). St. Rumbold (Cann and Pentridge) and St. Kenelm (Hinton Parva) were both shadowy Mercian saints of the 8C. St. Edwold (Stockwood), a 9C hermit of Cerne, and St. Wolfreda, the 10C mother of St. Edith of Wilton, both appear uniquely in Dorset. Also, St. Branwaleder occurs only at Milton Abbey and St. Wite only at Whitchurch Canonicorum. Dedications to St. Osmund and to the Holy Rood are both unusually frequent in Dorset.

Bere Regis, *St. John the Baptist.* The church has a complex architectural history dating back to the pre-Conquest period. It is chiefly noted for its superbly carved and decorated 15C wooden roof, which includes ten life-size figures. In addition, there are fittings and monuments of note. The church is built of alternating bands of stone and flintwork with brick restoration. It was restored in 1875 by G.E. Street.

The three-stage W tower dates from the 16C and has a stair turret in the NW corner and set-back buttresses. The top stage has three-light belfry openings, each with two transoms. There are battlements and square corner turrets with crocketed pinnacles. The three-light E window of the chancel dates from the 13C. Externally, most of the church dates from the 15C and 16C.

The nave is of five bays. The 13C E arch on the N side pierces walling which was part of a mid-11C church; it was the archway into a N transept but now leads into the 15C/16C E end of the N aisle. The aisles are otherwise 14C. The N arcade has mainly plain round columns and capitals of the late 12C. The S arcade has similar round piers but with square abaci; the capitals are decorated with scallops and a series of carved heads, including a man with his hand pressed to his head, a man opening his mouth, an animal attacking another, the head of a king and another figure of a man with hand on head. The last capital on the S side has shields at each corner. The wider W bays of both arcades are 13C extensions. The clerestory is late 15C. In the E wall of the nave there are further remains of the pre-Conquest church with some exposed long-and-short work and a small fragment of decorated arch voussoir. The chancel arch has a squint on each side. Above the squint on the N side is the opening for the entrance to the Rood screen, the staircase itself being in the N chapel. The chancel was totally rebuilt between the 14C and 16C. The wooden chancel roof dates from 1875. The tower arch has on its soffit 16 panels of twin trefoil arches. The N chancel aisle is the Morton chapel, for Cardinal Morton founded a chantry here, and the S chapel is the Turberville chapel.

It is, however, the roof of the nave which is the chief glory of the church. It dates from c 1485 and it has been suggested that it was paid for by Cardinal Morton, who was born in the parish. It is of oak and has five bays with six tiebeams, beneath which are arched braces which meet in carved bosses. The arched braces, which have trefoil decoration, have hammerbeams carrying life-size figures. Below these figures each arched brace continues down to the base of the wall post and the corbel. Above the tiebeams are a central kingpost, two queenposts and two further posts. Between the posts are cusped struts which support the purlins. The spandrels of the arched braces are filled with vertical struts. Between the beams, the secondary rafters have carved bosses and carved human heads where they join the purlins. The 12 life-size carved figures have been generally identified as the Apostles. The six central bosses include two coats of arms, two foliate designs, a Tudor rose and a bearded head. There are ten heads on the secondary rafters. The roof was repaired in 1875 by Harry Hems of Exeter and recolouring and gilding were executed by Clayton & Bell.

At the W end under the tower there is the circular Norman font, which has decoration consisting of interlaced arches with circles enclosing stars above. In the nave there are wooden pews with 13 reused bench-ends which date from the 16C. These have various carved panels. The octagonal wooden pulpit dates from 1875. Over the S door there is a pair of large iron thatching hooks for use in fires. The organ in the N aisle was built in 1901–03 by Bishop's of London. The reredos of the Morton chapel is made of Jacobean panelling with repeat pattern arches, from the former pulpit. The W end of the N aisle is screened and serves as a vestry.

In the chancel, against the N wall, there is the table-tomb of John Skerne (died 1593), the monument being erected in 1596. It consists of a tomb-chest which has four square panels on the front and one at each end, all of which are decorated with quatrefoils containing shields. At the corners are columns with capitals which carry the canopy and which continue as posts with finials. The canopy has a frieze of quatrefoil decoration and cresting above. Against the back panel are brasses of a kneeling male and female with an inscription and a shield between them. On the N wall of the Morton chapel is the memorial to Robert Williams (died 1631). The inscription is enclosed by attached Tuscan columns which support a pediment carrying a crest. Also in the N aisle, behind the organ against the N wall, there are the badly damaged remains of a 16C canopied tomb, with the indents for brasses of a kneeling knight, shields and an inscription. In the S wall of the S aisle is a recessed table-tomb set under an ogee arch. In the same place is a large canopied table-tomb, with twisted columns supporting the canopy which has quatrefoil decoration. The sides of the chest also have quatrefoil decoration with inset shields. Under the canopy are the remains of indents for two figures, inscriptions and shields. In the E wall is a brass to Robert Turbervyle (died 1559). Also against the E wall is a further large canopied table-tomb, the canopy having quatrefoil decoration; and once again only the indents for two brass crests, figures and inscriptions remain. This monument dates from the 16C and is to a Turbervyle (or Turberville).

All the stained glass is Victorian, much of it by John Hardman. In the four-light W tower window there are scenes from the life of St. John the Baptist. The N aisle windows show New Testament scenes. A S window has 20 heraldic shields in memory of the Turberville family. The S aisle E window depicts Christ with the Heavenly Host. On the N side of the chancel the windows depict Christ in the garden, Christ being condemned and Christ carrying the Cross. In the E window is depicted the Crucifixion. In the S wall the windows depict the Deposition, the Burial and Christ Risen.

There are new, sympathetically designed plans, 1987, to build an octagonal meeting room extending from the N door of the N aisle.

Blandford Forum, *St. Peter and St. Paul.* The present Georgian church was built in 1733–39 by John and William Bastard, who were also responsible for much of the rebuilding of the town after the disastrous fire of 1731 which had largely destroyed medieval Blandford.

The church has a W tower which has a pedimented window in each face and even, rusticated quoining up to the parapet, which comprises a balustrade with an urn at each corner. The tower is surmounted by a white cupola which was not designed by the Bastards; they had intended a spire. The W end has a projection which is wider than the tower, with a pediment which is broken by a clock-face. Under this there is a segment-headed window and the W door, which is set in an elaborate surround. The church is lit by large round-headed windows with exaggerated keystones. Each corner of the body of the church has even quoining. The N and S transepts, which have large doors with elaborate surrounds, are relatively small projections, pedimented and with urns above. At the E end the chancel was added in 1896 by Charles Hunt, the original apse being moved E on rollers to its present position. The parapets comprise alternating Portland stone panels and balustrades.

The nave is of six bays with narrow aisles. The third bay from the W is a double-bay, giving a N–S axis between the transepts. The pillars have tall, square bases and Ionic capitals. There is a richly decorated entablature and plaster vaulting which is much shallower in the aisles. The ribs have plaster decoration. The chancel and the apse have coffered vaults.

The church has notable fittings. The nave and aisles have box-pews, which were cut down from their original height in 1880. The W end has a gallery built in 1794 by Stephen Carpenter and Daniel Charmbury. It is one bay deep, and is supported on fluted wooden Ionic columns. Affixed to it are the arms of King George III. The organ, built by George Pike England in 1794, has a case with a fleur-de-lis and a crown on the top. In the nave, the Mayor's pew on the right comprises an ornate hooded chair flanked by two parallel benches which face one another. The pew dates from 1748. The hexagonal wooden pulpit came from St. Antholin's Church in the City of London in 1874. It is 17C, with raised panels with enriched borders. The base of six fluted Ionic columns and the stairs date from c 1895.

The present altar in the E bay of the nave was installed in 1971. The reredos at the E end has two fluted wooden Corinthian columns supporting a pediment. Two cherubs' heads are placed in the tympanum. The pediment carries urns and, in the centre, a Pelican in her Piety. The central panel below depicts Christ in Majesty. The E end of the S aisle is now used as a Lady chapel. Behind its altar is a wooden reredos with a segmental pediment and a painting of the Virgin and Child. At the W end of the S aisle stands the octagonal stone font of c 1739, whose wooden cover has a pine cone on the top. The pine cone was one of the motifs of the Bastard brothers. On either side of the doorways of both transepts there are benefaction boards. Flags hang from the balconies of the transepts, including those of the Royal British Legion and the Hood Battalion. E of the transept in the N wall there is a door to the modern Julian chapel. At the E end of this aisle there is a war memorial altar with a wooden reredos which has a central panel depicting the Crucifixion. The wooden altar front has three arches with fluted Ionic columns and with putti in the spandrels. Inset into the arches are painted figures of St. Edmund, St. George and St. Oswald. The stained glass of the church is early 20C. In the S aisle the windows depict, from the E, St. Matthew, St. Andrew and St. Mark. In the N aisle there are St. John, the Virgin Mary and St. James.

There is a remarkably large number of monuments, many to the Pitt, Bastard and Wake families. There is a brass plate in the N aisle to George Vince of the ship 'Discovery': he was a member of one of Captain Scott's expeditions to the Antarctic and lost his life in a fall from an ice cliff at Ross Island in 1902. There is a memorial in the S aisle to William and Amy Wake, the parents of William Wake, Archbishop of Canterbury in 1717–36. In the churchyard N of the church a table-tomb on a plinth, from one end of which an obelisk rises, commemorates John and William Bastard.

Canford Magna Church *(dedication unknown)*. The church is set in the grounds of what is now Canford School and is a school chapel as well as a parish church. It reveals work from pre-Conquest times onwards, with none of the phases paying much attention to the rest. The chancel is the nave of a late pre-Conquest church. The two-bay Norman nave of the present building has only responds between large sections of wall, supporting round-headed arches. Norman also is the three-stage N tower. The W extension of the nave (by David Brandon, 1876) looks more like the termination of an E end, with its triple-lancet windows and rose above. SW of the S porch is the tomb of Sir Henry Austen Layard (died 1894), who rediscovered Nineveh while he was envoy at Constantinople.

Cattistock, *St. Peter and St. Paul*. A church has stood on this site since the pre-Conquest period, but with the exception of a few minor medieval portions, the present building is the work of Sir Gilbert Scott and his eldest son, G.G. Scott, Jr, in 1857–74. It is a large and sumptuously decorated church with a very fine tower.

The church is built on a westward sloping site. The tower is its main feature, designed in 1874 by G.G. Scott, Jr and based on the tower of Charminster. It is of three stages, with set-back buttresses. The square-headed belfry windows rise through the full height of the middle and upper stages. They are pairs of two lights, each with two transoms, and blank in the lower part. A thin buttress rises up through the middle of the windows, finishing as a pinnacle above the pierced battlements. There are tall, square corner turrets with pinnacles. The turrets are panelled and start at the level of the hoodmould of the windows. Four large gargoyles project at the battlement stage. As for the rest of the exterior, the vestry, which is built S of the tower with a mullioned oriel window, appears at first-floor level from the road due to the lie of the land. The E end terminates in Sir Gilbert Scott's polygonal apse in 13C style (note the contrast to his son's use of Perpendicular). The walls of the transepts are medieval, both with 15C windows. The N porch has a statue of Christ over the outer arch.

The interior comprises a four-bay nave with three-bay aisles, an apsidal E end and a baptistery under the tower. The square marble font has a very tall wooden cover, rising almost to the roof, and highly decorated with stars and suns on a blue ground. There is wooden panelling with gilded filigree ornamentation, and the walls above are painted with patterns, texts and figures of saints, all attributed to Burlison & Grylls. On the S wall over the ogee doorway there is a statue of Christ and higher up a painting of St. George killing the dragon. In the nave, one S capital depicts a dog attacking a winged dragon and a bird attacking a serpent. At the E end of the S aisle there are a fragment of medieval carving and part of a 13C tomb-slab bearing a foliate cross. The S aisle serves as the Lady chapel and has a small altar and some 17C panelling. The polygonal stone pulpit has a figure of a saint in each face. The wooden lectern features a carving of a Pelican in her Piety.

The chancel arch has elaborate capitals and shafts of Purbeck marble. The chancel, raised on two steps above the nave, has a black and white tiled floor and a door in its N wall which leads into the pulpit. The sanctuary is raised on a further step. The N chapel is separated from the aisle by a stone screen, and there is also a stone screen between the baptistery and the nave.

The stained glass is 19C and 20C. In the nave the W window dates from 1857, depicts the Tree of Jesse and has been attributed to Burlison & Grylls. In the S aisle the two-light window with six angels in red and white robes against a blue background was by William Morris, 1882. The last window in the S wall, again two-light, is by Kempe & Co., 1916, and depicts the Annunciation. The windows in the chancel and apse depict the Prophets, St. Peter, Moses and Noah, the Crucifixion, the Ark of the Covenant, and St. Paul. The E window of the N aisle by R.A. Bell, 1923, depicts St. Dorothy.

Hinton St. Mary, *Roman Villa.* In 1963 a well-preserved 4C Roman mosaic floor, measuring 19ft by 28ft, was uncovered in this village next to the B3092 and about a quarter of a mile from St. Peter's Church. The floor was lifted in 1965 and has since been on display in the British Museum. It is unique in that it is the only known representation of Christ from Roman Britain and it is possibly the earliest from anywhere in the Roman Empire.

The floor consists of a larger square section and a smaller rectangular section, joined by a rectangular strip. The two sections correspond with two parts of a room, which was divided by a cross-wall. The main section has in its central medallion the clean-shaven portrait bust of Christ, set in front of a chi-rho monogram. On either side of this are pomegranates, symbols of immortality. In the four spandrels or quadrants are figures with pomegranates, possibly representing the Evangelists. These four busts are connected by diagonal arms, forming a cross, with panels of scrollwork formed by leaves. In three of the four semicircles are hunting scenes, while the fourth simply has a tree. The mosaic has a close parallel in a floor discovered in 1794 and recorded by Samuel Lysons at Frampton, which is of similar shape and has similar scenes and, in an additional apse, the chi-rho monogram. These mosaics were undoubtedly by the same mosaicists working probably from Dorchester (Durnovaria). It has been suggested that the double-rooms of Hinton St. Mary and Frampton, each having a mosaic floor of single design, might have been chapels.

Kingston, *St. James.* Set in a dramatic position atop a ridge dominating the skyline to the S of Corfe Castle, the church is the work of G.E. Street. It was built in 1873–80 at a cost of c £70,000 by the third

Earl of Eldon. It was one of Street's favourite works and among the largest of his churches. The church itself was the second built in the village in the 19C. The first, built in 1833 by the first Earl of Eldon, was made into the church hall. When Street's church was completed it remained, somewhat surprisingly, as a form of private chapel for the Eldon family. It was not until 1921 that Lord Eldon passed St. James's over to the Church Commissioners and the church was formally consecrated.

The church is built of Purbeck marble and stone. The dominant feature is the very tall central tower whose upper stage has three tall lancets in each face. Against the N side of the tower, in the NE angle of the N transept, rises a circular spire-capped stair turret, with ropework decoration in diagonal patterns. The idea for this was borrowed from Christchurch Priory. The slope of the site adds to the grandeur of the massing, notably of the transepts, of the two-storey vestries on the N side and of the apse at the E end, supported by four large buttresses. At the W end of the nave is a low narthex. The church is lit by lancets apart from a large rose window at the W end and two quatrefoils in the transepts. The roofs are stone-tiled.

Entrance is gained via the narthex. The nave is of four bays with piers of clustered Purbeck shafts and stiff-leaf capitals. The clerestory consists of eight lancets grouped in pairs. Between each pair there is blank arcading and between the windows, Purbeck shafts. The aisles have pairs of lancets too, with twin Purbeck shafts. The roofs of the aisles and nave are wooden, but the transepts, crossing and apse have rib-vaults with dogtooth decoration. The sanctuary is raised on a further three steps. All the fittings were designed by Street. The W door has ornate ironwork and elaborate handles. The font at the W end is quatrefoil in shape, supported on a cluster of Purbeck shafts. The pulpit is of iron openwork, as are the chancel screens. The altar rails are of brass and iron. The piscina and sedilia in the S wall of the apse are very elaborate.

The stained glass is all by Clayton & Bell. The large rose window in the W wall depicts the Lamb of God surrounded by the symbols of the Evangelists. In the N aisle the windows depict mainly Old Testament figures; the S aisle windows show Apostles and early saints (including the local St. Aldhelm). The transepts and chancel have a Passion cycle.

Against the N wall are two very elaborate marble monuments, one (by Sir Francis Chantrey) to the first Earl of Eldon (died 1838), Lord Chancellor, with a portrait medallion, and the other to Elizabeth, Countess of Eldon (died 1831), the Hon. William Henry John Scott (died 1832) and the Hon. John Scott (died 1805). In the S transept are marble plaques to John Scott, second Earl of Eldon (died 1852), and to Charlotte Elizabeth (died 1864), eldest daughter of the second Earl.

Lyme Regis

St. Michael the Archangel. Splendidly situated on the cliffs at the foot of the steep hill looking out over Lyme Bay, this large church has a complex architectural history. The tower and W porch are survivals of an early medieval church, which were retained at the W end of a new building of the late 15C, which comprises the present nave, aisles and chancel. The vestry was added in 1885.

The battlemented W tower and polygonal stair turret, along with much of the W porch, are cement-rendered. The tower has small lancets and larger louvred single openings above. The tower and the W porch are the remains of a 12C and 13C cruciform church, the porch being part of its nave and the tower once standing over the crossing. When the new church was built in Perpendicular style in the late 15C, it was added to the E.

Internally, two of the former nave's circular piers and double-chamfered arches are exposed on the N side of the W porch. In its S wall there are the remains of a 13C arch. The space beneath the tower, which is entered through a wide Perpendicular arch, now serves as the baptistery. The E arch of the tower is Norman, comprising responds of a half-roll which continues round the soffit, and an outer square-cut arch. In the N, W and S walls there are the remains of blocked arches, a little later in date. The spacious interior proper comprises a chancel and nave in one with N and S aisles. The slope of the site is such that having already risen a number of steps, the nave still slopes up to the E end. The nave is of four bays with very wide depressed arches and with piers set on square bases and having clustered shafts. The capitals are small, at the tops of the shafts, and mainly bear shields. Above the nave arcades there are triple-light Perpendicular windows. The two-bay chancel is structurally a continuation of the nave, as are the N and S chapels extensions of the nave aisles. The nave and chancel have wagon roofs; the two chapels are flat-roofed, that on the N being of c 1500 and that on the S 17C.

The octagonal font has a cluster of columns on an octagonal plinth. Its ornate wooden cover is dated 1846. At the W end a Jacobean gallery runs across the entire width of the church, one bay deep, supported on two wooden piers. An inscription records that it was erected in 1611 by John Hassard. The gallery houses an organ which was made by Hele & Co. and which was purchased from the church of St. Mary Major, Exeter in 1939. Also at the W end there are a Jacobean lectern and glass display cases in which are kept a 'Bad Bible' of 1653, a chained Breeches Bible and a copy of Erasmus's St. Luke's Gospel, 1559. Most of the pews are relatively recent, but there are odd sections of Jacobean carving, and the Corporation pew on the N side is 17C. The octagonal wooden pulpit dates from 1613. Its panels have two rows of arches set in foliate borders. Above it is a tester with the inscription: 'To God's glory, Richard Harvey of London, Mercer and Marchant Adventurer, 1613. Faith is by hearing'. Nearby there is the present lectern, a wooden eagle dating from 1898. The wooden Rood screen, with its centrally positioned cross, all in a Perpendicular style, was erected in 1889. The painting above, of the Raising of the Cross with Christ being led up the hill, is mid-19C. The high altar has a simple drape in place of a reredos. The N chapel, which has served as the Lady chapel since 1929, contains the ensign and bell from the Second World War ship, HMS 'Lyme Regis'. The arms of King Charles II are placed in the N aisle.

The stained glass is all of the 19C and 20C. A small lancet on the N side of the W porch depicts Thomas Coram (1668–1751), founder of the famous Foundling Hospital in London, who was born in Lyme Regis, along with three children. At the W end of the N aisle there is a four-light window in memory of Mary Anning (died 1847). She became famous, and made Lyme Regis famous, for her numerous fossil discoveries, including an Ichthyosaurus in 1812. The window, which shows the corporal acts of mercy, is by William Wailes. The E window of the Lady chapel is also by Wailes and depicts Jesus telling St. Peter to feed his sheep. In the S aisle, a four-light window towards the W end by James Powell & Sons depicts St. Michael, St. George, St. Nicholas and St. Gabriel, with panels of St. Michael slaying the dragon, war on land, war at sea and the Annunciation below them. The next window, with figures of David, Moses, Aaron and Elijah, c 1843, is by Wailes. The chancel E window, believed to be by Thomas Willement, shows St. Michael and the Lamb of God in the centre light, and decorative patterns in the remaining four; at the bottom appear the Evangelists and their symbols.

Mary Anning's grave is in the churchyard on the N side, opposite her memorial window.

Former Congregational Chapel. A handsomely proportioned Congregational Chapel in Coombe Street, built in 1750–55 by John Whitty, now serves as a dinosaur exhibition centre, a restaurant and a shop. Its main elevation has five bays with two arched ground-floor windows on each side of a square-headed doorway which is supported by fluted Doric pilasters. There are two hipped roofs with a valley between.

Milton Abbey, *St. Mary, St. Michael, St. Sampson and St. Branwaleder.* A church has stood on the site from as early as 938 when King Aethelstan, grandson of King Alfred the Great, founded a house of secular canons. It later became a Benedictine abbey. The present Decorated church, which consists of a choir, aisles, transepts and a central tower, was built after the previous Norman building had been struck by lightning in 1309 and burnt to the ground. From the 14C until the Dissolution in 1539 building was continuous, but the nave was not rebuilt. The materials used were Chilmark and Ham Hill stone, with some flintwork. The church became parochial at the Reformation, but in the late 18C was made the private chapel of the Earl of Dorchester. It passed back to the Diocese of Salisbury in 1933. Restoration took place in 1789 (by James Wyatt) and in 1865 (by Sir Gilbert Scott).

Set in parkland laid out by Capability Brown and next to the 18C mansion created by Sir William Chambers and James Wyatt, the church is some distance from the model estate village of Milton Abbas. The medieval town which formerly surrounded the abbey was demolished by the Earl of Dorchester in the 1780s. The tower is the dominant feature of the church. Each face has a pair of recessed, two-light bell openings; between them and at the corners there are buttresses which rise to become pinnacles. The parapet consists of a stone panel with a top row of quatrefoil openings. The choir is of seven bays with four flying buttresses rising over the aisle roofs. The buttresses each have a quatrefoil opening, and from their bases rise square turrets topped by small pinnacles. The aisles have parapets with pierced quatrefoils. The windows of the aisles and clerestory are mostly three-light, the middle light higher in each case, with all the lights merely cusped. The E end has five blocked arches with the remains of vaulting: all that is left of the Lady and ambulatory chapels. Above the blocked arches is a seven-light window. The N transept extends one bay N of the aisle and the S transept two bays from the S aisle. The N transept windows are Perpendicular, with an eight-light N window and very tall three-light E and W windows.

The S transept is 14C, but later than the choir. The tower's W face is a blank wall, with a porch designed by Sir Gilbert Scott in 1865 at its base. This has angle buttresses and a parapet of pierced quatrefoil decoration. The lower stage of the buttresses N and S of the porch show how the aisles of the projected nave were started but never continued.

The four massive tower piers have attached shafts rising to plain capitals which support simply moulded arches. The tower has a fan-vault of c 1500, with foliate and heraldic bosses. The transepts have lierne-vaults; the bosses are comparable with the tower's. The two tiers of E and W windows in the S transept are shafted; the catwalk of the clerestory has diagonal cusped panels. The choir aisles have quadripartite vaults with elaborate bosses of human heads, animals, angels and foliage. At the W end of the choir there is a stone pulpitum which, although restored, still contains much medieval work. Upon this stands the organ. The first two bays of the choir from the W have a stone screen on each side, with six small arches on Purbeck shafts in each bay. The shafts which rise to support the quadripartite vault of the choir start raised off the ground in these first two bays. The other bays alternate between arches and blank walls. At the E end there is a large Perpendicular reredos consisting of three rows of niches, the top two rows with canopies and plinths, designed to take 26 statues, which were destroyed at the Dissolution. The reredos dates from the end of the 15C and has an inscription in Latin in memory of Abbot Middleton (1482–1525) and Thomas Wilkin, Vicar of Milton, 1492. The screen was restored by Wyatt in 1789. To the S, the piscina and sedilia date from the early 14C, with elaborate canopies and pinnacles, formerly part of Abbot Middleton's chantry in the S transept.

The church is particularly rich in fittings. In the choir at the E end and hanging from the N wall there is a wooden pyx-canopy dating from the 15C. It is one of the very few pre-Reformation pyx-canopies to have survived. Although now plain, it was originally highly coloured. It is built in four stages. The bottom stage is square, the next two hexagonal, and the last is a slender recessed spire. The three lower stages are carved with tracery, pinnacles and battlements. A copy of Fox's 'Book of Martyrs', given by John Tregonwell in 1680, is on display in the Lady chapel in the S aisle. Also in the chapel there is a carving of St. James the Great, c 1500. In the N wall there is a painted niche with the base for a statue, and evidence of a former canopy above. Higher still there is a carving of a barrel (a tun) with a windmill, dated 1514, the rebus of Abbot Middleton (for Milton is a short form of Middleton), whose statue probably stood in the niche below. The wooden screen of the chapel is modern. Under the wooden canopies of the return stalls at the W end of the choir there are two 15C painted panels depicting King Aethelstan and (probably) his mother, Ecgwyn (or Egwynna). The items in the display cabinet under the pulpitum include a 1591 copy of the 1568 Bishops' Bible and the 15C Milton Abbey pectoral cross found in a tomb in the 19C. The large sculptural marble font by J.A. Jerichau stands in the N transept, just N of the W entrance. It consists of two life-size angels, one holding a cross, the other a palm, with the bowl between them. In the S transept there is a collection of carved fragments, medieval tiles and part of an abbot's tomb-slab, all against the W wall. In the S wall there is an ogee piscina and in the SE corner there are the remains of Abbot Middleton's chantry which was destroyed by Wyatt.

There are some fine monuments. In the N transept there is a large free-standing marble table-tomb, upon which lies the effigy of Caroline Sackville Damer (died 1775), the wife of Joseph Damer, first Baron Milton and Earl of Dorchester, whose semi-recumbent effigy, leaning on his arm, looks down at his sleeping wife. It was carved by Agostino Carlini. The panels of the chest, which has Gothick arches and niches, were designed by Robert Adam. On the E wall there is a marble tablet with Gothic detailing in memory of Caroline, Countess of Portarlington (died 1813, but the tablet erected in 1844). In the S transept there are numerous memorials to the Hambro family, owners of the mansion from 1852 to 1933. At the E end of the N choir aisle a large monument with Corinthian columns and a segmental pediment, and a female figure holding a skull and a book, commemorates Maria Bancks (died 1704). Nearby there is the canopied altar-tomb of Sir John Tregonwell (died 1565), who acquired the abbey at the Dissolution. On the wall below the canopy is a brass of the kneeling figure of Sir John in armour. The canopy is supported by two spiral columns. In the N wall of the sanctuary there is a 14C-style canopy designed by Scott to house the marble effigy of Baron Hambro (died 1877). A Purbeck marble grave-slab, probably of Walter de Sydelinge (died 1315), lies in the choir in front of the altar steps. It has indents for a large-scale figure of an abbot.

The choir E window has various heraldic stained glass fragments dating from the 15C, 16C and 17C, including the attributed arms of King Aethelstan and an angel holding a trumpet. The W window in the S wall of the S aisle has some 14C grisaille fragments. In the S transept the S window depicts the Tree of Jesse; it was designed by A.W.N. Pugin and made by John Hardman in 1847. The equivalent window in the N transept has some 18C heraldic glass.

On a hill 300yds E of Milton Abbey Church there stands St. Catherine's Chapel, a late 12C two-cell chapel which was restored for worship in 1901.

St. Aldhelm's Head, *St. Aldhelm's Chapel.* Remote on its headland 354ft above sea level with just the coastguard cottages and lookout for company, the small square chapel dates from the 12C. Internally, there is one massive square pier supporting roughly dressed vaults. There is a simple round-arched door on the NW side, a small round-headed window in the E wall and a blocked one in the S wall. Externally, the chief features are the massive buttresses and the pyramidal roof surmounted by a modern cross. The chapel was reopened for worship in 1881 after restoration at the expense of the third Earl of Eldon.

St. Aldhelm was the first Bishop of Sherborne in the year 705.

Sherborne Abbey, *St Mary the Virgin.* The large and magnificent abbey church has fabric from pre-Conquest times onwards. Much of it was rebuilt after 1420 in the Perpendicular style, despite a devastating fire in 1437. The site itself has been in use since at least 705, when it was made a See with St. Aldhelm as its first bishop. It remained a See until 1075, but the bishops of the new See of Salisbury (or Old Sarum) continued as Abbots of Sherborne until 1122. The monastery survived down to 1539. From 1925 Sherborne has once again become the title of (suffragan) bishops.

Externally, the N side, which was the site of the claustral buildings, now faces Sherborne School. The central tower has in each face two

two-light transomed and louvred windows, separated by buttresses which continue above the plain parapet as crocketed pinnacles. There are also corner pinnacles, making three to each face. At the W end, the rubble face of the aisles and of the nave below the nine-light W window is the core of the pre-Conquest cathedral's wall. The centrally positioned W door in the recess between the two buttresses has been shown to be the inner face of a pre-Conquest W tower. The Perpendicular W window was enlarged by the addition of the bottom two rows of lights during the extensive restoration of the 1850s by R.C. Carpenter and William Slater. The four responds are the remains of All Hallows' Church, which was the parish church until the Dissolution. On the S side of the W front is a plain Norman door. The parapet of the S aisle is a series of blank quatrefoils. The S porch is of Norman origin, but it was completely rebuilt in 1849, when the top storey was added. With the exception of a blocked Norman clerestory window in the E wall of the S transept, the whole of the rest of the S side of the abbey presents an unbroken Perpendicular picture. The nave clerestory consists of five large five-light transomed windows on each side. The choir has three six-light clerestory windows on each side, supported by flying buttresses which have quatrefoil decoration. On both choir and choir aisles the buttresses rise to crocketed pinnacles above the parapets, which have blank quatrefoil decoration. At the E end, what are now the chapel of St. Mary-le-Bow, the Lady chapel and the vestry were once used as the headmaster's house, hence on the S side the two 16C mullioned windows with carved shields in between, and the arms of King Edward VI set between twisted columns. In the gable above there is a sundial. The present E end, complete with two octagonal turrets rising above the parapet with quatrefoil decoration, is the work of W.D. Caroë and dates from 1921.

Internally, the piers of the nave are very thick and are simply the pre-Conquest piers encased in Perpendicular panelling. There are no capitals, the panelling continuing around the soffit of the arches of the five bays. Above the arcades are the large clerestory windows. There is a bottom blank panel and the splays have panelling similar to that of the nave piers. The chief feature of the nave, N transept and choir is the sumptuous stone fan-vaulting, with a large number of carved and painted bosses. The nave vaulting has been ascribed to William Smyth. At the W end of the N aisle there is a tall pre-Conquest doorway leading into a small room. The tower arch is Norman, as are the arches from the aisles into the transepts. The choir of three bays is entirely Perpendicular, with the piers having very small capitals on the attached shafts. The vaulting shafts rise uninterrupted from the floor to the roof, the splays of the arches being panelled with trefoiled tracery. Below the clerestory windows there are two tiers of blank panels, the lower in the spandrels of the arches. The fan-vaulting, which is the earliest in existence, is slightly different to that of the nave. In the E wall there is a nine-light window. Below this there are three rows of blank panels. All the painted decoration in the panelling and fan-vaults of the choir was designed by Clayton & Bell but painted by J.G. Crace. In the centre of the E wall is the reredos by R.H. Carpenter, 1884, with many niches and elaborate pinnacles. Under elaborate canopies, there is the figure of Christ Ascending, surrounded by the Disciples. Beneath this and behind three canopies, the Last Supper is depicted. The Lady chapel is largely Early English, with attached Purbeck marble shafts and capitals with stiff-leaf decoration.

In the N aisle there is the mechanism for a clock which cost £25 in 1740. The font is octagonal with quatrefoil decorated panels and dates from the 15C. In the choir amongst the Victorian stalls are ten with 15C misericords and elbow-rests. The rests on the N side include a woman with a scroll and a monk reading, and on the S a man with a sword, a woman feeding her dog from a pot, and an angel with a shield. The misericords on the N side depict a bust of a man between leaves, a man pulling his mouth open, Christ in Majesty, and a head in foliage. On the S they depict a woman praying, a monkey, a boy being beaten, an archer firing at a man on horseback with a man on a lion behind him, and finally a woman beating a man. In the N transept is the organ, built in 1856 by Gray & Davidson and restored most recently in 1986 by Bishop & Son. It has an elaborate dark case. The pulpit dates from 1899 and was designed by B. Ingelow. The carving of the panels was the work of J. Forsyth. In the Lady chapel is arguably the oldest brass chandelier in England. It is dated 1657 and came from Holland. The reredos of the Lady chapel consists of an engraved glass panel by Laurence Whistler, 1967–68. In the middle is a heart pierced by a sword, with a crown of lilies and roses and a burning rose in the centre. On either side of the heart are wings, and from the heart stem cornucopias, with wheat in one and grapes in the other. Around the edges is a border of stars. In the chapel of St. Mary-le-Bow at the E end of the S choir aisle is an octagonal 15C font. The screen has a Perpendicular base but is otherwise the work of W.D. Caroë. Around the church are standards of the Dorsetshire Regiment.

The church is particularly rich in monuments. In the Wykeham chapel, off the N transept, is the monument to Sir John Horsey (died 1546) and his son (died 1564). The father was the vendor of the abbey church to the town after the Dissolution. The monument has two recumbent effigies of knights in armour on a chest decorated with shields. At each corner a square decorated column supports the large entablature which in turn supports pediments surmounted by horses' heads. Against the back wall is a crest, set in a lozenge supported by two putti. In the N choir aisle there are two monuments: one is to Abbot Clement, c 1160, of Purbeck marble, with only the head and inscription round it preserved, and E of this is a damaged but otherwise fairly intact Purbeck marble effigy of a priest dating from the 13C. At the E end in front of the clergy vestry a brass plate records that near to the spot are the remains of Kings Ethelbald and Ethelbert, who were succeeded by their younger brother, King Alfred the Great. In the S choir aisle is another Purbeck marble effigy, of an abbot in vestments dating from the mid-13C. In the S transept against the S wall there is the large ornate Baroque monument to John Digby, third Earl of Bristol (died 1698). The monument is signed by John Nost and has the statues of the Earl and his two wives mounted on plinths and set under slender arches. This composition is framed by two fluted Corinthian columns which support an entablature and arch. Above there are urns and a centrally positioned crest. Under the arch and above the figures are carved drapes, and outside the pillars two small putti. To the S of the S transept is St. Katherine's chapel, which is dominated by the Leweston tomb. It is in memory of John Leweston (died 1574) and his wife Joan (died 1579). The tomb consists of their recumbent effigies on a tomb-chest with shields in the side panels. Six fluted Corinthian columns support an arched canopy which has putti at each corner; in the middle on the N and S sides the putti stand on top of rings supported by dolphins. Buried in the N transept is Sir Thomas Wyatt (died 1542), the famous Tudor courtier and poet.

There is a large range of stained glass. At the W end of the N aisle, in the small chamber through the pre-Conquest arch, is a three-light window with the image of St. Stephen Harding, by Frederick Cole, 1962. The nine-light W window has 27 figures of the Prophets and has been ascribed to A.W.N. Pugin and John Hardman. In the choir the E window depicts the Easter story. The windows in the clerestory of the choir are filled with figures of various saints and bishops of the early Church and those connected with Sherborne. These, along with the E window, are the work of Clayton & Bell. In the Lady chapel the four-light E window depicts the Virgin and Child with St. Aldhelm. Underneath are scenes of the angel appearing to Mary, and the Nativity. The window dates from 1957 and is by Christopher Webb. In the S transept the S window is a Te Deum with 96 figures. It is by Pugin and Hardman, 1851–52. In the S and W three-light windows of St. Katherine's chapel are 15C fragments of glass collected together and restored in 1925 by G.H. Fletcher. They include shields with heraldic devices, figures and heads.

The abbey has many famous associations. Its first bishop in 705 was St. Aldhelm. Two later bishops, Wulfsin (from 992) and Osmund de Seez (from 1078 at Sarum) were also to be canonised. One further monk who was born in Sherborne and educated at the abbey as a novice was St. Stephen Harding, who would go on to found the monastery at Citeaux. He is widely held to be the founding father of the Cistercian Order, for he taught its founder, St. Bernard. Sir Walter Raleigh used St. Katherine's chapel as a private pew when he owned the Manor of Sherborne (1592–1603).

Across the close to the S is the almshouse of St. John the Baptist and St. John the Evangelist, founded in 1438 and finished in 1448. The small chapel was built in 1442 and has fine medieval fittings.

Studland, *St. Nicholas.* This is Dorset's most complete and unaltered Norman church. It stands on the site of a pre-Conquest church, large parts of which are incorporated in the lower walls of the chancel. The pre-Conquest church was founded in the late 7C. It has a most beautiful setting, looking out across to the nearby sea. The nave is largely of the late 11C and the tower and upper parts of the chancel 12C. The church was restored in 1881.

Externally, the church, which is built of freestone with areas of ashlar dressing, is dominated by the centrally positioned, heavily buttressed tower, which is of three stages, the top stage being only partially built. On the S side is the 17C porch. The windows have largely been altered, with some 18C enlargements of existing windows and the addition of an Early English triple-lancet E window. The roofs are all stone-slated. Running around the nave is a corbel table with beasts and human heads.

Internally, the church consists of a nave, tower and chancel in line. The nave has a simple wooden raftered roof. At the W end is a gallery with an organ of 1937. The nave tower arch is of two orders with decorated scalloped capitals. The inner capitals have a chevron pattern on the abaci. These are carried on plain attached shafts. The tower space has a quadripartite stone vault carried on four angle shafts with decorated cushion capitals. The chancel arch is treated in a similar manner to the nave arch with decorated scallop capitals on attached shafts and chevron-patterned abaci. These support plain rolls. The chancel also has a quadripartite vault.

*The tower of the Norman St. Nicholas's. Note the tiny
chancel window (right), set in a larger surround*

At the W end there is a plain round font dating from the 12C. The
two hatchments on the N and S walls are 19C and of the Bankes
family. The octagonal pulpit and brass eagle lectern are 19C. There
are traces on the N wall of the nave, above the blocked door, of a 12C
wall painting. Over the nave arch is a 17C painted inscription of
Psalm LXXXIV, verses 1 and 2. In the chancel against the N wall
there is a table-tomb with a decorated Purbeck marble top.

There are a number of stained glass windows. On the N side of the
nave there is a small window with the Triumphant Christ, 1894. In
the S wall there is a larger window, signed by Thomas Willement and
installed in 1859, depicting the Raising of Lazarus. Under the tower

on the N side a small window dated 1883 depicts the Virgin Mary. St. Nicholas appears in a N chancel window.

Trent, St. Andrew. The church dates mainly from the 13C and has a 14C S tower and spire. There is a large number of fittings of note. The church was restored in 1840 and again in 1925. It is set in a well-tended churchyard, in the NE corner of which is the 15C chantry house built c 1440 by John Frankes. The tower of three stages has angle buttresses. The parapet has pierced quatrefoil decoration with a pinnacle at each corner, and below there is a row of cusped arch heads with gargoyles. Above rises the spire which was rebuilt in 1908–09. At the W end of the nave the polygonal vestry is Victorian and was built as a baptistery. At the same time the nave of c 1220 was lengthened. The N chapel also dates from c 1220. The porch on the S side dates from the 14C. The chancel is 15C.

Internally, the aisleless nave of four bays was restored in 1924. The wooden roof dates from the mid-19C, the ribs being supported by angels. The chancel is of two bays and has a painted vaulted ceiling. The most important fitting is the chancel screen. It was carved in the 15C and has been ascribed to the monks of Glastonbury Abbey. It consists of five arches rising to a vaulted canopy. Each of the arches, with the exception of the northernmost which contains a door to the former Rood loft, is divided into six cinquefoiled ogee lights. Above the canopy are three friezes of foliage. Between the N chapel and the nave is a low 17C wooden screen. In the nave the pews and bench-ends, carved with the symbols of the Passion, date from the early 16C. The wooden pulpit is Dutch, c 1650. It is octagonal and depicts the Annunciation, Nativity, Adoration, Presentation, Circumcision, Christ in the Temple and David. Hanging in the N chapel are two helmets from the 16C and 17C. In the S transept, which is the lower stage of the tower, is the octagonal stone font. The S transept became a baptistery in 1971.

In the N chapel in recesses are two 14C effigies. The first is a civilian, the second a knight, possibly Sir Roger Wyke (died 1380). On the E side of the arch between the N chapel and the nave is the monument to Ann Gerard (died 1633), restored 1792. It consists of two plain columns supporting an inscription and two angels holding a crest. Around the edge of the arch is an inscription, 'All flesh is grass and the glory of it is as the flower of the field'. On the S wall to the W of the arch is a monument to William Gerard (died 1604), consisting of pilasters on either side of a painted crest and inscription. In the W wall is the recumbent effigy of a Rector, William Henry Turner (died 1875), by W. Theed. It is dated 1853 and for 22 years the Rector kept it in the hall of Trent Rectory. In the S transept there is a slate tablet erected in 1974 in memory of Lord Fisher, 99th Archbishop of Canterbury, who retired to Trent Rectory and died there in 1972. (His grave is in the churchyard S of the tower.) In the nave is the monument to Sir Francis Wyndham (died 1716). It has a central inscription with four putti, one at each corner. This is enclosed by two Corinthian columns supporting a segmental pediment in which there is a relief portrait bust set against trophies.

The stained glass is largely Victorian. In the nave there are windows of the 1840s. In the S transept the three-light window dated 1871 is by Arthur O'Connor and depicts Christ in Triumph. In the N chapel the E window depicts St. George, St. Michael and St. Martin and has a memorial date of 1925. In the chancel two windows in the N and S walls depict the 12 Apostles, date from 1842 and are possibly the work of William Wailes. In the E window there is a collection of 16C and 17C glass from Germany and Switzerland, collected by William Turner.

Wareham

Of the seven parish churches of medieval foundation which Wareham once possessed, only three now stand and only two of these (Lady St. Mary's and St. Martin's) serve as churches today, Holy Trinity now acting as an art gallery. The two churches still in use stand at opposite ends of the town, St. Martin's standing on the pre-Conquest earthwork and Lady St. Mary's Church at the S end of the town by the River Frome. The churches possess rare fittings, pre-Conquest inscriptions, wall paintings and memorials.

Lady St. Mary. Lady St. Mary's Church was until the 1840s one of the largest surviving pre-Conquest churches, dating back to the 7C. However, in 1841–42 the nave was completely rebuilt by Professor T.L. Donaldson. The church and indeed the town are dominated by the large four-stage W tower of c 1500. It has a two-light window in each face of the top stage and is battlemented. The W porch and the vestry on the N side of the tower date from the 16C. The E end consists of the chancel and Becket chapel which date from the 13C and the 14C, St. Edward's chapel which dates from the 12C and, on the N side of the chancel, the organ chamber which dates from 1882.

Internally, the large nave has four bays with octagonal piers. The clerestory above has four two-light windows on each side. St. Edward's chapel is much lower than the chancel and is entered through a 12C arch and down six steps. The church has a wealth of fittings. At the W end of the nave there is an hexagonal lead font which has two arches on each face. Under each arch there is a figure, making 12 in all, one of which has been identified as St. Peter, so that the others are probably the remaining Apostles. At the E end of the N aisle there is a large collection of architectural fragments, stone coffins and inscribed stones. There are the remains of five stone coffins of various dates, one of which was allegedly used in 979 for the burial of the murdered King Edward the Martyr. There are three tomb-lids. The pre-Conquest inscriptions date from between the 7C and the 9C. They are: VIDCV … FILIUS VIDA … (7C); IUDNNE … FILI QUI … (late 7C); DENIEL FILIUS … AUPRIT.IACET (late 8C); GONGORIE (9C); and finally, set in the E wall of the N aisle, CATGUG.C … FILIUS.GIDEO.(7C). These inscriptions were discovered mainly when the pre-Conquest church was demolished in 1841–42. They are sub-Roman rather than English in origin, having affinities with Welsh examples. In the N wall of St. Edward's chapel is inset an icon brought from Moscow in 1917.

There are many monuments. In the chancel there are two cross-legged effigies of knights: by the N wall, Sir William d'Estoke (died 1294), and on the S, Sir Henry d'Estoke (died 1240). In the chapel of St. Edward, in the E wall on the S side, is a small opening with a glass panel, behind which are displayed bones, said to be of Crusaders. On the S wall is a memorial plaque to the Reverend John Hutchins (died 1773), who is famous for his 'History and Antiquities of the County of

Dorset'. On the W wall of the N aisle is a cartouche with putti in memory of Arthur Addams (died 1774).

The stained glass is Victorian or 20C. The E window in the chancel, of seven lights, depicts the Crucifixion and the Easter story. In the S aisle, working W, there are a two-light window with a memorial date of 1903, which depicts St. Birinus, St. Aldhelm, Alfred the Great and Edward, King and Martyr; a two-light window which depicts Catgug the Wise, Beorthtric, Ethelfleda the Abbess and a Benedictine Prior and Rector (1915); and the 'Soldiers' window' with a Roman, Viking, Crusader and Roundhead. In the W wall the three-light window depicts Faith, Hope and Charity.

At an unknown location in the church is buried Beorthric, King of the West Saxons, who died in c 800.

St. Martin. At the N end of the town is St. Martin's, which stands on the site of a church believed to have been founded by St. Aldhelm in 678. The present building dates largely from the 11C and 12C. It was restored and rededicated in 1936.

The church is set on a bank and is stone-built and stone-tiled. The church is basically a pre-Conquest, two-cell building, to which has been added a Norman N aisle and a 16C SW tower. The tower rises only just above the height of the nave wall and the gable likewise is only just taller than the pitch of the nave roof. The interior is tall and narrow. The nave and N aisle are divided by a two-bay arcade of round arches, with a square pier rising to a square capital with stiff-leaf carving. The E respond rises from two Purbeck marble shafts with stiff-leaf capitals; the W respond simply has a carved capital. On either side of the chancel arch there are two large squints. The church has a three-light Perpendicular E window, deeply splayed lancets in the N and S walls of the chancel (the S one wider) and a two-light Decorated window in the S wall of the nave.

There are wall paintings in the church. On the N wall of the chancel there is a 15C depiction of St. Martin of Tours. He is on horseback with the remains of part of another horse, part of his cloak and a naked beggar. There are two further mounted figures. Over the chancel arch are painted the arms of Queen Anne, 1713. In the N aisle there stands the large recumbent marble effigy of T.E. Lawrence (or 'Lawrence of Arabia'; died 1935), by Eric Kennington. He is depicted in Arab dress. Lawrence was buried at Moreton, eight miles E of Wareham.

Whitchurch Canonicorum, *St. Candida (St. Wite)* and Holy Cross. Set in rolling countryside near the Devon border, the church is chiefly of the Early English period. It is important for the intact shrine of St. Wite (or Wita), which is the only medieval English shrine other than that of St. Edward the Confessor in Westminster Abbey to survive complete with its relics. 'Whitchurch' derives from Wite, via a mistaken assumption that the Old English name Wite meant white. 'Candida' is simply the Latin for white. 'Canonicorum' refers to the canons of both Salisbury and Wells, who once received the greater part of the income of the benefice.

The church is dominated by the W tower of three stages, which was built in the early 15C. It has set-back buttresses rising to a battlemented parapet with corner pinnacles. On the S face, in the uppermost stage, there are two panels of 15C carving, depicting an axe and a ship. There are similar designs on the N face. The tower is built of ashlar, the rest of the church largely of freestone. The aisles and S porch are embattled. The S porch is 15C, but it shelters a Norman doorway. The N aisle was rebuilt in 1847–48, as was the E end of the chancel. The rest of the chancel, plus the transepts, are 13C. On the E end of the nave there is the rare survival of a medieval sanctus bell turret. Reused Roman tiles may be seen in the walls of the N transept and in the N wall of the chancel.

Internally, the nave has five bays on the N and four on the S (excluding the arches into the transepts). The wider W arch in each arcade was rebuilt by Henry Pitfield in 1738. The remaining arches show the development from Norman to Gothic. The S arcade has two round piers with different capitals of late 12C character. The second arch from the W is round, but also chamfered. The other arches are pointed. The N arcade presents a totally different picture, the four E arches being roll-moulded except for one with deeply cut horizontal zigzag, and their piers having attached shafts and stylised floral and leaf capitals. This is early 13C work. Above, the clerestory has recessed quatrefoil lights. The tall tower arch is Perpendicular, with the soffit panelled in eight pairs of traceried arches, a feature which is repeated in the transept arches. The chancel arch is Early English and has foliate capitals. On its S side there is a blocked doorway which originally gave access to the Rood loft. The chancel E wall has three tall, shafted lancets. Ringed shafts may be seen in the two transepts, more notably on the N. It should finally be noted of the fabric that the nave curves and that the walls lean both inwards and outwards.

Perhaps the single most important feature is the shrine of St. Wite against the N wall of the N transept. It consists of a plain 13C stone chest with three pointed-oval openings in its S face, and, above it, a stone coffin with a Purbeck marble top. When the shrine was opened in 1900, a lead box with a Latin inscription was found. Translated, it read: Here rest the remains of St. Wite. Inside the box were the bones of a woman aged about 40. St. Wite is thought to have been a local 9C martyr, who died at the hands of the Vikings. It has been suggested that the external carvings on the tower recount her story, and that the ship is a Viking ship. How did her shrine and relics survive the Reformation? It is possible that the incumbent at the time declined to interfere with them, or, having done so, had second thoughts and restored them. Subsequently, the plain shrine might have seemed to be an anonymous tomb, without objectionable features to reformers. The shrine was probably typical of many of the lesser medieval shrines in England.

In the nave, the Norman font is circular and has a band of continuous decoration at the top and interlaced arches below. The octagonal wooden pulpit is Jacobean and has two arches to each panel. The pews in the nave and aisles have 16C panels with carvings of fleur-de-lis and various coats of arms. In the S aisle there are two carved panels, possibly of pre-Conquest origin, in the S wall. On the E wall of the S transept there is an 18C hatchment. A few medieval stained glass fragments remain; in the chancel, the W window in the S wall has two panels of 15C glass including an angel, foliage and some initials.

There are some fine monuments. In the chancel against the N wall the larger of two prominent memorials is to Sir John Jefferey (died 1611). His effigy lies on a chest whose front is divided into two richly carved panels. Two fluted Corinthian columns rise from ornate bases at each end of the chest to support an entablature with cherubs' heads, small statues of Faith and Charity and the usual heraldry. In the spandrels of the arch above the chest there are angels. The arch itself bears cherubs' heads and flowers. The back wall below the arch has strapwork and a centrally positioned inscription. The smaller neighbouring monument is to John Wadham (died 1585). It consists of a base with panels of quatrefoils enclosing shields. Above, there are further panels with cusped arches and also a brass inscription. At the top there is a pediment with four circles cut into it. A plaque erected on the S wall in 1908 commemorates Admiral Sir George Somers, a shipmate of Sir Walter Raleigh and a coloniser of Bermuda, who died there in 1611 and is buried under the vestry. On the E wall of the S transept a painted wooden tablet commemorates Elizabeth Floyer (died 1667). In the S aisle there is a part of the indent of a brass to Thomas de Luda and Alianore his wife, of c 1320.

Wimborne Minster, *St. Cuthburga.* This large church reveals a complex architectural history. A church has stood on the site since c 713 and this was built over Roman remains. A nunnery was founded by St. Cuthburga and survived until 1013, when it was sacked by the Danes. The church was refounded in 1043 by King Edward the Confessor on collegiate lines and remained on these lines until the Reformation. In 1318 King Edward II made it a Royal Peculiar. The church possesses a wealth of important fittings and a notable chained library.

The town is dominated by the church with its W and central towers. It is set in a raised, lawned churchyard and reveals work from four architectural periods. The central tower has Norman windows and arcading in two of its stages. The E end, including the E window of three stepped lancets, is Early English. Much of the rest of the fabric is Decorated and Perpendicular. The W tower was built in 1464. In its N face, in the easternmost of the two louvred lancet windows, is the famous quarter jack, who is attired as a Grenadier guardsman of the Napoleonic period, and who strikes two bells every quarter of an hour. A jack was first installed in 1612 at a cost of ten shillings and was originally a monk. The low range of vestries on the S side was added in 1970. In the churchyard on the S side is a sundial and on the N side, the war memorial.

The nave shows how the original Norman church has been subsequently enlarged. The westernmost pair of piers is of the Decorated period, octagonal with moulded capitals. The next pair are half-Norman and half-Decorated. The two W pairs of arches are double-chamfered. There follow two pairs of circular Norman piers and finally a pair of larger circular Norman piers. The piers carry Transitional pointed arches with zigzag decoration. The nave has a Victorian hammerbeam roof of 1855–57. The aisles are Decorated. The central tower is supported by four large stepped Norman arches with paired shafts to the inner arches and single shafts to the outer, and with scalloped capitals. The nave and choir arches are wider. The tower itself has a first stage consisting of an arcade with Purbeck marble shafts and a wall passage. The arches are grouped into fours under pointed blank arches. Above are two round-headed windows in each wall, and then a flat wooden ceiling with four decorated bosses. The transepts display Norman work, but they were extended at a later date and therefore also have Geometrical features. The choir, presbytery and side chapels are wider than the nave but reveal the same architectural development. The choir has two bays and Transitional piers and arches. The presbytery of two bays is Early English, with a magnificent triple-lancet E window. Underneath the presbytery is the crypt, used as the Lady chapel. This is three bays by three bays and was built in 1340 in the Decorated style. On the N side of the choir and presbytery is St. George's chapel, again Decorated, as is Holy Trinity chapel on the S.

The church possesses many fittings, monuments and much Victorian stained glass. The oldest object is the small section of Roman tessellated pavement on display under the floor of the nave on the S side. On the S wall of the W tower a 24-hour astronomical clock shows the heavens moving around the Earth. It was built in c 1320 by Peter Lightfoot, a monk from Glastonbury Abbey, who also made three further clocks, one of which survives at Wells Cathedral. The two angels and three gilded cherubs are 18C and came from the old organ case in 1856. The octagonal font is of late Norman workmanship and has a wide central pillar, eight Purbeck marble shafts and a Victorian wooden canopy. Above the tower arch are the royal arms. The W bay of the N aisle, which formerly served as the consistory court and which now houses the gift shop, has a particularly fine monument to Thomas Hanham (died 1650). The monument has Ionic pillars supporting a pediment, and two kneeling figures of Thomas and his wife facing one another. Below them is a cartouche with a skull. Also in the former consistory court is a plaque on the N wall to Elizabeth Snodgrass (died 1836). It was this name, on this memorial, which Charles Dickens was supposed to have seen and noted for later use in one of his novels. Under the central tower, by the choir steps, is the large Victorian pulpit, carved by Thomas Earp and given in 1868, replacing a fine Jacobean pulpit, which now resides at nearby Holt Church. The brass eagle lectern is dated 1623.

In the N transept are the remains of three superimposed layers of wall painting from the 13C, 14C and 15C. There are parts of two Crucifixions, the Virgin and Christ and St. John. On the same wall are the remains of an early carved tomb-lid. In the S transept, above the entrance to Holy Trinity chapel, there hangs an English great bascinet helmet of c 1490–1500. There is also a memorial on the S wall to Edward Barnes (died 1926), who was the first Mayor of the Metropolitan Borough of St. Pancras in London. The Holy Trinity chapel has in its S wall, in an arched recess, the painted wooden coffin of Anthony Ettricke. He was somewhat eccentric and he was, it was said, so annoyed with the people of Wimborne that he at one time stated that he would not be buried within or without the church nor below or above ground. He got round this by building a recess in the wall. He was also convinced that he would die in 1693 and therefore had his coffin accordingly inscribed. This accounts for the altered figures on the side, for he did not in fact die until 1703. He was responsible for sending the Duke of Monmouth for trial in 1685. St. George's chapel was restored in 1935. It has a number of important fittings. The oldest is the massive solid wooden pre-Conquest chest, made from a single tree trunk. There is another medieval chest opposite. On the right-hand side of the altar there are the fairly well-preserved remains of a Crusader's tomb, with a knight in chain-mail armour. Against the N wall is the large marble and alabaster monument, by an unnamed Italian craftsman, to Sir Edward Uvedale (died 1606). His effigy, depicting him supporting his head on his arm with his eyes open, is on a tomb-chest. This supports two Corinthian columns and an entablature, which in turn carries the family crest framed by two obelisks. Also buried in the chapel are the two daughters of Daniel Defoe.

In the choir the stalls date from c 1600 and have a series of arches and pillars as part of their decoration. The presbytery, which is raised on a further seven steps, has three important monuments. Firstly, on the S side, there is the large marble tomb-chest, with life-size recumbent alabaster effigies, of John Beaufort, Duke of Somerset (died 1444) and his wife Margaret, who were the grandparents of King Henry VII. On the same side by the altar are the piscina and sedilia, all under a richly ornamented series of stone tabernacles dating from the Decorated period. On the N wall, by the sanctuary step, is a brass dating from c 1440 to King Ethelred, who died in 871 from wounds received from fighting the Danes at nearby Martin. This is the only brass to an English king. Near to this is the marble tomb-chest of Gertrude Courtenay, Marchioness of Exeter (died 1558). Arguably the greatest treasure of the church, however, is the justly famous chained library, built over the choir vestry next to the S transept and reached by a small spiral staircase. It was begun in 1686 by the Reverend William Stone and many of its books have their original chains, rings and rods. There are 240 books, most being theological. The books include a manuscript of 1343 of the 'Regimen Animarum' (Direction of Souls), three Breeches Bibles of c 1595, and a Polyglot Bible in nine languages of 1653–57. There is also a first edition (of 1562) of 'De Concilio' by Cardinal Reginald Pole, published by Paulo Manutius, son of the famous Aldus Manutius and who was made Director of Printing at the Vatican in 1562. There are a number of royal seals and many historical documents in the library.

Nearly all the stained glass is Victorian. The one exception is the E window. The central lancet has what is apparently 15C Flemish glass, which came from a Belgian convent as a gift from W.J. Banks, one of the great collectors from nearby Kingston Lacy. It represents the Tree of Jesse. Amongst the other glass are the single lancets in the N and S walls of the presbytery which represent the Evangelists. The N transept N window of four lights dates from 1891 and depicts four Wessex saints and scenes from their lives. They are St. Dunstan, St. Edward the Martyr, St. Richard and St. Sidwell. In the former consistory court is a two-light window depicting St. Luke and the church's patron saint, St. Cuthburga. The large six-light W window depicts the Apostles. The S transept S window was installed in memory of William Druitt (died 1892) and depicts Christ healing the sick.

The importance of Wimborne Minster is reflected in its historical connections. It was the pre-Conquest monastery on this site to which St. Boniface turned for assistance in getting missionaries to help him in Germany. In 871 King Alfred the Great buried his brother Ethelred in the church. King Henry VII's mother, Lady Margaret Beaufort, founded a chapel here and installed a priest 'To teach grammar to all comers' in 1496. In 1499, Hugh Oldham was Dean; he later became Bishop of Exeter and founded both Corpus Christi College, Oxford and Manchester Grammar School. Reginald, Cardinal Pole was also Dean of Wimborne in 1517, when he was only 17.

Wimborne St. Giles, *St. Giles*. The church is externally Georgian, rebuilt in 1732 and attributed to John and William Bastard (see Blandford Forum). It was given arcades and a N chapel by G.F. Bodley in 1886–87, and after a severe fire in 1908 Sir Ninian Comper was employed on its restoration and to add a N aisle. It is a treasure-house of Comper fittings and stained glass. It also has a very good collection of monuments of the Ashley family, Earls of Shaftesbury.

The church sits on the edge of the village green next to the almshouses built in 1624. The W tower has three diminishing stages has round-headed belfry windows and a balustraded parapet with urns at the corners. As at Blandford, there is even quoining. The W face has a pedimented porch and an additional round-headed window above it. Internally, the nave is of three bays with a narrow S aisle and a wide N aisle. The arcades have tall circular piers on octagonal bases, with plain octagonal capitals and simple shallow arches. The sumptuously decorated Rood screen which runs across the entire width of the church effectively separates the chancel and the Lady chapel, which are structurally continuations of the nave and N aisle, from the rest of the church.

At the W end Comper's wooden gallery stretches across the width of the church and is almost a bay deep. The gallery, which is supported by five octagonal piers, contains the organ which was built by Harrison & Harrison. In front of the gallery in the nave is the font which seems to be 17C. It has a circular bowl and an octagonal baluster and an ornate gilded canopy by Comper, supported on eight pillars with a tall tapering spire. The nave has a large brass chandelier and each of the pillars has attached two-light candelabra. The roof of the nave is highly decorated, the beams being supported by angels with unfurled wings. The magnificent Rood screen has arches with complex tracery and a vaulted canopy. Between each arch there is the figure of an Apostle set in a tabernacle. Above the figures is a continuous band of foliate carving. Over the chancel entrance are the Rood figures of Christ on the Cross flanked by the Virgin Mary and St. John, with attendant seraphim and dragons. On the S side the screen becomes part of the Ashley family pew. The reredos of the high altar depicts Christ on the Cross in the centre, flanked by St. Giles, St. Anthony, St. Benedict, St. Francis, St. Edward the Martyr, St. Osmund, St. Aldhelm and St. Rumbold. The soffit of the E window is decorated with ten shields under crowns and there are two figures in niches above the reredos. High over the altar above the E window is a tester which has a centrally placed Holy Dove.

In the N aisle there is a large memorial to the first Earl of Shaftesbury (died 1683, but the monument was not erected until 1732). It consists of a bust by J.M. Rysbrack above three female profiles in medallions. The monument to the third Earl (died 1712) consists of a niche containing a statue of a mourning female, underneath which is a sarcophagus. In the Lady chapel against the N wall is the large tomb of Sir Anthony Ashley, Bt. (died 1628) and his wife. It is painted and consists of their recumbent effigies upon a sarcophagus under an elaborate arched canopy. Kneeling by the side of the sarcophagus and facing E is the figure of their daughter. At Sir Anthony's feet is a hexagon believed by some to represent a stylised cabbage. Numerous Corinthian columns support a superstructure with two central arches, above which there are two inscription plates, heraldry and two allegorical figures. Over the S door is the large pedimented monument to Barbara, Dowager Countess of Shaftesbury (died 1811) by Rudolph Schadow, 1819. Also against the S wall is a recumbent stone effigy of a cross-legged knight, much restored, which is possibly that of Sir John de Plecey (died 1313). There is a memorial in the family pew to the most famous of the Earls of Shaftesbury, the seventh Earl (died 1885), the famous 19C philanthropist who is remembered by the statue of Eros in Piccadilly Circus, London, by Alfred Gilbert.

Nearly all the stained glass is by Comper. The only window not by him is the one in the W gallery which depicts St. Anthony, St. Anna, St. Simeon, St. Joseph and St. Giles. The large window in the N wall which depicts St. Christopher, St. Sebastian and St. Stephen is in memory of the seventh Earl. Beneath the main figures are scenes of the First Miracles, Baptism and the Boy Christ. Behind the tomb of Sir Anthony Ashley in the Lady chapel, the four-light window depicts King Charles I, St. Cuthburga (see Wimborne Minster), King Alfred the Great and a female saint largely obscured, possibly St. Elfuga. The E window of the Lady chapel is in memory of the first Duke of Westminster, who died at St. Giles's House (the home of the Earls of Shaftesbury) in 1899. The window dates from 1910 and depicts St. Gabriel and St. Michael flanking the Virgin and Child. The three-light E window of the chancel shows the Triumphant Christ surrounded by angels with David and the Prophets singing praises beneath. In the S wall the middle window has some 16C German or Flemish panels which show the Entry into Jerusalem and St. Andrew presenting a kneeling person to a figure on a throne.

THE ISLE OF ELY

The Isle of Ely was a separate administrative district for centuries. It was a county in its own right until 1965, when it was merged with Cambridgeshire. It encompasses not only the small cathedral city, but also all the land in the present county for over 20 miles to the N, reaching the borders of Lincolnshire and Norfolk, and includes too several miles S of the city. Large though this area may be, its acres of farmland lie deep in the Fens and there has never been any prospect of building many churches on this soft ground, except where the local greensand ridges have provided a solid island—such as one may find at Haddenham, Sutton and Manea. The county has four main centres, Ely in the S, March and Whittlesey in the centre of the true Fenland district, and the ancient seaport of Wisbech in the far N. The other settlements are little more than tiny clusterings of houses around a church or chapel, which were built as the waterlogged Fens were drained between the 17C and the 19C. Evidence of the great draining programmes may be seen in the parallel Bedford Rivers which were carved across the county, and in the drains and lodes found everywhere. These man-made rivers, banked above the dark, flat lands, much of which lie below sea level, together with the railways, form the major features of the area. Occasionally, however, a spire or an unusual tower built from imported stone catches the eye.

The greatest church of the district is, of course, Ely Cathedral, at one time isolated by the marshes, but always dominating the administration of the surrounding places of worship. It contains the oldest stone monument in the county—Ovin's cross—which dates from the 7C and commemorates an official of the foundress, Queen Etheldreda. Etheldreda (or Aethelthryth) was an East Anglian princess who, after two marriages, founded a monastery at Ely in 673. She died in 679. The fabric of Ely Cathedral is substantially Norman. Elsewhere, the most significant representatives of the Norman style are the columns and arches at Wisbech and the columns and capitals at Tydd St. Giles; Stuntney also retains work from this era. The Early English style may be seen in the well-preserved All Saints', Elm, and in its early or Transitional phase at Downham. Work of c 1300 is found at Haddenham. The tower at Wilburton and the detached tower at Tydd St. Giles should also be noted. The major examples of the Decorated period are included in the main text, but Chatteris may be added as an almost complete 14C church, and Stretham also, with its tower, spire and other features. The Perpendicular churches are once again covered by the main entries, with Wilburton providing an additional fine example, and Parson Drove with its tower and arcades. Of the Victorian period, mention should be made of Prickwillow by the local architect, R.R. Rowe, work at Littleport by S.S. Teulon, and at Tydd St. Giles by Sir Gilbert Scott.

The earliest figurative church decoration in the Isle must be the canopied carving at Wentworth of St. Peter with his key, dating from about the 12C. A late Gothic reredos survives at Coveney, dated c 1500 and carved in Germany, whilst Wilburton possesses a strange reminder of the great 16C Bishop of Ely, John Alcock, in the form of a wooden cockerel standing on a globe and suspended from the roof. At Prickwillow, there stands in a Victorian church the beautiful font which came originally from Ely Cathedral and dates from 1693. From the 19C, one should note the N aisle E window at St. Mary's, Doddington, by Morris & Co., dating from c 1865.

An interesting fact in the history of the Church in East Anglia is that Nicholas Breakspear, who was a curate at Tydd St. Giles in the 12C, rose to become Pope Adrian IV, the only English Pope.

Ely

St. Mary. Somewhat hidden by trees, St. Mary's stands to the W of Palace Green, and is the parish church of the whole of Ely. The building represents a fine example of Transitional architecture.

The exterior has been altered since St. Mary's was built by Bishop Eustace (1198–1215); the W tower and spire were added in the 14C, and the clerestory was added in the 15C together with aisle windows. The tower supports four pinnacles at the corners and an hexagonal spire with two tiers of dormers. To the S of the S aisle stands a late 13C chapel with a triple-lancet E window. The N porch is 14C, and inside is revealed the very fine doorway from c 1200 with its gently curved, spine-like arches, and the banded shafts with their stiff-leaf capitals. The doorway is Transitional Norman and leads into an interior of refined proportions in the earliest Gothic style.

The Norman columns of the seven-bay nave are of tall circular section with scalloped capitals, whereas the arches are in the Early English manner. Perhaps the pointed arches replace a slightly earlier, round-headed set, but it is also possible that the entire arcades date from the Transitional period when the two styles blended together. The broad, high 14C arch at the E leads into the 13C chancel with its four narrow lancets together with windows replaced at later dates. The Perpendicular E window with its sharply pointed arch is surely a respectful gesture from a later era to the builder of the dignified nave arcades.

The flat nave ceiling was painted to the designs of F. Franey in 1876. A fine Early English double piscina with a detached column exists in the S chapel. An Edwardian reredos of alabaster stands on the E wall of the S aisle. The E window is by C.E. Kempe, 1904. Outside in the churchyard, to the S, may be found an old pre-Norman font of Barnack stone with an inscription in lead lettering. On the SW buttress of the nearby tower, a plaque commemorates the five people hanged in 1816 as a result of 'divers Robberies' in the Littleport riots.

The half-timbered vicarage which stands on the NE border of the churchyard is known as Cromwell House, and was occupied by Oliver Cromwell when he was collector of tithes before proceeding to represent Cambridge in Parliament in 1640.

Prior Crauden's Chapel. This small chapel, at one time especially reserved for the Prior, lies S of the cathedral amongst the old monastic buildings which now form part of King's School.

The first half of the 14C saw a great programme of building at Ely, all of it inspired by the Sacrist, Alan of Walsingham. In 1321, the foundations of the Lady chapel were laid, but in the following year the massive Norman crossing tower fell, demolishing part of the choir, and the building of the Lady chapel was postponed whilst the magnificent octagon and lantern were constructed on the site of the former tower. During the early planning of these buildings, John

Prior Crauden's Chapel: a two-storey private chapel which is a famous example of the 14C Decorated style

Crauden, who was Prior in 1321–41, decided to build his chapel. Although the chapel is modest in size, being intended only for his private daily worship, the underlying pattern of the work has the ingenuity of a master craftsman, and many features indicate a common architect for the chapel and the contemporary cathedral work. Comparison of individual items may appear to indicate a dual purpose for this building. It is possible that the aim of a private chapel was coupled with the intention of constructing a model of experimental ideas in their built form. Many years of effort were about to be invested in the cathedral and it might have been considered prudent to attempt first a miniature replication of decorative designs.

The chapel of c 1321–25 occupies the first floor of a building adjoining the Prior's House and is supported by walls and vaults dating from the 13C which lie below the stringcourse. The chapel was constructed together with a new hall and study which were added to his lodgings; the study connected with the chapel by a wooden covered passage, but this was removed during the 19C. The grouping of these buildings conjures a scene of great antiquity and picturesque value. The three buttresses on the S wall divide it into two equal parts; the W half contains only one small, low window opening into the antechapel, whereas to the E, a pair of full-height twin-light windows was provided. The tall, elegant exterior composition is completed by a five-light E window having original Decorated tracery which makes fascinating use of the contemporary ogee curve; the E window is slightly higher than the side lights and breaks into the plain roof gable. Following the path leading to the W entrance one may see the low doorway to the undercroft, now a store. In the NW corner stands a spiral staircase which is separate from the main walls of the building and which actually opens onto an outside platform before leading through a small doorway in the N wall of the chapel. Above the staircase tower, an external opening, meant to contain a bell, lies empty.

The interior is small, no more than 31ft long by 15½ft wide, but the space is taut with the highly charged energy of much sophisticated, tightly controlled stone decoration. The N and S walls are divided into four compartments. The two E ones are occupied by tall two-light windows, the W one being plain ashlar with only the doorway breaking the NW corner. The remaining one on each side, second from the W, contains complex niches, one above the other and reaching the full height of the chapel walls, with ribs and shafts threading over and behind each other, interlacing three dimensionally and making bold use of the nodding ogee motif. The upper niche is empty but at one time probably held a statue, whilst the lower one contains a small window. The upper portions show such a close resemblance to the eight high niches on the octagon piers in the cathedral, as do the lower parts to the canopies in the Lady chapel, that the designer of all these motifs has long since been considered to be the same person. Again, not only do Prior Crauden's tabernacles match those in the cathedral in overall appearance but the sections of the masonry shafts have been demonstrated to be almost exactly the same. This would imply that the stone details in the chapel were designed a year or two before the octagon was undertaken in 1322–28 and 15 years before the Lady chapel was finally completed between the years c 1335–53. It is worth noting that the uncarved blocks of stone so clearly visible in the N tabernacle were left blank deliberately in the 19C restoration. The chapel had been deserted after the Reformation and converted subsequently into a dwelling, a fate which happily saved it from piecemeal destruction during the Civil War. A plan dated 1803 by William Wilkins shows the first conjectural view of the chapel without the additional two floors, and the walls and fireplaces used to form the interior of the house. The damaged stonework was restored in 1846 but the masons' original lines were maintained where replacement was necessary. Professor Willis, the architectural historian from Cambridge University, reconstructed the plan of the vaults of the wooden roof from the sections which were discernible in the wall shafts. Other details were restored including the heads of human figures on the tabernacle arches. The angles of the E wall contain two tall, blank arcades surmounted by ogee arches having two arches inserted beneath them, evidently to support statues and to form two further cubicles, namely the aumbry on the left and the piscina on the right. Around the walls of the chapel beneath the features described above runs a bench-table set at different heights from the floor emphasising the varied bases of the vault piers.

Special mention must be made of the remarkably complete tile pavement, formed in a mosaic arrangement of yellow and green glazed clay. The pavement is seen best today on the raised altar area where lies the large 'Temptation of Adam and Eve'. Eve, to the left, offers Adam an apple whilst he holds another of the same fruit. Between the two standing figures, the serpent is twined around the tree, his head level with that of Eve. Features such as eyes and leaves were added by hand-incised lines. The whole of this panel, which is over three feet long, has been considered too large for the overall design of the chapel floor and it has been suggested that the tiles might have been made for the Lady chapel but used here after its postponement in 1322. The pavement suffered some wear when in domestic use and is now protected permanently by a carpet. Heraldic beasts, including several lions passant and a wyvern, are the only other representational forms and these are stylised as though designed for a medieval banner. A medieval fresco painting of the Crucifixion on the SW wall faces the entrance; almost certainly the chapel was coloured throughout originally, but the painting which remains is much faded. The E window contains five panels showing figures of saints which are said to have come from Cologne Cathedral and which date from c 1850. These windows were given by Lady Smart and she also painted the 'Render unto Caesar' and 'Good Shepherd' scenes in the tracery above. The windows were installed during the restoration of the chapel, part of whose cost was borne by Lady Smart's brother.

March, *St. Wendreda.* March lies on the River Nene, and although a large marshalling yard for the railway has recently been closed, the town remains an important agricultural centre for the Fens. The church stands half a mile S of the centre. Early in the Middle Ages, St. Wendreda's was a chapelry to the church at nearby Doddington, but later became a place of pilgrimage for those seeking relief from sickness. The major architectural feature is the celebrated angel roof over the nave, arguably the finest in the country.

The oldest part of the present church, the N arcade, dates from c 1300. In 1343 a papal indulgence was obtained for building the Decorated features such as the lower parts of the tower, the S arcade and the chancel arch. The Perpendicular parts date from c 1500 and include the aisles with battlements, a variety of remarkable gargoyles over the apex of each window and the clerestory which has brick and flushwork decoration above the window arches with square panels between the windows, each displaying an individual pattern in flint. The slim tower and spire were completed between 1350 and 1380; at the SE corner a substantial stair turret reaches to the battlements, whilst the other corners are supported by gently stepping buttresses. Running N–S underneath the tower, an arched passage used to carry the road which now lies to the W of the church; notice the fine window with Decorated flowing tracery above the archway on the W side. The octagonal stone spire has two sets of four lucarnes on the cardinal faces. The E gable of the nave supports pinnacles to N and S and, over the central gable, a sanctus bellcote. The S porch dates from 1528 and is decorated with two gargoyles above the angle buttresses. The chancel was added in 1872 and possesses a tiled roof, in contrast to the nave which is lead-covered.

Inside, the N arcade dates from c 1300, about 50 years before its S counterpart; the two arcades differ mainly in the chamfering of the arches but the NW bay was narrowed when the tower was built. The aisles were renewed in the second major building period dating from c 1500; each three-light window is set within a shallow recess. The Perpendicular clerestory of nine tall windows over both the N and S arcades allows plenty of light onto the major and most exciting feature of the interior: the oak double hammerbeam roof which dates from the last quarter of the 15C or the first years of the 16C. There are 118 carved wooden angels altogether, most of them holding musical instruments. The three tiers of angels lie, at the lower level, on the corbels beneath the clerestory and, above these, on the ends of the twin hammerbeams. A fourth, less visible set are attached to the top of the collars which cross at the apex of the roof. In between the clerestory windows and above the angel corbels

15TH CENT'Y DOUBLE HAMMERBEAM ROOF
ST WENDREDA'S • MARCH •

Drawing by the Reverend Brian Roy

stand canopied figures of saints and Apostles displaying symbols of the Passion and martyrdom. The two easternmost statues represent **S** St. Etheldreda, the foundress of the abbey at Ely, and **N** St. Wendreda wearing a wimple. A further group of angels may be seen in the N aisle, whilst the S aisle contains strange carvings of distorted human figures.

The church contains few fittings of note. The Norman font has corners cut to an angle leaving circular carvings on only four of the eight faces. The octagonal pedestal is medieval. In the S aisle, one may see the brass to Anthony Hansard (died 1507) and his wife Kathryn, together with a depiction of the Annunciation. The Hansards probably contributed to the cost of the angel roof. The gallery within the tower arch is Jacobean and is used by the bell ringers, but before the organ was installed in the 19C it was used by the musicians. The interior is marred by a large boiler in the S aisle.

St. Wendreda was a 7C princess, a sister of both Etheldreda of Ely and Sexburgh, foundress of the monastery on the Isle of Sheppey. St. Wendreda practised her powers of healing at Exning in Suffolk and also at March, and when the story of her remarkable abilities was heard by King Cnut, he is said to have been converted to Christianity. Her shrine remained in the church until c 1545.

Wisbech, *St. Peter and St. Paul.* Wisbech lies on the River Nene. The prosperity of the port made possible the fine Georgian developments along the river banks which are known as the Brinks. Set within the Coronation gardens of 1953, the church of St. Peter and St. Paul has an unusual plan comprising two naves and two aisles which forms an interior of generous space but which is somewhat dark.

The church was begun in the 12C but from the exterior the only visible remains of this period are the buttresses of the old tower which may be seen on each side of the W door. To the southernmost buttress was added at a later date a narrow spiral staircase with a stone-capped hexagonal sanctus bellcote. Elsewhere the church remains 14C in appearance, with some windows replaced in the 15C. To the S of the Norman nave, a second nave was added in the 14C, and new aisles were built to N and S of this larger dual nave. The large W window of the S nave is a superb example of 14C Reticulated tracery. The N windows of the clerestory were replaced in the 15C, but on the S only some were replaced. Walking to the E one finds the steeper roof of the S chancel, which was constructed in the later 14C as a small side chapel and subsequently converted into a chancel for the new S nave. To the E of this chancel is a vestry dating from c 1500 which was once probably a guild chapel. It possesses square-headed windows and battlements which are elaborately decorated with coats of arms. To the N lies the main chancel of the 14C, comprising four bays, with a 15C clerestory to the SE, and a 19C E window. The Norman tower collapsed in c 1525; above the N entrance rises its replacement, a substantial Perpendicular tower which is actually detached from the N aisle by a few inches. The scheme of carving is beautifully detailed and contains some interesting imagery. The base of this well-proportioned tower contains a quatrefoil frieze, followed higher up by stringcourses running all the way around the walls and over the elegant bell openings, whilst the slim set-back buttresses give the impression of effortless support. Beside the clock-faces lie carved stone panels showing the arms of Bishop Goodrich of Ely (1534–54), the Sees of Ely and of Canterbury, the emblem of St. Katherine, and a depiction of a monstrance. The stepped battlements with pinnacles add a final light touch to the tower.

On entering through the W door, one notices the thick walls to N and S which indicate the position of the former 12C tower. The 12C N arcade leads the eye towards the wide arrangements of the E end. The unusual bend in the N nave arcade was constructed to accommodate the widened chancel which was enlarged in the 14C. To the N of the nave lies a 14C aisle, and to the S another nave lies beyond a Perpendicular arcade which was probably built after the collapse of the tower in c 1525. The N chancel is almost as long as the nave and compensates for the great width of the nave and aisles. One further architectural detail should be mentioned: the N door under the tower is 14C and finely carved with foliage and monsters.

One of the finest fittings is the royal arms at the W end of the S aisle. The supporting beasts are suitably showy, whilst the shield displays meticulous craftsmanship. The clerestory windows contain 15C glass, whilst Victorian glass was installed during the restoration of the church in 1856–58 by William Bassett-Smith, including the E window by John Hardman & Co. Inside the chancel there are a number of memorials including a large brass to Thomas de Braunstone, Constable of Wisbech Castle (died 1401) (beneath the carpet). The fine Parke memorial lies on the N wall and dates from the 17C. Edward Southwell was given a memorial with an obelisk by Joseph Nollekens, 1787. The reredos was designed by Bassett-Smith and was made from mosaic in 1885 by Salviati. Medieval misericords may be seen on the S of the chancel. The Lady chapel contains the organ by Harrison's, 1951, providing tone of a particularly high quality. The case dates from 1963, when the chapel was restored.

Thomas Clarkson was born and brought up in Wisbech and was an important leader during the slave trade reforms. Tablets to his parents may be found in the floor of the sanctuary. His own Gothic Revival monument, designed in 1881 by Sir Gilbert Scott, may be seen near the bridge in the town.

ESSEX

Essex is a fascinating county which is often underrated. It has over 350 medieval churches which are worth getting to know, and a rich variety of 19C and 20C churches. Essex is a county of contrasts in its landscape, its villages and its churches. There are miles of busy suburbs in the SW which make up 'London over the Border'. This conurbation grew out of old villages with churches of medieval foundation, like Barking, East and West Ham, Dagenham and Little Ilford. It is here that the 19C churches are prolific and where some of the best examples in the county may be discovered. The industrial and marshy Thames-side in the S looks over to Kent. This area is not always very picturesque but many of its churches are interesting, including West Thurrock, Rainham, Stifford, the Tilburys, Corringham and Fobbing. The Essex coastline and estuaries, with their marshes and islands, have a beauty of their own, with atmospheric places like Mersea, Brightlingsea, Burnham-on-Crouch, Paglesham and Bradwell-on-Sea. The N boundary with Suffolk, within reach of the beautiful Stour valley, has charming villages with an East Anglian flavour and churches like Dedham, Ardleigh and Great Bromley. There is the hilly NW, around Strethall, the Chesterfords and Chrishall, and the Hertfordshire borderland, with its farmsteads and rural scenery, where we find the occasional 'Herts spike' and endearing churches like Stanstead Mountfitchet, Roydon and the Hallingburys. Beneath is the forest area in the W, around Epping, High Beach, Chingford and Hatfield Broad Oak.

So much for the fringes of the county. Its heart is also fascinating, with green lanes and villages of great character, like the seven Rodings, the three Lavers, the Braxteds, the Notleys, the Easters, the Walthams and the Willingales, the latter with two churches in one churchyard. The old world market towns of Essex have some of its finest churches. Saffron Walden, Thaxted, Great Dunmow and Coggeshall are superb, and there are interesting churches at Halstead, Witham, Braintree and Rayleigh. The vast new towns like Harlow and Basildon have brought vast populations to former village parishes and in addition to their ancient churches, several imaginative modern ones have been built. The medieval parish church of Chelmsford has become the cathedral, its other churches being all 19C or 20C. Colchester, however, has seven medieval churches in its centre and three more in its suburbs.

In Essex we see a good representation of all periods. Its two pre-Conquest gems are the 7C chapel of St. Peter at Bradwell, and the 9C church at Greensted, with its wooden nave. In addition, the tower of Holy Trinity, Colchester, the churches at Rivenhall and Hadstock and at least a dozen other churches show pre-Conquest work. The use of Roman bricks and tiles may be seen in over 100 churches. Norman architecture is prolific, with several churches of this date remaining almost structurally unaltered. Rainham and Great Canfield are good examples, also Hadleigh, Great Clacton, Little Tey and Heybridge. Ambitious 12C craftsmanship may be seen at Castle Hedingham, Waltham Abbey and in Great Tey's massive tower. Although little premier Early English work survives here, many Essex churches are lit by lancet windows of this period and what could be more enjoyable than Tilty's simple 13C nave and its flamboyant 14C Decorated chancel? The latter style is gloriously represented in the chancels at Lawford, Great Sampford and Great Dunmow, and in several graceful arcades. The Perpendicular style is seen at its best in the great churches of Saffron Walden, Thaxted and Dedham; other good examples occur at Brightlingsea, Newport, Prittlewell, Great Yeldham, Great Bromley and Fingringhoe.

Of post-medieval work, the 18C gave Essex the little church at Shellow Bowells in 1754, the rebuilding of Ingrave in 1735, Thomas Hardwick's splendid Classical church at Wanstead (1787–90) and the Adam church at Mistley, of which only the towers remain. Several churches were refurbished in the 18C, including St. Peter's at Colchester, Debden, Lambourne and the tower at Terling. The early part of the 19C is represented by such churches as Harwich (M.G. Thompson, 1821) and the distinctive churches of St. Botolph, Colchester and Rowhedge (1837 and 1838, both by W. Mason). The Gothic Revival is well represented. There are many large and impressive churches in the 'London over the Border' area, like James Brooks' St. Andrew's, Plaistow, S.S. Teulon's ornate St. Mark's, Silvertown, the Cutts Brothers' churches of St. Edmund, Forest Gate and St. Alban, Ilford, F.T. Dollman's St. Saviour's, Walthamstow, James Bignell's St. Michael's, Walthamstow and Sir Herbert Baker's St. Andrew's, Ilford. In the county generally there are several 19C churches worth seeing. J.P. St. Aubyn designed two near Chelmsford, at Widford and Galleywood, G.F. Bodley designed the magnificent St. John's, Epping, Gilbert Scott designed Holy Trinity, Halstead and Greenstead Green and W.D. Caroë created the church of St. John at Stanstead Mountfitchet. The Southend area has several of interest—from Brooks' All Saints' to Sir Charles Nicholson's 20C churches of St. Alban, Westcliff and St. Margaret, Leigh and Sir Walter Tapper's mighty redundant church of St. Erkenwald. Clacton has a grand unfinished church of St. James by Temple Moore, Brentwood and nearby Bentley Common have distinctive churches by E.C. Lee and Great Warley Church is an Arts and Crafts extravaganza by C. Harrison Townsend. Interesting churches by local architects include Little Canfield, rebuilt in 1839 by its Rector, Charles Smith, and Rawreth, designed by the Reverend Ernest Geldart, who also transformed the interior of his own church at Little Braxted. Frederick Chancellor restored many churches and designed new ones at Pleshey, Steeple and Ford End. Interesting modern churches in new developments include St. Paul's, Harlow (1959), St. Martin's, Basildon (1962), the Ascension, Chelmsford (1962) and the 12-sided church of St. Gabriel, Pitsea (1964).

An important feature of Essex churches is the variety of building materials. In no other county are Roman tiles and bricks so widely reused in churches. Many churches are built of flint rubble and in some may be seen grey-brown septaria from the coast. Several churches in the S of the county use grey ragstone from Kent, particularly in their towers—Leigh on Sea, Fobbing, Rettendon, Canewdon and Prittlewell being among the finest. Essex must hold the record for the use of timber in churches, not only in porches, but also in belfries and complete towers, to say nothing of Greensted's pre-Conquest nave. The distinctive wooden belfries with their perky spirelets or pyramidal roofs not only have great rustic charm and character from the outside, but also usually rest upon sturdy timber frameworks inside the church. Many of these are medieval and they occur in more than 80 churches. In several other cases a stone or brick tower has been given a timber top, as at Marks Tey, Great Oakley, Upminster, Fyfield and others. The complete timber towers are mostly to be found in the area S of Chelmsford. These are remarkable constructions, with massive timber frameworks inside and usually receding stages outside, terminating in a spire. They occur at Navestock, Magdalen Laver, Blackmore, Margaretting, Stock, Ramsden Bellhouse, West Hanningfield and Mundon. Small wooden detached bell-houses may be seen at Wix and Wrabness. Unusual timber features include the six-bay arcade at Shenfield and the 15C font at Marks Tey. Needless to say, in this county of timber, we find many interesting roofs, fine medieval porches and ancient doors. The other material in which Essex excels is brick, which adds colour and charm to a church. Most of the brickwork is Tudor, of late 15C or early 16C date, although there are a few earlier examples from the 13C. Tudor brickwork may be seen in over 30 towers, including grand and lofty ones, like Theydon Garnon, Rochford, Ingatestone and Gestingthorpe, also c 22 porches, the best of which include Feering, Sandon and Pebmarsh. Parts of churches were rebuilt in brick, including the chancels at Greensted, Little Warley, Basildon and Langley, the fine clerestory at Great Baddow and arcades at St. Osyth and Blackmore. There are complete brick churches at Woodham Walter, East Horndon, Layer Marney and the fascinating church at Chignal Smealy, where the arcade and even the font are of brick. The 17C and 18C also produced craftsmanship in brick, with several towers and four complete churches.

Amongst notable furnishings are a rich variety of fonts, including several 12C and 13C ones and some good font covers, including Littlebury, Thaxted, Takeley, Fingringhoe and Pentlow. Over 100 churches have ancient timberwork in their roofs. In the N of the county are several hammerbeam roofs, including a rare 14C example at Tendring and late specimens by Thomas Loveday at Gestingthorpe, Castle Hedingham and Sturmer. Many of the ancient roofs have tiebeams with kingposts. Essex timberwork extends to a large selection of parish chests, including the fine 13C chest at Newport, but stalls are not so plentiful as in Norfolk and Suffolk. Although medieval timber screens, or parts of them, may be seen in c 50 churches, the most remarkable pieces of Essex screenwork are the two 14C stone examples at Great Bardfield and Stebbing. About 50 churches have medieval wall paintings and there are noteworthy examples at Copford, Great Canfield, Little Easton and Fairstead. Monuments of interest occur in several churches. The county comes first in England for effigies in oak, with ten examples in five churches (Little Baddow, Elmstead, Danbury, Little Leighs and Little Horkesley). Interesting brasses may be seen in c 150 churches. Three brasses (at Pebmarsh, Wimbish and Bowers Gifford) date from the first half of the 14C and other premier churches for brasses include Wivenhoe, Little Easton, Tilty, Chrishall, Writtle, Aveley, Harlow and Dagenham, also Chigwell, which has an Archbishop of York in cope and mitre—Samuel Harsnett, who died in 1631.

Amidst the infinite variety of churches in Essex are many of those atmospheric and unspoilt little gems which are off the beaten track but are well worth seeking out. Amongst these should be included Great Canfield, Aythorpe Roding, Tilty, Theydon Mount, Barnston, Little Dunmow, Faulkbourne, Elmstead, Layer Marney, Easthorpe, Bradwell-juxta-Coggeshall, and the remarkable 'Black Chapel' at Northend, on the Chelmsford–Dunmow road.

Two 17C associations are of interest. At Hempstead, William Harvey—the discoverer of the circulation of the blood—lies buried. Messing was the home of President Bush's forbears until they emigrated to North America in King Charles I's reign.

Blackmore, *St. Laurence.* Blackmore is a picturesque village, whose church stands at the end of an attractive street of pleasant old houses, in a neat churchyard. This is part of the church of an Augustinian priory, founded c 1155–62 and dissolved in 1527. The building has been greatly altered since it was first built in c 1170 and in its structure is craftsmanship of various periods. Its main claim to fame lies in its fascinating W tower, considered to be the finest of the timber towers of Essex.

This remarkable structure, with its well-proportioned receding stages and shingled recessed spire, is constructed entirely of local oak and dates from the 15C. Its lower stage has a sturdy timber framework, and a timber-framed four-light W window, with moulded jambs and mullions. Lean-to roofs link the boarded stages above, each considerably narrower than the stage beneath it. The top stage has simple two-light belfry windows and is crowned by a splay-foot spire. A look at the silhouette of the whole structure from the W shows how its excellent proportions create a united and uplifting whole. Internally the structure of the tower is a remarkable array of timbers. The lower stage has ten sturdy timber posts with arch braces, arranged like a nave and aisles. Above these is an array of cross-struts in two tiers. This superb skeleton supports the structure which carries a ring of five bells.

From the churchyard only the N side of the exterior is visible and several pieces of Norman stonework can be seen reused in its masonry. The nave and aisles are beneath one all-embracing roof. The N wall is pierced by two-light, square-headed windows of late 14C date, which were restored in the 19C, and in the roof are large dormers, dating from the 16C or 17C, with unusual timber-framed windows.

A fine 14C doorway beneath a much renewed timber porch, admits us to the interior. This comprises the nave and aisles of the former priory church, the present E wall having been built just after the Dissolution by Sir Thomas Smyth, who removed the priory chancel. The W end is of interest because it is the W wall of the Norman church, with two Norman windows, a small circular window and a handsome Norman W doorway, with three orders of shafts and scalloped capitals. At this end on each side are traces of the former Norman clerestory. The N arcade is 14C, with quatrefoil piers, but the S arcade is of early 16C Tudor brick. The roof was greatly restored and renewed under the direction of Frederick Chancellor in 1896–98, but the architect carefully removed and cleaned several original shields of c 1400 which had remained.

The octagonal font is of Purbeck marble and dates from the 13C. The N chapel was until 1900 the sealed family vault of the Crickett family. In the SE part of the church is the blocked doorway with what is thought to be a salamander carved above it. This probably led to the canons' living quarters. Nearby are the alabaster effigies of Sir Thomas Smyth (died 1594) and Margaret, his wife. Although these have suffered some damage, their faces have great character; he is in armour and she is wearing a most beautiful dress. There are some interesting memorial slabs in the floors of the church, including one of c 1400 to 'the just Prior', Thomas De Vere, and another to Simon Lynch, Rector of Runwell and Curate of Blackmore, who was 'sequestered, prosecuted and persecuted to the day of his death by Gog and Magog'! These were the Puritans, who made life difficult for him, but he lived to see the Restoration of the monarchy in 1660. There is a cresset stone in a glass case under the tower.

Bradwell-on-Sea, *St. Peter ad Murum.* This simple stone chapel, standing in isolation at the end of a long track near the Essex coast, is one of the earliest surviving places of Christian worship in England. It stands within the former Roman fort of Othona, which was built during the latter part of the 3C and which later became the centre of a small settlement called, in Old English, **Ythancestir.** It was to this community that St. Cedd came in 653 with a group of missionaries to convert the East Saxons to Christianity. St. Cedd himself had this church built for his missionary and monastic community and after he was consecrated Bishop of the East Saxons in 654, it became his cathedral. St. Peter's was built using materials from the old Roman fort, across the former wall of the fort, and is therefore known as St. Peter ad Murum—St. Peter's on the Wall. After Cedd's death the chapel continued to be used for worship and at the end of the 14C, when a new parish church was built for the people of Bradwell who had moved some distance inland, it became a chapel of ease. In the 17C it was converted into a barn and it continued as such until 1920 when it was reconsecrated. Since that time careful restoration has been carried out under Laurence King.

St. Peter's today is a fragment of what it once was. In 1442 it was reported to have a nave, chancel and a small tower above its W porch, containing two bells. The E end was apsidal and there were transeptal chambers to N and S. The nave was divided from the chancel by a triple arcade as at Reculver in Kent. These were probably demolished when it was converted into a barn and in the N and S walls of the surviving nave can be seen where the large entrances to the barn were cut. What is left today is a rectangular building, some 49½ft by 21½ft, with walls 24ft high. In the walls are a mixture of building materials, including septaria, Kentish ragstone, limestone tufa and Roman tiles. The N and S walls are pierced by rectangular windows and the W wall has a rectangular doorway with a single window of Roman tiles above it. In the E wall may be seen the remains of the arch to the former chancel again incorporating Roman tiles.

Inside, this ancient shrine has been left uncluttered and dignified. The roof was renewed in 1947 (with the exception of one tiebeam, which is considerably older). There are few architectural details remaining, apart from the fragments of the chancel arch, and the only piece of medieval decoration is a little red colouring—part of a scroll pattern—dating from c 1200 in a recess which was once a window opening near the E end of the N wall. Furnishings have been kept to a minimum; the altar is simple and above it is a very fitting Christus Rex on the E wall. The whole building, however, breathes antiquity and devotion. The visitor feels that he is a pilgrim standing upon holy ground, where people have worshipped for over 13 centuries. This is an unashamed place of pilgrimage. It is one of our few links with Celtic Christianity and many people follow in the footsteps of St. Cedd each year, either as lone visitors or on Quiet Days in organised parties, or even in their hundreds as they journey here for the great diocesan pilgrimage which takes place each year.

Castle Hedingham, *St. Nicholas.* This church stands in a quiet corner of its attractive village which is set in the Colne Valley. Above the village stands the great castle keep of the De Veres, the Earls of Oxford. It is only when we go inside this church that we fully appreciate its importance as one of the largest and finest Norman churches in the county. This is late Norman work of c 1180 and just after, and we see here the beginnings of the transition to Gothic architecture. From the E arch of the former Norman tower, the Norman church, with nave, aisles and chancels, is some 125ft in length.

St. Nicholas: a Norman chancel and a W tower of typical Essex brickwork

The building is set in a pleasant and cared-for churchyard, which contains a churchyard cross incorporating the shaft and base of an 11C cross, which is embellished with Norman and pre-Conquest style decorations. The exterior shows a variety of building materials and styles. The aisles, of flint rubble, have square-headed 15C windows. Most of the clerestory windows are lined with Tudor brick and above them are the De Vere badges of the boar and the mullet (or star). The nave and aisles are crowned with embattled parapets of Tudor brick and this material is also seen in the trim S porch (note its external stoup) and in the handsome W tower. This is a stately structure with buttresses, pinnacles, three-light belfry windows, a five-light W window and a prominent stair turret, rising above the parapet and crowned with an 18C cupola and vane. An inscription on the W face of the tower states that it was renovated by the master builder, Robert Archer, in 1616, but it is probably c 100 years older than this. Over the W window are stone carvings connected with the 13th Earl of Oxford, who died in 1512, including his chain of state as Lord Great Chamberlain. Three Norman doorways remain, each preserving an original door with 12C ironwork; one in the N aisle, the main S door and the doorway in the S chancel wall. Castle Hedingham's chancel is a rare and beautiful piece from c 1180–90. It has Norman pilaster buttresses and small Transitional windows with pointed arches and shafts with foliage capitals. Above the three lancets in the E wall is a beautiful wheel-window with eight circular shafts (each with carved capitals and bases) forming its 'spokes'.

Inside we soon become aware of the size and proportions of the Norman church. The sturdy six-bay arcade has semicircular arches (except in the E bays which have later pointed arches) resting upon large circular and octagonal piers with leaf capitals. The chancel arch is a magnificent piece of craftsmanship of c 1190, its pointed arch made up of three-dimensional zigzag ornament. The chancel itself shows stately Norman design. Its tiny windows have large Norman rere-arches and are interspersed by blank arches. The piscina and graduated triple sedilia were given their pseudo-Norman canopies in the 19C, but the large aumbry in the N wall is medieval. Narrow aisles flank a wide nave which is crowned by a superb double hammerbeam roof, believed to be the work of Thomas Loveday, a local builder, who may also have made the fine roofs at Gestingthorpe and Sturmer.

The beautiful oak Rood screen dates from c 1400 and has been tastefully restored. The delicate openwork tracery and the richness of the woodcarving make this screen one of the finest in Essex. The choirstalls have also undergone much restoration, but their 15C misericord seats survive, on the undersides of which are carvings which merit examination and include foliage, animals and human faces, also an intriguing carving of a fox carrying away a priest, with an animal blowing a trumpet preceding them (second from W on S). There is 17C panelling in the S chapel and in the N aisle hangs an unusual royal arms of King Charles II, which is believed to have come from the castle. The S chapel has a window with stained glass by Percy Bacon and the glass in the W window of the tower, assembled between 1895 and 1899, shows the Prophets and Apostles upon whom the Church is founded. The large-scale model of the church made by Percy C. Brown is as impressive and accurate as any of its type.

This was the parish church of the De Veres and although most of their monuments were at Earl's Colne Priory (and are now at St. Stephèn's Chapel, Bures) some are buried beneath the chancel here. On the N side of the sanctuary is the tomb of John, the 15th Earl (died 1539) and his wife. Their effigies and arms are deeply incised in the black marble top slab and their four named and kneeling daughters may be seen in the side of the tomb-chest.

Colchester, *Holy Trinity, Trinity Street.* This is the oldest of Colchester's medieval churches; it stands in a busy pedestrianised area in the town centre and in 1971–73 was given a new lease of life as a museum. Its three-gabled body and pre-Conquest tower form a pleasant contrast to the modern buildings nearby.

The N and S aisles stretch the entire length of the nave and chancel. The N aisle was added in 1886, when the church underwent restoration. The S aisle, however, has some attractive Perpendicular windows and the E window of the chancel has early 14C flowing tracery. There is much septaria in the masonry of the walls. The main item of interest here is the W tower—a noteworthy example of pre-Conquest work, dating from c 1000. It is unbuttressed and has quoins of Roman tiles. There are several haphazard courses of these tiles in the stonework; the windows, blank arches and W doorway are framed with them. Double-splayed windows may be seen in the lower part on the N and S sides, whilst on the W side is a triangular-headed doorway. Higher up are blank arches and small round-headed windows, including the double belfry windows. The summit is finished off with later brickwork and has a distinctive pyramidal cap.

The interest inside lies not only in the museum exhibits but in the church itself. In the porch is its medieval door and a small chest of considerable age. The S doorway has worn corbel heads. The arcades have three bays to the nave and two to the chancel. The S arcade is medieval, the N of 1885. The small corbels on the former are original and have been picked out in colour. The S aisle roof has medieval timbers, partly hidden by a plaster ceiling. The beautiful 15C font is still in place. Its bowl panels are exquisitely carved with foliage and shields. Behind it is the semicircular-headed pre-Conquest tower arch of brick. Modern investigation has revealed that the core of the nave is in fact a little earlier than the tower.

Copford, St. Michael and All Angels. This delightful Norman church, which is famous throughout England for its magnificent wall paintings, takes a little finding, but the search is very rewarding! It stands near Copford Hall, about a mile from where the Stanway–Marks Tey road passes through Copford village. The winding lane takes us to the long and atmospheric churchyard, at the end of which, beautifully set against a backcloth of cedars, is this picturesque church, with its Essex belfry and spirelet, both of which are shingled, and with its rounded apse and sweeping tiled roof, which embraces the Norman nave and later S aisle.

The exterior blends beautifully with its picturesque and unspoilt setting. In the warm-coloured walls, amidst brown stone and tiles, are Roman bricks and also early medieval bricks which appear to have been copied from the Roman ones. The low S aisle was added in the late 13C or early 14C and the pretty timber porch was added in the 19C. A walk round to the N side, however, reveals the Norman church, built c 1130, with nave, chancel and apse. This is lit by remarkably large Norman windows which have single shafts within and without. The N doorway has a fine Norman arch and has an ancient door with good ironwork. The W window, with Y-tracery, was added c 1300 to give more light to the nave.

A deep and mysterious devotional dusk pervades the interior, which is also bathed in subdued colour. A look at the nave walls reveals where its original stone tunnel-vault began and we can visualise what the simple, low Norman building must have looked like before later builders pierced the S wall with three odd arches (the centre arch being of brick) to add the S aisle. The old 12C external buttresses can be seen from the aisle. The trussed rafter roof dates from c 1400: towards the E it is strengthened by tiebeams and kingposts.

The late 12C font has a square bowl of Purbeck marble, with shallow blank arches. Sturdy 15C timbers support the belfry at the W end. Two of the three bells were cast in the 15C and the other in 1574. Note the pieces of human skin (believed to have come from sacrilegious Danes) taken from the door and now framed, with an explanation of their gory details! Near the N door are hatchments and a set of royal arms and beneath the central arch of the arcade is a 14C oak chest. The beautiful traceried Rood screen has survived from the early 15C. Copford Church also contains good 20C timberwork in the memorial benches which were given between 1951 and 1956, and the choirstalls which were made in 1963.

Most fascinating of all are the beautiful wall paintings which people come from far and wide to see. They cover the little vaulted apse and large areas of the other walls. Although Daniel Bell was responsible for much restoration of them in 1872, the year after their discovery, these masterpieces date from c 1140–50. We see in the sanctuary Christ in Majesty, surrounded by angels and the Apostles with their emblems. Around the arch which leads to the apse are the Signs of the Zodiac. The Raising of Jairus' Daughter on the N side of the nave is pleasantly unrestored (but cleaned in 1967), but portrays beautifully the anxious face of Jairus, who wears a Jew's black hat. Enough remains in the outer fragments to show that the walls of the entire building must have been covered with these paintings.

Danbury, *St. John the Baptist.* Danbury's 120ft spire is visible for miles around; it stands at the summit of a 365ft hill, above the valley of the River Chelmer. The site upon which the church stands is part of an ancient oval earthwork which was constructed c 500 BC.

The tower is 14C, with belfry windows inserted in the late 15C, of which date is the timber framework of the shingled spire. The N aisle is the oldest part of the church, its two-light windows dating from the late 13C. The S aisle was rebuilt during the general restoration of 1866, to the designs of Sir Gilbert Scott. He also added the S chancel chapel, which was rebuilt in 1951, together with the E end of the chancel, following war damage. To the N of the chancel is a 15C sacristy.

The interior contains pleasing ancient and modern workmanship. The three-bay arcades are early 14C and have quatrefoil piers. The nave has a kingpost roof which incorporates 15C timbers and the N aisle has a wagon roof, the framework of which may well be 13C. The wainscoting and the six faces along the embattled cornice are 15C. There is a squint from the aisle through the great thickness of the wall into the chancel and another gives a view of the high altar from the sacristy.

The glass tower screen was erected in 1978; the gallery balustrade above it incorporates the 17C communion rails. The fine benches are mostly copies (by Gilbert Scott, 1866) of the four 15C benches which remain at the rear of the nave. Near the entrance to the choir vestry is an interesting collection of pictures, one showing the church with its former S aisle. Over the S doorway is a piece of alabaster sculpture which may have been part of an Italian reredos. The glass in the E window is of 1955 by Carl Edwards.

The memorials here are of interest. In the N and S aisles, beneath arched recesses, are three oak effigies of knights, each one being cross-legged. The two in the N aisle date from c 1272–1307 and that in the S aisle may be a little later. These are probably members of the St. Clere family. A large burial slab in the N aisle, with indents of a brass cross, inscription and two shields, may have covered the body of Sir Gerard de Braybroke (died 1422).

East Horndon, *All Saints.* An isolated church in a magnificent position, perched above the Southend arterial road and with a commanding view towards Tilbury and the Thames valley. All Saints' is built almost entirely of mellow red Tudor brick. The Norman church which stood here was rebuilt in the 15C and the 16C by the Tyrell family of Heron Hall. It was declared redundant in 1970, since when it has been brought triumphantly back to life through the hard work of the All Saints' Society, and the Redundant Churches Fund which has had the care of it since 1972. The All Saints' Society acts as the agent to the Fund and its membership not only keeps the church clean and beautiful but also arranges services and concerts which take place here, greatly aided by the superb acoustics of the building.

There are fine panoramic views from the trim churchyard. The brick walls of the church, together with its quaint mixture of roof-lines, make this a very distinctive and memorable exterior of great character. The squat W tower, originally built by Sir Thomas Tyrell in c 1476, appears to have fallen some years later and a rebuild in the 17C gave it its present top stage, with large single belfry windows, angle turrets (of which the NE turret contains a staircase), stepped battlements and tiled pyramidal cap. The nave, chancel and transepts appear to have been constructed during the latter part of the 15C and the SE chapel was built with money left by Sir Thomas Tyrell in his will dated 1510. The S transept roof is lowered to embrace the adjacent porch which was built c 1540 and has a small brick niche above its entrance. It shelters a fine 15C Perpendicular stone doorway, with traceried spandrels, containing an original door with good ironwork and a grille.

The interior is bright and has great character. The nave roof has tiebeams and kingposts and the chancel has a boarded wagon roof which is studded with bosses, some of which are original whilst others are clever plastic replacements. The two transepts are most unusual because they are two-storeyed and the Tudor fireplace in the upper part of the S transept suggests that they may have served as living quarters for a resident priest. It may be that after the Reformation they served as manor pews—note the good sets of 17C rails which form gallery fronts. These transepts give a rustic feel to the interior; they contrast with the simple dignity of the two-bay 15C stone arcade which separates the Tyrell chapel from the chancel. This chapel retains its 16C roof.

All Saints' has several features of interest, although most of its former furnishings have now gone. A small piece of medieval glass in the S transept displays the Tyrell arms. A brick staircase gives access to the N transept chamber, where some interesting paintings of the church in former times may be viewed. The fine crucifix and candlesticks on the high altar, also the stone altar in the Tyrell chapel, were designed by Laurence King and installed in 1973.

The Tyrells have some interesting memorials here. On the N side of the chancel is their little chantry. Its walls are panelled with brick arches and it contains the tomb of Sir Thomas Tyrell (died 1476) and Anne Marney, his wife. In the chapel is a superb incised limestone slab with the effigy of Lady Alice Tyrell (died 1422), bordered by ten small figures, including her nine named children. There are two wall plaques on the chapel wall and in the floor are ledger-slabs—all to 17C and 18C Tyrells.

Epping, *St. John the Baptist.* The town of Epping, with its attractive main street on the A11, was originally known as Epping Street, or Epping Heath, in the parish of Epping Upland. A small chapel existed here from Norman times but Epping had no parish church until St. John's was built. The nave and chancel were consecrated in 1891, the N aisle was completed in 1908 and the tower was dedicated in the following year. The architects were Messrs. Bodley & Garner, who designed a noble and dignified church in the style of the 14C.

The E wall of the church, with its seven-light E window, flanked by angels in niches, borders the pavement of the High Street. The nave and chancel are under a single continuous roof, with N and S aisles stretching the full length of the church. The aisles, which are strengthened by gabled buttresses, are lit by three-light windows which, although not large, are uniform and graceful. A pair of tall three-light windows with Reticulated tracery pierces the W wall of the nave. The S porch has an openwork parapet and short pinnacles, a niche above its entrance and a groined ceiling. Epping's venerable 96ft tower is free-standing to the S of the chancel, to which it is connected by a vestry and passage. It is strengthened and enhanced by angle buttresses, each with an archangel or saint beneath a gable. There are recessed arches between small buttresses in a lower stage of the tower. The pairs of double belfry windows are set beneath deep arches and have stone openwork louvres. Above them are shields with the emblems of the Evangelists. An embattled openwork parapet crowns the tower, with vanes at its four corners. The splendid clock projects above the pavement; it was a gift from a former resident in 1908.

The interior is dignified, colourful and impressive, although the structure of the building is pleasantly uncomplicated. There is a feeling of height and space, also an atmosphere of devotion. The nave arcades have five bays, with a further two to the chancel. Above is the painted wagon roof, with inscriptions along the nave cornices, also along the chancel cornices which are deeper and have gold cresting. The SW corner is the baptistery, containing the font which has shields on its bowl and eight marble pillars round its stem.

The magnificent furnishings are mostly the work of G.F. Bodley. The handsome Rood screen has linenfold panels in its base and a coved canopy, above which is the Rood, with St. Mary Magdalen kneeling at the foot of the Cross. The pulpit is a fine piece of woodcarving in oak, with the figures of Moses, Elijah and John the Baptist, and the four Evangelists on its staircase. The lectern has linenfold panelling. The focal point is the splendidly adorned high altar, with its six Baroque-style candlesticks, also the sumptuous triptych reredos by Bodley & Hare. The wings of the reredos each have three angels and the central section has carved scenes beneath canopies, with Christ in Majesty and the Last Supper central, flanked by the Resurrection and Ascension, and the Annunciation and the Baptism of Our Lord. To the N of the chancel is Bodley's magnificent organ case in green and gold. The organ itself is a fine four-manual and pedal instrument by Messrs. Wordsworth & Co. To the S of the chancel is the Lady chapel. The aumbry here, containing the Reserved Sacrament, has a beautiful door. In a recess nearby is a modern bas-relief of the Virgin and Child, with a cat, made in fibreglass by Josephine de Vasconcellos. The two S windows of this chapel, and the W window of the aisle, contain glass by C.E. Kempe.

Finchingfield, *St. John the Baptist.* This picturesque church is delightfully set on a slight rise above the green of its picture postcard village. One entrance to its churchyard is beneath the timber-framed Guildhall, built c 1500. The church is an interesting building, showing craftsmanship of several periods, from Norman times onwards.

The W tower is bold and squat, giving an impression of great strength. Its lower stages are Norman work of c 1170 and there is a fine Norman W doorway, with three orders of shafts, scalloped capitals and zigzag moulding. It once had a tympanum and beneath where this fitted are beautifully preserved little faces looking inwards each side. The belfry stage and parapet are 15C, with two- and three-light belfry windows. There are corner figures at the base of the parapet and the tower is crowned by a 17C wooden cupola, which was rebuilt in 1966. The N and S aisles end in E chapels and the 15C nave clerestory is embattled. The chancel also has a clerestory, with impressive 15C windows. The small entrance to the S chapel has an arch of Tudor brick. The S porch is a handsome affair of stone, which is an 1865 rebuild of the 15C original. It shelters a fine 14C entrance arch, containing a pair of original traceried doors, on which may be seen carved the Crucifixion, the Pelican in her Piety and the dove of the Holy Spirit.

The interior has much of interest. The broad nave has five-bay arcades, the S with octagonal piers and large bases of the 13C; the N arcade is early 14C, each pier having major and minor shafts, except the two W piers which are later. It seems that work on them was resumed following the Black Death. The nave has a wide and almost flat roof which is dated 1561, resting upon good stone corbels. The chancel corbels are also noteworthy. A wide, unmoulded Norman arch leads to the tower base, which has unusual blank wall arcading and may have been the sanctuary of an earlier church or chapel.

The font bowl dates from c 1375 and has shields with the arms of families, including Helion, Colvile and De Vere. Over the tower arch are the arms of King Charles II. Beneath the chancel arch is one of the finest Rood screens in the county with exquisitely carved ogee openings backed by delicate tracery. This 15C screen was well restored in 1972 by Messrs. H. & K. Mabbitt. The screen to the S or Berners chapel is much earlier and parts may well be late 13C or early 14C. The more recent screen to the N or Kempe chapel was designed by the Reverend Ernest Geldart, Vicar of Little Braxted, who also designed the case of the fine three-manual organ—an instrument by Miller, which has 30 speaking stops. The Kempe chapel has a kingpost roof, a remarkable carving of 'Scandal', with asses' ears at the base of its E arch, a small panel of medieval glass in its E window and some hatchments of the Ruggles-Brise family. Here may also be seen the memorial to William Kempe (died 1628) and his wife.

The Berners chapel contains the magnificently carved tomb-chest of Sir John Berners and Elizabeth (died 1523), with figures beneath canopies in the sides and brass effigies on the top slab. In the chancel are memorials to the Marriott family. Richard Marriott (1703) has a tomb-chest on the N side, Thomas (died 1766) has a bust by W. Tyler (a pupil of Roubiliac) and Anne has an effigy in Grecian robes, carved by Sir Richard Westmacott in 1811.

Great Bardfield, *St. Mary the Virgin.* This church is pleasantly set on a rise, brooding over one of the many picturesque villages which grace this corner of Essex. St. Mary's is a sturdy building, whose nave and aisles were rebuilt c 1380. It has a devotional and cared-for interior in the Anglo-Catholic tradition and is dominated by its rare and magnificent stone screen.

Externally, the building is interesting and has some unusual features. The nave roof is lined with green copper and the sturdy W tower dates partly from the 12C. It is unbuttressed and is lit entirely by single windows, most of which have at least a hint of a pointed arch, suggesting the transition from Norman to Early English. The shingled spire is 18C and on the S side of the tower is an enormous diamond-shaped clock-face, dating from 1911. The aisles are lit by unusually large and tall three-light windows, which are flanked by interesting corbels. The clerestory windows of two lights have a similar pattern. The porch is also 14C and its two-light E window is flanked by quatrefoil openings. It shelters a fine pair of original traceried doors.

The interior has great dignity. The late 14C arcades have complicated piers, with polygonal and circular shafts (eight per pier), also fascinating corbels between the arches. The lofty nave has a tiebeam roof. Dominating everything is the amazing stone screen which fills the chancel arch and is thought to date from c 1380—a little later than the other Essex stone screen at Stebbing. The design and the elegance of the tracery are noteworthy, particularly the ogee-headed central arch. It is thought that the corbel faces each side of the screen are those of King Edward III and Queen Philippa. The Crucifix and figures of Our Lady and St. John were added by G.F. Bodley in 1896. The chapels at the E ends of the aisles were furnished with altars in 1949 to the designs of Laurence King, but their medieval piscinas remain; that in the N aisle has an ancient credence shelf and the S aisle has a small angle piscina. The windows are filled with 19C and 20C glass but there is medieval glass in the tops of some of the N aisle windows. One window has the figures of St. Stephen, Christ crucified and St. Lawrence, and in the W window are shields with arms of the Mortimer family. There is a large aumbry in the N chancel wall. Some experts believe the organ case to have been designed by A.W.N. Pugin. The high altar forms a colourful focal point to the chancel; the glass in the window above it was designed by G.F. Bodley.

Forming the seat of the sedilia on the S side of the sanctuary is the Purbeck marble tomb of William and Alienor Bendlowes of Place House (he died in 1584). The actual tomb may well be older but the top slab retains the brass figure of Alienor. William was a Member of Parliament and became Sergeant at Law in 1555 under Queen Mary I and, although a devout Catholic, was allowed to serve under Queen Elizabeth I also. He was a great benefactor, who founded almshouses here and in other villages on his estates, and a free school. His portrait (by Jeffery Courtney, 1984, copied from one at St. John's College, Cambridge) hangs above the tower arch, dressed in the scarlet robes of a Sergeant at Law.

Greensted, *St. Andrew*. It has been estimated that maybe as many as 100,000 visitors a year make their way to this small church in its peaceful and idyllic setting, which serves a tiny village near Ongar. The name 'Greensted' indicates a clearing in the great forest which once covered this part of Essex, and it is the timbers from ancient oak trees which have made this little church world-famous. In the unique log walls of Greensted's nave we have a national treasure—the oldest wooden church in the world. There is evidence that an earlier timber church, built in the 7C, stood upon this site, but the present timbers have been scientifically dated to c 845. The body of St. Edmund, the martyred King of East Anglia, is believed to have rested in this church in the year 1013, when it was being taken back from a period of safe-keeping in London to Bury St. Edmund's for final burial.

The setting is perfect, the churchyard is a picture and the building itself is a charming mixture of colours and textures from the building materials used in its construction. Of supreme interest is the low pre-Conquest timber nave, the logs being linked by unseen tongues of wood and bedded in a more recent sill and brick base. There were no windows in the pre-Conquest nave and two small eye-holes may be seen on the N side, one of which is placed in a recess beside the former pre-Conquest entrance (covered by the three flat logs to the E of it), which may have served as a holy water stoup. Three attractive dormer windows now light the nave each side. These are mostly 19C but are most attractive and are set in a sweeping roof of Tudor tiles. The timber porch was rebuilt in 1847; to the E of it is a stone coffin lid which is thought to have covered the body of a Crusader. In c 1500 the chancel was built of Tudor brick, upon the lower part (still visible) of the former chancel wall, which is believed to be Norman. Although the E section was rebuilt in 1847, the SW window and the priest's doorway beside it are attractive Tudor work. The white weatherboarded tower dates possibly from the 17C, but it has great character, with its simple belfry openings and more ornate W windows. It is crowned by a chamfered spire.

The homely and colourful interior contains ancient and modern work of charm and quality. The walls of the nave are lined with timber and the roof, which was much renewed in the 19C, is low enough to permit examination of its exquisitely carved spandrels in detail. These include the legendary wolf guarding the head of St. Edmund and were carved by James Barlow of Ongar, a man who suffered from asthma, but carried out most of the 19C restoration work here, and also carved the wooden lectern. The pulpit was given by Alexander Cleeve of Greensted Hall in 1698. One fragment of 15C glass survives and may be seen in the quatrefoil window at the W end of the nave; it is thought to portray St. Edmund. The other windows were designed in the 19C by Nathaniel Westlake. They show St. Andrew, St. Edmund, Jesus the Good Shepherd and, in the E window, the Last Supper and the Crucifixion.

Greensted has connections with the Tolpuddle Martyrs of Dorset who, after their period of transportation to Australia had been served, settled in the parish and at nearby High Laver for a time. One of them, James Brine, was married in this church. Today, St. Andrew's is a lively centre of Christian worship and witness. A herb festival is held here biennially, when this church is festooned with herbs of every description, which are used for medicinal, culinary and cosmetic purposes. The benefice now unites Greensted with Stanford Rivers, whose church of St. Margaret has a 12C nave and a Decorated chancel. Richard Mulcaster, the eminent Elizabethan schoolmaster whose pupils included Edmund Spenser the poet, was the incumbent from 1598 to 1611.

Hadstock, *St. Botolph.* A small and very attractive village at the foot of a hill near the Cambridgeshire border. The church is set at the top of a sloping churchyard, with pleasant views N into Cambridgeshire. Here we have an important pre-Conquest minster church, originally a small stone building, maybe of the 7C, which was rebuilt in the 11C. It was possibly St. Botolph's *Icanho*. The S transept was again rebuilt in the 14C, when its N counterpart was greatly altered. The porch and W tower were added in the 15C and the present chancel was built in 1884 to the designs of William Butterfield. Full-scale excavations beneath the floors in 1974 revealed much of the story of the building. A 7C origin was initially considered possible in the light of the excavations, but it has since been strongly argued that the findings point to a date in the early 11C for the first church, which would rule out a 7C link with St. Botolph, at least for this site.

The setting of the church is attractive, and there is beauty in the variety of craftsmanship in the exterior. High in the nave walls are pre-Conquest double-splayed windows of early 11C date. The N transept has a handsome three-light Decorated window and there are 14C windows in the S transept. The S nave doorway is 13C Early English, with two orders of shafts. Butterfield's chancel is built in the Decorated style, with flint and stone chequerwork in its upper parts. The 15C Perpendicular tower has a W doorway with carved corbels, a three-light W window and two-light belfry windows. There are gargoyles beneath its shallow embattled parapet. The porch is right beside the N transept. It shelters a bold and tall pre-Conquest doorway of c 1020, with one order of shafts supporting carved capitals. The abaci and the outer border of the semicircular arch are embellished with a carved decoration which has been described as honeysuckle moulding. The door itself is also 11C and may well be the oldest door still in regular use in the country. The discovery of some human skin beneath one of its hinges gives credence to the tradition that a Dane killed for sacrilege had his skin fixed to the door.

The interior is atmospheric and cared-for. The tall nave has a plaster ceiling, with tiebeams. The 15C tower arch is tall and elegant. The honeysuckle carving on the responds to the S transept arch show that they are 11C, although the arch is later. At the entrance to both transepts the pre-Conquest stone plinth has been revealed at the base of the walls. The chancel is very typical of William Butterfield, with tiled patterns on the walls and a reredos in the E wall, with coloured tiles. The font has a 14C bowl, supported by a stem which could be pre-Conquest. Excavations beneath it revealed the site of pits for casting bells in pre-Conquest times. The nave benches have 15C straight-headed ends and the simple lectern is also 15C, with a carved stem on an octagonal base. More 15C woodwork survives in the screen to the S chapel; this has a carving on one of its left-hand panels of a fox and geese. The chapel contains a pretty cinquefoil-headed piscina and a war memorial with names inscribed on old wooden panelling. In the N transept are the arms of King George I, painted on wood.

It is thought, on the strength of a reference in the Ely records, that St. Botolph may have built his monastery at Hadstock in 654, and was therefore buried here in c 680. The centre of his missionary activity is recorded as being at *Icanho* and Iken in Suffolk makes a justifiable rival claim to it. The excavations at Hadstock did reveal beneath the S transept floor a large empty pre-Conquest grave, marking the burial of somebody important and it is thought possible that this may have been the Saint's resting place.

Harlow, *Potter Street Baptist Church.* A small congregation of Baptists was formed in Great Parndon in 1662, but moved their place of worship to Potter Street in 1756, when their new chapel was built. This small rectangular building stands beside the old Harlow to Epping road at the NE end of Harlow, just S of Harlow Common. This is a good example of an 18C Nonconformist chapel, although its interior was remodelled and extended in 1973 because of an increasing congregation.

The chapel is built of red brick and has altered little externally at the front and sides. There are two tiers of rectangular windows and beneath the front gable is the inscription 'Baptist Chapel, Opened 1756'. The one ambitious piece of Classical craftsmanship in this otherwise humble exterior is the doorway, which is surmounted by an open pediment with scrollwork, supported upon brackets each side, which are adorned with foliage. Inside, the chapel has been extended at the front and equipped with a new communion table and pulpit, made by a member of the congregation. The side galleries have been removed and the old pews replaced by comfortable chairs. The original gallery at the back remains; it is supported by two circular columns. At the centre, beneath the floor, is the original baptistery for baptism by immersion.

Little Maplestead, *St. John the Baptist.* This is the latest of the four existing 'round churches' still in use in England. It consists of a circular nave with a rebuilt W porch and a chancel with an apsidal E end. It is an endearing building in a quiet rural setting about 2½ miles N of Halstead. A preceptory of the Knights Hospitaller was founded at Little Maplestead in c 1185 and it was these religious knights who built the distinctive nave in c 1325–40. This took the place of an earlier building and it may be that the core of the chancel was part of the Norman church. It is thought that the knights used the chancel as their chapel. We know that in 1338 there were two knights in residence here, also two chaplains, four clerks and several servants.

The exterior, in its lush and picturesque setting, is very distinctive and attractive. The circular nave is supported by buttresses and its conical roof terminates in a hexagonal wooden belfry with a tiled cap. The large two-light windows, with their impressive Decorated tracery, were renewed when the church was restored in 1851–57, but are faithful reproductions of the 14C originals. This restoration was supervised by R.C. Carpenter. He rebuilt the W porch and placed the little gabled ventilators in the roof. The W doorway has a 19C hoodmould and corbel heads but its beautiful arch, which is surrounded by four-petalled flowers, is original 14C work.

The interior is simple but has great dignity; it is airy and uncluttered and its shape produces splendid acoustics. The nave has six elegant 14C arches, with quatrefoil piers which have moulded capitals and bases. These form a circular 'aisle', which has six transverse arches resting upon 19C foliage capitals. The diameter of the central 'nave' part is 10ft and the total diameter, with the aisles, is 30ft. The chancel windows are 19C reproductions of 14C originals. Unusually, there are no windows in the apse. The oldest feature is the font, which is thought to date from c 1080, although some experts consider it pre-Conquest. Its bowl was originally square, but later its corners were cut away. On the four original sides are simple Romanesque carvings, including round-headed arches and the cross of St. Andrew. Hanging in the nave are framed prints of the church in 1765 and 1807, showing how quaint the building looked before Carpenter's restoration. On the nave walls are boards with the Ten Commandments. The church is simply and tastefully furnished and the pleasantly adorned high altar provides a worthy focal point.

Newport, *St. Mary the Virgin.* A large and stately church of flint and stone and some brickwork, slightly elevated above its village. The building is cruciform and may at one time have had a central tower. The earliest work here is 13C and additions were made during the 14C and 15C. The building was greatly restored in 1858–59 when the tower was rebuilt and all but the chancel was thoroughly restored to the designs of G.E. Pritchett of Bishop's Stortford. The chancel restoration took place in 1911, when the work was done by Bell & Son of Saffron Walden.

The exterior has considerable grandeur, its crowning glory being the large and stately tower, which has set-back buttresses, turret-pinnacles and large transomed three-light belfry windows. The chancel has a parapet and clerestory windows of Tudor brick. There are renewed early 14C Decorated windows in the S aisle and in the lower stage of the tower. In the N transept are two renewed 13C lancet windows. The handsome pinnacled 15C porch is two-storeyed, with a fine three-light upper window, above which is a sundial. The original timber framework of its lower ceiling survives.

The bright and spacious interior contains much 19C work, but much of interest also survives from earlier periods. The nave arcades have three bays, and there are also wider and earlier E bays at the crossing. The S arcade is early 14C, with octagonal piers; the N arcade has quatrefoil piers from a little later in the 14C. The corbels between the arches are worthy of inspection and there is nailhead ornament on the responds to the transept arches. The roofs, although restored, contain medieval timbers. The nave has a tiebeam roof with angels, the N transept roof is also of tiebeam construction and the chancel roof is late 15C and almost flat. The font has an unusual 13C bowl, embellished with trefoils beneath gables. Its simple 15C cover has four carved and crocketed ribs. The N transept has a small and pretty piscina, beside which is a larger arched recess.

The two lancet windows in the N transept contain early 14C glass which depicts St. Michael and St. Katherine. In the S transept is the great treasure of this church, a rare and beautiful late 13C chest of outstanding interest. Its front is exquisitely carved and its lid lifts to form a reredos, with five painted panels, showing the Rood group, and St. Peter and St. Paul. The ancient oak lectern has a traceried stem and tracery between its double bookrests. In the chancel are 15C ends to the renewed stalls. This was a collegiate church and so was probably equipped with a fine set of misericord stalls. The elegant screen contains much of its 15C timberwork. It has delicately traceried six-light openings on each side of its central arch. The pulpit is a 19C copy of one in Seville Cathedral. In the S aisle floor are the brass effigies of Thomas Brond and his wife, 1515 ('here lieth Thomas Brond whos soule god pardon'). The wall plaque to Dame Grace Brograve (died 1704), on the N chancel wall, is a good one, with its inscription on marble 'drapery'.

Radwinter, St. Mary the Virgin. The tall tower and slender spire of this wayside church are visible for some distance. They draw the visitor to a remarkable building—a very out-of-the-ordinary village church, thanks to its lavish restoration and almost total rebuilding which took place in stages between 1869 and 1888. This was inspired and the bulk of it was paid for by its Tractarian Rector, the Reverend F.J.W. Bullock. The architect was William Eden Nesfield, partner of Richard Norman Shaw, who produced a restoration of great quality and dignity. Outside, he produced the character of a medieval church of the 14C; inside, he created a lavish devotional paradise of exquisite craftsmanship, colour and beauty. The restored and extended nave and aisles and the rebuilt chancel and priest's vestry were rededicated in 1870. The rebuilt tower, the upper chamber of the porch and the N choir vestry were completed in 1887–88, by which time Eden Nesfield was a sick man and Temple Moore had taken over the direction of the work here. Father Bullock neverthe-less saw his 20-year task completed and remained here until 1916—a ministry of some 51 years in the parish.

St. Mary's has an attractive and inviting exterior. Its sturdy tower is supported by angle buttresses; it has distinctive pairs of double belfry windows and a staircase turret rising above the parapet. Its height is enhanced by its thin lead-covered spire. The walls of the church are faced with knapped flints, punctuated by bands of red tiles. The renewed windows are in the early 14C Decorated style. An attractive feature of the exterior is the remarkable two-storeyed porch. The lower section retains original sturdy 14C timbers. To this was added the attractive timber-framed upper chamber, which has an almost domestic appearance.

Inside, we have a beautifully preserved Tractarian interior, which has been largely unaltered, with its objects of devotion, its furnishings, metalwork and even its oil lamps still in place. The arcades, with the exception of the E bays, are medieval—the N arcade, with octagonal piers, is mid-14C, and the S, with quatrefoil piers, is a little earlier. The chancel arch has medieval stonework, although it was taken down and rebuilt further E when the nave was extended. The nave has a tiebeam and crownpost roof, parts of which are 14C, which rests upon intriguing stone corbel faces. There is medieval timberwork also in the N door. The real treasures of St. Mary's, however, are those from Eden Nesfield's and Temple Moore's restoration. The font has a tall wooden cover, carved with angels and Prophets, with the Virgin and Child at the top. The picture on the wall nearby, of Jesus and the Children, is by Alexander Gibbs and was the gift of the architect. There are large paintings of the Stations of the Cross, which are thought to be of German workmanship. Even Temple Moore's cupboards in the base of the tower show great taste and dignity. The screen beneath the chancel arch is a mass of intricate wrought ironwork and was made, to Eden Nesfield's design, by a Saffron Walden smith. Above it is a Rood beam with a Crucifix and 14 candles.

The chancel is a treasure-house of colour and craftsmanship. Its panelled roof is painted with monograms of the Blessed Virgin Mary and St. Alban. Seven sanctuary lamps hang before the high altar and the altar itself is painted with six angels (which are usually hidden behind frontals which have been in use for at least 60 years). Behind the array of tall candles on the gradine above the altar is the superb reredos. This is Flemish work of the early 16C and was purchased for the church in 1888. The carvings show scenes from the life of the Virgin Mary. The painted side wings were added by Temple Moore. Two large pictures hang on the chancel walls; these are copies of originals in the Vatican. Most of the stained glass in the church was made by the firm of Howard & Gibbs. The organ, which has a fine case, is a three-manual and pedal instrument by Miller of Cambridge. The tower contains a ring of eight bells.

Rivenhall, *St. Mary the Virgin and All Saints.* From a distance this church appears to be a total rebuild of the early 19C, with its stuccoed, embattled and turreted walls and its Y-traceried windows. It would be easy to dismiss it as an eccentric period piece from the most uninspired era of church building. It is only when we approach it more closely that we find not only an almost complete two-celled church of the early 11C, but also some of the most interesting medieval glass in any church in the E counties.

A careful archaeological investigation took place in 1971–78, when it was discovered that this church was built upon the site of a Roman villa. The land later became a Christian cemetery, upon which was built a 10C church of wood, to be replaced by the stone church which forms the core of the present building. Excavations have revealed that the Normans gave it an E apse, which was removed in the 14C when the church was restored. A tower, added in the 15C, collapsed in 1714 and was replaced in 1717 by a brick tower. In 1838–39 John Adey Repton was employed by Lord Western to give the building a facelift, resulting in the exterior we see today. In 1840, the Curate-in-charge, the Reverend Bradford Hawkins, purchased from the church at Chemi near Tours the remarkable glass which he set in the E window. He became Rector in 1853 and in 1877–78 commissioned Samuel Parmenter to restore the church. This involved a complete reordering of the interior, the opening up of two old windows and the erection of the S porch. In 1974 the new vestry was added on the N side to the designs of the Laurence King Partnership.

On the exterior, note the quaint Gothic work of 1839, also the foundations of the medieval tower and buttresses, the stonework of the walls where the stucco has been removed and the semicircular-headed windows in the chancel. The stone slab in the churchyard, not far from the porch, may have been the medieval altar slab, although no traces of its five crosses remain.

The interior is bright and cared-for, with much of interest. In the gallery at the W end is the organ which J.W. Walker built as a temporary instrument for St. George's Chapel, Windsor in 1904 and which, after a spell at Canford Magna, Dorset, was rebuilt here in 1981. The arms of King James VII and II over the S door are particularly noteworthy. The benches and floors date from Parmenter's 1877 restoration. On the N nave wall is preserved a fragment of medieval wall painting, moved here from the chancel; the lettering is probably 16C. The communion rails in the chancel are 18C.

Rivenhall's remarkable glass was mercifully taken and buried during the Second World War and thus escaped destruction when a German parachute mine exploded nearby in 1941. It was reassembled in 1948. In the E window we see four 12C roundels showing scenes from the life of the Virgin Mary, and two figures of French archbishops which are thought to be unique survivals. In the bottom of the S light is Robert Lemaire, a 13C knight on horseback. Later medieval glass (a dove of the Holy Spirit and a face) may be seen in the SE nave window, and some roundels of Flemish glass of the 16C and 17C appear in the opposite window.

There are several memorials of interest. On the S side of the sanctuary is the fine tomb of Raphe Wiseman (died 1608) and his wife Elizabeth (died 1594); she was the grand-daughter of Lord Rich, King Henry VIII's Lord Chancellor. Their effigies lie upon rush matting and on the side of their tomb-chest are their three sons and three daughters. Members of the Western family commemorated here include William (died 1729), who has a large wall monument with a black sarcophagus and an obelisk, also Baron Western (who instigated the 1838 restoration), who has a Gothic Caen stone memorial by Clarke of Wigmore Street; he died in 1844. There are two 13C coffin lids and an unusual 18C memorial of iron in the chancel floor, and some hatchments.

Saffron Walden, *St. Mary.* This is one of the largest and most magnificent churches in the county. It occupies a slightly elevated position at the N end of a busy market town which has many fine and picturesque buildings. A superb view of the church is obtained from the S end of the High Street, where we see the tower and spire and the embattled walls of this venerable building, dominating yet blending in so well with the fine townscape. The church is set in a quiet tree-shaded churchyard. It is built on a lavish scale and its features are large and commanding. Apart from the vaulted crypt beneath the S aisle and porch, the church was entirely rebuilt between 1450 and 1525, under the expert direction of John Wastell, who also designed (in part) King's College Chapel, Cambridge.

The exterior immediately impresses the visitor with its size and the quality of its architecture. The building is 183ft long and 80ft wide. The lofty spire, which was erected in 1832 to the designs of Thomas Rickman, rises to a height of 193ft. The tower dates from c 1470; its three-light belfry windows are set within rectangular frames (an Essex feature) and there are sturdy set-back buttresses at the corners. Tall turret-like pinnacles cluster round the base of the spire, to which they are linked by flying buttresses. The church has embattled parapets, punctuated by pinnacles. Beneath the nave parapets and sections of the aisle parapets are stone courses which are studded with foliage and faces. At the E end of the nave rise two turrets with crocketed crowns. The aisles are lit by enormous four-light windows, with five-light windows at the W ends. There are 13 clerestory windows in the nave, mostly arranged in pairs, and six in the chancel. The large S porch has six turret pinnacles. It is two-storeyed and inside is a vaulted ceiling.

The interior is noteworthy for the effect created by space, height, brightness and superb architectural design. There are carved span-drels flanking the arches of the seven-bay nave arcade and also the chancel arch. Above the nave arcades are stringcourses which are studded with carvings. The beauty of the clerestory windows may be further admired from inside. Stone shafts rise from the ground to support the arch-braced cambered tiebeam nave roof, which has bosses and some of its timber picked out in colour and has longitudi-nal arch-braces which frame the clerestory windows. The broad aisles are also crowned by tiebeam roofs. The three E bays of the N aisle have canopied recesses, thought to be 14C work reused. Above these are three handsome niches; two further niches may be seen in the S aisle.

The octagonal font is 15C. The tall screen and Rood loft beneath the chancel arch was made in 1923 to the designs of Sir Charles Nicholson. Much restoration took place here between 1860 and 1880, some of this being carried out under the supervision of William Butterfield. The only medieval glass remaining is the small head in the W window of the S aisle, which is thought to be of King Henry VI. There is some good 19C glass, including three windows in the N aisle by James Powell & Sons, a window in the S aisle by Lavers & Barraud and the E window of the N chapel, made in 1904 by Burlison & Grylls. The reredos in this chapel is a copy of Correggio's painting of the Madonna and Child with St. Jerome—the gift of Lord Howard in 1793. Of this date also is the heraldic glass in the E window of the S chapel, beneath which is the black Tournai marble tomb of Thomas, Lord Audley (Lord Chancellor of England), who died in 1544. The recesses in the N aisle wall now frame a series of nine brass effigies which were taken up from the floor. These include a 15C priest, above whom is a small brass of the Pelican in her Piety. Above the tower arch hang the arms of King Charles II.

The magnificent organ was originally built by John Vincent in 1824, and subsequent restorations and enlargements, culminating in a total rebuild by Hill, Norman & Beard in 1971, have produced a grand and versatile instrument with 64 ranks of pipes (3500 pipes in all). The tower contains a ring of 12 bells, eight of which were cast by Briant of Hertford in 1798.

Thaxted, *St. John the Baptist, Our Lady and St. Laurence.* This small and charming old town, a centre in medieval times of the cutlery industry, still preserves many of its ancient buildings. Magnificently set and majestically brooding over these buildings is what many experts describe as Essex's finest church. Its crocketed spire rises 181ft and is only 2ft shorter than the length of this great church, which grew between c 1340 and 1510. Its architecture and crafts-manship are superb, its proportions are satisfying and inspiring, and its interior is remarkably unspoilt and has through sympathetic care during our own century preserved an atmosphere of antiquity, prayer and devotion. Thaxted's church has seen much remarkable activity, not least since 1910, when the controversial Conrad Noel became its Vicar. He created here a centre for Anglo-Catholic worship in the Old English 'Sarum' tradition, and a place where crafts, music, dancing and folk religion have all played their part.

The view from the SE of the church rising above the town is as grand as any townscape in England. Approaching Thaxted from the W, we are faced with the superb tower and spire, which were erected c 1475—a masterpiece of design and proportion, with sturdy but-tresses, a fine W doorway, four W niches, double sets of two-light belfry windows and delicate flying buttresses linking the corner pinnacles to the spire. The embattled nave has large four-light clerestory windows; those in the chancel clerestory have three lights. Fascinating creatures and gargoyles peer down from the N aisle, which has pinnacles surmounting its buttresses. There are N and S transepts; their window tracery was blown out in a storm in 1764. The N and S chancel chapels were completed in c 1510; their four-light windows were ingeniously designed to fill all available wall space with glass. Both porches are large, handsome and two-storeyed. The S porch (built c 1380) has W, S and E entrance arches, and a fine tierceron star vault. Both porches shelter fine pairs of 15C doors. The N porch (built c 1445) is crowned by pinnacles with standing figures. Above its grand entrance are two compartments with the royal arms in stone, also a tall niche between its two upper windows. There are coats of arms in the bosses of its lierne-vaulted ceiling. This superb exterior offers so much to enjoy, both in the study of its many details and through standing back to view it as a whole from different angles.

The interior is a refreshing surprise—all superfluous seating has been removed, giving vast open spaces devoid of clutter. There is an endearing charm here, created by old pamment floors, unusual objects of interest and devotion in unusual places, an impeccable use of colour, many treasures from ancient and more modern times and exquisite medieval craftsmanship in the fabric of the building. The earliest work is a six-bay nave arcade, with fascinating corbel heads supporting the hoodmoulds over the arches, all dating from c 1340. The clerestory windows are work of the early 16C; their splays are lined with stone traceried panelling. The roofs are all medieval. Those in the nave and aisles have fine bosses and those in the chancel chapels have remains of canopies of honour above the altars. The chapels are divided from the chancel by four-bay late Perpen-dicular arcades, with arches flanked by open spandrels. There is some fine stonecarving to be appreciated here, including the ancient reredos in the E wall of the N transept, a niche in the N chapel and stone panelling and two niches in the walls of the S transept.

Although at first sight the interior may seem rather bare, it has many fittings of interest. The font is entirely encased in 15C wood-work, which continues upwards to form a cover. Some medieval carved screenwork survives at the E ends of the aisles and 17C screens are placed at the entrances to the chancel chapels. Fragments of 15C and 16C stained glass may be seen in several of the windows. The glass in the five-light E window is by C.E. Kempe. The communion rails date from c 1700 and the pulpit, with its grand staircase and sounding-board, dates from c 1681. Also of the 17C are the unusual benches with tall carved ends, to be seen in various parts of the church. There are two organs here: that in the N transept was brought here from St. John's Chapel, Bedford Row in 1858. Some authorities believe it to be the work of John Harris (c 1703), although others suggest that H.C. Lincoln built it in 1820. The organ beneath the tower by Cedric Arnold (1952) incorporates work by G.P. England of 1795. The church has surprisingly few monuments, the only one of interest being the brass of a priest (c 1450) in the chancel floor.

The Reverend Conrad Noel (Vicar, 1910–42) combined a crusading passion for Christian communism with a love of the old 'Sarum' worship and ceremonial. His head in bronze (by Gertrude Hermes) may be seen beneath the crossing. It was largely due to him that the church acquired its present internal decor. The furnishings of the high altar and of the Blessed Sacrament or N chapel, also the various pictures, the colourful banners in the chancel, the vast stella of candles hanging in the crossing (designed by Randall Wells) and the shrines and statues, nearly all arrived during his time here. He was a pioneer of the revival of Morris dancing and he developed here the medieval dignity of Sarum worship, with the people's High Mass at the centre of the worshipping life of the church. His tradition was maintained by his son-in-law, Jack Putterill, who was Vicar from 1942 to 1973. For a time Gustav Holst played the organ here and played a great part in developing the musical tradition of this church.

GLOUCESTERSHIRE

Gloucestershire is a large and satisfying county, both in the variety of its scenery and in the richness of its churches. The great River Severn bisects it, becoming in its lower reaches below Gloucester a wide estuary. E of the Severn Vale rises the steep escarpment of the Cotswold plateau, which slopes gradually down towards neighbouring Oxfordshire. In the Middle Ages the Cotswolds were one of the richest sheep-rearing areas of the country and the wealth of its merchants is reflected in the magnificence of several churches in the area. The Cotswolds produced a fine oolitic limestone which was easily worked and carved, then hardened and so lasted well. The major towns of Gloucestershire, Cheltenham and Gloucester itself, are in close proximity in the centre of the county; otherwise, medium-sized and small market towns predominate. W of the Severn is a remote, wild and beautiful area, the Forest of Dean, always a relatively poor area which produced few fine churches, with the notable exception of Newland, the 'Cathedral of the Forest'.

In the late 7C Christianity reached Gloucestershire under Mercian patronage. Gloucester was the first major centre, but the cathedral of the diocese was at Worcester. Minster churches, serving large areas, were set up throughout Gloucestershire. Deerhurst is the only surviving building, but the foundations of a large basilica have been excavated at Cirencester. The importance of the church at Deerhurst, with evidence of successive phases of building from the 8C to the 10C, is clear. Deerhurst boasts a second pre-Conquest building: Odda's Chapel of 1056. It survived only because it was encased in a later building and forgotten until 1885. It comprises a simple nave and chancel. Another two-cell building of which the fabric substantially survives is Coln Rogers (the details are mostly later). The nave fabric at Duntisbourne Rouse is pre-Conquest. Somerford Keynes has a narrow N door of early date (? late 7C), in a church otherwise much rebuilt. The interior arch has a lively early 11C carving of dragons' heads. At Bibury, a major pre-Conquest church largely rebuilt after 1130, the imposts and jambs of the chancel arch remain, carved with foliage. Daglingworth has pre-Conquest sculpture including a sundial, a crucifix on the chancel E wall (outside), a Crucifixion, and other pieces. At Wormington there is another Crucifixion, which may have come from Winchcombe Abbey. Beverston preserves a sculpture of the Resurrection, set into the S face of the (post-Conquest) tower.

Gloucestershire is especially rich in Norman churches. St. Wulfstan, Bishop of Worcester (1062–95), urged lords of the manor to build churches, having founded many himself. About 100 churches have surviving Norman parts. Norman on the grand scale are Gloucester Cathedral (monastic until the Reformation) and Tewkesbury Abbey. At the other extreme are some Cotswold churches of primitive design which lack an E window. Aston Blank is an example. It is remarkable that this deficiency was not rectified in later medieval times. Elkstone has the typical Norman plan of nave, central tower and chancel (but the tower fell in the 13C). Elkstone is one of a number of churches which have stone-vaulted chancels: others are Hampnett, Rudford and Kempley (St. Mary's). The chancel of Kempley is decorated with original frescoes of c 1130–40. Bishop's Cleeve was cruciform with a central tower. There is much Norman sculpture, especially in the form of doorways with beakhead ornament and carved tympana. Examples are at Elkstone (Christ in Majesty), Quenington (Coronation of the Virgin, and the Harrowing of Hell), Little Barrington and Eastleach Turville (Christ in Majesty, with angels), and Kempley (Tree of Life). At Harnhill the Archangel Michael fights a dragon; at Ruardean it is St. George. Elkstone has a corbel table with grotesque heads, and a central boss in the chancel which holds together grotesques. The best capitals are in the chancel of Leonard Stanley, illustrating the Nativity and the woman washing Christ's feet. The most remarkable sculpted survival is part of a 12C wooden Rood at South Cerney, including Christ's head, perhaps Spanish, brought back by a pilgrim to Compostela. The face is serene, Christ's eyes closed in death, but the work exudes a powerful and moving intensity.

Building work in the Early English period was mostly confined to the lengthening of chancels, but a few churches received more substantial work. At Berkeley the nave survives, with a graceful W end of five stepped lancets, and fine arcades. Slimbridge is more complete, and has interestingly carved capitals. At Teddington the tower arch and W window are Early English but were brought from Hailes Abbey in 1567 when the tower was built. They are the best-preserved parts of the abbey, but are too grand for the church. Several churches have Early English chancels with lancets at the E end. At Cherington the effect is almost of proto-tracery, with a grouping of round-headed window and lancets, and a quatrefoil above. At Wyck Rissington the effect becomes almost playful: pairs of twin lancets topped by concave-sided diamond windows, with a stringcourse meandering round them, and a straight-sided diamond in the gable. The Early English period produced some attractive bellcotes, more often on the E gable of the nave than the W. Examples are Boxwell, Harescombe, West Littleton and Acton Turville; the last is particularly splendid, the spirelet being supported by clustered shafts on corbelled feet.

The Decorated period provided mostly enlarged windows and distinctive spires. The most remarkable addition is the S transept at Minchinhampton, where the S wall and gable are filled by a huge window with a rose in the topmost part, and the sides are panelled by slim buttresses, closely set, with tiny windows between. The buttresses support an unusual stone vault. Longborough has a beautiful Decorated S transept with Reticulated tracery in the windows; and Eastleach Martin has a 14C N transept. St. Mary's, Cheltenham has many 14C features, including a rose window in the N transept and a central tower with a Decorated broach spire. Other spires of the period include Saintbury, Rodmarton and Standish. The Perpendicular period was the major phase of building after the Norman period. The style, indeed, originated at Gloucester Cathedral in the 1330s, and lasted about 200 years. This period also witnessed the growth of the wool trade, which reached the peak of profitability in c 1480. There were therefore many wealthy laymen; and since the responsibility of the laity was for the naves and towers of churches, it is hardly surprising that the major rebuildings usually involved those features. Fairford was perhaps unusual in being completely rebuilt (except for the central tower). Northleach, Chipping Campden and Cirencester received new naves between c 1460 and c 1530, with soaring arcades and a bold clerestory, and a distinctive 'Cotswold' window over the chancel arch. At least 40 Cotswold churches have Perpendicular towers, and there are others in the Severn Valley and near Bristol. The tower of Coates is amongst the earliest, c 1360; the tower of Thornbury, with battlements and pinnacles derived from Gloucester Cathedral, is the latest, c 1540. Lechlade is a great 'wool' church of the late 15C, wholly Perpendicular; Rendcomb is even later, completely rebuilt after 1517 by Sir Edmund Tame, who finished Fairford Church. Cold Ashton was rebuilt (except for the tower) in 1508–40 by the Rector, Thomas Key, right through the period of King Henry VIII's Reformation. Not every church received the same costly treatment, however, and at Upleadon is a rare timber-framed tower of c 1500, quaint rather than elegant. The N wall of the nave of Bledington has another oddity: two rows of square-headed windows, one above the other.

The Gothic style lingered for so long that its survival almost merged with its revival in the mid-18C. A remarkable number of towers were built in traditional style in the first half of the 18C. Before that, Gothic forms persisted in substantial 16C rebuildings at Naunton and Whittington. At Blockley the clerestory was rebuilt, and the S porch too, in the 1630s. Taynton, destroyed in 1643 during the Civil War, was a Parliamentary rebuilding of 1647–48. The nave of Newent was rebuilt in 1675 with segment-headed windows. Its builder, Edward Taylor, had worked for Wren in London. Painswick received its spire in 1632. The traditional Gothic 17C and 18C towers mostly have battlements and pinnacles; Dursley is modelled on the tower of Colerne, Wiltshire, with battlements and pinnacles after those of Gloucester Cathedral, and Blockley derives some of its details from Chipping Campden. Perhaps the parishioners of Tetbury were thinking in terms of tradition when in 1777 they requested a new nave of 'an elegant and regular Gothic plan', but what they received was Francis Hiorn's serious, impressive but rather unrestrained Gothic Revival church. The Classical style was not neglected in the 18C, appearing as early as c 1710 in the nave and S transept of Sapperton. The first major work was the church of St. John the Baptist, Gloucester, where all except the tower was rebuilt in 1732–34, with an impressive E end facing the street. At Bourton-on-the-Water the tower and nave were rebuilt in 1784; the tower survives, big and solid and stocky, with a rusticated base and a little lead-covered dome. Two completely Classical churches were added as appendages to great houses: Great Badminton, 1785, by Charles Evans, and Dodington, c 1799 by James Wyatt. Great Badminton has an interior inspired by St. Martin-in-the-Fields, London, therefore looking back to the early 18C; Dodington, more advanced, is cruciform with a central dome.

The 19C in Gloucestershire was an extremely prolific period of church building. Cheltenham entered its fashionable heyday early in the century, and has churches of a good range of style and date. St. Paul's, St Paul's Road, 1827–31 by John Forbes, is uncompromisingly Classical, the motifs Greek rather than Roman. There are enthusiastic pre-Ecclesiological Gothic churches, starting with George Underwood's Holy Trinity, Portland Street, 1820–23, and culminating in Christ Church, Malvern Road, 1838–40, by R.W. and C. Jearrad, with an imposing but somewhat stretched Perpendicular W tower. The Norman Revival made a brief appearance in S.W. Dawkes's St. Peter's, Tewkesbury Road, 1847–49, cruciform, correctly detailed and yet splendidly inventive, with a central circular lantern tower. John Middleton was one of the most accomplished local architects of the mid-19C, and he is represented by three churches in the town, including his finest work, All Saints', Pittville, 1868. Ewan Christian designed the interesting auditorium-church of

St. Matthew's, Clarence Street, in 1878–79; and for the Catholics, Charles Hansom built St. Gregory's, St. James's Square, in 1854–57. At Gloucester there is a brick-and-stucco Classical church of 1822 by Rickman & Hutchinson: Christ Church, Brunswick Square. Perhaps the most delightful and inventive pre-Ecclesiological church in the county is Richard James's Parkend, in the Forest of Dean, 1822, octagonal, with four arms and a W tower.

The more serious Gothic after c 1840 has many examples. A.W.N. Pugin is represented by the church of Our Lady at Woodchester, which he planned in 1845, but which was executed by Charles Hansom. J.P. Harrison designed Bussage for Thomas Keble (brother of John Keble) in 1846. G.F. Bodley enlivened the church with a S aisle and porch in 1854. Bodley also built France Lynch in 1855–57 and Selsley in 1861–62. William Butterfield designed Coalpit Heath, 1844–45, his first Anglican church, in 14C style. Sir Gilbert Scott is represented at All Saints', Gloucester, 1875, and elsewhere. G.E. Street's finest church in the county is at Toddington, 1873–79. S.S. Teulon designed the fine church at Woodchester, 1863–64, and the more inventive church at Huntley. Not far from Huntley is Henry Woodyer's superb Highnam, 1847–51, for which Thomas Gambier Parry provided the polychromatic decoration. J.L. Pearson's best church in the county is Daylesford, 1860. Outside Cheltenham, John Middleton built Clearwell in the Forest of Dean, 1866. The nave, S porch and N aisle of Bourton-on-the-Water were rebuilt c 1870–90 by Sir Thomas Jackson, better known for his work at Oxford. Of 20C churches, perhaps the most interesting is Randall Wells's St. Edward's, Kempley, 1903.

Gloucestershire is fairly rich in medieval furnishings, with one exception: Rood screens. Bishop Hooper ordered their destruction, along with the Roods which stood on them, in the mid-16C. He was burnt at the stake under Queen Mary Tudor, though not perhaps primarily for this offence! The best remaining wooden screens are at Fairford and Rendcomb (with almost identical detailing—both churches were built by the Tame family), Somerford Keynes and Ashchurch. Cirencester has several screens, enclosing side chapels as well as the chancel. The only stone Rood screen is at Berkeley, a broadly and boldly arched design with delicate openwork and modern wooden cresting. There are stone parclose screens to chapels in Tewkesbury and Cirencester. All surviving screens are 15C or early 16C, and most medieval pulpits are of this period also. About 20 stone pulpits remain, and these are of two types: the 'wine-glass' type, supported by a slender stem, and the bracketed type, built out from the wall.

15C wooden pulpits are found at Evenlode, Mitcheldean and Stanton. Two churches have late 15C brass eagle lecterns: North Cerney (a Flemish design) and Chipping Campden (East Anglian). There are many medieval fonts, mostly Norman and Perpendicular. Deerhurst's remarkable pre-Conquest font is exceptional. The most notable Norman font is probably Southrop's: niches round the bowl contain figures of Virtues and Vices and Moses with the tablets of the Law, flanked by Synagogue and Church. Above are little 'heavenly mansions' and florid and ornate interlace ornament. Similar in design but not in detail are the fonts at Rendcomb, Newnham-on-Severn and Mitcheldean (mostly now a copy), where the niches have figures of the Apostles. Gloucestershire has as many as six Norman lead fonts (Sandhurst, Siston, Tidenham, Oxenhall, Frampton-on-Severn and Gloucester Cathedral); all are late 12C and come from the same mould. Between bands of foliage is an arcade containing figures and scrolls alternately. The most interesting fonts from between the Norman and Perpendicular periods are at Bibury (13C), and Longborough, Leighterton, Staunton and Churchdown (all 14C). For the Perpendicular period there are about 70 examples, mostly of similar type, octagonal bowls decorated with quatrefoils or rosettes. Outstanding are Northleach (see entry), Abenhall (shields of the Free Miners and Free Smiths of the Forest of Dean), Abson and Barnwood (early 16C; winged angels hold shields).

At Northleach, in the sacristy, is a medieval stone altar. Others have been reconstructed at Forthampton and North Cerney (13C) and Daglingworth (Norman, now a credence table). The altar-top or mensa is preserved at Tewkesbury, Northleach, Edgeworth, Newland (where there are three), and Farmcote. Several churches have extensive medieval wall paintings. Those at St. Mary's, Kempley are perhaps the earliest, dating from c 1130–40. They are in fresco and cover the chancel. The theme of the ceiling is Christ in glory as told in Revelation; on the N and S walls are the Apostles, angels, laymen and buildings. Further paintings decorate the nave. Apostles feature also in a Doom painting at Stowell, late 12C. The subject of the main sequence at Stoke Orchard is the life of St. James of Compostela, c 1200, the only surviving example of this story in England. Ampney St. Mary has a painting showing that work on the Sabbath wounds Christ. There is a large and fairly well-known St. Christopher at Baunton, 14C. Of the same century, at Hailes, are St. Catherine and St. Margaret. The 15C embroidery at Chipping Campden has been mentioned in the text; Baunton also has a 15C frontal on display, and there are copes at Minsterworth, Little Dean and Winchcombe.

Several churches preserve 17C arrangements of furniture. Deerhurst's chancel, with seats on the N, S and E sides of the communion table, is now unique, but was once more prevalent. A similar effect has been recreated at Hailes, which also has 17C pews and pulpit in the nave, alongside some pre-Reformation seats. Farmcote has 16C benches, and an unsophisticated 17C pulpit with tester. Somewhat similar is the pulpit and desk at Teddington, dated 1655. It is inscribed with sober Puritan exhortations, 'Pray continually', and 'Quench not ye spirit, Despise not prophecying'. Appropriately, perhaps, its Commonwealth ideal is overborne by a huge royal arms of William and Mary, 1689, painted on a nearby wall. Buckland has interesting seats lining the walls of the aisles and chancel, those of the S aisle having testers above the panelling and hat-pegs. There is a 17C W gallery; another, extremely fine early 17C gallery is at Bishop's Cleeve. Several churches have early 17C pulpits—an attractive example, on a tall pillar-pedestal and with a tester, is at Oddington, and Windrush has a particularly ornate one. Unrestored 18C interiors, with the usual box-pews, triple-decker pulpit and Commandment boards, can be found at St. Lawrence's, Didmarton, Little Washborne and Temple Guiting. Late 17C or early 18C furnishings can be found in the Old Baptist Chapel at Tewkesbury, the Independent Chapel at Upper Cam, and the Unitarian Chapel at Frenchay. The most complete late 18C interior is at Tetbury. Notes on some of the best 19C interiors, such as Woodyer's Highnam, Teulon's Huntley and Bodley's Selsley, are found in the gazetteer. One of John Middleton's churches, Clearwell, has a quiet, unchanged interior of 1866, a feature of which are the brass candlesticks on the ends of the pews. G.E. Street's fine choirstalls at Kempsford are worth examining. At the end of the 19C, C.E. Ponting furnished Down Ampney with pews, pulpit, reredos and a fine Rood screen with Rood figures above. Sir Ninian Comper provided furniture for Stanton, c 1918–23. St. Edward's, Kempley, designed by Randall Wells in 1903, has furnishings from Ernest Gimson's workshop, Rood figures by David Gibb and an oak lectern by Ernest Barnsley, inlaid with mother-of-pearl. F.C. Eden designed a notable Rood loft for North Cerney in 1925; another screen by him is at Minchinhampton. Turkdean's screen is a very late addition of 1949, designed by Peter Falconer and brightly coloured on a white base.

Gloucestershire has a considerable amount of stained glass. The earliest schemes are at Cirencester, and the figures in the nave N windows of Arlingham, both c 1340. The small panel of St. Catherine at Deerhurst is contemporary. For the 15C, Fairford is of course preeminent, but the remains of ambitious schemes can be found at Rendcomb (with early Renaissance detailing, perhaps of c 1520) and Cirencester. At Tortworth, in the E window of the S aisle, is a portrait of King Edward IV; Bledington has some late 15C windows; and the E window of Buckland has three panels from a 15C Seven Sacraments window. Notable 19C stained glass includes the early Morris & Co. windows at Selsley, John Hardman & Co.'s windows at Cirencester and Fairford (upper section of the W window), and Clayton & Bell's at Daylesford.

Tewkesbury has by far the most extensive and grand display of medieval monuments; another church with a good collection is Berkeley. Brasses survive in several churches, particularly the great Cotswold 'wool' churches. For the early 17C there are interesting monuments by Samuel Baldwin of Stroud, at Berkeley, Avening, Painswick, Cirencester, Miserden and St. Lawrence's, Stroud. For the late 17C and 18C, Great Badminton has monuments of the Dukes of Beaufort, the first Duke by Grinling Gibbons, the second and third Dukes by J.M. Rysbrack. Rysbrack monuments can be seen also at Blockley and Sherborne. At Great Barrington can be seen Christopher Cass's attractive monument to the Bray children (died 1720). An angel takes them for a walk, hand in hand, over the clouds of Heaven. In Sherborne Church is the monument to James Lennox Dutton by Richard Westmacott the Elder, 1791. A rather buxom angel is supposed to be trampling Death underfoot, but seems rather to be tickling the amused skeleton with her foot!

Iron Acton has an early 15C outdoor or preaching cross, a square, open-arched structure topped by a pillar which once supported a cross. Of similar date is the beautiful and delicate churchyard cross at Ampney Crucis. At Bisley there is a late 13C cross known as the 'Poor Souls' Light', a hexagonal spirelet on trefoil-headed blank arcading, with recesses for candles lit at masses for the poor. It looks like a pinnacle from a 13C cathedral.

Chipping Campden, *St. James.* This is one of the great 15C Perpendicular churches built with the wealth of the wool merchants. The names of two benefactors, William Grevel (died 1401) and John Bradway (died 1488) are known, but there may have been others. Details of the 15C nave are so similar to details at Northleach that the same master mason must have designed both—possibly Henry Winchcombe, whose name appears at Northleach. Chipping Campden is notable for its tall nave, with typical 'Cotswold' window over the chancel arch, its splendid W tower, several brasses and monuments, and some fine medieval embroidery.

The church consists of nave and aisles, S porch, W tower, and chancel with N and S chapels. Of the 13C is the S doorway; the porch, with an ogee-arched niche over the entrance, is 14C. The chancel walls and the buttresses of the N and S aisles are also 14C. The transformation took place from c 1450. The aisles and chancel were given Perpendicular windows and pinnacled battlements. The nave was demolished and a new nave and clerestory were constructed. In his will, John Bradway left to 'the Bylding of the nave and body of the church one hundred marks'. The nave, like the aisles, is battlemented and pinnacled. The magnificent W tower is of three stages, with big diagonal corner buttresses rising to diagonal pinnacles. The second stage is decorated with blank tracery, ogee-headed and with leafy finials; the belfry stage has similar windows but with stiffer finials. The tower has openwork battlements. The most unusual feature is the pilaster decoration. It would be crude if the strips were not so slender. They rise the full height of the tower, three on each face, and at the top they form ogee arches, topped by small pinnacles. In the 16C, turrets with ogee domes were added to the NW and SW corners of the church.

The distinctive feature of the five-bay nave, apart from its great height, is the design of the arcades. As at Northleach, the piers and capitals are octagonal with concave faces, a design more unusual than elegant. But the piers are closely spaced, emphasising the height still more. The arches are shallow and four-centred. From the capitals, arches spring to surround the clerestory. The 'Cotswold' window above the chancel arch is wide and shallow, and its tracery is ingenious. The ceiling is flat and wooden. On the piers of the second bay from the E on the N side are stone brackets which would have supported a canopy, presumably covering a tomb. In the tower, which has a rib-vault, is a survival from the former church, a corbel of a muzzled bear. To the W of the S doorway is a 13C blocked window; and to the E is a trefoil-headed piscina. In the chancel there are a 13C tomb-recess in the N wall, 15C sedilia with fine details, and a 15C piscina with credence shelf, ogee-headed.

Half of an Early English font, carved from a Norman bowl, survives, fixed to the wall at the E end of the S aisle. The font in use is of 1839, copied from the 15C font in St. Mary Magdalen's, Oxford. The late 15C eagle lectern was given by Sir Baptist Hicks (Lord Campden) in 1618, who also gave the pulpit in 1612. In the N (St. James's) chapel are oak screens, communion rail, panelling and altar of 1945–48 by Norman Jewson.

The medieval embroidery is displayed in glass cases. This consists of a late 15C altar frontal, and two copes, one of c 1400 and the other 15C, of velvet, with saints in canopies. The E window has glass of 1920 by Henry Payne, with some medieval fragments in the tracery. John Hardman & Co. made the glass of the window over the chancel arch in 1878. In the S chapel is the monument of Lord Campden (died 1629) and his wife. The figures lie on a black marble tomb-chest, clad in robes of state and wearing huge ruffs, most intricately carved. 12 columns of Egyptian marble support the canopy. It may have been designed by Nicholas Stone. A wall monument of 1664 by Joshua Marshall commemorates Noel, Viscount Campden (died 1642) and Juliana his wife. The tomb doors are open, revealing two upright, shrouded figures. Amongst the brasses is a large one to William Grevel (died 1401) and his wife (died 1386); it somewhat immodestly states that he was 'the flower of the wool merchants of all England'.

Cirencester, St. John the Baptist. Cirencester is not only the largest parish church in Gloucestershire, but it is one of the largest and grandest in the country. Its outward appearance is gloriously Perpendicular, but inside it preserves a few fragments of the 12C and 13C. The nave is remarkably lofty. The church stood only yards S of an Augustinian abbey, but was clearly not to be outdone by its powerful neighbour. Both abbey and church were founded by King Henry I, 1117. Cirencester has the most opulent porch of any church in England, and some fine medieval furnishings.

The first sight which greets the visitor is the S porch, facing the Market Place, and the handsome W tower. The best view of the exterior, however, is gained from the churchyard E of the church. A typically Cotswold arrangement of gables is seen, but here the array is astonishing and impressive. The arrangement is most easily explained on examining the interior. Most parts are Perpendicular, with big windows of panel tracery: that is, the nave and its unusually wide aisles, the outer N aisle, the N chancel aisle and its outer chapel. The chancel and S chancel aisle are basically 13C. The lacy openwork battlements of the nave are particularly impressive. The nave was the last part to be completed, in 1515–30, largely the benefaction of prosperous townsfolk. The stringcourse has a representation of the Whitsun Ale procession, with figures and musical instruments. The tower is the earliest Perpendicular part of the church. It was built in c 1400–20, with funds donated by King Henry IV as a reward to the town for its part in quelling the Rebellion of the Earls in 1399. The royal arms are carved at the W door. The tower is of three stages, the middle stage being heavily modelled with blank panel tracery. It gives an effect of great solidity but loses some elegance. Above it, the belfry stage is lighter in effect. The panel tracery is again dominant, superimposing its uprights on the belfry windows. Tall corner pinnacles crown the parapets. The lower part of the tower is much plainer: it was not intended to be seen. The tower also suffers from having been shored up by two huge buttresses, which project diagonally outward and are half-absorbed by the W walls of the aisles. This happened soon after the tower had been built. The S porch was built in c 1490. Strictly speaking it was not part of the church, and was only annexed to it in the 18C. The abbey built it on its own land, for its own purposes. It was later called the Town Hall. It is a square building very intricately adorned. The sides are panelled, and the three-bay front has three oriel windows divided by mullions and transoms. Each light is arched. The buttresses are hollowed out and lined with (empty) niches. The openwork battlements are particularly beautiful. They have corner pinnacles and follow the canting of the oriels. The interior passage has a fan-vaulted ceiling.

The six-bay nave arcades are prodigiously high, dwarfing the tall mid-14C chancel arch. The piers are tall and slender, the arches small and shallow, a typical Cotswolds' Perpendicular fashion. Eight slim shafts encircle each pier, and each shaft has a tiny capital. On two sides of each pier, towards the nave and towards the aisle, are angels bearing shields or merchants' marks, commemorating the benefactors of the building. The lower part of the clerestory lights have blank panel tracery. More panel tracery surrounds the chancel arch, to the left of which is a blocked doorway, quite high up, which must have given access to a Rood loft well above any screen (the present screen is 16C). Over the substantial Cotswold window are carved the arms of King Henry VIII. Beyond the N aisle is the chapel of the Holy Trinity, an addition of c 1430–60, built for the Guild of

Weavers. It opens from the aisle by an arcade of four bays: on the apex of the arches are the Yorkist falcon and fetterlock. A stone screen encloses the chapel, and at the E end is an ornate reredos with canopied niches, which originally showed the arms of the House of York but now displays those of the Danvers family. At the E end of the S aisle is evidence of the Norman church, a blocked round-headed arch and a blocked window high up in the wall. The arch may have been for a recessed altar, since some 13C wall painting was discovered when it was opened. (There is also a round-headed doorway, once an exit from the church, standing between the St. Catherine's and Lady chapels.) The E bay of the S aisle is occupied by the Garstang chantry chapel, of c 1430–60, that is, of the same period as the N chapel. The Garstang family were Northerners who settled in Cirencester as wool merchants. The chapel is enclosed by an elaborate oak screen, with richly carved panels, tracery and openwork parapet, adorned with the Garstang arms and trademark. There is a wall tomb on the S side, and an altar dedicated to St. Edmund of Canterbury. Moving E, the visitor enters the chancel, which has on the S side evidence of a late 12C rebuilding. The piers of a two-bay arcade (one now blocked by the organ) survive. The arches are later. One pier is a Roman column reworked. The chancel was extended in the 13C and the E and flanking N and S windows are of this date. The S chancel aisle was rebuilt as St. John the Baptist's chapel. N of the chancel is St. Catherine's chapel, and beyond it the Lady chapel. Both were remodelled in the mid-15C into their present form. First, a new arcade was made on the N side of the chancel, below the 14C clerestory. Then in c 1450 the outer, Lady chapel was rebuilt, with Perpendicular windows and an arcade into St. Catherine's chapel. There was a stone screen between the two chapels. In c 1460 John Chedworth, Bishop of Lincoln, remodelled St. Catherine's chapel into a chantry of St. Catherine and St. Nicholas. The E wall was extended to the line of the chancel's E wall, making the NE window internal. Beside the altar are paintings of St. Christopher(N) and St. Catherine(S). The chapel was further enriched in 1508, when Abbot John Hakebourne heightened it and installed a pretty fan-vault. A small clerestory on the N side lights the vault. Two 15C oak screens enclose this and the Lady chapel at the W end. They have 17C cresting and 18C coats of arms.

The great Rood screen was completed only in the 1530s, when Henry Tapper, a merchant, left money for it. If the loft was finished it could only have stood a few years before the Reformation. The present canopy is by Sir Gilbert Scott. The screen in the S aisle is also 15C or early 16C; its canopy was added in 1906. The pulpit is 15C, of stone. It is wine-glass shaped, and formed of open traceried panels. The ogee arches are decorated with crocketed finials and pinnacles. The colouring was heightened by Scott in his restoration of 1865. There are two fonts, one Perpendicular, which was discarded in the 18C and brought back, much mutilated, in 1865; the other 18C, marble, and now in the Lady chapel. At the E end of the nave is a pair of brass chandeliers of 1701, by John Spooner of Bristol. The communion rails are of 1769; the reredos is of 1867, by Scott, painted and gilded in 1889. Scott also designed the organ case. The communion rails in St. Catherine's chapel are by Sir Ninian Comper; the reredos was carved in Oberammergau, Austria, and painted by William Butchart, 1905. In the Lady chapel the altar is by Stephen Dykes Bower, c 1948, with a frontal by Comper, c 1912.

Cirencester once had magnificent medieval stained glass,

comparable with Fairford's. Fragments survive in the tracery of many windows. By the end of the 18C the remaining glass hung so precariously that Samuel Lysons was commissioned to collect it and incorporate it in the E and W windows. The unused fragments languished in crates until c 1890, when by some incredible vandalistic mischance they were carted off to Oakley Hall and thrown into a ditch. Only one crate was overlooked, and F.C. Eden reset the assorted pieces in the SE window over the sedilia. The E window is still as arranged by Lysons in c 1800. The lower lights, a Virgin and Child flanked by St. Catherine and St. Dorothy, with donors below, were presented to Siddington Church in c 1480 by the Langley family, and were brought here at Lysons's rearrangement. Geoffrey Webb inserted the Child, which had been lost, in the 20C. Many medieval angels, some bearing shields, are in the other lights; Lysons supplemented them with angels and borders of his own invention. Most of the glass which had been collected into the W window was moved in 1946 to its original location, the S window of the S aisle. Panels show the Latin Doctors (but St. Augustine is lost); St. Catherine, St. Margaret and St. Dorothy (St. Ursula, lost); St. Zita, St. John of Beverley, St. William of York, St. Bathildis. Below are the kneeling donors. The period is late 15C. The N or Trinity chapel had an E window in honour of the House of York, of which only fragments remain. Geoffrey Webb brought the head of the Duke of York from the W window in 1939. Scott collected some fragments into the N windows of the Lady chapel in the 1860s, including crowned figures in canopies, c 1450. Most of the 19C glass is by John Hardman & Co., except for the E window of the N aisle, by C.E. Kempe, 1897, and Hugh Easton's S aisle W window of 1938.

There are many monuments worth examining. In the nave is a small brass to Philip Marner (died 1587). Scott collected many other brasses together in the Trinity chapel. The founders of the chapel, Richard Dixton (died 1438) and William Prelatte (died 1462), are commemorated, and also two 15C clergymen, Ralph Parsons (died 1478) and one unknown. Other wool merchants are Reginald Spycer (died 1442), who had four wives, and Robert Page (died 1434). The wall monument at the W end to the Bathursts, c 1776, has busts by Joseph Nollekens. The Garstang chapel has busts of Rebecca Powell, foundress of the local Powell's School, and her two husbands, c 1718. In the Lady chapel is the most sumptuous monument, to Humfry Bridges (died 1598) and his wife (died 1620). The recumbent effigies, with hands raised in prayer, are by Samuel Baldwin of Stroud. Two sons kneel at head and foot of the monument. Daughters and a son line the front of the chest. Above the main figures is an extravagant canopy with a coffered arch. Smaller side canopies, crowned with obelisks, cover the kneeling sons. St. Catherine's chapel has a recumbent effigy of a man in a N wall recess, said by Anthony à Wood to be Richard Osmund, purser to the abbey (died 1517). There is a 17C canopied tomb in St. John the Baptist's chapel, to George Monox (died 1638) and his wife. The figures are kneeling facing one another and two daughters kneel below.

The church possesses the gilt Boleyn Cup of 1535, made for the family of Anne Boleyn. It was presented in 1561 and is now displayed in the round-headed arch at the E end of the S aisle, which was opened up in 1968.

Deerhurst

St. Mary. This isolated spot in the Severn valley boasts not only a remarkably substantial pre-Conquest church but another pre-Conquest building also—Odda's Chapel. Deerhurst fell within the territory of the Hwicce, a people within the Kingdom of Mercia. Mercian kings appointed under-kings or earls to rule them. In 804 Ethelric, son of the Earl of the Hwicce, endowed Deerhurst and made it the largest landowner in the territory of his people. The monastery declined in importance in the 11C. In 1440 it became a cell of Tewkesbury Abbey. At the Reformation it became the parish church.

The church is substantially pre-Conquest. It is approached from the S; Priory Farm adjoins it at right-angles at the SE corner. The high nave has areas of characteristic herringbone work, now pierced with late Decorated clerestory windows. The aisle walls have later, large and rather unattractive square-headed windows. The tower is built of rubblestone with (high up) typical long-and-short work. The sequence of building is thought to have been as follows. The nave and a W porch were built. Then a semicircular E apse was added. Next, N and S porticus were built onto the sides of the nave. These porticus were then at least partly rebuilt, along with the upper parts of the nave walls and the upper storey of the W porch. The apse was subsequently rebuilt in polygonal form on the earlier foundations. Finally, more porticus were added to form virtual N and S aisles. The two-storey W porch was further raised to form the present tower. The various stages are traceable on the W face of the tower. The W door and the round-headed window above have projecting stones over them, a feature of other pre-Conquest churches such as Barnack. The apse, ruined since the 15C, can be seen by rounding the church on the N side and entering the farmyard. The walls survive to full height on the S side, and preserve, high up, a vigorous 10C sculpture of an angel. The dating of the fabric is much disputed, but c 800 and the late 10C seem probable for most of the pre-Conquest work.

The church is entered by the W door. At the inner door is a stone relief of the Virgin and Child. It has been called unfinished, but was probably painted with facial and other details. Inside, still part of the tower/porch, is a low narthex, and it opens by a round arch into the nave. This is remarkably but typically tall and narrow. It is pierced by attractive arcades of c 1200, with arches (on the S side) of alternate white and green stones, and capitals displaying stiff-leaf and other carvings. The W wall preserves, high up, a fine double opening with triangular heads and short fluted pilasters. It was probably the E window of a tower chapel. Below, a blocked doorway probably gave access to a W gallery; beside it is an early, plain triangular opening. Looking E, the pre-Conquest arrangement is clearly discernible. The chancel arch, now blocked, is 10C, and opened into the apse. It has an unusual hoodmould with beasts' heads as stops. To N and S are openings into the porticus, with simple doorways below and large round-headed openings above. In the S aisle, abruptly terminated attached columns seem to indicate an aborted vault. The church was restored by William Slater in 1861–63, and the wooden roof is by him, copied from a 15C model. The corbels are original.

Deerhurst has some notable furnishings. The font is late 9C. The bowl is enriched with a spiral pattern (which confirms a 9C date). Above and below are strips of vine scroll. The stem has comparable but less distinct patterning. Bowl and stem were rescued from secular use in the 19C. The chancel furnishings form a survival of the Puritan fashion of c 1600—seats surround the communion table on three sides, including the E. A fine communion rail separates chancel and nave. The pulpit, with naturalistic carving, is of 1861 by Slater, executed by James Forsyth. In the S aisle, the W pews are 15C; all the other pews are Slater's. In the N porticus are several brasses, one of c 1400 to Sir John Cassey and Alice his wife, most noteworthy perhaps for commemorating her dog, 'Terri', shown at her feet, the only pet named on a medieval monument. In the same chamber are two brasses of early 16C ladies. Medieval stained glass survives in the W window of the S aisle—St. Catherine with her wheel, c 1300–40; and (to the right) St. Alphege (a monk here in the 10C who became Archbishop of Canterbury and was martyred by the Danes). It dates from c 1450. The N aisle N window is by Clayton & Bell and shows the Ascension between St. Mary and St. John; the N aisle W window is of 1853 by William Wailes, in memory of Hugh Edwin Strickland, geologist.

Odda's Chapel. The survival of this chapel of 1056, SW of the church, was revealed in 1885, when repairs were made to the half-timbered Abbot's Court. In 1675 an inscribed stone had been found in the orchard, recording the erection of a royal hall by Earl Odda, the friend of King Edward the Confessor. The stone, which provides the very precise date of dedication, is now in the Ashmolean Museum, Oxford. It reads: ODDA DUX IUSSIT HANC/REGIAM AULAM CONSTRUI/ATQUE DEDICARI IN HONO/RE SANCTAE TRINITATIS PRO ANIMA GER/MANI SUI AELFRICI QUAE DE HOC/LOCO ASUMPTA EALDREDUS VERO/EPISCOPUS QUI EANDEM DEDICAVIT II IDI/BUS APRILIS XIIII ANTE ANNOS REG/NI EADWARDI REGIS ANGLORUM (Earl Odda ordered this royal hall to be built and dedicated in honour of the Holy Trinity for the soul of his brother Aelfric which was taken up from this place. Bishop Ealdred dedicated it on the second of the Ides of April in the fourteenth year of the reign of Edward King of the English), i.e. on 12th April, 1056. In 1885 an ancient window was discovered under the plaster, and the chapel was revealed. The nave had been a kitchen and the chancel had been divided by a floor. The chancel arch had been much damaged. The chancel was separated from the farmhouse only in 1965. Another inscribed slab, incomplete, was found in 1885 in use as a window-head. It was the altar slab. The inscription is probably 'In honour of the Holy Trinity this altar has been dedicated'.

The chapel, built of blue lias stone, now consists of a short nave and chancel, divided by an arch of square-cut stones. Part of the arch has been reconstructed. Two double-splayed pre-Conquest windows survive, one on the S side of the nave preserving part of a wooden window frame.

Fairford, St. Mary the Virgin. This sumptuous Perpendicular church, built in c 1491–97, preserves a remarkable set of stained glass windows of the finest quality of c 1500, probably from the school of Barnard Flower, King Henry VII's glazier. Every window is filled with glass illustrating the stories and tenets of the Christian faith from Adam and Eve to the Last Judgement. The church is a spectacular monument to its builder, John Tame, wool stapler and cloth merchant.

The exterior is grand and substantial. It has nave and chancel, aisles becoming chancel chapels, and a central tower. The tower, massive and strongly detailed, is partly older than the rest of the church. The base was raised by the Earls of Warwick, and is embellished with their arms and emblems. The corner buttresses are octagonal. Higher up they become canopied niches and then paired pinnacles, diagonally set. The parapet is pierced with quatrefoil openings. On the corner turrets of the buttresses are figures of warriors clutching swords. Other sculptures include the arms of successive Lords of the Manor who preceded the Earls of Warwick; the arms of John Tame; implements of local occupations (E face); and a 15C figure of Christ (W face). All the parapets of the church are battlemented over a stringcourse enriched with vigorous sculpture. On the S side the figure of a boy or jester is seen clambering over the stringcourse. Pinnacles rise at intervals along the parapets. The windows are large, with Perpendicular tracery, containing from three to seven lights.

The church is entered through the S porch, fan-vaulted. The original oak door, with its small postern, has survived. The NW and SW piers of the tower have earlier masonry. John Tame kept the old arches but heightened the stone vaulting and reinforced the structure with blocks of masonry. The arcades have slender, many-shafted piers and wide, four-centred arches. 69 angel corbels support the roofs. In the S or Corpus Christi chapel they hold emblems of the Passion, and one holds John Tame's arms. The E window of the N chapel (Lady chapel) is set very high because the sacristy is behind the wall. It is entered from the sanctuary by an original oak door. Opposite the door are sedilia with embattled canopies.

The font is 15C and survives from the previous building. One face has the badge of King Edward IV, the rose upon the sun-in-splendour. In the chancel is fine woodwork, choir and parclose screens, and stalls, erected by Sir Edmund Tame after his father's death. The screens have the emblem of Queen Catherine of Aragon. Over the founder's tomb on the N side, the screen becomes an arch. The stalls were brought here from elsewhere. There are 14 misericords, depicting a man and a woman draining a cider barrel, a drunkard, a woman belabouring her husband, and other subjects. The high altar, with riddel posts and curtains, is by Sir Ninian Comper, 1920, The Lady chapel reredos was designed by Geoffrey Webb and made by W.D. Gough, 1913: a delicate panelled piece, with figures of King David, St. Anne, the Virgin, the crucified Christ, St. John, St. Elizabeth and St. John the Baptist under canopies; in an upper tier, the Virgin and Child. The lectern in this chapel has 12C feet. In the S chapel is a communion table of 1626 and a 16C oak chest.

In the chancel, the founder's tomb has a brass showing John Tame (died 1500) in armour, and Alice his wife (died 1471). The prayer below the figures reads: 'For Ih[es]us love pray for me/I may not pray now pray ye/With a pater noster and an ave/That my paynys relessyd may be'. In the Lady chapel floor are set brasses of Sir Edmund Tame (died 1534), dressed in armour with a tabard and an impressive mantle, flanked by his first and second wives in long cloaks. Nearby, on the wall, another brass shows them kneeling. Above is a representation of the Trinity. In the corner of the Lady chapel is the table-tomb of Roger Lygon and Katharine his wife, widow of the second Sir Edmund Tame; erected 1560. There are many tablets, including one to John Keble (died 1835), father of the Oxford Movement leader. A tablet to John Keble the son (died 1866) was erected in 1966.

The glorious stained glass forms a cycle beginning in the N aisle,

just W of the Lady chapel screen. This window shows prefigurations
of the Incarnation from the Old Testament: Eve tempted by the
serpent (blue, with woman's head and bust and cat's paws!); Moses
and the Burning Bush; Gideon and the Fleece; Solomon and the
Queen of Sheba. In the Lady chapel, the first window shows the
parents, birth, presentation and marriage of the Virgin; the next
depicts the Annunciation, Nativity, Magi, and Presentation of Christ;
the E window has the Flight into Egypt, and Christ and the Doctors of
the Temple, with the Assumption between. The E window shows, in
the lower lights, the events of Holy Week from the entry into
Jerusalem to the bearing of the Cross; and, above, the Crucifixion.
The chancel S window has the Deposition, Burial, and Harrowing of
Hell (see the impenitent man behind the red bars). In the S chapel,
the E window shows Christ appearing to his mother (apocryphal
tradition) and to the women in the garden, with the Transfiguration
between. The next window shows the breaking of bread at Emmaus,
and the incredulity of St. Thomas; and the final window has the
miraculous draught of fishes, the Ascension, and the descent of the
Holy Ghost at Pentecost. The S aisle of the nave has the Apostles
holding scrolls with clauses of the Apostles' Creed. The westernmost
figures, St. Jude (or Thaddeus) and St. Matthias, were restored in
c 1864. In the N aisle are 12 Old Testament Prophets. The NW
window of this aisle shows the Evangelists; corresponding with it on
the S side are the Latin Doctors. The clerestory windows have, on the
S side, saints and martyrs, and (N) persecutors of the church, with
delightfully horrific demons above. The W windows depict judgement, on the S side David's Judgement of the Amalekite, and on the
N, the Judgement of Solomon. The great W window depicts the Last
Judgement, an astonishing *tour de force*, even if the top half is a
recreation of the original by John Hardman & Co. in the 1860s.
Above, Christ sits in the rainbow surrounded by swirling masses of
saints and angels. Below are souls being weighed in the balance,
with a devil clambering in to try to tilt it towards perdition. On the left
the blessed climb up to Heaven; on the right the wicked are dragged
off to Hell: a blue-bearded devil propels a wheelbarrow. Satan lurks,
fish-faced, in the lower right corner. Hardman has recreated the
drama, and the vivid colouring, but not the sparkle of the 16C glass.
All the glass was removed in the Second World War, and afterwards
replaced by Geoffrey Webb, with William Thurston as glazier. The
glass was cleaned and repaired and in some parts radically
reordered.

Gloucester, St. Mary de Crypt. The church, cruciform Norman in
plan, is substantially a Perpendicular building with a tall and sumptuous chancel. It was traditionally rebuilt by Henry Dene, Prior of
Lanthony from 1461 to 1501, but may be slightly earlier 15C.
St. Mary de Crypt has a nave and aisles under one roof, S porch,
tower and transepts, and a chancel flanked by chapels. The only
Norman evidence is in the crypt, where there are several blocked
arches. The W door is 19C neo-Norman, perhaps based on an old
example. There was a restoration in 1844 by Dawkes & Hamilton. In
the S chapel are some 13C lancets, and the E window of that chapel
is 14C Decorated. Decorated also are the aisle windows. The rest is
Perpendicular, including the two-storey S porch with its conical-
capped stair turret and the tower. The tower is very tall, the mullions
of the belfry windows continuing downward as blank panelling.
Until 1908 there were excessively high crocketed corner pinnacles.

The chancel was heightened in the 16C, when the clerestory was added.

The three-bay nave leads to the tall and narrow chancel, the most attractive part of the church. There were three-bay arcades, but the E bay is blocked. The pier supporting the open arches on either side opens out at the base to form an ogee-headed entrance to the side chapels. Perpendicular stone screens close these bays; 20C copies have been inserted at the W end of the chapels. Flanking the altar are elaborate canopied seats and niches: on the N a sedile and an Easter sepulchre, and on the S, triple sedilia and a piscina. The stringcourse is continued across the NE and SE windows, and the E wall has empty niches with huge canopies over them. The unusually tall E window must have been heightened when the clerestory was added. The wooden roof is carved with angels playing instruments. There are wall paintings in the chancel, thought to be early 16C, but they are mostly faded or obliterated. The tower has a lierne-vault.

Most of the furnishings are 19C and 20C; but the high altar has the medieval stone mensa, replaced there in 1844. The reredos dates from 1889 and encloses Venetian mosaics of Christ and saints in a Caen stone surround. The tester of the 18C pulpit is preserved in the church, and there is an 18C mace-rest of wrought iron, for visits of the Mayor and Corporation. The S chapel commemorates Robert Raikes, founder of the Sunday School Movement, and has oak panelling of 1939 by H. Stratton-Davis.

The E window, with figures of the Apostles, 19C, is supposed to copy the medieval stained glass at Drayton Beauchamp in Buckinghamshire. There are several interesting monuments. In the N aisle are brasses of William Henshawe (died 1519) and his first and second wives, removed from St. Michael's, Gloucester in 1959. In the N transept are 16C brasses (much restored) to John and Joan Cooke, founders of St. Mary de Crypt Grammar School in 1539. In the N chapel is Daniel Lysons's monument by Reeve of Gloucester. He died in 1681, and is shown kneeling, in an elaborate Classical surround, with florid cresting and female figures perched on the broken segmental pediment. On a windowsill is the bust of Richard Lane, Mayor of Gloucester (died 1667). The rest of his monument has disappeared. The S chapel contains, under an ogee arch, a monument thought to be that of Richard Manchester (died 1460); also a good 18C monument by Peter Scheemakers to Dorothy Snell (died 1746). A woman in mourning and a weeping cherub accompany a portrait of the contented-looking lady. Robert Raikes is commemorated by a box-wood profile, and his headmaster's desk, from the Crypt School.

Highnam, *Holy Innocents.* Thomas Gambier Parry's first wife died in 1848. Highnam is his memorial to her and several of their children. The result is one of the most ambitious and exciting early Gothic Revival churches in the country, with a remarkable decorative scheme conceived by Parry and executed by him also. He chose his friend, Henry Woodyer, fresh from William Butterfield's office, as his architect. Highnam was Woodyer's first church, and was erected in 1849–51.

Highnam is approached across parkland. It is set in a sort of arboretum with tall cypresses, Irish yews and monkey-puzzles. The magnificent W tower and spire soar over them. The tower has corner buttresses with crocketed pinnacles and many gables and set-offs. The belfry windows are tall, sturdy paired lancets with deep mouldings and a broad decorative band beneath. At the base of the S side is a strengthening arch, inserted when the idea for adding a spire was conceived. The spire is octagonal and plain, with lucarnes and corner pinnacles at the base and another set of tiny lucarnes near the top. The church has nave, aisles, S porch, chancel, S chapel and N vestry. The details are mostly Decorated, but there is much variety in the tracery of the windows. The porch, with heavy oak lattice doors, has an upper chamber with a relief of Christ the Holy Innocent being visited by the Shepherds and Magi. The clerestory is a series of tiny quatrefoils. They let in so little light that dormer windows were let into the roof to illuminate the Rood painting. The chancel S window is a series of slender lancets topped by quatrefoils with a spiky hoodmould over. The organ chamber on the N side, with its triangular dormer and round window in the gable, is surrounded by the vestry like a low cloister.

The interior, with stained glass everywhere, is very dim. Illuminated, the richness of Parry's decoration is revealed. The painting has an extraordinary pastel-like freshness: the colours have mostly lasted well, except where damp has penetrated. Parry devised a 'spirit fresco' medium to suit English conditions, and it has proved a triumphant success. The nave capitals have naturalistic carvings, symbolic of regeneration in baptism. W of the font are sinful thistles; E are oak leaves and acorns, vines and Rose of Sharon. The wooden roof of the nave is surprisingly stark and clumsy.

The architecture is really a backdrop to the rich furniture and fittings. Almost every available surface is adorned, even the floor, covered throughout in Minton tiles, and the radiators with their wrought-iron, pitched-roof covers by John Hardman & Co. At the entrance is the sumptuous font. Parry disliked the alabaster shafts, so he painted them blue and added fleur-de-lis. Hardman provided brasswork for the lectern, pulpit rail, and candelabra (now in the aisles and chapel). There is a Rood screen topped by a cross, and a fine wrought-iron screen to the S chapel. The stone reredos has elaborate canopied niches which Parry wanted to fill with statues. Nearby are triple sedilia with tall crocketed canopies. The painted decoration is (apart from the texts and diaper patterns) Parry's own work. He started in 1859 with the Last Judgement over the chancel arch. Christ in Glory is surrounded by saints and angels (with gilded plaster haloes!), while other angels descend the arch to summon the blessed with palms and crowns, or to expel the damned with flaming swords. The theme continues in the nave bays: to the right, Adam and Eve expelled from Eden, Abel the first victim, and suffering Job; to the left, the Annunciation, St. Stephen the first martyr, and St. John the Baptist, the forerunner. In the N aisle, a frieze of 1870–80 shows a Palm Sunday procession of New Testament worthies. Parry used friends as models, and the mother and child at the far right are his second wife and daughter. The S aisle is plainer and features texts. Further decoration is seen in the chancel: the E wall has roundels of angels, and the foliage, texts, emblems and shields have signs of crucifixion and torture. The ceiling is azure blue with stars. There is much fine stained glass. The E window, 1859, is by Clayton & Bell. It shows the Last Supper, Crucifixion, Transfiguration, Resurrection and Ascension, with roundels representing the Eucharist, Ordination, Marriage and Confirmation at the corners. The N aisle windows are by William Wailes, 1850: Gospel scenes in the lower lights, then Old Testament Prophets and New Testament writers who confirm their prophecy; at the top is the Old Testament scene relating to the lower lights. The theme is continued in the S aisle, with glass by John Hardman & Co. from A.W.N. Pugin's designs. Parry commissioned both artists in the hope that the competition would bring forth their best work. The other glass, in the W window, is by Michael O'Connor, 1850, and shows the Apostles' Creed with the false tradition that each Apostle was responsible for a clause. Near the font is a window of the Holy Innocents. By O'Connor also are the S chapel windows, showing the Prodigal Son and Christ washing the Apostles' feet; the E window depicts the Mocking of Christ and the Agony in the Garden. The tombs of Parry and his family are outside, under the E window. There is a brass to Parry (died 1888) in the S chapel, and a memorial to his son, Sir Hubert Parry (died 1918), the composer. On the eve of the consecration in 1851, Parry crept into the church at night carrying a bust of his dead wife and placed it in the niche in the S chapel, where it remains.

Huntley, *St. John the Baptist.* S.S. Teulon replaced the medieval church in 1862–63 under the patronage of Daniel Capper (Rector, 1839–65). He preserved only the 12C tower, and capped it with a spire. Teulon's church is built of rich red sandstone and grey Painswick stone, and is richly decorated inside, and little altered.

Huntley is modest in size. The W tower, with its plain broach spire of Painswick stone, provides the height necessary to compete with the tall ornamental trees of the churchyard. The church has a nave with S porch and N aisle, chancel and transepts. The S transept projects in a rather awkward position, its roof jammed against the E gable of the nave. Most of the windows are two- or three-light with Geometrical tracery; but the S transept is treated originally, with a trefoil-headed triangular window and almost Flamboyant tracery, and a panel of blank arcading below. On the N side of the church is a little turret with steps curving up inside to the vestry.

The internal decoration starts with the wall surfaces, which are striped in red and white stone, the white enriched with patterns in red mastic. The N arcade has vigorous stone carving by Thomas Earp. The piers have slender detached shafts of polished stone. Earp's capitals are a lush profusion of foliage. At the springing of the arches are bold figures of Prophets. In the spandrels, roundels hold the Evangelists; and their emblems are carved on the roof corbels above. Over many of the arches are painted texts: the nave arcade has verses from the Te Deum. The chancel is not long, but its decoration gives it an aura of depth. The roof, boarded and polygonal, has painted and gilded ribs. Over the sanctuary step is a large wooden arch, pierced with openwork and painted. Over the sanctuary are carved bosses. The capitals here, also by Earp, display the emblems of the Passion.

The lectern, pulpit and reredos, a set in alabaster, were carved by Earp to Teulon's designs. The reredos has a relief of the Last Supper and was shown in the Medieval Court at the Exhibition of 1862. The stained glass is by Lavers & Barraud. The distinctive nave and aisle windows were designed by Teulon. Their biblical scenes are drawn in outline on yellowish glass, enriched with grisaille surrounds, and with coloured borders.

Northleach, *St. Peter and St. Paul.* Northleach is a grand wool merchant's church of the 15C. Thomas Fortey (died 1447) is called (on his brass in the church) a 'renovator of roads and churches', and he probably erected much of the present building. His son, John (died 1458), continued the work, adding the great clerestory of the nave. The church possesses many medieval brasses.

The S porch of the church of St. Peter and St. Paul, one of the great 'wool churches' of the Cotswolds

It is approached from the E through a long churchyard and presents a wonderful profile of varied rooflines and huge Perpendicular windows. The chancel is steeply-pitched, and is flanked by wide aisles with flatter gables. Behind rises the gable of the nave, flatter still and pierced by a huge 'Cotswold' window; and the tower soars up, with battlements but no pinnacles. The W tower is the oldest part, c 1400; the ridge-mark of an earlier, taller nave is seen on its E side. The tower is plain until the belfry stage, where there is a graceful row of arches (the outer two blank) on each face, under ogee hoodmoulds with applied pinnacles. The motif continues on the buttresses as (empty) niches. All the windows of the church are Perpendicular, some sharply pointed and others with four-centred arches. The clerestory is battlemented, and nave and aisles have buttresses rising to crocketed pinnacles. The glory of the exterior is the two-storeyed S porch, taller than the aisle and crowned by very sumptuous crocketed pinnacles. One pinnacle on the W side, seemingly broken, conceals the chimney. The stair turret is capped by a spire, and there is a smaller flèche on the E side. The S door has a bold ogee hoodmould, which sweeps up into the central niche and supports a medieval statue of the Virgin. There are three more medieval statues, of the Trinity, St. John the Baptist, and St. Thomas of Canterbury.

The porch has stone vaulting and stone panelled walls with brackets and carved corbels. One depicts a cat fiddling to three mice. The interior is spacious but somewhat bleak. This is partly due to the huge window over the chancel arch, clear-glazed and letting light flood in, and giving an odd view of the steep chancel roof. The window seems to cry out for stained glass. The five-bay nave arcades are striking and unusual but rather inelegant: the piers and capitals are octagonal, with concave sides instead of the expected mouldings and shafts. The piers rise excessively high; over them spring small four-centred arches. The tower arch is more conventionally and subtly moulded. On the base of the SE pier is carved the name Henry Winchcombe (the master mason?); on the pier opposite is 'Edmunde' and 'God grant us his grace'. The roofs of the nave and N chapel are 15C; the S chapel has original corbels, one carrying the date 1489, and others representing King Henry VII and Elizabeth of York. The chancel roof is of the 1960s, by David Stratton-Davis. From the S or Lady chapel there is a squint to the high altar. S of this altar are triple sedilia, and on the N wall, high up, two sculpted croziers, perhaps marking the ownership of the church by the Abbey of Gloucester.

The church was extensively reordered in the 1960s. Some old fittings remain. The font, at the W end of the S aisle, is 14C, octagonal, vigorously carved with heads on the faces of the bowl, angels making music below, and demons skulking at the base. It is topped by an elegant openwork wooden cover, with a tall crocketed spire. In the nave is a 15C stone pulpit on a fluted stem. At the E end of the S aisle are the remains of a reredos with canopied niches and some traces of medieval colour. Near it is a 15C pillar piscina. The high altar of wood supports the original stone mensa, and has a frontal by Sir Ninian Comper and riddel posts by F.E. Howard. The E end is now the chapel of the Resurrection. The church was refurnished in 1877–84 by James Brooks, but now only his choirstalls survive, repositioned chapel-wise in the N aisle. In the 1960s a new nave altar, backed by a delicate wrought-iron screen, designed by L.W. Barnard & Partners, was installed, and new nave seating by Sir Basil Spence. A large painting by Ribera, 'Lord, whither goest thou?' hangs in the N chapel. There are fragments of medieval stained glass, including St Stephen, St. Lawrence with his gridiron, and possibly an Apostle, tracery lights of the S aisle, and further survivals in the N clerestory windows. The E window of 1963 by Christopher Webb depicts, amidst much plain frosted glass, the Resurrection.

The brass of John Fortey (died 1458), who completed the nave, is under the N arcade. Brackets of a former canopy still survive on the piers above. His initials and trade mark are in the wreaths of the border. He lies in a Gothic canopy, his feet resting on a sheep and a woolpack. Thomas Fortey (died 1447) is at the E end of the N aisle, with his wife Agnes and her first husband William Scors. The heads of Agnes and Thomas have been lost. An inscription exhorts the reader to 'pray for the children of Thomas Fortey' but another notes, less piously, 'these be the children of William Scors'. In the border are illustrations of a rose, a crab, dogs, a snail, a pig, a hedgehog and oak leaves. William Scors was a tailor and so a pair of scissors is shown at his feet. In the chancel, on the N side, is the brass of William Lawnder, priest (died 1530). He kneels on a faldstool in a surplice worn over a cassock. On the W wall of the Lady chapel are parts of a brass showing the children of William and Margaret Bicknell, who built the chapel. Also a brass to Mawd Parker, 1584, with acrostics on her name and that of her husband Thomas. In the S aisle are two more wool merchants: Thomas Bushe (died 1526), merchant of the Calais Staple, and Johane his wife, both with their feet on sheep and woolpacks; and John Taylour (died 1509), his wife Joane, with their 15 children. In the N aisle are a wool merchant and his wife, c 1400, she with a dog wearing a collar and bells at her feet. Nearby are William Midwinter (died 1501) and his wife, with feet on sheep. Another brass, 1501, commemorates Robert and Anne Serche and their children.

A carillon in the tower plays the tune 'Hanover' (O worship the King) every third hour.

Quenington, _St. Swithin._ Quenington has Norman N and S doorways with splendid tympana. The 12C N doorway, with three orders of chevrons and richly decorated abaci and capitals, frames an earlier tympanum showing the Harrowing of Hell. The S door and tympanum are of the same 12C date. Here the arch includes beakheads and heads of an ox and a horse. The scene is the Coronation of the Virgin. It may have been copied from a carving at Reading Abbey, which had the earliest known depiction of the subject.

The church, long and low, suffered much from restorers, particularly in 1882. The interior now presents a thoroughly 19C appearance.

Selsley, _All Saints._ The church was built in 1861–62 to the designs of G.F. Bodley to serve a portion of the parish of King's Stanley. The benefactor was Sir Samuel Marling, Bt., a cloth manufacturer, but Bodley's real patron was the Rector of King's Stanley, John Gibson. Selsley displays many of the features of Bodley's early churches and it is particularly notable for its complete scheme of stained glass by Morris & Co.

All Saints' stands prominently on a hilltop SW of Stroud. It comprises a nave, a lean-to N aisle, an apsidal chancel, NE vestry and a NW gabled tower. The S wall has three-light windows, which are set irregularly; the N aisle has two very small pairs of lancets. At the W end there are two two-light windows below a type of rose in which eight circles surround a much larger one. This W fenestration is to be found, in varying details, in most of Bodley's early churches. Below the W windows is a doorway, inserted in 1889. Previously, the entrance was under the NW tower. The tower itself is typical of Bodley's early designs in being gabled. The apse has five cusped lancets, each with a circle above, and there is one two-light window in the S chancel wall. Beneath this window is the tomb of Sir Samuel Marling, recessed and gabled. The position and form were probably copied from a medieval example at Bisley. The interior is divided by a two-bay arcade between the nave and N aisle and by a low stone screen between nave and chancel. The contrast with the elaborate painted wooden screens in Bodley's later churches is obvious. The arcade is of sharply accentuated arches, with a characteristic circle in the spandrels. Also characteristic of Bodley are the pairs of half-columns which support the chancel arch.

The font and the pulpit both bear Bodley's usual Greek cross. The plain, white stone font is square and has a flat cover. The pulpit is of marble. On the S wall there are no fewer than eight large, square memorial tablets to members of the Marling family. The stained glass is of special interest because it forms a complete scheme and is very early work of Morris & Co., which was founded in 1861. In the chancel S wall is the Annunciation by William Morris himself. The windows of the apse continue the cycle. They depict, from the S, the Visitation by Dante Gabriel Rossetti (the angel above by Morris); the Nativity by Ford Madox Brown (the angel by Rossetti); the Crucifixion by Brown (the angel by Sir Edward Burne-Jones); the Resurrection by Burne-Jones (the angel by Rossetti); and the Ascension, which is entirely by Morris. In the nave, the windows have relatively small areas of stained glass surrounded by much clear glass. From the E, they depict the Sermon on the Mount (by Rossetti); St. Paul preaching at Athens (by Morris) and Christ blessing children (by Burne-Jones). Note the Pelican in her Piety and the Agnus Dei in the tracery of the middle window; they are by Philip Webb. The windows at the W end represent the Creation (by Morris, but Adam and the Beasts by Webb). Webb designed the Evangelists' symbols in the N aisle. Under the tower are Adam and Eve, by Burne-Jones.

S.C.H.

Tetbury, *St. Mary the Virgin.* Tetbury is a very early and very serious Gothic Revival building, designed by Francis Hiorn of Warwick and built in 1777–81 to replace the decayed medieval church. The parish specifically requested 'an elegant and regular Gothic plan'. The old tower and spire were retained, but had to be rebuilt in 1891–93 by Waller & Son when the spire leant perilously. Hiorn's 18C work shows a real feeling for the spirit of Gothic, although enthusiasm triumphed somewhat over archaeological accuracy.

The exterior gives a misleading impression of the internal arrangement. There is a tall nave and a shallow chancel, in which huge four-light windows are set. The general effect is Perpendicular, but the details of the tracery are earlier Gothic. The parapets are castellated and punctuated with slender crocketed pinnacles rising from thin buttresses. Beneath the windows are low projections—aisles?—with groups of three lancets. The tower is of five stages, but is a stocky design. Over it soars the spire, with insignificant lucarnes at the base.

Entering by the NW door, the plan of the church is still not revealed. The supposed aisles are in fact long, low ambulatories, vaulted and extending round the N, W and S sides of the church. The visitor enters the church proper through a door in the centre of the W ambulatory. The interior is astonishingly high, a hall church with a shallow plaster vault, divided into seven-bay nave and aisles by remarkably slender clustered pillars, in wood. High box-pews fill the nave; the purpose of the ambulatories is now revealed. They provide, by means of doors in each bay, access to the pews in the aisles. There are N, W and S galleries, decorated, like the pews, with relentlessly repeated blind arcading. The E end has been raised to form a chancel.

In the nave are two huge and impressive brass chandeliers of 1781 (hung, perhaps, a little too low). The chancel screen of 1917, though light and inoffensive, obscures the E end. The reredos includes a picture of the Holy Family by Benjamin West. The altar rails are reconstructed from the originals. In the sanctuary are chairs in the Gothic style. There is a good collection of 18C wall monuments— draped urns, obelisks, and tablets—and some have been arranged in a pleasing pattern in the NE corner. Others line the ambulatories. One in the W ambulatory bears the inscription: 'In a vault underneath/lie several of the Saunderses,/late of this parish: particulars/the Last Day will disclose'. Medieval effigies from the old church lie along the N ambulatory.

The stained glass is 19C and rather gaudy. In the E window eight saints flank the Virgin, with angels over. On the N side are representations of the Crucifixion, the Ascension, and the Childhood of the Virgin. On the S side is depicted the parable, 'Well done thou good and faithful servant'.

Tewkesbury Abbey, *St Mary the Virgin.* Tewkesbury, a great Benedictine abbey church refounded by Robert FitzHamon before 1107, was bought by the townspeople in 1539 for £453. It has the grandest Norman tower in the country, an impressive Norman nave and W end, and a lovely Decorated ambulatory with a cluster of Decorated and Perpendicular chapels. Inside there are many notable medieval monuments, chantries and stained glass windows. The church, consecrated in 1121, had to be reconsecrated in 1471, after the Battle of Tewkesbury, when the Yorkists slaughtered some of the defeated Lancastrians in the church, where they had fled for sanctuary. The young Lancastrian Prince of Wales was slain in this battle and is buried in the church, traditionally under the central tower. After the Reformation the nave fell into disuse until the church was restored by Sir Gilbert Scott and his sons in the late 1870s. The proposals were so ruthless that they led William Morris to form the Society for the Protection of Ancient Buildings.

The great mass of the central tower dominates the exterior. The lower stage is plain and bears the outlines of the former, higher roofs of the church. Above are three stages which are richly ornamented with arcading, the middle stage blank and intersecting, the others pierced with belfry windows. The battlements and delicate openwork pinnacles are of 1660. The tower was built in the second quarter of the 12C, immediately after the completion of the nave. In the clerestory of the nave is original Norman blank arcading, now pierced at irregular intervals by Decorated windows. The aisle windows are Decorated also. The W end is a stupendous sight: a cyclopian Norman arch of six orders rises the full height of the nave, making even the 17C Perpendicular Revival window which fills it seem insignificant. The arch thrusts up through Norman blank arcading, which does not try to compete for effect. The parapet is now flat, and the front is crowned with two small Norman turrets, with later pinnacles and spirelets. The chapels which surround the E end have 14C Decorated windows, and at the E end remains are visible of the long-demolished Lady chapel. The Decorated windows of the ambulatory are more ornate and are crowned with gables and enriched with ballflower. Round the ambulatory an intricately pierced parapet runs. There was formerly a chapel at the end of the N transept, the Early English entrance to which (from the church) survives, and also the E arch, now filled by a Decorated window, which leads to St. Nicholas's chapel. The space between this chapel and the ambulatory was later filled by the chapel of St. James.

The nave has arcades with huge, high, circular Norman piers, close in style and date to those of Gloucester Cathedral, though there the arches are more finely moulded. The arcades are so high that they squeeze the triforium into insignificance, and the clerestory is mostly hidden by the lovely lierne-vault of c 1340. The 15 central bosses show scenes from the life of Christ. At the W end, solid walls N and S indicate an intention to provide W towers. The aisle vaults are of c 1300, but at the E end, at the crossing, there are remains of an earlier scheme to build half tunnel-vaults. The crossing still has all four Norman arches. The tower was designed as a lantern, but was filled in with another lierne-vault in the 14C. The transepts have vaults of the 14C, trying to be fan-vaults but not succeeding. The S transept has its original E apsidal chapel, but in the N transept this was replaced in the 14C by St. James's chapel, with a Decorated stone screen separating it from the ambulatory. Through this chapel, St. Nicholas's chapel is now reached. It has a good Early English wall arcade with stiff-leaf in the spandrels, and (originally) Purbeck marble shafts. In the apsidal chancel the arches rest on six Norman piers, now half the height of the nave piers, but probably originally the same height. In the 14C, Decorated capitals and arches were inserted at a new, lower level, and tall Decorated windows were inserted above. An intricate lierne-vault covered the new work, and this was liberally enriched with Yorkist badges in 1471. The ambulatory was similarly remodelled in the 14C. On the N side the first chapel is of St. Margaret of Scotland, separated from the ambulatory by a Decorated stone screen. Next is a chapel dedicated to St. Edmund and St. Dunstan. At the E end a blocked arch led to the Lady chapel. On the S side are, first, St. Faith's chapel, and then St. Catherine's (now a museum), and beyond it, the sacristy, the door extensively decorated with ballflower. The iron plates on the door came from armour worn by soldiers at the Battle of Tewkesbury.

The church is quite poor in furnishings but rich in medieval monuments. The stem of the font, with eight attached shafts decorated with ballflower, is 14C; the bowl is late 19C. At the W end, in the chapel of the Holy Child Jesus, between 18C boards listing benefactions, is a 16C altar painting after Innocenzo da Imola. John Oldrid Scott designed the wooden screen, W of the crossing, and Thomas Collins made it in 1892. Scott's stalls of 1875–79 are under the tower. They incorporate 14C misericords, many on the N side, and two on the S. The screen on the N side is 14C. Opposite stands the Milton organ, made in c 1580, the case and embossed tin pipes original. The maker was Thomas Dallam, and it was remade in the 17C by Robert Dallam. In the mid-17C it was in Hampton Court Palace, where Cromwell's secretary, the poet John Milton, almost certainly played it. In St. Nicholas's chapel, the painted reredos of c 1880 is by Thomas Gambier Parry. It formerly stood behind the high altar. St. Dunstan's chapel has a 15C Flemish altar painting. In the Lady chapel, off the S transept, there is a statue of the Virgin, 20C, by Alec Miller, and mosaic behind the altar of 1893 by Salviati of Venice.

The most sumptuous monuments are ranged around the ambulatory. On the N side, the first E of the crossing is the Beauchamp chantry, the most splendid in the church, of c 1430, two-storeyed, and ornately decorated. It was built for Isabel Despenser, whose first husband Richard, Earl of Worcester, died in 1421. She then married the Earl of Warwick. The lower level is enclosed with Perpendicular panelling, with angels bearing shields in the base parts. The W half of this storey has a fan-vault with pendants; the upper storey has lierne-vaulting. The chapel is crowned with intricate canopy work. Next E is the chantry of Robert FitzHamon (died 1107), founder of the abbey, a chapel of c 1395, fan-vaulted inside, and topped with a cresting of oak leaves. Nearest the altar, there are recumbent effigies in white alabaster of Hugh, Lord Despenser (died 1348) and his wife Elizabeth (died 1359). The canopy, in late Decorated style, is in tiers of open arches, with crockets, pinnacles and ogee gables. At the entrance to St. Margaret's chapel is the tomb of Sir Guy de Brienne, K.G., King Edward III's standard bearer at the Battle of Crécy. He died in 1390, aged 90, having prepared his tomb. At the entrance to the next chapel is Wakeman's cenotaph, commemorating John Wakeman (died 1549), last Abbot of Tewkesbury and first Bishop of Gloucester. The tomb is actually 15C, with a heavy canopy over an arched table, filled in below with delicate star-pattern tracery. On it reclines a cadaverous effigy in a state of putrefaction, upon which crawl worms, snakes, frogs, mice, snails and suchlike 'beasties'. Behind the high altar is the vault of the Duke of Clarence, brother of King Edward IV, drowned (it is said) in a butt of Malmsey, and buried here in 1478. Further on is the canopied tomb of Abbot Cheltenham (Abbot, 1481–1509). Opposite, behind the sedilia, is the tomb of Hugh Despenser (hanged 1325), associate of King Edward II, with many canopied niches, much mutilated by the Puritans. The coffin of Purbeck marble is not Despenser's, however, but that of John Cotes, Abbot in the 14C. W of it is Abbot Robert Forthington's tomb. He died in 1254. Nearby is an Early English style tomb, of Abbot Alan (died 1202), biographer of Thomas Becket. Under an arch of the choir is the Trinity chapel or Despenser chantry, built in 1375–80 for Edward Despenser (died 1375). It resembles the FitzHamon chapel opposite, and has Perpendicular screens and a fan-vault. On the roof, in a canopied niche, the kneeling figure of Despenser, painted and gilded, prays to the altar.

The seven large clerestory windows have glass of 1340–44, installed probably by Hugh Despenser as the gift of his mother, Eleanor de Clare. The E window shows the Last Judgement, with the Coronation of the Virgin in the quatrefoil of the rose window. At the base kneels the donor, naked, having forsaken all earthly goods. To left and right, windows show Prophets, patriarchs, kings and figures from Church history. The westernmost windows, remarkably, have men in armour, their mainly yellow and red surcoats bearing arms identifying them as Fitzroys, de Clares, Despensers, FitzHamon and Zouch, all connected with the abbey and with Eleanor de Clare.

Tewkesbury, *Old Baptist Chapel.* The Old Baptist Chapel stands in an alleyway off of Church Street. It is a 15C, timber-framed, three-bay hall house, which was remodelled for worship in the 17C and 18C. Its present appearance is the result of a restoration after 1976, which has aimed to revive its condition in c 1720. The building was in use by Baptists by the second half of the 17C. Many alterations were made in c 1720. The ceiling, tall windows and sunken baptistery all date from that time. A minister's room was also provided at the W end. In 1805 a new chapel was built elsewhere, and this one was reduced in size. Its present plan is that of a double-storey central bay, with galleries at either end. At the end of the alleyway is a burial ground.

S.C.H.

Winchcombe, *St. Peter.* Winchcombe is another 15C Cotswold wool church, but less ambitious than Northleach, Fairford or Cirencester. It is long and low, with an imposing W tower; its position close to the main street is impressive. The date of building was c 1465. The great Benedictine Abbey of Winchcombe stood to the NE and was entirely demolished after the Reformation. The abbot rebuilt the chancel of the church, the parishioners the nave.

There is no division between nave and chancel. Heavy castellated parapets terminate the clerestory and aisles. These had pinnacles at intervals, which have been removed in recent years. The removal is surely temporary. The parapets cry out for some vertical accents. The chancel roof was raised in 1690, and the continuous roofline and parapets were restored by J.D. Wyatt, 1872–73. The clerestory windows are paired, square-headed, and set remarkably close together. In the chancel they have more elaborate tracery. The aisles have windows with four-centred heads and Perpendicular tracery. On the N side an octagonal stair turret to give access to the Rood loft rises at the division between nave and chancel, and on the S side a similar turret is incorporated into the porch. The S porch is two-storeyed and castellated, and has pinnacles and a niche in the gable. The figure of St. Peter is of 1904 but the angel supporting the pedestal is medieval. The E end has N and S windows of four lights, and a broad E window of seven lights with panel tracery. Below it is a blocked door and evidence of a continuation (a vestry?). All the parapets have large corbels and gargoyles, human and animal heads. The W tower is tall and well-proportioned but sparsely decorated. No stringcourses or other divisions mark out its three stages. The parapet is castellated and has slim pinnacles.

The interior has arcades of eight bays, the piers octagonal and the arches four-centred and flattish. The arcades continue uninterrupted almost to the E end. The church is spacious but not lofty. 15C screens shut off the N and S chapels, and there is a great wooden chancel arch with traceried openings, which rests on big corbels. The screens N and S of the chancel are modern. In the chancel are 14C sedilia, a survival from the previous church. They have crocketed canopies and brackets, and niches for images between the seats. The piscina has a stone canopy bearing the arms of the Abbots of Winchcombe and Gloucester and of Sir Ralph Boteler. The tower, separated from the nave by a stone screen, has a stone vault.

Until 1872 the chancel was furnished Puritan-wise, like Deerhurst, but now only the 17C table remains, and the sanctuary has steps and a 19C reredos. The organ case, though enlarged in 1890, is basically of 1735. The octagonal stem of the font, and the cover, are of 1635, but the bowl is renewed. In the nave hangs a mid-18C brass chandelier, with a wrought-iron cross over it. King George III's arms, of 1778, are placed above the S door. In the N aisle is an almsbox with three locks, as ordered in the time of King Edward VI. A number of interesting objects are displayed in that aisle: a wooden door from Winchcombe Abbey, carved with the initials R.K., for Richard Kidderminster, Abbot 1488–1525; tiles from the abbey site; an altar frontal made from copes of c 1380 (fashioned in the time of Catherine of Aragon, and bearing her badge, a pomegranate); and a stringed instrument (from the parish orchestra?). There are a few fragments of medieval stained glass, but most of the glass is 19C and 20C. In the E window of the Lady chapel are panels showing the Agony in the Garden, the Bearing of the Cross, and the Women at the Empty Tomb, said to be 18C but looking very 19C. John Hardman & Co.'s E window of 1886 depicts Christ walking on the water. Other windows, in the N aisle and clerestory, are of the early 20C, by James Powell & Sons, and show saints and female personifications of Virtues, some of the colouring and modelling rather bad. The best monument is on the N wall of the chancel. It is to Sir Thomas Williams (died 1636): he is kneeling in armour before a double lectern on a pillar. Nearby is a monument to Dorothy Freeman (died 1818) and her sisters, by G. Lewis of Cheltenham. A female figure stands proudly beside a draped urn, clutching a cross.

Woodchester, *Our Lady of the Annunciation.* The Dominican priory, built for William Leigh of Woodchester Park in 1846–49, was demolished in 1970, but the church was preserved. Leigh turned first to A.W.N. Pugin for plans, but Pugin withdrew, and the work was entrusted to Charles Hansom. He built a fine, strong Decorated church, influenced by Pugin's plans, consisting of nave and aisles, chancel and chapels, and a SE tower with a curious spire, which starts as a 'Rhenish helm' but from which an octagonal top emerges. The chancel is divided from the nave by an elaborate screen with Rood figures above, and over the chancel arch is a wall painting of the Last Judgement, by Henry Doyle. The small S chapel is the chapel of the Forty Martyrs of Sebaste, and it houses the tomb of the founder (died 1873). His recumbent effigy is clad in the robes of a Knight of St. Gregory, and he holds a model of his church. The sculptor was Richard Boulton. The monument to Francis Nicholson, Carmelite Archbishop of Corfu (died 1855), is at the W end of the N aisle. The stained glass windows are by William Wailes and John Hardman & Co.

Hampshire

Much of Hampshire is made up of rolling chalk downland with sandy heathland in the NE and also in the SW, where it forms the New Forest. Along the shores of the Solent, the chalk disappears beneath layers of alluvial deposits. The county is therefore predominantly formed of chalk, with none of the bands of famous building stone found in neighbouring Dorset and Wiltshire. The indigenous building materials are therefore first and foremost flint, with large deposits of clay for the production of bricks and tiles. To a lesser extent harder forms of chalk have been employed. Large areas remain predominantly rural with the two major centres of population being on the coast, Portsmouth and Southampton. The only other large centres of population are Bournemouth, Winchester, Andover, Basingstoke and Aldershot.

The county has a wealth of pre-Conquest remains both in buildings and more importantly in sculpture. Pre-Conquest buildings of significance survive at Breamore and Boarhunt, with further work visible at Hambledon, Fareham, Headbourne Worthy and Titchfield amongst others. The group of over-life-size carvings of the Crucifixion at Romsey, Headbourne Worthy and Breamore is almost without parallel. The Norman period is exceptionally well represented, as befits the county which possessed in Winchester the one-time administrative capital of England as well as an important bishopric. Large Norman churches are Romsey Abbey and Winchester, St. Cross. Smaller churches of note include Portchester (a largely unaltered cruciform church), East Meon, with its magnificent central tower, Christchurch, Hambledon and Titchfield.

The transition from Norman to Early English can be seen at Winchester, St. Cross and in the nave of Romsey Abbey. Full Early English is best exemplified by the Garrison Church at Portsmouth, the parish church at Beaulieu and by work at Winchester, St. Cross and Christchurch. The succeeding Decorated period is singularly lacking in Hampshire, with no major buildings and little in the way of additions and alterations. The Perpendicular style is also not widely employed, but Winchester College Chapel is an example of the highest quality. The Tudor period provided in The Vyne what has been called one of the finest private chapels of the period in the country. There was also the total rebuilding of Southwick in 1556 in a continuing Perpendicular style.

The 18C and the Classical idiom is best represented by the large brick church at Avington, 1768–71. The 19C features buildings by most of the major national architects and also by regional architects. Amongst this wealth of work are a number of masterpieces, which include the magnum opus of Sir Arthur Blomfield, St. Mary's, Portsmouth, 1887–89, and William White's outstanding work, St. Michael's, Lyndhurst, 1858–70. All Saints', Hursley was built in 1846–48 by J.P. Harrison for John Keble. In Bournemouth there are two very large and outstanding churches, St. Peter's by G.E. Street and St. Stephen's by J.L. Pearson, 1881–98. Portsmouth also has J.H. Ball's St. Agatha's, Landport, built in 1893–95, which is famous for its internal decoration. The 20C is likewise well represented, with St. Philip's, Cosham, Portsmouth, 1937, being one of Sir Ninian Comper's masterpieces. Sir Charles Nicholson undertook a number of works including the Ascension at Southampton. At Burghclere, the

Sandham Memorial Chapel by Lionel Pearson (1927) is of importance for the paintings by Stanley Spencer (see below).

Fittings. Hampshire possesses four of the ten mid-12C black Tournai marble fonts in Britain, at East Meon; Southampton, St. Michael; St. Mary Bourne; and Winchester Cathedral. There is an impressive stone reredos dating from the middle of the 14C at Christchurch Priory. From the Perpendicular period there are notable wooden screens at Bramley, Ellingham, Fareham and Silchester. Also impressive are the stalls of The Vyne Chapel, the misericords of Winchester College Chapel and Christchurch Priory, and fragments of 16C Flemish tapestry in Winchester College Chapel. Wall painting is well represented, with an outstanding collection of 14C paintings in the tiny church at Idsworth. A good set of 13C paintings can be seen at Corhampton. Other churches with examples are Bramley, Catherington, Hurstbourne Tarrant, Romsey Abbey, Stoke Charity and Silchester. Medieval stained glass includes a number of examples which are among the very best of their period in Britain. At Winchester College Chapel and Grateley are 13C panels. Winchester College Chapel also possesses some magnificent glass dated 1393 and signed by Master Thomas of Oxford. St. Cross, Winchester has a series of 15C windows. Further examples of this period can be seen at Bramley. Fine 16C glass of Flemish origin is in the chapel of The Vyne.

Jacobean furnishings, especially pulpits, appear frequently in Hampshire, good examples being at Silchester, Idsworth and Ellingham. 18C and early 19C furnishings are numerous, with good collections at Avington, Bramley (where the Brocas chapel was designed by Sir John Soane in 1801), Ellingham, Idsworth and Southwick. The Victorian Age is represented by outstanding fittings at Lyndhurst, by St. Peter's and St. Stephen's at Bournemouth, and by St. Mary's and the Royal Garrison Church at Portsmouth. Of outstanding merit are the frescoes painted by Lord Leighton at Lyndhurst, the wall paintings by Clayton & Bell and Heaton, Butler & Bayne at St. Peter's, Bournemouth and the rare sgraffito murals by Heywood Sumner at St. Agatha's, Portsmouth.

For the 20C, Hampshire can offer two nationally important interiors of quite different style. The Sandham Memorial Chapel's sequence of paintings of scenes from the Macedonia campaign by Stanley Spencer, executed between 1927 and 1932, is of international importance. Comper's St. Philip's, Cosham, Portsmouth, has an ornate, richly decorated and gilded baldacchino set in an almost plain white interior.

Monuments of particular note are largely no earlier than the 16C, late enough to show the arrival of Renaissance details. The Draper and Countess of Salisbury's chantries at Christchurch are grand examples. There is, however, a fine collection of late medieval monuments at Stoke Charity, and brasses of note exist at St. Cross, Winchester (15C) and Bramley (early 16C). The best Elizabethan monument in the county is at Titchfield to the first and second Earls of Southampton, dated 1594. It is on a monumental scale and is by Gerard and Nicholas Johnson. Among 17C monuments is Nicholas Stone's small portrait bust of Sir Thomas Cornwallis (died 1618) at Portchester. A number of further notable 17C monuments are at Titchfield. Among the many Georgian monuments, of special note is Thomas Carter's monument in the chapel of The Vyne to Chaloner Chute, carved between 1775 and 1781. Also possibly by Carter is the large monument to Bernard Brocas (died 1777) at nearby Bramley.

Carter was responsible too for the monument to Viscountess Palmerston (died 1769) in Romsey Abbey. Avington has a good collection of smaller 18C and 19C monuments. From the end of the century, there are many good monuments by John Flaxman, including those at Romsey, Lyndhurst and Christchurch. Lyndhurst also has memorials by G.E. Street and S.P. Cockerell. Fareham has many 19C monuments, including work by Sir Richard Westmacott.

The county is extremely rich in 19C and 20C stained glass. Evans of Shrewsbury is represented at Winchester College Chapel. Morris & Co. glass is found at Lyndhurst, with work by Sir Edward Burne-Jones, William Morris himself, D.G. Rossetti, Philip Webb and Ford Madox Brown. Indeed, Lyndhurst is one of the best churches in the county for Victorian stained glass, with additional work by Clayton & Bell, Powell's and Henry Holiday. In Bournemouth, St. Peter's has work by William Wailes, Morris and Burne-Jones, Clayton & Bell and Comper. The stained glass of St. Stephen's, Bournemouth is all by Clayton & Bell. Hursley has a complete scheme by William Wailes. Hambledon has a number of windows by Ward & Hughes and Mayer & Co. Romsey Abbey has work by Clayton & Bell, Powell's and Kempe & Co. Comper designed windows at East Meon and Cosham. Contemporary with Comper's interwar work are the windows of the Ascension, Southampton by A.K. Nicholson.

The historical associations of Hampshire's churches go back to the days when Winchester was the city of St. Swithin and of many pre-Conquest kings. Most of the notable associations, however, are of the 18C and 19C. St. Peter's, Bournemouth has links with many prominent 19C figures; see the entry for details. Hursley was the home of John Keble, the leader of the Oxford Movement, in the mid-19C. The church of St. Cross at Winchester was the setting of a scandal in the 1850s over the misuse of charitable funds, which provided Anthony Trollope with a model for 'The Warden'. St. Mary's, Kingston, Portsmouth has been remarkable in the past century for its role in clergy training and for its distinguished incumbents. In the 20C, Romsey Abbey was closely connected with Earl Mountbatten. Amongst the many notable people buried in Hampshire churchyards and not mentioned under specific churches are Field Marshal Viscount Montgomery of Alamein (died 1976) at Binstead, Florence Nightingale (died 1910) at East Wellow, Charles Kingsley (died 1875) at Eversley, Harry Gordon Selfridge (died 1947) at Highcliffe, Sir Arthur Conan Doyle (died 1930)—the creator of Sherlock Holmes—at Minstead, Gilbert White (died 1793) at Selbourne and Thomas Lord (died 1832), the founder of the famous London cricket ground, at West Meon.

Avington, St. Mary. Avington is one of the most perfect of Hampshire's Georgian churches. It was built of red brick with stone dressings in 1768–71 and stands a short distance from Avington Park. The three-stage W tower dominates the setting. There are round-headed windows except for a Venetian E window. The entire church has battlements.

The undivided interior has a narrow gallery supported by wooden Ionic pilasters. The gallery contains a small 19C barrel organ, whose case has Gothick decoration, and bears the arms of King George III. The nave has box-pews of Spanish mahogany, with panelling to the walls. The manor pew opposite the pulpit has enriched panels. At the E end, the sanctuary has a metal rail with a wooden top, and a reredos with an open segmental pediment and the usual inscribed panels. On the S side of the nave the triple-decker pulpit is hexagonal and has a tester which is surmounted by a finial with a bird. The barrel-vaulted plaster ceiling has a central elliptical moulding from which hangs a brass chandelier. The font at the W end consists of a marble pillar with a bowl and a large scalloped base. All these fittings date from c 1770. The E window has four roundels of stained glass in the side lights, inserted in 1896, and a small panel in the centre. On the N side of the nave there are memorials to Elizabeth Peel (died 1865; depicting an angel carrying a girl, and carved by Thomas and James Nelson of Carlisle) and to the Duchess of Buckingham and Chandos (died 1836). A monument on the N side of the sanctuary commemorates Margaret, Marchioness of Carnarvon (died 1768), builder of the church. The monument has an obelisk back-plate with heraldry and swags, flanked by two urns, all above a long inscription. Opposite is a pedimented memorial to George Bridges (died 1751) and his wife Ann (died 1763), with Ionic columns, a sarcophagus and an urn. Finally, next to the pulpit there is a marble monument by W. Theed, with a relief portrait medallion, to John Shelley (died 1866), who was the brother of the poet, Percy Bysshe Shelley.

Bournemouth

St. Peter. This is the mother church of the town and despite being founded only in 1841, it is the second church on the site, built to the designs of G.E. Street from 1854 to 1879. The church and churchyard possess a wealth of details from the Victorian period onwards. The building of the church was due to the vision of the Reverend Alexander Morden Bennett, who was the first Vicar of Bournemouth between 1845 and 1880 and a staunch Anglo-Catholic.

Set in a large, well-wooded, sloping churchyard, the church is dominated by the tall W tower and slender recessed spire which rise to a height of 202ft. The tower was built in 1869–70 and the spire was added in 1879. The heavily buttressed three-stage tower has statues of St. Gregory, St. Augustine of Hippo, St. Jerome and St. Ambrose beneath the corner pinnacles. In between the pinnacles are parapets of blind arcading. From each pinnacle springs a flying buttress which supports the spire. The clerestory windows have plate tracery and polychromatic stone decoration.

Internally, the large six-bay nave is divided by octagonal piers which have moulded capitals. This was built in 1855–59. The W bays of the aisles are larger and taller and form W transepts. The S aisle is the only part not by Street; it is all that remains of the previous church, and was added by Edmund Pearce in 1851 to the original building of 1841–43 by John Tulloch. The clerestory has ten double-lights, with quatrefoils above, on each side. Between these are stiff-leaf corbels carrying slender Purbeck shafts which support the wooden roof. On either side of the nave the walls above the arches have paintings, six in all, depicting scenes from the Life of Christ. Each is set in a roundel with a floral border. Over the chancel arch the painting depicts the Crucifixion. All the paintings were executed by Clayton & Bell between 1873 and 1877. They have kept the brilliance of their colours due to the pigment having been mixed with a gelatine base instead of lime. The E end is very richly decorated. The chancel of two bays is raised on two steps and is separated from the nave by a low marble wall topped by a low metal screen. The columns of the chancel and the two-bay sanctuary have attached shafts of various marbles rising to stiff-leaf capitals. The chancel side arches are decorated with both foliage and dogtooth. Above are two recessed carved panels depicting the Annunciation and the Crucifixion. The arches are filled with metal screens which separate the chancel from the transepts. The S transept serves as the Keble chapel and the N as the chapel of the Annunciation, offices and vestries. The sanctuary is separated from the side chapels by three-bay alabaster and marble arcades. The effect is stunning and Street based the idea on a precedent at Lincoln Cathedral. The arcade on the S side also serves as sedilia. The sanctuary is rib-vaulted with the bosses and panels being decorated. The transepts have wooden barrel-vaults.

The fittings represent many great names in Victorian church design. In the S aisle is the octagonal stone font supported on a cluster of marble columns, designed by Street and installed in 1855. The wooden canopy dates from 1945. At the W end of the N aisle is the war memorial consisting of a large wooden crucifix with candlesticks on either side, designed by Sir Ninian Comper. At the E end is a panel of painting and mosaic depicting St. Paul in Athens. In the nave on the N side is the sumptuously decorated marble pulpit, designed by Street and carved by Thomas Earp. It was shown at the International Exhibition in 1862 before being installed in the church. It is supported on a cluster of short columns, with a large angel holding an inscription supporting the book rest. Opposite the pulpit is a large brass eagle lectern dated 1872. In the N transept in the W wall above a door is a carving by Earp of St. Peter receiving the keys from Christ. The organ is by Harrison & Harrison and was built in 1915 and rebuilt in 1975–76. The chancel has ornately carved wooden choirstalls. On the S side a brass plaque records that W.E. Gladstone, the famous Prime Minister, took his last communion in the church in 1898. The wooden roof above the choirstalls was designed by G.F. Bodley and has a Latin inscription which means, 'Thou art Peter and upon this rock will I build My Church.'

The S transept was turned into a chapel at the turn of the century by Sir Thomas Jackson. He placed the screen between the aisle and the transept. The walls of the transept are painted and are the work of Heaton, Butler & Bayne, as is the reredos in the chapel. The decoration was completed in 1907. The sanctuary is the most lavishly decorated part of the church. The vault has bosses and painting by Bodley. Suspended from the roof are seven silver sanctuary lamps. The floor of the sanctuary is of marble. The alabaster reredos by Earp was recoloured by Comper in 1929; it depicts the Triumphant Christ surrounded by angels. Either side of this are mosaic panels which depict three angels making music (N) and three censing angels (S). On the N and S walls are more panels. All were made in 1899 by Powell's. Above are images of saints by Sir Arthur Blomfield and painted by Clayton & Bell in 1886.

The stained glass of the church is of equally high standard. The windows of the S aisle are by William Wailes and date from 1852–57. They depict scenes from the life of St. Peter. The SW transept has a tall four-light window by Percy Bacon, dated 1896, which depicts scenes from the life of Christ. The S transept has a window which depicts the Te Deum; in the bottom right-hand corner is John Keble. Above the aumbry in the S wall is a window by William Morris and Sir Edward Burne-Jones, dated 1864. The large E window in the sanctuary is of five lights with two quatrefoils and a large rose above. It is by Clayton & Bell, 1866, and depicts scenes from the life of Christ with the Crucifixion in the central light. The chapel of the Annunciation has a two-light E window by Comper of the Annunciation, dated 1915. The N window is of five tall lancets depicting musical scenes, by Clayton & Bell, 1874. In the NW transept a tall four-light window depicting scenes from Revelation is by Clayton & Bell, 1880. The main W window of the Nativity was installed in 1880 and was heavily restored in 1948 after wartime bomb damage. In the S wall under the tower is a window known as the Founder's window, designed by Street in 1881 in memory of Morden Bennett. It depicts six great church builders with their churches, including Morden Bennett with a model of St. Peter's.

In the churchyard to the S on higher ground is the Chapel of the Resurrection built in 1925–26 by Comper as a war memorial. Since 1983 it has been a religious educational resources centre. The chapel has two two-light windows on each side. Over the W door is a finely carved Crucifixion. Internally, the chapel is painted white with four Tuscan columns supporting the blue-painted ceiling. The churchyard cross, designed by Street and carved by Earp in 1871, has a panel at the base depicting St. Peter being crucified upside down.

John Keble used the church in the last year of his life after retiring from Hursley 20 miles away. The famous musician Hubert Parry was baptised in the church. In the churchyard are the graves of Morden Bennett, the founder; Lewis Tregonwell (died 1832) who founded Bournemouth itself; Sir Dan Godfrey, who founded what was to become the Bournemouth Symphony Orchestra; General Richard Moody (died 1887), who founded British Columbia; and finally Mary Wollstonecraft Shelley (died 1851), who was the second wife of the poet Percy Bysshe Shelley and whose heart is buried with her. She is famous, of course, for creating Frankenstein.

St. Stephen. St Stephen's is considered by many to be the finest church in Bournemouth. It was built by public subscription in memory of Alexander Morden Bennett, the first Vicar of Bournemouth. He died in 1880 and the foundation stone was laid on October 11th 1881. The architect was J.L. Pearson. The church was completed in 1898, except for the NW tower which was built in 1907–08 under Pearson's son, F.L. Pearson.

The church is built of stone in a 13C style. Apart from the dominant tower, its roofline is punctuated by a series of turrets and by a flèche over the crossing. Pearson had intended a spire but this was never built. The tall tower has a low pyramidal cap. The emphasis on verticality is strengthened by the use of continuous set-back buttresses. The middle stage has two deeply-recessed double-light windows and the top stage has very tall pairs of double-light louvred openings. Above these is blind arcading. The W front has two corner turrets terminating in crocketed pinnacles, and three tall double-light windows which are deeply recessed and set under a single arch, the windows being separated by buttresses. Beneath the windows is the W door, surmounted by a niche containing a statue. There are very tall two-light nave clerestory windows. The aisles and transepts have gabled buttresses, emphasising the strong vertical lines. Set in the angles between the chancel and the transepts are two circular turrets. To the E of the S transept is the two-storey vestry. The E end has a buttressed apse, lit by triple-light windows. N of the chancel is the smaller Lady chapel which likewise finishes in a buttressed apse.

The interior gives a sense of size and grandeur. The nave of five bays is c 90ft long. The quatrefoil piers have demi-shafts which rise unbroken to carry the stone quadripartite vaulting. The E bay of the nave is canted inwards, which helps draw the eye towards the E end. Beneath the clerestory windows a gallery runs round the church. It has a parapet with pierced quatrefoil panels. At the W end a gallery fills the entire bay and is supported on stone rib-vaults. The aisles have rib-vaults too. The S transept differs from the N in that it has an upper floor supported on a rib-vault which carries the organ. Beneath this is the chapel of All Souls. The N transept has in its N wall four lancets and a large rose window. The chancel and sanctuary, raised on three steps, are dominated by the ornate high altar and triptych reredos. Behind the sanctuary runs an ambulatory. The ribs of the vault of the apse rise from slender attached shafts and are decorated with dogtooth. The Lady chapel opening off the E side of the N transept has a rib-vault, a smaller apse than that of the sanctuary, and tall lancet windows.

The fittings are of a sumptuous nature. Immediately next to the S porch entrance is the marble font, which consists of a circular tub carried on a cluster of columns, designed by Pearson and carved by Robert Davison of London. The font is flanked by two large metal candlesticks and is enclosed by metal screens designed by F.L. Pearson, made by White's of Winchester and installed in 1903. The ornate oak canopy with a crocketed spire was dedicated in 1892. In front of the chancel screen on the S side, under a tall canopy, is a painted statue of St. Stephen by Martin Travers. Opposite this is the pulpit, designed by Pearson and carved by Robert Davison and Nathaniel Hitch (the latter carved the figures). The three main panels depict Jesus preaching the Sermon on the Mount, St. Peter preaching and St. Paul preaching in Athens. Between these scenes are smaller figures beneath filigree panels. The ornate chancel screen and side screens are of wrought-iron, designed by Pearson and made by White's of Winchester. In the chancel the elaborate oak stalls have carvings of saints and poppyheads on the ends. The stalls were made by Moos Bros. of Winchester and the carving was by Nathaniel Hitch. The high altar and its magnificent triptych reredos form the central feature of the church. The panels on the altar represent the Adoration of the Magi, the Annunciation and Jesus being presented in the Temple. The triptych, restored in 1958, is finely gilded. The main panel is divided into three gabled sections by uprights on which stand four angels. The Crucifixion is the central image, set in an ornate arch with quatrefoils filling the space beneath the gable. Under smaller flanking gables are further figures. These are (left) Elijah with a raven and (above) St. Ambrose and St. Augustine. On the right are Isaiah and (above) St. Clement and St. Swithun. The left wing has figures of St. Stephen and Moses and the right wing St. John the Baptist and David. In front of the Lady chapel is an alabaster statue of the Virgin and Child by Benjamin Clemens.

All the stained glass is by Clayton & Bell. The windows form a grouping of the firm's work paralleled in scale only in Truro and St. Edmundsbury Cathedrals. Most of the windows depict the Apostles and other New Testament figures (note scenes from the life of St. Stephen at the W end), and saints of the early Church and of the Middle Ages.

The organ was built in 1898 by William Hill & Sons and rebuilt by Rushworth & Dreaper of Liverpool in 1951. Between 1930 and 1935 the great church musician and composer Percy Whitlock was organist and director of music. Indeed, the church has a strong tradition of music.

Breamore, *St. Mary (previously St. Mary and St. Michael).* Set in trees to the SE of the Elizabethan mansion, St. Mary's is a remarkably complete example of a large pre-Conquest church dating from the very late 10C or early 11C. It has a pre-Conquest inscription and the remains of a large-scale Rood. The chancel was restored in 1874 and the church as a whole in 1897.

St. Mary's from the SW: a cruciform pre-Conquest church with many later features

The church is constructed of flint, arranged in herringbone fashion, with stone dressings. There are also reused Roman bricks and tiles. The church is nearly 97ft long and consists of a long nave with a S porch, a large crossing space, a S transept and a chancel. The S transept is not very large and was matched on the N side until the 15C. The transepts originally served as side chapels. The porch is of two storeys, the lower stage being Norman and the part-timbered upper stage 15C. The porch has two Norman arches with the remains of a pre-Conquest Rood above the inner one. The tower and S transept have examples at each corner of long-and-short work, made up of large stone quoins. There are also examples of pilaster strips. A further pre-Conquest detail are the seven double-splayed round-headed windows, most of which have been partially altered. However, above the Norman doorway in the E wall of the S transept is a perfectly preserved example. A stone in the W wall of the S transept is inscribed, 'Avoid Fornication'.

The nave tower arch and the chancel arch are 14C insertions. Indeed, the chancel is largely of this period (with a three-light E window), although its lower walls contain much pre-Conquest work. The capitals of the chancel arch have very fine foliate carving with detailing of thistle leaves, acorns, oak leaves, vines and grapes. This sculpture has been tentatively ascribed to the same hand as work at Christchurch Priory. Above the chancel arch are the remains of a pre-Conquest inscription with the letters DES. The N transept arch is now blocked but the S transept is the purest pre-Conquest survival.

The arch has capitals made from two massive stones with a cable moulding carved on the angles. On the N face of the arch is the famous inscription, 'HER SWUTELATH SEO GECWYDRAEDNES THE' (Here is made plain the covenant to thee, which is from Titus 1, verse 3). The inscription, owing to the style of the lettering, has been placed in the reign of King Aethelraed II (979–1016). Above the arch is a pre-Conquest upper doorway.

The badly defaced pre-Conquest Rood figures in the S porch demand attention. Above the figure of the Crucified Christ with a sagging body is the Hand of God with the figures of the Virgin Mary, with a halo, and St. John, with a moon above him. Around the Rood are the remains of wall painting of a landscape with buildings and a church. On the W wall is the image of Judas hanged. There is no date ascribed to these paintings. Also on the N wall is a Norman medallion containing a carving of the Lamb of God. Against the S wall within is a wooden pedimented 18C door surround. On the sill of a window in the S wall of the nave is a bronze sculpture of the Flight into Egypt by Annette Yarrow. Twelve hatchments are placed beneath the tower. In the chancel on the S side are the piscina and a 16C chest. There are traces of painting on the E wall. The three-light E window is Victorian and depicts Christ with Peter, Gabriel appearing to Mary and the angel appearing to the women at the empty tomb.

Burghclere, *Sandham Memorial Chapel.* The Sandham Memorial Chapel designed by Lionel Pearson is a brick oblong box which adjoins one-storey almshouses. It is lit only by three tall rectangular windows in the W wall and is virtually devoid of any historical architectural vocabulary. Internally, it is famous for its sequence, round three walls, of paintings by Stanley Spencer dating from 1927–32. They are scenes of the First World War in Macedonia.

Cosham, *St. Philip.* St. Philip's is one of Sir Ninian Comper's masterpieces, reflecting his 'Unity by Inclusion' style, and is one of the more important interwar churches. The church, vicarage and parish hall were designed around three sides of a square to afford some protection for the church from the noise of the adjacent railway line. The church itself was consecrated in October 1937, having cost £15,894.

Externally, the church appears as a brick box with mouldings and dressings made of artificial stone. The roof of the nave, aisles and Lady chapel is continuous, with a Classical bellcote at the W end. The aisles each have three buttresses which rise above the roof and are capped with elongated pyramids. Between the buttresses and at the ends of the aisles are large three-light windows, with intersecting but uncusped tracery. The Lady chapel—in the normal position of a chancel—is lit by a very large six-light and fully Decorated E window and two smaller side windows. The W end has a projecting central bay which rises to the bellcote. On the N side at either end are the single-storey choir and clergy vestries.

Internally, the immediate impact is one of spaciousness and light. Entrance through the W door brings you under the choir gallery, which acts as a narthex. It is supported on four Tuscan columns. The ceiling of the narthex has six painted shields set in plaster frames. On the gallery is a Latin inscription which reads, 'Virgin aid the port, Nicholas cherish it, Thomas pray for it'. The nave and aisles are of four bays, the pillars being of hollow plaster, painted white. They rise to Corinthian capitals and simplified Gothic vaults. The effect of this plain white fabric is to draw the eye to the central feature of the church—the ciborium. Set in the E bay of the nave, its four gilded plaster columns with gilded Corinthian capitals carry the highly decorated arched canopy. The inner faces of the four arches have intricate gold arabesques. Above these are images of the Apostles. The vault of the ciborium is decorated with stars, a favourite Comper motif, and in the centre is the image of a dove supported by four angels. Over the front arch is a figure of the Triumphant Christ, and above each corner are eagles from whose beaks hang lamps. Angels appear on all four sides. The high altar under the ciborium is raised on three steps. The sanctuary is enclosed by an 18C-inspired wooden rail and there is similar sanctuary furniture. The Lady chapel behind has hangings designed by Comper. The large E window was planned to have stained glass but owing to financial restrictions only the top portion depicting the Risen Christ was completed, and this with £900 out of Comper's own pocket.

Immediately in front of the narthex is the octagonal font with its gilded canopy. This is the only other splash of colour along with the fine organ case above. The lower case set in the front of the gallery with dummy pipes has the images of St. Cecilia and St. Gregory. The organ by Harrison & Harrison is considered to be one of the finest organs in the S of England.

East Meon, *All Saints.* The church is in a superbly picturesque setting, surrounded by the South Downs and sitting above the village. It is basically an ambitious cruciform Norman church with an imposing central tower. It has many fittings and stained glass by Sir Ninian Comper, but its chief treasure is undoubtedly the Norman Tournai marble font.

The church's exterior is dominated by the stone-built central tower. It features three round-headed belfry windows which have shafts and zigzag decoration. Above this are three circular openings, again with zigzag. The tower is topped with a lead-covered broach spire. The only other exterior Norman features are the W door, the inner S door of the porch, which is not in its original position, and a number of round-headed windows. The church was much extended in c 1230 in the Early English style. This expansion can be seen in the W front where the join between the nave and the S aisle is easily discernible. It was at this time also that the Lady chapel was built. Most of the windows were replaced later, with the W window dating from the 14C and many others from the 15C. In 1869–70 the church was thoroughly restored by Ewan Christian.

Internally, the church presents a similar story. There is a three-bay nave and S aisle, separated by two octagonal piers with moulded capitals and three simple pointed Early English arches. In the wall above the E arch are the blocked remains of an original Norman nave window. The tower is supported by four massive Norman arches. The S transept shows how the later nave aisle affected the Norman fabric. The chancel of three bays and the Lady chapel were both extensively rebuilt in the 15C and much restored by Sir Ninian Comper in 1906–22. The arcade, however, is still of c 1200.

The most important fitting is the black Tournai marble font, situated in the W bay of the S aisle. It was made c 1150 and was probably a gift from Henry of Blois, Bishop of Winchester and brother of King Stephen, who held the manor. The font is one of just ten of this type in England, of which four are in Hampshire. It is square in shape with a shallow bowl. On the W side the Earth is represented as being flat and supported on typical Norman pillars. Above this is a frieze representing God's creation of animal life. On the N side is God creating man and woman, Eve being tempted by the serpent and Adam eating the forbidden fruit. The E side depicts Adam and Eve being barred from the Gates of Paradise, shown as a Norman palace by an angel wielding a sword. The angel is also shown teaching Adam to dig and Eve to spin. The S face is similar to the W face, with a row of pillars supporting the flat Earth, and above, the symbolic chase between doves representing good and dogs representing evil.

Over the S door are Jacobean royal arms and nearby is a Russian painting of the dead Christ. Opposite, in the NW corner of the nave, is a small organ built by Peter Wells and finished in 1983. In front of the tower crossing on the left-hand side is a wooden pulpit dated 1706, which came from Holy Trinity, Minories, in London. Comper's high altar with its riddel posts stands forward of the E wall to create a vestry space behind. Also by him are the wooden screen separating the chancel from the Lady chapel, the Lady chapel altar, and the reredos behind it which consists of four panels depicting the Nativity. The Lady chapel possesses many monuments, mostly 18C.

The stained glass is predominantly by Comper. His large five-light E window of 1920, which is a First World War memorial, consists of three tiers of figures, some of them unusual. In the top row are the Imperial Russian arms, Joan of Arc, St. Vladimir, St. Edward, St. David, St. Methodius, St. Catherine and the flag of the U.S.A. Below are St. Martin, St. Andrew, the Risen Christ, St. Patrick and St. Sebastian. At the bottom are St. Adrian, St. Michael, St. Nicholas, St. George and St. Quintyn. The Lady chapel E window has Comper glass of 1907.

Hursley, *All Saints*. A large stone church in the Decorated style, of which only the W tower is medieval. The rest of the building was rebuilt in 1846–48 by J.P. Harrison for John Keble, one of the key protagonists of the Oxford Movement. He was Vicar of Hursley from 1836 until his death in 1866 and paid for the rebuilding out of profits from his famous book, 'The Christian Year', which was first published in 1827, and also from 'Lyra Innocentium, Thoughts in Verse on Christian Children, their Ways and Privileges', which was published in 1846. Keble's grave and that of his wife lie in the churchyard W of the church.

Portchester, *St. Mary*. Set in the SE corner of the most perfectly preserved of the Roman Saxon Shore forts, diagonally opposite the Norman castle, the present church was built to serve an Augustinian priory founded by King Henry I in 1133. There is some evidence that it had been the site of a pre-Conquest church. What remains today is the greater part of an almost perfect cruciform Norman church. The priory remained on the site little more than ten years before moving N over Portsdown Hill to Southwick.

Apart from the Victorian flint-built NE vestry, the church is of stone. It has a low tower with a pyramidal cap. The W front is particularly impressive with two massive flat corner buttresses and a superb door of three orders. The inner order has zigzag decoration on the arch, the outer two have attached shafts with incised decoration and roll-mouldings. A further band of decoration consisting of circles containing various patterns adorns the middle arch, and bands of zigzag adorn the outer. Above the door are three round-headed arches. The outer two are blank, the larger middle one is glazed. All three arches have shafts, zigzag decoration, roll-mouldings and cushion capitals. The infill of the blank spaces is a repeat pattern of circles with inset quatrefoils. The S face of the tower reveals blocked windows and the roof pitch of the missing S transept. Likewise the E face reveals the roof pitch of the original Norman chancel as well as further blocked windows. The one jarring note externally is the very unsympathetically designed parish room of 1975, which is built of concrete breeze blocks and has been tacked on to the S wall of the nave. It does not sit at all well with its ancient surroundings.

The aisleless five-bay nave is entered from the W end. The S wall reveals two blocked Norman arches to the former cloister. The wide crossing has arches of two orders with roll- and billet moulding, and shafts with varying capitals. The N transept is a real *tour de force*. There is a blind arcade running round its walls at ground level. All the capitals are richly decorated with foliate designs. Most, if not all, of these capitals have been ascribed to the 19C but those of the N wall, which are more worn, have been suggested as dating from c 1200. The transept now serves as the Lady chapel. The chancel has the remains of blind arcading. Due to its late 16C rebuilding, there is a low wooden barrel-vaulted roof, instead of a higher stone vault.

At the W end of the nave above the wooden inner porch is a modern balcony supporting two very large and incongruous speakers. On the N side at the W end is the superbly carved Norman font. It is vigorously handled with a top band of animal and human figures and birds set in an acanthus scroll. Under this are intersecting arches. The W end also has choirstalls and a modern organ. The S door is now the entrance to the parish room. On the N wall is a large and elaborate panel of Queen Anne's arms put up after a fire in 1705, to mark a royal grant for restoration. Also in the nave are the brass lectern dated 1889 and the Victorian pulpit. The chancel has the remains of some Elizabethan bench-ends, a Roman child's stone coffin, and two medieval tomb-slabs with a sword cross and an abbot's staff carved upon them. Both slabs were discovered under the nave during restoration in 1885. Amongst the many monuments one of note set in the E wall of the chancel is a painted bust in a niche to Sir Thomas Cornwallis (died 1618), Governor of Portchester Castle. It was carved by Nicholas Stone. The stained glass includes the W window of Christ as the Good Shepherd (memorial date of 1907), and the Crucifixion in the E window.

Portsmouth

St. Mary, Kingston (also known as St. Mary's, Portsea). St. Mary's is the mother church of Portsea Island, excluding Old Portsmouth. The present church is the third on the site. The medieval church was demolished and rebuilt in 1843 and its replacement was succeeded in turn by the present magnificent structure of flint with stone dressings in 1889. The foundation stone was laid on August 9th 1887 by the Empress Frederick of Germany, the eldest daughter of Queen Victoria. The architect was Sir Arthur Blomfield and it is his masterpiece. It cost £44,000, which was provided by the First Lord of the Admiralty, the Right Hon. W.H. Smith, the son of the founder of the famous stationers. Besides being an architectural *tour de force* in the Perpendicular style, the church has an impressive list of connections with prominent churchmen.

The church and indeed much of the city is dominated by the massive W tower, 175ft high and of four stages. Above the ornate W door rises the large W window. In the third stage are two two-light windows and above are two tall two-light louvred openings in each face. It is surmounted by battlements and four large crocketed pinnacles. Each bay of the nave is marked by buttresses with pinnacles rising from them. The E end of the nave has octagonal turrets and the chancel terminates with two crocketed pinnacles rising from the set-back buttresses. On the N side is a two-storey vestry, which is balanced on the S by a chapel which now serves as a parish hall.

Internally, the impression is of height and width. The nave is 123ft long, 40ft wide and 78ft high, and is of six bays with octagonal piers and battlemented capitals supporting moulded arches. The clerestory consists of six pairs of double-light windows, all of which have clear glass. The hammerbeam roof is supported by shafts rising from above the nave arcades. The corbels consist of angels holding shields. The chancel is in reality a seventh bay of the nave, being of the same proportions but with different clerestory windows. There is a seven-light E window.

The church is rich in late Victorian fittings, with a handful from the previous churches. The stone pulpit on the N side of the nave is very large, with seven sides each decorated with three traceried arches. Above these is a continuous border of intricate floriate carving. It is supported on a cluster of columns. Rising above the pulpit and filling the N arcade of the chancel is the magnificent three-manual organ which was built by W. Walker & Sons in 1889–91. The case was designed by Blomfield. Beneath the organ is the chapel of St. Boniface. The imposing brass eagle lectern with lions at its feet was designed by Blomfield and made in 1889. S of this and S of the chancel, the metal screens of the former chapel of St. Stephen now stand in front of concrete breeze blocks which form the walls of the parish hall. The octagonal alabaster font has panels supported by angels which depict Moses striking the rock, the Baptism of Christ, Jesus blessing children and the baptism of the Ethiopian Eunuch. The ornate metal screen in the tower arch was originally the chancel screen. The chancel now has only a low marble wall enclosing it. The mosaic floors and the marble dado of the sanctuary are the work of Burke & Co. The large reredos is set into an arch, above which is blank arcading. The reredos has central panels depicting the Nativity and the Crucifixion. Flanking these are figures of saints and angels, all set under ornate tabernacles. It is the work of Buckeridge & Floyce. On the N side of the chancel is a large arched recess, housing a 13C stone coffin with a Crusader cross on the lid. In the S aisle is a roundel of the Virgin and Child attributed to Della Robbia. The many memorials date mainly from the 19C.

The stained glass is of the late 19C and early 20C and is largely by Burlison & Grylls. The E window depicts Christ in Majesty surrounded by saints and angels. Above what is now the parish hall are three windows depicting the Ascension, the Crucifixion and the Risen Christ. In the chapel of St. Boniface, a four-light window has figures set in clear glass of David, Solomon and the Nativity. In the N aisle the windows depict Old Testament scenes. The main W window depicts Christ teaching the children, John the Baptist baptising

Christ, and Noah and Moses. The windows in the S aisle are devoted to the New Testament.

Many clergy from St. Mary's have risen to the highest offices in the Church. Canon Jacob, who rebuilt the church, later served as Bishop of Newcastle and then of St. Albans. His place was taken in 1896 by Cosmo Gordon Lang, who rose to be Archbishop of York and finally Archbishop of Canterbury. He was noted as an active organiser. Cyril Garbett became Vicar in 1909. Under him the running of the parish with its many curates became a well-known model. In 1919 he became Bishop of Southwark, and eventually Archbishop of York in 1942. One of his staff was Philip ('Tubby') Clayton, who would later found the Toc H organisation. Later Vicars have left to become Bishop of Ripon, Dean of Salisbury and Bishop of Malmesbury.

Isambard Kingdom Brunel and Charles Dickens were baptised in the previous church on the site.

St. Agatha, Landport. Despite the grim appearance of the church, marooned between the naval base, main road and multi-storey car park, it possesses some internal decoration of distinction and has an important place in Church history. The church itself was miraculously spared during World War II but lost most of its parish. It was then used as a naval store from 1955 until very recently. In 1964 a fire destroyed the Lady chapel, which was subsequently demolished. Since then the church has often faced the threat of total demolition. Its future, however, is now secure with plans for a museum devoted to fittings, stained glass and the work of Heywood Sumner, St. Agatha's most famous decorator.

The church, built of brick in an Italian Romanesque style, was designed by J. Henry Ball. It took a year to build, being completed and consecrated in 1895, at a cost of £10,250. Some £3250 of this was spent on furnishings and decoration which included the now almost completely destroyed sgraffito decoration of the Lady chapel by Heywood Sumner. A marble high altar was added in 1898. The surviving Heywood Sumner sgraffito murals in the chancel apse followed in 1901, depicting Christ in Majesty, six large medallions containing Christian symbols, seven large figures of the Evangelists and Prophets, and texts. The figure of Christ is seated on a rainbow which utilises the shape of the apse and helps unify the composition. This scheme is at present boarded and caged off from the rest of the church, which is divided into a series of caged stores. The inserted upper levels of the store come to the level of the ornately carved capitals, designed by Heywood Sumner and carved by A.V. Heal, being completed in 1927. Of the other furnishings, the elaborate marble ciborium, designed by Ball and Sumner, was removed to St. Michael's Church where it was destroyed in 1960. The marble altar is now in Holy Trinity, Gosport and the wooden pulpit, designed by Ball and carved by Hoare of Southsea in 1902, was moved to St. John's, Rudmore, which has itself been made redundant.

The church owes its appearance to the vision of Father Robert Dolling, who came to the parish in 1885. He was strongly Anglo-Catholic and his ministry in one of the worst slums is justly famous. His congregation grew from a handful to hundreds and the need arose for a bigger church. Five months after the consecration his strong Anglo-Catholicism led him into trouble with the Bishop of Winchester. The cause was his saying of Masses for the dead. His successor, Father G.H. Tremenheere, continued the beautification of the interior.

Royal Garrison Church. This was the chapel of the Domus Dei (God's House), founded in c 1212. The present roofless nave was the result of bombing during the Second World War. The chancel is full of monuments and memorials to famous soldiers and sailors. The church was the scene of the marriage of Catherine of Braganza to King Charles II in 1662.

Romsey Abbey, *St. Mary and St. Ethelflaeda.* Romsey Abbey is one of the finest Norman churches in existence and, apart from the W end, is a pure example of Norman architecture. The site has been occupied by a church since 907, when Edward the Elder founded a nunnery for his daughter, Ethelflaeda or Elfleda. At the Dissolution the townsfolk purchased the monastery church. It possesses a wealth of fittings and monuments and is Hampshire's largest parish church.

Built of dressed stone, the church presents an almost perfect Norman appearance. The aisles, choir aisles and apsidal transept chapels have corbel tables, flat buttresses and round-headed windows with shafts and roll-mouldings. There is a further corbel table at clerestory level. The windows of the choir clerestory are flanked by blank arches. The S transept S wall is particularly fine with three rows of two arched windows, well separated by a central flat buttress. Against the W wall of the S transept and protected by a wooden canopy is one of the famous Romsey Roods. The large figure of the Crucified Christ with the Hand of God above dates from the 11C. To the left is a small rectangular niche probably used to place lit candles. Nearby is the fine Abbess's doorway, once the entrance from the cloister. It has two orders of shafts and rich decoration on the arch and hoodmould. The E end's two blank arches reveal where the Lady chapel once stood. The two large three-light windows date from the late 13C. The N porch was built in 1908 by W.D. Caroë. The low central tower is surmounted by a wooden octagonal belfry of 1624, which contains eight bells.

Internally, the appearance (the W end excepted) is one of outstanding Norman workmanship. The seven-bay nave has compound piers save for the easternmost pair, which are drum piers rising to triforium height, their capitals round and scalloped. The triforium arches in all bays subordinate the arches below, which appear inset between the piers. Each triforium bay has a pair of sub-arches, with no solid tympanum but instead a single small column standing above where the sub-arches join. Between each bay a shaft rises to the 19C wooden tunnel-vault installed by Benjamin Ferrey. The clerestory has triple arches, only the middle one glazed; the E bay is Norman, the rest Gothic. The crossing has four plain stepped arches. Above in the tower space are three pairs of small arches on each side. The S transept has at triforium level both in the W and E walls, above the aisle entrances, a large pier with a solid tympanum above. This does not occur in the N transept. With the exception of the 13C E windows, the three-bay choir is a pure example of the finest Norman architecture, built c 1120–40. The shafts of the lower arches have scalloped capitals as in the nave. The arches have zigzag decoration, as do those behind the altar which open into the retrochoir. The triforium and clerestory follow the scheme of the nave. The triple-light E windows fill what would have been the opening to the Lady chapel. The choir aisles and retrochoir have quadripartite stone vaulting. The S aisle serves as St. Anne's chapel, the N that of St. George. Some aisle capitals are carved: one in the S aisle shows a king holding a pyramid, and a seated figure holding a V-shaped scroll which frames a bearded head. The scroll is inscribed 'Robertus me fecit' or Robert made me. In the N aisle is a carving depicts two kings fighting and two angels intervening, signed 'Robert'.

The large font (1912) and the twelve-sided wooden pulpit (1891), which has figures of the Evangelists, are the work of W.D. Caroë. In the S nave aisle, covering the Abbess's doorway, is a large embroidery of 1966 by Mrs M. Helsdow and students of the Southampton College of Art, depicting saints. In the S choir aisle is the Threadgold Treasury, a cabinet displaying some of the abbey treasures: the bill of sale for the abbey in 1544, a 16C alabaster Pietà, a chalice dating from 1568, the Romsey Rose and the 15C Romsey Psalter. Behind the altar at the E end of the aisle is the second of the pre-Conquest Roods. This depicts Christ on the Cross with an angel on each arm of the Cross. Below the arms are the figures of the Virgin Mary and St. John, and below them two soldiers carrying the spear and the sponge. The Rood is set in a fragment of Perpendicular screen and serves as the reredos of St. Anne's chapel. In the retrochoir the N of the two bays serves as the chapel of St. Mary, the other as the chapel of St. Ethelflaeda. The chapel of St. Mary has some traces of 12C wall painting, restored in 1976. It was while this work was being undertaken that the Romsey Rose was discovered, an intact rose bricked up in the wall in the 12C. The painting is believed to depict scenes from the life of St. Nicholas. In the aisle are displayed a late 15C abbey cope made and embroidered by the nuns, a late 15C painting of a kneeling priest discovered in 1813, and some 14C floor tiles. Over the high altar the bas-relief of the Virgin and Child is by Martin Travers. The organ was made by J.W. Walker in 1858, rebuilt in 1888 and restored in 1975. The case was designed in 1858 by Ewan Christian. On the S side of the choir opposite the organ is the Broadlands Pew, used by the Mountbatten family. The transepts are blocked off from the tower space by wooden Victorian screens with the choirstalls in front.

Behind the screen in the N transept are exposed the curved foundation walls of the second church on the site which date from c 995. Behind the altar of St. Lawrence in this transept is a painted wooden reredos of the early 16C. The painting depicts Christ rising from the tomb, flanked by soldiers and angels. In the bottom left-hand corner is the image of an abbess, possibly Elizabeth Ryprose, who commissioned the reredos. In the top row are nine saints. The two flags at the W end of the nave were given by Earl Mountbatten of Burma and were his flags as Supreme Allied Commander of South-East Asia and as the last Viceroy of India.

Against the W wall of the nave are three monuments to the Palmerston family. The one to the second Viscount Palmerston (died 1802) is by John Flaxman. In the first bay of the nave is the tomb-chest and recumbent effigy of Sir William Petty (died 1687, but erected in 1858). Near the font is the tomb of Alice Taylor, with a figure of a young girl. In the S transept near the altar of St. Nicholas is the grave of Earl Mountbatten of Burma (died 1979). Nearby, against the E wall, is the painted monument to John St. Barbe (died 1658) and his wife Grissell. The monument consists of the frontal portrait busts of John and his wife, set in arched niches beneath the family crest in the pediment and above an inscription and the figures of their four children. The monument was restored in 1972. In the S wall is an elaborate 14C ogee arch sheltering the Purbeck marble effigy of an abbess of earlier date. In the S choir aisle is a marble monument to

John Storke (died 1711). It features Ionic columns and a relief carving of masted ships. In the retrochoir is a large marble memorial to Maud Ashley (died 1911) by Emil Fuchs and designed by Richardson & Gill. It depicts a female figure with two naked children.

The stained glass is 19C and 20C. The windows in the S nave aisle include the Crucifixion and two angels by Hugh Easton, and Jesus causing men to see, by Mayer & Co. The E window above the altar of St. Anne depicts the Nativity and is by Clayton & Bell, 1879. The window above St. George's altar is by C.E. Kempe, 1897, and depicts St. George and the Dragon. The E windows of the choir are by Powell's. In the N transept the three-light window in the W wall depicting St. Swithun was installed in 1951.

Silchester, *St. Mary the Virgin.* The present church from the medieval period is built partly of reused Roman material. It stands alone inside the impressive circuit of Roman walls. Excavation and research have revealed that S of the forum, near the centre of the site, there stood a small 4C church, thus making Silchester one of the oldest known Christian sites in England.

Southampton. *St. Michael's* is the only surviving medieval church in the city and possesses a number of very interesting features including a black Tournai marble font. S of this is the small church of St. Julian which is used by French Protestants. St. Mary's is the mother church of the city; the present very large church is basically the work of G.E. Street, 1878–84, but it was badly damaged in the war and was largely rebuilt in 1954–56 by R.B. Craze. In Bitterne Park on a steep sloping site is the church of the Ascension, designed by Sir Charles Nicholson in 1924–26.

Stoke Charity, *St. Mary and St. Michael.* Surrounded by fields and set in the middle of a turfed churchyard, this small flint church houses a notable group of monuments and brasses, and medieval wall painting and carving. The exterior is picturesque rather than architecturally interesting. At the W end is a bell turret surmounted by a splayed foot spire. All of this is tile-hung. The S porch has a Norman arch with zigzag decoration.

Internally, the dominant feature is the very large two-bay Norman arcade with a massive octagonal pier with scallop decoration on the capital and responds. The chancel arch has zigzag decoration and decorated capitals. N of the chancel is the Hampton chapel which dates from c 1250. The N aisle is the oldest part, dating back to the pre-Conquest period. The archway between the aisle and the Hampton chapel is of this period. The fittings and monuments are the chief glory of the church. In the nave, in a small arched recess on the S, is the tomb-chest of Thomas Wayte (died 1482). The chest is topped by a Purbeck marble slab into which is set a brass of a knight. At his head is the figure of Christ rising from a coffin.

Nearby, next to the chancel arch, is a wooden lectern with brass sconces. On the N side of the arch there is a double squint to the chancel and the Hampton chapel. In the chancel on the S side is a tomb-lid from the churchyard, upon which is carved a cross and four spheres. Opposite this are the medieval fragments of a pedestal and canopy. The sanctuary has simple wooden rails. There is a panelled seat against the S wall in place of the more usual stone sedilia. In the arch between the chancel and the Hampton chapel is the tomb of Thomas Hampton (died 1483). The tomb-chest is of freestone with a

Purbeck marble slab. Inlaid in the top of this are full-length brasses of Thomas and his wife Isabel. There are inscriptions below them and heraldic shields at each corner. Above the two figures is a representation of the Holy Trinity. Below the inscriptions are depicted their eight daughters. Against the N wall is a large Jacobean tomb-chest to Sir Thomas Phelipps (died 1626).

The floor of the N chapel has many medieval tiles. Against the wall is the tomb of John Waller (died 1526), with a Purbeck slab under a Tudor-style canopy. The front of the tomb has two panels containing shields inscribed with his initials. The outer panels depict St. Thomas of Canterbury and the Virgin and Child. On the floor is the mutilated brass to Richard Waller (died 1551) which consists of just two shields and an inscription. In the corner of the chapel is a unique medieval survival, that of a carving of the Mass of St. Gregory. It is dated to c 1500 and is the only intact depiction remaining. It was discovered in 1849 and put in its present position in 1900. It depicts St. Gregory kneeling and saying Mass. A large figure representing Christ has appeared showing his wounds. There is an assistant priest at one side. The altar is well-carved, depicting St. Gregory's mitre and a Bible. Either side of the figure of Christ, angels are holding back the drapes of a canopy. On the S wall of the chapel are the remains of a wall painting showing a male figure. It has been ascribed to the mid-13C and was discovered in 1966.

In the N aisle at the W end is the font which still has one of its iron staples *in situ* in the top, part of the measures taken to protect Holy Water. The staple dates from or soon after the decree on the matter in 1236. Near the font is the badly damaged monument to Sir James Phelypps (died 1652). What remains consists of a painted crest and a draped object above.

The E window has Victorian figures of St. Michael, St. Gabriel and the Virgin and Child, but the head of the Virgin and the various architectural details are medieval. In the Hampton chapel in the N wall is a three-light window with many medieval fragments collected together. Amongst them are parts of depictions of St. Margaret of Antioch, the Virgin and Child and St. Christopher with Christ on his shoulders.

The Vyne, *Chapel.* The chapel of The Vyne, which is in the care of the National Trust, has been rightly declared to be one of the most perfect late medieval chapels in Britain. It was built in 1518–27 by Sir William Sandys and has especially fine woodwork and early 16C glass.

The chapel is at the E end of the house and breaks up the symmetry of the N front. It has a polygonal apse and stone battlements which bear the arms of King Henry VIII, Catherine of Aragon, Lord Sandys, Sir Reginald Bray and the various members of the Order of the Garter. The two large, blind three-light windows were added in the 19C. The apse is lit by three three-light windows. On the S side there is a tomb chamber with a polygonal apse.

The chapel is entered through the antechapel which is in the style of Strawberry Hill. The chapel has a wooden ribbed roof. At the W end above the antechapel is a gallery separated by a wooden screen which came from Windsor Castle during the 19C. The tomb chamber has a plaster ceiling decorated with lozenges with inset quatrefoils, and wooden panelling with cusped arches.

The N, S and W walls have stalls with panelling behind, rising to a canopy which runs continuously above the stalls. Each rib on the underside of the canopy has carved heraldic badges, 32 in total. The cornice is carved with vine stems, foliage, flowers etc, interspersed with numerous putti playing games, hunting, supporting shields etc. The stall-ends finish with poppyheads of various designs, some being purely floral, while others have putti, figures and animals. The panelling has two tiers of cusped arches. Above the gallery screen is a frieze of putti riding scroll-work supporting a centrally positioned crest. The woodwork and carving dates from c 1527. On the walls of the gallery are *trompe-l'oeil* paintings of fan-vaulting painted by Spiridione Roma in 1771. They originally adorned the walls of the chapel and were moved in the 19C. In front of the sanctuary step and in front of the N and S stalls are encaustic tiles of various scenes and designs. They have been attributed to the workshop of Guido de

The chapel of The Vyne showing the exceptionally fine early 16C stained glass

Savino of Urbino, who was working in Antwerp in 1512. The tiles were found in heaps in the grounds during the 19C.

Above the altar the windows have transoms, making six panels in each window. The glass is unrivalled for its period, c 1520, being made in Basingstoke by a team of Flemish glaziers, including David Johns and Peter Coeck. The middle window depicts the Crucifixion and (below) King Henry VIII with his patron saint Henry II of Bavaria. The right-hand window depicts the Resurrection and (below) Queen Katherine of Aragon kneeling with her patroness, St. Katherine. The left-hand window depicts Christ carrying the Cross and meeting St. Veronica, and in the lower panel, Queen Margaret of Scotland with her patroness, St. Margaret.

In the tomb chamber the chief feature is the Classical marble tomb-chest designed by John Chute and carved by Thomas Carter between 1775 and 1781. It stands in the centre. The monument is in memory of the Speaker of the House of Commons, Chaloner Chute (died 1659), who is buried at St. Nicholas's, Chiswick. The tomb itself has a finely carved marble semi-recumbent effigy, the figure supporting his head with his hand, and lying on a pillow and a straw mat. In his other hand is an open book. The tomb-chest has free-standing fluted Ionic columns at the corners and two further attached demi-columns on either side. They support an entablature with swags and garlands. On both sides of the chest, at the ends, are heraldic devices with swags below them. A central panel contains the inscription. The ends of the chest have more shields with garlands. On the W wall is a large painting, 'The Holy Family with St. John and St. Elizabeth', attributed to Girolamo Sicciolante. The three-light window in the S wall has a painted glass panel of the Nativity by John Rowell. His too is the large painted E window, also depicting the Nativity. They were painted in 1730–31 at High Wycombe and bought by John Chute after the artist's death.

Winchester College, *Chapel.* The chapel was consecrated on July 7th 1395, the college having been founded in 1382 by William of Wykeham (Bishop of Winchester, 1366–1404) to ensure a regular supply of boys to be trained for the Church. The chapel is filled with fittings and glass of the highest merit.

The chapel is part of the S range of Chamber Court. The tower over the Thurbern Chantry chapel on the S side was built in 1476–85, the chapel beneath having been begun in 1473. In 1862–63 it became necessary to demolish the tower and it was meticulously rebuilt by William Butterfield. It is of four stages with large angle buttresses. The lowest stage has a large four-light window in the W face. The belfry has two openings with blank panels on each side and a row of four such panels below. There are three square corner pinnacles, a higher NE stair turret and a parapet of pierced arches. The chapel is entered through a small antechapel, above which is the E bay of the hall. The chapel itself is of six buttressed bays with tall three-light windows. Within, there is a fine wooden lierne-vault which is almost a fan-vault in appearance. The two-bay Thurbern Chantry chapel has a stone lierne-vault. Entry at the W end is under the gallery designed by W.D. Caroë in 1908. He was also responsible for the organ in the gallery. Running down both sides of the chapel are stalls and pews. Behind these the wooden panelling reaches the same height as the reredos at the E end. The panelling, pews and stalls are the work of Caroë, 1913–21. In the fourth and fifth bays the misericords are particularly fine and date from c 1390–95. On the N side are a dragon, a falcon with a mallard, and a shepherd. On the S side are a pelican, two goats, a dragon, and a man with a knife. The sanctuary has a stone reredos which dates from c 1470 and which was carefully restored in 1874–75 by Butterfield and altered again in 1920 by Caroë. It stretches across the E wall and continues round the N and S walls. There are three niches on the N and S walls and nine in the E wall, all under ornate crocketed canopies. The three in the centre rise above the others. The figures represent (in the middle) Christ with St. Mary and St. John on either side, and flanking them, the Apostles. On the S side the piscina and sedilia are under a similar canopy of crocketed pinnacles. The altar rail is by Edward Pierce and dates from 1680–83. In the N wall is a further organ case designed by S.E. Dykes Bower, 1948–49. On the S side the Thurbern Chantry chapel has two large panels of Flemish tapestry of c 1500 which are known as the Tapestry of the Roses. On the W wall of the antechapel is the Crimean War memorial, designed by William Butterfield and dating from 1858. This consists of five Early English style blank arches. Set in the floor of the sanctuary are six large figurative brasses, all of which are copies made in 1882 from medieval originals.

The stained glass is largely 19C. There is, however, some of the finest medieval glass in existence which is also, uniquely, dateable and signed. The E window of seven lights depicts the Tree of Jesse. Although dated to 1393, most of the glass was taken out in 1821 and replaced by the present glass dating from 1822–23 and made by Betton & Evans. Much of the medieval glass from the E window went to Ettington in Warwickshire, whence some of it was returned and placed in the four-light window in the W wall of the Thurbern Chantry chapel in 1951. The medieval glass is signed by Master Thomas of Oxford. In the same chapel the five-light window in the S wall has some medieval fragments dating from c 1500.

Winchester, *St. Cross.* Set amidst the meadows S of the cathedral and college, the Hospital of St. Cross presents a remarkable ensemble of 15C and 16C buildings round a large courtyard. On the S side is the large cruciform chapel started by the founder, Bishop Henry de Blois (Bishop of Winchester and brother of King Stephen), in c 1160. The hospital was founded in 1136 and the chapel was built between 1160 and 1290. It presents a textbook example of architectural development from Norman to Gothic and possesses a wealth of fittings, monuments and stained glass.

The E end is the oldest part and has three rows of paired Norman windows, a central flat buttress and outer buttresses which rise to become square turrets decorated with blank arcading. Inset into the gable end are two circular windows. Norman too are the chancel aisle windows and those of the transepts, except for the upper ones in the N transept. The nave is Norman to the E and Gothic in its W bay, including the N porch. The five-light W windows and the nave clerestory are 14C. The central tower has Perpendicular windows and blank arcading. On the S side of the S transept a small vaulted building known as the sacristy is all that remains from the earliest period of the Hospital.

The impact upon entry is one of extreme height and size. The church is 125ft long and 115ft wide across the transepts. The three-bay nave has massive drum piers with simple fluted or moulded capitals, and plain Transitional arches. Above are the gallery and clerestory. The crossing tower is immensely tall. The four arches with their clustered shafts and simple capitals are Transitional. The chancel of two bays and its aisles are rib-vaulted. The E end has two deeply-recessed windows both above the altar and in the clerestory; the triforium has four windows with intersecting arches. All the E windows have zigzag. In the N transept the first window in the E wall has unusual decoration consisting of bird beak and chevron pattern. Both transepts are rib-vaulted.

The church is exceptionally rich in notable fittings. In the nave the Victorian wooden pews each have a different carved design. At its E end there is a very fine wooden lectern which has the head of a parrot and the body of an eagle. Opposite this is a five-sided wooden pulpit dating from 1866. Inset into the tower arch is a wooden Rood beam and plain cross. The square font in the S aisle is Norman and came from St. Faith's, which was demolished in 1507. Around the font and throughout the church are patches of medieval tiles thought to date from c 1390. The S transept is largely taken up with the organ which dates from 1907. The N transept is divided off by a 15C screen. The chancel is separated from its aisles in the E bay by elaborate stone screens of the 15C which came from St. Faith's Church. The next bay on both sides is divided by fine wooden screens given by Bishop Fox and dated to c 1520. The altar rails of the S chancel aisle or Lady chapel are Jacobean, the altar is 16C and the triptych is Flemish, c 1535. The chancel has Victorian tiles and altar rails. In the N chancel aisle are the remains of 13C wall paintings, those on the S wall depicting figures under arches and in the SE corner a figure with a halo. In the S transept in a recess in the E wall is more 13C wall painting. The church has some fine monuments. In the N aisle in an arched recess is the large tomb of Peter de Sancta Maria, Master of St. Cross (died 1296). In the S aisle there is the marble wall monument to Charles Wolfran Cornwall (died 1789), Speaker of the House of Commons. It is pedimented and shows a sarcophagus and the Speaker's mace, and is by J.F. Moore. There are three magnificent brasses: to John Campedon (died 1410), just under 6ft in length, Richard Harward (died 1493), and Thomas Laune (died 1518).

The stained glass is 19C and 20C, with some 15C survivals. Hugh Easton designed the N windows of St. Christopher (1935) and St. Francis (1938). The remaining nave aisle windows have glass of 1873–75. The five-light W window depicts Old Testament figures and scenes. In the E wall of the N transept the first window is 15C and depicts St. Gregory. The glass in the chancel E windows dates from c 1495 and was possibly made at Michelmersh in Hampshire. They depict the Virgin Mary (bottom left), St. John (bottom right), St. Catherine (top right) and St. Swithun (top left). The windows of the N chancel aisle show in the N wall Justice and Fortitude and in the E window Christ with the Children.

The Hospital of St. Cross was widely known for the scandal involving Francis North, later Earl of Guilford, son of Bishop North of Winchester, who in 1807 appointed Francis as Master. His systematic abuse of the St. Cross revenues was the source of material for Anthony Trollope's novel, 'The Warden', and its Barchester sequels.

HERTFORDSHIRE

The gently undulating countryside of Hertfordshire with its ancient roads and prosperous villages provides a beautiful setting for the great variety of churches and chapels from Tring in the W to Bishop's Stortford in the E, and from Royston in the N to the outskirts of London in the S. Clearly, the county has been affected physically by the close proximity of the capital, and the presence of 'commuter land' is noticeable in the styles of much housing as well as in the frequent and convenient rail links heading S. The most historically significant settlement is St. Albans, and its beginnings as a major Roman centre are well displayed on their original sites in fine parkland settings. St. Alban's Abbey, which once served an immensely wealthy Benedictine house, became the cathedral of a new diocese in 1877. Its medieval abbots had jurisdiction over churches in the county and many controls also over the populace as a whole. There are almost 200 Anglican parish churches in Hertfordshire today, many built from the local flints found in the chalk and dressed either with clunch (Totternhoe stone) from Bedfordshire, or occasionally with limestone from counties to the N. Although brick had been employed by the Romans, it was not used again until the late Middle Ages, when pits were opened near St. Albans.

The pre-Conquest work at St. Michael's Church at St. Albans is mentioned in the main text. Westmill has a pre-Conquest nave, but also a Norman N arcade, whilst Reed has long-and-short work in the nave and tower. St. Mary's, Walkern possesses parts of a mid-10C nave and a Norman arcade and S doorway. Major Norman churches are St. Stephen's at St. Albans and St. Leonard's, Bengeo, which lies amongst suburban houses off the main road W of Ware, and which possesses a spacious apsidal chancel connecting with a nave. Bengeo has suffered little alteration except for the insertion of S windows in the nave during the 14C and 15C. The church of St. John the Baptist at Great Amwell possesses a Norman apse and chancel arch, whilst Great Wymondley and Great Munden have similar features. Holy Trinity, Weston has a completely preserved group of four crossing arches, and Holy Cross, Sarratt retains a Greek cross plan with Norman arches linking the four arms. Towers of the same period may be seen at Barley and at St. Nicholas', Stevenage, both with later upper stages.

Apart from the cathedral at St. Albans, the finest Early English work is at Anstey and Hatfield (both mentioned in the text), whilst Eastwick contains a rich chancel arch with Purbeck marble shafts, and similar work is at Standon. The chancel and crossing tower at Wheathampstead are both 13C. Decorated work is limited. St. Mary's, Baldock is perhaps the most complete church of the early 14C, but with 15C clerestory and roofs. Abbots Langley has a notable two-bay S chancel chapel, and at Benington the N chancel chapel of the early 14C has beautiful carving on the arcade; beneath one arch stands a contemporary knight's tomb surmounted by an ogee canopy. The wool trade provided new wealth, which is displayed in a conspicuous way at Watford, and in the large Perpendicular flint churches at Aldenham, Tring and Ware, this last with its fine 15C font. A curious survival at Sarratt is the 16C saddleback tower which presents the ridge of its roof at right angles to the nave. A note here on the local feature of the Hertfordshire spikes is appropriate; these thin lead spires, which are to be found throughout the county, are usually no more than short, thorn-like ornaments on top of the towers and date from the Middle Ages. Spikes are found in large numbers and a remarkable 55 such spirelets have been counted within a ten-mile radius of Hemel Hempstead (which is itself the possessor of the *ne plus ultra* of the spike). Variations are interesting: Baldock and Ashwell have polygonal drums at the base, Hitchin has herringbone leadwork, whilst Standon and Braughing have the more usual plain ribbing.

The major 17C building is St. Peter's, Buntingford, built on the Greek cross plan from brick, and with a 19C apse. The sole 18C 'mention' is Offley, which possesses a chancel dating from c 1750 and which was built by Sir Thomas Salusbury; the style is Classical, with stucco work and an elaborate baldacchino at the E end. The 19C saw a revival of church building and many restorations of existing buildings. A new chapel of considerable interest is that belonging to Ashridge near Little Gaddesden, at one time a monastery but rebuilt as a vast country house by the seventh Earl of Bridgewater, and now a management college. The house, a glorious Regency Gothic pastiche, was built between 1808 and 1821 by James Wyatt with additions by his nephew, Jeffry Wyatt (later Sir Jeffry Wyatville). The chapel, dated 1817, is the work of James Wyatt and employs a soaring antechapel which lies beneath the tower and spire; these form a major feature of the house from the outside. The chapel itself is collegiate in plan with stalls to N and S, whilst the tall windows lead up to fan-vaulting and a panelled ceiling. The interior fittings, including the stalls and organ case, were designed by Wyatville. St. Mary Magdalene's, Flaunden, 1838, was the first church of Sir Gilbert Scott. The chapel of St. Edmund's College at Old Hall Green near Ware is an important representative work of A.W.N. Pugin and dates from 1845–53, but the intended tower and spire were never built. The chapel is tall and was executed in the Decorated style; inside, the antechapel lies W of a Rood screen, with the main stalls E of the screen. The fittings are by Pugin, including much of the glass, but extensions were made to the chapel after his death, firstly the Schofield chantry (1862), whose entrance is along the passage S of the main building. Nobody knows who the architect was, but it may have been Pugin's son, Edward, and it must not be missed because it is taut with carved stone details in a very small space. Secondly, through doors W of Pugin's antechapel, is the Galilee; it is a spacious minimal Gothic structure by F.A. Walters (1922). An interesting group of buildings by the High Victorian William Butterfield may be seen at Hitchin. Holy Saviour, Radcliffe Road was built in 1865 in red brick with blue brick patterning and, inside, black stencil patterns on the stonework. Opposite the church, the Cloisters are picturesque, low, redbrick residences with slate roofs, lying around a central courtyard. Butterfield may also be seen at Barley (1872), whilst Richard Norman Shaw built Boxmoor (1874), and J.P. Seddon designed Ayot St. Peter (1875) in a rebellious early Arts and Crafts manner. The early 20C garden suburbs of Letchworth and Welwyn produced no outstanding church architecture, nor have the postwar London satellites of Stevenage, Hemel Hempstead and Hatfield New Town. Only at St. Martin's, Knebworth do we find a truly original approach worthy of its pioneering environment.

Items of interest surviving from the pre-Conquest era are rare, but a remarkable Rood showing Christ robed lies inside Walkern Church near the S porch, and a sculpted Norman capital of note survives at Great Munden. Of the 13C, a superb Purbeck marble effigy of a knight lies at Walkern, and the earliest brass is found at Albury (c 1340). Bengeo and Cottered contain fine medieval wall paintings, Albury a notable Perpendicular stone screen, Redbourn a 15C Rood screen and coving, and Barkway the remains of a late 15C Jesse window. At Buntingford, a remarkable 17C brass shows the interior of the church at about the time it was built, whilst important 18C sculptors appear at Flamstead (Flaxman), Hertingfordbury (Roubiliac), and Braughing (James 'Athenian' Stuart and Thomas Scheemakers). One major 18C fitting should be mentioned, the black basalt earthenware font by Wedgwood at Essendon, and one 19C monument, to the seventh Earl of Bridgewater (died 1823), by Sir Richard Westmacott, at Little Gaddesden. Later in the 19C, William Morris designed glass at Furneaux Pelham, 1866, and Kings Walden, 1867, whilst glass by C.E. Kempe may be found at High Cross, 1876. Ayot St. Peter contains a chancel arch by the Martin Brothers, c 1880, and Woolmer Green has furnishings of c 1900 by the celebrated Arts and Crafts designer, Ernest Gimson.

Several notable families have resided in the county, for example, the Salisburys, the Lyttons, the Bridgewaters, the Bacons, and the Strathmores, who are the Queen Mother's family and who still live at St. Paul's Walden. George Bernard Shaw owned 'Shaw's Corner' at Ayot St. Lawrence and Wren's assistant, Nicholas Hawksmoor, lived in the village of Shenley and is buried in the churchyard there.

Anstey, *St. George*. Anstey lies in remote countryside in the NE of the county but on no account should it be missed from a tour of Hertfordshire churches. A castle was built in the village in the 11C and it is considered that stone from this building was later used in the church; now only the castle mound remains. St. George's tower is late Norman Transitional and the main body of the church is a sumptuous display of the Early English style at its zenith; it is the rare quality of these features for such a small village which embellishes this place of worship with its special nature and importance.

The church is cruciform in plan with a central crossing tower of c 1200, and chancel and transepts date from a rebuilding of the late 13C. The nave is calculated to have been built in the early 14C, with additions in the Perpendicular period. The tower is crenellated only partly, with 14C openings of two lights and quatrefoils on each face; on top there is a leaded Hertfordshire spike. The S transept has triple lancets to the S and E, and a large stair turret in the SE corner. On the S side of the chancel are three two-light windows with quatrefoils above, whilst on the N side are two windows to half-height with exposed corbels beneath, presumably surviving from a low vestry. The Perpendicular E window has unusual pointed angular tracery. The N transept has old rendering amongst flint and red brick, with a square-headed, three-light N window and a blocked N door and W window. The S porch possesses a very worn Perpendicular doorway with shields in the quatrefoil spandrels; inside the porch lie triple-cusped windows together with a second Perpendicular door.

Inside, the quatrefoil piers of the four-bay nave support arches which have only a very shallow curve. The clerestory windows are 15C and are of the quatrefoil shape. The aisle windows are of the early 16C. The nave connects with the interesting tower arch with its spiral capitals and arches carved into a type of bobbin motif; these are repeated on the E archway of the tower, and all date from the late 12C. The S transept was at one time used as a chantry chapel, and a squint survives from the period when it was necessary to see the chancel altar. A column and bowl piscina also remain, together with a bracket to hold an altar. The excellent stonework of the chancel dates from the 13C, with a blank panel on each side of the E window and, on the S wall, the piscina and sedilia combined with the windows and a doorway.

The stalls in the chancel date from the 15C and have carved misericords depicting natural forms and human figures. Some wall painting, possibly medieval, may be seen on the walls of the chancel and there is against the S wall a good quality tomb dated 1635. The chancel also contains some graffiti which possibly originated on the stonework of the castle before it was built into the fabric of the church. Graffiti from the reign of Queen Elizabeth I may also be found. The transepts are, sadly, both now blocked—by an organ to the S and a reused medieval wooden screen to the N. Do not miss, however, the beautifully carved early 14C tomb-recess in the S wall of the S transept, displaying a woman's head in period head-covering; the effigy inside may be from elsewhere. The window in the S aisle was made in 1907 by Heaton, Butler & Bayne. The nave contains the late 19C pulpit and, at the W end near the S door, the rare and remarkable Norman font which shows four mermen, one for each side of the bowl, their hands grasping their tails; only one other font of this type survives in England—at St. Peter's, Cambridge.

The 15C lychgate has three sections all covered by a single roof; one of the bays was formed in 1831 into a brick-sided lock-up which remained in use until the First World War.

Arkley, *Poor Clare Monastery, Chapel.* The chapel of the Poor Clare Monastery, built in the late 1960s, hides in Galley Lane, a quiet backwater of Arkley on the outskirts of London to the W of Chipping Barnet. The exterior is characterised by its dark brick walls and the diving slope of its roof which supports a simple metal cross at the E end. Inside, the chapel is divided into three distinct areas, the rectangular congregational nave with free-standing pews, the raised altar space with its curved E wall, and the monastery chapel with its wooden stalls. The area containing the altar serves both the visiting worshippers' nave and the monastery chapel, which lie at right angles to one another. The latter is separated from the altar area by an aluminium screen. The walls throughout are of whitewashed rough plaster; the roofs have pale varnished wooden planks; and the floor is covered with brown earthenware tiles. The high sloping roof over the altar is supported by two full-height wall columns, one of which partly conceals a tall narrow stained glass window, which graduates from strong sunset hues at the top to pale purples and yellows beneath. Another, similar, window lies at the further end of the curved wall and may be seen only from the altar. The open nave contains imaginative Stations of the Cross in metal—simple, isolated shapes in space without the distractions of background details; in contrast, the heavy stone altar has a roughly chiselled surface to provide texture. The interest of this chapel lies in the uncluttered and pure interior, the sculptural use of space, and the apparent effect of excluding the outside world except for the reassuring light and colour of the windows, thus creating an environment which allows the mind to focus and concentrate.

Ashwell, *St. Mary the Virgin.* The village of Ashwell lies in the far N of the county. It came to prominence in the Middle Ages, when its wealth provided for both a weekly market and a large church. The ground-water springs surrounded by trees (which give the village its name) are the source of the River Cam which runs beside the colleges in Cambridge.

The main external feature of this 14C church is the unique shape of its tall W tower, 176ft high, which rises melancholy and ghost-like above the village and surrounding countryside. The tower is built of clunch and dates from c 1360. It is tall in comparison with its width; sturdy angle buttresses travel up three stages, and a leaded octagonal drum and coronet support a graceful spike and weathercock. The third stage provides especial vertical emphasis with two twin-light bell openings surmounted by deeply moulded arches on each face; beneath them lie a variety of moulded panel courses. The long nave (completed in 1381) and chancel (c 1340–68) are constructed of flint and clunch, the latter now somewhat weathered. The aisle windows are Perpendicular, but those of the clerestory keep to the Decorated style, as does the W window of the tower, which displays Flamboyant tracery. The chancel is crenellated; it has a blocked opening on the S side and gargoyles on the N side. The 15C N porch is single-storey, whilst the S porch, also 15C, is two-storeyed, having a priest's room above with access by an exterior turret staircase on the W face; the vault overhead dates from 1858. The wooden outer gates to the porch are 18C; the church doors themselves are 15C and they retain their original ironwork. The lychgate is a rare double-entrance type, probably dating from the 15C.

The plain, white interior gives the impression of a church which has lacked substantial endowment since the medieval period. The building suffered in the 16C at the hands of the Reformers and there has been little restoration since. The glass is plain and allows much light into the interior. Immediately noticeable are the buttresses of the tower which, unusually, are exposed internally on each side of the nave; they are decorated with two-light blind arcading running from floor to roof. The plain nave roof is 19C and the roofs over the aisles are 14C. The long chancel is lit by broad Perpendicular windows, and arranged without stalls and with the altar isolated from the congregation. Changes were made here in 1967 which intrude upon its antiquity and spaciousness; new stalls lie outside the entrance to the chancel. Notice the ogee arches over the 15C sedilia and piscina, and the fine pedimented slate and stone wall monument further W on the same side. The pulpit of 1627 once belonged to Pembroke College, Cambridge and stands in the S aisle before the Lady chapel, which is surrounded by a 15C screen. The E end of the N aisle contains the chapel of St. James, with an altar tomb probably belonging to John Harrison of Hinxworth, the founder of nearby Ashwell Chantry in 1462. The clerestory windows contain fragments of medieval glass which have been made into small roundels. The font is 19C except for the steps which are original to the church; notice the symbols of the Passion carved around the bowl.

The fascinating inscriptions which appear on the interior walls of the tower and on the nave arcading are of special importance to Ashwell. No exact dates can be given for these 'scratchings' but, judging by their style and content, they must have been produced in the 14C and 15C. On the N wall of the tower may be seen Old St. Paul's Cathedral, dating from c 1460. On the wall are recorded the extraordinary disasters which befell Ashwell in the years between 1349 and 1361. In translation: '100, three times 100, five times 10, pitiable, fierce, violent. The dregs of the people alone survive to tell the tale...' It was probably a monk who gave this graphic description of the plague which left the population depleted and the crops rotting in the surrounding fields. The wording continues: '...in the end a mighty wind, Maurus, thunders in this year in the world, 1361'. This storm began on January 15th, the feast of St. Maurice and, over the next few days, the wind caused much damage. Further inscriptions complain of unfaithful women and provide examples of medieval aphorisms.

Ayot St. Lawrence, *New Church of St. Lawrence.* St. Lawrence's maintains a striking stance as a white temple among the trees and fields of an unspoilt village. This early Greek Revival building with its direct historical references and severe proportions was part of a controversial movement which shocked 18C Palladian architects, and is the only complete building by Nicholas Revett.

Built in 1778, the church is seen across fields W of the village and was positioned to complete the vista from Ayot House, the large mansion nearby, whose owner, Sir Lionel Lyde, provided money for the new church and was apparently responsible for demolishing Old St. Lawrence's because it impeded a particular view from the mansion. The bishop prevented total demolition, but granted permission for a new, Classical church in the grounds of Ayot House. Its impressive exterior relies on the elegant symmetry of a white central portico flanked by small pavilions connected to the church by colonnades; the whole is raised on three steps. The front is coated in stucco and whitewashed, while the back is left plain brick. The whole building is reminiscent of those small contemporary neo-Classical structures built to adorn the newly landscaped parks around country houses and strategically placed for maximum effect. Revett's handling of the Greek Doric order in the façade is controlled by the then prevalent Palladian qualities of order and symmetry. The columns of the portico closely follow those at the Temple of Apollo at Delos, having no foot and displaying fluting around the top and bottom few inches only, thus leaving most of the column plain and smooth. These archaeologically correct details derive from Revett's visit to Athens with James Stuart, which resulted in the publication of 'The Antiquities of Athens' in 1762. The finance for this project came from the Society of Dilettanti, a group of wealthy intellectuals who were interested in the Antique. Sir Lionel appears to have had no connection with the society, and so his choice of a Greek Doric scheme must have been influenced either by his direct acquaintanceship with Stuart and Revett or indirectly through their writings.

On each side of the flanking colonnades, aedicules (or shrines) contain the rectangular funerary urns of Sir Lionel and his wife. It is said that Sir Lionel was not wholly content with his marriage and so he decided to separate symbolically in death his own monument from that of his wife by means of the church which had failed to unite them in life. I think it is more likely, however, that it was the marked current interest of the day in symmetry which dictated the partition.

The interior is light and spacious, with off-white walls and an ice-white ceiling, plainly detailed, and relying on simple spatial arrangements. A near-square room with small arched transepts to N and S opens into an E apse; and on the W side, an entrance vestibule projects beyond a screen of twin tapering columns which hold a heavy beam beneath an open lunette. The nave itself has a coffered ceiling with a deep cornice, beneath which lie recessed panels between pilasters. The apse continues this theme, wherein reflected light is provided by two concealed windows within small chambers to N and S. Black and white marble squares, laid on the angle, form a cross in the nave floor. Elegant benches facing N and S provide seating at the E end of the nave in contrast to the modern chairs to the W. To the N a box pulpit faces a smaller pulpit together with the original mahogany organ, which was restored in 1964 by Lord Brocket of Ayot House. A Classical urn in an arched niche in the N transept, dedicated to two members of the Williams family, forms an unusual monument; it would have been an architectural embellishment instead of being simply an interior fitting, had the pulpit been placed to one side to maintain the full visual effect. Two boards of the Commandments lie hidden on each side of the Victorian altar.

It is worth noting that this church was not admired by the Victorians; the 19C historian of Hertfordshire, J.E. Cussans, called it a 'heathen temple' and an example of 'disgraceful...ecclesiastical taste'. Few who see New St. Lawrence's today would agree with this harsh view.

Ayot St. Lawrence was the home of George Bernard Shaw from 1906 until his death aged 94 in 1950. Shaw's ashes were scattered in the garden of his house, 'Shaw's Corner' (now National Trust property), but there is no memorial in either of the churches. Shaw considered any commemorative cross to be an 'instrument of torture'.

Bishop's Stortford

St. Michael. Bishop's Stortford became prosperous during the 18C and 19C from its malting and tanning manufactories and later from the railway which brought a direct link to the capital. The town was associated with the London bishopric for 800 years, hence its name. This church is an eye-catcher from several viewpoints, especially from the suburb of Hockerill to the E. The church is a sturdy Perpendicular building with good quality original workmanship throughout, especially noticeable in the woodwork.

From a distance may be seen the full width of the low, crenellated, 15C flint church, with an upper stage of brick added to the tower in the early 19C. Close to, the typical Perpendicular features may be discerned, including the panel tracery of the depressed arches in the aisle windows and the square-headed openings of the clerestory. The chancel was extended in the 17C when a new roof was added; this roof was raised in the 19C to accommodate clerestory windows, whilst at the same time a new E window was fitted and the old one placed nearby in the S wall. The N chancel chapel was added in the 19C. S of the chancel, a tall vestry was added also in the 19C. The tower remains the most curious and dominant feature of the exterior, with sturdy 15C lower stages and 'Gothick' upper stages, the late medieval style having been lightly treated by the Georgian revivalists in 1812. The lower, Perpendicular portion of flint is supported by buttresses and is provided with an external stair turret and clock-faces, whilst the 19C belfry section is constructed in a pale red brick (originally rendered), also with buttresses and displaying all round the lowest stage blind arcading as a connecting feature to the old work. Tall bell openings above the arcading are followed by a narrow quatrefoil frieze beneath the crenellated parapet. Pinnacles on top of the four buttresses and a thin lead spire (at first slate-covered) complete the tower. High up on the upper stages, the builders left a message of their discontent: 'This tower was built by parish expense but a mean parish that gave the workmen nothing to drink'. The tower was restored in 1977. The two-bay N porch retains its Perpendicular roof and doorway, having spandrels with carved angels bearing a trumpet and censer. The label stops below the hoodmoulds on each side of the door (which is original) depict the symbols of the Evangelists.

The N door opens into the spacious nave of six bays with columns which each comprise four thin shafts of octagonal section with vertical coving dividing them. The 12 traceried braces supporting the roof rest on carved stone heads representing the Apostles, whilst the corbels in the aisles are of angels, grotesques and figures of everyday life such as a cook with a ladle; the nave roof and those of the aisles are original 15C work. The tall tower arch contrasts with the wide chancel arch, which was raised by Joseph Clarke in 1868, together with the chancel roof of 1660, in order to accommodate a clerestory; the E window also dates from the 19C restoration and so too, presumably, does the blank tracery of Perpendicular style on each side. This work follows on from a 17C extension, designed to hold the vault of the Denny family.

The principal fittings are the items of woodwork in the chancel, namely the screen and the 18 choirstalls. The 15C screen has four lights, two on each side of the central doors, and above is vaulting of 1885 by Arthur Blomfield. The chancel stalls also are 15C, with poppyheads on the front stalls and, at the back, superbly carved misericords depicting human heads, an angel and the forms of animals. The misericords are supposed to have been brought from Old St. Paul's Cathedral. The altar arrangement, together with the cross and candlesticks, were designed by S.E. Dykes Bower in 1964. Coats of arms on the bosses in the roof have been picked out in colour. The S window (1853) is by Powell's, the E window (1885) is by Arthur Blomfield. To the N, the Lady chapel was formed in 1928 out of the Victorian N chapel but work is in hand (1988) here and at the W end of the S aisle to improve the use of space. In the nave stands the pulpit of 1658, in a somewhat old-fashioned style and bearing quaint perspective scenes in architectural frames of a Classicising nature. Further W, in the S aisle, the ancient font of Purbeck marble dates from the mid-12C and is from an earlier church on this site; it was discovered in 1868 and was placed on an appropriate Roman-esque base, comprising a large pillar encompassed by four slender detached columns. The church has several 17C and 18C wall plaques, the most striking of which perhaps is the Maplesden monument on the S aisle wall, displaying in mathematical detail the death of an entire family from an outbreak of smallpox in the late 17C. Above the doors may be seen hatchments to the Denny family and to the Ducketts. Sir George Duckett and his engineer, Thomas Yeoman, made the River Stort navigable to the S, thus increasing the prosperity of the town in the late 18C by facilitating the transport of charred malt to London.

The W window (1877) under the tower is by C.E. Kempe, and was installed to the memory of the Vicar, the Reverend Francis William Rhodes, and his wife, the parents of Cecil Rhodes. He was their fifth son, born in 1853, who later became founder of Rhodesia and the De Beers Mining Co. and subsequently Prime Minister of the Cape. Unfortunately, the window is now partly obscured. His own memorial may be seen on the wall in the N aisle.

All Saints. On a hill overlooking the town, the suburb of Hockerill contains the church of All Saints by Stephen Dykes Bower. This church, built in 1937, replaced an earlier structure and lies within the old graveyard on Stanstead Road. The large, central W tower, like the rest of the church, is built of pale, rough-hewn stone and its roofs are covered with dark tiles. The tower's W elevation, facing the town, has three long lancet windows. The two steeply-pitched aisles contain the entrance doors and six pairs of lancet windows.

The interior is an exercise in extremes of contrasting proportions. The huge rose window and the altar's four giant Corinthian columns picked out in gold and red combine to dominate the E end, where other features such as the neo-Jacobean stalls in plain light oak and the picturesque oriel window in stone on the N wall of the chancel are of more usual scale. The five-bay nave includes substantial round piers. The nave has a roof of pale oak and a floor of stone flags which give it a light and spacious appearance. The fittings are few in number: a low-standing octagonal font, a silver sanctuary lamp and a cross over the tabernacle on the altar, and, providing an unusual revival after the First World War, a piscina and sedilia. An outsize silver processional cross completes the faintly surreal quality which might be felt in this most interesting church.

Hatfield, *St. Etheldreda.* The parish church stands at the top of the hill and holds a commanding position overlooking the old town of Hatfield; to its E is the Old Palace built by Cardinal Morton in the late 15C, which was the predecessor of Robert Cecil's great Jacobean mansion, Hatfield House. When the first church was built here, the village was held by the monastery of Ely which was founded by St. Etheldreda. From the time when Ely Abbey became a bishopric in 1109, Hatfield was a residence of the Bishops of Ely, hence the full name of 'Bishop's Hatfield'. The chief features of the church are the robust W tower and the various chapels dedicated to the families of several distinguished statesmen.

The 15C W tower, flint-faced and with buttresses up to the top stage, begins with a handsome W doorway displaying carved spandrels. Above this lies a broad, four-light window and, in the upper two stages, smaller two-light openings. The nave was rebuilt in 1871 on the lines of the previous 13C construction, but with a raised roof and incorporating some of the old oak beams into the N and S porches. The Decorated tracery in the windows also dates from 1871. The six dormers were designed to light the roof inside. The architect of all this work was David Brandon. The chancel walls and transepts date from the 13C. The S transept provides interest in the form of a blocked Early English lancet window in the E wall and by the little chapel which adjoins to the W, and serves the function of the E bay of an aisle in this aisleless church. To the E of the S transept, the Brocket chapel was rebuilt in the 15C. To the N of the chancel lies the Salisbury chapel, built of ashlar in 1618 by William, second Earl of Salisbury, as a resting place for his father, Robert Cecil (1563–1612). Immediately to the W lies the N transept. Modern rooms fill the place of a transept chapel to the W. The churchyard gates were brought from St. Paul's Cathedral and date from c 1710.

Looking E inside the Victorian nave, the various openings into the chancel, transepts and chapels may be seen. The chancel arch was narrowed in 1871 and has the family chapels on each side, whilst the transept entrances are provided with beams resting on corbels at the height of the nave roof. To the W lie the lower arches of their chapels. Moving into the S transept, the W arch, leading into the sub-transept, has trefoil responds displaying dogtooth mouldings in between the shafts, whilst the 14C E arch may be seen to have cut through a shallow, cusped-arched recess, and must have been built for the earlier chapel which preceded the present 15C Brocket chapel. Forming the arcade in the Brocket chapel, the columns each have four triple-shafts with angel capitals bearing shields of the Fortescue family of Ponsbourne which once owned the chapel; the corbels supporting the roof show the symbols of the Evangelists. The chancel betrays its 13C origins in the jambs of the E window and the fine piscina; the roof is early 14C. The Salisbury chapel opens to the N through the arcade of Shap granite Tuscan columns erected in 1618; a third column was added in 1875, indistinguishable from the others. At this time also a new roof was built and decorative additions were made.

The most important monument lies in the N chapel, the table-tomb to Robert Cecil, first Earl of Salisbury (died 1612), a great statesman and a crucial personality in the fortunes of Hatfield. The recumbent marble effigy rests on a black marble slab which is supported by four kneeling figures representing Faith, Justice, Fortitude and Prudence, each in flowing robes and bearing symbols of their virtues. Beneath the effigy displaying his worldly authority and success lies a reminder of death in the form of a skeleton on a straw mat. This tomb was commissioned by the second Earl from Simon Basyll, but the first Earl had already chosen the form of the monument before he died; the sculptures are by Maximilian Colt. The simple tomb of a knight nearby, showing his shield and armour, dates from the 13C. Close by, the shrouded figure which sinks gently into its marble base represents Sir Richard Curle, warden of the royal estates at Hatfield, which was carved by Nicholas Stone in 1617; it shows an uncommon subtlety of handling by an English craftsman for this date. In 1871, the third Marquess of Salisbury (the next Conservative Prime Minister after Disraeli) carried out a complete scheme of wall decorations, including marble blind arcading below the windows on the N and E walls, mosaics by Salviati of Venice and murals of four Apostles by Giulio Taldini; the latter are now in need of cleaning and re-lighting and, once this is undertaken, they will provide colour to this dark room. The beautiful W and S gates of the chapel are Flemish, 18C, and were brought from Amiens Cathedral by the third Marquess. The Marquess' own memorial (he died in 1903) may be seen in the SE corner; the bronze recumbent effigy by Sir William Goscombe John is a replica of that which lies on the Marquess' memorial in Westminster Abbey, designed by G.F. Bodley. The glass in the N windows, dating from the 1880s and 1890s, is by Burlison & Grylls; the E window, dating from 1872, is by Clayton & Bell. In the chancel, the reredos was designed by T.W. Earp in 1871 with a mosaic background by Salviati; the figures flanking the Crucifixion represent St. Etheldreda and St. Alban. The communion rails are 17C. The windows are by Clayton & Bell. The Brocket chapel contains tombs of owners of nearby Brocket Hall; the larger examples are of Sir James Reade and his son John, showing two busts by J.M. Rysbrack (1760) and, to the W, of Dame Elizabeth Brocket and her mother reclining one above the other (1612). The chandelier dates from the early 18C. The E window is by Temple Moore (and made by Burlison & Grylls, 1903). The S window of the S transept contains glass by Sir Edward Burne-Jones and was made by Morris & Co. in 1894. In the N transept, the hatchment commemorates the Marchioness of Salisbury, who died in the 1835 fire at Hatfield House. In this chapel the Cecil family at one time attended the church services. The pulpit in the nave is by Sir Albert Richardson, 1947. The Victorian font by Earp rests on the original 13C base. The N window, second from the W, is to the three sons of Lord William Cecil (Rector of Hatfield and later Bishop of Exeter) who were killed in the First World War. The window was designed by Christopher Whall in 1920 and shows three angels with youthful, pre-Raphaelite style faces.

The celebrated figure of Robert Cecil, first Earl of Salisbury and Lord Burghley's younger son, dominates Hatfield; it was he, whilst Lord High Treasurer, who exchanged his house at Theobalds near Cheshunt for the old Bishop's Palace then owned by King James and who began to build the present Hatfield House. He died before it was complete. The Salisbury graveyard at the W end near the Old Palace contains the remains of another famous Cecil, the third Marquess of Salisbury (1830–1903), who was three times Prime Minister. He chose not to take up residence in Downing Street but instead travelled into London each day in his private carriage on the railway. He constructed a viaduct approach from the house towards the station which lies beyond the statue of his seated figure at the end of the drive. Another of Queen Victoria's Prime Ministers, Lord Melbourne (1779–1848), is buried in the church. He lived at Brocket Hall. A memorial plaque is placed near the pulpit.

Hemel Hempstead, *St. Mary.* Second only to St. Alban's Abbey, this church is a fine example of Norman building in Hertfordshire. It lies on the sloping hillside below the High Street and above the river valley; the tall spire is unusual in this county of short spires.

The church remains largely in its Norman cruciform plan, built from flint and reused Roman bricks. The chancel was built together with the tower in c 1150, and the lead-roofed nave and transepts completed the cross about 40 years later. The nave possesses a contemporary clerestory (a rare survival from so early a period) where, connecting the hoodmoulds of the windows, a thin decorative frieze runs the length of the walls. The aisles are also 12C, but their two-light windows date from the 15C. The S porch was added 200 years after the main church was completed and the W porch is 15C with 20C outer doors. The W doorway into the nave betrays the thickness of the W wall, within which it is framed by a three-stepped arch, its voussoirs carved with zigzag and leaf mouldings dating from the late Norman period. The plain, undecorated transepts have low pitched roofs and deep-set Perpendicular windows, except in the S transept where the W window is Norman. The chancel has a single-light Norman window with shafts on each side; the S wall contains two tall 14C windows in which the tracery has been renewed. Extending N from the chancel is a narrow double-height chamber with a 14C loop light and original metal grille in the upper storey; beyond lie the Victorian vestries. The main accent, however, is the robust Norman central tower with its stair turret against the SE corner. Eight small round-headed windows feature in the lower stages and four more pairs open into the upper stage; a stringcourse joins these upper windows in a manner similar to that of the nave clerestory. The upper windows are surmounted by two blank arcades and a central roundel; a projecting parapet provides a plain horizontal. Soaring above the tower, the wooden 14C needle spire rises to almost 200ft. The spire is covered in chevron-patterned lead sheeting (renewed in 1987), and is topped by a gilded cross and weathervane. At the base of the spire, facing S, is mounted a blue clock-face with gilded Roman numerals (1783).

Inside, the handsomely proportioned nave boasts sturdy arcades resting on circular columns and scalloped capitals. Above each of the six arches stands a clerestory window with its round-headed arch, sloping sill and slender shafts. The timber roof is 15C and rests on plain stone corbels at clerestory level. The 12C doorway has a carved arch inside as well as out, and the internal capitals show carvings of Adam and Eve wrestling with a serpent, and in the background, the tree of life. To the E of the nave, a tall semicircular arch, one of four supporting the crossing tower and exhibiting especially fine capitals, opens into the chancel. This displays rare stone rib-vaulting resting on wall shafts, again with scalloped capitals. The Perpendicular E window provides light and height, and is set into the wall within a recessed rectangular panel. A blocked 15C archway in the N wall used to open into the chamber whose door now lies further W. The organ is seen through a modern, Norman-style arch, where its little chamber, like the chancel, is vaulted in two bays, the ribs resting on scalloped corbels. Below the 14C window in the N wall of the chamber, a doorway (perhaps contemporary with the window) leads today into the modern vestries, but may have been external. Both transepts have 15C wooden roofs with arched braces and spandrels, restored in 1880. The N transept contains the chapel of the Holy Spirit.

Modern pews fill the spacious nave, and the carved oak choirstalls date from the end of the last century. The reredos may have been carved at Oberammergau and was donated in 1880 together with the E window. The chancel walls and vaulting were painted in 1888 by G.F. Bodley, but they were considered a distraction and have been covered since with whitewash. The floor of the chancel is made of Minton tiles. The windows in its S wall are by Clayton & Bell, and date from 1858. On the E wall of the nave above the tower arch may be seen a painting of the Annunciation, dating from c 1900. On the W wall of the S aisle, notice the fine brass effigies to Robert and Margaret Albyn (c 1360). The font is probably Norman, with 19C carvings, and an oak cover with ironwork in the Norman style dates from 1956.

The Paston Cooper family, prominent in this church, derives its baronetcy from Sir Astley Paston Cooper (died 1841), a surgeon at Guy's Hospital, London. He was so honoured for performing a minor operation on King George IV, but he was remembered also as a major benefactor of Hemel Hempstead in founding there the original of the modern West Hertfordshire Hospital.

Hitchin, St. Mary. The quiet market town of Hitchin grew upon the prosperous wool trade during the later Middle Ages and retains both a street plan and a richly endowed church of the period. St. Mary's suffered several natural calamities in its early history which led to the replanned building which we see today, bordering the River Hiz to the E with its symmetrical landscaping centred about the church, and a group of shops partly encircling the spacious graveyard on the other three sides. The exterior is memorable for the fine Perpendicular S porch and the interior for its good quality fittings and monuments.

The church is built of flint rubble with stone dressings and over large areas is covered with cement mortar; much of this rendering has been removed, however, in recent years. The main body of the building follows a rectangular plan, the crenellated nave, aisles, chancel and chapels being of the same length and of roughly equal width. The squat tower, stair turret and thin spike provide a limited accent at the W end. The tower, together with the lower section of the nave, is 12C and is constructed of a conglomeration of materials, including some Roman bricks, reused stone, flint, and brick repairs of the 16C and 17C. The massive buttresses were added on top of thinner existing ones by the parishioners 'under pain of excommunication' when there was danger of collapse in the early 14C. The upper stage is lit by restored twin lancets and the lower one by a 15C window; a 13C doorway, having low proportions like the tower itself, lies on the W front; the mid-13C stair turret displays a sundial dated 1660. The nave dates from the first half of the 14C with the N aisle dating from about 20 years before the S aisle. An early 16C clerestory of three-light windows replaces the original one, whilst a small window on the W nave wall, also dating from the 16C, indicates the small change of level between the nave and chancel, which have, unusually, hipped slate roofs. The chancel chapels run E directly from the aisles, the S chapel dating from c 1450 and the N or Trinity chapel added soon after; at the same time, the chancel was extended to form an ambulatory comprising one bay behind the high altar. All the tracery in the windows originates from this 15C work. A double-height porch projects at the W end of each aisle; the more elaborate S porch was built in the late 15C. It is considered that the porch was donated by a rich wool merchant of the town, whose arms may be seen on the left-hand side of the entrance.

The well-lit spread of the interior—this is the largest parish church in Hertfordshire, 170ft long—displays the self-confidence of a town which was sure of the affluent position which it maintained throughout the Middle Ages and which endowed its place of worship generously. The four early 14C arches are supported by octagonal columns with moulded capitals. Above the clerestory lies the heavily restored 15C roof. The N aisle has a 14C roof at the E end which, judging by its proportions, probably came from the old chancel at the time of its extension in the mid-15C; the mouldings are of a high quality and the corbels represent an angel choir. The S aisle possesses a 15C doorway leading into the porch and a 14C door to the E which leads into the chamber over the porch. The broad tower arch, dating perhaps from the 13C, is probably the oldest architectural feature. The awkward chancel arch dates from two periods. The lower half-columns match the style and date of those in the nave (14C) whilst its Perpendicular shafts date from the time of the heightening of the chancel (15C). The chancel contains four arches of shafted columns, the easternmost arch being a little wider and dating from the mid-15C extension; the roof, together with those of the N and S chapels, is 15C. To the S, the chapel of St. Andrew was founded by a town guild and built in c 1450; its chief interest lies in the roof, displaying carved wooden angel supporters, some of which carry the insignia of the Staple of Calais. On the opposite side of the chancel, the Trinity chapel possesses another fine wooden roof, this time with wooden corbels.

The church acquired many fittings of high quality craftsmanship, including woodwork of especial refinement, and excellent monuments from all periods. Fittings of particular interest are the screens in the chancel and its chapel; an oak traceried example of high workmanship separates the Trinity chapel from the N aisle and, in the same position on the S side, the remarkable angel screen of c 1450 employs ogee arches and complex crocketing, with the row of angels which gives its name in relief on a beam at the top. In 1970, the medieval ambulatory behind the high altar was reinstated using a screen to separate the main chancel from what is now known as the chapel of St. John the Baptist. The S chapel is today the repository for many memorial brasses. Note also Sir John Sturgeon's memorial (1402) on the E wall, builder of the side chapels. The S chapel contains tablets to the Radcliffe family which owned Hitchin Priory, a nearby house converted from 14C Carmelite buildings. The chancel screen was removed in 1776, and all that remains is the doorway which led to the Rood loft. Near the S aisle stands the pulpit of c 1500. The main feature of the nave is the 15C font with its tall canopy of c 1896; the faces of the 12 Apostles were damaged by Cromwell's soldiers at the time of the Civil War. The oak tower screen, installed in 1952, is a successful example of revived Classicism carefully designed to suit a Gothic church and to allow the maximum light through the W window. In the N aisle may be seen a 17C Adoration of the Magi said to be from Rubens' studio; on the windowsills lie three medieval effigies, the westernmost of which is of Purbeck marble but which are all now whitewashed, unfortunately.

The S aisle contains on its W wall the memorial to Robert Hinde (died 1786), who is supposed to be the original of Thomas Sterne's Uncle Toby in 'Tristram Shandy' and who owned Preston Castle about three miles away. Hinde kept an 'army' of field-hands and children to commemorate the nation's successful battles and which would pass on to his fortified house; there the procession would fire a final salute, all observed in quietly resigned mood by the towns-people, I suspect.

London Colney, *All Saints' Pastoral Centre, Chapel.*The convent of All Saints, in the neo-Tudor style much favoured at the turn of the century by the Arts and Crafts movement, was built in 1899 by Leonard Stokes for the Society of All Saints, Sisters of the Poor. The complex of courtyard, refectory and ancillary buildings is pleasantly surrounded by a park with mature trees.

To the left of the entrance front stands the convent chapel, added in 1927. It was designed by Sir Ninian Comper. Comper, like his master G.F. Bodley, was interested in creating designs for buildings as a whole, including their fittings and interior details, to maintain homogeneity throughout. It follows the Gothic style, and is tall, long and narrow in the manner of Oxford and Cambridge college chapels. Completion was unhurried and work was further interrupted by the Second World War; the remaining three of the projected six bays were completed between 1960 and 1964 by Comper's son, Sebastian. The walls are brick, with tall windows and narrow stepped buttresses topped by sharp pinnacles with brick crenellations in between. Angle buttresses support both the W and E ends, and the Perpendicular and Early English styles combine to provide the fine window tracery. A tall niche with a canopy and pinnacles surmounts the apex of the E end wall, whilst a rose window of 20 outer lights and 10 inner lights provides the central punctuation of the W wall. Immediately below this window, a row of blind stone arches lies flush with the wall between two courses of stone, the central arch of which is used as a door for access from the interior onto a little balcony with a stone balustrade. Along the S side, a low side chapel, having a vaulted ceiling, abuts the two easternmost bays of the main building. A corridor flanking the length of the S wall leads to the convent buildings. On the N side, a single-storey side chapel with a broad window fills one bay at the E end.

The antechapel is entered from the NW door with the organ loft to the W, and a wooden screen to the E. The very light, white interior uses uncomplicated architectural features such as N–S arched divisions marking the position of each external buttress, with simple ribbed vaulting filling the spaces between arches. The three E bays were the work of Comper Senior and the others were completed in 1964 by his son, Sebastian. In the antechapel the arches support the organ loft which contains an instrument by Harrison's. At the opposite end, the high coloured window filling the E wall contrasts magnificently with the plain white of the walls and ceiling.

The floor is tiled white throughout, lying between the dark wood of the Jacobean-style stalls which form an enclosure in the manner of a college chapel at Oxford or Cambridge. Two statues on the W ends of the stalls in the antechapel represent St. Mary with the Christ child, and St. Alban, both under canopies. A hint of the Gothic in these essentially Classical stalls is suggested by the inclusion of crocketed finials over each seat. This fusion of styles is typical of Comper's later work. The E end centres on the altar which is covered by a baldacchino of four metal Corinthian columns. The entire structure is gilded and painted with winding flower stems on the columns, and blue and gold inscriptions around the cornice. This prominent feature emphasises the strong tenet which Comper practised concerning the importance of the altar in a church. Six tall candles, a silver crucifix over a sacrament ciborium and two hanging sanctuary lamps complete the arrangement. In the NE corner a painted statue of Mother and Child stands beneath a tall crocketed canopy of gilded wood. Wall sconces and hanging chandeliers supported by delicate wrought-iron brackets with fleur-de-lis decoration are all by Comper Senior.

St. Albans, *St. Michael*. St. Michael's is situated in a cluster of buildings in the middle of the Roman town of St. Albans or *Verulamium* near to the site of the Forum and about half a mile W of the present town centre. The church, and probably also the parish, together with St. Stephen's and St. Peter's, were founded in 948 by Ulsinus, Abbot of St. Alban's. The interest of St. Michael's lies in the ancient origins of the fabric, which is partly of pre-Conquest date, and also in the monument to Sir Francis Bacon, whose family home was at nearby Gorhambury.

The church is built of flint with stone dressings and some Roman brick, and has a lead nave roof and tiles elsewhere. The tower at the NW corner and the low vestry beneath the S nave wall were built in 1896. The medieval tower at the W end of the nave was demolished in that year, allowing the church to be extended to the W to provide extra accommodation. These works were undertaken by the rich lawyer, Lord Grimthorpe, who was an amateur architect and who restored St. Alban's Cathedral with his own money. Grimthorpe's alterations at St. Michael's appear to be less cumbersome than his designs for the cathedral. The S porch, which stands immediately E of Grimthorpe's vestry, was an earlier addition, by Sir Gilbert Scott, 1866. E of this porch stands the projecting early 13C Lady chapel, with its pair of square-headed 15C windows and its single lancet window; the buttresses at the corners were added in the 19C. The chapel's roof rises above that of the chancel. The nave and chancel walls are pre-Conquest, perhaps 10C. The N aisle is a Norman addition of the early 12C. A clerestory of six lancets was added to the nave in the early 13C. Pre-Conquest nave quoins are visible at the E end, and the chancel N door is also of the same period.

Inside the nave, the combined endeavours of the pre-Conquest and Norman builders may be seen where the walls from the 10C were pierced to form arcades in the 12C, ready for the construction of aisles. The N aisle has three arches, one fewer than in the S arcade (now partially blocked). It has been suggested that the former was completed by the Norman masons as a 'test' of the building's strength, before undertaking the bolder procedure of removing enough of the S wall to create four arches. It must have been found necessary to provide more light and space in the newly enlarged church, for the nave roof was heightened sometime in the early 13C and a thin lancet clerestory was inserted. To the E of the S nave wall, the lancets open into the Lady chapel, which dates from shortly after the clerestory. The nave roof with its stone corbels is 15C. The chancel, although partly rebuilt in the mid-14C, retains its pre-Conquest walls and blocked doorway on the N; it contains reused Roman brick from *Verulamium* and matches remnants of the pre-Conquest windows still visible in the nave walls. Also in the N wall of the chancel may be seen a 13C lancet window; the S wall contains one 15C and one 14C window (E and W), both with square heads; the E window is Victorian. In the Lady chapel the fine lancets are original, whilst on the E wall the central arch (now blank but for a circular opening) should have contained twin lancets which were almost certainly blocked to strengthen the wall; delicate shafts with moulded capitals support three arches around these windows. The N aisle contains a Decorated two-light window with fine tracery, three 15C windows under square heads, and a round-headed E lancet from the Norman period.

The church is furnished throughout with unusually fine Victorian pews, well-detailed and made from wood of a golden tone. The oak pulpit is late Elizabethan, with a hexagonal tester and book rests with carved brackets; there is also a 17C hourglass. The S clerestory lancets contain painted decorations on the jambs, whilst modern painting in the chancel shows four angels with instruments. The split organ at the W end of the nave was given in 1950 as a thank-offering for the church's millenary in 1948. On the N side of the chancel is situated the most celebrated monument in Hertfordshire, the seated, sleeping figure of Sir Francis Bacon (died 1626), philosopher and statesman, carved from alabaster, painted and set within the niche; *'sic sedebat'* as the inscription tells us ('thus he sat'). Other monuments include, in the S chapel, brasses to John Pecock (died 1330) and his wife (the arms show three peacocks), and, at the E end of the nave, a knight in armour of c 1400. In the S aisle an interesting panel shows the 'Doom' (by St. Michael's Sewing Group).

The most celebrated parishioner was Francis Bacon. Francis's father, Sir Nicholas Bacon, was Queen Elizabeth I's Lord Keeper of the Great Seal and built the nearby house of Gorhambury in 1568, where his two sons grew up. Francis became Lord Keeper like his father, and inherited Gorhambury in 1601. Later, he became Lord Chancellor and was created Viscount St. Albans in 1621.

Stanstead Abbots, *St. James.* The old church of St. James stands outside the village to the SE and has been taken into the care of the Redundant Churches Fund (the present parish church, St. Andrew's, lies to the NW and was built in 1880 by Alfred Waterhouse). St. James's chief interest lies in the 18C arrangements which are still maintained inside; its Victorian restorers did not reorder the interior, presumably because of the new church nearby. Further interest is provided by monuments dating from the 16C to the present day.

The exterior has a low, broad 15C W tower abutting a 12C nave, both carried out in flint rubble with stone dressings. The tower has two-light windows in the upper stage and angle buttresses up to window level. A stair turret stands at the SE corner and there is a small, lead-covered hexagonal spire with a weathervane. The chancel was increased to its present size in the 13C, and at the same time the nave windows were renewed as we see them today. A chapel was built in 1577 N of the chancel entirely of brick, but with

The W tower of St. James's, surmounted by a typical Hertfordshire spike

stone windows. The windows are still Gothic, cusped and straight-headed. Elsewhere in the church the windows are 15C with restored tracery of much later date. A low-pitched, tile-hung roof without a parapet covers both the nave (which has no clerestory) and the chancel. S of the nave, an open timber porch, also tile-hung, dates from the 15C, and is so built that its timbers appear quite massive when related to the small scale and simplicity of the structure.

Inside, the simple white interior with box-pews gives a rare impression of a plain, rural preaching house. The roof was plastered and whitewashed in the 18C, but the conspicuous kingposts betray its 15C origin. The nave and chancel form a long, unbroken compartment without a chancel arch. The N arches lead into, and are contemporary with, the chapel (1577). The arches with their octagonal columns of brick (wrongly plastered in the 19C), show no Classical influence. The chapel has two windows of two lights in the N wall and an E window of three lights, giving the church a sense of spaciousness appropriate to both the 18C furniture and the complete covering of whitewash throughout the building. At the centre of the box-pews along the S wall of the nave and illuminated by the cool N light, the preacher would have given his long sermon, his clerk seated beneath him, in his three-decker pulpit. The congregation sitting through his service would have kept the draughts away by closing the pew doors and would have been reminded of the Faith by the boards of the Lord's Prayer and Creed on each side of the altar and the Commandments positioned near the royal arms. Four hatchments, newly cleaned, add to the pre-Victorian wooden wall fittings. The glass is of limited interest. St. James and St. John by Jones & Willis may be seen W of the pulpit, and some Elizabethan glass (1573) is in the E window of the chapel. The 19C organ by Bevington stands under the tower arch.

The memorials which remain in the floor of the nave and on the walls cover a lengthy period. In the nave, a brass shows a man and his wife holding hands, c 1550. In the chancel, a standing stone slab shows a knight in armour dating from the late 15C. Also in the chancel, set in the floor, is the brass image of a young man, William Saxaye, who died in 1581. The inscription tells us that he was of Gray's Inn in London; the coat of arms indicates his local origin. A typical Elizabethan monument on the N chancel wall commemorates Sir Edward Baeshe (died 1587) and his family. In the chapel, a wall monument (1806) to Robert Jocelyn, Captain RN, and former owner of the nearby Stanstead Bury, commemorates the heroic days of the Royal Navy: a mast and sail, an anchor and a gun were chosen by the younger John Bacon, the sculptor, to represent Jocelyn's service.

A tablet to past members of the Trower family of Stanstead Bury on the W wall of the chapel was dedicated in 1987. It was designed by Stephen Dykes Bower.

KENT

Kent is a large county in terms of both area and population. Its modern boundaries are virtually coterminous with the most advanced of the early kingdoms, from which the conversion of England was begun under St. Augustine in 597 and which was heavily settled at an early date. It was the only English medieval county to have two cathedrals, at Canterbury and Rochester, both monastic and both founded in the early 7C. Before the Reformation these two cathedrals were the largest landowners in the county, and as they retained their estates in the 16C little former monastic property was available for redistribution to the new gentry. Kent is a county with no natural centre, Maidstone being the county town largely by accident and convenience, with few large landholdings but an exceptionally large number of medium-sized towns, the majority situated along the Channel Coast or Thames Estuary. In the medieval and early modern period industry and wealth was concentrated in the small towns of the Weald, such as Cranbrook and Tenterden. From the 18C the economic base shifted to the Medway Towns and the Isle of Sheppey, with their dockyards, and to the popular new seaside resorts in Thanet, Dover, Folkestone and even Gravesend. At the present time the industrial part of the county is confined to its NW corner bordering the River Thames, whilst the remainder is predominantly agricultural and horticultural, well known for many years as 'The Garden of England'.

The political and social structure of Kent is reflected in its churches, which are overwhelmingly medieval and generally rather small, frequently with nave and aisles under the same roof. Early foundations, many of them connected with members of the Kentish royal family, are quite common. After the Reformation the county was overwhelmingly Anglican and generally eschewed both Catholic and Protestant extremes. The number of recusants was very small and, with little Irish immigration in the 19C, Catholic expansion was very slow. In the early 17C many of the towns became strongholds of Puritanism and a leading member of the Kentish gentry, Sir Edward Dering, was one of the most learned of the Parliamentarians who sought to abolish episcopacy. However, after 1660 there were relatively few seceders to the dissenting sects and in the 18C little popular support for the early Methodists. Neither Evangelicals nor Tractarians were strong in the Established Church in Kent, and urban expansion, except on the fringes of London, was relatively modest in the period after 1800. The number of important post-Reformation churches is therefore small, and only the rebuilt church at Mereworth is of national significance. Most of the Victorian restorations and new buildings were entrusted to the more undistinguished, mostly local, architects.

The number of churches of early foundation, surviving either as existing places of worship or as fully excavated ruins, is impressive. In the former category there are the churches founded by the Abbesses Mildred and Sexburga respectively at Minster-in-Thanet and Minster-in-Sheppey, and by St. Ethelburga at Lyminge, all much altered over the years. At Folkestone the body of another royal abbess, St. Eanswythe, survives in a casket discovered in 1885 and her shrine has been restored. She is also commemorated in the dedication at nearby Brenzett, whilst the church at Bonnington is dedicated to St. Rumwold, son of the King of Mercia who allegedly cried 'Christianus Sum' at his birth and died three days later. St. Mary in Castro at Dover, though largely rebuilt in 1860–62, is another important pre-Conquest foundation. The churches that survive only as ruins include Stone-next-Faversham, St. Pancras' at Canterbury, and Reculver, where only the impressive W front remains of a church deliberately demolished by its then incumbent on account of its inconvenient position in 1809. As well as the important, and almost fully preserved, 12C churches still in use at Barfrestone, Brook and St. Margaret's-at-Cliffe, there are fine 12C fonts at Darenth and Newenden, and elaborate ironwork on the S door at Staplehurst.

Most Kent churches date from the 13C or 14C, and relatively few were rebuilt in the grand manner after 1400. The majority, even in the towns, are small in comparison with those of East Anglia or the West Country. The 13C chancel at Woodchurch, with its three lancets, is a particularly fine example of work of that period. There are extremely impressive 15C W towers at Charing and Tenterden. Among the most interesting post-Reformation churches are the 17C chapels-of-ease at Groombridge and Tunbridge Wells; Faversham, where the nave was rebuilt by the elder George Dance in 1754–55; and the only major 19C church, St. Augustine's at Ramsgate, built by A.W.N. Pugin in 1845–50 next to his own house, but given after his death to a community of French Benedictine monks. All other 19C churches and all other non-Anglican ones are of no more than purely local interest. A community of Anglican Benedictine nuns has provided Kent with its only dramatic piece of modern ecclesiastical architecture, the church at Malling Abbey, designed by Robert Maguire and Keith Murray and completed in 1966.

The general comments that apply to the fabric of churches in Kent can be repeated in the case of furnishings. There is, apart from the magnificent display at Canterbury Cathedral, little medieval glass, the best being found at a small group of churches in the Stour Valley: Boughton Aluph, Chartham, Chilham and Westwell. To the SE of this group, St. Mary's at Stowting has a splendid early 14C Virgin and Child in a nave N window, which is illustrated on the front cover of this book. Medieval woodwork is also thin on the ground and tends to be very simple in character. The exceptions are the virtually complete screens at Shoreham and Stalisfield, the 14C lectern at Detling (much admired by the Victorian ecclesiologists), and the handsome late medieval parish chests at Harty and Rainham. Many churches have late 16C or early 17C pulpits, one of the finest and earliest being that at Lenham; Trottiscliffe has a pulpit designed in 1775 for Westminster Abbey, its tester supported by a column in the form of a palm tree. There are virtually complete sets of 18C and early 19C fittings in the 'unrestored' churches of Badlesmere, Fairfield, Knowlton, Old Romney and Stelling. Apart from Kilndown there are ecclesiological ensembles at Boughton Malherbe and Frinsted, and the atmospheric restoration of a small and remote country church by G.F. Bodley at Bicknor. Two unusual survivals are the 15C cope at East Langdon, for long used as a pulpit hanging, and the 17C funeral pall at Hollingbourne, embroidered by the ladies of the Culpeper family and later used as an altar frontal.

The outstanding monuments are the brasses at Cobham, and many other churches contain at least one good medieval brass and sometimes later ones as well, including an exceptionally fine 17C one at East Sutton. By contrast medieval stone monuments, apart from those in the cathedrals at Canterbury and Rochester, are disappointing. After 1500, however, there are many monuments of high quality by major artists. Epiphanius Evesham is represented at Boughton-under-Blean and Otterden, Nicholas Stone at Wingham, J.M. Rysbrack at Chartham, Sir Henry Cheere at Otford, Sir Francis Chantrey at Chevening and Chilham. Victorian stained glass, though plentiful, is generally not of high quality. There is glass by William Morris and Sir Edward Burne-Jones at Langton Green and Speldhurst, by Henry Holiday at Westerham, by Thomas Willement at Ospringe and Selling, and a very exciting E window of 1896 at Wickhambreaux by Arild Rosenkranz, a rare Kentish contribution to ecclesiastical *art nouveau*. The most outstanding 20C stained glass is that by Marc Chagall at Tudeley and Patrick Reyntiens at Marden.

Biggin Hill, *St. Mark.* The present church was built in 1957–59 to the designs of Sir Giles Gilbert Scott, Son & Partner: a postwar building of modest detailing, which replaced an ageing 'tin tabernacle'. It is of interest only because it was built personally by the Reverend Vivian Symons, its Vicar from 1951 to 1966, with intermittent voluntary help. Even more surprising is the fact that in 1952–56, to secure the materials for the new St. Mark's, he had personally dismantled the church of All Saints, Davey Street, Peckham, in S London, again with intermittent voluntary help. The case of a clergyman dismantling one church and building another, very largely by himself, must be unique in 20C England. The first half of the task was described by Vivian Symons in 'The Moving Church', published in 1956.

S.C.H.

Brookland, *St. Augustine.* This is the most interesting of the many important churches on Romney Marsh, as significant for its varied fittings as for its fabric and for the unusual detached belfry which dominates the N side of the building. The church largely escaped the attentions of the Victorian restorer—as did several others in the area, e.g. Fairfield, Old Romney and Warehorne, and the interior is a pleasing jumble of rustic woodwork.

Externally, one must begin with the medieval belfry, which stands to the E end of the N aisle. It is constructed entirely in wood, built in three stages each with a shingled roof and is octagonal in plan. It has been described as resembling 'three candle-snuffers stacked on one another'. The exterior of the main building shows work of many periods and evidence of much patching in the 18C, including large aisle windows installed in 1790. The N porch, like the belfry, is entirely of timber and dates from the 14C.

Inside, the church is large and spacious with a wide nave and aisles completed in the 14C. The arcades between nave and aisles lean precariously outwards. There is no structural division between nave and chancel but the latter is a handsome construction of the mid-13C with lancet windows, piscina and sedilia. The roofs of the nave and S aisle are original, fine crownposts of the type found in many Kent churches. The relationship between the medieval fabric and its mostly post-Reformation fittings is exceptionally harmonious.

It is, however, the fittings for which the church is, after its belfry, most notable. Pride of place must be given to the 12C font, unique in England though similar to one at St. Evroult-de-Montfort in Normandy. It is cylindrical, of lead, with two series of carved vignettes under a row of arcading: one, labelled in Latin, shows the signs of the Zodiac; the other, inscribed in Norman French, illustrates the

Labours of the Months, scything in June, haymaking in July and so on. There are fragments of 15C wall paintings at the E end of the S aisle and of medieval glass in the E window of the N aisle. Also in the N aisle are three late medieval benches with simple rectangular ends. Otherwise most of the fittings date from the 18C and include several unusual items. There is a cut-down pulpit and reading-desk, altar rails and box-pews of c 1738. The curiosities are the tithe pen at the W end of the N aisle, a graveside shelter like a sentry box to keep the officiating clergyman dry during funerals and the scales, weights and measures, dated 1795, for the Hundred of Alloes Bridge. There is a small brass to Thomas Leddes, priest, who died in 1503 and a large number of 17C black ledger slabs and 18C wall tablets.

Canterbury

St. Martin. St. Martin's is a simple building of W tower, aisleless nave and chancel, which has long been acknowledged as probably the oldest church in continuous use in England. It has usually been accepted that it is the building to which Bede referred when he wrote that on the E side of Canterbury in St. Augustine's time, there 'stood an old church, built in honour of St. Martin during the Roman occupation of Britain, where the Christian Queen of whom I have spoken used to pray'. The Christian Queen was Bertha, the Frankish wife of King Aethelberht of Kent. In other words, it was believed in Canterbury in the 8C that St. Martin's had been built in Roman times and had survived to be used by Queen Bertha even before the conversion of the English began under St. Augustine. It is accepted that the present nave and W part of the chancel are no later than the early 7C, for they are both built in the late Roman technique and with Roman materials. The building could date either from the later years of the Roman province, in the 4C, or in the early 7C, when St. Augustine's party from Italy would naturally have used Roman methods. It is further accepted that the W end of the chancel is probably an earlier phase than the nave. A different theory claims, with less acceptance, that only the W end of the chancel is 4C and that the nave was added in the early 7C. The argument is therefore that St. Martin's was too small to be the church to which Bede referred, and that St. Pancras' (q.v.) was more likely the building which fitted the events he recounted. The objection to this is that we do not know what underlies the present nave of St. Martin's: might it not be a 7C replacement of a 4C one? Also, it is difficult to see how two churches could be confused within a century when their names—their obvious means of distinction—derived from Queen Bertha's and St. Augustine's own time. Only excavation will ever settle the argument.

The church stands in a large, rising churchyard near the street called Longport. St. Martin's is approached from the W and entered under the W tower. This tower, which dates from the 14C, is markedly plain, with two W buttresses and two lancet windows at different levels above, the lower being entirely renewed. At the E end of the church, which was remodelled in the 12C or 13C, the three stepped lancets are similarly modern. An air of antiquity is derived externally only from the obvious use of Roman materials and from two blocked doorways in the S wall of the chancel. There is a square-headed doorway with a large stone lintel, which could be late

Roman, and to the E of it a round-headed doorway which is later than the wall it pierces.

The interior is unexpectedly white-painted and bright. The overall dimensions are small. Only in odd places is the ancient fabric exposed to view. The W end of the nave reveals two round-headed windows which are enlarged versions of the originals. The internal S wall of the chancel is exposed and presents the round-headed door referred to earlier. Opposite, set into the N wall of the chancel, the traditional place of honour, is a tomb-recess, presumably of an unknown medieval benefactor. The cylindrical font of Caen stone at the W end is the one ancient fitting. It comprises a plain base, three tiers of blocks which have carved decoration of interlocking rings with pellets, and a rim with similar but smaller decoration. It has been convincingly argued by T. Tatton-Brown that most of this font is a former well-head from Christ Church Cathedral Priory which was made in the 12C and which was later taken apart and wrongly put back together. It will be seen that some of the rings are cut in half and should clearly have been placed so that they made a complete pattern. The three stepped E lancets have rere-arches and internal shafting, and are filled with 19C stained glass. In the top right-hand corner Queen Bertha and her companions worship in St. Martin's; below, St. Augustine and his party land in Kent. At top right, St. Augustine's party enters Canterbury and at bottom left, King Aethelberht is baptised. The Crucifixion fills the central light. Other windows feature St. Martin, St. Bede the Venerable and further early saints.

S.C.H.

St. Pancras. The ruins of St. Pancras' look insignificant next to the more spectacular ruins of St. Augustine's Abbey, but they are of very considerable antiquity and may, if one particular argument be accepted, represent the traditions and honours which have usually been applied to St. Martin's. There is no doubt that the ruins are of the 7C *at the latest.* In the Middle Ages it was said that the church was repaired for Christian use by St. Augustine after it had been used to shelter a pagan idol in the 6C. Its naming may be attributed to the influence of Pope Gregory I, who sent St. Augustine to England and is known to have been devoted to St. Pancras' memory. The ground-plan comprises a rectangular nave with chambers to N and S, a square-ended chancel which was originally apsidal, and a W porch. The building materials are Roman. The two chambers and the porch were later additions. A triple chancel arch once existed as at Bradwell, Reculver and Brixworth.

The theory that Queen Bertha's church was St. Pancras' rather than St. Martin's arises partly from the former being nearer to the Roman town and partly from the fact that, of the two fabrics, only St. Pancras' appears to be large enough to be considered a late Roman *church.* An excavation of St. Pancras' in 1965 by Frank Jenkins appeared to discern a pre-Augustinian phase of nave and chancel, whereas at St. Martin's opinion accepts only the W part of the chancel as Roman. Proof is ultimately dependent on a thorough excavation of St. Martin's and, for the reasons given under the entry for that church, it must be considered doubtful whether the traditional attribution of Bede's words should be changed.

S.C.H.

Chartham, *St. Mary the Virgin.* The church is a rare example of a medium-sized village church dating wholly from one period. There is documentary evidence that the church was being built in 1294 and it was probably begun and completed within the last decade of the 13C.

Externally the church is unremarkable: a short aisleless nave, shallow transepts and a comparatively long chancel of four bays, together with a W tower, remodelled in the late 15C. Internally the church was heavily restored by G.E. Street in 1873–75 and some of the fittings, notably the choirstalls and the tower screen, are his. Street, however, managed to preserve the fine tracery of the chancel windows and also much of their original late 13C stained glass. This is particularly remarkable, consisting largely of a series of grisaille patterns with coloured borders of leaves and flowers. All the windows in the chancel retain to a greater or lesser extent their original glass and where this has not been possible Victorian glass, repeating the original patterns, has been inserted. Recent restoration has been less kind to the interior, the neo-Jacobean screen which creates a wholly unnecessary narthex at the W end of the nave and the repositioning of the font in the S transept being particularly unfortunate. An important and unusual feature of the interior is the almost complete survival of the original roofs which meet at the crossing with four diagonal arches supported on a large boss of oak leaves.

The brasses and monuments are also notable. The life-size one to Sir Robert de Septvans, who died in 1306, shows him with a surcoat over his full armour and wearing *ailettes*, an early form of epaulettes. There are four less important 15C and 16C brasses, two to priests. The large monument to Sarah Young, who died in 1751, was designed by J.M. Rysbrack and a rather more modest tablet to Sir William Fagg, who died in 1792, by Thomas Scheemakers.

Cliffe-at-Hoo, *St. Helen.* The Hoo peninsula is a wild and marshy stretch of partly industrialised countryside between the Medway and Thameside towns of NW Kent. Cliffe is its largest village and is dominated by an exceptionally handsome church, much altered in a series of restorations between 1853 and 1884, though a good deal of damage caused then has been rectified by sensitive redecoration and reordering. In terms of the variety of its contents Cliffe is one of the most interesting and rewarding churches in the county.

The building is very large. Its core is a cruciform 13C church with a heavily buttressed W tower, heightened in the 14C when the chancel was rebuilt, the aisles widened and the two-storey S porch added. The church is even grander internally than it is externally. The tower space is vaulted, the nave piers are painted with red zigzags and the transepts are arcaded. In the chancel are elaborately carved and vaulted sedilia and piscina incorporated into the S wall when the chancel was rebuilt in the 14C. The other furnishings are of considerable interest. There are substantial remains of wall paintings, including the martyrdom of St. Edmund, on the E walls of both transepts, and substantial fragments of 14C glass in the windows of the chancel. The tower screen is 14C and the base of the Rood screen 15C. There are also medieval stalls with misericords in the chancel. The early 17C pulpit is complete with its wrought-iron hourglass stand, dated 1636. One of the most interesting features of the interior is the tiebeam across the E end of the nave, which replaces the chancel arch more usual in a building of this size.

For such a large church Cliffe has few monuments of significance.

There is a late 14C tomb-recess on the N side of the chancel and two small 17C civilian brasses.

Cobham, *St. Mary Magdalene*. Cobham is a rural oasis in the heavily industrialised NW corner of the county. It is an attractive village with a large collegiate church, a college of priests now serving as an almshouse and, at Cobham Hall, now a school, the former seat of the Lords Cobham, then the Dukes of Lennox and Richmond and latterly the Earls of Darnley, its grounds landscaped by Humphry Repton in 1790. The church itself is a fine 13C building, extended when it became collegiate, which houses the largest and most memorable collection of late medieval brasses in England.

Externally the church is relatively modest, as are so many, even of the larger medieval churches, in Kent. The college was founded in 1362 by Sir John de Cobham as a substantial chantry, consisting of a master and four priests. The college buildings were erected on the S side of the churchyard in 1370 and were adapted in 1598 to serve as 20 almshouses. Shortly after 1370 the church was enlarged with the addition of a W tower and the extension of the aisles by one bay so that they now flank the tower. New aisle windows, a clerestory to the nave and a vaulted N porch of two storeys, were added at the same time.

The interior is impressive. The nave and aisles date mostly from the late 13C. The chancel arch was reconstructed in 1860 when the church was restored by Sir Gilbert Scott. The wide chancel is the earliest part of the present church and is a noble early 13C construction. There are five tall lancets on the N and S sides and an E window of three lancets with Purbeck marble shafts. To signify the church's new collegiate status the chancel was given an exceptionally elaborate piscina and canopied sedilia in the late 14C. At the SE corner of the chancel are the remains of a spiral staircase which once led to a loft over the reredos, a very rare feature in England but occurring in several French churches. In the chancel are substantial remains of the original tiled floors.

Apart from the brasses and monuments, the fittings are less notable than the fabric and the restoration by Scott was a heavy one. However, there is a fine 13C font, an octagonal bowl on shafts, cut-down sections of medieval screens in the N and S arches of the W tower, and some remains of medieval woodwork in the stalls on the S side of the chancel. The stained glass in the E window, by Lavers & Barraud, dates from c 1863.

The brasses and monuments are outstanding, although the former fill virtually the whole of the chancel and make the high altar seem very remote from the rest of the building. Starting at the right of the E row they commemorate Joan de Cobham (early 14C), Thomas de Cobham (died 1367), John, third Lord Cobham (died 1408), the founder of the college, Margaret de Cobham (died 1398), Maude de Cobham (died 1380), Margaret de Cobham (died 1375), John, second Lord Cobham (died 1354), John Sprotte, priest (died 1498), Rauf de Cobham (died 1402), Sir Thomas Brooke (died 1529), Sir Reginald Braybrok (died 1405), Joan, Lady Cobham (died 1433), Sir Nicholas Hawberk (died 1407) and Lady Margaret Broke (died 1506). Virtually all the figures are life-size and most are canopied. The best of the 14 main brasses are those to Sir Reginald Braybrok and Sir Nicholas Hawberk, who were the two husbands of Lady Cobham. Elsewhere in the church are other brasses to three priests attached to the college: Reginald de Cobham (died 1402), William Tannere (died

1418), John Gladwyn (died 1450). To the E of the main brasses in the chancel and directly in front of the altar, further isolating it from the rest of the church, stands the large alabaster monument to Sir George Brooke, ninth Lord Cobham, erected in 1561. This and several of the brasses were damaged in the 18C when part of the chancel roof collapsed. They were repaired in 1839–40 and again in 1865–66. There are also a number of pleasing wall monuments, though greatly overwhelmed in a church which has the feel of a vast mausoleum. In the chancel there are four surviving tilting helms, two of which date from the early 15C.

Cranbrook, _St. Dunstan._ This largest and most distinguished of the quasi-urban churches of the Weald was almost wholly remodelled in the late 15C and early 16C from bequests by wealthy merchants and early industrialists, though over-restored by Ewan Christian and William Slater in the 1860s. Its one unique feature is a total immersion font, a kind of stone cupboard with a cover into which the baptismal candidate descends, situated near the S door. It was installed in 1710, in the pious though unfulfilled hope of converting the local Baptists by the Reverend John Johnson, author of 'The Unbloody Sacrifice' and one of the most learned, and in his time influential, of early 18C 'high churchmen' who remained loyal to the Anglican establishment.

Elham, _St. Mary the Virgin._ The main interest of this large medieval church, which contains work of all periods from the 12C to the 15C, is its extensive restoration by F.C. Eden in the early 20C. He retained the 17C painted texts on the nave walls, and added a mixture of modern and imported 'Classical' fittings. The sanctuary was paved in black and white marble in 1908, an organ loft installed at the W end of the nave in 1911; and other modern fittings include the sanctuary panelling in the style of Wren, wrought-iron altar rails, painted reredos, pews, screens and font cover. The imported fittings include a 17C French lectern, 15C and 16C stained glass, a 15C alabaster triptych to form a reredos in the S aisle and several paintings. The general atmosphere of the interior is extremely devotional.

Graveney, _All Saints._ This is an unusual church for Kent. Its spaciousness and generally 'unrestored' character would be much more typical in East Anglia. It stands somewhat away from the rather drab village in the middle of flat marshes between Faversham and Whitstable. The fabric is mostly 14C, but there are good fittings of many periods, including one exceptionally handsome late medieval brass.

The exterior of the church is homely as befits its setting, the walls a mixture of flints and rubble, the roofs tiled. The S porch is a mixture of stone and brick work. The tower stands at the W end of the N aisle. The interior is spacious with wide nave and aisles. The bases of the piers in the 14C nave arcades have been widened to form seats. The nave roof is contemporary with the fabric. The 12C chancel arch leads into a chancel somewhat narrower than the nave even though it was clearly remodelled in the 14C. The handsome piscina and sedilia date from the 15C.

The fittings are generally good and unobtrusive. As in some East Anglian churches, 18C box-pews have been grafted on to many of the surviving medieval benches. Across the chancel arch there is a 16C Rood screen, and there are further fragments of screens in the N aisle. The font, octagonal with alternating roses and shields, is of similar date to the Rood screen. There is a handsome late 17C pulpit on a 19C base. The church also retains, like a few others in this part of Kent (e.g. Harty and Rainham), a fine 13C parish chest. There are fragments of medieval glass in the chancel and the symbols of St. Luke and St. Mark in the E window of the N aisle. One of the surviving monuments is of more than local significance. It is a large brass with figures under canopies of John Martyn, Justice of Common Pleas (died 1436) and his wife. There are also two smaller and earlier brasses to members of the Feversham family.

Hythe, *St. Leonard.* The chancel of this otherwise fairly modest town church was ambitiously rebuilt in the 13C and raised over what was originally a processional way but later adapted to serve as a charnel house, a macabre display of quantities of skulls and bones arranged in racks and an unusual tourist attraction for at least two centuries. (Cf. Rothwell, Northamptonshire.) The interior of this chancel rises by nine steps from the crossing to the choir and a further three to the sanctuary, an enormously impressive arrangement similar to that at Wimborne Minster in Dorset. In the sanctuary is an elaborate double piscina and double sedilia, both with trefoiled openings under pointed hoods.

Ightham Mote, *Chapel.* Ightham Mote is the most substantial late medieval domestic building in Kent. It was begun by Sir Thomas Cawne between 1340 and 1374, added to in the 1470s, again in the 1520s and substantially restored in 1890–91. In 1953, then in a considerable state of decay, the house was purchased by an American businessman, Charles Henry Robinson, who refurbished it and bequeathed it to the National Trust. The house and its remarkable private chapel are open to the public on most days of the week between April and October.

The effigy of Sir Thomas Cawne, c 1373–74, in St. Peter's Parish Church, Ightham, wearing plate armour and chain mail. Sir Thomas was an early owner of Ightham Mote

The chapel is situated at first-floor level in the N range of the house. It is approached from the courtyard by its own staircase over which is a timbered bell turret. The chapel was built by the then owner of Ightham Mote, Sir Richard Clement, between 1521 and 1529, and largely rebuilt in the 1890–91 restoration. Externally it has no ecclesiastical appearance, with half-timbered frontages and large domestic windows.

Internally the chapel is divided into two roughly equal sections separated by a 16C screen. To the W of the screen was an originally unfurnished antechapel for the family servants, though this is now pewed. To the E of the screen are the original 16C returned stalls for the family and the canopied pulpit facing the stalls and entered from the W side of the screen. Behind the altar the wall, with doors leading to the chaplain's rooms and the main family rooms, has fine 16C linenfold panelling. Two E windows contain 16C German stained glass showing the Virgin and Child, St. George and St. John the Baptist.

Uniting both halves of the chapel is its remarkable wagon roof with faded paintings of royal badges, lozenges of white and green, roses and fleurs-de-lis, the castle of Castile and the arrows of Aragon. It is a rare and beautiful survival of a decorative scheme proclaiming the owner's passionate loyalty to the Tudor dynasty.

Kilndown, *Christ Church.* The church was begun in 1839 to designs by Anthony Salvin for Viscount Beresford, as a place of worship for the tenants on his estate. Externally, it is a typical small church of the period, a single-cell building, almost as broad as it is long, with lancet windows and its entrance under a W tower and spire. Internally, it was originally also typical of its period: low box-pews and on either side of the altar, a pulpit and reading-desk of almost equal height. All this was dramatically changed by the founder's stepson, Alexander Beresford Hope, one of the leading members of the Cambridge Camden Society, so that it is now one of the earliest and least altered examples of a church arranged according to ecclesiological principles.

Externally, Beresford Hope restricted himself to adding lucarnes to the spire and a parapet to disguise the low pitch of the roof. Internally, the transformation was considerable with virtually all the fittings replaced. Salvin designed a stone altar for a much refurbished sanctuary. A Rood screen, designed by R.C. Carpenter, was placed across the width of the church, with returned stalls on the chancel side. Immediately to the W of the screen high up on the S wall a new pulpit, designed by William Butterfield and modelled on the refectory pulpit at Beaulieu Abbey in Hampshire, was installed, reached by a staircase in the wall from the chancel. The lower parts of the walls were covered with red and yellow encaustic tiles and the upper parts with stencilled patterns in red, gold and blue. The box-pews were replaced by open benches. Butterfield also designed the brass lectern and two coronas for lighted candles on either side of the altar. With the exception of some of the stencilling all these fittings survive. So too do the original office books of 1843, sumptuously bound in red morocco with brass mounts.

An unusual feature is the stained glass in all the windows by Franz Eggert of Munich, specially commissioned by Beresford Hope. The E window has a Madonna and Child in the central light supported on either side by St. Peter and St. Paul. The windows on the N and S walls represent on one side the Saints of Britain and on the other the

Early Fathers of the Western Church. In the churchyard are monuments to both Viscount Beresford and his stepson.

Lullingstone, *St. Botolph.* Lullingstone is one of the earliest known sites of Christianity in England. The substantial Roman villa, fully excavated over the past 40 years, was altered in the 4C to include a chapel adorned with painted wall plaster showing Christians with their arms outstretched in prayer. Away from the villa and on the lawns of Lullingstone Castle, stands the present parish church, another family chapel much beautified by its Non-Juror patron, Percyvall Hart, who died in 1738.

The church dates mostly from the 14C and consists of a short nave and chancel with a bell turret on the W gable of the former. To this was added a 16C N chapel and 18C S porch. Most of the interior fittings are due to Hart. He added a Classical balustrade to the 16C Rood screen, handsome plaster ceilings in both nave and chancel and a black and white marble pavement in the latter. Other contemporary fittings include the open benches, pulpit, altar table and reredos and an unusual font set into a cupboard near the S porch.

There is some particularly interesting stained glass. That in the E window and the S window of the nave (the martyrdom of St. Erasmus, his entrails being extracted with a winch) is 16C. There are fragments of 14C glass in the N chapel. The two N windows in the nave contain glass of 1754 by William Peckitt of York. The N chapel contains a splendid array of monuments: three small late 15C and early 16C brasses; a canopied tomb of Sir John Peche who died in 1522; a wall monument to Sir Percyvall Hart who died in 1581; a tomb-chest for Sir George Hart who died in 1587; a hanging monument, surmounted by an obelisk, to Anne Dyke who died in 1763. The finest and most unusual monument is, appropriately, that to the church's 18C benefactor. It covers the whole of the N chapel's W wall, with Gothick arcading framed by bamboo-type shafts supporting palm fronds and a detailed inscription recording Hart's Non-Juror and Jacobite sympathies.

Maidstone, *All Saints.* This is the largest parish church in Kent and architecturally the most imposing religious building in the county after the cathedrals of Canterbury and Rochester. It was restored twice in the 19C: in the 1840s by the younger John Whichcord, who published a detailed study of its architecture, and in the 1880s by J.L. Pearson. It contains important monuments and some fittings of significance. The overall atmosphere is of civic pride, grandeur and opulence.

Externally, the church forms part of an important medieval complex of buildings on the E bank of the Medway cut off by an urban motorway from the main part of the town centre. To the N of the church stands the much repaired former palace of the Archbishops of Canterbury and to the E of this the former tithe barn now serving as a museum of carriages. It was Archbishop Courtenay who rebuilt the church in 1395–96, made it collegiate and established the college for a master and 24 chaplains, the remains of which stand S of the church. What impresses most is the breadth of the church. The nave aisles are spectacularly broad and there are aisles of about half this width to the chancel. There is a vestry with a parvise off the S chancel aisle and the tower stands over the S porch.

Internally, successive restorations, particularly Pearson's, have left their mark. The roofs have all been replaced. It was originally intended that most, if not all, the church was to have been vaulted but the intention was never carried out. The walls of the chancel are covered with paintings of saints, forming part of Pearson's refurbishment of the building. Although the building has been heavily restored, it is interesting as an example of a major church completely rebuilt within the space of a few years at the end of the 14C and beginning of the 15C.

Few pre-Victorian fittings survive. Exceptions are the magnificent late 14C sedilia in the chancel, four seats and a credence, all elaborately vaulted, and complete choirstalls, mostly with misericords, of roughly similar date. The font is unusual, an entirely medieval composition, octagonal with shields, but dating from the early 17C. Parts of the N parclose screen to the chancel are medieval, with parts added by Pearson, who designed a new Rood screen and a sumptuous reredos which fills much of the E wall. There is much Victorian stained glass though none of exceptional quality. The E window (1872) is by J.B. Capronnier, those on the S side by William Wailes and James Powell & Sons, those of the N side by Lavers & Westlake and the W window by Clayton & Bell.

The most important of the many monuments is that to John Wotton, the first master of the collegiate foundation, who died in 1417. Behind the tomb-chest on the back of the sedilia is a painting showing Wotton being presented to the Virgin Mary by the Company of Saints. Most monuments are to members of prominent local families, many of national political significance. That to Sir John Astley (died 1639), by Edward Marshall, has life-size standing figures in their shrouds. Those to Sir Charles Booth (died 1795) and Lt. Col. William Havelock (died 1848) are by Joseph Nollekens and the younger Richard Westmacott respectively.

In the early 18C an important parochial library was established in the church. In 1867 over 700 surviving volumes, including part of a 12C Bible, the other section of which is at Lambeth Palace Library, were transferred to Maidstone Museum, and thereafter in 1982 the library was placed in the care of the Kent Archives Office and a special trust is to be set up to administer it. In the 17C Maidstone was a centre of Puritan activity and many Puritans seceded from the Church of England after 1660. They worshipped in what is now the Unitarian Chapel in Market Buildings. This is a small square building of 1736 retaining its original pulpit and gallery. Similar Unitarian chapels, of 1716 and 1746 respectively, survive at Bessels Green near Sevenoaks, and Tenterden. William Hazlitt, the essayist, was born in Maidstone in 1778, his father being minister of the Unitarian Chapel at the time.

Mereworth, St. Lawrence. This is without doubt the finest 18C church in the county, despite internal alteration, and it is almost unbelievable that the architect is unknown. The former parish church was demolished and the present church built by the Earl of Westmorland in 1744–46.

Externally the church is dramatic, of the type to be found more normally in an urban than a rural setting. The E end has a large Venetian window with a lunette above. The W end has deep eaves, an elaborate steeple and a semicircular porch which gives it the appearance of being a mixture of St. Paul's, Covent Garden, St. Martin-in-the-Fields and St. Paul's, Deptford.

The interior is equally impressive. The broad nave and chancel are barrel-vaulted, the ceiling coffered. The shallow aisles have flat roofs. The columns separating the aisles from the main body of the church are painted to look like marble and support a frieze. On the W wall is a painted representation of an organ. There is some good 16C heraldic glass in the upper E window. Apart from the marble font none of the other original fittings has survived and the replacement woodwork is generally insipid but inoffensive.

The monuments from the former church have been grouped together on either side of the circular entrance vestibule below the steeple. They include a handsome canopied brass to Sir John de Mereworth who died in 1366 and a much smaller one to William Shosmyth who died in 1479. The finest monument is that to Sir Thomas Fane erected in 1639, 50 years after his death. Behind the reclining effigies are pairs of Corinthian columns, in between which are carved clouds with two gilded putti bearing a crown and palms.

New Romney, *St. Nicholas.* New Romney was a pre-Conquest planned town, once having, like Sandwich, three parish churches. The town was, however, as a result of coastal changes, in decline from the mid-13C, and today is little more than a large village. Only one church has survived and its conservative restoration in the late 1870s and early 1880s has prevented it from acquiring the over-restored grandeur of so many other large town churches.

The W parts date from the late 12C. They consist of a nave of four bays and the two westernmost bays of the original narrow aisles terminating in a W tower of five stages and the stump of a former spire. The aisles were at the same time extended along the N and S walls of this tower so that it is fully integrated into the body of the church, which is entered through a lavish W doorway as part of an elaborately arcaded 12C W front. In the early 14C a chancel of four bays, as wide as the nave, was added together with wide aisles to both the chancel and the two easternmost bays of the nave. The E end of the exterior is, as a result, most impressive, with three gables of equal height, over an E window of five lights, balanced by NE and SE windows of three lights, all preserving intact their elaborate Reticulated tracery. Internally the conservative restoration by John Oldrid Scott represents an early triumph by the Society for the Protection of Ancient Buildings. The society protested at plans to rebuild the 12C arcades which were, after an acrimonious correspondence published in the local newspapers, abandoned. The medieval fabric has been little altered and the interior has been allowed to retain its plastered roofs, uneven tiled floors set with handsome ledger stones and early 19C low box-pews. The tower screens date from 1602 and there are very handsome 18C altar rails and a chandelier dated 1745.

Postling, *St. Mary the Virgin and St. Radegund.* This small, though heavily restored, 12C church preserves on the N wall of the chancel its original dedication stone stating that it was dedicated in honour of Our Lady on the feast of St. Eusebius the Confessor, but omitting the exact year of the dedication. Very fragmentary remains of 12C wall paintings also survive.

St. Margaret-at-Cliffe, *St. Margaret of Antioch.* Kent has three important surviving 12C churches of which this is by far the largest. The other two, also in the E of the county, are Barfrestone and Brook. Barfrestone consists only of nave and chancel, the latter largely but sumptuously rebuilt in 1839–41 and preserving a remarkable display of intricate carving, especially in the S doorway and E wheel window. Brook is a little larger with a substantial W tower and is decorated internally with a well-preserved series of 13C wall paintings. St. Margaret's-at-Cliffe has both aisles and clerestory as well as a low W tower and both nave and chancel are of considerable height, length and width.

Externally what dominates is a complete series of original windows in the chancel of four bays, together with the original windows and arcading along the clerestories of the five-bay nave. On the N side this arcading is continued along the wall of the tower which is built into the body of the church and enclosed by the aisles. These originally had no windows but Ewan Christian, who restored the church in 1869, inserted windows, mostly though not wholly of a neo-Norman type. The W doorway of the tower, though much weathered, is elaborately carved. The N doorway, though less elaborate, is also contemporary.

Internally also it is the fabric that dominates. The furnishings have been entirely renewed over the last century and are generally unexciting and over-polished. The 12C chancel and tower arches are exceptionally tall though relatively simple in their decoration. The clerestory, surprisingly when contrasted with the exterior, has no decoration at all, but the piers of the nave arcades are alternately round and composite and they spring from substantial bases. These include the base of the original font, but the font itself has been replaced by one dated 1663. At the E end of the chancel there is a range of three lower windows with another above. The former have attractive glass, clearly modelled on some of the 13C glass in Canterbury Cathedral, of c 1860, but the other stained glass is much later and of poorer quality.

Speldhurst, *St. Mary the Virgin.* The church was entirely rebuilt by John Oldrid Scott in 1870–71 in an ambitious though derivative 13C style. The expensive furnishings include by far the most distinguished collection of late Victorian stained glass in the county. In the chancel the E and SW windows are by Sir Edward Burne-Jones, the NE and SE windows by Clayton & Bell. All the windows in the nave and N aisle are by Burne-Jones or William Morris, apart from the W window which is by C.E. Kempe. This complete glazing scheme was begun in 1873 and completed in 1905.

Stelling, *St. Mary the Virgin.* The interior of this small 13C–14C church was completely remodelled in c 1790, and it is now a rare surviving example of an Anglican T-plan interior, not dissimilar from Presbyterian ones in Scotland, in which most of the contemporary fittings survive. The two-bay arcade between nave and S aisle was demolished and replaced by a single broad arch. The aisle was then turned into a transept with central passageway from the S porch and box-pews on either side facing N. A gallery for schoolchildren runs along the S wall of the aisle. The three-decker pulpit, facing this gallery, is in the middle of the N wall of the nave with box-pews on either side from which it is also clearly visible.

Stone-next-Dartford, *St. Mary the Virgin.* The church is an outstanding example of an important medieval fabric enhanced by an exemplary Victorian restoration. The medieval work shows remarkable similarity to that in the choir chapels at Westminster Abbey and it is generally accepted that the church was built by the

Westminster masons and that some of the carving was done at Westminster and sent down to Stone already made up. The Victorian restoration was undertaken in 1859–60 by G.E. Street and there is a detailed account of the work carried out, by the architect himself, in both 'The Ecclesiologist' and 'Archaeologia Cantiana'.

The exterior is unremarkable and is entirely dominated by its unimpressive setting between a drab housing estate and a cement quarry. The nave has lean-to aisles all covered by the same steeply-sloping roof. The chancel is higher than the nave, even though both were built at the same time in the 13C. In the 14C a short tower was added to the nave and the aisles extended one bay W against its N and S sides.

Inside, the contrast is amazing. A humble exterior hides an interior of exceptional quality. The short nave of three bays has slender arcades and a narrow arch into the chancel. The chancel, almost as long as the nave but unaisled, is vaulted, the roof supported on Purbeck marble shafts. The walls are enriched with detailed and delicate internal arcading at their lower level, this representing the original work of the 13C. The upper parts of the chancel, the earlier vault of which was taken down in the 17C, were reconstructed by Street but clearly based on the original design after meticulous examination of the surviving evidence.

Had he wished, Street could have refurnished the church so that the fittings would have obscured and detracted from the purity of the fabric. Very wisely he chose restraint and his fittings are decent but simple. The only extravagant piece is the pulpit of carved stone, marble and alabaster by Thomas Earp. Apart from the E window of the N aisle, which is by William Wailes, all the stained glass was designed by Street to complement the building and is very typical of the type of unadventurous medievalist workmanship he favoured. It does, however, succeed in its aim; Stone is a church in which the fabric dominates throughout. There are substantial traces of 13C wall paintings in the N aisle, including a vibrant representation of the martyrdom of St. Thomas of Canterbury. The only monuments of note are a small brass to John Lumbarde, priest, who died in 1408 and the tomb-chest of Sir John Wiltshire, in the chantry chapel at the E end of the N aisle, built according to the instructions given in his will of 1526–27.

Tudeley, *All Saints.* The church was rebuilt in 1765, enlarged in 1876 and internally remodelled in 1967 by Robert Potter. Part of this remodelling included the insertion of a new E window to the memory of Sarah d'Avigdor-Goldsmid, drowned in a sailing accident at the age of 21. Marc Chagall was commissioned to design this window and was so pleased with the church that he offered to make glass for all its other windows and the scheme was completed in 1985. Tudeley is now one of only two churches in the world entirely lit by Chagall's brilliantly coloured glass. The E window recaptures the sailing accident with the figure of Christ suspended over the turmoil of the sea; all the other windows are entirely abstract in design though including the flora and fauna for which Chagall is famous. The windows are described in detail in 'Country Life', 6 March, 1986.

Tunbridge Wells, *King Charles the Martyr.* Tunbridge Wells became a fashionable watering place in the early 17C, but no place of worship was established there until a chapel was begun in 1676 and twice extended between then and 1690. The resulting building was virtually square and to this Ewan Christian added a short chancel in his conservative restoration of 1882. The original lists of subscribers to the chapel, mostly visitors taking the waters, are framed on the staircases to the N and S galleries.

The exterior of the chapel is of decidedly simple and domestic brickwork with a cupola on the SE gable. The interior is dominated by its handsome plaster ceiling. That over the SE part of the church, the original building, was designed and executed by John Wetherel, with a series of low circular domes, outlined by wreaths of fruit and the interspaces filled with crossed palms and putti heads. The NE extension was also designed by Wetherel but executed by Henry Doogood. Doogood then designed and executed the whole of the W ceiling, basically the same composition but with greater depth of style. Apart from the galleries and their seating, all the furnishings have been renewed but are generally in character with the original building. The present reredos is made up from 17C woodwork from the demolished Wren church of St. Antholin in the City of London, with the Creed and Lord's Prayer in gilded frames.

Westwell, *St. Mary the Virgin.* This complete 13C church has a remarkably handsome vaulted chancel entered from the nave through a tripartite stone screen, reaching right to the roof. The central lancet of the E window contains a complete Jesse Tree, the top half of which is contemporary with the fabric, the bottom half skilfully reconstructed in 1960 from remaining fragments. The piscina and triple sedilia are 14C insertions. Compared with the elaborate structure of the chancel, the nave, aisles and their E chapels are much more simple with the exception of the deeply moulded tower arch.

LONDON

Until the 17C, London was more or less what we now call 'the City'. This was the walled city of Roman times and of the Middle Ages. In recent years, archaeology has suggested that London in the 7C and 8C, the *Lundenwic* of early documents, lay outside the walled city on the W, in the vicinity of the modern Covent Garden. A move within the walls evidently came under King Alfred. Further W, Westminster Abbey existed from at least King Offa's time, the later 8C, and gradually the land between Westminster and the City was built on. The only suburb to the S was Southwark, at the southern end of London Bridge, which was the sole bridge across the Thames in London until as late as 1750. The river was for long a boundary. The Old English Kingdom of Essex, which encompassed the walled city of London and which was co-terminous with the original Diocese of London, lay entirely N of the river. The later County of Essex began E of the River Lea. To the W lay Middlesex, which surrounded (but did not include) the City of London. To the S, down to 1889 the County of Surrey ran up to the Thames as far E as Rotherhithe. The next place E, Deptford, lay in Kent. The County of London was formed in 1889. It was much enlarged in 1965, when its ruling body, the London County Council, became the Greater London Council.

For churches, therefore, the City *was* London until quite recent centuries. The rest, whether N or S of the river, encompasses either 17C to 20C churches of note, or older churches within historic villages which have been absorbed into the metropolis.

St. Mary Abchurch in the City of London, built by Sir Christopher Wren in 1681–86, one of the finest surviving Wren interiors, with a reredos by Grinling Gibbons

THE CITY OF LONDON

The archaeologists have concluded that London was founded by the Romans in about the year 50. Just over a decade later, Tacitus was able to refer to the new Londinium in his 'Annals' as 'full of merchants and famous for its commerce'. In the 8C, subsequent to the supersession of Roman Britain by the English kingdoms, St. Bede described London as 'the trading place of many nations coming by land and sea'. Later still, in the 12C, William Fitzstephen spoke of London in expansive terms as a fit setting for his hero, St. Thomas of Canterbury. All these comments reflect the fact that London has always been the richest and most important city in England. In the days of Roman Britain and for much of English history, it has also been an important seat of civil government. Its Christian history has therefore mirrored these circumstances. A Bishop of London called Restitutus attended the Council of Arles as early as 314. No evidence for a Christian church of Roman times has been found in the City, although in the 4C one or more churches almost certainly existed. Tradition puts forward the church of St. Peter-upon-Cornhill, which stands on part of the site of Londinium's basilica, but archaeology alone could confirm the story.

Over 100 parish churches were to stand in London by the end of the 12C, of which the vast majority stood within the city walls. In a number of cases, archaeology has shown that the first church on a site was built in the 12C itself. There is evidence of earlier foundation for relatively few City churches. All Hallows' by the Tower possesses a pre-Conquest archway, which might derive from the late 7C, when St. Erkenwald was Bishop of London, for the church was associated with Barking Abbey, which St. Erkenwald had founded. Excavations have shown that St. Alban's, Wood Street could indeed be a foundation by King Offa in the late 8C, as tradition claims. Documents speak of a handful of other churches before the Conquest. But the evidence in general is that most City churches were founded in Norman and early Plantagenet times, when the prosperity of London permitted the building of so many, but before ecclesiastical authority was strong enough to mould the parochial system to its own liking. The minute parochial divisions of early medieval London speak of the proprietory church, the church in private ownership, and not of episcopal government.

Of the 100 or more medieval parish churches, 37 still exist in Anglican use. Two are in non-Anglican use. In addition, there is the Temple Church, which is Anglican but non-parochial; the Dutch Church in Austin Friars; the City Temple, a United Reformed Church; and the chapel of the Mercers' Company in Ironmonger Lane. Most of these churches are stamped with the effects of the Great Fire of 1666 and, to a lesser extent, with the effects of the Second World War. No fewer than 87 churches were destroyed in the Great Fire. Untold riches vanished for ever in 1666. St. Helen's, Bishopsgate, one of the survivors, redolent of medieval piety and merchant wealth, provides a glimpse of what once existed throughout the City. The compensation for the losses of 1666 was that Sir Christopher Wren was commissioned to rebuild no fewer than 51 parish churches. Wren's works form the principal glory of the City churches today. Though reduced in number by 19C and early 20C demolitions, and by wartime destruction, and despite being overshadowed by modern and usually unsympathetic commercial buildings, they nevertheless remain ubiquitous and noticeable, precious reminders of that 18C London which Canaletto painted, a panorama of Classical steeples surrounding the great dome of St. Paul's Cathedral.

The population of the City began to fall in the early 19C, even before the coming of the railways. Churches were demolished as their parishioners departed and as commercial pressure to acquire their sites increased. The first such loss occurred as far back as 1781, when St. Christopher-le-Stocks was demolished to make way for an extension to the Bank of England. Most of the losses occurred in the later 19C. Towers were occasionally allowed to remain when these churches were demolished. Their fittings, however, were almost always saved and their availability has allowed postwar restorations to use many authentic furnishings.

The Second World War was severe, but not so catastrophic as the Great Fire. Of the churches which were completely gutted, all but eight have been restored to use. Ruins survive of two of the eight (St. Dunstan's-in-the-East and Christ Church, Newgate Street); a tower survives from a third (St. Augustine's, Watling Street); while a fourth (St. Mary Aldermanbury) has been rebuilt in its entirety, not in London but in Fulton, Missouri, U.S.A., where Sir Winston Churchill gave his 'Iron Curtain' speech in 1946. In the postwar years, fewer churches in the City have been allowed their own clergy. Two buildings have been handed over to German Lutherans and Scotch Presbyterians. Many of the rest have been made 'Guild Churches', that is, extraparochial churches which undertake special work such as running the Missions to Seamen at St. Michael's, Paternoster Royal.

Whereas the City's pre-Conquest remains are limited to those at All Hallows' by the Tower, Norman survivals are more substantial. The principal building is the church of St. Bartholomew the Great, which comprises the choir and crossing of the former priory church, partly rebuilt in the 19C and 20C but still preserving the authentic air of a 12C monastic building. Less well-known is St. Mary-le-Bow's crypt, whose arches or bows appear to have given the church its 'surname'. Finally, there is the Temple Church, one of England's four surviving 'round churches', which were built in imitation of the Holy Sepulchre Church in Jerusalem. It was consecrated in 1185. Its circular nave and W doorway are late Norman, but the church has some early Gothic elements too. The aisled chancel is of the 13C, with Purbeck marble piers, moulded capitals, a quadripartite rib-vault and graduated lancet windows. This work is exceptional in the City for its date.

The Gothic centuries generally have left little to discuss because of the Great Fire. The survivors of that catastrophe lie in the E and NE of the City. Most of what remains is very late medieval. St. Giles', Cripplegate and St. Andrew Undershaft are both fairly large 16C buildings, the latter incorporating a 15C tower. 15C too is the tower of St. Sepulchre's, foursquare and substantial, but much renewed. St. Olave's in Hart Street and St. Helen's, Bishopsgate are both predominantly 15C, but each offers earlier features. St. Olave's has a two-bay, rib-vaulted 13C crypt. St. Helen's has work of the 13C (blocked lancets and a N doorway) and the 14C (one chancel arch and a SE chapel). St. Ethelburga's, Bishopsgate has a 14C W doorway and a substantially 14C interior. It is also the only surviving representative of the numerous small churches in medieval London.

The early 17C, that is the 17C before Wren, has left one building which is of great interest as a mixture of Gothic and Classical styles, St. Katharine Cree Church in Leadenhall Street. Classical arcades were built alongside Gothic vaults and square-headed Gothic windows. Classical design before the Great Fire also appears in a doorway at St. Helen's (1633) and a gateway at St. Olave's (1658).

Wren's churches have been accorded many books to themselves. They form a very considerable group, built within about 50 years and many of them of the greatest individual interest. On the whole, Wren's churches follow medieval precedent rather more than one might expect. There were centralising plans, but the same churches can often be seen to have a longitudinal emphasis too. It is well-known that Wren considered his churches to be 'fitted for auditories'—that is, arranged for the hearing of the Word—but it was equally the case that the most sumptuous fitting in each was the reredos at the E end, standing behind, and giving honour to, the communion table. The fittings of Wren's churches often formed magnificent ensembles. It might be suggested that a typical Wren church had three visual levels. At ground level there was a grouping of darkly stained woodwork, comprising box-pews, the panelled bases of columns, a reredos, a pulpit with carved decorations and an ample tester, and doorcases. Occasionally there would be a screen (as at St. Peter-upon-Cornhill and St. Margaret's, Lothbury). The reredos would be divided into three; the centre would bear two panels of the Ten Commandments; and flanking them would be the Creed and the Lord's Prayer. Above all this woodwork would come a contrasting white level: white-painted columns and white-painted walls, pierced by round-headed, clear-glass windows with cobweb ironwork. No Classical Wren church was intended to have stained glass. Finally, there came a more colourful ceiling level, which might be a coffered or painted dome, a flat ceiling enriched by plasterwork with gilding, or a vault with similar enrichment. A Wren interior was most easily maltreated by moving or 'cutting down' the box-pews and by introducing stained glass. Both maltreatments were common in the 19C.

Of Wren's surviving churches, two are domed. The dome of St. Mary Abchurch surmounts virtually the entire interior and was elaborately painted in the early 18C; whereas the dome of St. Stephen's, Walbrook surmounts a Latin cross and is coffered. St. Mary at Hill, St. Anne and St. Agnes, and St. Martin's, Ludgate also have centralising plans, in which four columns are arranged within a roughly square interior to form a Greek cross. St. Sepulchre's, St. Andrew's at Holborn Circus and St. Magnus' are longitudinal churches in Classical dress. A few have a rectangular nave with only one aisle, such as St. Lawrence Jewry, St. Margaret Pattens and St. Margaret's, Lothbury. Wren always fitted his churches into the sites provided, however awkwardly shaped they might be. St. Michael's, Paternoster Royal and St. Nicholas Cole Abbey have structurally undivided interiors. The church of St. Mary Aldermary was designed by Wren in Gothic style, with a fan-vault.

Wren's steeples are justly famed for their individual qualities and for their collective contribution to London's skyline. The treatment he accorded each one was partly a matter of site and partly a matter of money. So the church of St. Clement Eastcheap was given the plainest of low towers, without a steeple, whereas St. Mary-le-Bow, an important church in Cheapside, one of the City's principal streets, received the most magnificent steeple of all. As a general rule,

Wren's towers have a belfry stage with pairs of pilasters on either side of a single, round-headed, louvred opening. The steeple proper varies greatly. There are 'medieval' spires (St. Margaret Pattens); square-cut open lanterns (St. Stephen's, Walbrook; St. James's, Garlickhythe; St. Michael's, Paternoster Royal); the 'wedding cake' of St. Bride's; the Baroque triangle with concave and convex stages at St. Vedast's (which one writer in 1989 has in fact re-attributed to Nicholas Hawksmoor); a Gothic crown at St. Dunstan's-in-the-East; and the foils to St. Paul's Cathedral which Wren gave St. Martin's, Ludgate and St. Augustine's, Watling Street.

A word needs to be said about Nicholas Hawksmoor in the early 18C. His most important churches were built in London outside the City, but within it he was responsible for two contrasting works. He designed a new Gothic tower for St. Michael's, Cornhill, a curiously unnoticed tower despite its height. The other work, the entire rebuilding of St. Mary Woolnoth in 1716–27, is far more important. It is monumental and strong, with rustication everywhere, elaborate and impressive niches in the otherwise blank N wall and a heavy, somewhat solemn interior.

The 18C in general looms unexpectedly large in the City's church building history. A number of churches which were spared in the Great Fire, on the City's N and E fringes, were rebuilt, mainly between c 1725 and c 1790. James Gold or Gould rebuilt St. Botolph's, Bishopsgate, in 1725–28; George Dance the Elder designed the new church of St. Botolph at Aldgate (1741–44); his son, the younger George, designed All Hallows', London Wall (1765–67); and Nathaniel Wright designed the new St. Botolph's, Aldersgate, in 1789–91. Further 18C churches were subsequently demolished in the late 19C and early 20C. Of all these 18C churches, All Hallows' in London Wall is easily the most distinguished. It has a lightness of design which stands out amongst the generally rather heavy 18C churches in and around the City.

New churches were very few indeed in the 19C City. Only one is of interest today—St. Dunstan's-in-the-West, by John Shaw, 1831–33. St. Dunstan's is an octagonal building which is surmounted by a substantial lantern tower on the lines of the medieval example at All Saints', Pavement, York. Later 19C work is entirely a matter of restoration and remodelling. Gothicising of Wren's work can be found at St. Michael's, Cornhill, where Sir Gilbert Scott introduced new window tracery, stained glass, a new Gothic porch and a marble reredos (in 1858–60). Most restorations, however, did not introduce a Gothic character so much as alter and detract from the existing Wren interior. The 'cutting down' of box-pews was widespread. This often had the effect of making the panelled bases of Wren's columns look absurdly high. Elsewhere, the testers of pulpits were quite needlessly removed. Stained glass was introduced into windows which were intended to be clear. In a few cases, curiously, some of Wren's churches were unexpectedly enriched through the demolition of other buildings and the transfer of their fittings.

The process of refitting continued in the early 20C. At St. Ethelburga's, Bishopsgate, Sir Ninian Comper introduced in 1912–14 a new chancel and parclose screens, and a W gallery, all in his attractive and detailed late Gothic style. In the 1920s, in St. Magnus' by London Bridge, Martin Travers turned Wren's interior into a lavish Baroque setting for the Anglo-Catholicism of the time. The reredos was heightened, additional altars were provided, and statues and candlestands were introduced. The result is a more elaborate (and darker) interior than Wren's, but one which is still entirely sympathetic to his architecture.

The destruction of the Second World War has prompted virtually all the postwar work. Most churches required some repair; a fair number required substantial restoration or rebuilding. Wren's churches have generally been restored in a simplified form, a more tepid Classicism than the original. Exteriors have remained the same, but interiors have often been given woodwork which is very lightly stained, giving a markedly different impression from the densely-packed, dark woodwork of the past. St. Andrew-by-the-Wardrobe (restored by Marshall Sisson) is an example. Two major churches, St. Bride's and St. Mary-le-Bow, were restored with much colour and re-arrangement. Both are successful and agreeable as new interiors but not as restorations of the old. St. Bride's was made collegiate in its seating plan, as was St. Vedast's, where the restorer, S.E. Dykes Bower, used genuine furnishings of Wren's time to refit the church. He also added to St. Vedast's a charming cloister N of the church and a Rectory of restrained Classical design. One blot on postwar restoration has often been the introduction of the most ghastly stained glass. Apart from the fact that Wren's churches were not intended to have any stained glass, the jagged style and obscure depiction of subjects in so much glass of the 1950s and 1960s were unfortunate, to say the least. An exception is the series of windows by Christopher Webb in St. Lawrence Jewry which is (unusually) a complete series for the church and is attractive. One new postwar church building deserves to be mentioned. The Dutch Church in Austin Friars was entirely rebuilt by Arthur Bailey in 1950–57. It has an aisleless, somewhat bare interior. It replaced the nave of a 14C friars' church, which the Dutch had received in 1550.

Of the fittings, the best collections from Wren's time are now in St. Margaret's, Lothbury, St. Magnus', St. Mary Abchurch, and St. Mary at Hill. Those at St. Magnus' owe as much to Martin Travers as to Wren, and those of St. Mary at Hill to W. Gibbs Rogers, a highly commendable 19C craftsman. St. Mary at Hill arguably has the most authentic Wren interior of those which are left. A very notable font cover is the one by Grinling Gibbons at All Hallows' by the Tower. His reredos at St. Mary Abchurch is also very notable. In practically all the City churches there are sword-rests, reflecting the days when the City's rich merchants lived there. (Cf. Norwich and York.) Almost all of them are of metal, with a holder for the sword and an heraldic back-piece. There are no fewer than six at St. Mary at Hill. St. Helen's, Bishopsgate and St. Mary Aldermary have wooden examples. An unexpected fitting is the Romanian icon screen in St. Dunstan's-in-the-West, introduced there in the 20C in connection with Romanian Orthodox worship. Apart from postwar work discussed above, stained glass is a 19C and early 20C matter. The largest collection is at St. Helen's, Bishopsgate. St. Michael's, Corn-hill, has good early Clayton & Bell glass.

Monuments divide into two broad groups: the surviving pre-Fire examples, which exist in relatively few churches, and the great number of commemorative wall tablets, usually quite modest, which date from between the late 17C and the early 19C. The earliest collection of monuments is in the Temple Church, comprising Purbeck marble effigies from the 12C and 13C of a number of secular and ecclesiastical worthies of the day. They were damaged in the Second World War and have been restored. The grandest collection of medieval monuments, however, is in St. Helen's, Bishopsgate (see gazetteer). St. Helen's also has a good collection of brasses, which only All Hallows' by the Tower can match. A famous Elizabethan, Sir Nicholas Throckmorton (died 1571), has a monument in St. Katharine Cree. In St. Bartholomew the Great there is the 15C monument to the 12C founder, Rahere: a conventional 15C tomb-chest with quatrefoils, with an effigy and a canopy over. St. Bartholomew's also has a monument to Sir Walter Mildmay, the founder of Emmanuel College, Cambridge, and a number of further 16C and 17C monuments of some interest. Two famous 17C individuals are commemorated in City churches: John Stow, the historian of London (died 1605), whose frontal bust is placed in St. Andrew Undershaft; and Samuel Pepys (died 1703), whose wife's bust looks down from the N arcade of St. Olave's to where his Navy pew used to be and near which his own 19C tablet is placed. The 18C and 19C offer only rather minor wall tablets. These have continued to some extent in the 20C. All Hallows' by the Tower has one larger 20C monument: a tomb-chest with effigy to Alfred Henry Forster, by Cecil Thomas.

Non-Anglican churches are practically absent today. Only the City Temple, a United Reformed Church, stands to recall the City's Free Church tradition. It is a 19C Classical work (by H.F. Lockwood, 1873–74), with a new postwar interior by Seely & Paget. In the 19C, Welsh Anglicans were given St. Benet's, Paul's Wharf, and in the 20C the church of St. Anne and St. Agnes has been used by German Lutherans, and the church of St. Nicholas, Cole Abbey by Scotch Presbyterians.

The historical associations of the City churches are legion, but showing a concentration between the 16C and 18C. Earlier associations of importance are few. King Offa was the founder of St. Alban's, Wood Street, according to Matthew Paris. St. Thomas Becket was baptised in St. Mary Colechurch and was once the priest of St. Mary at Hill. Henry Yevele, the famous 14C architect, was a worshipper at St. Magnus' and was buried there in 1400. A particularly notable medieval association is that of Richard Whittington with St. Michael's, Paternoster Royal: he rebuilt the church in the early 15C, founded a college of priests there, and was buried in it in 1423. Many associations have already been mentioned under monuments: those of Sir John Crosby and Sir Thomas Gresham at St. Helen's, Stow at St. Andrew Undershaft and Pepys at St. Olave's, Hart Street. In addition, Judge Jeffreys is connected with St. Mary Aldermanbury, Sir John Vanbrugh with St. Stephen's, Walbrook, John Milton with St. Giles' (burial in 1674), and William Hogarth with St. Bartholomew the Great (baptism in 1697). A whole host of 17C and 18C literary figures clustered around St. Bride's. Captain John Smith, the 17C pioneer of Virginia, had connections with both St. Mary-le-Bow and St. Sepulchre's. Also of American interest are the baptism of William Penn at All Hallows' by the Tower in 1644 and the marriage there of John Quincy Adams, the sixth President of the USA, in 1797. Benjamin Disraeli, the 19C statesman, was baptised in St. Andrew's, Holborn, in 1817. From 1892 to 1926, the founder of the Church Army, Prebendary Wilson Carlisle, served as the Rector of St. Mary at Hill. St. Sepulchre's has fostered close musical associations in the 20C; the ashes of Sir Henry Wood have rested there since 1944.

If their significant historical associations tend to be late in date, the City churches do have one element of high antiquity: their 'surnames'. These additional names, to distinguish churches of the same dedication, include a number of founders or early benefactors. There are Wulfnoth (St. Mary Woolnoth), Haakon (St. Nicholas Acon), and Orgar the deacon from the 12C at St. Martin Orgar, among others. The Eastcheap of St. Clement Eastcheap recalls the E market of the City, as Cheapside or Westcheap was the W market. St. Andrew by the Wardrobe is named after a medieval department of state, the King's Wardrobe. The names of the lost City gates nearly all survive in church 'surnames'. Of the dedications themselves, a rarity is the one to St. Ethelburga, who was the sister of St. Erkenwald, a late 7C Bishop of London. St. Olav or Olave, the 11C martyr-king of Norway, who is now represented by the church in Hart Street but once had up to five churches to his name in the City, attests to the Scandinavians in 11C and 12C London. St. Magnus, whom one may think of as the Viking Earl of Orkney, is probably an early Roman martyr, for the church stood long before the time of the Viking Earl. St. Bride or Bridget of Kildare, a 6C Irish saint, is represented in London almost certainly because Scandinavians from the W coast of Ireland brought her to London in late pre-Conquest times (cf. Bridekirk in Cumberland).

All Hallows by the Tower, Byward Street, EC3. The present church is substantially a rebuilding between 1948 and 1957 to the designs of Lord Mottistone and Paul Paget, after bombing in 1940. The tower, N and S walls, crypts and many fittings survived destruction and contribute notably to the church's character and interest. Many periods of art and architecture are thus represented, possibly from as far back as the earliest century of English Christianity, for All Hallows' possesses, uniquely for a church in London, traces of an aisleless church of perhaps the 7C, including an archway built of Roman bonding tiles. These remains survive from a church which apparently belonged from the beginning to Barking Abbey, whose founder was St. Erkenwald, Bishop of London from 675 to 693. Barking Abbey held the patronage until the Reformation and hence the church's ancient alternative name of All Hallows' Barking.

The church stands conspicuously where Byward Street meets Eastcheap. Its exterior is notable for its copper-covered spire at the W end, which was built to Lord Mottistone's design. The spire surmounts a brick tower, which is of rare Cromwellian date (1658–59, by Samuel Twyne) and from which Samuel Pepys, a resident of nearby Seething Lane, watched the Great Fire of 1666 ('became afeard to stay there long and down again as fast as I could'). At the E end of the church is a spacious garden. Entering by the N porch of 1884–95, one finds an interior of Gothic style, comprising the surviving, unplastered N and S walls of 14C and later date, and the postwar nave arcades of Painswick stone. The roofs are of reinforced concrete but are styled to blend with the Gothic stone fabric. There is no structural division between nave and sanctuary. The communion table, protected by postwar brass rails of 18C style, stands before an altar mural of the Last Supper by Brian Thomas. This splendid painting is at a very low level and it is somewhat crushed by the enormous postwar E window in the Perpendicular style, which is filled with clear glass. It has been said that the light admitted by this window is an advantage to the interior, but such a dominating window in a Gothic interior ought to contain stained glass. It would transform the atmosphere. The church possesses heraldic glass in the aisle windows by Reginald Bell and Michael Farrar Bell, and a baptistery window by Keith New. The glass of the S aisle reflects its role as a mariners' chapel.

The pulpit is of the age of Wren and comes from the demolished church of St. Swithin, London Stone. The benches in the nave have well-carved armorial ends which record their donors. More good craftsmanship in wood is to be seen in the internal doors at the W end and in the organ case above. A Restoration coat of arms is affixed to the organ gallery. Under the nave arcades stand the sword-rests of three parishioners who served as Lord Mayor in the 18C. The baptistery in the SE corner contains a famous limewood font cover of 1682 by Grinling Gibbons. The design is of a flat, circular tray with three putti supporting fruit and flowers, surmounted by a dove. Monuments include 17 brasses which date from 1389 to 1651; see a Flemish brass of c 1533 to Andrew Evyngar and his wife Ellyn. There is an effigy of Alfred Henry Forster of 1919 by Cecil Thomas, which serves as a memorial of the First World War, and on the nearby tomb of Alderman John Croke of 1477 stands another product of the Great War, the Toc H Lamp of Maintenance, which was made by the Bromsgrove Guild. 'Toc H' was the signallers' code for Talbot House, a wartime house of ministry near Ypres which was set up by the Reverend P.B. Clayton, who became Vicar of All Hallows' in 1922. The crypt has a 14C ribbed barrel-vault. Its altar, installed in 1925, came from the Crusaders' castle of Athlit. The crypt now contains a columbarium or funerary chapel. There are also substantial fragments of two 11C crosses, which presumably once stood in the churchyard.

In this church were baptised Lancelot Andrewes (1555), who became a saintly Bishop of Winchester (he called the church his 'nursing mother' in the Faith), and William Penn (1644), the founder of Pennsylvania. The church's proximity to the Tower led to its use as a place of burial for those who were executed nearby. The remains of John, Cardinal Fisher (1535), the Tudor poet the Earl of Surrey (1547), and of William Laud, Archbishop of Canterbury (1645), were buried here prior to translation elsewhere.

All Hallows, London Wall, EC2. The present church is a rebuilding of 1765–67 to the designs of George Dance the Younger (1741–1825), who designed the church at the age of 24 soon after returning from six years of study in Italy. It is a type of church which is otherwise lacking in the City of London. It is not a medieval survivor, nor a product of the Age of Wren; it is stamped neither by Victorian restoration nor by postwar reconstruction. Amongst churches of its own Georgian Age, it presents an unusual lightness of design, in the manner of Adam, which contrasts with the relatively monumental 18C churches which stand in and around the City. Dance's church escaped drastic 19C remodellings. Sir Arthur Blomfield undertook alterations in 1891–98, but the character of the original remained dominant even if the completeness of the Georgian interior was lost. The church was damaged in 1941 and was restored in 1960–62 by David Nye, preparatory to the arrival of the Council for the Care of Churches from Fulham Palace. The nave was used for exhibitions for some years. In 1975, however, the Council's library was moved into the nave from the adjoining offices.

The church has always stood against London's Roman and medieval wall. The semicircular shape of the N vestry reflects the plan of one of the wall's bastions. The street in which All Hallows' stands was very narrow until 20 years ago, when it became a dual carriageway where it passes the church. The stone-built W tower faces a small churchyard. A flight of steps leads up from the churchyard to a Tuscan doorway at the foot of the tower, which stands forward from the body of the church. The tower is of four unequal stages, comprising porch, ringing chamber, belfry and cupola. The belfry stage is plain in contrast to the thoughtful cupola. The external cornice is carried round the tower between the ringing chamber and the belfry. The S side of the brick-built body of the church, which is the only other part of the exterior which is easily visible, is remarkably plain. There are no nave windows proper, but three large, semicircular lunettes at clerestory level. The E end, which is apsidal, abuts turn-of-the-century parochial buildings which now serve as offices for the Council for the Care of Churches.

After the plain exterior, the interior is remarkable. It comprises an aisleless, barrel-vaulted nave, W gallery and coffered apse. There is no structural division between nave and chancel; the latter, which is still arranged for worship, is divided from the former by a low wooden screen of 1962. Fluted Ionic columns stand against the N and S walls. They support no cornice but there is a light frieze which encircles the church. The deep splays in the vault which are formed by the semicircular windows above the frieze give the impression of arcades resting on the Ionic columns. The vault has shallow coffering.

The apse contains a large painting by Nathaniel Dance, the architect's brother, after Pietro da Cortona. It represents Ananias restoring sight to St. Paul after the latter's conversion. The plain pulpit on the N side, the remnant of a former three-decker, may be entered only from outside the body of the church. A few Classical monuments are placed on the walls. The church's medieval predecessor was famous for its anchorites, of whom we particularly remember Simon the Anker for his authorship of 'The Fruyte of Redempcyon' in 1513. From 1890 to 1900 the Rector was Samuel John Stone, who wrote 'The Church's One Foundation' and who began a successful ministry to those City workers who arrived early each day on the cheap trains.

(Donald Findlay, 'All Hallows London Wall: A History and Description' (1985).)

St. Andrew Undershaft, St. Mary Axe, off Leadenhall Street, EC3. The church, which was built in 1520–32, is chiefly famous for the monument, in the NE corner, to John Stow (1525–1605). He was the author of 'The Survey of London' (1598), which was the first substantial historical work on the city. The alabaster monument is attributed to Nicholas Johnson. It shows a venerable figure in a ruff, sitting at a table and writing in a book, placed centrally in a Classical frame. Stow holds a real quill pen in his right hand. Each year, by arrangement of the London and Middlesex Archaeological Society, a City dignitary (until 1986, the Lord Mayor) changes the quill in a service of commemoration. Above the figure is the inscription: 'AVT SCRIBENDA AGERE/AVT LEGENDA SCRIBERE' (fortunate is he who is able to do things worth writing about or to write things worth reading about). The arms on top are those of the Merchant Taylors' Company, to which Stow belonged. A railing survives around the base.

St. Bartholomew the Great, West Smithfield, EC1. The church is very rare in London in being both monastic and substantially Norman. The building is the E portion of an Augustinian priory church which was founded by Rahere, a Prebendary of St. Paul's and courtier of King Henry I, in or possibly before 1123. At the Dissolution, the priory church was much reduced in size and was made parochial; but even then parts of it were turned over to unpalatable secular uses, until they were recovered in the late 19C and early 20C, and restored, most notably by Sir Aston Webb. The decidedly heavy architecture of the interior and its darkness give the building an atmosphere of antiquity and grandeur which no other City church can match.

The church is sited just beyond the hospital whose dedication it shares and which was also part of Rahere's 12C foundation. Only a 13C gateway, surmounted by a half-timbered building of 1595, is seen from West Smithfield. The statue of Rahere, placed high up, was given by Sir Aston Webb in 1917. Beyond is a fairly spacious churchyard, where once the medieval nave stood. The pathway through the churchyard follows the line of the demolished S nave aisle. It leads to a two-storey porch of 1893 by Webb, which stands against a modest 17C brick-built tower of three unequal stages, with restored window tracery and battlements and surmounted by a diminutive cupola and gilded vane. To the right is the E walk of the canons' cloister, largely rebuilt. To the left, the churchyard continues round the N side of the church.

Entering through the SW porch, the 12C entrance to the cloister is immediately on the right. The church proper comprises an apsidal choir, crossing, one bay of the medieval nave, N and S transepts, N and S choir aisles which join round the apse to form an ambulatory, and a Lady chapel at the extreme E end. The choir is massive and ponderous. Circular Norman piers support unmoulded arches which possess an outer ring of billet carving. Above is a Norman triforium, comprising four arched openings to each bay below, each opening formed by three scalloped columns under a blind arch. In the clerestory the architecture lightens. The two-light clerestory windows are of the 14C. At the E end they are almost continuous and admit the greater part of the church's light. The apse is a 19C rebuilding to the original plan; it had been straightened in the early 15C. The Lady chapel was completed in 1336, but its present fabric is substantially of the 19C. The E wall, windowless and with five empty niches for statues, is by Webb. The N and S transepts are largely of 19C date. The crossing is of interest because its E and W arches are round, but its N and S arches are pointed: an early example of the 12C transition from Norman to Gothic. On the S side of the choir, one bay at triforium level is occupied by an oriel window, which was inserted by William Bolton (Prior, 1506–32) in c 1517. It has one cusped light to each side and three to the front, all divided by a transom, with carving beneath. The central panel shows the Prior's rebus, a crossbow bolt through a tun or barrel.

The seating is arranged in collegiate fashion. Choirstalls are placed at the present W end, immediately in front of a screen with gallery above, in which the organ is housed. The screen was built in 1889. The floor of the sanctuary is of mosaic and marble. The high altar is of 1950 by Seely & Paget; the cross and candlesticks are by Omar Ramsden. On the N side of the sanctuary is the tomb of Rahere: *'Hic iacet Raherus primus canonicus et primus prior huius ecclesie'* (here lies Rahere, first canon and first prior of this church). The tomb was built in 1405, almost three centuries after Rahere's death in c 1145. A recumbent effigy lies on a table-tomb, whose front is ornamented with four large quatrefoils holding heraldic shields. An angel holds the arms of the priory at Rahere's feet. Above is a canopy of three bays, open to the sanctuary and clearly much restored. In the S choir aisle is an imposing monument to Sir Walter Mildmay (died 1589), the founder of Emmanuel College, Cambridge. It has an elaborate Classical frame, gilded and coloured and containing an inscription, which is surmounted by another, smaller frame surrounding an heraldic achievement. On the S side of the choir itself is a wall monument to Percival and Agnes Smalpace (died c 1558 and 1588). Two frontal busts are placed side by side in a Classical frame which sits a little awkwardly above further panels which bear inscriptions, including 'Behowlde youreselves by us, sutche once were we as you/ And you in thyme shal be even duste as we are now'. Opposite the monument may be seen a sword-rest. In the S transept stands a plain, octagonal 15C font, in which William Hogarth was baptised in 1697.

St. Bride, Fleet Street, EC4. The body of the present church was rebuilt in 1955–57 by W. Godfrey Allen after the bombing in 1940 of Sir Christopher Wren's church of 1671–78. The famous 'wedding-cake' steeple, which Wren added in 1701–03, survived the Second World War. The restored interior is far removed from the spirit of a Wren church; there is a complete absence of darkly-stained and closely-packed woodwork which is the hallmark of a Wren interior. Nevertheless, the postwar work is a worthy Classical composition, attractive and successful, and exceptionally light and colourful for a City church. The restoration was preceded by an excavation of the site. St. Bride's is first mentioned in the 12C, but the excavation revealed Roman remains and a pre-Conquest church of indeterminate date. It has been claimed that it is a 6C church which was named from the first after St. Bridget of Kildare. Far more likely is the suggestion that the present dedication was introduced by Danish settlers in the 10C or 11C after their migration from the W coast of Ireland.

The exterior remains much as Wren designed it. The church stands well back from Fleet Street. A narrow gap between buildings along the street reveals the steeple, which may be seen more comfortably from Ludgate Hill. A foursquare Wren tower, rising well above the body of the church, has a belfry stage whose round-headed, louvred windows are framed by Corinthian pilasters with entablature and segmental pediment above, and which is further ornamented by an attached Corinthian column at each angle. Above the belfry a panelled parapet covers the base of the steeple, which then rises in four diminishing tiers of open arches and a final short spire. The total height is 226ft. The body of the church is relatively plain, featuring Wren's usual round-headed and circular windows.

The interior is of five bays formed by Tuscan columns paired sideways, which support block entablatures and coffered arches. The barrel-vault forms deep splays with the oval clerestory windows. The E end projects slightly, but the impression of an apse derives entirely from the *trompe l'oeil* Glory painting by Glyn Jones. There are no galleries but a small balcony exists at the W end. All the windows contain clear glass. The collegiate seating is arranged in front of open screens which in turn stand in front of the arcades. The stalls have plaques which reflect the church's connections with the world of publishing. The nave is dominated by a free-standing reredos: a proud Classical composition which almost entirely blocks the view of the E window. Pairs of Corinthian columns support a segmental pediment; the entablature is interrupted for an oval stained glass panel of Christ and surrounding carvings of cherubs and swags.

Flambeaux surmount the pediment at the sides. The entablature of the nave's screens is carried round the E end and across the central part of the reredos itself, where it provides an upper frame for Glyn Jones's painting of the Crucifixion and for the candlesticks on the altar. At the W end, on top of the screens and flanking the nave, are figures of St. Bride and St. Paul by David McFall. Above, on the W wall, are royal arms of 1957, carved in stone. In the SW corner stands the diminutive font; its cover, made during the restoration, uses Wren's original design for the church's tower. The flooring of the church is of black and white marble.

At the NW corner is the staircase to the crypt, where the results of the postwar excavation may be seen alongside a substantial display on the history of the church and parish. In the 17C and 18C local residents included Dryden, Milton, Izaak Walton, Waller, Aubrey, Ashmole, Pepys (who was baptised in the church), Dr. Johnson, Boswell, Garrick, Goldsmith, Burke, Pope and Hogarth.

St. Helen, Bishopsgate, EC3. St. Helen's is a large medieval parish church which survived the Great Fire and which also preserves the church of a Benedictine nunnery. Two naves, each 25ft wide, stand side by side to recall the former dual use of the building. St. Helen's is notable too for its monuments, which are of unusual importance amongst the City churches. A number of them were brought from the nearby church of St. Martin Outwich, which was demolished in 1874.

The church stands in Great St. Helen's, an attractive City byway which is entered through an arch from Bishopsgate. The church has a symmetrical W front of two shallow-pitched and battlemented gables, with a slender wooden bell turret of the 17C between them. The two gables reflect the nuns' church to the N and the parish's to the S. The S side is quite asymmetrical. There are 20C vestries at the W end, then a Classical S doorway of 1633, with an eared frame, pediment and prominent keystone to the arch. A S transept and E chapels attached to it complete the S front. The W and N walls and those of the S transept are of the 13C; blocked lancet windows may be seen. The W door to the nuns' church is of the 16C, its parochial counterpart of the 14C.

Upon entering from the W end, down many steps from the modern ground level, the two naves are seen to be divided by a tall arcade of four bays of c 1475. The chancels, which are not structurally divided from the naves, are divided from each other by two lower arches, the W one of the 14C, the other of c 1475. The S transept opens off the parochial chancel. Two small SE chapels (the chapel of the Holy Ghost and the Lady chapel), of c 1374, fill the entire angle between the transept and the chancel. The roofs of the naves are of shallow pitch and are substantially of the 15C.

The parochial chancel has a wooden screen of 1892–93 by J.L. Pearson, who also introduced the sedilia, the splendid pavement of the chancel, the altar and the reredos. The rear stalls are of the 15C and came from the nuns' choir; the front stalls are of the 17C. On the S of the parochial choir is a wooden sword-rest of 1665, comprising two twisted columns which support an entablature and an angel-flanked coat of arms above. It recalls Sir John Lawrence, Lord Mayor in the Plague year of 1665, who lived in Great St. Helen's. A large and ornate pulpit, with tester, of the 17C, stands in front of the screen against the S wall. A 19C brass eagle lectern stands in front of the screen to the left. The S and SW doorcases, of c 1635, are both sumptuous pieces of woodwork; both seem grander by being at the

*St. Helen's, a medieval two-naved church with fine 17C
woodwork, good chancel fittings by J.L. Pearson and many
notable monuments*

top of flights of steps. The organ and its case, in the S transept, are by
Thomas Griffin, 1744. The font, of 1632, is of red and black marble
and stands on a baluster, at the W end of the nuns' church. Near the
W doorcase is a poor box, which rests on a 17C carving of a beggar,
holding out his hat. Against the N wall may be seen the nuns' night
stairs, which once led to the nuns' dormitory, and, to the E, the Easter
sepulchre of c 1525, which includes a squint, through which the nuns
could see their altar from outside the church.

The parochial E window of seven lights contains stained glass of
the Ascension, by Heaton, Butler & Bayne, 1868. The E window of
the nuns' church, of five lights, has stained glass by Powell's, 1866,
which shows St. Helen and the four Evangelists. High up in the N
wall the four three-light windows and one of the two-light windows
contain stained glass, which is either of re-arranged 17C fragments

or by Alexander Gibbs in the 19C. The two windows by Gibbs show Faith, Hope and Charity (to the W) and Christ healing the lame man and receiving children (to the E). The W window of the parochial church has stained glass of 1969 in its five lights, by John Hayward. It is symbolic of the Trinity: colourful, but more obscure than the 19C glass. The W window of the nuns' church, also of five lights, has stained glass of the worthies of St. Helen's, arranged in two tiers, by Heaton, Butler & Bayne, c 1868.

The most important monuments are at the E end. In the nuns' choir are two table-tombs, without effigies: the one to the N is of Sir Thomas Gresham (died 1579), founder of the Royal Exchange and of Gresham College; one of the most celebrated citizens of Elizabethan London. His device of a grasshopper may be seen. The neighbouring tomb is of Sir Julius Caesar Adelmare (died 1636), a judge. It bears a legal document which states that Sir Julius was ready to pay the debt of Nature. Immediately to the S, under the easternmost arch, is the tomb of Sir William Pickering (died 1574), Ambassador to Spain: a large marble composition, surrounded by a wrought-iron railing. In the corresponding position on the S side of the parochial chancel is the monument of Sir John Crosby (died 1476) and his wife. Sir John lived in a mansion called Crosby Place, which stood S of Great St. Helen's, but was removed for re-erection at Chelsea in 1910. The arcade of the church may have been built through his benefaction. To his S lies Sir John de Oteswich and his wife, from the early 15C. In the parochial nave, against the wall near the S door, is the monument to Sir John Spencer (died 1609), Lord Mayor (*Eques auratus civis & senator Londinensis*), and ancestor of the Marquesses of Northampton. Obelisks flank three figures, a daughter kneeling and the two parents recumbent, against a background of two arches and much Jacobean strapwork, and with heraldry above. Between the S and W doors is a wall monument to Alderman Richard Staper (died 1608), from St. Martin Outwich: 'the greatest merchant in his Tyme, the chiefest actor in discoveri [sic] of the trades of Turkey and East India'. The railed tomb under the second arch from the W is of William Kirwin (died 1594). He was a mason ('I have adorned London with worthy buildings'). On the N wall, near the W end, is a monument to Alderman John Robinson (died 1599), with nine sons and seven daughters depicted. To his E is Alderman Hugh Pemberton (died 1500), whose canopied tomb-chest was once accompanied by brasses of his family on the back wall. Further to the E is a wall monument of Francis Bancroft (died 1727), the founder of Bancroft's School. Finally, in the SE corner of the nuns' choir is a wall monument to Sir Andrew Judd (died 1558), Lord Mayor and founder of Tonbridge School. In addition to these monuments, St. Helen's possesses ten separate brasses, which date from between 1393 and 1633.

St. Katharine Cree, Leadenhall Street, EC3. The church was built in 1628–31, when William Laud was Bishop of London. It was consecrated by him on 16 January, 1631; during Laud's trial in 1644, his 'coming in a pompous manner' to St. Katharine's was held against him. The church is of architectural importance as a building of mixed Gothic and Classical styles and as a rare survivor in London of the period between the Reformation and the Great Fire. The name 'Cree' derives from Christ Church, a famous Augustinian priory which stood nearby from 1108 to 1531 (and which was better known as Holy Trinity Priory). St. Katharine's served as the priory's precinct church.

The church's future was uncertain in the 1950s, after the discovery of structural defects and beetle infestation, but repairs were undertaken by Marshall Sisson and the church was restored by 1962.

The church stands at the corner of Leadenhall Street and Creechurch Lane. The SW tower is of 1504; its upper part was rebuilt in 1776, when the present circular cupola was added. The S wall has five three-light, cusped windows under square labels: a very late Gothic style. Between the second and third windows from the E is a mural sundial, which was formerly inscribed MDCCVI (1706). On the street frontage beyond the E end used to stand a gateway, which was given in 1631 by William Avenon. It now stands against a new building N of the church. The W wall of the church, N of the tower, veers to the NE; it includes one large, blocked window with a shallow pediment over.

Interior of St. Katharine Cree built in 1628–31 in a mixture of Gothic Survival and Classical styles

The interior comprises a nave and N and S aisles. There are arcades of six bays, formed by Corinthian columns and round arches with rosettes in their soffits. Above, however, are two-light, square-headed Gothic clerestory windows, and, in both the nave and aisles, plaster rib-vaults. At the E end is a rose window, with five cusped lights below, all in a square frame which reaches from the reredos to the vault. There are four three-light, cusped windows to the N and five to the S. The E windows of the aisles are blocked. The aisles themselves are now screened off for offices, but well behind the arcades. There is no structural division between nave and chancel.

The reredos comes from St. James's, Duke's Place, which was demolished in 1874. It is of four fluted Corinthian pilasters, unevenly spaced, which support an entablature but no pediment. The usual inscribed boards are absent. The five lights above the reredos contain stained glass of 1880; they were blocked between 1962 and 1982, in favour of a canopy of honour for the altar, but the canopy has now gone. The stained glass of the rose is 17C; the predominant colour is yellow. The glass of the five lights is darker, but most attractive: Christ is preaching the Sermon on the Mount and below the scene is the text, 'Consider the lilies of the field, how they grow; they toil not, neither do they spin'. The window recalls the 'Flower Sermon' which was regularly preached in the church. In the S aisle is a window of 1963 by M.C. Farrar Bell, of Christ walking on the water. It commemorates those who died when the S.S. 'Lancastria', a troopship, was sunk on 17 June, 1940. The window of this very worthy commemoration is unfortunately in a jagged and rough style, less attractive than the lights above the reredos. The E end of the S aisle is the Laud chapel, which was restored by the Society of King Charles the Martyr in 1960. A portrait of Archbishop Laud, surmounted by the arms of Canterbury, hangs on the E wall. To the N of the chapel's altar is a small statue of King Charles I, who holds a copy of the 'Eikon Basilike' (kingly image), the book ascribed to him. The statue was made in 1964. Above the altar itself is the one monument of interest, to Sir Nicholas Throckmorton (died 1571; the date of 12 February, 1570 on the monument is according to the Julian Calendar). Sir Nicholas was an Elizabethan diplomat and courtier, after whom Throgmorton Street is named. His daughter, Elizabeth, married Sir Walter Raleigh. The monument comprises a recumbent effigy in a rectangular frame, flanked by two Tuscan columns; the inscription at the back is on a panel surrounded by much strapwork. A number of mural tablets are to be seen in the NW corner, surrounding the arms of King Charles II. The W gallery is large enough for only the organ, which was first built by Bernard Smith in 1686. The plain 18C pulpit stands to the N, under the second arch from the E. The 17C alabaster font bears the arms of Sir John Gayer, Lord Mayor, who, after being spared from a lion in the Syrian desert, founded an annual Lion Sermon on 16 October. The vaults have 17 large bosses, which are painted with the City arms (over the altar) and those of 16 livery companies. The ribs and also the capitals and arches of the arcades are all painted blue-grey.

St. Magnus the Martyr, Lower Thames Street, EC3. The church is a rebuilding of 1671–76 by Sir Christopher Wren after the Great Fire. A church had stood on the site since at least the reign of King William I (1066–87) and therefore its original patron was not St. Magnus, the Earl of Orkney, who was martyred in 1116 and canonised in 1135 and who is now accepted as the patron, but one of the earlier saints of the same name. For centuries, St. Magnus' stood prominently at the N end of Old London Bridge, but the opening of Rennie's bridge upstream in 1831 and the building of Adelaide House in 1921–24 have hidden the church. The building, whose minor damage in the Second World War was repaired by 1951, has a sumptuous interior of Wren's 17C style, but its atmosphere also owes much to the marked Anglo-Catholic tradition which has applied here since the 1920s.

The church stands on the S side of a major dual carriageway, to the E of Adelaide House. Lately, the exterior of the church has been cleaned to great advantage. The most prominent external feature is the steeple, 185ft high, which was added in 1703–06. The tower is surmounted by an octagonal lantern, which itself supports a lead dome and a small spire. Wren's design is clearly based on Francis Aiguillon's St. Charles Borromée, Antwerp, built in 1614–24. The clock which projects from the W front and which was visible to all travellers on Old London Bridge before 1831, was the gift of Sir Charles Duncombe, Lord Mayor. It is dated 1709 but now lacks the gilded figures which once surmounted the face. The passageway under the tower at the W end led directly onto Old London Bridge from 1763 to 1831. Before 1763 the tower was flanked by vestries at the W ends of the N and S aisles. These were removed and a passageway was made under the tower itself, as a result of the widening of the bridge in 1760. The removal of the W ends of the aisles made the N front asymmetrical. Of the original nine bays, only the central one survives intact, comprising the pedimented N door, which is surmounted by a circular window and a swag. The eight remaining bays once had round-headed windows under the straight hoods on corbels, but the windows were reduced to small circles in 1782, by John Tricker. Above are four oval clerestory windows. The E window is blocked.

The church has a nave, N and S aisles, W vestibule with gallery over, and a SW vestry. The nave is formed by tall, Ionic columns directly supporting the entablature. Originally, there was a wide space between columns in line with the N door, but this was filled by an extra pair of columns in 1924. The cross-plan was thus removed. The column bases are not panelled as is normal in a Wren church. The columns are painted white and their capitals are gilded (T.S. Eliot wrote in 1922: '...the walls of Magnus Martyr hold/Inexplicable splendour of Ionian white and gold'.) The nave is tunnel-vaulted. On the N side are seven circular windows. The westernmost window was brought from the former hall of the Plumbers' Company. The other six contain heraldic glass by Alfred L. Wilkinson. The S side has four full-length, round-headed windows. The glass is by Lawrence Lee and depicts SS. Magnus, Margaret, Thomas and Michael. St. Thomas was the patron of the chapel on Old London Bridge which served as a chapel of ease to St. Magnus'.

The grandest fitting is the reredos, which fills the entire E wall of the nave. The lower part is Wren's, including portraits of Moses and Aaron to the sides and a Pelican in her Piety above. The upper part was added by Martin Travers in 1924–25 in a style which entirely accords with that of Wren. At the very top is a Rood, with gilded figures, which would have seemed extraordinary to Wren but which is pleasing in its position. The wrought-iron rails around the sanctuary are of c 1705. In front of the second column from the E on the S side stand the pulpit and tester, tall and ornate, on a markedly slender stem. Next to the column on the opposite side is a sword-rest of 1708, but with the royal arms of 1800–16 added. The body of the church lacks the box-pews which Wren would have inserted, except in front of the W gallery. Next to the box-pew on the S side stands the font, whose cover resembles the dome of a telephone box. Behind it is placed a large benefaction board. The gallery houses the organ of 1712, by Abraham Jordan, the first swell organ in England. The N and S walls are panelled up to eye level. Affixed above are innumerable memorial tablets of the 18C and 19C. A statue of the Earl of Orkney, by Martin Travers (1925), stands against the S wall. Placed diagonally across the SE and SW corners are altars, each with a reredos made from reused doorcases. The one to the N serves the Lady chapel (which is also the Blessed Sacrament chapel); its reredos was once the NW doorcase. The chapel is further adorned by a statue of Our Lady of Walsingham. The altar table in the SE corner, now serving the chapel of Christ the King, was Wren's original high altar. The reredos, placed here in 1935, was the SW doorcase. Nearby, against the S wall, stands a large, 19C, mother-of-pearl crucifix, brought from Bethlehem.

In the pre-Fire church was buried Henry Yevele (died 1400), architect of the naves of Canterbury Cathedral and Westminster Abbey, and in the present church Miles Coverdale, translator of the Bible into English and Rector of the parish, was re-buried in 1840. A memorial to him is fixed to the E wall, to the right of the high altar. Anglo-Catholic worship was promoted at St. Magnus' by the Reverend H.J. Fynes-Clinton (1876–1959), Rector from 1922 to 1959; and hence the introduction of the English Baroque style by Martin Travers in the 1920s. A medieval Fraternity of Our Lady de Salve Regina, to which Henry Yevele had belonged, was revived in 1922.

St. Mary Abchurch, Abchurch Lane, EC4. The church is a rebuilding of 1681–86 by Sir Christopher Wren after the Great Fire. Damage by bombing in 1940 was repaired by Godfrey Allen. The excellence of the postwar repairs and the relative lack of Victorian alterations have left a substantially complete 17C interior, whose most notable feature is a painted dome.

St. Mary's stands in a narrow lane between Cannon Street and King William Street. The E end fronts the lane; the S side looks onto the former churchyard, which is paved in geometrical patterns. The church's exterior is of red brick with stone quoins; it was formerly stuccoed. The tower stands at the NW corner. It is surmounted by an ogee-shaped dome, an open lantern and a slender, lead-covered spire.

The interior is virtually a square and is structurally undivided. The whole is surmounted by a dome which rests on eight arches, which themselves rest on corbels. The corners of the church are groined to link the square ground plan with the slightly elliptical dome. The dome is not so grand as that of St. Stephen's, Walbrook, but it is enriched by a painting: the Divine Name in Hebrew (the tetragrammaton) is surrounded by a Glory and by the worship of Heaven. The painting is of 1708–09 by William Snow, a parishioner, who was paid £170 for the work, and it was restored after the bombing by Professor E.W. Tristram and Walter Hoyle. The E wall is of three bays. The central bay is filled by the reredos and the side bays each have a round-headed window surmounted by a circular one. The S wall has a very large central window, which is segment-headed and which is flanked by two smaller round-headed windows with portholes above.

The reredos has been proved to be by Grinling Gibbons. It is divided by two pairs of Corinthian columns, which support the ends only of a segmental pediment; the centre, above the usual inscribed panels, is filled with limewood carvings of fruit and flowers and by a Pelican in her Piety. An attic is surmounted by four urns. To the left is the pulpit with tester and stairs: a very fine original piece, by William Grey. The pews have been cut down except against the N and S walls and to the W. Affixed to the front pews are a lion and a unicorn, both original, and two sword-rests, made probably in the late 17C but adorned with the arms of parishioners who served as Lord Mayor in 1812 and 1814. The organ in the W gallery is housed in a case of 1717. In the SW corner, under the gallery, a railed enclosure houses the font, whose cover possesses carved figures of the four Evangelists in Classical niches. Large benefaction boards hang on the W wall. There are fine SW and NW doorcases. The former bears the royal arms of King James VII and II and the latter is surmounted by a gilded metal Pelican in her Piety, which was the church's vane before 1764. The only monument of much note is at the E end, under the window to the S of the reredos. It commemorates Sir Patience Ward (died 1696), Lord Mayor. Beneath the S side of the church is a small late medieval vault.

St. Mary at Hill, EC3. (This entry was written before fire destroyed the roof and damaged the fittings in May, 1988. The church is to be restored.) The church is a rebuilding of 1670–76 by Sir Christopher Wren after the Great Fire. Its present value is due to its preservation of closely-packed, darkly-stained woodwork, including (uniquely for a City church today) high box-pews, and to the clear glass of its windows. It is a sumptuous interior, whose 17C atmosphere is now unmatched for its completeness. Yet, curiously, the fabric was substantially rebuilt in the late 18C and early 19C: the W end is of 1787–88; much of the woodwork is of 1848–49; and the plaster ceiling in a light, Adam style is apparently of c 1826–27.

The exterior is largely hemmed in. The E elevation to the street called St. Mary at Hill has a pedimented central bay over a Venetian window, and an attractive projecting clock. The W front to Lovat Lane, including the plain tower, was rebuilt in brick in 1787–88 by George Gwilt the Elder.

Within, the almost square church is divided by four fluted Corinthian columns which form an inner square and which, with the help of pendentives, support a central dome and lantern. The columns also form a Greek cross, for their entablature is carried round the walls at the cardinal points. The E and W ends focus on the reredos and organ respectively, and the 'transepts' end in much larger windows than their neighbours in the N and S walls. In fact, the entablature actually divides the central N and S windows; the round-headed portions of the windows surmount it. All the windows are of clear glass, save for a few 19C roundels at the E end. The side walls were rebuilt in 1826 by James Savage. The ceilings were replaced at the same time. The fact that they were in a light, Adam style matters little; Wren's ceilings differ so much that this variation does not detract from the interior's general character. Savage undertook further restoration in 1848–49. In 1967 Seely & Paget restored the church, removing virtually all the 19C glass and cleaning and recolouring the interior.

The immense reredos is of three bays, surmounted by a segmental pediment and bearing the usual inscribed boards. Two capitals are gilded. The pulpit, with larger tester and fine stairs, stands to the left in the chancel; a reading desk is to the right. The W gallery is adorned with rich carving and houses the organ. Much of the carving in the church, including the decoration of the gallery front, the reading desk and parts of the pulpit, is not of the 17C but of 1848–49 by William Gibbs Rogers. His achievement was remarkable in reproducing completely accurate 17C woodwork. Amongst the box-pews at the W end are five sword rests, unusually ornate; a sixth is at the E end. The font stands to the SW. In the NE corner there is a bust of the Reverend William Johnson Rodber (died 1843) by Samuel Nixon. In the vestibule, in the NW corner of the church, is a relief of the General Resurrection, of c 1600. The Reverend Wilson Carlisle, the founder of the Church Army, was the Rector of this church from 1892 to 1926.

St. Mary-le-Bow, Cheapside, EC2. Sir Christopher Wren's costliest church, which was built in 1671–80 after its predecessor's destruction in the Great Fire, stands in Cheapside as proudly today, in the company of dreary postwar office blocks, as it did in the London of King Charles II. Its steeple is the most famous of Wren's many examples which once dominated the City's skyline. The church's interior was destroyed in 1941 and was rebuilt in 1956–64 by Laurence King in a style far removed from that of Wren. The woodwork is all lightly stained and, although in a worthy Classical style, diverges very widely from what a Wren interior would possess.

The famous steeple stands on Cheapside at the NW corner of the church, separated by a wide vestibule from the church proper. It was clearly placed to be noticed in the City's principal street and former market place ('Cheap' is the Old English word for market). An immense foursquare tower ascends from great rusticated, arched openings at its base: entrances of some grandeur amongst the City churches. Coupled pilasters frame the round-headed belfry windows above, and then follows the balustrade with what amount to stone coronae at the angles: four scrolls or volutes hold tall vases in the centre, vaguely reflecting the pre-Fire church's steeple. The steeple proper is built round a conical core; its base is a circle of columns, which supports an entablature and balustrade, and which is linked by volutes to a square stage of 12 small Aberdeen granite columns. At the very top is a final spire and a dragon vane, 8ft 10ins long and weighing 2cwt. The entire steeple reaches 230ft in height. In contrast to the Portland stone of the tower and steeple, the body of the church is built of red brick, with stone dressings. The W elevation is now viewed from a paved square, in which stands a statue of Captain John Smith (died 1631), the founder of Jamestown, Virginia, U.S.A. The E elevation fronts the narrow Bow Lane.

Entering under the tower and through the vestibule, the SW door of the church proper is reached. The body of the church is almost square, but it is divided longitudinally by two arcades of three bays, formed by square piers with attached Corinthian demi-columns. The latter support the transverse arches of the barrel-vault. The N and S aisles are very narrow—the S being narrower than the N—so that the impression is of one wide space. The E end has two attached Corinthian columns supporting block entablatures, with tall pedestals and urns above, the urns virtually reaching the vault. A large round-headed window separates the two columns. To the sides are two lower round-headed windows, with circular ones above. Clerestory windows make the usual breaks in the vault above the arcades. The internal architecture is a full restoration of Wren's design.

The woodwork is all by Laurence King. The usual Wren reredos is replaced by what was intended as a screen of honour for an episcopal chair, but the chair now stands on the N side of the sanctuary. A blue panel on the screen bears the opening words of St. John's Gospel in Latin, Greek and English. A gilded mitre and the Bishop of London's arms surmount it. The altar is free-standing. The sanctuary is defined not by rails but by a single step and by the hanging Rood above, which, in addition to the usual figures, includes the centurion and St. Mary Magdalen. It was designed by John Hayward and carved by Otto Irsara of Oberammergau. Also by John Hayward are the stained glass windows. Above the altar is a Christ in Majesty. To the left is the Blessed Virgin Mary, holding a model of the church and surrounded by depictions of other City steeples. The right-hand window depicts St Paul, patron of the City of London. The style of the glass, jagged and obscure in its detail, is not very attractive. It accords to some extent with the colouring of Laurence King's interior, but it must be recalled that Wren's windows were never intended to accommodate stained glass. There are two pulpits, one on each side of the nave: they have been used for lunchtime debates. To the SE and NE are good iron screens by Grundy Arnatt Ltd. The one to the S surrounds the Blessed Sacrament chapel, in which a tall sacrament house is surmounted by a Pelican in her Piety. The chapel to the N commemorates the Norwegian Resistance of the Second World War. At the rear of the church, above the doorcase, is the organ, housed in a worthy case by Laurence King. Modern royal arms surmount the W door. There is black and white flooring as in many postwar restorations of Wren's churches.

The 11C crypt is reached from the vestibule. The arches or 'bows' of its vault give the church its surname. They also named the Court of Arches, the provincial court of Canterbury, which has met here for centuries because St. Mary's was the principal peculiar of the Archbishop of Canterbury in London. Wren thought the crypt was a Roman structure, but its 11C date is obvious enough from the surviving Norman columns. The vault has been entirely renewed and so the crypt looks much less ancient than it did before 1941. The crypt is divided into three parts. The S aisle was re-opened in 1960 as the chapel of the Holy Spirit. It has an etched glass screen by John Hayward. The main part of the crypt is the Court of Arches. The N aisle is kept clear and serves as a vestibule.

The tower contains 12 bells, of which one is the Great Bell of Bow (recast 1956), the successor to one of medieval London's curfew bells. Birth within the sound of the bells is reckoned to define a Cockney. 'Bow bells' form the church's best-known association. Less well-known is the fact that the Society for the Propagation of Christian Knowledge (the SPCK) was founded in the old vestry in 1698.

St. Olave, Hart Street, EC3. The church is a building of c 1450 which was substantially restored by Ernest B. Glanfield in 1951–54 after severe damage by bombing in 1941. It is now the only church in central London dedicated to the first Christian King of Norway, St. Olaf or Olav (anglicised to Olave), reigned 1016–29, who had helped the English King Aethelraed II in 1014 against the Danes. He was martyred in 1030. The dedication reflects the important Scandinavian element in 11C London. King Haakon VII of Norway laid the commemorative stone of the restored church on June 15th, 1951. St. Olave's is famous, too, as the parish church of Samuel Pepys when he lived in Seething Lane and served in the Navy Office in the Restoration years.

The church, stone-built except for the brick-built upper stage of the tower, stands at the corner of Seething Lane and Hart Street. The E end comprises the shallow gable of the nave, a four-light E window with intersecting tracery, and low flanking aisles with almost flat roofs. A chimneyed 17C vestry projects from the SE corner of the S aisle. The W tower is seen to advantage from the churchyard. Its upper, brick-built stage, with simple Classical details and a projecting clock on the E face, is of 1731–32, by John Widdows. The cupola was restored in 1954. The fairly large churchyard is chiefly notable for its gate, dated April 11th, 1658, which is adorned with spikes above the segmental pediment and with skulls and crossbones in the tympanum. Dickens described it in 'The Uncommercial Traveller': '...the churchyard of St. Ghastly Grim ... with a ferocious strong spiked iron gate, like a jail ... the skulls grin aloft horribly, thrust through and through with iron spears'. The gate reproduces one in a Dutch copy-book of 1633.

The interior comprises a nave of just three bays, divided by quatrefoil piers from the N and S aisles. The sanctuary occupies the easternmost bay, without structural division or screen. To the SE is the 17C vestry, but with a 15C doorway (with quatrefoils in the spandrels) and door leaf. The vestry has panelling and a plaster angel on the ceiling. Below the church is a 13C crypt of two bays with ribbed vaults. The windows are largely Perpendicular: three-light windows under depressed arches to N and S, three-light windows at the E ends of the aisles and a 19C four-light one, in Decorated style, to the nave. The church's postwar glass was designed by A.E. Bass and was made by Goddard & Gibbs. The E window of 1953 depicts St. Olaf, Christus Salvator, Christus Victor and St. George. In the tracery lights are symbols of the Evangelists. In the N aisle, the E window comprises Queen Elizabeth I, St. Mary and St. Catherine. The S aisle's E window shows St. Clement in the central light: he is the patron of the Corporation of Trinity House, which gave the window. Over the S door is an armorial window by John Hayward, 1970, to the memory of Viscount Monsell (died 1969).

A low wall divides the sanctuary from the nave. To the left the wall includes a stone inscribed with a history of the church; to the right is King Haakon's stone and also a stone from the shrine of St. Olaf in Trondheim Cathedral. Placed on the wall are four sword-rests, representing parishoners who served as Lord Mayor in the 18C. Under the N arcade stands the 17C pulpit, brought from the demolished Wren church of St. Benet Gracechurch. It has no tester. There is a W gallery, which houses the organ. All the woodwork in the church is lightly stained, which is typical of postwar woodwork in the City churches. In the SW corner, used as a baptistery, there stands, behind a grille, a statue of St. Olaf by Carl Schou, a Norwegian sculptor.

A number of memorials were preserved through the Second World War. The most famous is that to Mrs Pepys (died 1669), by John Bushnell: a bust looks down from above the easternmost arch on the N side. Samuel Pepys himself (died 1703) is accorded a portrait medalion in Classical frame, surprisingly of 1883, and placed on the S aisle wall, where the Navy pew existed until the S gallery was removed in 1853. Wrapped around the easternmost N pier is a memorial to Andrew and Paul Bayning (died 1610 and 1616), Aldermen: kneeling figures in gowns and ruffs. Over the vestry door in the SE corner is a memorial to Sir James Deane (died 1608), divided into three parts by columns, with much heraldry above.

St. Stephen, Walbrook, EC4. St. Stephen's was rebuilt by Sir Christopher Wren in 1672–79 after the Great Fire. It is renowned for its plan, in which Wren showed the most masterly disposition of space in any of his City churches. Sixteen Corinthian columns are so placed that a rectangular space is divided into a nave, aisles, chancel, transepts and central space. Over the last rises a dome of wood and plaster, 45ft in diameter, which is rightly regarded as a miniature essay for that of St. Paul's Cathedral. The church may be considered to have either a centralised plan, formed from a domed Latin cross, or a longitudinal plan of medieval convention, in which the view from W to E was emphasised by the reredos, box-pews, aisles and by the fact that the nave is of two bays rather than one. A considerable change to the interior's appearance was made by F.C. Penrose in 1887–88. He replaced the box-pews by benches and chairs and laid down a mosaic floor. The loss of the box-pews seriously unbalanced the interior. The dark woodwork at ground level had deflected the eye from the considerable upward thrust of the 16 columns, whose bases now seem absurdly high. In addition, the placing of the blocks of box-pews contributed much to the longitudinal element in the church. The absence of the pews upsets the delicate balance which Wren had contrived. The church was bombed in 1941 and was restored by Godfrey Allen in 1949–54. A major restoration was carried out in 1978–87 under Robert Potter.

The exterior is partly hidden behind the Mansion House. It is very plain except for the NW steeple, which was added as late as 1713–17. The steeple compares closely with that of St. James's, Garlickhythe: both are of three stages, the lowest and square stage being especially adorned at the corners, the second stage repeating the first in miniature and the last being a diminutive lantern.

The church is entered by a W door beneath a garlanded oval window. A flight of steps leads up to a W apse, which is divided from the body of the church by an original doorcase. From the inner door the plan of the church unfolds. At the W end there is one bay of double arcades, forming a groined nave, flat-ceilinged aisles and narrow outer aisles. The rest of the church, which is virtually square, is divided by the remaining 12 columns, which are arranged in four groups of three. These groups of columns define both a square within a square and the arms of a Greek cross (which becomes a Latin cross within the whole church because of the second bay of the nave). The columns—which are all of equal height—support a straight entablature, which turns to define the four corners of the inner square and turns again to define the four arms of the cross. The chancel follows the nave in being groin-vaulted, but the transepts are tunnel-vaulted. The coffered dome, with lantern above, rests on eight arches (cf. St. Mary Abchurch); four of the arches span the arms of the cross, but the other four rest on arches which are placed diagonally across the corners. Each corner has a diagonal half of a bay of groin-vaulting and two segment-headed clerestory windows. The round-headed E window fills the entire E wall of the chancel above the reredos. It is flanked by two smaller round-headed windows at the E ends of the inner aisles and porthole windows at the E ends of the outer aisles. Small oval windows pierce the N and S walls.

The reredos at the E end is partly of the late 17C and partly by W. Gibbs Rogers in 1852. The upper part of the reredos was removed in 1776, to make room to put Benjamin West's painting of 'The Burial of St. Stephen' against the E window. The painting was moved to the N wall in 1852 and the reredos was restored. More recently, the painting has again been removed. The communion table is semicircular. The pulpit, with magnificent tester, stands to the right of the chancel. At the W end is a fine doorcase, with 17C royal arms and the organ above. The organ is of 1906, by William Hill, but it is housed in a case of 1765 which sympathises very well with the 17C doorcase. There is one wrought-iron sword-rest, of 1710 (but nevertheless bearing the crest of King George III). The font, which stands to the left of the entrance, is by Thomas Strong, with a cover by

William Newman (who also applied the carvings on the pulpit and reredos).

Sir John Vanbrugh (died 1726), architect, playwright and herald, was buried in the N aisle of this church. The famous epitaph suggested for him ('Lie heavy on him, Earth! for he/Laid many a heavy load on thee') is usually attributed to Dean Swift, but more probably came from Abel Evans. The Rector in 1556–57, Henry Pendleton, is well known as 'The Vicar of Bray', who changed his religious opinions to suit the tides of the Reformation. A more recent association is that the present Rector, the Reverend Chad Varah, founded the Samaritans at St. Stephen's in 1954.

In 1986 the churchwarden of St. Stephen's, Mr Peter Palumbo, with the support of the Rector, proposed to place a startling new altar under the dome. The altar, of 8½ tons and made of light-coloured marble, had been commissioned by Mr Palumbo from Henry Moore. Eight feet wide and 3ft 5ins high, or 4ft 3ins if one adds the steps on which it is mounted, it is intended to dominate the interior. New, light-coloured seating curves around it (rather than facing E). The Consistory Court of the Diocese of London heard the application for a faculty in 1986 and rejected it. The Chancellor considered the altar 'incongruous' with its surroundings, but ruled that the altar should be excluded from the church because it failed to meet, under Church law, the definition of a communion table. Early in 1987 the Court of Ecclesiastical Causes Reserved, in only the second sitting of its existence, upheld Mr Palumbo's appeal. The allowance of the altar as a communion table is no doubt legally sound, but aesthetically the result of the case is a disaster. An element which is alien to the spirit of Wren and disruptive of the church's Baroque interest has been introduced. The new altar is a blow to Wren's most splendid parish church.

The church architecture of London as a whole is characterised by a dearth of medieval fabric and by a large number of unusually important churches from between the 17C and the 19C. 'London North of the Thames', the title used in this book for those urban parts of the original Middlesex which surrounded the City of London, fits that pattern precisely. Medieval fabric comprises no more than four parish churches (of which two are restored almost out of recognition), plus fragmentary remains of a fifth; a couple of towers; four chapels of importance and the crypt of a fifth; the surviving parts of two monastic churches; and, last but far from least, Westminster Abbey. From the 17C onwards, however, churches of national importance by the leading architects of their day become numerous. Inigo Jones, Sir Christopher Wren, Nicholas Hawksmoor, James Gibbs, Thomas Archer and their 18C successors are all represented here more substantially than outside London. In the 19C London naturally had a significant share in that great wave of church building which coincided with an unprecedented rise in the national population. Important churches represent almost all the major 19C architects. There are also a number of notable early 20C churches and rebuildings of bombed churches after the Second World War.

Pre-Conquest remains are to be found only at St. Dunstan's, Stepney, where there are 10C or 11C carvings. The Norman period provides the earliest surviving buildings. One of the earliest and most important of all Norman structures is the White Tower of the Tower of London, whose chapel of St. John survives intact from the late 11C. It is an apsidal and galleried chapel in the usual heavy proportions of its period, but it is a building whose architecture stands remarkably clear of any distraction from fittings. Norman too are some parts of Westminster Abbey's surviving conventual buildings, the crypt of St. John's, Clerkenwell (where a Norman round nave is marked out in the roadway), and (a little uncertainly) some walling and two doorways at St. Pancras' Old Church. St. Pancras' also has a 13C sedile and a piscina. Sedilia of the same period exist in St. Dunstan's, Stepney. 13C too is the crypt of St. Stephen's chapel within the Palace of Westminster—one part of a two-storey private chapel which survived the fire of 1834. From the end of the 13C there remains a more or less complete two-storey chapel of the Bishops of Ely: St. Etheldreda's, Ely Place, Holborn Circus. The tracery there is intersecting and Geometrical, but not ogee. There is no 14C fabric of any consequence. St. Mary's, Stratford-le-Bow, dates from that time but is heavily restored. The chapel of the Charterhouse, which is an early 17C adaptation of a chapter house completed in 1414, also survives, but its worthy 17C fittings serve to make it seem entirely of that time. From the later Perpendicular age there are more significant survivals. St. Dunstan's, Stepney is almost entirely of the late 15C, but much repaired and 'scraped' in the 19C. St. Margaret's, Westminster is of the late 15C and early 16C and is the most prominent parish church in London to retain medieval fabric. St. Mary's, Stoke Newington has some 15C fabric amidst many later extensions. The old churches of Fulham (All Saints') and Hackney (St. Augustine's, in the same churchyard as St. John-at-Hackney) have retained 15C towers. From the early 16C there remain two chapels: the prominent chapel of St. Peter ad Vincula in the Tower of London, and the Savoy Chapel near the Strand.

The growth of London in the 16C and 17C was slow to be reflected in new church building. When it came, it was to be in the hands of the leading architects until the 18C. The earliest of these architects was Inigo Jones, the exponent of Palladio's Classicism in a London (and an England) which was still accustomed to the Gothic Survival. Jones designed the original St. Paul's, Covent Garden (1631–38), a Classical building in a setting thought to be so Italian that it is labelled a piazza to this day. St. Paul's was burnt in 1795 and was rebuilt on the old lines by Thomas Hardwick. Also by Inigo Jones is the Queen's Chapel (1623–27) in Marlborough Gate, opposite St. James's Palace. Although it is relatively little-known, it is the first wholly Classical English church, with pediments at the ends, a Venetian E window, and pedimented N and S windows. In view of the uncompromising Classicism of the Queen's Chapel, it is surprising to find attributed to Inigo Jones the contemporary Gothic Survival chapel of Lincoln's Inn (1619–23). At one time there was a plan to ask him for a design, but in the event the work was done—very differently—by John Clarke.

Whereas Wren's opportunity in the City of London resulted from the Great Fire of 1666, it was the growth of suburbs which led to church building to the W of the City in the late 17C and early 18C. Wren built or rebuilt three churches in London outside the City: St. James's, Piccadilly (consecrated 1684); St. Anne's, Soho (consecrated 1686); and St. Clement Danes (1680–82). St. Anne's was bombed and its surviving tower is not by Wren but by S.P. Cockerell (1801–03). St. Clement Danes, an ancient foundation which Wren rebuilt, was bombed too and it also has a tower and steeple by other hands. The steeple is unmistakably by James Gibbs, but the tower is pre-Wren: there is a doorway of the 1630s and windows with Y-tracery. St. James's in Piccadilly was an influential building, for it provided a model for the aisled and galleried church of the next century and a half. In addition to the three parish churches, Wren also designed the chapel of Chelsea Hospital, an unusually grand institutional chapel (completed 1687). Scattered throughout London and beyond are fittings from demolished Wren churches in the City: an example is St. Dionis', Parson's Green (1884–85), which houses fittings from St. Dionis Backchurch (demolished 1878).

Churches by Wren's immediate successors down to c 1730 are numerous, not merely because of the expansion of London but also because of the Fifty New Churches Act of 1711, which gave the opportunity to build some grand churches at Government expense. Mention has already been made of Gibbs's new steeple for St. Clement Danes. Just yards to the W of it in the Strand is St. Mary-le-Strand (1713–17), which Gibbs designed as one of the Fifty. It owes much to Wren, but it derives too from Roman Baroque, for Gibbs had trained in Rome. Further W is St. Martin-in-the-Fields (1721–26), where Gibbs designed a combination of steeple and W portico which was widely copied in the 18C. Also by Gibbs is a rare survivor of the 18C proprietory chapel: St. Peter's, Vere Street (1721–23), originally the Oxford Chapel. Benjamin Timbrell has been credited with the design of the slightly later Grosvenor Chapel in Mayfair (1730–31), an agreeable building which is quite distinct from the grand Classicism of its day. The Grosvenor Chapel is now a chapel of ease to St. George's, Hanover Square (1721–25), which is the one complete central London church by John James. To John James and Nicholas Hawksmoor jointly is credited the design of St. Luke's, Old Street (1727–33), now a ruin, whose famous feature is its obelisk spire. And so to Hawksmoor, the most original architect in the generation after Wren and whose churches in London are particularly monumental and striking. E of the City in Stepney he designed Christ Church, Spitalfields (1715–29), St. George's-in-the East (1715–23) and St. Anne's, Limehouse (1712–24); in Bloomsbury, he was responsible for St. George's (1716–31) near the British Museum. The steeples of the Stepney churches are in a class of their own, quite distinct from the tradition which goes from Wren to Gibbs, James, Flitcroft and beyond. Hawksmoor paraphrased Gothic in the octagonal lantern of St. George's-in-the-East and in the general design of the Spitalfields and Limehouse steeples. (He did of course design the two famous and fully Gothic W towers of Westminster Abbey and a Gothic tower for St. Michael's, Cornhill, in the City of London.) St. Anne's and St. George's-in-the-East have centralising plans, whereas Christ Church is basilican. The church in Bloomsbury is wholly Classical and looks convincingly ancient rather than an 18C derivative. It has a raised Corinthian portico which looks like the Pantheon's in Rome, a tower with a stepped pyramid which mirrors the Mausoleum of Halicarnassus, and a centralising interior. The only early 18C church architect who approached Hawksmoor in originality was Thomas Archer. His great work was St. Paul's at Deptford (see London South of the Thames), but N of the river he designed the exuberant Baroque St. John's, Smith Square (now a concert hall). It was consecrated in 1728. It has four corner towers, broken pediments and a plan which tends towards a Greek cross. Compare St. John's with St. Giles-in-the-Fields (by Henry Flitcroft, 1731–33) to see how far Archer had gone from the usual 18C model.

From the 1730s until the 1790s a number of churches were built or rebuilt on the fringes of London. They often replaced the surviving medieval churches of villages which were beginning to become suburbs of London. Their designs were usually by rather minor architects. An exception, perhaps, was St. Leonard's, Shoreditch (1736–40, by George Dance the Elder): a church close to the City and by the City Corporation's own architect. The steeple of St. Leonard's is very much in the Wren tradition. Also relatively near the City is St. James's, Clerkenwell (1788–92, by James Carr), which even at that date was given a Wren-inspired steeple. Further out of central London are St. John's, Hampstead (1745–47, by John Sanderson), St. Mary's, Paddington (1788–91, by John Plaw), and St. John-at-Hackney (1792–97, by James Spiller). The Hackney church is surprisingly large for a place so far from the 18C City.

A few significant non-Anglican churches remain from the 18C. They are significant chiefly for historical reasons. Wesley's Chapel in City Road (1777–78) stands next to the house where John Wesley lived in his last years. The present chapel took the place of a building which had been used for worship from 1739, from the earliest days of Methodism. The absence of a tower or a steeple is characteristic of non-Anglican buildings of its day. A former Methodist chapel which predates Wesley's and was built for French Protestants in 1700 remains in West Street near Cambridge Circus. From the other end of the religious spectrum there survives the church of Our Lady of the Assumption and St. Gregory (1788–90, by Joseph Bonomi) in Warwick Street, off Regent Street. It is the only Catholic place of worship to remain from the days of the embassy chapels, in this case the Portuguese and Bavarian Embassies of the 18C. Its reticent exterior recalls that the Gordon Riots had occurred less than a decade previously.

The next significant wave of church building after that of the Act of 1711 was occasioned by the two parliamentary grants of 1818 and 1824. The resulting buildings are the 'Commissioners' churches'. Many other churches were built in the same period under the terms of special Acts of Parliament. Stylistically, there is little to choose between the two groups. Classical buildings, often of Greek inspiration, were normal at first; and then, increasingly, Gothic churches were built, but usually with limited Gothic detail on a Georgian shell. What does distinguish the Commissioners' churches from the rest is the immense cost of some of the buildings which were paid for locally. St. Marylebone Parish Church (1813–17, by Thomas Hardwick) cost c £72,000; St. Pancras' New Church (1819–22, by W. & H.W. Inwood) cost c £82,000. By contrast, a typical Commissioners' church required between £13,000 and £20,000 (not all of which was necessarily paid by the Commissioners). St. Marylebone has three examples of Commissioners' churches in Classical style: Christ Church, Cosway Street (1822–24, by Philip Hardwick); St. Mary's, Bryanston Square (1821–23, by Sir Robert Smirke); and All Souls', Langham Place (1822–24, by John Nash). Each cost £19,000 or just under. St. Mary's copied Archer's St. Paul's, Deptford in combining a semicircular portico with a circular tower, sited to be seen from Wyndham Place. Similarly, Nash's All Souls' was placed to be seen up Regent Street, where there is a sharp curve into Langham Place. A Gothic Commissioners' church of the same period is St. Mary's, Eversholt Street (1822–24, by W. & H.W. Inwood). It has been regarded as a poor expression of Gothic, an unconvincing and inaccurate revival. This was the case with most Gothic Revival churches before 1840. An exception was St. Luke's, Chelsea (1820–24, by James Savage), which more nearly copied the Middle Ages than any of its contemporaries. It included a stone vault and flying buttresses. The shortcomings of St. Mary's, Eversholt Street are not surprising when it is considered that the Inwoods who designed it were better known as exponents of the Greek Revival. Their St. Pancras' New Church derived major features from the Tower of the Winds and the Erechtheion in Athens. A lesser-known Greek Revival church by the Inwoods is All Saints', Camden Street (also 1822–24), now used by the Greek Orthodox. Other prominent Greek Revival churches in central London are St. Peter's, Eaton Square (1824–27, by Henry Hakewill)—lately burnt and awaiting restoration—and St. Mark's, North Audley Street (1824–28, by J.P. Gandy-Deering), which has been redundant for some years.

After c 1840 two developments occurred which marked out the Victorian Age. Firstly, local church building schemes became numerous. Up to a dozen churches were built in a single district under the more ambitious schemes. Bethnal Green, Haggerston and St. Pancras witnessed such activity. The second major development was that the scholarly Gothic Revival emerged in the 1840s. Mere surface decoration, or versions of Gothic which would have been unknown in the Middle Ages, were now replaced by more or less accurate copies of medieval buildings. St. Stephen's, Rochester Row (1847–50, by Benjamin Ferrey) and St. Mary Magdalene's, Munster Square (1849–52, by R.C. Carpenter) were two Anglican parish churches which reflected the new spirit. The Catholic Church also turned to accurate medieval styles. A.W.N. Pugin, the earliest and most forceful proponent of scholarly medieval work, designed St. Thomas', Fulham (1847–49). J.J. Scoles designed the Jesuits' church in Farm Street, Mayfair (1844–49) in an elaborate Decorated style. Later in the century some Catholic churches veered back to the Classical. The London Oratory Church at Brompton (1880–84, by Herbert Gribble) was the major example. Anglican churches in London, however, remained Gothic for the rest of the century, but in all manner of medieval styles. William Butterfield contributed four tall redbrick churches, all of them important: All Saints', Margaret Street (1850–59); St. Alban's, Holborn (1861–63); St. Augustine's, Kilburn (1871–77); and St. Matthias', Stoke Newington (1851–53). Attempts at structural polychromy and saddleback towers were two distinctive features of his work. G.E. Street designed the significant churches of St. James the Less, Pimlico (1860–61) and St. Mary Magdalene, Paddington (1867–73). Their present surroundings, as with so many 19C London churches, are utterly different from those which once existed. Victorian architects so often faced restricted and difficult sites, which were later left high and dry by redevelopment. A church which was grandly sited and always prominent was Sir Gilbert Scott's St. Mary Abbots, Kensington (1868–72), his only major church in central London. The best London church by William White is St. Saviour's, Aberdeen Park (1865–66), which is now redundant, as is St. Stephen's, Haverstock Hill (1869–73), by the 'rogue' architect, S.S. Teulon. In Pimlico, Thomas Cundy designed a number of churches for the Grosvenor Estate, of which St. Barnabas' (1847–50) is the most important on account of its fittings and early associations with the Victorian High Church movement. James Brooks was responsible for many interesting churches in Haggerston, now so sadly depleted. To the N of Haggerston, at Dalston, St. Mark's is an interesting and spacious work of 1864–66 by Chester Cheston, with a later tower by E.L. Blackburne. G.F. Bodley designed St. Michael's, Camden Town (1880–81), St. Mary of Eton at Hackney Wick (1890–92) and Holy Trinity, Prince Consort Road, Kensington (1902–07). The last of these is an excellent example of Bodley's refined use of 14C and 15C styles. J.D. Sedding designed the Italianate Holy Redeemer, Clerkenwell (1887–88)—which from the beginning had a baldacchino over the high altar—and also Holy Trinity, Sloane Street (1888–90), whose fittings form an exceptional collection of the Arts and Crafts movement. St. Cuthbert's, Philbeach Gardens, Earl's Court (1884–88, by H. Roumieu Gough) likewise has exceptional fittings. Many of them were designed by William Bainbridge Reynolds, who worshipped at the church. In 1902–03 Sir Ninian Comper built St. Cyprian's at Clarence Gate, Regent's Park. He furnished it gradually, still working on it after the Second World War. Comper's aim was to recreate the 15C English church: tall, light, highly coloured, with a chancel screen and loft, a curtained altar with a canopy over, and further altars treated similarly. Much of Comper's work complemented the liturgical ideas of the Reverend Percy Dearmer, who was Vicar of St. Mary's, Primrose Hill, from 1901 to 1915. The 'English altar' was the linchpin of Dearmer's ideas and spread widely in subsequent years. Two more early 20C churches merit attention: the Annunciation, Bryanston Street, Marble Arch (1912–14, by Sir Walter Tapper), in a style dependent on Bodley's; and St. Barnabas', Shacklewell (1909–10, by C.H. Reilly).

Before leaving the Victorian and Edwardian periods, reference must be made to a few more non-Anglican churches. The Catholic Apostolic Church, a denomination which rapidly expanded in the early Victorian years (and which has almost disappeared in the 20C), built two exceptional churches. One was its 'cathedral', so to speak: the building now called Christ the King in Gordon Square,

Bloomsbury (1850–53, by J.R. Brandon), an impressive Gothic cruciform church which was never completed. The other—which is the only one in England still in use for worship by the denomination—stands in Maida Avenue. It was by J.L. Pearson, 1891, and is an example of Pearson's vaulted interiors. Amongst *Roman* Catholic churches, St. Dominic's in Southampton Road, Hampstead (1863–83, by C.A. Buckler) has an interesting plan of chapels to reflect the mysteries of the Rosary. Its style is Buckler's rather gaunt version of Early English. Also in N London is the Union Chapel, Islington, a United Reformed church of 1876 by James Cubitt. Finally, in central London the two most prominent Baptist and Methodist churches should be mentioned: the former a neo-Norman building in Bloomsbury of the 1840s and the latter a monumental French Classical building (the Central Hall, Westminster) of 1905–11 by Lanchester & Rickards.

Church building further into the 20C has naturally tended to be in outer London. Central London has chiefly seen restoration and rebuilding after bombing rather than new building. Perhaps the most distinguished restoration of a gutted church was that of St. Clement Danes in 1955–58 by Anthony Lloyd. Sir Giles Gilbert Scott and his brother Adrian Gilbert Scott restored St. Alban's, Holborn in a style very unlike that of Butterfield, but agreeable nonetheless. A total rebuilding of St. Paul's, Bow Common in 1958–60 by Robert Maguire produced a church which has often been cited as a model of postwar design. It is indeed a church which reflected the latest liturgical thinking, but even its admirers could not claim for it that it offers any ornamentation or details of interest. A more appealing church of similar date is Our Lady of the Rosary, Old Marylebone Road, opened in 1963. Its architect, H.S. Goodhart-Rendel, used a free medieval style which just manages to make agreeable a rather bare interior. In very recent years, Donald Buttress has undertaken a sympathetic restoration of part of Scott's St. Matthew's, Westminster. The church was burnt in 1977 and has had to be reduced in size.

Notable fittings are no earlier than the 16C and 17C. 16C Flemish glass is to be found at St. Margaret's, Westminster and St. George's, Hanover Square. The London Oratory Church has 17C statues of the 12 Apostles which were carved for Siena Cathedral by Giuseppe Mazzuoli. In addition, the altar of the Lady chapel comes from Brescia, where it was made for a Dominican church in 1693. English woodwork of the 17C may be seen in the chapel of the Charterhouse, where Ralph Symonds and Francis Carter provided splendid fittings (especially the W screen) in a Dutch style, and in St. James's, Piccadilly, where Grinling Gibbons designed the reredos and the font. The best-preserved 18C interior is probably that of St. Martin-in-the-Fields: darkly stained box-pews and galleries remain there. Innumerable distinguished items represent the 19C. Butterfield's fittings and decorations remain at All Saints', Margaret Street, many of them lately restored. St. Barnabas', Pimlico has a rich ensemble of fittings and stained glass which was formed over 50 years and more from its building. St. Augustine's at Kilburn and St. Mary Magdalene's at Paddington retain rich 19C interiors. The church of St. James the Less, Pimlico has an iron font canopy. St. Mary Magdalene's, Munster Square has an E window designed by A.W.N. Pugin and made by John Hardman. Also by Pugin is the high altar of the Jesuits' church in Farm Street, Mayfair. Holy Trinity, Sloane Street and St. Cuthbert's, Philbeach Gardens have exceptional collections of end-of-the-century fittings. Work by Sir Ninian Comper survives from the 1890s in the crypt chapel of St. Mary

Magdalene's, Paddington and in the Lady chapel of St. Matthew's, Westminster. His 20C work in St. Cyprian's, Clarence Gate is one of the great set-pieces of his career. Fittings by Comper exist too in St. Mark's, Regent's Park. St. Mary's, Bourne Street has fittings largely from the interwar years which represent the Continental or Italianising wing of the Anglo-Catholic movement. From after 1945, St. Etheldreda's at Holborn Circus has a notable scheme of stained glass by J.E. Nuttgens and by Charles Blakeman.

The history of monuments in this section of the book could well be written from Westminster Abbey alone, were that famous church to be within its scope. Westminster Abbey apart, notable monuments are relatively few. Perhaps the earliest monument of any distinction is that of John Holland, Duke of Exeter (died 1447), in the Tower of London's church of St. Peter ad Vincula. A rare monument of a monastic superior—of Prior Weston, head of the house of the Knights Hospitaller at Clerkenwell from 1527 to 1540—survives in the successor church there. His effigy is emaciated in the late medieval fashion. In the same church of St. John there is a monument to Don Ruiz de Vergara (died 1575) which was once at Valladolid. The tomb-chest seems truncated. In the nearby chapel of the Charterhouse there exists Nicholas Johnson's and Nicholas Stone's monument to Thomas Sutton (died 1611), the founder of the present almshouses and school. The railed monument has black marble columns and inscription plate; otherwise it is of alabaster. Also by Johnson is the monument of 1595 in Chelsea Old Church to Lord and Lady Dacre. The effigies lie in a recessed arch flanked by Corinthian columns, above which rise obelisks. The Dacres owned the former property at Chelsea of Sir Thomas More, who had erected a memorial in the same church in 1532 to his wife. It is a simple late Gothic work with a very long inscription. St. Dunstan's, Stepney has the table-tomb in a panelled recess of Sir Henry Collett, 1510, and also a number of 17C monuments. Elizabethan alabaster figures survive in St. John-at-Hackney. St. John's, Hampstead possesses 15C and 16C brasses, all minor. At St. Giles-in-the-Fields there is a memorial of 1634 to George Chapman which is attributed to Inigo Jones. It resembles an old milestone. Substantial groups of monuments survive in St. Margaret's, Westminster and in St. Pancras' Old Church. In the latter case they have been recoloured in recent years. None of them is of individual importance. Perhaps more interesting is Sir John Soane's memorial to his wife (1815) in St. Pancras' churchyard. Of interest from the 19C is the brass to the Reverend R.T. West in St. Mary Magdalene's, Paddington, but even that revived type is best represented in Westminster Abbey.

The older churches of central London naturally have numerous historical connections. St. Margaret's, Westminster is the burial place of Wenceslaus Hollar, William Caxton, Sir Walter Raleigh and Admiral Blake. John Milton was a parishioner. Samuel Pepys and Sir Winston Churchill married there in 1655 and 1908 respectively. Sir Winston's namesake and ancestor, the Sir Winston who died in 1688 and who was the father of the first Duke of Marlborough, was buried along the road at St. Martin-in-the-Fields. Other burials there were of Nell Gwynne, Thomas Chippendale and Nicholas Hilliard. Just to the E, at St. Paul's, Covent Garden, Grinling Gibbons, Thomas Arne (composer of 'Rule, Britannia!') and the artist Sir Peter Lely were buried, and W.S. Gilbert (of Gilbert & Sullivan) was baptised. Luke Hansard, the printer of parliamentary reports, and the 17C poet Andrew Marvell were both buried at St. Giles-in-the-Fields. J.C.

Bach lies in the churchyard of Old St. Pancras'. Another famous composer, Handel, was a parishioner of St. George's, Hanover Square. St. Luke's, Chelsea has two distinguished associations from the first half of the 19C: the first incumbent was the Duke of Wellington's brother and a few years later Dickens married there. The Brownings married in St. Marylebone Parish Church. St. John's, Hampstead is the parish church of numerous 19C artists and architects, including John Constable among the former. Sir Thomas More and his family were closely connected with Chelsea Old Church; a statue of Sir Thomas stands outside. Also in Chelsea, Madame Tussaud (died 1850), the proprietor of the famous wax-works, is buried at St. Mary's, Cadogan Street. John Wesley is buried behind the chapel in the City Road which was his headquarters. Across the road in Bunhill Fields lie Defoe, Bunyan, Isaac Watts and William Blake.

Unusual dedications are surprisingly few. St. Clement Danes is thought to reflect in both dedication and 'surname' a pre-Conquest Scandinavian settlement on the City's W side. St. Marylebone is a corruption of St. Mary-le-Bourne or St. Mary by the stream (the Tyburn). The early 18C churches of St. George in Bloomsbury, Hanover Square and Stepney owe their name to the Hanoverian Succession. St. Peter ad Vincula (or St. Peter in Chains) derives from the feast traditionally observed on August 1st and appropriately applies to the church on Tower Green. The rare dedication of St. Cyprian (a 3C martyr) was chosen for the church near Regent's Park by its founder, Charles Gutch, who had been impressed by the saint's writings.

Brompton, *The London Oratory Church of the Immaculate Heart of Mary, Brompton Road, SW7.* The London Oratory in Brompton Road was built in 1880–84 to the designs of Herbert Gribble. It is the second largest Catholic church in London after Westminster Cathedral and it is the most important Italianate church in the capital. It is served by a community of priests who belong to the Oratory of St. Philip Neri, which is an Order without vows and which pursues an essentially urban apostolate as laid down by its founder, who lived, mainly in Rome, from 1515 to 1595. St. Philip's Oratory was a feature of the Counter-Reformation and it was therefore to be argued in the 19C that its buildings in England should reflect that fact in Italian Renaissance dress and not seek to revive pre-Reformation Gothic. Cardinal Newman introduced the Oratory into England in 1848, but he chose to settle in Birmingham and the foundation of a house in London was left to Frederick William Faber, a fellow convert from the Church of England. The London Oratory began in King William Street, off the Strand, in 1849. It removed to Brompton in 1854, when a temporary church by J.J. Scoles was opened. The choice of Gribble to design the permanent church a generation later was the result of a competition in 1878, but it is thought to have owed much to the influence of the 15th Duke of Norfolk, who was a generous benefactor of the rebuilding. Gribble had worked with J.A. Hansom, who had designed the Duke's great church of St. Philip Neri at Arundel. The church of the London Oratory was consecrated in 1884, but its principal façade and its outer dome were not added until 1891–96. The total cost by then exceeded £100,000.

The church is a Latin cross, which is domed at the crossing. It is not orientated but faces N–S. Its principal or S façade is of two storeys, the upper one being much narrower and set back, for it covers only the nave and not its flanking chapels. The transepts and E end, however, are of two storeys. Four pairs of Corinthian columns and pilasters divide the narthex, which has a balustraded parapet. The upper storey, which is articulated by pairs of Corinthian pilasters, has volutes at the sides and a pediment above. The S façade was cleaned in 1984. The transepts are also pedimented. The outer dome is higher and steeper than Gribble originally intended, but this is agreeable as it is set well back from Brompton Road and needs to be substantial to be seen. To the W of the church's entrance is a memorial to Cardinal Newman, designed by Bodley & Garner and with a statue by L.J. Chavalliaud.

The interior comprises a three-bay nave, an apsidal E end, N and S transepts, a large NE chapel and three side chapels on each side of the nave and set at right angles to it. There are passageways between these chapels. The markedly wide nave is articulated by paired giant Corinthian pilasters in Plymouth marble, which stand against solid walling. The large arches to the side chapels spring from entablatures which are supported by paired Corinthian columns, which are half the size of the giant pilasters; the entablatures stretch from arch to arch, interrupted only by the giant pilasters. The chancel has a shallow dome, as does the middle bay of the nave. The first and third bays of the nave are groin-vaulted. Lanterns light the interior from above. On the W side, from S to N, the chapels are of the Sacred Heart, St. Joseph and the Seven Dolours; the W transept is the chapel of St. Philip Neri; to the E of the chancel is the chapel of St. Wilfrid; the E transept is the Lady chapel; and then follow the Calvary, St. Mary Magdalene's and St. Patrick's chapels towards the S. The baptistery occupies the SE corner. The Calvary chapel is smaller than the rest, for the portion of that bay which faces the nave is a singers' gallery.

The interior has greatly benefited from a restoration in 1984. The painting and gilding is now fresh and appealing. Many of the fittings predate Gribble's building. The altar rails, the choirstalls and the sanctuary flooring were all presented to the temporary church by the Duchess of Argyll in 1856. The seven-branched candlesticks in the chancel were designed by William Burges, whose patron, the third Marquess of Bute, was married here in 1872. Gribble had intended a baldacchino for the high altar, but this was never executed. The statues of the 12 Apostles, which flank the nave and transepts, were carved between 1679 and 1695 by Giuseppe Mazzuoli (1644–1725). They were made for Siena Cathedral, whence they were ejected in 1890. They were bought for the London Oratory in 1895. The statue of St. Peter under the singers' gallery is a copy of the one in St. Peter's in the Vatican. The pulpit is of 1930, by Commendatore Formilli. It has a stairway on each side and a huge tester. The altar of the Lady chapel was also rescued from rejection in Italy. It was made for the Confraternity of the Rosary in the church of San Domenico, Brescia, in 1693, under the supervision of Francesco Corbarelli and his two sons. They were personally responsible for the marble inlays, but the numerous statues were by several hands. These statues include four Dominican saints: St. Dominic himself (in the niche to the left of the altar), St. Catherine of Siena (niche to the right), St. Rose of Lima (left of the altar proper) and Pope Pius V (right). The decoration of the interior, although fully suggested by Gribble, was executed piecemeal by many artists. Gribble himself designed the altars of the chapels of St. Philip Neri and of the Seven Dolours. Underneath St.

Philip's altar lies a wax effigy of the saint, dressed in priest's vestments. Of special note is St. Wilfrid's chapel. Its high altar was made in the 18C for the church of St. Remy at Rochefort in Belgium. Also in this chapel is an altar of the English Martyrs (on the right by the doorway), which has a triptych of 1938 by Rex Whistler, featuring St. Thomas More and St. John Fisher and an execution scene.

(Michael Napier and Alistair Laing (Eds.) 'The London Oratory/ Centenary 1884–1984' (1984).)

Finsbury, *Wesley's Chapel, City Road, EC1.* The Mother Church of Methodism was built in 1777–78 for John Wesley himself (1703–91), who resided next door at 47 City Road for the last 12 years of his life. Wesley had felt his heart 'strangely warmed' in 1738 in Aldersgate Street, near the present Museum of London. In the following year he opened the Foundery Chapel nearby. Wesley's Chapel replaced it 40 years later. The building received a new portico in 1815 and underwent extensive restorations which were completed in 1880, 1891 and 1978. The chapel's character remains that of 1778. In 1984 a Museum of Methodism was opened in the crypt.

The chapel stands well back from City Road, forming the E side of an open courtyard. The chapel is of five bays, with the three central bays slightly projecting and pedimented. The portico has two pairs of fluted Doric columns. Vestibules to the left and right of the five bays are later additions. There are two tiers of arched windows, which continue along the N and S elevations. The E end has a stone-faced apse. Within, the chapel has a gallery on the N, S and W sides which is supported on polished jasper columns. Under the W end is a vestibule, separated from the body of the chapel by glass screens. The apse is framed by two polished Corinthian columns, set on high bases, which support a coffered arch. The apse itself has three tall arched windows, beneath which stands a curving tripartite Classical reredos, adorned with inscribed boards and with gilding. Some yards to the W, on the central axis, stands the pulpit, which is the top part of the original three-decker. The pews are of 1891. The ceiling is flat and has decorations in the Adam style. Stained glass fills most of the windows and is all of the 19C. A great many small memorials are affixed to the walls beneath the galleries. Of special note is the one in the vestibule to Jabez Bunting, a famous leader of Methodism in the early 19C.

The chapel's interior differs little from that of an 18C Anglican church. Wesley was himself an Anglican priest and saw his ministry as supplementary to that of the Anglican parishes, not rivalling them. Anglican clergy were in fact members of the chapel staff until as late as 1826. The chapel's exterior, however, differs from the Anglican pattern in its lack of a steeple and its lack of the grand portico which was given to so many 18C Anglican churches in London.

To the N of the chapel proper is the Foundery chapel, a low, lantern-lit room which houses some benches from the pioneering building of 1739 and possesses the chamber organ of Charles Wesley, John's brother, who was one of the most celebrated hymn-writers of all time. A door leads from here into the churchyard and so to John Wesley's tomb, which is a simple Classical monument of diminishing stages, surmounted by an urn. A long inscription speaks of Wesley's considerable ministry.

Church historians should not overlook Bunhill Fields, the burial ground on the other side of City Road, in which are buried some of the most famous members of the Nonconformist Churches. John

Bunyan, William Blake, Daniel Defoe and Isaac Watts are among those who lie here. In the adjoining Friends' Burial Ground lies George Fox, the founder of the Society of Friends or Quakers.

Holborn, *St. Etheldreda, Ely Place, EC1.* St. Etheldreda's is a rare survivor in London of work in the Decorated style from the end of the 13C. It was built between 1286 and 1297 as the chapel of the London house of the Bishops of Ely, with whose diocese it was continuously linked from 1286 until 1772. St. Etheldreda was the foundress in 673 of the monastery at Ely. The church in Ely Place is in the form of a typical two-storey medieval private chapel and is comparable with the famous Decorated chapel of Prior Crauden which survives at Ely itself. St. Etheldreda's was bought at an auction in 1874 by the Fathers of Charity, a Catholic Order which had been founded by Antonio Rosmini Serbati in 1828 (and thus known as Rosminians). Much restoration has occurred since the purchase, especially in the 1870s, in 1935 and in 1950–52. Despite much renewal of the stone-work, the church remains an authentic Decorated building. It is also notable today for its postwar stained glass, which is unusually attractive and sympathetic for glass of its date.

The church stands back from a quiet, gated street just a few yards from Holborn Circus. The gate is a memento of the former precinct of Ely House. The church's E end is practically the only part of the exterior which is visible. It is dominated by the five-light E window, whose intersecting tracery is enriched with sexfoils, cinquefoils and quatrefoils. The intersecting lights fall short of the apex, which is instead filled with a large sexfoil. Intersecting tracery is typical of c 1300, whereas Geometrical designs look back into the 13C; but the combination here, complex but not quite exuberant (or 'flowing'), seems to be on the verge of the fully Decorated tracery of the early 14C. To the left and right of the window are tall trefoiled niches. A blank quatrefoil is in the gable head. A doorway, well below the modern street level, gives access to the crypt. There were once polygonal corner buttresses, with traceried panels, which rose into pinnacles.

The church is entered through a passage on its S side and up a flight of steps. The interior is rectangular and aisleless, tall and divided only by a screen at the W end into an entrance bay or antechapel and five bays of the church proper. The five-light W window mirrors the E window, but with less complex tracery. The N and S windows are of two lights and trefoiled; between them are blank trefoiled niches with crocketed gables. The same gabled arches flank the E window. The roof is modern.

The W screen was designed by J.F. Bentley and was presented in 1897. Large statues of 16C and 17C English Catholic martyrs, by Mary Blakeman, are affixed to the N and S walls between the windows. A feretory stands on a ledge in the SE corner and contains a portion of St. Etheldreda's hand. Just outside the antechapel, in the passage, are finely carved wooden royal arms of the 17C. The interior is chiefly distinguished by the stained glass. The E window, whose size makes it a dominant feature, is arguably the most agreeable postwar window in London, and one which is wholly admirable in its sympathy for its setting. The central light depicts Christ the King, His right hand raised in blessing and His left holding an orb, the symbol of temporal sovereignty, surmounted by a cross, the symbol of spiritual precedence. Christ is crowned and is accorded the crossed nimbus to which He alone is entitled. He is shown against a background of the heavenly host and above Him is the dove of the Holy Spirit. To His left and right are the Virgin Mary and St. Joseph, the former labelled in Greek ('MP') and further distinguished by the title 'OY', which stands for *Theotokos* or God-bearer (Mother of God), given to her by the Council of Ephesus in 431. In the upper parts of the four outer lights are the Evangelists, each accompanied by the opening words of his Gospel in Latin and by his winged symbol: a man (Matthew), a lion (Mark), an ox (Luke) and an eagle (John). In the left-hand light, at the bottom, is St. Etheldreda, holding a staff and accompanied by no fewer than three shields of the Ely arms—of three gold crowns on a red background. A smaller scene above shows St. Etheldreda on her death-bed in 679, surrounded by her nuns as St. Bede describes. Below the three central panels is the Last Supper all the more appropriate for being just above the high altar. In the tracery lights may be seen the nine orders of angels; the alpha and the omega, the beginning and the end; the chi-rho symbol, the first two letters in Greek of the name of Christ; a triangular symbol of the Holy Trinity; and, at the very top, God the Father. The designer of this splendid window was Joseph E. Nuttgens and it was executed in 1952. All the other stained glass in the church was designed by Charles Blakeman. The W window of 1964 depicts those members of the London Charterhouse (sited half a mile away from Ely Place) who were martyred in 1535 under King Henry VIII. Smaller panels show the Passion of Christ and of the martyrs. The window bears the arms of Pope John XXIII at the apex and of the Spanish ambassador (bottom right), whose predecessor of the 1620s, Gondomar, lived in Ely House for a few years. The side windows of the church are of 1952–58 and show sequences of Old and New Testament scenes to S and N respectively. They also show the coats of arms and the names of pre-Reformation Bishops of Ely; three of the shields are those of cardinals and are thus surrounded by the red tassels of a cardinal's hat.

Medieval Bishops of Ely were of sufficient importance to bring fame to Ely House. Shakespeare's 'Richard II' and 'Richard III' both refer to it. John of Gaunt died there in 1399. In the Elizabethan period, Queen Elizabeth I forced Bishop Cox to lease part of his property to Sir Christopher Hatton, after whom the nearby street of the diamond trade is named. In modern times, the church has become known for the blessing of St. Blaise, which is given each year on the saint's feast, February 3rd. A blessing is given as crossed candles are held against the throat. A relic of the saint was given to the church in 1917.

Mayfair, *The Grosvenor Chapel, South Audley Street, W1.* The Grosvenor Chapel is a survivor of the 18C proprietory chapels which were once numerous in Mayfair and St. Marylebone. It was built in 1730–31, almost certainly to the designs of Benjamin Timbrell, a builder, who had previously worked on St. Peter's, Vere Street, and on St. Martin-in-the-Fields. Land for the chapel was leased for 99 years from Sir Richard Grosvenor, who had laid out Grosvenor Square just a few years before. (Its original name was Audley Chapel, from one of Sir Richard's forbears. His descendant became the first Duke of Westminster in 1874.) When the chapel's lease expired in 1829, the freehold was bought by the parish of St. George, Hanover Square, and under an Act of 1831 it became a chapel of ease to St. George's. This arrangement pertains today, although the chapel has always been run more or less as a distinct parish church.

In the 18C and 19C the congregation was markedly aristocratic and the chapel's income, from pew rents and burial fees, was substantial. Decline came at the end of the 19C. It was then proposed to demolish both the chapel and St. George's and to rebuild the parish church on the chapel's site. This proposal was finally vetoed by the second Duke of Westminster in 1912 and as a result the chapel was reordered in the following year by Sir Ninian Comper. His scheme was never completed and so the chapel's internal character today is that of the 18C with a stylistically sympathetic but incomplete E end of the early 20C.

The exterior, of yellow brick with contrasting white details, suggests New England or the Carolinas rather than Mayfair. Its W front faces South Audley Street and looks down Aldford Street opposite. This front is of five bays and is a somewhat muddled, though agreeable, composition. The tower, which projects slightly and is quoined, occupies the middle bay. Its lowest storey is hidden by a straight-topped Tuscan porch of four columns, which straddles the three central bays and has a door for each. Arched windows, recessed and eared, pierce each bay of the storey above the porch. The middle one, in the tower's W face, has a rectangular frame with Doric pilasters. The tower interrupts the pediment which would otherwise have surmounted the entire W front. An octagonal and very plain belfry stage sits awkwardly above the roofline, and above that is a very short and plain spire. A lantern and cupola, which were originally contemplated, would surely have been more appropriate. The N and S elevations have six bays, with two tiers of windows to reflect the internal galleries.

Within, the impression is one of dark woodwork below and whitened features above. There are N, S and W galleries on square Doric piers, with small Ionic columns above, all painted white. The nave has a segmental ceiling, but the aisles are groin-vaulted. The E end is at first sight strange and complicated. Two giant Ionic columns flank a white-painted screen, to the front of which are attached two Corinthian columns, which support an entablature above the level of the screen. The giant columns were to be parts of colonnades which would have divided the nave from the aisles after the removal of the galleries. Between the columns which were built is the Rood beam, with large gilded figures. The two small Corinthian columns were to be parts of a baldacchino, which was not allowed in 1913. So they now form a reredos for the altar, which stands in front of the screen. Behind the screen is the Lady chapel, which retains the original reredos (but without its inscribed boards) and also has a hanging pyx, which Comper would have placed under the baldacchino. Comper's arrangement of the altar, if completed, would have looked like that in St. Philip's, Cosham, Hampshire, or the one in the chapel of Pusey House, Oxford.

The galleries still retain 18C box-pews, but the nave has lost them and has also lost its three-decker pulpit. The original communion rails remain, brought forward from the E end. The organ in the W gallery was originally by Abraham Jordan; it has been rebuilt within its original case.

The Anglo-Catholic traditions, which began here in the later 19C, have been consolidated in the 20C. The chapel came to play a prominent role in the wider Church, especially between the Wars. Over the years a valuable ministry to young professionals was developed, notably through the William Temple Association.

(Ann Callender (Ed.), 'Godly Mayfair' (1980).)

Mayfair, *St. George, Hanover Square, W1.* St. George's was built in 1721–25 to the designs of John James as one of the Fifty New Churches under the Act of 1711. It was a trumpeting of the Hanoverian succession of 1714: it was part of the development of Hanover Square (laid out in 1716–20); it was named in reference to King George I; and it was originally intended that a statue of the king should surmount the W pediment. The church is a dignified Classical building, which shares with St. Martin-in-the-Fields and St. George's, Bloomsbury the distinction of being the first in London to have a hexastyle portico at the W end and a tower over the first bay of the body of the church. St. George's was altered by Benjamin Ferrey in 1871, by Sir Arthur Blomfield in 1894 and by his nephew, Sir Reginald Blomfield, in the 1920s.

The church stands in St. George Street, a few yards S of Hanover Square. Its S side is obscured and its N side looks onto the narrow Maddox Street. Only the W front is prominent. A hexastyle Corinthian portico stands in front of the church proper, but not quite as wide as the latter, just as at St. Martin-in-the-Fields. Behind the portico rises the tower, which is on a much smaller scale than those of other early 18C churches in London. A tier of clock-faces is surmounted by the belfry stage, in which a single louvred and arched window is flanked by pairs of Corinthian columns set across the chamfered angles. Two urns stand above the entablature of each angle to reflect the two columns below. This belfry is reminiscent of Wren's later steeples. Above the belfry is a small dome and a diminutive lantern. Here the cupola of Chelsea's Royal Hospital comes to mind. The small scale of St. George's steeple is much more appropriate to its position than that of the contemporary St. Martin-in-the-Fields; and yet it was the latter which was copied far and wide. The N front is treated in the strong, monumental style which brings Hawksmoor to mind rather than James. There are the usual two tiers of windows to reflect the internal galleries, the upper tier being placed in rectangular frames. Above the vestibules in the W bay are pedimented attics, which obviate the impression of the steeple sitting on the church's roof.

The interior has a nave which is divided from the N and S aisles by four-bay arcades which have square piers below and Corinthian columns above the galleries. The capitals of the columns are gilded; the rest of the columns and the walls are painted white. There is a straight entablature. There is no structural chancel but the sanctuary and the choir are clearly delineated by being raised on one step each. The ceiling is segmental. The N, S and W galleries are unaltered from the 18C. The E end is slightly recessed under a wide, depressed arch. It features a Venetian window.

The reredos is much larger than that of a Wren church. It fills the entire E wall up to the window and is not divided in the Wren manner. Instead, its centre is filled with a large, rather dark painting of the Last Supper by William Kent. The ends of the reredos are canted and each have two Corinthian columns, with gilded capitals and fluting. The E window above has 16C Flemish stained glass. It is attributed to Arnold van Nijmegen and comes from the church of St. Jacques, Malines, for which it was made in c 1525. It was adapted for St. George's by Thomas Willement in c 1843. The glass depicts the Tree of Jesse. In the central light, above Jesse, are medallions of St. George, Victory and Isabella. St. George was Willement's replacement for the Emperor Charles V, who gave the window with his wife Isabella to mark the return of the ship, 'Victoria', from

Magellan's circumnavigation. The figure of God the Father, which filled the top of the original window, was not used here and was placed instead in the church of St. Mary and St. Nicholas at Wilton in Wiltshire. The arrangement of the choir and its black and white marble floor are Sir Arthur Blomfield's. In 1926 Sir Reginald Blomfield added the screens which flank the choir and set up the NE chapel. He also designed the present font and arranged the baptistery in the NW corner in 1934. The pulpit is raised on six fluted, wooden Corinthian columns and has a fine wrought-iron stair rail. Its tester was removed by Benjamin Ferrey in 1871 and it was lowered by Sir Arthur Blomfield in 1894. Ferrey also cut down the former box-pews. On the gallery fronts and on panels in the galleries themselves are inscribed the names of churchwardens from the church's opening: a roll-call of the nobility and gentry, it will be noticed. The W gallery contains the organ, housed in a sumptuous five-towered case, which was originally built by Gerard Smith, 1725, but rebuilt by John Snetzler, 1761, by J.C. Bishop in the early 19C and most recently by Harrison & Harrison in 1972.

St. George's had the distinction of claiming George Frederick Handel as a parishioner from 1724 to 1759. He lived in Brook Street. He advised on the original organ and took part in the testing of candidates for the post of organist. The church has long been fashionable for weddings. Disraeli, Theodore Roosevelt, Asquith, Marconi, John Buchan, Shelley the poet, Joseph Grimaldi the clown and the Duke of Sussex (sixth son of King George III) were all married here.

St. Marylebone, *All Saints, Margaret Street, W1.* All Saints' was built in 1850–59 to the designs of William Butterfield. It was very largely a major benefaction of Alexander Beresford Hope, the second President of the Ecclesiological Society, whose 'model church' it was intended to be. It superseded the 18C Margaret Chapel, whose congregation, Tractarian by the 1840s, had wished to rebuild. This combination of the congregation's desire for a worthier building, the Ecclesiological Society's keenness to put its ideas into practice and Beresford Hope's willingness to pay ensured a formidable effort. The result was widely regarded as remarkable and earned praise from architects, ecclesiologists and from John Ruskin, whose writings had partly influenced the church's details. Drawbacks arose from the many arguments between Butterfield and Beresford Hope, and from the fact that in the end the decoration was not all of a piece. Nevertheless, the church is still an essential building for the church tourist in London. In the life of the Church in general, All Saints' became one of the great centres of Anglo-Catholic worship and remains noted today for its churchmanship, its music and for its role as a place of Christian education. The building and the adjacent clergy house are notable for their careful arrangement on a cramped site, and for their thoughtful use of Italian and German precedents, particularly in colouring. The church deserves to be seen when it is internally well-lit and in a thoroughly clean state, within and without; for wear and tear and gloom have so easily spoilt its effect on past commentators. It should be seen as a conscious early attempt in the Gothic Revival to adapt exuberant medieval, and especially medieval Italian, colouring to the 19C English scene.

The church stands a few hundred yards E of Regent Street, just N of its junction with Oxford Street. It is known as 'the cathedral of Oxford Circus'. Its site on the N side of Margaret Street is very cramped. Many 19C church builders in central London admittedly had to face such sites, but it was especially no easy place for a 'model church'. Butterfield designed the church without E and N windows and he had to provide a clergy house without obscuring the church too much. He chose to place the house along the street frontage of the site, divided on either side of a small courtyard. A gabled gateway stands in the middle. The church stands at the back, with neither its E nor W end visible from the street. A tall, thin W tower rises from behind the domestic building on the left and it is surmounted by a spire which rises to 230ft. The tower has pairs of very tall, two-light belfry windows. A gabled porch of some elaboration stands to the E of the tower. Just to the right of the porch rises a tall, decorated pinnacle, surmounted by a cross. This pinnacle leads the eye from the body of the church to the very considerable tower and spire. The chancel rises slightly above the level of the nave. The church is built of red brick, with bands of black brick and stone. The contrast of colours seems very mild today and it is difficult to see how critics could be startled by it in 1859. Butterfield became one of the principal users of 'structural polychrome'.

The interior comprises a three-bay nave, N and S aisles, a tall chancel with clerestory, and N and S chancel aisles. The baptistery occupies the SW corner, under the tower; its N wall takes the place of an arch in the W bay of the nave. The chancel has no Rood screen but a low marble wall with red and gilded gates. There is a chancel arch, but the chancel is as tall as the nave. The clerestory windows in the chancel have Geometrical tracery. To the N and S of the chancel there are arches filled with open tracery of three lights and with screens across the bases. A lightly stained screen stands at the E end of the S aisle. Both E and W ends have blind arcading. The W window, the largest in the church, is of five lights. The Lady chapel is at the E end of the N aisle.

The stained glass in the church was not considered to be entirely successful in the 19C, especially as it did not match the mural decorations. This arose from the disputes between Butterfield and Beresford Hope. Michael O'Connor designed the clerestory glass and the E window of the S aisle. Henri Gérénte was intended to be the designer of the major windows but he died, and his brother Alfred was commissioned instead. His were the original windows of the S aisle. These were replaced by Alexander Gibbs, whose designs depict the three archangels, St. Catherine and St. Alban, and St. Athanasius and St. Augustine. The W window, a Tree of Jesse, was also designed by Alfred Gérénte. Gibbs replaced it in 1877. By Gibbs too were the mural tiles on the N wall, 1873. The chancel's E wall was originally painted in the 1850s by William Dyce. Restoration was needed as early as 1864. In 1909 Ninian Comper executed the present paintings. There are seven panels in each of two tiers, under gabled arcading, plus a single panel at the top. Comper was also responsible for the paintings of the N and S walls of the sanctuary in 1914 and for the hanging pyx in 1930. The elaborate marble pulpit, which stands on three very thick, short columns, is Butterfield's. The screen in the S aisle is by Laurence King, 1962. Comper designed the fittings of the Lady chapel in 1911. All the paintings in the chancel were cleaned by Peter Larkworthy in recent years.

The residential choir school was closed in 1968, but the church's strong musical tradition continued. In 1970 an Institute of Christian Studies was founded, to provide a substantial education in the Christian faith for the laity.

St. Marylebone, *St. Cyprian, Clarence Gate, Glentworth Street,*
NW1. St. Cyprian's was built in 1902–03 to the designs of Sir Ninian
Comper. It is a very important building of the later Gothic Revival, a
worthy Anglo-Catholic interpretation in the early 20C of a late
medieval church from Norfolk or Suffolk. In Comper's career, it
stands out as one of the more complete examples of his early, purely
Gothic style, although it was to be fitted out over many decades. St.
Cyprian's was built nearly 40 years after the parish was founded. The
Reverend Charles Gutch began the work in 1866 at the other end of
what is now Glentworth Street by renting two houses, which G.E.
Street adapted to form a temporary chapel. Father Gutch worked in
the new district until his death in 1896 without being able to build a
permanent church, for the local landowner, Viscount Portman, disliked his High Churchmanship and refused to provide a site. After
Father Gutch's death, a site was rather grudgingly made available,
with strict conditions which were punctiliously met.

St. Cyprian's, Clarence Gate, built by Sir Ninian Comper
in 1902–03 and adorned by him in subsequent decades

The church stands at the N end of Glentworth Street, the opposite end to Father Gutch's temporary chapel, but on the very site of his clergy house. It is built of red brick, with large four-light windows separated by buttresses. It is long and low, with no tower but a tiny E bellcote instead. The W (or liturgical N) side has less tracery in its windows than the E side. The N (or liturgical E) elevation, which faces Ivor Place, has a chancel window of five transomed lights and four-light windows to the chancel chapels.

The interior of St. Cyprian's is strongly reminiscent of a 15C East Anglian church. There are seven-bay aracades with N and S aisles which run the full length of the church. The piers are thin and very tall, with the simplest of capitals. There is no structural division between the nave and chancel. Instead, there is an elaborate screen, painted and gilded, which stretches across both nave and aisles and whose position is mirrored in the roof above by a lower tiebeam. The interior as a whole is light and spacious, for although the windows at the E end have stained glass, those of the nave aisles have clear, bottle-end glass. The screen was completed only in 1924; the W end, including an organ gallery, dates from 1930; and the chapel of the Holy Name to the liturgical N of the chancel dates from 1938.

The great screen stands two bays from the E end. It has 32 painted figures in its panels and a particularly rich canopy. Above it is a Rood, with angels flanking the Virgin Mary and St. John, all gilded. In the chancel, the altar is an 'English altar', with angels atop riddel posts, a dossal behind and curtains to the sides. In later years, Comper preferred a baldacchino, and here in 1948 he moved in that direction by painting the canopy, which depicts Christ in Majesty. The altar in the Lady chapel, to the right, has no fewer than six angels. The altar in the chapel of the Holy Name is the one Father Gutch used in the 19C. The stained glass of the church shows Comper's typical blue and yellow colouring. The window over the high altar depicts, below, the appearance of the Risen Christ to St. Thomas, St. Cyprian and St. Cornelius, and above, St. Augustine, St. Peter, the Virgin and Child, St. Paul and St. Athanasius. These figures are surmounted by a bright light to represent the Holy Spirit, and a heavenly host surrounds them. The Lady chapel's main window, inserted in 1930, has as its principal subjects the Annunciation, St. Margaret of Scotland (left) and St. Etheldreda (right). The lectern, to the right of the nave, recalls the one in King's College chapel, Cambridge. The oak pulpit to the left has linenfold panels and a tester, in a style of c 1600. The W end, which features a vaulted stone gallery, is relatively bare. The one highly decorated fitting here is the font cover, tall, elaborate and gilded in the 15C East Anglian manner, but in this case including Classical as well as Gothic elements.

St. Pancras. The parish of St. Pancras achieved fame through the railway station which was opened in 1868 as the terminus of the Midland Railway. The parish was once of considerable size, reaching N to Hampstead and Highgate, but today it is limited to the vicinity of the Euston Road. There are in fact *two* parishes of the same name, for the ancient church of the district serves one parish and stands just N of the station, whereas the 'new' or early 19C church serves the other and stands prominently in Euston Road, further W. The saint himself suffered martyrdom in Rome in the early 4C under the Emperor Diocletian. The claims for an exceptionally early foundation of the church in London, which have been repeated so often, may be safely dismissed when the evidence is considered.

New Church of St. Pancras, Euston Road, NW1. New St. Pancras' was built in 1819–22 to the designs of William and Henry William Inwood under the terms of an Act of Parliament of 1816. The church is one of the most notable examples in London of the Greek Revival style. Elements of ancient buildings in Athens are directly copied here in the Euston Road. Henry William Inwood had travelled in Greece and had closely studied its buildings. St. Pancras', was one of the costliest of 19C churches; the sum of £82,000 was spent. Substantial restoration occurred in 1951–53.

The church stands in the angle of Euston Road and Woburn Place. Its W end has a hexastyle Ionic portico, behind which are three huge doors, the central one being slightly taller. These doors open into a vestibule, above which rises the tower. This is based on the Tower of the Winds at Athens. It is octagonal and of three receding stages, quite distinct among London's churches. It was once surmounted by a finial which copied a Corinthian column from St. Theodora's Church at Arta, but it now has a plain stone finial of 1952–53. The Ionic portico derives from the Erechtheion at Athens. The Greek original comprised a main block and two projections. One of these projections substituted for the usual columns a row of draped female figures or *caryatides*; an ancient survivor of them is now in the British Museum. The Inwoods copied this feature in the N vestry, which projects beyond the E wall of the church. There are two tiers of N and S windows to reflect the usual internal galleries. The tall upper windows taper towards the top and look Egyptian rather than Greek. The E end is apsidal.

The interior, 117ft long and 60ft wide, is undivided and preserves a fairly sumptuous late Georgian air. There is a flat, coffered ceiling. There are galleries and box-pews, with a very wide central alley. At the E end, at gallery height, there are six Ionic columns in scagliola, which stand away from the wall of the apse. More Ionic columns support the organ gallery at the W. The present scheme of blue, cream and white colouring is postwar, but appropriate. The pulpit, much decorated, stands on the right on four thin Ionic columns arranged in a square. The stairs to the pulpit are elaborate. Behind it the arrangement of the E end is late Victorian. An inscription states: 'This choir was enclosed, repaved, furnished and decorated, Christmas, 1889'. To the N of the choir, a glass screen of 1965 encloses a small chapel. The windows have stained glass by Clayton & Bell.

(Charles E. Lee, 'St. Pancras Church and Parish' (1955).)

Tower of London, *Chapel Royal of St. John the Evangelist, Tower Hill, EC3.* St. John's Chapel in the White Tower is the most important early Norman place of worship in London. It is placed in the SE corner of the White Tower, which was built between c 1077 and 1097 and which is the keep or citadel of the Tower of London. The chapel is a ponderous, two-storeyed work, almost entirely unornamented, which impresses by its strength and proportions. It is tunnel-vaulted and has an apsidal E end. The groin-vaulted aisles and tunnel-vaulted gallery curve round the E end as ambulatories. The arcades are of short, round piers, square abaci and unmoulded arches. The arches of the gallery are also unmoulded and they stand on square piers, directly above the round piers of the lower arcade. The sole ornamentation is in the capitals: simple scallop and T-cross designs.

Tower of London, *Chapel Royal of St. Peter ad Vincula, Tower Hill,*
EC3. The Chapel Royal of St. Peter ad Vincula is a building of the
early 16C whose interest lies chiefly in its monuments and in its
associations with prisoners of the Tower. It stands in the NW corner
of the inner ward, N of Tower Green and thus just N of the place of
execution. The building was completed in 1520 and there were major
restorations in 1876–77 and in 1970–71. It comprises a nave and a
slightly shorter N aisle, separated by a four-bay arcade, whose piers
have four attached shafts and hollows in the diagonals. The nave and
N aisle have five-light E windows, of clear glass; the S wall has five
three-light windows; but the hidden N wall has just one window. At
the W end there is a very thin, quoined tower, surmounted by an
agreeable lantern bellcote.

The early 16C chapel of St. Peter ad Vincula on Tower
Green, burial place of those beheaded nearby

Within, an organ of 1699 by Father Smith occupies the NE corner of
the aisle. The pulpit and seats were products of the last major
restoration. There are three large monuments. One, made in c 1620,
stands against the N wall of the sanctuary and commemorates Sir
Richard Blount, 1564 (right) and his son, Sir Michael Blount, 1596
(left), both Lieutenants of the Tower. Three Corinthian columns
divide two pairs of arches, each of which encloses kneeling figures. A
balustrade joins the column bases. There is much bright heraldry,
both above the figures in the arches and on top of the monument. In
the NW corner there is a large canopied monument to John Holland,
Duke of Exeter (died 1447), Constable of the Tower. This was
originally placed in St. Katherine's by the Tower. The monument
comprises a tomb-chest with three recumbent effigies (the Duke with
his first and third wives), surmounted by a huge canopy. The arch
of this canopy is cusped and sub-cusped and has angels in the
spandrels. There are very small figures on the uprights and larger
ones of angels in the frieze. Above are three painted helms and some
heraldry and a tall tier of empty niches. Under the second arch of the

central arcade from the W is a tomb-chest with the effigies of Sir Richard Cholmondeley (died 1544) and his wife. He was Lieutenant of the Tower under King Henry VIII. Notice the Tudor rose on his SS collar, just beneath his clasped hands.

Many of those executed on Tower Green were naturally buried in St. Peter's. They include Queen Anne Boleyn (1536), King Henry VIII's second wife; Queen Catherine Howard (1542), King Henry VIII's fifth wife; St. Thomas More (1535), Lord Chancellor, writer and saint of the Catholic Church; John Dudley, Duke of Northumberland (1553), the father-in-law of Lady Jane Grey; Edward Seymour, Duke of Somerset (1552), uncle of King Edward VI; Thomas Cromwell, Earl of Essex (1540), the ruthless overlord of the Dissolution of the Monasteries; James Scott, Duke of Monmouth (1685), the illegitimate son of King Charles II who rebelled against his uncle, King James VII and II; and three Scotch peers who were executed for their support of the Jacobite rebellion of 1745, namely the sixth Lord Balmerinoch and the fourth Earl of Kilmarnock (both 1746) and the 12th Lord Lovat (1747). Macaulay voiced the feelings of many when he said: 'In truth there is no sadder spot on earth'.

The name of the chapel means 'St. Peter in chains'. It is repeated in a number of English churches and in a famous church in Rome.

Westminster

St. Clement Danes, Strand, WC2. St. Clement's is a restoration of 1955–58 by Anthony Lloyd, after bombing in 1941, of Sir Christopher Wren's church of 1680–82. Wren's work did not include the tower, which had already been rebuilt by Joshua Marshall in 1669–70, and to which James Gibbs added a steeple in 1719–20. Anthony Lloyd's restoration is distinguished by its use of darkly stained woodwork, which is much closer to the woodwork of an authentic Wren interior than the very light woodwork used in other postwar restorations of Wren's churches. Since 1958 St. Clement's has been the central church of the Royal Air Force. Previously it was a parish church, whose origins apparently dated from the days of Danish settlement in London, perhaps in the 11C. The church's stonework was cleaned in 1982.

The church stands on an island site at the E end of the Strand, opposite G.E. Street's Law Courts. The junction of Aldwych and the Strand creates a large open space to the W of the church, which centres on a statue of W.E. Gladstone. The church has a tall W steeple which presents features of various dates. The W doorway is an early Classical composition and is similar to the S doorway of St. Helen's, Bishopsgate, which is dated 1633. Above the door comes an arched window with Y-tracery, then a 'porthole' of Wren's time and then another arched but Y-traceried window. It would appear that the Gothic tracery is of the same date as the doorway, in the 17C but probably before the Civil War. The upper part of the tower and its surmounting steeple are unmistakably by Gibbs. The louvred belfry windows each have a 'Gibbs surround'. The steeple proper is of three receding octagonal stages, with open arches and many urns. Embracing the tower at the W end are low, domed lobbies, the S one a staircase to the crypt, the other used as an office. Both have outer W doors with segmental heads and with porthole windows above. The body of the church has the two tiers of windows which are typical of a galleried interior: tall and arched above, small and segmental below.

The S side also has swags above the upper windows. Originally, the S side alone faced a busy street. The E end is apsidal. Beyond it, note the statue of Dr. Samuel Johnson, by Percy Fitzgerald, 1910. Dr Johnson lived in Gough Square, to the N of Fleet Street, not far E of the church.

Within, the church is a fine reproduction of Wren's interior. There are N and S galleries with square, panelled supports, above which rise Corinthian columns, their capitals gilded, which support block entablatures and the two arcades. There is a quadrant bay on each side between the E apse and the rest of the church, which has the usual effect of widening the E end. Below the church is a medieval crypt, reached from the SW corner.

The reredos has two arched panels, which were painted by Ruskin Spear to depict the Annunciation. They are subdued but successful amidst the darkly stained woodwork. Above is the E window by Carl Edwards, showing Christ in Glory. The two smaller windows to N and S are also by Carl Edwards. All the other windows in the church have clear Reamy Antique glass. The 17C pulpit, carved in the style of Grinling Gibbons, was preserved in St. Paul's Cathedral during the Second World War. The lectern, however, is a postwar work by Anthony Lloyd: much more agreeably ornate than other postwar examples. High above the E end of the nave, amidst the plasterwork of the ceiling, are the Stuart royal arms. Above the arcades are many gilded cherubim and coloured shields with gilded surrounds. The benches in the nave are telescopic and so the visitor will usually find a very wide central space. Set into the floor may be seen hundreds of R.A.F. squadron badges in slate. A more solemn reminder of the R.A.F. is the series of glass-fronted cabinets in the aisles which contain books of remembrance of former R.A.F. personnel. Each cabinet has small obelisks rising from the front angles and a domed top, surmounted by an eagle. R.A.F. flags hang in the galleries. Under the W gallery are further cabinets in which are displayed plate and other items with R.A.F. connections. In the gallery itself is the organ, built by Ralph Downes and given by the United States Air Force. It has four urn-topped towers and much gilding. The crypt is notable for two things: for the coffin plates which are affixed to the walls, and for the black granite font, which is surmounted by a Norwegian crown.

A 19C Rector of St. Clement's, William Webb-Ellis, is credited with the invention of the game of rugby in 1823. A claim with much longer roots is that the oranges and lemons of the traditional rhyme belong here. Fruit has indeed been distributed to children in modern times by virtue of the claim. The placing of the tradition here is highly questionable, for it would seem more probable that it originated at St. Clement Eastcheap in the City.

St. Margaret, Parliament Square, SW1. St. Margaret's is a rebuilding between c 1486 and 1523 of a typically placed precinct church, a parish church next to a monastery, in this case next to Westminster Abbey. The architects were Robert Stowell, master mason of the abbey, Thomas Redeman and his son Henry. Just as the abbey has always been of exceptional importance, so too has St. Margaret's been an unusually prominent church. It is the parish church of the House of Commons, with a special seat for Mr. Speaker, and has long been one of the most fashionable churches in London for weddings. In the 18C and 19C the fabric of St. Margaret's was much altered. John James virtually rebuilt the tower in 1735–37. Sir Gilbert

Scott altered the interior in 1877, more or less presenting the appearance which we see today. J.L. Pearson added the W and SE porches. The E end was extended by 6ft in 1905. In more recent years, the church has been substantially restored and cleaned.

The church stands on the S side of Parliament Square, to the N of King Henry VII's chapel in Westminster Abbey. The church's E end faces Westminster Hall. It stands free of all buildings, but it usually seems to be overshadowed by both the abbey and by surrounding trees. The church comprises a NW tower, nave, N and S aisles, a SE vestry, a W porch and a SE porch. Its W façade is perhaps the most conspicuous, seen from across the lawn to the N of the abbey. It comprises the gable of the nave, which is dominated by the large five-light W window with Perpendicular tracery and in front of which stands J.L. Pearson's porch of three pointed arches, with battlements and pinnacles above; the lean-to aisles, much lower than the nave and with shallow roof pitches; and, to the S, the tall tower, which has polygonal buttresses and transomed and louvred four-light belfry windows, set within huge rectangular frames. The aisle windows are of three lights. There is a pair of two-light clerestory windows for each bay of the interior. The nave and aisles have plain parapets. The E ends of the chancel and aisles, however, are surmounted by battlements. The small SE porch is by J.L. Pearson. All the external stonework looks much renewed.

The rectangular interior has no structural division between nave and chancel, which are separated from the N and S aisles by eight-bay arcades, six for the nave and two for the chancel. The tall, thin piers have four attached shafts, with mouldings between. The spandrels of the arcades are decorated with blank tracery. The walls are unplastered. The roof of the chancel is gilded.

The reredos is a triptych, whose central panel is a limewood carving of 1758 by Seffrin Alken. This panel is a copy in relief of Titian's painting of the Supper at Emmaus. It was placed above the altar as part of Kenton Couse's remodelling of the E end in 1758. The present sanctuary is panelled and the chancel is screened from the aisles. The E window contains early 16C stained glass, thought to have been made in the Netherlands, which was inserted here in 1758. The window is considered to have been given by Ferdinand and Isabella, King and Queen of Spain, either upon their daughter Catherine's betrothal to Prince Arthur, eldest son and heir of King Henry VII, or upon her marriage to King Henry VIII after Arthur's death. The Crucifixion occupies the central lights, with a bright blue background which is most attractive; the flanking lights depict, at the bottom, either Prince Arthur or King Henry VIII and Queen Catherine of Aragon. The W window of the N aisle, of four lights, by Clayton & Bell, commemorates John Milton: the blind poet is shown in the second light from the left, dictating 'Paradise Lost' to his daughter. Surrounding panels depict scenes from that work and from 'Paradise Regained'. The second window from the E in the N aisle is of 1888 by Edward Frampton and commemorates Admiral Blake, the 17C commander. Many S aisle windows have abstract stained glass of 1967, designed by John Piper and made by Patrick Reyntiens. It is jarring and unsympathetic in its effect. A painted pulpit stands against the N arcade. The font is by Nicholas Stone, 1641.

The church has many monuments, but none of them are of notable size. The largest is in the S aisle to Marie, Lady Dudley (died 1600), the daughter of Lord Howard of Effingham, the commander against the Spanish Armada of 1588. Her recumbent effigy lies in front of an arch. In the N aisle there are two memorials of special interest. One is of Cornelius Vandun (died 1577), a Yeoman of the Guard, depicted in a frontal bust. The other is of Wenceslaus Hollar (died 1677), the Bohemian artist whose famous panorama of pre-Fire London might be considered memorial enough. A tablet in his memory was unveiled in 1972. He is buried here.

St. Margaret's has many notable historical associations. Those who are buried in the church or churchyard include, in addition to Hollar, William Caxton, the first English printer (died 1491), Sir Walter Raleigh, the commander and adventurer (executed 1618), and Admiral Blake (died 1661). Amongst those married in the church were Samuel Pepys (in 1655) and Sir Winston Churchill (in 1908). In the 17C John Milton was a parishioner.

St. Martin-in-the-Fields, St. Martin's Lane, WC2. St. Martin's was built in 1721–26 to the designs of James Gibbs at a cost of nearly £34,000. The church replaced a building which had once been an isolated chapel between the City of London and Westminster, but which had become the parish church of a developed district by the early 18C. The rebuilding by James Gibbs was to be a most influential model in England and overseas. Despite this architectural importance, its site was actually much more obscure than it is today, until Trafalgar Square was laid out in 1826–30. Arguably, it has since been the most noticeable church in London. Its reputation for social work, for broadcasting and for music is even more recent, a product of the 20C. From the days when Dick Sheppard was Vicar (1914–27), the church assumed a position which it has retained, adding a national and international fame for its Christian life to its earlier architectural eminence.

The church stands at the NE corner of Trafalgar Square. Its W portico and W steeple are amongst London's most familiar landmarks. The building has often been likened to a Classical temple with a steeple mounted on its roof. In fact, the church proper is a plain rectangle, which begins to the E of the steeple. The steeple itself surmounts a vestibule, which is flanked by staircase lobbies. The portico is then attached to, but is not as wide as, the W end. It is a hexastyle Corinthian portico, reached by steps from St. Martin's Lane and from Duncannon Street. In its tympanum are the arms of King George I, for it is the parish church of St. James's and Buckingham Palaces. (King George I actually served as churchwarden when the church was new.) The entablature bears the inscription: D. SACRAM AEDEM S. MARTINI PAROCHIANI EXTRUI FEC. A.D. MDCCXXVI (the parishioners of St. Martin's have had built this sacred house of God AD 1726). The steeple has several receding stages, one with portholes, the next comprising louvred and arched belfry windows with 'Gibbs surrounds' and coupled pilasters at the angles, then one for clock-faces, next an octagonal lantern and finally an obelisk spire with four tiers of small openings. The N and S elevations have giant pilasters which mark out seven bays, but the E and W bays are distinguished by the addition of giant recessed columns. The windows are in the usual two tiers to reflect the galleries within, the upper ones all having 'Gibbs surrounds'. The E end has a central Venetian window. There is a balustrade on the N and S sides, which has never been surmounted by the innumerable urns which Gibbs intended for it.

The interior has two arcades of columns, with square bases and gilded Corinthian capitals, which support block entablatures and a segmental vault. The ceiling has much decorative plasterwork by Artari and Bagutti, which is gilded. The nave is very wide and the church therefore has a sense of spaciousness. There are N, S and W galleries. The E end has a sanctuary, to the N and S of which are vestries. The next bay W is canted and in the angles are special pews at gallery level: the royal pew to the left and the Admiralty pew to the right.

The fittings combine to preserve a dignified 18C atmosphere. The darkly-stained pews fill the body of the church. Above them, on the right, rises an elegant pulpit with a long stairway but no tester. The organ in the W gallery has a two-towered case. At the W end, on the N side, is the font of 1698, preserved from the previous church, and there is also a painting of St. Martin and the beggar, by Francesco Solimona. At the E end of the N aisle is a portrait of the church's architect, James Gibbs, by Jacopo Amigoni. The royal arms are depicted above the sanctuary arch.

The church has many associations. It is the burial place of Nell Gwynne, the Sir Winston Churchill who died in 1688 and who was the father of the first Duke of Marlborough, Thomas Chippendale the craftsman and Nicholas Hilliard the miniaturist. King Charles II was baptised in the previous church. The baptism of royal infants of more recent times is recorded in the registers, though the actual ceremonies have taken place at Buckingham Palace. In the 20C St. Martin's has become internationally known from the broadcasting of its services and from the spreading far and wide of the 'St. Martin's Review'. These were the initiatives of the Reverend H.R.L. ('Dick') Sheppard. Its social work too has become an established part of London's Church life and its place in musical history is assured through the Academy of St. Martin-in-the-Fields.

LONDON SOUTH OF THE THAMES

S London is a most atypical part of England for churches. It has no medieval church fabric of any significance beyond Southwark Cathedral, St. Mary's at Lambeth and the chapel of Lambeth Palace. A few towers are at least partly medieval, but no surviving parish churches other than St. Mary's at Lambeth are earlier in date than the 17C. There are a number of 18C churches of considerable interest and a very substantial number of 19C and 20C buildings, a few of which are important. There is no local building stone; since the 17C, brick and Portland stone have been the most usual materials.

Until very recent times, S London was not placed under a single administration, either ecclesiastical or civil. The County of London, which was formed in 1889, brought the district together under one civil authority for the first time. Previously, it was divided between Surrey and Kent. Ecclesiastically, the Kent portion had fallen for centuries within the Diocese of Rochester, and the Surrey portion in that of Winchester. The Diocese of Southwark was formed in 1905. The Catholic Church had formed its own Diocese of Southwark in 1850. It became an archbishopric in 1965.

Until the 18C, the entire district comprised scattered villages and hamlets, but only one town, Southwark, which was the ancient settlement at the foot of London Bridge. Until 1750 London Bridge was the only bridge in the capital, a fact which much influenced transport and development. The building of new bridges in the later 18C led to the development of extensive Georgian suburbs across Walworth, Camberwell, Brixton, Kennington and Clapham. The 19C greatly extended this development to the S.

Southwark first appears in recorded history as the *Suthringa Geweorc* of the Burghal Hidage of c 910: 'the defensive work of the men of Surrey' or a fortification opposite the walled city of London, to defend a river crossing. The fortification no doubt included a church, which is very probably the ancestor of Southwark Cathedral. Further churches followed in Southwark in the 11C and 12C. In the same centuries, the country villages beyond Southwark probably acquired their first churches. None of them today have pre-Conquest or Norman remains. Only St. Mary's at Lambeth was of much importance. It has the distinction of appearing in the Domesday Book as a landowner in its own right, its endowment deriving from the Danish kings of the 11C and from Countess Goda, the sister of King Edward the Confessor. Today, it is the only parish church with significant surviving medieval fabric S of the river within the districts included in the County of London in 1889. Restoration by P.C. Hardwick in 1851–52 has altered the details, but the fabric is still substantially that of c 1370. Next door, in Lambeth Palace, there is the even earlier survival of the 13C vaulted crypt of the chapel. Elsewhere, one has to go as far out as Putney to find original Gothic work other than in towers, in Bishop West's fan-vaulted chapel of c 1533. (Even further out, within the 20C's 'Greater London', the survival of early fabric becomes more frequent, but these are Surrey and Kent churches swallowed up relatively recently by modern London.) A number of early towers survive encased in later stonework: St. Nicholas', Deptford; St. Alfege's, Greenwich; St. Mary Magdalene's, Bermondsey; St. Mary's, Lewisham; and St. Leonard's, Streatham.

The 17C has bequeathed little more in S London than the Middle Ages. At Dulwich there is Christ's Chapel, which was built in 1613–

19. The chapel is part of Edward Alleyn's foundation of a school and almshouses; it forms the S wing of what is now known as the Old College. The buildings were much altered in the 19C. From the time of Wren in the later 17C, and indeed more than possibly designed by Wren himself, there survives the chapel of Morden College at Blackheath. The college was founded as almshouses for 'decayed Turkey merchants' in 1695 by Sir John Morden, who was himself a prominent trader with Turkey. The chapel, which is placed on the E side, deserves attention for its complete original furnishings. Another surviving chapel of the period is that of Boone's almshouses at Lee, dating from 1683. St. Mary Magdalene's, Bermondsey and St. Nicholas', Deptford also survive from the late 17C. Both were designed by Charley Stanton. St. Nicholas' (1696–97) was badly damaged in the Second World War but was reinstated. The two churches show a Classical centralising which mingles with the longitudinal precedent of the Middle Ages. The present elevation to Bermondsey Street of St. Mary Magdalene's is from a Gothick remodelling by George Porter in 1829–30. The contrast between this work and the 17C S elevation is marked. Slightly later than the churches at Bermondsey and Deptford is St. Thomas's, Southwark, by Thomas Cartwright, 1698–1704. This church, which ceased to be a parish church in 1898 and which served as Southwark Cathedral's Chapter House until 1988, is a formal and pleasing Classical work in red brick with stone dressings.

The 18C has left many worthy churches in S London. St. Mary's, Rotherhithe was largely built by John James in 1714–15; its W steeple was added by Lancelot Dowbiggin in 1747. It is built of brick with stone dressings, and has a shallow sanctuary and the usual two tiers of windows to reflect galleries within. The atmosphere is less 18C than 17C, and there is a strong reflection of the maritime past of Rotherhithe. St. Mary's has many similarities with the church of St. George the Martyr, Southwark, which is by John Price, 1734–36. The N and S elevations of the two churches are close in design, and there is the same shallow sanctuary. St. George's, however, retains all its galleries and a high (though altered) pulpit, so that it seems more decidedly 18C than St. Mary's. Downstream of Rotherhithe there are three major churches which were built with the help of the Act of 1711, the 'Fifty Churches Act'. St. Paul's, Deptford (by Thomas Archer, 1713–30) is the most distinguished. It was a daughter church of St. Nicholas', but it stands so proudly in the centre of modern Deptford that it is hard to believe that it was a new foundation on a new site less than three centuries ago. It is of architectural interest for its centralising plan and for its circular W tower set behind a semicircular portico. Not far to the E of St. Paul's comes St. Alfege's, Greenwich, which was built by Nicholas Hawksmoor in 1711–14. A medieval tower was left, but it was encased by John James in 1730. The church's most prominent feature is its E elevation, a pedimented composition of immense strength and solidity. The third church of the 1711 Act was St. Mary Magdalene's at Woolwich (by an unknown architect, 1727–39), which is a much plainer and less remarkable Classical work.

The later 18C has left a number of minor Classical churches: St. Mary's, Battersea (by Joseph Dixon, 1775–77); Holy Trinity, Clapham (by Kenton Couse, 1774–76); All Saints', Wandsworth (by William Jupp, 1779–80); and St. Mary's, Lewisham (by George Gibson, 1775–77, but retaining a late medieval tower). Many of their features are more colonial than metropolitan. Much grander in scale and detail is the chapel of the Royal Naval College at Greenwich. The college is of course a palace, which was originally the naval equivalent of Chelsea Hospital. Its chapel dates externally from 1735–43, but its interior is of 1779–89, when James Stuart and William Newton remodelled it after a fire. Greek taste is very apparent here as is to be expected from 'Athenian' Stuart.

None of the 18C parish churches mentioned above, except for St. Paul's at Deptford, were new foundations. It was not felt necessary to build additional accommodation in the form of new parish churches. Proprietory chapels were erected here and there, but even they were very few before the end of the 18C. New Nonconformist places of worship were by contrast legion down to 1800. They were almost all Classical structures, typically the gabled rectangle with just a little show on the W or entrance front. Hardly any have survived from before 1800. Only the Friends' Meeting House of 1778 in Wandsworth High Street is of architectural interest. A later one at Peckham (1826, now belonging to the Post Office) is equally attractive.

The 19C and the early 20C formed the heroic period of church building in S London. As a general rule, the Anglican Church had made do with the ancient parishes until the beginning of the 19C. Subdivision began in earnest in the 1820s. The parish of Newington was divided upon the opening of Sir John Soane's St. Peter's in Walworth (1823–25) and Francis Bedford's Holy Trinity, Newington (1823–24). Both churches were Classical, Soane's nearer the 18C tradition of a longitudinal church with a W tower over the main entrance, Bedford's more centralising in plan and more Greek in style. Bedford also designed St. George's (1822–24) in neighbouring Camberwell. St. George's was a St. Martin-in-the-Fields in Greek dress. It was very similar to the four contemporary churches which were named after the Evangelists: St. Matthew's at Brixton (by C.F. Porden, 1822–24), St. Mark's at Kennington (by D.R. Roper and A.B. Clayton, 1822–24), St. Luke's at Norwood (by Bedford, 1822–25) and St. John's at Waterloo (also by Bedford, 1823–24). St. Matthew's varies the usual plan by having a tower at the E, so that the W portico has no detraction. At Wandsworth, St. Anne's was built in 1820–24 to the designs of Sir Robert Smirke. It was given a tall circular tower, on the lines of the one at Smirke's St. Mary's, Wyndham Place, St. Marylebone. An even purer Greek style was to be seen in the same period in the Stamford Street Unitarian Church (1823), whose façade alone survives. Classical design barely outlived the 1820s in S London's Anglican churches. James Savage's St. James's, Bermondsey (1827–29) was the last notable example, and again Greek in style.

Classical churches already had Gothic rivals in the 1820s. Francis Bedford himself, perhaps the leading Greek proponent in S London, designed the Gothic St. Mary the Less, Black Prince Road, Lambeth in 1827–28 (now demolished). St. Michael's, Blackheath was built in 1828–29 with a notable spire: a well-detailed and attractive work. When the ancient parish of Rotherhithe was provided with no fewer than three new churches in 1838–40, Gothic was the accepted rule for all three. The Gothic of these pre-1840 churches was of a type subsequently considered 'incorrect', only loosely copied from medieval examples. The interiors would usually still have fittings which were closer to Georgian convention rather than a wholehearted medievalising scheme. The first Gothic church in S London which was obviously 'correct' in its architecture was Sir Gilbert Scott's St. Giles's, Camberwell (1842–44). Despite its 13C details, its proper chancel and substantial spire, the interior was still galleried and the E end still had the standard inscribed panels of 17C and 18C convention. A contemporary building which strove to be equally correct was A.W.N. Pugin's St. George's Cathedral, Southwark. Whereas Scott favoured the 13C style, Pugin preferred that of the 14C. St. George's was given two chantry chapels which are worthy of attention: the Petre chantry (by Pugin himself) and the Knill chantry (by his son, E.W. Pugin, 1856–57). The cathedral was bombed in 1941 and was substantially and worthily rebuilt in the 1950s by Romilly Craze. Other churches of the 1840s, of course, strayed well away from English Gothic precedents. Christ Church, Streatham (by J.W. Wild, 1840–41), employed an Italian style which has often been labelled Romanesque, but is nevertheless Pointed.

In the mid-19C, the Free Churches still employed Classical design. The Baptists in particular used it with some grandeur. The Metropolitan Tabernacle, which was built for Charles Haddon Spurgeon in Southwark in 1859–61 (by W.W. Pocock) was given a hexastyle Corinthian portico. A humbler Classical style was very widespread for Independent or Congregational buildings. By the last quarter of the 19C, however, the Free Churches were as thoroughly Gothic in their buildings as the Church of England, but towers and spires were not often provided. Exceptions were the commanding spire of Christ Church, opposite Lambeth North Station, which was built for the Congregationalists in 1873–76, and that of Emmanuel Congregational Church, Dulwich (1890–91).

The best-known architects of the High Victorian Gothic Revival contributed some buildings to S London, but proportionately rather few and on the whole much less notable than their works elsewhere. Apart from Sir Gilbert Scott's early church at Camberwell, mention must be made of J.L. Pearson's two fine churches at Vauxhall (St. Peter's, 1863–64) and Upper Norwood (St. John the Evanglist, 1878–87), which are both vaulted; G.E. Street's St. Paul's, Herne Hill (1858, a rebuilding after a fire) and his St. John the Divine, Vassall Road, Brixton (1871–74 and 1888–89), the latter a prominent landmark even from N of the Thames; the younger Charles Barry's two churches at Dulwich—St. Stephen's of 1867–68 and St. Peter's of 1873–74; William White's St. Mark's, Battersea Rise (1873–74); James Brooks's church of the Ascension, Lavender Hill (1876–83); and Norman Shaw's St. Mark's, Coburg Road, Camberwell (1879–80). G.G. Scott, Jr. contributed two churches which were of considerable importance beyond S London: St. Agnes' at Kennington Park (1875–77) and All Hallows', Pepper Street, Southwark (1879–80). St. Agnes' was perhaps the most important of all S London's 19C churches and one which influenced the design of many later churches, including Liverpool's Anglican cathedral. The building was added to and furnished by Temple Moore. It was bombed and the decision was made, unfortunately, to rebuild differently. Less prominent architects of the Victorian period sometimes designed notable churches. Of the many churches from the firm of Henry Jarvis & Son, that of St. Augustine, Lynton Road, Bermondsey (1875–82) is exceptionally grand and unexpected. Similarly, J.E.K. Cutts, whose buildings were widespread in S London, produced in St. Peter's, Clapham Manor Road (1878) a worthy and more interesting work. The very end of the 19C and the early years of the 20C bequeathed generally more modest buildings than the mid-19C, often lacking towers or being left incomplete in other ways. A noble portion of what was intended to be a very ambitious church, All

Saints', West Dulwich (by G.H. Fellowes Prynne, 1888–91) is of particular note. So is Temple Moore's All Saints' at Tooting (1904–06), a long, relatively low building.

Church building continued in the outer suburbs between the wars and occurred everywhere after 1945 to replace bombed buildings. St. Saviour's at Eltham (by Welch, Cachemaille-Day & Lander, 1932–33) was a watershed in S London's church design. The move away from the Gothic tradition did not resume in earnest until the 1950s and 1960s. Two Peckham churches—St. Mary Magdalene's (by Potter & Hare, 1961–62) and St. John's, Meeting House Lane (by David Bush, 1965–66)—serve to illustrate by their centralising plans, irregular fenestration and materials the substantial changes from before 1914. But perhaps the best postwar church is one which still retained more than a semblance of traditional design: H.S. Goodhart-Rendel's Most Holy Trinity Church at Dockhead, Bermondsey (1957–60). The brick-built church has a stately W front with two towers, a well-lit interior without the kind of random fenestration or glass walling which became fashionable in the 1960s, and some attractive fittings.

Fittings in S London's churches inevitably include few medieval ones. Only Southwark Cathedral's much-restored reredos of 1520 is exceptional. In the same place may be found a 17C fitting which is unique in S London but ubiquitous in the City: a sword-rest, a pointer to the City of London's former jurisdiction in Southwark. 17C fittings in general are represented by the chapel of Morden College at Blackheath (an unspoilt scheme), by the chapel of Lambeth Palace, by a Wren reredos from the City in St. Anthony's, Nunhead, and by surviving original woodwork in St. Mary Magdalene's, Bermondsey and St. Nicholas', Deptford. St. Mary's, Battersea has 17C glass by Bernard van Linge. Of note from the 18C are the fittings of the Royal Naval College's chapel at Greenwich, especially the pulpit and Benjamin West's painting of St. Paul's shipwreck; a font of 1729 by James Gibbs in Christ's Chapel at Dulwich; and the organ of 1764–65 in St. Mary's, Rotherhithe, by John Byfield II. The Victorian Age has left a tall tabernacle by A.W.N. Pugin in Southwark Cathedral (formerly in Ramsgate); a painting of St. Stephen by Sir Edward Poynter, 1872, in St. Stephen's, Dulwich; stained glass in the E window of St. Giles's, Camberwell, which was made by Ward & Nixon and which was designed by Edmund Oldfield with advice from John Ruskin; a good grouping of original fittings in St. Peter's, Vauxhall; and, from the very end of the period, fittings by Temple Moore in St. Agnes', Kennington, preserved from the previous bombed church. A recent notable item is Goddard & Gibbs's stained glass window of 1984 in St. George's Cathedral to commemorate Pope John Paul II's visit two years earlier.

The dearth of medieval fabric in S London is not surprisingly accompanied by a dearth of medieval monuments. Southwark Cathedral has the only significant group, including a 13C wooden effigy of a cross-legged knight, and a monument of considerable note to John Gower (died 1408). He was a poet and a contemporary of Chaucer. His monument now stands in the N nave aisle, a 15C canopied recess over a table-tomb, all brightly repainted. The canopy has three cusped ogee arches. The head of Gower's effigy rests on his three major books. Late medieval monuments of Gower's type are found in St. Mary's, Lambeth. The ogee arches of Gower's tomb have become wide, four-centred arches in the Lambeth examples. Later in the 16C, S London became the very centre for the design and execution of church monuments in England. The S bank of the Thames had long attracted craftsmen from the Low Countries, and in the 16C and 17C, a number of sculptors among them won a substantial market for their church monuments. The leading figures were William Cure I, his son Cornelius and his grandson William Cure II, Gerard Johnson and his two sons, Isaac James and Richard Stevens, who were all Flemish or Dutch craftsmen with anglicised names, and who collectively formed the *Southwark School*. To their number a distinguished English sculptor, Nicholas Stone, was added in the 17C; he was a pupil of Isaac James. A monument by the Southwark School will usually be a bust or a half-figure set within a Classical frame or, in larger examples, a canopied free-standing monument on the lines of that to Queen Elizabeth I in Westminster Abbey. Famous works of the Southwark School include Shakespeare's monument at Stratford-upon-Avon and John Stow's monument in the church of St. Andrew Undershaft in the City of London. Few of the School's monuments were installed in S London itself. The tomb of Lancelot Andrewes, Bishop of Winchester (died 1626), which is placed on the S side of the sanctuary in Southwark Cathedral, is possibly by Nicholas Johnson. (Its present appearance, however, owes much to Sir Ninian Comper in 1930.) Southwark Cathedral also houses the monument of Richard Humble, an Alderman of London (died 1616) and his two wives, by William Cure II, and the memorial in the N transept to Lady Clerke (died 1626) and her son, William Austin (died 1633), by Nicholas Stone, which represents various agricultural allusions in the Gospels. In the chapel of Trinity Hospital at Greenwich there exists a portion of Nicholas Stone's monument of the founder, Henry, Earl of Northampton (died 1614): a figure in a ruff kneels on a cushion, which rests on a tall base. The monument was originally larger and was made for Dover Castle. Further monuments by Stone exist in St. Mary's, Battersea, commemorating Sir Oliver St. John (died 1630) and his wife, and comprising two busts in a Classical frame, and in St. Luke's, Charlton, where there is a memorial of 1630 to Lady Newton. St. Paul's, Clapham contains the surviving parts of a distinguished late 17C monument by William Stanton to Sir Richard Atkins (died 1689) and his family.

Perhaps the most important 18C monument in S London is the one to Thomas Guy (died 1724) in the chapel of Guy's Hospital, Southwark (q.v.). It was sculpted by John Bacon, Jr. in 1779. St. Mary's at Lewisham has a group of notable late 18C monuments. The one to Mary Lushington (died 1797), by John Flaxman, is an interesting arrangement of two figures cleverly placed within a semicircular frame. St. Mary's at Rotherhithe has an elaborate tablet to Joseph Wade (died 1743), King's Carver in the Royal Dockyard at nearby Deptford. The maritime theme at Rotherhithe is also expressed in an early 17C memorial to Captain Anthony Wood, which incorporates a splendid carving of a contemporary ship. St. Mary's, Battersea has a mid-18C monument to the first Viscount Bolingbroke (died 1751) by L.F. Roubiliac. In St. Leonard's, Streatham there are memorials to Henry Thrale (died 1781), Dr. Johnson's friend, and to Mrs. Thrale's mother, both of which have inscriptions by Johnson. The same church also houses a Flaxman monument of 1824. From the late Georgian period there are memorials by Sir Francis Chantrey in St. Paul's at Clapham, St. Mary's at Lambeth and St. Luke's at Charlton. Notable post-Georgian monuments are few. The only category of interest is the continuing use of an effigy on a tomb-chest in the two S London cathedrals: Thomas Doyle, Provost (died 1879) and Peter

Amigo, Archbishop (died 1949) in St. George's Cathedral, and Edward Talbot, first Bishop of Southwark and later Bishop of Winchester (died 1934) in Southwark Cathedral. Talbot's monument is by Cecil Thomas.

The associations of S London's churches are numerous, but like their fabrics they are virtually all of the 16C or later. The only ancient association of importance is that St. Alfege, Archbishop of Canterbury from 1006 to 1012, was martyred (but not buried) at Greenwich on or near the site of the church which still bears his name. Otherwise, significant associations begin with Elizabethan and Jacobean times. At the very beginning of the 17C, in 1607, Edmund Shakespeare, the playwright's brother, was buried in St. Saviour's Church, the present Southwark Cathedral. Within the parish stood the Globe Theatre and William Shakespeare himself clearly knew St. Saviour's very well. In the same year of 1607 and in the same church, John Harvard was baptised. The son of a Southwark butcher, he became a Puritan minister and migrated to New England, where he founded the forerunner of Harvard University. Another American connection of the same period is the burial in St. Mary's, Rotherhithe in 1624 of Christopher Jones, the master of the 'Mayflower', which made a famous voyage to N America in 1620. Christopher Marlowe, the 16C dramatist who lost his life in a drunken brawl, is buried at St. Nicholas', Deptford. A more sober Elizabethan, the musician and church organist Thomas Tallis, was buried at St. Alfege's, Greenwich in 1585. The 17C botanist whose collections were to form the basis of the Ashmolean Museum in Oxford, John Tradescant, was buried in the churchyard of St. Mary's, Lambeth, as was his equally eminent father. The Tradescants' tomb lies to the SE of the church, just yards from another famous monument, that of William Bligh, master of the 'Bounty' in the late 18C and against whom some of his crew mutinied in the Pacific. A leading Anglican divine of the 17C, Lancelot Andrewes, was buried in Southwark Cathedral in 1626. St. Mary's, Battersea can claim two notable associations in the marriages of Edward Hyde, Earl of Clarendon, the 17C statesman, lawyer and writer, and William Blake, the 18C writer and painter. S of Battersea, the church of Holy Trinity at Clapham has distinguished connections with the Clapham Sect, a group of late 18C and early 19C Evangelicals with much influence in both Church and State. The great evangelist of the 18C, John Wesley, worked extensively in S London as elsewhere, but a particular link of some interest is that his wife, Mary Wesley, is buried in the churchyard of St. Giles's, Camberwell. Charles Dickens is indelibly associated with the church of St. George the Martyr, Southwark, which he knew when his father was held for three months in 1824 in the neighbouring Marshalsea Prison and which duly appeared in the story of 'Little Dorrit'. John Ruskin worshipped in the Beresford Chapel, Walworth, an Independent chapel whose minister, Dr. Edward Andrews, was a well-known preacher and writer. Beresford Street, in which the chapel was built in 1818, was renamed John Ruskin Street in 1937. Barely half a mile away, York Street was renamed Browning Street in 1921 as a result of a comparable connection. Robert Browning, the poet, worshipped in the York Street Independent Church, Walworth for many years in the early 19C. The Victorian soldier, General Gordon, who fell in Khartoum in 1885, was baptised in St. Alfege's, Greenwich in 1833. A famous Free Church preacher, the Baptist Charles Haddon Spurgeon, worked in Southwark and Walworth from 1854 until his death in 1892, chiefly in the Metropolitan Tabernacle. At the other end of the religious spectrum of Spurgeon's day was Arthur Tooth of St. James's, Hatcham, an Anglo-Catholic or 'ritualist' who suffered imprisonment under the Public Worship Regulation Act of 1874. Finally, amongst the numerous 19C Irish migrants who worshipped in S London's Catholic churches were the forbears of former President Reagan. His grandparents married in St. George's Cathedral, Southwark in 1851.

Camberwell, *St. Giles, Camberwell Church Street.* The present church was built between 1842 and 1844 to the designs of Sir Gilbert Scott to replace a medieval building which had been destroyed by fire in 1841. It is a major work of Scott's early career and a landmark in the Gothic Revival. Scott himself, alluding long after to the progress of the Gothic Revival, spoke of St. Giles's rather immodestly as 'the best church by far which had then been erected'. It is also a substantial town church which reflected Camberwell's development as a prosperous suburb. The church stands back from Camberwell Church Street, a few hundred yards E of Camberwell Green. The style is Early English. It is cruciform, with a broach spire of 207ft surmounting the crossing tower. The church is built of Kentish rag, faced in Sneaton and Caen stone.

Entering by the N porch, the visitor finds an aisleless nave of five bays, a substantial chancel and a markedly light interior which is nevertheless dominated by the stained glass in the five-light E window, of which more below. The interior differs from its Victorian aspect in lacking the galleries on iron columns which Scott supplied and in losing much 19C stained glass in the Second World War. Similarly, the reredos—now supplied with painted figures in its arches in High Victorian style—was originally filled with boards of the Commandments, Creed and Lord's Prayer as in 17C and 18C convention. The piers of the nave are alternately round and octagonal. High-pitched roofs cover the nave, transepts and chancel; the N porch and crossing tower are groined. In 1966 the interior was whitened.

The sedilia and piscina of c 1380 are survivals from the old church. They were placed on the S side of the sanctuary in 1916. The present high altar, which stands under the crossing, dates from 1974. The original chancel is now used as a Lady chapel. Its most important feature is the stained glass in the E window, which was designed by Edmund Oldfield and was made by the firm of Ward & Nixon. The central light and the tracery heads had been given their glass by the time of the consecration in 1844; the rest followed within about three years. The window is often attributed to John Ruskin, who was a parishioner, and although he undoubtedly prepared a design for the glass, his 'Praeterita' states clearly that he gave way to Oldfield in the matter. It is well known that Ruskin studied stained glass in N France for the purposes of St. Giles's, but it would be an injustice to Oldfield to conclude that he was not equally knowledgeable. The window, which was pieced together by 1950 after being shattered in the Second World War, follows the 13C French style, comprising rich purple and red medallions. The central light depicts the Nativity, Temptation, Crucifixion, Resurrection and Ascension. The two lights to the left show Old Testament scenes; the two to the right treat the Acts of the Apostles. Our Lord's Baptism and the Last Supper appear in the tracery lights. The S transept S window was designed by Sir Ninian Comper in 1956. It depicts St. Giles and St. Nicholas, two Bishops of Winchester, two Archbishops of Canterbury, a Bishop of

Rochester (Thorold) and the first Bishop of Southwark (Talbot, 1905–11). The icon in the S transept was given by the local Greek Orthodox congregation, who once worshipped here. The three-light W window contains 13C glass from Trier, which was acquired by the Reverend J.G. Storie, Vicar at the time of rebuilding, and repaired by Ward & Nixon. Comper was responsible for the colouring of Scott's reredos after the Second World War.

There are eight brasses which date from between 1492 and 1637 and which were preserved from the earlier church. They include Edward Scott (died 1538), whose figure is in fact that of a 15C knight reused, and John Scott (died 1532), Baron of the Exchequer, who kneels with his wife in the company of four of their 11 children. All the brasses are to be found in the S transept, where there is also a memorial to members of the First Surrey Rifles (the 21st County of London Regiment). In the N aisle there is a memorial tablet by Eric Gill to C.F.G. Masterman (1873–1927), writer and Liberal politician of the early 20C.

Mary, the wife of John Wesley, was buried in the churchyard in 1781. John Wesley's great-nephew, the 19C organist, Samuel Sebastian Wesley, was the organist of St. Giles's from 1829 to 1832. He designed the organ of 1844, which was built by J.C. Bishop. A worthy local priest, Father George Potter (died 1960), is commemorated by the chapel in the crypt, which was formed in 1964. The Reverend Festus Kelly, Vicar from 1880 to 1915, was the father of Sir Gerald Kelly, P.R.A.

Clapham, *Holy Trinity, North Side, Clapham Common.* Holy Trinity Church was built in 1774–76 to the designs of Kenton Couse to replace Clapham's original parish church of St. Mary, which stood in the Old Town (on the site of St. Paul's, Rectory Grove) and so away from the more fashionable quarter which had grown up around the Common. The fabric of 1776 has not been greatly altered. The W portico was extended to its present size in 1812 by Francis Hurlbatt. In 1902–03 A. Beresford Pite replaced the original shallow sanctuary by a more substantial chancel and designed a new Lady chapel and vestries. In the Second World War, much damage was done to the church and the Lady chapel was burnt out. Restoration was carried out under T.F. Ford.

The church stands completely detached in the NE corner of the Common. It is a simple Classical building, brick-built with stone quoins, with its whitened W portico and W steeple giving it a slight air of New England or the Carolinas. It is rectangular and has a pitched roof, a projecting chancel, a Lady chapel to the SE and vestries to the NE. The steeple sits above the central pediment of the W front. It comprises a square clock turret, which is unadorned except for the clock-faces; an octagonal belfry; a small dome; and a diminutive lantern and cross. The body of the church has the usual two tiers of windows to reflect the internal galleries: large and round-headed above, small and segment-headed below. The S or Venetian window of the Lady chapel was the E window of the sanctuary until Beresford Pite's remodelling of 1902–03. The E façade of his chancel is a robust composition of four Ionic pilasters and a pediment. This is in stone, but sits above plain brick walling and looks a little unrelated to the rest of the building.

The interior has fairly low galleries which are supported on fluted Tuscan columns. The arrangements otherwise are altered from those of 1776. The original box-pews were cut down and deprived of their doors by Arthur Blomfield in 1875. The three-decker pulpit, which stood centrally and which was markedly high, with a pagoda-like canopy on two columns, was dismembered and moved to the N side at the same time. The 18C reredos still survives at the E end, but with later adornments. The original communion table, 5ft 6ins wide, stands below the gallery in the SE corner. The organ which used to be in the W gallery was replaced by one of 1909, by A. Hunter & Son of Clapham, which is housed in a recess N of the chancel. The three E windows have stained glass of 1950 by Lawrence Lee, depicting the Crucifixion and members of the Clapham Sect. In the Lady chapel there is postwar stained glass by Marion Grant, of the Virgin and Child, the Lamb of God, and the Chalice and the Cross. There are three benefactors' boards in the vestibule.

Holy Trinity Church was the place of worship of the Clapham Sect (or 'the Saints'), a group of Evangelicals which had considerable influence in both Church and State in the late 18C and early 19C. Rich laymen for the most part, they strove particularly to secure the abolition of the slave trade and of slavery itself. The group included William Wilberforce, Zachary Macaulay, Henry and John Venn, John and Henry Thornton, Granville Sharp, Lord Teignmouth and Charles Grant. One of the group, the Reverend John Venn, was Rector here from 1792 to 1813. He is commemorated by a monument which was designed by John Bacon, Jr. The entire group is recalled by a tablet by H.P. Burke Downing, which was set up on the external S wall in 1919.

St. Paul's in Rectory Grove, which stands in the churchyard of Holy Trinity's predecessor, was built in 1815 to the designs of Christopher Edmonds. It contains monuments which came from Clapham's original parish church of St. Mary. The monument of Sir Richard Atkins (died 1689), by William Stanton, has five figures of very good quality. There is also a draped tablet, with cherubs and a portrait medallion of William Hewer (died 1715), the friend of Pepys. Pepys retired to Hewer's house in the then country village of Clapham in 1701 and died there two years later. A later monument is of J.B. Wilson (died (1835), by Sir Francis Chantrey.

Deptford, St. Paul, Deptford High Street. St. Paul's was built in 1713–30 to the designs of Thomas Archer as one of the new churches under the Act of 1711. It became the principal church of Deptford, replacing St. Nicholas', which remained to serve the riverside district. Deptford was long an important place as the site of a major naval dockyard, to which Samuel Pepys often travelled in the 17C. It was also the home of John Evelyn. St. Paul's is a proud Classical building in Portland stone, which successfully solved the problem of wedding a steeple to a W front. It has been splendidly restored in recent years through the energy and vision of its present Rector, Canon David Diamond, whose incumbency has been one of the most notable in its history. The church has been made a focus for Deptford's population.

The church stands on a podium and comprises an almost square nave, E apse, a semicircular portico at the W end and a circular tower rising from behind it. The portico is supported by four Tuscan columns and is surmounted by a balustrade. The way in which the semicircular portico agrees so well with the circular tower is often contrasted with the less happy arrangement at St. Martin-in-the-Fields, which, nevertheless, was copied far more frequently than St. Paul's. Thomas Archer had taken the idea from the church of St.

Maria della Pace in Rome, either directly or via the S portico of St. Paul's Cathedral. The steeple at Deptford has a square belfry stage with convex faces. The arched, louvred openings are small and have urns in front and clock-faces above. The next stage uses volutes to lead up to the short spire. The exterior has N and S pediments above the three slightly projecting middle bays, and many large arched windows, all set between rusticated pilasters.

The interior is galleried, spacious and rich in its Classical details. Giant Corinthian columns and semi-columns articulate the walls and divide the nave from the N and S aisles. Despite these aisles, the church is clearly no longitudinal building of medieval convention. The corners of the interior are canted to allow for vestibules and vestries. This has the effect of widening the sanctuary and countering the longitudinal influence of the aisles. The E apse has a Venetian window, which follows the curve, and which is fitted into an internal curving Tuscan screen. This has pilasters around the windows and ends in a column on each side. It is an attractive combination of windows and reredos, and very Baroque in its handling.

The pulpit, which is only a part of the 18C original by Joseph Wade, has iron stairs. The present neo-Norman font was given in 1897. The organ in the W gallery was built by Richard Bridge in 1748; Handel wrote of him in the following year: 'I very well approve of Mr. Bridge who without any objection is a very good organ-builder'. Memorials include one to the Reverend Charles Burney (died 1817), Rector from 1811 and the brother of Fanny Burney, and another, by Joseph Nollekens, to Vice-Admiral James Sayer (died 1776).

Greenwich

Royal Naval College, *Chapel of St. Peter and St. Paul, King William Walk.* The chapel has a grand and important interior of the late 18C, set within Sir Christopher Wren's late 17C Greenwich Hospital for aged and infirm seamen of the Royal Navy. The buildings which Wren designed form a riverside palace of monumental scale, which breaks to frame Inigo Jones's earlier Queen's House across Romney Road. The chapel occupies part of the Queen Mary Block (the SE block), the left-hand, domed block as seen from the river, and which was named after the wife of King William III, the founder of Greenwich Hospital. The chapel was burnt out in 1779 and most of its present interior is work by James ('Athenian') Stuart and William Newton. A redecoration was undertaken in 1954–55.

The chapel's exterior, although part and parcel of the whole set of buildings, is readily distinguished. There are three tiers of windows in eight bays to N and S. The lowest lights the crypt. Then come tall arched windows and finally smaller, segment-headed windows. In this case, therefore, it is the smaller windows which light the galleries, unlike the reverse which generally applies in parish churches. All the windows have clear glass. The domed tower stands at the W end, over the vestibule.

The interior is of considerable height and has a segmental vault. There are rather light and shallow N and S galleries, set high up, which are supported on curved brackets. The E and W ends are divided by two pairs of giant Corinthian columns. The E pair flank a huge painting in an arched frame of the 'Preservation of St. Paul after

Shipwreck at Malta', by Benjamin West. Above the picture, to left and right, are two angels in Coade stone, by John Bacon. The second painting just below the ceiling is of the Ascension by Biagio Rebecca. The altar comprises a marble slab which is supported by six cherubim in gilded Coade stone. The W end has a marble gallery on six Ionic columns to house the organ. Between the upper windows of the N and S walls are paintings of the Apostles and Evangelists, designed by West and executed by Rebecca. The pulpit, part of a three-decker which was moved from the centre to the S side only in 1952, stands on six fluted columns. The circular panels, made of Coade stone, depict scenes from the life of St. Paul and were designed by West. The semicircular sanctuary rails are of 1787.

Two memorial busts at the W end are of note: they are of Nelson's comrade, Admiral Sir Thomas Hardy (died 1839), by William Behnes and Admiral Sir William Keats (died 1834), who had served with King William IV ('the sailor king') and whose memorial was set up by the king himself.

St. Alfege, Greenwich Church Street. St. Alfege's is a distinguished Baroque rebuilding of 1712–18 by Nicholas Hawksmoor, with a W tower of 1730 by John James. The church was restored by Sir Albert Richardson after bombing in 1941. St. Alfege, Archbishop of Canterbury from 1006, was martyred at Greenwich by the Vikings on 19th April, 1012. His remains were afterwards enshrined at Canterbury.

The church stands on the W side of Greenwich Church Street. Its E façade is thus the most prominent and the one which Hawksmoor treated monumentally. It is articulated by four Doric pilasters and by two central columns, which frame the E window. This window is set behind a portico, which comprises the three central bays of the five-bay façade. An arch rises above the middle bay and breaks through the pediment above. Three substantial urns adorn the pediment. The entire composition, powerful and monumental, is unmistakably Hawksmoor's. The side elevations have nine bays, which are separated by giant Doric pilasters, with the three central bays projecting on each side. Each bay has a tall arched window above and a small, square window below, except in the projecting bays, where arched doors replace the lower windows. The W tower is partly a recasing of the one rebuilt in 1617. Its belfry portion is foursquare, with pairs of Ionic pilasters framing an arched, louvred opening in each face. Above come clock-faces set within arched panels, which are flanked by urns at the corners of the tower. These serve to connect the tower with the circular lantern and short spire which surmount it. The principal elements of the steeple are reminiscent of Wren's work: much tamer than Hawksmoor would have provided.

The galleried interior is dominated by the E apse. A tall, depressed arch frames a rich but somewhat dark *trompe l'oeil* painting, by Sir James Thornhill, restored after the Second World War by Glyn Jones. The ceiling of the apse (a half-dome) is made to look coffered. The pilasters of the chancel arch are also painted. The reredos comprises four small Corinthian columns and a straight entablature. Above this is the wide E window. To the left and right are groups of three giant, fluted, wooden Corinthian columns, set diagonally towards the centre. They support small triangular entablatures but nothing else: they merge imperceptibly into the dark ceiling and almost appear to support the arch of the window. The stained glass of the window is by Francis Spear, 1953. It depicts the Risen Christ, flanked by four angels who bear the Instruments of the Passion. Above them is the hand of God the Father and the dove of the Holy Spirit. Below are the figures of St. Alfege and Cardinal Morton, who represent the homage of the Church. Spear also designed the aisle windows (1956).

The organ console in the NE gallery is said to be at least partly a survival of one of 1552 which was used by Thomas Tallis. Tallis was buried in the previous church on the site; he is depicted in the window at the W end of the S aisle. The royal arms on the front of the S gallery are copied from the 17C originals which were destroyed in 1941. They mark the royal pew which has been maintained in the church since the rebuilding. The wrought-iron communion rails and the rails of the galleries to the N and S of the chancel area are attributed to Jean Tijou. Above these galleries are benefaction boards, which record an unusually splendid group of charities, including Queen Elizabeth's College (almshouses), Trinity Hospital (picturesque almshouses on the riverfront, founded in 1613), the Roan School, and finally the most splendid of all, the Royal Hospital for seamen, for which Wren designed a riverside palace and which is now the Royal Naval College.

John Morton, later Archbishop of Canterbury, was Vicar of St. Alfege's from 1444 to 1454. He was to become a supporter of King Henry VII, who built the palace of Placentia at Greenwich during his reign. The future King Henry VIII was baptised in the parish in 1491. In 1515, the king's sister, Mary Tudor, married Charles Brandon, Duke of Suffolk, in the palace chapel. General Wolfe, the conqueror of Quebec in the 18C, was buried here in 1759, and General Gordon, the 19C soldier and adventurer, was baptised here in 1833. All these individuals are commemorated in the aisle windows.

Lambeth, *St. Mary the Virgin, Lambeth Road.* St. Mary's is a building of 1374–77, whose aisles were rebuilt and extended in the early 16C and which was remodelled by P.C. Hardwick in 1851–52. It stands immediately next to the 15C gateway of Lambeth Palace, which has been the London house of the Archbishops of Canterbury since 1197. The church, however, has a prominent place in history from an even earlier period, for it has the distinction of appearing in Domesday Book as a landholding in its own right. Goda, Countess of Boulogne (died 1056), King Edward the Confessor's sister, had owned the manor. King Harthacnut, who preceded the Confessor and who was the son of King Cnut, had died at Lambeth at a feast in 1042. None of this notable past, however, saved the church from redundancy in 1972. The building was acquired a few years later by the Tradescant Trust for use as a Museum of Garden History. The fabric has thus been safeguarded, but can there be a more melancholy symbol of the withering of religion in the 20C than a redundant parish church of ancient foundation at the very gates of Lambeth Palace?

The church is built of Kentish ragstone, with limestone dressings. It comprises an aisled nave, a S porch, chancel, chancel chapels and SW tower. The tower has a polygonal SE stair turret, diagonal buttresses on the W side and pairs of two-light belfry windows. The top of the tower is of 1834. P.C. Hardwick refaced and reroofed the church and renewed its windows in 1851–52. The E and W windows are of five lights, the former with flowing 14C tracery, the latter with Perpendicular tracery. Within, the nave has five N bays and four S bays, comprising octagonal piers, octagonal moulded capitals and moulded arches. The walls are all stripped. In the chancel are two 16C tomb-chests, one to Hugh Peyntwyn, Archdeacon of Canterbury (died 1504) on the N, and the other to John Mompesson, a lawyer (died 1524) to the S. The tomb-chests both bear heraldic shields within quatrefoils, and both are surmounted by a four-centred arch which frames a recess.

A number of Archbishops of Canterbury have been buried in the church or churchyard. Also buried here are Elias Ashmole (died 1692), whose collection formed the origin of the Ashmolean Museum in Oxford; John Tradescant (died 1638), gardener to King Charles I, whose tomb lies to the E of the church; and Vice-Admiral William Bligh (died 1817), the famous master of the 'Bounty', whose monument in Coade stone, surmounted by a flaming urn, describes him as 'the celebrated Navigator who first transplanted the Bread Fruit Tree from Otaheite to the West Indies, bravely fought the battles of his country, and died beloved, respected and lamented'. He had lived in Lambeth Road. Rectors of the parish have included George D'Oyly (Rector, 1820–46), who was the founder of King's College, London, and Edmund Gibson (1703–17) and Beilby Porteus (1767–77), who became Bishops of London.

Lambeth Palace has a chapel N of the cloisters. The chapel proper was largely rebuilt in 13C style by Seely & Paget after bombing in the Second World War; it was completed in 1955. Beneath it, however, there survives a 13C crypt, whose vaulting of chamfered arches and ribs is supported by a central row of three Purbeck marble columns. There are four bays in two parallel lines. The chapel proper is entered through a surviving Early English W doorway. The round-headed doorway of three orders embraces two trefoil-headed door openings, divided by a single shaft. A quatrefoil in the tympanum bears the arms of the See of Canterbury impaling those of Archbishop Laud. The fittings are 17C in character, either original or restored. Also to be noted is the tomb-chest of Matthew Parker, Archbishop of Canterbury (died 1575), which suffered much damage in the 17C. Archbishop Parker had been consecrated in the chapel in 1559.

Rotherhithe, *St. Mary, St. Marychurch Street.* St. Mary's is a rebuilding of 1714–15 to the designs of John James. In the same years he rebuilt the church of St. Mary the Virgin at Twickenham, where he retained the 15C tower. Here, too, he left the earlier tower, but in this case it was replaced in 1747–48 by Lancelot Dowbiggin. The most important restoration was undertaken by William Butterfield in 1876. He left the exterior unchanged in appearance and, although he altered much within, nevertheless preserved the atmosphere of the original. In particular, St. Mary's still strongly reflects Rotherhithe's maritime past. Its setting in a narrow street very near the river, where it is surrounded by surviving warehouses and other historic buildings, reinforces its appeal.

The church comprises a W steeple, nave with N and S aisles, a NE vestry and a shallow projecting sanctuary. It is built of brick, with stone dressings. The N and S elevations reflect the original galleried interior. There are five arched upper windows, with smaller segment-headed windows below. On the S side the first and fifth bays have square-headed doors; there is also a blocked N door in the first bay from the W. The W tower has arched and louvred belfry openings, with clock-faces below and a balustraded parapet above, surmounted by a thin circular stage of Corinthian columns and a short obelisk spire. The steeple was rebuilt in 1861. Foundations of the old tower, which stood within the present nave at its W end, may be seen in the crypt. The projecting E end has a single large arched window.

The interior is of three unequal bays formed by tall Ionic columns. The columns rise from panelled octagonal bases, the height of whose panelling speaks of the box-pews which once surrounded them. The nave has a segmental, panelled ceiling. The roofs of the aisles are flat. There is still a W gallery, but the N and S galleries were removed by Butterfield in 1876.

St. Mary's by John James, 1714–15; the W end focuses on the organ by John Byfield II, 1764

Of the fittings, the most distinguished is the organ of 1764–65 by John Byfield II, which is housed in the W gallery. It has been much restored since it was built, but retains its original case and most of its early pipework. At the E end of the S aisle is an oil painting of King Charles I, which concerns the book attributed to the monarch, the 'Eikon Basilike' (the kingly image). The pulpit is the reduced version of the former three-decker, which stood centrally in the nave. The E window has 16C German stained glass of the Assumption, brought here c 1810. The reredos beneath the window is adapted from the original. The present arrangement is of dark panelling articulated by two pairs of fluted and gilded Corinthian pilasters to divide the reredos proper from the rest of the panelling, which continues around the three sides of the sanctuary. Paintings (copies of Old Masters) now adorn the panels which formerly proclaimed the Commandments, Creed and Lord's Prayer. Originally, there was a segmental pediment over the reredos proper, which was flanked on each side by an attached Corinthian column and a pilaster.

In the N aisle there is a brass memorial to Peter Hills (died 1614), the founder of the school whose attractive early 18C building survives opposite the S door of the church, complete with two Portland stone figures of charity children affixed to the façade. A second notable memorial is that of Captain Anthony Wood (died 1625), comprising an inscription below a fine carving of a contemporary ship. Next to it is a modern tablet to Christopher Jones, who was the master of the 'Mayflower', the famous ship which took the Pilgrim Fathers into exile in 1620. Also of nautical interest is the tablet to Joseph Wade (died 1743), King's Carver in the royal dockyard at Deptford. An 18C prince from the Pacific island of Belau, Lee Boo, is commemorated by a tablet within the church and by a tomb outside. He was brought to England in 1784 by Captain Henry Wilson of Rotherhithe, but died of smallpox at the very end of the same year. The East India Company placed the stone on the tomb (to the left of the S entrance), which reads: 'Stop reader, stop! let Nature claim a tear/A Prince of mine, Lee Boo lies buried here'. In 1892 a tablet was placed within the church, in the N aisle, by the Secretary of State for India, representing, in its quotation from the 'Acts of the Apostles' (chapter 28, v.2) the welcome which Captain Wilson and his crew had received on Belau in 1783: 'The barbarous people showed us no little kindness'.

Two 19C Rectors must be mentioned. One, Edward Blick (Rector, 1835–67) built four daughter churches and various schools. He is commemorated by the obelisk near the tower's S door. His successor, Edward Josselyn Beck (Rector, 1867–1907), saw three more daughter churches built and has left posterity in his debt by writing a history of the parish, entitled 'Memorials to serve for a History of the Parish of St. Mary, Rotherhithe' (1907).

Southwark

Chapel of Guy's Hospital, St. Thomas's Street. An almost square Classical chapel, with galleries and crypt, which forms the central part of the W wing of the hospital's front quadrangle. It was designed by Richard Jupp and built in 1774–77. The chapel's crypt is the burial place of the hospital's founder, Thomas Guy, who died in 1724 and whose foundation opened in 1726; he had originally been buried in St. Thomas's Church across the street. The chapel is of six bays in length, the easternmost being a screened vestibule, with gallery over, and the westernmost the sanctuary. The N and S galleries are supported on slender columns with silvered Ionic capitals. Columns rise from the galleries in turn to support groined vaults in the aisles. The sanctuary has Victorian altar rails, older choirstalls and, against the W wall, a marble arch by Louis Osman, 1956. Above are three round-headed windows which contain stained glass in memory of William Hunt, who died in 1829 and who was the most important benefactor after Guy. The windows depict Moses in the wilderness holding the serpent; Christ healing a sick man; and Peter at the gate of the Temple. Below the galleries are panels of mosaic and opus sectile of 1904 by James Powell & Sons. The panels depict Scriptural figures and commemorate those who have died in the service of the hospital. Against a shallow niche at the E end, between the two pairs of entrance doors and enclosed by a semicircular iron railing, stands a famous statue of Thomas Guy by John Bacon, 1779. It shows Guy welcoming a patient to the hospital, which appears in the background: '…he established this Asylum for that stage of Langour and Disease to which the Charities of Others had not reached … and rivalled the endowments of Kings'. Nearby is a small brass plate which commemorates W.E. Gladstone, the Liberal Prime Minister, who was a Governor of Guy's for 63 years.

St. George the Martyr, Borough High Street. St. George's is a rebuilding of 1734–36 to the designs of John Price. It was restored in 1807–08 by C.R. Cockerell and again in 1949–52 by T.F. Ford, after damage in the Second World War. The church is first mentioned under the year 1122 in the 'Annals' of Bermondsey Abbey. This date supports the view that its foundation occurred in the early 12C, when St. George's popularity in England rapidly grew, after his alleged intervention in favour of the English Crusaders during the siege of Antioch in 1097–98. The fame of the Southwark church derives substantially from its appearance in 'Little Dorrit'. John Dickens was held in the Marshalsea Prison, once sited a few yards N of the church, for three months in 1824, and his 12-year-old son, the future novelist, lodged in Lant Street, across the road to the S.

The church has an admirable location at a major crossroads about a quarter of a mile S of London Bridge, where the road anciently divided, one route heading for Canterbury and Dover (Watling Street) and the other going S to Chichester (Stane Street). The churchyard was much diminished by the extension of Tabard Street on the N side in 1902–05. St. George's is built of red brick, with Portland stone dressings, but its W end is almost entirely stone-faced. The tower sits above the W end, in the manner of St. Martin-in-the-Fields, but it more successfully combines the tower with the W front. The front is divided into three bays, the centre being framed by giant attached Ionic columns, which support a segmental pediment. This bay forms the lower W face of the tower. It is flanked by arched windows at gallery height and square-headed doors below. The parapet has a stone balustrade, which continues for one bay on the N and S sides, after which a plain brick parapet takes over. The N and S elevations reflect the galleries within, with an upper tier of arched windows, with ears, stone aprons and prominent keystones, and a lower tier of windows which are square but for their segmental heads. The tower itself is foursquare and masterful, with single arched and louvred openings in its first visible stage, above which it sharply recedes to a stage with four clock-faces, each clock being flanked by brackets and surmounted by small pediments. The remaining stages, ending in a short spire, are octagonal. The E end has a projecting sanctuary with a Venetian window.

Within, the church comprises a W vestibule under the tower, with a vestry to its S and a staircase lobby to its N, a rectangular nave with N and S aisles under galleries, a W gallery for the organ, a shallow sanctuary and small vestries to the NE and NW. There is a moulded plaster ceiling, on which are painted cherubim singing the Te Deum. This is a postwar restoration of a design of 1897 by Basil Champneys. The body of the church has box-pews (cut down but retaining their doors), over which presides a stately pulpit, raised very high on four fluted Ionic columns. There is no tester. A brass eagle lectern stands to the S. The royal coat of arms of the early 17C adorns the front of the W gallery. The Hanoverian royal arms are placed over the W door. The organ was built by Abraham Jordan in 1702 but is of course much rebuilt. The E window has postwar stained glass of the Ascension, flanked by St. Michael slaying the dragon and by St. George trampling on Diocletian's edict against Christianity, by Marion Grant. In the S aisle is a window brought from the Hanwell Residential Schools in 1933 and reset here in 1950. A brass tablet of 1618 commemorates Ethelred Reynell, wife of Sir George Reynell, Marshal of the King's Bench (and thus in charge of one of Southwark's prisons).

In 'Little Dorrit', Amy, the daughter of William Dorrit, 'Father of the Marshalsea', is baptised in the church (in chapter XIV) and marries Arthur Clennam there in chapter LXX. A notable marriage in reality was that of George Monk, future Duke of Albemarle, to Anne Clarges in 1654.

The Metropolitan Tabernacle, Elephant and Castle. The Metropolitan Tabernacle is a postwar restoration of a church which was first built in 1859–61 to the designs of W.W. Pocock for the famous Baptist pastor, the Reverend Charles Haddon Spurgeon (1834–92), 'the prince of preachers'. Spurgeon had become the pastor of New Park Street Baptist Church, Southwark, in 1854 at the early age of 20. His preaching there drew such large congregations that firstly Essex Hall and then the Surrey Music Hall in Walworth were hired for services. The Metropolitan Tabernacle was built as the permanent home of Spurgeon's vast congregation; it was planned to hold about 5000 people. In 1898 the Tabernacle was burnt down, but it was rebuilt on the old lines. Destruction came again in 1941 by bombing, after which a modern church was built behind the Classical 19C façade. The rebuilt church was opened in 1959, still with 1750 seats.

The principal façade is a hexastyle Corinthian portico, raised on a podium. The body of the church extends one bay to the left and right. The façade reflects the fact that the 19C Baptists patronised the grandest Classical style after the other Free Churches had turned to Gothic. The interior of Spurgeon's Tabernacle was arranged with two tiers of galleries which curved around the W end. All the seats, of course, focused on the pulpit.

MIDDLESEX

Despite its small area, Middlesex was formerly one of the most important counties in England, embracing all London except for the City. No fewer than four Roman roads radiated from London across the county, of which the most famous was Watling Street to the NW, which later became Edgware Road. In 1888, a separate County of London was formed, depriving Middlesex of its head and leaving it with a shapeless torso, largely urbanised or suburbanised and densely populated with only isolated pockets of country in the W towards Harefield and in the N around Enfield and South Mymms. It is this abbreviated area's churches we shall consider although even this area, apart from a small fringe bordering the River Thames transferred to Surrey and a small part in the N transferred to Hertfordshire, was absorbed into Greater London in 1965, and Middlesex is now thought of mainly as a postal address, a famous county cricket club and a well-known London hospital. The county is almost all clay, which compelled builders to resort to flint and rubble with stone dressings, although later brick came into regular use.

For medieval architecture, the loss of London's churches—apart from Westminster Abbey and St. Margaret's, Westminster—was no great deprivation as Middlesex was not rich in notable places of worship before the 17C. Nevertheless, there is much to see from Norman times including two above-average doorways at Harmondsworth and Harlington, the latter of four orders decorated with various motifs and the most elaborate example of Norman decoration in the county. Other doorways exist at Harrow, Friern Barnet and East Bedfont. There are seven Norman fonts comprising a notable one at Hendon which is large and has sturdy shafts supporting a heavy square bowl with interlaced arcading; the others are Hayes of c 1200, drum-shaped with coarse leaf decoration, Harrow (12C) which has a round bowl with scallop decoration, Ruislip, St. Mary's at Willesden, Harmondsworth and Harlington. Structurally the most interesting features are the arcades at Laleham with their short circular piers, and the chancel arch at East Bedfont with zigzag decoration—the only Norman one in Middlesex.

The 13C is best represented at Hillingdon where the chancel arch has stiff-leaf capitals on short shafts which rest on head corbels. Harrow's nave and chancel date from the same century, the chancel with lancet windows and the five-bay nave arcade supported on low round piers. Northolt has an early 13C nave and Hayes a late 13C chancel whilst Harefield's chancel also incorporates work of that century and St. Mary's, Willesden has two piers on the S side of the nave of the same period. Other items of contemporary date are the South Mymms chancel and the short nave arcade at Stanwell. Moving on to the 14C, Stanwell has a fine chancel housing the wall monument to Lord Knyvett (died 1622), who caught Guy Fawkes in the cellars at Westminster, and his wife, but the E end was rebuilt in the 18C. The 14C also dominates at Harefield, known for its varied collection of furnishings and its many monuments ranging from the 15C to the beginning of the 19C which create a crowded lovable hugger-mugger effect. A rewarding church for studying medieval architecture, furnishings and memorials in Middlesex is South Mymms which is a slow-growth construction stretching from the 13C to the early 16C. Uxbridge is mainly 15C but, apart from the roofs and especially the late 15C S aisle hammerbeam roof, the interior is not of great interest. Also 15C is the clerestory and roof of Harrow, the latter supported on wall posts carved with figures of Apostles which in turn rest on grotesque corbels.

Towers are plentiful and an appealing Middlesex custom is to provide some of them with a 18C top-knot in the form of an engaging little cupola (Harmondsworth, Hillingdon, Harlington, West Drayton, Uxbridge). Medieval spires number only two—Stanwell sheathed in shingles which leans six feet out of plumb and Harrow, sheathed in lead. On a smaller scale are the appealing weather-boarded bell-cotes at Perivale and on the old church at Greenford. Littleton has an early 16C brick tower heightened early in the 18C.

The early part of the 17C has not much to offer. Shepperton received a new church in 1614 of flint rubble with wide transepts, to which a battlemented oblong brick tower was added in 1710. The towers at Hillingdon and Staines date from 1629 and 1631 respect-ively, and the old church at Great Stanmore was consecrated by Archbishop Laud in 1632 (now only a picturesque ruin after being replaced by a new church begun in 1849). The 18C produced towers at Laleham (1732) and Sunbury (1752), a new church retaining an old tower at Twickenham (1714–15), and much work at Teddington (1753), but the major contribution was the rebuilding of Little Stanmore in 1715–20 by Lord (later the Duke of) Chandos. The early 16C brick tower remaining from the old church and the plain exterior leaves one quite unprepared for the lavish interior decorated from top to bottom and its retrochoir and Grinling Gibbons organ case appearing theatrically between two tall fluted columns of dark wood.

Examples of the style of 19C Commissioners' churches include St. Paul's, Mill Hill built in 1829–36 and St. John's, Hampton Wick in 1829–30. They are of the usual stock brick with tall narrow windows and interior galleries. There was no lack of Victorian work but, although most of the leading architects are represented, none of their major works appear. One of the best of the early Victorian buildings is St. Andrew's, Kingsbury. It was designed by S.W. Dawkes and John Hamilton and built in Wells Street, London but brought to Kingsbury in 1933. Sir Gilbert Scott designed Christ Church, Ealing (1850–52), which G.F. Bodley later decorated, and Christ Church, Southgate (1861–62), which was given some notable early Morris & Co. stained glass. Also in Ealing, S.S. Teulon recast the 18C St. Mary's in 1863–74 and gave it iron columns in the nave and remarkable open timber roofs. The Archbishop of Canterbury spoke of a change 'from a Georgian monstrosity into a Constantinopolitan basilica'. William Butterfield built All Saints', Harrow Weald (1849–52). Later works of note are All Souls', Harlesden, built in 1875–79 by E.J. Tarver as an unusual octagon, J.L. Pearson's St. John's, Friern Barnet (1891–1902), with a vaulted interior and Clayton & Bell glass, St. Peter's, Ealing begun in 1892 by J.D. Sedding and H. Wilson, also an original design with a very large W window, and St. Michael and All Angels, Bedford Park by Norman Shaw with its charming lantern and white timber balustrade. Sir Edwin Lutyens built two highly individual churches for the Hampstead Garden Suburb, one Angli-can and the other the Free Church. The parish church of St. Jude has an enormous roof starting close to the ground and a tall spire over the crossing, a conspicuous accent to the village from wherever one looks. Sir Giles Gilbert Scott designed the brick-built St. Alban's at Golders Green (1932). St. Thomas the Apostle at Hanwell was built in 1934 by Edward Maufe, with a Crucifixion by Eric Gill next to the E window, and a tall NE tower.

Furnishings. Furnishings include the fine oaken pulpit at Harrow of c 1675 supported on six scrolled brackets, the superlative oak font cover of c 1500 at Heston and, most notable of all, the 15C stalls from Winchester Cathedral at Littleton. South Mymms has the best screen and also the only pre-Reformation stained glass of note in the county. Wall paintings include a late 13C Christ in Glory in quatrefoil frame and a Crucifixion at East Bedfont, a large and partially restored St. Christopher at Hayes, and traces of painting of c 1500 from the life of a saint and others depicting St. Martin at Ruislip, which also has a well-carved bread cupboard with four shelves of 1697 in the N aisle. There are chests at Littleton, Ruislip, South Mymms (of hutch-type and possibly 13C, the earliest furnishing in the county) and Twickenham. St. Mary's, Willesden has a good Elizabethan communion table with bulbous legs and an attractive iron railing (ascribed to the 17C) to guard the weights of the clock. South Mymms has a 13C font with later base and at West Drayton there is a notable 15C octagonal font with carvings of the Crucifixion, Pietà, etc on the panels of the octagon. All Hallows' at Twickenham has fine late 17C furnishings, brought from a Wren church in the City which closed in 1938. St. John's, Hendon also has late 17C fittings from the City.

Brasses and Monuments. The best brasses are at Harrow, Hillingdon, Hayes, Enfield and St. Mary's, Willesden, where there is a set of six varying in size and ranging from 1492 to 1609. But it is in its 17C and later monuments that Middlesex has most to offer. The one at Harefield to the Countess of Derby (died 1636) and the canopied tombs to the two Henry Frowyks at South Mymms are the best. The other memorials at Harefield, mainly to the Newdigate and Ashby families, are described in the gazetteer. Other notable monuments which must be mentioned are those to Sir Roger Aston (died 1612) and his wife at Cranford, Lord Knyvett (died 1622) and his wife at Stanwell, and Sir Edward Carr (died 1657) and his wife at Hillingdon. These are all kneeling figures facing each other but, in the Hillingdon memorial, the children face outwards. The fine bearded marble figure of Sir John Wolstenholme (died 1639) at Great Stanmore is a recumbent effigy but Sir Edward Fenner (died 1612) at Hayes, Leonora Bennet (died 1638) at Uxbridge and Sir Nicholas Raynton (died 1646) at Enfield are shown semi-recumbent leaning on their elbows, Leonora Bennet on a tomb-chest which depicts a *memento mori* in the form of a charnel house. Other 17C memorials are the recumbent marble figures of Robert Clayton (stillborn 1665) at Ickenham showing the infant in swaddling clothes, a particularly poignant monument, and an especially fine large black marble slab on a low tomb-chest at Hendon to Sir Jeremy Whichcot of 1677 with no effigy but consisting of bold lettering, a large coat of arms and a border. At Hornsey, there is a delightful memorial to Francis Musters, who died in 1680 at the age of 15, showing him kneeling in prayer in clerical clothes with cherubs holding a crown above his head under a projecting pediment. From the 18C, Middlesex possesses the striking monument at Little Stanmore to the Duke of Chandos, depicting him standing bewigged in Roman costume between his two wives, designed by Grinling Gibbons some 27 years before the Duke died in 1744. In West Drayton, there is an inscription plate in the S aisle to Rupert Billingsley of HMS 'Royal George' (died 1720) with a vivid relief of the ship, a three-master, at the foot: at Hillingdon, a memorial to Henry Pagett, Earl of Uxbridge (died 1743) showing him in Roman clothes in a semi-reclining position on a tomb-chest and, at Great Stanmore, a monument to John Dalton of 1791 by John Bacon in the form of a woman leaning on an urn bearing his head in profile. The 19C has no especially good monuments to its credit. Speaking generally, apart from Baroque St. Lawrence's at Little Stanmore, brick St. Mary Magdalene's at Littleton and Lutyens's St. Jude on the Hill at Hampstead, Middlesex has more to offer in its monuments than in its ecclesiastical architecture.

Bedford Park, *St. Michael and All Angels, Bath Road.* The church is an integral part of this earliest planned garden suburb, started in 1875. Norman Shaw designed the principal group of church, inn and bank opposite the Common. The exterior of St. Michael's, dating from 1880, is distinctive for its large porch with palisaded gates and delightful lantern over the crossing. Inside, the eye is immediately drawn to the elevated high altar approached by a flight of seven steps through a tall open screen. A splendid roof, covering nave and chancel without interruption and spanning nave and aisles, gives a fine sense of spaciousness whilst the pale green tone used for the tall arcade and the pews add a cheerful note to the interior, enhanced by the balconies in front of the clerestory windows. Amongst many furnishings of interest, the font and sedilia may be singled out.

Ealing, *St. Peter, Mount Park Road.* The church was built in 1892–93 to a distinctive design by J.D. Sedding and his pupil, Henry Wilson. An enormous deeply-recessed W window is divided into three lights by buttresses rather than mullions, between narrow flanking turrets with spirelets. It has elaborate tracery used to good effect, but the circular window at the E end set above three blind arches of which the outer ones have thin lancets is not successful. A drawing of 1889 by Wilson shows three larger lancets within three arches and more elaborate tracery in the circular window. An E tower with spire originally planned was never built. St. Peter's is aisled with Lady chapel in the NE angle and has good modern furnishings.

Externally, the most striking feature is the manner in which the internal piers penetrate the roof and are completed with turrets which stick out halfway up and are connected by depressed arches. The interior has broad aisles supporting galleries on depressed arches; there are three clerestory windows above each arch. The bases of the huge piers are panelled and shafts run up to the roof. Nave and chancel have a continuous tall steep-pitched roof which is dominated by some very ordinary tiebeams.

The history of the building between its consecration and the Second World War was one of numerous additions of fittings. An excellent font in an attractive green colour and cover were installed and there is a large pulpit. Between 1911 and 1915, Kempe & Co. designed stained glass windows for the S transept, the Lady chapel and the E end of the S aisle. After the 1914–18 War, Cecil Hare, the inheritor of Bodley's practice, was responsible for the reredos, panelling and screen of the Lady chapel and for the choir and clergy stalls, the middle rows of which are enriched with carved angels having large wings at the ends. There are good altar rails.

Hampstead Garden Suburb, *St. Jude-on-the-Hill, Central Square.* Hampstead Garden Suburb grew out of the experiences of Mrs (later Dame) Henrietta Barnett and her husband, Canon Samuel Barnett, in Whitechapel and, as Dr. Winnington Ingram, Bishop of London, put it, 'the Garden Suburb was intended to be an exact contrast and antidote to all Mrs. Barnett had seen and known in Whitechapel'. St. Jude-on-the-Hill (named after St. Jude's in Whitechapel, of which

Canon Barnett was Vicar) is part of Central Square, the focal point of the Suburb; with the Free Church opposite and the Institute (Adult Education Centre) between, all designed by Sir Edwin Lutyens in 1908–10, it forms one of the most harmonious architectural groups in London. St. Jude's relates to the surrounding buildings by the use of similar materials (silvery-grey bricks with redbrick dressings plus some stone, and dark tiles for the roof). It is distinctive for its splendid tower with open belfry and 16-sided spire rising to a total height of 178ft, which display both Tudor and Byzantine motifs. Sweeping down over nave and aisles to within a short distance from the pavement is a vast roof, the surfaces of which are broken by large dormers to provide light within. The interior structure is Byzantine in character; rounded arches spring from brick piers supporting tunnel-vaults, but there are domes over the crossing, the sanctuary and the chapels; this combination assorts ill with the oak open-framed roofs over the aisles.

The whole surface of roof and walls is covered with murals painted in tempera on the prepared plaster by Walter Percival Starmer during the years 1920 to 1930. Starting on the Lady chapel the artist took as his theme for this part of the church 'the Women of the Bible', devoting the W section to the Old Testament and the E to the New, although the W dome includes Queen Victoria, Queen Alexandra, Florence Nightingale, Edith Cavell and Elizabeth Browning. Above the altar presides the Virgin and Child. The murals which cover the rest of the church are mainly concerned with the Life of Christ and incidents from the Bible, culminating in a representation of the Last Supper before the high altar.

Hampton Court, *Chapel Royal.* The inversion of noun and adjective in the name 'Chapel Royal' stems from the use of an old French word to describe the company of priests and singers who went with the king on his travels and performed religious offices for him. In course of time, 'Chapel Royal' was applied to the consecrated building which came into being as a part of a royal palace.

It seems probable that, sometime before 1525, Cardinal Wolsey rebuilt the chapel of the Knights Hospitaller of St. John of Jerusalem on the same site, he having rented their commandery or 'camera' at Hampton. Apart from glazing the new chapel, not much work appears to have been done after King Henry VIII took over the palace in 1529, until 1535–36, when the new vaulted roof was carved and installed. This was a major undertaking involving work on the carving for about nine months by close on 100 men. The task was carried out at Sonning near Reading, where suitable timber was available. The various sections had to be transported to Hampton by barge, continuing from August to December 1535, and the sections then assembled, this taking almost as long as the carving. It was not until the late summer of 1536 that the ceiling was ready for painting and gilding. Although constructed of wood and not of stone, the ceiling is a splendid creation with its lierne-vaulting and sumptuous pendants, each surrounded by four figures playing pipes, singing or bearing sceptres. Restoration in 1929 brought it back to its original state. Also in Tudor times, the floor was tiled and, although it is not certain that there were white as well as black tiles, it was renewed in 1711 in a chequer-board pattern to match what was believed to be the original design. In 1973 the floor was relaid. Alterations were made to the W gallery from which the King and Queen worshipped, to provide so-called separate Holyday Closets for them, and it was at this time that the stone tablets carrying the royal arms of King Henry VIII and Jane Seymour were painted and affixed to the wall on either side of the main entrance to the chapel.

The extensive early 18C alterations were made on Queen Anne's orders. Prior to this, sometime between April 1694 and March 1696, Grinling Gibbons took down the marble altarpiece and screen with the carved columns, ornaments and figures that stood in the chapel at Whitehall and transferred them by barge to Hampton Court where they were re-erected in the Chapel Royal. In 1706, however, the Dean and Chapter of Westminster demanded the return of the marble altarpiece, leaving the huge carved altar screen of Grinling Gibbons with cherubs and wreaths as a dominant, some might say overpowering, feature of the chapel. This was carved by Gibbons to Sir Christopher Wren's design and has coupled fluted giant Corinthian columns, a wide broken segmental pediment and plain marquetry oval, making a strong contrast with its broad curve to the Tudor roof. The painting above the screen is a copy of an Andrea del Sarto painting in Florence. Communion table, benches and a new organ were provided, the organ being built by Christopher Shrider, son-in-law of Bernard Smith, and the case was carved by Gibbons. Structural alterations included the panelling, the renewing of the floor, the transformation of the two Holyday Closets into the Royal Pew with a ceiling painted by Sir James Thornhill, and a new staircase. One Holyday Closet remains behind the Pew. Later changes embraced the replacement of the Wren windows in 1894 with copies of the old Tudor windows based on a part of an original window frame which had survived, the removal in 1973 of the centre pews placed in the nave in 1868, and the furnishing in recent years of a 17C font and cover which had originally been made for the church of All Hallows, Upper Thames Street, in the City of London. The brass altar cross was designed by Sir Edwin Lutyens and has a triangular base to harmonise with the older brass candlesticks.

Associations. Catherine Howard. On 2nd November 1541, Archbishop Cranmer handed to King Henry VIII when alone at his prayers in his Holyday Closet a document proving Catherine Howard's unfaithfulness. She was arrested shortly afterwards and confined to her room in Hampton Court. Over 300 years later, the gallery which led to the Closets became known as the 'Haunted Gallery' because a 'Grace and Favour' tenant at that time saw an apparition which she was convinced was that of Catherine Howard. It was probably then that the explanation was conceived that, while she was confined in her room, she slipped her guard and made her way to the Closet when the King was again alone at his devotions in the hope of seeing him and begging for her life to be spared. It was then stated that the guards refused her access and dragged the screaming 19-year-old Queen back to her room.

Fainting by young ladies. In the summer of 1831 a young lady fainted in the chapel, whereupon a hero from the Battle of Waterloo carried her to his apartment, laid her on a sofa and returned to his seat in the chapel. As the same thing happened with different young ladies on the following two Sundays, a notice was posted to say that, in future, any ladies so affected would be carried out by the dustman. No more fainting occurred.

Captain Robert Falcon Scott, who lost his life returning from the South Pole, was married in the chapel in 1909.

NB I am indebted to the comprehensive Paper No. 42 of the Borough of Twickenham Local History Society by G.D. Heath (September 1983, Second Impression) for much of the above information.

Harefield, St. Mary. On its own at the foot of a lane in one of Middlesex's few rural areas, the church is an historical record of the Newdigate and Ashby families, the chief landowners of the area, as seen in the array of monuments around the walls. Mainly 14C, this place of worship consists of nave, chancel, N and S aisles, N chancel chapel and a low 16C NW tower. The 16C N aisle and the low tower are both battlemented and terminate at the W end at the same point as the nave and S aisle, giving a picturesque three-roofed effect. Constructed mainly of flint rubble with stone dressings, part of the tower, in contrast, is refaced with brick. Attractive flint and stone chequerwork in the S aisle add to the general appeal of the building.

The interior has a 14C nave and 13C chancel, and the W wall may be partly Norman. The tower, N aisle and N chancel chapel are all early 16C. The general effect is one of spaciousness, despite the furnishings and monuments and one or two box-pews still remaining at various points. The nave arcades have quatrefoil piers with slender angle shafts. The chancel arch dates from the 18C. The nave furnishings are not of major interest but the chancel contains much that is above-average: a reredos luxuriously decorated with two kneeling angels above flanking two Commandment boards of frosted glass; and altar rails (possibly Flemish), also richly carved with foliage and scrollwork, with heads of a monk, a nun and cherubs. The pulpit beside the entrance to the chancel on the SE side is a fascinating piece. There are a few minor roundels of 16C glass in the E window of the N chapel.

The monuments, ranging in style from the small brass to Editha Newdigate (died 1444) to the massive four-poster tomb to Alice Spencer, Countess of Derby (died 1636) in the SE corner of the chancel, are the main attraction to the visitor. They chiefly commemorate members of the Newdigate and Ashby families. The grandest is the monument to the Countess of Derby who is carved lying in a four-poster on a tomb-chest, in the W wall of which (set in niches) are three kneeling daughters, all of whom married earls. The four columns with thick looped curtains of stone support a baldacchino with crests at the corners. The Countess wears a rich red dress and an ermine cloak; her delicate hands are at prayer and there is a crest by her neat little feet. Opposite the Countess in the NE corner is a Grinling Gibbons canopied monument to Mary (wife of Sir Richard Newdigate who died in 1692) and to Sir Richard himself. In complete contrast to the Countess's monument, it is all in white and shows the lady in a simple loose Roman robe in a reclining position. On the S wall of the chancel there is a recessed tomb-chest of c 1500, at the back of which are little brass kneeling effigies of John Newdigate (died 1545), his wife and 13 children. Above this are three large urns with varying inscriptions, one in Latin and two in Greek, and large identical niches, all to women—the mother and the two wives of Sir Roger Newdigate (founder of the Newdigate Prize who died in 1765). Other less important works to the Newdigate family are on the N wall of the chancel. In the N chancel chapel Sir Robert Ashby (died 1617) and Sir Francis Ashby (died 1623) are commemorated by routine kneeling figures with the children in relief below, but there is a more interesting memorial on the N side of the nave in the form of a rebus to William Ashby (died 1760). A fine portrait bust above a grey oval inscription tablet has white ash branches around and the letters BY in capitals at the foot of the oval. Other Newdigates are commemorated on the wall of the S aisle including brasses to John Newdigate (died 1528), his wife (died 1544) and 17 children against the E wall. Altogether, there are over 50 figures in brass.

Outside, on the N wall of the chancel, there is a tablet to William Ashby's gamekeeper, showing him with his gun and dog, and a long inscription starting with the words: 'In frost and snow, through hail and rain,/He scoured the woods and trudged the plain'.

Harrow-on-the-Hill, *St. Mary, Church Hill.* Archbishop Lanfranc began building in 1087 a church which was consecrated by his successor, St. Anselm, in 1094. Only the lower stages of the tower with N and S windows deeply splayed inside and a W doorway remain from this building. The 12C chancel was rebuilt except for the S wall by Gilbert Scott in 1846–49, but the chancel arch remains. Early in the 13C an Early English nave replaced the old Norman one but in the mid-15C the roof was removed and a clerestory erected in the Perpendicular style; also, the aisle windows were renewed. An upper storey was added to the tower and the lead-sheathed spire built, and a S porch with an upper room was provided. The poor condition of the fabric led to Gilbert Scott's restoration of 1846–49 when, apart from the reconstruction work in the chancel, battlemented parapets were added and the exterior except for the tower was re-faced in flint. A N porch in stone was built and the N chancel chapel and vestry were added.

The exterior on its lofty site is dominated by the spire, but the flint re-facing by Scott detracts from the overall appearance. The interior view from the W is made agreeable by the four-bay Early English nave with its arches set on low round piers and the well-proportioned original chancel arch. The flat-pitched mid-15C roof has cambered tiebeams on curved braces. The wall posts are carved with figures of Apostles and rest on grotesque corbels. The clerestory with its Perpendicular windows is also 15C.

The outstanding furnishings consist of a Norman font in the form of a round bowl with scallop decoration and a shaft with spiral fluting, a pulpit of c 1675 (although not given to the church until 1708) and an early 13C oak chest. The oak pulpit is supported on six scrolled brackets. Stained glass in the chancel lancet windows is by Kempe & Co.; the E window by Sir Ninian Comper dates from 1908.

The church has several brasses of note ranging in date from a small knight of c 1370 to the inscription of 1613 to Katherine Clerke of Ruislip, 13 in all, of which the best are in the chancel floor. A small brass against a pier of the N arcade commemorates John Lyon, founder of Harrow School, who died in 1592, and his wife, whilst above this is a memorial by John Flaxman to him, showing the teacher instructing his boys. Other monuments commemorate James Edwards (died 1813), with a portrait medallion, and J.H. North (died 1831), with a weeping female figure draped over an urn.

Hillingdon, *St. John the Baptist, Uxbridge Road.* Set effectively on the crown of a hill, the church is one of a small group of W Middlesex churches which are built with walls faced with trimmed black flints. The W tower is of 1629, the nave and its aisles are 14C, and the transepts, chancel and NE chapel are by Sir Gilbert Scott, 1847–48. Within, the chancel arch is a 13C survival, as the stiff-leaf capitals show. The aisle roofs are 15C. There are some interesting medieval corbels. In the S aisle is a large brass to John, Lord Strange of Knockin and his wife, erected in 1509. Lord in armour and lady in gown are represented under Gothic canopies with a minute daughter between them. In the chancel there are two notable monuments, the earlier one (of marble and alabaster) to Sir Edward Carr (died 1637) and his wife, a late version of the formerly well-established practice of showing the two figures kneeling opposite each other across a

desk, in this case adorned with a cherub. A delightful innovation is to
have the daughters Philadelphia and Jane facing outwards, the
younger with a posy in one hand and holding with her other the hand
of her elder sister who has a book. Above is a steep broken gable
with columns, draped curtains and allegorical figures. The later
monument is to Henry Pagett, first Earl of Uxbridge (died 1743)
showing him in Roman costume semi-reclining on a tomb-chest.

Kingsbury, *St. Andrew, Church Lane.* Two churches share the one
churchyard. Old St. Andrew's was the sole parish church of the district
until 1884, when it was replaced by William Butterfield's Holy
Innocents' Church of 1883–84 in Kingsbury Road. Some parishioners
refused to accept the arrangement, however, and eventually old St.
Andrew's was revived to serve a new parish of Neasden cum
Kingsbury. By 1932 the district had much expanded in population and
it was decided to transfer from Wells Street in London, W1 another
church of St. Andrew whose congregation had dwindled. St. Andrew's
in Wells Street had been built to the designs of S.W. Dawkes and John
Hamilton and it had been consecrated in 1847. It became one of the

*New St. Andrew's, Kingsbury, built by S.W. Dawkes and
John Hamilton in central London in 1847–48 and removed
to Kingsbury in 1933*

most famous of Victorian London's churches, for its third Vicar (1862–85) was Benjamin Webb, a leading Ecclesiologist. Almost every leading church architect and artist was called in to embellish the church. After the First World War, however, St. Andrew's was considered to have no future in central London, and instead of being demolished and lost, it was transferred in its entirety to Kingsbury, being consecrated in 1934. It inevitably superseded old St. Andrew's, but not until 1977 was the old church declared redundant. The Wembley History Society now maintains the old building.

The church of 1847 comprises a tall nave and chancel with N and S aisles, and a NW tower and spire. It stands well back from the road on slightly rising ground. The spire, which is visible from afar, is a broach spire, with one tier of gabled lucarnes. Pinnacles rise from the corners of the tower and lower ones in between. There are pairs of recessed belfry windows of two transomed lights. The belfry stage is narrower than the two lower stages, of which the lowest has a four-light, transomed W window. The main W window of the church is of five lights, set high above the W door, which is the main entrance. The E window repeats the W one, but with a transom, and flanking it are the four-light E windows of the aisles. The tracery is all Perpendicular. Perpendicular details were not favoured by Ecclesiologists in 1847, but the church was not built as their model church, no matter what it later became, and in any case, it is distinguished as it is. The aisles have their own pitched roofs. The fabric preserves the plan of Wells Street except for the aisle windows. In Wells Street there were no S windows and only one N window, which was inserted in 1873.

The interior is very tall and light. There is no structural division between nave and chancel, but there is a metal screen set on a low wall. The arcades are of five bays, in late medieval style. Two-light clerestory windows are placed above each arch. The chancel projects slightly beyond the aisles. At the W end a gallery extends across the church. The NW corner, under the tower, forms the baptistery. The Corpus Christi chapel is formed from the S aisle, the Lady chapel from the N.

The huge reredos of alabaster and Caen stone stretches right across the E wall of the chancel and also flanks the E window to the height of its tracery. The reredos was designed by G.E. Street and was made in 1865–72 by James Redfern, a sculptor whom Benjamin Webb had discovered when he was a curate at Sheen in Staffordshire. The canopied arches on the N and S walls of the sanctuary, including the sedilia, were added by J.L. Pearson in 1888 as a memorial to Benjamin Webb. The E window originally had stained glass made by John Hardman to A.W.N. Pugin's design. The present glass is by Goddard & Gibbs. G.E. Street designed the chancel screens and gates (in 1865 and 1871), and also the notable pulpit of metal openwork. All these were made by Hardman. All are largely painted black. The green and white marble flooring in the sanctuary is by Farmer & Brindley, 1907. On the S side of the nave, the brass lectern is by William Butterfield. The paintings on the W gallery are by Alfred Bell of Clayton & Bell. By the same firm is the stained glass in the N window (depicting the Transfiguration and the Magi) and at the W end. The font is by G.E. Street, 1878 (replacing an earlier one by Pugin), but the cover is by J.L. Pearson, 1887. The painting of the Baptism of Christ on the N wall of the baptistery is by Clayton & Bell. One distinguished fitting which is now on loan to the Victoria and Albert Museum is a litany desk, designed by William Burges in 1868. It was illustrated in 'The Ecclesiologist' in that year.

High up in the S wall there is set the canopied tomb-recess of the second Vicar (1847–62), James Murray. Burges was the designer. The recumbent effigy is shown in cassock, surplice and stole. The recess, which has huge cusping, is surmounted by a Pelican in her Piety. In the central nave aisle there is a brass to Vicesimus Knox (died 1855), an early example of an art the Victorians revived.

In its days in Wells Street, the church was known for its music and for its dignified liturgy. Sir Joseph Barnby was its organist and choirmaster from 1863 to 1871. Alexander Beresford Hope, President of the Ecclesiological Society and Webb's patron, became its church-warden when he tired of All Saints', Margaret Street, for which he had been chiefly responsible.

S.C.H.

Kingsbury, *Old St. Andrew's, Church Lane.* From the evidence of excavations, the old church seems to have originated in c 1200. For most of the Middle Ages it belonged to the Knights Hospitaller of St. John of Jerusalem. At the Dissolution, it passed to the Dean and Chapter of St. Paul's. Restoration took place in 1840, 1870 and 1888. The building is rectangular, aisleless and without internal structural division. There is a 15C W window of three lights, heavily restored; a doorway of Norman design, also much restored; two 15C windows in the S wall; and a wooden belfry at the W end. On the N wall at the E end there is a brass to John Shepard (died 1520), his successive wives, Anne and Maud, and their 18 children.

S.C.H.

Laleham, *All Saints.* There is reason to believe that monks from Westminster Abbey built the first church at Laleham, from which the nave piers of c 1150 survive. The church today presents a 19C appearance except for the tower and the NE (or Lucan) chapel built of diapered brick. The nave arcades and a large painting of Christ on the sea with St. Peter by G.H. Harlow are the main internal features. Externally dominant is the tower, a massive brick construction of 1732 with wide quoins surmounted by capitals and a heavy parapet. The brick NE chapel has four moulded three-light windows. A 17C map shows that, before the tower was built, the church had a steeple with a wooden spire.

Internally, the tune is called by the three-bay Norman nave arcades, although the N aisle was rebuilt in 1827 and the S was blocked up when the aisle was demolished (date unknown). Galleries were removed in 1910, at which date the altar rails, pulpit, panelling and chancel marble floor were all installed. The nave capitals are scalloped and the NE arches have been replaced in brick. In the S wall are some reset pieces from a former Norman doorway. A later medieval feature is an altar slab with all five crosses set in the W wall. The reredos was erected in 1926. The stained glass—originally intended for the E window—was moved following protests by parishioners. In the W window is an unusual representation of St. Christopher by Wilhelmina Geddes, 1926. The painting by G.H. Harlow of Christ on the sea with St. Peter is a large one against the W wall of the N aisle and dates probably from c 1810.

Laleham is closely linked with Thomas Arnold and his son, Matthew. Thomas taught at Laleham from 1819 before moving to Rugby in 1828 where his methods earned him great praise. Matthew was born in Laleham in 1822 and was buried in the churchyard in

1888. Matthew's three sons are also buried here, all dying before they had reached the age of 18.

Little Stanmore, *St. Lawrence Whitchurch, Whitchurch Lane.* Baron (later the Duke of) Chandos, after amassing a fortune as Paymaster-General to the Duke of Marlborough, launched a building programme for a lavish mansion on his Canons Estate, and rebuilt a medieval church which was to serve more or less as his private chapel, although remaining a parish church. In 1715–16, the old church was demolished except for the W tower and the Duke enlisted artists and craftsmen to decorate the interior of the new church in a Continental Baroque style. The family fortune was dissipated by the second Duke and the mansion soon disappeared but the unique unaisled Baroque church remains. This has been restored by conservators from Tübingen in Germany who completed their work in 1984; the dark Victorian varnish had earlier been removed from much of the woodwork, which resumed its original golden oak colour.

Once a pleasant rural area, Little Stanmore has been engulfed by suburbanisation but the church itself stands in a spacious churchyard with a park and playing fields adjoining. As so often with Baroque churches, the exterior gives no hint of the exuberance within. The W tower, built of stone with brick battlements and dating from c 1500, is all that remains of the medieval predecessor but a circular window and doorway were inserted during the rebuilding—probably to provide a more lordly entrance. The 18C round-headed windows are undecorated and there are broad Tuscan corner pilasters.

The interior is very much a personal statement of the Duke, described on his monument as 'religious without enthusiasm'; he could sit in splendour with his retainers in the W gallery, approached by a staircase with a wrought-iron balustrade, under a freely rendered copy of Raphael's painting of the Transfiguration by Antonio Bellucci. There, he could listen to the playing of Handel, who worked for the Duke in 1717–18 as composer in residence, on an organ appearing behind the altar in stage fashion through pairs of fluted wooden Corinthian columns supporting a segmental arch. The gallery is divided into three compartments, for the Duke and his entourage in the middle and his retainers on each side. The central part of the church filled with box-pews is more restrained but the walls and ceilings are covered with paintings, the walls in grey (or grisaille) with Virtues, Evangelists and St. Peter and St. Paul, and the ceilings in sepia with eight panels by Louis Laguerre representing Biblical scenes, mainly miracles. The painting most Baroque in feeling is the one on the ceiling above the altar of the Adoration of Jehovah (who is represented in Hebrew letters) with swirling limbs and draperies, also by Laguerre. Flanking the altar are 'Our Lord's Nativity' and 'The Descent from the Cross' by Bellucci and on either side of the organ 'The Ten Commandments' and 'The Sermon on the Mount' by Verrio.

In 1966, a Lady chapel was fitted into the ground floor of the tower. The NW box-pew has been converted into a baptistery with an elegant marble fluted font presented by the Duke in 1716. The wrought-iron altar rails of 1715 and the pavement are original 18C work but the altar itself and choirstalls date from c 1900. The organ case, carved by Grinling Gibbons, is the outstanding furnishing, the cherubs being particularly delightful. The keyboard on which Handel played with white and black notes reversed is preserved, the organ itself being built by Gerard Smith, nephew of Father Smith. Gibbons also carved the two gilded panels above the pictures on either side of the altar.

From the NE of the nave one enters the Antechamber, originally added by the Duke as his monument room; this also has 18C paintings (not yet restored) but, when his second wife died in 1736, he built the larger Mausoleum, designed by James Gibbs. At the top of the steps, one can see through the wrought-iron gates the Duke's monument, showing him bewigged and in Roman toga with hand on chest standing proudly between his first two wives, Mary and Cassandra, who kneel on each side; the figures are separated by elegant pilasters with urns on top, between which is a kind of canopy. In addition, the Mausoleum contains on the S wall two monuments, one to Mary (died 1738), the first wife of the second Duke, and the other to Margaret (died 1760), first wife of the third Duke.

In the churchyard, there is a gravestone E of the church with hammer and anvil erected in 1863 to William Powell (died 1780)— parish clerk and village blacksmith. His name is erroneously linked with Handel's 'The Harmonious Blacksmith'.

Littleton, _St. Mary Magdalene, Squires Bridge Road._ Lying next to one of London's largest reservoirs is the mainly redbrick church of Littleton. It consists of a tall 16C tower (heightened in the 18C), 13C nave and chancel, 13C aisles, 16C clerestory, early 18C vestry and adjoining family mausoleum, the E wall of which is built to a chequerboard design of light and dark coloured brick. This church is chiefly noted for its furnishings, particularly the richly traceried and panelled choirstalls from Winchester Cathedral (15C) and the sumptuously carved Flemish altar rails (17C). In addition, there are 15C nave pews, a medieval font with beautifully carved 15C cover, a chancel screen which came from Westminster Abbey in the 17C, and an 18C pulpit plus two chests, one plain but the other with fine studded leatherwork.

The tall church stands invitingly as viewed from the road. Although very bricky in appearance, the exterior is built mainly of ragstone, ironstone, chalk and flint with Reigate stone dressings and later redbrick additions. The N aisle shows rough weathered stone bound together by massive short brick buttresses which are also found on the S side, including one angle buttress where the S aisle meets the chancel with a small narrow lancet window in a diagonal wall about one foot wide. The porch has rough crenellation but interesting roof beams within. The 18C uppermost stage of the tower has roundels on each side. In the clerestory, there are two pairs of windows with nearly square heads. An interesting detail is the hoodmould on the three-light E window with its two well-carved monk's (?) head label stops.

The interior is charming with a village atmosphere. The two-bay nave arcades have wide arches divided by central piers (round drum-shape on the S dating from c 1200 and octagonal 13C on the N) with responds at each end. The aisles are low with small windows, those on the S side containing richly-coloured glass in the form of patterns, shields and angels. The 17C Westminster Abbey screen separates the nave from the longer but lower chancel; this screen has been restored and, above it, is a Rood designed by Martin Travers in 1941. He also designed the small window dating from 1939 in the N aisle— 'In memory of the monks of Chertsey Abbey who served the church from 1135 to 1308'. Behind the pulpit is the small lancet window seen outside; it is approached by steps and contains glass representing St. Michael with scales. In addition to providing light for the pulpit it may have given access to the Rood. The inside of the tower is octagonal, although square outside, with walls 24 to 30 ins thick. This might indicate that the outer walls were built around an earlier tower.

The 15C choirstalls are of exceptional interest with their cusped ogee arches, richly traceried backs and handsome panelling along the walls. They have canopied ends with carved figures but no fronts, leaving the chancel space uncluttered. The 17C Flemish altar rails are carved in high relief with four panels and a central gateway making a fifth panel when closed. Among the subjects depicted are the Resurrection, the Pelican in her Piety, the horns of the altar of sacrifice and the stone tablets; on the gateway are the Cherubim worshipping the Host and Chalice in radiance. The 15C cover of the font is adorned with foils containing flowers which diminish in size towards the top. There is a double piscina in the chancel, the E one with shelf. Of the two chests, the larger one with fine studded leatherwork is in the SW corner. In the sanctuary are four carved wood aumbries of 17C date; they are Flemish with carved figures and tracery. Beside the N pier of the chancel arch is a post-1927 tablet to members of the Bouwens family, Lords of the Manor for many centuries who at one time were patrons of the church; two were army officers who fought at Waterloo and in the Crimea. Of two brasses, one dates from 1533; the other is a palimpsest dated 1509, bearing on one side an inscription with roses and arms to Blanche Vaughan and the other commemorating five local sisters. Of eight hatchments, one at the W end shows the 'White Bull', the emblem of the Wood family.

Outside, near the porch, is a group of tablets commemorating various members of the Dyer family with the poignant reminder of the insecurity of life in the early 19C; Edward, the father, died at the age of 44 in 1816 and three daughters aged between six and nine died within five days of one another in 1818. Two more children died in their teens or early twenties.

South Mymms, *St. Giles.* The church retains its village character. Consisting of 13C chancel, 14C W tower, nave with early 16C octagonal piers and four-centred arches giving access to the N aisle, chantry chapel of 1439–47 (now Lady chapel) and modern porch, the history of St. Giles' goes back to 1136. It is chiefly noted for its Frowyk monuments and brasses, its early 16C parclose screens and its large chest which may go back to the 13C and therefore may be the earliest piece of church furniture in the county. Externally, St. Giles' presents a very flinty appearance, although the NE former chantry chapel is of brick. The W tower has a battlemented parapet and a SE stair turret, square in outline, rising above it. One enters by the S porch built by G.E. Street.

The interior is darkened by the ancient yew trees on the S side and is not helped by the glass installed by G.E. Street in 1877 and G.C. Grey in 1899 nor by Street's chancel screen and the large Rood of 1910 above. Nevertheless, the N nave arcade of 1527 with its octagonal piers, concave capitals and four-centred arches gives it a distinctive appearance and the various monuments and furnishings provide much of interest to the visitor. A staircase to the old Rood is preserved in the S wall. The early 16C parclose screen of 15 and 10 traceried bays with steep gables divided by buttresses and with two fine doorways which surrounds the Lady chapel is of fine workmanship. The 17C candelabrum in the chancel, plain 13C font and trefoil-headed piscina are all of interest, as is Sir Ninian Comper's font cover of 1938 with eight gleaming columns supporting a pyramidal top. Comper also designed the E window of the Lady chapel which includes the unusual device of the Virgin Mary holding the infant Christ in one hand and the Host in the other. There is a little stained glass dating from 1526 showing kneeling figures in the Lady chapel and N aisle. A fine organ of 1889 by Bevington is currently being rebuilt by Bishop & Son of London.

The two Frowyk monuments are of considerable interest as they cover the transition from Gothic to Renaissance. The one to Thomas Frowyk (died 1500) in the Lady chapel with recumbent effigy is purely Gothic and is covered by a canopy with four-centred arch; it is enclosed by tall corner posts with shaft-rings. The other monument, which is in the sanctuary, is to the father who died later in 1527. It has no effigy but has a Renaissance cornice with traceried roof and shafts supporting it which develop in their upper parts into bulbous acanthus leaf-covered Renaissance balusters. In addition, there are two brasses to members of the Frowyk family (Henry—died 1386—in the chancel and Thomas—died 1449—under the tower). Thomas has disappeared but his wife Elizabeth and 19 children remain. Elizabeth wears a draped head-dress and flowing gown with a tiny dog in its folds. There are also two shield brasses, one just below the chancel step with the arms of the Haberdashers' Company and the other in the Lady chapel with the arms of the Eastlands Company.

In the 20C South Mymms has been associated with Frederick Brittain (1893–1969), a native of the district who became a well-known character at Cambridge. Amongst his many books was 'South Mymms, the Story of a Parish' (1931).

Twickenham, *St. Mary the Virgin, Church Street*. Many Thames riverside churches are dedicated to St. Mary and the one at Twickenham bears a close link with St. Mary's, Rotherhithe in that they were both rebuilt in 1714–15 by John James. The previous church at Twickenham had actually collapsed except for the 15C tower which was retained.

The W tower of Kentish ragstone with a SE stair turret rising above the battlemented parapet offers a striking contrast to James's building, for which he used brick of the finest quality. He concentrated his main efforts on the N and S sides facing the town and river, which are given prominence by wide projections covering three bays with large pediments supported on broad Tuscan pilasters. The E end also projects and has a circular window and a pediment. ·

The rectangular interior is brightened by colouring and gilding, and by its furnishings. The ceiling of Wedgwood blue with Adamesque decoration and in the form of a large circle contained in a rectangle is particularly pleasing. The chancel also rises to the roof and there are impressive spacious galleries on each side. The glass is all postwar due to bombing. The present E window embodies symbols of the Virgin Mary. The side windows contain coats of arms of patrons of the living and other notable persons associated with the church. Many of the 17C and 18C furnishings (wooden reredos, table in the N aisle, metal altar rails, pulpit and chest) are retained but are not especially noteworthy. The font at the W end and organ in the S gallery are particularly attractive.

This church will long be remembered for its close links with Alexander Pope and Sir Godfrey Kneller, the court painter. The latter was churchwarden from 1713–16 and it was at his instigation that the church was rebuilt. Neither had a monument in the church erected at the time of his death. Pope did not want a monument and was content to have the date of his death (1744) inscribed on his parents' monument in the N gallery. Bishop Warburton, however, had a monument erected to Pope in 1761 in the form of an obelisk in relief with portrait medallion, also in the N gallery. Other monuments of note are two fine Jacobean ones in the tower to Sir Joseph Ashe and to General Lord Berkeley of Stratton; to Francis Poulton (died 1642) and his wife to the right of the pulpit, made of baked clay with the top half missing, and whose figures are frontal demi-figures with their right hands clasped over a skull; to Admiral Sir Chaloner Ogle (died 1750), signed by J.M. Rysbrack in the N gallery with a cherub holding a wreath amid war trophies; to George and Anne Gostling with a mourning female figure kneeling on a pedestal, which dates from 1800 and is by John Bacon, Jr; and to Lady Mary Wildman (died 1825) by Sir Richard Westmacott. Beyond the fine Jacobean door to the vestry is the oldest memorial, a stone slab with small metal inscription commemorating Richard Burton (died 1443), cook to King Henry VI.

A brass plate given by three American scholars (members of the Faculty of English of Yale University) in 1962 is set in the floor to the left of the chancel step to mark Pope's burial place, the stone above being incised with the letter 'P'. At the end of the N aisle is a window with the arms of Sir Godfrey Kneller who is buried here but whose monument was too big to go in the church and was therefore erected in Westminster Abbey. In the next window are the arms of King Edward III, patron from 1347 to 1375 and beyond that those of St. George's Chapel, Windsor, patron since 1562.

Outside on the NE wall are tablets to Mary Beach, Pope's nurse, and to Kitty Olive, a well-known stage figure at the time. Henry Tyron is also commemorated here; he was Governor of New York when the American War of Independence started.

Willesden, *St. Mary, Neasden Lane.* This pleasant medieval survival is set in a spacious churchyard but in uninspiring urban surroundings. Consisting of nave, chancel and S aisle with low SW tower attached, chancel chapel and 19C N aisle, the church is chiefly noted for its set of six brasses in the chancel ranging in date from 1492 to 1609, its Norman font and Elizabethan altar. The door in the S porch dates back to 1315 and has fine blank tracery. The walls are built of ragstone rubble with some flint. The building composes well when viewed from the E although, when in leaf, a tree masks the low grey tower which has L-shaped buttresses. A board on the E wall states that St. Mary's was founded by King Athelstan in 938, although this is open to doubt.

The interior has an attractive village atmosphere with a 13C S arcade with round piers and simple abaci; the arches vary in width. The chancel was renewed in the 14C and the chancel chapel beyond the S aisle dates from the early 15C. Further interest is afforded by the well-restored 17C wall tablets in the chancel and the numerous ledgers in front of the chancel step; these are mainly to members of the Roberts family, one of whose American descendants has been generous in providing funds for various needs, including a substantial contribution towards the fine Walker pipe organ at the W end

Behind the 12C font is a charming railing to guard the clock weights although the two outer ones are now dummies and only the central one activates the mechanism. They have been painted red in the restoration of the 60s. The most notable furnishing is, in fact, the font dating from 1150 and made of Purbeck marble; it has a downward tapering bowl with abstract decoration and stands on a large central shaft with four slender corner shafts. Next to it is a wooden altar table dating from 1539, part of the old high altar, and behind it an attractive iron railing with coloured rosettes on the top. A more important altar table of Elizabethan date with typical bulbous legs of the period is placed at the end of the N aisle. In the E chancel chapel there is an Easter sepulchre on the S side and a curtained aumbry. On the other side carved in limewood by Catherine Stern is a statue of the Black Virgin of Willesden which harks back to a medieval shrine destroyed at the Reformation. The Walker organ was installed in July 1983 and contains 1127 pipes.

The monuments have much social interest. Wall tablets in the chancel to members of the Paine and Franklyn families commemorate 'Ric Paine, J.P. & Corum' (died 27 December 1606 in his 95th (sic) year) and Margerie, his wife (died 23 February 1595 aged 72); he was 'Gent Pentioner to 5 Princes HY 8 & EY 6 QM, Q Eliz & our Soveraigne K. James'. To the S of the altar, another commemorates Sir John Francklyn in an elaborate tablet with scrolls on the top of black colonettes which stand on lions' heads and states that he died at the age of 48, by which time his wife had presented him with ten sons and seven daughters. 'He was wiser in ye opinion of others than his owne'. The brasses ranging from 1492 to 1609 include Bartholomew Willesden who died in 1492 and one of his two wives, Margaret Roberts, who died in 1505, and a group to Edmund Roberts, his wives and children of Queen Elizabeth's time.

The church includes among its associations the fact that William Gladstone used to read the lessons when he was staying at Dollis Hill. Charles Reade, the author of 'The Cloister and the Hearth', is buried in the churchyard.

NORFOLK

Could any other English county offer so much with which to thrill the church enthusiast? Norfolk has over 650 medieval churches and, if we add the many ruined churches, we cross the 700 mark. This county is punctuated by market towns which form useful centres from which to see its many churches, and what indeed could be more splendid than the great churches of Wymondham, Attleborough, Fakenham, Swaffham and North Walsham? The town of Thetford, which is steeped in ecclesiastical history, is in the S of the county and King's Lynn, with its two enormous medieval churches, is in the W. Great Yarmouth has one of England's largest parish churches, Cromer has the county's tallest church tower and Norwich, the jewel in the crown of East Anglia, has more medieval churches than any other English city.

The countryside presents a pleasing variety: the woodland and heathland of Breckland, the flat fens of the Marshland with their huge and glorious stone churches, the royal estate of Sandringham, with its varied churches which incorporate much local brown carstone, the exquisitely beautiful Broadland, which has some of the county's real gems, like Ranworth, Ludham and Barton Turf, and a coastline which is quite different from any other part of the country. Within easy reach of the Norfolk coast are some of its finest towers and grandest churches—Winterton, Happisburgh, Ingham, Martham, Hickling, Walcot and Southrepps, then on through Cromer, past Runton, Beeston Regis upon its cliff, pre-Conquest Weybourne, light and lofty Salthouse and then to the glorious trio of Blakeney, Cley and Wiveton. Wherever one goes in Norfolk there are clusters of churches—often within a mile of each other—each with its individual charm. In almost every part of the county, the map reveals shoals of them, in quiet villages, in lush parkland and occasionally across fields and up tracks, well away from their villages. Norfolk has an abundance of large, 'big-boned' churches, with lofty naves, fine clerestories, and aisles lit by large Perpendicular windows. Thirty three of these larger churches have windows in the E wall of the nave, above the chancel arch. Sanctus bell turrets occur in 21 Norfolk churches. Flint is the main building material, and the 15C gave Norfolk some superb examples of flint and stone flushwork panelling in parapets, buttresses and porches, and probably seen at its very best at St. Michael at Coslany, Norwich and in Redenhall's superb tower. Other building materials include brown carstone, which is found mostly in the NW of the county, and the grey oolitic limestone from Lincolnshire and Northamptonshire, which is used in the great Marshland churches.

Norfolk towers are many and varied, but spires are few. The majority of England's round towers are in this county; 119 in all (plus eight visible ruins), of which 78 are thought to be of pre-Conquest origin. Many have been heightened and beautified with octagonal belfry stages in later centuries. Three Norfolk towers are octagonal throughout. Many of the square towers are lofty and of stately proportions. About 20 exceed 100ft in height, the tallest being Cromer (160ft), Wymondham (142ft) and Winterton (130ft). A feature peculiar to the county is the 'Norfolk sound-hole'—a rectangular aperture at ringing-chamber level for the purposes of lighting and ventilating this stage of the tower, rather than to let out sound. These are filled with stone tracery in a variety of patterns and form an attractive feature of about 95 Norfolk towers.

The main pre-Conquest feature is the round tower. Other features occur in barely a dozen churches. Weybourne, Great Dunham and Newton by Castle Acre have important remains. Norman work is better represented and over 70 Norfolk churches have good Norman doorways. Premier work of this period includes arcades at Wymondham, Walsoken and Tilney All Saints, the fine central tower at South Lopham and the churches at Castle Rising, Burnham Overy and Gillingham. Early English architecture has a few noteworthy examples: Blakeney, Burgh next Aylsham, Rushall and Wramplingham have attractive chancels of this period; and the grand W front at Binham, and the towers at Walsoken, Tilney All Saints and St. Nicholas's, King's Lynn, have fine Early English work. The grand Marshland church at West Walton exhibits superb and ambitious work of the period. The Decorated style is seen in many Norfolk churches and several chancels in particular show beautiful Decorated craftsmanship. Some good examples built predominantly in this style occur at Snettisham, Elsing, Harpley, Great Walsingham and Hingham.

It is in Perpendicular architecture that Norfolk churches excel, although in some cases exquisite Decorated tracery continued to be designed in the late 14C and early 15C and churches may have windows of similar shape showing both Decorated and Perpendicular tracery. From the 15C comes what might be termed the typical Norfolk church, with tall nave and aisles, large three or four-light Perpendicular windows and possibly also an E window beneath the nave gable. From this period also come many of the magnificent roofs, including the hammerbeam roofs at Trunch, Gissing, Knapton, Wymondham, etc., or roofs where the hammerbeams hide beneath carved coving as at St. Peter Mancroft, or Ringland. The Red Mount Chapel, King's Lynn is a most unusual 15C building.

The county is rich in church furnishings. There is a fine selection of fonts from most periods, including a group of Norman fonts in the area W of Fakenham, several 13C Purbeck marble fonts, beautiful 14C ones at Yaxham, Stalham and Blofield, and superb 15C Seven Sacrament fonts, of which Norfolk has 25. There is even a font made of Tudor brick at Potter Heigham. There are many ancient font covers, including 13 or so from the 15C and about 40 from the 17C. Screens are a speciality here, with over 200 churches possessing remains of them, of which over half are more or less complete, and several have their painted panels remaining. The screens at Ranworth and Attleborough are among the finest in the land. 15C benches are seen in abundance and several churches have complete sets. There are c 20 medieval pulpits and many 17C examples, also a dozen or so medieval lecterns, several of which are in the Lynn area. With so many churches it is difficult to catalogue their myriad items of interest. To say that over 100 have monuments of note, over 120 have brasses of interest and about 126 churches contain fragments at least of their medieval glass, shows something of the magnitude of interest here and the scope for the church enthusiast.

Post-medieval churches are relatively scarce. Of the 17C is the delightful brick church at Hoveton St. Peter (1624). The 18C gave us the Classical churches of North Runcton (1713), St. George's, Great Yarmouth (1714) and Gunton (1769), also the Gothic churches of Sisland (1761) and Thorpe Market (1796), the latter being a remarkable 'Gothick' period piece. Amongst Norfolk's few noteworthy 19C Gothic Revival churches are J.P. Seddon's St. James's, Great Yarmouth (1870), J.D. Sedding's church at Edgefield (1883), Anthony Salvin's St. John's, King's Lynn, and Frederick Preedy's St. Edmund's, New Hunstanton. The extravaganza by the Reverend Whitwell Elwin at Booton is the most spectacular (1875 et seq.) and at Pirnough is a rather unusual church, designed in 1856 by the Reverend W.E. Scudamore. R.M. Phipson built pleasing churches at Harleston and Whittington and Thomas Jekyll designed new churches for Great Hautbois and Thorpe St. Andrew. Of the 20C examples, the most interesting include Dilham, rebuilt in 1931 by C.G. Hare and the most remarkable Pilgrimage Church at Walsingham, by Milner & Craze (1931–37). One of the most interesting 19C restorations is that by A.W.N. Pugin at West Tofts, in the Stanford Battle Area, where this Roman Catholic architect designed a new chancel, chantry chapel and furnishings for this Anglican church.

Apart from their imposing Early English cathedral at Norwich, the Catholics have some interesting churches. The Slipper Chapel at Walsingham is a beautiful 14C building. In the gardens of Oxborough Hall is a beautiful chapel (1835) by A.W.N. Pugin. The small village of Gillingham has an impressive Catholic church (by F.E. Banham, 1898) and the Catholic church in Great Yarmouth is a Gothic building by J.J. Scoles.

Attleborough, *The Assumption of Our Lady.* A large, impressive and commanding church, comprising the nave, aisles, N porch, central tower and transepts of a former collegiate church, the chancel of which was demolished in 1541. It is worth a visit, not only for its Norman and Decorated architecture, but also for its magnificent screen, complete with Rood loft, which stretches from one side to the other.

Externally, the squat yet bulky tower is at the E. Its base is Norman and its upper part is 13C, with large pairs of lancet windows, above which are circles in plate tracery. Sadly the E and S windows have lost their details. The N and S transepts were built as chapels; the former by Thomas Chaunticlere in 1378 and the latter by Sir William Mortimer in 1297. The nave and aisles were completed between 1378 and 1405, but their excellent windows still use the Decorated style of architecture. These are tall, of three lights, with fine tracery. The W front has a large five-light window. There are plain stone parapets with gargoyles. The large two-storeyed porch was built by Sir John Ratcliffe who died in 1441. Its N face has niches and is crowned by figure pinnacles. Inside is a tierceron star-vaulted ceiling.

The great height of the interior is impressive and is emphasised by the fact that there is no structural chancel. The tall five-bay arcades have great dignity and the aisles also have blank arches in their walls. The roofs of the nave and aisles are medieval and rest upon wooden corbels. The 15C arch to the porch staircase contains an original traceried door. The base of the tower now forms the sanctuary and it has four sturdy Norman arches which are beautifully shafted. In the wall above the W arch are two Norman windows, one above the other.

Dominating the interior is the truly magnificent screen, which was built c 1475 by members of the Ratcliffe family. It is 19ft in height and its great length of 52ft covers the entire width of the church. At its centre is the unusually wide opening to the chancel, each side of which are sets of three painted figures (Our Lady and the two St.

Johns to the N, and St. Thomas Becket, the Trinity and St. Bartholomew to the S), which formed reredoses to the side altars. Then
there are the entrances and screens to the two transept chapels.
Above is the loft, which has vaulting on its underside and displays
shields with the arms of the 24 bishoprics existing at that time. These
had been overpainted after the Reformation with texts, parts of which
remain. At the very top is an Elizabethan text from the Book of
Proverbs. The 15C font, which stands in the Lady chapel, came here
only in 1975. The pulpit is believed to have been carved by Ver
Brugen, an assistant of Grinling Gibbons, in the 18C for the Broad-
way Chapel, Westminster. The unusual cast-iron lectern, dating from
1816, came from St. Nicholas's, King's Lynn. Amongst the other
noteworthy features are the consecration crosses in the walls, the
wall painting of St. Christopher over the S doorway and the series of
wall paintings above the screen, showing Moses, David, angels and
other figures around what was a central cross. There is a 17C
almsbox and a fine three-manual organ by Norman & Beard, with 32
speaking stops. Two stained glass windows in the S aisle and one in
the N aisle are by Heaton, Butler & Bayne.

Bale, *All Saints*. A delightful and unprepossessing small village
church, which has a neat embattled early 14C tower, with two-light
windows and a pretty ogee-headed niche beneath the W window.
The nave has 15C Perpendicular windows and the chancel has a
beautiful four-light E window of the Decorated period. The nave
retains its medieval arch-braced roof, at the E end of which is the
pulley block for raising the light in front of the Rood. The chancel has
a single-framed rafter roof and in the S sanctuary wall is an angle
piscina of c 1300. The font dates from c 1470; around its bowl are
foliage panels and emblems of the Passion, the Trinity, the cross of St.
George and a tilting shield. There is an iron-bound chest of c 1500
and the royal arms date originally from c 1660, although the monarch's initials and date have been subsequently changed. On the
walls are seven consecration crosses, some with foliage borders, also
a faint wall painting of St. Christopher. Of supreme interest in this
church is the 14C and 15C glass which fills the SE nave window,
having been salvaged from other windows of the church and
assembled here by Dennis King in 1938. In this three-light window
are several angels, parts of at least five scenes of the Annunciation,
also Prophets, an abbess, part of a Trinity scene and the bearded
figure of St. Philip. Four shields, one with the Wilby arms, may be
seen at the bottom of the window.

Booton, *St. Michael and All Angels*. Booton is totally eccentric, in
fact it is unique! It is the brainchild of its Rector in the years 1849–
1900, the Reverend Whitwell Elwin, who demolished most of the
medieval church and replaced it with this most remarkable building.
Local people have called it the Cathedral of the Fields, Sir Edwin
Lutyens called it 'very naughty but in the right spirit' and its reverend
architect wrote, 'I had but one end in view, which was to give the
church the aspect of a House devoted to Prayer'. The building grew
between 1876 and 1900. The Rector had no training as an architect—
just a burning zeal and a good library of architectural books from
which to gain ideas.

The stately and lavish exterior rises above the Norfolk countryside;
its twin towers, placed at odd angles to the W end, form a distinctive
landmark. These are faced with stone panelling, have large openings

higher up and terminate in clusters of crockets and pinnacles. The windows of the church are in the Decorated style. The tall nave is lit by three-light windows inspired by those in Temple Balsall Church. Its four-light window was copied from one at Old St. Paul's and the doorway beneath it from Glastonbury. The curious central pinnacle looks almost oriental, whilst the flamboyant pinnacles on the E nave and chancel gables look more in keeping with a Gothic church. The buttresses of the nave and the chancel terminate in pinnacles, the S vestry looks more like a small chapel and the N porch contains a genuine 14C statue of the Virgin and Child.

The interior is stately and impressive. The W part of the nave is a baptistery, divided by a tall arch. The nave itself has a vast hammer-beam roof, with tall wall posts resting upon huge stone capitals and angels with upturned wings. Instead of a pulpit, Elwin provided a stately canopied throne from which to preach. Above the chancel arch is a huge triangular opening containing three trefoils in circles. The angels in the chancel roof were made by a carver of ships' figure-heads. The chancel walls are very thick because inside them are the medieval walls of the former chancel. The chancel and sanctuary are richly adorned with wall arcading and diapering, although the sanctuary feels rather sombre and lifeless. The glass is a feature of this church. Some of the chancel windows were designed by a Mr. Buckley, but the rest are the work of glaziers named Booker & Purchase. There is a wall plaque from the old church to Peter Elwyn (died 1798), beneath which is a simple plaque to the parish priest, architect and donor of this unforgettable church.

Burnham Thorpe, *All Saints.* People come from far and wide to Burnham Thorpe because about a mile to the SE of the church is the site of the Rectory where Admiral Lord Nelson was born. The church which he attended, and where his father, the Reverend Edmund Nelson, was Rector, has an isolated setting, away from its small village in the N Norfolk countryside.

The elegant pinnacled tower, of late 14C date, has a good flush-work parapet. Many of the windows in the church are late 14C or early 15C, but the W windows of the aisles have cusped Y-tracery of c 1300. The best feature of the exterior is the E wall of the chancel. The three-light Perpendicular E window is flanked by canopied niches, with a third above it, and the entire wall is embellished with flint and stone chequered flushwork, using two distinct patterns. This may have been the gift of Sir William Calthorpe, who died in 1420. Inside, the four-bay arcade, with circular piers, takes us back to the 13C, although the roofs and most of the furnishings are Victorian. The Purbeck marble font bowl is also 13C, with the characteristic pairs of shallow arches. In the chancel is a fine set of 15C sedilia and piscina beneath cusped ogee arches, resting upon angel corbels, all beneath a square hoodmould which is studded with flowers and faces. In the N aisle is a squint through to the high altar.

The finest memorial is the brass in the chancel floor to Sir William Calthorpe (died 1420), who is portrayed in his armour and wearing the 'SS' collar. The inscription reads: *quonda(m) d(omi)n(u)s manerij et patronus eccl(es)ie de Burnham om(n)i(um) s(an)c(t)o(rum)* (sometime lord of the manor and patron of All Saints' Church at Burnham). Also in the chancel floor is the ledger slab of Nelson's parents. His father has a plaque on the S wall nearby, beneath which is the bust of the Admiral himself, which was erected in 1905. At the W end is a framed account of his funeral from a contemporary newspaper.

Several other items relating to Nelson and to the Navy may be seen, not least the lectern and the cross on the Rood beam which are made from timbers which came from H.M.S. 'Victory'.

Cawston, *St. Agnes*. The vast bulk of Cawston's bold and lofty tower dominates the surrounding countryside and rises 120ft above the community clustered beneath it. This is one of Norfolk's grandest churches—a large and stately building, magnificent outside and in, and with a host of interesting features. Although the chancel and S transept are at least a century earlier, the tower, nave and aisles were built largely through the generosity of Michael de la Pole, Earl of Suffolk, who died in 1414.

The exterior is imposing although the chancel is rather humble compared with the rest. It is work of c 1300, and its large five-light E window has intersecting tracery. Also of this date are the two S windows and the priest's doorway. The S transept has a three-light window with later Decorated tracery, also two square-headed 15C E windows, with intricately sub-cusped tracery. To the N of the chancel is the 15C chapel of St. John the Baptist and a medieval sacristy. The soaring nave and aisles show 15C craftsmanship. Over the E gable of the nave is a sanctus bell turret. The clerestory is lit by six large three-light windows each side and the windows in the aisles have attractive Perpendicular tracery. The aisles have shallow stone parapets and some good gargoyles, as does the porch, which is two-storeyed, with tierceron-vaulted ceiling and a fine S face. The great tower is faced with stone and is a magnificent piece of craftsmanship, although it lacks a parapet or pinnacles. The quality of the workmanship may be seen in the elaborate double basecourse (which is also visible inside the church, leading some experts to believe that it predates the present nave and aisles), also the mighty W doorway, flanked by tall niches, with a wild hairy wodewose and a dragon in its great spandrels. Above it is a frieze of shields and a tall four-light W window. The belfry windows are large and lofty and somehow compensate for the lack of a parapet.

The interior is bright and majestic. Tall six-bay arcades separate the aisles from the nave; their piers are octagonal and the W arches are wider than the others. The tower arch is tall and graceful. Beneath it is a 15C ringers' gallery, with sturdy corner posts, and tower screen, bearing the inscription 'God spede the plow and send us all corn enow our purpose to make at crow of cok of ye plowlete of Sygate, be mery and glade wat good al yis work made'. Clearly this was erected from the proceeds of 'church ales'. The 15C font has a bowl panelled with window tracery and a beautifully traceried stem. Its cover was given in 1958. Crowning the nave is a superb hammerbeam roof, its wall posts resting upon stone corbels. There are angels along the cornices, on the hammerbeams and also at the apex, in addition to traceried spandrels and an array of carved bosses. The floors are a mixture of bricks, pamments and burial slabs. The S transept was the chapel of Our Lady of Pity and has a fine roof, studded with bosses. The faint traces of a wall painting may have depicted the Virgin, or possibly St. Agnes. The piscina here has a wodewose and a dragon in its spandrels. A two-bay arcade separates the chancel chapel, now an organ chamber and vestry. The chancel roof is greatly restored; it is also of a hammerbeam construction. In the sanctuary is a double piscina, also three 15C misericords and 17C communion rails.

Beneath the chancel arch stands the tall and handsome Rood

screen, with lofty openings and with its doors still in place. The dado is adorned with 20 painted panels, executed c 1504, and showing the 12 Apostles, the four Latin Doctors, and St. Agnes, St. Helen and John Schorne. Note that St. Matthew is wearing spectacles! Most of the benches in the church are 15C, with simple poppyhead ends. Several benches in the aisles are backless and the rear bench-ends have animal armrests. The pulpit, with its three-light traceried panels, is 15C and has been remarkably well-preserved. Some 18C wainscoting may be seen in the N transept and N chancel chapel. Amongst the other features here are a little medieval glass, a 15C poor box and a sturdy medieval chest. The only monuments of real antiquity are two stone coffin lids with effigies in the floor of the S transept.

The church has the unusual dedication to St. Agnes, who is depicted with a lamb (*agnus* is the Latin for lamb) and appears on the screen, on the roof and in the E window.

Cley Next the Sea, *St. Margaret.* A grand church, superbly set above a pretty green and looking out across what in ages past was a busy harbour, but now is green meadows. The exterior is superb. The 13C tower, with lancet windows in its base, stands at the end of the N aisle. It is quite lofty but is somewhat dwarfed by the tall clerestory and roof of the long nave. The clerestory windows alternate between large circles with cinquefoils and two-light early Decorated windows—a masterpiece of the early 14C. The aisles are lit by large 15C windows. At the W end of the nave is a mighty six-light window and a small W porch which shelters a sumptuous 14C W doorway with a cinquefoil-headed arch which is sub-cusped. Also of the 14C is the S transept which has been in ruins for over 300 years but is still beautiful; its gabled buttresses have niches, its crocketed roof gable is flanked by pinnacles and its S window has exquisite tracery. The chancel is humble in comparison with the lofty nave and has windows of c 1300, except the five-light Perpendicular E window which appears to have replaced a set of Early English lancets. The two-storeyed S porch shows 15C work of high quality. It has an openwork parapet; the S face has a pair of three-light windows with a niche between them. There are niches in the buttresses and the grand shield-studded entrance arch has the emblems of the Trinity and the Passion in its spandrels. The porch has a tierceron-vaulted ceiling, with several bosses, including a woman chasing a fox. The 14C S doorway is superb, with cusps and sub-cusps.

Inside, the church is lofty, light and airy. Above the six-bay arcade on the S side are niches with canopies and panelled and coloured pedestals resting upon intriguing corbel brackets, including musicians, a lion and St. George fighting the dragon. There is an atmosphere of unspoilt antiquity here, with old floors and many ancient and beautiful things. The mid-15C font shows the Seven Sacraments in the panels of its bowl. There are 15C benches with poppyheads or figures on their ends and in the chancel are six misericord stalls which are carved with coats of arms, including the initials and merchant's mark of John Greneway, a 16C Cley merchant. The pulpit dates from 1611 and the altar table, also 17C, stands upon the pre-Reformation altar slab. On the tower wall are 17C royal arms painted over with Queen Anne's initials. The Lord's Prayer, Creed and Commandments, once over the high altar, are now in the S aisle.

There are several interesting brasses here. In the N aisle is the

Rector, John Yslington (c 1460), holding the chalice and host and dressed in his doctor's cap and gown. The S aisle contains brasses of John and Agnes Symonds (died 1511 and 1508), dressed in shrouds, with their children beneath them. On the wall are John Symondes (1505) and his two wives, also the palimpsest brass of John Tayllar (died 1578), which has canopy work from a 14C Flemish brass on its reverse side.

Cromer, *St. Peter and St. Paul.* A large and stately church in the heart of this popular seaside resort, the tower of which rises to a height of 160ft. The church is entirely work of the 15C except for the two E bays of the aisles and the chancel, which were pulled down c 1681 and rebuilt in 1887–89 to the designs of Sir Arthur Blomfield. The resort became very fashionable in the late 19C and early 20C, and the church's restoration reflected the improving fortunes of the town.

The glory of Cromer Church is in its exterior and its enormous size and grand proportions. The tower is a truly magnificent piece of building construction, strengthened by set-back buttresses which extend just above the pairs of two-light belfry windows, and capped by a richly carved stone parapet, with pinnacles and spirelets at the corners. The ringing chamber is lit by intricately carved sound-holes. Beneath the great W window are a porch, with a panelled parapet, a stone W face with niches and worn shields bearing the emblems of St. Peter and St. Paul (only St. Peter's keys now remain) and inside a tierceron-vaulted ceiling. The N and S porches are two-storeyed, with stair turrets. The N porch has flushwork and a pair of 15C traceried doors; the S porch has a single niche and a vaulted ceiling, and shelters a fine doorway with quatrefoils surrounding its arch. This is an exterior which rewards standing back and viewing as a whole. Surrounding the base of the church is a band of stone shields and flowers and there is flushwork panelling beneath the windows. The aisle windows are large, each of four lights and divided by transoms, and taking up the maximum amount of wall space. Between them are elegant buttresses which have niches with canopies and pedestals. The nave and aisles have plain parapets, beneath which are stringcourses and gargoyles. Blomfield's 19C work blends well with the medieval craftsmanship; his chancel has tall two-light N and S windows and a large seven-light E window.

The interior is noteworthy because of its size and the magnificence of its structure. It is like a vast hall of stone and glass—light and airy, with a feeling of tremendous height and space. The height of the tower and chancel arches is immense, and the six-bay nave arcades are tall and uplifting, drawing the eye upwards to the great 19C hammerbeam roof, resting upon its stone corbels. A further two bays divide the aisles from the chancel. The E end of the N aisle is filled with Cromer's magnificent organ—a four-manual and pedal instrument by Norman & Beard, originally in Bath Abbey and erected here in 1897. Since then it has been restored and enlarged and now has 49 speaking stops. Its W case (facing the N aisle) came from Southwell Minster. The font is a 19C copy of the 15C font in Yaxham Church. Nearby is a memorial to Henry Blogg, GC, BEM, who died in 1954 and was the famous coxswain of the Cromer lifeboat. The lifeboat which was named after him is depicted in the Clarke memorial window in the S aisle. The four panels of 20C glass in this window and those in the Rudland window further E show places and items which are linked with Cromer and the sea. The E window has good pre-Raphaelite figures and the W window, showing the Ascension, was made in 1959. There are several wall plaques but few memorials of great interest or antiquity. The small brass of Margaret Cornforth, who died in 1518, survives on the wall near the chancel arch. The royal arms in the N aisle are Hanoverian.

Cromer Church has long been renowned for its lively Evangelical worship and for its excellent musical standard.

East Dereham, *St. Nicholas.* This large and venerable church stands pleasantly aloof from the centre of its busy but atmospheric country town, in a large and sloping churchyard. It is a building which has been altered and added to at various periods since Norman times. The original central tower collapsed and the present one was built to the W of it. This is a parish church of considerable size and importance, consisting of nave, with aisles and S porch, double transepts to N and S, each with an E chapel, and a central lantern tower, to the E of which is one bay and then the chancel.

A noble exterior graces a fine setting here. Near the E end of the chancel stands the detached bell tower, built during the early years of the 16C, with its large entrance arch, three-light belfry windows and enormous clock-face. It lacks a parapet, but contains a fine ring of eight bells. The core of the chancel is probably Norman, although its S windows date from the second half of the 13C, when Early English was beginning to change to Decorated; it has two S doorways. The windows of the N aisle have Decorated flowing tracery and the S aisle windows are Perpendicular. The W window is early 14C. The central lantern tower is also 14C, with set-back buttresses and graceful pairs of Decorated windows. A later cupola on its roof contains the sanctus bell. Of the 15C is the S porch, with a remarkable array of creatures crouching upon its buttresses, a base course with shields, two holy water stoups, a pair of niches and Our Lady and the Angel Gabriel in the spandrels.

The interior has a definite slope upwards towards the E. The five-bay nave arcades have a mixture of piers—quatrefoil, octagonal and circular. The nave has a restored roof and there are old timbers in the aisle roofs. The central tower rests upon four sturdy arches and there are three arches each side beneath the windows which light it. The transept chapels have beautifully painted and panelled 15C roofs. Each side of the chancel arch are Norman spiral fluted columns—the earliest surviving work to be seen here. The chancel roof has ancient tiebeams and kingposts. In the S sanctuary wall are 13C triple sedilia and a restored double piscina, embellished with dogtooth ornament. Opposite is a large aumbry which may have served as an Easter sepulchre. The reredos of five cusped arches is Victorian and its four painted figures were added in 1929.

The fine Seven Sacrament font dates from 1468 and cost £12 13s 9d. The Sacraments and the Crucifixion are set beneath canopies; there are eight figures round the stem of the font and more at its foot. The chest in the N transept is 16C Flemish work and was presented in 1786. It bears a carving of the Nativity beneath the large lock. Above the chancel arch are the royal arms of King George III (1782). The brass lectern dates from c 1500 and rests upon three lions. The screen and Rood beneath the chancel arch is a war memorial, but in the N transept is the medieval screen (c 1480) from Oxborough Church and one of its painted figures shows St. Withburga, Dereham's local saint. The stained glass windows include two in the chancel by William Wailes, the Cowper memorial window by

Heaton, Butler & Bayne and a window showing St. Withburga, made in 1957. There are two small 15C brasses in the floors of the church, also several ledger slabs. William Cowper's unusual memorial in the N transept is by John Flaxman. He died in 1800 and is buried here. A churchyard cross near the E end of the chancel commemorates the Reverend Benjamin Armstrong, the Tractarian diarist, who was Vicar here from 1850–88. To the W of the church is St. Withburga's Well. She was the sister of St. Etheldreda and she founded a convent at East Dereham in 654. She was originally buried here, but was later re-buried at Ely. The church at Holkham in Norfolk is named after her.

East Harling, *St. Peter and St. Paul*. A delightful church of the 14C and 15C, situated at the W end of the village, and containing fine medieval glass, good monuments and a host of treasures.

The elegant tower has gabled buttresses and the W ones are pierced with niches which have crocketed canopies resting upon carved faces, and pedestals carved with foliage. The W window and belfry windows show that this tower dates from c 1300. The 15C builders gave it a stone openwork parapet and pinnacles and it is crowned by a regal lead-covered flèche. There are 14C windows in the S aisle (visible from inside) and in the chancel, but the majority of the windows are Perpendicular. The imposing stone-faced clerestory is lit by nine triple Perpendicular windows. A small doorway in the N chapel has unicorns in its spandrels. The 15C S porch has flushwork on its S and E faces and a niche above its entrance. Its roof timbers are original and the large doorway which it shelters has the remains of a vine-trail pattern carved into the head of its arch.

The interior is a treasure house of beautiful things and its structure is elegant and uplifting. The N aisle is considerably narrower than the S and both are divided from the nave by five-bay arcades, with graceful quatrefoil piers. The nave has a fine single hammerbeam roof with an unusually steep pitch. Its spandrels are beautifully carved with openwork and the E tiebeam has the pulley for the rowel light which lit the Rood. The unicorn and the bull from the arms of the Harling family can be seen in the spandrels of the 15C S aisle roof. The 15C font has a broad panelled stem and flowers in quatrefoils round the bowl; its cover is 17C. Over the modern tower screen is a medieval beam with traces of colour, above which are 17C gallery rails. Near the N doorway is an internal stoup like a small font, set beneath a trefoil ogee arch. Near the W end of the nave is the base of what must have been a superb Rood screen of c 1510. Each side has three panels and a door panel. Although there are no painted figures surviving, the woodcarving is excellent, with quatrefoils containing shields, a helm and crest, the Cross as the Tree of Life and a beautiful 'IHS' monogram. More glorious still is the parclose screen in the S aisle with vaulted coving at the top, three-light openings and much of its original colour. There are several 15C bench-ends, particularly in the S chapel, where the E bookrest has a beautifully carved front, maybe incorporating part of another screen. There are remains of a wall painting in the N aisle and the arms of King Charles II (1660) are at the W end of that aisle. In the chancel are six misericord stalls, four of which have carvings (coats of arms) on the underside of their seats. Note the superb creatures on the armrests, including a unicorn and a wodewose. There are fragments of 15C glass in the clerestory and S aisle windows, but resplendent above the altar and forming a focal point in the church is the superb glass in the E window. This was made in Norwich in the 15C. There are 20 panels, telling the story of the life of Christ from the Annunciation to Pentecost, also figures of the donors—Sir Robert Wingfield and Sir William Chamberlain. Note the lovely Ascension scene at the bottom in the centre, with the footmarks on the summit of the Mount of Olives and the feet ascending.

Amongst the monuments here are two in the sanctuary to members of the Lovell family, who died in the 16C, above which hang 17C helmets. On the N side of the chancel is the magnificent tomb of Sir William Chamberlain (died 1462), through which we can see into the N chapel (now a vestry) and also through it could be seen the N chapel altar and the high altar by means of squints E and W. Sir William's father-in-law, Sir Robert Harling (died 1435), lies with his wife upon a tomb-chest in the S chapel, set beneath a fine ogee-arched recess with angels and a pelican amongst the carvings on the ends of its many cusps. To the W of this we see Sir Thomas Lovell (died 1604) and his wife Alice, with a bundle of feathers and a saracen's head at their feet, beneath a canopy supported by three columns.

East Raynham, *St. Mary.* A beautiful parkland setting in the grounds of Raynham Hall. The church was totally rebuilt in 1868, using the Perpendicular style. The architects were Clark & Holland. Several features retained from the medieval church may be seen inside. The greatest treasure is the magnificent Easter sepulchre, which is also the tomb of Lady Townshend. Her will of 1499 bequeathed money for this monument 'upon the tomb to be cunningly graven a Sepulchre for Easter Day'. A glorious piece of stonecarving this is, despite a considerable amount of restoration work. The tomb-chest is panelled with three shields set in tracery. The recess is backed by five niches, with exquisite canopies and even fragments of the original figures which occupied them.

Elsing, *St. Mary the Virgin.* A small and pretty village, with a church built in one piece by Sir Hugh Hastings and his wife Margery c 1330. It is a noble example of Decorated architecture and has the widest unaisled nave in East Anglia. Sir Hugh's brass, in the chancel, is one of the most noteworthy in the country.

The nave and chancel have embattled parapets with good gargoyles. Their windows have beautiful flowing tracery, including the splendid five-light E window. The embattled and pinnacled W tower also has good Decorated windows. The porches have trefoil ogee-headed outer entrances and the N porch, by which we enter, shelters a trefoil-headed and sub-cusped doorway.

Inside we can appreciate the enormous width of the nave—39½ ft—all under a vast roof which was rebuilt in 1781. In comparison, the chancel arch appears narrow, as does the tall tower arch. The 14C font has an octagonal bowl, surrounded by an undulating pattern. It is crowned by a handsome cover, which some authorities claim to be 14C also and therefore very early of its type, with intricately carved tabernacle work and some original colour remaining. In the sanctuary are triple sedilia and a piscina beneath trefoil-headed arches. The base of the 15C screen survives and although its painted figures are now very faint, the ogee canopies are richly and beautifully carved. Over the N door are the arms of King George III (1794). In a S chancel window is some beautiful 14C glass, assembled here in 1901 and including figures of the Apostles Matthew, Jude and Philip, dating from c 1375 and set beneath canopies. In the chancel floor in the centre—a fitting place for the founder of the church—is the brass of Sir Hugh Hastings, who died in 1347. The effigy, in armour, is 5½ft long. The head rests upon a pillow supported by angels, beneath a traceried and gabled arch, where we see a small scene of angels receiving Sir Hugh's soul and a circle containing a scene of the knight on horseback. In the borders are his relations mourning his loss and at the very top is the Coronation of the Virgin in two panels.

Great Walsingham, *St. Peter.* Great Walsingham is the small village with its church on the hill, above the larger village of Little Walsingham in the valley, to which pilgrims come from far and wide. This is a dignified Decorated church, built during one period (c 1320–30). Unfortunately, the chancel was lost in the 16C and so the building comes to rather an abrupt end, with only fragments of the chancel walls remaining.

The bold W tower has a plain parapet with gargoyles, two-light belfry windows and a very beautiful three-light W window. The aisles are lit by windows which have Reticulated tracery, filled in turn with small flowing tracery. The clerestory has sets of seven quatrefoil windows in circles. There is a low-side window in the fragment of the chancel wall which remains. The S porch is the only Perpendicular addition; it has flushwork and niches flanking its entrance arch. Its N counterpart is, in fact, a vestry of 1860.

The interior is bright, atmospheric and unspoilt. The four-bay arcades have quatrefoil piers and the nave has a medieval arch-braced roof. Both aisles have ancient roofs and trefoil-headed piscinas and in the N aisle is an aumbry with its original oak door, complete with hinges and locks. The large font has double traceried

The painted altarpiece of the Lady chapel in St. Peter's

panels in its bowl and is crowned by a 17C cover which has later paintwork. The Rood loft staircase remains complete. The great treasure of the church is its complete set of 15C benches, which stand on their original curbs. There are 40 benches in all, with traceried backs and poppyhead ends. Those in the N aisle have figures of saints on their armrests, whilst the S aisle bench-ends have strange animals and creatures crawling up them. There is linenfold panelling in the front benches. Original glass remains in the tracery of the windows, including a small figure of the Virgin Mary and the head of Christ in the E window of the N aisle. The pulpit is 15C but it was restored, altered and painted in 1613. Also of the 15C is the poor box, which is bound with iron strapwork and is secured by three locks. The arms of King George I may be seen over the N door.

The three bells were cast for this tower when it was built and they form one of the oldest sets of three bells for the same tower in England. They were cast by William Silisden of Lynn in the 14C.

Great Yarmouth, St. Nicholas. This giant church, standing squat and fortress-like in its large churchyard to the N of the Market Place, is a claimant to be England's largest parish church; its floor area covers 25,023 sq. ft. What began as a simple Norman cruciform church gradually grew through a series of extensions and alterations over the medieval period into the massive and complex building which we now see. It was founded by Bishop Herbert de Losinga in 1101 and was consecrated in 1119. Some 12C work remains in the tower beneath the belfry windows. St. Nicholas's was gutted by incendiary bombs in 1942 and remained a roofless shell for 16 years. It has been gloriously resurrected to the designs of S.E. Dykes Bower by Messrs. Rattee & Kett of Cambridge and was reopened in 1961. This is therefore a fine example not only of a medieval church of national importance, but also of a tasteful, sympathetic and dignified 20C remodelling.

It is the great width and bulk of this church, rather than its height, which is so striking. The exterior is distinguished by flint and stone walls, tall copper roofs and an amazing number of turrets and spirelets. The W front is 121ft wide and is a remarkable sight with its four turrets and spirelets, the narrow nave with its triple 13C lancets and grand W doorway and the much wider aisles with their three pairs of late 13C windows. These aisles are 39ft wide and are considered to be the widest in the country. Most of the windows in the church were renewed in the 19C, when the church underwent restorations in 1847 by J.H. Hakewill and in 1862 by J.P. Seddon. They are nevertheless very worthy—of three lights in the aisles and a superb seven-light Decorated window in the S transept. Only the S chancel chapel shows pure Perpendicular work. The N and S doorways are original early 13C and the S porch, with its groined ceiling and its pairs of triple Decorated windows, although restored, shows fine 14C craftsmanship. The central tower has a stone-faced belfry stage, pierced by three lancet windows each side. The parapet and pinnacles were renewed in 1882. Until the Blitz, this tower carried a tall spire.

Inside this vast building, we are aware of its tremendous space. Everything is beautifully light and colour has been used with great taste. The wide aisles and narrow nave are crowned with panelled roofs framed with Canadian red cedar. Dykes Bower altered the original building effectively by doubling the number of arches in the choir arcade and halving the number in the nave. Further arcades divide off the N and S chancel chapels. There is a central altar beneath the tower, above which is a painted panelled ceiling. The chancel roof is also painted and the sanctuary is equipped with a piscina and sedilia. Behind the high altar is a sacristy which has two original 15C doorways which are bordered with quatrefoils.

There are many items of beauty and interest here. Two medieval tomb-recesses survive in the aisle walls. That in the S aisle is of Sir John Fastolf, who built Caister Castle. The small font, with a Norman bowl and 13C stem, was brought from the disused church at Highway, Wiltshire. Suspended above it, and now serving as its cover, is the sounding-board from the early 18C pulpit of St. George's Church in the town. The pulpit, with its inlaid panels and fine staircase, stands towards the E end of the nave. Some 18C pews from St. George's may also be seen in the nave. St. Andrew's chapel, to the S of the chancel, has a fine iron screen, designed by S.E. Dykes Bower, and made by Eric Stevenson. This was donated to the church by Erie Technological Products of Pennsylvania, USA. The Lady chapel (N of the chancel) has a carved wooden reredos, made by Rattee & Kett in 1910 and presented by them to the church. The stained glass was designed by Brian Thomas and was made at the Whitefriars Studios. Of particular note is the Colman window in the S transept. The N transept houses S.E. Dykes Bower's magnificent organ case. The organ itself came from St. Mary's, The Boltons, Kensington and was built by William Hill. It was rebuilt here by John Compton and has three manuals, pedals and 59 speaking stops. The tower contains a fine ring of 13 bells, cast at the Whitechapel bell foundry; the tenor bell weighs 30½ cwt.

Hales, *St. Margaret.* The far SE corner of the county has a lovely selection of tiny rustic churches in rural settings, many with round towers and a variety of Norman doorways. Hales is one of the most delightful of them all. It has been described as the perfect Norman church, although its tower is older still. The church is totally isolated and is set quite high. It ceased to be used for regular services in 1967 and is now in the care of the Redundant Churches Fund.

The circular W tower has a variety of windows, including Norman slit windows at the W, and several lancet windows of c 1200; the flint and stone chequer parapet is a later addition. The nave and the chancel, with its rounded apse, are both thatched. The Norman window in the nave was probably blocked when the larger windows were inserted c 1300. The S doorway, with two Mass dials, shows fine 12C craftsmanship, but the N doorway is even grander, with a rich variety of Norman ornamentation, including zigzags, bobbins and stars, also a hoodmould studded with 17 wheels, each with eight radiating spokes. Even the capitals are exquisitely decorated with stars and patterns. In the jambs of the doorway are several pilgrim crosses. The chancel has Norman buttresses, a stringcourse with a simple pattern, blocked single and double Norman windows, later Early English lancets and a two-light Y-traceried window of c 1300.

The interior is devotional and atmospheric, yet has few airs and graces. A little restoration took place c 1867, by H.J. Green of Norwich. Beneath the tower are two blocked circular apertures of pre-Conquest date and in the stage above is a blocked triangular-headed opening. These date the tower to c 950–1000. The deep tower arch is hidden behind an 18C musicians' gallery, from which a good view of the interior may be obtained. The bowl of the 15C font is adorned with Tudor roses and angels bearing shields; it has a simple 17C cover. The Rood loft staircase remains, and behind the 17C pulpit is a 14C wall painting of St. James with his pilgrim staff. The upper portion of a 15C St. Christopher appears on the S wall and over the E window is a scroll of foliage. The base of the Rood screen is in position; this is now very worn and only one of its panels retains its beautiful carving. Simple niches flank the E window in the apse and the SE lancet windowsill is lowered to form a sedile, with a tiny piscina drain on the adjacent ledge. The aumbry in the N wall has its original shelf. The altar slab is the medieval one and is marked with its small crosses.

King's Lynn, *The Priory Church of St. Margaret, with St. Mary Magdalene and all the Virgin Saints.* This great church, which speaks clearly of the medieval importance of the town, is some 235ft in length and consists of a nave with aisles, two W towers with a small chapel (now the entrance) to the N, a crossing with shallow transepts, and a chancel with N and S aisles which stretch to its E end. The building has had a chequered history and is a mixture of several periods. A Norman church was started in the mid-12C, of which the lower parts of the two W towers remain. This church was enlarged in the 13C and work of that period remains in the crossing, transepts and chancel. The S chancel chapel was added c 1433 and the chancel clerestory is also 15C. In 1452 the foundations beneath the N tower gave way and the town paid for a new tower to be built. In 1741, a gale caused the spire on the S tower to crash into the church, destroying much of the nave, transepts and the central lantern tower over the crossing. Much of this area was rebuilt in a Gothic style by Matthew Brettingham by 1744 and was further restored by Sir Gilbert Scott in 1875. The addition of the reredos by G.F. Bodley in 1899 and the central altar in the 1960s make St. Margaret's a grand and glorious assortment of styles and traditions.

The exterior is massive and impressive. Its E end has flanking turrets and a most unusual E window—a 19C replacement of a medieval rose window. The chancel clerestory has ten triple Perpendicular windows and the chancel aisles also show 15C work. The central tower is no more than a stump; until 1741 it had a tall octagonal lantern, after the fashion of Ely Cathedral. The nave and aisles are mostly of the 1745 rebuilding—a very fair attempt at Gothic for this period. To the N of the NW tower is part of a former chapel which now serves as an entrance vestibule. It is thought that this is what remains of an outer N aisle; it is 15C Perpendicular. The glory of the exterior is the W front, which has a grand W window of seven lights with a niche above and an embattled porch below, which has traceried panelling (like four-light windows) in its two sides. The S tower has a Norman base, with broad shafted buttresses and intersecting wall arcading. Further up it develops through the Transitional trefoil arcading to Early English work with plate-traceried windows and finally 13C belfry windows with bar-tracery. Note the painted moon-clock, given by a 17C churchwarden, which shows not only the phases of the moon, but also the times of the local high tides. The letters read 'LYNN HIGH TIDE'. Note also the water marks of previous floods on the W wall. The NW tower is 15C; it is wider and has three-light Perpendicular windows, and also niches in its W buttresses.

Inside we are aware of the church's great length, also of the pleasing mixture of styles to be seen. The W towers are supported upon their original sturdy Norman arches. The five-bay nave arcades are of 1745–46, using the bases of the 13C piers. Magnificent 13C work is seen in the arches of the crossing and the chancel arcades, with their foliage capitals and hoodmoulds which rest upon intriguing corbels. There is an internal walkway beside the 15C clerestory windows. The E window looks very effective above G.F. Bodley's mighty reredos of 1899, with its array of figures and foliage in what is now rather subdued colour.

The chancel has a fine set of misericord stalls, dating from c 1370, with carved heads on the armrests and a variety of carvings beneath the seats, including one of the Black Prince and his 'shield for peace'. Backing the stalls and extending E beneath the chancel arcades is handsome screenwork of the 14C and, to the S of the sanctuary, a 15C screen with an exquisitely carved door opening. The two screens beneath the crossing are later; the N one dates from 1584 and behind it is the historic organ. Its case was built by Snetzler in 1754, to the directions of Dr. Burney, the organist, who was the father of Fanny Burney and a friend of Mozart. In the chancel is the 15C eagle lectern. The pulpit is a grand piece of early Georgian work, with inlaid marquetry panels, a tester and a fine staircase. Over the W crossing arch are the arms of King Charles II. The modern nave altar of aluminium was designed by Colin Shewring and stands in a specially made sanctuary, which also contains the bishop's throne of teak, installed in 1963. Amongst the other items of modern craftsmanship in the church is the W window in the N porch, by Geoffrey Clarke, and a list of incumbents on slate, designed by John Skelton.

In the S chancel chapel are two of the largest monumental brasses in the country. They are rectangular and measure approximately 9ft by 5½ft. The W brass shows Robert Braunche (died 1364) and his two wives. Beneath their feet is shown the Peacock Feast which Robert, as Mayor of Lynn, gave for King Edward III on a visit to the town. The other brass shows Adam de Walsokne (sic) (died 1349) and his wife. He was also Mayor and at the bottom of his brass is a contemporary country scene, with a post-mill.

North Runcton, *All Saints.* This attractive building is a pleasing example of early 18C craftsmanship and design. In 1701, the tower of the medieval church collapsed, destroying most of the building. The new church was completed in 1713 and its architect, Henry Bell, lived in the village.

The W tower also forms a porch. It has a sundial, is crowned by Classical vases and from its summit rises a wooden cupola and spirelet. The nave has shallow central projections to the N and S, containing large Classical windows. These are flanked by smaller windows, with oval windows above them. The chancel E window is only visible from the outside. The organ chamber was added in 1894.

The entrance vestibule contains the arms of King George I (1719), with flanking angels, the hatchment of Harriet Gurney (died 1837) and the arms of the Reverend Edward Rudd (1720). The interior of the church has great atmosphere and contains craftsmanship of quality. Four Ionic columns support a beautiful domed ceiling, from which hangs a central chandelier. The Classical font, of polished marble, came in 1907 from St. Margaret's, King's Lynn. There are three chancel arches, with double columns. The focal point of the chancel is the reredos, with its large paintings of the Evangelists by the Florentine artist, Lamponi, presented to the church in 1899. Lamponi's central Resurrection painting arrived two years later. The framework of the reredos was designed by Henry Bell for St.

Margaret's, King's Lynn. Many of the furnishings, which are well in keeping with the design of the church, arrived during the internal reordering which took place in 1887, under the direction of H.J. Green.

Norwich

This is indeed the city of churches. There are more medieval churches within its walls than in any other town in the United Kingdom, including London. In the Middle Ages there were 56 parish churches; now there are 31, in addition to the cathedral, the great Dominican church now known as St. Andrew's Hall, and the remains of St. Benedict, St. Peter Southgate and St. Bartholomew in Ber Street. Of the 31 churches, ten are still in regular use for Anglican worship, St. John Maddermarket is now used by the Orthodox Church and St. Clement's is open daily as a church where people may go to pray. Alternative uses for many of the others include a puppet theatre, a museum of church treasures, a scout headquarters, a night shelter, a thriving centre for rest and refreshment, and several temporary uses. Thanks to the Norwich Historic Churches Trust, all the churches are preserved intact for posterity.

Most Norwich churches are faced with flint, although a few are wholly or partly faced with dressed stone. Several are large and very magnificent buildings. Others are small, atmospheric and compact, like St. Peter Hungate and the tiny rebuilt church of St. Julian, where pilgrims come to visit the former home of the anchoress and mystic, Julian of Norwich. Work of most periods may be seen in these churches. The round tower of St. Mary at Coslany is pre-Conquest, there is Norman work in St. Etheldreda's and St. Julian's, and 14C craftsmanship in the tower of St. Margaret's, in the E window of St. Andrew's Hall and in the church of St. Mary the Less. It is 15C Perpendicular which predominates here. Fine examples include the churches of St. Peter Mancroft, St. Andrew, St. George Colegate, St. Clement, St. Gregory, St. John Maddermarket, St. Laurence, St. Giles, St. Michael at Coslany (fine flushwork), St. Peter Parmentergate and St. Stephen. Perpendicular towers abound, including St. Giles's (126ft), St. Andrew's (96ft), St. John de Sepulchre (c 90ft and set very high), St. Laurence's (112ft), St. George Colegate, St. Michael at Coslany and St. Clement's. Nine of these towers have 'sound-holes'. St. Augustine's has a brick tower of 1687. 17 of the churches have two-storeyed porches and 14 have medieval roofs.

Although several of the interiors have drastically altered since redundancy, some still in use retain interesting furnishings. St. George Colegate has many of its Georgian fittings. St. Helen's has a remarkable interior, with box-pews, a central two-decker pulpit, and the altar in a vaulted transept. St. John Maddermarket and St. George Tombland have fine Georgian reredoses. Devotional and colourful Anglo-Catholic interiors may be savoured at St. Giles's, St. Julian's, St. John Timberhill and St. George Tombland; 30 years ago no less than 12 of the churches were of this tradition. An unusual feature is the superb variety of civic sword and mace rests. Fourteen churches have memorials of quality and interest, the finest being those in the Suckling chapel at St. Andrew's, the Pettus monuments at SS. Simon and Jude, and the Berney monument at St. Peter

Parmentergate. 12 churches possess brasses of note, including a large array at St. John Maddermarket.

There are several 19C and 20C churches in the suburbs, including three (Christ Church, Catton, 1841, St. Mark, Lakenham, 1844, and St. Matthew, Thorpe Hamlet, 1851) by the local architect, John Brown. Imaginative Gothic Revival churches include Holy Trinity (1861) by William Smith and Christ Church, Eaton (1873) by J.H. Brown & Pearce. The 20C produced St. Alban's (1932) by Cecil Upcher, St. Catherine's (1935) by Caroë & Robinson and the fine refurbishing of the gutted church of St. Thomas (originally of 1886, by Ewan Christian).

The Free Churches have several interesting places of worship. The Octagon Chapel (1756) is of premier importance and nearby is the Old Meeting House, built in 1693 and also good of its period. The Friends' Meeting House in Goat Lane was erected in 1826 and Princes Street United Reformed Church is a large building by E. Boardman, built in 1869. St. Mary's Baptist Chapel is a pleasing building by S. Wearing of 1951. The Roman Catholics have their vast cruciform Cathedral of St. John, which dominates the city skyline and was begun in 1882 to the designs of G.G. Scott, Jr and J. Oldrid Scott. The church of St. George, by Sebastian Comper (1962), is also worth a visit.

Octagon Chapel, Colegate. This remarkable chapel, built in 1766, was originally a Presbyterian chapel, but in 1820 its congregation became Unitarian and the building acquired the title of the Octagon Chapel. The architect was Thomas Ivory—a man greatly influenced by James Gibbs.

This chapel stands back from the street in its attractive courtyard. It is a sturdy octagon of brick, with a tiled octagonal roof. There are two tiers of windows in the walls, the upper ones being taller and arched. In the roof are attractive dormers, with circular windows. The large semicircular-headed entrance shelters beneath a stately portico, the pediment of which rests upon Ionic columns. To the W of the chapel is a small graveyard which provides a hidden haven of peace.

The subdued exterior conceals a grand and elegant interior, with exquisite detail and beautiful original fittings. The octagon is punctuated by eight Corinthian columns supporting semicircular arches. Above is a panelled ceiling which is lit by the small dormer windows. The pews fill the centre of this preaching auditorium and then rise in tiers at the sides. Between the columns are galleries where the seats also rise in tiers. The pulpit was altered in 1887–89, when the small original pulpit was extended to form a rostrum, with rails on three sides. Behind it is a panelled and pedimented back and above this is the organ, with its attractive case. There are several 18C and 19C wall tablets, including one by John Athow to the Reverend William Enfield (died 1759) and another by Thomas Rawlins to Sarah Petty (died 1751). Five Mayors of Norwich from this congregation are recorded on the sword and mace rests.

St. Peter Mancroft. At the heart of this city of churches and gracing the N side of the Market Place, is the grandest and greatest parish church, its ancient dedication being St. Peter and St. Paul in the Magna Crofta, or Great Meadow. This long and lavish building was erected in one piece between 1430 and 1455. It has been described as the Norfolk church par excellence—Perpendicular architecture at its very best.

The exterior is almost entirely faced with stone, with a little flushwork in the lower part of the tower. The churchyard slopes downwards towards the E, making the E end of the church very lofty. There is a passage beneath the sanctuary and a three-storeyed vestry to the E. A single unbroken roofline crowns the nave and chancel and the aisles embrace all but the E bay. The magnificent clerestory has 17 triple windows. The aisles are lit by four-light windows and there are short N and S transepts. The E wall is filled with an immense seven-light window and is flanked by turrets with cupola-like crowns. Around the aisles is a flushwork basecourse and a frieze of stone shields. Their elegant buttresses have canopied and pedestalled niches which rise to form short pinnacles. The S porch is small and neat; the N is two-storeyed, with three tall canopied niches, shields with the emblems of St. Peter and St. Paul and a pair of external holy water stoups. The massive W tower, which was restored to the designs of G.E. Street by his son, A.E. Street, in 1891–95, is almost covered with shallow traceried panels and niches on all four sides, including the buttresses which rise to the level of the parapet. The basecourse, the noble five-light W window, the three processional arches and the large three-light belfry windows, are most impressive, as is the richly carved parapet and the four octagonal turrets at the corners, of which the SE is larger, for the staircase. The elegant flèche, designed by Street, was made by John Downing & Sons of Norwich and the height from the ground to its summit is 146ft.

The interior is a masterpiece of craftsmanship and design and the visitor is struck by its size, height and space, also by its brightness and the excellent use of colour. The church is 212ft long and the eye is directed upwards to the splendid roof which stretches unbroken from the tower arch to the E end. This is superb 15C timberwork, its hammerbeams being hidden behind elegant ribbed coving each side. The tall wall posts between the clerestory windows rest upon a series of carved faces which peer outwards. Between the arches of the tall eight-bay arcade are canopied niches and the tower arch is itself surrounded by niches. Again we can appreciate the beauty of the window tracery from inside, particularly the E windows of the aisles and chancel.

Many of the furnishings date from the restoration in the 1850s by R.M. Phipson, although the magnificent reredos was made by Harry Hems of Exeter to the designs of J.P. Seddon in 1886. Its five lower figures and the colour scheme of blue and gold are the work of Sir Ninian Comper in 1930. The font was given by John Cawston, a grocer, in 1463 and was a Seven Sacrament font until the Puritans defaced it. The remarkable canopy has its original 15C corner posts and roof, but its upper parts are a careful reconstruction of 1887. In a frame nearby are displayed the Articles of the Norwich Ringers Association in 1716. There are 13 bells in Mancroft tower and the tenor weighs about two tons. There are chapels in the E ends of the aisles. The Jesus chapel in the N aisle is used for small services. St. Anne's chapel in the S aisle has glass in its E window by H. Hendrie, inserted in 1921 as a war memorial. The most magnificent glass in this church is in the E window, which is almost filled with 15C glass of the Norwich School of glass painters. Of its 42 panels which show stories from the life of Christ, only seven (mostly in the central light) are 19C replacements by Clayton & Bell. This great window is the focal point of the church and blends well with the altar and reredos, and the two doors leading to the sacristy behind. The S chapel contains part of the case of the original organ made by Renatus

Harris in 1707. The present instrument in the W gallery was built by Peter Collins in 1984. There are some fine sword and mace rests. The N transept has recently been made into a treasury, where some of the superb plate and other items of interest are on display.

Several Norwich worthies are commemorated here and the best monument is that in the Jesus chapel to Francis Windham, who died in 1592. A wall plaque in the chancel commemorates Sir Thomas Browne (died 1682), the physician, antiquarian and writer, whose statue is in the Haymarket, to the S of the church.

Mancroft provides a varied Sunday and weekday ministry. Its bells and ringers are famous in the ringing fraternity throughout the country, and its musical tradition is of a very high standard.

Old Hunstanton, *St. Mary.* A tranquil and very picturesque setting, away from the main road and from the fashionable holiday resort and near the entrance to the Hall—the home for centuries of the Le Strange family. The present church was erected during the late 13C and early 14C. It underwent a very thorough restoration in 1857 to the designs of Henry Styleman Le Strange, who also painted the nave roof of Ely Cathedral.

The exterior, with its tall, steeply-pitched roofs, shows much 19C renewal of considerable quality and dignity and mainly in the Decorated style. The five-light E window is particularly grand. The interior is dignified and colourful; its excellent 19C work blends well with the medieval craftsmanship which has been preserved. The font is Norman; its square bowl, with colonettes at the corners, rests upon four columns and a central shaft. Beneath the chancel arch is the tall early 16C Rood screen, which was restored and given its coved top by G.F. Bodley. The dado has original painted figures of the Apostles. The pulpit nearby is an ornate structure of stone and alabaster, with pillars of green and red marble and figures of Jesus and the four Evangelists. In the sanctuary is an angle piscina and windowsill sedilia. The stained glass in the E window is by Frederick Preedy, who designed St. Edmund's Church at New Hunstanton. It was inserted in 1867 in memory of Henry Styleman Le Strange (1815–62), who is also commemorated by a brass tablet on the S wall of the chancel. The window comprises 15 scenes arranged in three tiers in the five lights, plus nine further scenes in the tracery lights. The Passion provides the theme for the principal scenes. On the N side of the sanctuary is the vast canopied monument of Henry Le Strange (died 1485). It has a stone-panelled back wall and a canopy with shields in elaborate quatrefoils. It is clear that this tomb was also designed for use as an Easter sepulchre and a very grand one it must have made. In the N aisle is a richly-carved tomb-chest of Sir Roger Le Strange (died 1506), upon which is his brass, where he is seen beneath a glorious canopy and helm, with eight members of his family portrayed in the supports to the canopy. Near the S doorway is the brass of Sir Edmund Grene and his wife (c 1490).

Oxborough, *St. John the Evangelist.* A pretty setting, near the entrance to Sir Edmund Bedingfield's splendid late 15C Hall. This was a fine Perpendicular church until 1948, when its 150ft tower and spire collapsed into the nave and S aisle, mercifully leaving the chancel and Bedingfield chapel. The N aisle has survived, with its fine arch-braced roof. Its W window and the N porch are 14C and earlier than the rest of the church.

The chancel has been made into a comfortable and devotional place of worship. It contains a fine 15C set of sedilia and piscina, with a frieze of tiny angels, preserving some of their original colour, also little flowers, in the square-topped surrounding frame. There is traceried panelling in the backs of the sedilia. The lectern, made c 1530, was given by the Rector, Thomas Kypping, as an inscription shows. On the N wall is a memorial to Charles Parkyn (died 1765), Rector for 40 years, who was a famous 18C historian of Norfolk.

The Bedingfield chapel contains two sumptuous and ornate Renaissance terracotta monuments, both probably of Flemish workmanship. From the tomb-chests rise ornate pilasters which support arched canopies. Margaret Bedingfield, in her will of 1513, asked to be buried in the chapel which she wished to be erected. The chapel was duly built and her tomb is magnificent, with an entrance arch attached, forming what could be described as a W screen. The other fine tomb is situated between the chapel and the chancel. On the E wall is the large black wall monument, with alabaster adornments, to Sir Henry Bedingfield (died 1704). Another Sir Henry Bedingfield (died 1583) has an alabaster memorial here, with an inscription surrounded by gilt strapwork.

Pulham, *St. Mary the Virgin.* A fine church, beautifully situated above the road and approached by an avenue of lime trees. Much of what we see here is 15C, although early 14C Decorated work remains in some windows, particularly the E window, which has Reticulated tracery of c 1330. The tower is supported and enhanced by diagonal buttresses, has good two-light belfry windows and is crowned by a flushwork parapet and pinnacles. The glory of the exterior is the lavish 15C two-storeyed porch. The entrance arch, flanked by pairs of niches, has the Annunciation in its spandrels. Above is a frieze of shields, with motifs which include the Passion emblems and the Trinity. The pair of two-light windows in the upper chamber are set amidst five canopied niches and the porch is crowned by an openwork parapet of quatrefoils, with animal pinnacles and a cross-legged wodewose at the centre. There is flushwork in the buttresses (which also have niches) and on the side walls. The porch has a fine 15C oak roof.

Inside, the nave is impressively wide and the position of the tower and chancel arches suggests that it was widened southwards at some time and then the S aisle added, its four-bay arcade resting upon unusual quatrefoil piers, the four sections being polygonal in shape. The nave has a tiebeam and arch-braced roof of the 15C which was well restored in 1886, and the E bay of which formed a canopy of honour to the Rood. The aisle roof has beautifully traceried spandrels and the chancel roof has been tastefully repaired and painted, probably during the restoration which took place in 1886 under G.F. Bodley. It has shields at the feet of its wall posts and bosses at the intersection of the beams. The font is of the typical 15C East Anglian pattern, with seated figures round the stem, angels beneath the bowl and in the bowl panels the four Evangelists and angels bearing shields with the emblems of the Passion. This too was tastefully restored and given a pretty cover by Bodley. The sanctuary contains work of a much earlier period; in its S wall is a superb double piscina which dates from the mid-13C and has intersecting arches. Beside it are three graduated sedilia and opposite, in the N wall, is a double aumbry.

Amongst the treasures of this church is the fine Rood screen, dating from c 1450 and carefully restored by Bodley, who gave it its vaulted coving. The base, with its ten painted figures of Apostles, is original. There are sets of 15C benches on one side of the nave and in the S aisle. The poppyhead ends are short and most of the figures have gone. The rear bench has a traceried back, but the rest were originally backless and their present back-rests are 17C woodwork. Some ancient bench-ends are also incorporated in the chancel stalls. On the W wall are the arms of King Charles I. The organ case in the chancel was designed by Bodley and the marble slab on the high altar was given by a relation of W.E. Gladstone. Medieval glass remaining in the tracery includes part of a 14C Coronation of the Virgin in the NE nave window, 15C figures of SS Mary Magdalene, Barbara, Cecilia and Catherine in the SE chancel window, and in the centre window of the nave N side are the 12 Apostles in two rows.

Ranworth, *St. Helen*. A beautiful Broadland church, serving a small village, and much visited by holidaymakers, who come to climb its tower for the superb views and to enjoy its truly magnificent screen.

Ranworth's tower is 96ft high, with a chequered base course, pretty sound-holes and tall two-light belfry windows. The embattled nave has large Perpendicular windows and the chancel has a beautiful three-light E window of c 1330, with Reticulated tracery. There are fine traceried 15C sets of N and S doors.

Although its plan is simple, comprising an aisleless nave and chancel, the interior is lofty, stately and is filled with light. The nave roof was made new in 1901, but the chancel roof, despite a fire in its former thatched covering in 1963, still retains its 14C timbers. Beneath the chancel arch is Ranworth's famous Rood screen—a masterpiece of c 1450—with much of its original colour remaining. More than this, the screen stretches the full width of the church and incorporates small parclose wings, also reredoses to the side altars which flank it. The woodcarving is exquisite, with graceful openwork divisions and the vaulted base of the Rood loft. The saints and figures painted in its panels merit detailed examination. The central panels show the Apostles with their emblems, the N parclose wing has SS. Stephen, George and maybe Felix, whilst its S counterpart has SS. Thomas of Canterbury, Lawrence and Michael. On the N reredos are SS. Etheldreda, Agnes, John the Baptist and Barbara and the S (Lady chapel) has SS. Mary Salome, Mary the Virgin, Mary Cleopas and Margaret of Antioch.

Other features of interest in the church include sets of return stalls with misericords, an Easter sepulchre and 17C communion rails in the chancel. In the nave are some 15C bench-ends, a linenfold pulpit, a medieval cantor's desk and a rare and beautiful antiphoner—an illuminated service book inscribed by the monks of Langley Abbey c 1400. During the winter months this is displayed in Norwich Castle Museum.

Salle, *St. Peter and St. Paul*. To many people this is the finest church in Norfolk, yet Salle (pronounced Saul) has less than 200 inhabitants and never was a large community. Here we have a prize example of a building which was not set up to be filled with people but was built for the Glory of God. Its mighty walls and soaring tower dominate the countryside. It is glorious without and within and looks magnificent from wherever one chooses to view it.

The building grew during the 1400s and the exterior shows Perpendicular architecture at its best. The stone-faced, 126ft high tower is elegant and graceful, with angle buttresses, large and exquisitely traceried sound-holes and tall three-light belfry windows; then a richly panelled parapet, with corner pinnacles and spirelets. Beneath the four-light W window is the great W doorway, with a frieze of shields above it (including the arms of King Henry V when Prince of Wales from 1400–13) and fine niches flanking it. Its deep arch is framed by spandrels containing angels with censers, and the massive traceried doors are the originals. The two-storeyed N and S porches both have prominent staircase turrets; both have vaulted ceilings with carved bosses and both shelter pairs of 15C traceried doors. The body of the church has panelled and embattled parapets and the chancel also has pinnacles. The building is lit by handsome Perpendicular windows (although some on the N side have had replacement intersecting tracery). The five-light window in the S transept is noteworthy, also the enormous seven-light E window.

The church of St. Peter and St. Paul, widely regarded as the most interesting of Norfolk's larger medieval churches

The interior of this 170ft long church contains so much which is beautiful and of interest. The soaring arcades of six bays are particularly graceful and lift the eye upwards to the tall clerestory and to the magnificent nave roof, which is 15C and retains much of its original colour. Its span is immense and it is studded with carved bosses. The aisle roofs are also original, the transept roofs are exquisitely panelled and the chancel roof is resplendent with bosses showing scenes from the life of Christ, and also 159 of its original angels. Beneath the tower arch is the 15C ringers' gallery from which a huge carved beam projects to carry the weight of Salle's tall and graceful 15C font cover. The font itself was given by the Luce family in the 15C and its bowl panels show the Seven Sacraments and the Crucifixion, each angel beneath the bowl having in its hands a symbol of the Sacrament above it. It is worth climbing the staircase to the chamber above the N porch. This is the Lady chapel, with a piscina and an aumbry, also a splendid groined ceiling with bosses, including one of the Coronation of the Virgin. The chancel is 59ft long, over 25ft wide, and is dominated by its enormous E window. This part of the church was probably built c 1450 by John Nekton, the Rector. It is furnished with a fine piscina and sedilia. The S transept is thought to have been added by Thomas Brigg and his initials appear upon two of the roof bosses. The N transept (restored in 1912 by the Jodrell family) was the chapel of Thomas Rose, who died in 1441.

There are 15C benches, with poppyhead ends, in the nave. The elegant 15C wineglass pulpit was converted into a three-decker arrangement in 1611, when its back and sounding-boards were added. The N aisle contains the royal arms of 1790, several hatchments and a 17C box-pew. The N transept has a beautiful image niche, with some of its original colour remaining. The S transept has medieval floor tiles, a pretty piscina, a Jacobean altar table, a bier and a sturdy iron-bound chest. At the entrance to the chancel is the base of what must have been a very fine Rood screen, with eight of its painted panels, showing the Latin Doctors and four Apostles. The chancel is equipped with its original stalls, with 26 misericords, carved with birds, animals and human heads. The great E window has much original glass in its tracery and more 15C glass may be seen elsewhere, including six figures in a transept window. The glass in the N transept is by H. Bryans of London.

There are several brasses in this church, including one to Geoffrey and Alice Boleyn (he died in 1440, and was the great-grandfather of Anne Boleyn) and a bracket to Thomas Rose (died 1441) in the N transept, which also shows his wife and 12 children. The blocked N window in this transept contains the memorial to Edward Hase, who died in 1801—a wall plaque which is good of its period, but which was erected without the Rector's permission and was the subject of subsequent litigation.

(W.L.E. Parsons, 'Salle' (Jarrold and Sons Ltd, 1937).)

Sandringham, *St. Mary Magdalene.* This little building has been so greatly altered and beautified during the 19C and 20C that little of the 15C work remains. The first restoration took place in 1857–58 by S.S. Teulon and there was another restoration in 1890 by Sir Arthur Blomfield. Nevertheless, shoals of visitors come to see it for its royal associations and the craftsmanship inside is of the highest quality. The neat exterior is faced mostly with local carstone in small blocks. The tower has a pretty parapet and pinnacles; its single belfry windows have simple pierced tracery. In the windows of the 15C porch are 15C glass figures of St. Catherine and St. Etheldreda.

The interior is richly and lavishly adorned. The nave has a 19C arch-braced roof and the chancel a hammerbeam roof. The walls are panelled and wainscoted and the chancel walls have stencilled colouring. The marble font, given by King Edward VII, was made in Florence. An American, Mr. Rodman Wanamaker, presented the oak and silver pulpit in 1924 and the silver-lined altar in 1911; both were designed by Barkentin & Krall. Kempe & Co. created the reredos in 1920 and the glass in the E window in 1911. The processional cross is a Spanish 15C piece and near the chancel arch is a beautiful ivory and aluminium statuette of St. George, made by Alfred Gilbert in 1892. Beautiful Norwich-made 15C glass remains in the tracery of two of the windows, one in the nave and the other in the N aisle, each with six figures of saints. The figures of St. Francis and St. Ignatius are thought to be unique in England.

Saxlingham Nethergate, *St. Mary the Virgin.* A charming and idyllic village setting in a picturesque churchyard approached from a small green, with the Elizabethan Hall on one side and the Rectory of 1784 by Sir John Soane on the other. The church completes the picture—a pretty building, with tower, nave, S porch and chancel, and also a wide 19C N aisle out of view.

The tower is slender and tapering, with a brick and flint chequer-work parapet and four carved figures at the corners, graceful two-light belfry windows, and a single-handed clock, with a sundial beneath it. The short nave has a pair of three-light late Perpendicular windows and a low-side window. An early 14C window may be seen in the chancel. The porch shelters a medieval S door, which has two iron quatrefoil openings.

The interior contains much work from the 1867 restoration by J.S. Benest, when the N aisle was built and the church was reseated. The font is 15C and on its bowl are lions, with angels bearing shields displaying the Trinity, the Instruments of the Passion, the three crowns and the Blessed Sacrament emblems. The reredos is made out of part of a 15C screen. The great feature is the remarkable medieval glass, dating from the 13C to c 1500. In the SE chancel window is the oldest glass in Norfolk—four medallions, dating from the mid-13C and showing St. John and St. James, a saint being beheaded, and two panels with St. Edmund. The window to the W of it has St. Philip with his basket of loaves and St. James the Less with his fuller's club in the tracery, both of late 14C date, and in the little low-side window is a roundel of c 1500 of the Virgin and Child. Other old glass in the chancel includes scenes of the Apostles at Pentecost and the Ascension, two of the Latin Doctors (NW window: St. Jerome in his red cardinal's hat and St. Ambrose to his right), and in the N aisle E window, St. Edward the Confessor.

Shelton, *St. Mary.* A pleasant rural setting for this fine example of late Perpendicular architecture. Apart from the earlier tower, the building is entirely the work of 1480–90, erected through the generosity of Sir Ralph Shelton. It is like a great Norfolk church in miniature and is built mainly of mellow Tudor brick, with dressings of stone.

The W tower, of flint rubble, is 14C, as is also the W window in the S aisle beside it. The rest is Sir Ralph's 1480 rebuild. The aisles of Tudor brick (displaying the diaper pattern, using darker coloured bricks) extend to the E end of the church. Their plain stone parapets have good gargoyles and the windows have impressive Perpendicular tracery. The clerestory is stone-faced and has nine triple windows. Beneath the tall E window is the sacristy—an unusual position for it.

The interior is bright and elegantly proportioned, although in some ways it feels but a shade of its former glory. The original roof was removed in the 18C and the present plaster ceiling substituted for it. The stone angels bearing shields which once supported its wall posts remain and beneath the clerestory windows is blank panelling which continues down to the arches of the six-bay arcade. Between the arches are niches, each flanked with pinnacles and shields. We are reminded several times that this is the Sheltons' church, because their arms (a gold cross on a blue ground) and the rebus of Sir Ralph (an R, a shell and a tun or barrel) appear in several places.

There is a 15C East Anglian font and in its bowl panels are lions, and also angels with shields showing the Passion, the Trinity, the three crowns and the Blessed Sacrament emblems. The lower portion of the 15C screen, which stretches the entire width of the church, retains its handsome traceried panels. The impressive set of carved royal arms over the tower arch are those of King William III. The lectern is made up of medieval woodwork, a small 15C bench remains in the N aisle and the 17C communion rails have been reused as fronts to the chancel stalls. The E window contains much of its original glass, as do the E windows of the aisles. Depicted here are Sir Ralph Shelton and his wife, also Sir John Shelton and his wife, together with the Shelton arms impaling those of several Norfolk and Suffolk families. There are also pictures in glass of two English Kings—Edmund of East Anglia and Henry VII. Near the E end are three 16C tomb-chests, bearing coats of arms. That to the N of the altar has the Shelton arms and the beginning of what was to have been a splendid canopy. In the S aisle is the monument to Sir Robert Houghton (died 1623) upon which are the kneeling effigies of himself and his family.

Sir Ralph Shelton's son, Sir John, married the aunt of Anne Boleyn, and when Anne was beheaded, her daughter (the future Queen Elizabeth I) is believed to have hidden in the tower of this church to avoid arrest by court conspirators.

Snettisham, *St. Mary.* A fine church in a commanding rural setting away from the main road and the village centre. It is considered to be the most ambitious church of the Decorated style in the county, built c 1340, when this style of architecture was producing craftsmanship of great beauty and intricacy. St. Mary's was a cruciform church, although its chancel (which was some 40ft in length) has disappeared, the altar now being beneath the tower.

Externally it is glorious, especially when approached from the W, or viewed across the green with the surrounding trees. The nave has a six-light W window with beautiful and lavish tracery, flanked by sturdy turrets with spirelets. The aisles have three-light windows, with several patterns in Decorated tracery. The clerestory is a satisfying combination of alternating two-light windows and circular windows with traceried patterns. There is a five-light window in the S transept and opposite, on the N side, is what appears to be the earliest work in the building, with Y- and intersecting traceried windows of c 1300. The E window in the blocked tower arch is 19C. The tower is broad and sturdy, with short two-light belfry windows, flanked by blank arches, with panelling beneath. It has corner pinnacles with spirelets, linked by flying buttresses to the soaring and graceful spire, which is the finest of Norfolk's very few stone spires. This spire, which has two tiers of lucarne openings, was carefully rebuilt in 1895 and rises to 175ft.

The interior again shows the beauty of Decorated architecture. The five-bay arcades are tall and have composite piers with wide bases which formed seats. The arches are framed by hoodmoulds resting upon a variety of corbels. The crossing tower rests upon four similar arches, and half-arches span the E ends of the aisles. The arch-braced roof is steeply pitched and although much restored, has some of its original timbers.

The octagonal font, although restored in 1856, has a medieval bowl. Near the SW corner of the church is a fireplace marking the position where an oven was situated in which wafers were baked for use at Mass. Nearby is the old sanctus bell, its long waist showing its very early date; it may well be 13C and therefore older than the present church. The pulpit was much renewed in the 19C. Its repainted panels depict the five great preachers of righteousness. The sounding board is 20C, by Cecil Howard of South Walsham, who also made the choirstalls, communion table and reredos. The eagle lectern, however, is a treasure from the 15C; at its feet are lions. The glass in the E window is by William Warrington, installed in 1848 and showing Old Testament scenes. The W window of the S aisle has glass of 1861 by O'Connor and another window in this aisle shows the Virgin and Child in glass of 1969, designed by Paul Jefferies.

Two interesting brasses may be seen at the W end. On the N side is the brass of John and Elizabeth Cremer (he died 1610) and their family. In the S aisle is a palimpsest brass with a figure of c 1495 on one side and a lady of 1570 on the other. In the N chapel, the alabaster effigy of Wymond Carye, who died in 1612, rests upon a stately tomb; it is believed that he was responsible for taking down the chancel.

South Creake, *St. Mary.* A delightful setting in a quiet and picturesque corner. This is a large and venerable church, the core of which dates from the late 13C and early 14C. Then, c 1510, the clerestory, aisle windows and sacristy were added. It is the interior here which is so memorable—a beautiful combination of ancient craftsmanship with tasteful and devotional Anglo-Catholic fittings of the present century.

The proportions of the exterior are grand. The long chancel is entirely work of c 1300 or just after, with Y-traceried windows and a five-light E window with intersecting tracery. To the N of it is the sacristy, added c 1410. The aisles are lit mostly by Perpendicular windows although their E and W windows are 14C Decorated. The broad and sturdy tower is supported by angle buttresses and its W window has Reticulated tracery of c 1330; the belfry windows are of a similar date. The tower has an unfinished appearance because it lacks a parapet.

The interior is remarkable for its devotional atmosphere. It feels like a holy and prayerful place and medieval churches were after all designed to bring folk to their knees. It has been well restored and furnished with great care. It is a bright building and colour has been tastefully used in the altars and the many aids to devotion here. Beneath the massive 14C tower arch is a screen which came from a convent at Brancaster Staithe. The five-bay 14C arcades have piers on broad bases which acted as seats. The nave roof is a well-restored single hammerbeam, with painted angels. The 15C aisle roofs have carved spandrels and good stone corbels. To the right of the 14C chancel arch is the entrance to the Rood loft stairs. The N chapel piscina has a stone with a consecration cross in its rear wall and the S chapel has a 14C piscina. To the S of the high altar is a piscina and a set of 15C sedilia with angels in its richly carved canopy.

The 15C font, elevated upon two steps, has the Seven Sacraments (now sadly mutilated) in the panels of its bowl; its wooden cover is 19C but nevertheless attractive. The pulpit dates from the early 15C and there are remains of colour in its double traceried panels. Of similar date is the handsome screen, although traces only now remain of its once magnificent paintings. The 19C Rood group above it came here in 1982 from the church of St. Mary at the Walls, Colchester. In the chancel are several 15C bench-ends; there are more of these in storage, awaiting restoration and reuse. The priest's stall is made up of medieval woodwork. Other items of note include a bier of 1688 and two fine old chests—one totally iron-bound. A considerable amount of ancient glass remains in the windows, including coats of arms, angels, the Betrothal and Coronation of the Virgin, a Crucifixion scene and, in a N aisle window, saints and Apostles.

Two brasses may be seen at the W end: one of a priest in a cope, made c 1400 and the other of John Norton (died 1509) and his parents. Beneath the N chapel altar is a memorial to the Reverend Henry Ventham (Vicar 1927–44). He and the Reverend Leonard Smith (Vicar 1944–77), who is commemorated in one of the windows, did much to make this church the colourful shrine that it now is. It is a credit to this small community. The beautifully adorned altars, statues and shrines and the ever-present savour of incense, combined with the atmosphere of centuries of prayer and devotion, make this ancient building very much a place where Heaven and earth meet.

Swaffham, *St. Peter and St. Paul.* A market town, with a market cross erected in 1783 and a stately church which took its present form in the second half of the 15C. The building is cruciform and is 173ft long. Much restoration took place during the 19C but the church, with its graceful tower and distinctive lantern spire, has preserved its grandeur and contains much of beauty and interest.

The tower was built by the early 16C. It is faced with Barnack stone and is elegant and beautifully proportioned, with set-back buttresses, an openwork stone parapet, pinnacles and three-light belfry windows. There are small sound-holes in the ringing chamber and the tall five-light W window has canopied niches in its splays. The deep-set W doorway is flanked by niches and holy water stoups and the tower has a stone basecourse. The attractive spire was rebuilt in 1897 and the height to the weathercock at its summit is 173ft. The aisles are lit by large four-light windows, above which is the fine clerestory with its 13 triple windows. On the nave's E gable is a sanctus bell turret. The chancel has 19C windows in the Decorated style, but very pleasing. 14C work remains in the E window of the S transept and the W window of the S aisle. W of the S transept is a small projecting chapel. The two-storeyed vestry is medieval. The S porch is crowned with pinnacles, with a dog at the centre and inside it has a hammerbeam roof.

Entering by the W door, we see that there was once a vaulted ceiling beneath the tower. The tower arch is lofty and the ringers' gallery beneath has 17C rails. The seven-bay nave arcades rest upon quatrefoil piers and there are wall arcades in the aisles. A superb double hammerbeam roof crowns the nave, with two tiers of angels on the cornices, angels on the hammerbeams and at the apex—over 190 in all. The aisles have arch-braced roofs, as do the chancel and transepts. The S transept has angels on its roof and a beautiful piscina with foliage in the spandrels. Much of the restoration work took place in 1876 and 1888–95, including the installation of many of the furnishings. The architect was William Milne.

The two clergy stalls have excellent 15C carved ends. The N stall has figures of a local merchant's family and its S counterpart has men with packs on their backs and muzzled dogs beneath them. The glass in the E window of 1853 is by William Wailes and the window in the tiny Corpus Christi chapel (now the War Memorial chapel) is by the firm of William Morris. A little medieval glass remains in the N aisle windows. The three-manual organ was built by Bishop & Sons in 1876 and has 30 speaking stops. In the chamber above the vestry is a parochial library of some 400 volumes. The font was made in 1851.

Beneath the cinquefoil-headed arched recess in the sanctuary is the effigy of John Botright, Rector here 1435–74, who was responsible for the rebuilding of the church. The shields on the tomb-chest show the emblems of the Blessed Sacrament, the Trinity, three boats and three augers (for boatwright). In the S transept is the brass of Sir John Audley (c 1530) and a wall monument to Catherine Steward (died 1590), who was Oliver Cromwell's maternal grandmother.

Portrayed in various places in this church is John Chapman, the 'Pedlar of Swaffham', and his dog. He was in fact a very wealthy man, who was a great benefactor to the rebuilding of the church in the 15C.

Terrington St. Clement, *St. Clement.* A great and majestic Marshland church, which grew during the late 14C and early 15C on the site of an earlier building. Of Barnack stone, it is 167ft long and 47ft wide, with a lofty nave, aisles, transepts and chancel, a S porch, and a mighty detached bell tower.

The exterior is magnificent and is worth admiring as a whole. The 15C tower gives the impression of great strength. It is supported by diagonal buttresses and terminates in a stone-panelled parapet with slender pinnacles, rising to a height of 97ft. It has a basecourse of quatrefoils, a large W doorway with three carved heads, a four-light W window and three-light belfry windows. Although detached, the tower stands very close to the N aisle and the view of the W front of the church is impressive. The W window of the nave is flanked by niches, with a further niche above it. The nave has W turrets, as do the aisles. The nave and aisles have panelled and embattled parapets and slender crocketed pinnacles. Fine sets of 14 clerestory windows each side light the nave. The flying buttresses near the W end are a later addition. The S face of the S transept has a fine array of six three-light windows. The chancel has a five-light E window and a brick clerestory with six three-light windows. The NE window has late 13C bar tracery and remains from the earlier church.

Inside, there are arcades of seven bays and a large crossing space with four sturdy arches. Between the clerestory windows are canopied niches which rest upon a variety of carved figures. Above the crossing arch at the E end of the nave is a grand array of seven canopied and pedestalled niches. The nave roof was renewed in 1829, but incorporates earlier bosses. The spacious chancel was restored and refurnished in 1879. In the floor near the entrance to the chancel are three stone altar slabs; another is in the floor beneath the high altar, which is raised upon several steps because there is a vault beneath it. The double piscina and triple sedilia show craftsmanship of the 13C, with trefoil-headed arches, embellished with dogtooth ornament. These survive from the earlier church. The 15C font has a most remarkable 16C cover, the lower section of which opens out to reveal Flemish paintings of the Baptism of Jesus, also scenes from the Temptations story, with a red-robed devil. Above, in the clouds, are the four Evangelists. The bottom section is mostly 17C work; above is an elegant 16C openwork spire. At the W end of the nave is a large oak screen erected in 1788 at a cost of £13, with a central gallery supported by cast-iron pillars. In the S vestry enclosure are two medieval stone figures of St. Clement and of St. Christopher carrying the Christ Child. Over the N door are the arms of Queen Anne. In their original positions in the transepts are fine 17C boards, with the Creed and the Lord's Prayer, surrounded by strapwork decoration and dated 1635.

Trunch, St. Botolph. St. Botolph's has many features which make a visit to it rewarding. There is evidence of early 14C work in the tower and chancel and it is thought that the nave and aisles were rebuilt in c 1380. The splendid roof, screen and font canopy were added in the late 15C or early 16C.

Trunch's tower is elegant and quite slender, with clearly diminishing stages. There are diagonal buttresses and four corner gargoyles at the base of its plain parapet and graceful two-light Decorated belfry windows. The aisle windows have pleasing Decorated and Perpendicular tracery and the clerestory and chancel windows are Perpendicular, the E window being tall and graceful. The unusual small porch (with a buttress starting from its roof) on the S side of the chancel shelters an early 14C priest's doorway. On the 15C main porch are two Mass dials, and a third (which predates the porch) is on the E side of the S doorway.

The nave has four-bay arcades with octagonal piers and octagonal moulded capitals and is crowned by a fine single hammerbeam roof, which was carefully restored in 1897. There are angels on the hammerbeams and fine tracery in the spandrels. The font, which has a traceried bowl of c 1350, stands beneath a remarkable wooden canopy, dating from c 1500. It is supported upon six columns, each carved with foliage and vine-leaf patterns. These rise to a vaulted roof, which is a mass of exquisite woodcarving. Above it is a hexagonal carved top, from which radiating ribs rise to form a crown. The handsome Rood screen dates from 1502. Beneath its openings is an inscription set in a trail of carved foliage and in the dado are the figures of the Apostles, including St. Paul, with their symbols. In the chancel, backing on the screen, are six stalls with misericords. Amongst the other interesting items in the church are a few old bench-ends, a little 15C glass in the clerestory windows, the medieval arched support to the ringers' gallery and a small heart brass of c 1530 in the central aisle.

Walpole St. Peter, St. Peter. They call it the 'cathedral of the Fens' and the 'Queen of the Marshlands', and this vast church (which was a pioneer of our modern Flower Festivals) is certainly the finest of the great churches which punctuate the flat marshy scenery hereabouts. St. Peter's dates almost entirely from the late 14C and 15C. Only the tower survives from the early 14C and the earlier church which was attached to it was destroyed by a great sea flood in 1337. The present nave also included the chancel until c 1425, when a new chancel was added to the E of it. Finally c 1450 the S porch was added.

It is worth standing back to admire the superb exterior as a whole. The nave, aisles, chancel and porches have embattled parapets with stone panelling, and a multiplicity of carved figures and gargoyles. The aisles are supported by gable-topped buttresses and are lit by large three-light windows with transoms. Above is the array of 13 clerestory windows. The E nave gable is flanked by stone-panelled turrets with crocketed spirelets and terminates in a beautiful sanctus bellcote. The chancel has five three-light windows each side and an enormous seven-light E window. Beneath the sanctuary is a passage-way, known locally as the 'Bolt Hole'; this has a groined ceiling with carved bosses. The S porch is two-storeyed and is unusually long. It has a magnificent S face and inside is a tierceron-vaulted ceiling with bosses, including the Assumption and the Last Judgement. This rests upon niches at the corners, with figures which include a Pietà at the NW corner. The church is entered through a pair of medieval traceried doors.

Inside one is immediately impressed by the space and size of this great church, which is 161ft long. Light floods in through the clear glass of the windows and the absence of seating in the W part enables us to appreciate the grandeur of the proportions here. The seven-bay arcades (the three E bays were in the former chancel) have sturdy quatrefoil piers. The floors, with their ancient slabs and tiles, enhance the atmosphere of unspoilt antiquity. The nave and N aisle roofs contain much of their original timberwork although the chancel and S aisle were reroofed in 1812. The chancel is lined with arcaded wall seats, with a variety of carved and vaulted canopies. Above these are canopied niches between the windows. The sedilia and piscina have lost their once magnificent vaulted canopies. The E angles are recessed with canopies, flanking the E window. The most satisfying feature must be the position of the high altar, ten steps above the chancel floor and 14 above the level of the nave.

This is a premier church for furnishings and fittings. The grand W screen was made c 1630 and the nave benches are of similar date. The benches in the S aisle are 15C and (unusually) they face N. These have beautifully carved ends and also incorporate some 17C woodwork in places. More medieval benches may be seen in the N aisle. The handsome octagonal font is dated 1532 and bears the name of the Reverend John Wheltholme (Rector 1525–37). Its cover, made c 1600, has unusually tall and spectacular woodcarving for the period. The base of the Rood screen remains at the entrance to the chancel. It has painted figures, including St. Catherine and several Apostles. A fine parclose screen separates the S aisle chapel, which now contains the organ. The corresponding chapel in the N aisle has a fine piscina and a collection of medieval glass fragments in its N window. The great chandelier suspended in the nave dates from 1701. The eagle lectern, with three lions at its feet, is a treasure from the early 16C. The pulpit was made c 1605. The chancel stalls incorporate fine 15C woodwork, including carvings of a camel, an antelope, the wolf guarding St. Edmund's head, and two misericords on the N side. Amongst the many other fascinating items is a poor box dated 1639, a shelter looking like a sentry box to keep the priest dry at funerals and an early 19C inscription in the porch, requesting people to remove their pattens in church.

Walsoken, *All Saints.* This dignified church is quietly and sedately set among trees, pleasantly apart from its main centre of population, which has become part of Wisbech suburbia. This is a late Norman church of considerable merit, although most of the Norman work is only visible inside. Good Early English work may be seen in the tower. The church was also greatly refurbished in the 15C and in the 19C.

The handsome stone W tower is basically 13C, with sturdy poly-gonal buttresses and arcading which encircles its exterior. The W doorway has Early English stiff-leaf capitals but retains the Norman pattern of a semicircular arch. The arcading has plain and trefoil patterns and there are lancet windows. To this lower part the belfry stage with its two-light windows was added in the 14C, also the recessed stone spire. The outline of the tower is satisfying, with its receding stages, turret pinnacles and its spire which is nicely proportioned without being lofty. The rest of the church externally is mostly Perpendicular, with an embattled and pinnacled clerestory lit by three-light windows. 13C work remains in the N aisle corbel table and the S porch. The aisles terminate in N and S chancel chapels. At the E end of the nave is a large sanctus bellcote.

Inside we see the glory of the 12C work, chiefly in the superb Norman arcades with their rich zigzag mouldings and the multiplicity of designs in their capitals. There are seven bays in the nave and two more in the chancel, which are slightly later in the 12C. Above the latter are blocked Norman windows. The chancel arch shows the transition between Norman and Early English architecture, with elaborate zigzag ornamentation to its pointed arch and eight shaft-rings in the supporting shafts each side. The nave has a fine 15C roof, with standing figures beneath canopies on the wall posts and angels on the small hammerbeams. In the chancel is an arch-braced roof and the chancel chapels have good medieval carving in their roofs. Above the 13C tower arch is a 17C wooden figure of King Solomon, surrounded by a painting of his judgement; above the chancel arch is a figure of King David.

The Seven Sacrament font is a fine example and is less mutilated than many of the others. The Sacraments and the Crucifixion are beneath vaulted ogee canopies and around the stem are eight identifiable saints. The inscription at the foot requests prayers for S. Honyter, his wife and John Beforth, Chaplain, 1544, and has shields with the Instruments of the Passion. Several 15C bench-ends remain, each with two figures and a central figure in a niche. 15C parclose screens divide off the chancel chapels, that to the S being the more elaborate, with two tiers of intricate tracery. The chancel stalls have new seats, but have good 15C faces on their armrests. The 16C communion table now stands at the W end of the N aisle. There is glass by T.F. Curtis of Ward & Hughes and by Jones & Willis in the S aisle, and two windows in the N aisle are by William Glasby.

The one monument of special note is in the N aisle; it is a trefoil-headed recess containing a pair of hands holding a heart and it marks the site of a heart burial. It dates from c 1350.

West Walton, *St. Mary the Virgin.* The distinctive detached bell tower at the entrance to the churchyard and the remarkable church behind it were built between c 1225–40 and are excellent examples of Early English architecture. The building was largely financed by Sir William de Warenne, Earl of Surrey.

The great campanile is a little later than the church, which appears rather humble in comparison. At the four corners of the tower are bulky polygonal buttresses in receding stages, which are embellished with blank arcading and gable-topped niches in the lower stages. These terminate in short corner pinnacles with crocketed spirelets. The four open arches at the base of the tower are decorated with dogtooth ornament. Above them are tall triple arches, behind which is a passageway. The double bell openings are large and tall, almost filling the wall each side. They are set under embracing arches, with dogtooth decoration, with a circle of plate tracery above the two lancets. Above this is more arcading and a later stone-panelled parapet. The tower was built on the firmest land in this Marshland parish and houses a ring of five bells.

The church's exterior is a rustic mixture of alterations and enlargements, but its core is 13C Early English work, which is seen in the clerestory, a plate tracery window and a doorway in the S aisle, the N doorway, which is flanked by blank arches, and the great double W doorway, beneath a massive arch, with five shafts each side. Superb Early English work also occurs in the porch, which has kept its wide entrance arch, its arcaded flanking turrets with spirelets and its arcaded inner walls. It shelters a fine Early English S doorway. Later periods added the pretty two-light Decorated windows in the S aisle, also the Perpendicular W and S windows and the sanctus bell turret over the E nave gable. The N aisle is remarkably wide and has rather crude windows, which were probably inserted after the Reformation. The chancel was shortened in 1807, when it received a new E window.

The interior is spacious and light; it has an unspoilt and almost rustic atmosphere. The six-bay arcades are fine examples of Early English work. They have circular piers, each with four detached shafts of dark Purbeck marble, and beautiful stiff-leaf capitals. Above them is the clerestory with its single lancet windows (blocked on the N side) interspersed with blank arches. The 15C nave roof has tiebeams and hammerbeams, the latter having carved angels with shields bearing the Instruments of the Passion. The S aisle also has an ancient roof. The chancel arch is good Early English, as are the blocked chancel arcades of two bays, and the wall arcading in the sanctuary.

The simple but very pleasing 15C font has a slender stem and quatrefoils in the bowl. Some 15C bench-ends may be seen incorporated in the chancel stalls. There are faint traces of wall paintings between the clerestory windows. Between the arches in the nave are 17C painted shields, representing the 12 Tribes of Israel. At the E end of the N aisle are two table-tombs. One has a brass inscription dated 1552 remaining, but the border and several shields are missing. The other has the effigy of a priest in vestments of Purbeck marble. The figure may represent Prior Albert, or possibly Hugh of Northwold, Bishop of Ely, both of whom are traditionally linked with the foundation of the church.

Wiggenhall

St. Germans. Set beside the river, the slender tower at St. Germans is Early English at its base and Perpendicular above. The nave has a stone-faced clerestory with a panelled parapet and three-light Perpendicular windows, also a sanctus bell turret. The disused S porch is of Tudor brick. Inside are 15C arcades and a 13C tower arch with dogtooth ornament. The pulpit, made in 1631, retains its hourglass, and the reading desk is also 17C. The superb bench-ends are the main feature here, with poppyheads, figures each side and saints with their emblems beneath niches. Some of the small figures are worth finding, including a priest blessing a person and a couple of lovers.

St. Mary Magdalene. A very handsome and stately exterior. The noble 14C tower is of stone; the rest of the church is 15C and mostly of Tudor brick. The grand nave and aisles have large windows, also E turrets and a sanctus bellcote. The two-storeyed porch shelters a fine entrance, flanked by shields in flowers and foliage. The lofty arcades are 14C and there is a good 15C roof with tiebeams and queenposts, and small hammerbeams with angels. Panels of the Rood screen painted with emblems of the Evangelists are at the W end and parts of a 15C parclose screen now enclose the NW vestry. There are some medieval benches in the nave. The 'weeping' chancel has a 13C piscina, also an aumbry and sedilia. Carved 17C panelling lines the E wall. In the tracery lights of the N aisle windows are 40 figures of saints, popes, bishops, etc., in 14C and 15C glass. Some have labels which identify them and many of the figures are rarely depicted elsewhere, making this collection of glass important and very interesting.

St. Mary the Virgin. A lonely and peaceful setting for this sizeable church, now in the care of the Redundant Churches Fund. The sturdy tower, which has much brick in its walls, has two W staircase turrets. The porch of c 1400 has a sundial dated 1742 and is tunnel-vaulted inside. The N and S doorways are 13C and the corbels flanking the windows of the aisles are worth examining. The interior has a superb array of 15C or early 16C benches, which are beautifully preserved and magnificently carved, with openwork traceried backs and excellent ends. Each end has a poppyhead, flanked by seated figures, with a standing saint beneath an ogee canopy at the centre. These provide a fine catalogue of saints and their emblems. The pulpit with hourglass stand and the almsbox are 17C. The font cover was made in 1625 and has a pelican at its summit. The base of the Rood screen has painted figures of female saints and St. John the Baptist. The name of its donor, Humphrey Kervile, who died in 1526, also appears on the screen. Part of the parclose screen divides off the S aisle chapel, which contains the fine monument of Sir Henry Kervile (died 1624), with the effigies of the knight and his lady, and on the side of the tomb-chest, their daughter and a tiny chrisom baby. In the floor is the heart brass of his ancestor, Sir Robert Kervile, who died in 1450.

Wilby, All Saints. Beautiful Decorated work may be seen in the chancel, particularly in the E window, with its flowing tracery. The tall tower is also of this period. The nave windows are mostly 15C, although its N doorway, which has an ogee arch, is 14C. The interior was refitted after a fire in 1633, making it a 17C period piece. The ringers' gallery (1637) has turned balusters. The chest near the door, the arms of King Charles I, the almsbox (1629), the nave benches with their simple fleur-de-lis ends, the three-decker pulpit with back and sounding boards, the box-pews to the E of it, the chancel screen, the fine set of communion rails and the altar table are all 17C. There are also older features which survived the fire. In the sanctuary is a 14C piscina, a windowsill sedilia and three aumbries. The nave has another piscina, a wall painting of St. Christopher, two 13C coffin lids and a 14C font. Robert Wilton's ledger slab in the sanctuary has his own arms and those of his two wives. The 17C shields on the walls show the arms of the Wilton and Bell families.

Wymondham, St. Mary and St. Thomas of Canterbury. Two great towers with the roofline of the church between them form an unusual landmark. This massive building faces quiet open countryside. It is the parochial nave and aisles of the abbey church founded by William D'Albini in the 12C. The Norman church grew between 1107 and 1130. The E tower was built by the monks in the 14C at the W end of their conventual church and in 1448 work began on the massive W tower which was built by the parishioners and may have been the work of James Woderofe. After the Dissolution, the monastic church, E of the former tower, disappeared, and only a few remains are left. The parishioners, however, asked for the lantern tower which contained the bells to be kept, also the S aisle which had belonged to the abbey, and these requests were granted.

The E tower is now gaunt and open to the sky, yet is lofty and stately, with a 60ft tall E arch in its square base and large 14C windows in its two octagonal upper stages, which are buttressed on their four intermediate faces. The W tower rises to a height of 142ft. It has panelled polygonal buttresses and a large W doorway, flanked by niches, above which is a frieze of shields and a four-light W window. The pairs of belfry windows are set beneath embracing ogee hoodmoulds which terminate in finials. The S aisle (a reconstruction of 1544–60) is lit by Y-traceried windows. The N aisle was widened in 1440–45 by Sir John Clifton and has a fine array of seven Perpendicular and two Decorated windows. The clerestory has flushwork panelling and majestic windows with finials at their summits. The two-storeyed N porch has a parapet of quatrefoils. Its wide entrance arch has the Annunciation in its spandrels, above which is a frieze of shields in quatrefoils. Inside is a tierceron star-vaulted ceiling with bosses, carved with the Nativity, Resurrection and Ascension of Christ, and other subjects.

After the 14C and 15C exterior, the interior is a glorious surprise, for here we have grand Norman work. The nave is tall and majestic, yet tasteful work of this century has made it a homely and comfortable place of worship. The bold Norman six-bay nave arcades have sturdy piers and a variety of mouldings round the arches. Three more arches flank the chancel but on the S side two at the E are blocked. Above are sets of Norman triforium arches and then the 15C clerestory which provides a pleasing contrast. The nave, which is 112ft long and 65ft high, is crowned by a single hammerbeam roof. There are angels at the base of the arch braces, on the hammerbeams and on the cornices, and some 45 bosses. The wide N aisle roof is also a single hammerbeam, but this roof is panelled too and its E bays form a canopy of honour over what is now the Lady chapel. Here may be seen parts of the old organ gallery remodelled as communion rails, and a fine candelabrum presented in 1712. The 15C font stands at the W end of the aisle. It is a good example of the East Anglian pattern, with the four Evangelists round the bowl, alternating with angels bearing shields with the emblem of the Trinity, the Blessed Sacrament and the three crowns of Ely. There are lions and wodewoses round the stem. The tall font cover was designed by Cecil Upcher and made in 1962. The organ gallery at the W end was erected during a restoration in 1901–05. It houses one of Norfolk's finest organs, built by James Davis in 1793. In the tower above is a fine ring of ten bells. The E end has no window; it is simply a wall against which has been placed Sir Ninian Comper's sumptuous and substantial reredos—a mass of carving and a blaze of colour, blue and gold predominating. Two rows of figures beneath intricate Gothic canopies flank a central figure of Christ in Majesty, with the Virgin and Child beneath. Projecting from it is a tester, forming a canopy over the high altar. Above this is a beam with the Rood group. The reredos was Wymondham's First World War memorial. On the S side of the sanctuary is part of a terracotta monument which now serves as a sedilia. This is beautiful Renaissance work and may be from the tomb of Eligius Ferrers, the last abbot of the monastery, who died in 1548. There are various memorials on the walls, including two noteworthy ones to John Drake (died 1767) and his wife Sarah (died 1793) in the S aisle.

OXFORDSHIRE

Part Home Counties, part Midlands, Oxfordshire's character is diverse and not easy to define. Oxford is undoubtedly the chief place in the county, yet its influence on the architecture of the area has been less than might be supposed. The city is dominated by the University, and the University has been, architecturally at least, introspective and conservative for long periods of its history. Oxford University is the oldest in England; it had its origins in the 13C. Oxfordshire traditionally straggled in several directions, with Oxford as its centre. Its S boundary was the wandering River Thames. In 1974 the county was much enlarged when a great tract of land S of the Thames was severed from Berkshire. But for the old county, Oxford was the pivot: to the SE is a long stretch of the Chilterns with Thame in the N and Henley in the S; to the NE is the Otmoor level, ending at Bicester; to the N, the Cherwell Valley leads to Banbury; and to the NW and W are the Cotswolds, with Burford and Chipping Norton as the chief towns. In its demand for building stone, however, Oxford did reach out into the county. Taynton and Burford supplied the best stone, a grey limestone. To the N, a rich brown ironstone predominates. From Stonesfield came limestone roof-slates, much prized for Oxford buildings, but unobtainable since 1909. In the Chilterns, flint was abundant and found widespread use. Oxfordshire provides examples of every style of architecture from pre-Conquest times to the present, but no characteristics. Langford for pre-Conquest, Iffley for Norman, Dorchester Abbey for Decorated, and so on, but nothing which can be identified as uniquely or typically 'Oxfordshire'.

Oxfordshire's major pre-Conquest remains are the tower and sculptures of Langford, and the tower of St. Michael-at-the-North-Gate, Oxford. The Oxford tower is of typical pre-Conquest shape and ornament: tall, unbuttressed, rubble-built, and with two tiers of twin openings high up in each face. The lower part of a pre-Conquest tower survives at Caversfield; North Leigh's W tower was a late pre-Conquest central tower; and at Bampton, the central tower was the pre-Conquest W tower. Waterperry has a pre-Conquest chancel arch partly filled by a 14C arch. For the Norman period there is much more to see, though no other churches approach Iffley in completeness and quality of decoration. In Oxford the W doorway of St. Ebbe's has survived, and St. Cross has a plain chancel arch; but the main survival is the crypt of St. Peter-in-the-East. It is an evocative place, with stocky columns and low, groin-vaulted roofs. In NE Oxford, St. Andrew's, Headington has a fine chancel arch, and in the SE, St. James's, Cowley has a reset S door and the capitals and responds of the Norman chancel arch, which have retained their original coloured patterning of spirals and lozenges. Similar to Iffley in arrangement, but earlier and plainer, are Cassington (which has a good corbel table) and Stanton Harcourt (though the chancel is 13C and there are later additions). Cuddesdon was cruciform from its first building: a good W door and the tower arches survive. The simplest Norman form, aisleless and terminated by an apse, survives at Swyncombe (with some 19C alterations) and at Checkendon, where there is a fine compartmental interior. Of the old church of Heythrop, the chancel survives as a mortuary chapel. Many churches have Norman carved tympana: at Middleton Stoney and Brize Norton the Tree of Life is portrayed, and at Fritwell this motif is flanked by beasts. Kencot has Sagittarius hunting a monster, and Church Hanborough shows St. Peter, the *Agnus Dei* and the lion of St. Mark.

In the SW, a group of churches—Langford, Little Faringdon and Kelmscott—has Transitional arcades: the arches still round, but the capitals Early English, with stiff-leaf. At Fulbrook the process is more advanced: the arches are pointed. A little Purbeck marble was being used at this period, and can be seen as shafts in some of the chancel windows of Ipsden, and in the tower arches of Iffley. There is not much of the Early English period in Oxford: the N arcade of St. Peter-in-the-East; fine high arcades and several single and grouped lancets at St. Giles's, and the chancel of St. James's, Cowley. There are few complete churches of this period, but many buildings were extended and remodelled. At Thame, the chapel of the Prebendal House, near the church, was restored in the early 20C. It is virtually unaltered from c 1250. Toot Baldon and Stonesfield (though spoilt by a N aisle of 1876) are substantially Early English. The impressive cruciform church at Witney is Early English (with later additions). It has a tower topped by an imposing spire with large pinnacles and gabled lucarnes. The spire is close in style to that of Christ Church Cathedral, but grander in scale. Thame is cruciform and substantially Early English, but altered later; and Bampton is cruciform also, with attractive groups of triple lancets and a tower and spire of imaginative design, with corner statues replacing pinnacles. The most impressive Early English bellcote—a massive double example which needed 17C buttresses to prop it up—is at Forest Hill. Among Early English chancels Langford and Stanton Harcourt are outstanding.

The chancel of Great Haseley spans the late Early English, Geometrical and early Decorated periods, and has an impressive E window. The finest Geometrical windows are in Merton College chapel, 1290–96. They are almost a textbook of the style, with a variety of tracery motifs in the side windows, and a huge seven-light E window. There is not much of the Decorated period in Oxford (the spire of St. Mary the Virgin is 14C but was twice restored, quite drastically, in the 19C). In the county, however, the story is quite different. If Merton's chapel is the textbook of Geometrical tracery, Dorchester Abbey is the place to study Decorated windows. The pre-Conquest cathedral (the See was transferred to Lincoln after the Conquest) became an Augustinian abbey in 1170. The chancel was rebuilt in the 14C on a magnificent scale, glorious and original Decorated tracery filling the windows rather than being confined to the heads. This is remarkable, but the decoration of the tracery with figures is astonishing. The N window is populated by a complete Tree of Jesse (who lies on the sill). Only the Virgin and Child, which was at the top, has gone. The E window has figures illustrating the Passion and Resurrection (William Butterfield restored the head of the window in 1846–53). The S window is late Decorated, almost Perpendicular. On the transom are saints and monks bearing the bier of St. Birinus (whose relics were brought here in 1225). There are also splendidly canopied sedilia and piscina, with—an unusual feature—windows behind them. Decorated windows with figures incorporated into the tracery are found also at Bloxham (N aisle W window) and Ducklington (N aisle E window). The N aisle of Ducklington was rebuilt in the mid-14C as a chantry chapel, with fine tracery and tombs of the founders under ogee-arched canopies, richly decorated with figures and foliage. There are few substantially Decorated churches. The best is probably Cropredy, but even here the tower, porch and S aisle are Perpendicular. Some fine towers and spires were built in this period: Adderbury and Bloxham are notable, and others are Cassington and Newington. At the base of Bloxham's tower, over the W door, is a sculpture of the Last Judgement. There are elaborately carved piscina, sedilia and an Easter sepulchre at Piddington.

In the 15C several Oxford colleges built chapels in Perpendicular style, first New College, then All Souls', and finally Magdalen. They all adopted the T-plan which had evolved at Merton; All Souls' has an original reredos of many canopied tiers which entirely fills the E wall; New College's reredos is mostly 19C, having been mutilated in the late 18C; Magdalen's is a 19C creation. The statues in all of them are 19C. At Magdalen, too, the tall and striking bell tower was built. It impresses by its height and delicacy; Merton's (completed in the 15C) by its massiveness and strong detailing. At St. Mary the Virgin, the nave and chancel were rebuilt in Perpendicular style. Outside Oxford, the best Perpendicular work is perhaps the chancel of Adderbury, rebuilt in the early 15C. Richard Winchcombe, who later built the Divinity School in Oxford, was the mason, and he was probably responsible for the Wilcote chapel at North Leigh, a work of very high quality. Winchcombe may also have designed the Milcombe chapel at Bloxham, striking with its tall windows, whose mullions and transoms extend over the walls in a grid pattern. At Stanton Harcourt is the less elaborate Harcourt chapel, built c 1470, perhaps by William Orchard, who has been suggested as the mason of Magdalen College. Substantially 15C churches can be found at South Leigh and Ewelme. In the W the Cotswolds rise, and the area shared in the wool wealth of the late medieval period. Grand additions were made to several churches: Burford and Chipping Norton are the chief examples. Chipping Norton's nave was rebuilt c 1485, with a 'Cotswold' window over the chancel arch. At two churches, new naves were provided, the piers having the pronounced concave mouldings which are a feature of 15C Gloucestershire. The churches are at Church Hanborough (c 1400) and Eynsham (c 1490). Burford and Church Hanborough have Perpendicular spires, and another fine example is at Kidlington.

The Gothic style persisted in Oxfordshire until the middle of the 17C. In the University it was deliberately maintained as the traditional way of building. In the 1660s, the remarkable fan-vault of Brasenose chapel was being erected at the same time as Sir Christopher Wren was designing the Sheldonian Theatre in the Classical style. Wadham chapel (1610–13) is still completely Perpendicular, but the window tracery of Oriel, University, Lincoln and Brasenose contain oval lights and other elements which show that the designers were losing their way somewhat. Even when such a non-Gothic feature as the S porch of St. Mary the Virgin was added in 1637, a fan-vault was provided. Several country churches had towers rebuilt in the 16C and 17C in Perpendicular style, using flint and stone in chequer patterns: Henley-on-Thames (early 16C), Dorchester (1602) and Warborough (as late as 1666). At Deddington the tower was being rebuilt after 1634, was interrupted by the Civil War, and was completed in the same style in 1685. The N porch is domed and fan-vaulted in a style close to the vault of the hall staircase at Christ Church, 1640. At Burford the chapel of the Priory is of 1662, and shows the same confused approach to Gothic as some of the 17C Oxford college chapels.

When the Classical style arrived in Oxford, it produced two buildings of strength and boldness: Trinity College chapel and All

Saints' Church (now Lincoln College Library). The designer of Trinity, built in 1691–94, is not known; All Saints' was probably the design of Henry Aldrich, Dean of Christ Church. It was built in 1706–08. The chapel of Queen's, part of the impressive Classical Front Quad, was built in 1714. The architect is not known but Hawksmoor has been suggested. It is remarkable that none of these three accomplished Classical buildings can be attributed with certainty. After Queen's there is no important ecclesiastical architecture in Oxford until the 19C. Outside Oxford, there are some notable Classical buildings, of which the chapels of Cornbury Park by Hugh May (c 1677) and Blenheim Palace by Nicholas Hawksmoor (1726–31) are outstanding. North Leigh has a N aisle in Tuscan style (c 1700) by Christopher Kempster, one of Wren's masons at St. Paul's Cathedral. In 1764 Lord Harcourt and James 'Athenian' Stuart designed the church in Nuneham Park, Nuneham Courtenay, more for picturesque effect than for practical convenience. It is a domed temple flanked by porticoes, one blank, on either side. Banbury Church was rebuilt by S.P. Cockerell from 1790, but it did not receive its striking W front, a semicircular portico with a round tower rising from it, until 1818–22. Cockerell's son, C.R. Cockerell, was the architect. John Yenn rebuilt the tower at Woodstock in 1785. The tower of Benson is an 18C mixture of styles, for the base was rebuilt in Classical style in 1765–71, and the top was added in Gothic in 1781. In 1789 Mapledurham House received a Gothic chapel, and in 1796–1800 the chapel at Stonor Park was remodelled internally. Both are in the flimsy Gothic of the 18C. In Oxford, the pre-Victorian 19C produced two churches, one proudly Classical, the other self-consciously and oddly neo-Norman. The Classical church, St. Paul's, is now a restaurant. It is of 1836 by H.J. Underwood, and has a badly-weathered fluted Ionic giant portico. St. Clement's, 1828 by D. Robertson, has extraordinary, over-sized Norman windows. There is better Gothic at Churchill (1826) by James Plowman: a competent 14C and 15C design with an ambitious W tower, a scaled-down version of Magdalen College's tower. Inside, the Oxford theme continues, with a hammerbeam roof copied from the hall of Christ Church. Thomas Rickman, who gave the classifications by which Gothic architecture is still 'discriminated', designed Albury in 1830. It is not a very competent advertisement for his writings.

The first major Victorian Gothic Revival work in Oxford was Scott & Moffatt's N aisle of St. Mary Magdalen's (1842), built, like Scott's Martyrs' Memorial of 1841 which it faces, in late 13C style. In 1854 Scott rebuilt Exeter College chapel, a soaring, serious imitation of the Sainte Chapelle in Paris. Greater Victorian originality was provided by William Butterfield's polychrome Balliol chapel of 1856–57, built with bands of pink and brown stone, and the same architect's Keble College chapel, 1868–70. It is a *tour de force* as soaring as Scott's Exeter, and built mostly of brick. The decorative and polychrome possibilities of this medium are at Keble utilised to the full. The city was expanding in the later 19C and some memorable churches were designed. G.E. Street's St. Philip & St. James's, 1860–66, towers over the comfortable villas of N Oxford, with polychrome stonework and a bold tower and spire. Arthur Blomfield's St. Barnabas', 1869–89, presides over the poorer area of Jericho. The style is Italian Romanesque, with a prominent campanile. St. Frideswide's, Osney, is an eccentric building of 1870–72, with a short octagonal central tower. The architect was S.S. Teulon. Of later church and chapel building, several examples are outstanding: G.F. Bodley's St. John the

Evangelist's, Cowley, 1894–1902; Sir Thomas Jackson's chapel at Hertford College, 1908—not Gothic; and Temple Moore's Pusey House chapel of 1911–14. Outside Oxford, Scott designed the notable church at Leafield, c 1860–74. With its central broach spire and 13C details, it is remarkably similar in conception to Street's St. Philip & St. James, Oxford, built at about the same time. Scott's restoration of Adderbury is quite sensitive, but at Clifton Hampden (1844) it amounted to a virtually total rebuilding. It was, however, apparently an improvement on the old church, and has a striking spired turret. Butterfield built a brick church with his usual polychrome decoration at Horton-cum-Studley, 1867. Street's best church is perhaps Milton-under-Wychwood, 1854; others of interest are at Filkins, 1855–57 and Wheatley, 1856–68, which has a forceful W tower and spire. J.L. Pearson's fine church at Freeland, 1869–71, has a saddleback tower and apse.

The oldest fittings of interest, as elsewhere, are fonts. Dorchester Abbey has a late 12C lead font of the highest quality, featuring an arcade which houses seated Apostles. Hook Norton has a circular Norman font which bears primitive but animated figures of Adam and Eve and Zodiac signs. Warborough has a lead font, later than Dorchester's and less remarkable. St. Giles's in Oxford has a heavy 13C font with dogtooth decoration, and there are 13C fonts at Aston Rowant (of Purbeck marble) and Littlemore (where the bowl, from St. Mary the Virgin, Oxford, is decorated with trefoil arches and fleur-de-lis). The same century produced the Rood screen at Stanton Harcourt (c 1250), which is one of the oldest in the country. Chinnor's screen is of c 1300; and there are good 14C examples at Broughton (of stone) and Cropredy (part only survives, on the N side of the chancel). A 13C aumbry survives at Langford. 14C misericords remain in the chapel of New College, Oxford, and at Kidlington. Interesting fonts from the 14C occur at Shilton (with Passion scenes on the sides of the square bowl, and the Evangelists at the corners), Tadmarton (the bowl also square, with low-relief fleur-de-lis, intersecting tracery and roundels, and below, an octagonal stem decorated with trefoils), and at Wroxton. Burford's font was recut in the 14C with the Crucifixion and figures of saints.

The earliest wall paintings to survive are 13C, at Checkendon (Apostles, with Christ in Majesty above) and at Black Bourton. At South Newington there are remarkably fine and accomplished wall paintings of c 1330 in the chancel, depicting the Virgin, saints and martyrs. A later and less accomplished group of Passion scenes is in the nave. A very complete but faded 14C scheme survives at Chalgrove. Further medieval painting may be seen at Horley (a good 15C St. Christopher), North Stoke (14C), Combe (15C, including a Last Judgement over the chancel arch), Shorthampton (14C and 15C scenes), South Leigh (a restored 15C Last Judgement), Northmoor (14C figures) and Swalcliffe (a 14C St. Michael).

Late medieval fittings are more numerous. There are stone reredoses from the beginning of the 15C at Somerton and Bampton, which depict the Last Supper. Stone pulpits survive at Combe (late 14C), Cornwell and Shipton-under-Wychwood (both 15C). Church Hanborough has 15C traceried wooden panelling in its pulpit. Begbroke possesses a 15C aumbry. 15C screens extending across chancel and aisles survive at Ewelme and Church Hanborough, and at Kidlington screens divide the chancel and side chapels. Adderbury has a screen thought to be of Winchester craftsmanship. Charlton-on-Otmoor's early 16C screen is the most complete in

Oxfordshire, and retains its Rood loft. The colouring, though renewed in 1889, is thought to reproduce the original scheme. There are sets of 15C misericords in the chapels of All Souls' and Magdalen at Oxford, and among the best bench-ends are those in the chancel of Stanton St. John (early 16C), carved with human and monstrous heads, and at Wood Eaton (15C), with emblems of the Passion. Medieval brass eagle lecterns survive only at Cropredy (15C) and in the chapel of Corpus Christi College, Oxford (early 16C). Bampton has a fine 15C Easter sepulchre. At Sandford-on-Thames there is an early 15C alabaster relief of the Assumption, and Yarnton has four 15C alabaster panels depicting the Magi, the Betrayal of Christ, the Carrying of the Cross and the Pietà. Notable late medieval fonts are found at Ewelme (with a towering oak cover), Church Hanborough and Taynton.

Rycote Chapel has notable 17C fittings, especially two large, special pews and an altarpiece. They are not from one scheme. The chapel at Water Eaton has fittings mostly of the 17C, including a screen. Yarnton's Spencer chapel of 1611 is enclosed by elaborate Jacobean screens. In Oxford, almost every college chapel has a W screen dividing it from the antechapel. The earliest is at Wadham, c 1613, and Lincoln's may date, with the other furnishings, from the 1630s. The screen of Brasenose, mostly reconstructed in the 19C, dates from the 1660s. Corpus Christi, Jesus and Oriel have late 17C screens. Of the many 17C pulpits, there are notable examples at Horspath, where the spaces under the arches are inlaid with perspective views; and at Towersey, where the spaces have foliage and scrolls. Cassington and Merton have 17C choirstalls which were brought from Oxford in the 19C. Much of the woodwork at Wroxton (16C and 17C) is a 19C insertion, too. Late 17C furnishings may be seen in the chapel of Cornbury Park, and in the chapels of Trinity and University Colleges at Oxford. Also in 17C Oxford, a veritable flight of eagles appeared on chapel lecterns, at Magdalen, Balliol and Exeter in the 1630s, Oriel in 1654, Queen's in 1662 and Wadham in 1691. Brasenose and University Colleges received theirs in the early 18C and St. John's acquired one as late as 1773.

Blenheim Palace's chapel has an early 18C character, but this is due mostly to Sir Thomas Jackson's alteration of the 1890s. The chapel of Queen's College, Oxford, has early 18C fittings contemporary with the building. Well-preserved 18C and early 19C interiors with box-pews, triple-decker pulpit and W gallery are at Chislehampton, Wheatfield and Widford. Fittings of similar date remain at Short-hampton. L.N. Cottingham provided the chapel of Magdalen College, Oxford, with many new fittings in 1829–34. In the Victorian period, Sir Gilbert Scott designed most of the furnishings for his new chapel at Exeter College (1854–60; where there is also a tapestry of the Adoration of the Magi by Sir Edward Burne-Jones, 1890) and for his new chancel at Clifton Hampden, which was reconstructed in the 1840s as a burial chapel for G.H. Gibbs and where only the reredos (made in 1873 by Clayton & Bell to Charles Buckeridge's design) is later. A fine font and reredos by William Butterfield may be seen at Horton-cum-Studley. He also designed the pulpit and E end tiles at Dorchester Abbey and the furnishings in the chapel of Keble College, Oxford, where, however, they are pushed into insignificance by the richness of the decoration. J.L. Pearson's Freeland is as notable for its unchanged interior as it is for its exterior. There are font, pulpit and wrought-iron Rood screen, an alabaster reredos and wall paintings in 13C style. At Middleton Stoney the reredos, pulpit and choirstalls were designed by G.E. Street. Henry Woodyer provided the bold Early English-style screen at Toot Baldon, 1865.

The most remarkable 19C decorative schemes, apart from that at Keble College, are found in the 18C college chapels of Pembroke and Worcester. At Pembroke C.E. Kempe introduced a lush neo-Renaissance scheme in 1884. William Burges, 20 years earlier, had 'hotted up' James Wyatt's cool, Classical chapel at Worcester College with Italianate decoration of the walls and ceiling, an inlaid floor, and a delightful menagerie of small carved animals on the bench-ends. Much of Sir Arthur Blomfield's Romanesque and Italianate decoration survives in St. Barnabas' Church, Oxford.

20C fittings include various works by Sir Ninian Comper: an altar at Ewelme in 1902, a pulpit at Iffley in 1907 and the gilded baldacchino of 1937 in the chapel of Pusey House, Oxford, which strikes a strident note among Temple Moore's quieter furnishings of 1911–14. St. Margaret's, Oxford has a remarkably large and ornate reredos of 1908 by Cecil Hare. Lawrence Dale designed the screen and Rood loft at Horley, 1949.

The pre-Reformation stained glass of Oxfordshire has fortunately been recorded in detail by Dr Peter Newton in the 'Corpus Vitrearium'. Outside Oxford, there are numerous fragments, mostly tracery lights, 14C and 15C in the main, but a few from the 13C. Oxford's college chapels, on the other hand, contain a wealth of stained glass of all periods, including parts of original medieval schemes and much 17C glass. The earliest medieval glass in Oxfordshire includes four late 13C panels in St. Michael-at-the-North-Gate, Oxford (see gazetteer), which are almost contemporary with the windows in Merton's chapel (c 1295); and a roundel of c 1250 in Dorchester Abbey, showing St. Birinus receiving his cross-staff from Pope Honorius (N aisle E window). Dorchester also has good 14C glass in its chancel, especially in the E window and in the N (Tree of Jesse) window, whose iconography is complemented by the tracery and carved figures. From the 14C also there is interesting glass at East Hagbourne (including an attractive Virgin and Child and Nativity), Beckley (including a St. Edmund), Chinnor (St. Lawrence and St. Alban and parts of a Corporeal Acts of Mercy scheme), Asthall (heraldry), New College's chapel at Oxford by Thomas Glazier, c 1380–86; Biblical figures), and in the Latin chapel of Christ Church Cathedral. Kidlington has surviving 13C–15C glass collected into the chancel windows (in 1829). Yarnton has a good collection of 14C–17C panels but they are mostly from elsewhere and were installed by Alderman William Fletcher in 1813–16. Mapledurham has some 14C and 15C figures in its E window. Begbroke has 15C fragments and Flemish roundels of the 16C and 17C, all given in the 19C, as at Yarnton, by Alderman Fletcher. The antechapel of All Souls', Oxford, has mid-15C glass by John Glazier, skilfully restored by Clayton & Bell in 1876–79. St. Michael-at-the-North-Gate in Oxford has a rare 15C lily Crucifixion. Further good 15C glass may be seen at Burford, Combe and Shiplake, where five windows from St. Bertin's at St. Omer, France, were bought by the incumbent and installed in 1828 and 1830.

In Oxford, the early 16C windows of Balliol were reused in William Butterfield's chapel of the 1860s, as were 16C windows in the early 18C Queen's chapel. Oxford is especially rich in glass of c 1620–40, the work mostly of Bernard and Abraham van Linge. Bernard van Linge did windows at Wadham (1622) and the side windows at Lincoln (1629–30). The E window, in Flemish style, may be his also.

Abraham van Linge did windows at Balliol (N side of chapel, 1637), Queen's (1635) and University College (1641), his finest work in Oxford. Other early 17C windows, probably by Robert Rudland of Oxford, 1616, are in Wadham (side windows), and at Magdalen the antechapel is filled with remarkable grisaille windows probably by Richard Greenbury, 1632. There is some interesting 18C glass, mostly at New College, where the S windows are by William Price, 1735–40, and the N windows by William Peckitt of York. New College also has Sir Joshua Reynolds's noteworthy W window. There is another Peckitt window, the Presentation of Christ in the Temple, in Oriel chapel, 1767. Queen's has early 18C glass by Joshua Price in the E window. The chapel of Stonor Park has glass of 1800 by Francis Eginton.

The main 19C designers and firms are well-represented throughout the county. John Hardman & Co. provided two windows at Dorchester (S choir aisle) and two at Henley (N chapel), and also executed A.W.N. Pugin's window for Danesfield (Buckinghamshire), which was installed in Sacred Heart Church, Henley, in 1936. Hardman also made two windows to Pugin's designs for St. Mary the Virgin, Oxford, and provided windows in Magdalen chapel (1857–60) and All Souls' chapel (W window, 1861). Clayton & Bell appear in several places, notably in J.L. Pearson's Freeland (1869–71), G.E. Street's Filkins (1855–57; E windows), and in Oxford at Exeter chapel, St. Edmund Hall chapel (side windows), St. Mary the Virgin (Keble window), St. Thomas's (N aisle E window), and St. Philip and St. James's (apse and aisle windows). Morris & Co.'s—mostly Burne-Jones's—windows are at St. Edmund Hall (1865, E window), the cathedral, and Manchester College (1893–98), all in Oxford, and outside at Bloxham (E window, 1869), Bicester (E window of S chapel, 1866) and Lewknor (chancel NE and SE windows). Henry Holiday designed the windows of Worcester's chapel (1864–65, made by Lavers & Barraud) and all the glass in the chapel of Summerfields School, Oxford, 1895–1914. Alexander Gibbs provided windows for Keble chapel, Oxford, and excellent ones for William Butterfield's Horton-cum-Studley, 1867. Butterfield himself designed the rose window in the chancel of Dorchester, 1847–48, which was executed by Michael O'Connor; and O'Connor designed the E window in University College's chapel, 1864. Thomas Willement did much work in Oxfordshire, including the chancel windows at Forest Hill, 1847. James Powell & Sons provided stained glass for the chapel of Trinity College, Oxford. Work by C.E. Kempe may be seen in the chapels of Pembroke and St. John's (E window), and outside Oxford at Burford and Cuddesdon. Broughton has a good chancel S window by Burlison & Grylls. Finally, in the antechapel at Wadham College, Oxford, there is work of 1838 onwards by Betton & Evans of Shrewsbury, designed by John Bridges.

In the 20C, there is a big window by Sir Ninian Comper at Pusey House (1937). More recently, John Piper and Patrick Reyntiens provided windows for Pishill (1967), Nettlebed (1970), Sandford-on-Thames (1974) and the chapel of Nuffield College. At Checkendon there is a window by Laurence Whistler, 1960, not stained but engraved.

The Oxford colleges are so rich in monuments that only a few general points can be made here. The more prominent ones are noticed in the gazetteer. It must suffice to say that three college chapels, Magdalen, Merton and New, are particularly rich in medieval brasses; that the antechapels of many chapels contain numerous memorials, mostly wall tablets of the 16C to the 20C, and that they are characterised by a restraint which kept them small in scale. The same applied to the city's churches; the best series is in the University Church. Mention should be made of one special memorial: St. Frideswide's shrine in the cathedral, a late 13C canopied tomb-chest, reconstructed in the late 19C. For ostentation and splendour in monuments, the visitor must look beyond Oxford. There is a particularly fine monument of c 1280 to a knight at Dorchester (S choir aisle). Dorchester has other medieval monuments, including a 14C judge, probably John de Stonor; an alabaster effigy of a knight of c 1400 on a tomb-chest; and the 14C shrine of St. Birinus, reconstructed in the 20C. Another 14C shrine, that of St. Eadburg, survives at Stanton Harcourt. Broughton is good for medieval monuments, including John de Broughton, early 14C, in a carved recess, all overpainted in 1846; a noble brass figure of Lady Philippa Bishopsden, and two alabaster figures on a chest, seemingly husband and wife, but actually an early 15C lady and a late 15C knight. The 14C effigy of a lady lies in a recess at Asthall. At Northmoor, figures in recesses are topped by traces of wall paintings showing the souls being borne to Heaven. In Ewelme Church, the alabaster effigy of Alice, Duchess of Suffolk (died 1475), who was related to the Yorkist kings, bears the insignia of the Garter. Medieval brasses include fine examples to Sir Robert Bardolf (died 1395) in the S aisle at Mapledurham and to Lord Robert de Grey (died 1387) at Rotherfield Greys, and groups at Chinnor (14C and 15C) and Ewelme (15C and 16C).

The earliest Renaissance monument is of 1559, to Lord Williams of Thame in St. Mary's, Thame. One of the finest is the free-standing Tanfield monument of 1628 at Burford (where there is a good collection of monuments from the 15C to the 17C). Further fine 17C monuments are at Rotherfield Greys—one to the Knollys family, 1605 with later additions, whose canopy is supported by six marble columns; at Yarnton (where two are by Jasper Hollemans and John Nost); Brightwell Baldwin (to the Stone family, c 1670); at Spelsbury (to the Lee family, later Earls of Lichfield, in a series which extends into the 18C); at Wroxton (to the Pope family, Earls of Downe); at Great Milton; and at Swinbrook, where two large monuments to the Fettiplace family each have three shelves of semi-reclining effigies.

In the early 18C came some big Baroque monuments, but none quite so overwhelming as the Duke of Marlborough's (by William Kent and J.M. Rysbrack) at Blenheim Palace. Bicester has some interesting 18C monuments. Stanton Harcourt, where there is a fine series of monuments from the 15C to the 19C, has one 18C memorial with an epitaph by Alexander Pope and another which is attributed to James 'Athenian' Stuart. Notable too are William Tyler's monument (to Henry Keene's design) to the third Earl of Lichfield (died 1772) at Spelsbury, featuring a cherub clambering in an oak tree, and John Bacon's to Sir John Morton (died 1780) at Tackley, showing an accomplished figure of Justice. The Earl of Guilford (better known as the Prime Minister, Lord North), has a monument at Wroxton which depicts Britannia and a lion. Substantial in scale is Sir Francis Page's monument at Steeple Aston, by Henry Scheemakers, 1730. Page was a judge and is shown reclining in full legal robes. Monuments by Peter Scheemakers are at Wheatfield (1739) and Hampton Poyle (1742). At Mongewell, John Sanders (died 1731) is shown lounging against a tomb and a pyramid, wearing a turban.

In 1834, Sir Francis Chantrey was responsible for the monument to Mary Boulton (died 1829) at Great Tew, which shows a pensive figure on a couch. 19C memorials, however, increasingly revived medieval styles. Thomas Knowles's monument to Alderman William Fletcher (died 1826) at Yarnton comprised a brass on a tomb-chest. There are two recumbent effigies at Stanton Harcourt, one of which is of Archbishop Harcourt of York (died 1847). Sir Gilbert Scott designed the monument to G.H. Gibbs at Clifton Hampden. Another eminent Victorian designer, William Morris, was commemorated in a monument of 1896 by Philip Webb at Kelmscott. Finally, Sir Joseph Boehm designed a good effigy of Sir Edward Jodrell (died 1882) at Lewknor.

Among Oxfordshire's historical associations, John Hampden, the 17C parliamentarian, was born and buried at Thame. Sir Winston Churchill was born at Blenheim Palace and is buried at nearby Bladon. Cardinal Newman built the church at Littlemore, outside Oxford, and made the beginnings of an informal Anglican community there, before his secession to Rome in 1845. William Morris, the 19C designer, lived at Kelmscott, which gave its name to his famous private press. Rare dedications are of St. Eadburg, a 7C abbess, at Bicester (and she is remembered too in the name of Adderbury—'Eadburg's burh'); St. Britius, St. Martin's successor at Tours in the 4C, at Brize Norton; St. Kenelm, a 9C Mercian prince, at Enstone and Minster Lovell; and St. Etheldreda, the 7C foundress of Ely Abbey, at Horley.

Adderbury, *St. Mary the Virgin*. A big medieval church with a tall spire. It is less grand than nearby Bloxham, which has carving by the same unknown 14C sculptor. Although much restored in the 19C, its spaciousness and details are impressive.

The W tower was an addition of the early 14C. It is sturdy, of four stages, and has belfry windows with intersecting tracery. The termination is rather abrupt, though softened by a parapet of open trefoils and by large gargoyles. Above rises the octagonal spire, not too tall, with lucarnes and corner pinnacles. The spire was twice rebuilt, first in the 17C, when it collapsed, and again in the mid-18C after damage in an earth tremor. The W door preserves original 14C ironwork. Also in the 14C the aisles were rebuilt and widened. They too have carved friezes: on the S, grotesque animals and human heads; on the N, musicians with medieval instruments. In 1407–19 New College, Oxford rebuilt the chancel and vestry in sumptuous style. The mason was Richard Winchcombe and the stone was Taynton freestone. Buttresses rising to crocketed pinnacles separate the large Perpendicular windows. Over the E window are the head and arms of William of Wykeham (died 1404), founder of New College. The two-storey vestry on the N side has an attractive oriel window. During the 18C the church fell into extreme disrepair, and nearly all the tracery was removed from the windows in 1788. J.C. Buckler restored the chancel in 1831–34, in a successful and convincing way. In 1866–70 Sir Gilbert Scott restored the nave and aisles, using old views of Adderbury and existing work at Bloxham. The restoration was completed in 1886 by John Oldrid Scott.

The interior is big and broad. The four-bay nave has standard 14C piers and arches, but retains 13C capitals. The clerestory is late 14C, and vigorous stone and wooden corbels support a wooden roof of 1886. Just W of the crossing are carved lions' heads, which may have supported a beam. In the transepts remains of the 13C can be seen—

blocked lancets, especially in the E wall, and narrow blind arches flanking the N and S windows. When the aisles were widened, the W walls of the transepts were opened out and supported by double arches and a central, slim pier. Both piers have energetically carved capitals: on the S, knights' heads with interlaced arms, and on the N, the heads of four women. The transepts were heightened in the 15C. In the chancel, the roof corbels and hoodstops have heads of bishops and kings. At the E end, niches with crocketed pinnacles in canopied panels flank the window. The roof is 19C but the bosses are medieval, and include angels, a bearded man, an old woman blowing a fire with bellows, and a shepherd shearing sheep.

Adderbury preserves its 15C Rood screen. In the 17C the tracery was taken down and stored in the tower. It was reassembled in 1870 by Scott, who added the loft. The screen may have been made by the craftsmen who rebuilt the chancel. Buckler restored the small, canopied medieval reredos and filled it with figures. He added a stone altar, and removed a tomb which had badly damaged the piscina and sedilia, and elaborately reconstructed them from the fragments which remained. The choirstalls are 19C, with misericords on the S side of 1870, based on the E one which is said to be medieval. Those on the N side were added in 1905. In the transepts is panelling from pews of c 1650, which were dismantled in 1906. The N transept has a 17C communion table, removed from the chancel in 1831. The stone altar in the S transept is medieval and was found under a pew. It stands on 14C tiles recovered from the vestry floor. The font of 1831 is by John Plowman.

There are two 14C tomb-recesses in the aisles, and in the S aisle a cusped and gabled canopy, possibly restored. In the S transept is the monument to Thomas More (died 1586) and his wife. On the E wall of this transept is a brass to Jane Smith who died, apparently, on 30th February, 1508. The stained glass is 19C. In the E window are scenes from the life of Christ, with the childhood of Christ and the Annunciation below. The N transept E window is by Ward & Hughes, showing the Annunciation and the Adoration of the Shepherds; the N transept N window is by Clayton & Bell, 1877, depicting the life of Christ. In the S transept S window is glass of 1905 by C.E. Kempe, which shows Faith, Hope, Charity and Patience. The tower houses a carillon which plays a different melody every three hours during the day.

Banbury, *St. Mary.* Banbury's medieval church was demolished in 1790. To replace it, S.P. Cockerell designed a bold Classical building, which was built in 1790–97. His son, C.R. Cockerell, completed the portico and tower in 1818–22 to a modified design.

The church is built of a rich orange stone. The contrast with the green copper of the domes of the portico and tower is exotic. The combination of a tall, round tower with a semicircular portico is unusual. The portico has Tuscan columns supporting a triglyph frieze, which continues across the W wall of the church. From the dome, the tower rises in three stages. The belfry stage has elongated, engaged columns separating the windows. The parapet has a balustrade. The smaller top stage is domed. The side walls are rusticated and have simple round-headed windows.

The vestibule is circular and domed. Cockerell's interior was centrally planned, with 12 Ionic columns, eight of them supporting a shallow dome, and galleries on all four sides. The E gallery was removed in 1858, and in 1873 Arthur Blomfield created an apsidal chancel within the standing walls. The original pews (lowered in 1864) were saved from removal in 1987. An application to remove them was rejected by the ecclesiastical courts. An Act of 1790 had allotted rights to pews in perpetuity, and the descendants of some of the original owners objected to the removal. The pulpit is by Blomfield, 1864. Heaton, Butler & Bayne did the chancel painting, of Christ in Majesty, in 1876, and also installed the stained glass windows.

Blenheim Palace, *Chapel.* Blenheim Palace was conceived as a national monument to John Churchill, first Duke of Marlborough, and the chapel as a setting for the Duke's monument. The chapel makes no contribution to the remarkable Baroque ensemble designed by Sir John Vanbrugh with the assistance of Nicholas Hawksmoor, but is hidden away behind one of the colonnades flanking the palace's forecourt. The chronology of Blenheim Palace is briefly thus. After Marlborough's victory at Blenheim in 1704, Queen Anne granted him the royal manor of Woodstock and Parliament voted funds for the palace. Work went on until 1712 when the Duke and Duchess fell from favour and moved into exile. The funds were stopped; when work restarted in 1716 it was at the Marlboroughs' expense. The Duke was incapacitated by a stroke, the Duchess was in control, and Vanbrugh was dismissed. In 1722 the Duke died, leaving funds to the Duchess to complete the work. Hawksmoor was recalled, and the chapel was completed in 1726–31 to his designs. His design for the monument was rejected in favour of William Kent's, which was executed by Michael Rysbrack. In 1732 the Duchess wrote approvingly: 'The Chapel is finish'd and more than half the Tomb there ready ... in short everything that could do the Duke of Marlborough Honour and Justice. This is all uppon the wall of one side of the Chappel. The rest of it is finish'd decently, substantially and very plain'. She was thankful that her chapel contained none of the 'Wonderful Figures and Whirligigs I have seen Architects finish a Chappel withal, that are of no manner of Use but to laugh at'. It may however be admitted that 'Wonderful Figures and Whirligigs' are just what Kent provided in the extravagant monument to the Duke.

The chapel is a tall rectangular room painted in pale apricot with the architectural details and plasterwork picked out in white. It is lit by tall round-headed windows at the (ritual) E end and on the (actual) S side. The S windows are in a large round arch decorated, under the arch, with a band of coffering. An identical arch, in which the monument stands, answers it on the N side. The walls are embellished with fluted Corinthian pilasters, coats of arms, a sunburst with cherubs' heads over the altar, an elaborate frieze, and other enrichments. The ceiling has bands of plasterwork.

The monument, in white and patterned marble, is set against an obelisk of grey marble, and this is backed by a neutral marbled wall flanked by trophies. At the top of the main pile the Duke stands, in Roman costume. The seated Duchess gazes approvingly at him. Their two sons (who died young—the title descended through a daughter) accompany them. Below, angels recline against the sarcophagus, one trumpeting, the other sculpting the cartouche with a quill pen! At the base is a bas-relief of Marshal Talland's surrender to Marlborough at Blenheim. The furnishings, sensibly, do not compete with the monument for swagger. They were designed by T.G. Jackson in c 1890 in a late 17C style, replacing a remodelling of

S.S. Teulon of 1857–59, completed by David Brandon in c 1870. Jackson's pulpit is a charming wine-glass shape with a big, ogee-domed tester. There are two other monuments: a relief figure of the seventh Duke (died 1883) and a figure of Lord Randolph Churchill (died 1895), the father of Sir Winston.

Bloxham, *Our Lady of Bloxham.* Bloxham is one of the great medieval churches of Oxfordshire, with a proud, soaring spire, taller and finer than nearby Adderbury's. There are many similarities with Adderbury, and it is clear that the same group of masons worked on both churches. There is much vigorous carving on capitals, corbels and friezes, including a Last Judgement over the W door. Fragments remain of a 12C church, but the nave was rebuilt in the 13C, the chancel, aisles and N and S porches in the 14C, and the Perpendicular S chapel was added in the 15C. In the 15C also, the large E windows of the aisles were inserted, and the nave clerestory added. The N aisle has a mid-14C corbel table with vigorous carvings of men in combat, a pig and piglets, and various mythical animals. The best view of the exterior is from the churchyard to the E.

The tower looms over the main street. It was built in the early 14C. It has four stages, with triple-lancet belfry openings, the central one being a canopied niche. Above is an octagonal stage, decorated with a traceried band and carved heads of men and beasts. At the corners rise sturdy pinnacles, almost detached. Then the spire soars up to 198ft, with lucarnes at its base. The Last Judgement was added over the W door after the tower was finished. The doorway is decorated with leaves, birds, heads and ballflower, and the hoodmould features the 12 Apostles seated on thrones, with Christ presiding above amidst angels and the Instruments of the Passion, flanked by depictions of the saved and the damned.

The 13C nave is of four bays. At the S door, steps rise to an upper chamber above the porch, and then higher, to a second-floor room. The N aisle has interesting early 14C tracery, especially the W window, which has a curious and inelegant wheel design, with carved figures, including Christ at the centre. The N transept is entered by a double arch divided by a slender pier (cf. similar piers at Adderbury), the capital decorated with heads and shoulders with interlaced arms. In the chancel, rebuilt in the 14C, are reset fragments of the Norman church. The N door (to a vestry of 1866) has a richly decorated tympanum. The arches of the windows preserve, remarkably, Norman beakhead and other carving. The side windows have 14C tracery but the E window dates from G.E. Street's restoration of 1864–66. He also designed the piscina and sedilia. In the S aisle are vigorous corbels, two ladies' heads, a king and queen, and a bishop. The 15C S or Milcombe chapel is entered through two four-centred arches. The tall Perpendicular windows with panel tracery bathe the chapel in light. The E window has clear glass, in contrast to the opaque cathedral glass of the other windows. The panelling continues downwards from the windows, and at the E end is formed into a reredos with arched niches. The E window of the chapel, and that of the S aisle, have the remains of tall canopied niches on either side. The statues date from 1894. The chapel's mason is unknown; it is suggested that Richard Winchcombe, who worked at Adderbury, may have been responsible.

The font is 15C, an octagonal tub with Perpendicular tracery. It has a stocky 17C conical cover. 15C also is the Rood screen, of wood, five bays wide, with traceried heads. The lower panels have original painted figures of Doctors of the Church and symbols of the Evangelists, but the colouring of the top and the wooden cornice are modern. Street provided the pulpit, the choirstalls and the reredos, an over-elaborate concoction of stone, marble and Minton tiles, in 1866. In the N transept is a 17C table, an arched wooden reredos (war memorial) and an old wooden chest with two locks. There are fragments of a 15C Doom painting over the chancel arch, 16C scenes from the life of a martyr in the Milcombe chapel and a St. Christopher over the door in the N aisle. In the N aisle windows are pieces of 14C glass. There are several 19C and early 20C windows. The four-light E window is by William Morris and Edward Burne-Jones, 1869, the sky designed by Philip Webb. In the lower row of figures are St. Alban and St. Stephen, Kings Alfred and Louis, St. James, Bishop of Jerusalem, and St. Augustine, and St. Cecilia and St. Catherine. In the upper row are angels with censers, Gabriel and Raphael, St. Peter and St. James, Ezekiel and St. John the Baptist. In a dark window on the S side of the chancel, by C.E. Kempe, 1886, are Melchizedek and St. John the Baptist. Burne-Jones designed the tiny low-side window, a powerful depiction of St. Christopher, 1868. The N aisle E window, a memorial to the 1914–18 War, is by J.H. Dearle. It shows St. Denys, the Virgin and St. Martin (the figure by Burne-Jones), and, below, Galahad, St. George and St. Joan of Arc. In the Milcombe chapel are several monuments to the Thornycroft family, including the large monument by Andrew Carpenter to Sir John Thornycroft (died 1725). He reclines languidly under an obelisk enclosed in an arched and columned frame.

Burford, *St. John the Baptist.* Burford is a grand church mostly of the 15C, in a town which grew rich on the wool trade. The church, away from the main street and close to the river, has a commanding central tower and spire, and a splendidly ornate three-storey S porch. It was extensively restored by G.E. Street in the 1870s; William Morris's fears that it and other buildings might be ruined by over-restoration led him to found the Society for the Protection of Ancient Buildings. The Vicar, undaunted by Morris's criticisms, replied: 'The church, Sir, is mine, and if I choose to I shall stand on my head in it'.

It is an extensive building with many additions, but its basic shape is cruciform. Originally it was Norman, with a long low nave, tower and apse. Of the Norman building, the tower and the W wall of the nave survive. At the W end is a big round-headed doorway with orders of beakhead, zigzag and beading in the arch, the door still possessing delicate ironwork of the late 12C. The lower part of the central tower is clearly Norman, with single round-headed windows in the first stage, and above, a more complicated design of double openings under an arch with extensive zigzag, flanked by lower blank arcading. The course of rebuilding and enlargement can be described, but there is little external work to be seen, the whole fabric having been remodelled and consolidated in the 15C. First, in c 1200, a S aisle and transept were added. Then in the 13C a N transept was built, the S transept was enlarged, and the chancel was lengthened. In the churchyard to the SW, the merchants built a Guild chapel, detached and at an angle to the main fabric. In the 14C a chapel of St. Thomas was built W of the S transept. In c 1396 John Cakebred, a wealthy merchant, left money for the heightening of the tower. The belfry windows of the higher stage are an elegant design: under an ogee head are two cusped lights with a canopied niche between. The tall spire is octagonal, with tiny lucarnes at its base.

The top of the spire fell in 1707. The S porch was added after the middle of the 15C (since it bears a shield of the Earl of Warwick, who became Lord of the Manor in 1449). It is tall, and topped with crocketed pinnacles. The arched doorway is sharply pointed, and the wall surface is covered with deep-cut panel tracery, in which are set canopied niches and windows. The old statues in the niches—the Virgin, St. John the Baptist and St. John the Evangelist—were given new heads in 1962, sculpted by Edgar Frith and Vivienne Jenkins. Under the parapet is a frieze of angels bearing shields. Later in the century, the Guild chapel was added to the church, shortened at its W end but extended E to the S porch. In its N wall are still two original 13C lancets and a blocked, round-headed door. The S door is Early English, and has a relief of the Crucifixion, now much worn, above it. Four large 15C windows were inserted in the chapel's S wall with slender tracery and crenellated transoms. At the SW corner is a stair turret. Windows throughout the church were renewed in the 15C in Perpendicular style. A S chapel ('newly built' in 1486) was added to the chancel, also a vestry and chapel on the N side. The N transept was shortened, and a N aisle built. A clerestory was raised over the new arcade of the nave.

The porch is lined within with panel tracery and has a beautiful fan-vault. The nave is tall and light, and more light streams in through the Guild chapel. The five-bay arcades have quatrefoil piers. The hoodstops here, and in the clerestory and N aisle, have well-carved heads in early 15C dress, probably representing merchants who paid for the work and masons who executed it. The W window is large, with panel tracery. Over the tower arch can be seen outlines of two previous roofs. At the SW corner of the nave, beside the tower arch, is a puzzling stair turret, which breaks into both nave and aisle. It is thought to have been part of an earlier, pre-12C church. The tower arches are late 12C, elliptical and low. The masonry above has sagged visibly since the spire was added, and it is thought possible that the arches may have been reconstructed. NW of the tower are two later buttressing arches, and SW, on the N wall of the turret, is a blocked door to the former Rood loft. Under the tower can be seen blank arcading, Norman arches in two tiers, the openings mostly filled as a support for the spire. The only remaining part of the 12C S aisle and transept is the arch between them, in Transitional style. Capitals on the N side of the arch have stiff-leaf. Over the arch can be traced the low roof of the aisle. The 15C arches from the tower to the transepts are smaller replacements for 13C ones. The transepts have 13C remains: a piscina to the S, and to the N a blocked lancet can be seen in the NW corner. The 14C St. Thomas's chapel is raised over a crypt, and is reached by steps from the aisle. The chapel has a 14C piscina and a credence shelf. The chancel has a large, five-light E window flanked by niches containing statues of the Virgin and the Archangel Gabriel, 1901. 13C remains in the chancel include the double piscina with a shelf, all under a trefoiled arch, restored sedilia, and a (blocked) arch to the N chapel. The arches to N and S chapels are 15C. The N chapel has a niche in its E wall, rib-vaulted and with a squint to the altar. The Guild chapel, now the Lady chapel, opens from the S aisle by two arches. A window looks into it from the porch, strong evidence that the latter was built before the chapel was integrated into the church.

The earliest furnishing is a sculpture high up on the S side of the tower turret, a pre-Christian carving, perhaps representing Epona, a Celtic fertility goddess. It shows a horse-goddess and two male supporters with mask-like faces. The font in the NW corner could be a Norman bowl recut. It is round, and features St. Mary and St. John at the Crucifixion (S side); St. John the Baptist and St. Catherine (W side); St. Andrew (N side); the rest unrecognisable. On the lead top are Civil War graffiti. Leveller rebels were held in the church in 1649, and one carved 'ANTHONY SEDLEY, PRISNER, 1649'. G.E. Street made the pulpit (1878) out of medieval tracery panels. Some original colour remains. Close to the pulpit is a small nave chapel enclosed by a medieval wooden screen (the dado is 19C). It was originally Holy Rood chapel, then for long the pew belonging to Burford Priory, and from the 1870s, when Street restored it, St. Peter's chapel. The altar stands under a stone canopy. There is some medieval colour, but its roof was painted in 1877–78 under Street's direction. In 1878 a Rood painting by Clayton & Bell was placed over the tower arch. They also provided the high altar reredos, showing the Adoration of the Magi. The wooden screens to the N and S chapels are 15C; another 15C screen, with battlements, is in St. Thomas's chapel. The altar, reredos and stone screen of the Lady chapel were given in 1911 by J. Meade Faulkner and Sir John Noble (they gave the statues beside the high altar too). The work was designed by E.B. Hoare and sculpted by Esmond Burton. C.T. Cheatle added the statues in 1950. Meade Faulkner also presented the medieval altar frontals which are preserved in a case (behind a curtain) in the N aisle. In the N transept is the frame (made after 1660) and mechanism (renewed) of the clock which was formerly in the tower. In a glass case is a model of the interior arrangement of the church from 1827 until the 1870s.

Some fragments remain of 15C stained glass. In the tracery of the W window are pieces collected together in 1826–28, including St. George and the Dragon, St. Barbara, St. Margaret, and seraphim. The main part of this window is by C.E. Kempe, 1869. In the N transept N window is a 16C shield showing the arms of King Edward the Confessor, a late 15C female head inscribed 'sancta dei' and a mid-15C head of St. James the Great. The tracery work is mostly 19C. In the chancel E window are restored 15C canopies and 15C lights in the tracery, including St. John the Baptist, St. Barbara, St. Christopher, and Gabriel at the Annunciation. The rest of the glass in the E window is by John Hardman & Co., 1886. The N aisle windows are by Kempe, and so is the St. Thomas's chapel window. The S transept S window is of 1907 by Christopher Whall, and the windows of the Lady chapel are by F.C. Eden, 1939 and earlier.

The earliest surviving monument is a brass to John Spicer (died 1427) and his wife Alice at the E end of the nave, under the Rood which he had given. The kneeling figures remain, and an inscription recording their benefaction. In the S transept is a 15C tomb-chest, from which the brass has been lost. Three more unidentified tomb-chests are in the S chapel. In the Lady chapel are five chests to the Sylvester family, 1568–1626, starting with Edmund Sylvester. Not surprisingly, this part of the church was for long known as the Sylvester aisle. Paul Sylvester was the last to be buried here, in 1904. Also in the Lady chapel are a wall monument to John Osbaldeston (died 1624) and his wife, in brass; a tablet decorated with swags and fruit, to John Warren (died 1659), with female supporters of its pediment; and a grander memorial to Richard Sindrey (died 1661). In the N aisle, Edmund Harman (died 1569) is commemorated in a tablet which features, amazingly, American Indians, the earliest portrayal of this race in England, copied from a book of French proverbs of c 1540. Harman was barber to King Henry VIII, witnessed the King's will and was left a legacy by him. Below are rows of children. In the S chapel (once called the Bartholomew aisle) are several late 17C and early 18C wall monuments to the Bartholomew family. In St. Thomas's chapel is an old-fashioned monument to John Harris (died 1674), a painted half-figure in a Classical frame; and in the S transept a wall monument to Christopher Kempster (died 1715), with grieving putti. Finally, the grandest monument is to Lord Chief Justice Tanfield (died 1625) and his family. In 1628 the churchwardens repaired the N chapel and Lady Tanfield immediately commandeered it for her own use. The monument fills the chapel. It has been attributed to Gerard Christmas, and is an accomplished work. The effigies lie under an arched canopy, with corner obelisks and heraldry, supported by six columns of black marble. The monument is mostly of alabaster. At the head is the Tanfields' daughter Elizabeth, at the foot their grandson Lucius, second Lord Falkland. In the open basement is a carved skeleton, a grim *memento mori*. On the canopy, at the corners, are carvings of Virtues. Lady Tanfield added a long and tedious Latin inscription, lamenting that her husband had not been given a nobler burial place; she also added some equally tedious verses of her own composition. In the churchyard is the tomb of J. Meade Faulkner (died 1932), benefactor to Burford Church and a well-known writer.

In 1649 a group of Leveller mutineers was imprisoned in Burford Church by Oliver Cromwell. Several were shot in the churchyard on his orders. Speaker Lenthall, who opposed King Charles I in the House of Commons on the King's attempt to arrest the Five Members, lived in Burford, and died in 1662. He was buried in the N transept, but the stone is now lost. In his will Lenthall stipulated that the stone should bear two brief words only: *'Vermis sum'* (I am a worm [and no man]) from Psalm 22.

Chislehampton, *St. Katherine.* St. Katherine's was built in 1762 to replace a medieval chapel of St. Mary. It is a small and unpretentious building, which preserves its original fittings. The design, which has been attributed to Samuel Dowbiggin, includes some curious Classical details. The church was built at the expense of Charles Peers, a porcelain merchant from London, who also rebuilt Chislehampton House in 1768. One of his descendants, Sir Charles Peers, was Surveyor of the Fabric of Westminster Abbey. The church stands beside the drive to the house. It was declared redundant in 1977 and passed to the Redundant Churches Fund in 1978.

The church, whose exterior is stuccoed, is a rectangular building with slightly projecting chancel. The entrance, plainly moulded, is at the W end. The corners are boldly quoined, and are crowned above the parapet with stone urns. The gable ends in curious scrolly volutes at the top. Above rises an over-large turret of two stages, the lower a clock-stage framed with vermiculated quoins, and the upper an open arched stage. There are round-headed windows on the S side of the church only.

Inside, the windows on the S are balanced on the N by blank arches. Between them rise pilasters springing from brackets above the pews. The cornice breaks forward over the pilasters to suggest capitals. The chancel recess is framed by a segmental arch with keystone, supported by plain pilasters. The furnishings are well-made and restrained. They are exactly what is expected in an unaltered 18C church: box-pews, a triple-decker pulpit on the N wall, a W gallery on plain Tuscan columns, an altar rail of turned balusters enclosing the altar on three sides, and a wooden reredos with Commandment boards. The pulpit is, however, early 17C, saved perhaps from the earlier church. It is decorated with the usual blank arches. The reredos is enriched with Rococo garlands of flowers and ribbons; the higher central section has a broken segmental pediment flanked by volutes. Benches for children are provided at the sides of the altar rail. Three handsome brass chandeliers hang above the central aisle, and there are candle brackets on the walls and pulpit.

Cornbury Park, *Chapel*. Cornbury Park was for centuries a hunting lodge in the royal forest of Wychwood. After the Restoration in 1660, the rangership and house were granted to Edward Hyde, Earl of Clarendon, the king's chief minister. Clarendon obtained plans for the rebuilding of Cornbury from Hugh May. These included a chapel. Clarendon fell from favour in 1667 and went into exile; the house and chapel were completed by his son after 1677. The chapel, though externally plain, has the finest late 17C Oxfordshire interior, excluding college interiors. It projects from the S wing of the house into the courtyard, and has plain, round-headed windows, shallow niches at the altar end, and a projecting cornice.

The interior has the features and atmosphere of a college chapel, with its coved plasterwork ceiling and oak panelling and furniture. The chapel is entered under a gallery which is supported by columns of black marble with white capitals. Between the columns are gates and screens with inverted arch tops. The stalls are arranged in a single row along the walls, with benches in front, making a spacious 'nave'. There are carved bench-ends. The ceiling has an oval central section surrounded by palms, foliage and flowers. A balustraded rail surrounds the altar on three sides. Behind the altar is a carved reredos with coupled, fluted pilasters and festoons of flowers. It was made to contain a larger painting than the present altarpiece. Above are the arms of Clarendon, flaming urns and more festoons.

John Evelyn, the diarist, may have had a hand in the design, since he visited Cornbury with May in 1664, and wrote 'we design'd a handsom chapell'. There is, however, no conclusive proof that May's design was used when the chapel was eventually built.

Ewelme, *St. Mary the Virgin*. The church was mostly rebuilt in c 1432 by Alice Chaucer, Duchess of Suffolk. Alice was the granddaughter of Geoffrey Chaucer, the poet, and married William de la Pole, Earl of Suffolk (created Duke, 1448). Ewelme is notable for its woodwork, monuments and painted decoration, all carefully preserved during the Civil War in the 17C by the local Parliamentarian, Francis Martyn.

The exterior is unaccented. The low tower, heavily buttressed on its W side, is early 14C and survives from the previous church. It has Y-tracery in the belfry windows, and an inserted 15C W window. The 15C body of the church is built of stone and flint (set in a chequer pattern at the E end), with brick castellations. It has a continuous nave and chancel, flanked by aisles and a S chapel. Most of the windows are slightly arched and have bar-tracery, but those of the clerestory are square-headed and simpler. The N porch has original arches but was rebuilt in 1832; the S porch is original and oak-built, the side-lights traceried and the lower panels filled with brick in a herringbone pattern. The doors on the W and N sides of the church are 15C.

There is no chancel arch, so the arcades continue uninterrupted almost to the E end. The N arcade is more ornate, the spandrels being terminated by angels holding shields and a king's head. The E part of the S arcade continues this decorative scheme, but the rest is plainer, with blank shields as terminations. The S chapel (St. John's) is the chapel of the almshouses (which were founded in 1437). Under arches between it and the chancel are Chaucer monuments. The wall painting, an endless repetition of the IHS symbol, is 15C, but was much restored in 1843. Flanking the altar are empty canopied niches. The wooden roof is decorated with angels and a further outbreak of the IHS symbol.

On entering, the almost over-ornate font cover confronts the visitor. It was presented by the second Duke of Suffolk, probably in c 1485–91. Tiers of close-packed, gabled and crocketed arches tower up ten feet or more. The counterbalance is decorated with a Tudor rose. There is a similar cover at Ufford, Suffolk. The font is octagonal, carved with blank shields, on a base with blank tracery. The other nave furnishings are of 1832. 15C screens run across the church, dividing off the E parts. They are formed of many closely spaced uprights linked at the top with ogee arches. The screens were lowered in 1844 but restored to their original height in 1925. The S chapel has 15C tiles with heraldic devices, and an 'English altar' of 1902 by Sir Ninian Comper, with a fine frontal of saints and angels entwined with holly on a gold ground, and a reredos of a holly-twined Crucifixion. In the E window of this chapel are 14C and 15C stained glass fragments, mostly saints and heraldic roundels. The great E window of 1882 is by Clayton & Bell and shows the Crucifixion.

There are several brasses, notably that of Thomas Chaucer, the poet's son (died 1434) and his wife Matilda, on the tomb-chest under the arch between the chancel and the S chapel. There are two Rectors in the nave: John Bradstane (died 1458) and Henry Morecote (died 1467); and two Masters of the Hospital (William Branwhait (died 1498) and John Spence (died 1517)) in the S aisle. In the chancel are kneeling figures of Thomas Palmer (died 1599) and his wife. E of the Chaucer brass is the ornate tomb of Alice, Duchess of Suffolk (died 1475). Her recumbent effigy is on a tomb-chest which has been shortened: it is suggested that it was formerly free-standing. The effigy is stiff, of alabaster, and she wears the Garter on her sleeve. At the head is a rich canopy. On the chest, under canopies, are angels bearing shields. The base is open, and through the traceried arches a shrivelled, partly shrouded corpse can be glimpsed. Much of the original colouring of the monument survives. The tomb was inserted into a square-headed aperture, panelled and topped by a frieze of angels, quatrefoils and cresting. From it on each side rise four slender pinnacles topped by wooden statues of angels and monks. There are several other monuments and tablets, the most curious a memorial to Henry Howard (died 1647). From an urn, two angels haul his hefty shrouded figure heavenwards.

Jerome K. Jerome is buried in the churchyard here.

Iffley, *St. Mary the Virgin.* Iffley is a splendid Norman church, unchanged in plan and little altered in detail from when it was built, possibly by Robert de St. Remy in c 1175–82. The plan is of an aisleless nave, tower and chancel in line. There is much rich original carving, but some details derive from 19C restoration.

The W front is a fine 12C design, partly reconstructed in the 19C. The lowest stage has a doorway of many orders of continuous mouldings, including beakhead and zigzag, flanked by tall, narrow blank arches. The doorway's hoodmould has symbols of the Evangelists and signs of the Zodiac. Above, there is a round window with zigzag, by J.C. Buckler, 1858, but based on Norman evidence. In the gable there is an arcade of three windows, all recessed and with orders of beakhead and zigzag, and divided by paired shafts, with single shafts on the outsides. The gable was restored in 1823 by Robert Bliss, for in the 17C part of it had been destroyed, the side windows being cut off below the capitals. Bliss added the little blank window below the apex.

The nave has a W pair of Norman windows, original N and S doorways, and an E pair of three-light Perpendicular windows. The S doorway is more sumptuously decorated than the W one. There is a continuous inner order of a roll embellished with animal and other carvings, and two outer shafted orders of zigzag. The shafts have capitals of Samson and the lion, knights, a centaur with her offspring and animals fighting, symbolic of Good (right) and Evil (left). As is usual, the N doorway is relatively plain. The nave has a corbel table of squared blocks; only on the S side was any carving attempted. The battlemented S parapet is dated 1612. The nave roof was also lowered then; it was raised again in 1844 by R.C. Hussey.

The three-stage battlemented central tower is big and mostly unbuttressed. The lowest stage has Perpendicular N and S windows in the original openings. Above the plain middle stage, the belfry has pairs of widely spaced round-headed windows, separated by flat pilaster strips. The SW window alone has zigzag and beakhead carving. The corbel table, with small arches alternately round and pointed, has uncarved square blocks. There is a stair turret on the NW side. The chancel has one Norman W bay and a 13C E bay with single lancets and buttresses. At the E end the buttresses have angle-shafts. There was a 13C anchoress here called Annora, whose anchorage might have connected with the church through the blocked arch in the S chancel wall. It has been suggested that she paid for the 13C extension. The E gable has a reused small Norman window with zigzag.

The interior is narrow and compartmental. The two chancel bays have quadripartite vaults, the W one with zigzag. The 13C windows have internal shafts. The sedilia, piscina and aumbry are also 13C. The main interior features, however, are the two tower arches. All faces have zigzag, and there is also a floral design on the W side of both arches. The W sides additionally have a pair of octagonal Purbeck shafts.

There is 15C/16C stained glass in the nave windows. On the S side there are fragments including 15C heraldry of John, second Duke of Suffolk (see Ewelme). The N tracery lights have more medieval glass, mainly of angels. The E window is by Christopher Webb, 1932. The square 12C font has three original supports with spiral decoration and one of the 13C. The pulpit is by Sir Ninian Comper, 1907, and the arcaded reredos was installed by J.C. Buckler, 1864.

The sum of £107,000 was spent on restoration here in 1975–84. A plan for housing on the adjoining glebe (1989) is arousing much opposition.

S.C.H.

Langford, St. Matthew. Oxfordshire is not richly endowed in pre-Conquest or Saxo-Norman building and sculpture, and the tower and S porch carvings of Langford are perhaps the finest examples.

The church consists of nave and aisles, S porch, central tower and chancel. The tower has large and unusual double belfry openings which may date from just after the Conquest. They are round-headed and roll-moulded, and have semicircular shafts with acanthus bands in the place of capitals. There is a later corbel table above. The lower stages of the tower, presumably earlier than the belfry, have conventional pilaster strips and small round-headed windows (one on the N side is now covered by the 13C gabled tower stair). On the S side of the tower there is a low relief carving of two bearded men whose raised arms once supported a sundial. The aisles and S porch were added in c 1200. Two pre-Conquest sculptures were reset in the porch. On the E wall is a figure of Christ triumphant (the 'Langford Rood'), headless now, with outstretched hands, clad in a robe of which the carved folds are still visible at the sides. The relief over the S entrance has been wrongly reset. Christ's arms are reversed, and the Virgin and St. John face outwards. The nave and aisles have a variety of windows. There are lancets at the W end; the windows W of the N and S doors are late 15C, square-headed. E of the doors are Decorated windows, that on the S having Reticulated tracery. Next to this is a small round-headed lancet. The Norman buttresses at the W end are topped with pencil-like 16C pinnacles. Two flying buttresses of 1574 (according to an inscription) prop up the N wall. The chancel is a grand yet rather charming 13C addition. It was once probably longer, since the priest's door is now at the E end of the S side, and the windows of the E end are badly reassembled. The windows are as unusual as the belfry openings (though Wyck Rissington, Gloucestershire has similar examples). They are paired lancets topped by concave-sided lozenges, a primitive essay in plate tracery which escapes ugliness through the slight, whimsical ogee effect of the window arches, emphasised by the stringcourse. The priest's door is set in a tall, shallow gable. The chancel was badly restored in 1829, when the lozenges were blocked and a flat roof installed, by Richard Pace; Ewan Christian returned it to its former state in 1864.

The nave arcades of c 1200 still have high, round piers and round arches, but the details are Early English—stiff-leaf capitals and roll-mouldings. Over the S door of 1200, which has nailhead in the hoodmould, is a blocked door reached by a recessed staircase, which led to an upper room of the porch. The pre-Conquest arches of the tower lead to the tall, light chancel. The rather plain W arch is unchamfered and has squared imposts and a surrounding pilaster strip. The E arch, seen from the chancel, is finer, very high, and roll-moulded, with semicircular shafts which continue round the soffit. The plain chamfered capitals have neck moulds. The tunnel-vault in the tower has been thought pre-Conquest, but it is more probably 13C. In the chancel there is a rare 13C aumbry of six compartments under three gables on the N side of the altar. Opposite is a contemporary piscina; another, later piscina is W of this.

The 15C font has the usual octagonal bowl with blank shields in quatrefoils. Parts of a 15C wooden screen with panel tracery are at the E ends of the aisles. The pulpit, once larger, was made by Thomas Whiting in 1673. At the altar is a brass to Walter Prunes (died 1594) and Mary his wife (died 1609). There is a monument of 1691 in the S aisle to the Howse family, with a bewigged head and the quaint inscription 'Within this little howse three howses lie'. John Howse was a churchwarden.

Oxford

Oxford has so many architectural splendours that it is difficult to know where to begin and where to end in describing them. Most visitors come to see the college chapels. It should be pointed out that many colleges restrict access and that afternoons are the best times for visiting their chapels.

S from Carfax, along St. Aldate's, is **Christ Church**, founded by Cardinal Wolsey in 1525 and refounded by King Henry VIII in 1546. It is unique in England in that its chapel, formerly the Priory Church of St. Frideswide, is also the cathedral of the Diocese of Oxford, and as such falls outside the scope of this guide. Opposite Christ Church is **Pembroke College**, founded in 1624. The chapel is in the second or Chapel Quad. It is a simple rectangular building of 1728–32, probably by William Townsend, restrained and coolly Classical on the outside, but rich and slightly riotous inside, with a neo-Renaissance decorative scheme of 1884 by C.E. Kempe. The windows, of course, are his, but so are the pedimented marble altarpiece, the figures on brackets and under canopies, and the Raphaelesque painting of the ceiling and walls. Remaining from the 1730s are the fine screen and the stalls.

Back up St. Aldate's and right along Blue Boar Lane, the visitor reaches Oriel Square. **Oriel College** (1326) has its chapel opposite the gateway in Front Quad. It was built in 1637–42. The window tracery is part-Gothic and part-17C, not yet Classical; a rather unhappy compromise. Most of the woodwork is of c 1640–70. T.G. Jackson moved the screen W in 1884, and designed the organ case and openwork fronts of the gallery. The SW window—the Presentation of Christ in the Temple—is by William Peckitt of York, 1767. Nearby in Merton Street is **Corpus Christi College** (1517). The chapel is in the SE corner of Front Quad. Like the college, it is small and intimate, and dates from the foundation. The plain stalls and panelling of c 1677 resemble Oriel's. William Townsend may have designed the Classical W screen, c 1701–05. Corpus Christi has the only pre-Reformation brass eagle lectern in Oxford, given in the early 16C by the first President.

Next to Corpus Christi is **Merton College**, founded before 1264. It has the finest medieval chapel in the University, with a splendid Perpendicular tower, stockier than Magdalen's, but more richly detailed. It was also a parish church until 1891. The original plan was for nave and aisles, but these were never built, and the plan of chapel and W transepts became the model for other Oxford chapels. The main chapel was finished by 1297. The windows have good examples of late 13C tracery, especially the huge seven-light E window. The crossing and S transept are 14C (but the latter with 15C windows); the N transept and the tower are 15C. By this time plans for a nave were given up, and a large W window was inserted. The interior is spacious and tall, and the crossing, with its huge piers composed of many orders of shafts, is imposing. The ceiling of the main chapel is by William Butterfield, 1850, painted by J. Hungerford Pollen. Against the W window is the organ, in a case of 1968 by Robert Potter, in a Georgian Gothic style and standing on a raised gallery. Behind it the window is blocked by A.W. Acworth's *trompe l'oeil* conceit of a nave vista. Butterfield provided stalls, sedilia, piscina and a font. The other font, of green Siberian marble, was the gift of Tsar Alexander of Russia in 1816. The chapel has a remarkable brass lectern of c 1500, with two desks. The W screen is by Sir Christopher Wren, 1671–73, but was dismantled and dispersed c 1850 and only partially restored to the chapel in 1960. Amongst many monuments is one in the N transept to Sir Thomas Bodley (died 1613) by Nicholas Stone. He founded the Bodleian Library.

On the S side of the High Street the visitor reaches *University College* (mid-13C). The chapel, opposite the gate in Front Quad, is entered by the left-hand door of the centrepiece—the other leads to the hall. The quad was started in 1634 and the chapel was consecrated in 1666. The windows have 17C late Gothic tracery with an oval in the head, as at Oriel. The main features of the interior are Abraham van Linge's stained glass windows of 1641, richly coloured and illustrating Biblical episodes in landscape settings. Most of the woodwork is late 17C. Sir Gilbert Scott altered the chapel in 1862, providing the E window, roof and rich corbels, and the sedilia. The E window is by Michael O'Connor, 1864, and the SE by Clayton & Bell, 1866.

At the E end of the High Street is *Magdalen College* (1458), its tall and gracious bell tower of 1492–c 1509 a focal point for the street. The chapel is at the entrance to the cloister. It was built in 1474–80 to the usual T-plan. The W window is very broad, with 17C tracery. The other windows are of three lights with Perpendicular tracery. Much of the detail of the interior (rib-vaulting, stone screen, stalls, reredos and stone panelling round the altar) are by L.N. Cottingham, 1829–34. The sculpture over the altar, *noli me tangere*, is by Sir Francis Chantrey, c 1835, and the ranks of statues were carved by Thomas Earp to Clayton & Bell's designs, 1865. N of the altar is a chantry chapel with a fan-vault, much now of Cottingham's time, intended for the tomb of the college's founder. It houses the monument to his father, Richard Patten, brought from Wainfleet in Lincolnshire in 1833. The lectern is a fine brass eagle of 1633. Hardman did the stained glass of the main chapel in 1860, but the antechapel has interesting and unusual grisaille glass of 1632 by Richard Greenbury, with large and sombre figures of prophets and saints. In the antechapel also there are medieval stalls with misericords, an early 14C chest, and several brasses. One brass is 19C, designed by J.C. Buckler and made by Hardman & Co., to Martin Routh, President for 64 years, who died in office in 1854 aged 99. The modern bronze sculpture, *noli me tangere*, is by David Wynne, 1963.

Along High Street to Queen's Lane, and *St. Edmund Hall*. It was the last of the medieval halls—hostels rented by Masters to house and teach students—but became a full college in 1957. The chapel is opposite the gateway in a five-bay range built in 1680. It projects beyond the range and is reached by a central door and passage. The main feature is the E window, by Morris & Co., 1865. The theme is the Crucifixion and events surrounding it. Sir Edward Burne-Jones did most of it but the Women at the Tomb and the Men of Galilee are by William Morris, and the rest is by Philip Webb. Next, in the High Street, is the *Queen's College* (1340). The Front Quad, with the chapel and hall facing the entrance screen, is the grandest piece of Baroque architecture in Oxford. Hall and chapel were built in 1714. They may be by Nicholas Hawksmoor, who designed the entrance screen, but this is not certain. They form a strong ensemble, with arched windows separated by stocky pilasters, topped by a heavy entablature and balustrade, and linked by an attached, pedimented portico over which a domed, Wren-like tower soars. The chapel, to the right, is apsed. The interior is high, and the walls are articulated with pilasters, those in the apse marbled. The apse has a ceiling painting of the Ascension, 1716, by Sir James Thornhill. The splendid screen, the stalls and the panelling, and the wrought-iron communion rail, are of 1715–20. The brass eagle lectern predates the chapel: it was made by William Borroghes in 1662. Also earlier are many of the windows. Four windows on each side (starting beside the E window) are by Abraham van Linge, 1635. They are his finest surviving works. On the S side are the Ascension, Resurrection, Adoration of the Shepherds, and Pentecost; on the N are the Last Judgement (two windows), Last Supper and Crucifixion, Annunciation, and Visitation. The other side windows contain figures and shields of 1518; the E window, showing the Rest on the Flight, is by Joshua Price, c 1718. He reset the other windows.

Further along High Street is *All Souls' College* (1438). It is unique in the University in having no students, only Fellows. The chapel, in Front Quad opposite the gateway, dates from 1442. Like New College chapel, it is T-plan, with two-bay W chapels, broader to the S than to the N, because it abuts on to Radcliffe Square. Also like New College, it has a many-tiered reredos covering the E wall. The figures are all 19C, by E.C. Geflowski, 1872; but the richly carved framework, bristling with crocketed canopies, is mid-15C, as are the shallow hammerbeam roof and the stalls (but the upper parts are 19C). There is a good set of 24 misericords. The screen was installed in 1664 and altered by Sir James Thornhill in 1716 with fluted Corinthian columns and a tall central arch topped by a pediment. In c 1664 Isaac Fuller painted a huge Last Judgement which covered the reredos; a few large boards with figures survive in the antechapel. The antechapel has much 15C stained glass, mostly figures of saints and kings. It was well-restored and completed by Clayton & Bell. The central W window is by John Hardman & Co.

Passing along the E side of Radcliffe Square, *Hertford College* (refounded 1874) is reached. The college was mostly rebuilt by Sir Thomas Jackson. His chapel, in the SE corner of Front Quad, dates from 1908. There is a small polygonal tower with a dome supported by eight columns, and a short, two-bay cloister. The interior has a Renaissance feel, but many of the elements of the design, especially the windows, are Jackson at his most inventive. The side windows, two-light and round-headed under a single round arch, are divided by attached columns. The E window, a development of the Venetian window, looks splendid from New College Lane, but is filled with clear glass which admits a too dazzling amount of light. The stalls are copied from the late 16C seats in Ypres Cathedral, which were destroyed in 1914.

New College chapel is described separately. At the beginning of Parks Road is *Wadham College* (1610). Its buildings were designed and built in one campaign and finished in 1613. The chapel is at the NE corner of the Front Quad. It is the typical Oxford T-plan, but this is only apparent when the building is entered, such as the ingenious way in which this shape is fitted into the façade. The window tracery, very late Gothic going Classical, is found in several other Oxford buildings of this period. The spacious interior has a fine screen designed by John Bolton in 1613, and a pulpit, communion rail and brass eagle lectern all from the 17C. The reredos and stalls are of 1832 by Edward Blore. Sir Thomas Jackson designed the organ case. The stained glass in the E window is by Bernard van Linge, 1622, and the side windows are thought to be by Robert Rudland of Oxford. One is dated 1616. The antechapel has glass of 1838 and a good monument to Sir John Portman (died 1624), a young man reclining in an architectural frame, flanked by paired black columns. On the broken pediment are putti and statues, and on a higher pediment stands Father Time.

Back into Radcliffe Square: opposite All Souls' is **Brasenose College** (1509). The E end of the chapel looks onto the square. It was built in 1656–66, at the time of the Commonwealth. The E window tracery, though still Gothic, is Gothic of a very self-conscious form, the central motif of the tracery being an elongated oval. Above, going Classical, is a scrolly open pediment, but higher still is more Gothic, a crocketed parapet with urns. The chapel is reached through Old Quad and a passage to the left, along a cloister under the library. It is the usual T-plan. The interior is notable for its plaster fan-vaulted ceiling of 1665, complete with pendants like the chancel ceiling of the cathedral. The big screen and organ case are mostly by Sir Thomas Jackson, who built the new range of the college on High Street. The pulpit is 17C. The lectern, given in 1731, is another brass eagle. The many-marbled reredos is c 1740. In the W window are figures painted by J.R. Mortimer in 1776 to James Pearson's design.

In Turl Street, at the High Street end, is **Lincoln College** (1427). The impressive Classical church of All Saints is now its library. The chapel is by contrast a small and delightful building of 1629–31, which closes the second quad. The exterior is late Perpendicular. Through the screen is a charming, intimate space. The 17C woodwork is finely carved, and on the stall-ends is a series of small statues. The glass is 17C too, 12 panels in the E window depicting New Testament episodes and Old Testament prefigurations; and in the N and S windows, Prophets and Apostles, attributed to Bernard van Linge, c 1630.

Towards Broad Street is **Jesus College** (1571). The chapel is a simple structure of c 1620–36, entered by a pedimented doorway of c 1700. The windows are still Perpendicular. Many of the furnishings are by G.E. Street, 1864, but the late 17C screen and early 17C pulpit remain. There is a bust of T.E. Lawrence (of Arabia). Opposite is **Exeter College** (1314). The chapel, by Sir Gilbert Scott, is a *tour de force*, a soaring structure based on the Sainte Chapelle in Paris, and built 1854–60. Unfortunately it is quite out of scale with the rest of the quad. Scott intended it to go into the centre of the E range, opposite the gateway. It is apsidal, with large windows filled with Geometrical tracery of various designs, and heavy gabled buttresses with statues at the top under canopies. Rising above the roof is a slender, lead-covered flèche. The S doorway is elaborately carved with figures and foliage. The interior is high and vaulted, religiously dim, the windows filled with splendid glass by Clayton & Bell. Sadly, one window was left undone, and it is a glaring, gaping hole. The furnishings are ornate and produce a crowded interior. There is a stone screen from the antechapel, with gates of brass and iron by Francis Skidmore. G.F. Bodley designed the canopies for the stalls. Round the apse are mosaics by Salviati of Venice. There is a lovely Morris & Co. tapestry designed in 1890 by Edward Burne-Jones, depicting the Adoration of the Magi. The eagle lectern is a survival of 1637 from the old chapel.

Across Broad Street, **Trinity College** chapel is the late 17C at its best. It is described separately. In Trinity Front Quad is a view of the E end of William Butterfield's chapel of **Balliol College** (1282). The chapel dates from 1856–57. Butterfield used attractive polychromatic banding of pink and brown stone for the exterior. The windows have late 13C Geometrical tracery. In Balliol's Front Quad, the chapel might have seemed as insensitively high as Scott's at Exeter, but Alfred Waterhouse's huge and brutal entrance front manages to dwarf it. There is a rose window in the high W gable and a thin and jaunty SW turret. Inside, several features of the earlier chapel were retained: the E end panelling, the pulpit and lectern of the 1630s, and many stained glass panels. In the E window, given in 1629, are scenes from the Passion to the Ascension; on the S side, a window of 1529 illustrating the legend of St. Catherine, and another with figures of saints; on the N side, panels from various 15C, 16C and 17C windows, and windows by Abraham van Linge (first two from the E end, and the antechapel), given in 1637. There is a recumbent effigy of Benjamin Jowett, a well-known 19C Master of Balliol.

Into St. Giles, and then along Beaumont Street to *Worcester College* (refounded 1714). The chapel and hall project from the early 18C façade, probably by George Clarke of All Souls'. The chapel has a Venetian E window. The interior was completed by James Wyatt in 1791, but is dominated by William Burges's lush decoration of 1864. The floor is inlaid with mosaics with an early Christian theme. Henry Holiday designed the friezes, ceiling paintings and stained glass. Burges's stalls are inhabited by a menagerie of strange animals, even a dodo. The ornate lectern is of alabaster.

In St. Giles is *St. John's College* (1555). The chapel, in Front Quad, is externally plain and internally mostly 19C remodelling. The exception is the Baylie chapel on the N side, of 1662, with a good fan-vault, as late as that at Brasenose. The Baylie chapel is filled with monuments to Richard Baylie (died 1667) and others. There is a good eagle lectern of a remarkably late date, 1773. Along St. Giles and then Keble Road, is *Keble College* (1868), the Oxford Movement's tribute to John Keble and William Butterfield's redbrick masterpiece. The tall chapel, as dramatic as Scott's Exeter but more easily accommodated in the spacious quad, is decorated on the outside with an array of decorative motifs in stone and brick, with bands and diaper and chequer patterns. The windows are set remarkably high: the visitor almost expects an underchapel. There are vestigial transepts and a SW portal rising to a statue-topped gable. The entrance, however, is through the cloister at the W end. There is high blank arcading round the walls, inside and outside. Inside, bands of brick and tile decoration run through it. The wall surfaces are extremely rich, even if the elements—brick patterns, mosaics, and stained glass by Alexander Gibbs—are rather discordant. Butterfield designed the pulpit and brass lectern. In a side chapel is William Holman Hunt's painting 'The Light of the World'. It is worth noting that Keble was the first college to abandon the chapel-wise arrangement of the seats: the pews face E, giving due Tractarian emphasis to the altar.

Selected churches in Oxford are described below in alphabetical order. St. Mary the Virgin, the University Church, is described separately.

All Saints, High Street is now the library of Lincoln College and has been transformed internally. It is not open to the public. This imposing Baroque building of 1706–08 is supposed to have been designed by Henry Aldrich, Dean of Christ Church. The body of the church is articulated by paired Corinthian pilasters, with a heavy cornice separating the round-headed windows of the lower section from the smaller, segment-headed windows of the attic. There are pedimented porticos at the NW and SW corners. The W tower starts as sturdily as the body of the church, but rising from the balustrade above the belfry stage is a more dainty spire-capped rotunda. Nicholas Hawksmoor probably had a hand in designing this feature.

St. Aloysius, Woodstock Road. Built in 1873–75 by J.A. Hansom & Son, the church is set back from the street. It is a large church with an E apse flanked by top-lit side chapels. The apse has a notable reredos, with two tiers of statues by Farmer & Brindley, 1879, then a frieze of angels, and higher still a tier of busts in roundels.

St. Barnabas, Cardigan Street, Jericho. The Italian Romanesque campanile is prominent in views of Oxford from the W. The church was started in 1869 and finished in the 1890s, financed by Thomas Combe and designed by Arthur Blomfield. Rubble, cement-rendered, was used for the walls, and this has weathered in a rather dreary way. It is relieved with ornamental bands of brick. The SE campanile of 1872 was originally free-standing but was connected to the church in 1887. The great feature of the interior, which has round-arched arcades and an apse, is the decoration, designed by Blomfield: gold and mosaics in the apse, and figures of martyrs on the N wall, between the clerestory windows. The S wall was never done. Capitals at the W end are carved with heads including those of Combe, Blomfield and Bishop Wilberforce.

St. Cross, St. Cross Road. Mostly medieval, with a chancel arch of c 1160 and a W tower a little later. The N aisle, which was Perpendicular, was rebuilt in 1838, reusing old materials, and the S aisle was rebuilt in 1843 by J.M. Derick. There is a brass of 1622 to Mrs Franklin, showing her in bed.

St. Giles, St. Giles Street. Standing at the intersection of Banbury Road and Woodstock Road, in a fine churchyard, St. Giles's retains the air of a country church. It is substantially 13C, that is, the tower, nave, aisles and S porch. The chancel is late 13C, and the S chapel is of 1850–52, reusing old materials, including the Geometrical E window. There is a good range of lancet windows. The N aisle is a series of projecting gables, as if built separately as a series of small chapels. There is a good 13C square font, decorated with dogtooth. The church was restored by Sir Charles Nicholson in 1920.

St. John Evangelist, Iffley Road, by G.F. Bodley, 1894–96 (tower 1902), was the church of the Cowley Fathers, and is now cared for by St. Stephen's House, an Anglican theological college. The interior has a monastic emphasis on the chancel. The painted wagon roof of nave and chancel is continuous. The style is mainly Decorated (the nave arcades, W window), but there are E lancets and features of other styles. Bodley designed the pulpit, screen and organ case; C.E. Kempe was responsible for the E, W and NE windows.

St. Martin, Carfax. Only the tower survives. The church was demolished in 1896. The clock has quarter-jacks and an 'Oxford' chime composed by Sir John Stainer.

St. Mary Magdalen, Magdalen Street. St. Giles's closes one end of the street and St. Mary Magdalen's the other. On a constricted site it has become wider than it is long, with nave and broad aisles, and an outer S aisle. The church was much restored by Scott & Moffatt in 1842. The 14C outer S aisle has Reticulated tracery and buttresses whose crocketed niches hold 19C statues. In the E window of this aisle is flowing tracery. Scott & Moffatt altered the E end of the nave, removing the Norman chancel arch and continuing the Perpendicular arcades eastward. The stocky tower was rebuilt in 1511–31. The N aisle is entirely by Scott & Moffatt, and was the first archaeologically 'correct' example of the Gothic Revival in Oxford. The church has an ornate and splendid Perpendicular font.

St. Michael, Cornmarket Street. The tall, unadorned W tower is
early 11C pre-Conquest, the oldest in Oxford. It has two tiers of twin
belfry windows in each face. The church is 'at the North Gate' of the
city; the gate was demolished in 1772. The chancel is 13C, and the
nave was remodelled in Perpendicular style in the 15C. The Perpendicular font has moved twice, as churches in the city closed: it was
first at St. Martin's, Carfax, and then at All Saints', High Street. In the
N chapel is a Decorated reredos, with figures of 1942. The church has
the earliest surviving stained glass in Oxford: four panels in the E
window show the Virgin and Child, St. Michael, St. Nicholas and St.
Edmund of Abingdon, late 13C.

St. Peter-in-the-East, Queen's Lane. This fascinating medieval
church is now the library of St. Edmund Hall, and only the crypt is
open to visitors. It is approached through the college. Nave and
chancel are Norman, but nearly all the windows are later. The crypt
is beneath the chancel, and is an evocative space. Two rows of
columns, some with vigorously carved capitals, support groin-vaults.
At the W end are three doorways, two with stairs leading to the
church, and the central one to a small relic chamber. The chancel has
buttresses against its E wall which rise to circular, spire-topped
turrets. Remains of Norman blank arcading are visible on the S wall,
and parts of the original corbel table survive on the N. The E window
is four-light Perpendicular. On the N side is a 13C chapel with lancet
windows to the E and a Decorated window to the N. The N aisle has
two Decorated windows with flowing tracery; the NW tower tapers
towards the top. The upper stage is Perpendicular and is finished
with a flat parapet of quatrefoils. Similar parapets are on the nave
and chancel. The S wall of the nave provides a variety of windows of
13C to 15C date. The two-storey porch of c 1500 covers a reset
Norman doorway, decorated with beakhead and zigzag.

St. Philip and St. James, Woodstock Road. This superb church by
G.E. Street is now a centre for Mission Studies. It was built in 1860–
62, and the tower and broach spire were added in 1864–66. The style
is 13C, and Street used red sandstone in decorative bands throughout the building. The tower is placed over the chancel at the E end,
with only the apse projecting. The belfry openings are twin lancets,
deeply and strongly moulded. The W front is an attractive design:
gabled door, three lancets over it, and a rose window above. Most of
the furnishings were by Street, and there is Clayton & Bell glass in
the apse and in the aisles. C.E. Kempe did the W windows and
Burlison & Grylls the clerestory and S transept lancet windows.

St. Mary the Virgin, High Street. A building of much splendour,
well-positioned between Radcliffe Square and the High Street. It is
mostly 15C, but the tower and spire, prominent in many views of
Oxford, are older. From the top of the tower a fine prospect is
obtained. The church consists of nave with aisles, S porch, chancel,
tower centrally placed on the N side, with a chapel to its W and
former University buildings to its E.

In Radcliffe Square the tower (which forms the N entrance)
confronts the Radcliffe Camera, an early 18C rotunda. The tower
dates from c 1300; the spire was added in c 1315–25. It is sumptuous
but somewhat heavy. A profusion of pinnacles, gables and lucarnes
clusters round the main spire. The details, of 1894–96, are T.G.
Jackson's attempt to recreate the medieval appearance after J.C.
Buckler's drastic and inaccurate restoration of 1848–52. The original
statues, much worn, now stand in New College's cloisters. The body

of the church is best viewed from the S, in the High Street. It was rebuilt in the late 15C in a lively Perpendicular style, with crocketed pinnacles rising above the parapets. The nave and aisles, with four-centred windows and castellated parapets, are of c 1485–95; the more chaste chancel, aisleless and with taller windows, is of 1463. The S porch, a splendid addition of 1637, was provided by Dr Owen Morgan, Archbishop Laud's chaplain, and designed by Nicholas Stone. The niche holds a statue of the Virgin and Child: this 'Popish' innovation was held against Laud at his trial in 1644. The porch's façade, with twisted columns (a motif derived from St. Peter's in Rome), scrolls and segmental pediment, is Classical, but inside the Gothic style persists in the fan-vault.

Within, the six-bay nave, with well-proportioned arcades and wooden roof supported on canopied niches (without statues), is separated from the five-bay chancel by Thomas Plowman's tripartite Gothic stone screen of 1827–28. Plowman's also are the font in the S aisle, the wooden pulpit, and the Gothic W casing of the organ. At the W end, under the gallery, is an early 19C throne for the Chancellor of the University. Beyond the N aisle is the Brome chapel, built by Adam de Brome in c 1328, but with 15C Perpendicular windows. His tomb-chest is here, but only the lid is original. In this chapel the Chancellor held his court. The narrow chancel, with its tall windows, is lighter than the nave. It has 15C stalls with small poppyheads. At the E end are the remains of a 15C reredos, a row of canopied niches (with 19C statues). Under it is wooden panelling of c 1693, with Corinthian pilasters. The altar rail of 1673–75 has panels of open-work foliage.

The stained glass is mostly 19C, but there are fragments of 15C and 16C glass in the upper lights of the E window. The chancel is otherwise clear-glazed. In the S aisle, the E window and a S window were designed by A.W.N. Pugin and executed by John Hardman. The Keble memorial window is by Clayton & Bell. C.E. Kempe designed the large W window in 1891 as a memorial to Dean Burgon. There are many monuments. In the chancel, there is a large tablet with scrolled pediment and urn to Charles Holloway (died 1679), by William Stanton. In the S aisle there are a half-figure preaching, to Joe Wallis (died 1703), and a lively bust and a relief of three putti wielding astronomical instruments, to David Gregory (died 1708). In the N aisle is a monument to Elizabeth Cary (died 1723), a bust in an oval frame set against black drapery; and John Flaxman's Indian and allegorical figure of 1801 to Sir William Jones. The Brome chapel has Westmacott's tablet to Dorothy Eveleigh (died 1799). The tower porch has a brass of a small kneeling figure with St. Catherine, to Edmund Croston (died 1507); and J. Townsend, Jr's early Gothic Revival monument to Henrietta Fermor, Countess of Pomfret (died 1762).

The former University buildings are E of the tower. They are two-storeyed. The lower room was the Congregation House until c 1488. Here University business was done and degrees were conferred. The low, rib-vaulted room, dating from the 14C, is now a chapel. Over it was the original University Library, built in c 1320–30 to house Bishop Cobham's library. The library moved across Radcliffe Square to the Duke Humphrey Library in 1488.

In St. Mary's in 1554, three leading Reformers, Archbishop Cranmer and Bishops Ridley and Latimer, were subjected to lengthy disputations and trials, before being burnt at the stake in what is now Broad Street. A pillar on the N side of the nave with its moulding cut away was the site of the platform on which Cranmer was condemned. In 1833 John Keble preached his Assize Sermon here, criticising the suppression of Irish bishoprics and expressing fears for the future of the Church of England. This sermon is held to be the starting-point of the Oxford Movement and of the Catholic revival in the Anglican Church. Under John Henry Newman, its Vicar in 1828–43, St. Mary's became the centre of this revival.

New College, Chapel. When William of Wykeham, Bishop of Winchester, founded New College in 1379, it was as novel and ambitious in its statutes and educational plan as it was in its architectural layout. He founded, too, the sister establishment, Winchester College, in 1382, which was to produce students for his Oxford college. The chapel of New College, which survives much as Wykeham planned it, is one of the largest and most spacious in Oxford. It has notable 18C stained glass and a remarkable painted window by Sir Joshua Reynolds.

The approach along New College Lane, with its sharp right-angled turnings, is memorable. A sharp turn to the left inside the gateway brings the visitor to the chapel. It occupies one half of the N side of the quadrangle, the other half being the hall. The tall windows of the N and S sides, separated by huge buttresses, contain Perpendicular tracery of 1380–86. The windows are of four lights. The chapel is T-shaped, that is, it has a transeptal antechapel at the W end. The plan derives from Merton College, where a nave was planned but never built. The T-plan became the usual Oxford plan throughout the medieval period. The windows of the antechapel, also Perpendicular, are variously of four, six and (in the W window) seven lights.

The antechapel is two bays deep, the bays separated by tall shafted piers, with capitals on the shafts only. The timber roofs of both antechapel and main chapel are by Sir Gilbert Scott, 1877–81, replacing plaster vaults by James Wyatt, 1789–94. The noble proportions of William Wynford's design are still apparent, despite the lateness of most of the furnishings. Wynford was Wykeham's master mason.

At the E end, Wynford provided a spectacular tiered stone reredos, filling the entire wall. What we now see is Scott's recreation of the reredos, for Wyatt had replaced it with a stucco concoction in the 18C. It has five levels of closely-packed statues—Prophets, English ecclesiastical worthies, Apostles, angels and Christ in glory—under crocketed canopies. The marble reliefs above the altar are by Sir Richard Westmacott. Scott also replaced the W screen (keeping some old doors, spandrels and panels) and the stalls. Of these the elbow-rests and misericords are 14C and original. The misericords are well-carved and inventive, featuring complicated scenes as well as simple naturalistic motifs. The organ case on the screen, harsh and angular but not unsuited to its setting, is by G.G. Pace, 1968–69. In the antechapel is Jacob Epstein's tall and impressive sculpture of Lazarus, 1951. In the floor of the antechapel are many 15C to 17C brasses. There is late 14C stained glass, reset in c 1899, in its windows, all with large figures under varied canopies. The theme of figures under canopies was continued by William Price in the S windows of the chapel proper, 1735–40. Indeed, he incorporates some 14C glass. The figures are of saints, patriarchs and bishops. William Peckitt did the N windows in c 1770, with figures of Prophets and Apostles. Then in 1778–85, Thomas Jarvis painted the W window to designs by Sir Joshua Reynolds. The seven Virtues occupy the lower lights, and a Nativity is above. Reynolds portrayed himself as a shepherd on the left of the scene, and he glances at the visitor as if seeking reassurance about the effect of his work. Horace Walpole, for one, was highly critical, condemning the 'washy colours' of the Virtues. Shades of brown predominate. The atmospheric effects are smoky and mysterious, not at all what is expected in ecclesiastical coloured glass. Reynolds was greatly disappointed by it. The most astonishing thing about it is that it has survived the 19C and the restoring energies of Scott. There are several monuments in the antechapel, including two half-figures in black marble niches, to Hugh Barker (died 1632) by Nicholas Stone, and to Robert Pinke (died 1647), probably by Stone. James Wyatt designed, and Richard Westmacott the Elder executed, the small tablet to John Oglander (died 1794). The monument to Charles Bulson (died 1836), with a large prostrate female figure in mourning, is by Humphrey Hopper. Eric Gill executed the two war memorials to C.H. Holden's designs, in 1921 and 1930.

At the W end is a sequestered cloister of c 1400, with three-light Perpendicular tracery in its unglazed windows. It leads nowhere, except to the bell-tower on the N side; it was not planned as a thoroughfare but as the bounds of a burial ground and a place for quiet contemplation. The walls are lined with monumental tablets, mostly 18C to 20C, and along the walks stand eight weathered statues from the tower of the University Church.

Trinity College, Chapel. This is the finest late 17C ecclesiastical building in the county. Outside Oxford, Cornbury Park's chapel is comparable in date and style; but Trinity's chapel far exceeds Cornbury in the beauty of its setting, the nobility of its architecture, and the richness of its interior and fittings. It was built in 1691–94. The architect is not known. Trinity College had been Durham College, an establishment maintained by the Benedictines of Durham Cathedral Priory, from c 1286 to 1544, when it was suppressed. It was refounded in 1555 by Sir Thomas Pope, Treasurer of the Court of Augmentations, who had acquired the sites of several dissolved monasteries. His monument is in the chapel, but half-hidden by the late 17C designer in a glazed cabinet, like an antique curiosity.

The setting is unmatched in Oxford. The old quadrangle of the college lies back from Broad Street, at the end of an avenue in a miniature parkland setting. The chapel, on the S side of the quad-rangle, faces Broad Street side-on, five bays long. The W bay is the gateway to the quadrangle. The gate is round-arched, with pilasters. Above is a window, the round arch of which is filled with a cartouche and other carved decoration. Two larger cartouches flank it. Above the cornice and parapet there is a tower of one stage, with a balustraded parapet and statues of Theology, Geometry, Astronomy and Medicine crowning the corners. The four bays E of the gateway are of the chapel proper. Tall, round-arched windows fill the bays: they are divided by pilasters. The heavy, balustraded parapet is enlivened by urns. The N façade in the quad is identical.

The chapel is entered from the quad. Passing through the ante-chapel under the organ loft, the visitor is struck by the height and lightness of the chapel, and the richness of the dark woodwork. This not only looks good but smells good too: the result of centuries of polishing. The woods used were oak and juniper, and lime for the

The chapel of Trinity College, 1691–94, with contemporary fittings

carving. The reredos fills the E wall and dominates the interior. Fluted Composite columns flank the centre and carry an over-heavy segmental pediment. On the pediment sit two reclining figures. The centrepiece, where a painting might be expected, is a subtle IHS in a sunburst, all in marquetry and veneer. Around it hang heavy festoons of almost freshly plucked fruit and foliage. With wood carving of such amazing virtuosity and date it is almost irresistible to think of Grinling Gibbons, but there is nothing beyond a hint by Celia Fiennes to link him with the work. Where the woodcarver stops, the stuccoist takes over, and the upper walls and ceiling are a *tour de force* of the late 17C style: swags, cartouches, bands of foliage, scrolls and flourishes, and inset painted panels by Pierre Berchet. The largest panel portrays the Ascension. The walls are panelled up to the level of the windows, and the stalls, restrained in mood, have little urns on their bench-ends. The screen at the W end picks up the motifs of the reredos. Stephen Dykes Bower designed the triangular projection of the organ on the screen. The sides of the screen have opulent openwork panels. James Powell & Sons provided the stained glass in 1885. It is in a quiet, Renaissance style which does not get in the way of enjoyment of the 17C splendours. The monument to Sir Thomas Pope and his wife is of alabaster: the effigies are recumbent on a tomb-chest. It is in the cupboard on the N side of the altar.

Pusey House, Chapel. Of the three early leaders of the 19C Oxford Movement in the Church of England, John Keble, John Henry Newman and Edward Bouverie Pusey, it is perhaps Pusey who is least known today. He was Regius Professor of Hebrew and a Canon of Christ Church, and on him devolved the leadership after Newman seceded to Rome in 1845 and Keble died in 1866. Pusey died in 1882 and Pusey House was established as his memorial in 1884. It is not a University college but a 'house of sacred learning', with a chapel and theological library, and its chapter of clergymen are called 'Priest Librarians'. The buildings were designed by Temple Moore, and the chapel—a surprisingly large and impressive interior—was the first part to be built, in 1911–14.

The chapel occupies the N side of the quadrangular site. The details are Perpendicular. On the E side is a large, five-light window, with bar tracery but no transoms. There is a similar but smaller window at the W end, with a deeply moulded doorway under it. On the S side, seen from the quadrangle, is a small tower at the junction of 'nave' and 'chancel', with a large S window to throw light onto the Rood. The roof is continuous. 'Nave' windows have four-centred heads; the larger 'chancel' windows are pointed. Below the windows run what seem to be low aisles.

The aisles are in fact long, winding, vaulted passages, running the length of the chapel. The entrance is from the E. There are in fact two chapels, of contrasting appearance, but both are high and light and vaulted in concrete, with stone ribs and bosses of Prophets and Evangelists. The E chapel is the Blessed Sacrament chapel or chapel of the Resurrection. It is entered by a door under the Rood screen. It is narrower than the 'nave' chapel, and the oak stalls are arranged E–W as in a college chapel. The stalls have plain misericords and are backed by high panelling. Above are stone panels, pierced as a sort of triforium; and the vaulting shafts terminate in angels bearing shields. To the left of the altar, under a shallow arch, is a recess for confessions, and to the right, above the door, is a gilded and coloured statue of the Virgin and Child under a convex, gabled and pierced canopy. The ogee-arched sedile is in a frame panelled with quatrefoils and decorated with Tudor roses. All this is Temple Moore's design, quiet and sober; but in 1937 Sir Ninian Comper installed the gorgeous but rather flashy gilded baldacchino of Corinthian columns, topped by figures of the Resurrection, the ceiling painted with the Holy Spirit as a dove, and scrolls naming the Seven Gifts issuing from it. The gilt-bronze frontal of the altar has, amongst scrolly foliage, the Annunciation. The E window above, also by Comper, is a Tree of Jesse commemorating Pusey, with figures of Old Testament Prophets and Fathers of the Church, representing some of his areas of study, surrounding Christ in Majesty and the Virgin and Child. The figure of Pusey can just be seen, kneeling at the base of the second light from the right: remarkably, he is wearing a cope. The early leaders of the Oxford Movement were not Ritualists.

After the intimacy of the Blessed Sacrament chapel, the nave chapel is surprisingly austere. The walls are lined with blank arches, suggestive of aisles. Above them runs a band of quatrefoils, and a miniature gallery (conveying the heating apparatus) pierces the shafts. The organ is borne on a canted gallery at the SW end. A stone screen divides the chapels, with small doors at either side of the altar. On the screen are gilded and painted Rood figures by Temple Moore. The cross-arms bear emblems of the Evangelists. The reredos, showing the Adoration of the Shepherds and Magi in cameo reliefs on backgrounds of pale pink and blue, is subdued, and looks particularly fine in its setting. It was in fact made for St. Philip and St. James's Church, Woodstock Road, and was brought here in c 1980. In the passage are windows commemorating Temple Moore (died 1920) and his son, Richard Temple Moore (died 1918).

Charles Gore (1853–1932) was the first Principal of Pusey House; he founded the Community of the Resurrection at Mirfield and was successively Bishop of Worcester, Birmingham and Oxford.

Rycote, *St. Michael and All Angels*. Rycote has never been a parish church. It stands in a secluded parkland setting three miles W of Thame, at the end of a narrow lane, and close to Rycote Park, of which it was until 1952 the private chapel. It is now in the guardianship of English Heritage. Rycote was founded in 1449 by Sir Richard Quatremayne and Sibyl his wife, as a chantry for three priests. Its architecture is unaltered from then; but it is chiefly remarkable for its opulent 17C furnishings.

It is a narrow building, consisting simply of nave and chancel in one, with no additions, and a W tower as wide as the nave. The side walls have five windows of two lights under stiff, angular pointed hoodmoulds. The buttresses rise to little pinnacles (one on the N side contains a chimney); there is no parapet. The N door is decorated with quatrefoils in the spandrels. Shackled creatures sit atop the E buttresses. The window is of five lights, with panel tracery. The battlemented tower has a three-light W window, and two-light belfry openings, under the same angular hoods. Between them is an empty canopied niche. The W and S doors are pointed.

The interior is scarcely changed from 1700. It is dominated by the two large enclosed pews which stand at the E end of the nave and which mostly block the view into the chancel. At the W end is a delicate balustered gallery carried on columns, painted black to simulate marble, with Ionic capitals. It is reached by a stair in the SW corner which rises higher, to a tiny quatrefoil peep-hole and then to a priest's room, with fireplace, in the tower. Under the gallery is the font, with panelled base and wooden ogee cover of the 15C; but the bowl may be recut from a 12C original. Under the tower is an incomplete reredos of 1610, with Commandment boards divided by Ionic columns, and foliage in the spandrels. The nave pews date from the 15C and were probably installed at the foundation. The church has a painted wagon roof, and at the W end its 17C decoration, gold stars on a blue ground, has been restored. The pulpit is square and early 17C, with panels of blank arcading. Above it is a flat tester, panelled on the underside. In front of the pulpit is an 18C reading-desk. The two huge pews differ in design. The N one is supposedly the Norreys family pew. Its arcading, with black-painted columns, continues the design of the screen on its E side. Inside, stairs to the former Rood loft lead to a musicians' gallery with panels of exquisite filigree work. The pew has a ceiling of painted stars and clouds; on the N panels are remains of landscapes and figures in oval frames. The S pew was traditionally made for the visit of King Charles I in 1625, but since it was once crowned with a statue of the Virgin and Child, with other images at the corners, it would seem more likely that it was a Laudian installation of the 1630s. The arcading is lower than in the N pew; above the door, in the spandrels, is foliage and strapwork. Over the arcade is another tier of black columns supporting an ogee canopy. Inside, part of the ceiling has been repainted with red ribs and gold stars in a blue sky. The screen has remains of its 15C predecessor in the jambs of the central arch and the flanking panels. The rest is early 17C, an arcade with strapwork over the central arch.

James Bertie, first Earl of Abingdon (died 1699), refurnished the chancel in 1682. The rough tiles of the nave floor give way to elegant black and white marbling. The 15C stalls, with traceried fronts and poppyheads, were retained. The altar rails are of 1682, with twisted balusters. Abingdon erected the grand reredos. It has four compartments with the usual texts, under triangular and segmental pediments. The columns are Corinthian. Over all is a big segmental pediment filled with swags of fruit and flowers. Abingdon's monument in the chancel was erected in 1767. His bust is placed in a niche surrounded by coronet and sword and palms. The monument to Alfred Hamersley (died 1929) has its inscription carved by Eric Gill.

Stonor Park, *Chapel of the Holy Trinity.* The Stonor family has held Stonor Park since the 12C, and perhaps earlier. They have been staunch Catholics, and Stonor Park is one of the few places in England where the Mass continued to be celebrated through penal times. The private chapel, which is attached to the house, is a medieval building and operates under licences granted in the medieval period. It was established in the late 13C but was enlarged in the mid-14C. The consecration was in 1349, when Sir John Stonor obtained a licence for a dwelling for six chantry priests. James Thorp remodelled the interior in Gothic style in 1796–1800. It was renovated and restored to its 1800 appearance in 1960 by O.S. Chesterton and J.A. Hanley, with advice from John Piper and Osbert Lancaster.

The chapel is attached to the E end of the S front of the house. The connection is by a brick tower of c 1416–17 (one of the earliest uses of brick in the region). It stands on the N side of the chapel, and has a pyramidal roof and an 18C wooden lantern. The chapel is of flint, with stone dressings. The entrance is at the W end. The windows are simply pointed, without tracery.

Inside, the simple plaster vault, supported by angel corbels, is of 1800. James Thorp also installed the W gallery, the front decorated with a blank arcade of pointed arches, and the simple Gothic iron communion rail. The altar, of various marbles, was presented by Henry Blundell of Ince Blundell, Lancashire, father-in-law of Thomas Stonor. Blundell recommended the glass painter, Francis Eginton, and the subjects of the side windows, the Fathers of the Church, were copied from pictures at Ince Blundell. One window has perished. The E window is a rather feeble representation of the Saviour of the World, based on a painting by Carlo Dolci at Burghley House.

Witney, *St. Mary the Virgin.* Witney is a splendid medieval church with a magnificent 13C tower and spire, 150ft high. The church incorporates parts of its Norman predecessor. It was much restored by G.E. Street in the 1860s.

The church is cruciform. Of the Norman building the only external evidence is the late 12C N porch, between the N transept and the NW chapel. A Norman porch is an unusual feature. Both outer doorway and inner door are round-headed. The chancel is 13C, with original lancets N and S, and three E lancets inserted by G.E. Street in 1865–67. One window on the N side was altered in the medieval period and has Decorated flowing tracery. The belfry has three lancets in each face, and above it soars the spire, with elongated lucarnes at its base, each of two lights and with carvings above them, and huge octagonal pinnacles at the corners. The transepts have W aisles, a rarity in this part of the country. The N transept was built in the 13C but was remodelled in the 14C and has an impressive N window with flowing tracery. The S transept was also of the 13C but was extended S in the 15C. The S window has Perpendicular panel tracery. In the 14C the NW chapel was added. The windows are mostly Decorated: only one has been altered in Perpendicular style. The exterior has buttresses with canopied niches for figures, and an ogee-headed doorway. The nave clerestory is Perpendicular, as is the W end of the nave, with a large five-light window with panel tracery. There was a 15C chamber over the N porch, perhaps for a chantry priest.

The four-bay nave has 13C arcades without capitals. The tower arches and transept arcades are similar, but the N transept piers have a narrow moulded band at the level of the capital. Above the nave N arcade can be seen the heads of two Norman windows of the earlier, aisleless church, and from the N aisle a small, round-headed lancet can be seen. A door in the W wall of the N transept led to the upper chamber of the porch. This transept probably had a crypt (see the two doors in the N wall), and a raised chapel such as survives at Burford. In the E walls of both transepts are remains of the original, shafted lancets. The S transept has a blocked arch indicating the entrance to a former chapel.

Most of the fittings date from G.E. Street's restoration of 1865–67. Several tomb-recesses survive from the medieval period. In the NW chapel is the recess of the (unknown) founder's tomb. The effigy is of a priest. The screen to this chapel is of the late 14C. In the N transept are two recesses under the N window, square-headed, with flowing tracery. Its W aisle has a stone reredos with four ogee arches, containing a modern statue of St. George. The aisle was made into a chapel of St. George in 1957. In the E wall of this transept there is a 13C reredos with a band of cinquefoils and three niches above. Nearby is an Early English piscina with stiff-leaf hood-stops. There is another 13C piscina in the S transept, and in the SW corner of the transept, a Perpendicular tomb-recess. The chancel sedilia and piscina are by Street; the reredos of 1884 is by Clayton & Bell, based on Street's design. It incorporates statues in alabaster of Christ, the Virgin Mary, St. John, St. Mary Magdalene and St. Peter. By Clayton & Bell also is the E window of 1879 and the other stained glass, except for one N window by John Hardman & Co. and for the W window by William Wailes, 1867. In the S transept is the monument to Richard Wenman and his two wives. It is a tomb-chest, dated 1501, with brasses set into a slab of Purbeck marble. In the NW chapel is the wall monument to Sir Francis Wenman (died 1680), with plenty of Baroque swags, cherubs and lions' heads in a columned and pedimented frame.

SOMERSET

This county is said to have more variety of scenery than any other county in England. There is the wild expanse of Exmoor, the delightful coastal scenery on either side of Porlock, fen country around Athelney, the hill country of the Mendips (with Cheddar Gorge and Caves) and the Quantocks, seaside resorts such as Minehead and Weston-super-Mare, and innumerable villages with their churches. The number of ancient churches is c 470, which is about the same number as in Devon, although that is a much larger county. We have been referring to the original Somerset before Avon was carved out of it. Avon is partly Somerset (with Bath) and partly Gloucestershire (with Bristol). In cricket we still refer to Somerset and Yorkshire. Has anyone ever heard of a match between Avon and Humberside?

We also particularly refer to the original Somerset as all the grand Perpendicular church towers ranging from c 1380 to 1541 are within it. There are some 60 of them and we have no hesitation in stating that for beauty and perfection they are unrivalled. The masons who built them apparently only went outside their county boundaries twice, to Chittlehampton in Devon and to Probus in Cornwall. So that the serious student of churches may be able to visit and enjoy all the very finest towers we give a list at the end hereof in alphabetical order (in addition, of course, to the many included in the text). Moreover, as the county has more of interest in churches than any other county in England, except possibly Norfolk and Suffolk, we give a second alphabetical list of churches of outstanding interest either for their architecture or their fittings, but of course every ancient church is usually worth visiting. In Somerset, much church building occurred in the 15C and on the very eve of the Reformation in the 16C. 240 bells in the county's church towers are pre-Reformation, and more than 200 Elizabethan chalices are used in its churches.

Why are there such fine towers in Somerset? Simply because the county had wealth (it produced about a quarter of the woollens made in the whole country), and it had good building stone. Somerset is the only county where these two factors are found together. Sandstone is available S of Bristol, in the Quantocks and on Exmoor; limestone in the Mendips; oolite in the E of Somerset (Bath down to Bruton) and also around Crewkerne; and lias is found between Ilchester and Shepton Mallet in the SE. Exmoor is the great physical feature on the W side of the county. At the N end there is the River Avon. The Rivers Axe, Parrett and Yeo flow through the centre.

Of the early Christian history of Somerset, parts of the county fell under English rule and settlement in the 7C only after the Kings of Wessex had become Christian. King Cynegils, the son-in-law of St. Oswald, was baptised in 635. King Ina, who succeeded in 688, played an important part in the early history of Glastonbury. In his day, St. Aldhelm worked in Somerset. Wells became a bishopric only in 909, and Bath in 1088.

Rare dedications in Somerset include St. Julian at Wellow, St. Vigor at Stratton-on-the-Fosse (one of only two cases in England), St. Cyriac and St. Julitta at Tickenham, and St. Bridget (or Bride) at Chelvey and Brean. The place-name, Congresbury, derives from St. Congar. St. Hugh of Lincoln was Prior of the Charterhouse at Witham from 1176 to 1186.

Churches with grand towers. Batcombe, Chewton Mendip, Evercreech (and roofs), Huish Episcopi, Isle Abbots, Kingsbury Episcopi, Kingston St. Mary, Leigh-on-Mendip (and roof), Long Sutton (and pulpit, screen and roofs), Mells, North Petherton, Staple Fitzpaine, Weare, Winscombe (and glass), and Wrington.

Other notable churches. Axbridge (ceiling); Brushford (aisle by Sir Edwin Lutyens, 1926); Brympton d'Evercy (near Montacute) (the church with bell-cage adjoins the Tudor manor house and medieval chantry house); Buckland St. Mary (by Benjamin Ferrey, 1853–63, with Clayton & Bell glass); Cameley (charming, homely interior of 18C fittings); Carhampton (screen); Crewkerne (complete Perpendicular church of golden Ham Hill stone); Croscombe (Jacobean woodwork); Crowcombe (benches); Culbone (the smallest complete medieval church, 35ft x 12ft; its solitude is a good tonic for today); Dundry (the church tower built on the top of Dundry Hill by the Merchant Venturers of Bristol in 1484 as a landmark for shipping; there is a wonderful view over Bristol; the tower has amazing parapet, pinnacles and spirelets based on Gloucester Cathedral); Hinton St. George (notable monuments); Kingsweston (by C.E. Giles, 1855, in 13C style); Langport (medieval glass); Lullington (doorway of c 1100); Martock (roof with 768 carved panels); Monksilver (woodwork and gargoyles); Muchelney (abbey, priest's house, and church with painted roof); Nettlecombe (glass and Seven Sacrament font); North Cadbury (a perfect Perpendicular church adjoining the Elizabethan manor house); Shepton Mallet (the roof has 350 carved panels, all different, and over 300 bosses; medieval stone pulpit; the earliest of the grand towers and from which all the others were probably derived); Somerton (roof with 640 carved panels); Stogursey (Norman work); Swainswick (14C ogee work); Templecombe (a painting, apparently of Christ, of the late 13C or 14C, hangs on the S wall); Watchet, St. Decuman (up the hill away from the port; roofs); Wellington (remarkable monument to Sir John Popham, Chief Justice, and wife, 1607: no less than 28 charming figures); Wellow (full of interest); and Yeovil ('the Lantern of the West'; early Perpendicular).

Banwell, *St. Andrew.* We first notice the early Perpendicular tower which is one of the grand ones of Somerset. It has three belfry windows on each side, except on the S owing to the higher stair turret with a spirelet at the SE corner. Only the central belfry window is perforated for the sound of the bells, the others having blank tracery. There is a straight-topped pierced parapet and corner pinnacles. This is the type that is found around the W Mendips. On the W face of the tower there is a representation of the Annunciation with a lily. The pierced parapets (a Somerset feature) continue round the aisles, porch and clerestory, but the chancel lacks them. There are Rood stair turrets with pyramidal caps on both sides. In the porch is a medieval Rood loft, which might have been used in the Palm Sunday procession.

Inside, the five-bay arcade has tall slender piers of four shafts and four hollows, with small circular gilt foliate capitals on the shafts. The nave roof is a fine wagon roof. The principals stand on shafts which rest on angels and a trefoil moulding. Between the moulding and the three-light clerestory windows there is blank panelling. The aisle roofs are panelled, and the chancel roof is again a wagon roof, elaborately painted. The inside of the tower, as so often, has a stone lierne-vault.

The church contains almost everything connected with a medieval church. The gilt Rood screen takes pride of place. The fan-vaulting remains on both sides with cornice and cresting. There is a coloured coat of arms upon it which proves the date of 1522. The doors of the screen are carved from single blocks. The font is Norman, but the carvings upon it are 15C. The cover is Jacobean, consisting of a low recessed spire. The benches of c 1500 are plain and have simple poppyheads which are usually only found in East Anglia. The fine Perpendicular stone pulpit of c 1480 is one of about a dozen in this area. It has two-light blank tracery, cresting and a panelled stem. Above it is an octagonal tester on which the date of 1621 is inscribed. The upper part of the W gallery is Elizabethan. There are fragments of medieval glass in the E windows of both aisles: that of the S aisle shows a child in a boiling cauldron, which is an incident in the life of St. Nicholas. Well-arranged are a number of roundels of old Flemish glass depicting the story of Tobit and his son Tobias. We see Tobias giving alms with his parents looking on, the marriage of Tobias and Sara, and their journey home with a delightful camel caravan. There are also roundels of the Conversion of St. Paul, and Christ writing on the ground in the Temple. The rest of the stained glass is Victorian. The chancel has 19C tiles and a substantial reredos painted mainly white but with added red, black and gilt. There are two small brasses W of the Rood screen, and on the S aisle wall is the brass to John Martok (died 1503), shown in a cope.

Bishop's Lydeard, _St. Mary the Virgin._ In the churchyard is a 14C cross, with a base decorated with the 12 Apostles and Christ risen and enthroned, and on the shaft is a figure of St. John the Baptist. The whole church is of beautiful red sandstone, with a tall grand Somerset tower of a type found around the Quantock Hills. There are double belfry windows of three lights with transoms, with single windows below flanked by niches; set-back buttresses; pierced battlements and pinnacles; and a higher stair turret at the NE corner. There is a W door and a W window of five transomed lights above. It will be noted how the enrichment increases with height, which is as it should be. The S aisle is battlemented, and there is a Rood turret. The great studded door has an immense lock (the key weights 1lb 4oz).

Inside, there are four-bay Perpendicular arcades. The tower arch is markedly tall. The wagon roof has painted panels to form a canopy of honour over the Rood. The panels and the Rood figures on the screen were added by Sir Ninian Comper in 1948. The screen itself, which is very fine and dates from the early 16C, runs across nave and S aisle, with vaulting, an inscription (the Apostles' Creed in Latin) and a carved cornice. The aisles continue one bay E of the screen. The octagonal font is Perpendicular, with rosettes on the bowl. The Jacobean pulpit is also fine, with blank arches and rose and thistle decoration. The early 16C benches are also notable, with carved ends, backs and fronts. Particularly notable is one with a windmill with the miller and his horse, and doves, no doubt representing the Holy Spirit by which all life is powered. Another famous one is a three-masted ship. Note also marks of the Passion, a Pelican in her Piety, a stag, a fleur-de-lis on a shield with a large crown above supported by two lions rampant, and dogs chasing rabbits, which is particularly homely. A number of plants are also carved, including oak, holly, ragged robin, and even pea plants (showing that the countryman of those days was keen on his garden). The backgrounds of the bench-ends are painted red or blue. Recent glass, very light with yellow and blue predominating, indicates the work of Sir Ninian Comper . By him are the E window (depicting the Virgin and Child in the centre) and the E window of the S aisle (showing the Annunciation). The high altar with four gilded angels on riddel posts and with a painted canopy above, is also his, dating from 1925. There is a brass plate to Nicholas Grobham and his wife and five children, 1585: an inscription, an angel trumpeting and a boy blowing bubbles. Richard Grobham, eldest son of Nicholas, founded the village's almshouses in 1616. Note also a memorial to Thomas Slocombe, 1801, by Thomas King of Bath: two women in white stand by an urn.

Brent Knoll, *St. Michael.* A grand Perpendicular tower with three belfry windows (only the centre one perforated), a straight-topped pierced parapet, pinnacles, and higher stair turret at the NE corner. The W doorway is flanked by niches. The church is mainly Perpendicular, but the S doorway (with old door) is Norman (as also is the pillar piscina in the church), and the S porch and S transept are early 14C. The N aisle has a pierced parapet as on the tower. There is no S aisle.

Inside, the N aisle arcade of six bays is of usual Perpendicular form. The aisle has a fine panelled roof, and the nave has a wagon roof. The bench-ends form the main feature of the church. They have poppyheads of lozenge shape. In addition to a Pelican, the Lamb and Flag, and symbols of the Evangelists (lion, ox, eagle and angel), most visitors come to see the animal fable of Reynard the fox on three bench-ends. (i) He is disguised as a mitred abbot with pastoral staff, and three pigs in cowls and many birds pay respect to him; at the foot two monkeys roast a pig on a spit, and above is a chained ape with a money bag. (ii) The fox is foot-cuffed and is put into the stocks, with a monkey with an axe guarding him; his mitre hangs on the wall. (iii) The fox is hung by triumphant geese, all pulling the rope, and two watch-dogs are barking with joy. What is the meaning? We must remember that the medieval Churchman usually had a sense of humour (if only there could be a little more today!). The great Bishop Grosseteste, Bishop of Lincoln, wrote in the 13C: 'Three things are needful to keep one in bodily health—food, sleep, and a jest'. So the meaning may be a jest upon monasteries in general and possibly Glastonbury in particular.

There are two other features of note. The pulpit is of 1637, with blank arches in two tiers. The big coloured monument against the S wall is fascinating. It is to John Somerset, 1663; he is a three-quarter figure in an oval niche, flanked by two twisted columns, with his two wives to left and right in very different headgear: there are two reliefs below—in one kneels his family and in the other he is seen rising in his shroud from his tomb. All is beautifully and brightly recoloured.

Bruton, *The Blessed Virgin Mary.* There is a superb view of this fine church from the railway between Westbury and Taunton (yet how many people see it?). The W tower is Perpendicular at its best and it is one of the grand ones of Somerset, with three belfry windows (each one perforated for the sound of the bells, unlike those farther W in the W Mendips where the side windows are blank arcading), battlements and pinnacles. The W face has a large square-headed door with a six-light, transomed window over it and five niches. The tower on the N side is somewhat altered owing to the stair turret at

A famous bench-end, poking fun at an abbot as a fox, at St. Michael's

the NE corner (which however does not rise above the tower). The tower and nave are 15C, but older are the crypt below the chancel and the three-storey N porch tower with projecting turret, both of the 14C. The clerestory is 16C, with pierced parapets repeated over the aisles.

Inside, the arcade is of five bays with piers of four shafts and four hollows. The fine nave roof of typical Somerset tiebeam type, resting on shafts with stone niches filled with modern figures, was erected with the clerestory: the shield of Bishop Fitzjames of London, 1506–22, is on the roof. The aisle roofs are of the same date. The tower arch is tall and the vaulting is fan-vaulting of the 19C. Two sets of Rood stairs may be seen. There is a fine First World War memorial altarpiece at the E end of the N aisle. By great contrast, the chancel was rebuilt in 1743 to the designs of Nathaniel Ireson, and it is certainly handsome for its date, in white and pale blue picked out in gold. There is no E window, but a large altarpiece with a Glory. There are Corinthian columns and Rococo decoration. The roof is a plaster groin-vault with leaves as ribs. The altar rails and stalls are of the same date. The wooden chancel screen harmonises with the chancel. It was erected in 1938 (by W.H. Randoll Blacking) and has six Corinthian columns which separate four side bays and a wider central opening. The screen under the tower is dated 1620. The pulpit is typical Jacobean with the usual round blank arches. Some of the benches are also Jacobean and end with shell-tops. Other items of interest are a long 13C chest, a fragment of a medieval cope (at the W end), and the arms of King Charles II (over the N door). Modern glass vividly shows the angels, Michael and Gabriel (S aisle, second window from E). The stained glass of the W window is by Clayton & Bell. Effigies of Sir Maurice Berkeley and his two wives, 1585, lie on a tomb-chest in a deep niche on the N side of the chancel. Opposite is a bronze bust to William Godolphin, 1636. The tablet to Captain William Berkeley, 1749, is by Peter Scheemakers. A large damaged tomb-chest at the W end of the nave is said to be of John Luttrell (died 1430). It has large quatrefoils enclosing shields.

Cheddar, St. Andrew. Numerous tourists visit the famous Gorge, but how many walk beyond the ancient market cross to the church? There is the usual grand Perpendicular W Mendips tower (but taller than usual) with three belfry windows (but only the central one perforated), straight-topped pierced parapet and pinnacles. There is a higher stair turret with a spirelet at the NE corner. Above the W window is a window flanked by original figures of the Annunciation. The N aisle, porch, and clerestory (which is 14C and is earlier than usual) have pierced parapets. There are large chancel chapels and an elaborate chapel is placed E of the S porch.

Inside, as the two-light clerestory windows are 14C, so are the nave arcades of five and a half bays. The piers are octagonal. The arches from the chancel to the chapels are also 14C, but the arch from the aisle into the outer S chapel is late Perpendicular and is elaborately panelled: on its E side are three richly decorated and canopied niches with modern figures of St. Stephen, St. Augustine, and St. John the Baptist. In a smaller niche by the window is the original figure of St. Erasmus. This outer S chapel is known as St. Nectan's chapel or the Fitzwalter chantry. The roofs of nave and aisles are original, that on the nave being panelled. The tower has a stone lierne-vault.

The font is 13C, a pillar piscina is slightly earlier and a double one slightly later, and there is an old iron-bound chest. The Rood screen and parclose screens have mostly béen reconstructed. The 15C stone pulpit with colour is notable: there are small canopied niches, and busts of angels on the underside. Some of the bench-ends are original, with plain tracery. The communion table of 1631 with its bulbous legs is very fine. The painting of Christ at Emmaus in the outer S chapel is by Jan Erasmus Quellinus (1629–1715). The glass in the same chapel is mostly 15C and is well-arranged—St. Barbara, St. Catherine, the Annunciation, a priest, some angels and heraldic. At the W end, under the tower, there are large 18C paintings of Time and Death, looking like medieval wall paintings. On the N side of the chancel there is a tomb-chest with canopy and with a brass to Sir Thomas Cheddar in armour (died 1442), and, on the floor below, a brass to his wife, Isabel (died 1474).

In the churchyard is the grave of William Chatterton Dix (died 1898), author of many hymns, including 'As with gladness men of old' and 'Alleluia! sing to Jesus'.

Dunster, *St. George.* Every traveller here will obtain an unforgettable picture of Old England—the octagonal market cross which was a yarn market built c 1589 by the Luttrells; the Luttrell Arms Hotel, a residence of the Abbots of Cleeve Abbey; a partly 14C, tile-hung house known (misleadingly) as the Nunnery; and, high up on its hill, Dunster Castle, purchased by the Luttrells in 1376 and owned by them until it was vested in the National Trust in 1976.

St. George's is a fine cruciform building with a central tower and was formerly the Benedictine Priory Church, serving a daughter house of Bath Abbey. The W side of the crossing piers and the W doorway prove that there was a Norman church. The chancel is 13C (with restored triplet of lancets at the E end), but otherwise the church is Perpendicular. The tower with diagonal buttresses and with higher stair turret at the NW was erected in 1443 (the contract still exists). There is an embattled S porch and a Rood stair turret. The W window is a good example of Perpendicular.

Inside, the S arcade is of six bays and the N arcade is only of four bays (due to monastic buildings) with typical Perpendicular piers. An arch of curious shape which leads from the S transept into the S chancel aisle is the result of a 16C widening of a 13C arch. The chancel aisles are of two bays. There are original wagon roofs with many bosses, but the S aisle has a panelled ceiling with small bases. Particularly fine is the Perpendicular Rood screen of 14 bays across nave and aisles in the second bay W of the crossing, with blank panels below, tracery, and then ribbed and panelled vaulting and carved friezes. The screen was erected in 1499 to divide the church between monks and parishioners. The monks had the E part. The side screens to the N and S chapels are also fine and have traceried panels and a broad frieze of foliage on the cornices. Beneath the crossing the altar has a folding, painted reredos. The late Perpendicular octagonal font in the SW corner has shields, Instruments of the Passion, and the five wounds of Christ. Its tall cover is 19C. The arms of King Charles II, 1660, painted on a large wooden panel, are placed on the N nave wall. The brass chandelier is of 1740. The painting of the Brazen Serpent is attributed to Sir James Thornhill. The E window has stained glass by Clayton & Bell. The firm also seems responsible for the four-light W window.

The S transept houses a grave-slab of Adam of Cheddar, who was Prior here from c 1345 to 1355. In the adjoining S chancel aisle the alabaster slab commemorates Lady Elizabeth Luttrell (died 1493), and the huge Jacobean alabaster monument has effigies of Thomas Luttrell (died 1571) and his wife Margaret, and of their son, George (died 1629) and his wife Joan. George is shown kneeling. The monument dates from 1613. In the chancel itself an ogee recess on the S houses an effigy of a woman of c 1300. On the N side a tomb-chest decorated with quatrefoils enclosing shields bears the effigies of Sir Hugh Luttrell (died 1428), a veteran of Agincourt, and his wife.

East Brent, *The Blessed Virgin Mary.* The church and village are situated on the E side of Brent Knoll Hill, as the church and village of Brent Knoll are situated on its W side. An ancient stone spire may seem rare in Somerset, but there are 18 and this one is particularly elegant. The tower has a W doorway and window, above which are three niches, all fortunately retaining their original figures: in the lowest are the Virgin and Child, in the middle niche the Trinity—the Father holding the crucified Son—and in the highest Christ enthroned crowning St. Mary. There is a pierced parapet and square pinnacles. The N aisle has large windows, pinnacles and a pierced parapet. The S side is plainer, with a small chapel E of the porch. The S door with tracery and its handle are 15C.

Inside, there is a N aisle of five bays and a two-bay S chapel, but what will first be noticed is the nave roof of embossed plaster: it is dated 1637 and it can be said to be early Gothic Revival. The chancel was rebuilt in the early 1840s, but the sedilia are probably medieval. The pulpit is dated 1634 and has blank arches in two tiers. The W gallery is a year later and may have formed part of the chancel screen. It was placed in its present position and altered in 1824. There is a bier in the S chapel, inscribed 1734. The royal arms over the S door are of King George IV, 1825. The wooden eagle lectern is 15C, as are the benches, with plain poppyheads. There are a Pelican in her Piety, the symbols of the Evangelists, blank tracery and the initials of John Selwood, Abbot of Glastonbury from 1457 to 1493, who built a house N of the church.

The glass in the E window of the N aisle is mostly medieval and it is a gem. There are nine scenes, and above each panel is a Latin inscription explaining the scene below: **Top left**: The Betrayal: Judas is kissing Christ and St. Peter strikes off the ear of Malchus. **Top right**: Christ before Pilate, who prepares to wash his hands. **Top centre**: Christ before King Herod. **Middle left**: The Scourging: what awful faces the men have compared with the calm dignity of Christ. **Middle centre**: The Crucifixion: St. Mary is swooning and St. John the Evangelist supports her; Longinus pierces Christ's side, from which blood flows, and when he touches his eye with this blood his temporary blindness is cured; the centurion was suddenly converted and he is seen behind with his inscription declaring *filius Dei est iste* (this is the Son of God). **Middle right**: The Deposition or taking down from the Cross: for the first time all the persons are Christ's friends: St. Mary and St. John the Evangelist kneel at the foot of the Cross, a servant in socks of different colours unnails the Body of Him who has borne the weight of the world's sin, and the Body is reverently held by Nicodemus and St. Joseph of Arimathea. **Bottom left**: The Entombment: here St. Mary, St. John the Evangelist, St. Joseph of Arimathea, Nicodemus, and possibly St. Mary Magdalene surround a coffin in which they have laid a Christ of unutterable peace. **Bottom centre**: The Ascension: just the feet of Christ appearing under His robe as He ascends (*hic elevatus est dominus*: here ascends the

Lord). **Bottom right**: The Coronation of the Virgin by the Father and the Son, with the Dove above. The NE window of the N aisle has three large 15C figures of saints in yellow stain—St. James the Great, St. John the Evangelist and St. John the Baptist. The N aisle windows are otherwise 19C and depict the Apostles.

There are two decayed mid-14C effigies of priests, in the S chapel and in the N aisle, and a Gothic Revival tablet in the S chapel of c 1869 to the children of the Reed family, erected by George and Sarah Reed and signed by Casentini & Co.

The name that will always be connected with East Brent is that of Archdeacon Denison, Rector for 51 years in the last century, who was a notable High Churchman. He lies buried SW of the S porch. The parish claims that it was the first to introduce the Harvest Festival, started by Archdeacon Denison in 1857. (But cf. Morwenstow, Cornwall.)

Glastonbury, *St. John the Baptist.* The abbey was founded in c 700, but legend takes us back still further, when St. Joseph of Arimathea arrived with the Holy Grail, sent by St. Philip to evangelise Britain. Legend also affirms that King Arthur was buried here. The monastic remains are inspiring, and the abbey had influence and splendour second only to St. Alban's. The visitor will then visit the other medieval church, St. Benign or Benedict, mainly early 16C, and will then walk to the top of the Tor, 500ft high, for the marvellous view, and to see the most conspicuous object in Somerset, the tower of St. Michael's, 13C and 15C. There are seven niches on the W face and on either side of the doorway are panels showing a woman milking a cow and St. Michael weighing souls.

Now to the fine Perpendicular church of St. John the Baptist, with its grand tall Somerset tower, 134½ft high. It has double belfry windows, much panelling, stringcourses carried round the receding set-back buttresses, and very elaborate parapet and pinnacles, all based on Gloucester Cathedral. There is a large W doorway and W window with niches. The W door is Perpendicular with elaborate tracery. The S side of the church is embattled, and the porch of two storeys has niches with modern statues of St. John the Baptist and St. George and a lierne-vault. All the aisle windows are large (four-light) and with the clerestory windows give plenty of light. The E window is of seven transomed lights. The sanctus bell turret is over the E end of the nave. It was rebuilt by Sir Gilbert Scott in 1856–57.

Inside, the arcade is of seven bays with typical Perpendicular piers. The two E arches are lower than the rest. Angel-busts carry shafts which support the Somerset roof of 1500. The tower arch is panelled. The organ occupies the NW corner. There is a restored screen to the S transept (St. George's chapel): it has St. George, Tudor roses, the *Agnus Dei* and a Pelican in her Piety. The restoration was by F. Bligh Bond, 1927. The altar in the chapel has a 15C German painting of the Crucifixion flanked by the Church Triumphant and the Synagogue with broken staff. A number of copies of Italian Old Master paintings hang elsewhere in the church. The font and the pulpit are both by Sir Gilbert Scott. There is a cupboard of c 1500, and a chest has the arms of the Courtenay family. The arms of King Charles II in the N aisle are well-carved. The church possesses part of the cope of Abbot Whiting, made into a pall in 1774. It is displayed in the N transept, placed over the 15C tomb of John Alleyne, and it is surrounded by an exhibition of some plate, Erasmus' *Paraphrases*, a Breeches Bible, and Abbot Whiting's gremial or silk apron. On the N side of the chancel are some 15C pieces of stained glass put together, with kneeling figures at the foot. The N window of the N transept has stained glass of 1936 by A.J. Davies of Bromsgrove, which depicts the legend of Joseph of Arimathea. Other 19C glass is by N.H.J. Westlake (S chancel aisle; main E window) and Clayton & Bell (E window of N chancel aisle). On the N and S of the chancel there are the tomb-chests of Richard and Jane Atwell (died 1476 and 1485), with brasses lost, but with weepers between panels. The tomb-chest with alabaster effigy in the S transept is of John Cammell (died 1487), lay treasurer of Glastonbury Abbey. Four weepers and five camels adorn the sides of the tomb-chest.

Ilminster, *The Blessed Virgin Mary.* A grand church dominated by one of the finest of the grand Somerset towers, in this case a crossing tower. There are three square-headed windows in each of its two storeys (the upper ones perforated), numbers of pinnacles, and a stair turret with spirelet at the NW corner, and all in the lovely golden Ham Hill stone. The whole church is Perpendicular with large windows, but even so the N chapel is the most splendid part. It is described as a glasshouse and was probably built by a bequest of Sir William Wadham in 1452. It has a five-light N window and three-light windows to E and W, all transomed. The parapet is decorated and pinnacled. The S porch has an ogee gable and blank panelling. With a central tower, a large W window is possible.

Inside, the three-bay arcades have been altered, but the piers are original. The arches are notably wide. The nave has a typical Somerset roof, and that of the chancel is 15C. Under the fine crossing is a fan-vault. The very tall crossing arches are panelled. There are large squints into the chancel. An altar of 1976 stands beneath the tower. The S transept serves as the Lady chapel.

The octagonal font is Perpendicular. The screen to the N chapel (in the N transept) is Jacobean. The modern reredos has figures of saints. The chandeliers are 18C. The E window is by Burlison & Grylls, depicting St. Gabriel, St. John the Evangelist, the Virgin and Child, St. Athanasius and Isaiah. By Heaton, Butler & Bayne are nave windows which show the Magi (S, first from E), Christ among the Doctors (S, second from E), the Ascension (N, first from E) and the Crucifixion (N, second from E). The N window of the N transept (the Wadham chapel) is by Christopher Webb, 1964. The N transept houses two significant monuments of the Wadham family. One is of Sir William Wadham and his mother with her little dog, 1452: fine brass figures on a large tomb-chest with empty nodding ogee niches and at one end, two small figures kneel below a seated figure of Christ. The other (against the N wall) commemorates Nicholas Wadham and his wife Dorothy (founders of Wadham College, Oxford, died 1609 and 1618): also fine brass figures on a tomb-chest with a wall plate flanked by black columns. Note that the inscription is reversed so that it may more easily be read. In the S transept there is a wall monument of Humphrey Walrond (died 1580).

Milborne Port, *St. John the Evangelist.* This church is quite different to all the other churches mentioned in this county. It is not predominantly Perpendicular for there is much pre-Conquest and early Norman work. Definite pre-Conquest features can be seen in the chancel S wall, such as pilaster strips, horizontal bands and arcading, which are typical of that period. Moreover, the chancel has the tall profile of a pre-Conquest church. Nevertheless, there are shafted windows in the chancel which seem early Norman. It is instructive to see the two periods side by side. There are also some lancets of 13C date. The church has a central tower, which is Norman in its lower parts. The upper part is Perpendicular. The N chancel chapel is also Perpendicular. The S transept is Norman, but it has been refaced. In the angle between the transept and the S side of the church there is a Norman stair turret. The S doorway is also Norman, and although it has been restored, its tympanum is original, showing two fierce beasts. The nave, wide N aisle and N transept were all rebuilt in 1867–69. There is no S aisle.

Within, the five-bay N arcade has octagonal piers and large capitals. The crossing has four substantial arches, the N and S still entirely Norman, the E and W pointed but resting on Norman shafts. Each arch has three orders. A nave altar beneath the crossing was dedicated in 1984. It was one part of an extensive reordering by Oswald Brakspear. Above there is a fine panelled ceiling. The sanctuary has a boarded and painted ceiling of 1908, which was inserted during a restoration by Sir Walter Tapper. To the left and right of the E window the tall medieval niches contain statues of St. John the Evangelist and the Virgin and Child, by John Skelton, 1972.

The Rood screen is Perpendicular with the usual arches, tracery and mullions, but, rather unusually, it is straight-topped (not vaulted). The octagonal font is Norman. Much of the stained glass is by Clayton & Bell: the W window, S nave windows and the E window of the S transept. The E window of the chancel is by William Bainbridge Reynolds, 1908. A painted board of the arms of King Charles II, 1662, is suspended from the N aisle's roof. A recess in the S transept has a worn female effigy, c 1290. At the E end of the N aisle there is a large Gothic wall tablet to Sir William Medlycott, 1835, by Humphrey Hopper. High up in the N transept there are a number of hatchments.

The name *Port*, incidentally, is an Old English word for a town. It suggests an early importance for the place and provides a context for a substantial church.

Minehead, *St Michael*. Usually approached up a number of steep steps, with thatched cottages on either side. The church is in a superb position on North Hill with wonderful views. The tall 15C W tower has three-light belfry windows, set-back buttresses, battlements and a higher stair turret at the SE corner. On the S face of the tower is a representation of the Holy Trinity, God the Father holding Christ Crucified with the Dove, and on the E face is shown St. Michael weighing a soul which a devil is trying to weigh down, but St. Mary is just successful. There is a niche on each side of the W doorway. The embattled S side has quatrefoils in the battlements, a S porch and a Rood turret. The N chapel proceeds as far as the chancel itself. In the NE corner there is a vestry (formerly a chapel) and so the E end has three gables.

Inside, the 15C N arcade is of seven bays with octagonal piers and double-chamfered arches. The arch into the N vestry, most unusually, is of wood. The nave roof is a replacement of 1886 by J.P. St. Aubyn. The octagonal font is 15C with a panelled base and figures with legs dangling below the bowl. The fine 15C Rood screen across nave and aisle with vaulting and foliage friezes is similar to so many that still exist in Devon. On top is a painted clock-jack who formerly held a hammer to strike the hours. He is mentioned in the churchwardens' accounts of 1641. The wooden communion table in the N chapel is very fine. It is Elizabethan, with bulbous legs and two angels who support the top. Slightly later is the carved pulpit of the mid-17C. The brass chandelier is dated 1727. There are no fewer than three sets of royal arms: Queen Anne (1704) and King George II (1743) side by side on the N wall, and King Charles II over the S door. The usual inscribed boards from an altarpiece, plus paintings of Moses and Aaron, are fixed to the N wall at the W end. They are of the 1630s. In a case at the W end is a missal which belonged to Richard Fitzjames (Bishop of London, 1506–22), who was Vicar here in 1485–97. It was given to the church in 1949. There are several early 20C windows by Henry Holiday. Monuments include a brass to Mary Quirke in a high horned head-dress of c 1440, and a 15C effigy of a priest under a fine canopy (placed between the sanctuary and the N chapel); he holds a chalice and has two angels at his head, and at his feet a dog sleeps with his paws on a bone. He may be Richard of Bruton, Vicar here in 1401–06.

Selworthy, *All Saints*. All tourists in this area visit this delightful village of whitewashed thatched cottages around a village green. On the way to the church the shaft of the medieval cross in the churchyard will be noticed. This churchyard must be one of the most beautiful sites in England, being situate on a hill, with a marvellous view looking across the valley to Dunkery Beacon, the highest point on Exmoor, 1707ft.

The church is equally delightful. The font is Norman and the lowest part of the low tower is 14C, otherwise all is Perpendicular. The tower has a stair turret with cap at the NE corner. The two-storeyed S porch has a doorway with panelling, and the door is original with linenfold panels. The S aisle is embattled with particularly fine windows. The N aisle is plainer, but its E window is of the fine type with some fragments of old glass. The exterior is painted white, and the E end terminates in three gables, as usual in the West Country.

The interior is as a church should be, with its tall slim piers and large windows. The glory of the church, however, is the S aisle; a capital gives the date 1538. All the wagon roofs are original, and, of course, particularly elaborate is that of the S aisle. It has richly decorated wall plates with angels holding shields, and large bosses with the face of Christ and Instruments of the Passion. The coloured bosses of the nave roof are also remarkable, the Holy Trinity surrounded by saints.

The restored pulpit has some early 16C panels, a 17C sounding-board and an hourglass stand. The altar rail is of c 1700 with turned balusters. There is a 14C wooden chest strongly bound with iron bands. The W gallery is dated 1750 and is supported on Doric pilasters. The squire's pew of the early 19C is the upper storey of the porch. The E window has stained glass in nine panels by Clayton & Bell. There is a Perpendicular tomb-chest in the chancel, without effigies. There are two identical monuments at the W end of the S aisle by Sir Francis Chantrey—to C.R. Dyke Acland (died 1828) and C.B. Dyke Acland (died 1837)—each with a portrait medallion and a draped altar. There is also a memorial on the S wall to William Blackford (died 1730), with heads of cherubs at the foot. The ashes of Francis C. Eeles, the founder and first Secretary of the Council for the Care of Churches, lie near the tower.

*St. Mary Magdalene's: one of the finest of the many fine
15C and 16C Somerset towers*

Taunton, St. Mary Magdalene. Seen from the railway, Taunton is dominated by two grand Perpendicular church towers—St. Mary Magdalene's and St. James's. Both towers have been rebuilt, but almost exactly as they were. St. Mary Magdalene's is 163ft high, the highest in the county, and it is the most elaborate in England. It has double windows of three transomed lights in its three upper stages (the bell stage being taller), a large W window, a W doorway flanked by niches, large battlements and very tall pinnacles, all pierced like lace, crowning the top. The stair turret at the NW corner does not rise above it. The tower was built by c 1514 and was rebuilt in 1858–62 to the old design. The S porch is dated 1508: it is of two storeys and has three niches above the doorway and a lierne-vault inside. Modern figures fill the niches. The aisles have Perpendicular windows and there is a pierced parapet on the S side.

Inside, there are double aisles of six bays. The arcade between the two N aisles is 13C, the only survival of the previous church. The capitals of the piers and of the tower arch are angel-busts. In the tower there is a fine fan-vault. The tower arch is panelled. The 15C roof has tiebeams and kingposts with angels. The angels are gilded, as are innumerable further carvings on the panels above (the gilding dating only from 1968), and the tiebeams are painted red and blue. 19C statues of the 12 Apostles fill niches between the clerestory windows. The reredos of Mansfield stone and Caen stone is by G.E. Street, 1872. The octagonal font is Perpendicular; its tall canopy is of 1845. There are some pieces of ancient glass in the S chapel and in the clerestory windows. The seven-light E window has stained glass to commemorate Queen Victoria's Golden Jubilee in 1887. The E window of the S aisle, by A. Moore, has stained glass depicting ten Somerset worthies, including Robert Blake (the admiral), King Ina (a 7C King of Wessex) and King Alfred. There are monuments to Thomas More, 1576, a plate divided into six panels with shields, at the W end of the inner S aisle; and to Robert Graye, 1635, with a life-size, painted standing figure in alabaster, flanked by columns and placed high up on the N wall.

Trull, All Saints. The church is comparatively small, but it is one that must be visited because of its fittings. The W tower is not the usual Perpendicular, but late 13C, as is proved by the W window of three lancets and the absence of a W doorway. The remainder of the church is however Perpendicular. The S aisle and porch are battlemented.

Inside, the S arcade is slightly earlier than that on the N. Both are of three bays. The nave's wagon roof and the tower roof are original. The 15C or 16C wooden pulpit is outstanding. It has its original large figures of the Latin Doctors (St. Gregory, St. Ambrose, St. Jerome and St. Augustine of Hippo) and St. John the Evangelist with a chalice. These figures are said to have been buried and hence their preservation. Angels appear in the upper panels and there are two small saints between each of the larger figures. The Rood screen must have been very fine when complete. Now only the base, vaulting with leaf decoration, and very rich cornice remain. There is a tympanum of plaster on a beam above the screen. The side screens are similar to each other with linenfold panelling and the names of the donors over the doors. The benches of c 1510 are a large and interesting collection. As usual there are the Instruments of the Passion (one bench-end showing a Tree Cross, lantern, pincers, hammer, cock, ladder and three scourges), leaves, plants, tracery, and Renaissance profiles and vases, but what is unique is a religious procession over five bench-ends—a priest in a cope, a man with a processional cross, a man with a shrine, a man with a candle, and a man with a book. The bench against the back wall with linenfold panelling is dated 1560 and has the name of Simon Warman as its maker. The 15C glass is also notable. In the chancel E and S windows are fine examples of St. Mary and St. John the Evangelist (part of a Rood group), and the three saints associated with dragons—St. Michael, St. Margaret and St. George. In the N aisle, the NW window is by C.E. Kempe, 1899 (depicting St. Martin, St. Machar—who evangelised Mull and Aberdeen—and St. Nicholas) and its W window by Kempe & Co., 1913 (depicting St. James the Greater, St. Elizabeth and St. Peter). The E window in the S aisle wall, which is of 1876 by Lavers, Barraud & Westlake, shows the Corporal Works of Mercy. The W window of the same aisle shows St. Luke, St. Paul and St. Mark, by John Bucknall, 1968.

Wells, *St. Cuthbert*. A very rare dedication in the S of England, but the original church was probably founded by King Alfred, who granted a resting place at Chester-le-Street, County Durham, for the body of St. Cuthbert. It is the largest parish church in Somerset with one of the biggest of the grand towers, 122ft high, with most striking pairs of three-light belfry windows continued into the stage below, and prominent main and minor pinnacles. There are five niches on its W face. For more than a century until 1561, there was a second, central tower. The plan is of a six-bay nave with N and S aisles; a S porch, opposite which is a 13C treasury or sacristy (now a choir vestry); N and S transepts, both 13C; outer N and S chapels which are placed W of the transepts; a three-bay aisled chancel; and a projecting sanctuary. The church was lengthened to W and to E in the 15C. The clerestory, S porch (note the boss with pig and litter), aisles, transepts, and chancel, all with parapets, seem to be Perpendicular, but the treasury on the N, the S transept's E window and the S doorway are of c 1300 or earlier. The numerous large 15C windows all have five lights, including the clerestory. The parapets have blank arcading.

Inside, the nave piers are 13C, heightened by the 15C masons. The tower has a lierne-vault with bosses, and the broad tower arch is panelled. Between the clerestory windows wall shafts rise on demi-angels to support the typical Somerset tiebeam roof with more demi-angels. Its restoration was completed in 1963 and it is now very beautiful. The N transept proper is St. Catherine's chapel. To its W is Holy Trinity chapel, which was long connected with the civic life of Wells. The S transept was the Lady chapel (or Tanner's chantry). The chapel to its W was St. Cuthbert's. The S chancel chapel was of St. Martin and All Saints.

Fragments of reredoses remain in the transepts and they must have been very fine: that on the S was a Tree of Jesse, made by John Stowell in 1470. The contract survives. The figure of Jesse can still be recognised. The reredos in the chancel is by James Forsyth, 1867, depicting the Last Supper. The chancel also has 19C floor tiles. The notable pulpit is dated 1636, with rich carvings of Old Testament scenes (Jacob and the Angel, David and Goliath, Samson and the Lion, Jonah in the Whale, and Daniel in the Lion's Den). It is supported on bird brackets. The royal arms are of 1631, placed over a doorway in the N nave aisle. The E window has stained glass by William Wailes, and the other chancel windows and the E window of the S chancel aisle are also 19C, by Joseph Bell of Bristol. In the S transept there are numerous monuments, including a brass to Francis Hayes (died 1623).

Westonzoyland, *St. Mary the Virgin*. The place is well known as being the site of the Battle of Sedgemoor in the Duke of Monmouth's rebellion, July 6th, 1685. Many rebels were imprisoned in the church, where five died of their wounds; and then followed Judge Jeffreys' Bloody Assize. The parish register states: 'The Ingagement began between one and two of the clock in the morning. It continued nearly one hour and a halfe'.

The church's tall Perpendicular tower is one of the grand Somerset ones with three belfry windows in the top of its four stages, only the centre one perforated; there are battlements and pinnacles and a number of niches; the stair turret is at the NE corner, but it does not rise above the tower. The S side of the nave is all embattled—aisle, clerestory, two-storeyed porch (whose roof rests on busts of angels) and S chapel. The initials of Richard Bere, Abbot of Glastonbury, 1493–1524, appear on a buttress. The medieval door bears tracery. The chancel is earlier, being 14C (Decorated). The N side is a plainer version of the S. Note the tall, transomed, three-light N window of the N transept.

Inside, the nave arcades are of six bays with typical Perpendicular piers. Note the tall panelled tower arch (the whole height of the nave), which opens into a fan-vault. The chancel arch is also panelled. The roof is one of the finest even in this county of fine roofs. Ornamented tiebeams supported on wall posts with angels support more angels and kingposts. There are numerous bosses. Just think how it was all carved some 500 years ago. The roof of the S transept is also fine, panelled with angels and bosses. The Rood screen with loft and Rood, as every church had originally, is of 1939. Some benches are square-headed with tracery motifs as usual, but there are also some poppyheads (rare in the West Country), one with the initials of Richard Bere, Abbot of Glastonbury (as on the buttress and on a fragment of glass). The Elizabethan communion table, now placed at the E end of the nave, is fine with bulbous legs. The font is Perpendicular, octagonal and arranged in layers. All the windows have clear glass, except for a few roundels and for some panels in the W window. In a recess in the N transept there is an effigy of a priest of c 1300.

SUFF0LK

This charming county of contrasts has been known for years as 'Silly Suffolk'—a very apt title, because it is really 'Selig', or Holy, Suffolk—hence no doubt its array of just over 500 medieval churches, one of the grandest selections in England. Follow its picturesque coastline to Orford and Aldeburgh (of Benjamin Britten fame) and on to Walberswick, Southwold, Kessingland, Lowestoft and Corton, all with fine churches, their towers visible for miles over land and sea. Hunt out the pretty villages among the Waveney valley, which forms its N border, with their flint churches, some with round towers, like Syleham and Weybread, others of considerable size and grandeur, like Beccles, St. Mary's at Bungay and Hoxne. Likewise the idyllic scenery and settlements along the Stour valley in the S, where Suffolk and Essex meet—to Nayland, Bures and Sudbury (a town with three glorious churches) and on through Cavendish and Clare. There is grand, yet gentle scenery in the valleys of the Rivers Deben, Orwell and Alde. St. Botolph built his monastery at Iken, overlooking the Alde, and the church there contains a pre-Conquest cross-shaft which may have been his memorial. Suffolk's greater churches number among the best-known in England—Lavenham, Long Melford, Southwold and Blythburgh—yet the county also has its share of those rustic little gems with charming and often isolated settings and unspoilt interiors, like Shelland, Badley, Withersdale and Thornham Parva.

Most Suffolk churches are faced with flint or flint rubble, because durable dressed stone had to be imported from Northamptonshire and Rutland. The flints, which are either whole or knapped to expose their dark cores, give the walls a pleasant colour and texture. Flint and stone are used in beautiful flushwork panelling, which is seen in parapets and buttresses, also towers (e.g. Eye) and over 70 porches, of which Woodbridge is one of the finest. Several E Suffolk churches incorporate chunks of greyish-brown septaria, which was dug from near the coast between Orford and the Naze. This is not a very durable building material and some towers built of it have collapsed. Two towers near Orford (Chillesford and Wantisden) are built of yellow-buff coralline crag which was mined in the immediate vicinity. Over in the far W the chalky and often much-weathered clunch may be seen in doorways, windows and fonts. When Tudor brick came into fashion in the late 14C and 15C, Suffolk pressed this into service in some 15 towers, a dozen or so porches, windows, doorways and the S aisle at Kenton. Timber is also attractively used for bell turrets in 14 churches and in porches, including the superb 14C N porch at Boxford.

Suffolk has a pleasing variety of towers, usually of flint. The tallest is Lavenham (141ft), followed by Stoke-by-Nayland and Mildenhall (120ft). Other lofty flint towers include Woodbridge, Eye, Southwold, Stradbroke, Laxfield, Kessingland, Bungay and Hoxne. Grand towers with double sets of belfry windows and fine flushwork parapets trace the churches at Mendlesham, Horham, Stonham Parva, Falkenham and St. Nicholas', Ipswich. The majority of the Tudor brick towers are in the E half of the county, as are most of the porch-towers which are a feature of the area within a 12-mile radius of Ipswich. There are 42 round towers (also two ruins) and at least 25 of these are pre-Conquest. Many occur to the N and E, although six are in the W, including the handsome Norman round tower at Little Saxham.

Apart from the round towers, only a handful of Suffolk churches have visible pre-Conquest remains. A group to the N of Ipswich, including Claydon, Hemingstone, Gosbeck and Debenham, have long-and-short quoins indicating pre-Conquest structures. Norman work is more abundant and the county is quite rich in Norman doorways. Churches with large amounts of Norman work include Polstead, Wissington, Orford (chancel), Fritton, Ousden, Oulton and the magnificent bell tower at Bury St. Edmund's. Early English architecture is somewhat sparse and is seen at its best in the chapels at Lindsey and St. Stephen's, Bures, in the chancels at Troston and Kesgrave and in parts of the churches at Hunston, Little Whelnetham, Lydgate, Rumburgh, Little Wenham and South Elmham St. James. Late 13C work is seen at its best in the chancels at Ashbocking and Great Barton and early Decorated work of c 1300, with simple 'Y' or intersecting tracery abounds in many churches; Westerfield and Westleton being two where work of this period predominates. Later Decorated architecture is particularly note-worthy at Cotton, Dennington, Raydon, Burstall, Rickinghall Inferior, Coney Weston, Bramfield and Redgrave, also several churches (e.g. Eriswell and Icklingham All Saints) in the far W of the county. It is the Perpendicular style in which Suffolk really excels; in the great churches like Lavenham, Long Melford, Lowestoft, St. Mary's at Bury, Woodbridge, Southwold and Blythburgh and in smaller churches like Denston, Stowlangtoft and Gipping Chapel. Features of this period include fine clerestories, low-pitched roofs, large spacious windows, ornate porches and beautiful flushwork.

The Classical period is scantily represented, although the remodelling of Euston Church in 1767, the restorations at Brightwell (1656–57) and Shelland (1767), and the 18C chancel at Shotley are worth seeing. There are towers of this period at Gislingham, Grundisburgh, Cowlinge, Drinkstone and Redgrave.

A few new churches were built (mostly of white Suffolk brick) in the 1840s, of which W. Ranger's St. John's, Bury St. Edmund's, J.M. Clark's St. John's, Woodbridge and T.M. Nelson's small church at Stowupland are noteworthy. The Gothic Revival is represented by a variety of architects. There are restorations by William Butterfield at Great Waldingfield, St. Peter and St. Gregory, Sudbury and St. Mary Stoke, Ipswich. Leiston Church was almost entirely rebuilt in a very eccentric manner by E.B. Lamb and Elveden Church was given a grand and lavish early 20C enlargement by W.D. Caroë. Several restorations were done by J.H. Hakewill and E.L. Blackburne, but few of the new 19C churches are by nationally famous architects. The best of these include Higham Green by Sir Gilbert Scott, Hopton (near Lowestoft) by S.S. Teulon, St. Agnes', Newmarket by R.H. Carpenter and the churches of St. John at Ipswich and Felixstowe by A.W. Blomfield. Several 19C churches and many restorations are by local architects. R.M. Phipson rebuilt St. Mary-le-Tower, Ipswich, and designed the fine church at Great Finborough. Frederick Barnes designed the new church at Melton, did many restorations and designed several Nonconformist churches. E.F. Bisshopp designed St. Michael's, Ipswich and was responsible for some versatile restorations in the Ipswich area, from the fine Gothic chancel of St. Clement's, Ipswich to the neo-Classical chancel at nearby Holy Trinity. Several churches were restored by H.J. Green of Norwich, who rebuilt the tiny churches at Darmsden and Willisham. J.S.

Corder towards the end of the 19C produced some very attractive restoration work, particularly the unusual tower at Swilland. One of Suffolk's grandest 19C churches is St. Bartholomew's, Ipswich, begun in 1896 to the designs of Charles Spooner. This tall and dignified building was built for Anglo-Catholic worship on a large and lavish scale.

Of the 20C are three Ipswich churches by H. Munro Cautley, an authority on medieval churches and on royal arms in churches. St. Thomas', Ipswich is by N.F. Cachemaille-Day, and St. Francis', Ipswich and Chelmondiston are by Basil Hatcher.

Suffolk interiors are rich in interest and craftsmanship. The quality of medieval roofs is superb and in Suffolk churches one must never forget to look upwards. There are fine open timber roofs of the 14C, like Dennington's and St. Peter's, Ipswich. There are several tiebeam and kingpost roofs, particularly in the area NW of Ipswich, around Barking, Flowton and Nettlestead. The 15C arch-braced cambered tiebeam roofs abound and Blythburgh's roof retains most of its original colour. Most glorious of all are the hammerbeam roofs, either single, as at Badingham, Earl Soham and Westerfield, or double, as at Grundisburgh, Cotton, Woolpit and Gislingham. Some of these roofs have original or restored angels and others have remains of canopies of honour over their E bays. Most remarkable of all is the unique roof at Needham Market.

This is a county for fine screenwork; out of about 150 examples, some 65 are more or less complete and several (like Bramfield, Eye, Westhall, Somerleyton and Southwold) have original painted panels of saints and Apostles—each one an Old Master. A few parclose screens survive, and the two at Dennington are complete with their original lofts.

A few Norman fonts survive (e.g. Kettlebaston and Preston) and several octagonal Purbeck marble fonts of the 13C may be seen, but the majority follow the typical octagonal late 14C and 15C East Anglian pattern, with lions and sometimes with hairy wodewoses round the stem, angels with outstretched wings beneath the bowl, and in the bowl panels usually the Evangelists' emblems, alternating with lions or with angels bearing shields carved with emblems and symbols. This type culminated in the 14 fonts (mostly in the E) which show the Seven Sacraments around the bowl. Good examples of these may be seen at Woodbridge, Westhall, Melton, Badingham and Great Glemham. A few pre-Reformation font covers have survived. Ufford's 18ft tall cover is exceptionally fine and other good examples occur at Hepworth, Worlingworth, Bramford and Sudbury St. Gregory.

Although medieval pulpits are scarce (15 or so remain), there are in the region of 117 17C examples. There are hundreds of 16C bench-ends, with poppyheads and fascinating armrests. Fine sets of these remain at Woolpit, Stowlangtoft, Fressingfield, Ufford, Dennington and Ixworth Thorpe. About 26 churches have carved chancel stalls and those at Stowlangtoft and Sudbury St. Gregory are almost complete.

Monuments abound here; the churches of Hawstead, Hengrave and Kedington have a great many of them, and Framlingham and Wingfield have excellent sets. This is also an important county for brasses, which can be seen in just over 100 churches, including premier examples at Playford, Acton, Burgate and Sotterley.

Most Suffolk villages possess a 19C brick Nonconformist chapel. Ipswich has some larger stone-built chapels, but the finest Nonconformist buildings are the Unitarian churches at Ipswich (1699–1700) and Bury St. Edmund's (1711–12) and the Congregational Chapel at Walpole (1607 and 1847). Interesting Roman Catholic churches are at Bury St. Edmund's (1837), Bungay (1892) and Beccles (1889).

Treasure houses of furnishings and features exist at Dennington, Hessett, Kedington, Mendlesham and Denston. Particularly atmospheric smaller interiors may be enjoyed at Badley, Boxted, Brent Eleigh, Ramsholt, Cretingham, Gislingham, Thornham Parva and Withersdale. Clusters of attractive smaller churches are those in the Lothingland peninsula above Lowestoft, or in the 'Saints', S of Bungay (comprising the six South Elmhams and the four Ilketshalls). There are a group of rural shrines along the Deben valley above Wickham Market, including Hoo, Letheringham, Easton and Kettleburgh. There are picture postcard villages in W Suffolk (and the church usually 'makes' the picture)—like Kersey, Cavendish, Monks Eleigh, Brent Eleigh, Chelsworth, Boxford and Stoke-by-Nayland. Over in the far W Mildenhall's great church looks across the Fens and Elveden, Eriswell, Lakenheath, Brandon and Santon Downham are near or in the well-wooded Breckland.

Suffolk's market towns have great character and fine churches. Eye, Framlingham, Bungay, Beccles, Woodbridge, Clare and Hadleigh are well worth seeking out. Suffolk also has its share of the unusual. There are the two Trimley churches in one churchyard, the great fragments of vast churches, with tiny churches in the ruins, at Walberswick and Covehithe. There is Hengrave's idyllic church, with its pre-Conquest tower, set beside the Hall, which is now the church of the Reconciliation—a Roman Catholic church which is used by people of many denominations for retreats and conferences.

Acton, All Saints. This church has a charming approach and there are good views W from the churchyard towards Long Melford. The rendered, embattled S aisle has Y-traceried windows of c 1300; it was extended E in the 18C to form a SE chapel. The E window of the chancel is original, with intersecting tracery of c 1300. The N aisle has two good Perpendicular windows and a two-light late 14C window with good Decorated tracery beneath a depressed arch. The base of the tower, with its sturdy W buttresses, appears to be 13C, but the upper part, which had been taken down as unsafe in the 19C, was attractively rebuilt by 1923 to the designs of A.A. Hunt and G.C. Coates. The embattled porch has a large 15C outer entrance and a smaller but elegant inner entrance, beside which is a cinquefoil-headed stoup.

The interior is bright, colourful and cared-for, with 14C arcades of three bays to the aisles and two bays to the S chancel aisle. A few 14C timbers remain in the simple nave and N aisle roofs, while the S aisle has a fine 15C roof, with carved bosses, and the chancel has a wagon roof, with recently painted panels. The church was thoroughly restored in 1885–86 by W.M. Fawcett, when the N aisle received its handsome E window, with glass by Heaton, Butler & Bayne.

The present font at the W end is 19C, but the bowl of the original font may be seen in the S aisle. Many of the benches have their original 15C poppyhead ends. The rear benches also have traceried backs. Over the N door is a small Hanoverian royal arms, carved in wood. There are three steps up to the small chancel, which retains some old woodwork in its stalls. The altar rails are of the 17C.

On the N side of the chancel is a superb Decorated tomb-recess, with a magnificent ogee canopy which has two sets of cinquefoils, sub-cusped with more cinquefoils, also tiny flowers in the border, crocketed pinnacles and a finial. Beside it is a doorway with well-preserved corbel heads. The N chapel contains a series of brasses, including the famous one of Sir Robert de Bures (died 1331): the third oldest in the country but the best preserved and the finest military brass. His 6½ft effigy is in armour, over which is worn a sleeveless, belted surcoat. His feet rest upon a lion. The shield is thought to have been added later and, indeed, it is suggested that Sir Robert's shield was added to an earlier figure which had been intended for another knight. Also in the N chapel is the fine brass of c 1435 of Alice de Bryan, whose effigy is set beneath a canopy, and three 16C brasses. There are some good ledger slabs with coats of arms. At the E end of the S aisle is the little chapel built for the monument to Robert Jennens, who died in 1725 and was ADC to the first Duke of Marlborough. He reclines on a mattress, his bewigged head supported by his hand, with his sorrowing wife watching over him. The monument is framed by fluted Corinthian pilasters, which support a pediment.

Aldeburgh, St. Peter and St. Paul. This squat and solid church, with its noble tower and long porch, stands upon a slight rise overlooking the seaside and the town. Much of its fabric was rebuilt and reordered in the early 16C, and is therefore rather late medieval.

The N and S aisles reach to the E end of the chancel and as there is no clerestory the church appears remarkably wide when viewed from the E. The body of the building is lit by large Perpendicular windows. The W tower, which is a little earlier than the rest, is handsome and well-proportioned, with a SE staircase turret rising above the embattled parapet. There are fine two-light belfry windows and a good W doorway. The S porch is unusually long and has E and W arches in order to facilitate outdoor processions. In the spandrels of the niche above the S entrance are the emblems of the church's patron saints.

The proportions of the interior are unusual; the nave and aisles are very broad and the chancel, by contrast, is rather short. There are five-bay arcades. The nave roof, with its array of painted shields, is an exact copy, made in 1934, of its 16C predecessor. The 15C East Anglian font bowl (now moved to the E end of the N aisle) has traces of its original colour.

There is much 19C and 20C work here, but treasures from earlier periods include a medieval chest with three locks, a W gallery of 1735, which incorporates woodwork from the former Rood screen, the arms of King Charles II, a 17C reading desk and a superb pulpit, an oak octagon, made in 1632. A few medieval traceried bench-ends may be seen in the choirstalls and in the S chapel. Of the more recent work, the communion rails (1911) and the reredos (1950) are noteworthy. The E window contains Hardman glass of 1891 and the S aisle E window has glass by A.K. Nicholson (c 1929). The Benjamin Britten memorial window in the N aisle (1979) contains vivid red, green and blue glass by John Piper and Patrick Reyntiens, depicting three of the composer's operas. Twelve attractive 19C brass candelabra stand under the arcades. A beautiful plan, elevations and sections of the church, all by E.F. Stacey, 1977, hang on the S wall.

Amongst the memorials here are some 16C brasses in the S aisle, and in the floor beside the altar rails are three unusual 17C memorials to the Elyot family, in the form of wooden coffin-lids. Also commemorated here is George Crabbe (1764–1832), the poet, who was a doctor in Aldeburgh and was Curate here. The bust of him at the E end of the N aisle is by Thomas Thurlow, 1847. Benjamin Britten (1913–76), the composer, is buried in the far N section of the churchyard.

Blythburgh, *Holy Trinity.* One of Suffolk's finest Perpendicular churches which, apart from the lower part of the tower, grew during the 15C, as a variety of bequests towards its construction testify. The W window of the tower remains from the 14C, but the remainder of the building seems to have been built as one piece on a grand and lavish scale, with an unbroken nave and chancel and aisles reaching only one bay short of the E end. The exterior, in its setting across heathland to the S and the estuary of the River Blyth to the N, is superb and unforgettable; it looks particularly impressive at night when the whole building is floodlit. The interior has been altered as little as possible during the 19C and 20C and so preserves an atmosphere of antiquity, although some of its treasures are timeworn and a little mutilated. The church had become so dilapidated in the 1870s that the bishop ordered its closure because it was dangerous. G.E. Street made a report upon its condition just before his death and A.W. Blomfield took over the supervision of its careful and sympathetic restoration.

In the exterior we see Perpendicular architecture at its zenith. It has a long unbroken roofline, sets of 18 uniform clerestory windows, large three-light windows in the aisles taking up much of the wall space, and a graceful five-light E window, above which is a representation of the Holy Trinity in stone, flanked by corner pinnacles, and beneath which is a frieze of letters and motifs in superb flushwork. The S aisle has an openwork parapet of stone quatrefoils, punctuated by a variety of grotesque creatures which serve as pinnacles. In the stringcourses beneath the parapets are a variety of angels, shields, flowers and animal heads, also fine gargoyles. Small N and S doorways are set beneath cut-away buttresses towards the E ends of the aisles; note the large and clear Mass dial in the S buttress. The two-storeyed S porch has a fine parapet and beside its entrance is a huge Holy Water stoup, looking like part of a small font, with carved angels and a traceried shaft. The porch has a vaulted ceiling and shelters a pair of 15C traceried doors—the N doorway also has its original doors. The tower seems rather plain but is in fact well-proportioned and quite lofty. One imagines how grand the exterior would look with the tracery of the belfry windows replaced, the tower parapet made good and the bricked-up windows in the sanctuary opened up.

The atmosphere of the interior is superb. It has height, brightness and space; grandly soaring arcades, whitewashed walls and pleasant vistas. It feels uncluttered and unspoilt. The floors are a haphazard mixture of bricks, pamments, medieval tiles and a vast assortment of burial slabs (at least 19 of which once carried brasses—this would have been a brass-rubbers' paradise!). The church is 127ft long and stretching the entire length of nave and chancel is one long glorious unbroken arch-braced cambered tiebeam roof, which retains much of its medieval colour and is punctuated by large central hovering angels. The medieval aisle roofs, with their carved spandrels, rest upon an array of stone corbel faces. The impressive eight-bay arcades rest upon quatrefoil piers. The great font once had the Seven Sacraments carved upon its bowl. At its base the emblems of the

Evangelists remain. It is raised upon two steps and the inscription around the top step tells us that John and Katherine Masun gave it. The stone stools for priest and sponsors are a rare survival. The priest's room above the SW porch is furnished as a small and homely chapel.

There are many fittings worthy of examination here. The nave benches are 15C and have fascinating carvings which graphically depict the Seven Deadly Sins, also an array of characters, dressed in similar hats and pleated coats, illustrating the seasons of the year. The stalls in the chancel are also medieval. Their fronts have carved figures of the Apostles and St. Paul. The pulpit shows good 17C craftsmanship. The wooden lectern, with its buttressed stem, dates from c 1450. The Rood screen is mostly 19C, but the screens to the N and S chapels contain much original work. The spacious sanctuary has a piscina and triple sedilia. The modern altar frontal adds a welcome splash of colour here. Nearby is the superb panelled and canopied tomb of John and Thomasin Hopton. Note also the Swillington tomb in the N aisle, which now displays sordid specimens of the effects of death watch beetle. In the N chapel is an almsbox of 1473. The Jack O'Clock in the chancel dates from c 1652—he is still equipped to take a good swipe at his bell with his axe! The only stained glass is what remains of the original 15C glass in the tops of some of the aisle windows.

Much has been done during recent years to maintain the church and preserve it intact and beautiful. The people of this small community care for it admirably and visitors are made to feel expected and welcome.

Bures, *St. Stephen's Chapel.* This small building takes some finding and involves a journey of about one third of a mile along the road to Assington and then turning right into a track which, after about a quarter of a mile, leads to this small chapel in an idyllic position, with fine views across the Stour valley. This still comparatively unknown little gem was consecrated in 1218 by Archbishop Stephen Langton. It stands upon the spot where St. Edmund was crowned King of the East Angles in 855. For many years it was known as Chapel Barn, but it was tastefully restored in the 1930s and was re-dedicated for Christian worship in 1940.

St. Stephen's is a rare example in Suffolk of pure Early English architecture. It is a single-celled building with a thatched roof. Its N and S walls are pierced by single lancet windows and the E window is a triple lancet. A small vestry of brick and plaster has been built onto the N side, above which is a gallery. At the W end is a timber extension, reminding us of its former use as a barn.

Inside, this little church is atmospheric and greatly cared-for. There are consecration crosses upon its walls and the three lancets which form its E window have detached internal shafts. The communion rail incorporates 18C woodwork. In the S sanctuary wall is a piscina, and the aumbry on the N side has old woodwork in its door. The chapel is crowned by a simple open timber roof. The base of a 15C font remains and in some of the windows are fragments of medieval glass. The E window was given new glass in 1934.

The chapel contains the magnificent monuments of the De Veres, Earls of Oxford, which were transferred here from Earls Colne Priory in Essex in 1935. The effigy of Robert De Vere (died 1296), the fifth Earl, rests upon a superb tomb-chest which was made c 1340 for somebody else and has excellent niches. The tomb of Thomas, the eighth Earl (died 1371) has canopied niches, occupied by 'weepers' (or mourners) in pairs. Upon another tomb lies Richard, the eleventh Earl (died 1417) and Alice his wife; he fought at Agincourt and she wears a horned head-dress and has pet dogs at her feet. Also note here the remains of a coffin-lid, with part of an effigy, thought to be that of Alberic De Vere, who died in 1141.

Bury St. Edmund's

St. Mary, Crown Street. This great church was almost totally rebuilt between 1424 and 1446 and only the core of the chancel and a few reused features survived from the previous building, apart from the massive flint tower which was erected in c 1395–1403. The 15C work has been attributed to William Layer (died 1444).

The embattled exterior of this 213ft long church is grand and dignified, particularly when viewed from the S, where the elegantly-buttressed S aisle, ashlar-faced and with fine gargoyles and tall windows, stretches almost the entire length of the church. Its E section (the Lady chapel) was added just after 1463 and the corresponding N chapel (the Jesus chapel) was added a little earlier. Above the aisles rises the handsome and uniform embattled clerestory with 20 two-light windows. The E end of the nave has octagonal staircase turrets with crocketed spirelets. The sanctuary was added to the earlier chancel in the second half of the 15C. The W front is grand. The five-light W window is enormous and has four-light aisle windows each side of it. The W doorway is flanked by two canopied niches. The tower stands beside the N aisle and, although not tall in proportion to the nave, is a massive and sizeable structure, with angle buttresses and large three-light belfry windows. The N or Notyngham porch, built from a bequest of John Notyngham, a grocer, in 1440, is a superb piece of 15C stonework. An inscription over the entrance asks prayers for the donor. Both its buttresses have stoups and there are three fine canopied niches. Four beast-pinnacles surmount the parapet. The stone-panelled ceiling inside radiates from a central pendant, shielding an intriguing carving of God the Father, surrounded by angels. The inner doorway is 14C, reused from the previous church.

The interior is vast, spacious, airy and lofty. The tall ten-bay nave arcades draw the eye upwards to the magnificent angel roof—one of the grandest in East Anglia. This masterpiece of 15C woodcarving deserves careful examination, preferably with binoculars. 42 standing figures support the wall posts and at the ends of the hammer-beams are superb hovering angels, several illustrating the various duties performed at a High Mass and arranged in pairs down the church. There are two rows of angels on the cornices and fine tracery may be seen above the collar-beams. The E bay was a canopy of honour to the Rood. The aisle roofs are also splendid, with fascinating carvings in the spandrels (we see in the S aisle a fox and goose, a hairy wodewose and a mermaid) and also carved bosses. Above the 14C chancel arch is a 15C window with tracery of 1840 by L.N. Cottingham and stained glass of 1844 by Thomas Willement. There are two Rood loft staircases. The chancel has a beautifully painted and panelled wagon roof, studded with many bosses, one of which shows a fox, crozier in hand, preaching to a cockerel and a hen! Arcades of four bays separate the chancel from the chapels and an

E arch divides the sanctuary from the chancel. St. Mary's was agreeably restored in 1840–47 by L.N. Cottingham, when work was done to the nave roof (woodcarving by E. Nash of London) and the stonework of the windows. The arcaded reredos was also inserted at this time. The nave benches, by Arthur Blomfield, were made in 1867. The choirstalls, although much restored and reconstructed, incorporate 15C woodwork, including some ancient carved ends. The N chapel (now known as the Suffolk chapel) was tastefully furnished by Sir Ninian Comper in 1913 as a chapel for the Suffolk Regiment. Near the octagonal font is an interesting painting of c 1710 showing the interior before the 19C restoration. The tower has a squint into the N aisle which enabled the sexton, who had his quarters in the tower, to see what was taking place in the church.

St. Mary's has a rich variety of stained glass, including some by Heaton, Butler & Bayne in the great W window (1854) and in several S aisle windows, and by Clayton & Bell in the SE window of the Lady chapel, which was donated by Queen Victoria to commemorate Mary Tudor, Duchess of Suffolk, King Henry VIII's sister. She is buried beneath a stone N of the high altar. Amongst the other monuments is a tomb in the S aisle, with a cadaver effigy of John Baret, a clothier (died 1467). Near the altar rails are the tombs of Sir William and Lady Margaret Carewe (died 1501 and 1525) and Sir Robert Drury (Speaker of the House of Commons, died 1536) and his wife Anne. The brass of John Fyners, Archdeacon of Suffolk (died 1509), may be seen in the Suffolk chapel, and in the Lady chapel is a brass believed to be of Jankyn Smith (died 1481) and his wife. He is thought to have paid for the sanctuary, a chantry chapel in the N aisle and the N chancel chapel.

St. Mary's is known for its lively Evangelical worship and has a fine musical tradition.

Unitarian Chapel, Churchgate Street. The chapel is an early Georgian building of some distinction, bearing the date 1711 on its rainwater heads and retaining many of its original fittings. The roof was repaired by the Department of the Environment in 1975 and the interior was thoroughly restored in 1987–88 by Philip Orchard of the Whitworth Co-partnership. The building remains in use for Unitarian worship but also serves as a public meeting-hall.

It presents to Churchgate Street a S elevation of red brick laid in English bond. Four pilasters divide the façade into three bays. Tall arched windows flank a doorway which is surmounted by an open segmental pediment. Above the door is an oval window. There is a parapet which is raised in the central bay and which is further raised in the centre of that bay in the form of a small arched capping for the parapet's sundial. The E and W walls have two tiers of windows, the upper ones arched, which reflect the galleries within. The N wall has two very large arched windows which are separated by two small oval windows, which are typically placed to light the pulpit.

The E, W and S galleries have original seating more or less throughout. The pulpit, reached by a curving, balustered staircase and surmounted by a large tester, is also original, but slightly reduced in height. The box-pews which the chapel would have had at ground level are absent. The spaces under the galleries are now open to the centre, having been encased by early 20C screens until 1987. The clock on the S gallery's front is notable. The chapel is lit largely by uplighters. There is a central pillar to support the valley of the double-hipped roof.

S.C.H.

Clare, St. Peter and St. Paul. A noble, all-embattled market town church which incorporates flint rubble, brick and some Roman tiles in its masonry. Its proportions are grand and it contains craftsmanship from a variety of periods.

The lower portion of the sturdy W tower is Early English work of the 13C, which is seen in the single lancet windows and the W doorway, which is embellished with dogtooth ornament. The W window and the frieze of quatrefoils beneath it, and the three-light belfry windows, are 15C. The nave and aisles were rebuilt in c 1460. The aisles are lit by three-light Perpendicular windows and have stone courses beneath their parapets, studded with flowers and gargoyle faces. The clerestory has six three-light windows each side and at the E end of the nave are a pair of very distinctive staircase turrets, capped by crocketed spirelets. The chancel was restored in 1617, when its lofty windows were renewed. The E window has five lights and a transom. The S porch is attached to a small chapel. Above its entrance is a sundial of 1790, but its windows are 14C and it has a groined ceiling with carved bosses. The inner entrance arch contains 15C traceried doors, as does the N doorway and the small S priest's doorway.

The interior is light, airy and lofty. The six-bay arcades incorporate 14C piers, which were rebuilt and reused a century later. Over the arches, and the chancel arch, are unusual but very attractive crocketed hoodmoulds. The medieval arch-braced cambered tiebeam nave roof was restored in 1804 and the chancel roof, with its distinctive shields, was renewed in 1617. The stringcourses beneath the clerestory windows are studded with angels, flowers and foliage.

The 15C screenwork in the S aisle was part of the Rood screen. Nearby is the ringers' jar, made in 1729. The small chapel beside the S porch has been fitted with a 17C gallery. Beneath this chapel is a vaulted crypt or bone-hole. A great treasure of this church is its early 16C eagle lectern of latten, which is amongst the finest in the country. Note the doors to the two Rood loft staircases. The chancel is equipped with a set of Jacobean stalls, dating from 1617, of which date also are the communion rails and the heraldic glass in the E window. The church was restored in 1876–83 to the designs of J.P. St. Aubyn; the present floors and benches date from this time. The organ was brought here from the redundant church of St. Peter, Ipswich in 1977. There is a brass memorial tablet to Prince Leopold, first Duke of Albany (died 1884), Queen Victoria's youngest son, in the N nave aisle.

Dennington, St. Mary. This sturdy and dignified church, which is almost 150ft long, rises majestically from its large churchyard at the S end of the village centre. The structure grew during the 14C and 15C and the chancel is a fine example of late Decorated architecture of c 1330. The great interest at Dennington lies inside, where we may enjoy as grand a collection of treasures as may be found in any church of similar size in the land. Fine medieval craftsmanship blends with work of the 17C and 18C and also worthy craftsmanship from our own century.

Although externally this church lacks some of the airs and graces of the grand Suffolk churches, it is a noble building of great dignity.

There was an earlier church here and some pieces of stone from this earlier building have been reused. The visible work in the nave and aisles dates from the late 14C. The aisles are lit by triple Perpendicular windows and the narrow clerestory above has double windows of similar date. Money was left for building the tower in 1383. This is sturdy and well-proportioned, with large two-light belfry windows, three fine niches in its W face and a NE embattled staircase turret, which rises above the tower parapet to a height of 82ft. During the 15C the S aisle was extended E to form the Bardolph chapel, and the N porch, with its elegant niches, was erected. The chancel is entirely work of c 1330, with gabled buttresses and fine windows with Reticulated tracery and a fascinating array of corbel heads. The S priest's doorway has a mitred bishop at its apex. N of the chancel is a two-storeyed sacristy of late 15C Tudor brick.

A solid medieval door (most of the doors here are medieval) admits us to Dennington's fascinating interior. There are 14C arcades of five bays and the wide nave is crowned by a vast single-framed and braced roof of c 1430. The timberwork of the aisle roofs is mostly ancient and the roofs all rest upon an array of stone corbel faces. The chancel arch is mainly 14C but its foliaged corbels incorporate 13C work. The chancel contains much carved stonework worthy of examination. The windows are flanked by an array of fascinating 14C faces and the capitals of the internal shafts are carved with foliage, birds, animals, etc. The priest's doorway has corbels showing a bishop and a Pope, also an amazing carving at its apex, incorporating three different subjects. There are two distinct sets of sedilia and piscina in the S wall, which are exquisitely carved. The sanctuary was refurnished and the church restored by W.H. Randoll Blacking in the 1950s and the N and S chapels were refurbished in the 1960s by Eric Sandon, the modern work being entirely executed by East Anglian craftsmen.

It would take much space to catalogue the treasures here, but they include 76 intricately carved 15C bench-ends, with a variety of carved figures on their armrests and on one of the ends the mythical sciapod, basking under the shade of his enormous foot. The 15C font cover terminates in a finial with leaves and fruit being pecked by a bird. The large three-decker pulpit was made in 1625–28 and the E half of the nave is equipped with 17C and 18C box-pews. The chapels are set within glorious 15C parclose screens, with their richly traceried lofts complete and intact; sadly, only the base of the Rood screen remains. In the N aisle is a 14C iron-bound safe, a 19C sand-table where local children learned to write, and part of the 17C clock workings. In the chancel is a 14C Peter's Pence box, communion rails of 1750 and, suspended above the high altar, the only medieval pyx-canopy (c 1500) which has been restored to its rightful use. There is richly-coloured medieval glass in the tops of several chancel windows, and one window has glass by M. & A. O'Connor. The glass in the N aisle is of unusual design and colour—the work of E. Woolnough, plumber and glazier, of Framlingham, made in 1858. In the S chapel is the fine alabaster tomb of William Phelip, Lord Bardolph and the Lady Joan. He fought at Agincourt. On the wall nearby are the effigies of Sir Thomas Rous (died 1603) and his wife. The S window of this chapel also forms a tomb-recess, lavishly decorated with carved stonework and with pedestals for votive lamps.

The organ is a two-manual and pedal instrument by 'Father' Henry Willis, which was brought here second-hand in 1967 and fitted into the early 19C case already here. The tower contains a fine ring of six bells.

Eye, *St. Peter and Paul.* In a quiet corner of Church Street, we are suddenly faced with Eye's soaring tower, which rises to a height of 101ft and is one of the grandest in Suffolk. To really enjoy Eye Church in its setting, it is worth climbing the castle hill (visible to the W) and being rewarded by a glorious view, looking down upon it.

The tower is strengthened by polygonal buttresses which rise in diminishing stages and terminate in elegant corner pinnacles. These and the W face display a mass of flushwork panelling from top to bottom. Only the steep and stone-panelled parapet provides a contrast to this kaleidoscope of flushwork in stone and knapped flint. The basecourse, with shields in sexfoils, is also of stone, as is the frieze of shields in quatrefoils above the W doorway, which has a deep arch and is flanked by niches. Above the tall and graceful four-light W window are two double windows and the clock-face; then come the pairs of double belfry windows. This masterpiece of craftsmanship took shape during the 1460s and 1470s.

Of similar date is the magnificent S porch, which was even grander when the stone panels covering its E and W faces were filled with flints, rather than the present bricks and tiles and when its parapets and stone corner turrets were complete. There is still much to admire in this porch, however, including the remains of a fine stone base-course, the motifs (e.g. coats of arms, lions, IHS and MR emblems) to be seen in the stone-panelled polygonal turrets, the fine entrance arch, with friezes of panelling above, and the lateral windows with their carved spandrels. The porch shelters a 13C Early English S doorway, which has dogtooth moulding. The aisles are pierced by three-light Perpendicular windows and have chequered and pan-elled flushwork in their parapets, also good gargoyles which are near enough to the eye to be enjoyed in detail. The E ends of the aisles form chapels; the N chapel has a brick parapet and the S chapel's parapet is of Tudor brick with terracotta panels. The small doorway to the S chapel is entered beneath a cut-away buttress.

We pass through the fan-vaulted base of the tower into the lofty, bright and colourful interior, where craftsmanship from our own century has blended with the more ancient treasures to produce a place of worship which is tasteful, dignified and devotional. The church is 120ft long. At the W end is the stone-fronted ringers' gallery and on the tower wall are the arms of King George III. The arcades of five bays in the nave, with octagonal piers, and two bays in the chancel, with quatrefoil piers, are 14C. The nave has an arch-braced roof, with angels in the cornices, carved figures jutting out at the sides and carved bosses. The E bay is painted as a canopy of honour to the Rood, with IHS monograms. The aisle roofs have fine bosses and wooden corbels. The arch-braced chancel roof has many details beautifully picked out in colour. The roofs retain much of their original timberwork, but they were carefully restored in 1869, during the general restoration of the church. The architect for this was J.K. Colling and the benches were inserted at this time, as was the font, which is now resplendent with its delicate and tall blue and gold openwork cover, added in 1932 and designed by Sir Ninian Comper.

In the N aisle wall is a fine 14C ogee recess, with a crocketed hoodmould, finial and flanking pinnacles. This now provides an ideal canopy for the beautiful and memorable woodcarving of Our Lady and her Son—the work of Lough Pendred in 1973 to commemorate

Canon Donald Rea, who was Vicar here for 32 years. In the S aisle is a 17C communion table and at its E end is a chapel where the Blessed Sacrament is reserved. The altar here has a medieval stone mensa. Dominating the interior is Eye's glorious screen, resplendent with medieval colour and dating from c 1480. In 1925, Sir Ninian Comper restored this screen to its former medieval glory by adding the delicately-carved Rood loft and the Rood group, with their flanking angels. The old and new work blend perfectly. The paintings on the richly-carved panels of the dado (base) are superb: 15C Old Masters, which reward careful study. They show (working from N to S): a king; St. Helena; St. Edmund; St. Ursula; King Henry VI; St. Dorothy; St. Barbara; St. Agnes; St. Edward the Confessor; St. John the Evangelist; St. Catherine: St. William of Norwich; St. Lucy; possibly St. Thomas Becket and possibly St. Cecilia.

The chancel is bright and lofty and its furnishings are a tribute to the 20C. The light oak screens on the N side, the rails, the altar, and the gradine of Polish granite, were made in 1969. The small mensa stone set in the top of the altar was consecrated by Pope Pius XII. The cross and candlesticks, and the beautiful sanctuary lamps, are by Sir Ninian Comper. He also designed the glass in the E window in memory of the Reverend John Polycarp Oakley, who died in 1927. We see the priest kneeling beside St. Polycarp in the far right-hand light of the window. The door to the vestry is 15C, as is the beautiful arch which frames it. The organ was built by Norman & Beard in 1911; it has two manuals, pedals and 21 speaking stops.

Amongst the memorials are two very similar tomb-chests, with canopied recesses above them. One, in the N aisle, is for Nicholas Cutler (1568) and the other, in the S chapel, is for William Honyng (1569).

Felixstowe, *St. John the Baptist.* A rare Suffolk example of 'seaside High Church' in all its glory! It was built to cater for the growing resort which was developing out of two slightly inland villages. St. John's stands on one of the highest points in the town and its 175ft high spire is a prominent landmark. The church is built of red brick and Bath stone and uses mainly the Early English style of architecture. The nave and lean-to aisles were completed in 1895, the chancel and S chancel chapel were added in 1899 and the SW tower and spire rose in 1914. The architect was Sir Arthur Blomfield. This is one of his large, functional and reasonably cheap redbrick churches and it was said of him that he 'excelled in the charitable and unremunerative art of keeping down the cost'. It is nevertheless an impressive church of great dignity.

The exterior blends well with its surroundings. The building has a pleasing mixture of rooflines. The almost horizontal aisle roofs allow maximum light to enter the clerestory windows and accentuate the steeply-pitched gables of the nave, chancel and chapel. The cinquefoil-headed lancet windows are single in the aisles, and in groups of three (in the chapel E window) or four (in the great W window). The clerestory windows are cinquefoil in circles, alternating with sexfoils in unusual three-cornered openings. The three-light E window, with its Geometrical tracery, is the one example of pure Decorated architecture. Dominating the exterior is the stately tower and spire of 1914, which are modifications by Charles Blomfield of his father's design. The tower is cleverly positioned at the SW corner; had it been placed at the W end of the nave, it would have been totally out of proportion, but here its height is accentuated successfully. The large angle buttresses add dignity and make the tower appear broader than it actually is. The judicious use of Bath stone is most effective in the crocketed hoodmould of the large S doorway, the hoodmoulds above the pairs of lancet windows which pierce the walls, and in the parapet, with its turret-pinnacles and spirelets. The stone spire is elegant and well-proportioned.

The interior has preserved its Tractarian atmosphere of stillness and mystery. Just enough light streams through the lofty W windows and the clerestory, but an atmospheric 'devotional dusk' increases the further E we go. The internal walls are faced with red brick as are the piers of the five-bay nave arcade. This led Sir John Betjeman in his poem 'Felixstowe' to mention 'the redbrick twilight of St. John's'. The broad nave has a tiebeam and kingpost roof, rising to a height of some 60ft. The lofty chancel is divided from the S chapel by a two-bay arcade. The high altar is backed by a mosaic reredos framed in ornamental alabaster, showing the Last Supper which was given by Canon F. Pretyman.

The 12-sided font stands at the W end of the N aisle. On the windowsill is a remarkable model of a ship, made from the breast-bone of a Christmas turkey by a member of the crew of the Cark lightship. The handsome pulpit and Rood screen were designed by Gerald Cogswell and were given in 1903 and 1910 respectively. The furnishings of the Lady chapel were designed and made by Wippell & Co. in 1926–28. Its small lectern is the work of a local doctor and was carved in 1943. The Sacrament is reserved in the Lady chapel, 'where the white light burns with steady glow' as in Betjeman's poem. The excellent glass in the windows is almost entirely the work of James Powell and his firm. Two windows in the Lady chapel are the work of Goddard & Gibbs. One is of St. John the Baptist, to mark a death in 1971; the other is of St. Thomas More, following a death in 1982. The E window of the Lady chapel shows St. Edmund, St. Felix and St. Fursey: East Anglia's martyr-king and two of the region's early evangelists.

The church possesses a Bible, Prayer Book and two other service books, all bound in leather and embellished with silver fittings, which were presented to it in 1899 by Augusta Victoria, Empress of Germany and inscribed by her. These were in regular use until 1914 when, for obvious reasons, they were put into mothballs!

Framlingham, _St. Michael._ A large and prosperous town church, situated a few hundred yards from the castle of the Bigods and serving one of Suffolk's most attractive market towns, St. Michael's is noted for its fine organ (the oldest in the county) and for the superb set of monuments which are found towards its E end and mostly in the large chancel chapels. These chapels were added, and the chancel lengthened, by the third Duke of Norfolk and the work was not completed until c 1553.

The exterior is distinctive and the building has a feeling of great strength and solidity. The chancel and its flanking chapels are wider and a little longer than the nave and aisles. They are lit by large Perpendicular windows. The aisle windows have Decorated tracery, set under square heads and are possibly late 14C. The fine flushwork-faced clerestory has sets of five triple Perpendicular windows and money was left for this in 1464 and 1520. Above the clerestory is a most unusual inscription from the Psalms in lead, punctuated by angels over gateways. This is not ancient and is believed to have been copied from a church in Paris. The great W tower is bold and sturdy and 96ft high. There is flushwork in its basecourse and buttresses and it has massive four-light belfry windows to release the sound of the eight bells inside. The embattled porch is said to date from c 1780.

Inside, we are aware of the church's considerable length, its unusual proportions and, as we go E, a remarkable amount of space. There are five-bay arcades in the nave and four-bay arcades in the chancel. The crowning glory of the nave is its fine roof of single hammerbeam construction, but the hammerbeams are hidden behind elegant ribbed coving each side. The chancel has a wagon roof and its walls retain their William Morris-type stencil decoration. The chancel chapels are particularly bright and spacious.

The 15C font is of the typical East Anglian variety, crowned by its original spire-like cover, with crocketed ribs. The nave benches, in medieval fashion, are worthy pieces of 20C carving. At the W end on its stately gallery is the organ, made by Thomas Thamar of Peterborough in 1674 for Pembroke College, Cambridge. Above the N arcade is part of a 14C wall painting of the Holy Trinity. The arms of King Charles II hang near the S entrance. The space in the large chancel has been wisely used. A central altar stands E of the chancel arch and there is clear space between this and the high altar in the sanctuary, which is backed by an early 18C reredos with a 'Glory' (the IHS in rays) in the centre and the Ten Commandments each side. Note also the ancient chest near the S chapel screen and, in the S chapel, a most unusual long bench, which was for the use of the residents of Hitcham's Almshouses.

At the E end is a superb set of mid-16C Renaissance monuments, commemorating members of the Howard family, the Dukes of Norfolk. These great tomb-chests, which are elaborately and sumptuously carved, are noteworthy as fine pieces of architecture in addition to their interest as monuments. Commemorated here are Henry Fitzroy, the illegitimate son of King Henry VIII, and his wife, Lady Mary Howard, also Thomas Howard, third Duke of Norfolk, and his wife, and the two wives of the fourth Duke. On the N side of the N chapel is the excellently recoloured monument of the poet, Henry Howard, Earl of Surrey, who was beheaded in 1547, and nearby a small tomb-recess commemorates the fourth Duke of Norfolk's little daughter Elizabeth. Commemorated in the S chapel is also Sir Robert Hitcham, who died in 1636.

Hadleigh, *The Blessed Virgin Mary.* The setting is beautiful; a peaceful and pretty churchyard which is pleasantly away from the main street of the market town, containing this great flint church, which makes a perfect picture with the 15C timber-framed guildhall to the S and the majestic Deanery Tower—a masterpiece of Tudor brickwork—to the W. Hadleigh was a 'peculiar' of the Archbishops of Canterbury, as was the Essex living of Bocking. Both incumbents are co-Deans of Bocking.

Hadleigh's W tower was begun in the early 13C, with Early English lancet windows in its base. It was completed in c 1300 and has three-light belfry windows with intersecting tracery. It is crowned by a tall lead-covered spire, also of c 1300. The tower is 64ft high and the spire rises a further 71ft. There are eight bells in the tower, but the oldest bell (which may well be 13C) hangs beneath a small gable outside the spire. The rest of the church is embattled and has good gargoyles beneath the parapets. The aisles stretch the entire length of the building and have uniform late 14C windows.

The E wall is quite spectacular, with its vast seven-light E window and large three-light E windows in the aisles. N of the chancel is a two-storeyed medieval sacristy. The S porch has pairs of tall two-light lateral windows and three niches above its wide entrance. Inside we can see that it was once vaulted. The S doorway has a pair of sturdy 15C traceried doors.

Inside we are aware of the vastness of this church, which is 163ft long and 64ft wide. There are wide five-bay nave arcades, also a further two bays to the chancel chapels, which have interesting corbels between the arches. The roofs of the aisles are medieval and the chancel has a 15C panelled roof which has several bosses, with figures each side of the beams at the apex. The sanctuary piscina and triple sedilia have been restored, but opposite is a beautiful tomb-recess which probably also served as an Easter sepulchre.

The font is a fine piece of 14C stonecarving. In its stem and bowl are shallow canopied and vaulted recesses. Its tall openwork cover was made in 1925 to the designs of Charles Spooner. At the W end are several hatchments, also the 18C ringers' jug, or 'Gotch'. There are 15C traceried screens to the N and S chapels and in the S chapel is a seat made up of two 15C bench-ends. One has a creature and the other the legendary wolf guarding the head of St. Edmund. Three small squints pierce the wall of this chapel, giving a view of the high altar. Much of the N chapel is taken up by the organ, the upper part of whose case is by 'Father' Smith and dates from 1687. Much of the 19C work here dates from the restoration which took place in 1871 under the supervision of J.D. Wyatt. The pulpit is by Farmer & Brindley and the lectern is by John Hardman. Much of the 19C glass is by Ward & Hughes, including the E window and the S aisle windows, of which three are signed by T.F. Curtis (in 1897, 1899 and 1908). The E window of the aisle contains interesting glass by George Hedgeland, of 1857. In the S aisle wall is a 14C ogee tomb-recess. Several brasses may be seen on the walls. One brass inscription (a palimpsest) commemorates the Reverend Rowland Taylor, who was burned to death in 1555 for his Reformation principles. He is further commemorated in a window in the S chapel.

Ipswich, *Unitarian Meeting House, Friars Street.* Set in a quiet courtyard near the town centre is this remarkable building, which is one of the finest and most unspoilt meeting houses in the country. It was built by Joseph Clarke, a local house carpenter, in 1699–1700 and was opened as a Presbyterian chapel. It cost £257! By the end of the 18C the congregation had become Unitarian and it has been used by the Unitarians ever since. The building is excellent of its type and period and most of its furnishings are not only original, but also of very high quality. Daniel Defoe wrote of it: 'As large and as fine a building of that kind as most on this side of England, and the inside the best finished of any I have seen, London not excepted'.

This is a timber-framed building with plaster walls. It has a double-hipped roof. On three sides are two tiers of rectangular windows and there are attractive oval windows over the three doorways. On the S side are larger semicircular-headed windows, with circular windows above them. The doorways (containing original doors) are master-pieces of design, with handsome carved brackets supporting their pediments. The tiny spy hole in the E door (facing the passage to St. Nicholas Street) is a reminder of the times when Nonconformists were persecuted and their services disrupted.

After the simple dignity of the exterior, the interior is majestic, with an unspoilt atmosphere, created by the beautiful original furnishings. The building is a rectangle, measuring 60ft by 50ft. Across the centre are four tall circular columns of wood rising from the floor to the ceiling. Galleries, with panelled fronts and resting upon circular columns, occupy three sides of the building. These contain seats which rise in tiers. The chapel is furnished at ground level with original box-pews. The circular communion table stands in the central space, behind which is the reading desk and the magnificent pulpit, with its grand staircase and fine woodcarving in the style of Grinling Gibbons, which is thought to be by one of his pupils. Above the organ, at the opposite end, is a hexagonal one-handed clock, which was placed here in 1700, but is in fact older than this. Suspended at the centre of the building is a fine three-tiered brass candelabra which was made in Holland during the 17C and weighs over 200lbs. Pegs for wigs survive in the galleries.

Kersey, *St. Mary.* From its splendid elevated position, this pictur-esque church dominates and broods over one of England's most picturesque villages, which was a centre for clothmaking in medieval times. The village street ascends both sides of the valley and is crossed by a ford at the bottom. It is this perfect setting which is one of the greatest features of this church, which displays good 14C and 15C work.

The exterior is imposing and the fine tower, completed in 1481, has a flushwork parapet, tall belfry windows, a W window flanked by niches and a good entrance arch, containing a pair of original doors. The N and S porches are both noteworthy; the N is smaller, but both have gabled buttresses and superb proportions. The S porch has excellent flushwork, niches and a handsome entrance arch. The 14C N aisle has a chequerwork parapet and pinnacles, also fine gargoyles. The chancel was rebuilt in 1862.

Inside, the tall nave is separated from the N aisle by a remarkable seven-bay arcade, the elegant arches being framed with foliage. It is incomplete at the W end and maybe work stopped at the Black Death. The nave has a 15C arch-braced and single hammerbeam roof; the hammerbeams are headless figures and beneath them are beautifully carved spandrels. Traces may be seen in the E bay of a painted canopy of honour to the Rood. The aisle roof is panelled and the walls supporting it are topped by richly-carved stone cornices. In the N wall is an arched recess, elaborately carved and retaining a little of its original colour. Amongst the stone fragments which it now displays is part of an alabaster carving of the Trinity. The chapel at the E end of the aisle (known as the Sampson chapel) has a richly canopied sedilia and piscina, from which there is a squint to the high altar. Two niches, which are now but a shadow of their former glory, flank the E window here and six panels of a 15C screen in the chapel depict Prophets and kings in medieval colour. They include St. Edmund, holding an arrow (second from the left).

The font is 15C and now rather worn, but it has fine carvings of angels and traceried patterns. The nave wall has traces of a wall painting of St. George. The lectern has a carved 15C base, support-ing an eagle which is also of considerable age, but believed to be from a different source.

The chancel contains mostly 19C work, although much of its roof timbering is older. The reredos was sympathetically and imag-inatively repainted in 1958 by Jack Penton. The church was reseated in 1888 to the designs of J.P. St. Aubyn.

Lavenham, *St. Peter and St. Paul.* This magnificent 15C and early 16C church, which retains its earlier 14C chancel, is pleasantly situated on a rise, a sedate distance away from the centre of the small and picturesque medieval town which it was built to serve. Three generations of the Spring family, who were wealthy clothiers, and also John De Vere, the 13th Earl of Oxford, were prominent among its many benefactors. The mullet (or star) of the De Veres and the chevron between three mascles of the Springs may be seen many times in the stonework of the church.

The view of the exterior across the large and well-tended churchyard is unforgettable. The chancel (c 1340) has large E and S windows with fine Decorated tracery; E of it is the vestry, built by Thomas Spring II in 1444. The nave, aisles and E chapels are faced with dressed stone (unusual in Suffolk churches; the stone here is from Casterton). These have beautifully carved battlements with openwork decoration, fine gargoyles, buttresses which are embellished with foliage and ogee arches and large windows. The nave and aisles were rebuilt during the second half of the 15C. The tall clerestory has a dozen large three-light windows on each side. The staircase turret, with its crocketed spire, at the E end of the nave, was wisely retained from the 14C church. The S chapel, which is higher than the S aisle, was built by Thomas and Alice Spring in 1523–25. It has three transomed four-light S windows, a transomed five-light E window and an embattled parapet, but the details of these features differ from those of the S aisle. The chapel's N counterpart was erected by Simon and Elizabeth Branche in c 1500. Both chapels have inscriptions asking prayers for their donors. The S face of the stone porch (built by John De Vere) is a mass of stonecarving. The porch has a fan-vaulted ceiling and the S doorway contains a pair of 16C linenfold doors.

Lavenham's mighty tower, rising 141ft (the tallest in Suffolk) was begun in 1486 and was finished shortly after 1523. This massive structure of knapped flint has great beauty and dignity, with elegant set-back buttresses which are embellished with niches and traceried panels, a grand W doorway with ogee canopy and flanking pinnacles, a large four-light W window with a fine arch, which is studded with lions' faces and foliage, and large three-light belfry windows. The rather short parapet and square corner terminations suggest that the tower may be unfinished, yet its proportions are excellent and many experts agree that a more complicated parapet and taller turrets would be superfluous.

Lavenham's interior is dignified and devotional. The church is 173ft long and 68ft wide. As in the exterior, the stonecarving is glorious, particularly in the arcades of six bays and the mass of stone panelling between these and the clerestory windows. The panelling is of lozenges with shields. The spandrels are decorated with quatrefoils containing blank shields.

The glass in the W window, designed by J.M. Allen and made by Lavers & Barraud, appeared in the International Exhibition in 1862. It depicts St. Peter. The base of the tower is lined with stone wall seats, backed by trefoil-headed arches. The wide nave and aisles are crowned by well-restored 15C roofs, with standing figures on the wall posts. The cambered tiebeam nave roof has a canopy of honour in its E bay. The octagonal Purbeck marble font is now very worn and probably dates from the 14C. Over the S doorway are three sets of royal arms. Those of King George III are carved in relief, King George II's are painted, and at the centre are the arms of our present

Queen. Towards the E end of the N aisle is the sumptuously carved Renaissance Spring parclose screen, very darkly stained, made in c 1525, which encloses the tombs of Thomas Spring III (died 1523), 'the rich clothier', and his wife Alice. Another chantry screen may be seen in the S aisle, possibly for the Spourne family. The ancient tomb which it now encloses was brought here from the churchyard in 1908. The Rood screen, with its beautiful openwork tracery, is 14C; it retains its original doors—a rarity in East Anglia. The parclose screens to the chapels are 15C.

The Spring or S chapel provides a beautiful and intimate place for prayer. It has a fine roof and a 17C communion table. Note the band of stonecarving beneath the sills of the windows. The glass in the windows here is early 19C and is particularly colourful. The E window is exceptionally attractive and shows, in the upper lights, Christ blessing children of both Biblical and late medieval times, and in the lower lights, the donors of the church present their gift alongside the woman who poured her precious ointment over Christ. The Branche or N chapel has wall seats and fragments of medieval glass in its windows. Nearby is the organ, a Conacher instrument, rebuilt by Arnold, Williamson & Hyatt in 1962, with 20 speaking stops.

The chancel arch is 14C, as is the core of the chancel and its two windows. It is equipped with a set of 15C stalls, which have traceried fronts and carved poppyhead ends. The five misericords which remain are worth examining; they include the Pelican in her Piety, a man squeezing a pig under his arm to make it squeal, and a man's ears being pulled by an ibis and a spoonbill. The sanctuary contains much work of the 19C, including the reredos, the restored sedilia and the richly coloured red and blue glass in the E window, designed by J.M. Allen in 1861 for Lavers & Barraud. The three-light S window in the chancel is of 1861, by Frederick Thompson. The 19C restoration at Lavenham progressed in stages from 1860 onwards. The architect for much of this work was Francis C. Penrose. The present seating in the nave and aisles, and also the chancel roof, dates from this time. Much restoration of the chancel woodwork was carried out by Henry Ringham of Ipswich. The reredos of 1890 has seven crocketed gables, the central one being larger than the rest, with pinnacles at the two ends.

Amongst the memorials of note is the wall monument in the sanctuary to the Reverend Henry Copinger (died 1622), which shows effigies of him, his wife and children. In front of the communion rail is the tiny chrisom brass of the baby, Clopton D'Ewes, who died in 1631.

Long Melford, *Holy Trinity.* Long Melford is aptly named; its main street stretches for some two and a half miles. Suffolk's longest parish church, sedately set across a green at its N end, stretches about 250ft from W to E, of which 70ft is taken up by the E Lady chapel, which is itself considerably larger than several Suffolk churches! Most of this great church was erected between c 1467 and c 1497 and the vestry was completed by 1507. This is Suffolk Perpendicular in flint and stone at its very best.

Its noble exterior, of vast scale and proportions, is a mass of flushwork panelling, with great windows occupying an incredible amount of wall space. The aisles stop short of the chancel's E bay. These have elegant buttresses and the majority of the three-light windows are arranged in pairs. Above them rises the tall embattled clerestory, with 18 three-light windows each side. The N aisle has

Holy Trinity Church, one of the most famous of Suffolk's late medieval 'wool churches', with a tower rebuilt by G.F. Bodley, 1903

fine gargoyles and on this side rises the embattled Rood loft staircase turret, in mellow Tudor brick. The tall and airy S porch has lofty lateral windows and a wide entrance arch, flanked by niches, and with three fine canopied niches above it. The inner S doorway has a handsome 15C arch which is studded with flowers and is flanked by corbel heads. Between the N aisle and the Lady chapel is the tiny Clopton chantry, with its seven-light E window. In a corresponding position on the S side is the vestry. The Lady chapel, with its distinctive three gables, a long and low structure, is an entity in itself, built in 1495–96, with flushwork tracery and uniform three-light windows. Around the exterior are inscriptions asking prayers for the souls of many of the benefactors by whose generosity parts of this church were built. These include the Clopton family of Kentwell Hall and the Martyn family of Melford Place.

The sturdy tower (rising 118ft) is comparatively modern, although it blends well with the rest of the exterior. What we see today is the work of G.F. Bodley (completed in 1903) who encased the brick tower with flint and stone and gave it new windows producing the Gothic structure which graces the exterior today.

The interior will be remembered not only for its many treasures, but also for its all-pervading atmosphere of brightness and spaciousness, its grand vistas and noble proportions. Graceful nine-bay arcades (of which the six W bays are 14C work) draw the eye upwards to the bright clerestory and to the long unbroken arch-braced cambered tiebeam nave roof, which is glorious simply for its size and length, not to mention its traceried spandrels and the host of standing figures on the wall posts. This and the aisle roofs are 15C. The major 19C restoration here took place in 1868–69 under Henry Woodyer. The benches were modelled upon Sir Gilbert Scott's seating for St. James's, Bury St. Edmund's.

The huge font shows 15C craftsmanship in Purbeck marble and is crowned by a 20C cover. The arms of King George I hang over the S door and nearby hangs the Savage hatchment (1635) which is the oldest of its kind in Suffolk. More hatchments may be seen on the tower walls. In this aisle is glass by Ward & Hughes. The windows of the N aisle contain one of the finest displays of 15C glass to be seen in England. Here we see portrayed in rich colours a host of benefactors, Melford worthies, saints, Apostles and emblems. Particularly beautiful is the tiny roundel above the N door, with three rabbits' faces, each having two ears, but with only three ears between them! In the wall towards the end of this aisle is an alabaster panel, of 14C date, showing the Wise Men visiting a giant-sized reclining Virgin Mary and her infant Son. The E ends of the aisles form chapels, each with a piscina. In the N chapel are brasses to members of the Clopton family, also the tomb, with effigy, of Sir William Clopton (1446). In the E wall of this chapel, on the S side, is a fascinating double squint, which penetrates two walls to give a view of the high altar. The S chapel contains brasses to members of the Martyn family.

From the E end of the N chapel, a door admits us to a vestibule (with a pretty traceried ceiling) leading to the Clopton chantry chapel, which John Clopton in his will of 1494 called 'My lytell chapell in Melforde Churche, there my grave is redy made'. This intimate chapel is a tiny and devotional spot. Piercing its S wall is John Clopton's tomb, which also served as an Easter sepulchre. On the underside of its arch are exquisite mural paintings, including one of the risen Christ. In this chapel we see some fine sedilia, a piscina, canopied niches built to contain the 12 Apostles, a remarkable roof with two long poems painted on scrolls around the cornices, and, in the E window, the lovely lily crucifix (Christ crucified upon a lily, the emblem of the Virgin Mary) in 15C glass.

The sanctuary is dominated by Farmer & Brindley's grand Caen stone reredos, erected in 1877. Light pours in above it from the great five-light E window. N of the altar is the handsome monument of Sir William Cordell (1580), who built Melford Hall, and was Speaker of the House of Commons and Master of the Rolls. His recumbent effigy is guarded by figures representing Prudence, Justice, Temperance and Fortitude. Pairs of black columns support two large coffered arches.

We enter the remarkable Lady chapel from outside. This has a central worship area surrounded by processional aisles. Its pretty arcades, fine original roof and canopied niches are noteworthy. There are fragments of medieval glass in its windows, an early 18C Chinese-style clock by Thomas Moor of Ipswich, and a multiplication table carved in the E wall, which survives from the days when this chapel was used as a village school.

('A Sermon in Stone/The 500th Anniversary Book of Long Melford Church (1983)'.)

Orford, *St. Bartholomew*. This little town of great charm, from which the sea has receded to leave the remarkable spit of land known as Orford Ness, is dominated by two historic buildings. The massive castle keep was built for King Henry II between 1165 and 1173 and the parish church was begun later in the 12C as a chapel of ease to Sudbourne Church. This building is a fine example of 14C Decorated architecture, with important Norman work remaining in its ruined chancel. It was once cruciform, and its aisled chancel was used as the conventual church of a priory of Augustinian Canons. This part had fallen into decay by 1720 and was abandoned. The great tower partly collapsed in 1830 and stood in ruins until it was restored in 1962 and 1971.

The church stands nobly in its large churchyard, behind the houses of the town square. The tower is massive and in its lower parts we see 14C work, with a splendid W doorway, containing carved doors which were made by a local archdeacon in 1928. In the masonry of the lower stages is much brown septaria, which was probably the cause of the tower's downfall. The nave and aisles are tall and sturdy, with elegant tracery in the three-light windows of ʻc 1320–30 and circular quatrefoil windows in the clerestory. The porch, which has the emblems of the Passion and the Trinity in the spandrels of its entrance arch, is a 15C addition and shelters a beautiful 14C S doorway. The E wall of the church was refaced and remodelled in 1896 by J.T. Micklethwaite. The Norman chancel ruins have two beautiful arcades, with massive piers and semicircular arches.

The great height of this impressive, airy and spacious interior is enhanced by the absence of a structural chancel. The nave is punctuated by lofty five-bay arcades of c 1320–30. The roofs were part of J.T. Micklethwaite's 1890s restoration. At the E end of the N aisle is the Norman arch which led to the former N transept of the cruciform church, also the sturdy 12C pier which may have supported the central tower. An inscription tells us that the beautiful 15C East Anglian font was given by John and Katherine Cokerel. There are lions and wodewoses round the stem and in the bowl panels are the four Evangelists' emblems, the Passion and Trinity emblems, also Our Lady of Pity and part of a Trinity scene.

There are many items of interest here. In the W part of the building are 18C benefaction boards, a 15C bench, a chest dated 1634, three of the church's five bells, interesting old pictures of the church, the parish stocks and 18C paintings of Moses and Aaron, which once were part of an altarpiece. The handsome screen and Rood were carved by Lawrence Turner in 1921, to the designs of Sidney Tugwell of Bournemouth. He also designed the choirstalls, behind which on the N side is a panelled screen of 1712, with the arms of King William III, which once surrounded the mayor's pew. Parts of a 16C screen may be seen in the sanctuary. There are two fine paintings at the E end; that above the high altar is 16C, by Bernardino Luini, and the other, of the Holy Family, in the Lady chapel, is by Raffaelino del Colle, a pupil of Raphael. The glass in the E window (1921) is by Clement Bell.

The wall monument in the Lady chapel has the kneeling effigy of the Reverend Francis Mason (died 1621). In the floors of this church are no fewer than 11 brasses, dating from c 1480 through to 1613.

Southwold, _St. Edmund, King and Martyr._ This superb 15C Perpendicular church was built as a single entity between c 1450 and 1500, much of the fabric having been completed by 1460. The small chapel of ease to Reydon Church which it replaced had burned down c 1430.

St. Edmund's is magnificent outside and in. It is 144ft long, 56ft wide and its massive tower soars to a height of 100ft. The exterior exemplifies late Perpendicular architecture and Suffolk flint and stonework at their very best—it is elegantly proportioned and majestic. The aisles embrace all but the E bay of the chancel. They are pierced by large uniform Perpendicular windows and are supported by elegant buttresses. The walls are the nearest that the builders dared go towards providing walls of glass! The stringcourses beneath the parapets are punctuated by angels, faces, little flowers and gargoyles. The clerestory has a stone parapet and two-light windows each side. Above it stretches one long green copper roof, punctuated only by the elegant pinnacled and copper-covered flèche, which is a 19C replacement of the original sanctus bell turret. At the W ends of the aisles are embattled staircase turrets. The N doorway has foliage and a little bird in its arch moulding and on this side is the abutment for the Rood loft staircase. The W tower is sturdy and lofty, with much flushwork. The great W doorway is flanked by crowned lions and has a variety of carvings in its arch, as does the deep arch of the W window, above which is the inscription 'SCT EDMUND ORA P NOBIS' (St. Edmund, pray for us) in crowned letters. The window is flanked by two fine vaulted and canopied niches. The pairs of double belfry windows are tall and graceful and give the tower great character and beauty, although this tower does lack the lovely embattled parapets and pinnacles of other fine Suffolk towers. The flint and stone flushwork which graces this exterior is seen at its best in the S porch, where we see chequerwork on its E and W faces, a basecourse with arched panels and 'AMR' motifs, also a variety of panelling on the S face and parapet. The S parapet is of stone, with traceried panels. The porch is two-storeyed and between its pair of upper windows is a fine canopied niche. The entrance has traceried spandrels and the Lamb of God emblem in its arch moulding. The stained glass in the windows of the porch (by Clayton & Bell) was saved from the tracery of the Lady chapel window, which was blown out in 1943. The porch has a vaulted ceiling, with beautiful bosses. Its inner doorway has a richly moulded arch and superb 15C traceried doors.

Southwold's interior is lofty and bright. Light floods in through the clear glass of many windows, highlighting the beauty of the colourful work with which our own century has adorned this stately church. A judicious restoration took place here in the mid-1860s to the designs of R.M. Phipson, but so much of the original medieval craftsmanship survives here to be admired. There are seven-bay arcades and a handsome tower arch, but there is no chancel arch to impede our view of the glorious single hammerbeam and arch-braced roof, which extends the full length of the church. Its wall posts rest upon stone corbel faces and there are angels at the ends of the hammerbeams. The E bay of the nave roof is a canopy of honour to the Rood. The chancel roof has been boarded, ceiled and gloriously coloured. The aisle roofs have been tastefully restored and their bosses are worthy of note.

At the W end stands the fine 15C font. This is still beautiful, but is only a shadow of its former glory, having lost the Seven Sacraments which adorned the panels of its bowl, although their canopies remain. The tall and elegant font cover, designed by F.E. Howard, was made in 1935. Overlooking the font from his pedestal by the tower arch is Southwold's Jack, with his bell. He is dressed as a man-at-arms of c 1480, when he was made. On the tower arch are some of the many masons' marks to be found in the church. The glass in the

W window is by Lavers, Barraud & Westlake (1880). The tower houses a ring of eight bells. Over the N doorway are the arms of King George III (1783) and nearby is a fine medieval chest with a traceried front and a carving of St. George. The fine traceried pulpit is 15C and was tastefully re-coloured in 1930. In the S aisle is the old Elizabethan communion table. The lectern is a copy of the medieval lectern in the church of All Saints, Pavement, York. The painting on Southwold's glorious screen (which stretches the full width of the church) was completed in c 1500. Along its dado, in panels which are lined with golden 'gesso' plasterwork, we see in the N section the emblem of the Trinity and various orders of richly-feathered angels and archangels. In the central section are the Apostles, with their emblems, and the S section has characters from the Old Testament. The chancel is equipped with some of its original 15C misericord stalls, which have fascinating creatures on their armrests and on the undersides of the seats. These are backed by superbly carved parclose screens. Behind the high altar is F.E. Howard's noble and colourful reredos, installed in 1930. The great E window above it has stained glass by Sir Ninian Comper, made in 1954. The window to the N shows St. Edmund in incised glass by John Hutton (1974). The arches of all three windows in the sanctuary are embellished with a variety of carvings. In the S wall is an unusual piscina, with three small recesses, and a fine sedilia, with a canopy above and stone shields beneath. The organ was built by J. Walker in 1887 and rebuilt in 1966 by Arnold, Williamson & Hyatt.

Stoke-by-Nayland, _St. Mary the Virgin._ This large and stately church, most of which dates from 1421–81 (although parts of the porch and N chapel are 14C) has a length of 168ft and a grand position on high ground overlooking the picturesque valley of the River Stour, in a charming village. Its noble exterior, which was the subject of a painting by John Constable, is dominated by a magnificent W tower which rises to a height of 120ft. This is one of Suffolk's outstanding churches and, although it underwent considerable restoration in 1865, when many of its internal fittings were replaced, it remains a grand example of Perpendicular architecture, with fine proportions, and contains several memorials to the Tendring and Howard families who helped to rebuild it.

The grand tower is a landmark for miles. There is much brickwork in its masonry, its buttresses are embellished with niches and it is crowned by stocky pinnacles with spirelets. There is a stone basecourse with shields and in the grand W doorway are the arms of the Tendring and Howard families, also sturdy original doors. The body of the church is long and embattled, with three-light windows in the aisles and a set of 13 clerestory windows in the nave, and more in the chancel. Of note on the N side is the small 14C chapel (St. Edmund's chapel, c 1318), also the pleasing mellow Tudor brick N porch. The two-storeyed S porch retains some 14C work. It has a vaulted ceiling with carved bosses, and shelters what must be the finest pair of 15C traceried doors in the county.

The interior is lofty, spacious and dignified, showing fine proportions and superb medieval stonework. The nave arcade of six bays is particularly impressive; its piers have attached shafts and the arches are framed by hoodmoulds resting upon corbels. A stringcourse beneath the clerestory is studded with carvings of angels and flowers. Simpler arcades of two bays separate the chancel from the chapels which flank it. Most glorious of all is the mighty W tower arch, which is very tall and remarkably satisfying, showing the beauty and grandeur which can be created by a Gothic arch. The arch-braced cambered tiebeam roof of the nave rests upon large corbels. The great five-light E window almost fills the E wall; it contains colourful glass made by J.B. Capronnier of Brussels in 1876. His work also appears in the E windows of the N and S chapels.

The font stands upon three steps and is a fine piece of 15C stonecarving, showing the Evangelists and some curious figures in the panels of its bowl. There are 15C screens to the N and S chapels, and seven carved stalls with misericords, thought to date from the 14C, may be seen in the nave. The memorials are mostly to be seen in the E chapels. The S chapel contains the excellent brass, 6ft long, of Sir William de Tendring (died 1408) in his armour, his head resting upon a helm, with a crest of feathers. Also in this chapel is the brass of Lady Katherine Howard (died 1465), the great-grandmother of Anne Boleyn and of Catherine Howard, who were Queens of England. On the S wall is the alabaster monument of Lady Anne Windsor (died 1615) with her effigy dressed in a red fur-lined mantle and her three children kneeling at her head and feet. To the W is the monument of her mother, Lady Waldegrave (died 1600), and in the chapel floor is a slab with a baby in a chrisom robe—this was John Windsor, who died in 1588. The N chapel contains the monument (thought to be by Nicholas Stone) of Sir Francis Mannock of Gifford's Hall, who died in 1634. His fine alabaster effigy is well-preserved and the inscription is well worth reading.

Thornham Parva, *St. Mary*. A tiny church, which is living proof that 'small is beautiful', with a beautiful rural and pastoral setting in a meadow. This humble and rustic building of flint rubble consists only of a nave and chancel under the same roof and a W tower. The roof is thatched and even the tower has a perky thatched pyramidal cap. This is a gem of a church, which incorporates work of most periods from pre-Conquest times to the present day and contains much which is of beauty and interest.

The exterior is humble in size and proportions, but contains a variety of windows and doorways. Here we see from the 14C Y-tracery, flowing tracery and (in the E window) Reticulated tracery. There are also square-headed 15C Perpendicular windows. The N and S doorways are Norman; the former is small, plain and remarkably narrow and the latter a little larger, with scalloped capitals and roll-moulding. The masonry of the nave walls is almost certainly pre-Conquest and at the W end (visible from inside) is a small circular double-splayed window.

The interior is homely and full of atmosphere. Although the people of this tiny parish keep it spotless, and tasteful work of modern times may be seen here, one is aware that people have worshipped here for a thousand years. At the W end is the 18C bow-fronted musicians' gallery, which affords a good view of the interior. The font beneath it has a pretty 14C traceried bowl. On the N and S walls are considerable remains of the 13C wall paintings which once covered them. It is thought that these told the story of St. Edmund, the martyred King of East Anglia. On the N side is a medieval cart and scenes of the saint's coffin being carried by monks, the legendary wolf which guarded his head, also the skeleton of the saint, with his crowned head. The paintings on the N wall were restored in 1980, those on the S in 1984. The SW nave window contains a little medieval glass and two anels of engraved glass made in 1980 by Laurence Whistler. The pulpit is 17C and the oak Rood screen is two centuries older. The altar is backed by 17C panelling, above which is the exquisite 14C triptych retable, which is thought to have come from the Dominican monastery at Thetford, because amongst its painted figures are St. Dominic and St. Peter Martyr, who was a Dominican Friar. Also depicted upon it are Our Lord, His mother and other saints. In the chancel may be seen a 14C chest and a copy of the Bible which was printed in 1640.

In the churchyard E of the church is the grave of Sir Basil Spence (1907–76), who was the architect of Coventry Cathedral.

Walpole Chapel. This fascinating building was one of the first Congregational chapels to be opened in England. The building began life in 1607 as a pair of cottages (although some think that it may have been a tannery). It was converted for use as a chapel in 1647, during the Civil War.

The exterior has preserved its domestic appearance, with its double roof gable, two tiers of windows and two simple S doorways. These windows are very similar to cottage windows. Only in the N wall do we see a pair of taller, arched windows. The building is of brick, with rendered walls, and is set in an attractive graveyard.

The interior is rustic and unspoilt; it has changed very little over the centuries and has preserved the unassuming simplicity of a rural 17C Nonconformist place of worship. It has brick floors, a plaster ceiling and 17C fittings of great character. On three sides of the rectangular interior are galleries, supported by square and circular columns. Beneath the E gallery are the vestries. A large central wooden column, which was once a ship's mast, reaches from floor to ceiling in the centre of the building. The seating is made up of box-pews and the simplest of benches. At the front is the reading desk, which is backed by the 17C pulpit, with sounding-board above it. The simplest of chandeliers hangs at the centre and further lighting is provided by four paraffin lamps which were once in the parish church.

This chapel, although not now in regular use, is still cherished, cared-for and clean. It has a homely atmosphere and few airs and graces, yet has a charm of its own, which is not easily forgotten.

Woolpit, *The Blessed Virgin Mary.* A village of considerable charm, with an elegant and well-proportioned church, whose stone spire forms a landmark in the neighbourhood. Much restoration and refurbishing took place here in the 15C, but a considerable amount of Decorated architecture from the first half of the 14C remains in this much cared-for church, which is noted mainly for its superb roof and benches.

An attractive setting and a stately exterior here, where work of different periods blends well. The tower and spire, each 70ft high, were rebuilt in 1853–54, after the former tower and spire were struck by lightning. The architect was R.M. Phipson and the new structure is attractively faced with pebbles. Beneath the openwork parapet is an inscription and the pinnacles are linked to the spire by elegant flying buttresses. The windows in the S aisle show graceful flowing tracery of the 14C and the E window of the chancel, of five lights, has Reticulated tracery of c 1330. The priest's doorway could well be 13C and in the masonry of the chancel we can see Norman stonework reused. There are good niches in the E chancel buttresses. Above the aisles rises a superb 15C clerestory, with flushwork panelling and a set of ten Perpendicular windows. The glory of this exterior, however, is the tall and lavish S porch, for which money was left between 1430–55. A further bequest in 1473–74 provided for images to fill its niches. The porch is two-storeyed; its E wall is faced with flint and stone chequerwork and its S wall with dressed stone. This has lavish decoration, with stone traceried panels, also a superb entrance arch and five canopied niches. It is crowned by an openwork parapet of stone, with pinnacles. Inside is a lierne-vaulted ceiling, studded with bosses.

The interior has five-bay arcades with octagonal piers and octagonal moulded capitals, separating its very narrow aisles from the broad nave. Crowning the nave is a magnificent double hammerbeam roof, erected in 1439–51 and restored in 1844 by the Ipswich woodcarver, Henry Ringham, who skilfully replaced many of the angels that the Puritans had destroyed. This roof is a superb tribute to the medieval woodcarvers. There are angels beneath the wall posts, standing figures beneath canopies against the wall posts, two tiers of angels in the cornice, angels at the ends of the hammerbeams and more at the very summit of the roof. It is further embellished with a wealth of intricately carved fretwork cresting in the cornices and beams, exquisitely carved spandrels, and central bosses. The aisle roofs are also 15C. Above the chancel arch is a most unusual canopy of honour, which has five coved compartments; its colouring and lettering are 19C. Above it is a three-light window, similar to those in several Norfolk churches. At the E end of the S aisle is a piscina in the angle of the window splay. The sanctuary has a double piscina and a windowsill sedilia.

In the nave are 52 superb bench-ends. Those towards the front are excellent 19C copies of the ancient ones behind, for which money was left in 1494. The backs of the benches are carved and their poppyhead ends have a fascinating array of creatures. At the W end are interesting pictures of the church, including one drawn after the fall of the tower. The tall pulpit (1883) was designed by G.G. Scott, Jr. The brass eagle lectern, however, dates from the early 16C and is a rare treasure. The screen is mostly 15C, although its panels were repainted in the 19C and show Biblical characters and East Anglian saints. The doors into the chancel are early 17C and the date 1750 at the top of the screen records the replacement of some ancient woodwork here. In the chancel are some medieval carved stall-ends and the priest's stall is a misericord. Fragments of medieval glass may be seen in the tops of the chancel windows and in the upper part of the E window, which also contains later glass of 1962.

SURREY

Apart from the beauty of its scenery and proximity to London, Surrey had little to recommend it in the Middle Ages. The exposed land of the Downs, the impenetrable Weald and the hungry soil deterred settlers and only in the river valleys did people reside in any number. As late as 1831, the population was only just over 150,000. The drawings of Charles Thomas Cracklow made in the 1820s show that, apart from the town churches, the character of Surrey's places of worship had a rustic quality, many looking more like chapels than parish churches. The county was not devoid of building stone but this was not of the first quality, although the calcareous Reigate or firestone from the Upper Greensand was used in old London Bridge, the Abbey and Palace of Westminster, Windsor Castle and St. Mary Overy Priory at Southwark. The best material is Bargate sandstone with its warm brown and yellow tints found in the Godalming area and heath or Sarsen stone found in isolated boulders in the sandy soil of the Bagshot Beds. With the opening of the London to Woking railway line in 1838, the character of the county was transformed, for proximity to London and its scenic beauty brought ever-increasing numbers of prosperous commuters to Surrey, many with very decided views on the form of worship they favoured. This led to enlargements and restorations and the building of new churches. Although much of the restoration has been criticised as insensitive and as trying to preserve the spirit of the Middle Ages without the substance, some of the new buildings are of high quality and are an adornment rather than the reverse.

Pre-Reformation. Of the 64 Surrey churches recorded in Domesday, 61 were rebuilt soon after the Normans took over. Pre-Conquest remains are therefore scarce, the most interesting being the tower of St. Mary's, Guildford. The good Bargate stone masonry of Compton tower may also be pre-Conquest. Norman survivals are more extensive but there is nothing on the scale of Shoreham or Steyning in Sussex. Norman arcades are to be found at Chobham, Walton-on-Thames (with pointed arches), Fetcham and especially Compton with its double sanctuary; and Norman chancels at Addington and Ripley. Towers are relatively uninspired, the best being at Godalming, Limpsfield and Wotton (of the two-stage pyramid type seen mostly in the Welsh Border country). There are good doorways at Old Woking (W with good iron scrollwork) and Ewhurst (S). Farleigh, St. Nicholas', Pyrford and Wisley make an attractive trio of village churches.

The 13C was not a productive period and there was no evolution of a local style encouraged by the monasteries, owing to the lack of important quarries which might have produced a local school of masons. At Reigate, the nave piers (skilfully rebuilt by Sir Gilbert Scott) show early leaf decoration and at Ockham there is an almost unique medieval example of a seven-light lancet E window. St. Mary's, Guildford and Stoke D'Abernon were provided with vaulted chancels but the best example of a 13C chancel is at Chipstead. Towers are minor, the most pleasing being the one at Thames Ditton with its lead-sheathed spike; Godalming, however, received a tall lead-sheathed spire—a rarity in this part of the country. Oakwood in the Weald and Wanborough afford examples of 13C hamlet chapels but the former was spoilt by the addition of a N aisle in 1879. The most consistent Early English church is Byfleet, but there have been unfortunate Victorian additions. Notable 13C sedilia survive at Old Coulsdon.

The Black Death in the 14C saw the beginning of the demise of the medieval monastery but, before that, Chertsey Abbey—the most important monastic foundation in Surrey—enjoyed the rule of Abbot Rutherwyke, the abbey's most famous leader, described by Eric Parker as 'an ardent and admirable landlord and a prelate of enduring energy and wisdom'. Evidence of his benevolent influence is to be seen in the chancels of Egham and Great Bookham where, in beautiful Lombardic lettering, it is recorded that he had the chancels rebuilt in 1327 and 1341 respectively. Other chancels were extended, Lady and other chapels formed, but there is little to see of window tracery, for which the Decorated style is particularly noted. A splay-footed spire was added at Compton and a tower with spire built at Lingfield. Fetcham has a notable N arcade but the church where the Decorated style is most in evidence is Cranleigh.

The Perpendicular period is poorly represented. There was a certain amount of trade in cloth in Guildford and Godalming but not nearly enough to produce great wool churches. There is no major Perpendicular church, the best being Lingfield which is quite small, has no clerestory and where the tower was built in the 14C in the Decorated style. The abundance of timber, however, produced a large crop of timber-framed bellcotes and bell turrets, some with spires (Alfold, Byfleet, Crowhurst, Horley and Thursley) and some-times complete belfries rising from the ground in Essex fashion (Burstow, the best, Great Bookham, Newdigate—much restored—and Tandridge). Most unusually, Horley's bell chamber is shingled as well as the spire and Thursley's bellcote is supported on a timber cage over what is now the middle of the nave, the latter having subsequently been extended westwards. Bisley, Egham, Merton, Oxted, St. Nicholas's, Pyrford, and Send have attractive porches but roofs are generally plain. Among private chapels there are the Loseley chapel at St. Nicolas's, Guildford, the Norbury chapel at Stoke D'Abernon and the Slyfield chapel at Great Bookham; later examples are the Cecil chapel at St. Mary's, Wimbledon and the Weston chapel at Holy Trinity, Guildford. St. Andrew's, Farnham has an impressive tower (Victorian upper windows and crown) of Somerset type. The tower of Mortlake, apart from the top storey and the lantern, was built on King Henry VIII's order. A rare example of a complete church built in the middle of the 16C of chalk and flint blocks, is St. George's, Esher, noted for its later Georgian furnishings including the Newcastle pew.

Post-Reformation. Surrey was no exception to the general lull in church building after the Reformation. Brick 17C churches were added at Malden (flint chancel) and Morden, and an attractive brick tower at Thorpe. In the Georgian period, new churches were built at Kew and Richmond, and Petersham received a N transept. Most of the new places of worship in this period are to be found in the area hived off from Surrey to the new county of London in 1889 and the only substantial one erected further afield was Holy Trinity, Guildford. The early 19C saw the building of various Commissioners' churches (Addlestone, St. James's, Croydon, St. Peter & St. Paul, Mitcham, St. John the Divine, Richmond and All Saints', Upper Norwood), none of which are of architectural consequence, but the church of St. John the Baptist at Egham, built in 1817–20, is a period piece with many associations and a notable monument.

The London–Woking railway, completed in 1838 one year after

Queen Victoria's accession, introduced large numbers of new residents, and there was a great demand for more space in existing churches and for new churches. Every Victorian ecclesiastical architect of note is represented, although William Butterfield now has only the admirable Guards Chapel at Caterham to his name and G.F. Bodley Holy Innocents', S Norwood and a small village church at Valley End, near Windlesham. Augustus Pugin redecorated in 1839 the S transept of the old church in Albury Park and worked at Peper Harow in 1844. The early years of the reign, however, belong to Benjamin Ferrey whose churches include Hale (bizarre neo-Norman), Kingswood (replica of Shottesbrooke in Berkshire), Shalford, Christ Church, Esher Green, and Brockham. The ubiquitous Sir Gilbert Scott built three major churches—St. Matthias', Richmond of 1858, St. Bartholomew's, Ranmore Common (faced entirely with cobbles and boasting a fine octagonal tower and spire) a year later and, in 1865, St. Mary's, Shackleford—all notable and each improving on its predecessor. He also rebuilt St. John the Baptist's, Croydon after the 1867 fire. Butterfield's pupil, Henry Woodyer, practised extensively in Surrey. His work was uneven but he has to his especial credit a town church (St. Martin's, Dorking) and a village church (Hascombe). Built in 1864, the latter is an outstanding example of original Victorian work using Bargate stone and respecting the vernacular with a shingled bellcote.

William Burges built a most enjoyable place of worship at Lowfield Heath in 1867 (now unfortunately hemmed in by the Brighton Road and a Gatwick Airport runway). J.L. Pearson designed several churches. Weybridge from his earlier days (1848) and Hersham (1887) from his later are not particularly distinguished but St. Michael's, Croydon (1880–83) and St. John the Evangelist, Upper Norwood (1881–87) are two of his finest products. Pearson was also involved in rebuilding St. John's, Redhill in 1889–95 with a soaring steeple of Midlands type. G.E. Street designed Headley tower, Long Ditton (1878–80) and Holmbury St. Mary, one of his last churches and built at his own expense, extremely competent but lacking warmth. Sir Arthur Blomfield built a noteworthy church at Surbiton of yellow and red brick. Of lesser mortals, the eccentric E. Buckton Lamb built Addiscombe, 1868–70 (more roof than wall) and Englefield Green, 1859 whilst Sidney Barnsley designed the extraordinary Byzantine church at Lower Kingswood (1891–92) dedicated to the Wisdom of God.

The turn of the century saw work by Sir Arthur Blomfield and his nephew at Carshalton (1893–1914), in which Sir Ninian Comper and G.F. Bodley co-operated on some of the furnishings. In 1903 Sir Edwin Lutyens erected one of his rare ecclesiastical buildings at Pixham near Dorking, attractive and original with a massive round-headed entrance door and radiating pattern in tiles. Two other 20C churches of note, apart from Guildford Cathedral—outside the scope of this book—are All Saints', Weston Green (near Esher) by Sir Edward Maufe, reflecting his love of tall windows and cool, uncluttered and spatial interiors. The other is St. Paul, Woldingham of 1933 by Sir Herbert Baker with a marked East Anglian flavour including a flushwork W tower.

Fittings. As one would expect in a county which was not highly regarded until the Victorian Londoners moved into it, Surrey is richer in 19C than in medieval furnishings.

Fonts. Norman fonts include massive, decorated examples at Alfold and St. Martha-on-the-Hill, Chilworth; one in the form of a

block capital at Thames Ditton and another in the form of a tapered
bowl at Thursley. Another which stands out is the lead font at
Walton-on-the-Hill. Dated c 1150–60 and probably the oldest surviving lead font in the country, it has a frieze at top and bottom and, in
between, eight delicately modelled, seated figures in high relief,
placed under round-headed arches. They wear haloes and hold
books. Many of the 13C fonts are of routine square shape with four
narrow corner shafts and a central supporting stem; Shere has the
best. Rare wooden examples survive at Ash and Chobham from the
17C (possibly 15C in the case of Chobham). Of Victorian fonts, the
outstanding example is at Ranmore Common (of polished brown
marble); other good ones are at Long Ditton (oval-shaped fluted
design in green marble), Oakwood (black marble), Hersham (of
Caen stone, richly carved and supported on columns of red and
green Devonshire marble) and St. Bartholomew's, Haslemere (of
black and red marble). St. Nicolas, Guildford's font has a soaring font
canopy of gilded and painted wood completely enveloping the font.
Of modern fonts, the Church of the Good Shepherd at Pyrford has
one of unusual design carved from a single block of Ancaster
limestone.

Pulpits. No pre-Reformation pulpits survive but, as a result of the
1603 edict stating that every church should be provided with 'a
decent and comely pulpit', Jacobean pulpits are to be found—West
Molesey, St. Nicholas's, Pyrford and especially Stoke D'Abernon
(1602). Chaldon has a rare Cromwellian example of 1657, Mickleham
a Belgian one of c 1600 with ornate decoration, Petersham a two-
decker and St. George's, Esher a three-decker of the 18C. St.
Martin's, Dorking has one which may have been brought from the
Netherlands c 1837 with a panel (probably 17C) of St. Martin and the
beggar. The most striking Victorian fonts are Betchworth, St. Michael's, Croydon and Ranmore Common (of variegated alabaster).

Stained glass. Although Chiddingfold was the main centre in the
Middle Ages for the making of white glass in England, Surrey has not
a great deal to offer for the stained glass enthusiast. The best
medieval example is the 14C window in the N wall of the village
church of Buckland, depicting St. Peter and St. Paul in dark reds and
blues. Also of this century are a handsome St. George at Wimbledon,
figures at Worplesdon, several fragments at Shere, a quatrefoil
tracery light at St. Nicholas's, Pyrford and probably the Evangelists
in the E window tracery lights of Oxted. Of earlier date is the
charming 13C roundel in the E window of Compton and the small
13C medallions in the N and central lancets of the E window of West
Horsley. Of later date are the 15C tracery figures on the S side of the
chancel and the 18C painted glass of various dates on the S side of
the nave at Ockham, also the 15C Flemish or German scenes in the E
window of Great Bookham (parts of a larger window). Stoke D'Abernon has both 15C and 16C work, English and Continental, spread
around the church, of which two roundels in the nave of the Virgin,
one smiling and the other weeping, both French, are particularly
interesting. 17C heraldic glass is to be seen at Compton, similar to
that at Abbot's Hospital, Guildford. Victorian glass is too numerous to
list but some of the better firms such as Clayton & Bell (Loseley
chapel in St. Nicolas's, Guildford) and Morris & Co. (Busbridge,
Milford and Nutfield) are well represented. Finally, coming right up-
to-date there is excellent work by Lawrence Lee (Abinger, Byfleet,
Thorpe).

Seating. Apart from the early pews at Dunsfold, box-pews are to be found at Petersham. Lingfield has misericords of conventional type with some very fine heads; it also has a bench on the N side of the chancel which is decorated with Renaissance panels of medallion heads and the royal arms. St. Mary's, Guildford has an early 17C armchair in St. John's chapel.

Screens, Lofts and Roods. Surrey can only offer Charlwood with cresting above a line of angels and dragons holding initials and a vine trail below, a former nave parclose screen used as a chancel screen at Chelsham, a much renovated screen at Nutfield and a mutilated one at Send. At Compton, however, there is a 12C guard rail to the upper sanctuary which can claim to be the oldest piece of ecclesiastical woodwork in the country. At St. Nicholas's, Pyrford the celure which used to provide a canopy of honour for the Rood remains and, at Shere, the ends of sawn-off beams used to support the Rood, and the corbels on which the Rood beam rested are to be seen. From the 19C there are the wooden screen inserted by Henry Woodyer at Grafham for allegedly structural reasons against the Bishop's wishes and at Hascombe a richly and attractively painted example of 1864. The most notable example, however, from any age is the Art Nouveau composition made of iron and dating from 1897–99 at Busbridge, designed by Lutyens and executed by J. Starkie Gardner.

Wall paintings. At Chaldon a painting of c 1200 on the W wall on a subject akin to the Ladder of Salvation has been restored and one is easily able to follow what is happening. One of the most important English wall paintings of its date, the symbolism is well set out in detail in the church guide. Warlingham and West Horsley (the latter discovered in 1972) have St. Christophers. Charlwood has a faded example of the Three Living and the Three Dead, which became popular after the Black Death, but showing the three princes only. This church also has paintings depicting the legend of St. Margaret. St. Nicholas's at Pyrford has an interesting example of a double painting where the original mid-12C painting has had scenes of Our Lord's Passion superimposed only 60 years later.

Other furnishings. Mention can be made of the 18C wrought-iron altar rails in the Lady chapel of All Saints', Carshalton and the wooden rails at Ewhurst which exceptionally embrace three sides of the altar. Shere has a modern altar rail in stainless steel by Louis Osman. Amongst chests, the early dugout example at Betchworth, the large early 13C chest at Shere, and the 14C/15C one at Stoke D'Abernon are notable. At Thursley there is a Jacobean example (dated 1622) and at Leatherhead a leather-bound chest with stud patterns (dated 1663).

Brasses/monuments. Surrey is distinguished in having at Stoke D'Abernon one of the oldest brasses in the country, to Sir John D'Abernon (died 1327); the one to his son, also Sir John (died 1350), is not so good; there are others to Anne Norbury (died 1464), Ellen Bray (died 1516) and a priest (a replica of one to John Prowd—died 1497). Horley has two brasses on each side of the chancel, the one on the N being a large and dignified female brass under a well-designed ogee canopy. To these should be added the fine early 15C set at Lingfield. There are also small ones of note to John, Lord Audley (died 1491) at Shere (but only the top half and inscription are original) and to a former Rector at Byfleet dating from c 1480.

The best of the medieval stone monuments are those to members of the Cobham family at Lingfield dating from 1381 and 1446. The Lumley monuments at Cheam date from the end of the 16C and beginning of the 17C. A small memorial to John Goodwine (died 1618) and his wife at Horne retains much of its original colouring. At Egham there is a notable but macabre wall monument to Sir John Denham (died 1638) showing him with reconstituted body rising above the charnel house with his unfortunate wife left behind; it is a work of great skill. Subsequent monuments are too numerous to itemise but the following deserve special mention: (a) the grand one to Sir Robert Clayton (died 1707) and his wife at Bletchingley. He is carved in a standing posture with his wife but the swagger is offset by the pathetic figure at the foot in embroidered clothes of their still-born child; it is stated that the statue was completed before Sir Robert's death; (b) the monument to Sir Ambrose (died 1713) and Lady Crowley (died 1727) with profile portraits in a medallion by J.M. Rysbrack at St. Peter and St. Paul, Mitcham; (c) the memorial by the same sculptor to Lord King (died 1734) at Ockham; (d) the highly individual monument to Richard Boyle (died 1740) by L.F. Roubiliac at Walton-on-Thames, showing this famous soldier against a background of tent, gun and flags with the seated figure of his disconsolate daughter beautifully carved at the base on the right-hand side.

Albury. The small village of Albury used to be dominated by Albury Park mansion—so much so that a former owner (Admiral Finch) made life so difficult for the villagers that they moved a mile W to Weston Green. This left the old church of St. Peter and St. Paul without a congregation and it eventually fell into disrepair until rescued by the Redundant Churches Fund in 1974. Prior to this, however, a later owner of the mansion, Henry Drummond, who succeeded to the estate in 1819, decided to place the family mortuary chapel in the S transept and he engaged Augustus Pugin to design the present lavish decoration with windows filled with stained glass by William Wailes and the wall and ceiling decoration by T. Earley.

Drummond was a supporter of Edward Irving, the founder of the Catholic Apostolic Church, and Albury became its spiritual centre. A new church for the sect designed by William McIntosh Brooks was built next door to the house in Commissioners' Gothic style in sandstone and carstone with a large W tower and an octagonal chapter house on the N side.

Bletchingley, St. Mary the Virgin. St. Mary's, much altered over the years, has an outstanding early 18C monument to Sir Robert Clayton (died 1707) and his wife by Richard Crutcher, showing them both standing under a soaring aedicule. The vast composition fills the whole of the E wall of the S chapel and the larger than life figures are dressed magnificently—Sir Robert in the robes of the Lord Mayor of London—but their swagger is offset by the pathetic figure of the small baby in embroidered clothes between their feet, their child who had died over 40 years earlier in the 1660s. Sir Robert had this huge monument put up during his own lifetime in 1705 in honour of his wife. A very different representation of the same child in swaddling clothes may be seen in a small marble monument at Ickenham, Middlesex.

Burstow, St. Bartholomew. Lying in a quiet lane surrounded by trees but close to the M23, the church is famed for its timber tower built up from the ground in Essex style; it is a separate construction, there being a W wall. The main body of the building is constructed of yellow-hued Wealden sandstone with firestone dressings and is mainly Perpendicular although two small Norman windows (one, very small, in the nave is blocked) survive. The furnishings are minor, consisting of a large chest of c 1600 and a 15C font of the usual octagonal type but with quatrefoil and leaf decoration.

The exterior is dominated by the tower. It is of three stages, weatherboarded and tiled below followed by a belfry stage having a pronounced batter, rising to a splay-footed spire with delicate corner pinnacles, all delightfully shingled, giving the tower a most distinctive appearance. The external weatherboarding and shingling may be 18C but the framing is medieval, probably either 15C or 16C. The Perpendicular windows have four lights, restored with stone different from the local material previously used, but the small square-headed priest's door on the S side is original. There is pleasing Victorian bargeboarding on the S porch.

The relatively unrestored interior is chiefly interesting for the tower framing. The structure rests on four corner posts and has much diagonal reinforcement. On the W, N and S sides there are projections with lean-to roofs, within which buttresses stand. The chancel arch is framed by a pair of niches. Piscinas indicate various medieval altars. Beneath the sill of the chancel NE window is a recess with two trefoiled openings separated by a mullion which may have been used as an Easter sepulchre. The tower arch is a comparatively recent insertion within a medieval four-centred arch.

John Flamsteed, the first Astronomer Royal, was Rector of Burstow from 1684 until his death in 1719 and is commemorated in the E window and by a sculptured plaque presented in 1975 to mark the tercentenary of his appointment as Astronomer Royal.

Busbridge, *St. John the Baptist.* This is a worthy church respecting its Victorian surroundings whilst preserving the Surrey vernacular style in its pleasing shingled central tower and its use of the local Bargate stone, which Sir Edwin Lutyens put to such good effect in the many delightful houses he built in the neighbourhood. His influence is apparent in the church and churchyard; he designed the dramatic combined Rood and chancel screen which fills the upper parts of the chancel arch, and the war memorial as well as tombs to Gertrude Jekyll (died 1932)—his patron—and other members of the family in the churchyard. The Rood and chancel screen were made of iron by J. Starkie Gardner and are influenced by Art Nouveau motifs. It is a dominating feature in an otherwise unexciting interior although there is Burne-Jones glass with its familiar blues and greens in the W and E windows made by the Morris works.

Chaldon, *St. Peter and St. Paul.* This is a small flint building of the late 12C/early 13C in an isolated situation, containing one of the most important wall paintings of the 12C in the country. Measuring 11 x 17ft it covers most of the upper half of the W wall and is divided into two tiers with a ladder running vertically through the centre, thus forming four equal quarters. The theme is the Ladder of Salvation and the painting depicts in much detail the struggle of those trying to reach Heaven and the torments of those in Hell, with fearsome devils and tall slender angels in hieratic pose whilst little naked figures represent the humans. The figures appear against a background of dark ochre. It was discovered beneath coats of whitewash in 1870. Preservatives were applied after discovery and no further restoration is recorded, although the detailed description in the 'Surrey Archeological Collections' (Volume 72) states, 'some of the red ground appears somewhat refreshed'. This volume describes the technique, style and iconography of the painting at length. The church also possesses a rare Cromwellian pulpit of 1657.

Charterhouse School, *Chapel.* Amidst the spacious and open grounds of Charterhouse School which moved to Godalming in 1872, the chapel by Sir Giles Gilbert Scott is easily recognisable by its lofty proportions and the fact that it is open to the playing fields on the S side. It was built as a War Memorial chapel in 1922–27.

Externally, the building is conspicuous for its tall lancets, widely spaced, which rise above the eaves with separate gables. Internally, the chapel is distinguished by its proportions and its notable apse. All the fittings were designed by Scott, including the reredos which sits easily in front of the E window.

Cheam, *Lumley Chapel.* Originally the chancel of the old church, built of flint, the Lumley Chapel is well-known for its monuments to members of the Lumley family including John, Lord Lumley (died 1609). He was the son-in-law of the Earl of Arundel who completed Nonsuch in 1556 and it was he who sold the palace to Queen Elizabeth in 1592. His monument has no figures and consists of an inscribed wall plate between two black columns, with a coat of arms above. The other major monuments are to his two wives, Jane (died 1577) and Elizabeth (died 1603). Both memorials were designed in 1592, in Jane's case well after her death and in Elizabeth's before. Jane's monument is incomplete and consists of a table-tomb with alabaster panels with kneeling figures; Elizabeth's is a well-carved monument with recumbent effigy.

There are also several small 14C and 15C brasses and a palimpsest with Thomas Fromonde (died 1542) and his wife on one side, and on the other, St. John the Evangelist dating from c 1420.

The chapel was beautifully redecorated in plaster in 1592, and even the tiebeams were plastered with fruit. There is a ribbed tunnel-vaulted ceiling above with large pendants.

Chipstead, *St. Margaret.* Situated beside a triangular green on high ground S of scattered suburban development, the church is a large cruciform building of the late 12C/early 13C, constructed of flint with Reigate stone dressings. Although much altered during the 19C and suffering severe war damage, this is Surrey's best example of medieval Early English ecclesiastical architecture, chiefly noted for its rows of lancet windows, particularly those on the N side of the chancel. It possesses early stone seats and a rare Surrey example of a font in the Decorated style. From pre-Conquest times until the Dissolution the church belonged to Chertsey Abbey.

The nave roofs sweep down over the aisles, masking the clerestory windows which can only be seen from within. The S transept, destroyed earlier by fire, was rebuilt in 1855. The N aisle was added in 1883 by Norman Shaw, who also designed the attractive W doorway and W window in neo-Perpendicular style, resetting the original 12C doorway with dogtooth moulding in the N aisle. The crossing tower is dated 1631.

The interior is as impressive as the exterior. The well-proportioned arcades in Reigate stone have circular piers and a clerestory of small quatrefoil windows above. The lancets in the chancel and transepts have unusual triangular heads, a feature which also occurs on the doorway inside the N transept. Well-executed rib-vaulting is to be seen under the tower with a lively central boss. The E window is a replica of one destroyed in the war with, apart from the four figures in the upper part inserted in 1851, glass consisting of 15C fragments collected by the Rector from various parts of the church; he executed most of the work himself. The S transept window has 13C and early 14C fragments.

The stone seats, dating from c 1200, are ranged along the N and S walls of the chancel and have decorated curved arms at the ends. The large 14C font is octagonal with tracery decoration; its base dates from 1827. Other furnishings include a Jacobean pulpit and reading desk, and 15C chancel screen with early 19C royal arms above, probably King George III's. There is a noteworthy monument by Westmacott the Elder to the Reverend James Tattershall (died 1784), with a large urn in front of an obelisk. On the N wall of the nave, Sir Edward Banks (died 1835), who built the former London Bridge as well as Waterloo and Southwark Bridges, is commemorated by a monument on which the three bridges are represented. A brass commemorates Katherine Roper who died in 1614.

Compton

St. Nicholas. The church is probably one of the best-known in Surrey because of its double sanctuary. Well restored by Henry Woodyer in the 19C, this is a good example of a Norman village church with a tower of fine Bargate masonry which many consider to be pre-Conquest. It lies on a small knoll well above the road, with the tower raised even higher because of the many previous burials in its area, and is approached from the E by a steep path. Apart from the interest of its double sanctuary, St. Nicholas's has an early Norman square-bowled font, Jacobean altar rails, pulpit with tester, and 17C screen under the tower arch (removed from the chancel arch) and a charming 12C/13C stained glass roundel of the Virgin and Child in the E window of the lower sanctuary.

A cat-slide roof with dormers sweeps down over the aisles with a change of slope on the S side due to the insertion of taller Perpendicular windows in the 15C. The tower is unbuttressed and is completed with a splay-footed shingled spire of the 14C. Entry is through a modern porch but the zigzag-ornamented Norman doorway of c 1165 remains.

To this date belong also the three-bay nave arcades, the tower, the chancel arch (unfortunately less well restored and with a plaster moulding below) and the N doorway. Local crimped plaster decoration has been added around the chancel arch to provide extra ornamentation. The nave arcade arches, strikingly white from the use of clunch or chalkstone, are slightly pointed; they have short round columns with some capitals scalloped and others with foliage. The famous double sanctuary consists of a groin-vaulted chamber below, surmounted by a separate chapel with reset piscina open to the chancel but with a guard rail of nine semicircular arches carried on thin posts which have faintly discernible crocketed capitals. This rail is cut from a single plank and is probably among the earliest church woodwork in the country. The purpose of the upper chapel is not known. Contemporary with the late 12C sanctuary is a small room to the S with a Norman window which may have been a cell for an anchorite or an oratory. On the S side of the chancel arch, which is bordered by nook-shafts, the figure of a knight (late 12C) is scratched on the stonework.

The square-bowled font, shaped like a capital, is supported on a large circular stem with a ring between, and is early Norman. The Jacobean altar rails, pulpit with tester and screen date from c 1620. The stained glass roundel in the E window of the lower sanctuary shows the Virgin with a flowering sceptre in her hand and the infant Christ in a green robe. Although small, it is a delightful example of 12C/13C work. A small fragment of early glass can be seen in the N chancel window. This was given by the restorer of the Dutch 16C glass depicting the Baptism of Christ near the font in the W wall of the S aisle; he replaced the original which was destroyed by bomb damage during the 1939–45 War with a replica. In 1966 the lozenge mural over the chancel arch was uncovered.

The main monument, which is inside the porch, is a handsome tablet with urn to Edward Fulham (died 1694) and family, not erected until 1778. In the N aisle there are two 14C decorated arches of sophisticated design which once covered tombs.

Watts Chapel. The late Victorian painter and sculptor of the well-known equestrian statue of 'Energy', G.F. Watts, lived at Compton. In 1896, his wife designed his redbrick cemetery chapel on a steep site above the road. It is in the form of a Greek cross with curved walls between the arms and has an open belfry. Celtic motifs in terracotta are used outside for decoration, but inside, which was decorated later, there is a riot of Art Nouveau designs covered with gesso (fibre soaked in plaster of Paris) including tall angels in sombre colours writhing over its surface. This startling decoration accords ill with the structure, the plan of which is a circle with four deep embrasures.

Croydon, *St. Michael and All Angels.* A short step from the Whitgift Centre in modern Croydon, this is Surrey's finest 19C church, designed by J.L. Pearson and built in 1880–83. It is justly praised for its noble interior. The furnishings, including font, pulpit, organ case, choirstalls and hanging Rood are in keeping with the distinction of the architecture.

Externally, French influence is evident in the apse clasped by turrets with pyramidal caps and in the copper flèche over the crossing. There are transepts and a SE Lady chapel but the intended tower and spire never materialised. Only the base of the SW tower was erected. The material used for the exterior was red brick.

The interior is a *tour de force*. There is no chancel arch and the whole is dominated by the huge hanging Rood designed in 1924 by Cecil Hare. Mostly of brick of a light brown colour with high, wide, stone-ribbed vaults, the strong vertical emphasis and the exquisite proportions combine to provide a noble place of worship. The best view is from the narrow ambulatory which encircles the apse looking towards the crossing and the SE Lady chapel, which has its own nave and aisles separated by slender quatrefoil columns. Pearson's love of the Early English style is demonstrated in the lancets and plate tracery.

Font, pulpit, richly gilded organ case and clock in the N transept were all designed by G.F. Bodley. The font, presented in 1904, has enriched towering and canopied cover by F.L. Pearson, J.L. Pearson's son; the pulpit, erected in 1898, is beautifully carved and bears the inscription—'*Praedica Verbum*' (preach the Word). The choirstalls were by L. Temple Moore and the nave pews by F.L. Pearson (1938).

There is Clayton & Bell glass; other glass dating from 1895 and later in the W and E windows of the N chapel is by C.E. Kempe.

Dunsfold, *St. Mary and All Saints.* Situated on high ground about half a mile from Dunsfold, the church is a notable example of a Surrey village church of the late 13C, cruciform but aisleless, and transitional between the Early English and Decorated styles. The masonry shows a sophistication which puts it above the average of such churches in the county and this is probably due to it being under the patronage of the Rector of Shalford, a Crown living, at the time of the main building work and thus benefiting from the skill of royal masons. It is exceptional in its harmony of style, its main fittings being the old oak pews, the double piscina and sedilia, and the ironwork of the S door. Dunsfold was the country church most highly regarded by William Morris.

St. Mary and All Saints: the late 13C transition between the Early English and Decorated styles

The remoteness of the site may be due to the need to build above the flood level of a tributary of the River Arun, plus the fact that it may well have been a pre-Christian burial ground, the mound on which the church stands being thought artificial; it is also near a holy well with a reputation for miraculous cures of eyes. Except for the rebuilt and slightly later W window of three lights, intersected and cusped, the windows are late Geometrical (the E window being raised in the 19C). The outer walls are constructed of Bargate stone (Surrey's best building material) which, as late as 1882, had ironstone chips inserted in the mortar (a traditional local practice known as galleting). The 15C shingled bell turret together with the W window and wall were all rebuilt in 1892. The S porch may be as early as the 13C but the outer doorway is Tudor.

The interior is cruciform, with transepts at different levels, both containing piscinas and the S used as a Lady chapel. There are no aisles but there are indications that a S aisle may have been contemplated. A stringcourse runs right round with delicate mouldings in the chancel. The chancel arch was much altered in the 19C and now has no capitals.

Dunsfold Church is famous for its early 13C pews, probably the oldest in the country, although the seats have been widened and the backs filled in. The ends are carved into delicate whorls with cusps below and pricket holes for candles above. At floor level, holes were cut in the walls to enable water to be sluiced through for cleaning and three of the ducts can be seen externally; although blocked up on the inside, the old wooden plugs secured by chains are still in place. The double piscina with shelf serving as a credence table above and the three stepped sedilia are of particular interest; the mouldings are delicately carved and the seats are separated by shafts of Sussex marble (Winkle stone). The S door has long plain iron strap-hinges, closing ring, key escutcheon and large oak lock case; there is also an arched fillet of iron strengthening the top, a rare feature. The key is 12½ins long and continual use has caused the wards to turn almost at right angles to the stem. The Sussex marble font is of uncertain date and has a 17C cover. The well-preserved arms of King George IV are dated 1828.

Esher, St. George. This endearing church overlooks the busy High Street and is a rare example of a place of worship built in the latter years of King Henry VIII's reign or shortly afterwards. It was used by Princess Charlotte and her husband Prince Leopold of Saxe-Coburg when they came to live at Claremont in 1816. There is a monument to her in the N chapel but the main interest lies in the 18C furnishings in the nave, including Surrey's only three-decker pulpit, the reredos and the Newcastle family pew on the S side.

This pew, the most interesting of the furnishings, was built in 1725–26, probably by Sir John Vanbrugh, for the Duke of Newcastle. It can only be entered from outside and was used by the Princess. At the back are box-pews for the household servants with seats for their superiors in front, all of deal. The Duke at first shared the pew with his brother, Henry Pelham, but later it was divided, the E half being reserved for Esher Place and the W for Claremont. The front of the pew looking into the church has four white Corinthian columns, surmounted by a pediment, all made of pine.

Farnham Castle, Chapels. The manor of Farnham was granted to the Bishops of Winchester in 688 but the oldest visible masonry dates from the building work of Bishop Henry of Blois, brother of King Stephen. It remained an episcopal seat until the new Diocese of Guildford was formed in 1927, the domestic part being converted to a conference and retreat centre and the keep taken into State guardianship.

Of the two chapels, the old chapel has 12C round-headed lancets on the S side. A N aisle of two bays with circular piers and abaci was added in 1254 but later removed. In c 1680 a new staircase was built E of the hall, leading to the later chapel which was sumptuously refitted by Bishop Morley. Of main interest are the identical panels, separated from one another by a cherub and carvings of fruit. The pulpit, which is entered from the back, is placed between the panels.

Great Bookham, St. Nicholas. In medieval times, the church came under Chertsey Abbey and the chancel, as recorded in a beautifully cut stone slab in Lombardic writing at its E end, was rebuilt by the illustrious Abbot Rutherwyke in 1341. The Slyfield chapel was formed at the E end of the S aisle in the mid-14C and the N aisle was rebuilt in 1841–45 when considerable other changes were made. The nave, however, is 12C Transitional with the S arcade dating from c 1140 and the N from c 1180. The most striking feature is the weatherboarded W tower—with flint below—of the Essex type (cf. Newdigate and Burstow), built up from the ground and with a shingled splay-footed spire. Of furnishings, the main interest lies in the monuments and the six panels of Flemish or German glass in the E window. The memorials include many brasses of which the late one to Robert Shiers (died 1668) on the floor of the S aisle shows him dressed as a Bencher of the Inner Temple. He is also commemorated in a stone monument in the N aisle with his wife (died 1700) and his son (died 1685), where they appear in three busts with an elaborate surround. In the same aisle is a monument to Colonel Thomas Moore (died 1735), Overseas Paymaster, depicted as a semi-reclining figure but, better than either, is the monument on the other side in the S aisle to Cornet Geary (died 1776 in the American War of Independence), an admirable composition with a relief showing his death in an ambush. The E window glass consists of six panels acquired in 1954 from a set of 40 smuggled out of a French church during the French Revolution and bought for the chapel of Costessey Hall, Norfolk. A framed panel beside it describes the scenes portrayed.

Guildford. The three churches situated either on or near Guildford High Street are completely different in style, ranging from the late 12C Transitional of St. Mary the Virgin, through the Georgian brick of Holy Trinity to the High Victorian of St. Nicolas's. St. Mary's is one of Surrey's most attractive town churches, greatly enhanced by the rise from W to E due to the rise of the ground, its main features being the early tower going back to pre-Conquest times and its rib-vaulted chancel. It was the original parish church and, when the Court was at the castle, may well have been used by royalty. Holy Trinity retains the Weston chapel at the W end, dating from 1540, with chequerboard flint and freestone exterior, but otherwise the church is mid-18C and as altered in Victorian times. It is a prominent feature at the top of the High Street opposite Abbot's Hospital, founded by one of Guildford's most famous sons, George Abbot, Archbishop of Canterbury, who has an elaborate memorial in the S transept. St. Nicolas's, at the foot of the High Street, also retains a late medieval chapel—the Loseley chapel—where Sir William More, who built 16C Loseley House, and Lady Margaret More are buried. The interior is bright and cheerful and is famed for its painted and gilded towering font canopy of 1891 by Henry Woodyer, which completely envelops the font. He also executed the fine wrought-iron screens.

Ham House, *Chapel*. The chapel, which is in the NE corner of the ground floor, was created from what previously had been a living room. The work was carried out in the 1670s, from which time date the pews and wainscoting, also the carved details and furnishings. The altar table is original and is still covered by the cloth of 'crimson velvet & gould & silver stuff with gould & silver fringe', a rarity. The almsdish and candlesticks are of Flemish origin. The whole, panelled in dark wood and with rose-red drapes at the upper window level, makes an harmonious ensemble.

Lingfield, *St. Peter and St. Paul*. Approached through a small square of attractive buildings, the church at the N end helps to form one of the most attractive churchscapes in Surrey. It is a mainly Perpendicular building but the SW tower and splay-footed spire are 14C and there is no clerestory so that it is only a modest example of the style used to such glorious effect elsewhere. It was, however, made collegiate in 1431 and has the best set of brasses and stone monuments in the county. These are mainly to members of a branch of the Kentish Cobham family, although not as fine as those at Cobham, Kent itself. There are also interesting stalls, some with misericords and other late medieval furnishings.

The church is aisled, with the N aisle extended by the Lady chapel to create a two-nave effect, one of which may have been collegiate and the other parochial; the S aisle, on the other hand, is comparatively short, being closed at the W end by the tower and at the other by the vestry. There are no transepts. The walls are built of Tunbridge Wells sandstone but subsequent restoration has been with Sussex sandstone from West Hoathly; the roofs are mainly of Horsham slates. The tower has a projecting parapet but no pinnacles.

The spacious interior, apart from the two-nave effect, has the

The font canopy by Henry Woodyer, 1891, in S.S. Teulon's and Ewan Christian's St. Nicolas's, Guildford

unusual feature of a transverse arcade running from N to S embracing the chancel arch. The arcades have typically slender Perpendicular piers and the roof is of the arched-brace type with panels. At the E end is an undercroft with vaults entered from the N side.

The late medieval fittings include a 15C font with ogee-shaped wooden cover, a double-desk wooden lectern of uncertain date with a chained Bible bought in 1688 on one slope, and stalls of note. Five of the original 16 stalls have been replaced by a bench with Renaissance panels of medallion heads and eight have misericords. From a later date, the royal arms on the N wall of the nave are those of Queen Anne and the brass chandelier is 18C. Three of the five brasses in the Lady chapel commemorate members of the Cobham family, the remaining two being a small demi-figure of Katerina Stocket (c 1420) and the other of John Hadresham in military costume. There are five more in the chancel, all—except for one small figure—to priests connected with the college who died between 1445 and 1503. The monuments consist of four table-tombs (three in the Lady chapel) to members of the Cobham family. The earliest is to Sir Reginald, first Baron Cobham (died 1361) and the latest to another Sir Reginald, third Baron Cobham. These two have effigies; the others have—for the second Baron—just a slab of Purbeck marble with brass figure inlaid and, in the fourth case, nothing to indicate with certainty whom it commemorates. The first Baron's tomb is of Caen stone with the effigy in Reigate stone; it shows him with open face dressed in full plate armour with a helmet supported by two angels under his head and a Saracen with a long beard and a doleful, expression at his feet. Sir Reginald was born in 1295 and fought with distinction in France and Flanders between 1327 and 1360; he was Marshal of the Black Prince's army at Poitiers in 1356 and died of the plague in 1361. The tomb of the third Baron of firestone with effigies in alabaster occupies the central position in the chancel; at the head is another helmet with angels but instead of a Saracen there is a sea wolf at the foot with a wicked expression. It was this Sir Reginald who founded the college and rebuilt the church. Born in 1382, he fought at Agincourt; he is dressed in plate armour except for the head and hands.

Ockham, All Saints. The small village of Ockham will always be remembered as the probable birthplace of William of Ockham (or Occam) (c 1285–1349), the great medieval theologian who, despite crossing swords with the Pope, survived. The church lies in leafy solitude at the end of an approach road and next to the stables of Ockham Park (destroyed by fire in 1948). Basically 13C, the elegant two-bay nave arcade and the wide well-proportioned chancel arch as well as the E window date from this period; the S wall of the nave was rebuilt in the following century. The tower is Perpendicular, possibly post-Reformation, and the King chapel on the N side was added c 1735. This church is chiefly noted for its seven-light lancet E window, and for J.M. Rysbrack's monument to Lord King (died 1734) in the King chapel.

The building material except for the brick King chapel is flint and ironstone rubble with freestone and chalk dressings; thin bricks are worked into the tower and buttresses. The E window is immediately visible as one approaches. A priest's door on the S chancel wall was blocked up in 1834 and one's attention is soon drawn to the fine 14C curvilinear windows in the nave wall. Entrance is by the NW porch although there is a more substantial W doorway consisting of a pointed arch in a square surround.

The interior is harmonious with the two bays of the N arcade separated by a slender pier with circular abacus. The famous E window dated c 1250 is easily seen through the wide chancel arch. Plain externally, the inside arches are decorated with dogtooth moulding and have Purbeck marble shafts with excellent stiff-leaf foliage capitals, all different but based upon a common motif. The stepping-up from side to side is most skilfully contrived. The glass, designed by Sir Thomas Jackson and made by Powell's, dates from 1875. The King chapel beyond the N aisle has a vaulted bay, entered through a coffered arch. The roofs of nave and aisle are of the wagon type above tie and camber beams respectively with diamond-panelled ceilings. The tower arch is of uncertain date.

Other furnishings—apart from the King monument described below—include a canopied niche at the E end of the N aisle enclosing a delicately carved 14C female head with hair in two plaits under a close-fitting cap, a double piscina to the right of the altar plus a single one to the right of the chancel arch, and 15C stalls. The stained glass, other than that in the E window, includes 14C and 15C fragments in the chancel and indifferent Dutch 18C glass of various dates in the nave windows but the top tracery light of the SE window contains a striking piece of original glazing of c 1360, showing five stars on a blue diapered background; the SE window in the chancel includes a small pane in the right-hand light showing a mushroom inserted sideways. In 1985, on the 700th anniversary of William of Ockham's believed year of birth, a fine commemorative window, designed by Lawrence Lee, was dedicated at the W end of the N aisle.

The notable King monument in white marble by Rysbrack shows him in his robes of office as Lord Chancellor, with his wife Ann; the finely carved figures are seated on either side of a large urn. In the same chapel are a bust to Peter, seventh Lord King (died 1833) by Richard Westmacott the Younger and a simple monument containing the ashes of the second Earl (died 1906) and Countess of Lovelace by C.F.A. Voysey.

Brasses include one to Walter Frilende (c 1376 and Rector c 1350), a demi-figure 15ins high and the earliest of a priest in Surrey, on the N side of the altar, and, on the other, one to John and Margaret Weston (died 1483 and 1475 respectively); he is in armour with a hound at his feet and she wears a close-fitting gown and butterfly head-dress. There are also small brasses to Robert Kellett (Rector from 1485–1525)—N wall of chancel—and to John Westcombe with a rhyming Latin inscription dating from c 1390—S wall of N aisle, now in the vestry.

Petersham, *St. Peter.* The church is the product of many alterations and additions but is essentially Georgian in appearance both within and without. The interior has typical 18C fittings—box-pews, two-decker pulpit and a corresponding raised reading desk. There are galleries to the wide transepts. On the N wall of the chancel lie the stiffly reclining but gaily coloured recumbent effigies of George Cole (died 1624), his wife and, below the main structure, their grandson. An imposing tablet on the chancel S wall commemorates Sir Thomas Jenner (died 1707). Petersham's most celebrated son, Captain George Vancouver, RN, who circumnavigated the world and discovered Vancouver Island, is buried in the churchyard under a perfectly plain grave. Among marriages here was that on 16th July 1881 between the parents of Queen Elizabeth the Queen Mother.

Shere, St. James. Familiar to many visitors because of its attractive situation, the church is a notable building in its own right. It is basically Transitional of the late 12C with a large central tower heightened in the mid-13C and a splay-footed spire of the late 14C. The original cruciform shape has been changed by the shortening of the N transept and the extension of the S aisle. Furnishings include a font of c 1200 in Purbeck marble, fragments of medieval glass, a large early 13C oaken chest and an unusual set of chancel fittings in metal designed by Louis Osman in 1956. There are also two Norman Transitional doorways of note.

The approach through a small funnel-shaped square of attractive cottages is one of Surrey's most picturesque views. The churchyard is entered through a lychgate designed by Sir Edwin Lutyens and roofed with Horsham slates. The massive tower and spire and the large roofs may be thought overwhelming, but the tower has fine bell openings towards the W. The windows are of varying periods ranging from Norman to Perpendicular. The shortage of good building stone in Surrey is underlined by the variety of materials used— Bargate stone and rubble, ironstone, flints, Caen stone, reused Roman tiles, clunch, Horsham slab and Tudor brick, not to mention Purbeck marble inside.

One enters through a noteworthy early 13C W doorway, the door itself dating from 1626. The S doorway is earlier, being Transitional in style with Petworth marble shafts and a rough oak, well-studded door, said to date from c 1200. The interior is wide and spacious, particularly the large uncluttered chancel, reminiscent of East Anglia; this had been extended in the mid-14C followed a little later by the St. Nicholas chapel added N of the crossing. The round arches of the crossing may then have been replaced by the present pointed ones except for the S arch which was probably altered in 1275. Prior to this, c 1300, the S aisle was extended E to form the Bray chancel (the Bray family were Lords of the Manor from 1487); the entrance is through a fine Norman doorway with zigzag decoration. On the N side of the chancel can be seen the traces of an anchoress's cell (quatrefoil and squint cut into the wall). Post-Reformation additions include a W gallery in 1749; a fairly gentle restoration was carried out in 1895–96.

The furnishings include a font of c 1200 in Purbeck marble with central stem and four corner shafts with stiff-leaf capitals; many fragments of medieval glass, including three red roses and one white in St. Nicholas's chapel and a richly coloured eagle in the S aisle E window. The unusual Louis Osman fittings include an altar cross and candlesticks in iron, plated copper and gilt, a fine silver ciborium, an aumbry cast in bronze and a stainless steel altar rail. On a respond NW of the Bray chancel is a tiny 13C Madonna and Child, only two inches high, discovered in 1880; on the E side of the SW respond of the crossing is a carving of St. James.

There is a memorial to William Bray in the Bray chancel and brasses to John, Lord Albury (died 1491) on the floor of the chancel, a 20in figure, finely executed; to Robert Scarcliffe, Rector (died 1412), a 12in figure; and to John Redford (date of death unknown) in S aisle.

Stoke D'Abernon, _St. Mary the Virgin_. Although insensitive Victorian restoration has given this church a 19C look, it has more to show the visitor than any other Surrey place of worship. Situated next to the Manor House, it has close associations with the D'Abernon, Norbury and Vincent families who were Lords of the Manor and was more of a private chapel than a village church.

Inside, there is a wealth of interesting features—the Perpendicular Norbury chantry chapel with its coloured Vincent effigies; the large D'Abernon brasses on the chancel floor, of which that to Sir John D'Abernon (died 1327) is one of the oldest complete brasses and one of the finest in the country; a set of 17C furnishings in the chancel, which is a notable example of vaulted 13C work encircled by stone seats; considerable quantities of stained glass of varying dates; a late 15C font; a magnificent Elizabethan pulpit and a 17C lectern; a late 12C/early 13C chest probably used to collect money for the Crusades; a mid-15C Flemish panel used as a reredos in the sanctuary and part of a 13C mural in its E wall.

The unfortunate 1866 restoration stripped the exterior rendering, exposing the field flints and Roman tiles of the structure, and added the NW tower, N transept and an extension of 15ft to the nave. The church was also re-roofed. After rounding the SW corner, however, one can see high up on the S wall the well-dressed jambs and stone lintel of a 6ft upper door once reached by an external wooden staircase which led to a wide W gallery reserved for the thane and his family. This type of structure is typical of early rather than late pre-Conquest work and many believe it goes back to the late 7C.

Inside, the nave consists of two bays supported by circular columns with pointed arches dating from c 1190 and is separated from the chancel by an arch of 1866. The chancel is also of two bays and dates from 1240 when the pre-Conquest apse was squared off in favour of the noble vaulted chancel we see today with its well-moulded ribs carried on stone shafts rising from stone seats. The lancet windows are original. The Perpendicular Norbury chantry chapel was added in the NE corner c 1490. It is entered through wrought-iron 17C gates of Italian workmanship and contains the coloured Vincent effigies (Sir Thomas Vincent (died 1613) and his wife on the N and Lady Sarah on the E wall). They lean on their elbows with rather wooden expressions. In the SE corner is a kneeling figure of Sir John Norbury in Carolean armour with a brass inscription below; it replaces his destroyed tomb. In the E wall is a more recent addition—a small Roman cinerary urn of the 2C from the Catacombs, containing the ashes of Viscount D'Abernon (died 1941) and who was once ambassador in Paris. On the N wall is a rare pre-Reformation fireplace to enable the families to worship in comfort.

The 17C furnishings in the chancel include a Laudian altar table with movable top, credence table, Carolean chair, stool supported by carved figures, altar rails with twisted balusters and, of special interest, an aumbry let into the wall, of Baroque design and decorated with cherubs, stylised pelican etc., which may have come from a private recusant chapel; it is made of oak. The brass candelabrum is also 17C.

The lavishly adorned pulpit, seven-sided and of walnut, was given by Sir Francis Vincent in 1620; it is supported on a base adorned with volutes and strange caryatid figures, part animal and part human; the canopy, the standard of which bears the Vincent arms, is supported by elaborate and very fine wrought-iron stays. On one of the sides the words—'*Fides ex auditu*'—(faith comes from what is heard) is inscribed. The 17C lectern is of unusual type with salomonic (barley sugar) stem. Beside the pulpit is a notable chest with the stiles prolonged to raise it off the ground and carved roundels on the front. The mid-15C Flemish panel used as a reredos depicts the Annunciation and the 13C mural, in the sanctuary E wall, shows the Adoration of the Lamb. The font is late 15C and a statue near the lectern dates from c 1480. The large quantity of 15C to 17C glass is of varying origins. Most notable are the Trier panels of the Virgin with St. Anne, the group of three connected panels of Rhenish (?) glass in the E window and the two central roundels of the Virgin in the S part of the nave. The centre light of the E window depicts Christ before Herod, the Nailing to the Cross and the Resurrection—a colourful group well portrayed. It came from Costessey Hall, Norfolk (cf Great Bookham). The roundels of the Virgin are French and show her both smiling (the Queen of Heaven) and weeping. Other motifs to be found are Susanna before the Elders, the consecration of the Temple and heraldry and saints.

Apart from the monuments and brasses already mentioned, there is a later brass of 1592 on the S wall of the Norbury chantry chapel to Thomas and Frances Lyfeld with their daughter Jane whose effigy, as Lady Vincent, is in the tomb opposite. It is in a handsome alabaster memorial. The other four brasses are quite small.

Among the many associations of St. Mary's is a record of the earliest English honeymoon which was spent in the manor. This was described in Norman-French in the contemporary poem of 1189, 'L'Histoire de Guillaume le Marechal', on the occasion of the marriage of the Earl of Pembroke's heiress to the future Regent of England and guardian of King Henry III.

Walton-on-the-Hill, *St. Peter.* This church has suffered much from Victorian attentions, although the tower erected in 1895 is a great improvement on the earlier one. The feature which brings visitors to St. Peter's is its lead font dated c 1150–60. Only 20ins in diameter and 13¾ins deep, it has a frieze of foliage at top and bottom enclosing eight (possibly 12 originally) figures in high relief; delicately modelled, they are seated under round arches, wearing haloes and holding books, either to their breast or on the left knee. The number 12 suggests the Apostles but it is believed that the figures represent the Latin Doctors repeated.

Witley, *All Saints.* This is a church with a history stretching back beyond Domesday with a central tower capped with a shingled spire and 17C pinnacles. Together with the adjoining cottages, it makes one of Surrey's most attractive vignettes as viewed from the main road. In 1889, early 12C wall paintings were uncovered on the S wall of the nave, executed with the fresco technique of painting while the plaster was still wet and therefore of particular interest. Unskilled early conservation work has now been abandoned for more modern techniques and there are to be seen three tiers of paintings, the two lower of which probably represent episodes from the life of Christ, with the middle tier the easiest to see. In the bottom tier, the event at the W end is the post-Resurrection draught of fishes and the next scene may be the call to Peter to feed the sheep. The middle tier, viewed from the W, is the Harrowing of Hell, followed probably by Christ appearing to the three Marys and then the three Marys at the Sepulchre. The upper tier is less well-preserved; a surmise is that above the three Marys at the Sepulchre is the Feast of Dives and his death with part of the torment in Hell.

Woking, *St. Peter's Convent, Chapel.* This notable example of the work of J.L. Pearson was designed by him shortly before his death in 1897 and was built by his son (F.L. Pearson) over the next ten years. The chapel is Perpendicular in style, except that the two arches between the nave and the choir are respectively Norman and Early English. The E end rises to the full height of the chapel from the crypt with a Rood on the top of the gable carved by Nathaniel Hitch. There are apsidal projections on each side of the choir. The building materials are basically brick and stone, but many different marbles are used inside, both for the structure and for the furnishings.

The chapel consists of nave, choir, N chapel (St. Andrew's) and Lady chapel in the crypt (the most beautiful part), the N chapel being completed first. The interior is vaulted. The marbles used in the main sanctuary and Lady chapel range in colour from red to green, yellow, mauve and grey and come from many European countries. They provide a beautiful variety. The altar and baldacchino are finely carved in alabaster of oyster and pink shades; the supporting piers of the baldacchino and the altar table itself, plus one of the steps, are of African red marble, a particularly beautiful stone of volcanic origin never before used in England. On the pinnacles of the baldacchino's piers are eight figures of saints and, below the centre of the upper roof, the Holy Spirit in the form of a dove with outstretched wings looks directly down on the altar. The work is by Nathaniel Hitch. The three steps to the sanctuary are symbolic in that the bottom one is black, representing our sinful state, the middle red, representing man's redemption through the blood of Jesus Christ, and the top white, representing the forgiveness of God, enabling us to ascend and partake of the Communion. The Lady chapel altar is made of Carrara marble with pale green piers of Connemara marble at the corners; other attractive stones are set for decoration. The reredos is of gold leaf on copper. The mosaic work was carried out by Italian craftsmen in 1908. The stained glass is mainly by Clayton & Bell to Pearson's designs. A bronze plaque in a frame on a pier in the S aisle of the nave was brought from the catacombs of Rome in 1920; in the top left-hand corner is depicted the cock which crowed after Peter's denial of his Master.

SUSSEX

The churches of Sussex are of particular interest for three periods: the late pre-Conquest and early post-Conquest years, the 13C, and the 19C. Many churches are pre-Conquest, or are alleged to be pre-Conquest, but almost all of them are of the 11C. It is very difficult in Sussex to distinguish between, say, a church of 1050 and one of 1120. This stylistic continuity is referred to as the 'Saxo-Norman overlap'. The undisputed Norman style has some valuable examples, not least Chichester Cathedral. There are also some splendid instances of Early English work, whose simpler form is very frequent in the county. The later medieval centuries, plus the 17C and 18C, are rather thinly represented. As elsewhere in England, however, the 19C saw a massive wave of church building. Two particular factors in Sussex may be mentioned. Firstly, the development of coastal resorts was very important; towns such as Brighton, Eastbourne and Worthing overtook the old inland towns such as Lewes and Horsham. Secondly, improved communications have drawn Sussex more into London's orbit in the 19C and 20C. It is commonly stated that Sussex was once isolated by the forests of the Weald in the N and by marshland to the E. The argument has probably been overstated and has ignored the historic shipping links of Sussex's river ports (Rye on the Rother, Newhaven on the Ouse, Shoreham on the Adur and Littlehampton on the Arun) and the medieval Cinque ports in the E, which counted Hastings as the leading member.

In common with other SE counties, Sussex has little good building stone, but it is not totally absent. The main geological feature is the chalk of the Downs, which provides ubiquitous flint. There is also sandstone in the Weald. In some early churches the reuse of Roman materials is apparent. In the 18C and 19C Lewes and Brighton made use of the glazed brick or 'mathematical tile', but stucco superseded it in those towns. Beach pebbles have been used in some places.

Sussex was a distinct Old English kingdom whose earliest traditions were preceded only by those of Kent. The early power of the Kings of Sussex soon faded, however, and for most of the pre-Conquest period the rulers of Mercia and Wessex held sway. It was probably under the Mercian king, Wulfhere (died 675), that Christianity first made headway in Sussex. A few years later, in the 680s, St. Wilfrid conducted his famous mission during his exile from Northumbria. St. Wilfrid has been regarded as the Apostle of Sussex ever since, not least because of the claims made for him in the 'Life' attributed to Eddius Stephanus. St. Bede naturally refers to Wilfrid's work, but also mentions an Irish mission at Bosham. Selsey in SW Sussex was the county's ecclesiastical capital from St. Wilfrid's time until 1075, when the bishopric was moved to Chichester. The See of Selsey or Chichester has always been co-terminous with the county. It has long been divided into two archdeaconries, of Chichester and Lewes, which have corresponded with the civil E and W Divisions. Since 1974 the two divisions have been technically separate counties.

The principal pre-Conquest churches are Holy Trinity, Bosham; St. Mary's, Sompting; and St. Nicholas', Worth. All three were built late in the pre-Conquest period. Bosham is notable for its tall W tower and for its chancel arch, which is of horseshoe shape and is the most powerful feature of the church's interior. Sompting is famous for its 'Rhenish helm', once considered pre-Conquest but now shown to be Norman. The church nevertheless possesses much pre-Conquest fabric and carvings. Worth is a transeptal church whose nave walls are pierced with the type of windows normally used for pre-Conquest belfry openings. Other early churches of note are St. Botolph's at Botolphs; All Hallows', Woolbeding; St. Mary Magdalene's at Lyminster; and the ruined church at Bargham, which has a W apse. The 'Saxo-Norman overlap' has left many two-cell churches which have tall and narrow naves and chancels in pre-Conquest fashion but which were probably built in Norman times. St. James's at Selham, St. Mary's at Stopham, St. Botolph's at Hardham, St. Mary's at Stoughton and the church of St. John the Baptist at Clayton are good examples. The details of their architecture are as simple as their plans. In view of the 'Saxo-Norman overlap', indisputably Norman work necessarily dates from well into the 12C. Examples are Shipley (the central tower), Newhaven (a central tower and an apsidal chancel), Bishopstone (a W tower), New Shoreham (the crossing and remains of the nave), Old Shoreham, Boxgrove (the W parts), Amberley (a chancel arch with zigzag), Tortington (a S door and a chancel arch with beakhead) and North Marden.

The nave at Steyning and the chancel at New Shoreham both lead us into the Transitional style. Then follow the numerous examples of the fully-fledged Early English style. The chancel at Boxgrove is a well-known instance, and there are Bosham (the E end), Tangmere, Pevensey, Oving, the Greyfriars' church at Chichester, Burpham (chancel), Ashurst (chancel), Chidham and Climping. Shingled broach spires begin in this period and form a recurring feature (Catsfield, Bury, Bosham, Wisborough Green, etc.). (Otherwise the low pyramidal cap is common, or in the humblest church, a W bellcote only.) The later Middle Ages present an anti-climax in Sussex. The church of the old Cinque port of Winchelsea is a splendid Geometrical building, erected in a new town of the late 13C. The chancels of Sutton and Felpham are notable Decorated works. Etchingham is mid-14C. Alfriston is a mixture of Decorated and Perpendicular styles of c 1370. The full Perpendicular style of the 15C is to be seen at Arundel, where St. Nicholas' was rebuilt from 1380 as a collegiate foundation, and also at Pulborough (except the chancel), in the two Hastings churches of All Saints and St. Clement and in the chancel at Westbourne. The very end of the Gothic centuries is represented by the De La Warr chantry at Boxgrove, where Gothic mingles with the Renaissance.

The 17C, 18C and early 19C produced few notable buildings. Classical works are sparse: there are St. Mary's at Glynde (1763–65), St. Paul's at Worthing (1812), St. John's at Chichester (1812–13, now redundant), and St. Bartholomew's, also at Chichester (1832). Early 19C Gothick is represented at St. Peter's, Parham. Tillington, on the edge of Petworth Park, has a corona or open Gothic spire of 1807, designed to be seen from the park. St. Alban's, Frant, of 1819–22 by John Montier, is more seriously Gothic. From only a little later comes St. Peter's, Brighton (1824–28, by Sir Charles Barry), a new parish church to replace St. Nicholas'. At the same time in Hastings, however, Joseph Kay designed the Classical St. Mary-in-the-Castle (1828) as the centrepiece of Pelham Cresent; and back in Brighton in 1820, the Unitarian Church was built in a pure Greek style by A. H. Wilds. Earlier non-Anglican buildings had generally been neither Classical nor Gothic, but domestic. Worthy of note are the Friends' Meeting Houses at Ifield (1676) and at Thakeham (1691, known as 'Blue Idol': see gazetteer); the Unitarian chapels at Billingshurst

(1754) and Horsham (1721); the Westgate Chapel at Lewes; and Providence Chapel, Chichester (1809).

The serious Gothic Revival has left many major examples in Sussex, partly because it coincided with the rise of the coastal resorts. H.M. Wagner (Vicar of Brighton, 1824–70) and his son, Arthur (Vicar of St. Paul's, Brighton, from 1850), built numerous churches in that resort. Among them were St. Paul's (1846–48, by R.C. Carpenter) and St. Bartholomew's (1872–74, by Edmund Scott). St. Bartholomew's is a noble building of immense height. St. Paul's has a dark and uninspiring exterior. Its designer, however, Richard Cromwell Carpenter, was a most capable early exponent of an accurate medieval style. The best example of his work in Sussex is St. Peter's, Chichester (1848–52). His son, R.H. Carpenter, designed the impressive chapel at Lancing College, the 'cathedral' of the Woodard schools. Also in Brighton is St. Michael's, first built in 1861–62 by G.F. Bodley and considerably extended in 1893–95 to the designs of William Burges. Bodley's part reflects the influence of Continental models in the 1850s. Bodley also designed St. Wilfrid's at Haywards Heath (1863–65) and All Saints' at Danehill (1892), and restored Holy Trinity at Cuckfield from 1855. There he employed C.E. Kempe, a Sussex man, to paint the roof and to insert stained glass. Bodley's close contemporary, G.E. Street, designed the church of St. Saviour in Eastbourne (1865–67)—a redbrick church with a tall spire—and the chapel of St. Margaret's Convent at East Grinstead (1879–83). Other notable 19C Anglican churches are William Butterfield's St. Mary Magdalen's, West Lavington (1850); the chapel of All Saints' Hospital at Eastbourne, by Henry Woodyer, 1869; and J.L. Pearson's All Saints', Hove, 1890–91. The Catholic tradition of W Sussex found dramatic expression in J.A. Hansom's huge church in 13C style at Arundel (1870–73). C.A. Buckler built a number of slightly frugal Catholic churches in 13C style and designed the new chapel in Arundel Castle in the 1890s. The church of St. Mary Star of the Sea at Hastings, built in 1882 by Basil Champneys, has an impressive profile including a tall, polygonal E end. At the very end of the century, F.A. Walters designed the agreeable churches of the Sacred Heart at Petworth and Our Lady of Ransom at Eastbourne. At Parkminster a French architect, M. Norman, built the only modern Charterhouse in England in 1877–83. A notable 20C church is St. Wilfrid's, Brighton (1933–34), by H.S. Goodhart-Rendel, in a modern but quite individual style, which has (surprisingly) already been declared redundant.

On the subject of fittings, perhaps the most precious possessions of any Sussex church are the 11C or 12C carvings in Chichester Cathedral, which represent the Raising of Lazarus and Christ meeting Martha and Mary. These carvings are in a class of their own. Sompting Church also has some early sculpture (see gazetteer). Of great significance in the 12C are the wall paintings which survive at Hardham, Clayton, Coombes and Plumpton. These paintings form a group which derived from the Cluniac Priory of St. Pancras at Lewes. 13C wall paintings survive at Wisborough Green, 14C ones at Preston and Rotherfield, and 14C and 15C examples at Arundel. Battle has a significant series of paintings about the legend of St. Margaret of Antioch. From the end of the Middle Ages, both Boxgrove Priory and Chichester Cathedral have 16C decorative painting by Lambert Barnard. Medieval fonts of note are a mid-12C carved stone one in St. Nicholas', Brighton, lead examples at Pyecombe (12C), Edburton (13C) and Parham (14C), and a 15C stone

one in St. Clement's, Hastings, which is carved with the Instruments of the Passion. Didling Church has some medieval benches. Medieval tiles survive at Poynings. St. Mary's at Shipley long possessed a Limoges enamel reliquary of the 13C; it was regrettably stolen in 1976. Medieval stained glass is found at Sutton, North Stoke, Ticehurst, Battle and Yapton. At Arundel there is a substantial 15C stone pulpit, but its present appearance owes much to the early 19C. St. Mary's Hospital, Chichester, a 13C almshouse in which residents live in the 'nave', has 24 original misericords in its chapel. Misericords from the 14C survive at Etchingham. West Tarring has late medieval misericords.

Penhurst and Ashburnham have collections of 17C fittings. From late in the same century the chapel of Petworth House has carvings which have been attributed to John Selden. Botolphs Church has a notable pulpit of 1630 and Lurgashall a font of 1661. 17C communion rails around three sides of the altar exist at Poynings. Twineham Church has a particularly ornate 17C box-pew. Burton possesses elaborate painted arms of King Charles I, 1636 (with the Scripture: 'Obey them that have the rule over you') and painted texts of the same period. Rotherfield has a sumptuous 17C pulpit by Francis Gunby of Leeds, brought to Sussex in the late 19C. 18C fittings remain at East Guldeford, Kingston Buci, and at Tortington, where the box-pews are carved with the names of local houses. Similar inscriptions survive at Shermanbury. 19C fittings and stained glass of note may be seen at Cuckfield (a Bodley screen, Kempe glass and roof painting), Rotherfield (a Morris E window), in St. Andrew's, Worthing (stained glass and other work by Kempe), and in the Brighton churches of St. Michael and St. Bartholomew. Well-known mid-20C works of art are to be found in Chichester Cathedral: a *noli me tangere* by Graham Sutherland and a famous tapestry by John Piper. At Berwick there are paintings of the 1940s by Duncan Grant and by Vanessa and Quentin Bell.

Monuments of note begin with the pre-Conquest slab in St. Peter's, Bexhill. From the 12C there survives in St. John's, Southover, Lewes, a particularly precious memorial: that of Gundrada, the wife of William de Warenne I, who was the founder of Lewes Priory. The Tournai marble slab has palmettes and a long inscription. Winchelsea Church has three anonymous 14C monuments. At Bepton there is a 14C tomb-recess whose crockets take the shape of flames. Amongst medieval brasses, the most famous is that of Thomas Nelond, Prior of Lewes (died 1433) at Cowfold. The Camoys brasses at Trotton, from the 14C and 15C, are equally important. Other notable brasses exist at Etchingham (to 14C and 15C members of the Echyngham family) and at Fletching (to 14C members of the Dalyngrige family). Arundel Church has a significant group of late medieval monuments, mostly of the Fitzalans, Earls of Arundel. The change from Gothic to Renaissance may be studied there. The famous De La Warr chantry at Boxgrove, of the 1530s, is an agreeable blend of Gothic and Renaissance.

Notable groups of later stone monuments are at Ashburnham, Broadwater (of the De La Warr family), Thakeham (the Apsley family), West Firle (the Gage family), Friston (the Selwyn family, 16C and 17C), Withyham (the Sackville family) and Isfield (the Shurley family, 16C and 17C). Of note from the 19C are Bertel Thorwaldsen's monument to the Earl of Newburgh (died 1814) in the Catholic church at Slindon, E. H. Baily's seated statue of the third Earl of Egremont (died 1837) at Petworth, and Sir Gilbert Scott's monument of Walter Farquhar Hook, Dean of Chichester (died 1875) in Chichester Cathedral. Finally, it should be remarked that the Sussex iron industry has left many cast iron tombstones, mainly 16C to 18C, most notably at Wadhurst.

The historical associations of Sussex's churches form a worthy group. Bosham is mentioned by Bede as the base in the 7C of an Irish missionary called Dicul. In the 11C Bosham Church became closely associated with King Cnut; his daughter was buried there. Later in the 11C Bosham played a famous part in the Norman Conquest. It was from its shores that Harold, Earl of Wessex, set sail in 1064; his shipwreck on the coast of Normandy was a crucial antecedent of the events of 1066. Bosham Church therefore has the distinction of appearing (in stylised form) on the Bayeux Tapestry. Battle Abbey, N of Hastings, was of course the scene of King William I's victory; the abbey itself was his foundation. One other place of pre-Conquest note is Steyning, where King Aethelwulf of Wessex, the father of King Alfred, was buried in 858.

Amongst medieval Bishops of Chichester, mention must be made of St. Richard de Wych (or St. Richard of Chichester), Bishop from 1245 to 1253, who was canonised in 1262 in recognition of his exceptional pastorate. In the early 17C the See was held briefly by Lancelot Andrewes, who sought to emphasise the Catholic heritage of the Church of England. A contemporary who stood at the opposite or Puritan end of the spectrum, John Harvard, the founder of the American university, married the Vicar's daughter at Ringmer in 1636. The Deanery of Chichester was held from 1859 to 1875 by Walter Farquhar Hook, who had formerly been a distinguished Vicar of Leeds. Walter Hussey, the Dean from 1955 to 1977, was particularly notable as a rare ecclesiastical patron of significant contemporary art in recent times. The 19C Ecclesiologist and Church historian, John Mason Neale, was Warden of Sackville College at East Grinstead from 1846 to 1866. A further ecclesiastical connection of interest is that Cardinal Manning, the 19C Archbishop of Westminster, had begun his career in the Church of England as the incumbent of West Lavington and as Archdeacon of Chichester. The modern Catholic Church of which Cardinal Manning was a significant leader has long had an important centre at Arundel, where the Earls of Arundel and Dukes of Norfolk have remained loyal to Rome, with very few exceptions, since the Reformation. Philip Howard, the 13th Earl, was canonised by Pope Paul VI in 1970. Five years earlier, the huge church which the 15th Duke had built in 1870–73 had become the cathedral of the new Catholic Diocese of Arundel and Brighton.

Literary connections include the burial of the 18C historian, Edward Gibbon, at Fletching, and the burial of the 20C writer, Hilaire Belloc, at the church of Our Lady and St. Francis, West Grinstead. In the churchyard at Ovingdean is the tomb of C.E. Kempe (died 1907), one of the most prolific of Victorian stained glass artists. He was the son of Nathaniel Kemp (sic), the builder of Kemp Town in Brighton.

Rare dedications in Sussex include St. Wulfran at Ovingdean, St. Agatha at Coates, St. Ledger or Leodegar (a 7C Bishop of Autun in France) at Hunston, and St. Cosmas and St. Damian at Keymer. St. Pancras is unusually frequent in Sussex, no doubt because of the Cluniac Priory of St. Pancras at Lewes. St. Lewinna, who was supposedly a convert of St. Wilfrid and later suffered martyrdom, is traditionally connected with Seaford. Steyning was the home of St. Cuthman, an 8C hermit. Finally, in Arundel Cathedral, there are relics which some consider to be the remains of St. Edmund, the 9C English martyr-king.

Arundel, *St. Nicholas*. St. Nicholas' dates from the late 14C, when a college of secular canons replaced an earlier priory at the instance of the third and fourth Earls of Arundel. Richard Fitzalan, the third Earl, who died in 1376, provided endowments. His son, also Richard, secured consent from King Richard II in 1380 to dissolve the priory and to provide an entirely new church for his college. The college proper was the E part of the present church, now known as the Fitzalan chapel, but the parochial nave was also rebuilt at the same time. The college lasted until 1544, when King Henry VIII conveyed its property to Henry Fitzalan, 12th Earl of Arundel, whose heirs, the Earls of Arundel and Dukes of Norfolk, have owned it ever since. The fact that those heirs have been Catholics has entailed a separation between the Fitzalan chapel and the parochial nave, for the latter became an ordinary Anglican church at the Reformation. Restoration of the parish church took place in 1874 under Sir Gilbert Scott. The Fitzalan chapel was restored in 1886.

The church stands on high ground N of Arundel's centre, but it is overshadowed on one side by the castle and on the other by the 19C Catholic Arundel Cathedral. St. Nicholas' comprises a nave with N and S aisles, W, N and S porches, a crossing tower, N and S transepts, and, at the E, the Fitzalan chapel, which in fact comprises the chapel proper, a Lady chapel and a sacristy to the N of it and two smaller rooms to the S. The nave aisle windows are of three lights, with Perpendicular panel tracery. The clerestory windows are quatrefoils set within circles. These continue in the upper walls of the transepts. The W window is of five lights. The low crossing tower has a recessed pyramidal cap and two tiers of recessed two-light windows. The windows of the Fitzalan chapel are grander, four-light to the S, with five quatrefoils in the heads, and culminating in the seven-light E window, which comprises two groups of three lights joined by an emphasised central one.

The nave of five bays has tall piers of four attached shafts and four hollows, and arches with two hollow mouldings. The arch from the nave to the crossing is huge. Beyond may be seen a lower, glazed arch which separates the parish church from the Fitzalan chapel. A 19C reredos stands in front of that arch, with choirstalls arranged diagonally to its W, under the crossing. Behind the reredos there survives a screen of Sussex iron, an important piece of medieval metalwork. At the E end of the nave there is a newer, central altar, raised on three steps. To the S of it stands a canopied stone pulpit, made for the new church after 1380 but repaired and altered in the 19C. It has three openings, with crocketed gables above. There is a gallery in the W bay, which is screened off below. In front of it stands the 14C font of Sussex marble, octagonal, with two-light tracery on each face. On the wall of the N aisle, wall paintings may be seen. There are 14C depictions of the Seven Deadly Sins (with a central figure surrounded by dragons) and the Corporal Works of Mercy (with seven scenes surrounding an angel), and a 15C painting of the Coronation of the Virgin. The stained glass is by various designers. John Hardman & Co. was responsible for the window of 1882 in the S aisle which commemorates Henry Holmes. The W window of 1875 is by Mayer of Munich. The St. Nicholas window is by Burlison & Grylls, 1886.

The Fitzalan chapel has to be entered from outside, quite independently of the parish church. It was thoroughly restored in 1886. The present oak vault dates from then, although it incorporates some late medieval bosses. The E window has stained glass by John Hardman & Co. Stalls are placed at the W end. Visually dominant in the chapel proper and in its N and S annexes are the numerous monuments, which form an important collection. They divide into three main groups. Firstly, there are the tombs of Earls of Arundel between the early 15C and the late 16C. Secondly, there are 19C and 20C monuments of the Dukes of Norfolk and their kinsmen. Thirdly, there are seven late medieval brasses and the matrices of three more.

A word might be written here on the various titles of the owners of Arundel Castle. The Earldom of Arundel descended in the Fitzalan family until the death of Henry, the 12th Earl, in 1580. His daughter and heiress, Lady Mary Fitzalan, had married Thomas Howard, fourth Duke of Norfolk, a man who was at the very centre of high politics and intrigue in the Tudor period. The Duke was beheaded in 1572 and his own titles were suspended. Their son, Philip, became the 13th Earl of Arundel, the first of the Howard line. The Earldom has continued in the Howard family ever since, but upon the restoration of the Dukedom of Norfolk in 1660, it has been a subsidiary title only. The Dukedom itself dates from 1483, when King Richard III granted it to Sir John Howard by virtue of his descent from the earlier Mowbray Dukes of Norfolk.

In the Fitzalan chapel proper, the large tomb in the centre at the W end is that of Henry, 15th Duke (died 1917), by Sir Bertram Mackennal. It comprises a black marble tomb-chest with a bronze effigy in Garter robes. To its E and also in the centre is the tomb of Thomas, fifth Earl (died 1415) and his wife (died 1439). The entirely alabaster monument has two effigies on a tomb-chest. The Earl died from dysentry contracted in King Henry V's French campaigns of 1415. His wife was a daughter of King John I of Portugal. The effigies have elaborate head canopies. No fewer than 28 small figures of ecclesiastics surround the tomb-chest, to recall the College of Arundel. On the S side of the sanctuary there is the monument of William, the ninth Earl (died 1487). It is in fact a chantry, an enclosed space of which the monument is just a part. There is a three-bay canopy of Sussex marble, with twisted columns acting as flying buttresses. The canopy itself is square-topped, with cresting and pinnacles above and with crocketed gables decorating each bay. Low arcading divides the monument from the chapel. There is a vault with pendants. The tomb itself carries effigies of the Earl and of his wife Joan, who was the sister of Warwick the Kingmaker. On the opposite side of the sanctuary there is a similar canopied monument to three successive 16C Earls—the 10th (died 1524), the 11th (died 1544) and the 12th (died 1580). It was erected by John, Lord Lumley, in 1596; those commemorated were his wife's forbears. The canopy is similar in size to its 15C counterpart, but it is heavier and incorporates Classical motifs. The 12th Earl has a second monument just E of the ninth Earl's chantry. Under an arch which separates the chapel proper from the Lady chapel there stands the tomb-chest of John, the seventh Earl (died 1435). Like the fifth Earl, he was much involved in the French wars of the early 15C. His tomb-chest has open sides, the three arches of each long side being subdivided into two cinquefoil-headed openings with a pendant between. On the lower slab of Sussex marble rests a cadaver in a shroud, a standard 15C *memento mori*. On the upper slab is a rather stiff effigy in armour.

In the Lady chapel to the N there are two large tomb-chests in the centre. The E one is of John, sixth Earl (died 1421), with sub-cusped quatrefoils on the side but without an effigy. Its W neighbour commemorates Lord Henry Howard (died 1824). It also lacks an effigy, but the tall black marble chest with coloured shields has a solemn and dignified air. Against the N wall of the Lady chapel there is a Classical monument to Robert Spyller (died 1634), who was the steward to Anne, Countess of Arundel. To the S of the chapel proper there is a separate room for the tombs of Henry, 14th Duke (died 1860) and his wife (died 1886). Both tombs comprise Purbeck chests with white marble effigies.

Of the brasses, one at the W end of the chapel proper commemorates William White (died 1420), Master of the College of Arundel. Further E are brasses to John Threel (died 1465), in armour, and to Agnes Salmon (died 1418), who has a noticeably large head-dress. Both of these brasses have long inscriptions. In the Lady chapel there is a full-length brass of John Baker (died 1456), a priest of the College of Arundel, shown in his vestments. But perhaps the most splendid brass is the most recent: the one to the 16th Duke (died 1975). Designed by Christopher Ironside, it was unveiled in 1979. The Duke is shown in his coronation robes against a background of dark Belgian marble.

Bishopstone, *St. Andrew*. Bishopstone lies a mile or so N of the road between Newhaven and Seaford. The manor was anciently held by the Bishops of Chichester and hence its name. St. Andrew's comprises a W tower, a nave with a N aisle, a S porch, a chancel and a sanctuary. The S porch and much of the nave date from sometime between the 8C and the 10C. The porch was originally a chapel or *porticus*, which could be entered only from the nave. The present S doorway is Norman, no doubt inserted when the Norman W tower abolished a pre-Conquest W door. Norman too are the N aisle and the E parts. The chancel might appear to suggest an intended crossing tower, but it was probably no more than a rebuilding of the small pre-Conquest chancel, to which a square-ended sanctuary was added. The N aisle windows seem genuinely Norman, but the N arcade is later, perhaps of the early 13C. The arch from the nave to the chancel is clearly 13C.

The pre-Conquest fabric is built of knapped flints with sandstone quoins. The SW quoin of the nave survives intact. The S porch is tall, with one later window in its W wall. The round-headed doorway is set within a gabled projection. There is a single shaft to each side, with scalloped capitals, and the arch has interlaced zigzag decoration. Above the gable is a sundial which is inscribed '+EAD/RIC'. The W tower is of four unequal and slightly receding stages, which are separated by stringcourses. It has a corbel table and a shingled, pyramidal cap. A carving of an animal's head projects from above the W window of the second stage. The N aisle has small, round-headed windows, apparently Norman, set very low in the buttressed wall. The sanctuary is very low and narrow in contrast to the body of the church. Most of the windows in the nave, chancel and sanctuary were renewed, either in the 13C or the 19C, but three small circular windows are original Norman, two in the E wall of the chancel and one in the gable of the sanctuary.

Within the S porch there is an ornate late medieval niche in the E wall. It has an ogee trefoiled gable. The doorway from the porch into the church is narrow, round-headed and unmoulded and could be the original opening into the porch. The nave has a two-bay N arcade with one round pier, semicircular responds and pointed arches with two slight chamfers. The tower arch is low and round-headed, with a roll-moulding. To the E there are two arches, one from the nave to the chancel which has Early English stiff-leaf capitals, and the other from the chancel to the sanctuary, which has earlier, 13C shafts with scalloped capitals but also a pointed arch and dogtooth moulding. The chancel has two arches to both N and S, those on the N opening into the N aisle. The E arch on each side has zigzag decoration, the W ones only a roll-moulding. The sanctuary is vaulted, but the vaulting is clearly a modern renewal. The E window looks renewed too.

Bosham, _Holy Trinity_. Holy Trinity Church may claim to be on or near the site of the earliest known Christian church in the county. In the 7C, before St. Wilfrid's mission to Sussex, an Irish missionary called Dicul is recorded by St. Bede as working at Bosham. Whatever structure Dicul may have built, there was certainly an important church on the site by late pre-Conquest times. It achieved fame through being the residence of King Cnut and later of Earl Godwin, the father of King Harold II. It is the reputed burial place of a daughter of King Cnut and was undoubtedly the place from which Harold set sail for Normandy in 1064, a fact which gave the church the distinction of being depicted on the Bayeux Tapestry. Subsequently it became collegiate and remained so until 1548. The W tower and W part of the chancel are 11C, the nave and E end are 13C, and the aisles were widened in the 14C. A major restoration took place in 1865.

The church stands next to the millstream and overlooking the attractive Quay Meadow and Bosham Channel, which is a branch of Chichester Harbour. The unbuttressed pre-Conquest W tower is surmounted by a shingled broach spire, an agreeable combination which is the focus of so many pictures of Quay Meadow. The rest of the church comprises a nave with N and S aisles, a S porch, a chancel, a NE vestry and a crypt under the S aisle. The high-pitched nave roof of 1865 continues down at a different angle over the aisles, which have battlemented parapets. There are two-light Decorated windows in the nave walls, with three-light windows at the E ends of the aisles. The long and much lower chancel is pre-Conquest at its W end, then Norman and finally Early English at its E end, with an E window of five stepped lancets. In the N wall one pre-Conquest window is visible. The churchyard gates at the E end are by Grey Wornum.

Entering through the S porch, the church is seen to have four-bay nave arcades with pointed, double-chamfered arches on round piers, which have very wide moulded bases. Three small circular windows above the N arcade have been claimed as pre-Conquest, but could equally be later. The N aisle has 14C windows, but those to the S are 19C imitations. The S aisle, to the E of the S door, is raised up above the crypt. The raised portion forms the chapel of All Hallows. The crypt itself is of two groined bays and was perhaps intended as a charnel. All these features, however, seem insignificant in the presence of the pre-Conquest chancel arch, which is a tall, wide, horseshoe arch, presenting an impression of strength and dignity, worthy of the church of King Cnut and King Harold II. It has roll-mouldings which are mirrored below the abaci as shafts. At the W end, the unmoulded tower arch is pre-Conquest, featuring simple long-and-short work, and above it is a triangular-headed doorway, which once led into a gallery, and also a window yet higher up, set asymmetrically. The Early English work in the chancel is very notable. The lancets all have internal Purbeck marble shafting and rere-arches.

In the nave floor, to the right of the chancel arch, there is a memorial slab to King Cnut's daughter. Tradition held that she was about eight years old when she drowned in the millstream. An excavation in 1865 revealed the grave of a child of that age. An inscribed slab was presented by the children of the parish in 1906; this was recut, and a new tile of a black Danish raven added, in 1959. A worn 14C effigy of a woman is placed on the N side of the chancel. A tomb-chest within a recess of perhaps the same date is placed by the steps to the crypt. In the E wall of the N aisle is a trefoiled 13C piscina, whose drain is a 12C pillar-piscina. There is a double piscina in the chancel, each opening being trefoiled with a diminutive column standing in between. The octagonal font, in the SW corner, is of c 1200 and rests on a thick central pillar and four thinner shafts. There are four 15C Flemish roundels in the S window of All Hallows' chapel. They depict the Instruments of the Passion and came from Norwich Cathedral.

Boxgrove, *Priory Church of St. Mary and St. Blaise.* Boxgrove Priory is the largely 13C surviving portion of a monastic church which served a Benedictine house founded in c 1115. In style and in the plan of the remaining fabric, Boxgrove compares with New Shoreham, and in style it also compares with the retrochoir of Chichester Cathedral. The present church comprises the medieval choir and its aisles, a crossing tower, N and S transepts, one bay of the medieval nave, a N sacristy and a SW porch. It is a substantial building, even as it is, for the small village in which it stands.

The priory church of the 12C is represented today by the transepts, the crossing and the remaining bay of the nave. The E end of the nave had round piers and scalloped capitals, but its late 12C W extension, as may be seen from the ruins W of the present church, had piers with attached shafts and foliate capitals. The nave had a S aisle but no N aisle until it reached W of the cloister. The low crossing tower has battlements, a recessed pyramidal cap and a pair of round-headed and roll-moulded belfry openings in each face. The transepts are virtually as tall as the surviving bay of the nave, whereas the choir is taller than both. The choir has one tall single-light clerestory window in each bay, two smaller lancets in the aisles (but Reticulated aisle E windows), corbel tables, three flying buttresses to N and S, and three stepped lancets at the E end.

Entering by the 14C SW porch, the one surviving bay of the nave is seen to be a double bay, with two pointed arches under a rounded superarch. The bay has a quadripartite vault with dogtooth decoration on the ribs. So this vault was a 13C addition to the 12C nave. The corresponding part of the S aisle has vaulting in two bays. The present W end is an adaptation of the medieval pulpitum. The crossing arches are late 12C remodellings, wide and much moulded, and rest on clustered piers with enriched scalloped capitals. The transepts are divided into two storeys and have 15C wooden screens to the crossing. The choir follows the same pattern as the nave: four double bays of two pointed arches under a round one (with a quatrefoil between the lower arches); quadripartite vaulting with dogtooth on the ribs; and eight vaulted bays in the aisles, twice the number in the choir. All this is work of c 1220, a most attractive essay in the Early English style. The piers are variously octagonal, round and clustered. There is a clerestory gallery with Purbeck marble shafts standing forward of, and repeating the width of, the lancet windows. The recessed E lancets have Purbeck shafts with one shaft-ring each. The vault is painted after the manner of Chichester Cathedral's Lady chapel. The work was done by Lambert Barnard in the early 16C for Lord De La Warr. It comprises heraldic shields and much foliage. In the second bay from the E, on the S side, is the De La Warr chantry, an enclosed chantry chapel which was built in 1532 for Thomas, ninth Lord De La Warr (died 1554). The chapel is of mixed Gothic and Renaissance styles. A substantial canopy is supported on four corner columns and one half-way along the N and S sides. The canopy is vaulted beneath, with large pendants. Ten small niches, arranged in five vertical pairs, adorn the N and S canopy faces. Between them are heraldic shields. On the N side there is a gate of Sussex iron.

The reredos of three gabled arches is 19C, by Sir Gilbert Scott. So too is the stained glass in the E lancets, designed by Michael O'Connor in memory of Charles, fifth Duke of Richmond (died 1860). The military and agricultural subjects from the Bible which are depicted in the window allude to the Duke's interests. In the S transept, which serves as a chapel of St. Blaise, there is a 20C statue of the saint by Professor Tristram. St. Blaise was a 4C Bishop of Sebaste who has long been a patron of woolcombers and thus of appeal to shepherds of the South Downs. At the E end of the S choir aisle, which is the chapel of St. John the Baptist, there are some 16C floor tiles.

The church has a number of monuments. One, in the N transept, commemorates Mary, Countess of Derby (died 1752). The designer is not known. In the S aisle there is a recumbent effigy of Admiral Philip Nelson-Ward (died 1937), by Cecil Thomas, a worthy 20C monument in a medieval style. Various table-tombs stand in the S transept, decorated with quatrefoils in circles, a 15C style.

Brighton

St. Bartholomew. The church was built in 1872–74 to the designs of Edmund Scott, a local architect. It was founded by the Reverend Arthur Douglas Wagner, who was the great patron of the Anglo-Catholic movement in Victorian Brighton. It is a most striking church, chiefly because of its exceptional height: 135ft to the roof-ridge, or 144ft to the top of the cross.

The church stands in a district which still comprises comparatively low houses. It is a rectangle, 170ft in length, which faces N–S. It has no tower, transepts or aisles, but the way in which the walls are strengthened gives the impression of aisles, especially within. The side walls are 90ft in height to the pierced parapet. There are nine bays, each of which has a huge lancet window in the recessed upper part and a smaller window below. Gabled buttresses separate the upper windows. The liturgical W front has a wide, arched doorway, above which is a canopied statue of St. Bartholomew; then four widely spaced lancets; then a huge circular window; and finally a long, square-headed belfry opening which is divided by three thin columns. The W front has much white stone banding to contrast with the red brick.

Within, the impression of aisles is strong at first sight, because the upper walls are supported on internal arcades. Each sharply pointed arch creates a shallow side chapel. The extreme width is 58ft, which reduces to 46ft between the arcades. Above the arcades, the impression of a triforium is given by small openings, three to a bay. The upper lancets form a clerestory. There is a wagon roof with plain tiebeams.

*The high altar (1899–1900) by Henry Wilson in
St. Bartholomew's*

Apart from the dramatic scale of its architecture, St. Bartholomew's is chiefly notable for the fittings which were designed in the 1890s and early 1900s by Henry Wilson. His are the baldacchino of 1899–1900, 45ft high, flat-topped, with huge arched openings, white alabaster capitals and a ceiling in gold mosaic and mother of pearl; the two giant marble candlesticks; the door of the tabernacle; the choirstalls; the polygonal pulpit of 1906, made of green and red marbles on a black plinth; the altar of the Lady chapel of 1902; the W gallery of 1906; and the baptistery of 1908. The octagonal font is made of dark green marble and beaten copper and stands on a black marble plinth. The statue of St. John the Baptist was designed by Sir Giles Gilbert Scott and was made by W.D. Gough in 1925. The high altar itself is the original one, with paintings by S. Bell.. The crucifix is of 1912, by McCulloch of Kennington. The sanctuary lamps by Barkentin & Krall were installed in 1915. Above the baldacchino is a huge cross, designed by S. Bell, which comprises encaustic tiles and painting. The Stations of the Cross, of 1881, are placed in gabled panels which are set into the brick piers between the arches. Kempe & Co. provided four stained glass windows, which depict the Virgin and Child (above the Lady altar), St. John the Evangelist, Malachi and St. John the Baptist (over the baptistery). J.C.N. Bewsey designed the window of St. Mary Magdalene.

St. Michael and All Angels. St. Michael's was originally built in 1861–62 to the designs of G.F. Bodley, and comprised a nave with N and S aisles. In 1893–95 Bodley's N aisle was removed and a much larger and taller nave with a new N aisle were added, to the designs of William Burges. The first St. Michael's was one of Bodley's important early works. It represents Bodley's reaction against the style with which he had worked as a pupil in Sir Gilbert Scott's office. Bodley wrote in 1896: 'St. Michael's, Brighton, was a boyish antagonistic effort. Not believing in what one saw at Scott's one went in for a violent reaction. One had seen bad mouldings, and so would not have any, and inane crockets—one felt 'away with them'—which was but the weakness of youth'. St. Michael's is also an example of the influence of Continental Gothic on English architects in the 1850s, and is notable for its early work by Morris & Co. The architecture and fittings of Burges' additions are less notable and lack an intended campanile and cloister, but contributed to what was by the turn of the century a substantial and important building within Brighton's well-known Anglo-Catholic traditions.

St. Michael's is built of red brick and stands at the S end of a block of property which rises to the N. The main entrance is up a good number of steps and through a SW narthex. The lean-to S aisle is dwarfed by Bodley's tall nave, which has a steeply-pitched roof. Plate-traceried windows of two lights form a tall clerestory. At the same level, at the W end, is a pair of two-light windows, with a type of rose above. This comprises seven large circles set around a slightly larger central one. This arrangement of windows at the W end is typical of Bodley's early churches. The red brick is interspersed with lighter stone bands. A tall, thin flèche rises from the E end. Burges' church to the N is huge in contrast to Bodley's. It is built in the same materials. Its principal external features are huge E and W windows, which look strident and showy after Bodley's.

Bodley's four-bay nave has short, circular piers; heavy square capitals; sharply accentuated and unmoulded arches; and large stone roundels in the spandrels. The chancel arch is also sharply accentuated. The surviving S aisle is very narrow and dark, for the S wall is windowless. The E window is set high up in the wall. Burges' church is of cathedral dimensions, having a triforium and clerestory above the arcades, and differs from Bodley's in being internally faced in stone. The style is of the 13C. The capitals are lavishly carved. The tracery of the clerestory windows is repeated in inner openwork tracery. There is an organ gallery at the W end, between whose two arches is a carving of St. Michael. The details of Burges' work are thought to have been much altered by John Sidney Chapple.

The stained glass is of considerable interest. The lights at the W end depict the archangels. On the left are St. Michael (by Ford Madox Brown) and St. Raphael (by William Morris); and on the right are St. Uriel (by Brown) and St. Gabriel (by Morris). The left-hand tracery light depicts St. Michael fighting Lucifer, by Peter Paul Marshall; its equivalent to the right shows the Annunciation, by Morris. Above, in the rose, is a Virgin and Child, surrounded by angels who carry bells, by Sir Edward Burne-Jones. All these W windows show a loss of linework and enamel, due to the excess borax in the original paint. In Bodley's S aisle, the W (or baptistery) window depicts the Baptism of Christ. At the E end of the aisle, in the former organ chamber, the Women at the Tomb appear in the E window and the Flight into Egypt is depicted in the S window. The E window of Bodley's nave is by Clayton & Bell. In Burges' church, there are four windows by C.E. Kempe and one by Jones & Willis, all in the N aisle, and a Tree of Jesse in the E window of the nave, by H.W. Lonsdale.

The font is of grey Devonshire marble and was designed by Bodley. The original pulpit, of verde antique and alabaster, was moved into the new nave in the 1890s. Bodley's E end now has a 15C Flemish wooden triptych, gilded and coloured, which presents scenes of the Passion. The reredos of the present high altar is of 1900, by Romaine Walker. Christ is surrounded by the four Latin Doctors and by several other saints, including St. Nicholas (the patron of Brighton's oldest church), St. Wilfrid (the Apostle of Sussex) and St. Richard of Chichester. Also by Walker are the wrought-iron screens, the low marble walls and the Rood.

Unitarian Church. The Unitarian Church in New Road was built in 1819–20 in a pure Greek style to the designs of Amon Henry Wilds. It presents four fluted Doric columns and a pediment to the street. Originally, there was a Greek inscription on the entablature. There are four round-headed windows to N and S. The congregation traces its history to a split which occurred in 1793 in a Baptist church in what is now Bond Street; those who would not accept the belief in everlasting Hell were expelled. The present building was erected under the influence of Dr. Morrell, a Classical tutor in Brighton. It is interesting to note that as early as 1827, the 'Royal Brighton Guide' discussed the church as 'built after the manor of a heathen temple'; already, presumably, only Gothic was felt to be satisfactory.

The interior once had box-pews, with side aisles but no central aisle, and a pulpit centrally placed against the E wall. The present interior was completed in 1968, by Kenneth S. Tayler.

Chichester, St. Peter the Great. The church of St. Peter the Great was built in the Decorated style in 1848–52 to the designs of R.C. Carpenter. The building is a remarkably accomplished essay of the Gothic Revival for so early a date, perfect in its proportions and pleasing in its details. It comprises a nave, with wide S aisle and narrow N aisle, a chancel, and a later W porch that amounts to a narthex. There are steeply pitched roofs with gable crosses. Buttresses separate the windows.

The church stands just across the road from Chichester Cathedral. It was built to house a congregation which had worshipped for some centuries in the cathedral's N transept and which formed a parish known either as St. Peter's or as the Subdeanery. It is thought that the parish might be the successor of a pre-Conquest minster of St. Peter, which existed here before Chichester superseded Selsey as the seat of the bishopric in 1075. So this relatively recent building may in fact represent the oldest parish in the town. Now, alas! the building is in secular use as St. Peter's Shopping Arcade, but its exterior is intact and its interior, although divided, is not structurally altered.

Clayton, *St. John the Baptist.* St. John's is substantially an 11C 'Saxo-Norman' building, which is notable for its chancel arch and for its extensive 12C wall painting. It is flint-built and partly rendered. It is a small, two-cell building, tall and narrow in its proportions, with a low wooden belfry sitting on the roof at the W end. There is a N porch of c 1500, which shelters the original N door, and a SW vestry. There were once N and S transepts, extending from the E end of the nave. One blocked 13C window may be seen on the exterior of the chancel's N wall. It was revealed only in 1983. The chancel has two elongated lancets in its N and S walls and three stepped lancets to the E. The nave has a two-light window to both N and S and a square-headed 14C W window of two trefoiled ogee lights. Many of the windows were altered in the 19C. Old prints show round-headed 11C windows.

The interior is dominated by the vigorous chancel arch. There are semicircular rolls on the E and W faces and reveals of the jambs, and round the E and W faces and soffit of the arch. The impost blocks are thin, square slabs, chamfered below. Flanking the chancel arch are round-headed recesses, which are apparently blocked 13C openings into the chancel. On the N and S walls, at their W ends, may be seen the low, blocked openings into the former transepts. At the W end, large wooden struts provide support for the belfry above. The nave roof is 15C. The N and S lancets of the chancel have single internal shafts with foliate capitals. On the S wall of the chancel is affixed a brass of Richard Idon (died 1523), priest, who was the incumbent of the parish.

The wall paintings appear in two tiers on the E, N and S walls of the nave. The lower tier is only fragmentary. They concern almost entirely the Last Judgement. On the E wall, Christ appears above the chancel arch in a vesica surround, which is supported by angels. To the left and right are the Apostles, all white-robed. In the lower tier, on the left, St. Peter is seen receiving the keys of Heaven, and on the right, St. Paul is receiving the book. Clayton Church belonged from the late 11C to the Cluniac Priory of St. Pancras at Lewes, where there was a particular devotion to St. Peter and St. Paul. On the N and S walls, in the upper tiers, there are long processions of figures, including kings and bishops, all tall and thin, with rather small heads. On both walls, an angel may be seen giving the Last Trump. To the N, in the lower tier to the W of the window, may be seen the weighing of souls. Towards the W end of the S wall the Cross is held by angels, to symbolise judgement. Horses from Revelation appear on the N wall. The paintings were executed in true fresco, that is, painted on to fresh plaster.

East Grinstead, *Sackville College, Chapel.* Sackville College is a group of almshouses which was founded under the will of Robert Sackville, second Earl of Dorset, who died in 1609. The buildings, comprising two-storey ranges around a quadrangle, were completed by 1622. The chapel stands in the middle of the E range. Its present character derives from its restoration in 1846–50, latterly by William Butterfield, who re-roofed the chapel, extended it to the E and gave it a new three-light E window. The fittings also date very largely from that time. They included a new screen, the stalls, the piscina, the aumbry, stained glass in the E window and the raised altar. On the screen is fixed an original inscription, which reads: 'PRAY GOD BLES MY LORD OF DORSET AND MY LADIE AND AL THEIR POSTERITIE AN DO 1619'.

Butterfield was commissioned by the Reverend John Mason Neale, who served from 1846 to 1866 as the most notable Warden in the College's history. He was a co-founder in 1839 of the Cambridge Camden Society, which had a considerable influence on 19C church building and furnishing. He was also a pioneering student in England of the Eastern Churches, and a noted hymn-writer. More locally, he founded the Sisterhood of St. Margaret, which moved to East Grinstead in 1856. His High Churchmanship was opposed by the then Bishop of Chichester, who formally inhibited him from 1847 to 1863. Neale received no preferment from the Church but was honoured instead for his scholarship by the Tsar of Russia and by Harvard University. He is very widely remembered today, not least by a stained glass window in Chichester Cathedral.

(A.G. Lough, 'John Mason Neale—Priest Extraordinary' (1976).)

Hardham, St. Botolph. St. Botolph's is a two-cell building which, like so many in Sussex, could be either pre-Conquest or post-Conquest. The church is notable chiefly for its extensive series of wall paintings, which dates from the early 12C and which is considered to be the work of artists from the Cluniac Priory of St. Pancras at Lewes.

The church comprises an aisleless nave and square-ended chancel, with a bell turret placed over the E end of the nave, and a N porch. A blocked S doorway, visible only from outside, is an original feature. Against the S wall of the chancel an anchorite's cell was built in the 13C. A squint used by the anchorite may be seen within. The bell turret and the porch are 19C. The church is built of local sandstone, firestone rubble and reused Roman materials. The walls are rendered and painted white, but stone quoins remain visible. The N and S nave walls have one small original window, set high up, and one larger, later lancet. The S wall of the chancel has one original window and a two-light window in Decorated style. The 13C E window is of two lights. At the W end there is one large, untraceried window, with the glass arranged in small square panes.

The interior has a wide, unmoulded chancel arch and open timber kingpost roofs. It is visually dominated by the wall paintings, which have been uncovered gradually since 1866. The surviving paintings are arranged in two tiers. Red and yellow are the predominant colours, but some figures have a bluish-green nimbus. Nativity and Infancy scenes are to be seen in the upper parts of the N, S and E nave walls. The most distinct scenes are the Annunciation and the Visitation, which are depicted on the upper part of the E wall of the nave, to the S of the chancel arch. The Archangel Gabriel and the Virgin Mary each have a bluish-green nimbus. N of them, a roundel over the chancel arch depicts the Lamb of God, flanked by two censing angels. The right-hand angel is both well-preserved and well-designed. N of the arch is Christ among the Doctors. In the lower tier, on the E wall, the baptism of Christ may be discerned on the S. On the S wall, in the upper tier, from E to W, are shown the Nativity, the Adoration of the Magi, the Journey of the Magi, and the Adoration of the Shepherds. The series continues on the N wall, showing the Magi presenting their gifts, the Dream of St. Joseph, the Dream of the Magi, the Flight into Egypt, the Fall of the Images and the Massacre of the Innocents.

In the lower tier of the N wall, W of the door, are shown scenes concerning St. George, which are particularly interesting. One view is of St. George appearing at the siege of Antioch in 1097–98, during the First Crusade. In addition there are views of St. George's trial and of an attempt to break him on a wheel. On the W wall are depicted the torments of Hell in four scenes.

The paintings in the chancel are less well-preserved. The upper tier shows figures of Apostles and Elders. A Passion cycle is partly preserved in the lower tier. The Last Supper may be seen on the N wall. On the W wall are Adam and Eve and their labours after the Fall. Eve is receiving the forbidden fruit from the Serpent (which looks more like a dragon) in the Tree of Knowledge.

Lancing, *College of St. Mary and St. Nicholas, Chapel.* Lancing College was founded by Canon Nathaniel Woodard (1811–91) in 1848. It was the first of many schools within the Woodard Corporation, and its chapel was built to be their 'central minster'. The foundation stone of the chapel was laid in 1868; the crypt was built in 1871–75; the E apse was ready by 1885; the building was dedicated, with an incomplete W end, in 1911; and finally, the W end and various details were added in 1957–78. The original architect of the college was R.C. Carpenter, but he died before work began. He was succeeded by his son, R.H. Carpenter, who oversaw the building until his own death in 1893. The chapel was his major work. Additions were then made down to the 1920s by Temple Moore. In 1951, S.E. Dykes Bower, the foremost Gothic architect of the mid-20C, was appointed to oversee the completion of the building, and it is to his credit that the great W rose window was finished by 1978. Amongst the builders, Billy Woodard, the founder's third son, worked heroically to see the original plan materialise. The materials were local, including stone from the college's own quarry at Scaynes Hill near Haywards Heath.

The chapel is one of the grandest institutional chapels in England. It is built in a 13C style, with a French Gothic emphasis on height and with a French apsidal E end. The external height is 150ft at the E end, and 90ft within from the floor to the vault. The W rose is 36ft in diameter. The side elevations are dominated by the flying buttresses, which support the formidable height of the main walls and rise into pinnacles. There are two larger E pinnacles where the nave and apse meet. At the W end, the great rose window is placed within a traceried square. There are two flanking pinnacles which reach up to the height of the W gable. The First World War memorial cloister, which is placed S of the chapel, was built in 1921–27 to the designs of Temple Moore.

The interior is undivided from W to E. The E end has tall windows around the apse. At the W end the rose is placed above a tier of arcading and above two large pointed arches, which lead through into a narthex. On the S side towards the E end is the founder's chantry, by Temple Moore. The recumbent effigy of Nathaniel Woodard is by P. Bryant Baker. The chantry on the N side, also by

Temple Moore, commemorates Billy Woodard. The stalls were designed for Eton College Chapel in 1851 by Sir Gilbert Scott and were presented to Lancing in the 20C. The large tapestries were designed by Lady Chilston in 1933 and were made at Merton Abbey. They depict Christ in Glory and the patron saints of the various Woodard schools. The stained glass of the W rose, which represents the arms of the Woodard schools, was made by Goddard & Gibbs.

Lewes, Southover, *St. John the Baptist.* St. John's was originally a church for the layfolk who came to live near the Cluniac Priory of St. Pancras, which was founded by William de Warenne I and his wife Gundrada in 1077. William was the first Norman lord of Lewes and his foundation was the first Cluniac house in England. Some ruins of the priory survive nearby, but its most precious survival, Gundrada's tombstone, is now placed in St. John's. The church had moved to its present site by the 13C, apparently by converting an existing *hospitium* or guest-house.

The church stands in Southover, a suburb of Lewes to the S. Its fabric has been greatly altered over the centuries. A tower and a spire stood at the E end until they collapsed in 1698. A new tower was subsequently built at the W end. Only in the later 19C did the E end reach its present plan. The present fabric comprises a 12C arcade, a 14C N wall, a 16C S aisle, a battlemented W tower of 1714–38, a neo-Norman S chapel of 1847 (by J.L. Parsons), a chancel of 1884, and a SE vestry. Within, the four-bay arcade consists of cylindrical piers in Caen stone, which support three unmoulded, round arches (whose stonework has been plastered) and a 15C E arch which is not *in situ*. The E window has stained glass of 1930 by Jessie M. Jacob. It depicts the presentation of the priory to the Abbot of Cluny by William de Warenne and Gundrada, and also shows St. John the Baptist, St. Pancras and St. Benedict, and the arms of Cluny, the town of Lewes and the families of de Warenne and Fitzalan. Other windows are by C.E. Kempe (second from E in S aisle), Morris & Co. and (perhaps) Henry Holiday.

The S chapel was built to house the bones of William de Warenne I and Gundrada, which had been found in leaden caskets in 1845, during the building of the nearby railway line. The bones were reburied beneath Gundrada's original grave-slab. The leaden caskets were placed in niches in the S wall of the chapel. The grave-slab itself had been found in Isfield Church in 1775, where it had formed part of a table-tomb in the Shurley chapel. The grave-slab is of Tournai marble and dates from the mid-12C. Gundrada had died in 1085. The design comprises strips of inscription round the edges and lengthwise down the middle. The remaining space is filled by 16 plant designs, which are linked by lions' heads. It was once thought that Gundrada was King William I's daughter and, although this view is not accepted today, it remains the case that the tomb in La Trinité, Caen, Normandy, of King William's wife, Matilda, provided the model for the arrangement of the inscription on Gundrada's tombstone.

New Shoreham, *St. Mary de Haura.* St. Mary's is the greater part of an impressive cruciform building, which dates from two separate periods of the 12C, the earlier one Norman, the later one Transitional. The present fabric comprises a choir, N and S choir aisles, a crossing tower, N and S transepts and one aisleless bay of the nave, which now forms the W porch. The rest of the six-bay nave seems to have been lost in the 17C. Of the surviving fabric, the transepts and the crossing tower are of c 1130–50. Excavations in 1915 showed that originally the transepts had E apsidal chapels and there was also an apsidal, aisleless chancel. These were replaced in the last quarter of the 12C, when the present aisled choir was built. The church was about 210ft in length by the 13C. The additional name, *de Haura*, means 'of the harbour'.

The crossing tower has two tiers of louvred windows in each face. The upper windows are pairs of three very narrow, round-headed lights, but they are placed under a pointed superarch. The transepts have surviving 12C Norman windows, which are flanked by single external shafts. The S window of the S transept, of three lights, is Perpendicular. The W faces of the transepts bear the markings of the former lean-to nave aisles. The choir aisles have neo-Norman windows of 1876–79, but these are overshadowed by the two huge 13C flying buttresses on each side. The E windows have been restored in the 19C and 20C. They comprise two tiers of three tall lights. The parapet of the choir is Perpendicular.

Within the church, the porch is immediately next to the crossing. All four arches are Norman, unmoulded and unchamfered, except for the W one which has roll-mouldings and is particularly tall and impressive. The two transepts are substantially Norman, with single internal shafts to the 12C windows, but there are later windows too. The five-bay choir is the glory of the interior: a rich essay in the Transitional style, harmonious to the eye but in fact composed of widely differing details. On the N there are alternating octagonal and cylindrical piers, very thick and standing on large plinths, with rich foliage capitals and moulded arches. The S arcade has compound piers with moulded arches. The choir has a quadripartite vault. The vaulting shafts on the N begin above the arcade, but those on the S rise from the ground. The choir aisles are also vaulted, and have round-headed blank arcading along the outer walls. The gallery has paired openings on the N, single on the S.

The font of Sussex marble is Norman, with a square bowl supported on a central column and four angle shafts. Two late medieval brasses are placed on the S choir aisle wall.

Petworth House, Chapel. Petworth House is a remodelling of 1688–93 by an unknown architect for the sixth Duke of Somerset (died 1748). Its E elevation speaks of the earlier house of the Percy family, which the Duke of Somerset acquired by marriage. The chapel, which is placed towards the NE corner, is substantially a survival of that earlier house. Its exceptionally thick N and S walls mask the fact that its alignment is askew to that of the surrounding rooms. Its character is of two quite different periods: the 13C and the late 17C. Of the 13C, that is of the Early English style, are the wall arcades and the windows. Moulded arches and Sussex marble shafts divide the walls and frame recessed pairs of windows. The E window is of three lights, in the same style, but its details have been renewed. The plaster tunnel-vault is of the late 17C. Except for the 14C eagle lectern, the fittings are of 1685–92. The notable carvings were executed by John Selden. In each bay the panelling has a cherub's head beneath a pediment, and in front of each wall shaft stands an urn on a pedestal, which overhangs the stalls. At the W end is the family pew, placed above the doorway in a gallery on Ionic columns. It is surmounted by a theatrical arch, which is painted and carved to resemble drapery and which bears a huge coat of arms of the Duke of Somerset.

Petworth House was transferred to the National Trust in 1947.

Rye, St. Mary the Virgin. St. Mary's is a cruciform building of many periods from Norman times onwards, whose tower presides over this ancient Cinque port, which is the easternmost place of importance in Sussex. The church comprises a nave with N and S aisles, a central tower, N and S transepts, a chancel and N and S chancel aisles. Many of the details date from the 14C and the 15C, as a result of repairs after French raids. Considerable alterations were made in 1860 and in 1882–84.

The church stands S of the High Street. Its central tower is battlemented and has a very low recessed pyramidal cap, with a tall weathervane of 1702. On the N side there is a clock of 1560 (made by Lewys Billiard of Winchelsea), but the clock-face and two quarter-jacks date from 1760. The aisles have battlements and window tracery from the 14C and 15C. The E window and the main transept windows are Perpendicular. The five-light W window has elaborate Decorated tracery. To the W of the S transept there stands a two-storey vestry which was originally a chantry.

There is a wide nave of five bays. The piers are round, except for an octagonal one (second from the W), with moulded capitals. The arches are mostly only just pointed. Dogtooth decoration may be seen on the hoodmould. Above, there are lancet clerestory windows—all renewed in 1882–84—and a clerestory wall passage. The nave aisles are spacious. Wide rounded arches lead from them into the transepts, which are still substantially Norman. The crossing is 15C. There are three-bay arcades in the chancel, of which the N is Early English (two bays) and Perpendicular (one bay), the S entirely Perpendicular. The chancel chapels are 13C; they have lancets, but on the N they are paired, with a circle above.

The font is a 19C copy of one in Newenden Church, Kent. The arms of Queen Anne, 1704, are placed over the chancel arch. Other fittings of interest are the pulpit, with 16C linenfold work; 15C oak screens between the transepts and the chancel chapels; and a chandelier of 1759 in the chancel. The stained glass is all of the late 19C and 20C. The W window, by James Powell & Sons , was given in 1937 by E.F. Benson, the novelist who served as Mayor of Rye in 1934–36, in memory of his parents. (His father was Edward White Benson, Archbishop of Canterbury, 1882–96.) His brother, A.C. Benson, who wrote 'Land of Hope and Glory', is commemorated by the Benedicite window of 1928 in the S transept, by James Powell & Sons. A.C. Benson himself appears in the lower corner of the fifth light. Two windows in the S aisle are by C.E. Kempe, c 1882 and 1889. The N aisle has a window of 1886 by Clayton & Bell (illustrating the 23rd Psalm) and one of 1897 by Sir Edward Burne-Jones in memory of Mary Tiltman. The main E window is by Christopher Webb, 1952. The E window of St. Clare's chapel was dedicated in 1912 in memory of a churchwarden, Edward Henry Liddell, the brother of the original 'Alice in Wonderland'.

John Fletcher, the dramatist, was baptised here in 1579. His father was the minister.

Sompting, St Mary. St. Mary's is famous for the Rhenish helm spire which surmounts its W tower. A close study in 1984 showed that the lowest stage of the present tower is the W end of a pre-Conquest nave, and that the parts above are Norman additions of the late 11C. Carbon dating has assigned the present helm spire to the early 14C, although it is probable that it repeats one of the 11C. St. Mary's is distinguished too for its tower arch and for the pre-Conquest carvings which are preserved throughout the church. The aisleless nave, chancel and N and S transepts are late Norman and Transitional in date, built after the Templars had acquired the church in 1154. Restoration took place under R.C. Carpenter in 1854. A parish room was added N of the nave in 1971, in an almost hidden position, where a N chapel had stood from the 14C until the Reformation.

The church stands on rising ground just N of the A27, to the NE of Worthing. The W tower has four gables, from which rise the steep pyramidal, shingled roof. A pilaster strip runs vertically in the centre of each face, crossing a decorated stringcourse at about the height of the nave walls. The strips are flat below the stringcourse, semicircular above it. High up on the E and W faces there are pairs of single gable-headed openings, divided by the pilaster strip. On the N and S faces there are two pairs of two-light, round-headed openings, the lights of each pair separated by a shaft. The W face has a blocked Norman window in the lowest stage and, to the S of it, a later trefoiled window and a Perpendicular doorway.

The S transept has two square-headed windows and a 16C porch on its S side. On its E side a chapel projects. The N transept has an E aisle whose two bays have separate gabled roofs at right angles to that of the transept proper. The aisle has Norman windows, one to the N, two to the E.

Entering by the S porch, the impression of a N–S orientation is given by the size of the two transepts. The nave and chancel are aisleless and are no wider than the tower. There is no chancel arch. The S transept has an E arch of two square-cut orders, the outer with a single shaft. The N transept has a single round pier, semicircular responds, scalloped capitals and pointed arches. A blocked N doorway may be seen in the nave. The tower arch is of much interest. It has a square-cut outer order, with capitals in the form of spirals or volutes enclosing bunches of grapes. The semicircular inner order or soffit roll has very simple leaf capitals. The arch has been seen as a faint reflection of Classical design.

The pre-Conquest carvings are scattered. In the S transept there is a figure of an abbot or a bishop, nimbed and with a crozier standing unsupported next to him. A 13C Christ in Majesty, carved on the back of a pre-Conquest fragment, is placed on the N side of the nave. The triangular-headed piscina incorporates two strips of pre-Conquest carving, possibly from a frieze. The 12C font, round and plain, stands in the E projection of the S transept. On the N side of the chancel there is a monument to Richard Burré (died 1527) and his wife, which presumably served as an Easter sepulchre. 19C stained glass fills the chancel windows (the Magi, S; Christ amongst the Doctors, N; the Ascension, E) and the Norman windows of the N transept's E aisle.

Thakeham, *The Blue Idol, Friends' Meeting House.* This Friends' Meeting House has a site of marked isolation, at the end of a lane off the A272 between Billingshurst and Coolham. It is a half-timbered domestic building of two storeys, converted for worship in 1691. William Penn belonged to the congregation at that time, but the benefactor was John Shaw.

The external timbers divide the façades into more or less square panels. The interior is a single room which goes up two storeys. There is a simple ministers' gallery and other plain fittings. The W end was extended in 1927 to serve as a guest-house. The name, 'Blue Idol', is thought to refer to the building's former blue wash and to the fact that it was unused from 1793 to 1869. 'Idol' is thus a corruption from 'idle'. Its formal name is Thakeham Meeting House.

Tillington, All Hallows. All Hallows' is chiefly notable for the crown on its tower of 1807. It is a design which mirrors those of the cathedrals at Newcastle and Edinburgh. Four flying buttresses spring from the corner pinnacles to hold the spire in the centre. The tower, uncommonly placed S of the chancel, was built at the expense of the third Earl of Egremont (died 1837), the owner of nearby Petworth House, one of whose guests was the painter J.M.W. Turner. In view of Turner's training as an architect and the inclusion of Tillington's new tower in Turner's views of Petworth Park, the tower has been attributed to him. Unfortunately, Turner did not visit Petworth until 1809, two years after the tower had been built. The available sources allow no attribution to be made.

All Hallows' has the distinction of having been painted not only by Turner but also by John Constable, whose attractive view of it is held in the British Museum.

Worth, St. Nicholas. St. Nicholas' is one of the most important pre-Conquest churches in Sussex. Worth looked more to Surrey than to Sussex in the 11C and may have been built under the influence of Chertsey Abbey. Substantial restoration took place in 1871 under Anthony Salvin. On 8th September, 1986, the church suffered considerably from a fire; restoration under Geoffrey Claridge was finished in 1988.

The church comprises a nave with N and S transepts or *porticus* towards its E end, a S porch, a lower apsidal chancel and a NE tower. The tower was built in 1871 by Salvin. It has a shingled broach spire. The porch is also Victorian, built in 1886. The rest of the church is late pre-Conquest, of the 10C or the 11C. The nave has pilaster strips on the W and S sides, which rise to a stringcourse. This stringcourse, which survives on the N side too, serves as the sill level of the original windows, two to the N, one to the S. These windows each have two lights, separated by a markedly wide shaft. Pictorial evidence suggests that these windows were much restored in the 19C. The W front has one three-light 14C window with flowing tracery, above a doorway of similar date. The S transept has a blocked pre-Conquest window with a monolithic head on the W side and pilaster strips on the E side (partly of 1871). Just E of the transept is a trefoiled ogee lancet, very attractive. The walls of the transepts rise only to the level of the nave's stringcourse. The apsidal chancel has pilaster strips of 1871 and a stringcourse, lower than the nave's, above which Salvin placed renewed lancets. The two-light window below the stringcourse on the S side is 13C. Note the original double plinth.

Within, there is a wide chancel arch of late pre-Conquest character, with semicircular responds, double imposts with a horizontal emphasis, and an unmoulded arch. The arches to the transepts are lower but fairly wide. The S doorway and the blocked N doorway are by contrast very tall and narrow. The church has a 13C stone square font, a very frequent type in Sussex, and a carved wooden pulpit of 1577, of German origin. There are attractive 17C and 19C wall tablets in the transepts. The W gallery is 17C.

THE ISLE OF WIGHT

The Isle of Wight, geologically and scenically, is similar to parts of Hampshire and Dorset, with a backbone of chalk downland running across the island from the Needles in the W to Culver Cliff in the E. Flint has therefore been widely used for building. Besides the chalk there is much sandstone, with deposits of limestone in the N of the island at Binstead and Quarr. The island is still predominantly rural, but the N and SE coastal resorts have developed apace since the 19C, when the presence of Queen Victoria and the royal family at Osborne did much to popularise the island.

The majority of the churches serve small rural communities. Many of them have medieval origins and show the various architectural phases as well as a wealth of fittings and monuments. Norman work appears in a number of churches. An 11C W doorway, tall and relatively narrow, survives at St. George's, Arreton. St. Edmund's, Wootton, has a 12C S doorway with zigzag and billet moulding and single scalloped shafts. The church of St. John the Baptist at Yaverland also has a Norman S doorway in addition to a (renewed) Norman chancel arch. St. Michael's at Shalfleet has a Norman W tower and a S doorway with sculpture in its tympanum. St. Mary's, Carisbrooke, formerly a priory church, has as its core an aisleless Norman building. The 13C is much represented in the Isle of Wight, as in Hampshire. St. Mary's at Brading is a classic example. Work of the same period occurs at Niton, Newchurch, Calborne and Freshwater. At Binstead, the chancel is of the 13C, whereas the nave is of

The tympanum of the Norman N doorway at Shalfleet

1844 in 13C style. Recessed spires, usually short, became frequent from that time in the Isle of Wight. Perpendicular renewal and additions, to towers, clerestories and windows, are also frequent in the Island as elsewhere. Two late medieval wall paintings must be mentioned: a St. Christopher at Shorwell and a lily Crucifix at Godshill (see gazetteer). The 17C has left a number of pulpits and altar rails, of which the canopied pulpit at Northwood deserves special mention. Significant work in quality and quantity then resumes in the 19C. In its early years, John Nash designed a W tower at St. Mary's, Cowes in a Greek style. For Victorian work, in addition to St. Mildred's, Whippingham (see gazetteer), there is of particular note the large church of All Saints at Ryde, by Sir Gilbert Scott (1868–72, the steeple of 1881–82). St. Thomas's, Newport is a large town church of 1854–55 by S.W. Dawkes. In the 20C, the major ecclesiastical building is Quarr Abbey, built after 1908 by Dom Paul Bellot. The church is built entirely of brick, angular in style and unusual in plan. Emphasis is given to the long choir, which leads to the sanctuary under an E tower. The short nave at the W is at a lower level than the choir.

Royal memorials are naturally numerous at Whippingham, the estate church for Osborne. In addition, St. Thomas's, Newport has the tomb of Princess Elizabeth (died 1649), daughter of King Charles I. The monument was erected by Queen Victoria. Amongst older memorials, two brasses might be noted: one to William Montacute, Earl of Salisbury (died 1379) at Calbourne, and the other (now headless) to Harry Hawles (died 1430), a veteran of Agincourt, at Arreton. Tombs of the prominent family of Oglander form a notable series at Brading. The Leighs and the Worsleys, also leading landowners, are represented at Godshill and Shorwell.

As to historical associations, the church of St. Mary the Virgin at Brighstone can lay claim to fame through three of its Rectors having risen to the rank of bishop: Thomas Ken, Rector 1667–69, later Bishop of Bath and Wells; Samuel Wilberforce, Rector 1830–40, son of William Wilberforce, who became Bishop of Oxford and then of Winchester; and finally, George Moberly, Rector 1867–69, who became Bishop of Salisbury. Alfred Tennyson lived at Farringford, near Freshwater, from 1853. The poet himself is buried in Westminster Abbey, but the churchyard of All Saints', Freshwater includes his family vault. In the 20C, Mottistone has had a close link with John Seely, second Lord Mottistone (died 1963), the well-known architect (of the firm of Seely & Paget), who undertook much work on churches.

Dedications on the Isle of Wight include St. Blasius at Shanklin, St. Radegund at Whitwell, St. Boniface at Bonchurch and St. Olave, the 11C Norwegian martyr-king, at Gatcombe.

Godshill, *All Saints*. Godshill is the number one picture postcard view of the Isle of Wight, with thatched cottages clinging to the sides of the hill, below the church and its surrounding churchyard. Indeed, it is believed to be one of the most-visited churches in England. Its setting commands wide views in all directions. The present church dates from the 14C and is the largest medieval church in the Isle of Wight. It has a number of impressive monuments but its chief claim to fame is the mid-15C wall painting of Christ crucified on a triple-branched lily plant, on the E wall of the S transept.

Internally, the church consists of two naves and chancels which are continuous, and N and S transepts. The N nave and chancel formed the medieval parish church proper, the S side being reserved for the use of Appuldurcombe Priory. The naves and chancels are divided by a six-bay arcade of octagonal columns on square bases with moulded capitals which date from the late 14C. The N transept was rebuilt in 1741. Despite the many monuments and fittings, the church has a spacious quality and this is enhanced by many of the windows being clear-glazed.

Above the door to the porch are the arms of Queen Anne, dated 1707. In the W bay of the S nave is a white-painted, late Georgian organ which was bought for the church in 1814. Nearby, at the W end, is a catafalque dated 1853 with the initials W.M. and J.F. The S transept, which is dedicated to St. Stephen, is enclosed by metal gates, painted blue and dated 1937. The main feature of the transept and indeed of the church is the wall painting dating from the middle of the 15C, on the E wall above the altar. Christ is depicted crucified on a triple-branched lily plant. On either side of this are painted curtains. Between these and the Crucifixion are a number of inscriptions, and above the Crucifixion are two angels. The painting was restored by Mrs Eve Baker in 1966. The wooden beams above have carved springers depicting female heads, which in turn are carried on carved stone corbels, that above the wall painting being an angel. The transept is now used for the Reserved Sacrament. Immediately outside the transept is a modern wooden pulpit designed by Laurence King. In the S wall is the medieval Rood loft doorway. There is a modern (1948) Rood beam with brightly coloured figures. On the S wall below the Rood loft entrance are the remains of a medieval consecration mark and what appears to be a symbolic representation of the hand of God. In the N chancel the altar rails are 17C. In front of the chancels are two brightly painted modern statues of the Virgin and Child and St. George. The N nave has a large oil painting, a copy of Rubens's 'Daniel in the Lion's Den', given by the first Lord Yarborough in the early years of the 19C. Also on the N wall, at the W end, is a large depiction of St. George and the Dragon, by Heywood Sumner, dating from 1894.

The church is particularly rich in monuments. At the W end behind the organ is a massive sarcophagus, apparently many tons in weight, standing on giant lion claw feet, which rest on a very high plinth. It is to Sir Richard Worsley (died 1805), who was a great traveller and collector of antiquities. Against the S wall of the S chancel is the tomb of Richard Worsley (died 1565). It has no figures but consists of a central inscription set between two pairs of pillars, which carry an elaborately decorated entablature and which in turn supports a centrally placed family crest. On either side of this are two urns with animal heads. Above, suspended from the wall, are a helmet and gloves. On the E wall to the left of the high altar is the memorial tablet to Stuart Worsley (died 1708), with a crest and skull. Between the N and S chancels, in the last bay of the arcade, there is the large Caen stone table-tomb with recumbent effigies of Derbyshire alabaster of Sir John Leigh (died 1529) and his wife Agnes. A rare feature is that beneath the soles of his feet are two small carved figures of monks with their rosaries, otherwise known as bedesmen. They and his feet rest on a pig or boar. Against the N wall of the N chancel is the monument to Sir James Worsley (died 1536) and his wife Anne (died 1567). It consists of the two kneeling figures facing E at desks which bear their respective crests. The figures are set between two Ionic pilasters which support a decorated frieze and a pediment, which is surmounted by three putti bearing shields. The figures of this tomb, along with the crests on the tombs of Sir Richard Worsley and Sir John and Agnes Leigh, have been repainted with very bright modern colour paints. Lady Worsley was the daughter of Sir John and Lady Leigh and by her marriage brought the Worsleys to Appuldurcombe House, just SE of Godshill. The N wall of the N transept is taken up almost entirely with the very large monument to Sir Robert Worsley who died in 1747. The monument was erected in 1741, partly in memory of his brother, Sir Henry Worsley, who died that year. Above the monument are two faded flags which were the colours of the Isle of Wight Volunteers and which date from 1806.

The church has a number of stained glass windows. The E window of the S chancel depicts the Virgin and Child flanked by St. Gabriel and St. Michael. It has a memorial date of 1927 and is by Percy Bacon. The E window of the N chancel depicts Christ on the Cross flanked by the two Marys. The two-light window in the N wall of the N chancel depicts the Immaculate Conception and is by Morris & Sons of Kennington, with a memorial date of 1933.

Shorwell, *St. Peter.* Positioned beneath the downs on a sloping site, the church is set amongst beautiful rural scenery. The church is rectangular in plan with nave and aisles of equal length, a W tower and N and S porches. The reason for the rectangular plan is that for some considerable time there were in fact two adjacent churches, the N aisle and chancel being served by Carisbrooke Priory, the nave and S aisle being served by a Vicar. The church possesses a large number of interesting fittings.

Externally, the church reveals a largely 15C character, being built of rubble masonry with dressed stone details. At the W end the crenellated tower carries a recessed spire. The weather vane atop the spire depicts a cockerel and is dated 1617. In the N wall are two of the earliest features of the church, a blocked doorway and a lancet window. The S door has chevron moulding and like the lancet window and blocked N doorway dates from the Early English period. In the S wall is a large Perpendicular four-light window which has a Tudor rose carved in one of its spandrels.

Internally, the church slopes upwards from the W end. There are five bays, the E two bays serving as the chancel, which (along with the corresponding bays of the aisles) is raised on two steps. The nave piers are octagonal with simple octagonal capitals. The chancel piers are round. The tower has a tierceron star vault. In the N aisle, above the N porch door, is one of the most important features of the church, a large wall painting of the life of St. Christopher, dating from the middle of the 15C. The left-hand image depicts St. Christopher riding with the Devil, and his renouncing of the Devil. The central image is of St. Christopher carrying the infant Christ on his shoulder across the water and holding a large staff. Between St. Christopher's feet are depicted fishes, one of which has taken the bait of a man fishing on the bank. There are also various boats illustrated. From Christ's mouth issues forth a label inscribed *Ego sum alpha et omega* (I am the alpha and the omega—the beginning and the end). On the right-hand side is St. Christopher's martyrdom, in a similar fashion to St. Sebastian's. Above this, looking on, are a king and an executioner.

In the nave the stone pulpit is built against one of the piers and dates from the mid-15C. It is five-sided and has blind arcading. Above it is a highly decorated Jacobean wooden tester, dated 1620. Fixed against the pier is an hourglass and its iron stand. Above the chancel arch, the beam is designed like a Rood beam, except that the central figure is of Christ in Majesty, with the figures of St. Michael and St. Gabriel on either side. The beam itself carries the inscription *Gloria in Excelsis Tibi Domine, Alleluia, Amen* (Glory to you in the Heavens, Lord, Alleluia, Amen). The beam is carried on two carved corbels, one depicting Sin and the other Death. The free-standing high altar, dedicated in 1961, stands in front of a stone blind arcade.

In the S aisle the W bay formerly served as a gun chamber, where the parish gun was kept. It now serves as a vestry. On the S wall is an oil painting depicting the Nativity. The wooden carved font cover, which dates from the early 17C, is surmounted by a carving of the Holy Dove. Around the cover is carved the inscription, 'And the Holy Ghost descended in a body shaped like a Dove upon him. Luke 3.v.22'. The small wooden altar at the E end has carved sides and was used by General Sir Willoughby Gordon in the Peninsular War of 1809. Behind this the painting is a copy of the altarpiece of 1836, brought from Thingvellir Church in Iceland. The original was presented to the church in 1899 and in 1974, on the occasion of the 1100th anniversary of Icelandic Christianity beginning at Thingvellir, it was handed back and the copy given to Shorwell.

In the Leigh chapel on the N wall are three monuments. That to Sir John Leigh (died 1629) and his great-grandson, also John Leigh, who died aged only nine months in the same year, consists of the kneeling figures of Sir John and the tiny figure of the infant, facing W. This would indicate that they were originally designed to be on the opposite side of the church and therefore facing the altar. The figures are set under a Classical canopy. Next to this is the tomb of Elizabeth Leigh (died 1619). This consists of a centrally placed inscription with a cherub's head above. This is set between Classical columns which carry an entablature supported by a central crest flanked by putti. Nearby is the monument to John Leigh (died 1688) and his daughter-in-law, Anna (died 1719). Behind the altar is the brass to the two wives and children of Barnabas Leigh. It depicts Mrs Elizabeth Bampfield (died 1615), who bore all 15 children and who stand behind her. Next to Elizabeth is his second wife, Mrs Gartrude (sic) Percevall (died 1619). In front of the high altar is the brass to Richard Bethell (died 1518), who was Vicar from 1478 to his death in 1518. It is of a priest in his robes, with an inscription below. On the S wall is a pre-Raphaelite-inspired tile image of St. George and the Dragon, which is a memorial to Mark Leigh Goldie (died 1915).

The chancel window is of four lights and depicts two central images of Jesus with the inscriptions, 'Feed my Sheep' and 'Lord Save me', flanked by the Apostles.

The church has links with Algernon Charles Swinburne who wrote part of 'Atalanta in Corydon' at nearby North Court.

Whippingham, *St. Mildred.* This is the estate church for Osborne and as such is unparalleled amongst parish churches for royal connections, memorials and tombs. It is the third church on the site, the first being founded in pre-Conquest times. The second church was built by John Nash and the present church was built in 1854–55 and 1860–62. It was designed by Albert Jenkins Humbert and the Prince Consort.

It is set in a well-kept churchyard, with views down to the River Medina and the lines of anchored yachts. The lychgate was given by Queen Victoria. Externally, the rubble-built church is dominated by the large central tower of dressed stone and by the central octagonal lantern spire rising from a blunt pyramid. The tower has large square turrets at the corners and each wide face has arcading pierced by six lancets. The profile and details of this tower are thus most unusual. By the S porch is a large Calvary. At the E end is Queen Victoria's private entrance. Her arms are carved over the door. Rich marble columns and capitals support a highly decorated Norman style arch.

Internally, the chancel is Early English in style, the nave and transepts neo-Norman. The transepts have rose windows. In plan the church has a four-bay aisleless nave but the chancel has N and S aisles. At the W end, the gallery houses the organ built by Henry William in 1861–62. Also at the W end is the font, which consists of a large central pillar and bowl, possibly by Nash, with the later addition of four further supporting piers. The carpet to surround the font was designed and made by Princess Louise, Duchess of Argyll, and Princess Beatrice. The nave and transepts have wrought-iron triple-branch candelabra with glass shades, presented by Queen Victoria. Under the tower space are the priest's chair and the five-sided pulpit, richly carved with the Beatitudes. On either side of the chancel arch are two paintings. That on the left is a copy of 1893 by Anif Richardson of 'Beati Angelica'. On the right is 'The Great Sacrifice' by James Clark. High up in the lantern of the tower is a representation of the Order of the Garter. The sanctuary has an elaborately carved alabaster reredos depicting the Last Supper, set in a coloured marble surround. This was presented to the church by King Edward VII as a memorial to Queen Victoria. The chair in the sanctuary dates from c 1650 and was presented by Princess Louise, Duchess of Argyll. The chancel roof has three angels on each side, bearing shields carrying the word Holy on each. The N chancel aisle or Battenberg chapel has metal screens in an Art Nouveau style by Sir Alfred Gilbert, which fill the six small Early English style arches. A plaque in the arcade wall contains a copy of Queen Victoria's handwriting to state that she gave the screens in 1897 as a memorial to her son-in-law, Prince Henry of Battenberg. In the chapel are three display cases, of which the central contains the silver spoon used to administer Queen Victoria's last communion at Osborne. There are also photographs of Victoria and Albert, and Prince Henry and his wife, Princess Beatrice. The right-hand case contains a Bible and photographs of Princess Beatrice and Lord Mountbatten. The left-hand case contains a Bible richly decorated with jewels, which was presented to Princess Beatrice upon her marriage by 'The Maidens of England'. At the E end is an altar with a marble carving of the figure of Christ on the Cross with a large winged angel, designed by Princess Louise. There are further figures of angels on each side of the altar. In front of the E end of the tomb, on a chair, is a crocheted hassock made by Queen Victoria. At the W end hang Prince Henry's Garter regalia, and a furled full Admiral's banner, given to Prince Louis of Battenberg by his ship's company upon his promotion in 1907. On the N wall hangs Lord Carisbroke's Garter banner. On the S side is the royal pew, again separated by an arcade of six small Early English style arches.

The church is full of monuments. In the Battenberg chapel is the large white marble tomb-chest of Prince Henry of Battenberg (died 1896). Princess Beatrice was laid to rest with him in 1945. To the right of the altar is a memorial plaque to the Russian royal family. In the N wall are three caskets of ashes, those of the Marquess and Marchioness of Carisbrooke and of David Mountbatten (died 1970). On the W wall is a plaque to George, second Marquess of Milford Haven (died

1938), which was placed there by his sister, Queen Louise of Sweden. In the S chancel aisle or royal pew are a number of royal memorials, including a monument erected by Queen Victoria in 1886 in memory of Prince Leopold, Duke of Albany (died 1884), her youngest son. A memorial by F. Theed to Princess Alice (died 1878) was erected by Queen Victoria in 1879. It depicts two grieving angels holding a portrait medallion. On the W wall is a large monument by Humbert and W. Theed, executed in 1864, in memory of Prince Albert (died 1861). It also has two angels holding a portrait medallion. Beneath this are three arches, two containing crests of Prince Albert. In the N transept is a memorial to William Arnold, father of the famous headmaster. In the nave by the S door is a memorial tablet to 90 Hessian soldiers killed by an outbreak of typhus in 1794.

The single-light W window of St. John the Baptist was designed by Pace, who also designed a single light of the Madonna and Child with three angels in the S wall near the font. These windows were paid for by Princess Beatrice. The three-light E window depicts the Resurrection, Crucifixion and Ascension. Above this is a circular window containing a representation of the Holy Dove. In the Battenberg chapel, the three single lights depict St. Henry, St. Beatrice and St. Maurice (all name-saints of the family).

The church was the royal family's place of worship while in residence at Osborne for the last 40 years of the 19C. The church was also the scene of the wedding of Prince Henry of Battenberg to Princess Beatrice in 1885. The churchyard contains one further royal burial and one other burial of note. The royal tomb is that of Louis Alexander Mountbatten, Admiral of the Fleet (died 1921), and his wife Victoria (died 1956), Earl Mountbatten's parents. Nearby is the tomb of Uffa Fox (died 1972), the famous sailor, naval architect and inventor of the wartime rescue lifeboat.

WILTSHIRE

Although the county is predominantly one of chalk, including the justly famous areas of the Marlborough Downs and Salisbury Plain, there are large deposits on the W side of the county of good building stones, forming part of the Jurassic Limestone belt which runs up the country from the Dorset coast. Amongst the best of these stones are those which have been extensively quarried in and around Box and Corsham. The N and NW of the county are in effect part of the Cotswold stone belt. In the SW Chilmark was the source of the grey-coloured stone used for many churches including Salisbury Cathedral. The Marlborough Downs have produced the unique Sarsen stone. The chalk, of course, has provided flint in large quantities. The SE of the county and part of the Savernake Forest have good deposits of clays which have been used for brick, tile and pottery making. With the exception of Swindon, and to a lesser extent Trowbridge and Melksham, the county has no significant industrialisation and is predominantly rural with stunning scenery of rolling downland with deep valleys and vales.

From the pre-Conquest period, the county possesses at Bradford-on-Avon an intact and virtually unaltered building which houses the remains of two carved angels, once part of a life-sized Rood scene. From Norman Wiltshire, Malmesbury Abbey is an impressive large-scale fragment, the nave of an important Benedictine church. Also on a large scale is the church of St. John, Devizes. Far more humble is the small but almost perfectly preserved church at Manningford Bruce. Other notable Norman remains can be seen at Tisbury and Chippenham. The Early English period is well represented in churches, which is not surprising considering the influence of Salisbury Cathedral. The two best examples, Potterne and Bishop's Cannings, were owned by the cathedral. A further fine example is the S chapel at Boyton. The Decorated period is best represented by Bishopstone and the chancel of Urchfont. In Edington the county possesses a church which is of national importance in showing in one building the step from Decorated to Perpendicular. For the Perpendicular period, fine examples are Steeple Ashton, Calne, Lacock, Cricklade, St. Mary's at Devizes, the Beauchamp chapel at St. John's, Devizes, St. Thomas's, Salisbury and Seend.

During the 17C most building or rebuilding was still in the Gothic idiom, the rebuilding of the tower and the spire at Chippenham being a good example. After the collapse of the crossing tower at Calne in 1638, the chancel was rebuilt with Classical columns. Dating from c 1698 is the Zion Baptist Church at Bradford-on-Avon. At Farley the large brick church built in 1689–90 was possibly in part designed by Sir Christopher Wren. From the 18C the two finest churches are Hardenhuish (1779), designed by John Wood of Bath and Wardour Castle chapel, designed by James Paine and Sir John Soane. For 19C churches Wiltshire is not particularly rich. The chapel at Bowood by C.R. Cockerell, 1821–24, is in a Classical style. At Wilton there is a large-scale essay in Italian Romanesque, 1841–45, by Thomas Henry Wyatt and David Brandon. The only other large-scale church of note is Bodley & Garner's Marlborough College Chapel of 1883–86.

At Ramsbury there is an impressive collection of carved pre-Conquest stones, crosses and memorials. Pre-Conquest carvings exist at Britford and Codford St. Peter (both 9C). For the Norman period it is to Malmesbury Abbey one needs to look, with pride of place going to the impressive sculptures in the S porch. A further example of Norman sculpture can be seen at Knook, where there is a carved tympanum. At Stanton Fitzwarren there is a particularly fine carved 12C font. The major medieval wall painting is the famous Doom painting of c 1475 at St. Thomas's, Salisbury. There are further wall paintings at Lydiard Tregoze. For medieval woodwork Mere is the finest church with notable Perpendicular screens. The church also possesses a number of stalls with carved misericords. There are misericords, too, at Edington. Avebury has a rare 15C Rood loft. Also of Perpendicular date are the stone screens at Compton Bassett and in the aisles at Malmesbury Abbey. Of late medieval origin is the rare penitential seat at Bishop's Cannings. Bishopstone has a number of carved panels of English and Continental origin, from the late Middle Ages onwards. The communion rail at Tisbury is made up of fragments of a Perpendicular screen. The pulpit at Potterne is 15C.

Of Jacobean furnishings, Edington has some unusual communion rails, a reredos in the Lady chapel and in the nave a fine pulpit. Tisbury possesses a pulpit, font cover and pews of the period. At Lydiard Tregoze is the very unusual and rare painted triptych memorial dating from 1615 and contemporary pews, pulpit and screen. For the later 17C, the church at Farley has a complete set of furnishings contemporary with the building of the church. At East Knoyle, where Sir Christopher Wren was born and baptised, his father (who was Rector) designed the plasterwork scheme for the chancel walls in 1639. St. Thomas's, Salisbury has a good Classical reredos of 1724. The church also has the former cathedral organ dating from 1792. At Chippenham the sumptuous organ and organ case were built in 1752. Dilton retains a complete set of 18C fittings. By far the most impressive 18C interior is, however, that of the Roman Catholic chapel at Wardour Castle, most of the fittings of which are of Continental origin. From the 19C, the fittings of Marlborough College Chapel are of merit. At Calne, the reredos was designed by J.L. Pearson in 1890. At Calne also, the magnificent and ornate wooden organ case was designed by C.R. Ashbee in 1908 and made by the Campden Guild. This same combination was responsible for the reredos in the chapel of the Epiphany and St. Edmund.

For monuments, the finest churches are Edington and Lydiard Tregoze. At Edington there are two cross-legged effigies of 14C knights and an impressive coloured, canopied, late medieval tomb-chest. At Malmesbury Abbey is the 15C tomb of King Aethelstan, who lived in the 10C. At Stourton a fine range of monuments includes a good 15C female effigy. At Lydiard Tregoze the small church is almost overwhelmed by the monuments of the St. John family, which date from between 1592 and 1748. Amongst these the largest is the work of Nicholas Stone in 1634 and is considered to be one of the finest monuments of the period. Other fine Tudor and Jacobean monuments can be found at Lacock, Chippenham, Edington, Stourton and St. Thomas's, Salisbury. Representing the 18C, Urchfont has a monument of 1753 by Peter Scheemakers, and Lydiard Tregoze, Bradford-on-Avon (Holy Trinity) and Maiden Bradley have memorials by J.M. Rysbrack. From the 19C, Edington has a life-size monument by Sir Francis Chantrey, 1815. At Hardenhuish there is the Classical monument to David Ricardo by William Pitts. Richard Westmacott the Elder is represented at St. John's, Devizes, and Sir Richard Westmacott at Farley. There are a number of memorials by Thomas King of Bath at St. John's, Devizes and at Steeple Ashton. Bishopstone has a Gothic monument of 1844 designed by A.W.N. Pugin.

Amongst medieval brasses, Mere has two large figures of knights and Lacock has a 16C family group. Medieval stained glass is best represented at Wilton which has the finest collection including French 12C, 13C and 14C glass, German 14C and 16C glass, Dutch 16C and 17C and English 15C and 16C. There is some good 15C glass at Edington, Crudwell, Westwood, Oaksey and at Mere. Other fragmentary glass can be seen at Lydiard Tregoze and St. Thomas's, Salisbury. At Lydiard Tregoze the 17C glass is by Abraham van Linge and dates from c 1633. 19C glass abounds, with good collections at Marlborough College Chapel, Mere, Chippenham and Wilton. William Wailes appears at Wilton, Urchfont, Bishop's Cannings and Bishopstone, the latter's glass being designed by A.W.N. Pugin. Morris & Co. worked at Marlborough. Clayton & Bell are represented at Mere and Manningford Bruce. Chippenham has examples by Lavers & Westlake and Burlison & Grylls. Mere also has work by Henry Holiday, Kelly & Co., Powell's, and Ward & Nixon. There is much work by C.E. Kempe in the county. 20C glass is represented by Christopher Whall at Chippenham, Sir Ninian Comper at East Knoyle, Christopher Webb at Mere and Martin Travers at Cricklade.

Amongst the many figures of historical note associated with Wiltshire's churches are King Aethelstan (reigned 924–939), who is buried at Malmesbury Abbey; St. Aldhelm, Abbot of Malmesbury and founder of a church at Bradford-on-Avon; St. Osmund, Bishop of Salisbury (Old Sarum), who encouraged Aldhelm's cult; George Herbert, Vicar of Bemerton, who married at Edington (1629); Sir Christopher Wren, who was baptised at East Knoyle in 1632; Francis Kilvert, the diarist, who was born at Hardenhuish; George Crabbe, Vicar of St. James's, Trowbridge, where he was buried (1832); General Pitt-Rivers, the early archaeologist, who is buried at Tollard Royal (1900); and finally, Ian Fleming (died 1964), buried at St. Andrew's, Sevenhampton.

Bishop's Cannings, *St. Mary the Virgin.* Despite the name of the village and the implication that the church was formerly the possession of the Bishops of Salisbury, it was in fact under the control of the Dean and Chapter of Salisbury. Their ownership resulted in a large and impressive cruciform church, chiefly of the Early English and Perpendicular styles.

The church is situated below the rolling Marlborough Downs, at the W end of the Vale of Pewsey. Externally, the imposing central tower of two stages is Early English, the lower stage having two lancets in each face, and the upper stage three tall belfry lancets, a trefoil frieze and a corbel table of carved heads beneath the plain parapet. The stair turret rising above the parapet at the NE corner and the recessed spire are 15C additions. The clerestory of the nave and the aisle windows are Perpendicular. Each bay of the nave is supported by a buttress which rises to a pinnacle above the battlements. The W end has a triple-lancet Early English window. In the N aisle the W window is the only external evidence of the Norman building. The chancel, transepts and chantry chapel have tall recessed lancets, but the windows on the S side of the chancel are 14C alterations. The S porch has a 15C upper room; below, the S door is round-arched and has shafts with stiff-leaf decoration and thus shows the development from Norman to Transitional.

The nave is of four bays, the piers being circular, late Norman. The capitals have simple scallop decoration, but on the S side at the E end they show a development towards stiff-leaf. The arches are pointed. The present Perpendicular clerestory consists of three-light windows. The tower arch is deeply if plainly moulded. Above it is the door to the tower space, which is inset between the buttresses of the tower. The crossing has a 15C lierne-vault with carved bosses. The N transept is now used as a vestry and also houses the organ. In its N wall the triple-lancet windows have attached shafts with foliate capitals. The E wall has clusters of such shafts and capitals supporting two ribbed arches, each containing two recessed lancets. In the S transept the E wall is treated in a similar manner. The S arch leads into the chantry chapel. The long, low, three-bay chancel is a very good example of Early English architecture, the lowness being explained in part by the quadripartite stone vault. The triple-lancet E window has attached shafts of Purbeck marble with foliate capitals.

The nave and aisles have Victorian wooden pews, the ends being carved by Harry Hems of Exeter and installed during the restoration of 1883–84. The wooden roof of the nave is supported by five carved heads on each side and has some beams dated 1670. By the S door there is a wooden offertory box dating from the 17C. In the nave at the W end is the 14C octagonal stone font with quatrefoil panels. The choirstalls have been moved into the E bay of the nave and the altar, which is Elizabethan, has been placed under the crossing. In the N transept there is the organ with a wooden case and gilded pipes, dating from 1809, the work of George Pike England. In the S transept there is a rare medieval penitential seat dating from the 15C, with later additions. The back panel is painted and depicts a giant hand with various short quotations on each finger. Beneath this are two longer passages, one being held in the beak of a bird. A metal gate encloses the chantry or Ernle chapel, the altar of which is dated 1709. In the chancel the altar and reredos date from c 1830. In the S wall are two piscinas and the remains of two-arched sedilia with a carved head in the centre. Throughout the church there are the remains of wall paintings, some as late as the 17C.

In the chantry chapel there are two monuments to members of the Ernle family. On the E wall behind the altar is a large marble monument with a broken pediment supported by two Corinthian columns and a crest, in memory of Edward Ernle (died 1656). Against the N wall of the chapel is the elaborate stone altar-tomb to John Ernle (died 1571). The chest has three panels with shields bearing coats of arms and a Tudor arched canopy over. Above the arch is the family crest and a helmet. The stained glass is Victorian. The E window by William Wailes is dated 1860, the centre light depicting the Last Supper, the Betrayal, the Crucifixion, Christ Risen and the Ascension. The two other lights depict scenes from the Old Testament.

Bishopstone, _St. John the Baptist._ The village was a living of the Bishops of Winchester, which resulted in a large and impressive cruciform church mainly in the Decorated style. The church is set in idyllic rural surroundings in a large well-tended churchyard. It is built of grey stone with flint infill, much of which has been rendered. The central tower has a two-light louvred window in each face and is capped by simple battlements. The S wall of the S transept has attached to it a heavily buttressed passage open at both ends with two arches on its S side. It shelters a tomb. The Perpendicular S porch (rebuilt 1884) has an upper storey which has two lancets on either side of a canopied niche. The chancel S door has an elaborate ogee canopy with pinnacles and miniature stone vaulting. The S transept has a parapet consisting of pierced quatrefoil panels.

Internally, the aisleless nave of three bays rises to a wooden beamed roof. The chancel is of two bays, rib-vaulted. Against the S wall are very fine stone sedilia with pinnacles and crockets. In the N transept there is a large cusped arched recess. The S transept, which is largely taken up by the organ, has a rib-vault with carved bosses. There is a canopied piscina and a large canopied arched recess containing a tomb.

The octagonal stone font is Perpendicular. The pews are a mixture of 20C and Victorian together with bench-ends from different periods from the Continent. The octagonal wooden pulpit is Baroque in style and has carved garlands, putti, saints and the figure of Christ. All of this has traces of gilding. The main altar frontal comes from Westminster Abbey and was used at the Coronation of Queen Elizabeth in 1952. There is a good range of monuments. In the N transept are two foliate cross-slabs, one inset in the wall under the arched recess, the other immediately in front set in the floor. On the W wall are monuments to the Throope family with coloured crests. There is also an anonymous Jacobean monument of c 1630 of a figure between pilasters. In the S transept, in the S wall, is the tomb of George Augustus Montgomery, Rector here and Rural Dean of Wilton (died 1842), designed by A.W.N. Pugin in 1844. Over the S door is a marble pedimented monument to Michael Throope (died 1737). The stained glass includes the three-light window in the S wall of the S transept, designed by Pugin and made by William Wailes.

Bradford-on-Avon, *St. Lawrence.* The tiny church is one of the most famous pre-Conquest buildings in this country. Its importance lies in its almost complete survival without any great later alteration or addition. The church has been argued to be the building erected by St. Aldhelm at the end of the 7C (an 'ecclesiola'), but it is more likely to date from the beginning of the 10C, on stylistic grounds. It appears to have been built and completed in a very short space of time. That the church survived is due in part to a larger church being built opposite soon after the Norman Conquest. St. Lawrence's was used for some time as a charnel house and in the later medieval period it was surrounded by other buildings and gradually altered. The nave was turned into a schoolhouse with the insertion of an upper floor, and the chancel was turned into a cottage with a chimney being put in place of the chancel arch. The church remained hidden from view until 1856 when a chance discovery of the remains of two carved angels led the Vicar of the neighbouring church, Canon Jones, to research the origins of the building. In 1871 restoration commenced first under J.T. Irvine and then under C.S. Adye, a local architect.

The stone-built church has a nave only some 25ft in length, 13ft in width and 25ft high. The chancel is just over 13ft in length, 10ft wide and 18ft high. The N *porticus* survives, but of the S *porticus* only the roofline and two large buttresses remain. Externally, the nave and chancel have long pilaster strips. Running around the entire building is a blind arcade, whose arches are hewn out of the walls in relief, but the stones of the bases of the arches are part of the structure of the wall and show that the decoration was planned from the beginning. The tall narrow round-headed doorways are typical of pre-Conquest

St. Lawrence's, a complete pre-Conquest church

style. Internally, the emphasis is one of height created by the proportions of the building. The very narrow chancel arch has placed over it the two carved figures of angels which are all that remain of what would once have been a large Rood. The chancel floor is possibly pre-Conquest. There are three original small windows, double-splayed. The small altar in the chancel is partly made up of carved pre-Conquest stones and was constructed in 1970. Above the altar are the remains of a pre-Conquest cross.

Calne, *St. Mary the Virgin.* From the outside the church appears as a large and impressive Perpendicular building. Internally, however, it reveals work from the pre-Conquest period to the 20C, including an impressive array of fittings with some outstanding work by C.R. Ashbee and the Campden Guild. The dominating four-stage tower of 1628 is on the N side of the church. At each stage are pinnacles, rising from set-back buttresses. The top of the tower is battlemented, as are the aisles, porches and nave. Each bay of the nave is flanked by a buttress which rises above the battlements as a pinnacle. The walled churchyard has a scatter of tombs and avenues of yew hedges.

The nave is of five bays with Norman circular piers and scalloped capitals carrying round arches. The clerestory has three-light windows dating from the 15C. The corbel table above has alternating bishops' and saints' heads supporting the wooden roof. Above the arch of the third bay in the N arcade are the remains of a pre-Conquest arch. The N porch door is Norman. The transept arches and the two-bay chancel have Tuscan columns and date from after 1628. The S chapel and transept were rebuilt in 1864 by William Slater.

At the W end of the nave is the octagonal Perpendicular stone font which has the usual quatrefoil decoration. In the N aisle, the first bay forms a vestry whose screen was erected in 1900. An arch filled with wooden panelling in the same aisle leads to the choir vestry which was once St. Edmund's chapel. Inset in the panelling of the choir vestry arch is a cross made from nails of the destroyed Coventry Cathedral. At the end of the N aisle is a large oak chest dated 1579. Against the N wall of the N transept are two angels by C.R. Ashbee from the echo chamber of the organ and on the E wall of the transept are framed drawings by Ashbee for the organ case. At the E end of the nave, the pulpit of 1891 has carvings of the 12 Apostles. S of the S aisle is the chapel of the Epiphany and St. Edmund. The wooden screens date from 1907. The reredos depicting the Three Kings offering their gifts to the infant Jesus was designed by Ashbee and carved by the Campden Guild. The N chancel aisle is filled with the magnificent organ and organ case, the latter designed by Ashbee in 1908 and made by the Guild. The organ itself was made by P. Conacher & Co. of Huddersfield and was originally a five-manual instrument, now reduced to four. In the chancel the reredos was designed by J.L. Pearson in 1890, altered in 1936 and restored after damage in 1971. It has a series of ornate canopied scenes of the Nativity, Crucifixion and Ascension, with saints in between. The monuments include a large marble monument over the door to the vestry to Benedict John Angell Angell (died 1856), which has two angels and a portrait medallion.

The W window depicts scenes from the Life of Christ and has a memorial date of 1867. In the N aisle, the W window of c 1907 shows Christ preaching. In the N aisle N wall the windows show scenes from the Life of Christ, the Last Supper, the Crucifixion and the Ascension. In the S aisle the W window with a memorial date of 1865 depicts St. Paul. In the chapel of the Epiphany and St. Edmund two windows depict the Three Kings offering their gifts, and John the Baptist. The five-light E window of the chancel depicts Christ in Majesty with the three archangels surrounded by saints and prophets.

The church has a number of important historical and religious connections. In 978 Archbishop Dunstan and the Witan of England met at Calne. Robert Grosseteste was Vicar in 1221 and rose to become Bishop of Lincoln in 1235. Finally, Edmund of Abingdon (c 1175–1240), also Vicar here, later became Archbishop of Canterbury and in 1246 was canonised as St. Edmund of Canterbury.

Chippenham, *St. Andrew*. A church has stood on the site since pre-Conquest times. The present building has evidence of its Norman predecessor but it is largely the result of 14C and 15C expansion and the restoration and enlargement in 1875–78 by R. Darley. The church is set in a large churchyard which expands out from a narrow gap between buildings. The W tower is of three stages with large clasping buttresses. The parapet consists of trefoil-headed arches, with square turrets at the corners surmounted by pinnacles. The upper stage and the spire date from 1633. On the S side the aisle and the S or Hungerford chapel are 15C Perpendicular, with crocketed pinnacles rising above the battlements. Above the S door is a sundial dated 1705. The N aisle is part of Darley's extensive restoration.

The large five-bay nave has slender piers rising to foliate capitals. Above the Perpendicular arches, the clerestory consists of five triple lights on each side. The W end has a large Decorated tower arch with traces of earlier rooflines above. The large side room which is now the baptistery was once the chapel of the Fraternity of St. Katherine, built by the local clothiers' guild. The chapel was on the first floor, now gone, but evidence remains in the beam sockets, the piscina at first floor level and the stairs in the S wall. The chancel has in the second bay on the N side a re-erected and supposedly Norman chancel arch, looking as fresh as the day it was carved, with scalloped capitals and zigzag ornamentation. One further Norman work is the small deeply-recessed round-headed window in the N wall of the chancel. In the S wall is a recess with a stone frieze of crocketed pinnacles used as sedilia. The chancel, like much of the rest of the church, was altered during 1875–78. The Lady chapel on the S side of the chancel is of two bays' length.

The brass eagle lectern dates from 1874. The wooden pulpit and tester are of 1926. The present altar and rails were installed in front of the chancel screen in 1985. In the N aisle is an exceptionally fine 13C chest, whose front panel has carved on it the Lamb of God in a medallion between two doves which have olive branches in their beaks. Also depicted is a fox with a pastoral staff who is preaching to birds. The large wooden Perpendicular-style chancel screen has a traceried bay on each side of the central arch. It was erected in 1921 to the designs of F.E. Howard of Oxford and made by Mowbray's. In the chancel the altar rails are 18C and have twisted balusters. The Lady chapel screen consists of three cusped arches supported on slender piers with traceried panels at the bottom. The canopy has a band of foliage supporting three crests of the Hungerford family. The screen was erected in memory of Canon Rich (died 1913). At the end of the N aisle is a large 18C organ with an ornate case, built by the Seede family in 1752. The case has detailed Corinthian capitals, the pipes acting visually as pillars, with two angels blowing trumpets on either side of a segmental pediment above. In the baptistery, laid out in 1907, the octagonal font has panels with quatrefoil decoration.

In the N aisle is a marble tablet with an urn above by Thomas King of Bath, to Henry Singer (died 1778). In the Lady chapel there are an upright carved slab depicting a woman, dating from the 13C, and in the SE corner is a large tomb-chest to Sir Edward Baynton (died 1570). In the S aisle the first monument is to Anthony Martyn (died 1731). It consists of a pedimented tablet with fluted Corinthian pilasters and an urn above which contains a crest. The most impressive monument is that of Sir Gilbert Prynne (died 1627), consisting of the figures of Sir Gilbert and his wife kneeling in prayer and facing one another under two arches, with their coats of arms above. Beneath the main figures are carvings of their seven children, of whom two boys and three girls carry skulls, signifying their death during infancy. Beneath this is the inscription.

The stained glass is 19C and 20C. In the N aisle at the E end a three-light window of c 1900 depicts Joshua, St. Patrick and David, and is by Lavers & Westlake. The four-light window depicts angels flanking St. Paul and St. Andrew and four scenes of the Corporal

Works of Mercy (1882 by Burlison & Grylls). The main E window depicts Christ in Majesty and the Te Deum, by Lavers & Westlake, 1878. The E window in the Lady Chapel, dated 1901, is also by Lavers & Westlake and shows the Tree of Jesse. In the baptistery the E window of three lights by Burlison & Grylls, 1907, depicts Christ with a child and St. Katherine and St. Nicholas. In the S wall the four-light window of 1918 by Christopher Whall depicts four archangels with a weeping woman below, portraits in the background of three brothers killed in the war, and scenes of war with buildings on fire.

Cricklade, *St. Sampson.* A church has stood on the site since c 890 and its dedication to St. Sampson (a 6C Celtic monk-bishop) is unusual. The chief glory of the church is the elaborate Perpendicular central tower, which dominates the surrounding countryside. Each corner of the tower has large octagonal turrets which rise a stage higher than the rest of the tower. These are battlemented and are capped with spires. These turrets and the faces of the tower are decorated with blind arcading, composed of tall narrow arches. In the lower stage each face of the tower is pierced by a three-light window. The battlements are of openwork. The tower was paid for chiefly by John Dudley, Duke of Northumberland, who was beheaded under Queen Mary in 1553. Excepting the tower which is built of dressed stone, the church is largely built of freestone, with stone tiled roofs. On the S side, the SE corner of the S chapel is supported by an arched buttress which carries a pinnacle. The S aisle reveals its comparatively recent workmanship, being rebuilt by Ewan Christian in 1864. The N wall has two three-light windows with unusual tracery.

Internally, the three-bay nave has on the N side rectangular piers with large attached demi-shafts and leaf capitals. The S arcade has quatrefoil piers of eight shafts. Evidence of the pre-Conquest building can be seen in the remains of a pilaster above the S arcade. From the S aisle there is a large squint which is matched on the N side. The nave tower arch has elaborate stone decoration comprising three blank trefoil arches each side with large quatrefoils above. The tower has an intricate lierne-vault. Over the chancel arch, there are three carved shields and flags supported in bulbous heart shapes. The nave and aisle roofs date from the 1864 restoration by Ewan Christian.

In the N aisle at the W end is the Perpendicular octagonal stone font. Set into the S wall of the N porch, above the door, are two pre-Conquest stones with interlace decoration. There are further carved stones set in the N wall of the S aisle. In the tower space stand the choirstalls and, in the N transept, the organ. The S transept is screened off. All this woodwork has a rather unfortunate light brown coating of paint. In the sanctuary the altar has a frontal of 1982. Behind this is a reredos with a central panel containing the IHS monogram. There are riddel posts and light blue drapes. The posts support rather coy, naked, kneeling angels holding candlesticks. The work is by Martin Travers. In the chancel the large two-tiered brass candlelabrum dates from 1733. On the S side the Hungerford chapel has a wooden reredos which depicts the Crucifixion, by Martin Travers. In the N aisle at the E end above the altar are a number of mainly 18C monuments. Against the N wall in a Decorated recess is a worn female effigy which has been identified as Agnes Lushill (died 1442). The stained glass is mostly 19C. The W window of the N aisle, dated 1888, is by C.E. Kempe. In the N wall a window dated and signed by Martin Travers, 1934, depicts St. Nicholas. To the W of the N porch, St. Christopher is also by Travers, and so too is the E window of the chancel, which depicts the Crucifixion.

Devizes, *St. John.* St. John's is a large Norman church which was substantially rebuilt in the 15C. It was built c 1130 by Bishop Roger of Salisbury, Chancellor to King Henry I. The church is dominated by the very large central tower of three stages. The top stage has a blind arcade of five arches in the E and W faces with the second and fourth arches being pierced by two-light louvred windows. The E face also has a clock above the arcading. The tower is battlemented and has large turrets and pinnacles at each corner. Both the N and S transepts have blocked Norman windows. High up in the S wall of the S transept is a Norman arch with chevron pattern and two pillars with plain capitals. The E end of the chancel has four large buttresses and a large Norman window with a smaller one higher up. The rest of the church is Perpendicular in appearance. The W end of the nave with its five-light window dates from 1861–62 and is by William Slater. The aisles, nave and porches are all genuinely 15C. Perhaps the most elaborate feature, however, is the S chancel or Beauchamp chapel which was erected in the 1480s. It has pinnacles rising above the battlements and attached to each stage of the buttresses. The battlements have decorated panels. At the apex of the gable at the E end is a pinnacled and canopied niche. There is an elaborate carved canopy over the S door.

Internally, the nave has six bays with square piers, semicircular attached shafts and moulded capitals. The doors of both the N and S porches date from the 15C. The tower's nave and chancel arches are exceptionally wide and have zigzag patterning. The arches to the N and S transepts are pointed and have chevron decoration. The arch to the Beauchamp chapel is Perpendicular and has traceried panels. In the S wall, in between the two very large four-light windows, is an empty canopied niche and a canopied priest's door. On either side of the E window are further canopied niches containing statues of the Virgin Mary and St. John the Baptist. On the N wall is the Norman corbel table which was once external. The chancel of two bays is Norman, with a low stone rib-vault carried on shafts with foliate and scallop capitals. The E wall has six interlaced arches, the N and S sides four. Above the arcading is a triple arch with richly decorated columns and scallop capitals. Only the larger central light is pierced. The N chancel chapel, now used as a vestry, has a four-light window in both the E and N walls.

In front of the tower arch on the N side is the Perpendicular wooden pulpit; the panels have carvings of crocketed pinnacles rising from traceried arches. On the S side is the brass eagle lectern dating from 1901. Under the crossing are Victorian choirstalls. The N transept is largely taken up with the organ, which is an 18C instrument housed in a 17C case. In the chancel the wooden altar rails have Norman-style arches. There is a large number of mostly 18C and 19C monuments. Over the N porch door is a large pyramid-shaped monument with a mourning figure leaning on an urn, in memory of James Sutton (died 1784). Also in the N aisle is a memorial to another James Sutton (died 1788), by Thomas King of Bath. Over the S porch door is the memorial to a third James Sutton (died 1801), by Sir Richard Westmacott. It shows a female figure in mourning against a pillar, set on a pyramid-shaped tablet with the figure inset under an arch. The whole tablet is supported on lions' heads. In the floor of the Beauchamp chapel is a large brass cross to Mary Malkell (died 1847). The stained glass in the W window has a memorial date of 1900 and depicts Christ as the Light of the World. In the N aisle a three-light window designed and painted by George Harris in 1877 depicts the Sermon on the Mount. In the Beauchamp chapel the E window depicts the Crucifixion and has a memorial date of 1918. The E window of the chancel shows the Lamb of God and symbols of the Eucharist.

To the W of the church, in the churchyard, there is an obelisk recording a tragic boating accident in 1751 when five people were drowned.

On the E side of the town is the church of St. Mary which was also built by Bishop Roger. Although largely rebuilt in the 15C in the Perpendicular style, with a W tower, the chancel is very similar to that of St. John's, with interlaced arcading and a low stone vault.

East Knoyle, *St. Mary the Virgin.* The church has work from the pre-Conquest period onwards, but the chief feature is the plasterwork decoration of the chancel walls which was designed by the Rector, Dr Christopher Wren, in 1639 and executed by Robert Brockway. Dr Wren was the father of Sir Christopher Wren, who was born in the village and baptised in the church in 1632. The E window is by Sir Ninian Comper, 1934.

Edington, *St. Mary, St. Katherine and All Saints.* This priory church is a complete building erected in a relatively short space of time, 1352–61, and has been virtually unaltered since. It was sympathetically restored in 1887–91 by C.E. Ponting. There is a wealth of fittings and the church has connections with a number of historical figures. The church was founded to be the home for the Bonshommes (Augustinians) by William of Edington, Bishop of Winchester.

The cruciform church is set against the scarp face of the chalk downs of Salisbury Plain in a well-tended churchyard with a medieval cross which was restored in 1891. The church represents possibly better than anywhere else the changeover from Decorated to Perpendicular. It is completely embattled. Two buttresses rise above the W gable as turrets with crocketed pinnacles. There is a Perpendicular eight-light W window. Beneath this the W doors are separated by a central pillar supporting two cusped arches with blank, trefoil-headed, arched panelling above. The W windows of the aisles are Decorated. The S porch is of three storeys and there is a stair turret in the SW angle. The windows are mainly Decorated with some Perpendicular motifs. The buttresses of the transepts and chancel rise above the battlements as turrets topped by crocketed pinnacles. The middle buttress of the S wall of the chancel has an arch in its lower stage and the buttress W of the S door contains a window. The central tower has a two-light louvred window in each face and is battlemented. The N transept is similar to the S and contains a stair turret in the NW angle. In its N wall there are four niches with shell heads possibly dating from the 17C, which prove that the neighbouring mansion house gardens originally butted against it. The N aisle has at its E end a former entrance to the claustral range which was sited to the N. The windows here are also smaller and finish much higher up than those in the S aisle. Immediately beneath them is a drip course for the cloister walk roof.

Internally, the nave of six bays has moulded capitals carrying simply-moulded arches. Between the clerestory windows are the plain corbels which carry the wall posts. In each of the six bays of the roof are a further eight divisions with plaster decoration of geometric patterns. It dates from c 1663. Under the crossing the plaster roof is in imitation of fan-vaulting. The chancel is of three bays and has a Gothick plaster ceiling of c 1790. In the S wall an ogee gable surmounts a doorway and there are the remains of the sedilia. Between the windows there are empty niches with pinnacled canopies; the bases have superb carvings dating from c 1330. Similar niches flank the E window. The hoodmoulds of the windows all terminate with carved heads.

At the W end of the S aisle is the royal crest of 1631 which came from Imber Church in 1952 along with various other fittings and monuments. The W bay of the N aisle is the baptistery. The octagonal stone and marble font is set on a circular marble plinth surrounded by a mosaic depicting fish and four roundels of John the Baptist baptising Christ, and Christ with children. The base of the font is Perpendicular; the wooden cover dates from 1826. In the nave the octagonal wooden pulpit is Jacobean and has plain panels. A curved stair of c 1720 with turned balusters gives access to it. There is also an octagonal tester. In the sixth bay of the nave stands the altar erected in 1891. In front of the organ, in the N aisle, is the 17C altar of St. Giles which came from Imber Church. Also in the N aisle is a large painted benefactors' board of 1852. The chancel screen is in reality a pulpitum and dates from c 1500, although much restored on a number of occasions. The altar rail dates from the early 17C and has alternating turned balusters and fretwork. The top of the rail has pairs of obelisks between turned, urn-shaped finials. The altar and reredos date from 1936, being designed by W.H. Randoll Blacking. In the N transept, which is the Lady chapel, the altar has 18C rails and a Jacobean wooden reredos which consists of two arches set between fluted pilasters. Flanking this are two Doric fluted columns which support the decorated entablature.

The church has some magnificent monuments. At the W end of the S aisle there are two medieval stone effigies of cross-legged knights, both of which came from Imber Church. One has the arms of the Rous family. In the fifth bay between the the S aisle and the nave is the monument to Sir Ralph Cheney (died c 1401) and his wife. It may well have originally been a chantry chapel. The tomb-chest has three quatrefoil panels on each side with inset shields. On the top is a Purbeck marble slab with indents for brasses of male and female figures with inscriptions and shields. Above is a canopy with niches. There is an ogee-arched door with pinnacles to the W side. Against the S wall of the S transept is a painted monument dating from the 15C, whose subject is unknown despite the intials T.B. or J.B. It was restored and recoloured in 1969–70. It consists of a tomb-chest with four quatrefoil panels, inset into which are two barrels and a Tudor rose. The recumbent effigy is of a man in a blue robe with his head on a pillow and his feet resting against a barrel with the intials T.B. or J.B. Over this is the vaulted canopy with quatrefoil openings in the spandrels, and an angel holding a shield with a barrel and branch motif. At each side is a niche with pinnacled canopies over statues of St. Peter and St. Paul. In the chancel on the S side is the tomb of Sir Edward Lewys (died 1630) and his wife, Lady Anne Beauchamp (died 1664). In front of the tomb-chest are five children, two sons and three daughters, who are kneeling facing E. On the chest are the recumbent figures of Sir Edward with his head on a pillow and feet on a lion, and, slightly raised, Lady Anne, whose feet also rest on a lion. The canopy is supported by two large columns with Ionic capitals. These columns have carved drapes tied around them and pulled back to reveal a suspended angel holding a crown. On the back wall is the inscription set in a frame. Above the entablature is a central crest set in its own architectural frame and flanked by two putti holding shields. Against the N wall is a monument by Sir Francis Chantrey to Sir Simon Richard Brissett Taylor (died 1815). The monument consists of a marble tomb-chest on which three life-size figures carved in relief depict a dying man on a couch being comforted by two grieving women. In the N transept is a floor slab recording the restoration of the transept by the Friends of Edington Priory Church, 1957–64, carved by David Kindersley.

In the W window of the S aisle and an adjacent S wall window are medieval stained glass fragments from Imber Church. In the N transept the E window is filled with 14C stained glass depicting the Crucifixion. The clerestory of the nave on the N side has remains of six saints dating from the 14C. That in the W window depicts St. William of York. The others have been identified as St. Stephen or St. Paul, St. Christopher, St. Cuthbert, St. Audon and St. Leodegar.

In 1629 the poet George Herbert was married in the church. It is famous today for its annual festival of music.

Lacock, St. Cyriac. Besides the unusual dedication the church is notable as a Perpendicular structure with 14C transepts. There are a number of fittings of note including a monument of national importance. The church was restored in 1861 by Sir Arthur Blomfield and the chancel in 1903 by Harold Brakspear.

It is set in a picture-postcard village which is in the hands of the National Trust. The Perpendicular W tower has two-light louvred windows, battlements with square turrets and pinnacles at the corners, and a recessed spire. At the base of the tower is the late 15C battlemented porch which has a fine tierceron-vault with carved bosses. Beneath the battlements around the church are excellently carved gargoyles. The transepts are very plain in comparison with the rest of the building. The E gable of the nave has a six-light window above the chancel arch. The chancel has a parapet of pierced quatrefoil decoration. The buttresses rise above the parapet as turrets, finishing in crocketed pinnacles. Internally, the church is very light and spacious. The three-bay nave has tall slender piers with attached shafts and small individual capitals rising to simply-moulded wide arches, above which is blank arcaded panelling. The chancel was rebuilt in 1902–03 by Harold Brakspear as a memorial to William Henry Fox-Talbot, the pioneer photographer. The arch into the N or Talbot chapel (now the Lady chapel) has carvings in the soffit. The two-bay chapel dates from c 1430 and contains striking lierne-vaulting with carved bosses and a pendant. On the N wall are niches with canopies and bases, that on the E side with a carved head under the base. Flanking the four-light E window are further canopied niches.

The nave and aisles have Victorian pews. At the W end of the nave is the octagonal font standing on four Purbeck marble legs and dating from 1861. In the N transept the organ with a Gothick case dates from c 1800 and was made by William Bates of London. The chancel has Victorian stalls and a reredos of 1902 consisting of three canopied niches and attached shafts with foliate capitals.

In the Lady chapel is the outstanding monument to Sir William Sharington (died 1553). It is a tomb-chest with three panels containing the Sharington badge, a scorpion, above which flanking pilasters carry a depressed arch and a decorated entablature. A centrally placed crest supported by two putti stands above, and is itself capped by a shell panel and by vases with flowers. Inset under the arch is a strapwork cartouche. In the S transept are two painted wooden monuments to Ursula Baynard (died 1623) and Edward Bainard (died 1575 but monument dated 1623). In the floor are the brasses of a knight and his wife with their 13 sons and five daughters below. It is to Robert Baynard (died 1501) and his wife Elizabeth.

Lydiard Tregoze, *St. Mary.* The small Perpendicular church is memorable for the sheer wealth, range and quality of its monuments. Set in parkland to the N of the mansion, the church has a three-stage W tower with diagonal buttresses. The parapet has pierced quatrefoil panels and at each corner a square turret topped by a pinnacle. At the base of the parapet are gargoyles. The S aisle and porch are battlemented. Over the S chancel door is a large crest dated 1633. Above the nave E gable is a bellcote with a small spire.

Entrance to the church is under the tower. The nave has a N arcade of four bays with piers without capitals. With the exception of one bay which is 15C, the arcade is 13C. The S arcade has three bays with octagonal piers, dating from the 14C. The wagon roof is of wood and plaster, six wooden heads supporting it on each side. The S chancel chapel is a two-bay E extension of the S aisle and is largely filled with monuments. Internally it was altered in 1633 when the arcade to the chancel was replaced by three columns with Doric capitals and the roof of the chapel was painted with clouds, sky and stars. The chancel has a coved painted ceiling depicting clouds, sky, the sun and stars.

The box-pews start under the tower and are a mixture of Jacobean, Georgian and Victorian. In the nave they have finials in the form of crosses. On the S side of the nave and extending into the S aisle is the Bolingbroke family pew which is Jacobean and has foliate carvings, animals and figures. The pulpit is Jacobean, with carved arches in the panels on three sides. The chancel screen is also Jacobean, being divided into three sections. Above the middle arch are the Stuart royal arms. Flanking this are two pediments with bulbous finials. At the W end of the nave is the stone font which is octagonal and dates from the 13C. At the E end above the arcade is a 16C helmet. In the chancel the altar rails are very ornate; being gilded wrought-iron of c 1700. They have foliate decoration with birds, garlands, stars and cherubs' heads. Flanking centrally positioned gates are urns with trailing garlands. The altar stands in front of a flat painted reredos dating from the 18C. Inscribed panels and the figures of Moses and Aaron are divided by Corinthian columns. Against the N wall of the chancel, there is a large and rare family triptych memorial, with an entablature supporting a pediment surmounted by an eagle. Inset in the pediment is a portrait of a female and two flanking crests. When closed the triptych depicts on four panels and on the inside of the two outer panels a very detailed family tree. When opened, the triptych reveals a painting of Sir John St. John (died 1594) and his wife kneeling facing one another on top of a sarcophagus. On the left are the standing figures of his son Sir John, who put up the memorial in 1615, and his wife. On the right are six other children. All these figures are framed by two pillars and set in a very acute perspective. In the S aisle is the oldest monument in the church (1592), that of Nicholas and Elizabeth St. John, who were the grandparents of the first Baronet. It is painted and consists of two kneeling figures under a richly decorated arch. The plinth of the monument has various coats of arms and above the monument the arms of Walter St. John, the first Baronet's elder brother who drowned in 1597.

Over the S chapel door is the so called 'Conversation Piece' monument to Katherine (died 1633), wife of the infamous Sir Giles Mompesson. They face one another under arches, he holding a book, she holding a skull. They are framed by Corinthian columns supporting a large entablature and a small centrally-positioned pediment set within a larger broken pediment. Also on the S wall of the chapel is the monument to John, Viscount St. John (died 1748), by J.M. Rysbrack. It consists of an urn in front of a plain obelisk, with his crest supported by two angels. The S chapel is mostly taken up with the large and sumptuous monument to the first Baronet, Sir John St. John (died 1648, but the monument was erected in 1634). It is believed to be the work of Nicholas Stone and is regarded as one of the most important monuments of its time. The plinth consists of panels of inset circles and squares of contrasting colours. On this base is the raised effigy of Sir John flanked by his two wives. At their feet are three daughters and at their heads five sons, all kneeling. There are further children depicted in medallions, 13 in all. Over these figures eight black columns with Corinthian capitals support the complex arched canopy. The four pillars at each end support entablatures which carry allegorical statues at the corners and raised broken pediments at the W and E ends with centrally-positioned helmets. Behind these are shields supported by obelisks. The central arch carries four ribs which in the centre support an eagle. Around the monument are contemporary railings. Against the N wall of the chancel is the so-called Golden Cavalier monument to Edward St. John, who died from wounds received at the Battle of Newbury in 1645. It consists of a plinth with trophies on either side supporting a cartouche with Edward's arms. The figure is set under a draped canopy which is held back by two page boys.

The church has fragments of wall painting dating from the 13C and 14C which were first uncovered in 1901. On the N wall of the nave there is part of the scene of the murder of St. Thomas Becket, depicting a soldier. Also shown are part of a landscape, St. Christopher and over the chancel arch a centrally-positioned cross, busts and texts which date from after the 16C. On a pier of the S arcade is a painting of the Risen Christ and above this St. Michael weighing souls, with the Virgin Mary. In the S porch is a head of Christ.

There is a good range of stained glass from medieval to Victorian. In the tower W window there is the Ascension by Alexander Gibbs, 1859. The N aisle windows all have medieval fragments in the tracery. In the S aisle the middle window has the remains of six medieval figures in the tracery and tabernacles in the top of each light. In the S chapel in the S wall, a window has a number of medieval heraldic shields. The single light in that chapel has 12 medieval fragments including three heads, one whole figure of a king and various architectural features. The E window has a medieval angel in the top quatrefoil and three shields in one of the lights. The E window of the chancel is filled with glass by Abraham van Linge, c 1633, who was also responsible for the painted glass in the mansion. In the centre light is an olive tree with six crests and in the outer, St. John the Baptist and St. John the Evangelist. In the flanking lights are the Nativity and Christ in the Garden.

Malmesbury, *St. Peter and St. Paul.* This large and tantalising fragment of what must once have been a magnificent church and at one time boasted a spire taller than that of Salisbury Cathedral is, today, largely a Norman edifice. It contains a host of important features, such as the famous sculptured S porch, and has connections with a number of historical characters. A church has stood on the site from as far back as c 640. By the time of the Dissolution the E end and the transepts were in ruins due to the collapse of the crossing spire in c 1500. The nave and the W tower remained intact until c 1662 when the tower collapsed, removing most of the first three bays of the nave. Between 1900 and 1928 extensive repair and restoration work was undertaken.

The SW part of the W front remains with a four-stage stair turret. On the W face of the bottom stage is interlaced arch decoration which is repeated on both the W and S faces of the three stages above, with the arcading becoming progressively finer. The former internal S nave arcade reveals Norman piers and the triforium and clerestory. The cloister garden to the N affords a good view of the N side. The six bays have massive buttresses dividing the aisles. These in turn carry the pinnacled flying buttresses. Both cloister doors survive. At the present E end are the N transept crossing arch and the large infilled nave crossing arch. The W wall of the S transept extends for two bays at triforium height. On the S side the nave appears for the full nine bays. The tall Decorated clerestory windows are glazed in the six E bays. The third window from the W is traceried but open, and the two W windows are empty. The flying buttress between the two W bays is also missing. The aisle has Perpendicular windows in recessed Norman arches, with the exception of two bays towards the E end which have large Decorated windows. The parapet is of pierced trefoils at both nave and aisle level. The large two-storey porch fills most of the width of three bays and has very large buttresses and outer arch. Internally, the porch contains one of the most important groups of Norman carvings in England. The arch is of eight orders, all decorated. Three of the orders have figurative carvings, the inner two of these depicting Old Testament scenes, the outer New Testament scenes. Inside the porch are four blank arches on each side with the pillars missing. The lunettes above the arcading are filled with carvings of the 12 Apostles, six to each lunette, seated on a bench with an angel horizontally positioned above them. The tympanum over the inner door depicts Christ in Majesty, seated on a rainbow, with a book held in his left hand. The door has three bands of decoration.

Inside, the nave is of six bays, with the S aisle running its full original length of nine bays as a result of the restoration carried out in 1928. The nave has massive drum piers and circular capitals with scallop decoration. From these spring pointed arches which have mouldings of beakheads and centrally placed animals' heads. Above this the triforium has bays of four small arches with scalloped capitals and plain columns under a larger round arch with attached shafts, scalloped capitals and zigzag decoration. The fourth bay of the S side of the triforium contains a box-like cubicle, the purpose of which is unclear. From the nave piers rise attached shafts to clerestory level, where the stone lierne-vault springs from foliate capitals. The vaulting has a series of carved bosses. The E end of the nave terminates in a solid wall filling the crossing arch. At the W end a very tall six-light window is set into the wall which was built after the destruction of the W tower and the W three bays in c 1662. Both aisles have rib-vaults and the remains of blind arcading running along the outer walls.

At the E end the present chancel is the last bay of the original nave. The altar rails are of c 1700 and have twisted balusters. Behind the altar, the stone screen (or pulpitum) has a blocked central Perpendicular arch and the arms of King Henry VIII on the cornice. Inset into the arch is an IHS monogram. In the nave at the E end is the large wooden pulpit with carved traceried panels and a tester above, a 20C work in 16C style. At the E end of the S aisle is a Perpendicular stone screen with six divisions, traceried arches and traceried panels beneath. The middle two panels have an archway inserted into them. The enclosed bay now serves as St. Aldhelm's chapel. In the S aisle are some medieval tile fragments and the parish chest, dated 1638. At the W end of the nave is the 18C font supported on a large baluster.

The chief monument is the late medieval tomb of King Aethelstan (died 939), situated in the N aisle. It consists of a tomb-chest with plain panels, on top of which is the recumbent effigy of the king with a lion at his feet and an ornate tabernacle above his head.

In the parvise over the porch are housed the abbey treasures. These include a collection of medieval manuscripts, Bibles, prints of the abbey, etc. The abbey has many connections with historical figures, not only King Aethelstan. In 676 St. Aldhelm was the first Abbot and he was buried here in 709. In 1010 a monk named Elmer became the first recorded English aviator by constructing glider-shaped wings and then launching himself off one of the towers, only to break his legs on landing. William of Malmesbury, c 1090–1143, the great medieval chronicler and historian, was trained here and lived in the monastery.

In the churchyard is an ordinary gravestone with a bizarre tale. It records that on 23rd October 1703 Hannah Twynnoy, aged 33, was mauled and killed by a tiger from a visiting circus.

Marlborough College, Chapel. The chapel sits on the right-hand side of the entrance on a bank above the main road. It is the work of G.F. Bodley and Thomas Garner and dates from 1883–86.

Built predominantly of Bath stone, the building is of eight buttressed bays plus an apse. At the W end above the W door is a statue of the Virgin and Child. Over the meeting point of the nave and the chancel is a flèche. The S entrance leads into the narthex which runs across the whole width of the building. Entering from the narthex under the gallery at the W end, the impact is one of height and length. Each side of the nave has six raised ranks of benches and stalls. Each bay has a three-light, deeply recessed window and between each bay rise piers supporting simple capitals. The chancel is of two bays' length.

Behind the stalls and benches runs continuous wooden panelling with a canopy. Inset into this panelling are 12 painted panels by J.R. Spencer Stanhope, 1872–79, which came from the previous chapel. Flanking the W window are four painted figures set in elaborate frames. The large reredos was designed by Bodley in 1866 and has scenes depicting the Nativity and the Crucifixion, and a figure of the Risen Christ. Behind the reredos the apse has figures of angels on a bright blue background. The scheme was designed by Sir Ninian Comper in 1950.

There is a painting of Lord Fisher of Lambeth, Archbishop of Canterbury, who was an assistant master here in 1911–14. There are plain white memorials in the narthex to William Morris and Sir John Betjeman.

Mere, _St. Michael the Archangel._ This church of exceptional interest dates mainly from the 13C, 14C and 15C, and is uncommonly rich in furnishings, monuments and glass. The 15C W tower is of three stages with large octagonal clasping buttresses rising above the battlements and finishing as tall tapering pinnacles. In the top stage is a three-light louvred window in each face. The battlements have panels of quatrefoil decoration. At the E end of the S aisle is the Bettesthorne chapel which has a large polygonal stair turret. The parapet of the chapel, which continues round the turret, is pierced by keyhole-like openings. The chapel dates from c 1350; its E window is Perpendicular but has a Decorated hoodmould with four carved heads. The N or Still chapel was built c 1325 and has Decorated windows on the N side and a Perpendicular E window. In a niche over the N porch is a statue of St. Michael killing the dragon which dates from c 1160.

The five-bay nave has Perpendicular piers with the usual four shafts. The wall plates of the nave roof have angels with outstretched wings. The Perpendicular tower arch has eight pairs of panelled arches on its soffit. The chancel of three bays has Decorated arcades to the two chapels. Evidence of the 13C chancel comprises the two-light window now opening into the N chapel and the doorway below it.

The pews in the nave date from 1640. The 15C chancel screen has three traceried arches of six lights and a gallery above, which was reinstated in the 19C. At the E end of the N aisle over the screen are the arms of King Charles II, dated 1684. In the S aisle at the E end the octagonal font with panels of quatrefoil decoration dates from the 15C. In a niche in the S wall are the remains of wall painting and above this is a further niche containing an unfortunate modern sculpture of 'Our Lady Great with Child' by Greta Berlin. In the chancel the Victorian choirstalls have some 15C as well as Victorian misericords. On the N side are depicted St. Michael, an angel, an angel with a lute and an angel with a shield, the last three being medieval. On the S side there are a head with its tongue poking out, the Tudor Rose, a floral design and an angel. Under the Vicar's stall is depicted a fox. The altar, which is on two steps, has riddel posts surmounted by angels. In the N chapel on the S wall are two charity boards, hatchments and a clock. Most of the chapel is taken up with the organ loft, the carved panels of which date from 1904.

In the Bettesthorne chapel in front of the altar is the 4ft 3in brass effigy of Sir John Bettesthorne (died 1398). On the altar step is a large fragment of brass, again depicting a knight, possibly Sir John Berkeley (died 1426). In the E arch between the chapel and the chancel is a large tomb-chest with a Purbeck marble top and quatrefoil panels with inset shields on the sides. It is believed to be the tomb of John, first Lord Stourton (died 1463). The church possesses a wide range of stained glass. In the W wall of the N aisle, the three-light window of 1865 is by Henry Holiday and depicts the Women at the Tomb, Christ appearing to Mary, and Christ with the Disciples. In the S aisle the W window (c 1862) is partly the work of Holiday. In the S wall of the S aisle are three windows which depict King David, St. Mary and St. John, 1909, by Clayton and Bell. The next window is etched with a view of the church and a scene of the induction of the Vicar in 1981. It is by John Finnie, 1983. The final window in the S aisle depicts Christ with children and was made by Kelly & Co. of London, 1909. In the Bettesthorne chapel in the S wall is a five-light window in which are set four raised quatrefoil lights of c 1330 which depict St. Nicholas, St. Martin, St. Christopher and a Pope. Also in the S wall is a window of c 1838 which depicts the Life of Christ, by Ward & Nixon. The E window of the chapel is dated 1859 and was designed by H. Moberley and made by Powell's. In the chancel a window in the S wall of 1933 by Christopher Webb depicts St. Michael, the Virgin and Child and St. Martin.

Potterne, *St. Mary.* The church is a textbook example of a cruciform 13C church with a large and magnificent 15C central tower. The quality of the workmanship and the large size of the building are due to the fact that Potterne was held by the Bishops of Salisbury. The church was restored in 1871–72.

The church stands on a sloping ridge, set above most of the village and main road. The transepts and chancel are of the same length and together with the nave are lit by simple tall lancets. The N and S porches are of a slightly later period but otherwise the nave, transepts, chancel and lower stage of the tower are Early English. The top stage of the tower is a fine example of Perpendicular architecture, capped by pierced battlements with three pinnacles to each face. The aisleless nave rises to a wooden raftered roof, the W end is lit by a triple-lancet window and the N and S walls are each pierced by four recessed lancets. In the nave tower arch there are traces of a doorway which formerly led to the Rood loft. The N transept serves as the Lady chapel and the S is taken up by vestries and the organ. The chancel has three recessed lancets in the N and S walls. The E end has a magnificent recessed triple-lancet window with two blank lancets on either side. To these lancets have been added six attached shafts of Purbeck marble, reminiscent of work at Salisbury Cathedral.

The church has two fonts: below the W window is a pre-Conquest tub with a Latin inscription from Psalm 42 ('As a Deer longs for the running brooks, so longs my soul for you, O God'); and the other font in the nave dates from the 15C. At the W end there are two painted panels of Moses and Aaron, and panels of the Creed, Lord's Prayer and Commandments, which are the remains of an altarpiece given in 1723. Below the W window are placed the arms of King George I. The N door has its original wooden 13C door leaf. Under the tower is a wooden chest dated 1639. The 15C wooden octagonal pulpit has six carved panels with pinnacled traceried arches. The S transept's organ case and vestry screens were designed in 1938 by Sir Charles Nicholson, on whose advice the walls of the church were painted white in 1936.

The monuments are chiefly of the 18C onwards. Against the S wall of the nave is a marble tablet in the shape of a sarcophagus to Henry Kent (died 1759), signed by Joseph Nollekens. Also on the S wall is a large marble tablet of a female figure leaning against a partially draped urn, to John Spearing (died 1831), by E.H. Baily.

The stained glass in the W window depicts St. John the Baptist baptising Christ. The nave windows largely show scenes from the boyhood of Jesus. In the E wall of the N transept the three lancets have scenes from the Parables. In the chancel the windows depict scenes from Jesus's adult ministry.

Salisbury, *St. Thomas of Canterbury.* This is the principal parish church of Salisbury. A church is believed to have stood on the site from 1219, when Bishop Richard Poore built a wooden chapel. With the town moving from Old Sarum to the present-day site in 1220, the church was rebuilt in 1226. In 1400 a bell tower was built on the S side as a free-standing tower. In 1447 the choir collapsed, taking with it the chapel of St. Stephen. Rebuilding of the chancel and the S chapel commenced and a large N chapel was added. To the N of this a three-storey vestry dates from c 1450. The nave aisles were added c 1465. The church has many fine features and chief amongst these is the famous Doom painting which is the largest extant in England.

The tower on the S side rises two stages above the aisle. On the E face is the clock which was restored in 1983; it has Tudor quarter jacks. The tower is surmounted by battlements with decorated panels and a low pyramidal roof. The nave and chancel are battlemented and the nave has large four-light clerestory windows. The W end has a battlemented gable and is capped by a foliate cross. Beneath this is a large seven-light Perpendicular window filling the space completely between the nave wall buttresses.

Internally, the nave is of five bays with slender quatrefoil piers, whose shafts have mostly foliate capitals. Above the moulded arches are panels of blind arcading with cusped arches. The tracery is continued up into the clerestory windows. Between the windows, shafts rise from the nave piers to the corbels, on which stand the wooden wall posts of the roof, which is a particularly good example of a Somerset-style roof, adorned with many carved and painted angels. There is a modern glass and wooden screen at the W end. The aisles are lit by five very large four-light windows. The chancel of four bays has quatrefoil piers with finely carved foliate capitals. High above are six three-light clerestory windows.

The most visually arresting feature in the church is the justly famous Doom painting which covers the wall above the chancel arch. It dates from c 1475 and is possibly the work of Flemish artists. It depicts in the upper part Christ in Majesty seated on two rainbows, showing his wounds; angels holding the Instruments of the Passion and the Virgin Mary and St. John, all of whom flank Christ; the 12 Disciples in a line below Christ; and a stylised representation of the City of Heaven in the two corners at the top. To the left of the arch people rise from their graves, with the angels sounding trumpets. Below, under a canopy, is a depiction of St. James the Great with a book in his hand. To the right of the arch is a depiction of the Devil with one foot painted on the arch, being offered an ale pot by a woman with an elaborate head-dress, possibly representing a prostitute. Behind her a group of chained people are being driven by demons towards the mouth of Hell, which is represented as a whale's mouth. Beneath the scene of Hell, under a canopy and matching the figure on the other side, is St. Osmund, crozier in hand. The whole Doom painting was discovered under whitewash in 1819 and covered up again, not being fully uncovered until later in the century when it was extensively restored by Clayton & Bell.

On the N side of the nave below the chancel arch is the stone pulpit designed by G.E. Street in 1876. The nave and aisles have Victorian pews. In the S aisle at the W end is a medieval chest and over the tower door in that aisle are the arms of Queen Elizabeth I. On the S wall is a richly carved oak panel dated 1671, which depicts angels, sheep and soldiers with an inscription which tells us that it was the work of Humphrey Beckham and serves as his memorial. At the E end of the N aisle is the altar of St. George which has been made from a medieval tomb-chest. Behind this and filling much of the N chancel chapel is the large organ which was presented to the church in 1877, being restored in 1897, 1930 and 1969. In the S chancel aisle which serves as the chapel of Our Lady and St. Stephen there are traces of wall paintings which depict red drapery suspended by rings from a rod. On the drapery are lilies and shields of St. George. In the spandrels above the arches are depictions of the Annunciation, the Visitation and the Adoration of the Magi. All of these are dated to the late 15C. The wrought-iron railings and the wooden reredos in this chapel were erected in 1724. The reredos consists of a tall central section with a segmental pediment and a crest, supported by Corinthian fluted pilasters, and lower side sections. Set at angles in the corners above the reredos are two fine Jacobean monuments to the Eyre family; once highly coloured and positioned in the chancel, they were moved here and painted to match the other woodwork when the Eyre family altered the chapel to make a vault. Also in the chapel are Georgian mayoral mace stands. In the chancel the arches of the sedilia and piscina contain Victorian painted panels of angels which are repeated on the N side. All these panels are set in stone screens which are surmounted by more angels. Against the E wall, the reredos depicting the Crucifixion was carved by Thomas Earp in 1868 to the designs of G.E. Street who was responsible for the restoration of the chancel.

The church is rich in monuments from the 18C and 19C. In the Lady chapel the monument to Christopher Eyre (died 1628) and his wife to the left of the reredos has kneeling figures facing one another under arches. Above them a large entablature carries family crests and is supported by three Corinthian columns. The monument on the right also has two kneeling figures facing one another across a prayer desk, Thomas Eyre (died 1628) and his wife. Beneath the figures are depictions of their six sons, five daughters and four dead infant children. On the floor of the chancel by the Lady chapel entrance is a large brass with the figures of John Webbe (died 1570) and his wife, with their six children beneath them. In the N chancel aisle there is a large marble pyramidal monument with urns to Sir Alexander Powell (died 1786), by Richard Earlsman the Younger.

The stained glass is 19C apart from medieval fragments. In the Lady chapel the second window from the W in the S wall has a medieval fragment, possibly of St. Thomas, which was restored in 1985. The next window eastwards has medieval fragments restored in 1966 which have been tentatively ascribed to the workshop of Thomas of Oxford, who was active between 1386 and 1422. In the E window there are further medieval fragments. Finally, the chancel E window was designed by G.E. Street and depicts Christ surrounded by the Disciples. In the tracery above are angels.

Before the Victorian restorations the church had galleries and high pews and was the source for Thomas Hardy's church setting in 'Jude the Obscure'. The church can also claim the third oldest Sunday School in the country, started in 1785.

Steeple Ashton, St. Mary. Despite the name of the village the impressive church has lacked its 93ft spire since it fell during a storm in 1670. This collapse did much damage and repairs were completed in 1675. The present structure is Wiltshire's finest example of a Perpendicular building. It was also designed from the outset to be built totally of stone, although the nave vaulting was eventually constructed of wood. One other feature of note is the Samuel Hey Library.

The church is dominated by the tall four-stage W tower, which has set-back buttresses rising to pinnacles. Above the W window are five empty canopied niches. The top stage is capped by battlements. The nave, chancel, aisles and porch also have battlements with pinnacled buttresses. The chancel was rebuilt in 1853 by Henry Clutton, replacing Early English work. The exterior is considerably enlivened by a series of carved gargoyles. The S porch of two storeys has large diagonal buttresses which continue as corner turrets and finish as pinnacles.

Internally, the impact is one of spaciousness and lightness. The four-bay nave has piers with attached shafts and moulded capitals supporting much-moulded arches. Above the nave arcades are large four-light windows. Between each window slender attached shafts rise to decorated corbels above which there are stone springers. From this point the rest of the lierne-vault of the nave is of wood; recently it has been suggested that it was a 17C replacement of the original stone vault rather than that the vault was always wooden. The rest of the vaulting throughout the church is of stone. In the aisles the vaulting comes down to springers which consist of tabernacled niches, all of which are empty. These in turn are supported by large busts. Most of the bosses of the vaulting are foliate but in the N aisle, in the N chapel, the E boss depicts the Assumption of the Virgin and the W boss shows Christ surrounded by the Prophets. The nave and aisles have Victorian wooden pews. In the W bay of the S aisle is the octagonal stone font which dates from 1841. Nearby is an early 15C chest with iron straps. In the nave at the E end the large, wooden, seven-sided pulpit has a stone pillared base and was designed by Clutton. It was erected in memory of Richard Crawley who was Vicar for 41 years. On the N side of the chancel and taking up part of the N chapel is the organ which was presented in 1875.

The church has a very large number of mostly 18C and 19C memorials. On the W wall of the S aisle is a large pedimented marble monument to John Smith (died 1775) and his wife, Ann. On the N wall is a monument with an urn to Thomas Beech (died 1771), by Thomas King of Bath, who was responsible for a further four monuments including one to Archibald Colquhoun, Lord Register of Scotland. Over the S porch door is a Gothic marble tablet by Reeves & Son of Bath to Samuel Hey (died 1828), Vicar here (see below). There is a palimpsest brass which on one side has the remains of the depiction of Queen Anne, Prince George and two bishops standing next to scales weighed down by a Bible. There is part of the title at the top, 'and the Divil overballanced by he bible'.

Many of the aisle windows have fragments of medieval glass depicting the White Rose of York, the shields of St. George, St. Andrew and St. Swithun, and various monograms, crowns, lions' heads and fleur-de-lis. In the tower, the W window of 1879 has eight figures in two rows. In the top row from left to right are St. Elizabeth, St. Anne, St. Mary and St. Mary Magdalene and below are St. Martha, Salome, Dorcas and Eunice.

Over the S porch is the Samuel Hey Library, named after the Vicar between 1787 and 1828. He left 1100 books which remained intact until 1941, when they were sorted for wartime salvage purposes. The remaining 200 or so volumes were retained in the vicarage until 1968 when they were moved to the church. Included are works dating from the 15C to the 19C.

Old Counties

SCOTLAND

NORTHUMBER-
LAND

CUMBERLAND   DURHAM

WEST-
MORLAND   North Riding

YORKSHIRE
East Riding

West Riding

LANCASHIRE

Lindsey

CHESHIRE   DERBY   LINCOLN

NOTTS

ENGLAND   Kesteven

STAFFORD   Holland

NORFOLK

LEICESTER

1

SHROPSHIRE   2   3

SUFFOLK

WALES   WARWICK   West   East

NORTHAMPTON

WORCESTER   4

HEREFORD   HERTFORD   ESSEX

GLOUCESTER   OXFORD   BUCKS

GREATER
LONDON

BERKSHIRE   KENT

WILTSHIRE   SURREY

HAMPSHIRE   SUSSEX
West   East

SOMERSET

DEVON   DORSET

CORNWALL

ENGLISH COUNTIES

1. RUTLAND
2. HUNTINGDON AND PETERBOROUGH
3. CAMBRIDGE AND ISLE OF ELY
4. BEDFORDSHIRE

Post 1973-75
Reorganisation of Counties

SCOTLAND

NORTHUMBER-
LAND

1

DURHAM
2

CUMBRIA

NORTH YORKSHIRE

LANCASHIRE

WEST
YORKSHIRE

HUMBERSIDE

4

5

3

CHESHIRE

DERBY

NOTTS

LINCOLN

ENGLAND

STAFFORD

SHROPSHIRE

LEICESTER

NORFOLK

WALES

6

HEREFORD
AND
WORCESTER

WARWICK

NORTHAMPTON

CAMBRIDGE

SUFFOLK

7

GLOUCESTER

OXFORD

BUCKS

HERTFORD

ESSEX

GREATER
LONDON

AVON

WILTSHIRE

BERKSHIRE

SURREY

KENT

SOMERSET

HAMPSHIRE

WEST
SUSSEX

EAST
SUSSEX

DEVON

DORSET

8

CORNWALL

ENGLISH COUNTIES

1. TYNE AND WEAR
2. CLEVELAND
3. SOUTH YORKSHIRE
4. MERSEYSIDE
5. GREATER MANCHESTER
6. WEST MIDLANDS
7. BEDFORDSHIRE
8. ISLE OF WIGHT

INDEX OF ARCHITECTS, ARTISTS AND CRAFTSMEN

INDEX TO CHURCHES AND CHAPELS